Stan Lee PRESENTS

ESSENTIAL CAPTAIN AMERICA

VOL. 2

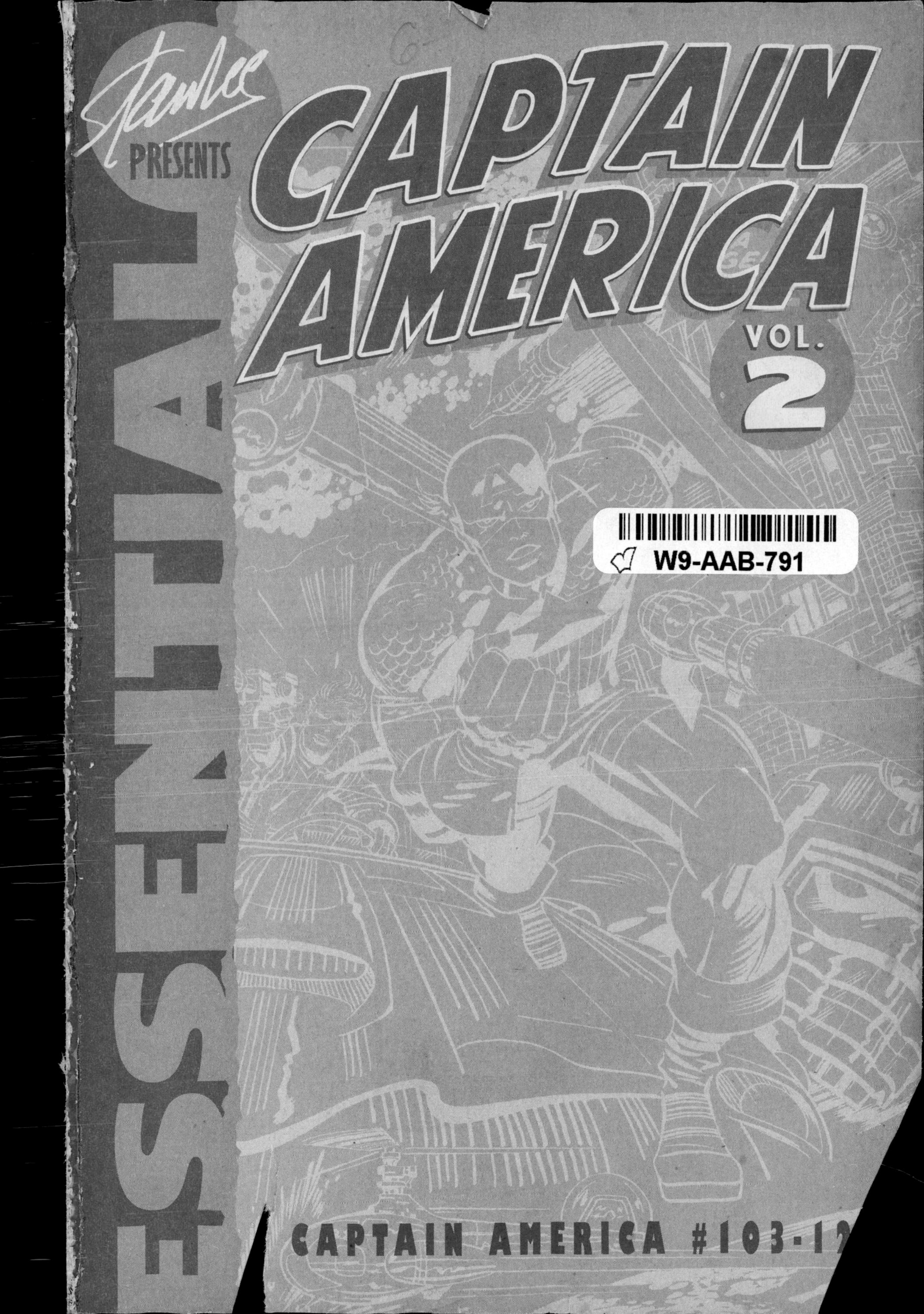

CAPTAIN AMERICA #103-12

ESSENTIAL CAPTAIN AMERICA VOL. 2

CAPTAIN AMERICA #103

WRITER: STAN LEE
PENCILER: JACK KIRBY
INKER: SYD SHORES
LETTERER: ARTIE SIMEK

CAPTAIN AMERICA #104

WRITER: STAN LEE
PENCILER: JACK KIRBY
INKER: DAN ADKINS
LETTERER: ARTIE SIMEK

CAPTAIN AMERICA #105

WRITER: STAN LEE
PENCILER: JACK KIRBY
INKER: DAN ADKINS
LETTERER: SAM ROSEN

CAPTAIN AMERICA #106

WRITER: STAN LEE
PENCILER: JACK KIRBY
INKER: FRANK GIACOIA
LETTERER: SAM ROSEN

CAPTAIN AMERICA #107

WRITER: STAN LEE
PENCILER: JACK KIRBY
INKER: SYD SHORES
LETTERER: ARTIE SIMEK

CAPTAIN AMERICA #108

WRITER: STAN LEE
PENCILER: JACK KIRBY
INKER: SYD SHORES
LETTERER: ARTIE SIMEK

CAPTAIN AMERICA #109

WRITER: STAN LEE
PENCILER: JACK KIRBY
INKER: SYD SHORES
LETTERER: ARTIE SIMEK

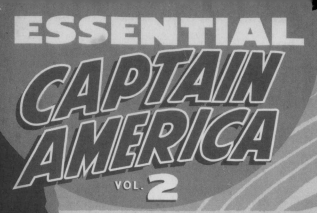

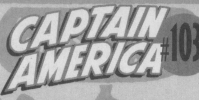

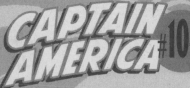

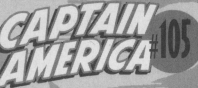

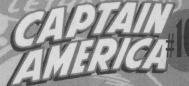

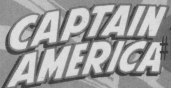

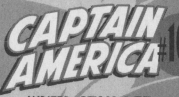

CAPTAIN AMERICA #110

WRITER: **STAN LEE**
PENCILER: **JIM STERANKO**
INKER: **JOE SINNOTT**
LETTERER: **SAM ROSEN**

CAPTAIN AMERICA #111

WRITER: **STAN LEE**
PENCILER: **JIM STERANKO**
INKER: **JOE SINNOTT**
LETTERER: **SAM ROSEN**

CAPTAIN AMERICA #112

WRITER: **STAN LEE**
PENCILER: **JIM STERANKO**
INKER: **GEORGE TUSKA**
LETTERER: **ARTIE SIMEK**

CAPTAIN AMERICA #113

WRITER: **STAN LEE**
PENCILER: **JIM STERANKO**
INKER: **TOM PALMER**
LETTERER: **ARTIE SIMEK**

CAPTAIN AMERICA #114

WRITER: **STAN LEE**
PENCILER: **JOHN ROMITA**
INKER: **SAL BUSCEMA**
LETTERER: **HERB COOPER**

CAPTAIN AMERICA #115

WRITER: **STAN LEE**
PENCILER: **JOHN BUSCEMA**
INKER: **SAL BUSCEMA**
LETTERER: **SAM ROSEN**

CAPTAIN AMERICA #116

WRITER: **STAN LEE**
PENCILER: **GENE COLAN**
INKER: **JOE SINNOTT**
LETTERER: **SAM ROSEN**

CAPTAIN AMERICA #117

WRITER: **STAN LEE**
PENCILER: **GENE COLAN**
INKER: **JOE SINNOTT**
LETTERER: **SAM ROSEN**

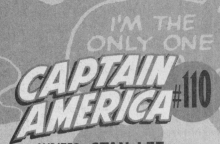

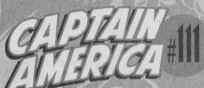

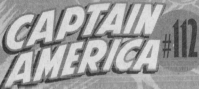

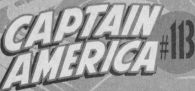

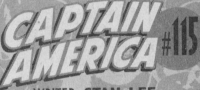

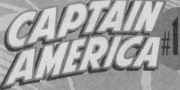

ESSENTIAL
CAPTAIN AMERICA
VOL. 2

REPRINT CREDITS

CAPTAIN AMERICA #125

WRITER: **STAN LEE**

PENCILER: **GENE COLAN**

INKER: **JOE SINNOTT**

LETTERER: **SAM ROSEN**

CAPTAIN AMERICA #126

WRITER: **STAN LEE**

PENCILER: **GENE COLAN**

INKER: **FRANK GIACOIA**

LETTERER: **SAM ROSEN**

CAPTAIN AMERICA #127

WRITER: **STAN LEE**

PENCILER: **GENE COLAN**

INKER: **WALLY WOOD**

LETTERER: **ARTIE SIMEK**

CAPTAIN AMERICA #128

WRITER: **STAN LEE**

PENCILER: **GENE COLAN**

INKER: **DICK AYERS**

LETTERER: **ARTIE SIMEK**

COVER ART
JIM STERANKO

COVER COLORS
TOMMY CHU

COVER & INTERIOR DESIGN
JOHN 'JG' ROSHELL OF COMICRAFT

PRODUCTION ASSISTANT
CORY SEDLMEIER

ASSISTANT EDITOR
MIKE FARAH

COLLECTIONS EDITOR
MATTY RYAN

MANUFACTURING REPRESENTATIVE
FENTON ENG

DIRECTOR-PUBLISHING OPERATIONS
BOB GREENBERGER

EDITOR IN CHIEF
JOE QUESADA

PRESIDENT & COO PUBLISHING, CONSUMER PRODUCTS & NEW MEDIA
BILL JEMAS

ESSENTIAL CAPTAIN AMERICA® VOL. 2 Contains material originally published in magazine form as CAPTAIN AMERICA #103 - 126. First printing, January 2002. ISBN # 0-7851-0827-0. Published by MARVEL COMICS, a division of MARVEL ENTERTAINMENT GROUP, INC. OFFICE OF PUBLICATION: 10 EAST 40th STREET, NEW YORK, NY 10016. Copyright © 1968, 1969, 1970, 2002 Marvel Characters, Inc. All rights reserved. Price $14.95 in the U.S. and $23.95 in Canada (GST #R127032852). No similarity between any of the names, characters, persons, and/or institutions in this publication with those of any living or dead person or institutions is intended, and any such similarity which may exist is purely coincidental. This publication may not be sold except by authorized dealers and is sold subject to the conditions that it shall not be sold or distributed with any part of its cover or markings removed, nor in a mutilated condition. CAPTAIN AMERICA (including prominent characters featured in this publication and the distinctive likenesses thereof) is a trademark of MARVEL CHARACTERS, INC. Printed in Canada. PETER CUNEO, Chief Executive Officer; AVI ARAD, Chief Creative Officer; GUI KARYO, Chief Information Officer; STAN LEE, Chairman Emeritus.

10 9 8 7 6 5 4 3 2 1

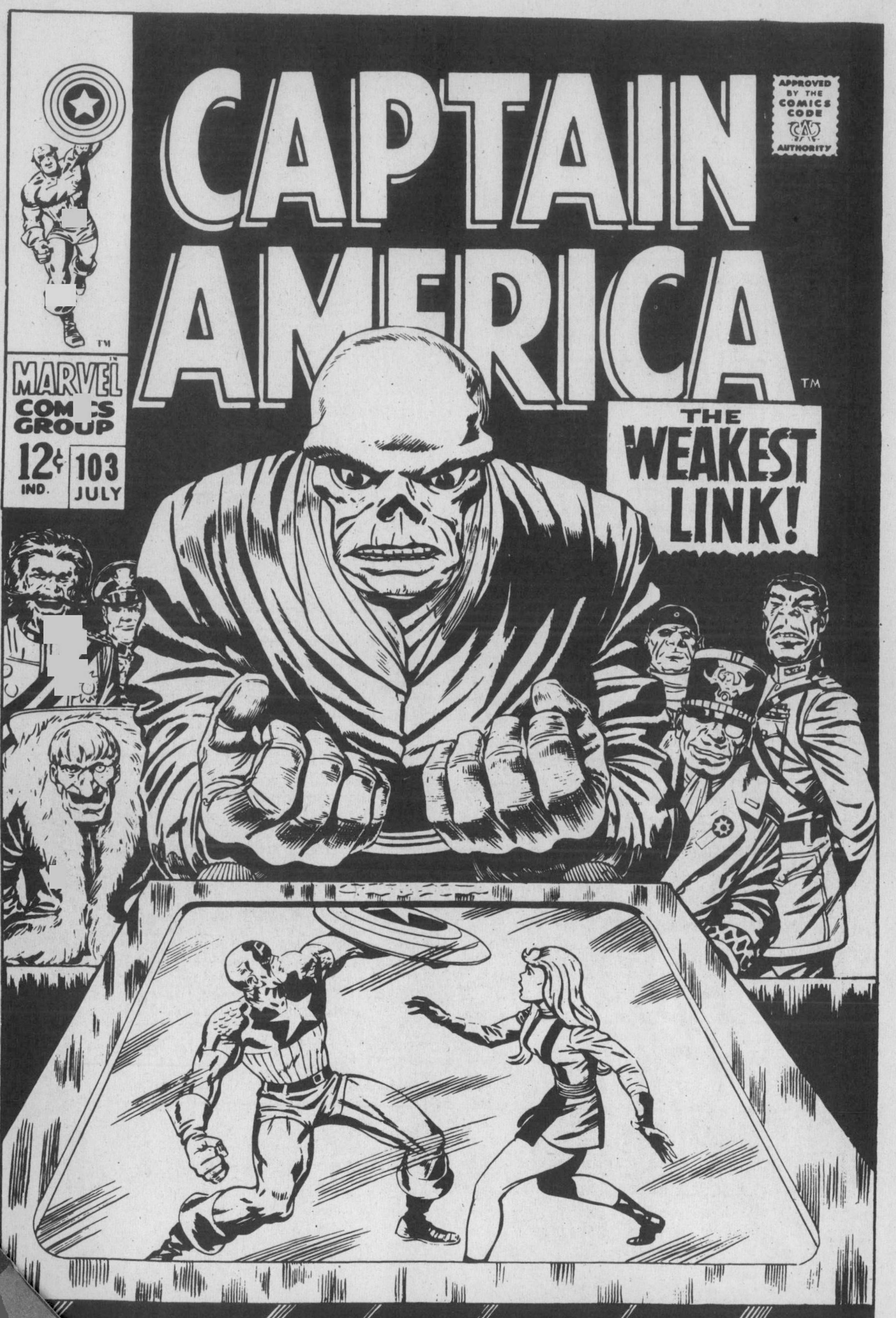
CAPTAIN AMERICA
TM
APPROVED BY THE COMICS CODE AUTHORITY
MARVEL COMICS GROUP
12¢ IND.
103 JULY
THE WEAKEST LINK!

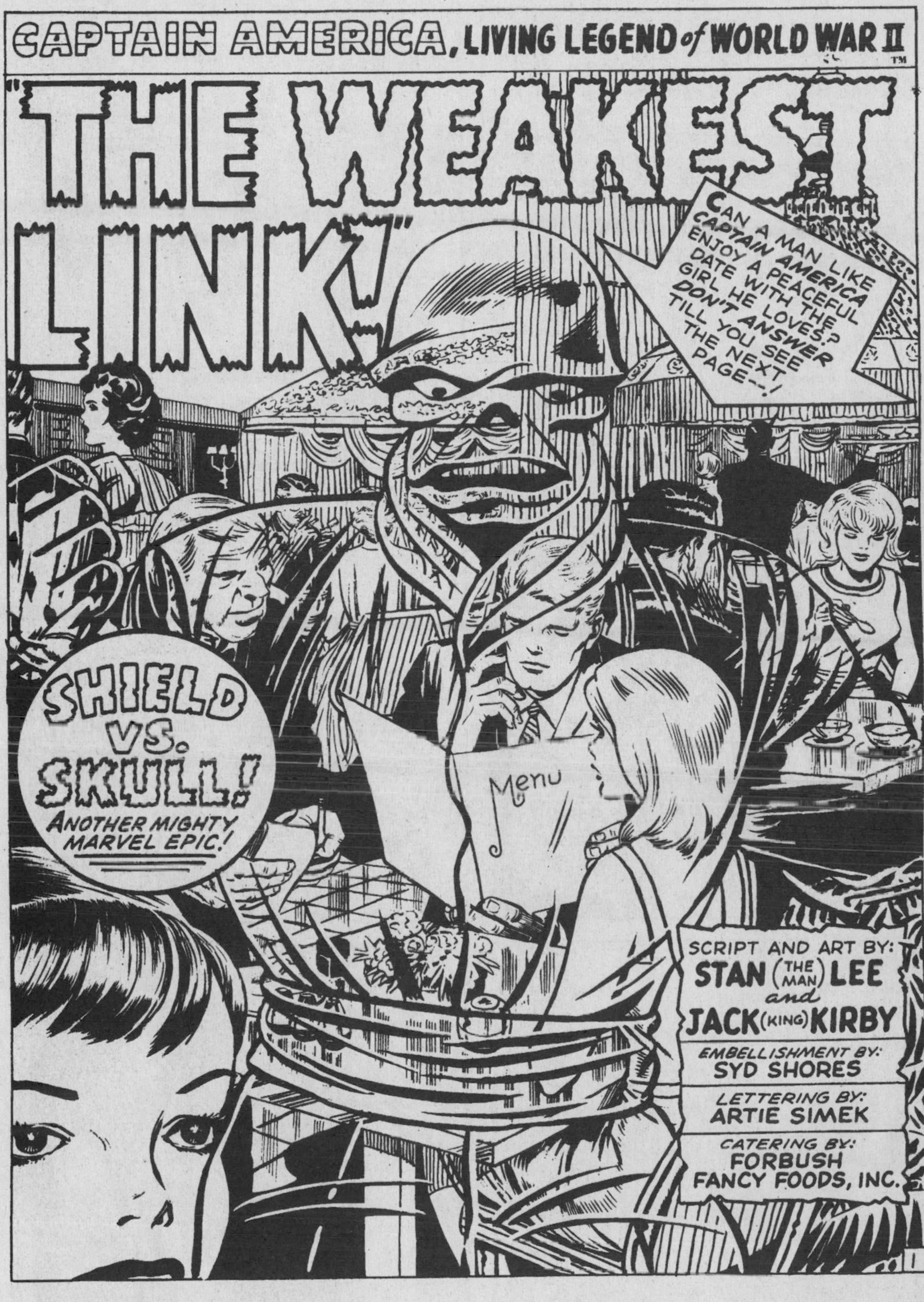
CAPTAIN AMERICA, LIVING LEGEND of WORLD WAR II
TM
"THE WEAKEST LINK!"
CAN A MAN LIKE CAPTAIN AMERICA ENJOY A PEACEFUL DATE WITH THE GIRL HE LOVES? DON'T ANSWER TILL YOU SEE THE NEXT PAGE--!
SHIELD VS. SKULL! ANOTHER MIGHTY MARVEL EPIC!
Menu
SCRIPT AND ART BY: STAN (THE MAN) LEE and JACK (KING) KIRBY
EMBELLISHMENT BY: SYD SHORES
LETTERING BY: ARTIE SIMEK
CATERING BY: FORBUSH FANCY FOODS, INC.
1

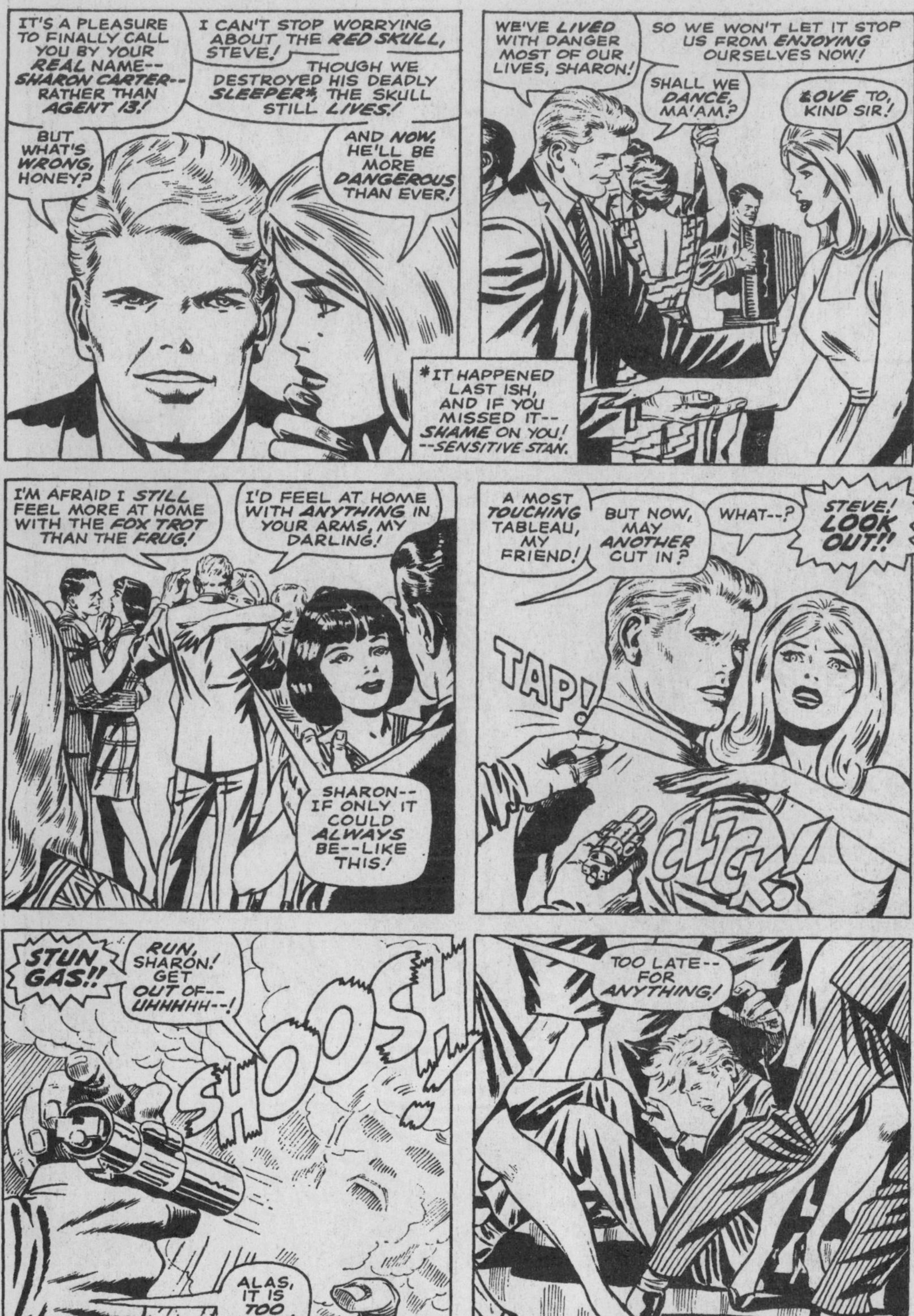
IT'S A PLEASURE TO FINALLY CALL YOU BY YOUR REAL NAME-- SHARON CARTER-- RATHER THAN AGENT 13!
I CAN'T STOP WORRYING ABOUT THE RED SKULL, STEVE!
THOUGH WE DESTROYED HIS DEADLY SLEEPER*, THE SKULL STILL LIVES!
BUT WHAT'S WRONG, HONEY?
AND NOW, HE'LL BE MORE DANGEROUS THAN EVER!
WE'VE LIVED WITH DANGER MOST OF OUR LIVES, SHARON!
SO WE WON'T LET IT STOP US FROM ENJOYING OURSELVES NOW!
SHALL WE DANCE, MA'AM?
LOVE TO, KIND SIR!
*IT HAPPENED LAST ISH, AND IF YOU MISSED IT-- SHAME ON YOU! --SENSITIVE STAN.
I'M AFRAID I STILL FEEL MORE AT HOME WITH THE FOX TROT THAN THE FRUG!
I'D FEEL AT HOME WITH ANYTHING IN YOUR ARMS, MY DARLING!
SHARON-- IF ONLY IT COULD ALWAYS BE--LIKE THIS!
A MOST TOUCHING TABLEAU, MY FRIEND!
BUT NOW, MAY ANOTHER CUT IN?
WHAT--?
STEVE! LOOK OUT!!
TAP!
CLICK!
STUN GAS!!
RUN, SHARON! GET OUT OF-- UHHHHH--!
SHOOOSH
ALAS, IT IS TOO LATE!
TOO LATE-- FOR ANYTHING!

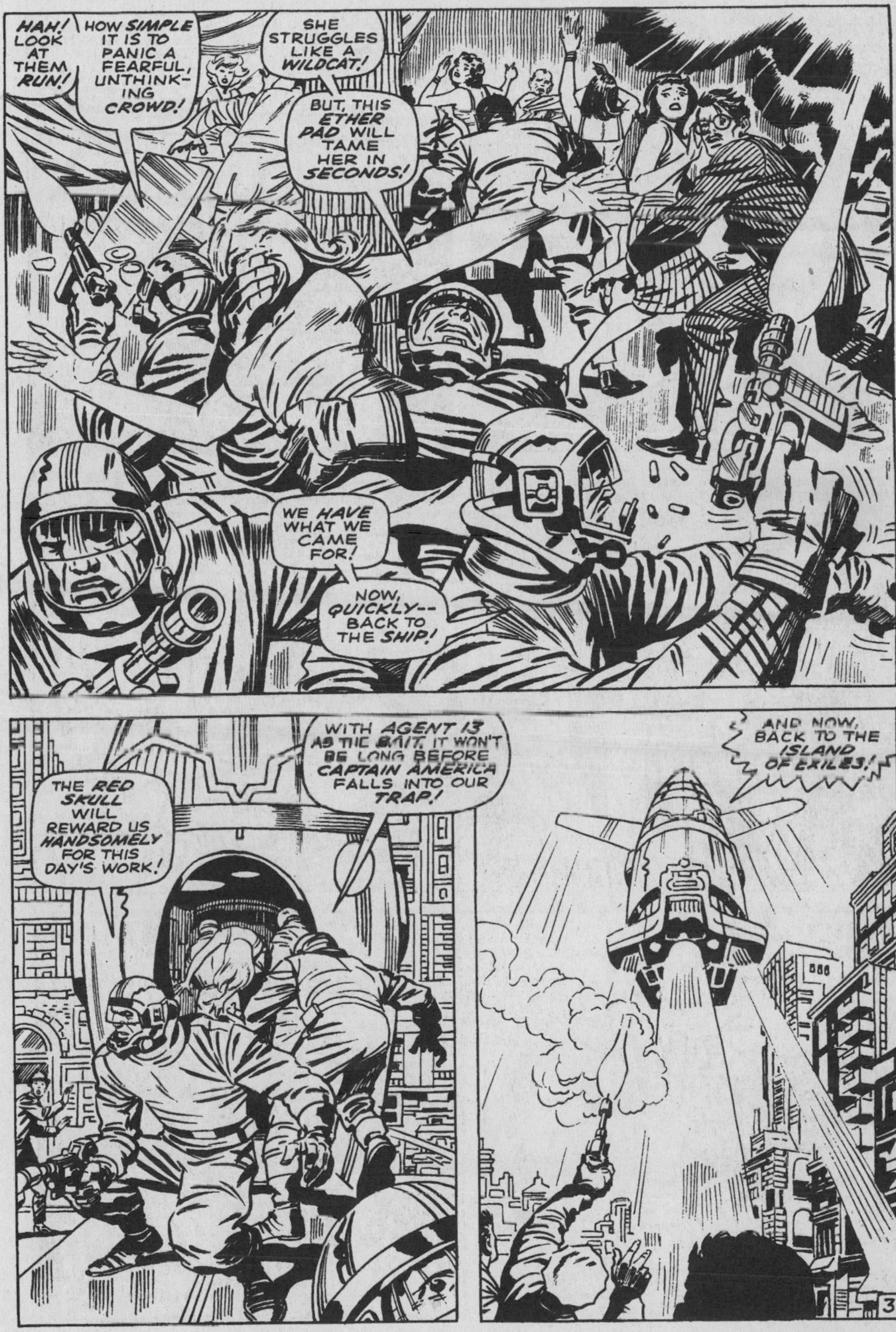
HAH! LOOK AT THEM RUN!
HOW SIMPLE IT IS TO PANIC A FEARFUL, UNTHINKING CROWD!
SHE STRUGGLES LIKE A WILDCAT!
BUT, THIS ETHER PAD WILL TAME HER IN SECONDS!
WE HAVE WHAT WE CAME FOR!
NOW, QUICKLY-- BACK TO THE SHIP!
THE RED SKULL WILL REWARD US HANDSOMELY FOR THIS DAY'S WORK!
WITH AGENT 13 AS THE BAIT, IT WON'T BE LONG BEFORE CAPTAIN AMERICA FALLS INTO OUR TRAP!
AND NOW, BACK TO THE ISLAND OF EXILES!
3

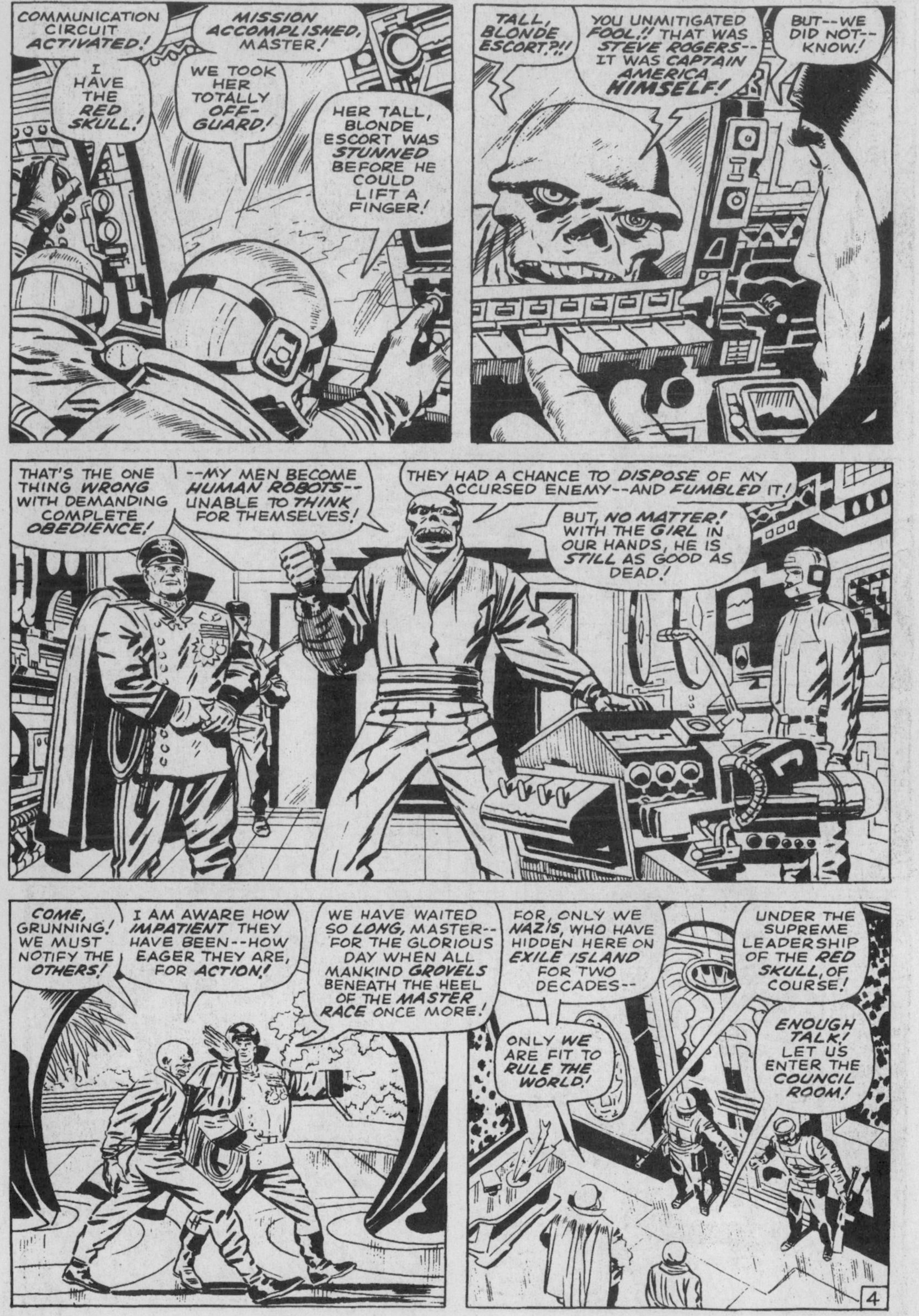

COMMUNICATION CIRCUIT ACTIVATED!
I HAVE THE RED SKULL!
MISSION ACCOMPLISHED, MASTER!
WE TOOK HER TOTALLY OFF-GUARD!
HER TALL, BLONDE ESCORT WAS STUNNED BEFORE HE COULD LIFT A FINGER!
TALL, BLONDE ESCORT?!!
YOU UNMITIGATED FOOL!! THAT WAS STEVE ROGERS-- IT WAS CAPTAIN AMERICA HIMSELF!
BUT--WE DID NOT--KNOW!
THAT'S THE ONE THING WRONG WITH DEMANDING COMPLETE OBEDIENCE!
--MY MEN BECOME HUMAN ROBOTS-- UNABLE TO THINK FOR THEMSELVES!
THEY HAD A CHANCE TO DISPOSE OF MY ACCURSED ENEMY--AND FUMBLED IT!
BUT, NO MATTER! WITH THE GIRL IN OUR HANDS, HE IS STILL AS GOOD AS DEAD!
COME, GRUNNING! WE MUST NOTIFY THE OTHERS!
I AM AWARE HOW IMPATIENT THEY HAVE BEEN--HOW EAGER THEY ARE, FOR ACTION!
WE HAVE WAITED SO LONG, MASTER-- FOR THE GLORIOUS DAY WHEN ALL MANKIND GROVELS BENEATH THE HEEL OF THE MASTER RACE ONCE MORE!
FOR, ONLY WE NAZIS, WHO HAVE HIDDEN HERE ON EXILE ISLAND FOR TWO DECADES--
ONLY WE ARE FIT TO RULE THE WORLD!
UNDER THE SUPREME LEADERSHIP OF THE RED SKULL, OF COURSE!
ENOUGH TALK! LET US ENTER THE COUNCIL ROOM!
4

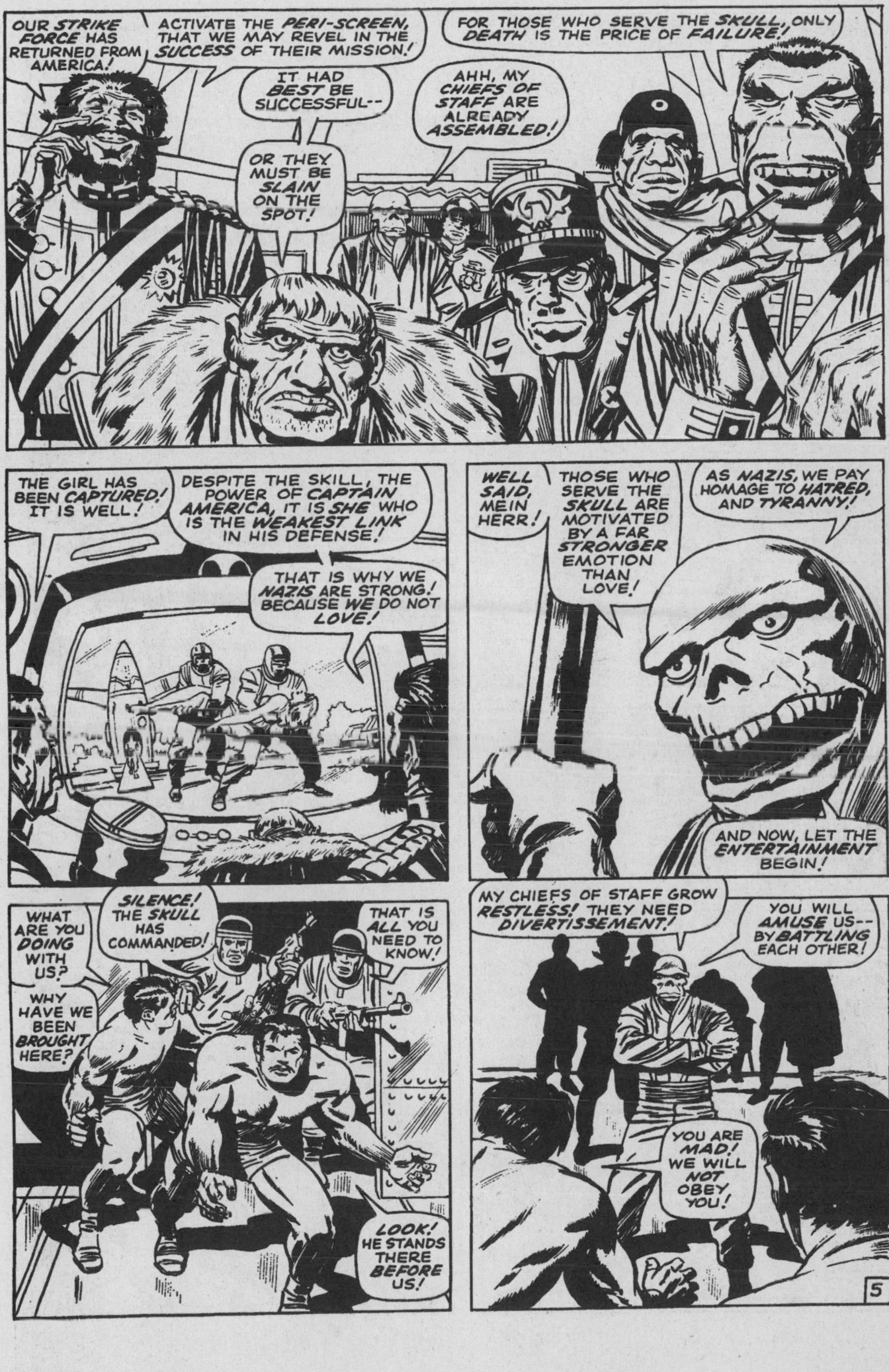
OUR STRIKE FORCE HAS RETURNED FROM AMERICA!
ACTIVATE THE PERI-SCREEN, THAT WE MAY REVEL IN THE SUCCESS OF THEIR MISSION!
FOR THOSE WHO SERVE THE SKULL, ONLY DEATH IS THE PRICE OF FAILURE!
IT HAD BEST BE SUCCESSFUL--
OR THEY MUST BE SLAIN ON THE SPOT!
AHH, MY CHIEFS OF STAFF ARE ALREADY ASSEMBLED!
THE GIRL HAS BEEN CAPTURED! IT IS WELL!
DESPITE THE SKILL, THE POWER OF CAPTAIN AMERICA, IT IS SHE WHO IS THE WEAKEST LINK IN HIS DEFENSE!
THAT IS WHY WE NAZIS ARE STRONG! BECAUSE WE DO NOT LOVE!
WELL SAID, MEIN HERR!
THOSE WHO SERVE THE SKULL ARE MOTIVATED BY A FAR STRONGER EMOTION THAN LOVE!
AS NAZIS, WE PAY HOMAGE TO HATRED, AND TYRANNY!
AND NOW, LET THE ENTERTAINMENT BEGIN!
WHAT ARE YOU DOING WITH US?
WHY HAVE WE BEEN BROUGHT HERE?
SILENCE! THE SKULL HAS COMMANDED!
THAT IS ALL YOU NEED TO KNOW!
LOOK! HE STANDS THERE BEFORE US!
MY CHIEFS OF STAFF GROW RESTLESS! THEY NEED DIVERTISSEMENT!
YOU WILL AMUSE US-- BY BATTLING EACH OTHER!
YOU ARE MAD! WE WILL NOT OBEY YOU!
5

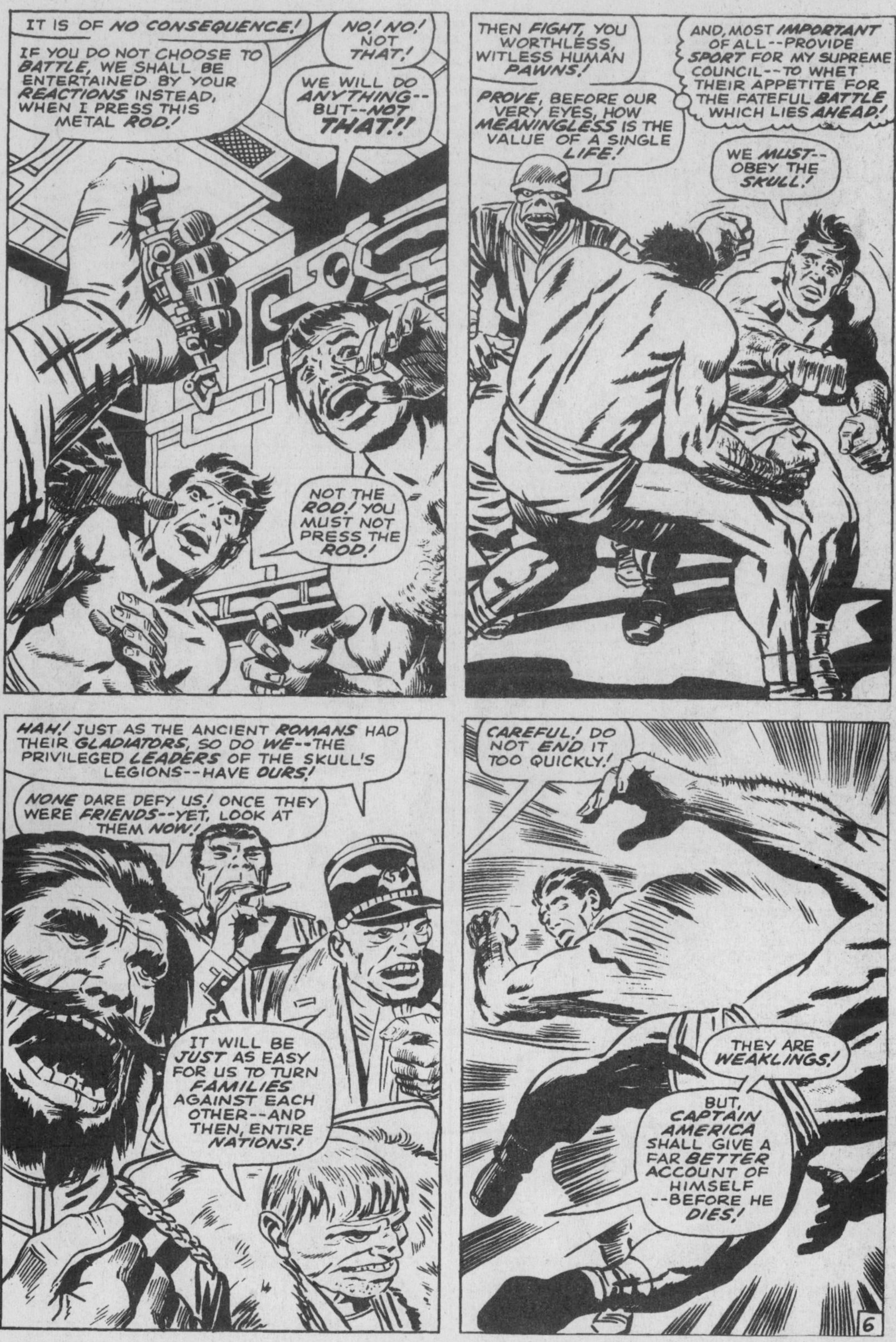
IT IS OF NO CONSEQUENCE!
IF YOU DO NOT CHOOSE TO BATTLE, WE SHALL BE ENTERTAINED BY YOUR REACTIONS INSTEAD, WHEN I PRESS THIS METAL ROD!
NO! NO! NOT THAT!
WE WILL DO ANYTHING-- BUT--NOT THAT!!
NOT THE ROD! YOU MUST NOT PRESS THE ROD!
THEN FIGHT, YOU WORTHLESS, WITLESS HUMAN PAWNS!
PROVE, BEFORE OUR VERY EYES, HOW MEANINGLESS IS THE VALUE OF A SINGLE LIFE!
AND, MOST IMPORTANT OF ALL--PROVIDE SPORT FOR MY SUPREME COUNCIL--TO WHET THEIR APPETITE FOR THE FATEFUL BATTLE WHICH LIES AHEAD!
WE MUST-- OBEY THE SKULL!
HAH! JUST AS THE ANCIENT ROMANS HAD THEIR GLADIATORS, SO DO WE--THE PRIVILEGED LEADERS OF THE SKULL'S LEGIONS--HAVE OURS!
NONE DARE DEFY US! ONCE THEY WERE FRIENDS--YET, LOOK AT THEM NOW!
IT WILL BE JUST AS EASY FOR US TO TURN FAMILIES AGAINST EACH OTHER--AND THEN, ENTIRE NATIONS!
CAREFUL! DO NOT END IT TOO QUICKLY!
THEY ARE WEAKLINGS!
BUT, CAPTAIN AMERICA SHALL GIVE A FAR BETTER ACCOUNT OF HIMSELF --BEFORE HE DIES!
6

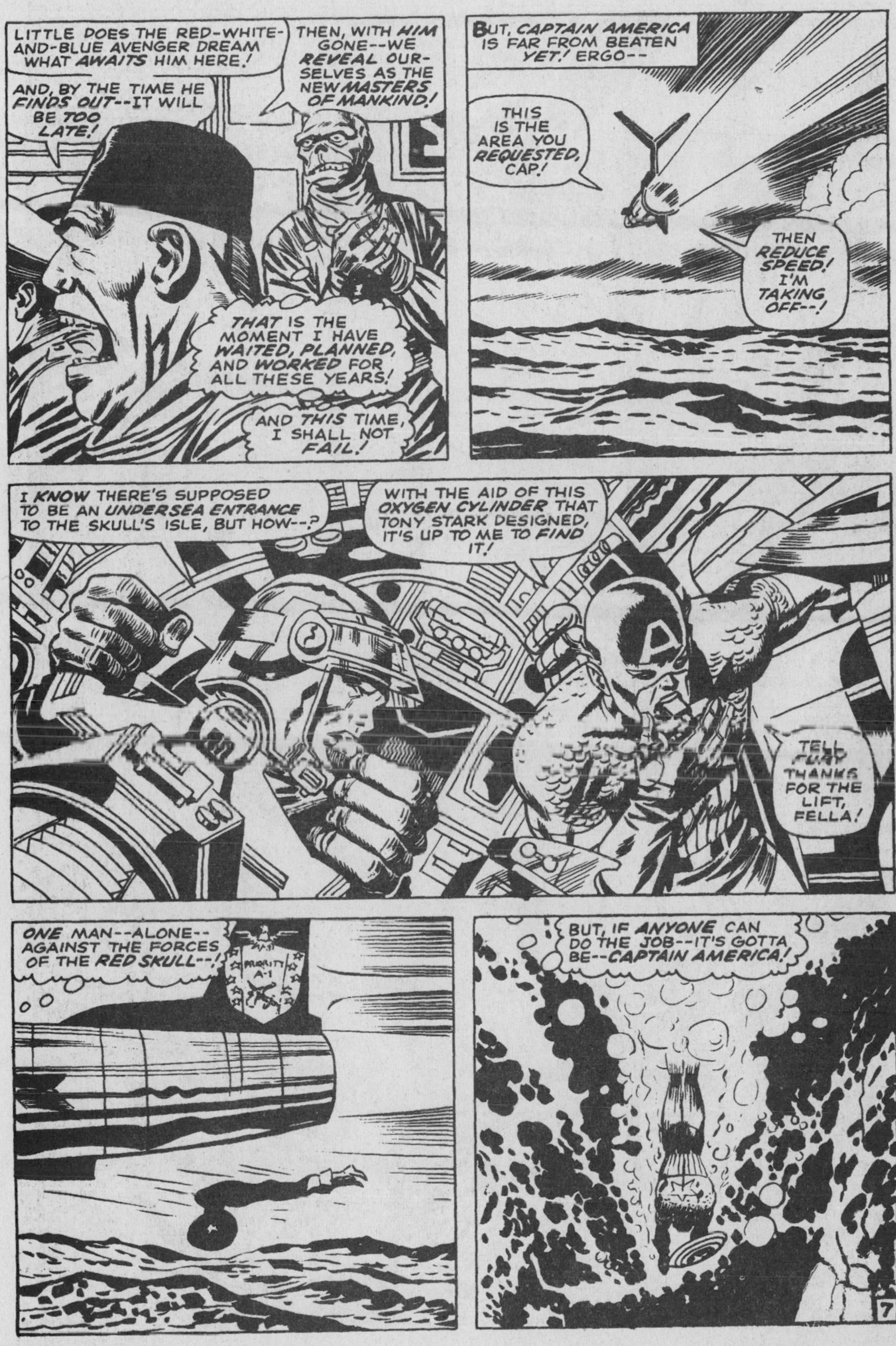
LITTLE DOES THE RED-WHITE-AND-BLUE AVENGER DREAM WHAT AWAITS HIM HERE!
AND, BY THE TIME HE FINDS OUT--IT WILL BE TOO LATE!
THEN, WITH HIM GONE--WE REVEAL OURSELVES AS THE NEW MASTERS OF MANKIND!
THAT IS THE MOMENT I HAVE WAITED, PLANNED, AND WORKED FOR ALL THESE YEARS!
AND THIS TIME, I SHALL NOT FAIL!
BUT, CAPTAIN AMERICA IS FAR FROM BEATEN YET! ERGO--
THIS IS THE AREA YOU REQUESTED, CAP!
THEN REDUCE SPEED! I'M TAKING OFF--!
I KNOW THERE'S SUPPOSED TO BE AN UNDERSEA ENTRANCE TO THE SKULL'S ISLE, BUT HOW--?
WITH THE AID OF THIS OXYGEN CYLINDER THAT TONY STARK DESIGNED, IT'S UP TO ME TO FIND IT!
TELL FURY THANKS FOR THE LIFT, FELLA!
ONE MAN--ALONE--AGAINST THE FORCES OF THE RED SKULL--!
PRIORITY A-1
BUT, IF ANYONE CAN DO THE JOB--IT'S GOTTA BE--CAPTAIN AMERICA!
7

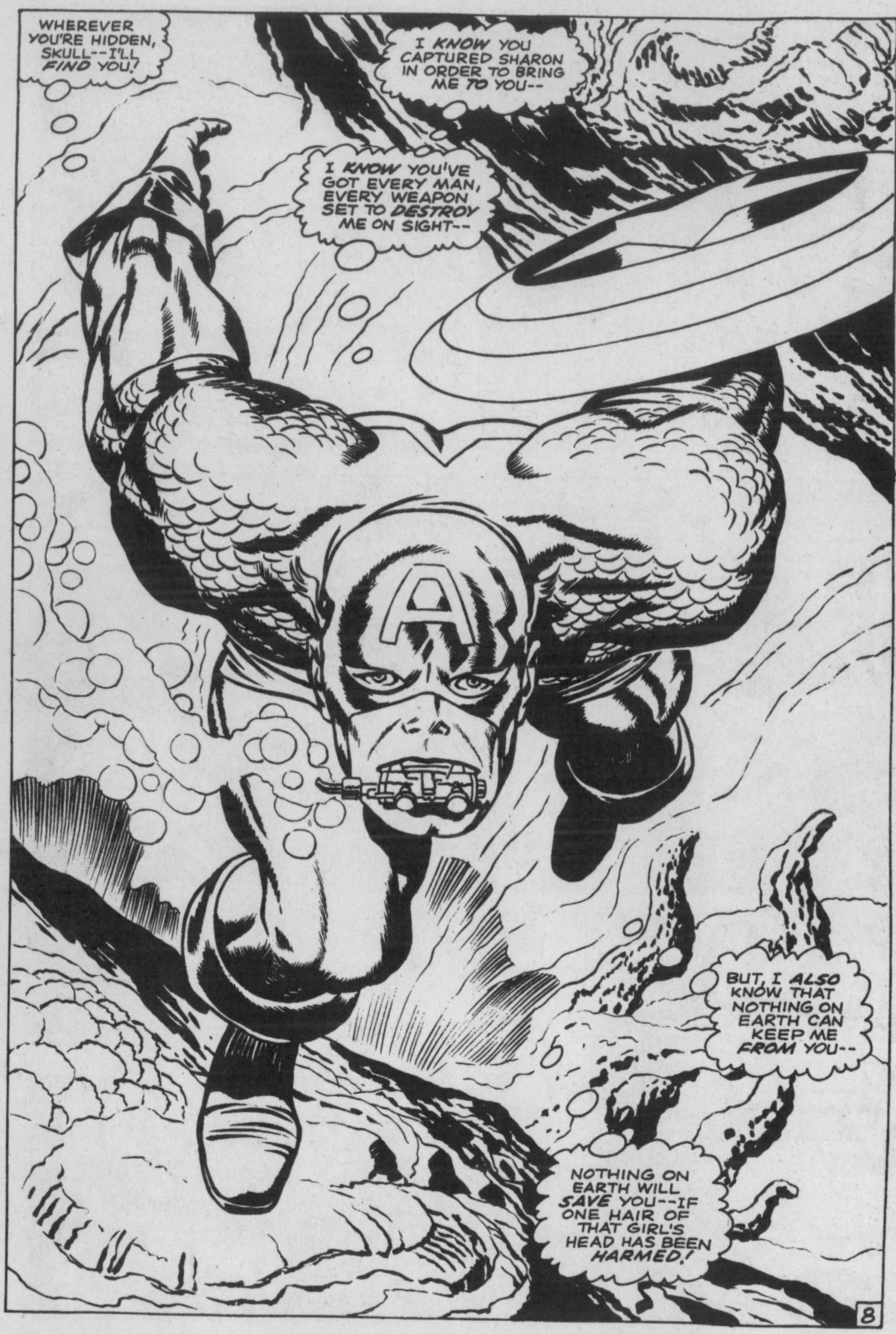
WHEREVER YOU'RE HIDDEN, SKULL--I'LL FIND YOU!
I KNOW YOU CAPTURED SHARON IN ORDER TO BRING ME TO YOU--
I KNOW YOU'VE GOT EVERY MAN, EVERY WEAPON SET TO DESTROY ME ON SIGHT--
BUT, I ALSO KNOW THAT NOTHING ON EARTH CAN KEEP ME FROM YOU--
NOTHING ON EARTH WILL SAVE YOU--IF ONE HAIR OF THAT GIRL'S HEAD HAS BEEN HARMED!
8

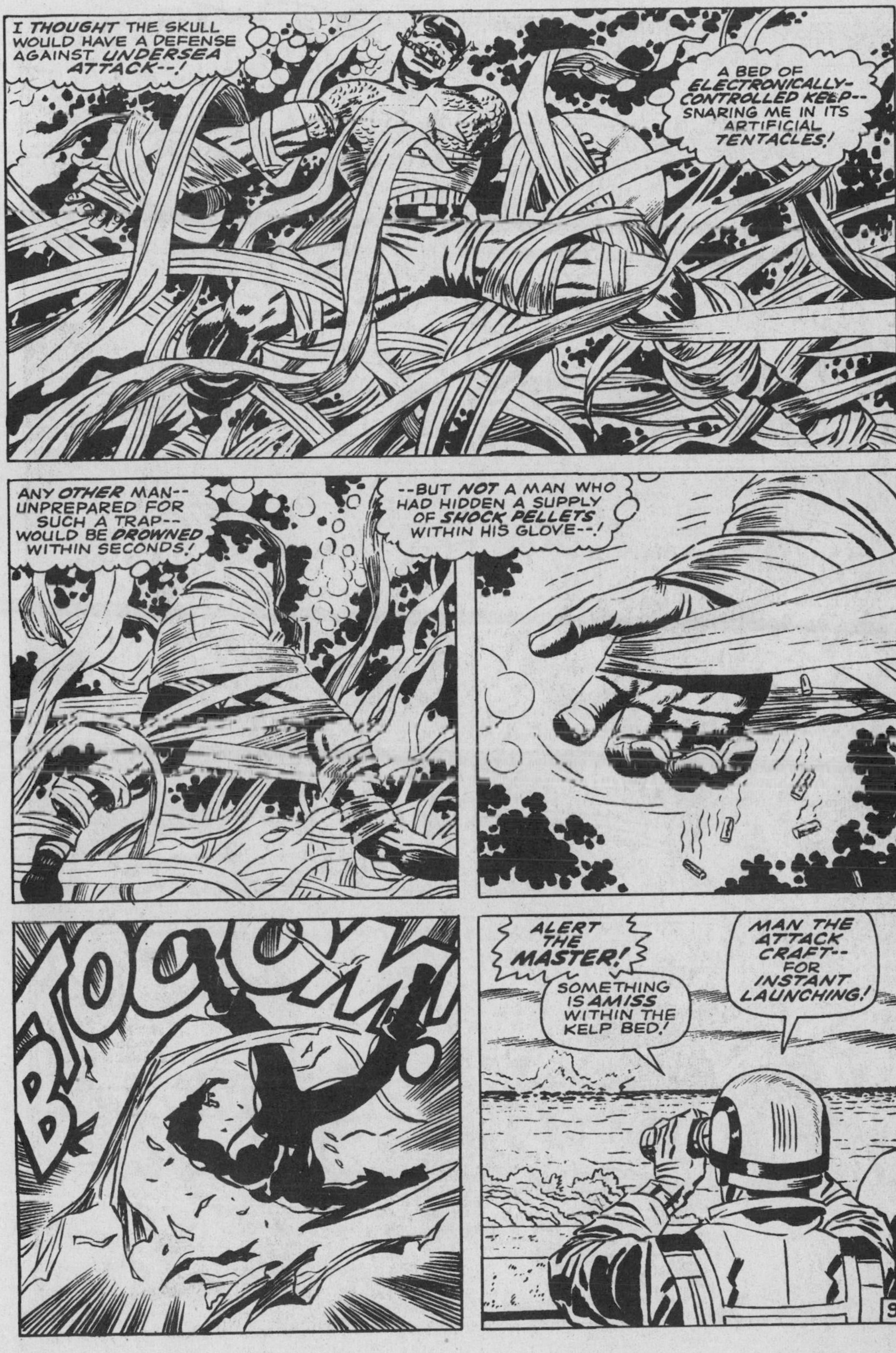
I THOUGHT THE SKULL WOULD HAVE A DEFENSE AGAINST UNDERSEA ATTACK--!
A BED OF ELECTRONICALLY-CONTROLLED KEEP--SNARING ME IN ITS ARTIFICIAL TENTACLES!
ANY OTHER MAN--UNPREPARED FOR SUCH A TRAP--WOULD BE DROWNED WITHIN SECONDS!
--BUT NOT A MAN WHO HAD HIDDEN A SUPPLY OF SHOCK PELLETS WITHIN HIS GLOVE--!
BOOOOM!
ALERT THE MASTER!
SOMETHING IS AMISS WITHIN THE KELP BED!
MAN THE ATTACK CRAFT--FOR INSTANT LAUNCHING!
9

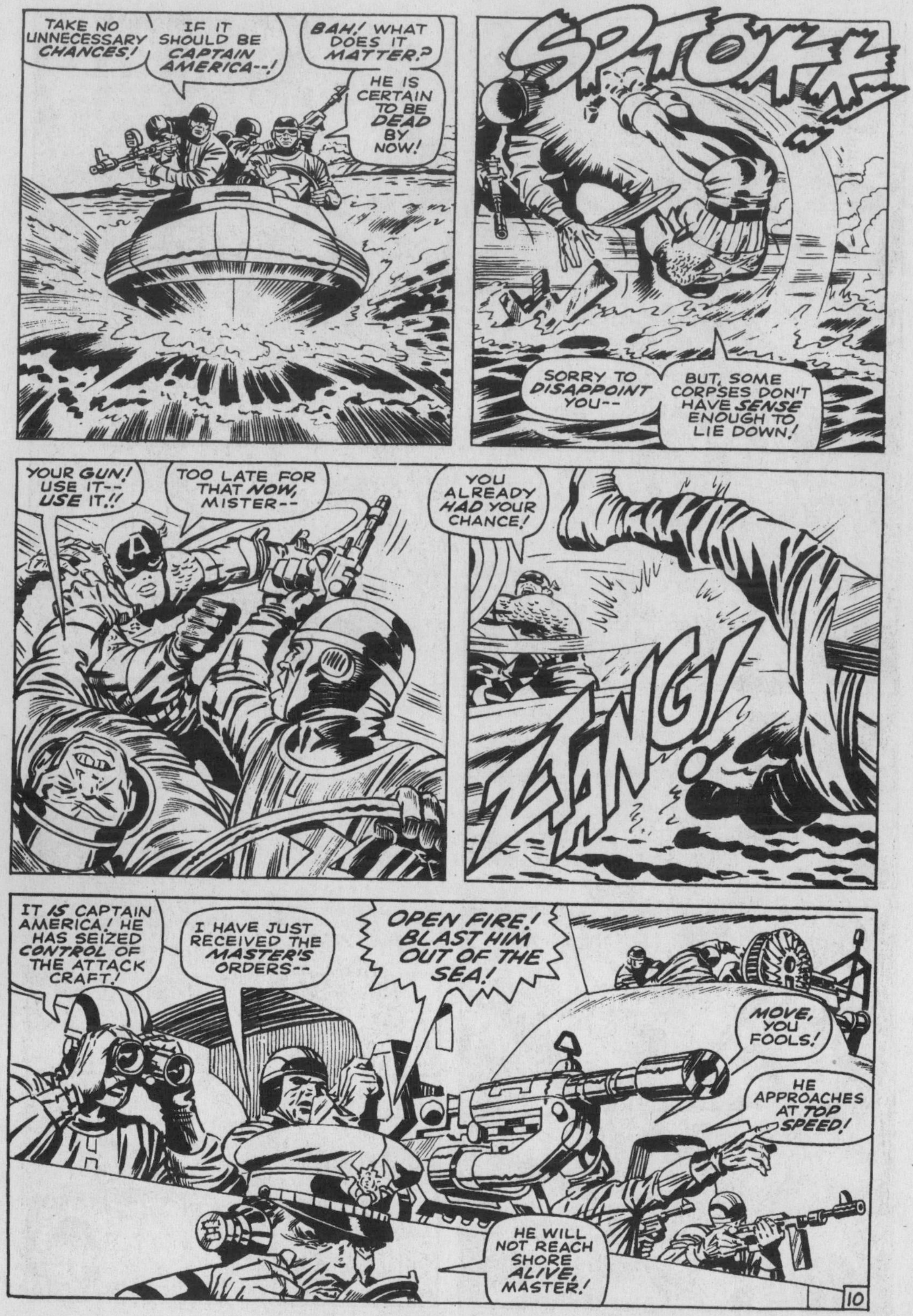
TAKE NO UNNECESSARY CHANCES!
IF IT SHOULD BE CAPTAIN AMERICA--!
BAH! WHAT DOES IT MATTER?
HE IS CERTAIN TO BE DEAD BY NOW!
SPTOKK
SORRY TO DISAPPOINT YOU--
BUT, SOME CORPSES DON'T HAVE SENSE ENOUGH TO LIE DOWN!
YOUR GUN! USE IT-- USE IT!!
TOO LATE FOR THAT NOW, MISTER--
YOU ALREADY HAD YOUR CHANCE!
ZANG!
IT IS CAPTAIN AMERICA! HE HAS SEIZED CONTROL OF THE ATTACK CRAFT!
I HAVE JUST RECEIVED THE MASTER'S ORDERS--
OPEN FIRE! BLAST HIM OUT OF THE SEA!
MOVE, YOU FOOLS!
HE APPROACHES AT TOP SPEED!
HE WILL NOT REACH SHORE ALIVE, MASTER!
10

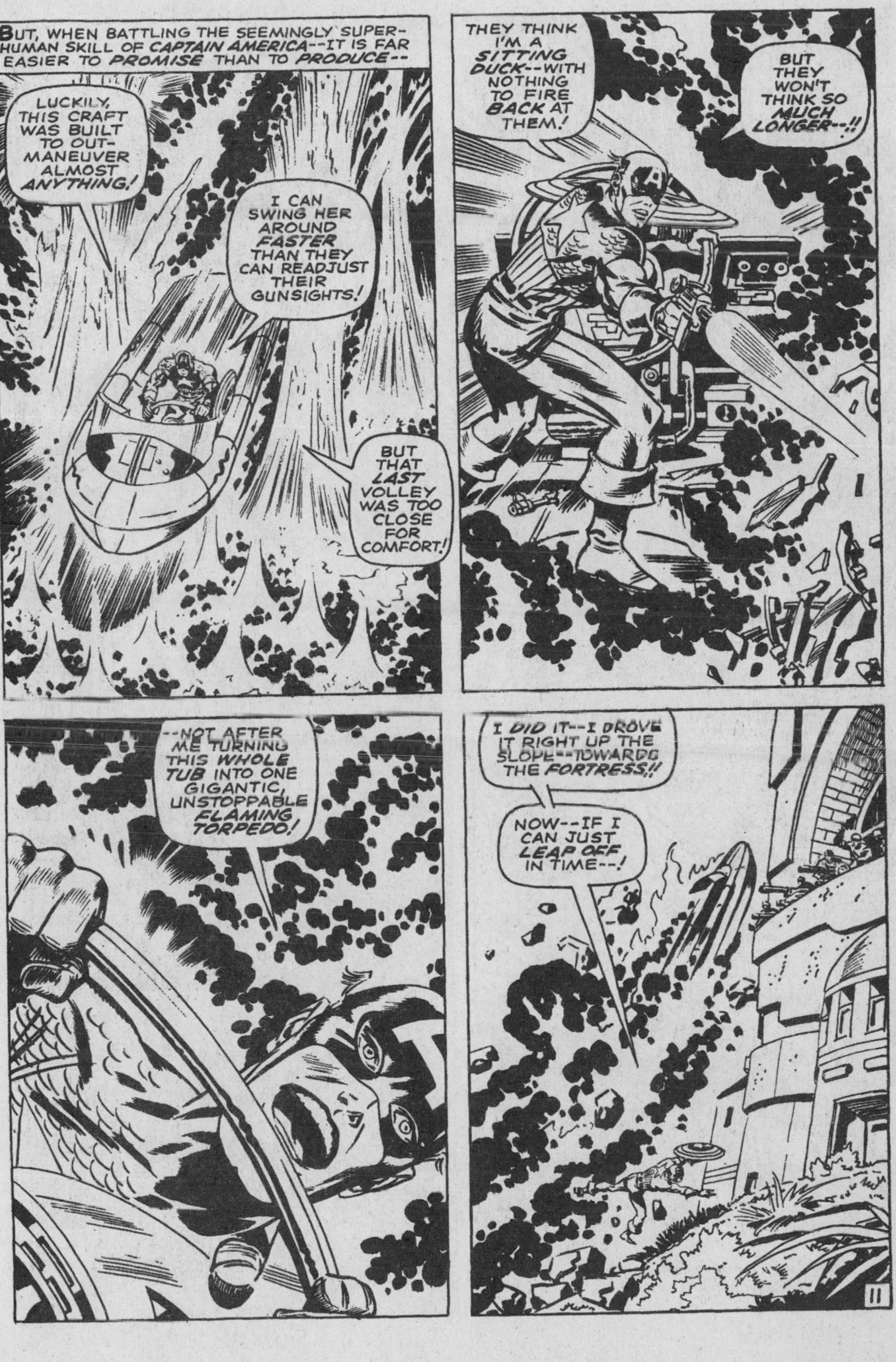

BUT, WHEN BATTLING THE SEEMINGLY SUPER-HUMAN SKILL OF CAPTAIN AMERICA--IT IS FAR EASIER TO PROMISE THAN TO PRODUCE--
LUCKILY, THIS CRAFT WAS BUILT TO OUT-MANEUVER ALMOST ANYTHING!
I CAN SWING HER AROUND FASTER THAN THEY CAN READJUST THEIR GUNSIGHTS!
BUT THAT LAST VOLLEY WAS TOO CLOSE FOR COMFORT!
THEY THINK I'M A SITTING DUCK--WITH NOTHING TO FIRE BACK AT THEM!
BUT THEY WON'T THINK SO MUCH LONGER--!!
--NOT AFTER ME TURNING THIS WHOLE TUB INTO ONE GIGANTIC, UNSTOPPABLE FLAMING TORPEDO!
I DID IT--I DROVE IT RIGHT UP THE SLOPE--TOWARDS THE FORTRESS!!
NOW--IF I CAN JUST LEAP OFF IN TIME--!

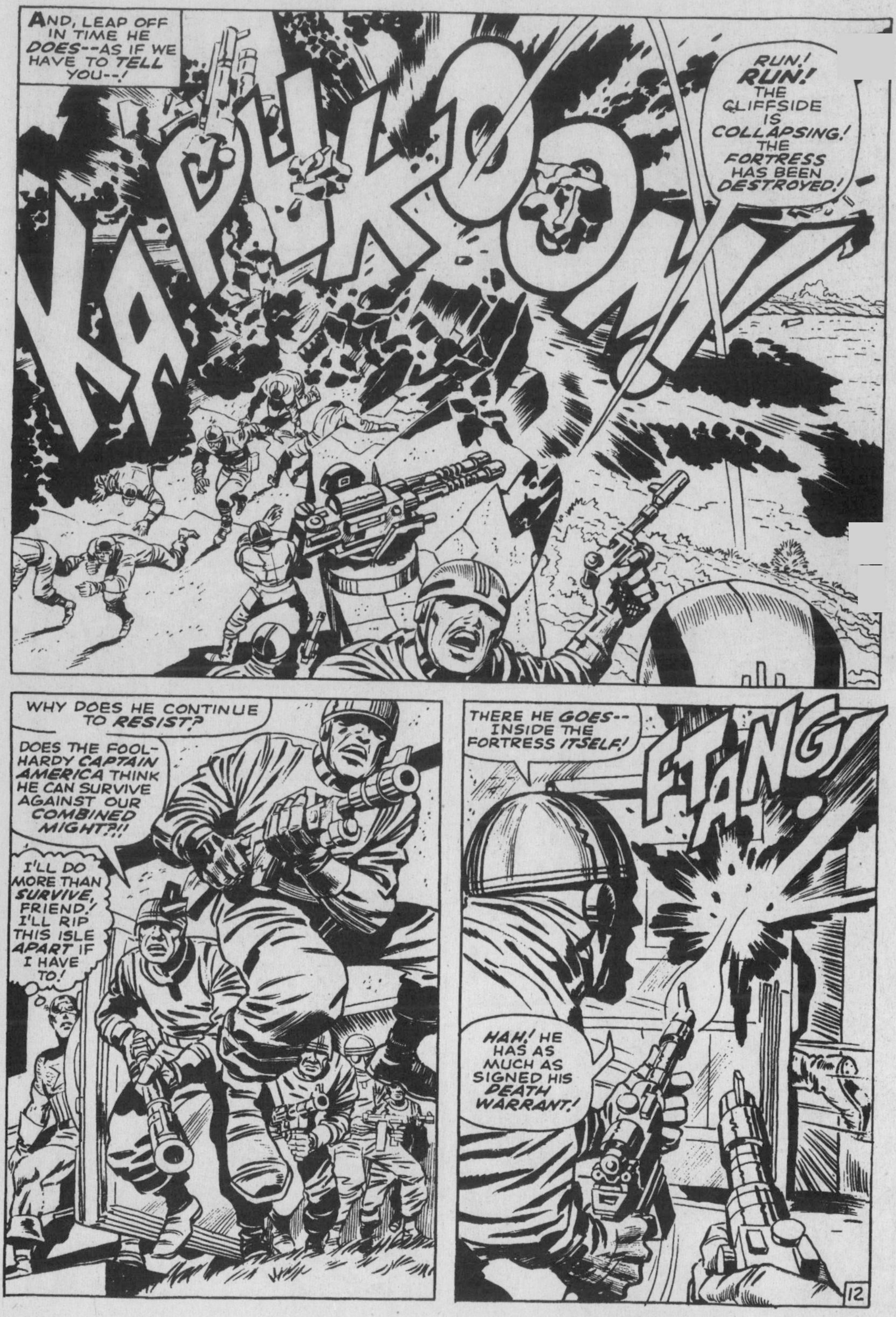
AND, LEAP OFF IN TIME HE DOES--AS IF WE HAVE TO TELL YOU--!
KA-PL-KOOM!
RUN! RUN! THE CLIFFSIDE IS COLLAPSING! THE FORTRESS HAS BEEN DESTROYED!
WHY DOES HE CONTINUE TO RESIST?
DOES THE FOOL-HARDY CAPTAIN AMERICA THINK HE CAN SURVIVE AGAINST OUR COMBINED MIGHT?!!
I'LL DO MORE THAN SURVIVE, FRIEND! I'LL RIP THIS ISLE APART IF I HAVE TO!
THERE HE GOES-- INSIDE THE FORTRESS ITSELF!
FTANG!
HAH! HE HAS AS MUCH AS SIGNED HIS DEATH WARRANT!
12

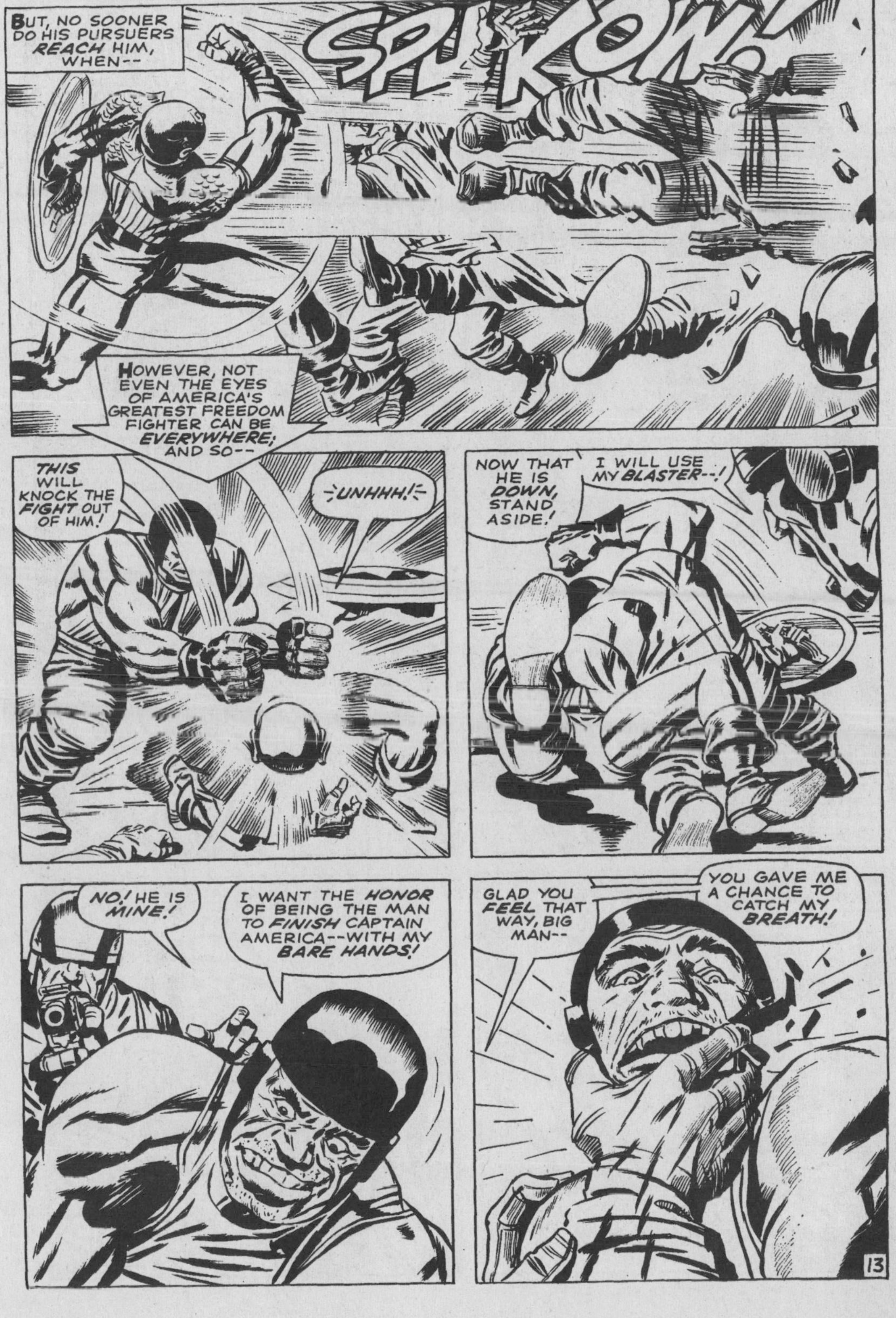
BUT, NO SOONER DO HIS PURSUERS REACH HIM, WHEN--
SPLKOW!
HOWEVER, NOT EVEN THE EYES OF AMERICA'S GREATEST FREEDOM FIGHTER CAN BE EVERYWHERE; AND SO--
THIS WILL KNOCK THE FIGHT OUT OF HIM!
UNHHH!
NOW THAT HE IS DOWN, STAND ASIDE!
I WILL USE MY BLASTER--!
NO! HE IS MINE!
I WANT THE HONOR OF BEING THE MAN TO FINISH CAPTAIN AMERICA--WITH MY BARE HANDS!
GLAD YOU FEEL THAT WAY, BIG MAN--
YOU GAVE ME A CHANCE TO CATCH MY BREATH!
13

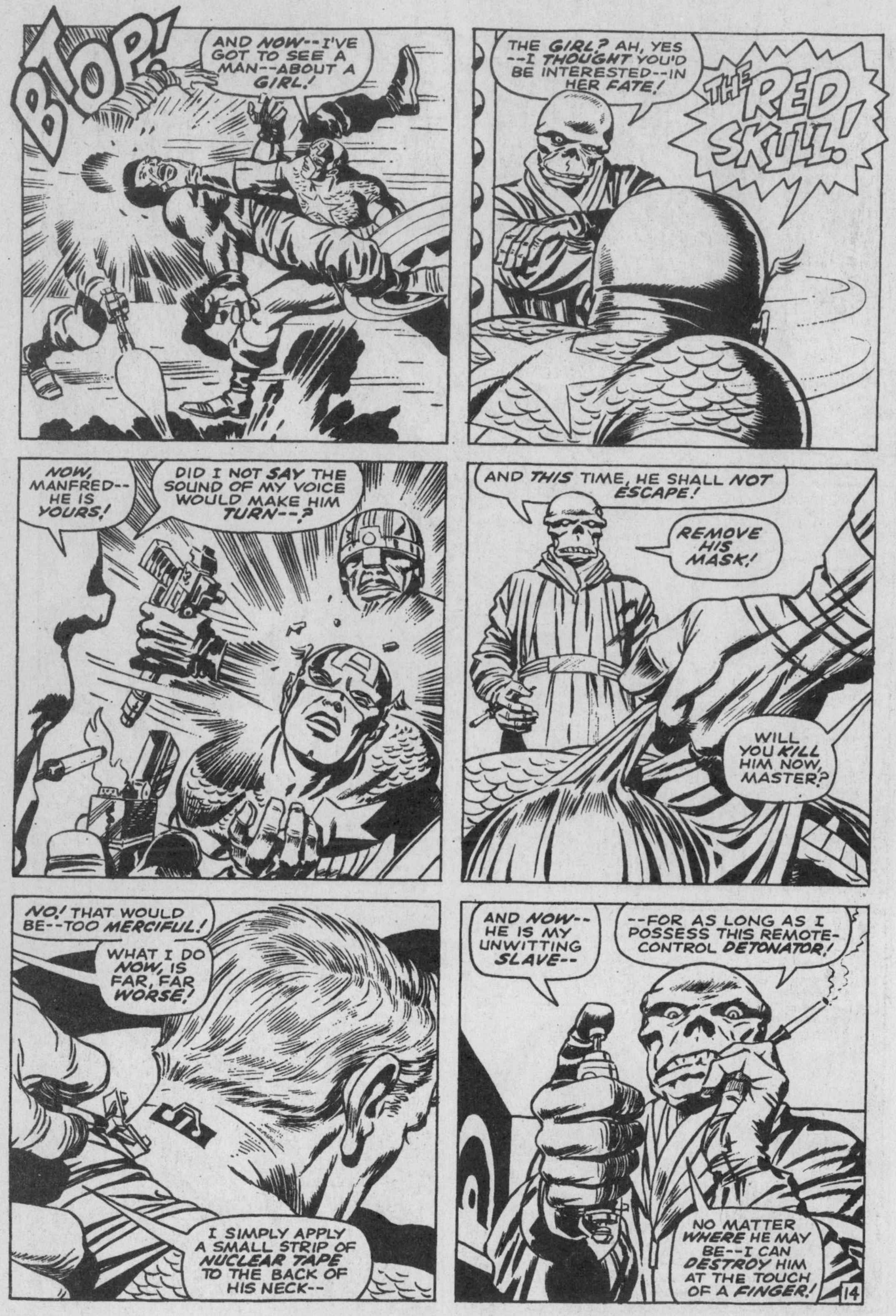
BTOP!
AND NOW--I'VE GOT TO SEE A MAN--ABOUT A GIRL!
THE GIRL? AH, YES --I THOUGHT YOU'D BE INTERESTED--IN HER FATE!
THE RED SKULL!
NOW, MANFRED--HE IS YOURS!
DID I NOT SAY THE SOUND OF MY VOICE WOULD MAKE HIM TURN--?
AND THIS TIME, HE SHALL NOT ESCAPE!
REMOVE HIS MASK!
WILL YOU KILL HIM NOW, MASTER?
NO! THAT WOULD BE--TOO MERCIFUL!
WHAT I DO NOW, IS FAR, FAR WORSE!
I SIMPLY APPLY A SMALL STRIP OF NUCLEAR TAPE TO THE BACK OF HIS NECK--
AND NOW--HE IS MY UNWITTING SLAVE--
--FOR AS LONG AS I POSSESS THIS REMOTE-CONTROL DETONATOR!
NO MATTER WHERE HE MAY BE--I CAN DESTROY HIM AT THE TOUCH OF A FINGER!
14

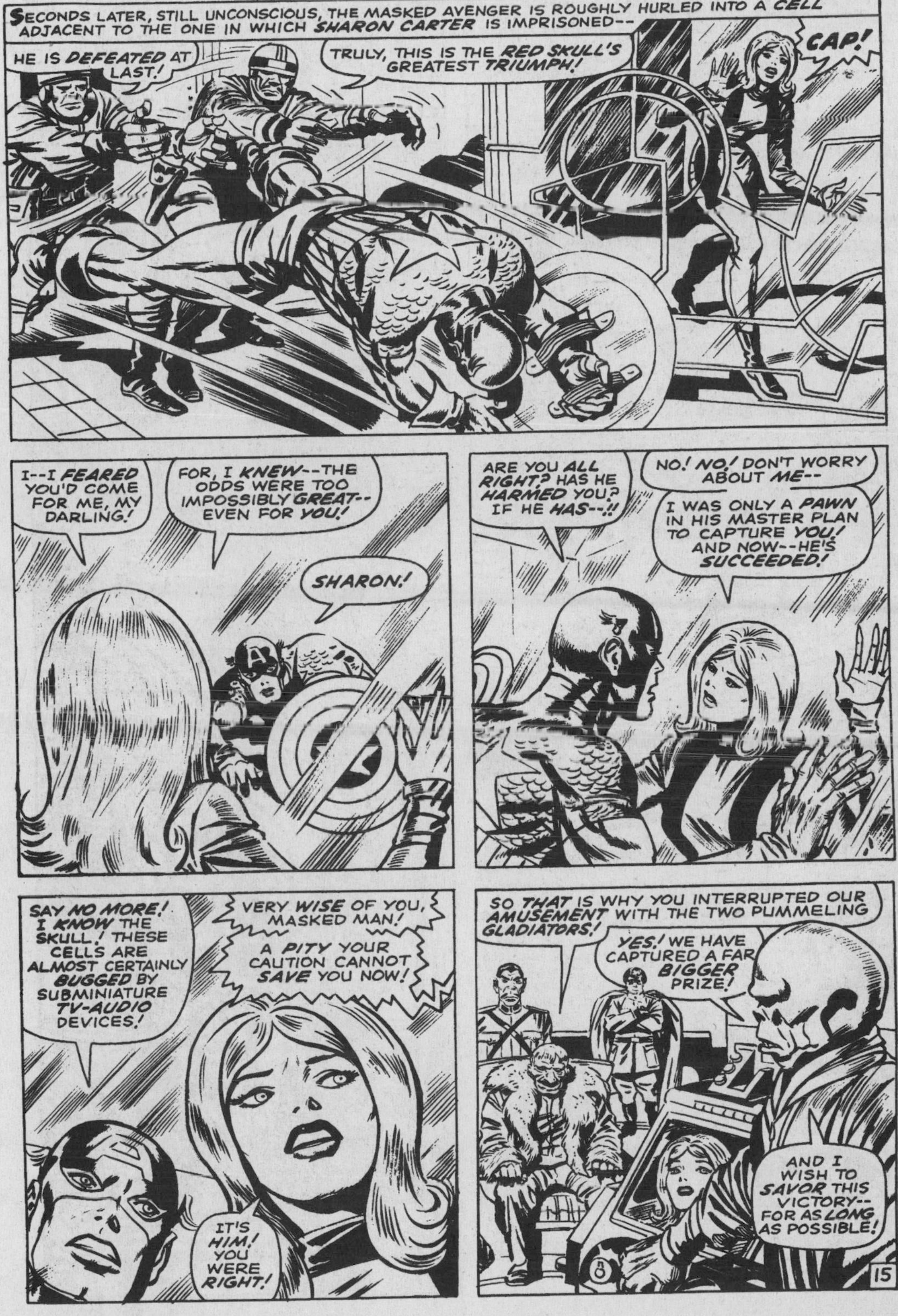
SECONDS LATER, STILL UNCONSCIOUS, THE MASKED AVENGER IS ROUGHLY HURLED INTO A CELL ADJACENT TO THE ONE IN WHICH SHARON CARTER IS IMPRISONED--
HE IS DEFEATED AT LAST!
TRULY, THIS IS THE RED SKULL'S GREATEST TRIUMPH!
CAP!
I--I FEARED YOU'D COME FOR ME, MY DARLING!
FOR, I KNEW--THE ODDS WERE TOO IMPOSSIBLY GREAT--EVEN FOR YOU!
SHARON!
ARE YOU ALL RIGHT? HAS HE HARMED YOU? IF HE HAS--!!
NO! NO! DON'T WORRY ABOUT ME--
I WAS ONLY A PAWN IN HIS MASTER PLAN TO CAPTURE YOU! AND NOW--HE'S SUCCEEDED!
SAY NO MORE! I KNOW THE SKULL! THESE CELLS ARE ALMOST CERTAINLY BUGGED BY SUBMINIATURE TV-AUDIO DEVICES!
VERY WISE OF YOU, MASKED MAN!
A PITY YOUR CAUTION CANNOT SAVE YOU NOW!
IT'S HIM! YOU WERE RIGHT!
SO THAT IS WHY YOU INTERRUPTED OUR AMUSEMENT WITH THE TWO PUMMELING GLADIATORS!
YES! WE HAVE CAPTURED A FAR BIGGER PRIZE!
AND I WISH TO SAVOR THIS VICTORY--FOR AS LONG AS POSSIBLE!
15

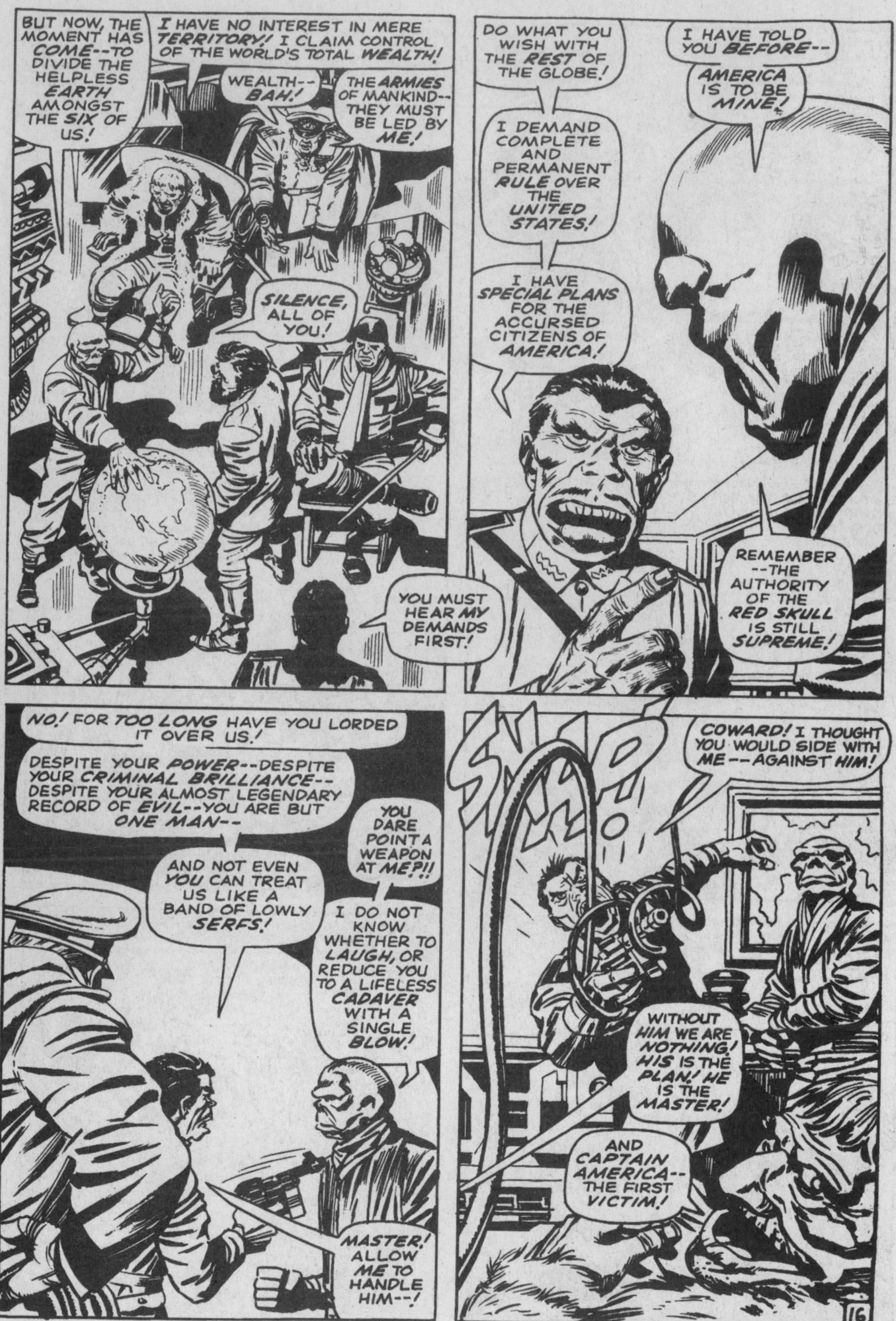

BUT NOW, THE MOMENT HAS COME--TO DIVIDE THE HELPLESS EARTH AMONGST THE SIX OF US!
I HAVE NO INTEREST IN MERE TERRITORY! I CLAIM CONTROL OF THE WORLD'S TOTAL WEALTH!
WEALTH-- BAH!
THE ARMIES OF MANKIND-- THEY MUST BE LED BY ME!
SILENCE, ALL OF YOU!
YOU MUST HEAR MY DEMANDS FIRST!
DO WHAT YOU WISH WITH THE REST OF THE GLOBE!
I DEMAND COMPLETE AND PERMANENT RULE OVER THE UNITED STATES!
I HAVE SPECIAL PLANS FOR THE ACCURSED CITIZENS OF AMERICA!
I HAVE TOLD YOU BEFORE--
AMERICA IS TO BE MINE!
REMEMBER --THE AUTHORITY OF THE RED SKULL IS STILL SUPREME!
NO! FOR TOO LONG HAVE YOU LORDED IT OVER US!
DESPITE YOUR POWER--DESPITE YOUR CRIMINAL BRILLIANCE-- DESPITE YOUR ALMOST LEGENDARY RECORD OF EVIL--YOU ARE BUT ONE MAN--
AND NOT EVEN YOU CAN TREAT US LIKE A BAND OF LOWLY SERFS!
YOU DARE POINT A WEAPON AT ME?!!
I DO NOT KNOW WHETHER TO LAUGH, OR REDUCE YOU TO A LIFELESS CADAVER WITH A SINGLE BLOW!
MASTER! ALLOW ME TO HANDLE HIM--!
SNAP!
COWARD! I THOUGHT YOU WOULD SIDE WITH ME -- AGAINST HIM!
WITHOUT HIM WE ARE NOTHING! HIS IS THE PLAN! HE IS THE MASTER!
AND CAPTAIN AMERICA-- THE FIRST VICTIM!
16

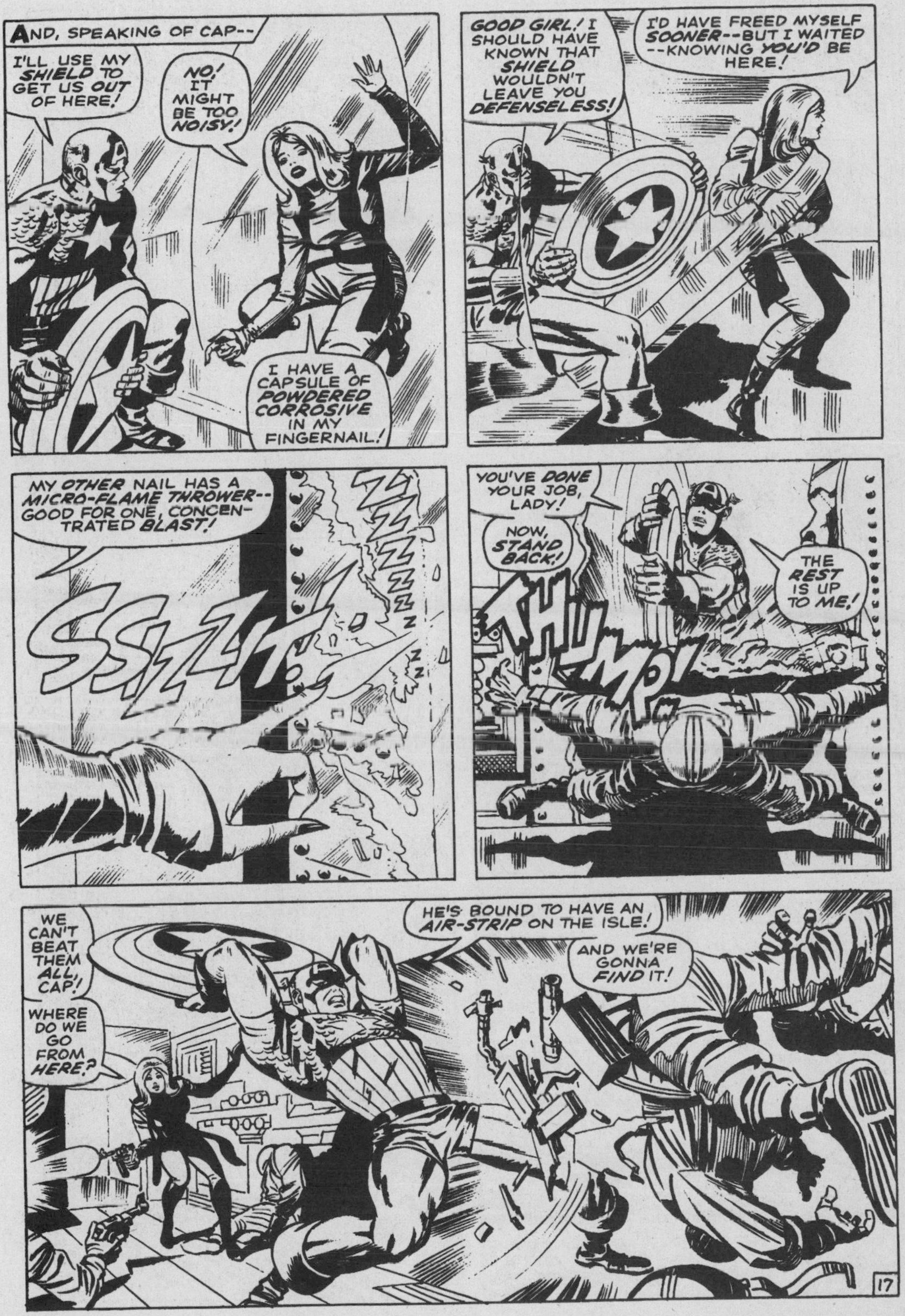
AND, SPEAKING OF CAP--
I'LL USE MY SHIELD TO GET US OUT OF HERE!
NO! IT MIGHT BE TOO NOISY!
I HAVE A CAPSULE OF POWDERED CORROSIVE IN MY FINGERNAIL!
GOOD GIRL! I SHOULD HAVE KNOWN THAT SHIELD WOULDN'T LEAVE YOU DEFENSELESS!
I'D HAVE FREED MYSELF SOONER--BUT I WAITED --KNOWING YOU'D BE HERE!
MY OTHER NAIL HAS A MICRO-FLAME THROWER-- GOOD FOR ONE, CONCENTRATED BLAST!
ZZZZZZZZ
SSZZZT!
YOU'VE DONE YOUR JOB, LADY!
NOW, STAND BACK!
THE REST IS UP TO ME!
THUMP!
WE CAN'T BEAT THEM ALL, CAP!
WHERE DO WE GO FROM HERE?
HE'S BOUND TO HAVE AN AIR-STRIP ON THE ISLE!
AND WE'RE GONNA FIND IT!
17

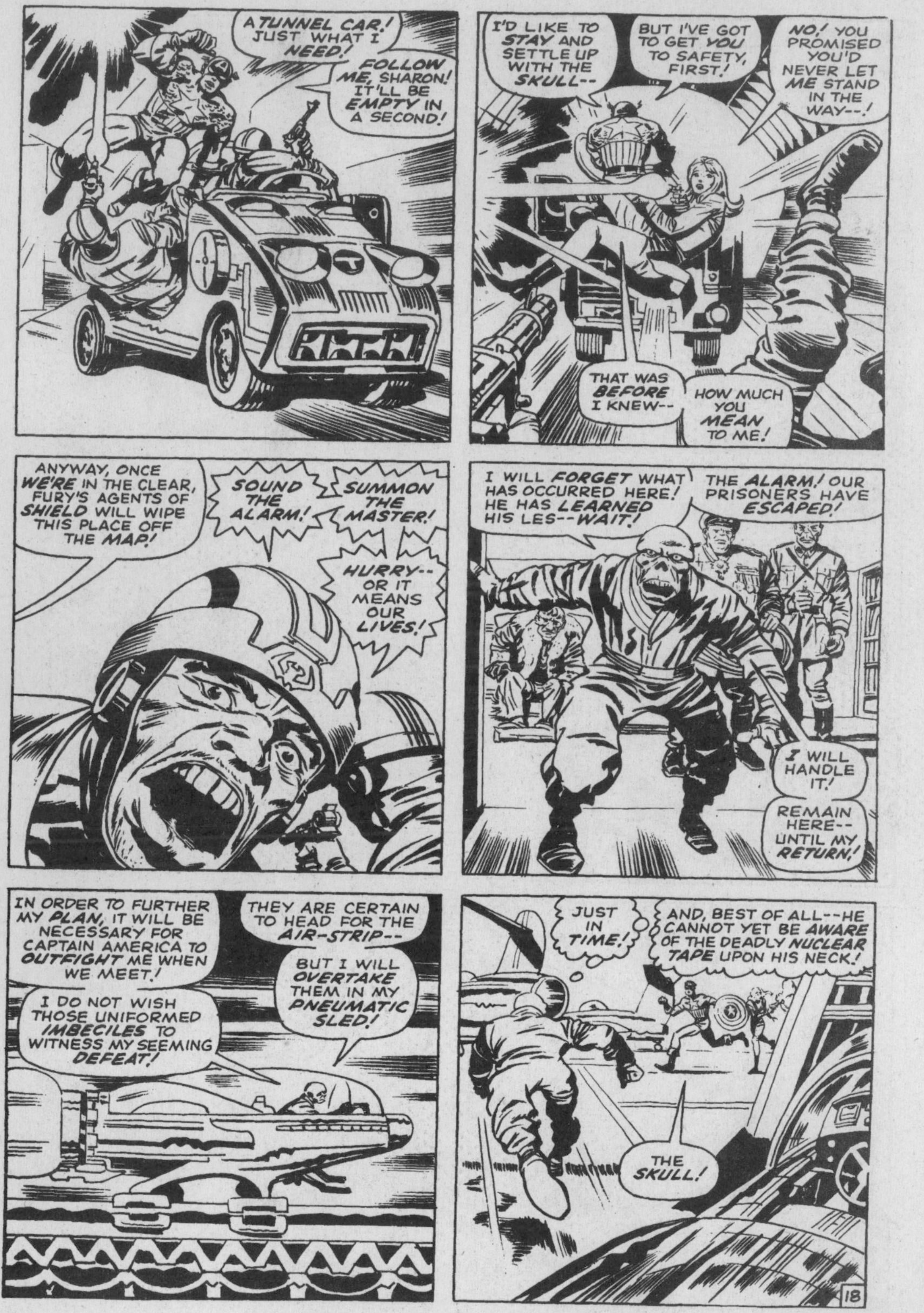
A TUNNEL CAR! JUST WHAT I NEED!
FOLLOW ME, SHARON! IT'LL BE EMPTY IN A SECOND!
I'D LIKE TO STAY AND SETTLE UP WITH THE SKULL--
BUT I'VE GOT TO GET YOU TO SAFETY, FIRST!
NO! YOU PROMISED YOU'D NEVER LET ME STAND IN THE WAY--!
THAT WAS BEFORE I KNEW--
HOW MUCH YOU MEAN TO ME!
ANYWAY, ONCE WE'RE IN THE CLEAR, FURY'S AGENTS OF SHIELD WILL WIPE THIS PLACE OFF THE MAP!
SOUND THE ALARM!
SUMMON THE MASTER!
HURRY-- OR IT MEANS OUR LIVES!
I WILL FORGET WHAT HAS OCCURRED HERE! HE HAS LEARNED HIS LES-- WAIT!
THE ALARM! OUR PRISONERS HAVE ESCAPED!
I WILL HANDLE IT!
REMAIN HERE-- UNTIL MY RETURN!
IN ORDER TO FURTHER MY PLAN, IT WILL BE NECESSARY FOR CAPTAIN AMERICA TO OUTFIGHT ME WHEN WE MEET!
I DO NOT WISH THOSE UNIFORMED IMBECILES TO WITNESS MY SEEMING DEFEAT!
THEY ARE CERTAIN TO HEAD FOR THE AIR-STRIP--
BUT I WILL OVERTAKE THEM IN MY PNEUMATIC SLED!
JUST IN TIME!
AND, BEST OF ALL--HE CANNOT YET BE AWARE OF THE DEADLY NUCLEAR TAPE UPON HIS NECK!
THE SKULL!
18

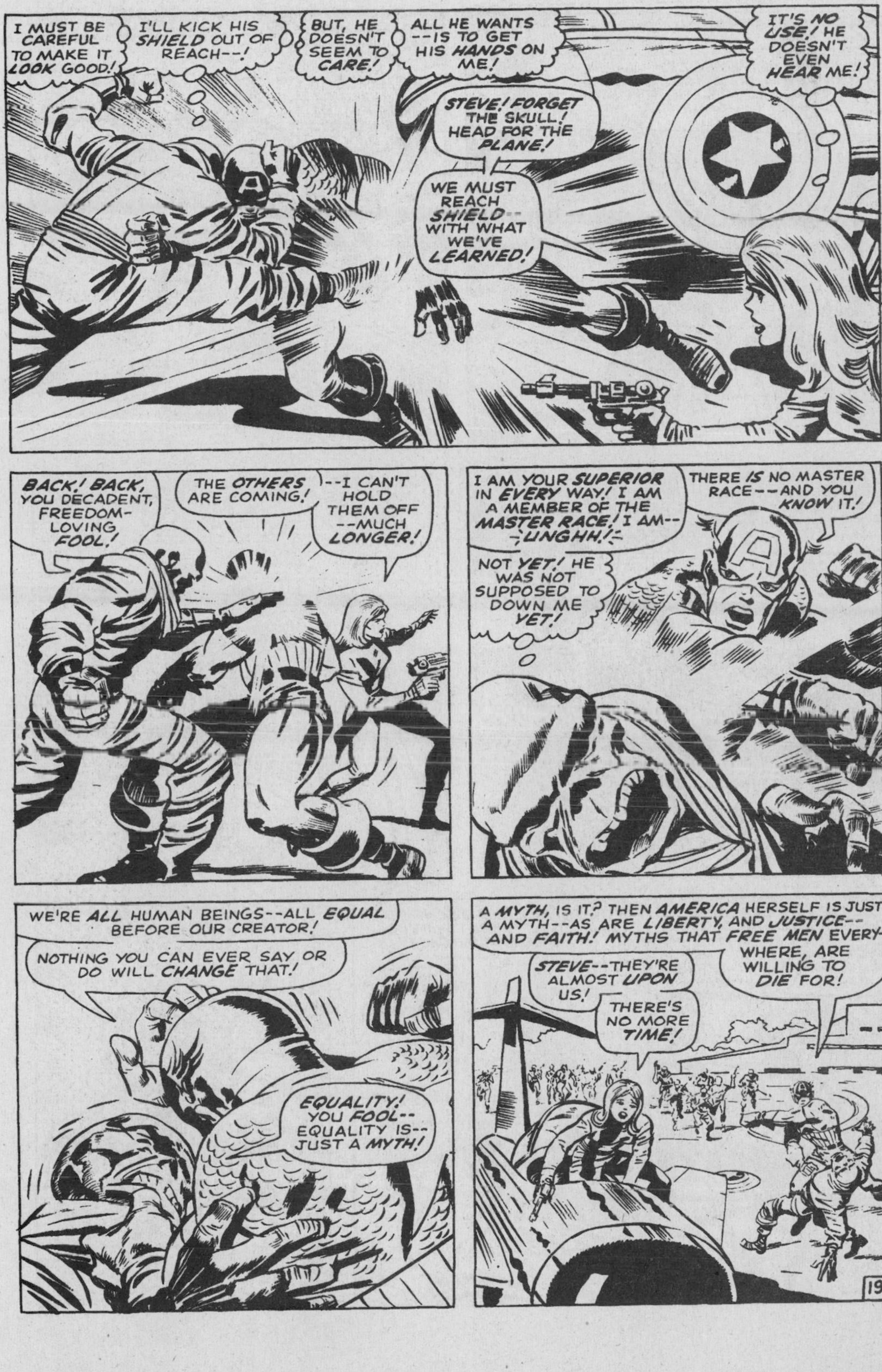

I MUST BE CAREFUL TO MAKE IT LOOK GOOD!
I'LL KICK HIS SHIELD OUT OF REACH--!
BUT, HE DOESN'T SEEM TO CARE!
ALL HE WANTS --IS TO GET HIS HANDS ON ME!
IT'S NO USE! HE DOESN'T EVEN HEAR ME!
STEVE! FORGET THE SKULL! HEAD FOR THE PLANE!
WE MUST REACH SHIELD-- WITH WHAT WE'VE LEARNED!
BACK! BACK, YOU DECADENT, FREEDOM-LOVING FOOL!
THE OTHERS ARE COMING!
--I CAN'T HOLD THEM OFF --MUCH LONGER!
I AM YOUR SUPERIOR IN EVERY WAY! I AM A MEMBER OF THE MASTER RACE! I AM-- --UNGHH!
THERE IS NO MASTER RACE--AND YOU KNOW IT!
NOT YET! HE WAS NOT SUPPOSED TO DOWN ME YET!
WE'RE ALL HUMAN BEINGS--ALL EQUAL BEFORE OUR CREATOR!
NOTHING YOU CAN EVER SAY OR DO WILL CHANGE THAT!
EQUALITY! YOU FOOL-- EQUALITY IS-- JUST A MYTH!
A MYTH, IS IT? THEN AMERICA HERSELF IS JUST A MYTH--AS ARE LIBERTY, AND JUSTICE-- AND FAITH! MYTHS THAT FREE MEN EVERY-WHERE, ARE WILLING TO DIE FOR!
STEVE--THEY'RE ALMOST UPON US!
THERE'S NO MORE TIME!
19

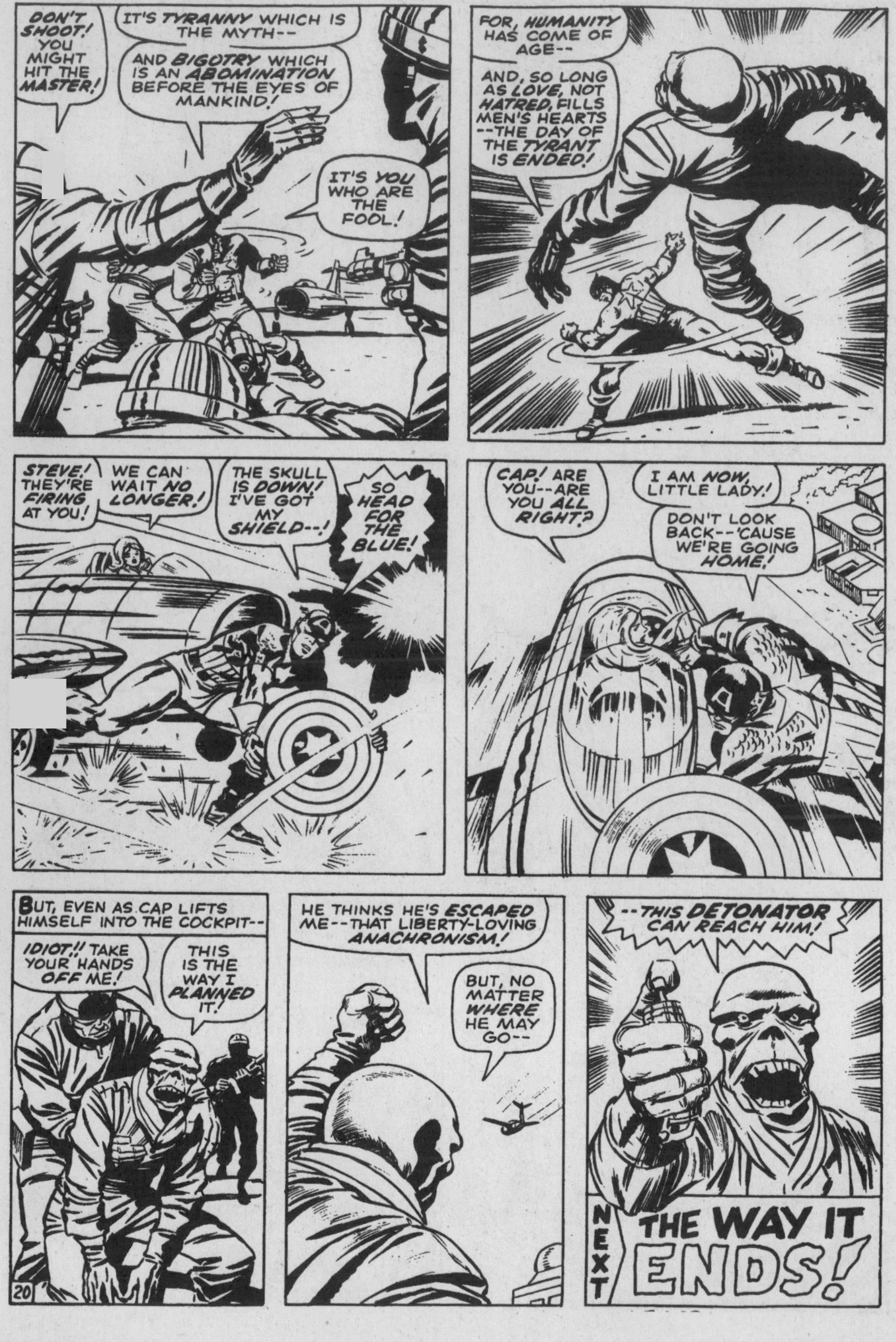
DON'T SHOOT! YOU MIGHT HIT THE MASTER!
IT'S TYRANNY WHICH IS THE MYTH--
AND BIGOTRY WHICH IS AN ABOMINATION BEFORE THE EYES OF MANKIND!
IT'S YOU WHO ARE THE FOOL!
FOR, HUMANITY HAS COME OF AGE--
AND, SO LONG AS LOVE, NOT HATRED, FILLS MEN'S HEARTS --THE DAY OF THE TYRANT IS ENDED!
STEVE! THEY'RE FIRING AT YOU!
WE CAN WAIT NO LONGER!
THE SKULL IS DOWN! I'VE GOT MY SHIELD--!
SO HEAD FOR THE BLUE!
CAP! ARE YOU--ARE YOU ALL RIGHT?
I AM NOW, LITTLE LADY!
DON'T LOOK BACK--'CAUSE WE'RE GOING HOME!
BUT, EVEN AS CAP LIFTS HIMSELF INTO THE COCKPIT--
IDIOT!! TAKE YOUR HANDS OFF ME!
THIS IS THE WAY I PLANNED IT!
HE THINKS HE'S ESCAPED ME--THAT LIBERTY-LOVING ANACHRONISM!
BUT, NO MATTER WHERE HE MAY GO--
--THIS DETONATOR CAN REACH HIM!
NEXT
THE WAY IT ENDS!
20

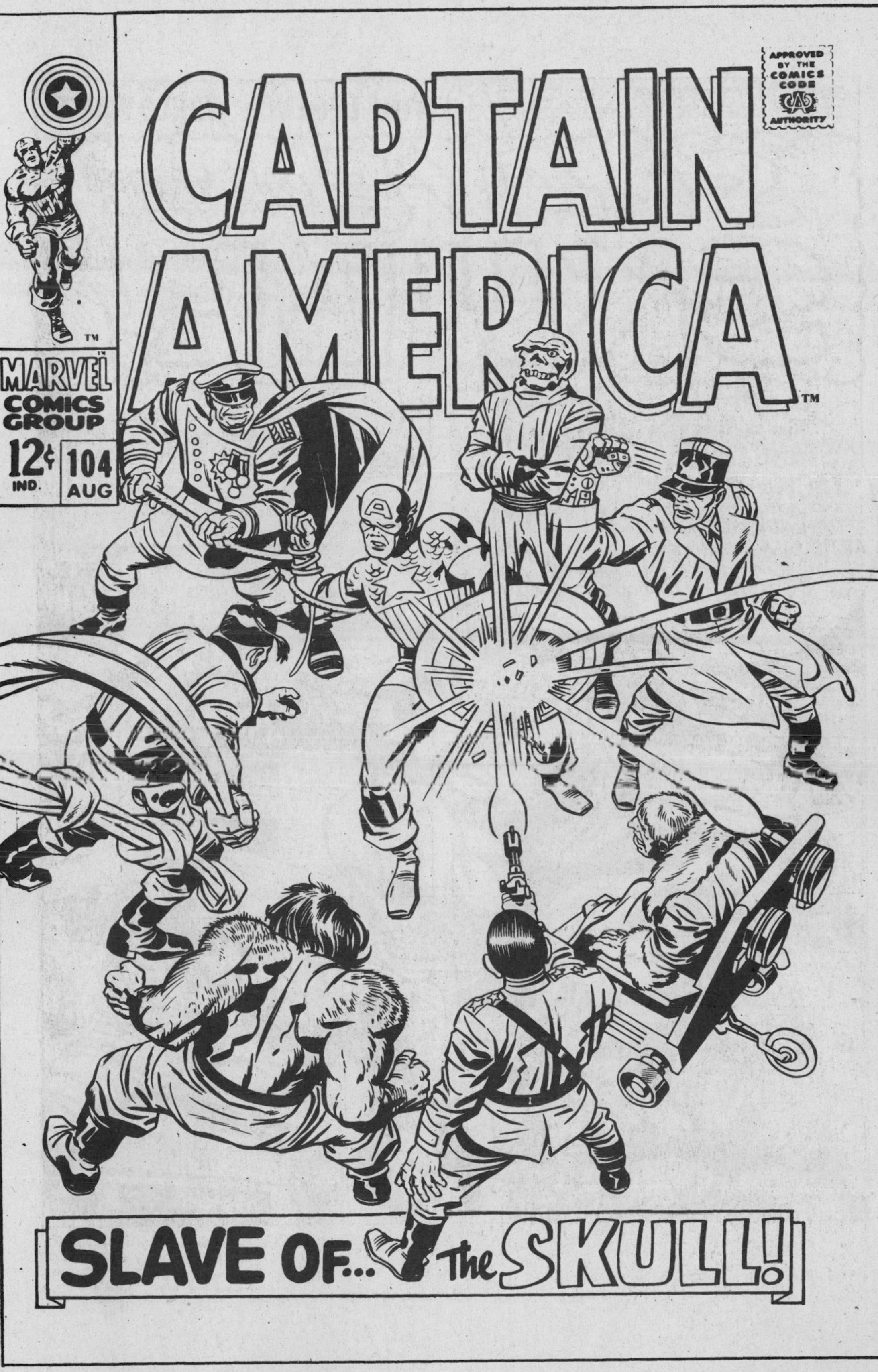
CAPTAIN AMERICA
APPROVED BY THE COMICS CODE AUTHORITY
MARVEL COMICS GROUP
12¢ IND.
104 AUG
SLAVE OF... the SKULL!

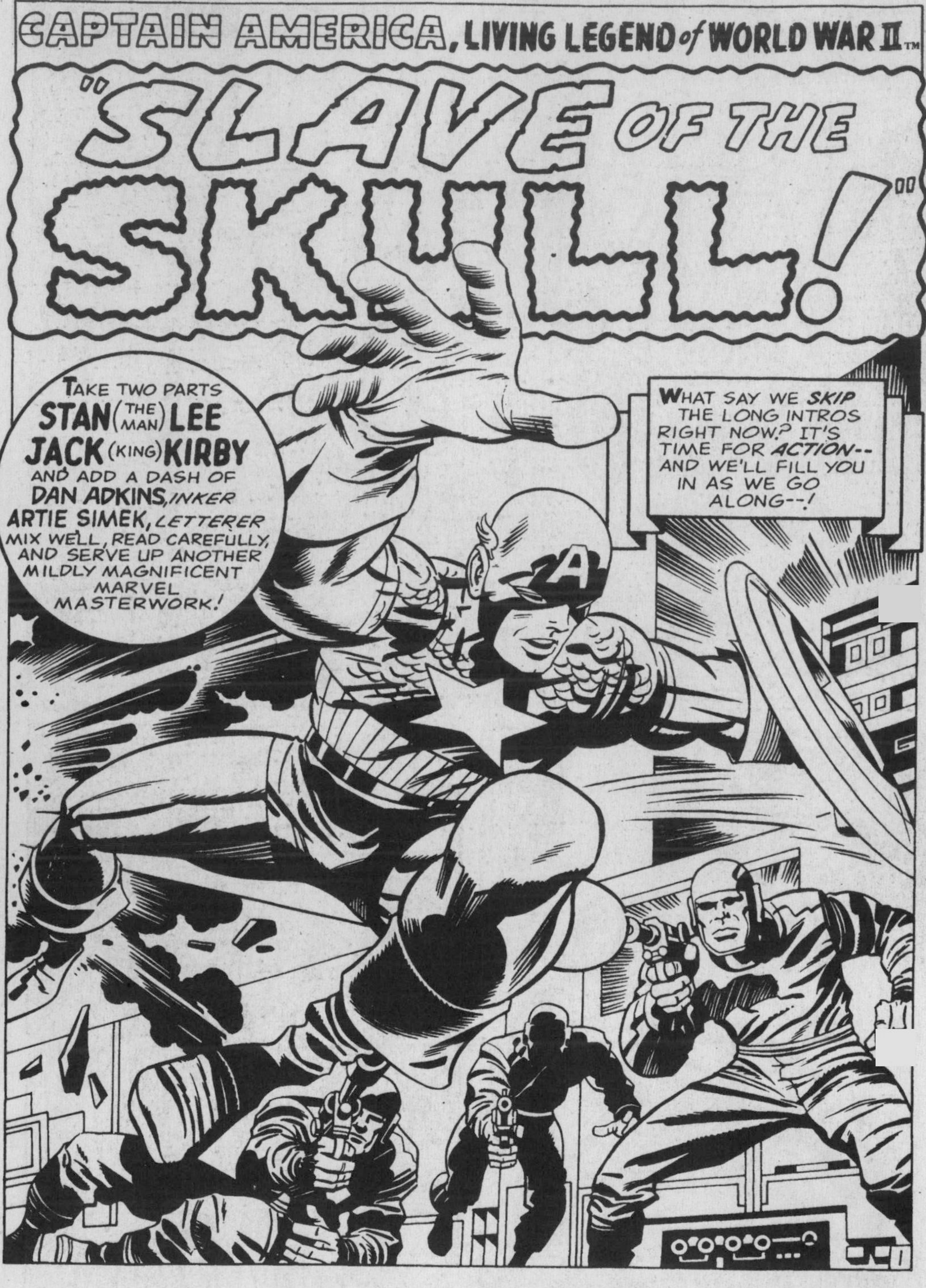

CAPTAIN AMERICA, LIVING LEGEND of WORLD WAR II™
"SLAVE OF THE SKULL!"
TAKE TWO PARTS STAN (THE MAN) LEE JACK (KING) KIRBY AND ADD A DASH OF DAN ADKINS, INKER ARTIE SIMEK, LETTERER MIX WELL, READ CAREFULLY, AND SERVE UP ANOTHER MILDLY MAGNIFICENT MARVEL MASTERWORK!
WHAT SAY WE SKIP THE LONG INTROS RIGHT NOW? IT'S TIME FOR ACTION-- AND WE'LL FILL YOU IN AS WE GO ALONG--!

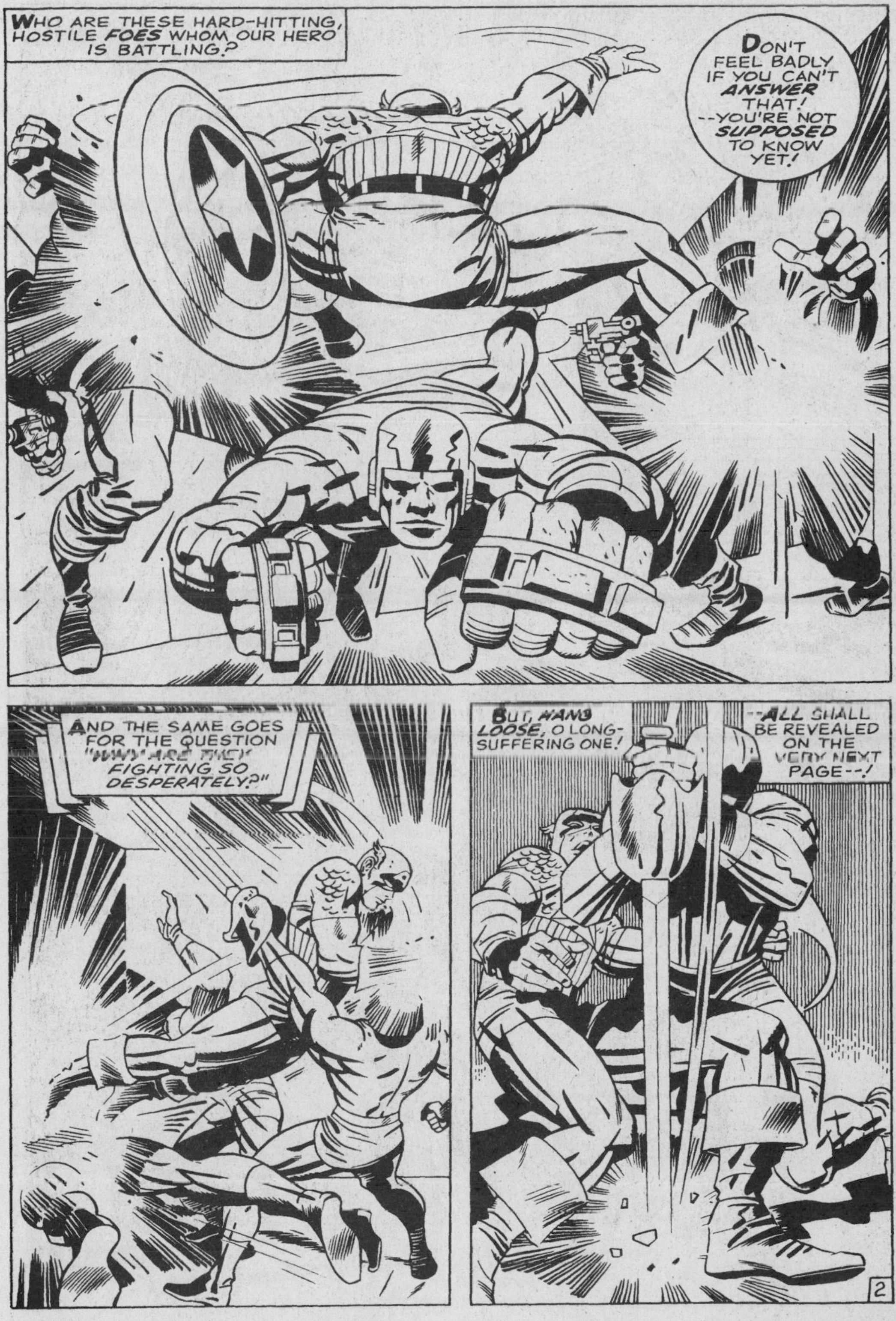
WHO ARE THESE HARD-HITTING, HOSTILE FOES WHOM OUR HERO IS BATTLING?
DON'T FEEL BADLY IF YOU CAN'T ANSWER THAT! --YOU'RE NOT SUPPOSED TO KNOW YET!
AND THE SAME GOES FOR THE QUESTION "WHY ARE THEY FIGHTING SO DESPERATELY?"
BUT, HANG LOOSE, O LONG-SUFFERING ONE!
--ALL SHALL BE REVEALED ON THE VERY NEXT PAGE--!
2

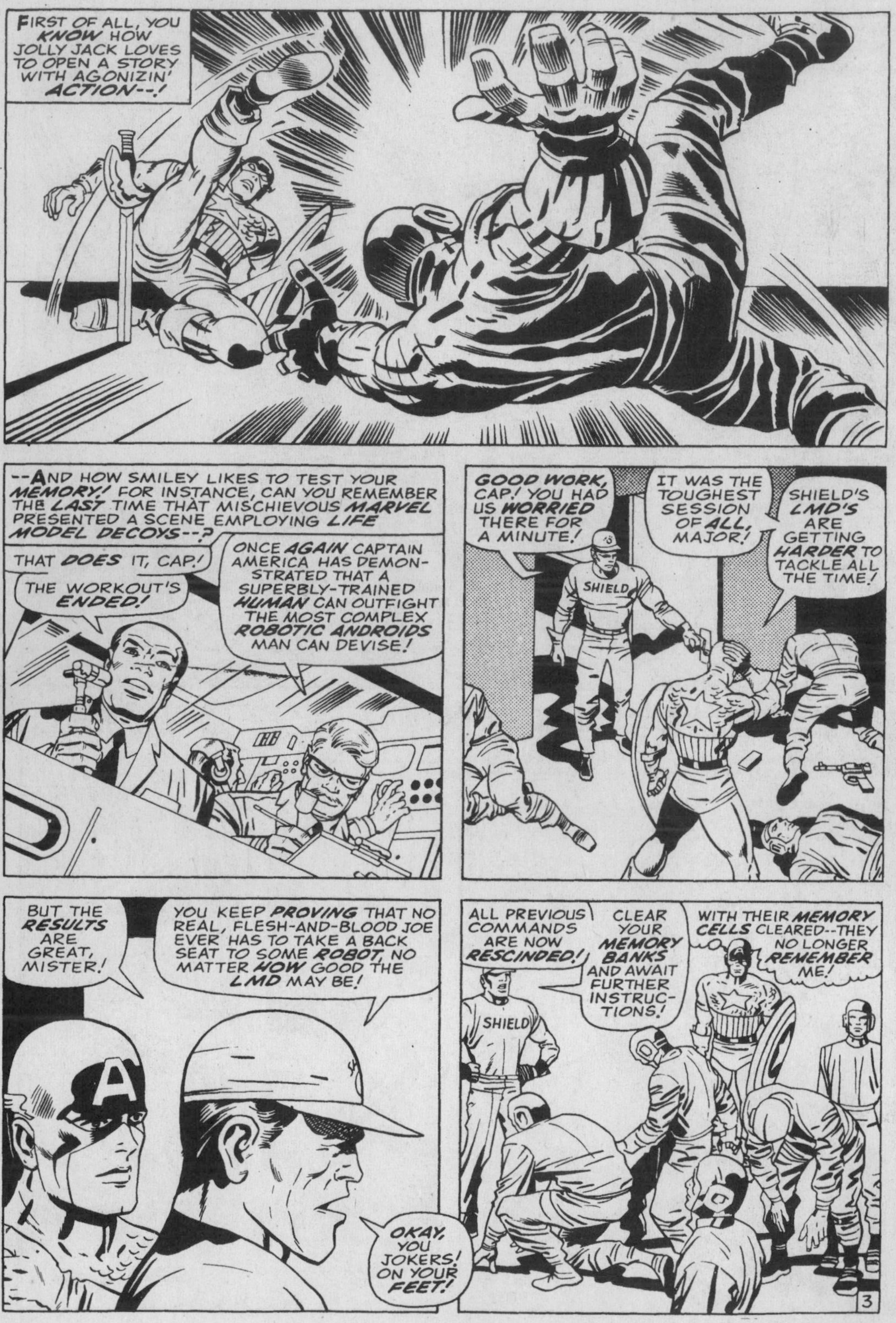
FIRST OF ALL, YOU KNOW HOW JOLLY JACK LOVES TO OPEN A STORY WITH AGONIZIN' ACTION--!
--AND HOW SMILEY LIKES TO TEST YOUR MEMORY! FOR INSTANCE, CAN YOU REMEMBER THE LAST TIME THAT MISCHIEVOUS MARVEL PRESENTED A SCENE EMPLOYING LIFE MODEL DECOYS--?
THAT DOES IT, CAP!
THE WORKOUT'S ENDED!
ONCE AGAIN CAPTAIN AMERICA HAS DEMONSTRATED THAT A SUPERBLY-TRAINED HUMAN CAN OUTFIGHT THE MOST COMPLEX ROBOTIC ANDROIDS MAN CAN DEVISE!
GOOD WORK, CAP! YOU HAD US WORRIED THERE FOR A MINUTE!
IT WAS THE TOUGHEST SESSION OF ALL, MAJOR!
SHIELD'S LMD'S ARE GETTING HARDER TO TACKLE ALL THE TIME!
SHIELD
BUT THE RESULTS ARE GREAT, MISTER!
YOU KEEP PROVING THAT NO REAL, FLESH-AND-BLOOD JOE EVER HAS TO TAKE A BACK SEAT TO SOME ROBOT, NO MATTER HOW GOOD THE LMD MAY BE!
OKAY, YOU JOKERS! ON YOUR FEET!
ALL PREVIOUS COMMANDS ARE NOW RESCINDED!
CLEAR YOUR MEMORY BANKS AND AWAIT FURTHER INSTRUCTIONS!
WITH THEIR MEMORY CELLS CLEARED--THEY NO LONGER REMEMBER ME!
SHIELD
3

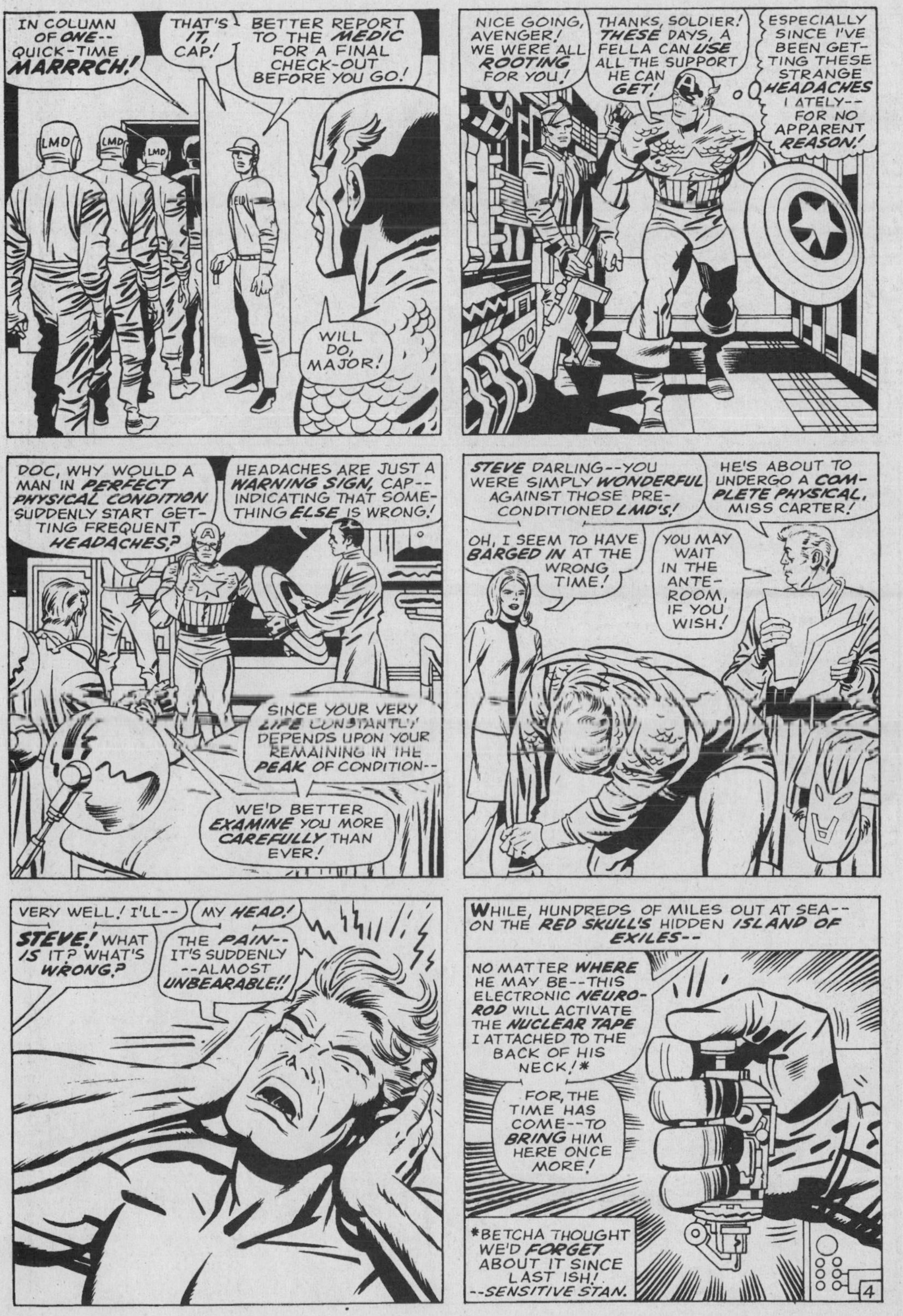
IN COLUMN OF ONE-- QUICK-TIME MARRRCH!
THAT'S IT, CAP!
BETTER REPORT TO THE MEDIC FOR A FINAL CHECK-OUT BEFORE YOU GO!
WILL DO, MAJOR!
NICE GOING, AVENGER! WE WERE ALL ROOTING FOR YOU!
THANKS, SOLDIER! THESE DAYS, A FELLA CAN USE ALL THE SUPPORT HE CAN GET!
ESPECIALLY SINCE I'VE BEEN GETTING THESE STRANGE HEADACHES LATELY-- FOR NO APPARENT REASON!
DOC, WHY WOULD A MAN IN PERFECT PHYSICAL CONDITION SUDDENLY START GETTING FREQUENT HEADACHES?
HEADACHES ARE JUST A WARNING SIGN, CAP-- INDICATING THAT SOMETHING ELSE IS WRONG!
SINCE YOUR VERY LIFE CONSTANTLY DEPENDS UPON YOUR REMAINING IN THE PEAK OF CONDITION--
WE'D BETTER EXAMINE YOU MORE CAREFULLY THAN EVER!
STEVE DARLING--YOU WERE SIMPLY WONDERFUL AGAINST THOSE PRE-CONDITIONED LMD'S!
HE'S ABOUT TO UNDERGO A COMPLETE PHYSICAL, MISS CARTER!
OH, I SEEM TO HAVE BARGED IN AT THE WRONG TIME!
YOU MAY WAIT IN THE ANTE-ROOM, IF YOU WISH!
VERY WELL! I'LL--
MY HEAD!
STEVE! WHAT IS IT? WHAT'S WRONG?
THE PAIN-- IT'S SUDDENLY --ALMOST UNBEARABLE!!
WHILE, HUNDREDS OF MILES OUT AT SEA-- ON THE RED SKULL'S HIDDEN ISLAND OF EXILES--
NO MATTER WHERE HE MAY BE--THIS ELECTRONIC NEURO-ROD WILL ACTIVATE THE NUCLEAR TAPE I ATTACHED TO THE BACK OF HIS NECK!*
FOR, THE TIME HAS COME--TO BRING HIM HERE ONCE MORE!
*BETCHA THOUGHT WE'D FORGET ABOUT IT SINCE LAST ISH! --SENSITIVE STAN.
4

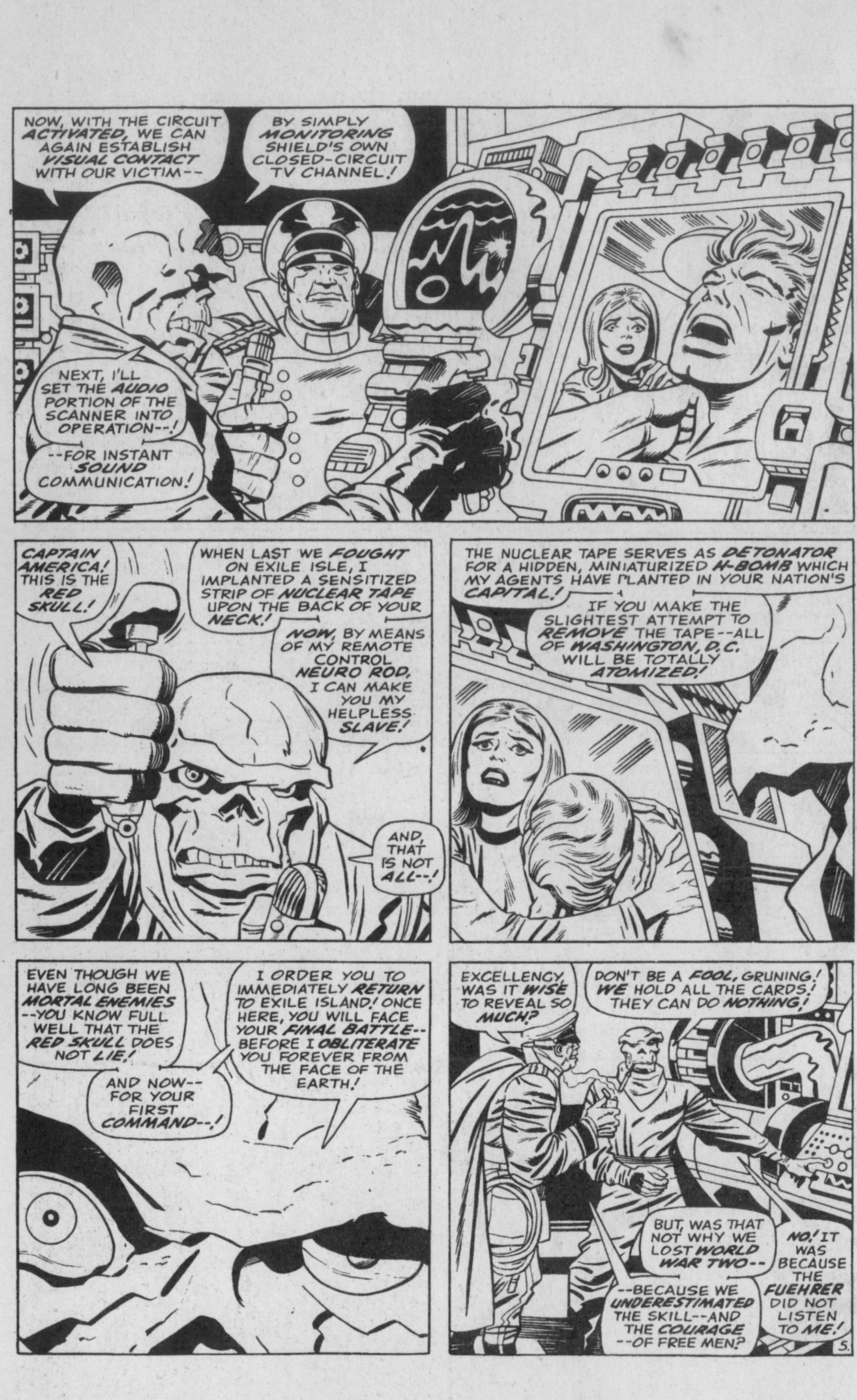
NOW, WITH THE CIRCUIT ACTIVATED, WE CAN AGAIN ESTABLISH VISUAL CONTACT WITH OUR VICTIM--
BY SIMPLY MONITORING SHIELD'S OWN CLOSED-CIRCUIT TV CHANNEL!
NEXT, I'LL SET THE AUDIO PORTION OF THE SCANNER INTO OPERATION--!
--FOR INSTANT SOUND COMMUNICATION!
CAPTAIN AMERICA! THIS IS THE RED SKULL!
WHEN LAST WE FOUGHT ON EXILE ISLE, I IMPLANTED A SENSITIZED STRIP OF NUCLEAR TAPE UPON THE BACK OF YOUR NECK!
NOW, BY MEANS OF MY REMOTE CONTROL NEURO ROD, I CAN MAKE YOU MY HELPLESS SLAVE!
AND, THAT IS NOT ALL--!
THE NUCLEAR TAPE SERVES AS DETONATOR FOR A HIDDEN, MINIATURIZED H-BOMB WHICH MY AGENTS HAVE PLANTED IN YOUR NATION'S CAPITAL!
IF YOU MAKE THE SLIGHTEST ATTEMPT TO REMOVE THE TAPE--ALL OF WASHINGTON, D.C. WILL BE TOTALLY ATOMIZED!
EVEN THOUGH WE HAVE LONG BEEN MORTAL ENEMIES --YOU KNOW FULL WELL THAT THE RED SKULL DOES NOT LIE!
I ORDER YOU TO IMMEDIATELY RETURN TO EXILE ISLAND! ONCE HERE, YOU WILL FACE YOUR FINAL BATTLE-- BEFORE I OBLITERATE YOU FOREVER FROM THE FACE OF THE EARTH!
AND NOW-- FOR YOUR FIRST COMMAND--!
EXCELLENCY, WAS IT WISE TO REVEAL SO MUCH?
DON'T BE A FOOL, GRUNING! WE HOLD ALL THE CARDS! THEY CAN DO NOTHING!
BUT, WAS THAT NOT WHY WE LOST WORLD WAR TWO--
--BECAUSE WE UNDERESTIMATED THE SKILL--AND THE COURAGE --OF FREE MEN?
NO! IT WAS BECAUSE THE FUEHRER DID NOT LISTEN TO ME!
5.

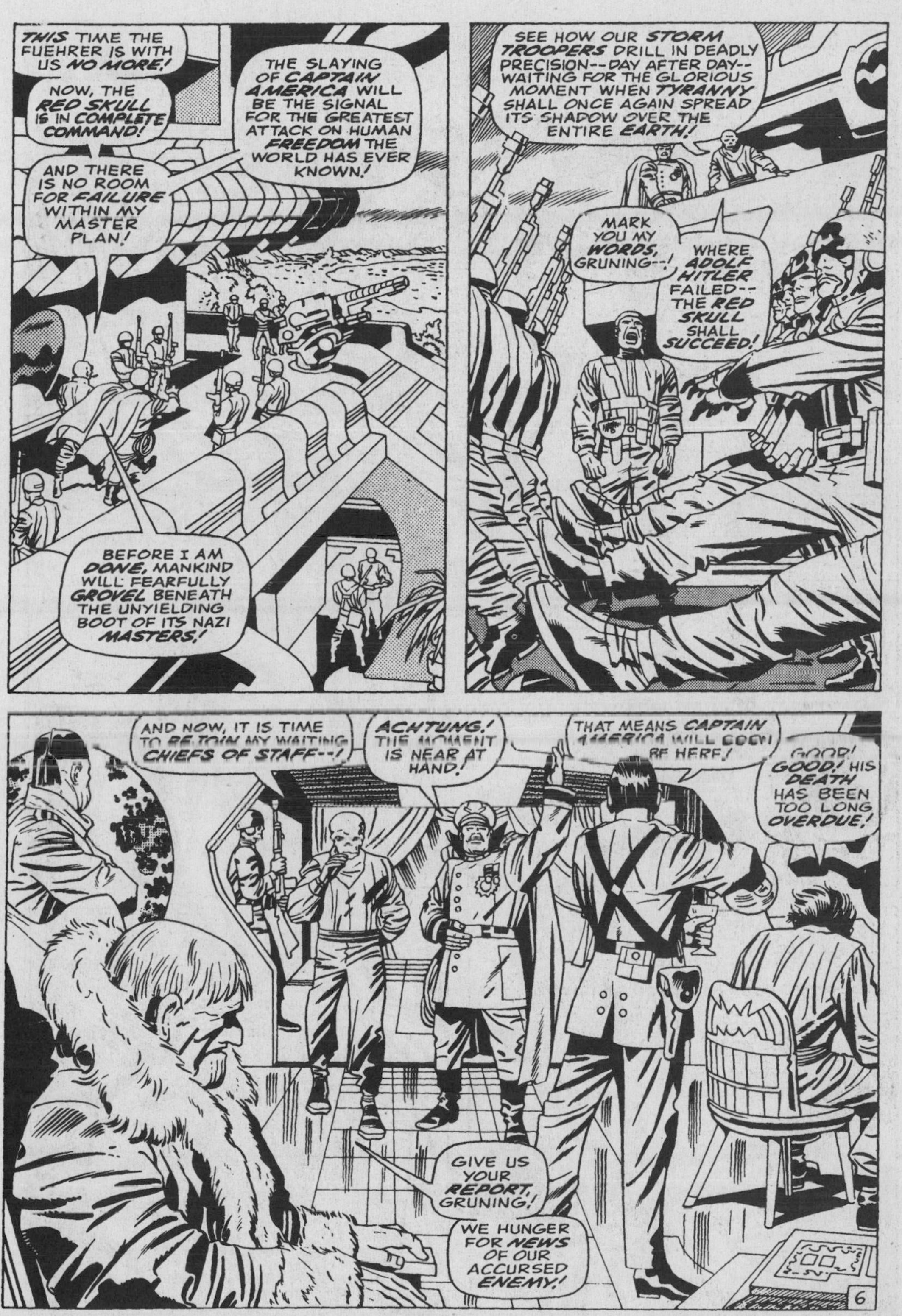
THIS TIME THE FUEHRER IS WITH US NO MORE!
NOW, THE RED SKULL IS IN COMPLETE COMMAND!
AND THERE IS NO ROOM FOR FAILURE WITHIN MY MASTER PLAN!
THE SLAYING OF CAPTAIN AMERICA WILL BE THE SIGNAL FOR THE GREATEST ATTACK ON HUMAN FREEDOM THE WORLD HAS EVER KNOWN!
BEFORE I AM DONE, MANKIND WILL FEARFULLY GROVEL BENEATH THE UNYIELDING BOOT OF ITS NAZI MASTERS!
SEE HOW OUR STORM TROOPERS DRILL IN DEADLY PRECISION--DAY AFTER DAY--WAITING FOR THE GLORIOUS MOMENT WHEN TYRANNY SHALL ONCE AGAIN SPREAD ITS SHADOW OVER THE ENTIRE EARTH!
MARK YOU MY WORDS, GRUNING--!
WHERE ADOLF HITLER FAILED--THE RED SKULL SHALL SUCCEED!
AND NOW, IT IS TIME TO RE-JOIN MY WAITING CHIEFS OF STAFF--!
ACHTUNG! THE MOMENT IS NEAR AT HAND!
THAT MEANS CAPTAIN AMERICA WILL SOON BE HERE!
GOOD! GOOD! HIS DEATH HAS BEEN TOO LONG OVERDUE!
GIVE US YOUR REPORT, GRUNING!
WE HUNGER FOR NEWS OF OUR ACCURSED ENEMY!

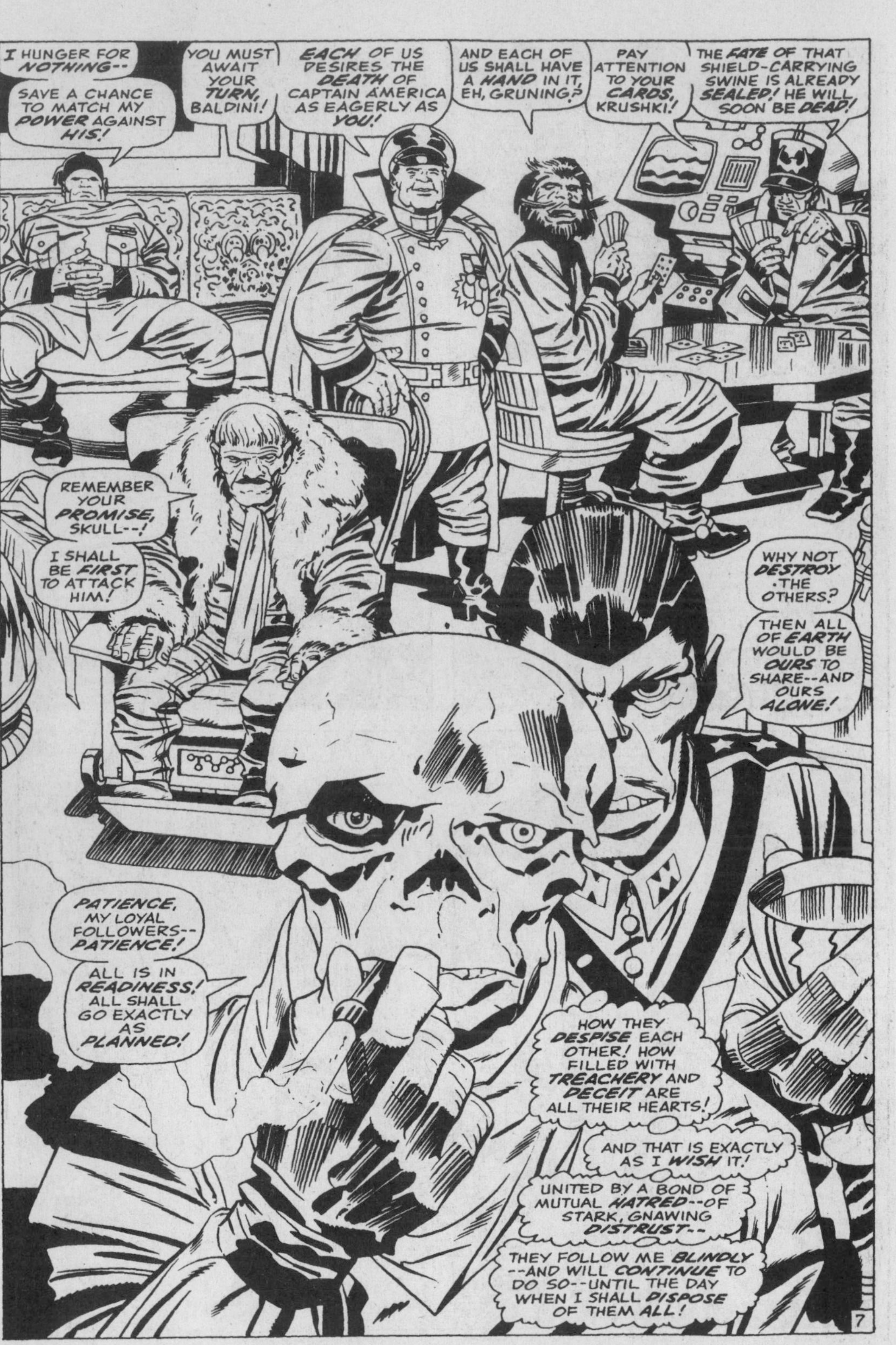
I HUNGER FOR NOTHING--
SAVE A CHANCE TO MATCH MY POWER AGAINST HIS!
YOU MUST AWAIT YOUR TURN, BALDINI!
EACH OF US DESIRES THE DEATH OF CAPTAIN AMERICA AS EAGERLY AS YOU!
AND EACH OF US SHALL HAVE A HAND IN IT, EH, GRUNING?
PAY ATTENTION TO YOUR CARDS, KRUSHKI!
THE FATE OF THAT SHIELD-CARRYING SWINE IS ALREADY SEALED! HE WILL SOON BE DEAD!
REMEMBER YOUR PROMISE, SKULL--!
I SHALL BE FIRST TO ATTACK HIM!
WHY NOT DESTROY THE OTHERS?
THEN ALL OF EARTH WOULD BE OURS TO SHARE--AND OURS ALONE!
PATIENCE, MY LOYAL FOLLOWERS--PATIENCE!
ALL IS IN READINESS! ALL SHALL GO EXACTLY AS PLANNED!
HOW THEY DESPISE EACH OTHER! HOW FILLED WITH TREACHERY AND DECEIT ARE ALL THEIR HEARTS!
AND THAT IS EXACTLY AS I WISH IT!
UNITED BY A BOND OF MUTUAL HATRED--OF STARK, GNAWING DISTRUST--
THEY FOLLOW ME BLINDLY--AND WILL CONTINUE TO DO SO--UNTIL THE DAY WHEN I SHALL DISPOSE OF THEM ALL!
7

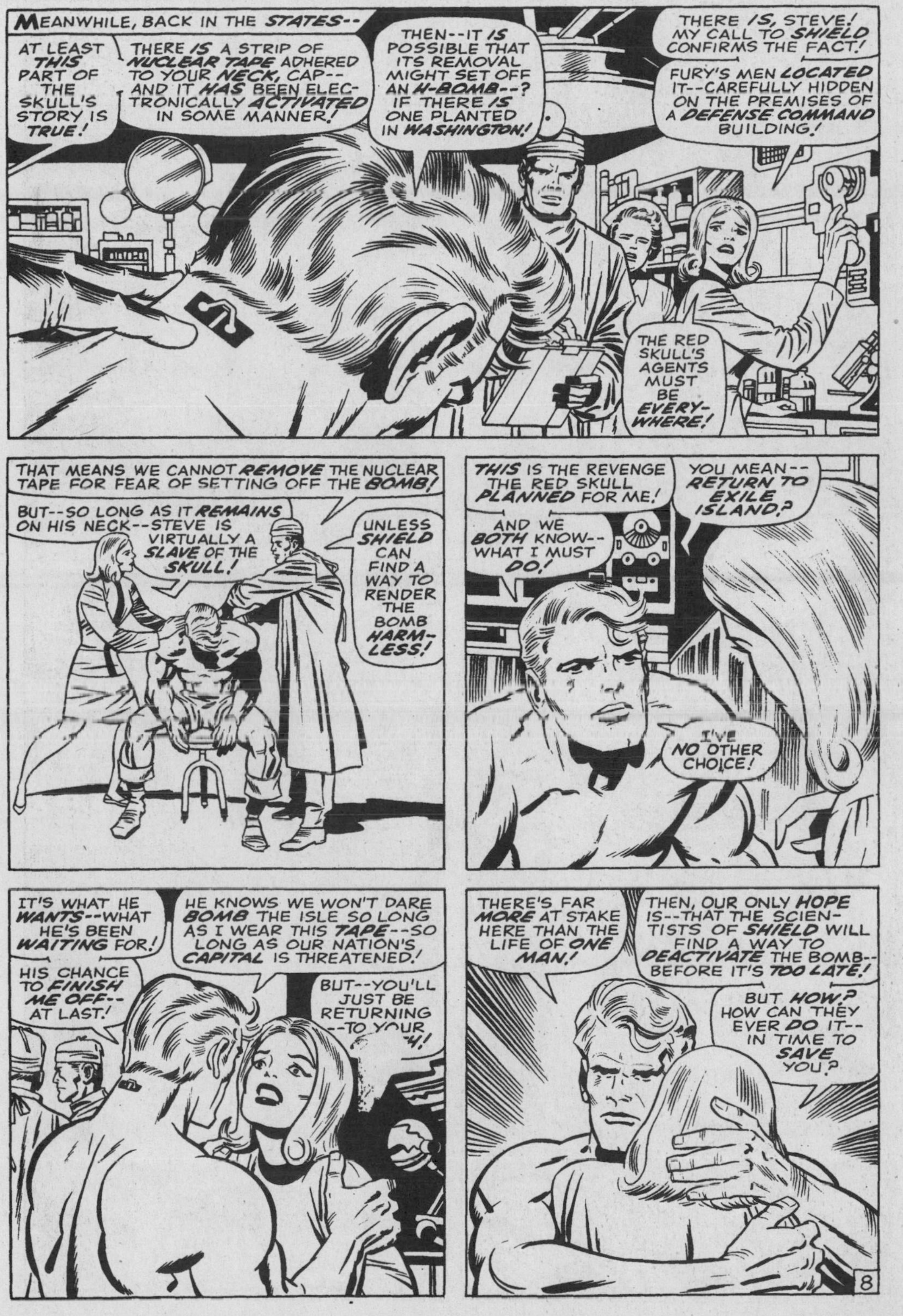
MEANWHILE, BACK IN THE STATES--
AT LEAST THIS PART OF THE SKULL'S STORY IS TRUE!
THERE IS A STRIP OF NUCLEAR TAPE ADHERED TO YOUR NECK, CAP-- AND IT HAS BEEN ELECTRONICALLY ACTIVATED IN SOME MANNER!
THEN--IT IS POSSIBLE THAT ITS REMOVAL MIGHT SET OFF AN H-BOMB--? IF THERE IS ONE PLANTED IN WASHINGTON!
THERE IS, STEVE! MY CALL TO SHIELD CONFIRMS THE FACT!
FURY'S MEN LOCATED IT--CAREFULLY HIDDEN ON THE PREMISES OF A DEFENSE COMMAND BUILDING!
THE RED SKULL'S AGENTS MUST BE EVERY-WHERE!
THAT MEANS WE CANNOT REMOVE THE NUCLEAR TAPE FOR FEAR OF SETTING OFF THE BOMB!
BUT--SO LONG AS IT REMAINS ON HIS NECK--STEVE IS VIRTUALLY A SLAVE OF THE SKULL!
UNLESS SHIELD CAN FIND A WAY TO RENDER THE BOMB HARM-LESS!
THIS IS THE REVENGE THE RED SKULL PLANNED FOR ME!
AND WE BOTH KNOW-- WHAT I MUST DO!
YOU MEAN-- RETURN TO EXILE ISLAND?
I'VE NO OTHER CHOICE!
IT'S WHAT HE WANTS--WHAT HE'S BEEN WAITING FOR!
HIS CHANCE TO FINISH ME OFF-- AT LAST!
HE KNOWS WE WON'T DARE BOMB THE ISLE SO LONG AS I WEAR THIS TAPE--SO LONG AS OUR NATION'S CAPITAL IS THREATENED!
BUT--YOU'LL JUST BE RETURNING --TO YOUR
THERE'S FAR MORE AT STAKE HERE THAN THE LIFE OF ONE MAN!
THEN, OUR ONLY HOPE IS--THAT THE SCIENTISTS OF SHIELD WILL FIND A WAY TO DEACTIVATE THE BOMB-- BEFORE IT'S TOO LATE!
BUT HOW? HOW CAN THEY EVER DO IT-- IN TIME TO SAVE YOU?

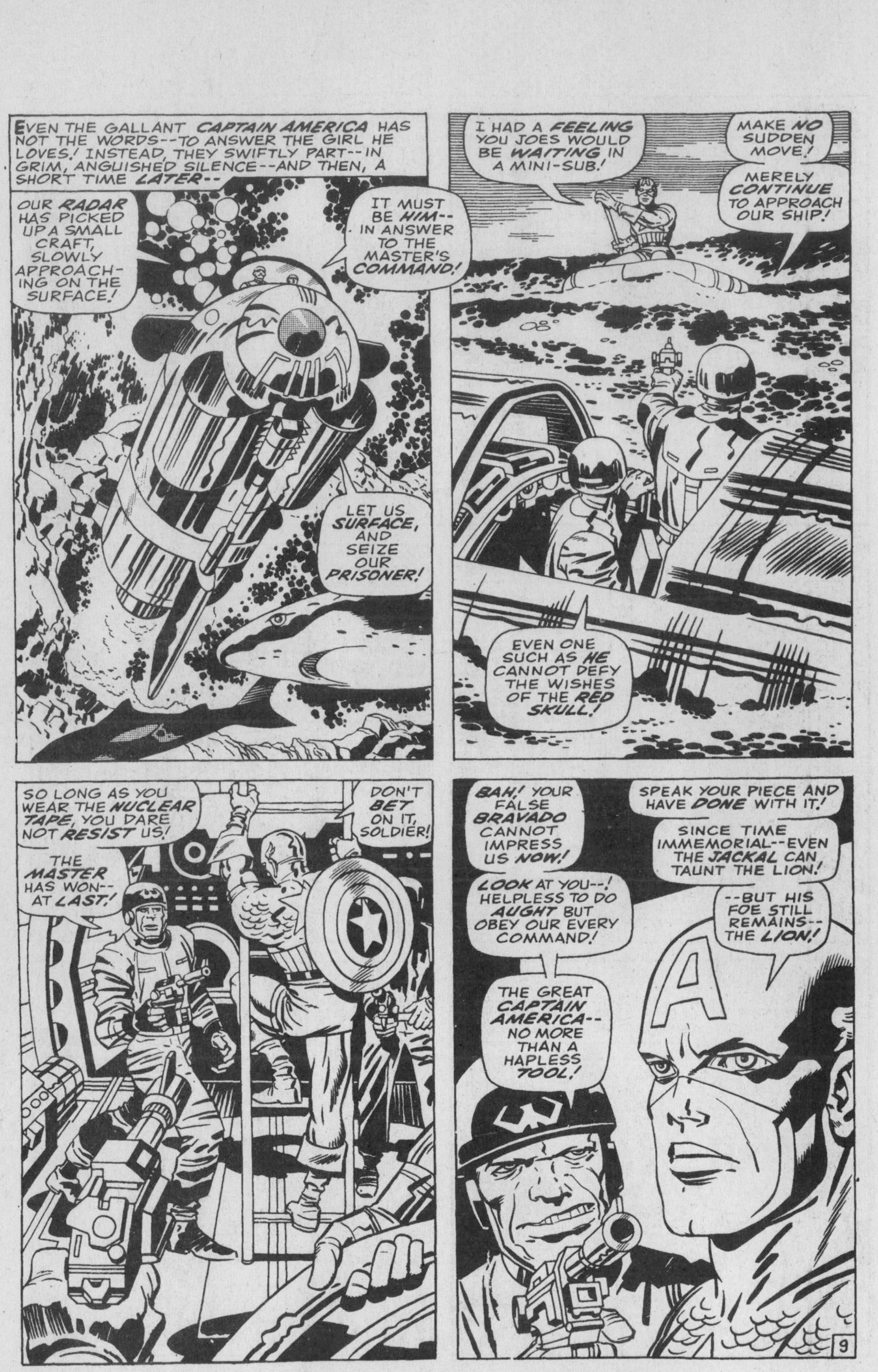

EVEN THE GALLANT CAPTAIN AMERICA HAS NOT THE WORDS--TO ANSWER THE GIRL HE LOVES! INSTEAD, THEY SWIFTLY PART--IN GRIM, ANGUISHED SILENCE--AND THEN, A SHORT TIME LATER--
OUR RADAR HAS PICKED UP A SMALL CRAFT, SLOWLY APPROACHING ON THE SURFACE!
IT MUST BE HIM--IN ANSWER TO THE MASTER'S COMMAND!
LET US SURFACE, AND SEIZE OUR PRISONER!
I HAD A FEELING YOU JOES WOULD BE WAITING IN A MINI-SUB!
MAKE NO SUDDEN MOVE!
MERELY CONTINUE TO APPROACH OUR SHIP!
EVEN ONE SUCH AS HE CANNOT DEFY THE WISHES OF THE RED SKULL!
SO LONG AS YOU WEAR THE NUCLEAR TAPE, YOU DARE NOT RESIST US!
THE MASTER HAS WON--AT LAST!
DON'T BET ON IT, SOLDIER!
BAH! YOUR FALSE BRAVADO CANNOT IMPRESS US NOW!
LOOK AT YOU--! HELPLESS TO DO AUGHT BUT OBEY OUR EVERY COMMAND!
THE GREAT CAPTAIN AMERICA--NO MORE THAN A HAPLESS TOOL!
SPEAK YOUR PIECE AND HAVE DONE WITH IT!
SINCE TIME IMMEMORIAL--EVEN THE JACKAL CAN TAUNT THE LION!
--BUT HIS FOE STILL REMAINS--THE LION!
9

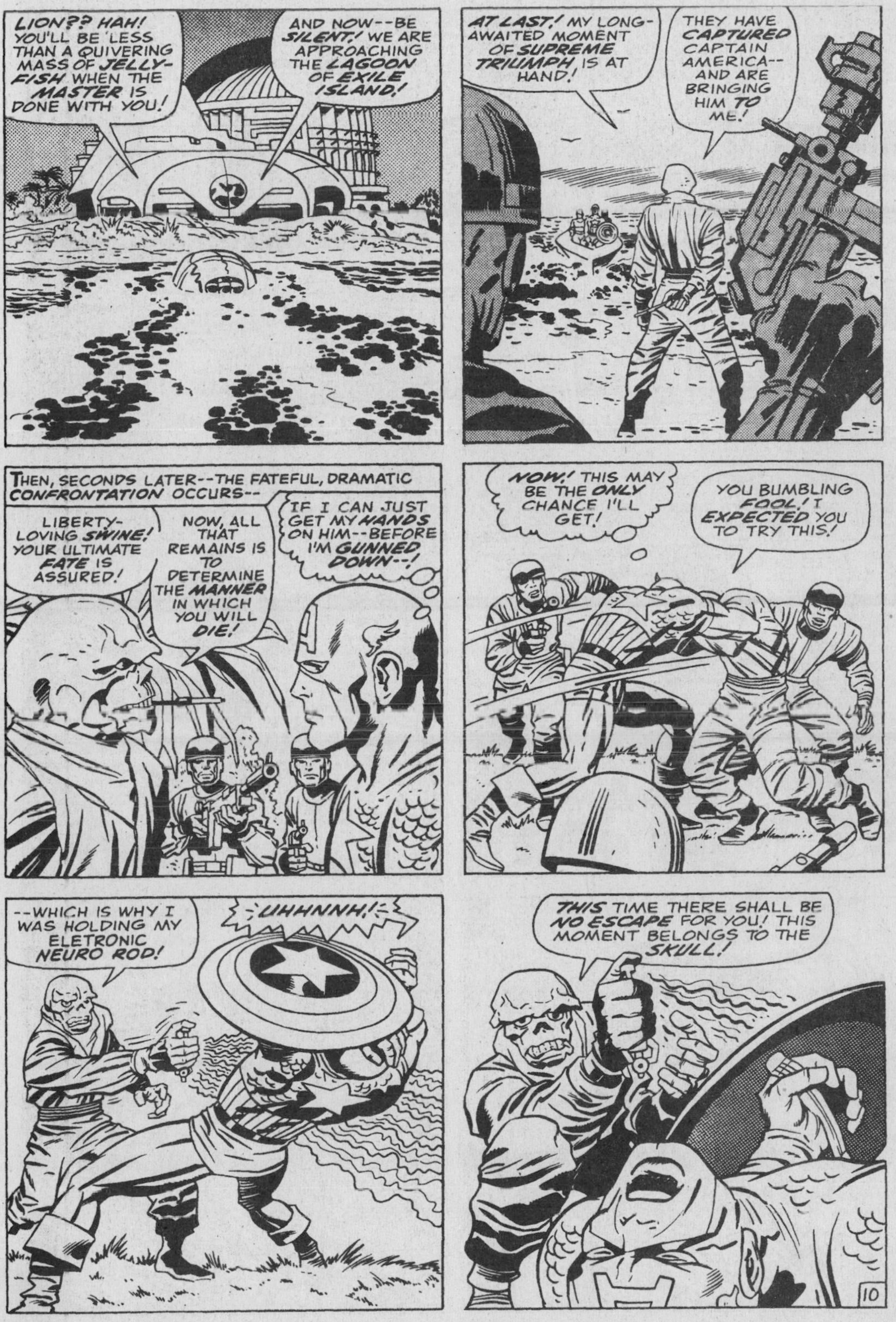
LION?? HAH! YOU'LL BE LESS THAN A QUIVERING MASS OF JELLY-FISH WHEN THE MASTER IS DONE WITH YOU!
AND NOW--BE SILENT! WE ARE APPROACHING THE LAGOON OF EXILE ISLAND!
AT LAST! MY LONG-AWAITED MOMENT OF SUPREME TRIUMPH IS AT HAND!
THEY HAVE CAPTURED CAPTAIN AMERICA--AND ARE BRINGING HIM TO ME!
THEN, SECONDS LATER--THE FATEFUL, DRAMATIC CONFRONTATION OCCURS--
LIBERTY-LOVING SWINE! YOUR ULTIMATE FATE IS ASSURED!
NOW, ALL THAT REMAINS IS TO DETERMINE THE MANNER IN WHICH YOU WILL DIE!
IF I CAN JUST GET MY HANDS ON HIM--BEFORE I'M GUNNED DOWN--!
NOW! THIS MAY BE THE ONLY CHANCE I'LL GET!
YOU BUMBLING FOOL! I EXPECTED YOU TO TRY THIS!
--WHICH IS WHY I WAS HOLDING MY ELETRONIC NEURO ROD!
UHHNNH!
THIS TIME THERE SHALL BE NO ESCAPE FOR YOU! THIS MOMENT BELONGS TO THE SKULL!
10

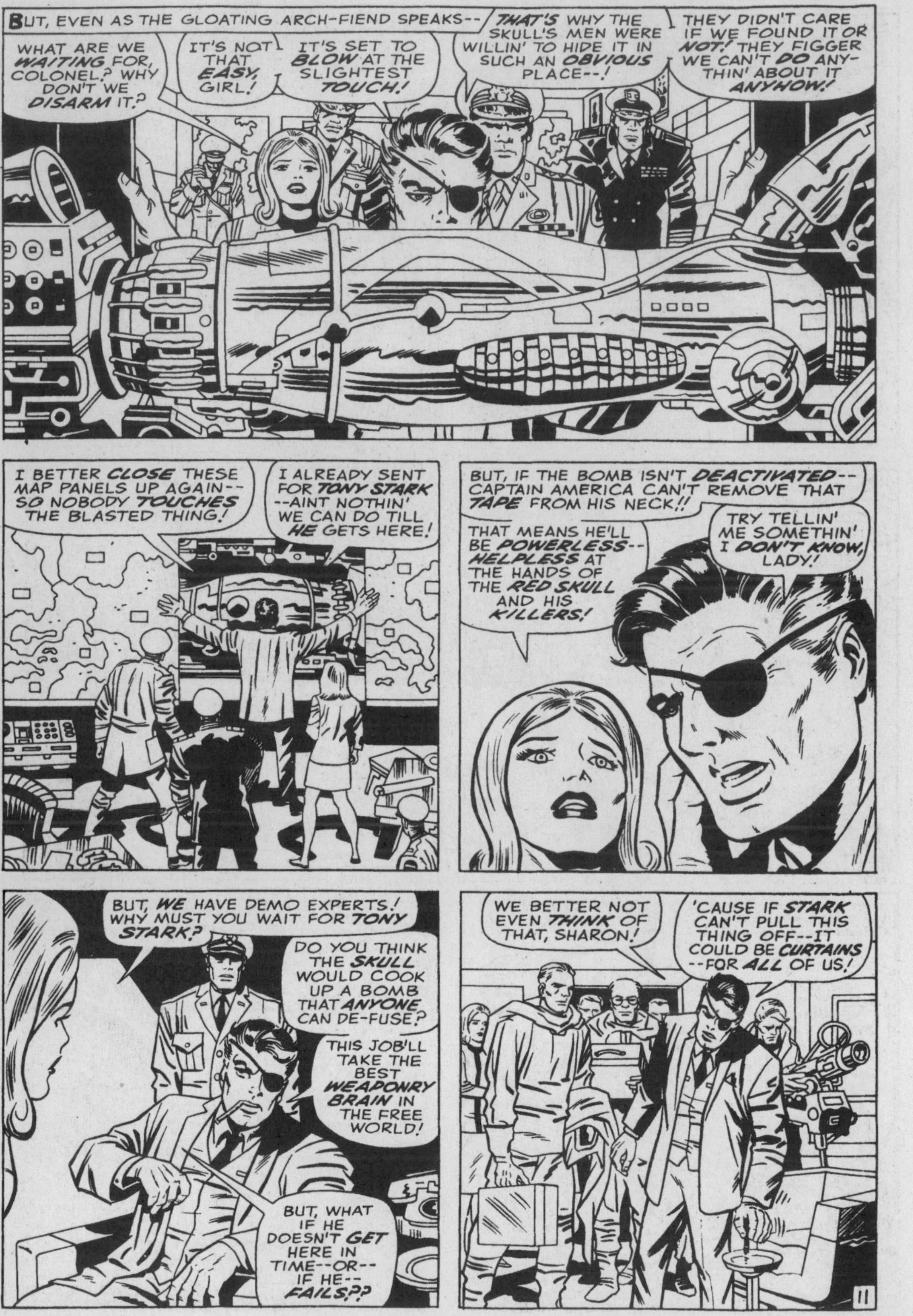

BUT, EVEN AS THE GLOATING ARCH-FIEND SPEAKS--
WHAT ARE WE WAITING FOR, COLONEL? WHY DON'T WE DISARM IT?
IT'S NOT THAT EASY, GIRL!
IT'S SET TO BLOW AT THE SLIGHTEST TOUCH!
THAT'S WHY THE SKULL'S MEN WERE WILLIN' TO HIDE IT IN SUCH AN OBVIOUS PLACE--!
THEY DIDN'T CARE IF WE FOUND IT OR NOT! THEY FIGGER WE CAN'T DO ANYTHIN' ABOUT IT ANYHOW!
I BETTER CLOSE THESE MAP PANELS UP AGAIN-- SO NOBODY TOUCHES THE BLASTED THING!
I ALREADY SENT FOR TONY STARK --AINT NOTHIN' WE CAN DO TILL HE GETS HERE!
BUT, IF THE BOMB ISN'T DEACTIVATED-- CAPTAIN AMERICA CAN'T REMOVE THAT TAPE FROM HIS NECK!!
THAT MEANS HE'LL BE POWERLESS-- HELPLESS AT THE HANDS OF THE RED SKULL AND HIS KILLERS!
TRY TELLIN' ME SOMETHIN' I DON'T KNOW, LADY!
BUT, WE HAVE DEMO EXPERTS! WHY MUST YOU WAIT FOR TONY STARK?
DO YOU THINK THE SKULL WOULD COOK UP A BOMB THAT ANYONE CAN DE-FUSE?
THIS JOB'LL TAKE THE BEST WEAPONRY BRAIN IN THE FREE WORLD!
BUT, WHAT IF HE DOESN'T GET HERE IN TIME--OR-- IF HE-- FAILS??
WE BETTER NOT EVEN THINK OF THAT, SHARON!
'CAUSE IF STARK CAN'T PULL THIS THING OFF--IT COULD BE CURTAINS --FOR ALL OF US!
11

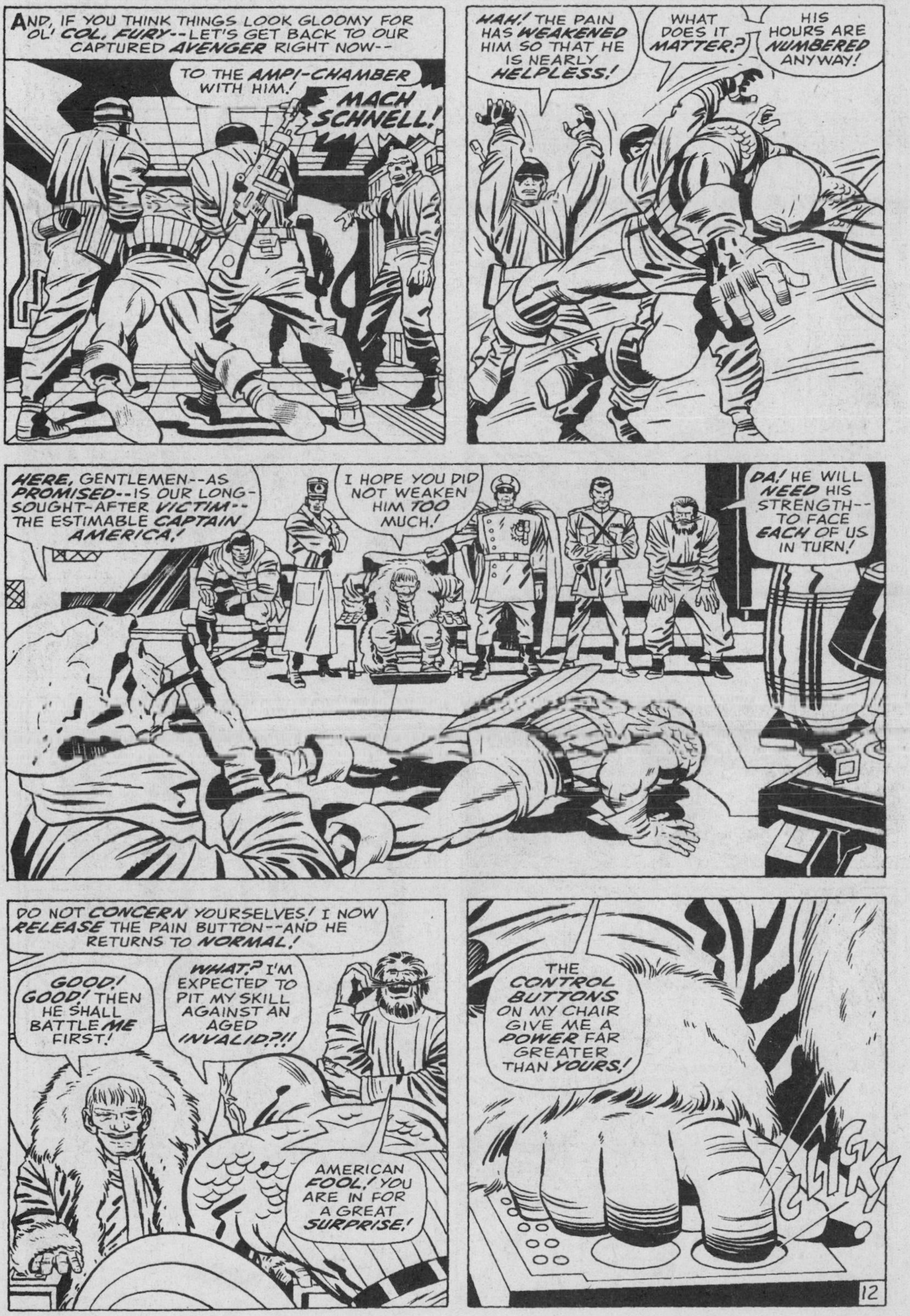
AND, IF YOU THINK THINGS LOOK GLOOMY FOR OL' COL. FURY--LET'S GET BACK TO OUR CAPTURED AVENGER RIGHT NOW--
TO THE AMPI-CHAMBER WITH HIM!
MACH SCHNELL!
NAH! THE PAIN HAS WEAKENED HIM SO THAT HE IS NEARLY HELPLESS!
WHAT DOES IT MATTER?
HIS HOURS ARE NUMBERED ANYWAY!
HERE, GENTLEMEN--AS PROMISED--IS OUR LONG-SOUGHT-AFTER VICTIM--THE ESTIMABLE CAPTAIN AMERICA!
I HOPE YOU DID NOT WEAKEN HIM TOO MUCH!
DA! HE WILL NEED HIS STRENGTH--TO FACE EACH OF US IN TURN!
DO NOT CONCERN YOURSELVES! I NOW RELEASE THE PAIN BUTTON--AND HE RETURNS TO NORMAL!
GOOD! GOOD! THEN HE SHALL BATTLE ME FIRST!
WHAT? I'M EXPECTED TO PIT MY SKILL AGAINST AN AGED INVALID?!!
AMERICAN FOOL! YOU ARE IN FOR A GREAT SURPRISE!
THE CONTROL BUTTONS ON MY CHAIR GIVE ME A POWER FAR GREATER THAN YOURS!
CLICK!
12

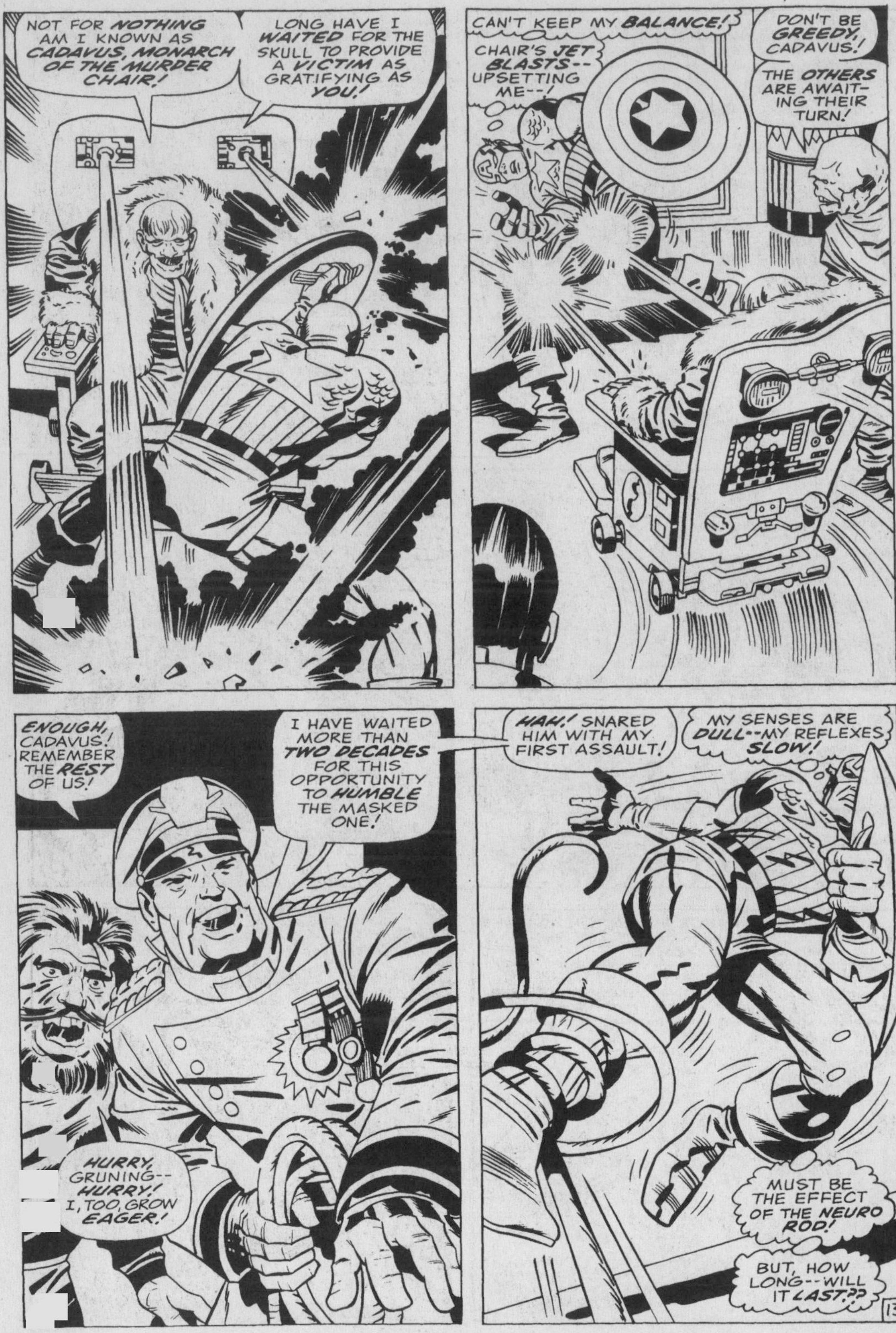
NOT FOR NOTHING AM I KNOWN AS CADAVUS, MONARCH OF THE MURDER CHAIR!
LONG HAVE I WAITED FOR THE SKULL TO PROVIDE A VICTIM AS GRATIFYING AS YOU!
CAN'T KEEP MY BALANCE!
CHAIR'S JET BLASTS-- UPSETTING ME--!
DON'T BE GREEDY, CADAVUS!
THE OTHERS ARE AWAITING THEIR TURN!
ENOUGH, CADAVUS! REMEMBER THE REST OF US!
I HAVE WAITED MORE THAN TWO DECADES FOR THIS OPPORTUNITY TO HUMBLE THE MASKED ONE!
HURRY, GRUNING-- HURRY! I, TOO, GROW EAGER!
HAH! SNARED HIM WITH MY FIRST ASSAULT!
MY SENSES ARE DULL--MY REFLEXES SLOW!
MUST BE THE EFFECT OF THE NEURO ROD!
BUT, HOW LONG--WILL IT LAST??
13

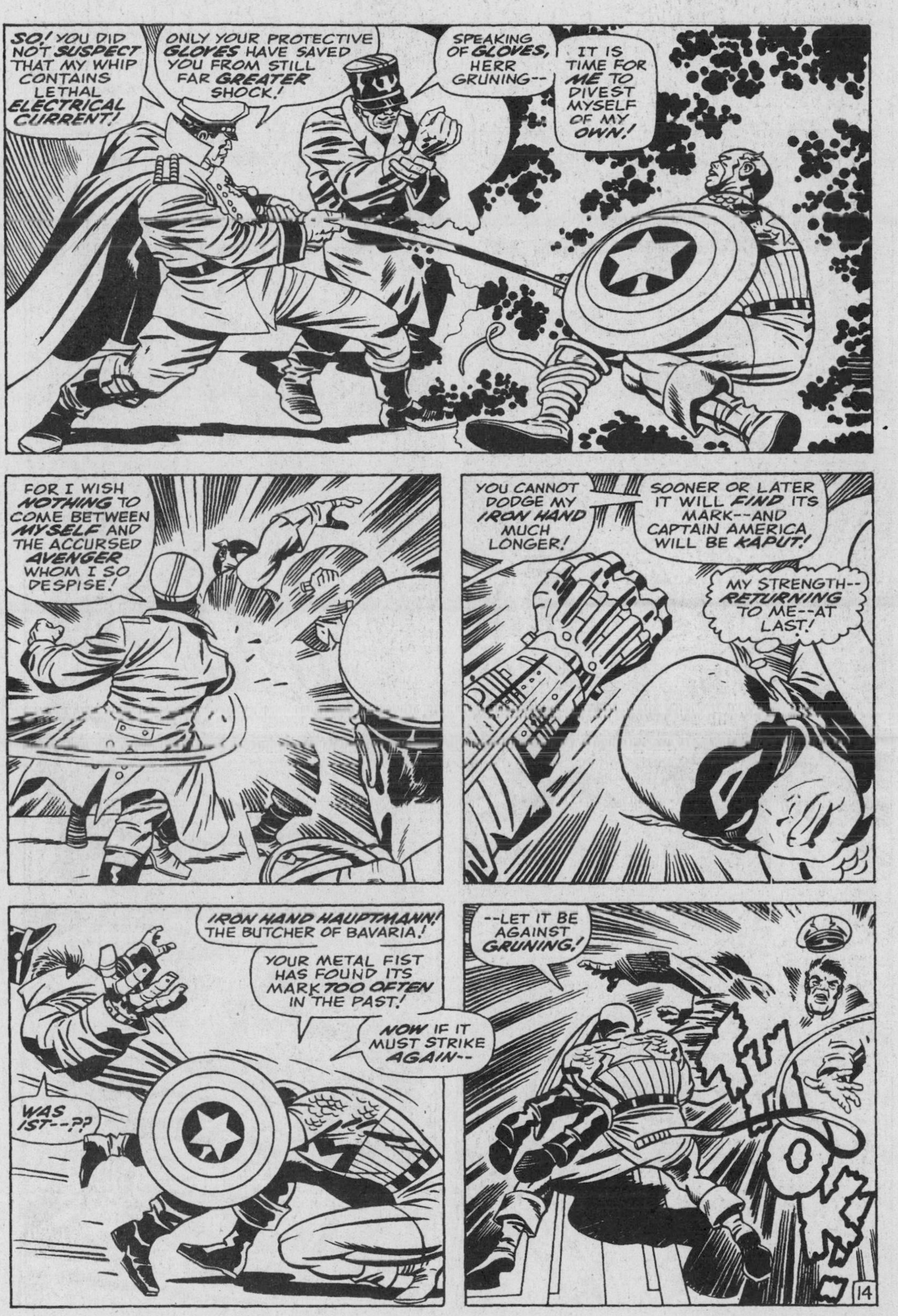
SO! YOU DID NOT SUSPECT THAT MY WHIP CONTAINS LETHAL ELECTRICAL CURRENT!
ONLY YOUR PROTECTIVE GLOVES HAVE SAVED YOU FROM STILL FAR GREATER SHOCK!
SPEAKING OF GLOVES, HERR GRUNING--
IT IS TIME FOR ME TO DIVEST MYSELF OF MY OWN!
FOR I WISH NOTHING TO COME BETWEEN MYSELF AND THE ACCURSED AVENGER WHOM I SO DESPISE!
YOU CANNOT DODGE MY IRON HAND MUCH LONGER!
SOONER OR LATER IT WILL FIND ITS MARK--AND CAPTAIN AMERICA WILL BE KAPUT!
MY STRENGTH-- RETURNING TO ME--AT LAST!
IRON HAND HAUPTMANN! THE BUTCHER OF BAVARIA!
YOUR METAL FIST HAS FOUND ITS MARK TOO OFTEN IN THE PAST!
NOW IF IT MUST STRIKE AGAIN--
WAS IST--??
--LET IT BE AGAINST GRUNING!
SOCK
14

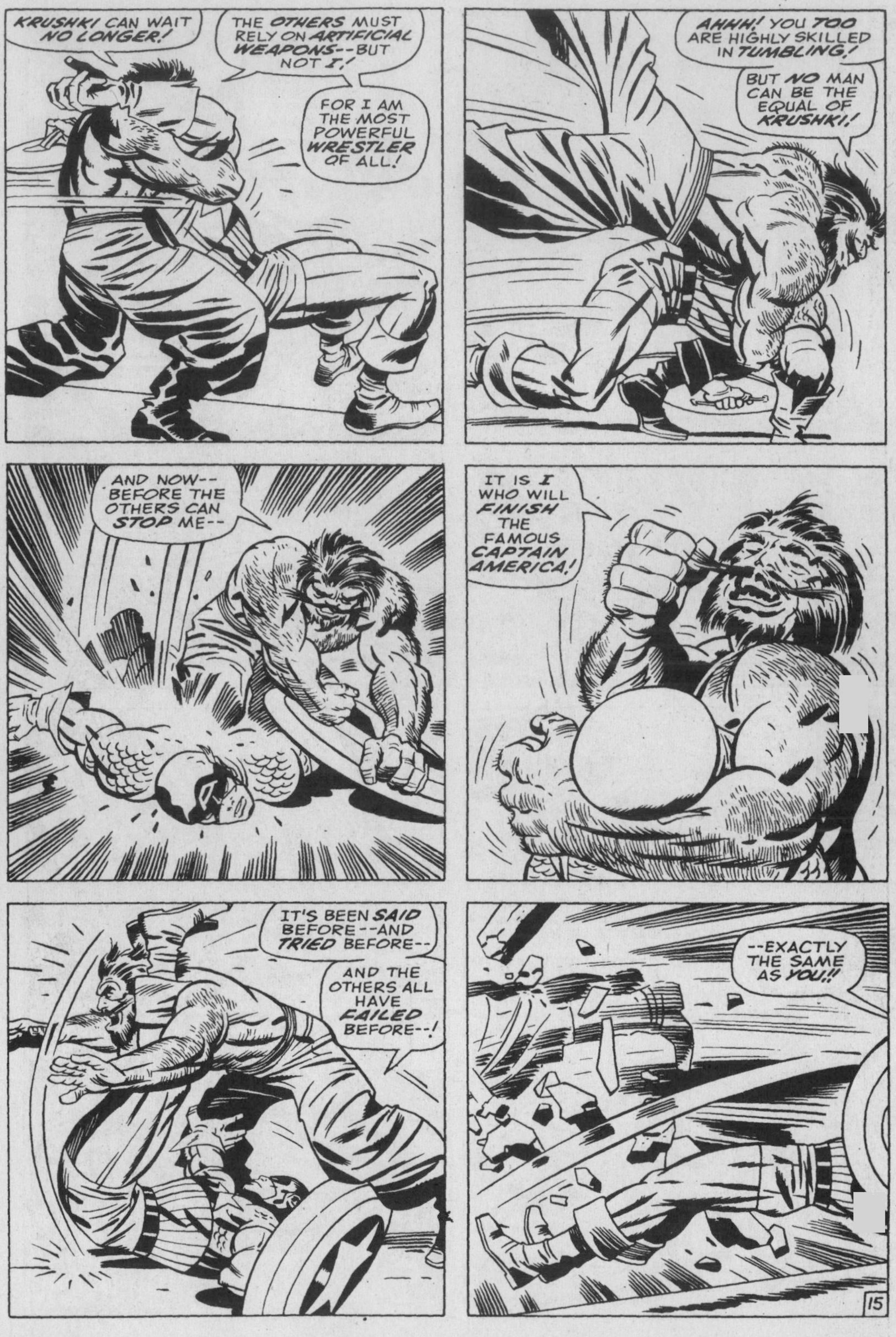
KRUSHKI CAN WAIT NO LONGER!
THE OTHERS MUST RELY ON ARTIFICIAL WEAPONS--BUT NOT I,!
FOR I AM THE MOST POWERFUL WRESTLER OF ALL!
AHHH! YOU TOO ARE HIGHLY SKILLED IN TUMBLING!
BUT NO MAN CAN BE THE EQUAL OF KRUSHKI!
AND NOW--BEFORE THE OTHERS CAN STOP ME--
IT IS I WHO WILL FINISH THE FAMOUS CAPTAIN AMERICA!
IT'S BEEN SAID BEFORE--AND TRIED BEFORE--
AND THE OTHERS ALL HAVE FAILED BEFORE--!
--EXACTLY THE SAME AS YOU!!
15

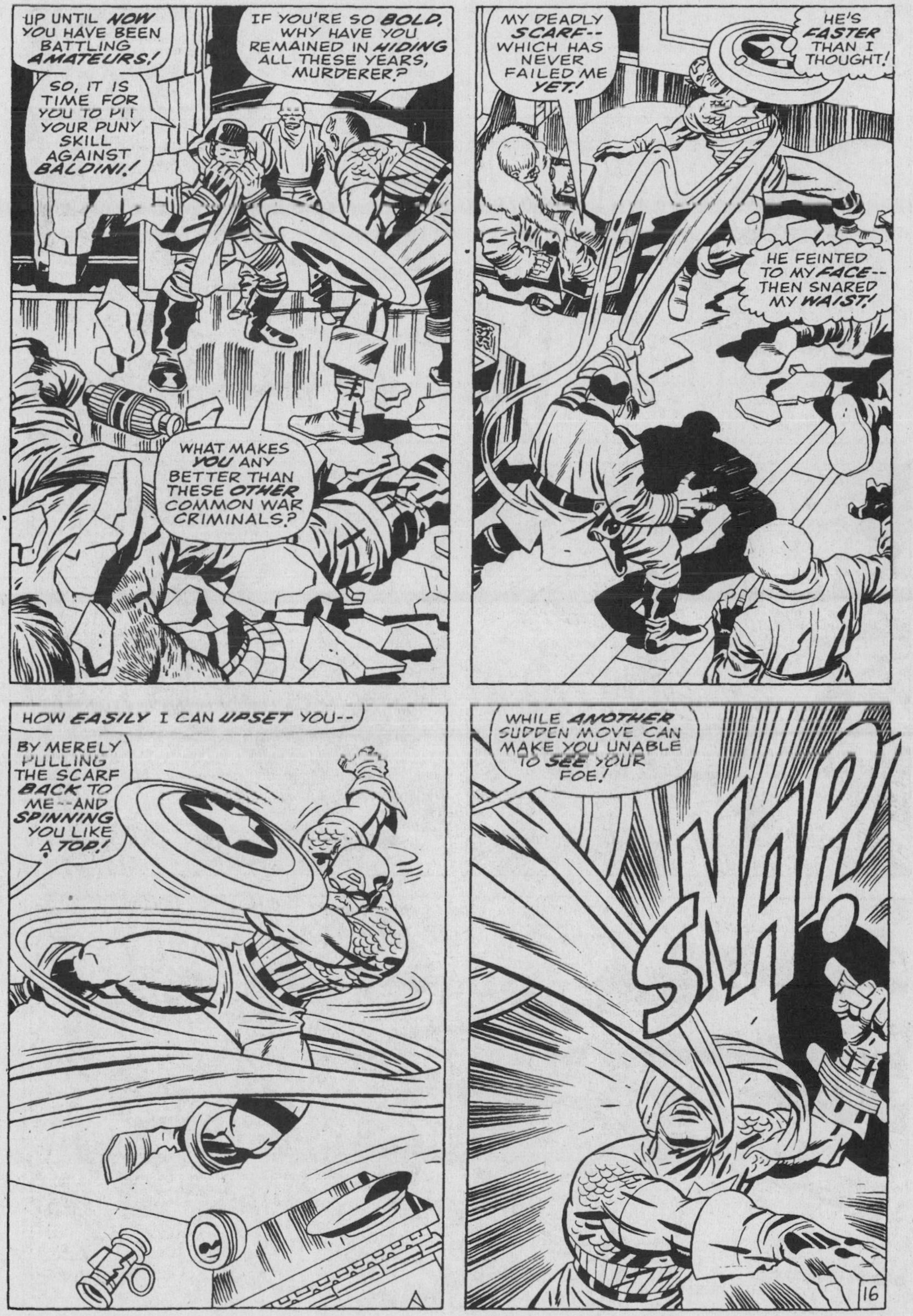
UP UNTIL NOW YOU HAVE BEEN BATTLING AMATEURS!
SO, IT IS TIME FOR YOU TO PIT YOUR PUNY SKILL AGAINST BALDINI!
IF YOU'RE SO BOLD, WHY HAVE YOU REMAINED IN HIDING ALL THESE YEARS, MURDERER?
WHAT MAKES YOU ANY BETTER THAN THESE OTHER COMMON WAR CRIMINALS?
MY DEADLY SCARF-- WHICH HAS NEVER FAILED ME YET!
HE'S FASTER THAN I THOUGHT!
HE FEINTED TO MY FACE-- THEN SNARED MY WAIST!
HOW EASILY I CAN UPSET YOU--
BY MERELY PULLING THE SCARF BACK TO ME--AND SPINNING YOU LIKE A TOP!
WHILE ANOTHER SUDDEN MOVE CAN MAKE YOU UNABLE TO SEE YOUR FOE!
SNAP!
16

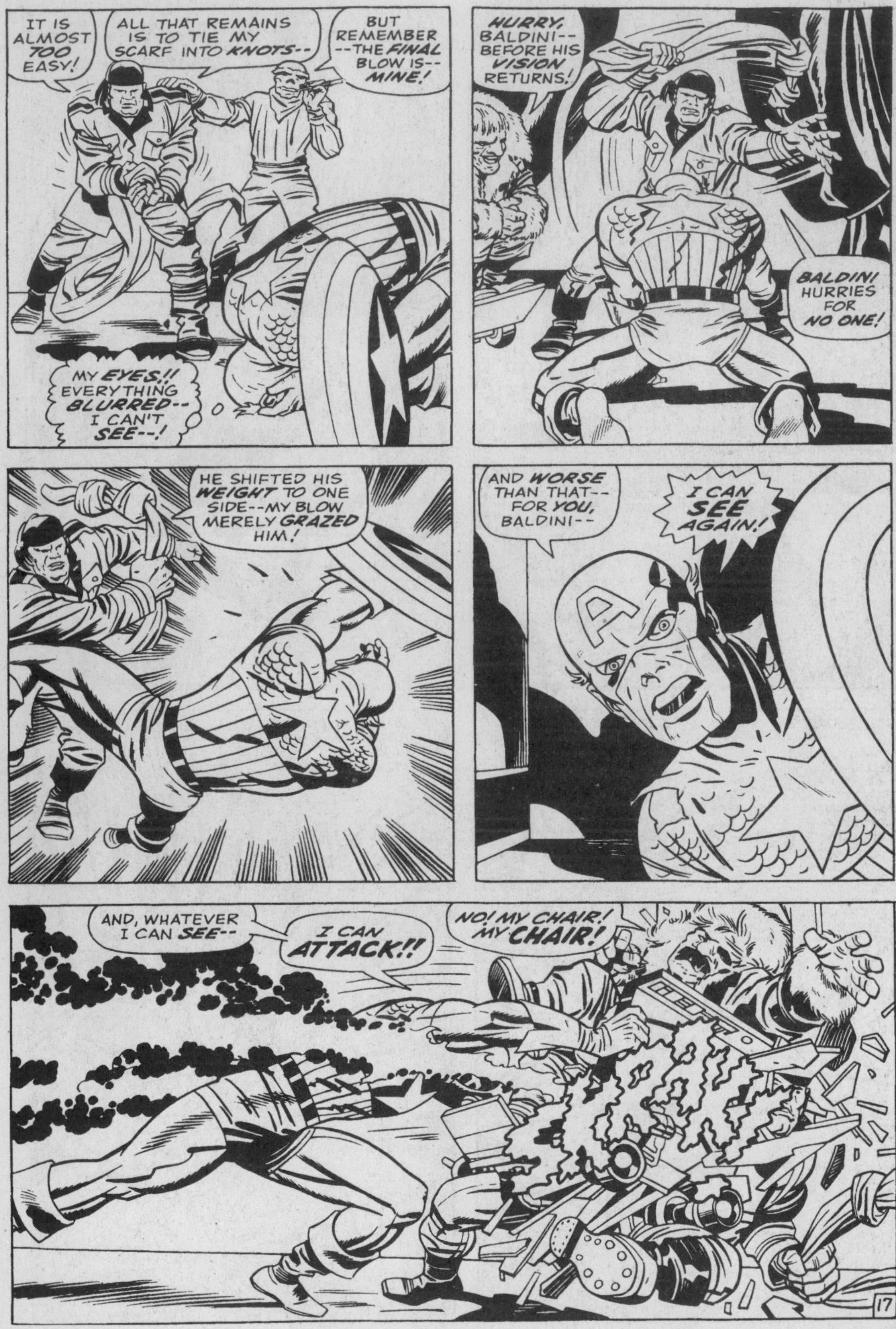

IT IS ALMOST TOO EASY!
ALL THAT REMAINS IS TO TIE MY SCARF INTO KNOTS--
BUT REMEMBER --THE FINAL BLOW IS-- MINE!
MY EYES!! EVERYTHING BLURRED-- I CAN'T SEE--!
HURRY, BALDINI-- BEFORE HIS VISION RETURNS!
BALDINI HURRIES FOR NO ONE!
HE SHIFTED HIS WEIGHT TO ONE SIDE--MY BLOW MERELY GRAZED HIM!
AND WORSE THAN THAT-- FOR YOU, BALDINI--
I CAN SEE AGAIN!
AND, WHATEVER I CAN SEE--
I CAN ATTACK!!
NO! MY CHAIR! MY CHAIR!
17

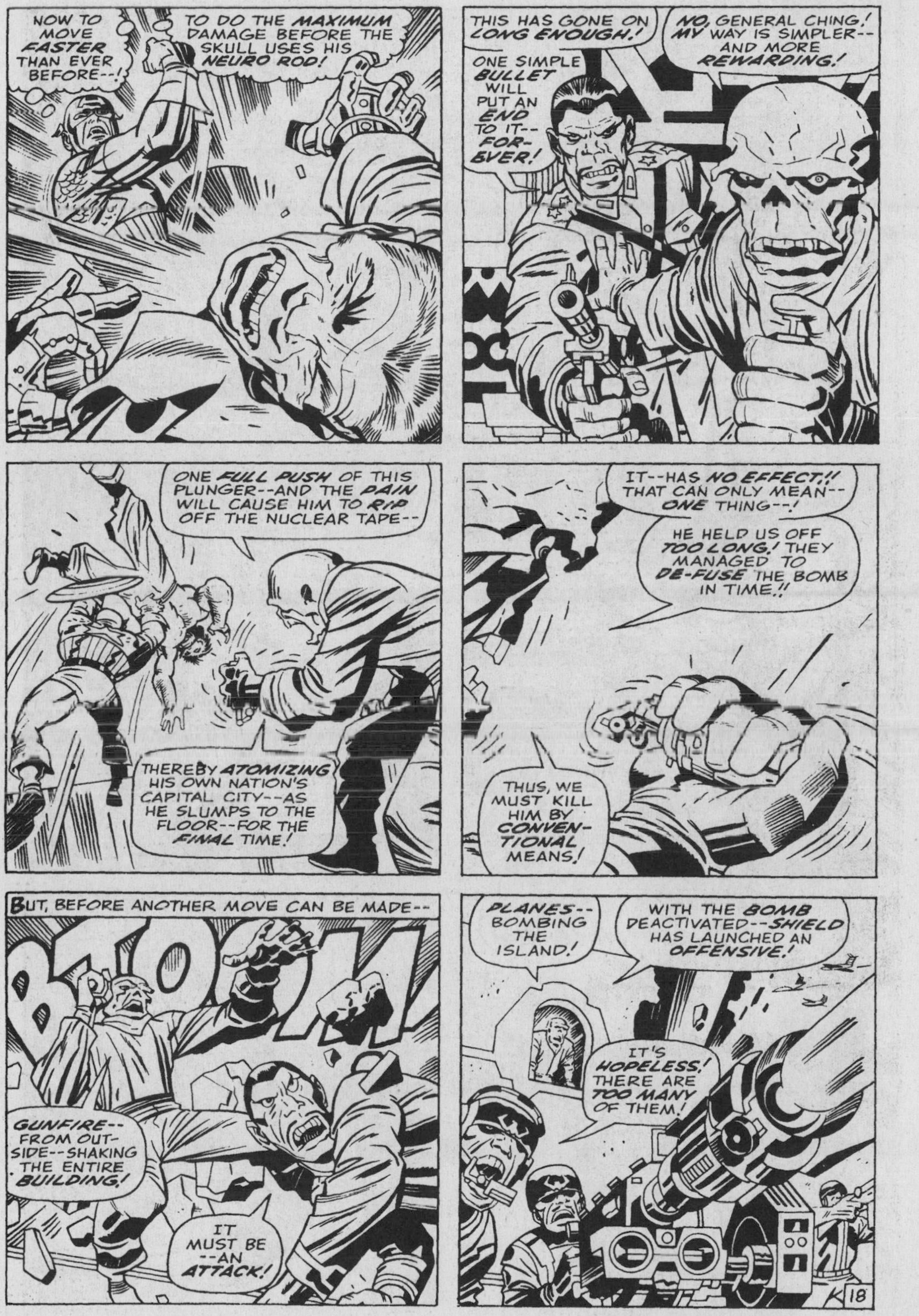
NOW TO MOVE FASTER THAN EVER BEFORE--!
TO DO THE MAXIMUM DAMAGE BEFORE THE SKULL USES HIS NEURO ROD!
THIS HAS GONE ON LONG ENOUGH!
ONE SIMPLE BULLET WILL PUT AN END TO IT--FOR-EVER!
NO, GENERAL CHING! MY WAY IS SIMPLER--AND MORE REWARDING!
ONE FULL PUSH OF THIS PLUNGER--AND THE PAIN WILL CAUSE HIM TO RIP OFF THE NUCLEAR TAPE--
THEREBY ATOMIZING HIS OWN NATION'S CAPITAL CITY--AS HE SLUMPS TO THE FLOOR--FOR THE FINAL TIME!
IT--HAS NO EFFECT!! THAT CAN ONLY MEAN--ONE THING--!
HE HELD US OFF TOO LONG! THEY MANAGED TO DE-FUSE THE BOMB IN TIME!!
THUS, WE MUST KILL HIM BY CONVEN-TIONAL MEANS!
BUT, BEFORE ANOTHER MOVE CAN BE MADE--
BTOOM
GUNFIRE--FROM OUT-SIDE--SHAKING THE ENTIRE BUILDING!
IT MUST BE --AN ATTACK!
PLANES--BOMBING THE ISLAND!
WITH THE BOMB DEACTIVATED--SHIELD HAS LAUNCHED AN OFFENSIVE!
IT'S HOPELESS! THERE ARE TOO MANY OF THEM!
K 18

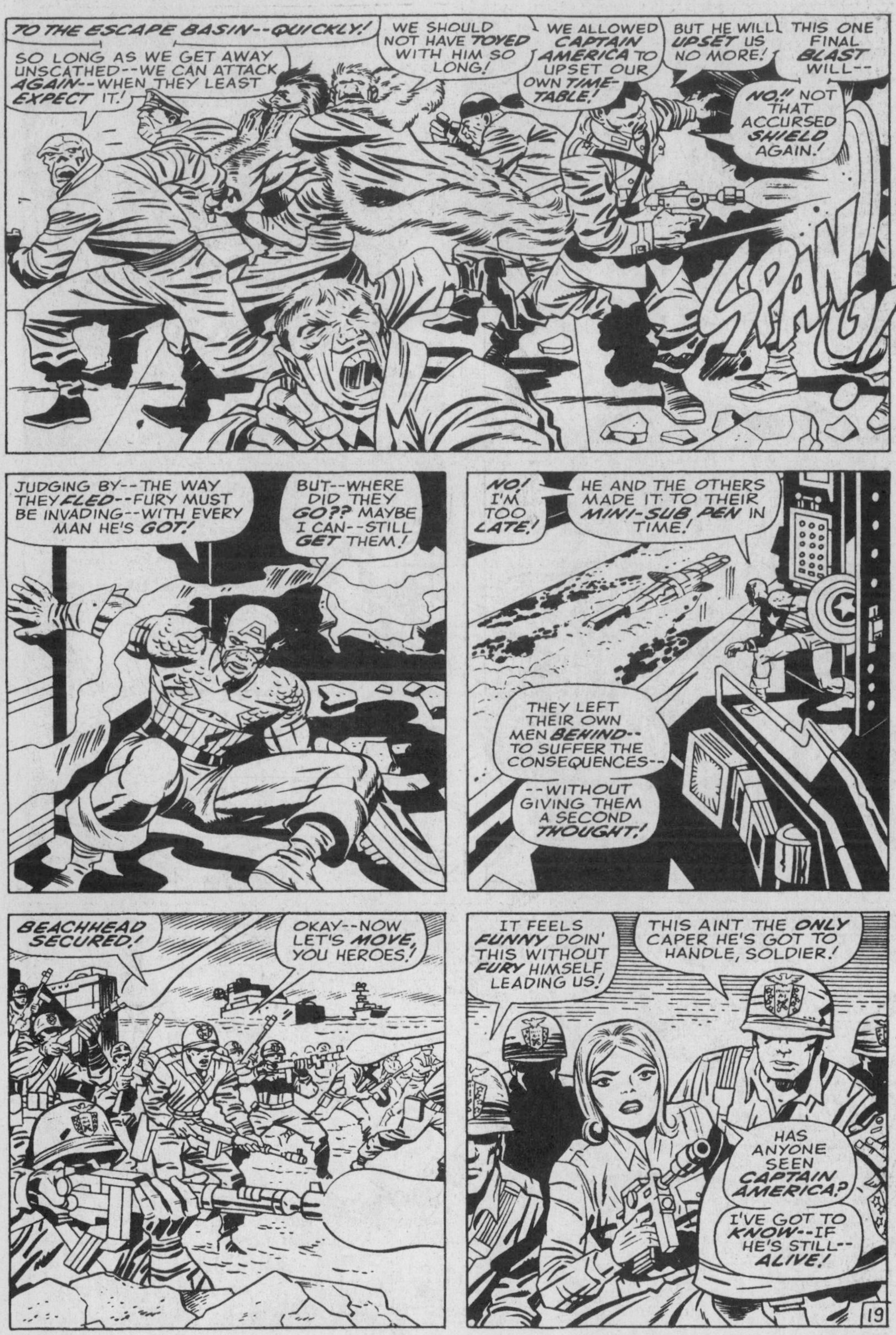
TO THE ESCAPE BASIN--QUICKLY!
SO LONG AS WE GET AWAY UNSCATHED--WE CAN ATTACK AGAIN--WHEN THEY LEAST EXPECT IT!
WE SHOULD NOT HAVE TOYED WITH HIM SO LONG!
WE ALLOWED CAPTAIN AMERICA TO UPSET OUR OWN TIME-TABLE!
BUT HE WILL UPSET US NO MORE!
THIS ONE FINAL BLAST WILL--
NO!! NOT THAT ACCURSED SHIELD AGAIN!
SPANG!
JUDGING BY--THE WAY THEY FLED--FURY MUST BE INVADING--WITH EVERY MAN HE'S GOT!
BUT--WHERE DID THEY GO?? MAYBE I CAN--STILL GET THEM!
NO! I'M TOO LATE!
HE AND THE OTHERS MADE IT TO THEIR MINI-SUB PEN IN TIME!
THEY LEFT THEIR OWN MEN BEHIND--TO SUFFER THE CONSEQUENCES--
--WITHOUT GIVING THEM A SECOND THOUGHT!
BEACHHEAD SECURED!
OKAY--NOW LET'S MOVE, YOU HEROES!
IT FEELS FUNNY DOIN' THIS WITHOUT FURY HIMSELF LEADING US!
THIS AINT THE ONLY CAPER HE'S GOT TO HANDLE, SOLDIER!
HAS ANYONE SEEN CAPTAIN AMERICA?
I'VE GOT TO KNOW--IF HE'S STILL--ALIVE!
19

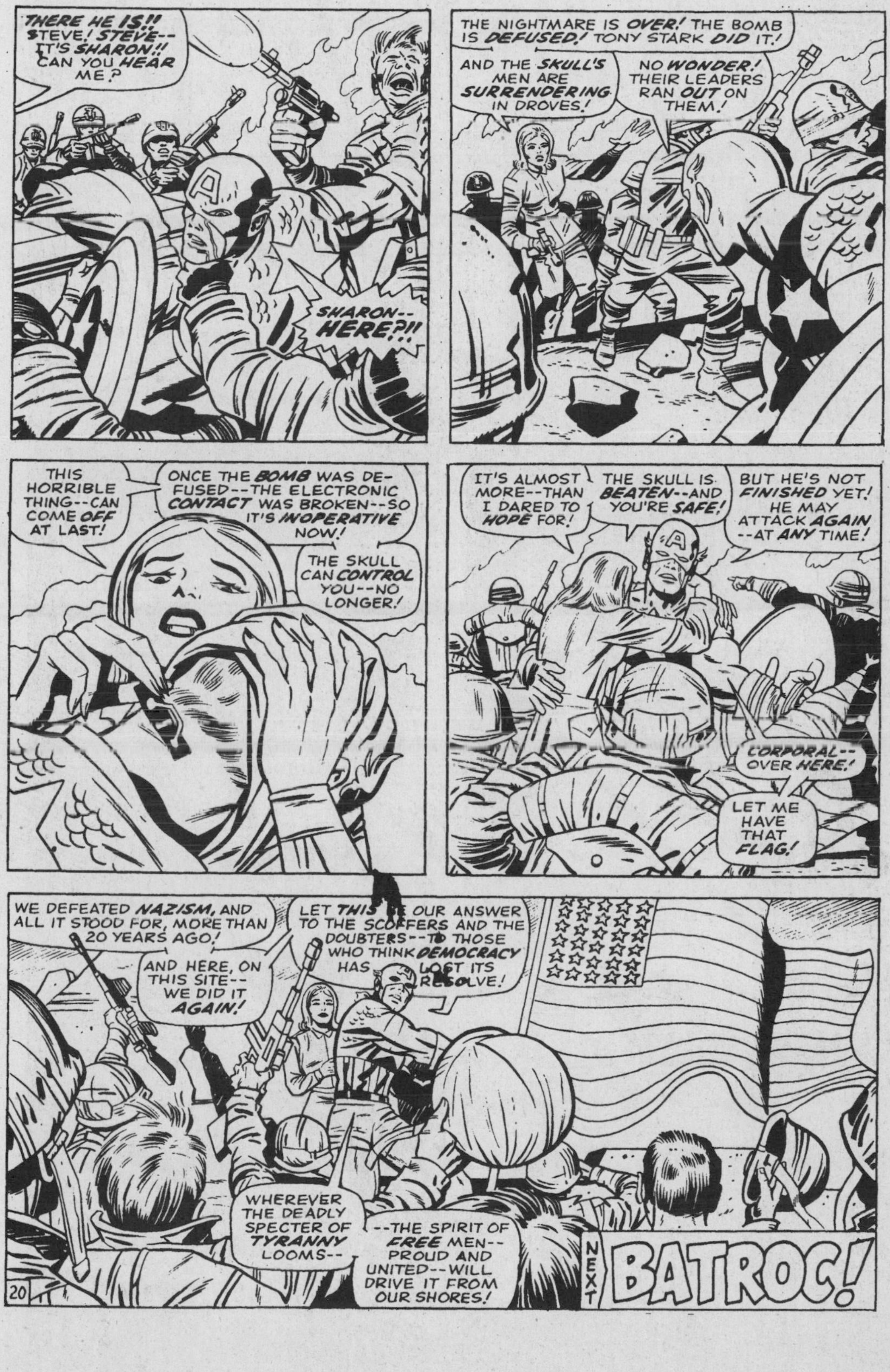
THERE HE IS!! STEVE! STEVE-- IT'S SHARON!! CAN YOU HEAR ME?
SHARON-- HERE?!!
THE NIGHTMARE IS OVER! THE BOMB IS DEFUSED! TONY STARK DID IT!
AND THE SKULL'S MEN ARE SURRENDERING IN DROVES!
NO WONDER! THEIR LEADERS RAN OUT ON THEM!
THIS HORRIBLE THING--CAN COME OFF AT LAST!
ONCE THE BOMB WAS DE-FUSED--THE ELECTRONIC CONTACT WAS BROKEN--SO IT'S INOPERATIVE NOW!
THE SKULL CAN CONTROL YOU--NO LONGER!
IT'S ALMOST MORE--THAN I DARED TO HOPE FOR!
THE SKULL IS BEATEN--AND YOU'RE SAFE!
BUT HE'S NOT FINISHED YET! HE MAY ATTACK AGAIN --AT ANY TIME!
CORPORAL-- OVER HERE!
LET ME HAVE THAT FLAG!
WE DEFEATED NAZISM, AND ALL IT STOOD FOR, MORE THAN 20 YEARS AGO!
AND HERE, ON THIS SITE-- WE DID IT AGAIN!
LET THIS BE OUR ANSWER TO THE SCOFFERS AND THE DOUBTERS--TO THOSE WHO THINK DEMOCRACY HAS LOST ITS RESOLVE!
WHEREVER THE DEADLY SPECTER OF TYRANNY LOOMS--
--THE SPIRIT OF FREE MEN-- PROUD AND UNITED--WILL DRIVE IT FROM OUR SHORES!
NEXT BATROC!
20

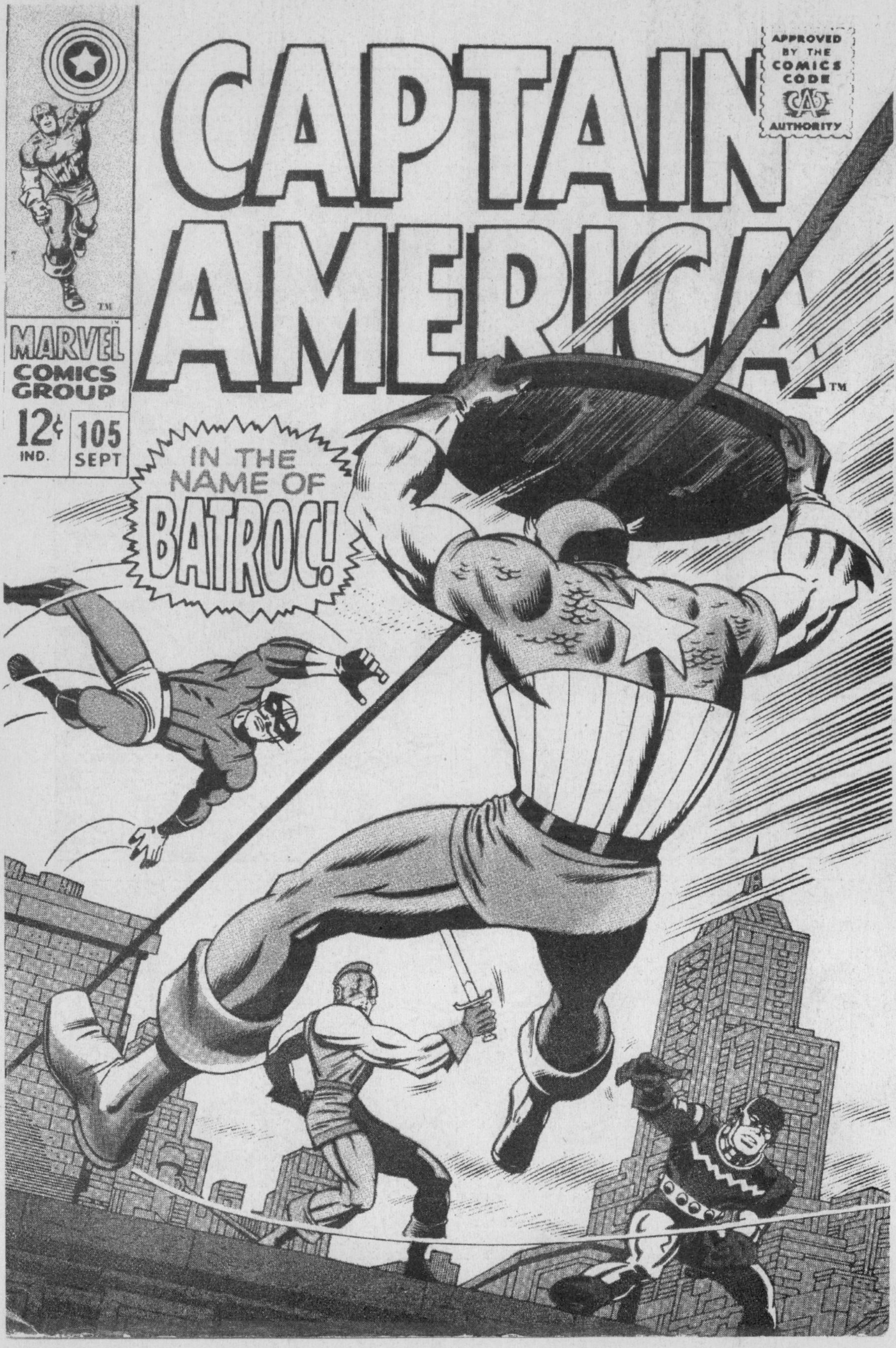
CAPTAIN AMERICA
MARVEL COMICS GROUP
12¢ IND.
105 SEPT
APPROVED BY THE COMICS CODE AUTHORITY
IN THE NAME OF BATROC!

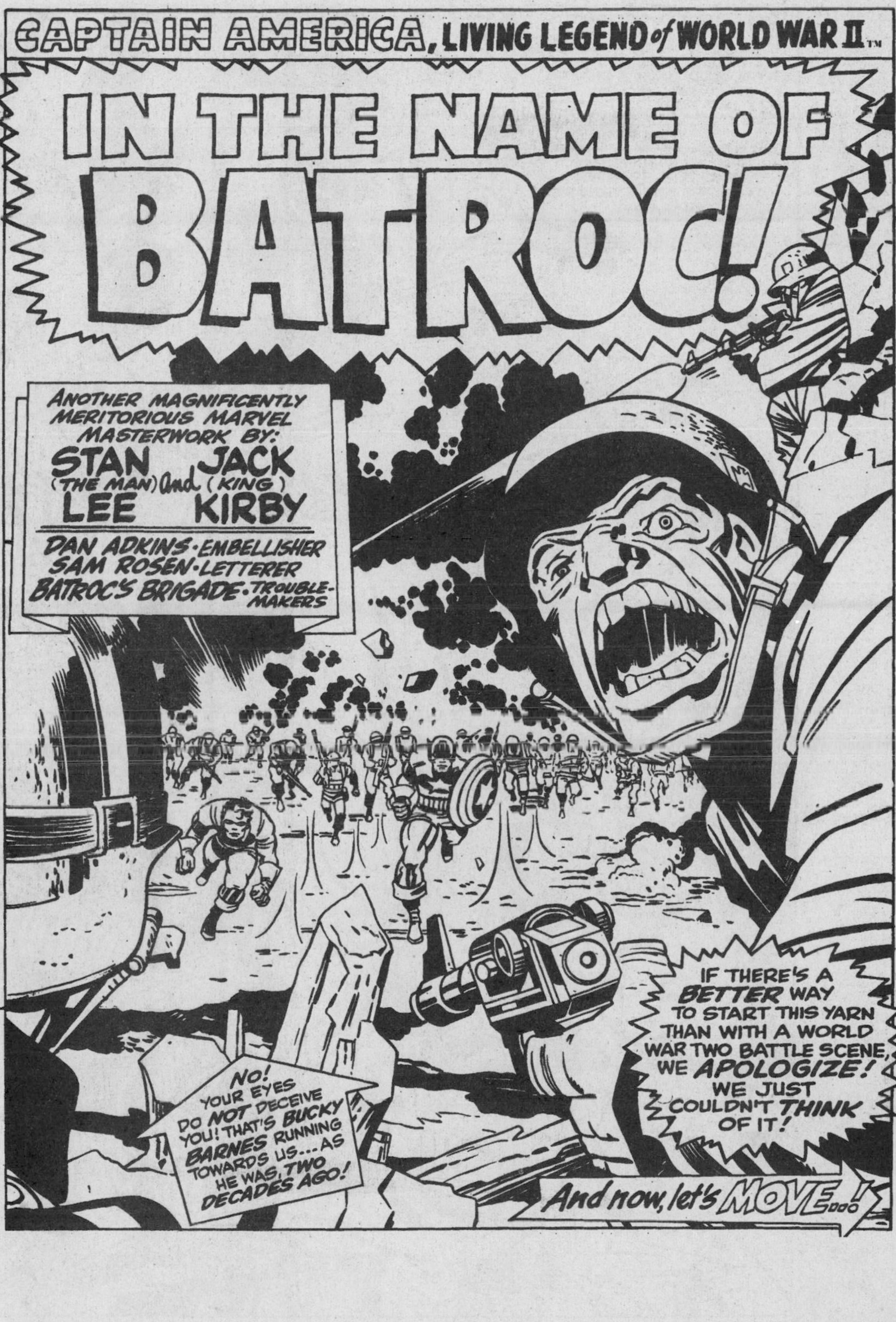
CAPTAIN AMERICA, LIVING LEGEND of WORLD WAR II TM
IN THE NAME OF BATROC!
ANOTHER MAGNIFICENTLY MERITORIOUS MARVEL MASTERWORK BY:
STAN (THE MAN) LEE and JACK (KING) KIRBY
DAN ADKINS·EMBELLISHER
SAM ROSEN·LETTERER
BATROC'S BRIGADE·TROUBLE-MAKERS
NO! YOUR EYES DO NOT DECEIVE YOU! THAT'S BUCKY BARNES RUNNING TOWARDS US...AS HE WAS, TWO DECADES AGO!
IF THERE'S A BETTER WAY TO START THIS YARN THAN WITH A WORLD WAR TWO BATTLE SCENE, WE APOLOGIZE! WE JUST COULDN'T THINK OF IT!
And now, let's MOVE...!

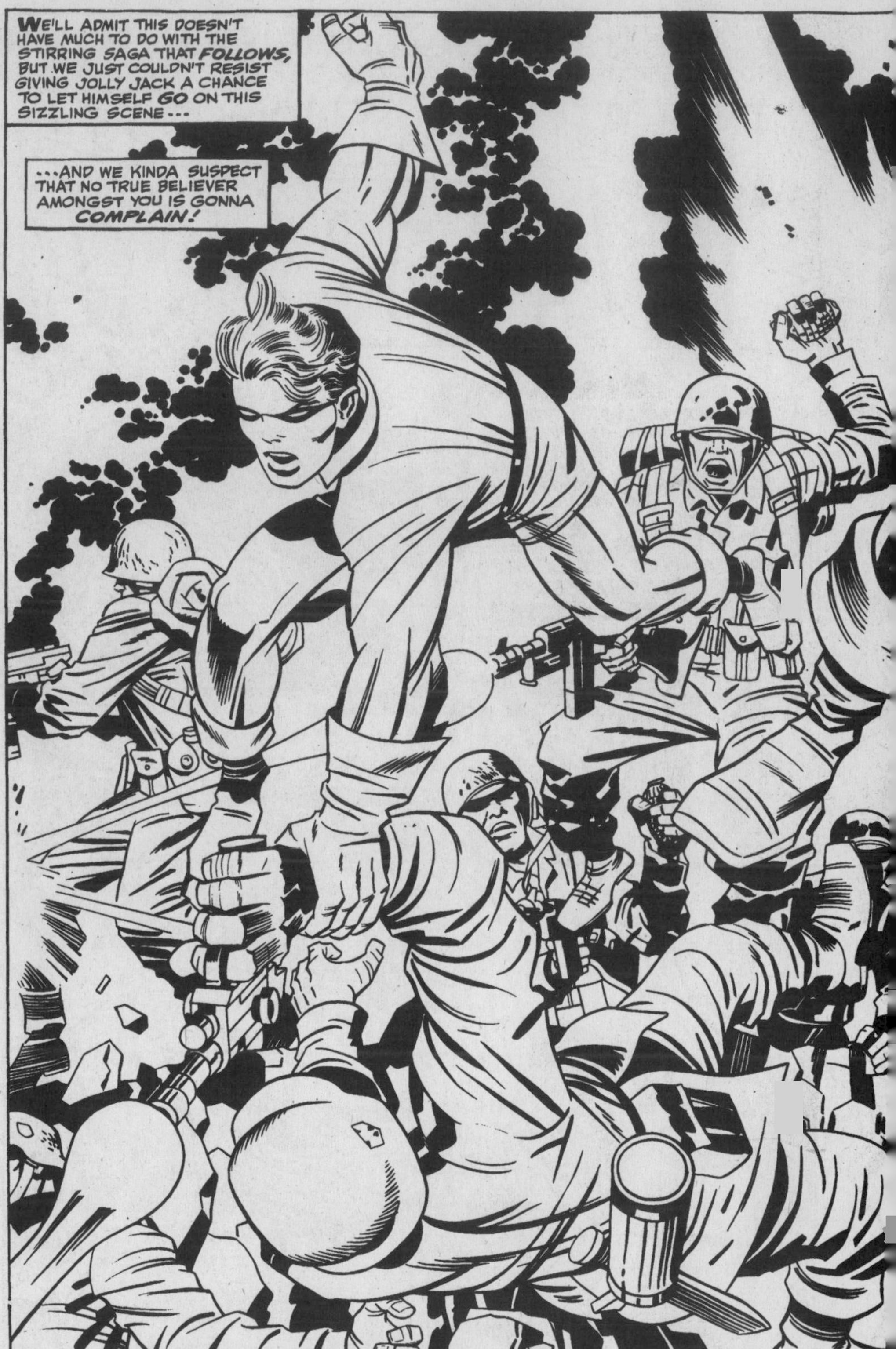
WE'LL ADMIT THIS DOESN'T HAVE MUCH TO DO WITH THE STIRRING SAGA THAT FOLLOWS, BUT WE JUST COULDN'T RESIST GIVING JOLLY JACK A CHANCE TO LET HIMSELF GO ON THIS SIZZLING SCENE---
...AND WE KINDA SUSPECT THAT NO TRUE BELIEVER AMONGST YOU IS GONNA COMPLAIN!

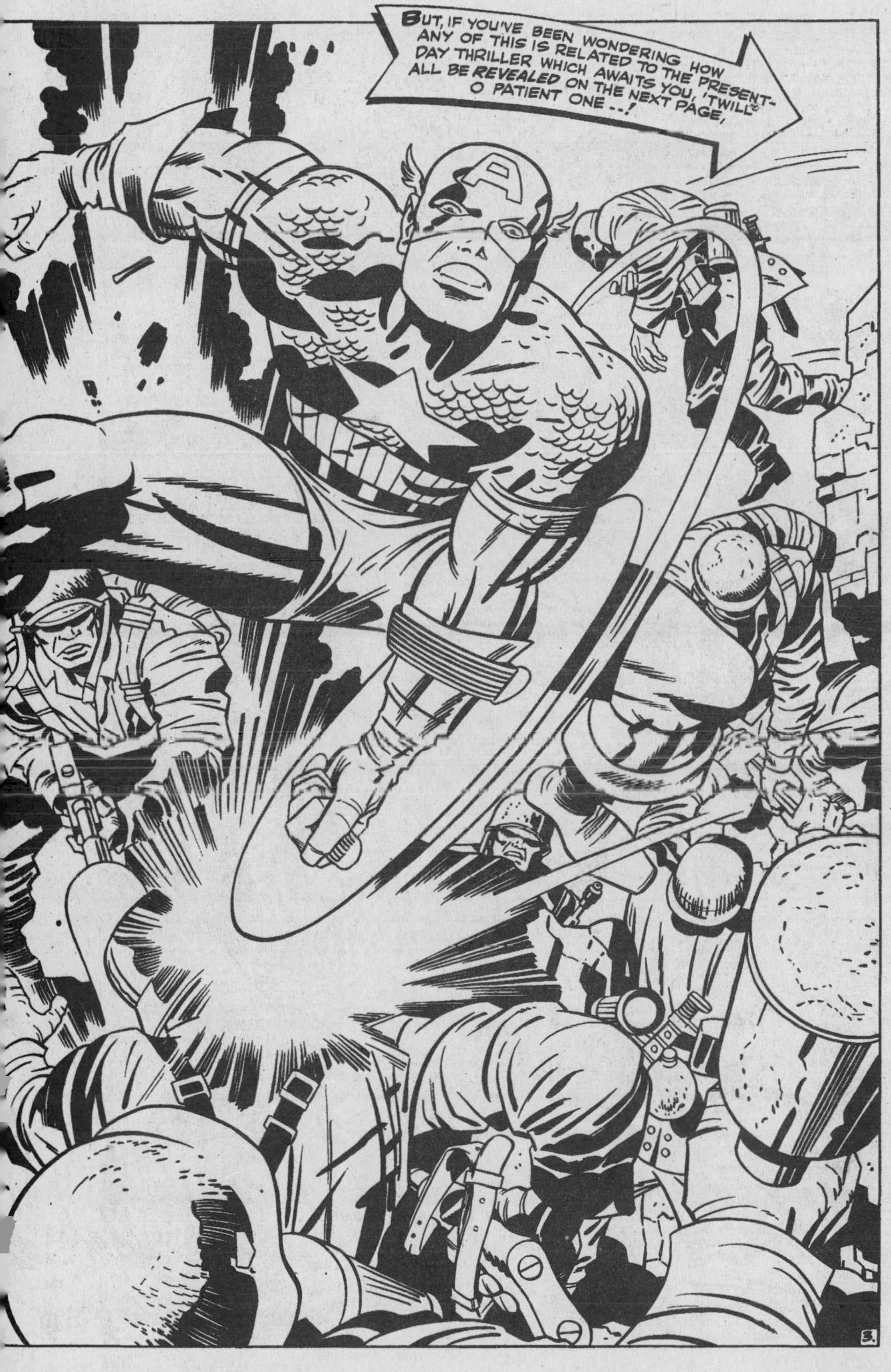
BUT, IF YOU'VE BEEN WONDERING HOW ANY OF THIS IS RELATED TO THE PRESENT-DAY THRILLER WHICH AWAITS YOU, 'TWILL ALL BE REVEALED ON THE NEXT PAGE, O PATIENT ONE..!
3.

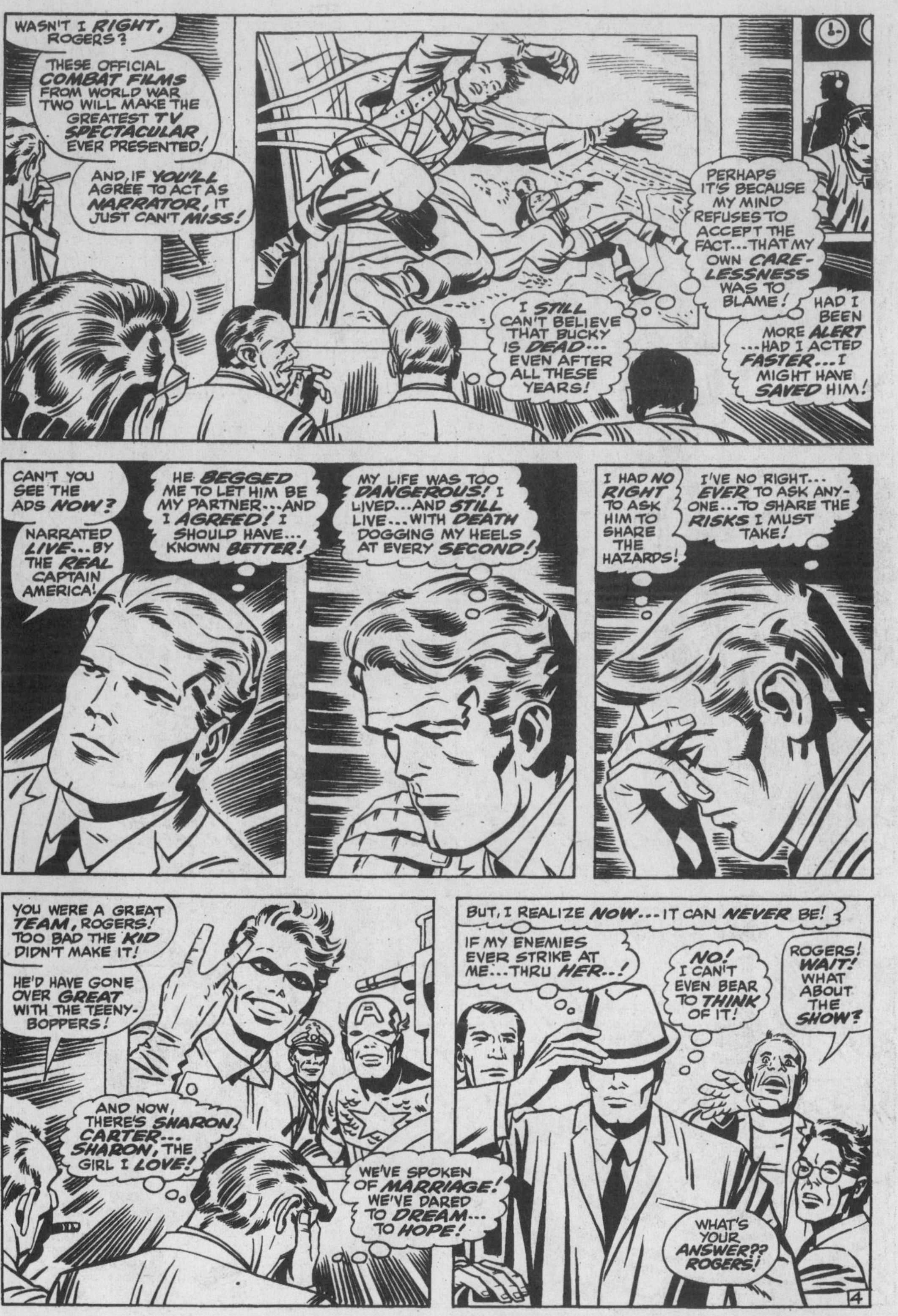
WASN'T I RIGHT, ROGERS?
THESE OFFICIAL COMBAT FILMS FROM WORLD WAR TWO WILL MAKE THE GREATEST TV SPECTACULAR EVER PRESENTED!
AND, IF YOU'LL AGREE TO ACT AS NARRATOR, IT JUST CAN'T MISS!
I STILL CAN'T BELIEVE THAT BUCKY IS DEAD... EVEN AFTER ALL THESE YEARS!
PERHAPS IT'S BECAUSE MY MIND REFUSES TO ACCEPT THE FACT...THAT MY OWN CARE-LESSNESS WAS TO BLAME!
HAD I BEEN MORE ALERT ...HAD I ACTED FASTER...I MIGHT HAVE SAVED HIM!
CAN'T YOU SEE THE ADS NOW?
NARRATED LIVE...BY THE REAL CAPTAIN AMERICA!
HE BEGGED ME TO LET HIM BE MY PARTNER...AND I AGREED! I SHOULD HAVE... KNOWN BETTER!
MY LIFE WAS TOO DANGEROUS! I LIVED...AND STILL LIVE...WITH DEATH DOGGING MY HEELS AT EVERY SECOND!
I HAD NO RIGHT TO ASK HIM TO SHARE THE HAZARDS!
I'VE NO RIGHT... EVER TO ASK ANY-ONE...TO SHARE THE RISKS I MUST TAKE!
YOU WERE A GREAT TEAM, ROGERS! TOO BAD THE KID DIDN'T MAKE IT!
HE'D HAVE GONE OVER GREAT WITH THE TEENY-BOPPERS!
AND NOW, THERE'S SHARON CARTER... SHARON, THE GIRL I LOVE!
WE'VE SPOKEN OF MARRIAGE! WE'VE DARED TO DREAM... TO HOPE!
BUT, I REALIZE NOW... IT CAN NEVER BE!
IF MY ENEMIES EVER STRIKE AT ME...THRU HER...!
NO! I CAN'T EVEN BEAR TO THINK OF IT!
ROGERS! WAIT! WHAT ABOUT THE SHOW?
WHAT'S YOUR ANSWER?? ROGERS!
4

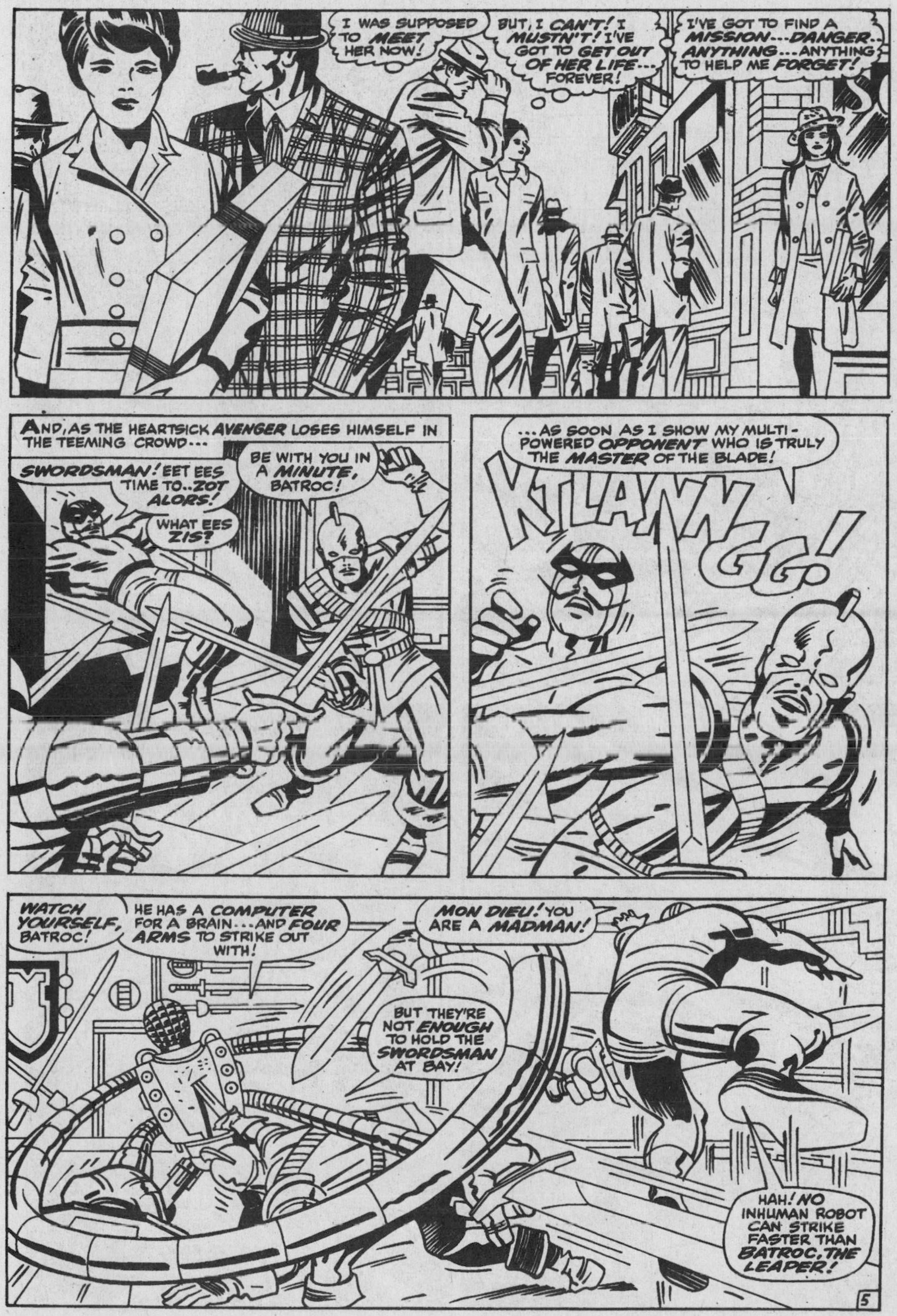

I WAS SUPPOSED TO MEET HER NOW!
BUT, I CAN'T! I MUSTN'T! I'VE GOT TO GET OUT OF HER LIFE... FOREVER!
I'VE GOT TO FIND A MISSION...DANGER... ANYTHING...ANYTHING TO HELP ME FORGET!
AND, AS THE HEARTSICK AVENGER LOSES HIMSELF IN THE TEEMING CROWD...
SWORDSMAN! EET EES TIME TO..ZOT ALORS!
WHAT EES ZIS?
BE WITH YOU IN A MINUTE, BATROC!
...AS SOON AS I SHOW MY MULTI-POWERED OPPONENT WHO IS TRULY THE MASTER OF THE BLADE!
KTLANNGG!
WATCH YOURSELF, BATROC!
HE HAS A COMPUTER FOR A BRAIN...AND FOUR ARMS TO STRIKE OUT WITH!
MON DIEU! YOU ARE A MADMAN!
BUT THEY'RE NOT ENOUGH TO HOLD THE SWORDSMAN AT BAY!
HAH! NO INHUMAN ROBOT CAN STRIKE FASTER THAN BATROC, THE LEAPER!

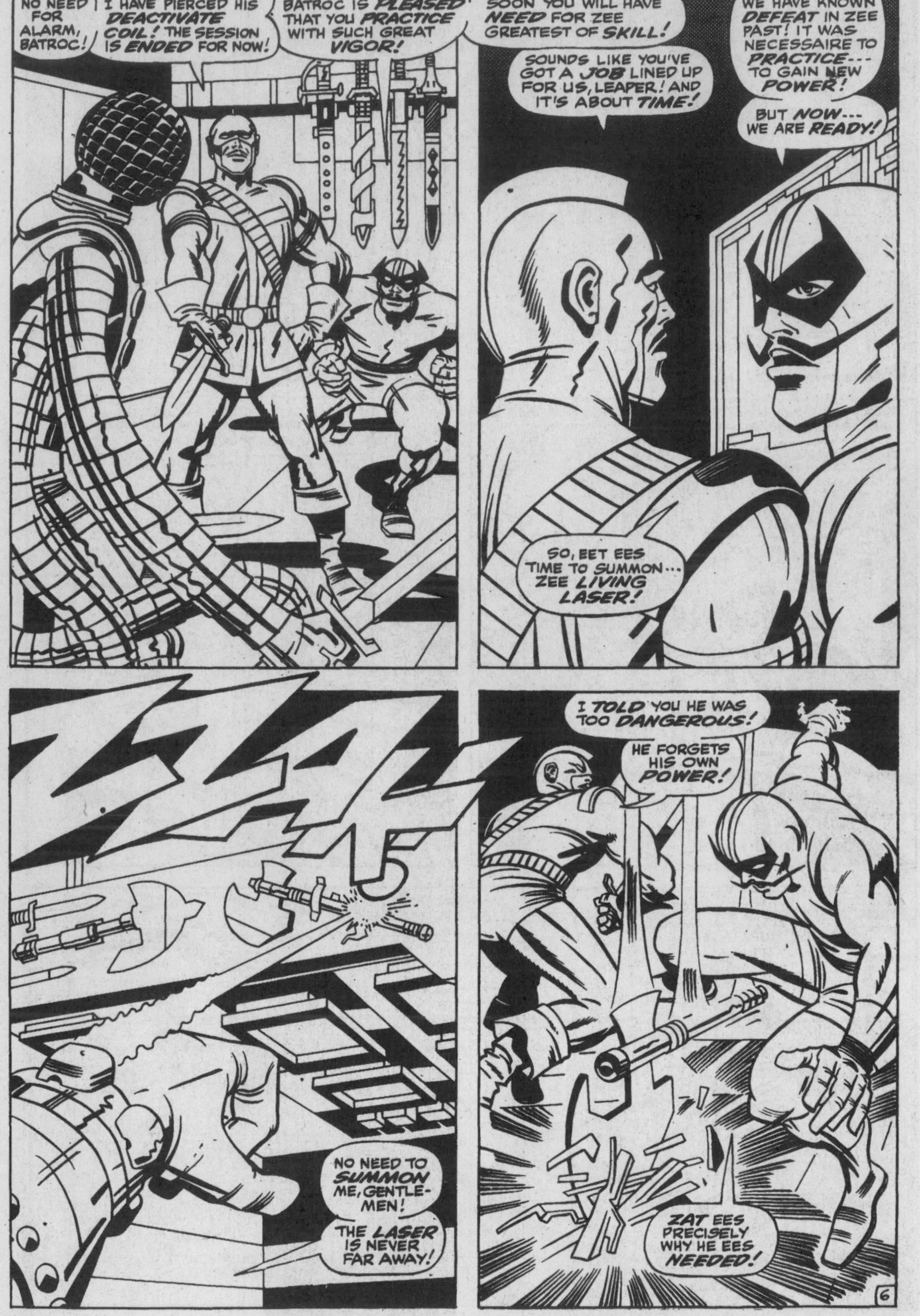
NO NEED FOR ALARM, BATROC!
I HAVE PIERCED HIS DEACTIVATE COIL! THE SESSION IS ENDED FOR NOW!
BATROC IS PLEASED THAT YOU PRACTICE WITH SUCH GREAT VIGOR!
SOON YOU WILL HAVE NEED FOR ZEE GREATEST OF SKILL!
SOUNDS LIKE YOU'VE GOT A JOB LINED UP FOR US, LEAPER! AND IT'S ABOUT TIME!
WE HAVE KNOWN DEFEAT IN ZEE PAST! IT WAS NECESSAIRE TO PRACTICE--- TO GAIN NEW POWER!
BUT NOW... WE ARE READY!
SO, EET EES TIME TO SUMMON... ZEE LIVING LASER!
ZZAK
NO NEED TO SUMMON ME, GENTLE-MEN!
THE LASER IS NEVER FAR AWAY!
I TOLD YOU HE WAS TOO DANGEROUS!
HE FORGETS HIS OWN POWER!
ZAT EES PRECISELY WHY HE EES NEEDED!
6

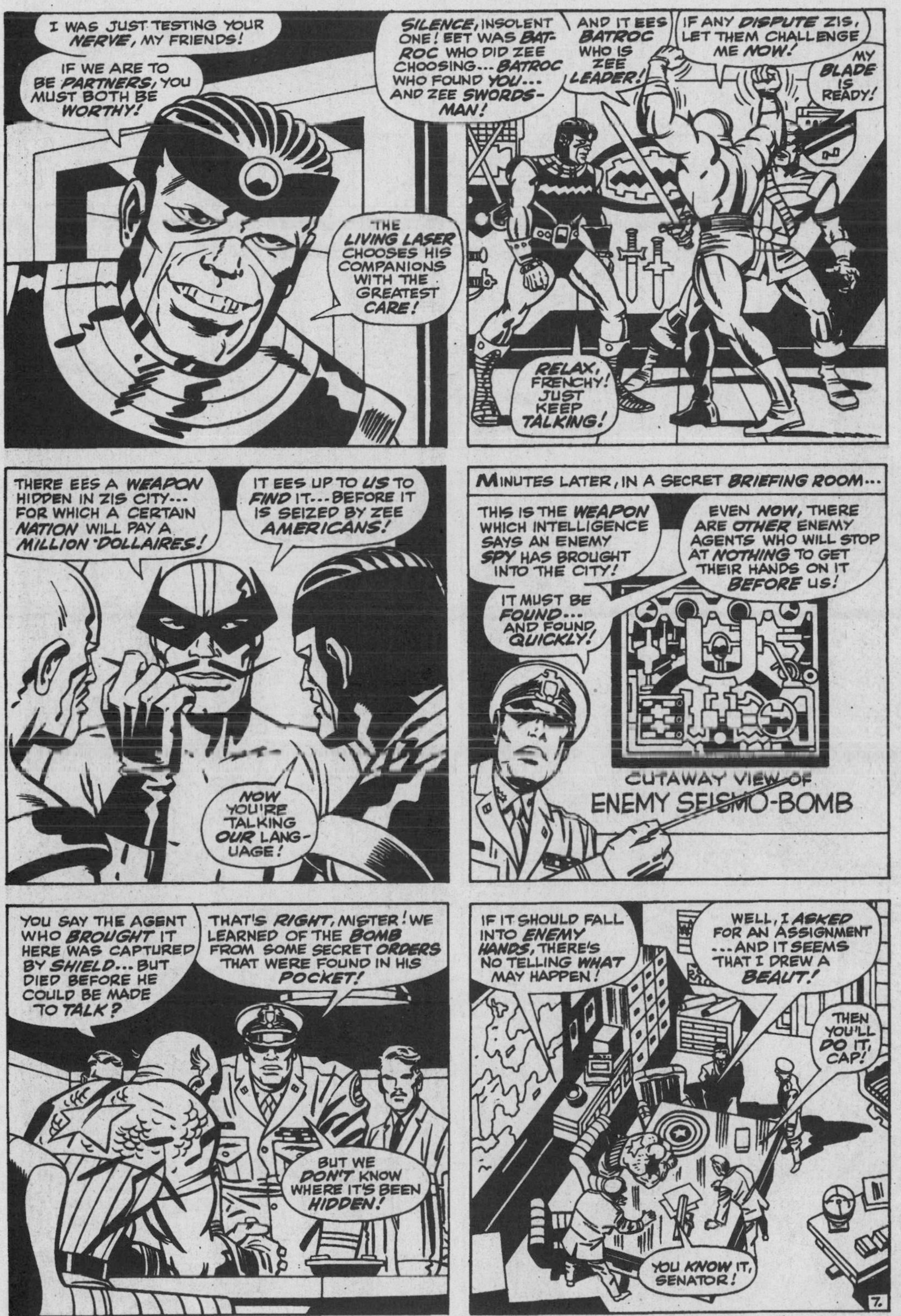
I WAS JUST TESTING YOUR NERVE, MY FRIENDS!
IF WE ARE TO BE PARTNERS, YOU MUST BOTH BE WORTHY!
THE LIVING LASER CHOOSES HIS COMPANIONS WITH THE GREATEST CARE!
SILENCE, INSOLENT ONE! EET WAS BATROC WHO DID ZEE CHOOSING... BATROC WHO FOUND YOU... AND ZEE SWORDSMAN!
AND IT EES BATROC WHO IS ZEE LEADER!
IF ANY DISPUTE ZIS, LET THEM CHALLENGE ME NOW!
MY BLADE IS READY!
RELAX, FRENCHY! JUST KEEP TALKING!
THERE EES A WEAPON HIDDEN IN ZIS CITY--- FOR WHICH A CERTAIN NATION WILL PAY A MILLION DOLLAIRES!
IT EES UP TO US TO FIND IT--- BEFORE IT IS SEIZED BY ZEE AMERICANS!
NOW YOU'RE TALKING OUR LANGUAGE!
MINUTES LATER, IN A SECRET BRIEFING ROOM...
THIS IS THE WEAPON WHICH INTELLIGENCE SAYS AN ENEMY SPY HAS BROUGHT INTO THE CITY!
EVEN NOW, THERE ARE OTHER ENEMY AGENTS WHO WILL STOP AT NOTHING TO GET THEIR HANDS ON IT BEFORE US!
IT MUST BE FOUND... AND FOUND QUICKLY!
CUTAWAY VIEW OF
ENEMY SEISMO-BOMB
YOU SAY THE AGENT WHO BROUGHT IT HERE WAS CAPTURED BY SHIELD... BUT DIED BEFORE HE COULD BE MADE TO TALK?
THAT'S RIGHT, MISTER! WE LEARNED OF THE BOMB FROM SOME SECRET ORDERS THAT WERE FOUND IN HIS POCKET!
BUT WE DON'T KNOW WHERE IT'S BEEN HIDDEN!
IF IT SHOULD FALL INTO ENEMY HANDS, THERE'S NO TELLING WHAT MAY HAPPEN!
WELL, I ASKED FOR AN ASSIGNMENT ...AND IT SEEMS THAT I DREW A BEAUT!
THEN YOU'LL DO IT, CAP!
YOU KNOW IT, SENATOR!
7.

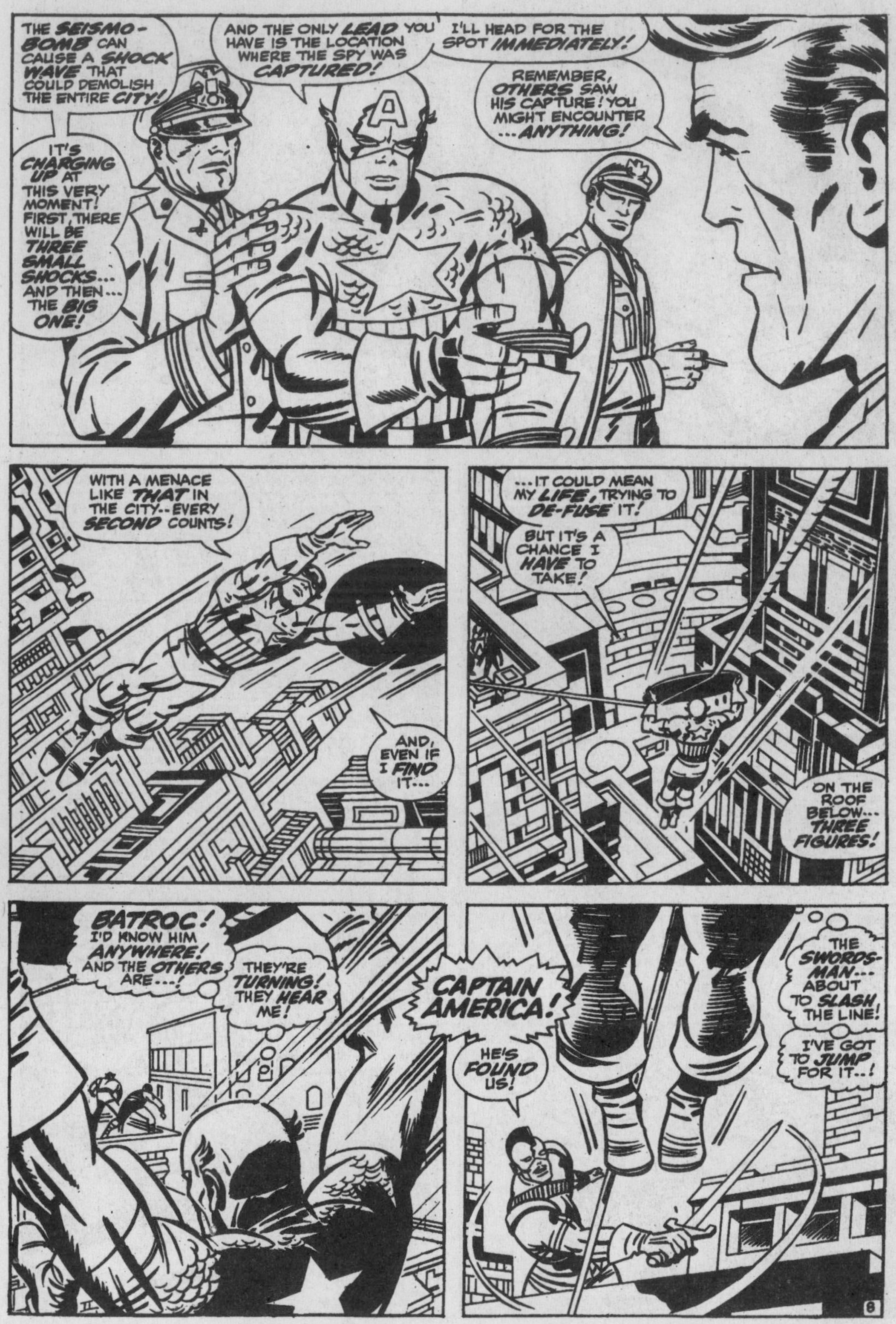
THE SEISMO-BOMB CAN CAUSE A SHOCK WAVE THAT COULD DEMOLISH THE ENTIRE CITY!
IT'S CHARGING UP AT THIS VERY MOMENT! FIRST, THERE WILL BE THREE SMALL SHOCKS... AND THEN... THE BIG ONE!
AND THE ONLY LEAD YOU HAVE IS THE LOCATION WHERE THE SPY WAS CAPTURED!
I'LL HEAD FOR THE SPOT IMMEDIATELY!
REMEMBER, OTHERS SAW HIS CAPTURE! YOU MIGHT ENCOUNTER ...ANYTHING!
WITH A MENACE LIKE THAT IN THE CITY--EVERY SECOND COUNTS!
AND, EVEN IF I FIND IT...
...IT COULD MEAN MY LIFE, TRYING TO DE-FUSE IT!
BUT IT'S A CHANCE I HAVE TO TAKE!
ON THE ROOF BELOW... THREE FIGURES!
BATROC! I'D KNOW HIM ANYWHERE! AND THE OTHERS ARE...!
THEY'RE TURNING! THEY HEAR ME!
CAPTAIN AMERICA!
HE'S FOUND US!
THE SWORDS-MAN... ABOUT TO SLASH THE LINE!
I'VE GOT TO JUMP FOR IT..!
8

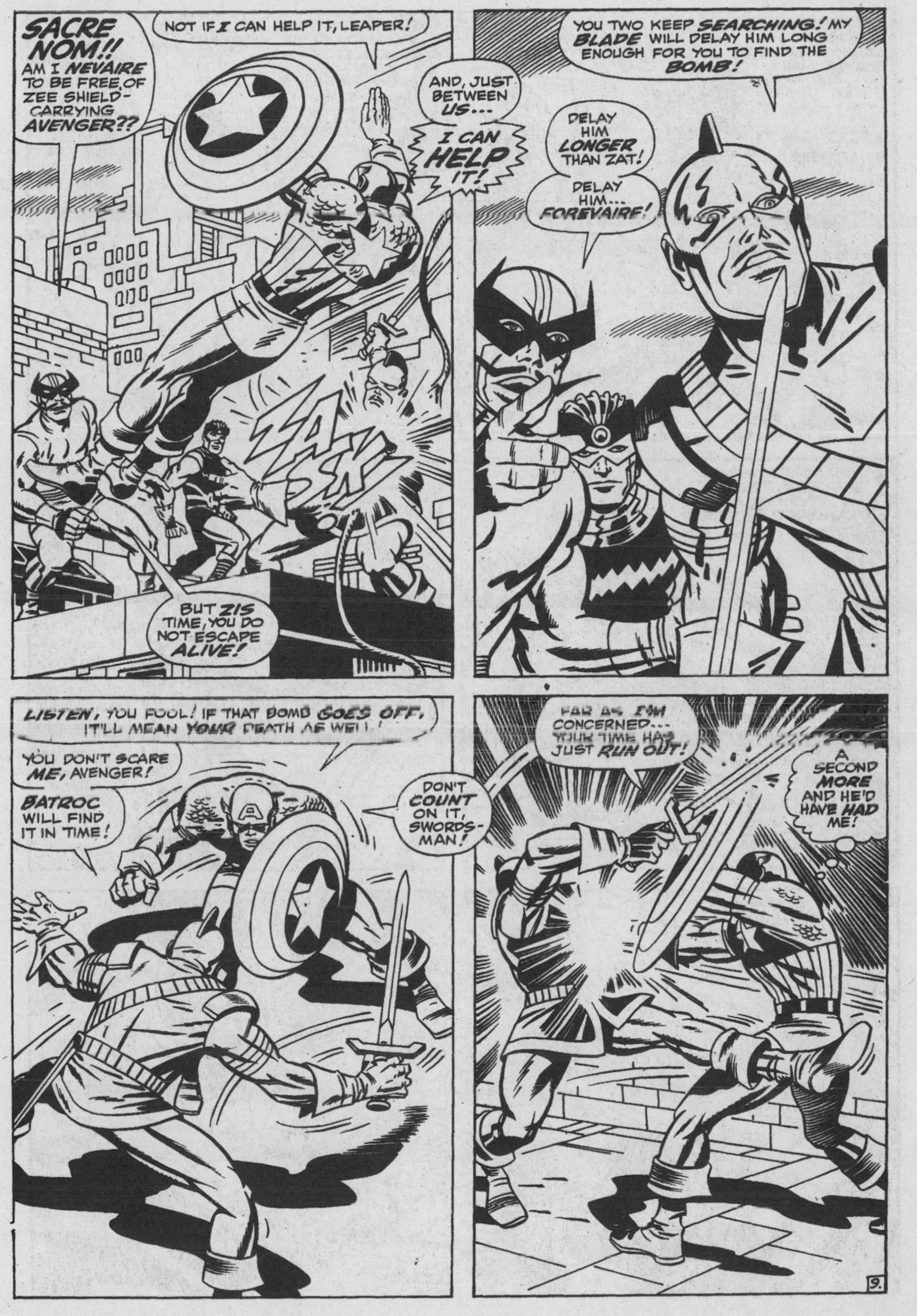

SACRE NOM!! AM I NEVAIRE TO BE FREE OF ZEE SHIELD-CARRYING AVENGER??
NOT IF I CAN HELP IT, LEAPER!
AND, JUST BETWEEN US...
I CAN HELP IT!
ZAK
BUT ZIS TIME, YOU DO NOT ESCAPE ALIVE!
YOU TWO KEEP SEARCHING! MY BLADE WILL DELAY HIM LONG ENOUGH FOR YOU TO FIND THE BOMB!
DELAY HIM LONGER THAN ZAT!
DELAY HIM... FOREVAIRE!
LISTEN, YOU FOOL! IF THAT BOMB GOES OFF, IT'LL MEAN YOUR DEATH AS WELL!
YOU DON'T SCARE ME, AVENGER!
BATROC WILL FIND IT IN TIME!
DON'T COUNT ON IT, SWORDSMAN!
FAR AS I'M CONCERNED... YOUR TIME HAS JUST RUN OUT!
A SECOND MORE AND HE'D HAVE HAD ME!
9.

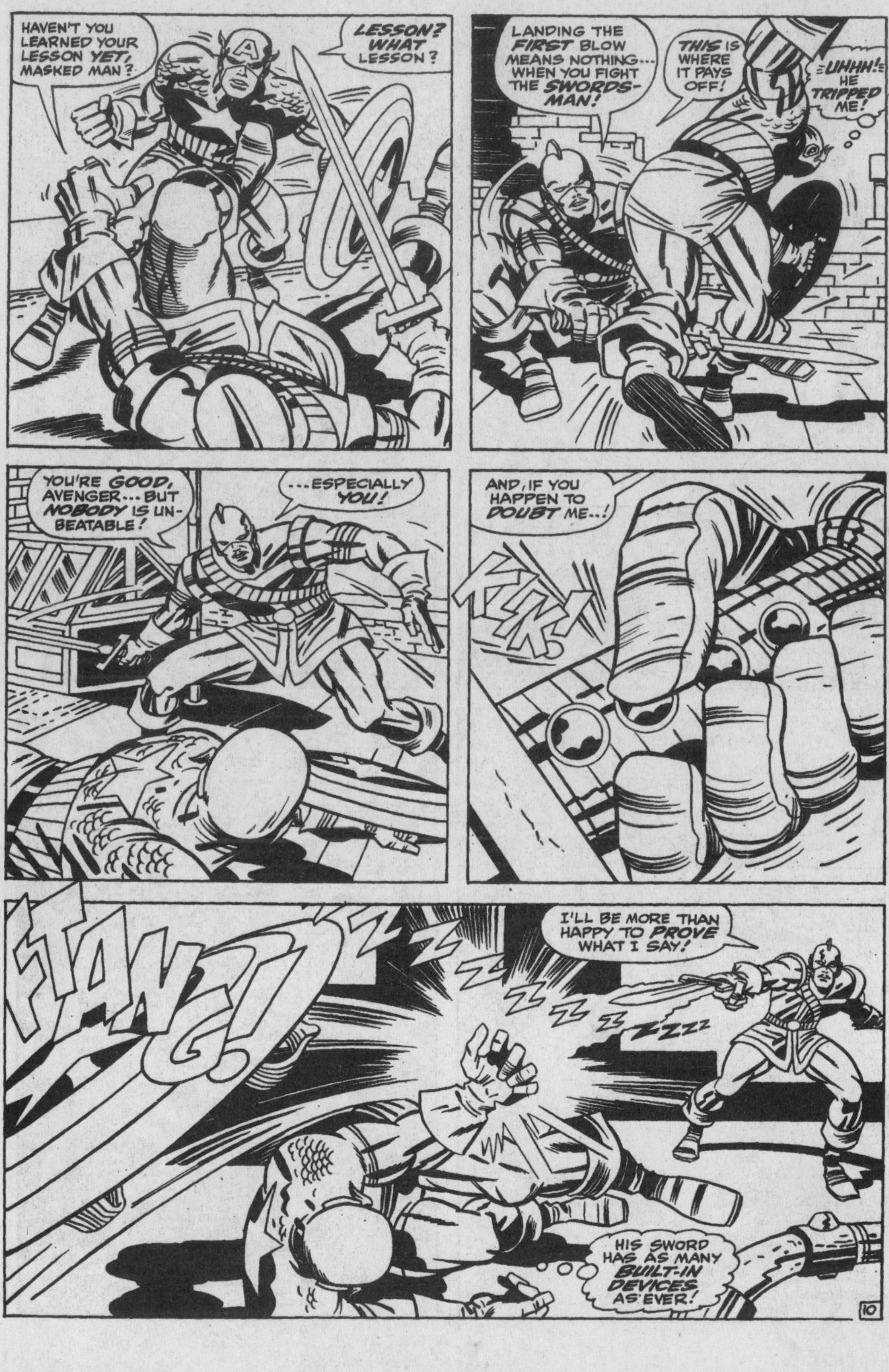
HAVEN'T YOU LEARNED YOUR LESSON YET, MASKED MAN?
LESSON? WHAT LESSON?
LANDING THE FIRST BLOW MEANS NOTHING... WHEN YOU FIGHT THE SWORDSMAN!
THIS IS WHERE IT PAYS OFF!
UHHH! HE TRIPPED ME!
YOU'RE GOOD, AVENGER... BUT NOBODY IS UNBEATABLE!
...ESPECIALLY YOU!
AND, IF YOU HAPPEN TO DOUBT ME...!
KLIK!
I'LL BE MORE THAN HAPPY TO PROVE WHAT I SAY!
FTANG!
HIS SWORD HAS AS MANY BUILT-IN DEVICES AS EVER!
10

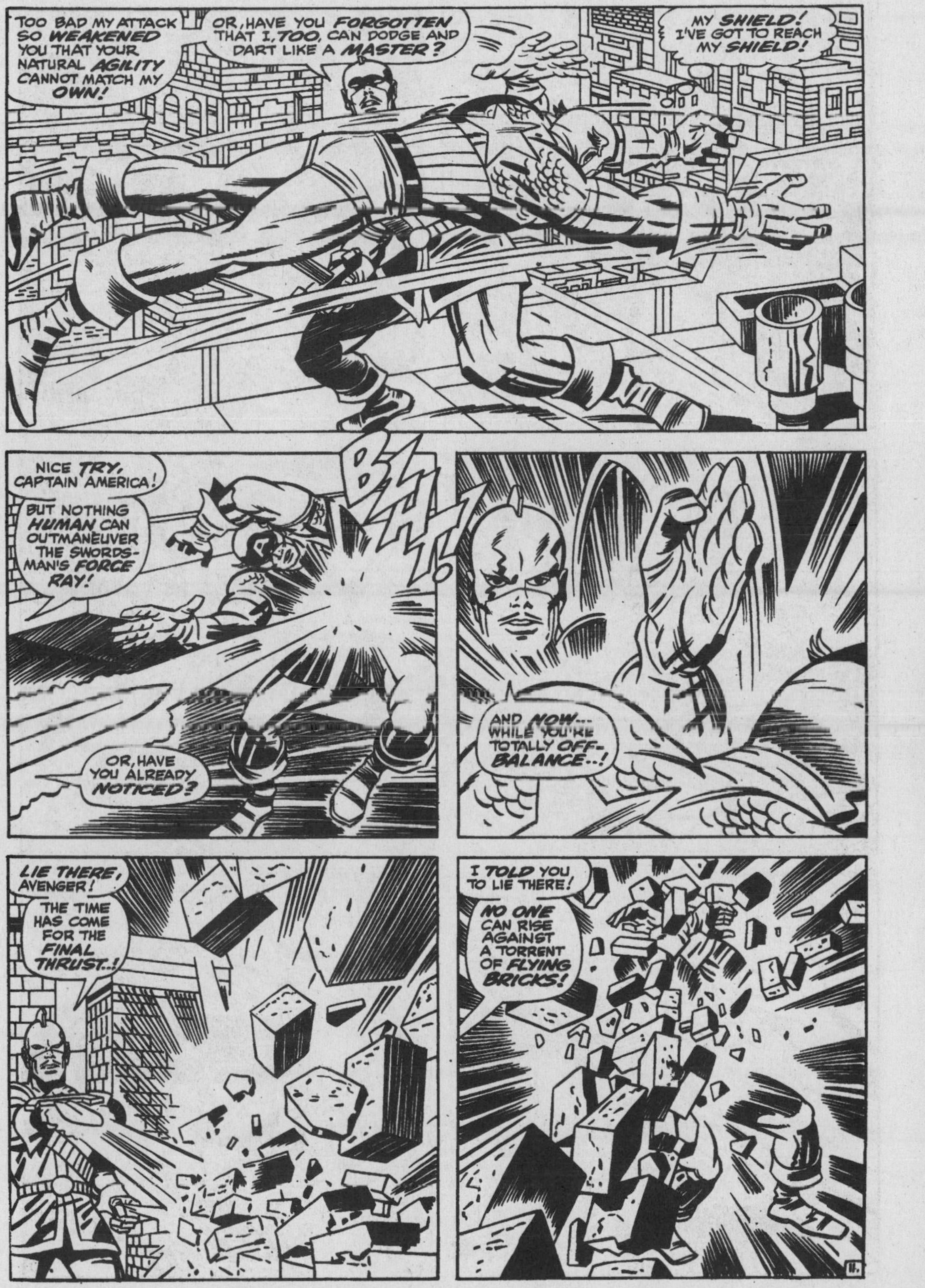

TOO BAD MY ATTACK SO WEAKENED YOU THAT YOUR NATURAL AGILITY CANNOT MATCH MY OWN!
OR, HAVE YOU FORGOTTEN THAT I, TOO, CAN DODGE AND DART LIKE A MASTER?
MY SHIELD! I'VE GOT TO REACH MY SHIELD!
NICE TRY, CAPTAIN AMERICA!
BUT NOTHING HUMAN CAN OUTMANEUVER THE SWORDS-MAN'S FORCE RAY!
BLAM!
OR, HAVE YOU ALREADY NOTICED?
AND NOW... WHILE YOU'RE TOTALLY OFF-BALANCE..!
LIE THERE, AVENGER!
THE TIME HAS COME FOR THE FINAL THRUST..!
I TOLD YOU TO LIE THERE!
NO ONE CAN RISE AGAINST A TORRENT OF FLYING BRICKS!
11.

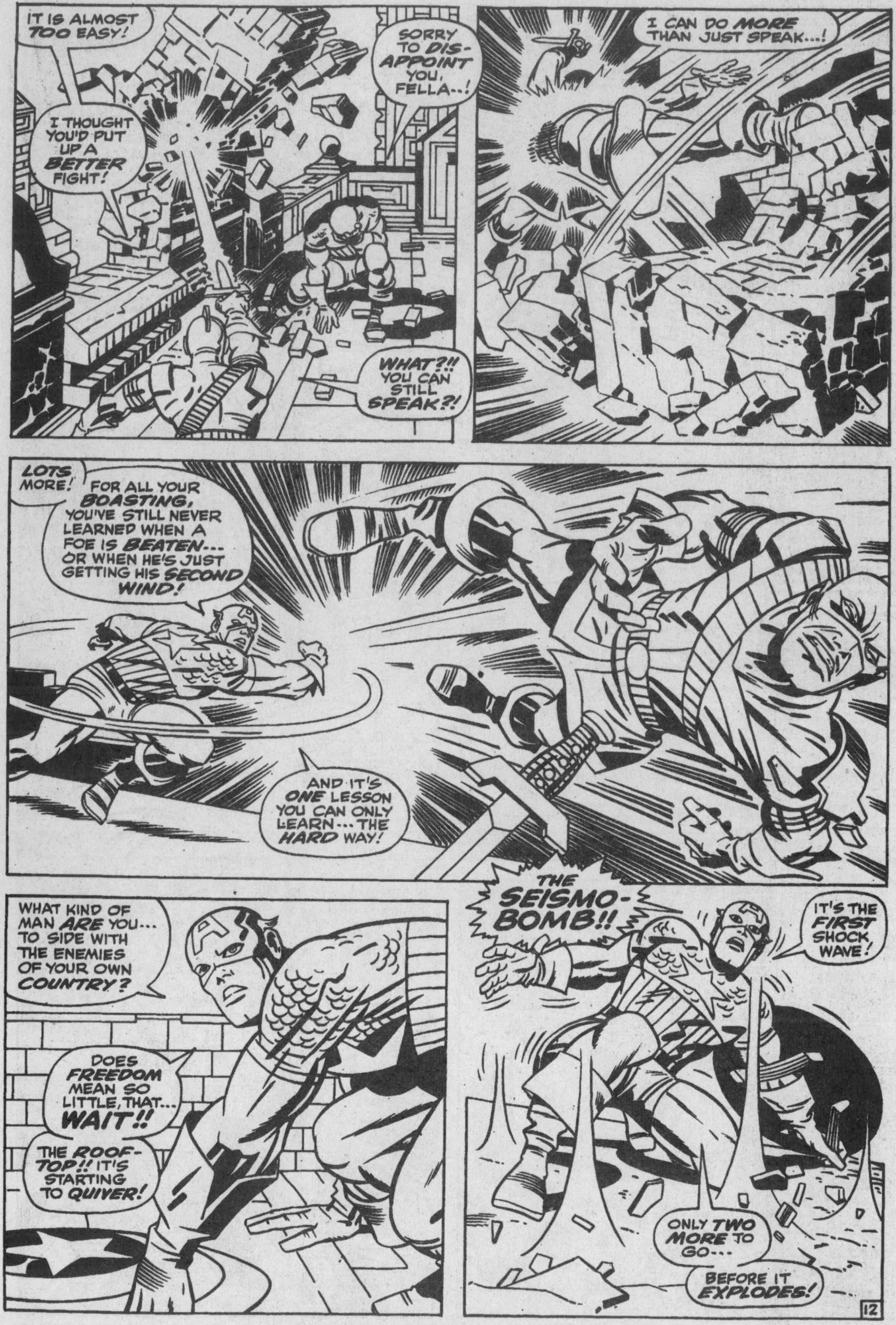
IT IS ALMOST TOO EASY!
I THOUGHT YOU'D PUT UP A BETTER FIGHT!
SORRY TO DIS-APPOINT YOU, FELLA..!
WHAT?!! YOU CAN STILL SPEAK?!
I CAN DO MORE THAN JUST SPEAK...!
LOTS MORE!
FOR ALL YOUR BOASTING, YOU'VE STILL NEVER LEARNED WHEN A FOE IS BEATEN... OR WHEN HE'S JUST GETTING HIS SECOND WIND!
AND IT'S ONE LESSON YOU CAN ONLY LEARN... THE HARD WAY!
WHAT KIND OF MAN ARE YOU... TO SIDE WITH THE ENEMIES OF YOUR OWN COUNTRY?
DOES FREEDOM MEAN SO LITTLE, THAT... WAIT!!
THE ROOF-TOP!! IT'S STARTING TO QUIVER!
THE SEISMO-BOMB!!
IT'S THE FIRST SHOCK WAVE!
ONLY TWO MORE TO GO---
BEFORE IT EXPLODES!
12

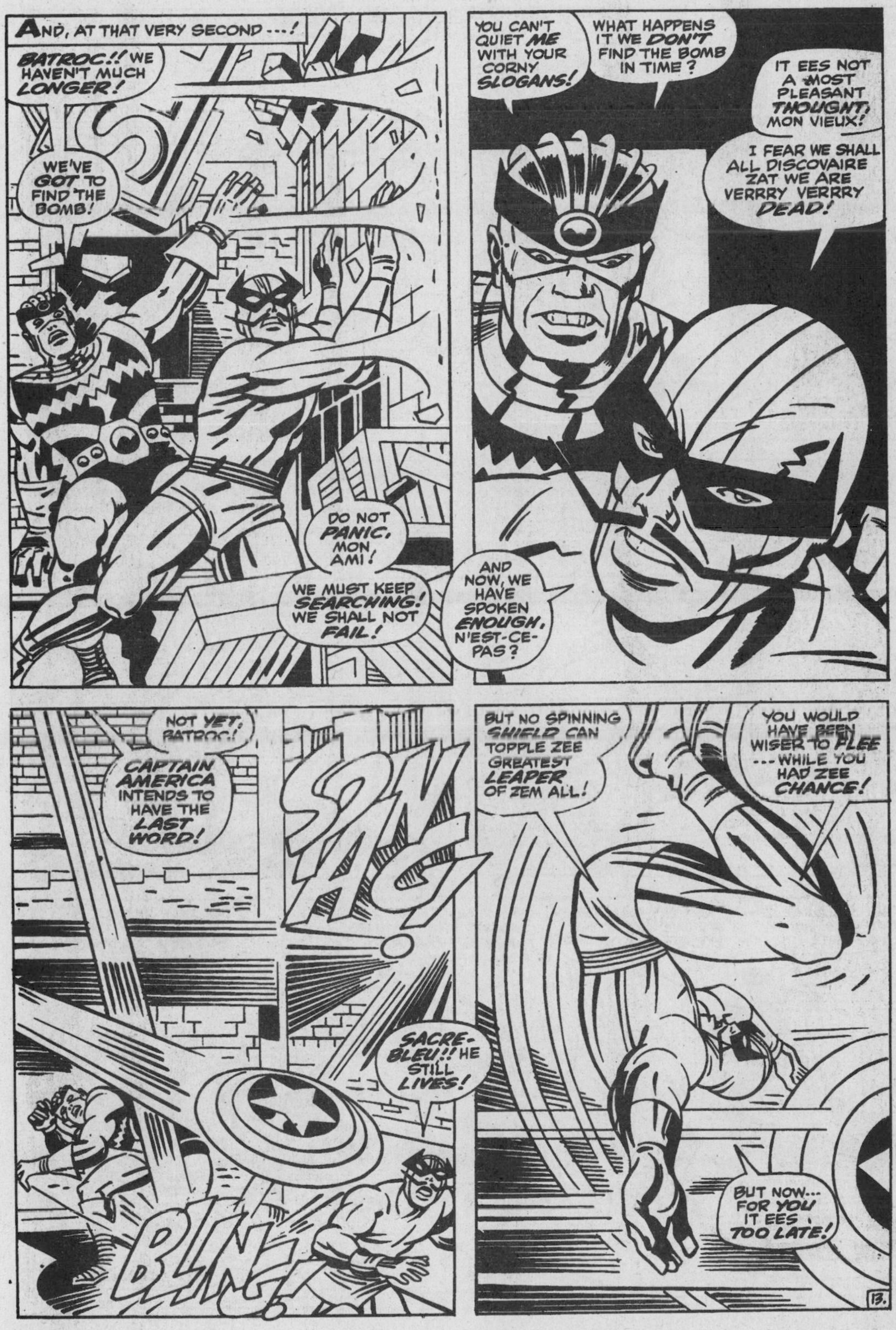
AND, AT THAT VERY SECOND ---!
BATROC!! WE HAVEN'T MUCH LONGER!
WE'VE GOT TO FIND THE BOMB!
DO NOT PANIC, MON AMI!
WE MUST KEEP SEARCHING! WE SHALL NOT FAIL!
YOU CAN'T QUIET ME WITH YOUR CORNY SLOGANS!
WHAT HAPPENS IF WE DON'T FIND THE BOMB IN TIME?
IT EES NOT A MOST PLEASANT THOUGHT, MON VIEUX!
I FEAR WE SHALL ALL DISCOVAIRE ZAT WE ARE VERRRY VERRRY DEAD!
AND NOW, WE HAVE SPOKEN ENOUGH, N'EST-CE-PAS?
NOT YET, BATROC!
CAPTAIN AMERICA INTENDS TO HAVE THE LAST WORD!
SPANG!
SACRE-BLEU!! HE STILL LIVES!
BLING!
BUT NO SPINNING SHIELD CAN TOPPLE ZEE GREATEST LEAPER OF ZEM ALL!
YOU WOULD HAVE BEEN WISER TO FLEE ---WHILE YOU HAD ZEE CHANCE!
BUT NOW... FOR YOU IT EES TOO LATE!
13.

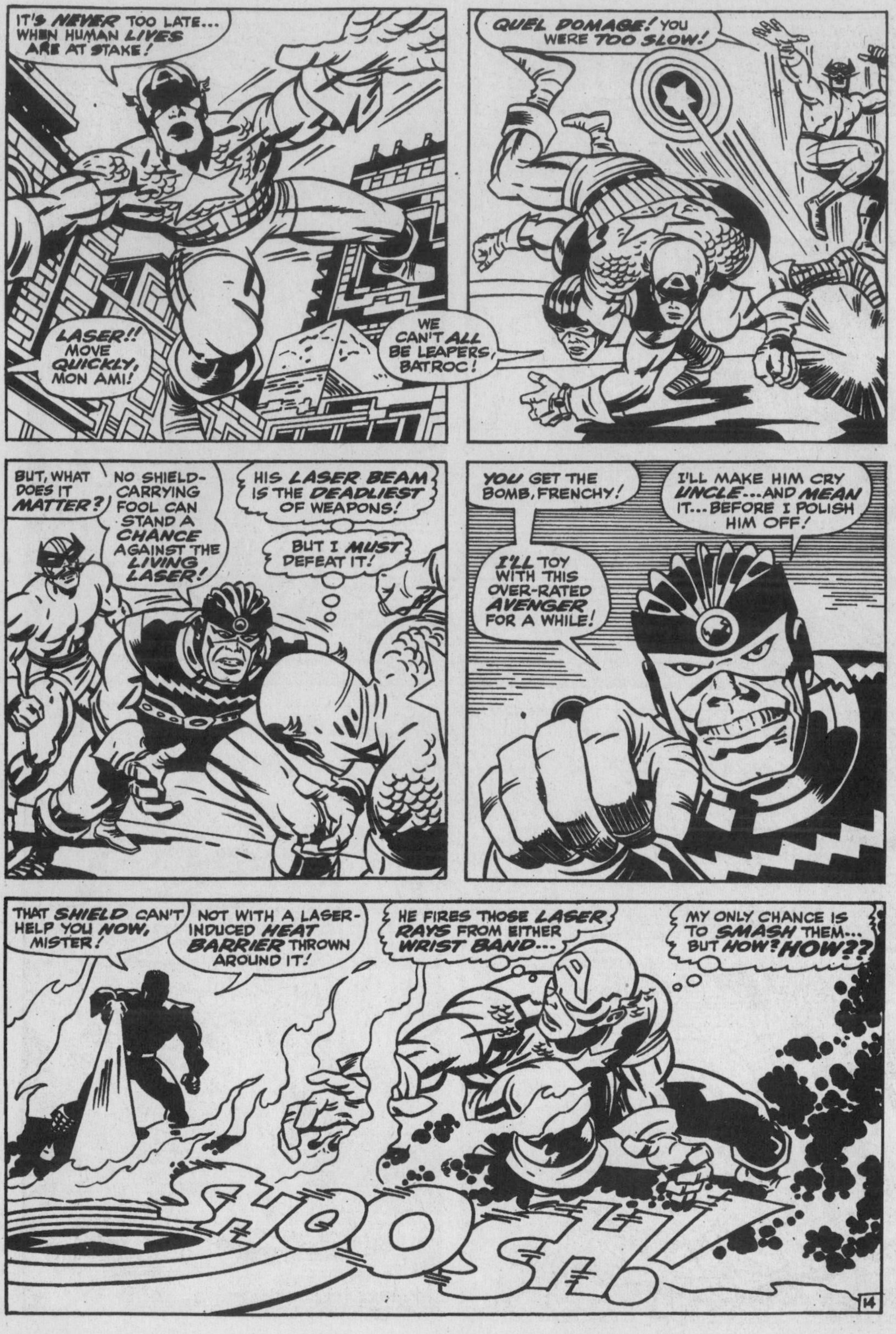
IT'S NEVER TOO LATE... WHEN HUMAN LIVES ARE AT STAKE!
LASER!! MOVE QUICKLY, MON AMI!
WE CAN'T ALL BE LEAPERS, BATROC!
QUEL DOMAGE! YOU WERE TOO SLOW!
BUT, WHAT DOES IT MATTER?
NO SHIELD-CARRYING FOOL CAN STAND A CHANCE AGAINST THE LIVING LASER!
HIS LASER BEAM IS THE DEADLIEST OF WEAPONS!
BUT I MUST DEFEAT IT!
YOU GET THE BOMB, FRENCHY!
I'LL TOY WITH THIS OVER-RATED AVENGER FOR A WHILE!
I'LL MAKE HIM CRY UNCLE...AND MEAN IT...BEFORE I POLISH HIM OFF!
THAT SHIELD CAN'T HELP YOU NOW, MISTER!
NOT WITH A LASER-INDUCED HEAT BARRIER THROWN AROUND IT!
HE FIRES THOSE LASER RAYS FROM EITHER WRIST BAND...
MY ONLY CHANCE IS TO SMASH THEM... BUT HOW? HOW??
SHOOSH!
14

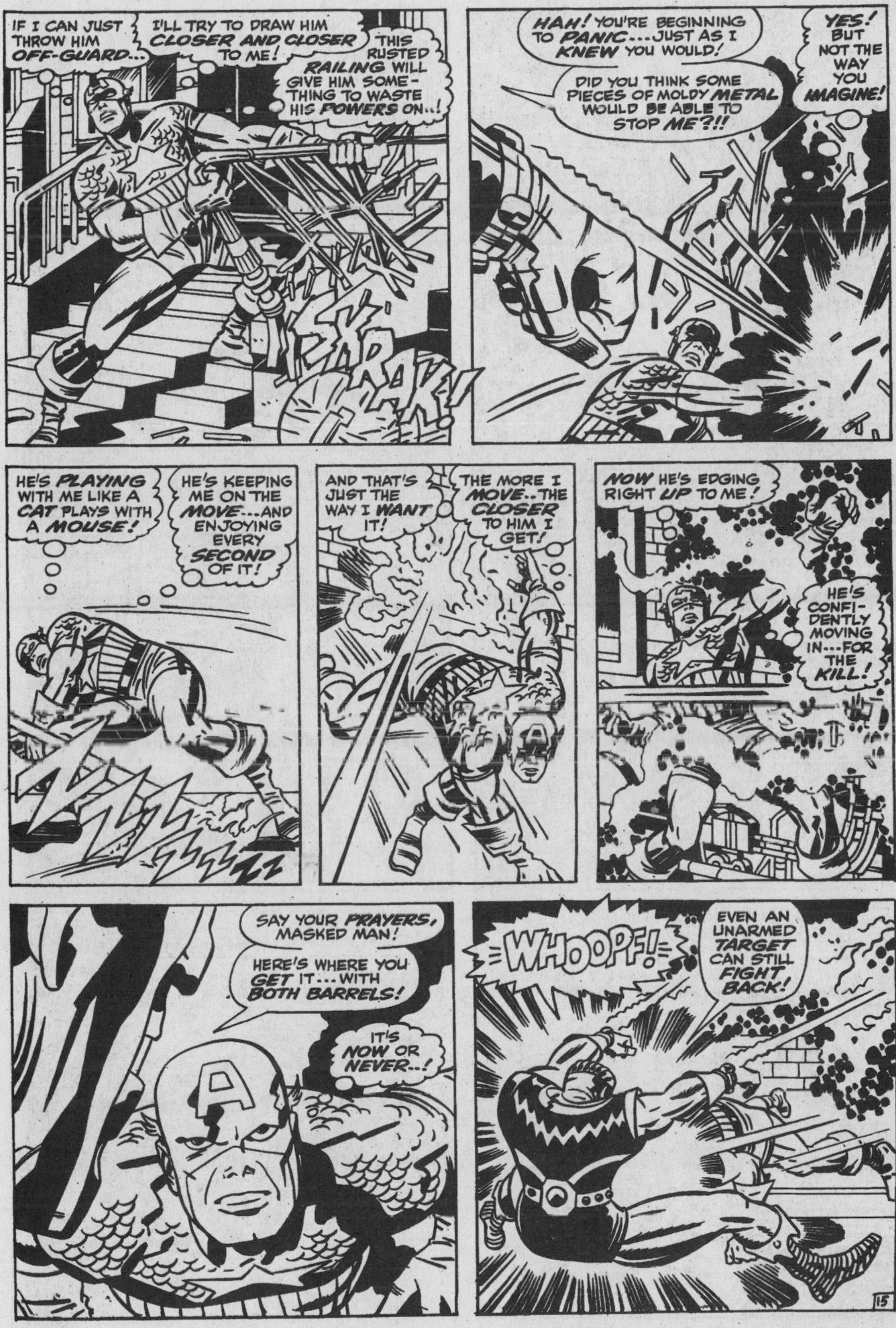
IF I CAN JUST THROW HIM OFF-GUARD...
I'LL TRY TO DRAW HIM CLOSER AND CLOSER TO ME!
THIS RUSTED RAILING WILL GIVE HIM SOMETHING TO WASTE HIS POWERS ON...!
SKRRAKK!
HAH! YOU'RE BEGINNING TO PANIC... JUST AS I KNEW YOU WOULD!
DID YOU THINK SOME PIECES OF MOLDY METAL WOULD BE ABLE TO STOP ME?!!
YES! BUT NOT THE WAY YOU IMAGINE!
HE'S PLAYING WITH ME LIKE A CAT PLAYS WITH A MOUSE!
HE'S KEEPING ME ON THE MOVE... AND ENJOYING EVERY SECOND OF IT!
AND THAT'S JUST THE WAY I WANT IT!
THE MORE I MOVE.. THE CLOSER TO HIM I GET!
NOW HE'S EDGING RIGHT UP TO ME!
HE'S CONFIDENTLY MOVING IN... FOR THE KILL!
SAY YOUR PRAYERS, MASKED MAN!
HERE'S WHERE YOU GET IT... WITH BOTH BARRELS!
IT'S NOW OR NEVER...!
WHOOPF!
EVEN AN UNARMED TARGET CAN STILL FIGHT BACK!
15

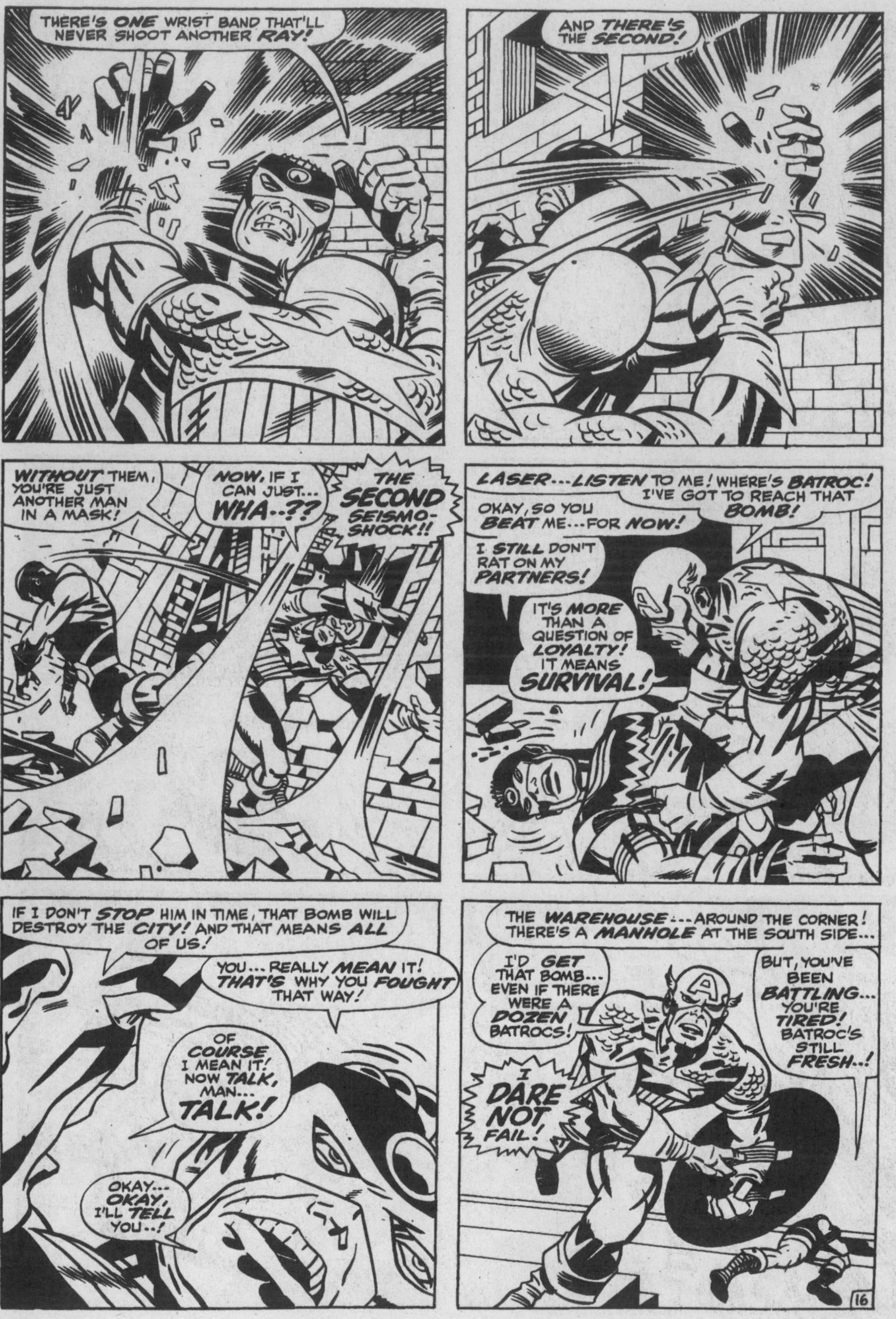
THERE'S ONE WRIST BAND THAT'LL NEVER SHOOT ANOTHER RAY!
AND THERE'S THE SECOND!
WITHOUT THEM, YOU'RE JUST ANOTHER MAN IN A MASK!
NOW, IF I CAN JUST... WHA..??
THE SECOND SEISMO-SHOCK!!
LASER... LISTEN TO ME! WHERE'S BATROC! I'VE GOT TO REACH THAT BOMB!
OKAY, SO YOU BEAT ME... FOR NOW!
I STILL DON'T RAT ON MY PARTNERS!
IT'S MORE THAN A QUESTION OF LOYALTY! IT MEANS SURVIVAL!
IF I DON'T STOP HIM IN TIME, THAT BOMB WILL DESTROY THE CITY! AND THAT MEANS ALL OF US!
YOU... REALLY MEAN IT! THAT'S WHY YOU FOUGHT THAT WAY!
OF COURSE I MEAN IT! NOW TALK, MAN... TALK!
OKAY... OKAY, I'LL TELL YOU..!
THE WAREHOUSE... AROUND THE CORNER! THERE'S A MANHOLE AT THE SOUTH SIDE...
I'D GET THAT BOMB... EVEN IF THERE WERE A DOZEN BATROCS!
BUT, YOU'VE BEEN BATTLING... YOU'RE TIRED! BATROC'S STILL FRESH..!
I DARE NOT FAIL!
16

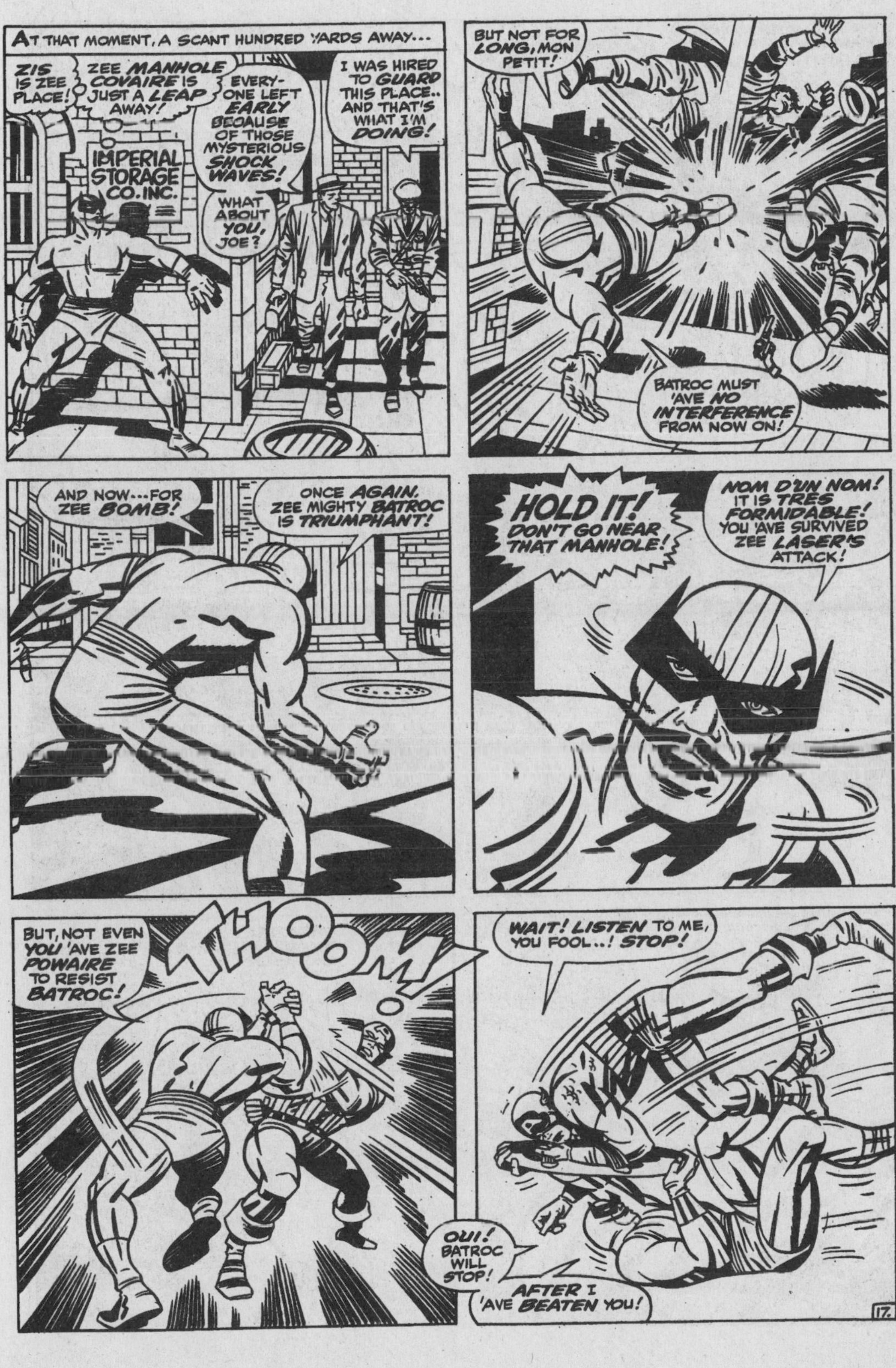
AT THAT MOMENT, A SCANT HUNDRED YARDS AWAY...
ZIS IS ZEE PLACE!
ZEE MANHOLE COVAIRE IS JUST A LEAP AWAY!
IMPERIAL STORAGE CO. INC.
EVERY-ONE LEFT EARLY BECAUSE OF THOSE MYSTERIOUS SHOCK WAVES!
WHAT ABOUT YOU, JOE?
I WAS HIRED TO GUARD THIS PLACE.. AND THAT'S WHAT I'M DOING!
BUT NOT FOR LONG, MON PETIT!
BATROC MUST 'AVE NO INTERFERENCE FROM NOW ON!
AND NOW...FOR ZEE BOMB!
ONCE AGAIN, ZEE MIGHTY BATROC IS TRIUMPHANT!
HOLD IT! DON'T GO NEAR THAT MANHOLE!
NOM D'UN NOM! IT IS TRES FORMIDABLE! YOU 'AVE SURVIVED ZEE LASER'S ATTACK!
BUT, NOT EVEN YOU 'AVE ZEE POWAIRE TO RESIST BATROC!
THOOM!
WAIT! LISTEN TO ME, YOU FOOL..! STOP!
OUI! BATROC WILL STOP!
AFTER I 'AVE BEATEN YOU!

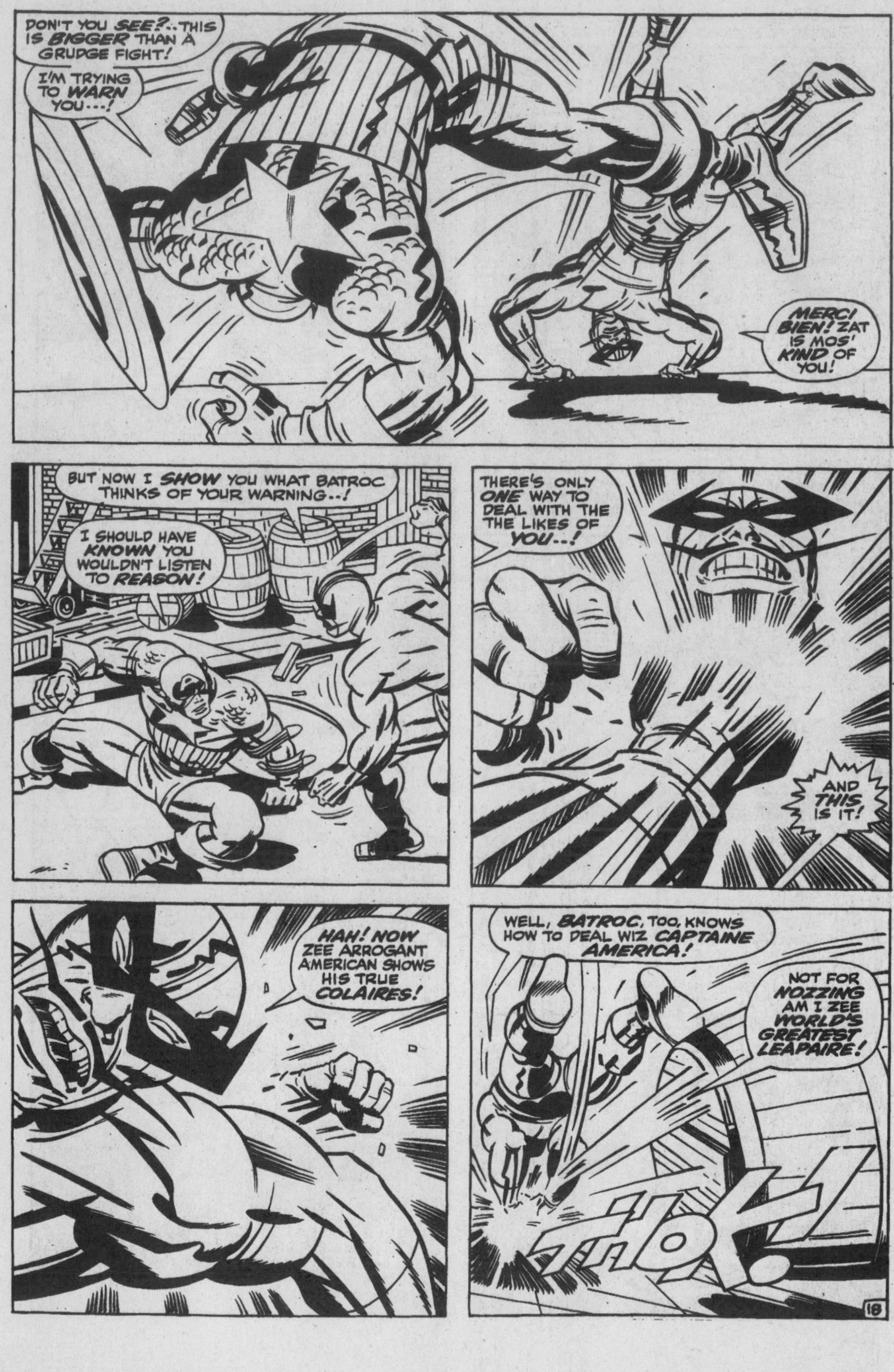
DON'T YOU SEE?..THIS IS BIGGER THAN A GRUDGE FIGHT!
I'M TRYING TO WARN YOU...!
MERCI BIEN! ZAT IS MOS' KIND OF YOU!
BUT NOW I SHOW YOU WHAT BATROC THINKS OF YOUR WARNING..!
I SHOULD HAVE KNOWN YOU WOULDN'T LISTEN TO REASON!
THERE'S ONLY ONE WAY TO DEAL WITH THE THE LIKES OF YOU...!
AND THIS IS IT!
HAH! NOW ZEE ARROGANT AMERICAN SHOWS HIS TRUE COLAIRES!
WELL, BATROC, TOO, KNOWS HOW TO DEAL WIZ CAPTAINE AMERICA!
NOT FOR NOZZING AM I ZEE WORLD'S GREATEST LEAPAIRE!
THOK!
18

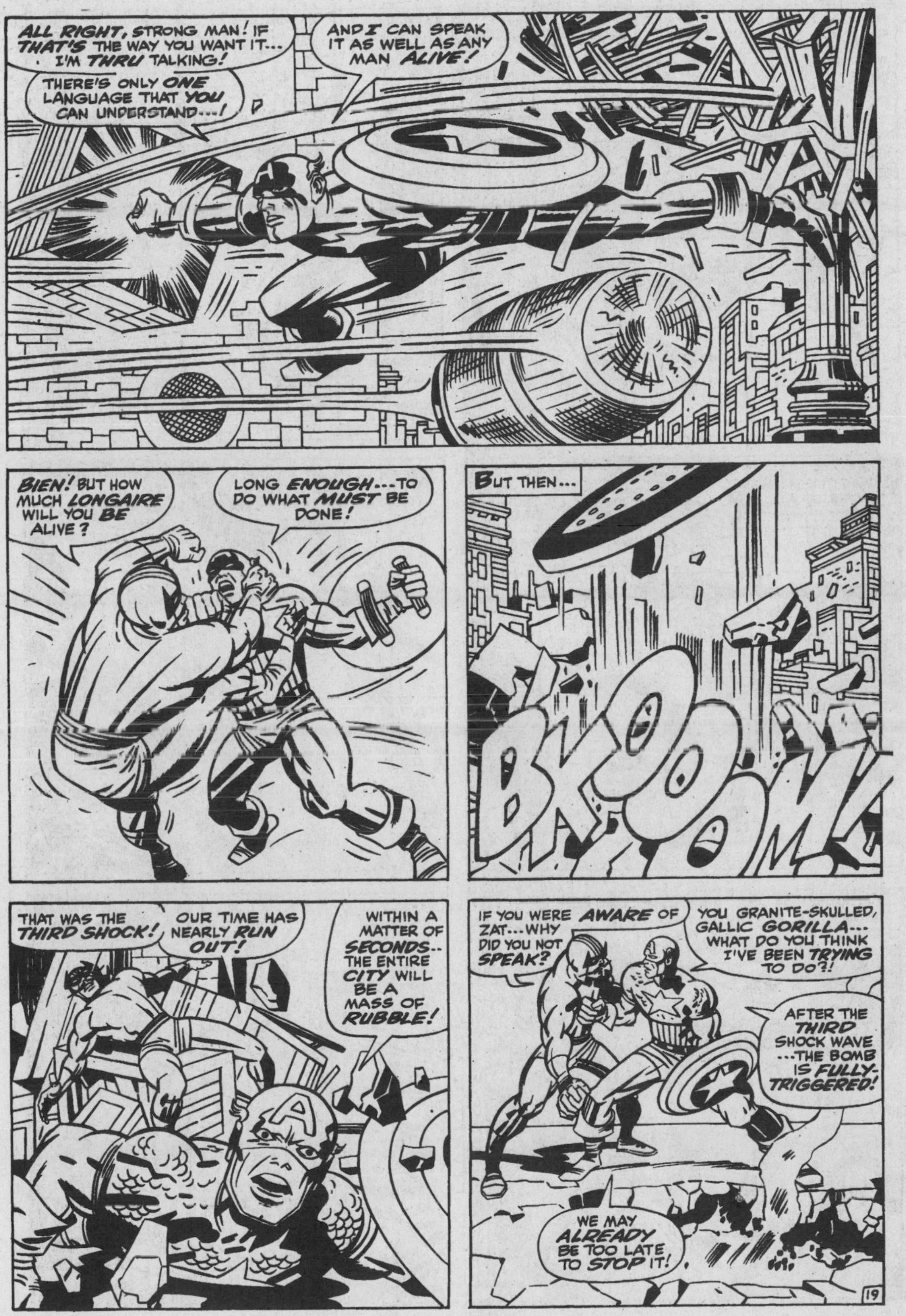

ALL RIGHT, STRONG MAN! IF THAT'S THE WAY YOU WANT IT... I'M THRU TALKING!
THERE'S ONLY ONE LANGUAGE THAT YOU CAN UNDERSTAND...!
AND I CAN SPEAK IT AS WELL AS ANY MAN ALIVE!
BIEN! BUT HOW MUCH LONGAIRE WILL YOU BE ALIVE?
LONG ENOUGH---TO DO WHAT MUST BE DONE!
BUT THEN...
BKOOOM!
THAT WAS THE THIRD SHOCK!
OUR TIME HAS NEARLY RUN OUT!
WITHIN A MATTER OF SECONDS.. THE ENTIRE CITY WILL BE A MASS OF RUBBLE!
IF YOU WERE AWARE OF ZAT...WHY DID YOU NOT SPEAK?
YOU GRANITE-SKULLED, GALLIC GORILLA... WHAT DO YOU THINK I'VE BEEN TRYING TO DO?!
AFTER THE THIRD SHOCK WAVE ...THE BOMB IS FULLY-TRIGGERED!
WE MAY ALREADY BE TOO LATE TO STOP IT!
19

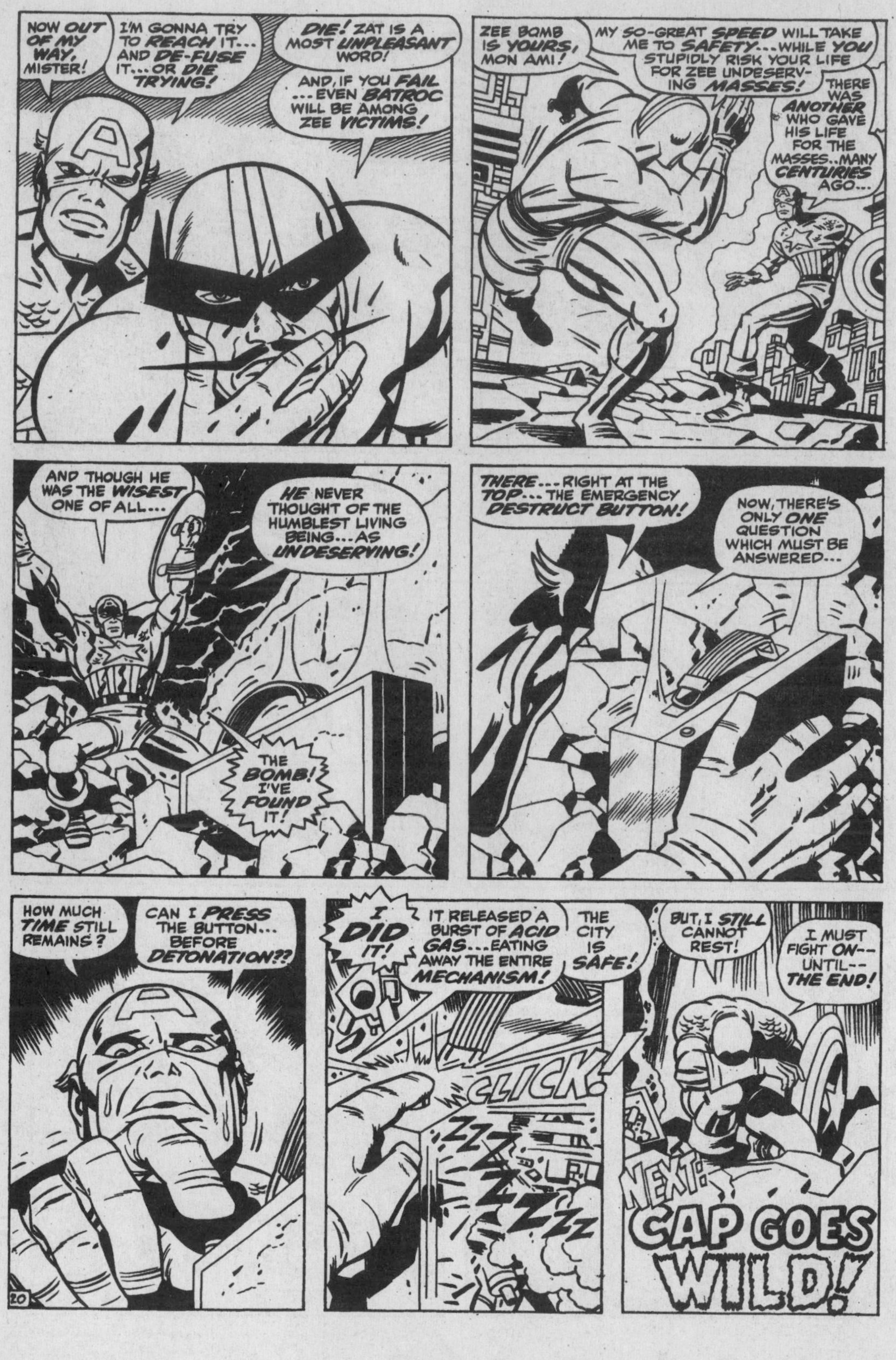
NOW OUT OF MY WAY, MISTER!
I'M GONNA TRY TO REACH IT... AND DE-FUSE IT... OR DIE TRYING!
DIE! ZAT IS A MOST UNPLEASANT WORD!
AND, IF YOU FAIL ...EVEN BATROC WILL BE AMONG ZEE VICTIMS!
ZEE BOMB IS YOURS, MON AMI!
MY SO-GREAT SPEED WILL TAKE ME TO SAFETY...WHILE YOU STUPIDLY RISK YOUR LIFE FOR ZEE UNDESERVING MASSES!
THERE WAS ANOTHER WHO GAVE HIS LIFE FOR THE MASSES..MANY CENTURIES AGO...
AND THOUGH HE WAS THE WISEST ONE OF ALL...
HE NEVER THOUGHT OF THE HUMBLEST LIVING BEING...AS UNDESERVING!
THE BOMB! I'VE FOUND IT!
THERE...RIGHT AT THE TOP...THE EMERGENCY DESTRUCT BUTTON!
NOW, THERE'S ONLY ONE QUESTION WHICH MUST BE ANSWERED...
HOW MUCH TIME STILL REMAINS?
CAN I PRESS THE BUTTON... BEFORE DETONATION??
20
I DID IT!
IT RELEASED A BURST OF ACID GAS...EATING AWAY THE ENTIRE MECHANISM!
THE CITY IS SAFE!
CLICK!
ZZZZZZ
BUT, I STILL CANNOT REST!
I MUST FIGHT ON-- UNTIL-- THE END!
NEXT: CAP GOES WILD!

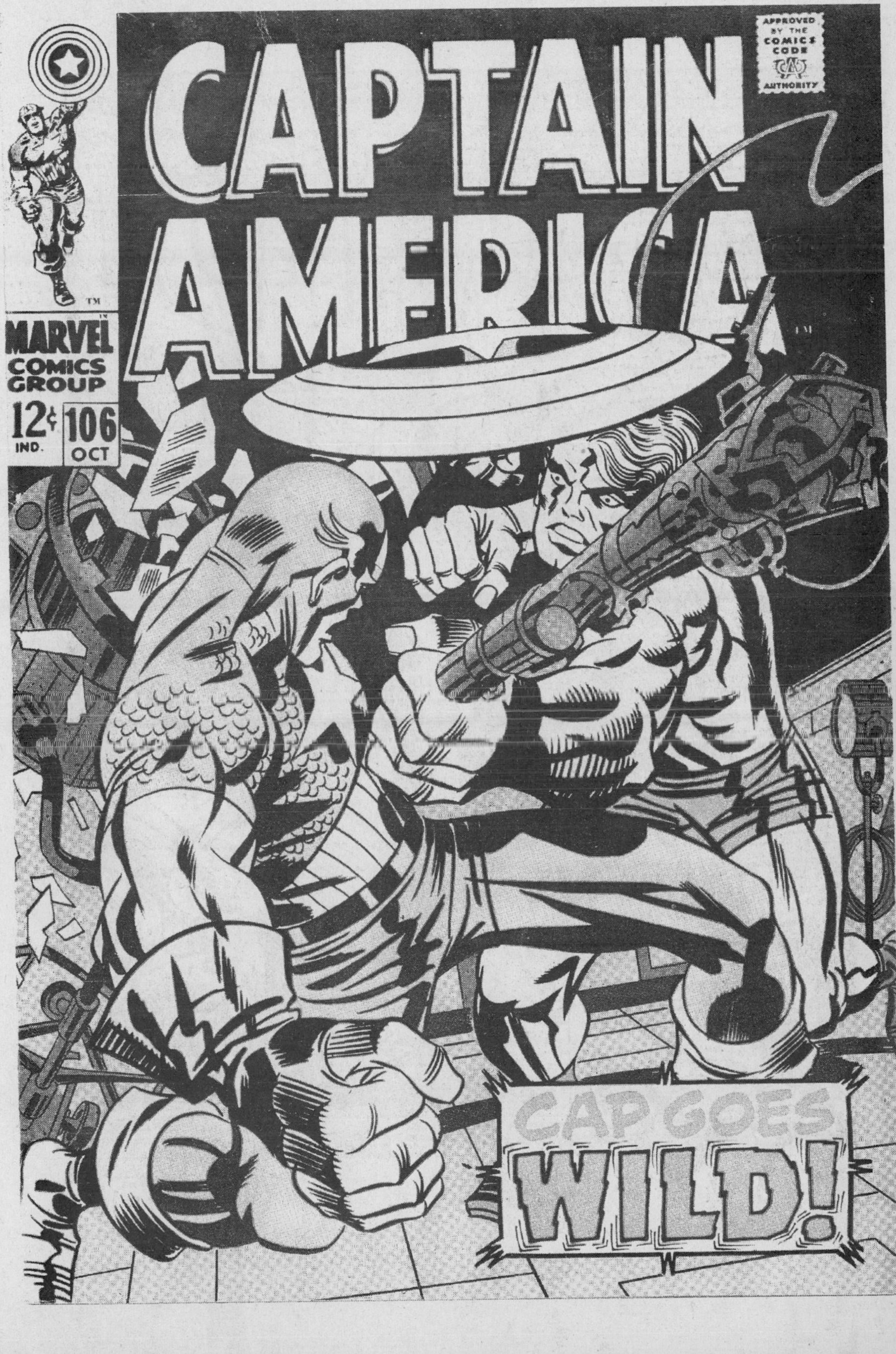

APPROVED BY THE COMICS CODE AUTHORITY
CAPTAIN AMERICA
MARVEL COMICS GROUP
12¢ IND.
106 OCT
CAP GOES
WILD!

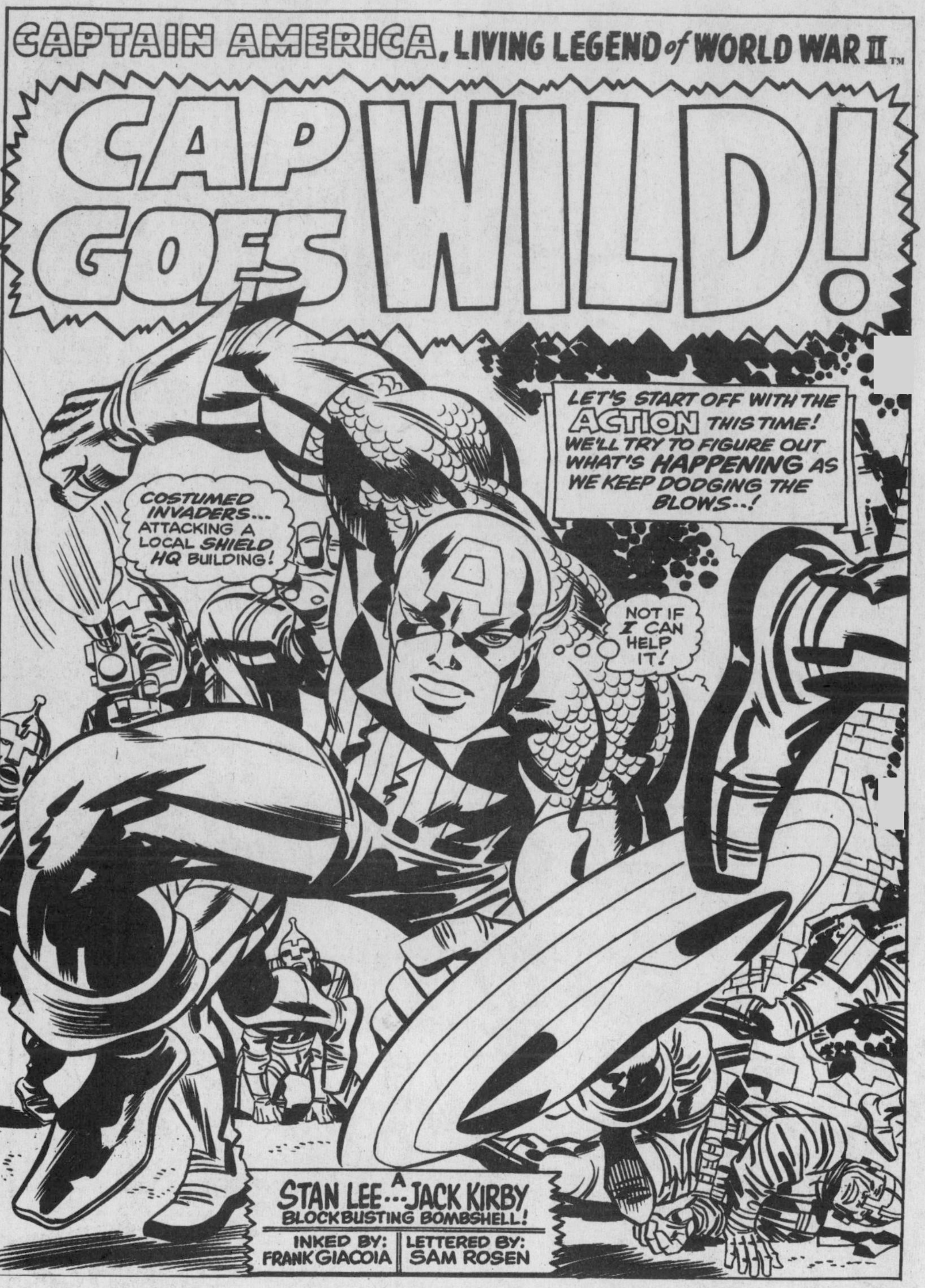
CAPTAIN AMERICA, LIVING LEGEND of WORLD WAR II™
CAP GOES WILD!
LET'S START OFF WITH THE ACTION THIS TIME! WE'LL TRY TO FIGURE OUT WHAT'S HAPPENING AS WE KEEP DODGING THE BLOWS--!
COSTUMED INVADERS... ATTACKING A LOCAL SHIELD HQ BUILDING!
NOT IF I CAN HELP IT!
STAN LEE--A--JACK KIRBY BLOCKBUSTING BOMBSHELL!
INKED BY: FRANK GIACOIA
LETTERED BY: SAM ROSEN

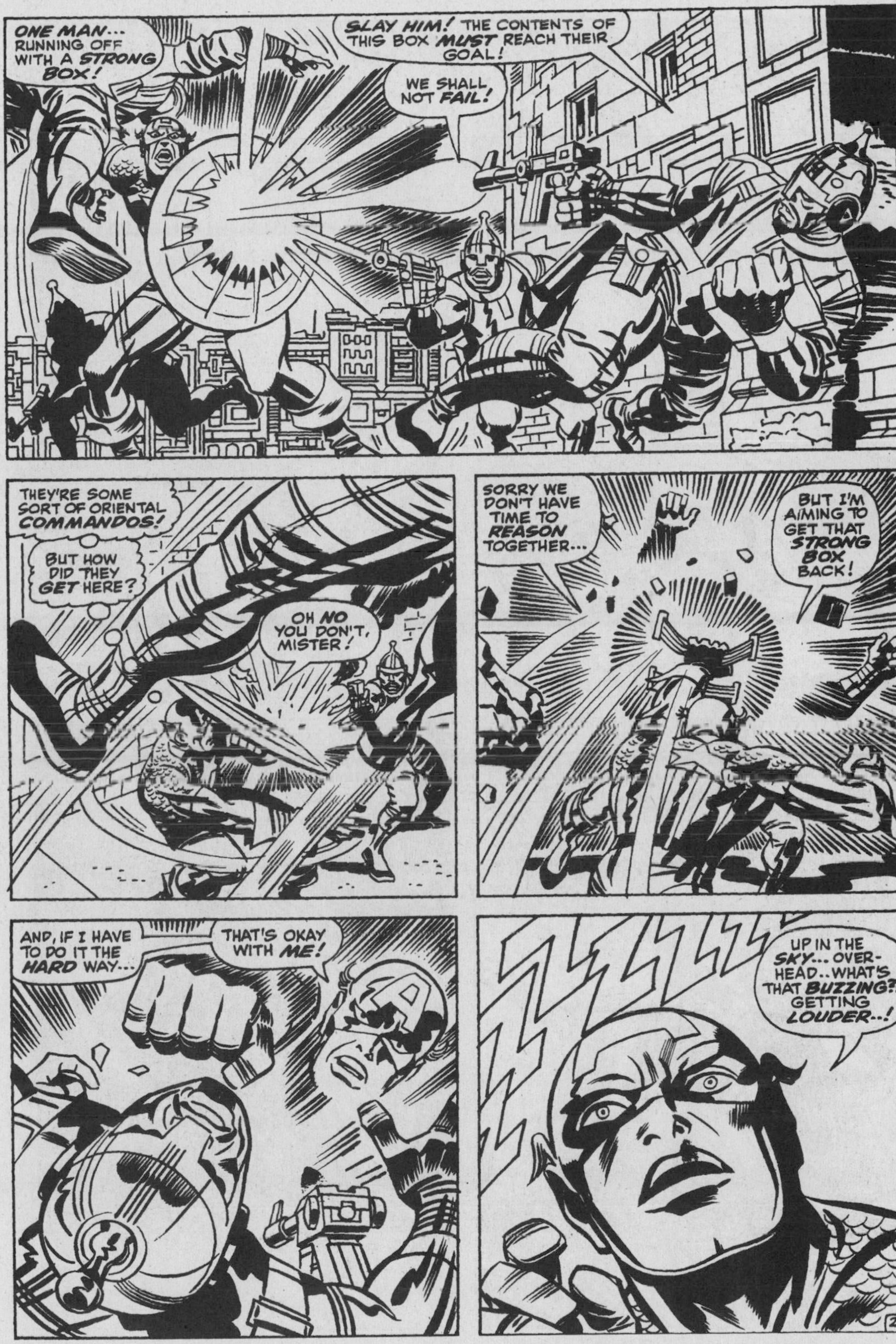
ONE MAN... RUNNING OFF WITH A STRONG BOX!
SLAY HIM! THE CONTENTS OF THIS BOX MUST REACH THEIR GOAL!
WE SHALL NOT FAIL!
THEY'RE SOME SORT OF ORIENTAL COMMANDOS!
BUT HOW DID THEY GET HERE?
OH NO YOU DON'T, MISTER!
SORRY WE DON'T HAVE TIME TO REASON TOGETHER...
BUT I'M AIMING TO GET THAT STRONG BOX BACK!
AND, IF I HAVE TO DO IT THE HARD WAY...
THAT'S OKAY WITH ME!
UP IN THE SKY... OVER-HEAD... WHAT'S THAT BUZZING?? GETTING LOUDER..!
2.

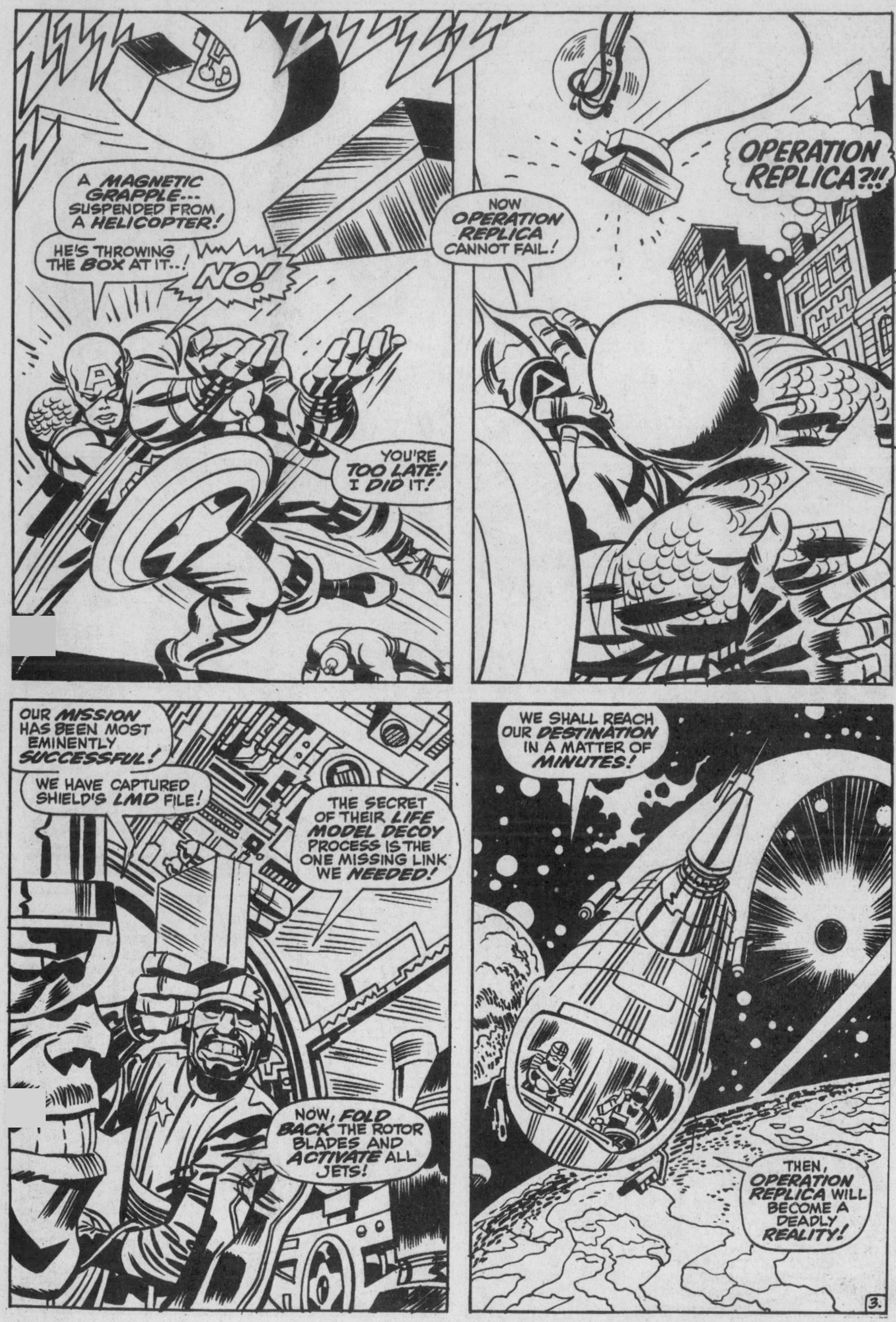
A MAGNETIC GRAPPLE... SUSPENDED FROM A HELICOPTER!
HE'S THROWING THE BOX AT IT..!
NO!
YOU'RE TOO LATE! I DID IT!
NOW OPERATION REPLICA CANNOT FAIL!
OPERATION REPLICA?!!
OUR MISSION HAS BEEN MOST EMINENTLY SUCCESSFUL!
WE HAVE CAPTURED SHIELD'S LMD FILE!
THE SECRET OF THEIR LIFE MODEL DECOY PROCESS IS THE ONE MISSING LINK WE NEEDED!
NOW, FOLD BACK THE ROTOR BLADES AND ACTIVATE ALL JETS!
WE SHALL REACH OUR DESTINATION IN A MATTER OF MINUTES!
THEN, OPERATION REPLICA WILL BECOME A DEADLY REALITY!
3.

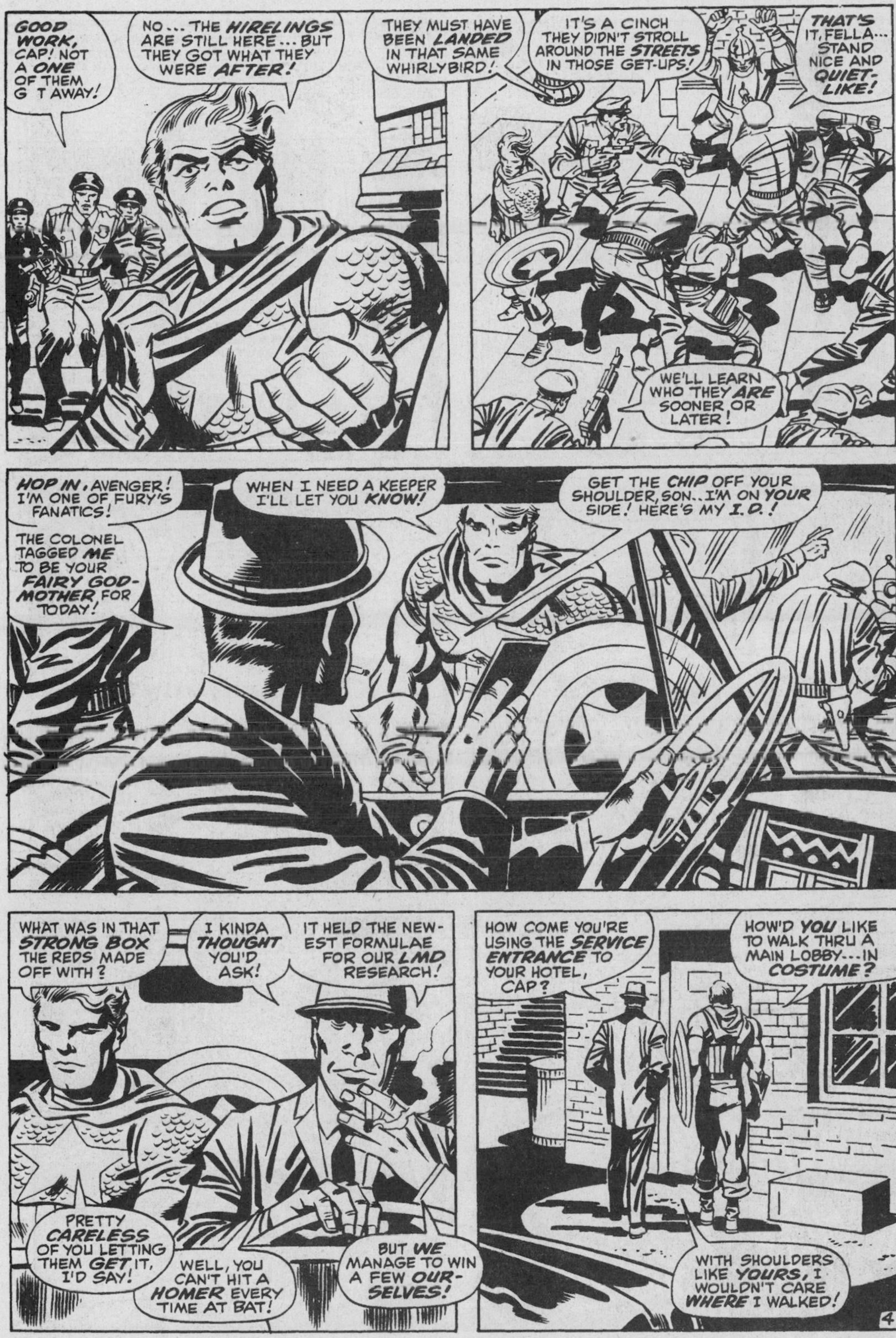

GOOD WORK, CAP! NOT A ONE OF THEM G T AWAY!
NO... THE HIRELINGS ARE STILL HERE... BUT THEY GOT WHAT THEY WERE AFTER!
THEY MUST HAVE BEEN LANDED IN THAT SAME WHIRLYBIRD!
IT'S A CINCH THEY DIDN'T STROLL AROUND THE STREETS IN THOSE GET-UPS!
THAT'S IT, FELLA... STAND NICE AND QUIET-LIKE!
WE'LL LEARN WHO THEY ARE SOONER OR LATER!
HOP IN, AVENGER! I'M ONE OF FURY'S FANATICS!
THE COLONEL TAGGED ME TO BE YOUR FAIRY GOD-MOTHER FOR TODAY!
WHEN I NEED A KEEPER I'LL LET YOU KNOW!
GET THE CHIP OFF YOUR SHOULDER, SON.. I'M ON YOUR SIDE! HERE'S MY I.D.!
WHAT WAS IN THAT STRONG BOX THE REDS MADE OFF WITH?
I KINDA THOUGHT YOU'D ASK!
IT HELD THE NEW-EST FORMULAE FOR OUR LMD RESEARCH!
PRETTY CARELESS OF YOU LETTING THEM GET IT, I'D SAY!
WELL, YOU CAN'T HIT A HOMER EVERY TIME AT BAT!
BUT WE MANAGE TO WIN A FEW OUR-SELVES!
HOW COME YOU'RE USING THE SERVICE ENTRANCE TO YOUR HOTEL, CAP?
HOW'D YOU LIKE TO WALK THRU A MAIN LOBBY---IN COSTUME?
WITH SHOULDERS LIKE YOURS, I WOULDN'T CARE WHERE I WALKED!
4

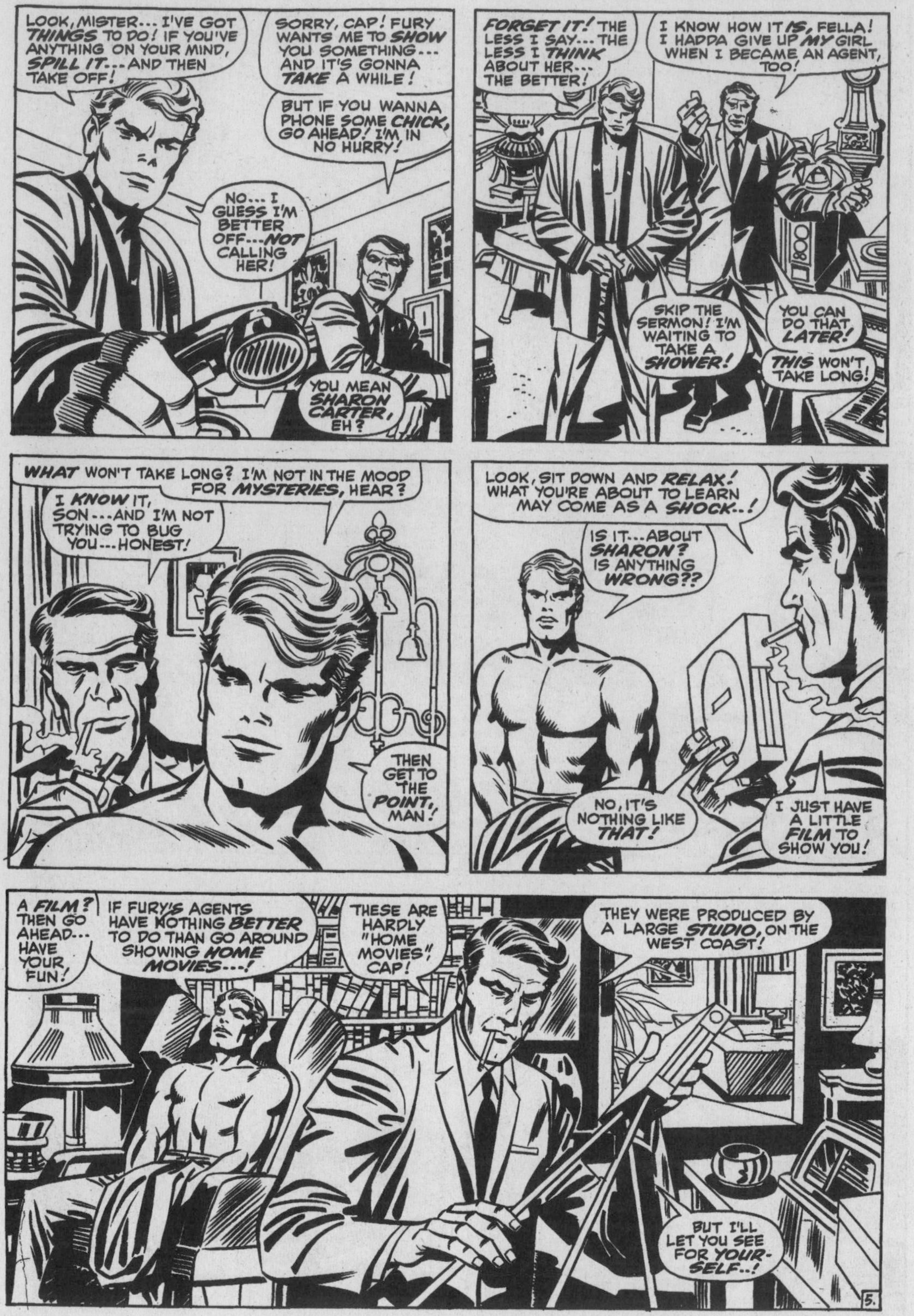
LOOK, MISTER... I'VE GOT THINGS TO DO! IF YOU'VE ANYTHING ON YOUR MIND, SPILL IT... AND THEN TAKE OFF!
SORRY, CAP! FURY WANTS ME TO SHOW YOU SOMETHING... AND IT'S GONNA TAKE A WHILE!
BUT IF YOU WANNA PHONE SOME CHICK, GO AHEAD! I'M IN NO HURRY!
NO... I GUESS I'M BETTER OFF... NOT CALLING HER!
YOU MEAN SHARON CARTER, EH?
FORGET IT! THE LESS I SAY... THE LESS I THINK ABOUT HER... THE BETTER!
I KNOW HOW IT IS, FELLA! I HADDA GIVE UP MY GIRL WHEN I BECAME AN AGENT, TOO!
SKIP THE SERMON! I'M WAITING TO TAKE A SHOWER!
YOU CAN DO THAT LATER!
THIS WON'T TAKE LONG!
WHAT WON'T TAKE LONG? I'M NOT IN THE MOOD FOR MYSTERIES, HEAR?
I KNOW IT, SON... AND I'M NOT TRYING TO BUG YOU... HONEST!
THEN GET TO THE POINT, MAN!
LOOK, SIT DOWN AND RELAX! WHAT YOU'RE ABOUT TO LEARN MAY COME AS A SHOCK..!
IS IT... ABOUT SHARON? IS ANYTHING WRONG??
NO, IT'S NOTHING LIKE THAT!
I JUST HAVE A LITTLE FILM TO SHOW YOU!
A FILM? THEN GO AHEAD... HAVE YOUR FUN!
IF FURY'S AGENTS HAVE NOTHING BETTER TO DO THAN GO AROUND SHOWING HOME MOVIES...!
THESE ARE HARDLY "HOME MOVIES," CAP!
THEY WERE PRODUCED BY A LARGE STUDIO, ON THE WEST COAST!
BUT I'LL LET YOU SEE FOR YOURSELF..!
5.

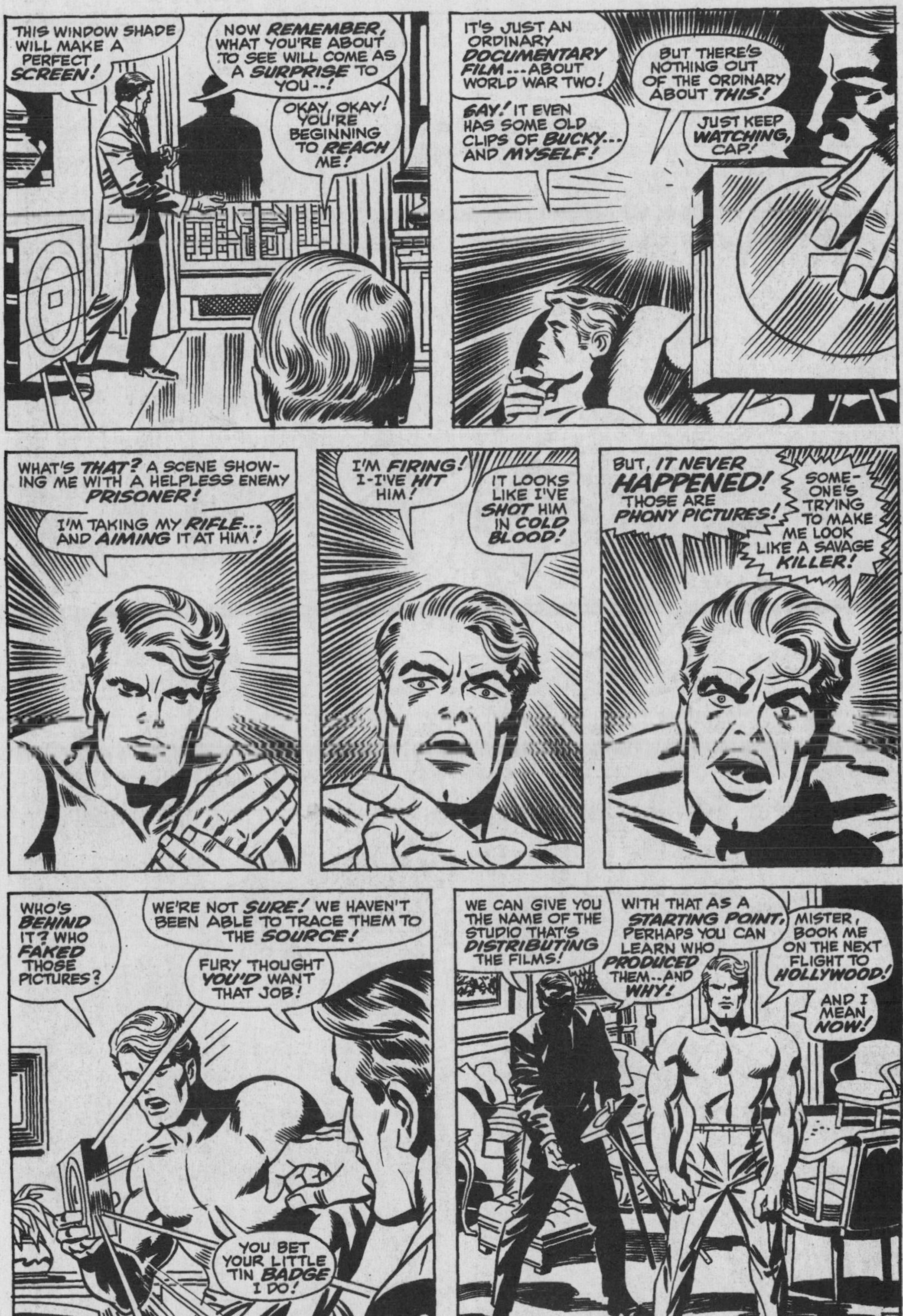
THIS WINDOW SHADE WILL MAKE A PERFECT SCREEN!
NOW REMEMBER, WHAT YOU'RE ABOUT TO SEE WILL COME AS A SURPRISE TO YOU--!
OKAY, OKAY! YOU'RE BEGINNING TO REACH ME!
IT'S JUST AN ORDINARY DOCUMENTARY FILM...ABOUT WORLD WAR TWO!
SAY! IT EVEN HAS SOME OLD CLIPS OF BUCKY... AND MYSELF!
BUT THERE'S NOTHING OUT OF THE ORDINARY ABOUT THIS!
JUST KEEP WATCHING, CAP!
WHAT'S THAT? A SCENE SHOWING ME WITH A HELPLESS ENEMY PRISONER!
I'M TAKING MY RIFLE... AND AIMING IT AT HIM!
I'M FIRING! I-I'VE HIT HIM!
IT LOOKS LIKE I'VE SHOT HIM IN COLD BLOOD!
BUT, IT NEVER HAPPENED! THOSE ARE PHONY PICTURES!
SOMEONE'S TRYING TO MAKE ME LOOK LIKE A SAVAGE KILLER!
WHO'S BEHIND IT? WHO FAKED THOSE PICTURES?
WE'RE NOT SURE! WE HAVEN'T BEEN ABLE TO TRACE THEM TO THE SOURCE!
FURY THOUGHT YOU'D WANT THAT JOB!
YOU BET YOUR LITTLE TIN BADGE I DO!
WE CAN GIVE YOU THE NAME OF THE STUDIO THAT'S DISTRIBUTING THE FILMS!
WITH THAT AS A STARTING POINT, PERHAPS YOU CAN LEARN WHO PRODUCED THEM...AND WHY!
MISTER, BOOK ME ON THE NEXT FLIGHT TO HOLLYWOOD!
AND I MEAN NOW!
6

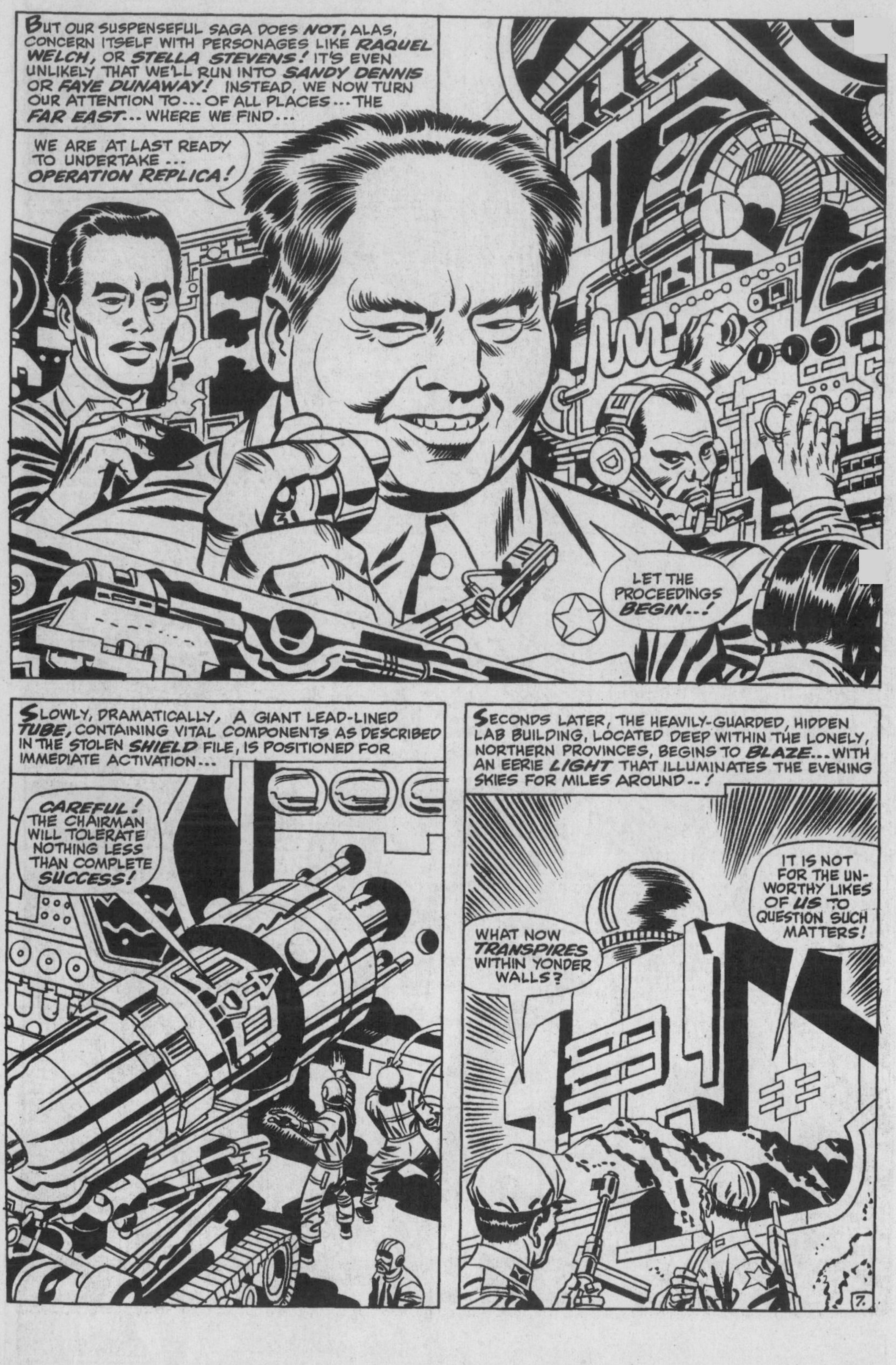
BUT OUR SUSPENSEFUL SAGA DOES NOT, ALAS, CONCERN ITSELF WITH PERSONAGES LIKE RAQUEL WELCH, OR STELLA STEVENS! IT'S EVEN UNLIKELY THAT WE'LL RUN INTO SANDY DENNIS OR FAYE DUNAWAY! INSTEAD, WE NOW TURN OUR ATTENTION TO... OF ALL PLACES... THE FAR EAST... WHERE WE FIND...
WE ARE AT LAST READY TO UNDERTAKE ... OPERATION REPLICA!
LET THE PROCEEDINGS BEGIN..!
SLOWLY, DRAMATICALLY, A GIANT LEAD-LINED TUBE, CONTAINING VITAL COMPONENTS AS DESCRIBED IN THE STOLEN SHIELD FILE, IS POSITIONED FOR IMMEDIATE ACTIVATION...
CAREFUL! THE CHAIRMAN WILL TOLERATE NOTHING LESS THAN COMPLETE SUCCESS!
SECONDS LATER, THE HEAVILY-GUARDED, HIDDEN LAB BUILDING, LOCATED DEEP WITHIN THE LONELY, NORTHERN PROVINCES, BEGINS TO BLAZE... WITH AN EERIE LIGHT THAT ILLUMINATES THE EVENING SKIES FOR MILES AROUND..!
WHAT NOW TRANSPIRES WITHIN YONDER WALLS?
IT IS NOT FOR THE UNWORTHY LIKES OF US TO QUESTION SUCH MATTERS!
7.

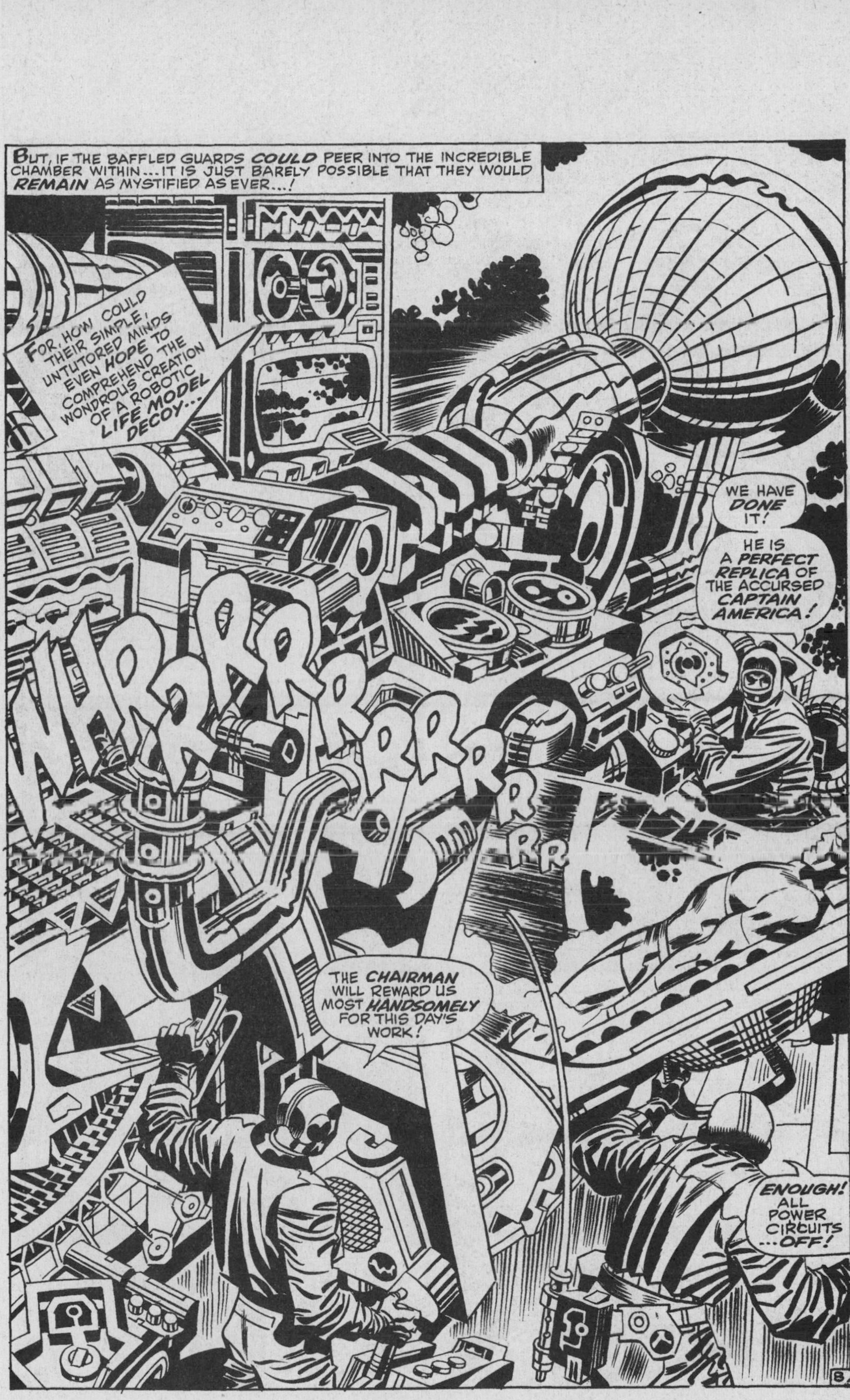
BUT, IF THE BAFFLED GUARDS COULD PEER INTO THE INCREDIBLE CHAMBER WITHIN... IT IS JUST BARELY POSSIBLE THAT THEY WOULD REMAIN AS MYSTIFIED AS EVER...!
FOR, HOW COULD THEIR SIMPLE, UNTUTORED MINDS EVEN HOPE TO COMPREHEND THE WONDROUS CREATION OF A ROBOTIC LIFE MODEL DECOY...
WE HAVE DONE IT!
HE IS A PERFECT REPLICA OF THE ACCURSED CAPTAIN AMERICA!
WHRRRRRRRRRRR
THE CHAIRMAN WILL REWARD US MOST HANDSOMELY FOR THIS DAY'S WORK!
ENOUGH! ALL POWER CIRCUITS ...OFF!
8

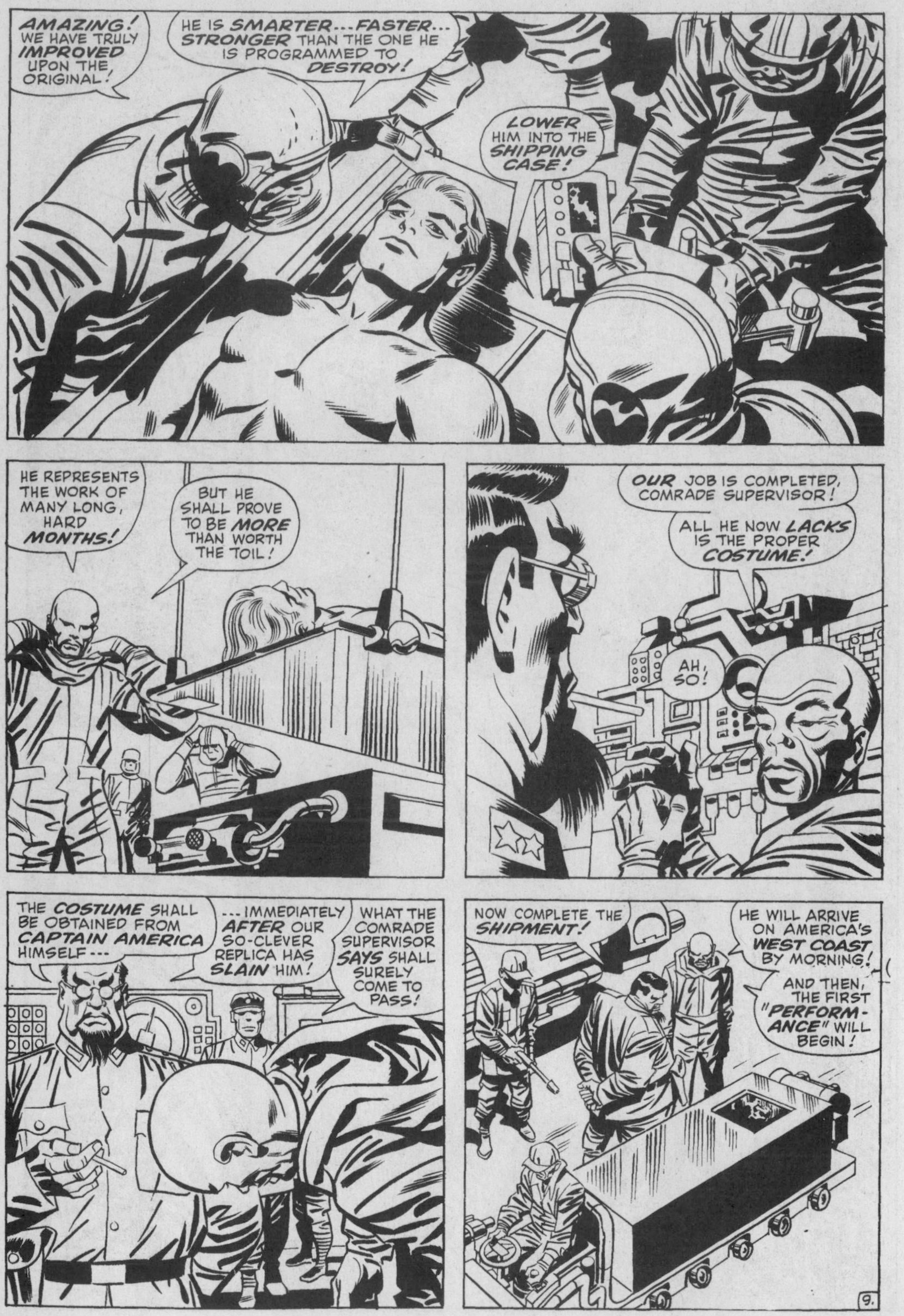
AMAZING! WE HAVE TRULY IMPROVED UPON THE ORIGINAL!
HE IS SMARTER...FASTER... STRONGER THAN THE ONE HE IS PROGRAMMED TO DESTROY!
LOWER HIM INTO THE SHIPPING CASE!
HE REPRESENTS THE WORK OF MANY LONG, HARD MONTHS!
BUT HE SHALL PROVE TO BE MORE THAN WORTH THE TOIL!
OUR JOB IS COMPLETED, COMRADE SUPERVISOR!
ALL HE NOW LACKS IS THE PROPER COSTUME!
AH, SO!
THE COSTUME SHALL BE OBTAINED FROM CAPTAIN AMERICA HIMSELF---
---IMMEDIATELY AFTER OUR SO-CLEVER REPLICA HAS SLAIN HIM!
WHAT THE COMRADE SUPERVISOR SAYS SHALL SURELY COME TO PASS!
NOW COMPLETE THE SHIPMENT!
HE WILL ARRIVE ON AMERICA'S WEST COAST BY MORNING!
AND THEN, THE FIRST "PERFORM-ANCE" WILL BEGIN!
9.

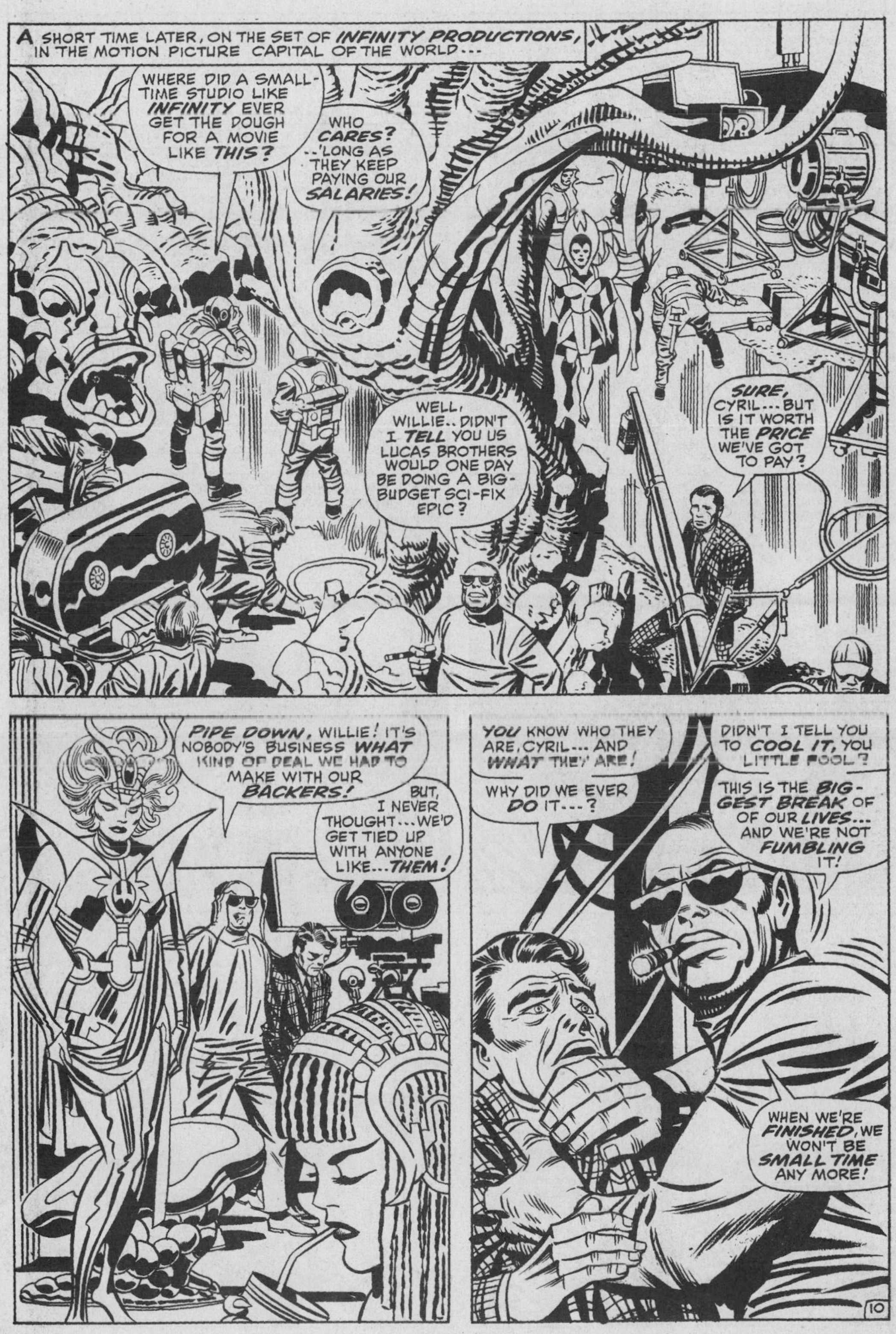
A SHORT TIME LATER, ON THE SET OF INFINITY PRODUCTIONS, IN THE MOTION PICTURE CAPITAL OF THE WORLD---
WHERE DID A SMALL-TIME STUDIO LIKE INFINITY EVER GET THE DOUGH FOR A MOVIE LIKE THIS?
WHO CARES? --'LONG AS THEY KEEP PAYING OUR SALARIES!
WELL, WILLIE.. DIDN'T I TELL YOU US LUCAS BROTHERS WOULD ONE DAY BE DOING A BIG-BUDGET SCI-FIX EPIC?
SURE, CYRIL... BUT IS IT WORTH THE PRICE WE'VE GOT TO PAY?
PIPE DOWN, WILLIE! IT'S NOBODY'S BUSINESS WHAT KIND OF DEAL WE HAD TO MAKE WITH OUR BACKERS!
BUT, I NEVER THOUGHT... WE'D GET TIED UP WITH ANYONE LIKE... THEM!
YOU KNOW WHO THEY ARE, CYRIL--- AND WHAT THEY ARE!
WHY DID WE EVER DO IT---?
DIDN'T I TELL YOU TO COOL IT, YOU LITTLE FOOL?
THIS IS THE BIG-GEST BREAK OF OF OUR LIVES... AND WE'RE NOT FUMBLING IT!
WHEN WE'RE FINISHED, WE WON'T BE SMALL TIME ANY MORE!
10

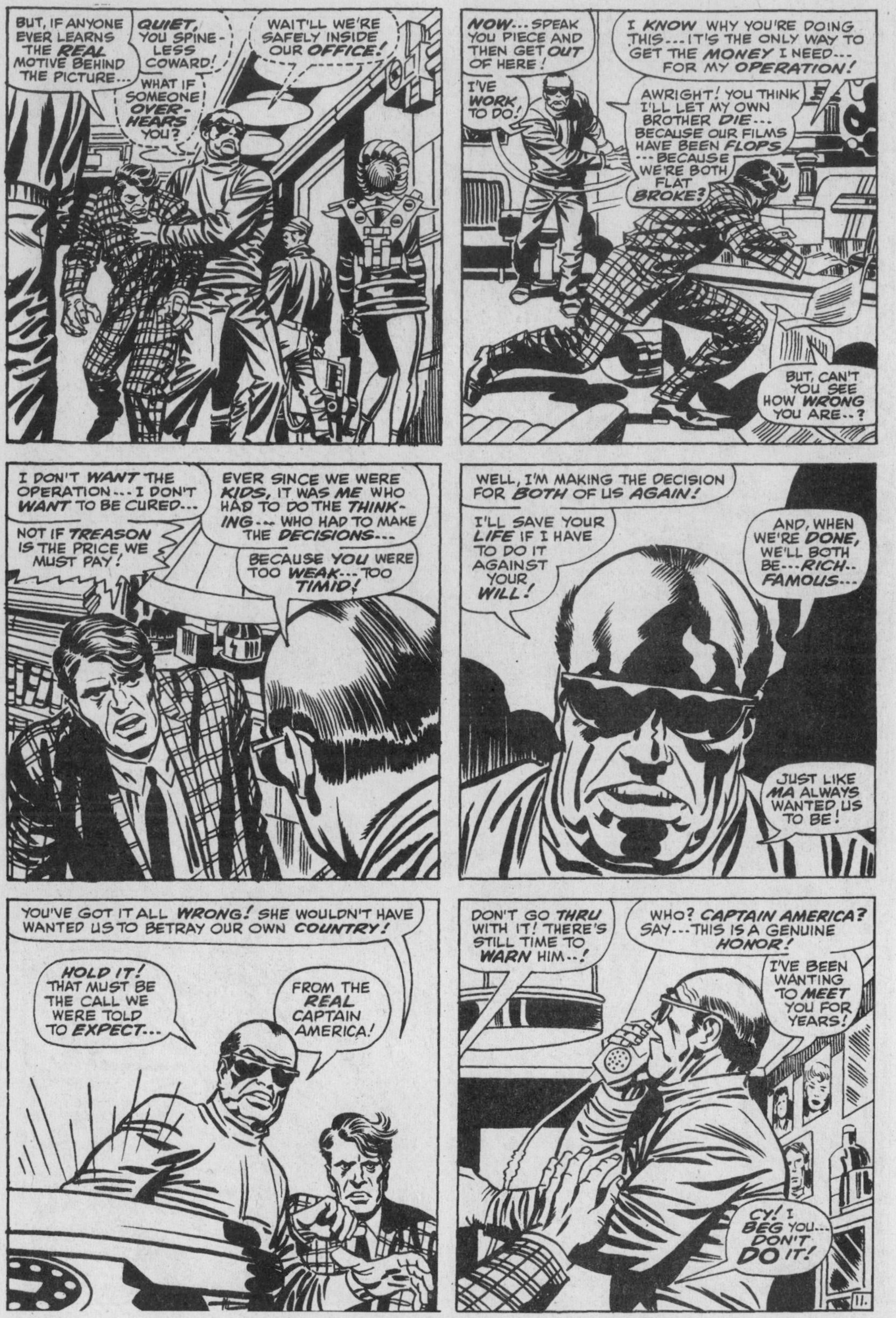
BUT, IF ANYONE EVER LEARNS THE REAL MOTIVE BEHIND THE PICTURE...
QUIET, YOU SPINE-LESS COWARD! WHAT IF SOMEONE OVER-HEARS YOU?
WAIT'LL WE'RE SAFELY INSIDE OUR OFFICE!
NOW... SPEAK YOU PIECE AND THEN GET OUT OF HERE!
I'VE WORK TO DO!
I KNOW WHY YOU'RE DOING THIS--- IT'S THE ONLY WAY TO GET THE MONEY I NEED--- FOR MY OPERATION!
AWRIGHT! YOU THINK I'LL LET MY OWN BROTHER DIE--- BECAUSE OUR FILMS HAVE BEEN FLOPS --- BECAUSE WE'RE BOTH FLAT BROKE?
BUT, CAN'T YOU SEE HOW WRONG YOU ARE--?
I DON'T WANT THE OPERATION--- I DON'T WANT TO BE CURED...
NOT IF TREASON IS THE PRICE WE MUST PAY!
EVER SINCE WE WERE KIDS, IT WAS ME WHO HAD TO DO THE THINK-ING--- WHO HAD TO MAKE THE DECISIONS---
BECAUSE YOU WERE TOO WEAK--- TOO TIMID!
WELL, I'M MAKING THE DECISION FOR BOTH OF US AGAIN!
I'LL SAVE YOUR LIFE IF I HAVE TO DO IT AGAINST YOUR WILL!
AND, WHEN WE'RE DONE, WE'LL BOTH BE---RICH-- FAMOUS---
JUST LIKE MA ALWAYS WANTED US TO BE!
YOU'VE GOT IT ALL WRONG! SHE WOULDN'T HAVE WANTED US TO BETRAY OUR OWN COUNTRY!
HOLD IT! THAT MUST BE THE CALL WE WERE TOLD TO EXPECT...
FROM THE REAL CAPTAIN AMERICA!
DON'T GO THRU WITH IT! THERE'S STILL TIME TO WARN HIM--!
WHO? CAPTAIN AMERICA? SAY--- THIS IS A GENUINE HONOR!
I'VE BEEN WANTING TO MEET YOU FOR YEARS!
CY! I BEG YOU... DON'T DO IT!
11.

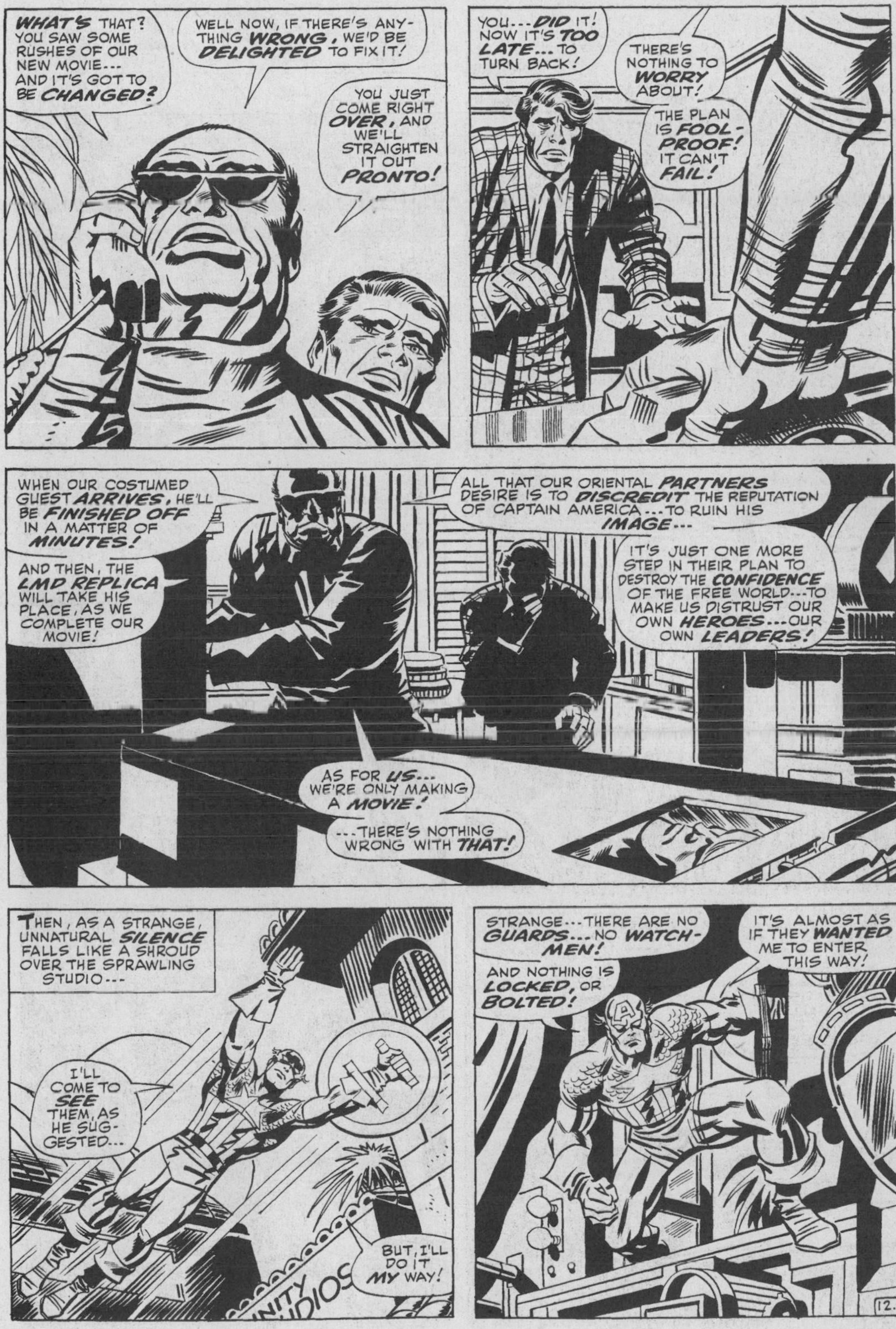
WHAT'S THAT? YOU SAW SOME RUSHES OF OUR NEW MOVIE--- AND IT'S GOT TO BE CHANGED?
WELL NOW, IF THERE'S ANY-THING WRONG, WE'D BE DELIGHTED TO FIX IT!
YOU JUST COME RIGHT OVER, AND WE'LL STRAIGHTEN IT OUT PRONTO!
YOU---DID IT! NOW IT'S TOO LATE... TO TURN BACK!
THERE'S NOTHING TO WORRY ABOUT!
THE PLAN IS FOOL-PROOF! IT CAN'T FAIL!
WHEN OUR COSTUMED GUEST ARRIVES, HE'LL BE FINISHED OFF IN A MATTER OF MINUTES!
AND THEN, THE LMD REPLICA WILL TAKE HIS PLACE, AS WE COMPLETE OUR MOVIE!
ALL THAT OUR ORIENTAL PARTNERS DESIRE IS TO DISCREDIT THE REPUTATION OF CAPTAIN AMERICA---TO RUIN HIS IMAGE---
IT'S JUST ONE MORE STEP IN THEIR PLAN TO DESTROY THE CONFIDENCE OF THE FREE WORLD---TO MAKE US DISTRUST OUR OWN HEROES---OUR OWN LEADERS!
AS FOR US--- WE'RE ONLY MAKING A MOVIE!
---THERE'S NOTHING WRONG WITH THAT!
THEN, AS A STRANGE, UNNATURAL SILENCE FALLS LIKE A SHROUD OVER THE SPRAWLING STUDIO---
I'LL COME TO SEE THEM, AS HE SUG-GESTED...
BUT, I'LL DO IT MY WAY!
STRANGE---THERE ARE NO GUARDS---NO WATCH-MEN!
AND NOTHING IS LOCKED, OR BOLTED!
IT'S ALMOST AS IF THEY WANTED ME TO ENTER THIS WAY!
12.

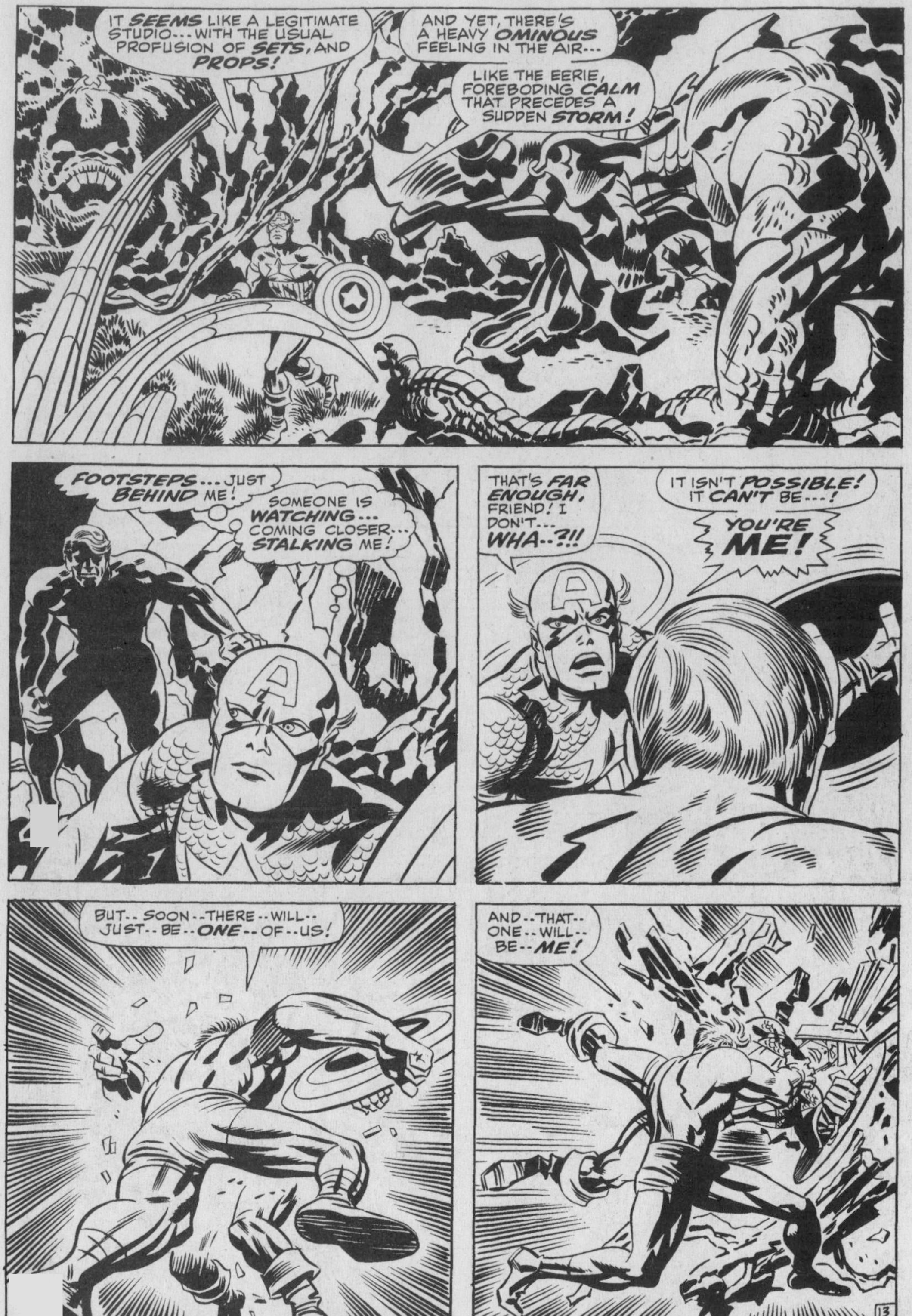
IT SEEMS LIKE A LEGITIMATE STUDIO--- WITH THE USUAL PROFUSION OF SETS, AND PROPS!
AND YET, THERE'S A HEAVY OMINOUS FEELING IN THE AIR---
LIKE THE EERIE, FOREBODING CALM THAT PRECEDES A SUDDEN STORM!
FOOTSTEPS... JUST BEHIND ME!
SOMEONE IS WATCHING... COMING CLOSER... STALKING ME!
THAT'S FAR ENOUGH, FRIEND! I DON'T... WHA--?!!
IT ISN'T POSSIBLE! IT CAN'T BE---!
YOU'RE ME!
BUT-- SOON--THERE--WILL-- JUST-- BE--ONE--OF--US!
AND--THAT-- ONE--WILL-- BE--ME!
13

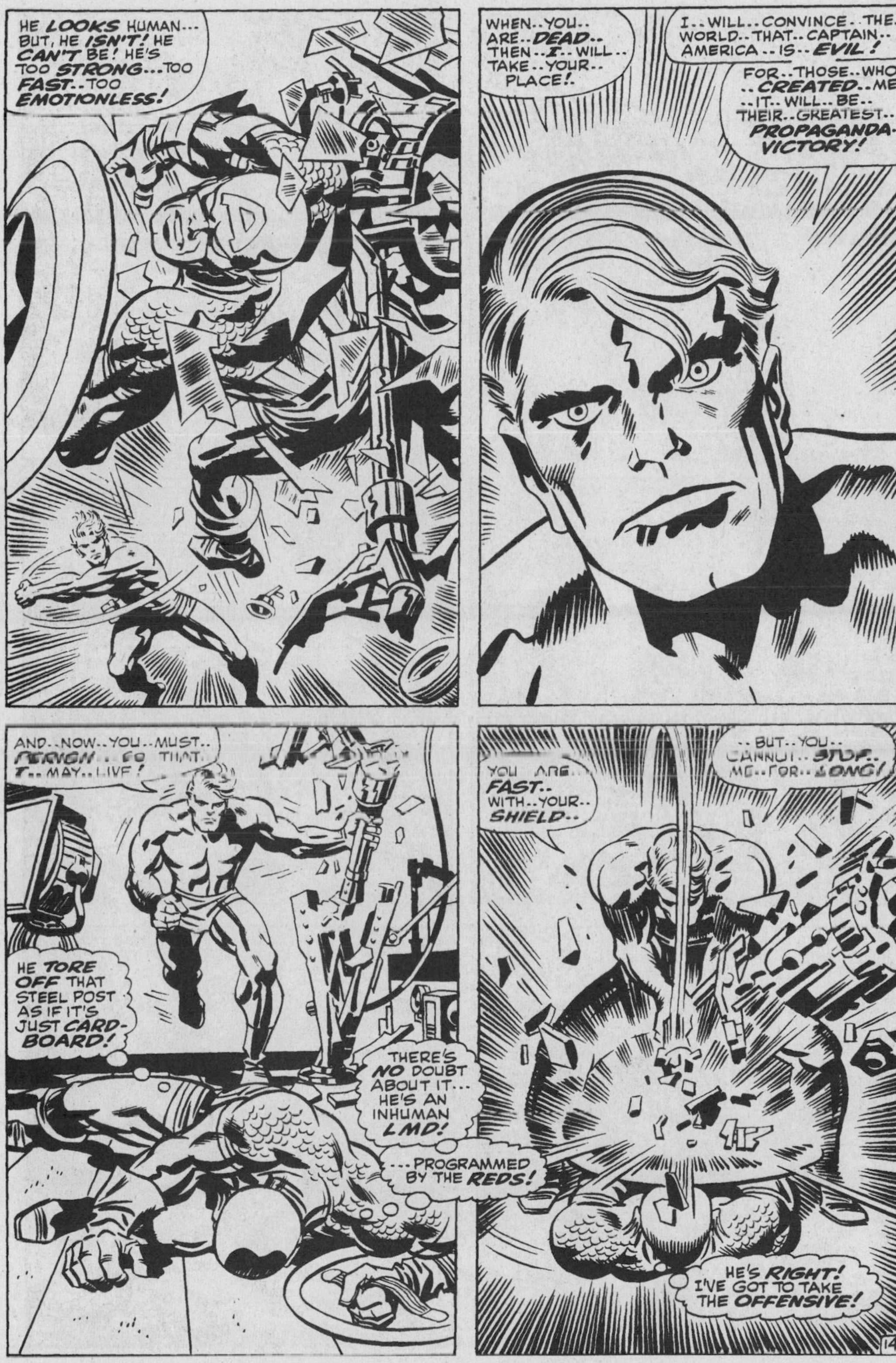
HE LOOKS HUMAN... BUT, HE ISN'T! HE CAN'T BE! HE'S TOO STRONG...TOO FAST..TOO EMOTIONLESS!
WHEN..YOU..ARE..DEAD..THEN..I..WILL..TAKE..YOUR..PLACE!.
I..WILL..CONVINCE..THE..WORLD..THAT..CAPTAIN..AMERICA..IS..EVIL!
FOR..THOSE..WHO..CREATED..ME..IT..WILL..BE..THEIR..GREATEST..PROPAGANDA..VICTORY!
AND..NOW..YOU..MUST..PERISH..SO THAT..I..MAY..LIVE!
HE TORE OFF THAT STEEL POST AS IF IT'S JUST CARDBOARD!
THERE'S NO DOUBT ABOUT IT...HE'S AN INHUMAN LMD!
...PROGRAMMED BY THE REDS!
YOU ARE..FAST..WITH..YOUR..SHIELD..
..BUT..YOU..CANNOT..STOP..ME..FOR..LONG!
HE'S RIGHT! I'VE GOT TO TAKE THE OFFENSIVE!
14

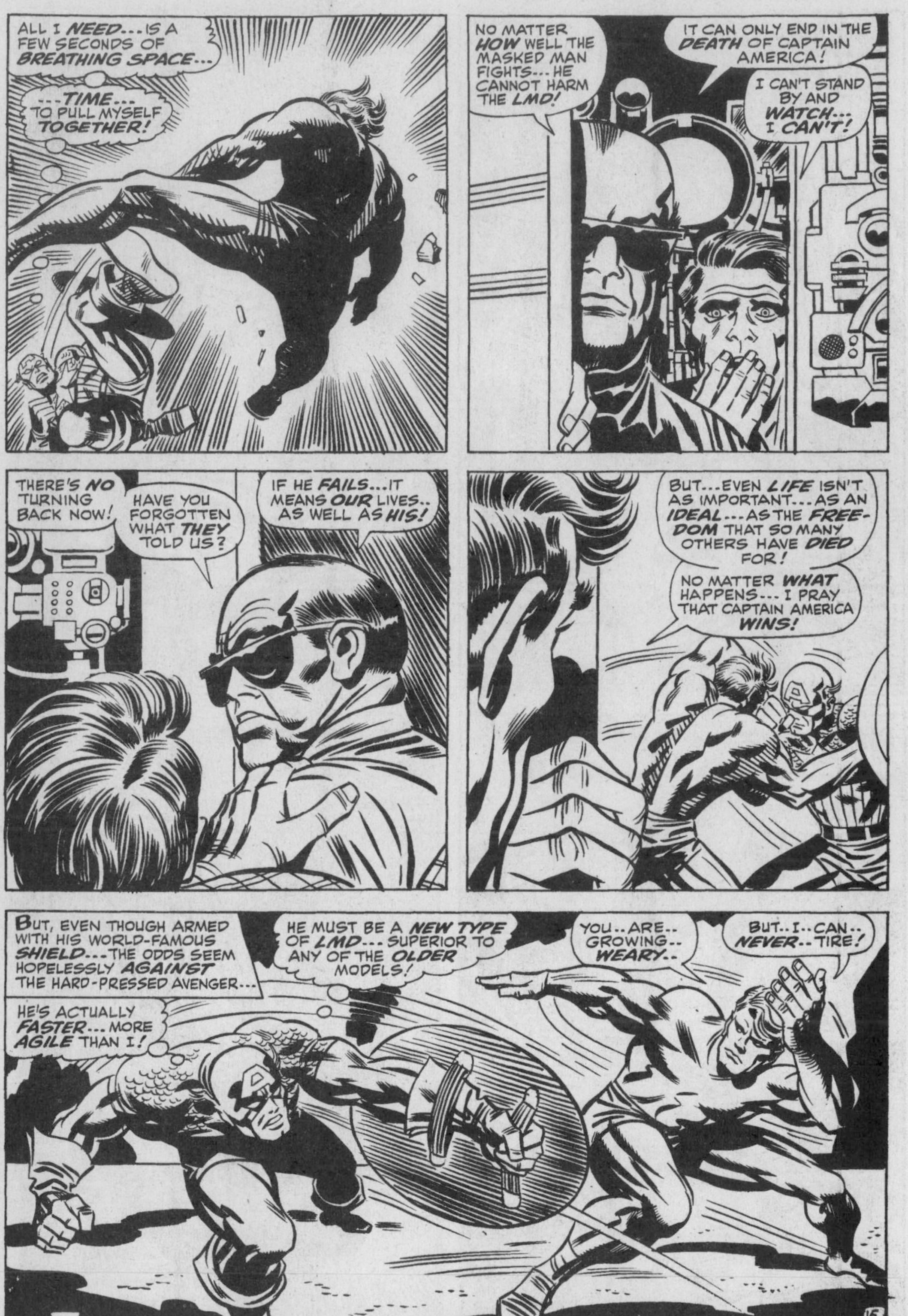
ALL I NEED...IS A FEW SECONDS OF BREATHING SPACE...
...TIME...TO PULL MYSELF TOGETHER!
NO MATTER HOW WELL THE MASKED MAN FIGHTS...HE CANNOT HARM THE LMD!
IT CAN ONLY END IN THE DEATH OF CAPTAIN AMERICA!
I CAN'T STAND BY AND WATCH...I CAN'T!
THERE'S NO TURNING BACK NOW!
HAVE YOU FORGOTTEN WHAT THEY TOLD US?
IF HE FAILS...IT MEANS OUR LIVES.. AS WELL AS HIS!
BUT...EVEN LIFE ISN'T AS IMPORTANT...AS AN IDEAL...AS THE FREE-DOM THAT SO MANY OTHERS HAVE DIED FOR!
NO MATTER WHAT HAPPENS...I PRAY THAT CAPTAIN AMERICA WINS!
BUT, EVEN THOUGH ARMED WITH HIS WORLD-FAMOUS SHIELD...THE ODDS SEEM HOPELESSLY AGAINST THE HARD-PRESSED AVENGER...
HE MUST BE A NEW TYPE OF LMD...SUPERIOR TO ANY OF THE OLDER MODELS!
HE'S ACTUALLY FASTER...MORE AGILE THAN I!
YOU..ARE..GROWING..WEARY..
BUT..I..CAN..NEVER..TIRE!
15.

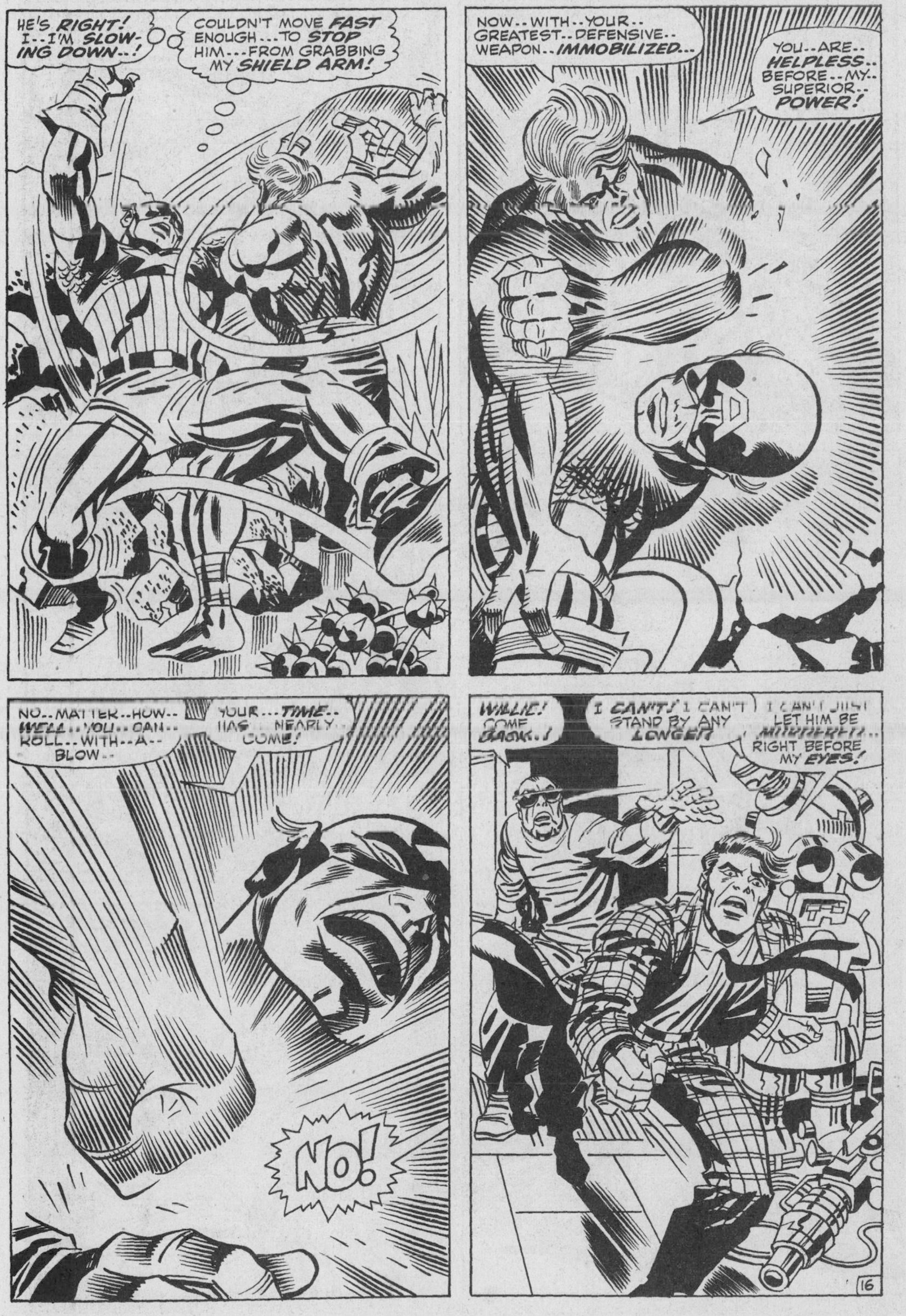
HE'S RIGHT! I--I'M SLOWING DOWN--!
COULDN'T MOVE FAST ENOUGH---TO STOP HIM---FROM GRABBING MY SHIELD ARM!
NOW--WITH--YOUR--GREATEST--DEFENSIVE-WEAPON--IMMOBILIZED...
YOU--ARE--HELPLESS--BEFORE--MY--SUPERIOR--POWER!
NO--MATTER--HOW--WELL--YOU--CAN--ROLL--WITH--A--BLOW--
YOUR...TIME--HAS NEARLY COME!
NO!
WILLIE! COME BACK..!
I CAN'T! I CAN'T STAND BY ANY LONGER!
I CAN'T JUST LET HIM BE MURDERED... RIGHT BEFORE MY EYES!
16

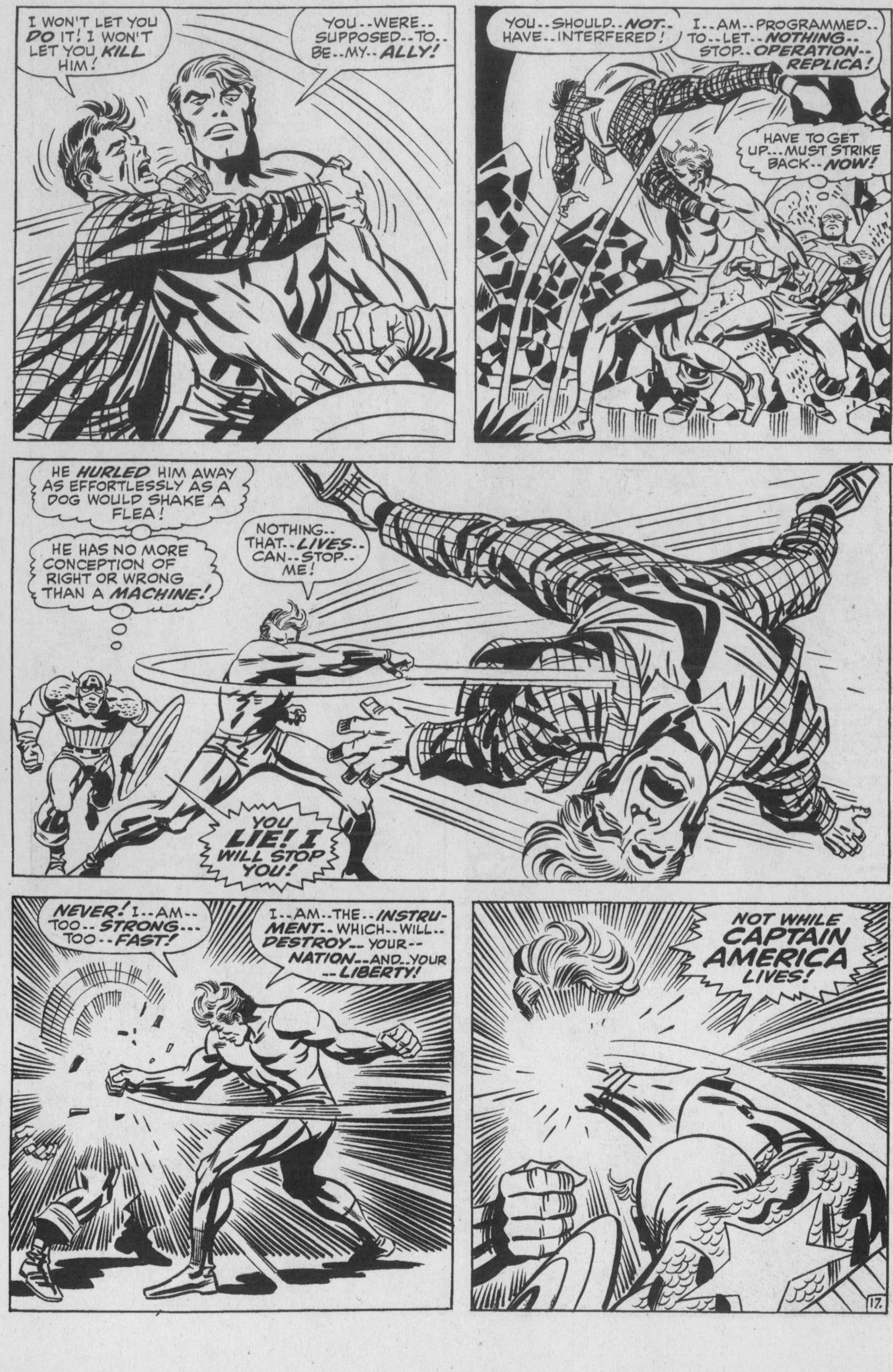
I WON'T LET YOU DO IT! I WON'T LET YOU KILL HIM!
YOU--WERE--SUPPOSED--TO--BE--MY--ALLY!
YOU--SHOULD--NOT--HAVE--INTERFERED!
I--AM--PROGRAMMED--TO--LET--NOTHING--STOP--OPERATION--REPLICA!
HAVE TO GET UP...MUST STRIKE BACK--NOW!
HE HURLED HIM AWAY AS EFFORTLESSLY AS A DOG WOULD SHAKE A FLEA!
HE HAS NO MORE CONCEPTION OF RIGHT OR WRONG THAN A MACHINE!
NOTHING--THAT--LIVES--CAN--STOP--ME!
YOU LIE! I WILL STOP YOU!
NEVER! I--AM--TOO--STRONG---TOO--FAST!
I--AM--THE--INSTRUMENT--WHICH--WILL--DESTROY--YOUR--NATION--AND--YOUR--LIBERTY!
NOT WHILE CAPTAIN AMERICA LIVES!
17.

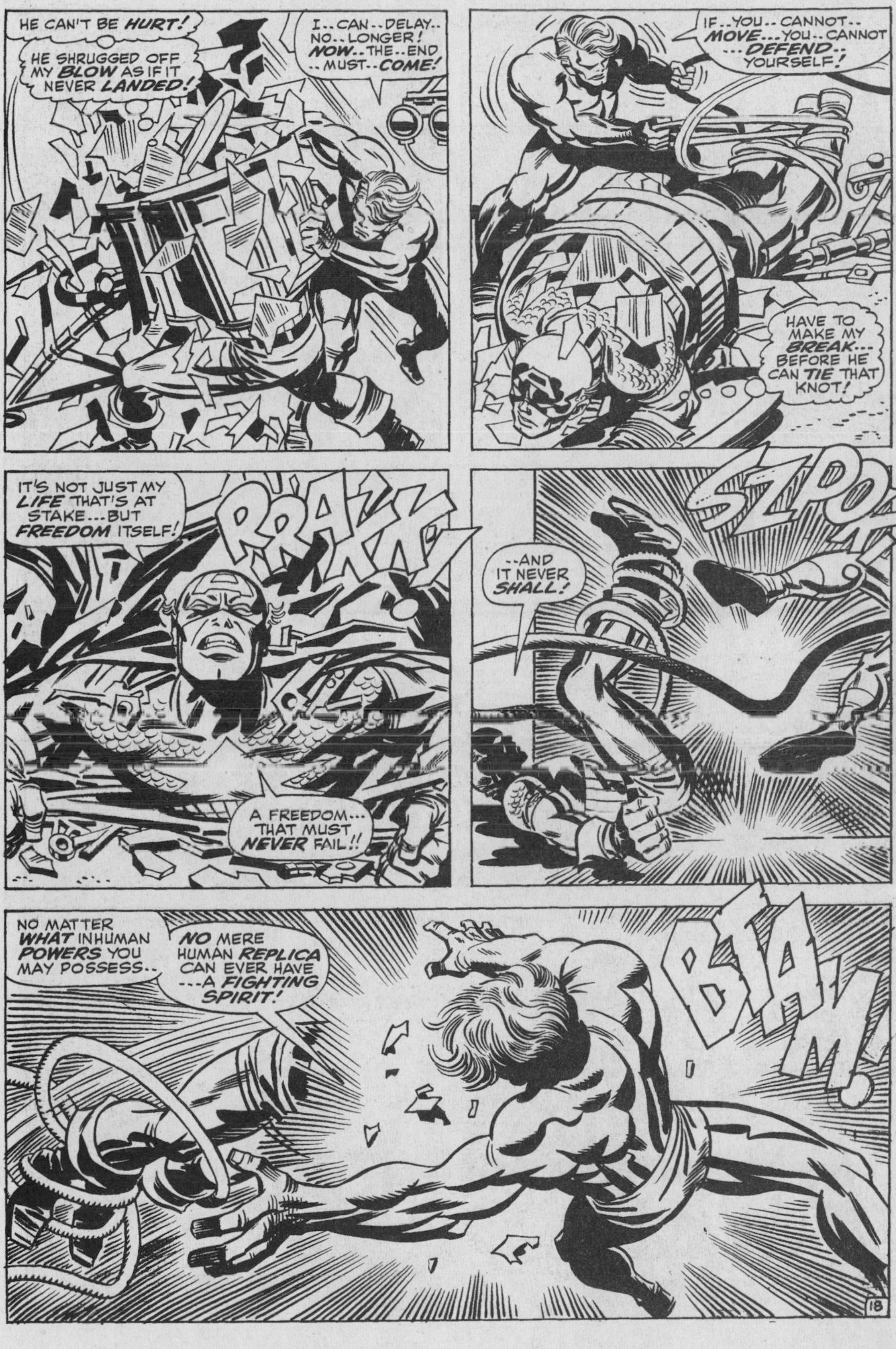
HE CAN'T BE HURT!
HE SHRUGGED OFF MY BLOW AS IF IT NEVER LANDED!
I.. CAN.. DELAY.. NO.. LONGER! NOW.. THE.. END .. MUST.. COME!
IF.. YOU.. CANNOT.. MOVE... YOU.. CANNOT ... DEFEND.. YOURSELF!
HAVE TO MAKE MY BREAK... BEFORE HE CAN TIE THAT KNOT!
IT'S NOT JUST MY LIFE THAT'S AT STAKE... BUT FREEDOM ITSELF!
RRAKK!
A FREEDOM... THAT MUST NEVER FAIL!!
SZPOK!
--AND IT NEVER SHALL!
NO MATTER WHAT INHUMAN POWERS YOU MAY POSSESS..
NO MERE HUMAN REPLICA CAN EVER HAVE ---A FIGHTING SPIRIT!
BTAM!
18

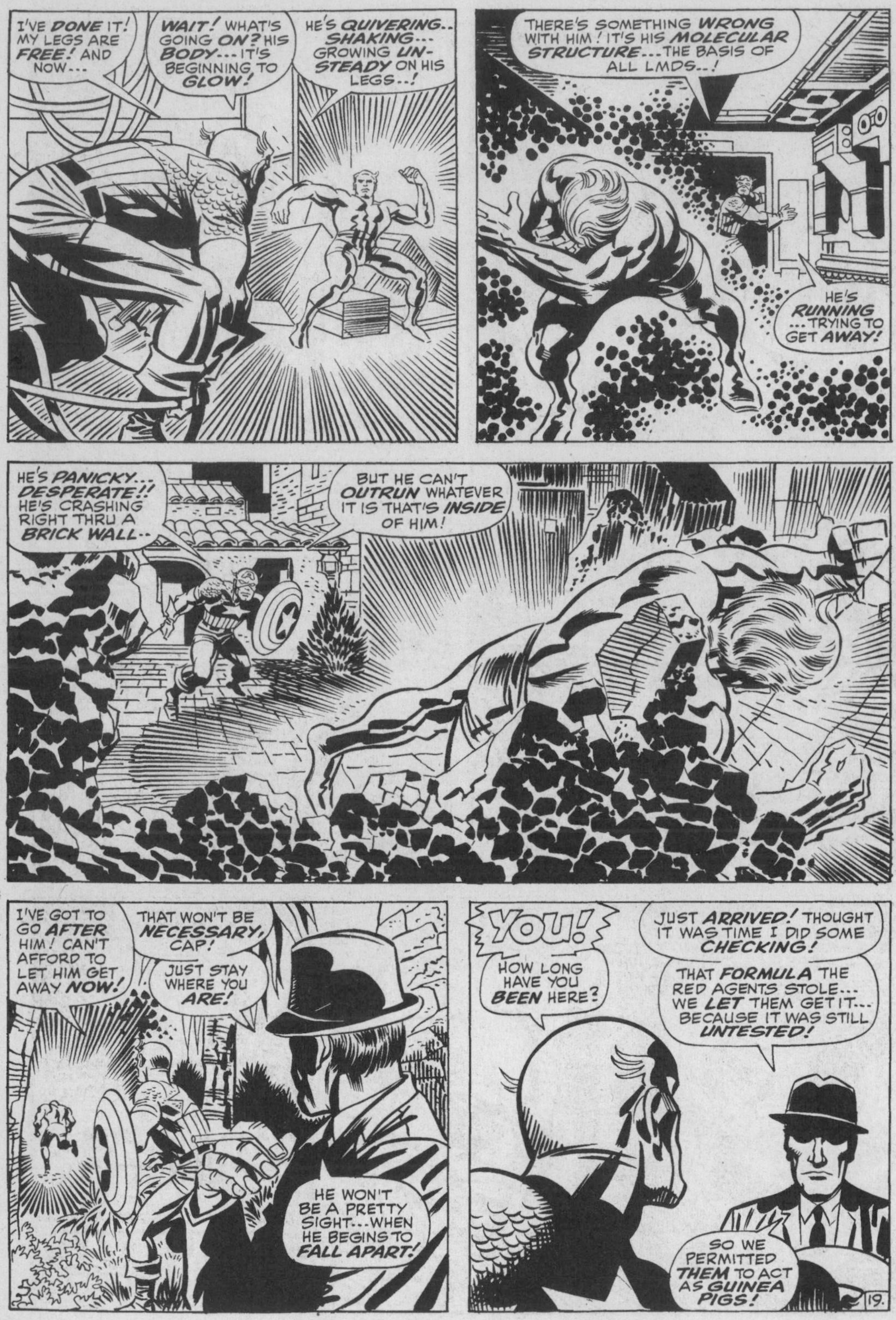

I'VE DONE IT! MY LEGS ARE FREE! AND NOW---
WAIT! WHAT'S GOING ON? HIS BODY--- IT'S BEGINNING TO GLOW!
HE'S QUIVERING.. SHAKING--- GROWING UN-STEADY ON HIS LEGS..!
THERE'S SOMETHING WRONG WITH HIM! IT'S HIS MOLECULAR STRUCTURE--- THE BASIS OF ALL LMDS..!
HE'S RUNNING ...TRYING TO GET AWAY!
HE'S PANICKY... DESPERATE!! HE'S CRASHING RIGHT THRU A BRICK WALL..
BUT HE CAN'T OUTRUN WHATEVER IT IS THAT'S INSIDE OF HIM!
I'VE GOT TO GO AFTER HIM! CAN'T AFFORD TO LET HIM GET AWAY NOW!
THAT WON'T BE NECESSARY, CAP!
JUST STAY WHERE YOU ARE!
HE WON'T BE A PRETTY SIGHT---WHEN HE BEGINS TO FALL APART!
YOU!
HOW LONG HAVE YOU BEEN HERE?
JUST ARRIVED! THOUGHT IT WAS TIME I DID SOME CHECKING!
THAT FORMULA THE RED AGENTS STOLE--- WE LET THEM GET IT--- BECAUSE IT WAS STILL UNTESTED!
SO WE PERMITTED THEM TO ACT AS GUINEA PIGS!
19.

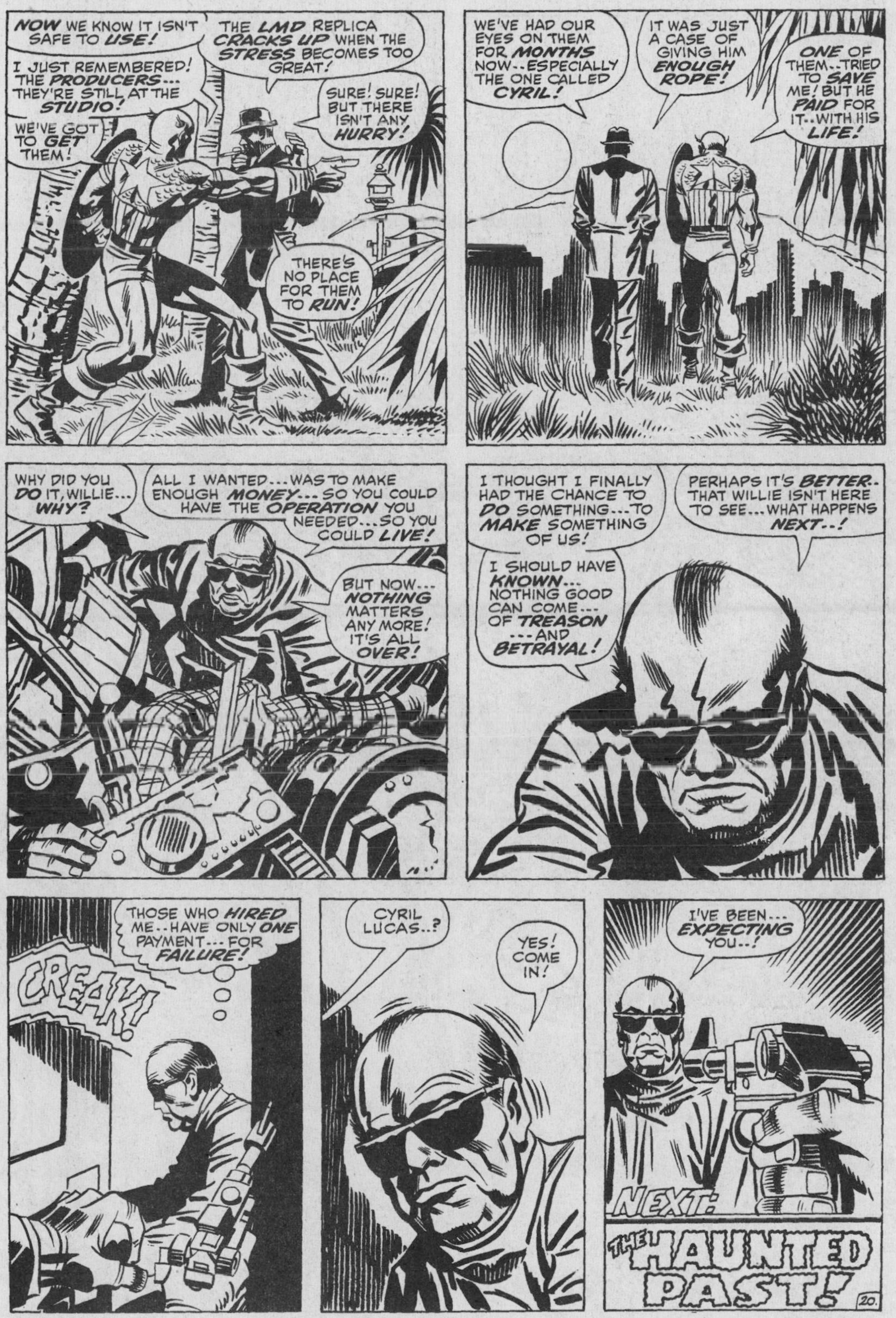
NOW WE KNOW IT ISN'T SAFE TO USE!
THE LMD REPLICA CRACKS UP WHEN THE STRESS BECOMES TOO GREAT!
I JUST REMEMBERED! THE PRODUCERS... THEY'RE STILL AT THE STUDIO!
SURE! SURE! BUT THERE ISN'T ANY HURRY!
WE'VE GOT TO GET THEM!
THERE'S NO PLACE FOR THEM TO RUN!
WE'VE HAD OUR EYES ON THEM FOR MONTHS NOW--ESPECIALLY THE ONE CALLED CYRIL!
IT WAS JUST A CASE OF GIVING HIM ENOUGH ROPE!
ONE OF THEM--TRIED TO SAVE ME! BUT HE PAID FOR IT--WITH HIS LIFE!
WHY DID YOU DO IT, WILLIE... WHY?
ALL I WANTED... WAS TO MAKE ENOUGH MONEY... SO YOU COULD HAVE THE OPERATION YOU NEEDED... SO YOU COULD LIVE!
BUT NOW... NOTHING MATTERS ANY MORE! IT'S ALL OVER!
I THOUGHT I FINALLY HAD THE CHANCE TO DO SOMETHING---TO MAKE SOMETHING OF US!
PERHAPS IT'S BETTER.. THAT WILLIE ISN'T HERE TO SEE... WHAT HAPPENS NEXT--!
I SHOULD HAVE KNOWN... NOTHING GOOD CAN COME--- OF TREASON ---AND BETRAYAL!
THOSE WHO HIRED ME--HAVE ONLY ONE PAYMENT--- FOR FAILURE!
CREAK!
CYRIL LUCAS..?
YES! COME IN!
I'VE BEEN... EXPECTING YOU--!
NEXT:
THE HAUNTED PAST!
20.

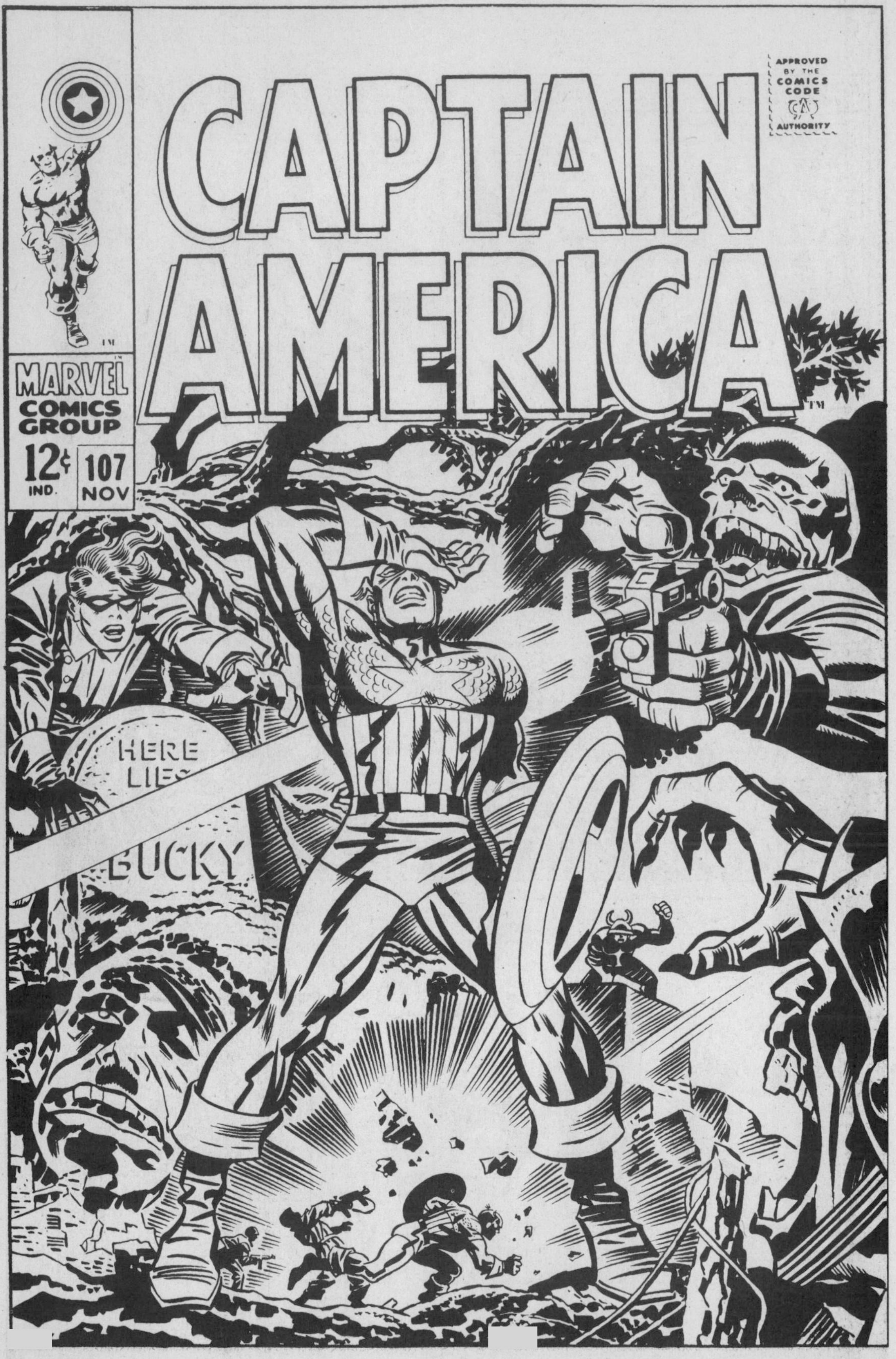
CAPTAIN AMERICA
MARVEL COMICS GROUP
12¢ IND.
107 NOV
APPROVED BY THE COMICS CODE AUTHORITY
HERE LIES
BUCKY

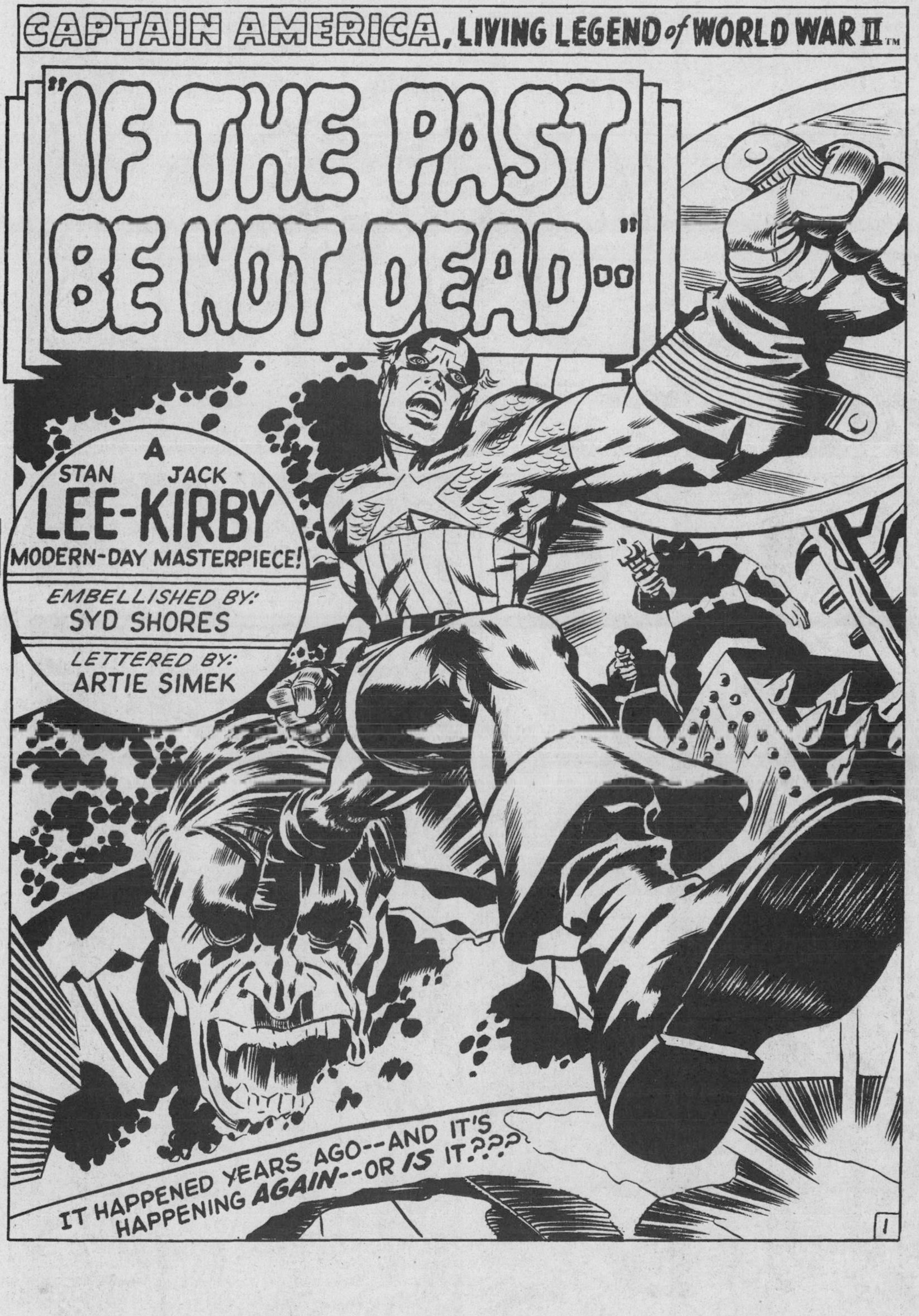

CAPTAIN AMERICA, LIVING LEGEND of WORLD WAR II TM
"IF THE PAST BE NOT DEAD--"
A STAN JACK LEE-KIRBY MODERN-DAY MASTERPIECE!
EMBELLISHED BY: SYD SHORES
LETTERED BY: ARTIE SIMEK
IT HAPPENED YEARS AGO--AND IT'S HAPPENING AGAIN--OR IS IT???
1

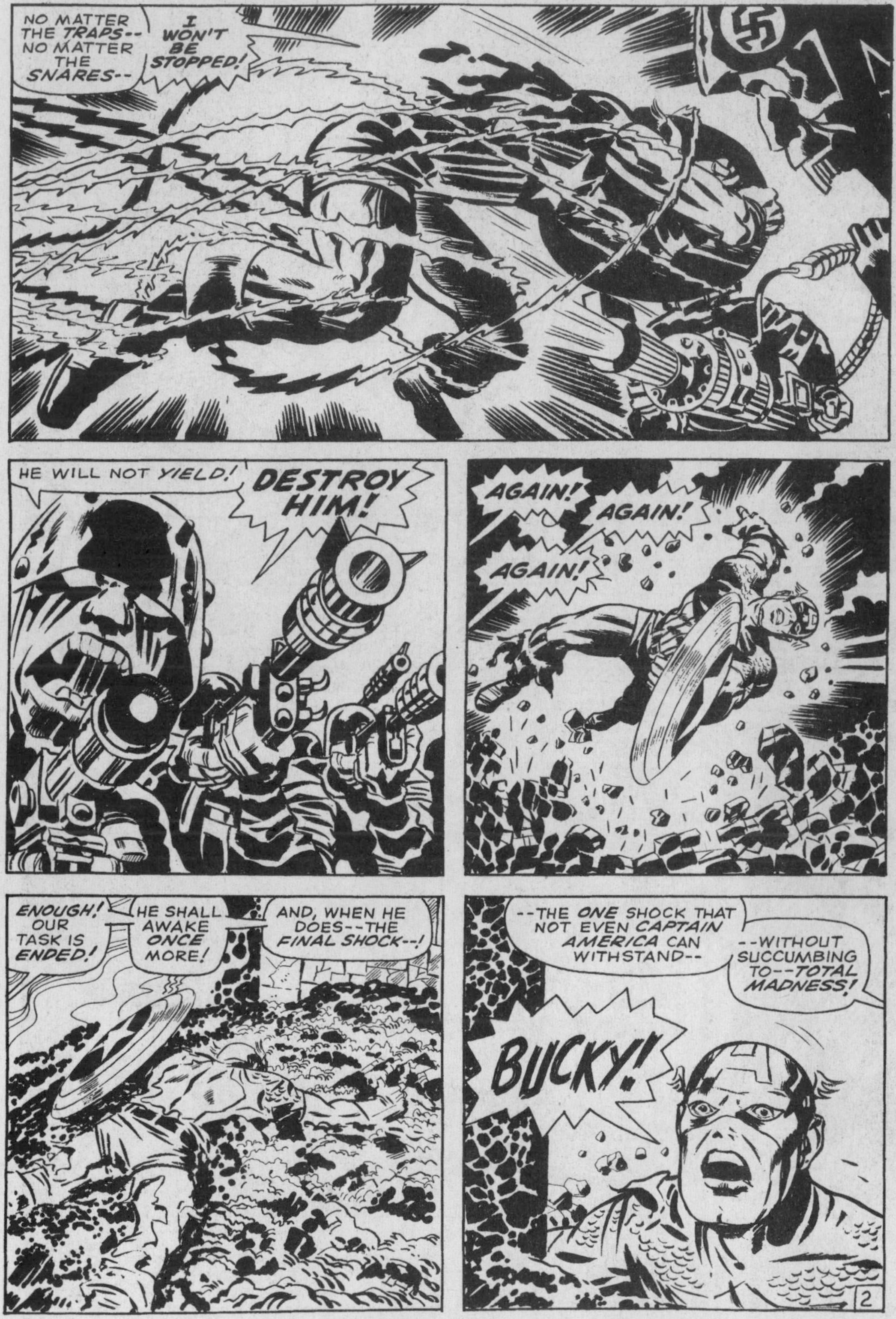
NO MATTER THE TRAPS-- NO MATTER THE SNARES--
I WON'T BE STOPPED!
HE WILL NOT YIELD!
DESTROY HIM!
AGAIN!
AGAIN!
AGAIN!
ENOUGH! OUR TASK IS ENDED!
HE SHALL AWAKE ONCE MORE!
AND, WHEN HE DOES--THE FINAL SHOCK--!
--THE ONE SHOCK THAT NOT EVEN CAPTAIN AMERICA CAN WITHSTAND--
--WITHOUT SUCCUMBING TO--TOTAL MADNESS!
BUCKY!
2

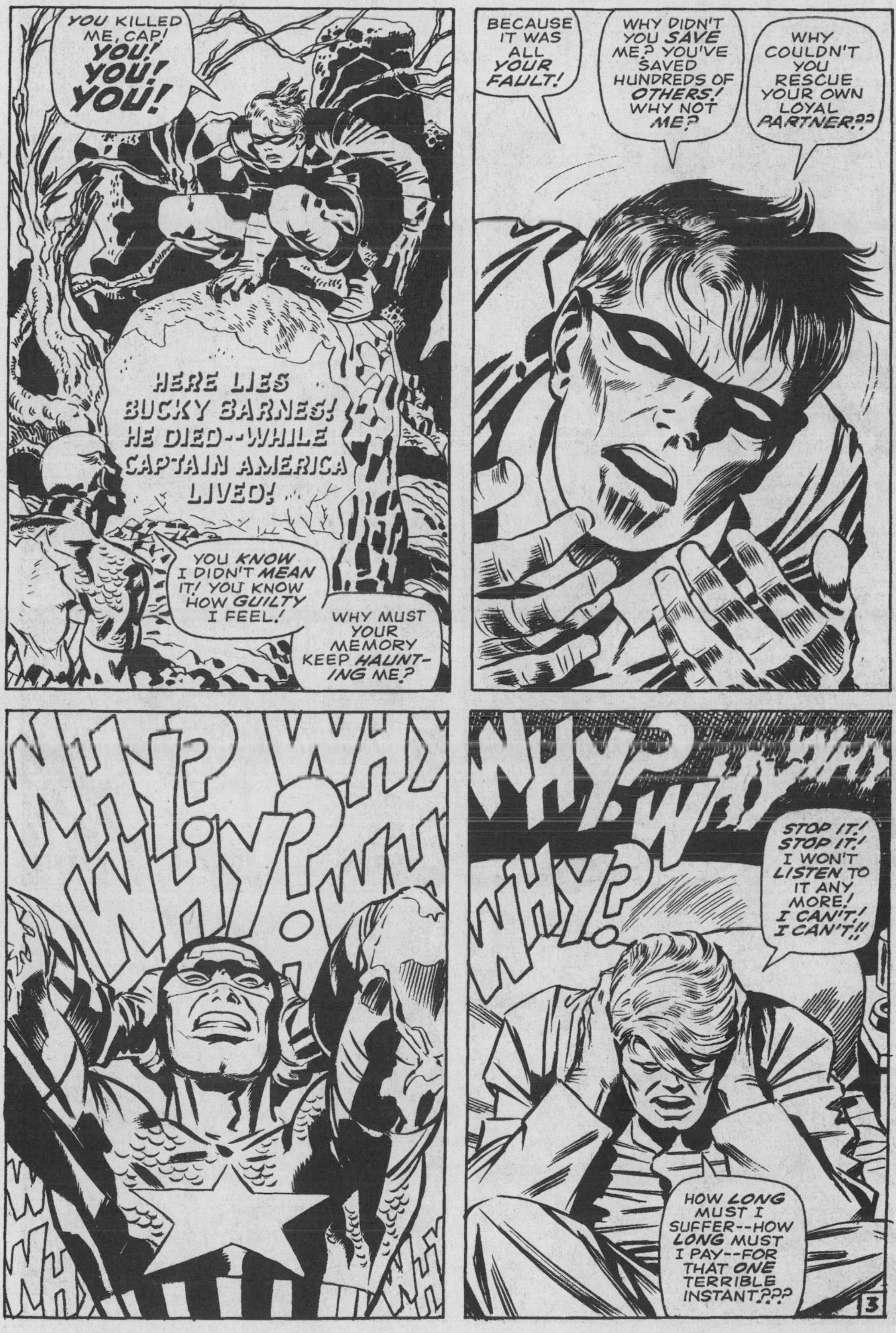
YOU KILLED ME, CAP! YOU! YOU! YOU!
HERE LIES BUCKY BARNES! HE DIED--WHILE CAPTAIN AMERICA LIVED!
YOU KNOW I DIDN'T MEAN IT! YOU KNOW HOW GUILTY I FEEL!
WHY MUST YOUR MEMORY KEEP HAUNTING ME?
BECAUSE IT WAS ALL YOUR FAULT!
WHY DIDN'T YOU SAVE ME? YOU'VE SAVED HUNDREDS OF OTHERS! WHY NOT ME?
WHY COULDN'T YOU RESCUE YOUR OWN LOYAL PARTNER??
WHY? WHY WHY? WHY?
WHY? WHY? WHY?
STOP IT! STOP IT! I WON'T LISTEN TO IT ANY MORE! I CAN'T! I CAN'T!!
HOW LONG MUST I SUFFER--HOW LONG MUST I PAY--FOR THAT ONE TERRIBLE INSTANT???
3

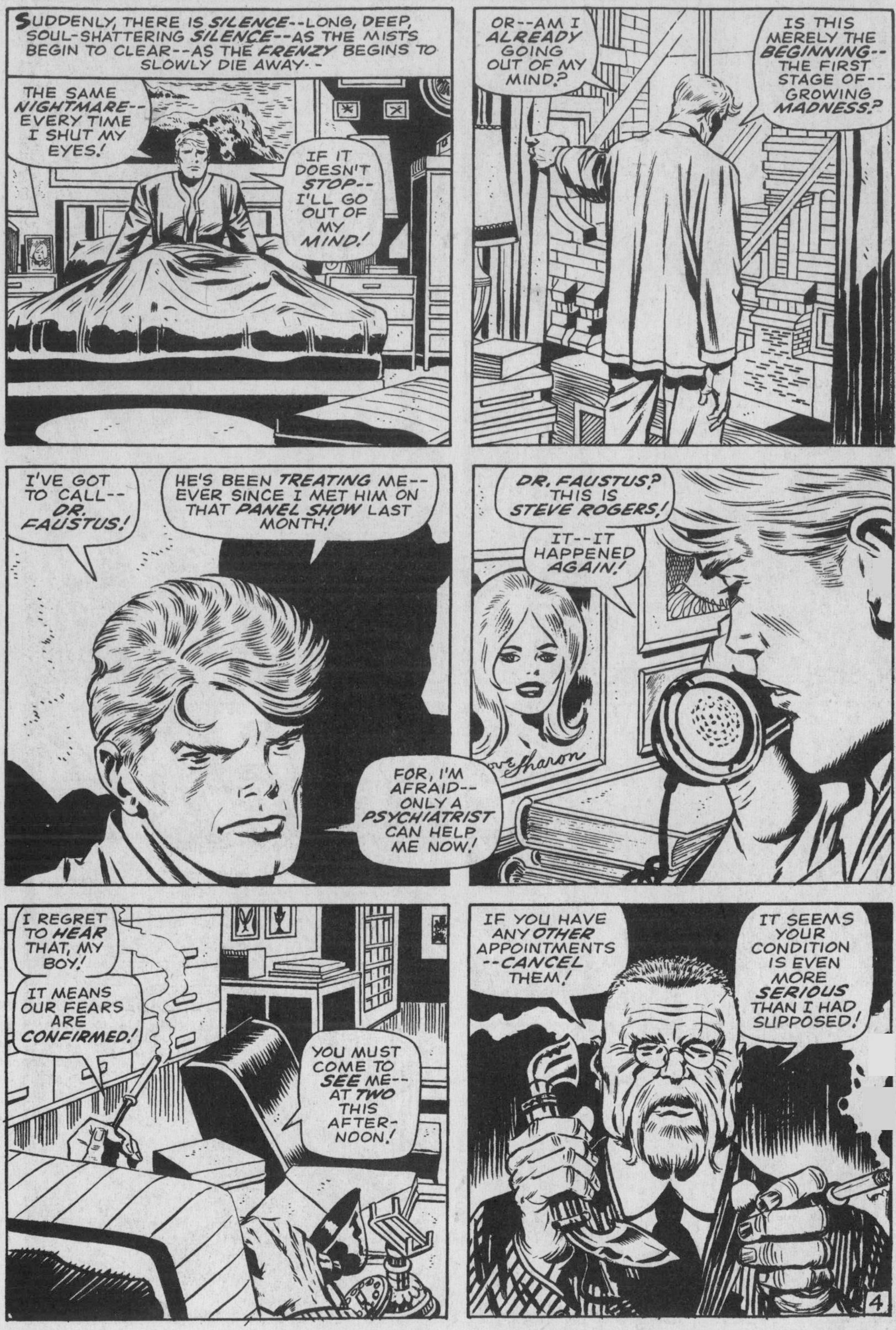
SUDDENLY, THERE IS SILENCE--LONG, DEEP, SOUL-SHATTERING SILENCE--AS THE MISTS BEGIN TO CLEAR--AS THE FRENZY BEGINS TO SLOWLY DIE AWAY--
THE SAME NIGHTMARE-- EVERY TIME I SHUT MY EYES!
IF IT DOESN'T STOP-- I'LL GO OUT OF MY MIND!
OR--AM I ALREADY GOING OUT OF MY MIND?
IS THIS MERELY THE BEGINNING-- THE FIRST STAGE OF-- GROWING MADNESS?
I'VE GOT TO CALL-- DR. FAUSTUS!
HE'S BEEN TREATING ME-- EVER SINCE I MET HIM ON THAT PANEL SHOW LAST MONTH!
FOR, I'M AFRAID-- ONLY A PSYCHIATRIST CAN HELP ME NOW!
DR. FAUSTUS? THIS IS STEVE ROGERS!
IT--IT HAPPENED AGAIN!
Love Sharon
I REGRET TO HEAR THAT, MY BOY!
IT MEANS OUR FEARS ARE CONFIRMED!
YOU MUST COME TO SEE ME-- AT TWO THIS AFTER-NOON!
IF YOU HAVE ANY OTHER APPOINTMENTS --CANCEL THEM!
IT SEEMS YOUR CONDITION IS EVEN MORE SERIOUS THAN I HAD SUPPOSED!
4

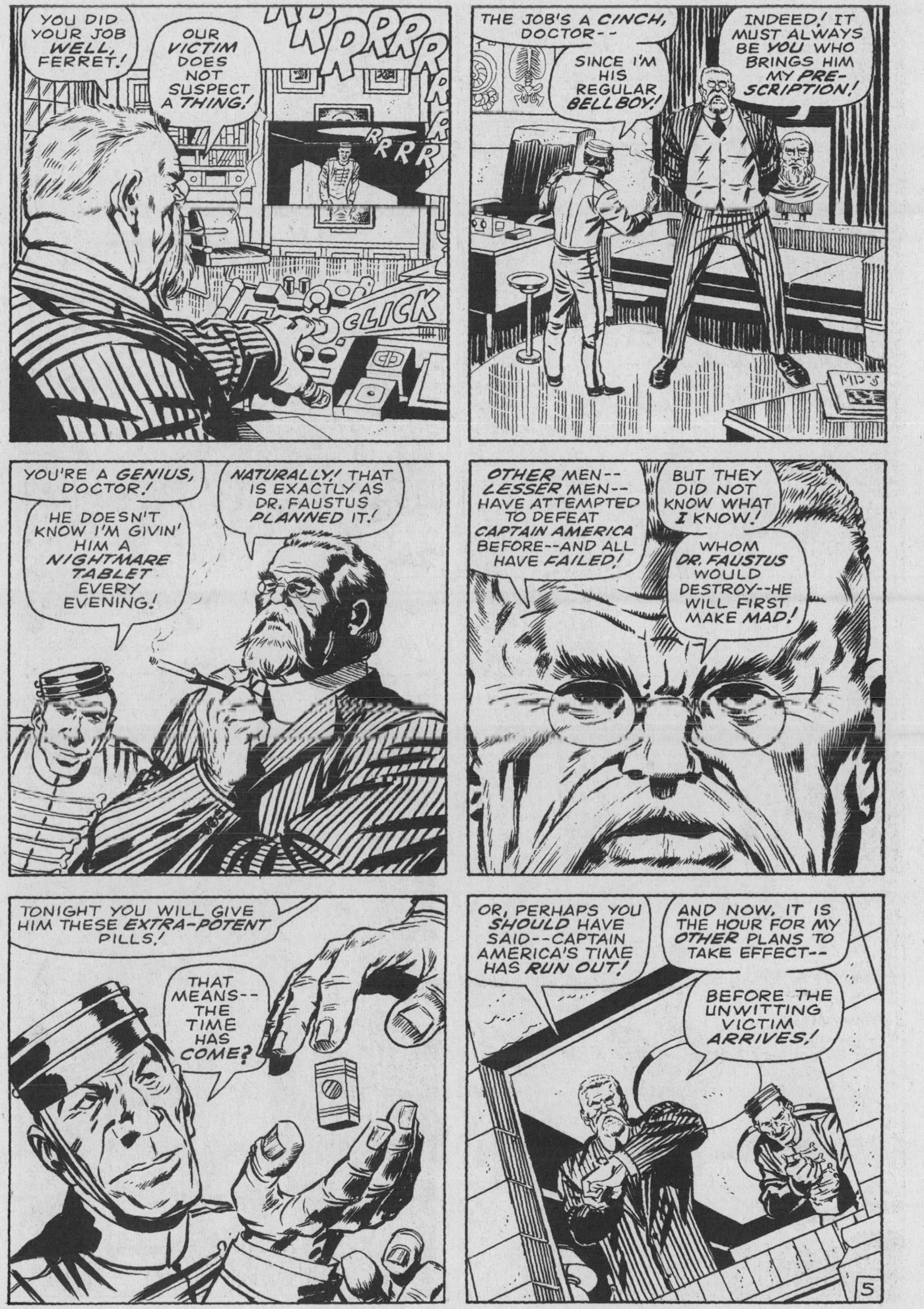

YOU DID YOUR JOB WELL, FERRET!
OUR VICTIM DOES NOT SUSPECT A THING!
RRRRRRRRRRRR
CLICK
THE JOB'S A CINCH, DOCTOR--
SINCE I'M HIS REGULAR BELLBOY!
INDEED! IT MUST ALWAYS BE YOU WHO BRINGS HIM MY PRE-SCRIPTION!
YOU'RE A GENIUS, DOCTOR!
HE DOESN'T KNOW I'M GIVIN' HIM A NIGHTMARE TABLET EVERY EVENING!
NATURALLY! THAT IS EXACTLY AS DR. FAUSTUS PLANNED IT!
OTHER MEN-- LESSER MEN-- HAVE ATTEMPTED TO DEFEAT CAPTAIN AMERICA BEFORE--AND ALL HAVE FAILED!
BUT THEY DID NOT KNOW WHAT I KNOW!
WHOM DR. FAUSTUS WOULD DESTROY--HE WILL FIRST MAKE MAD!
TONIGHT YOU WILL GIVE HIM THESE EXTRA-POTENT PILLS!
THAT MEANS-- THE TIME HAS COME?
OR, PERHAPS YOU SHOULD HAVE SAID--CAPTAIN AMERICA'S TIME HAS RUN OUT!
AND NOW, IT IS THE HOUR FOR MY OTHER PLANS TO TAKE EFFECT--
BEFORE THE UNWITTING VICTIM ARRIVES!
5

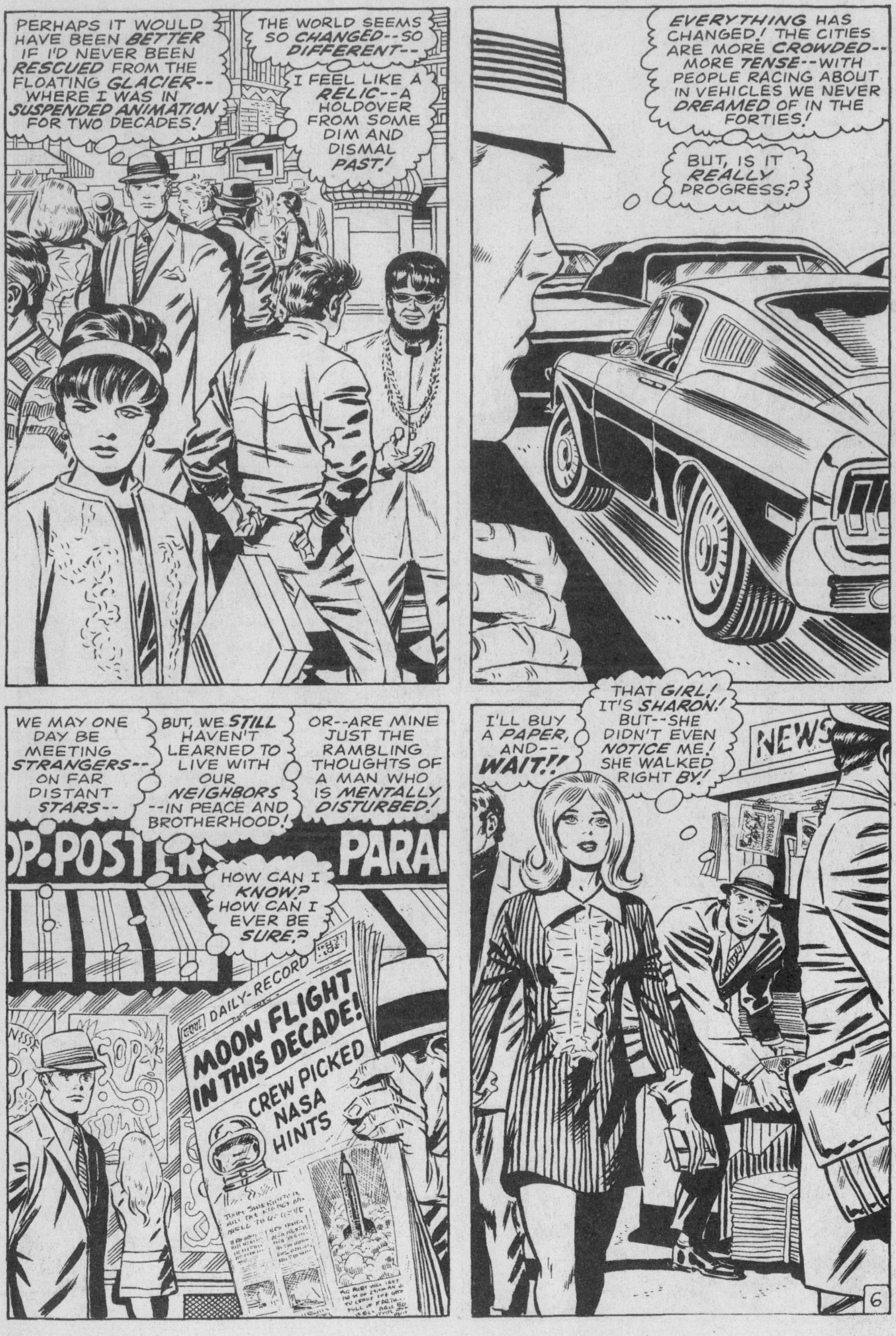
PERHAPS IT WOULD HAVE BEEN BETTER IF I'D NEVER BEEN RESCUED FROM THE FLOATING GLACIER-- WHERE I WAS IN SUSPENDED ANIMATION FOR TWO DECADES!
THE WORLD SEEMS SO CHANGED--SO DIFFERENT--
I FEEL LIKE A RELIC--A HOLDOVER FROM SOME DIM AND DISMAL PAST!
EVERYTHING HAS CHANGED! THE CITIES ARE MORE CROWDED-- MORE TENSE--WITH PEOPLE RACING ABOUT IN VEHICLES WE NEVER DREAMED OF IN THE FORTIES!
BUT, IS IT REALLY PROGRESS?
WE MAY ONE DAY BE MEETING STRANGERS-- ON FAR DISTANT STARS--
BUT, WE STILL HAVEN'T LEARNED TO LIVE WITH OUR NEIGHBORS --IN PEACE AND BROTHERHOOD!
OR--ARE MINE JUST THE RAMBLING THOUGHTS OF A MAN WHO IS MENTALLY DISTURBED!
OP·POSTERS
PARA
HOW CAN I KNOW? HOW CAN I EVER BE SURE?
DAILY-RECORD
MOON FLIGHT IN THIS DECADE!
CREW PICKED NASA HINTS
I'LL BUY A PAPER, AND-- WAIT!!
THAT GIRL! IT'S SHARON! BUT--SHE DIDN'T EVEN NOTICE ME! SHE WALKED RIGHT BY!
NEWS
6

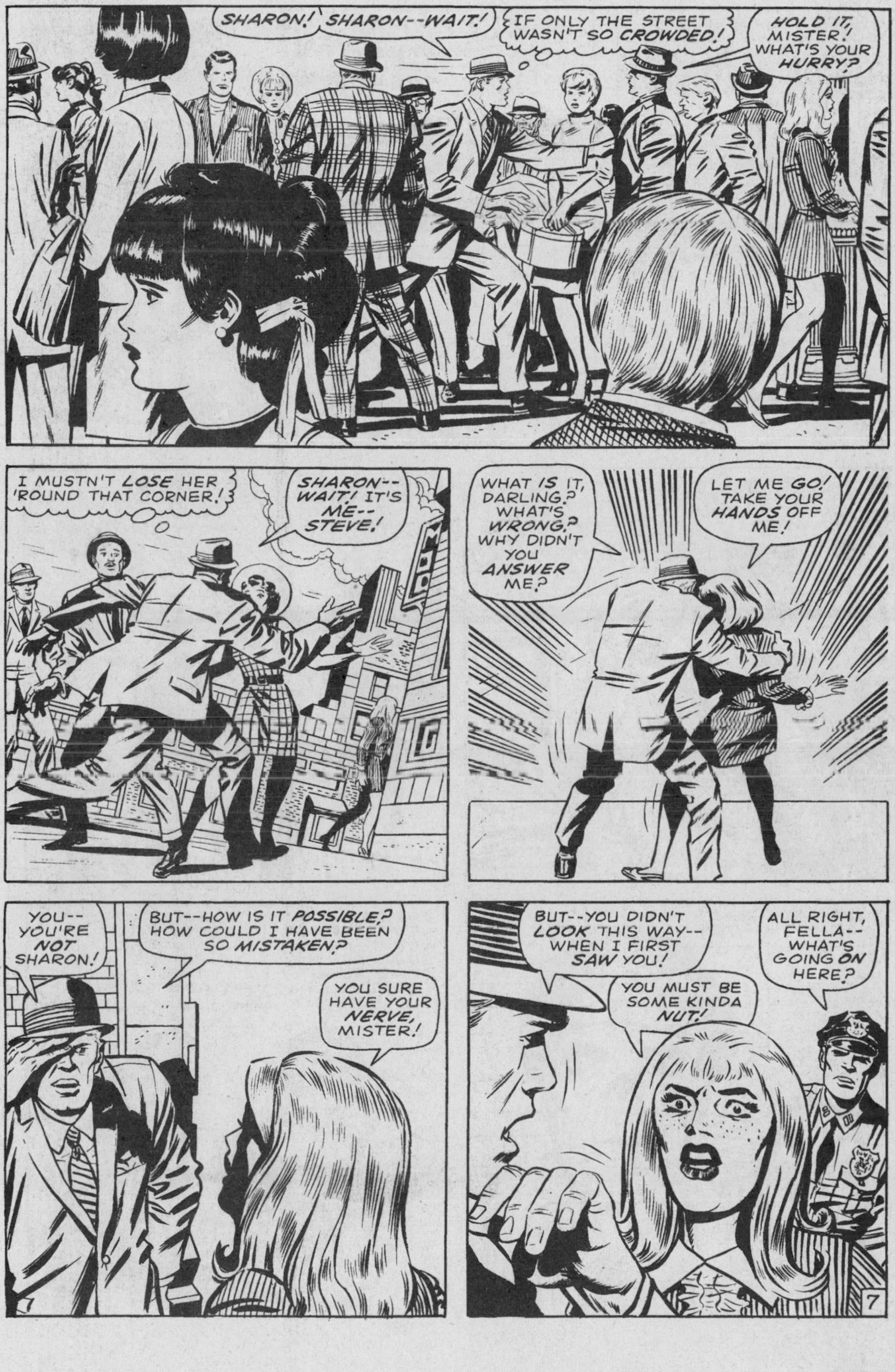
SHARON! SHARON--WAIT!
IF ONLY THE STREET WASN'T SO CROWDED!
HOLD IT, MISTER! WHAT'S YOUR HURRY?
I MUSTN'T LOSE HER 'ROUND THAT CORNER!
SHARON-- WAIT! IT'S ME-- STEVE!
WHAT IS IT, DARLING? WHAT'S WRONG? WHY DIDN'T YOU ANSWER ME?
LET ME GO! TAKE YOUR HANDS OFF ME!
YOU-- YOU'RE NOT SHARON!
BUT--HOW IS IT POSSIBLE? HOW COULD I HAVE BEEN SO MISTAKEN?
YOU SURE HAVE YOUR NERVE, MISTER!
BUT--YOU DIDN'T LOOK THIS WAY-- WHEN I FIRST SAW YOU!
YOU MUST BE SOME KINDA NUT!
ALL RIGHT, FELLA-- WHAT'S GOING ON HERE?

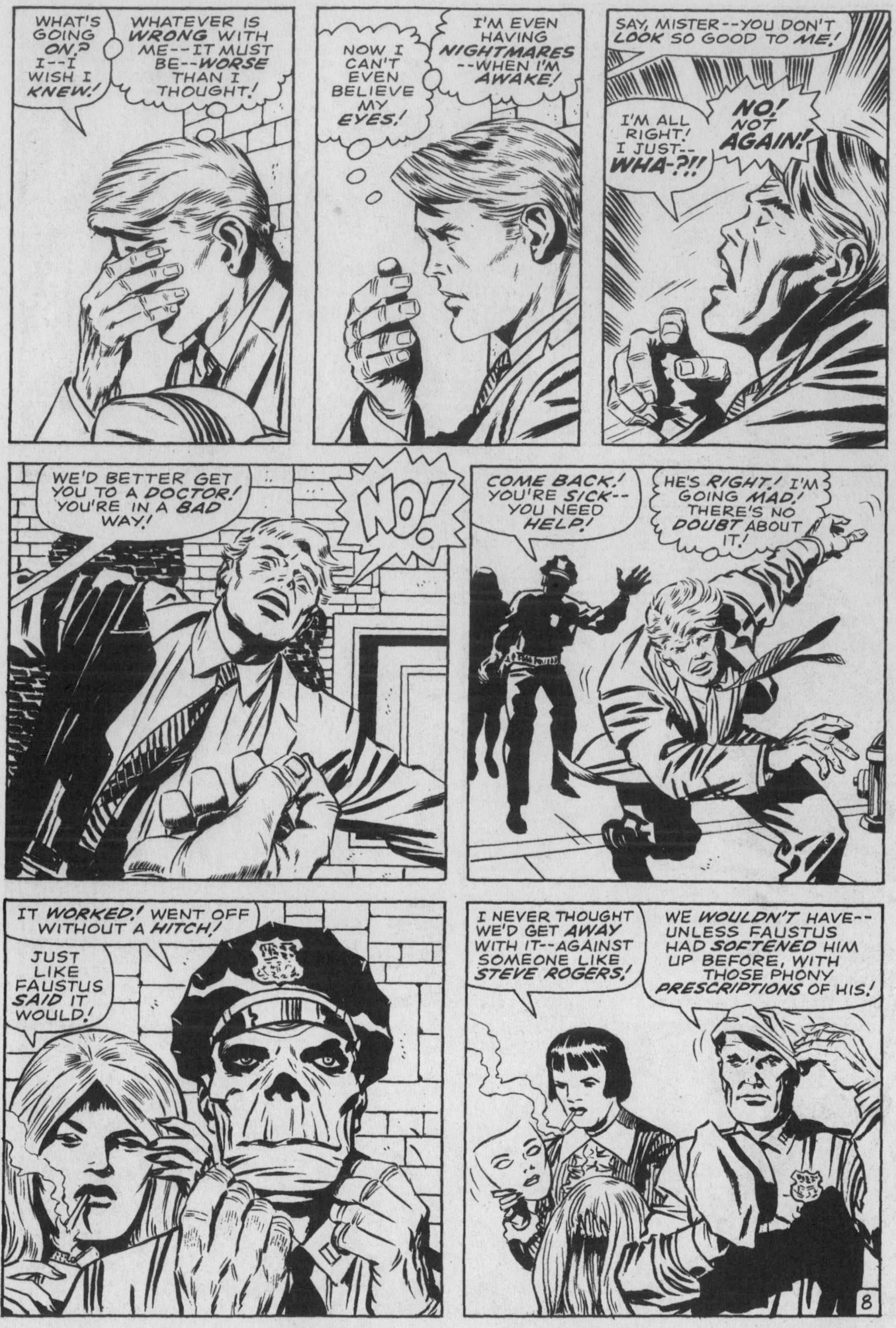
WHAT'S GOING ON? I--I WISH I KNEW!
WHATEVER IS WRONG WITH ME--IT MUST BE--WORSE THAN I THOUGHT!
I'M EVEN HAVING NIGHTMARES --WHEN I'M AWAKE!
NOW I CAN'T EVEN BELIEVE MY EYES!
SAY, MISTER--YOU DON'T LOOK SO GOOD TO ME!
I'M ALL RIGHT! I JUST-- WHA-?!!
NO! NOT AGAIN!
WE'D BETTER GET YOU TO A DOCTOR! YOU'RE IN A BAD WAY!
NO!
COME BACK! YOU'RE SICK-- YOU NEED HELP!
HE'S RIGHT! I'M GOING MAD! THERE'S NO DOUBT ABOUT IT!
IT WORKED! WENT OFF WITHOUT A HITCH!
JUST LIKE FAUSTUS SAID IT WOULD!
I NEVER THOUGHT WE'D GET AWAY WITH IT--AGAINST SOMEONE LIKE STEVE ROGERS!
WE WOULDN'T HAVE-- UNLESS FAUSTUS HAD SOFTENED HIM UP BEFORE, WITH THOSE PHONY PRESCRIPTIONS OF HIS!
8

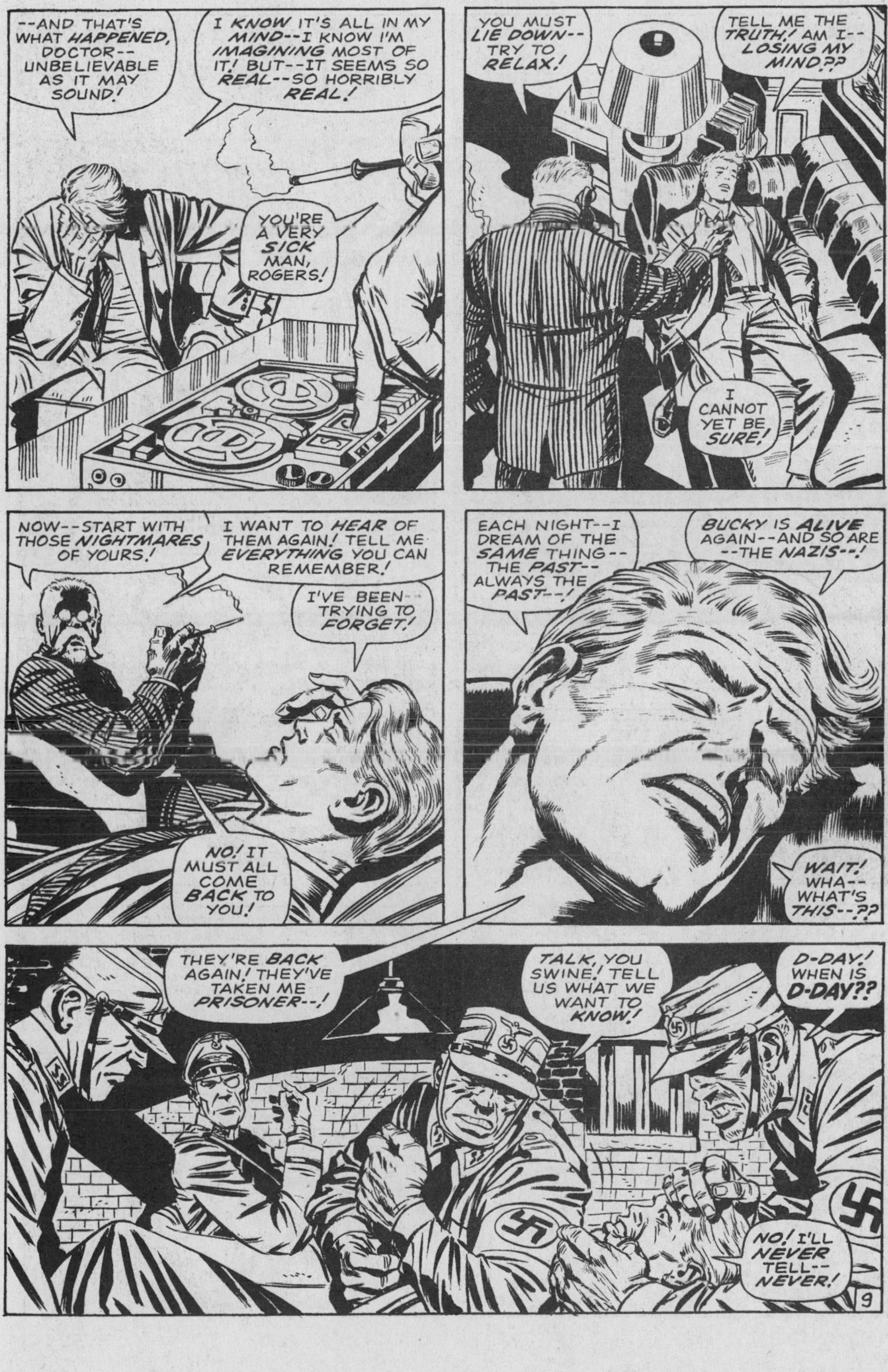

--AND THAT'S WHAT HAPPENED, DOCTOR-- UNBELIEVABLE AS IT MAY SOUND!
I KNOW IT'S ALL IN MY MIND--I KNOW I'M IMAGINING MOST OF IT! BUT--IT SEEMS SO REAL--SO HORRIBLY REAL!
YOU'RE A VERY SICK MAN, ROGERS!
YOU MUST LIE DOWN-- TRY TO RELAX!
TELL ME THE TRUTH! AM I-- LOSING MY MIND??
I CANNOT YET BE SURE!
NOW--START WITH THOSE NIGHTMARES OF YOURS!
I WANT TO HEAR OF THEM AGAIN! TELL ME EVERYTHING YOU CAN REMEMBER!
I'VE BEEN-- TRYING TO FORGET!
NO! IT MUST ALL COME BACK TO YOU!
EACH NIGHT--I DREAM OF THE SAME THING-- THE PAST-- ALWAYS THE PAST--!
BUCKY IS ALIVE AGAIN--AND SO ARE --THE NAZIS--!
WAIT! WHA-- WHAT'S THIS--??
THEY'RE BACK AGAIN! THEY'VE TAKEN ME PRISONER--!
TALK, YOU SWINE! TELL US WHAT WE WANT TO KNOW!
D-DAY! WHEN IS D-DAY??
NO! I'LL NEVER TELL-- NEVER!
9

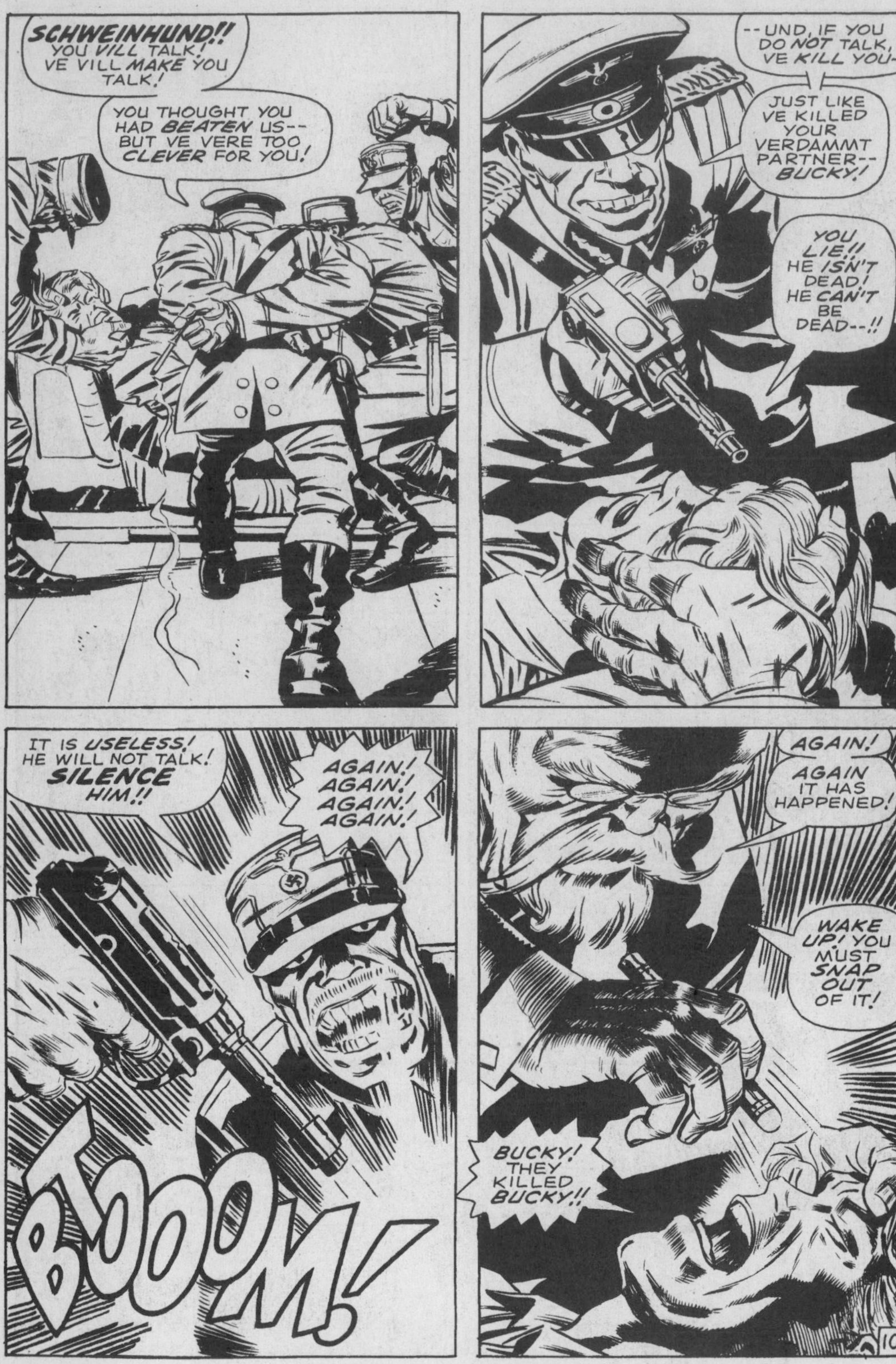
SCHWEINHUND!! YOU VILL TALK! VE VILL MAKE YOU TALK!
YOU THOUGHT YOU HAD BEATEN US-- BUT VE VERE TOO CLEVER FOR YOU!
--UND, IF YOU DO NOT TALK, VE KILL YOU--
JUST LIKE VE KILLED YOUR VERDAMMT PARTNER-- BUCKY!
YOU LIE!! HE ISN'T DEAD! HE CAN'T BE DEAD--!!
IT IS USELESS! HE WILL NOT TALK! SILENCE HIM!!
AGAIN! AGAIN! AGAIN! AGAIN!
BLOOOM!
AGAIN!
AGAIN IT HAS HAPPENED!
WAKE UP! YOU MUST SNAP OUT OF IT!
BUCKY! THEY KILLED BUCKY!!
10

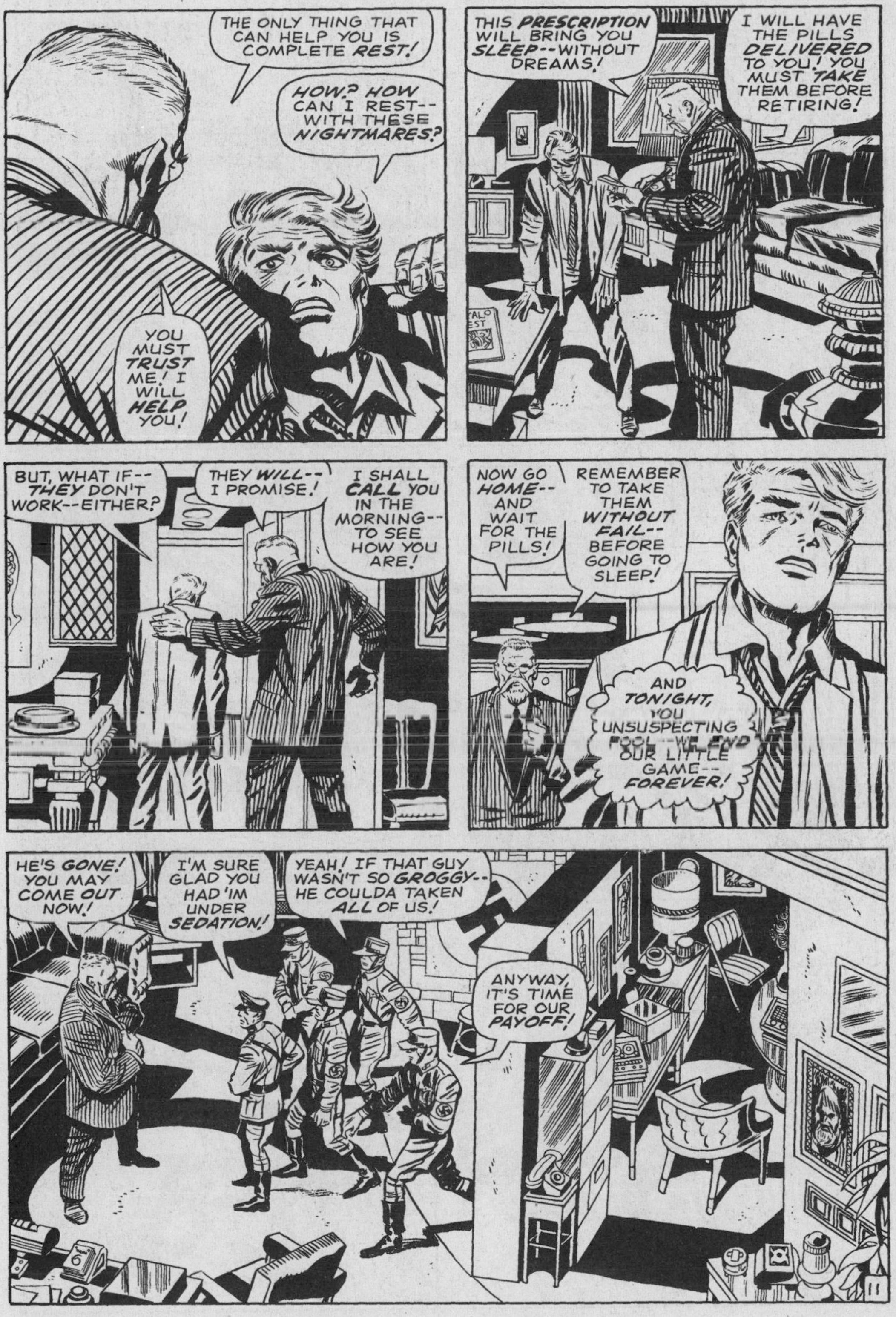

THE ONLY THING THAT CAN HELP YOU IS COMPLETE REST!
HOW? HOW CAN I REST--WITH THESE NIGHTMARES?
YOU MUST TRUST ME! I WILL HELP YOU!
THIS PRESCRIPTION WILL BRING YOU SLEEP--WITHOUT DREAMS!
I WILL HAVE THE PILLS DELIVERED TO YOU! YOU MUST TAKE THEM BEFORE RETIRING!
BUT, WHAT IF--THEY DON'T WORK--EITHER?
THEY WILL--I PROMISE!
I SHALL CALL YOU IN THE MORNING--TO SEE HOW YOU ARE!
NOW GO HOME--AND WAIT FOR THE PILLS!
REMEMBER TO TAKE THEM WITHOUT FAIL--BEFORE GOING TO SLEEP!
AND TONIGHT, YOU UNSUSPECTING FOOL--WE END OUR LITTLE GAME--FOREVER!
HE'S GONE! YOU MAY COME OUT NOW!
I'M SURE GLAD YOU HAD 'IM UNDER SEDATION!
YEAH! IF THAT GUY WASN'T SO GROGGY--HE COULDA TAKEN ALL OF US!
ANYWAY, IT'S TIME FOR OUR PAYOFF!

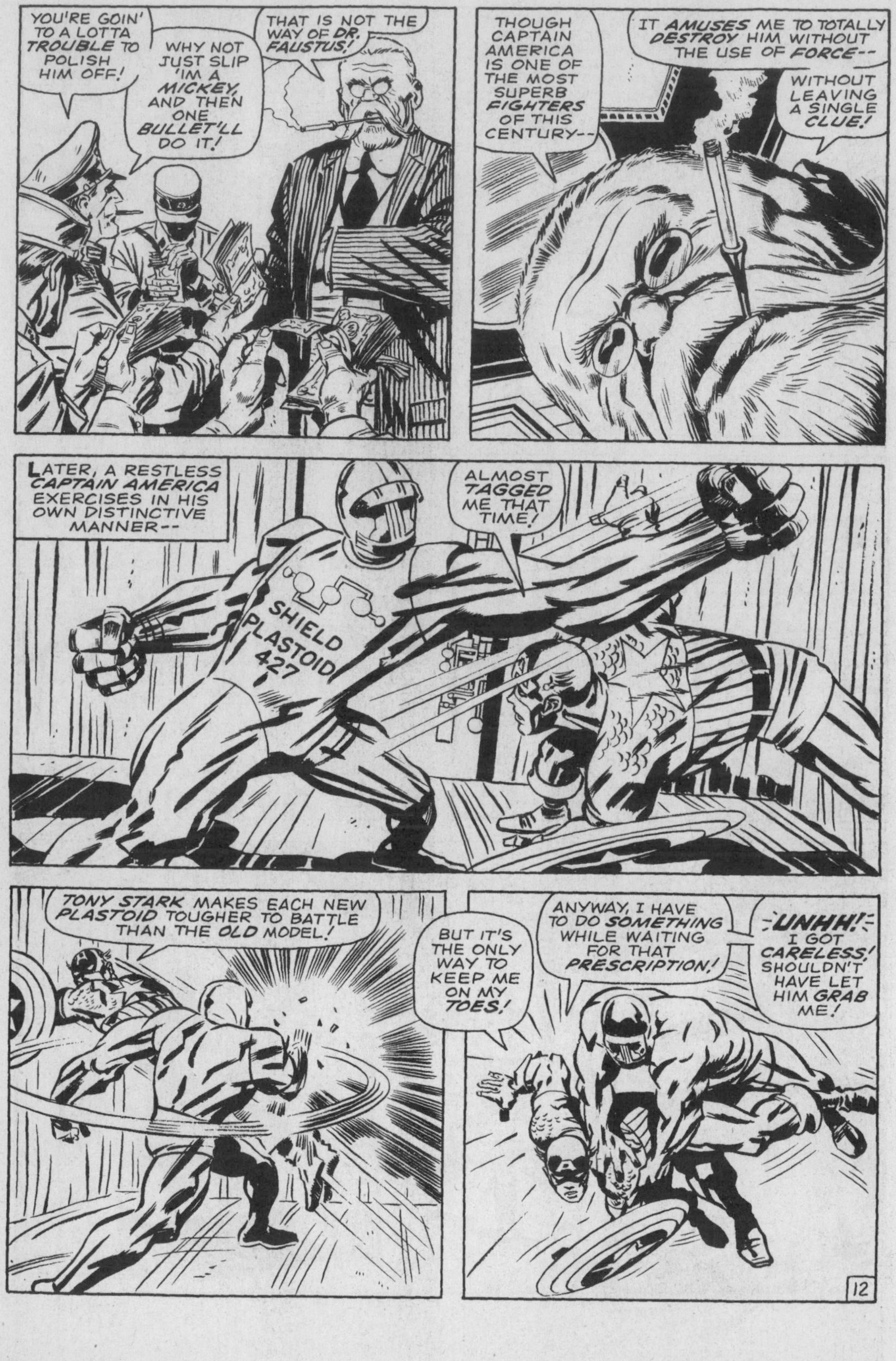
YOU'RE GOIN' TO A LOTTA TROUBLE TO POLISH HIM OFF!
WHY NOT JUST SLIP 'IM A MICKEY, AND THEN ONE BULLET'LL DO IT!
THAT IS NOT THE WAY OF DR. FAUSTUS!
THOUGH CAPTAIN AMERICA IS ONE OF THE MOST SUPERB FIGHTERS OF THIS CENTURY--
IT AMUSES ME TO TOTALLY DESTROY HIM WITHOUT THE USE OF FORCE--
WITHOUT LEAVING A SINGLE CLUE!
LATER, A RESTLESS CAPTAIN AMERICA EXERCISES IN HIS OWN DISTINCTIVE MANNER--
ALMOST TAGGED ME THAT TIME!
SHIELD PLASTOID 427
TONY STARK MAKES EACH NEW PLASTOID TOUGHER TO BATTLE THAN THE OLD MODEL!
BUT IT'S THE ONLY WAY TO KEEP ME ON MY TOES!
ANYWAY, I HAVE TO DO SOMETHING WHILE WAITING FOR THAT PRESCRIPTION!
UNHH! I GOT CARELESS! SHOULDN'T HAVE LET HIM GRAB ME!
12

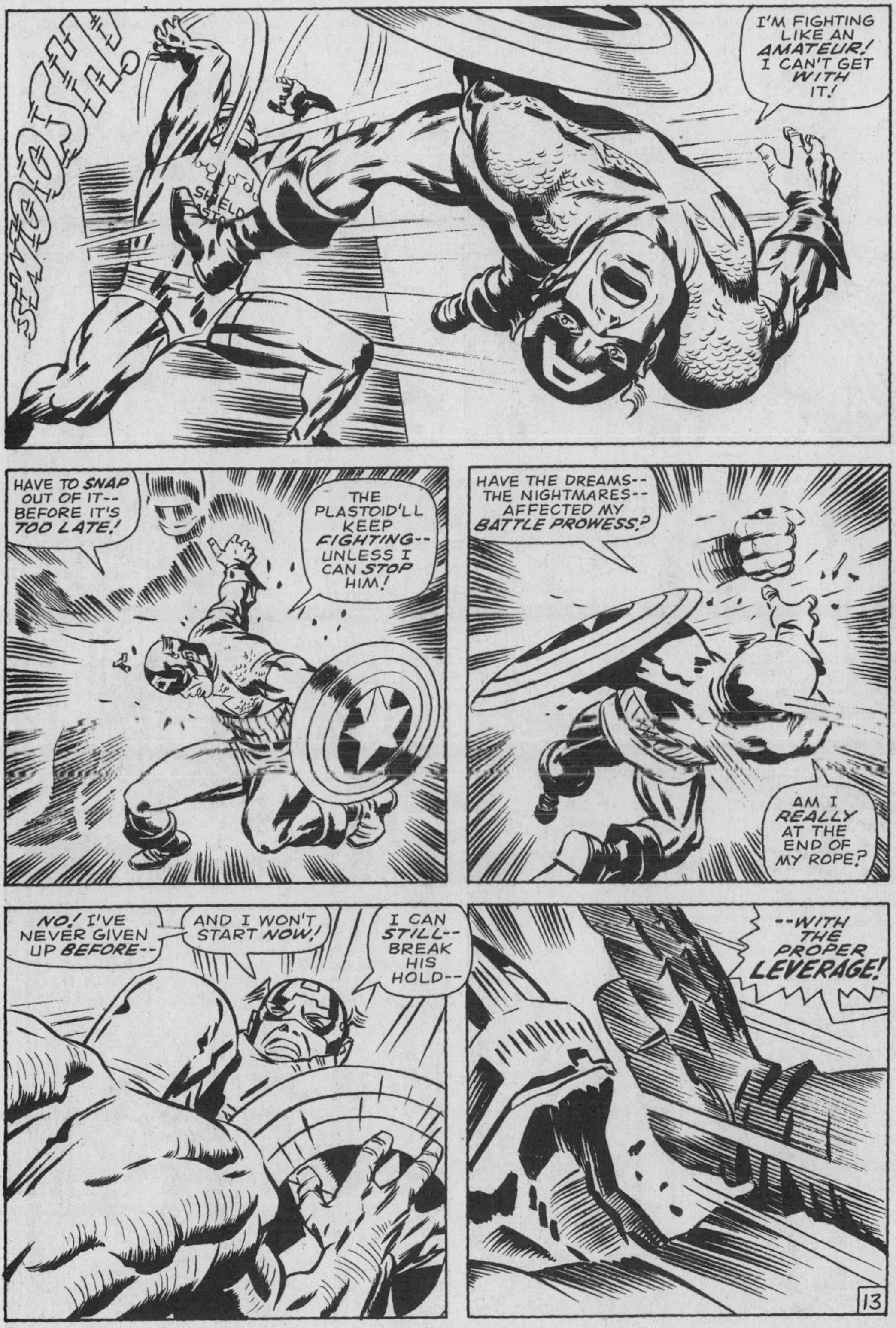
I'M FIGHTING LIKE AN AMATEUR! I CAN'T GET WITH IT!
HAVE TO SNAP OUT OF IT-- BEFORE IT'S TOO LATE!
THE PLASTOID'LL KEEP FIGHTING-- UNLESS I CAN STOP HIM!
HAVE THE DREAMS-- THE NIGHTMARES-- AFFECTED MY BATTLE PROWESS?
AM I REALLY AT THE END OF MY ROPE?
NO! I'VE NEVER GIVEN UP BEFORE--
AND I WON'T START NOW!
I CAN STILL-- BREAK HIS HOLD--
--WITH THE PROPER LEVERAGE!
13

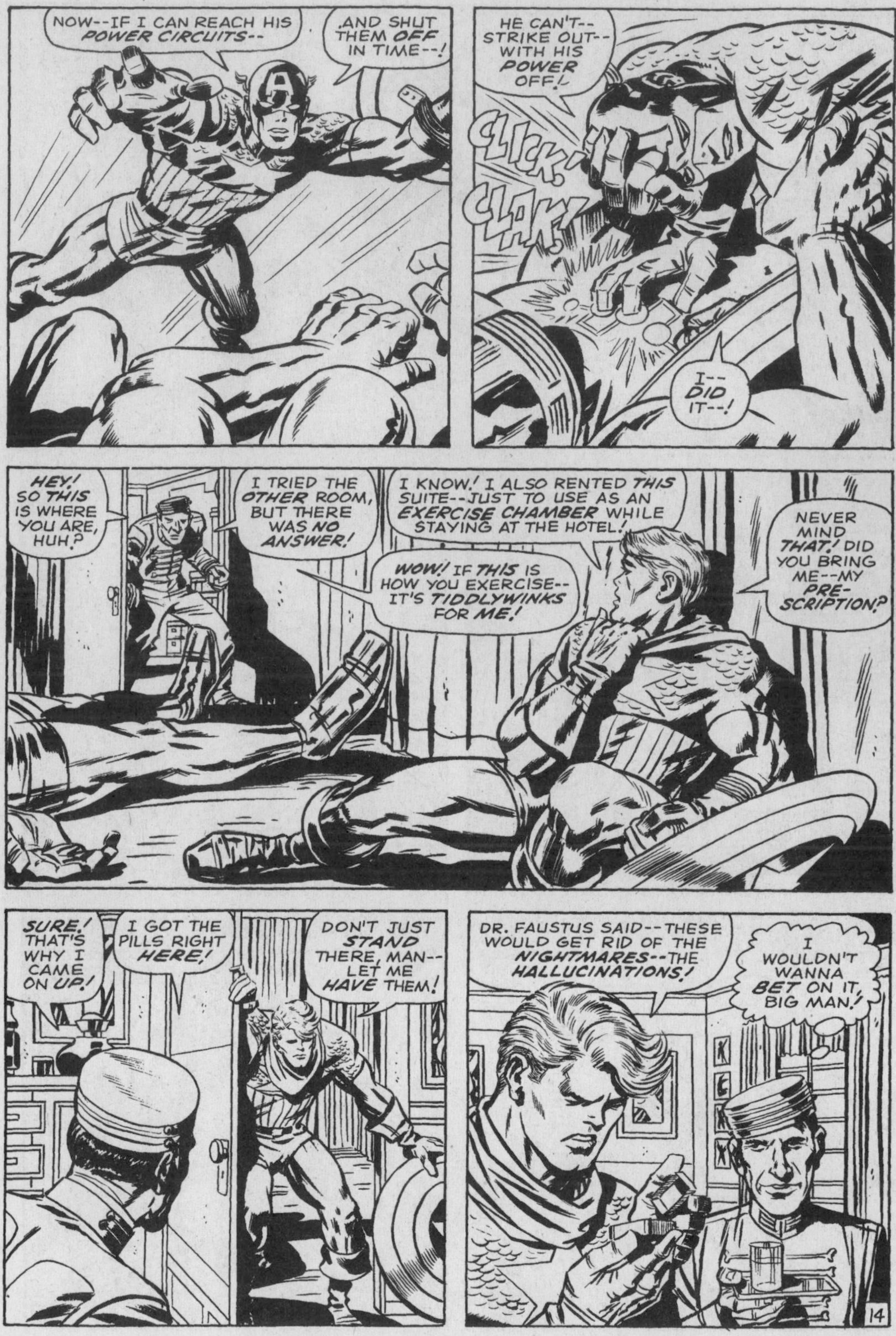
NOW--IF I CAN REACH HIS POWER CIRCUITS--
..AND SHUT THEM OFF IN TIME--!
HE CAN'T--STRIKE OUT--WITH HIS POWER OFF!
CLICK!
CLAK!
I--DID IT--!
HEY! SO THIS IS WHERE YOU ARE, HUH?
I TRIED THE OTHER ROOM, BUT THERE WAS NO ANSWER!
I KNOW! I ALSO RENTED THIS SUITE--JUST TO USE AS AN EXERCISE CHAMBER WHILE STAYING AT THE HOTEL!
WOW! IF THIS IS HOW YOU EXERCISE--IT'S TIDDLYWINKS FOR ME!
NEVER MIND THAT! DID YOU BRING ME--MY PRE-SCRIPTION?
SURE! THAT'S WHY I CAME ON UP!
I GOT THE PILLS RIGHT HERE!
DON'T JUST STAND THERE, MAN--LET ME HAVE THEM!
DR. FAUSTUS SAID--THESE WOULD GET RID OF THE NIGHTMARES--THE HALLUCINATIONS!
I WOULDN'T WANNA BET ON IT, BIG MAN!
14

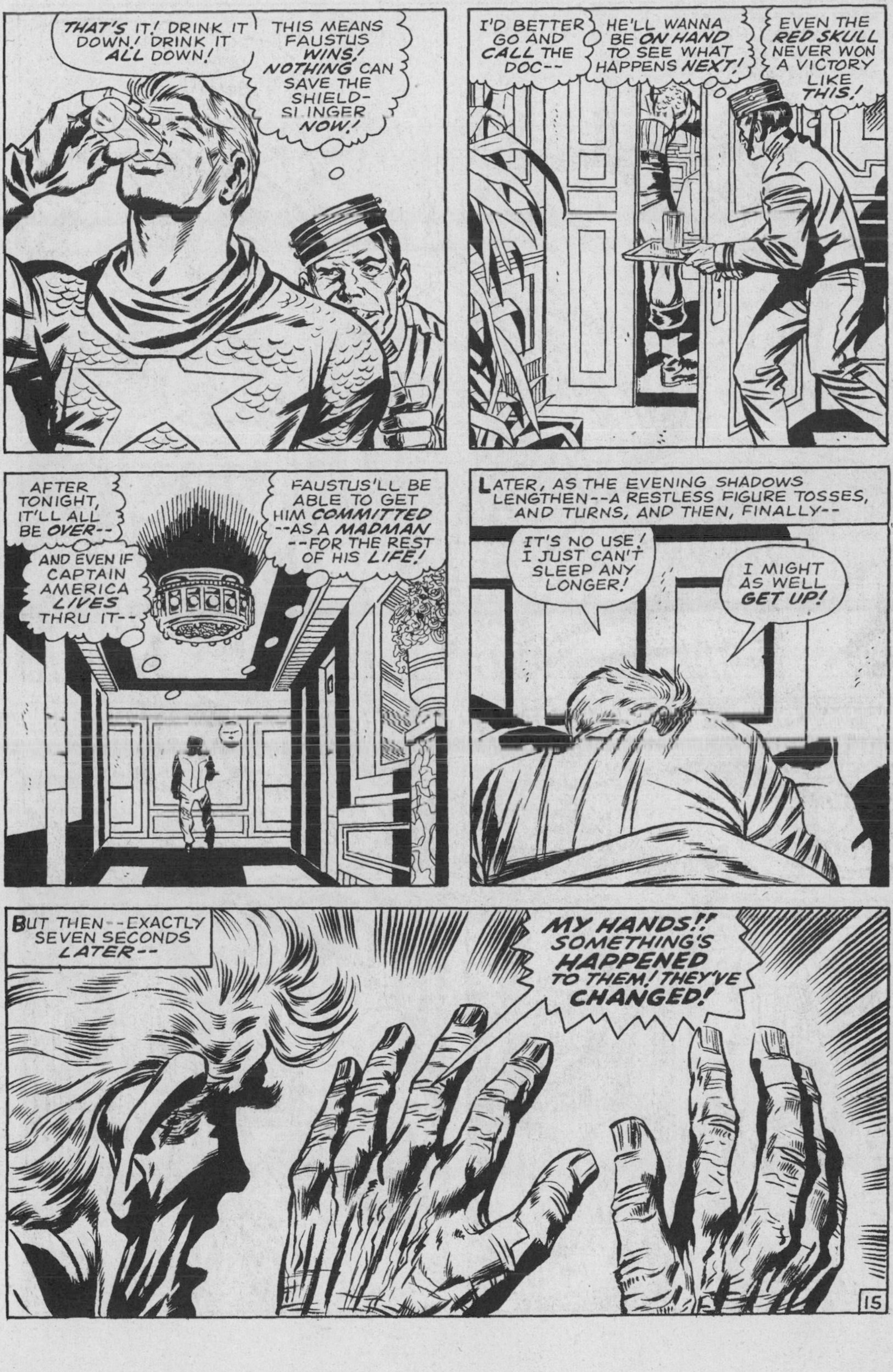
THAT'S IT! DRINK IT DOWN! DRINK IT ALL DOWN!
THIS MEANS FAUSTUS WINS! NOTHING CAN SAVE THE SHIELD-SLINGER NOW!
I'D BETTER GO AND CALL THE DOC--
HE'LL WANNA BE ON HAND TO SEE WHAT HAPPENS NEXT!
EVEN THE RED SKULL NEVER WON A VICTORY LIKE THIS!
AFTER TONIGHT, IT'LL ALL BE OVER--
AND EVEN IF CAPTAIN AMERICA LIVES THRU IT--
FAUSTUS'LL BE ABLE TO GET HIM COMMITTED --AS A MADMAN --FOR THE REST OF HIS LIFE!
LATER, AS THE EVENING SHADOWS LENGTHEN--A RESTLESS FIGURE TOSSES, AND TURNS, AND THEN, FINALLY--
IT'S NO USE! I JUST CAN'T SLEEP ANY LONGER!
I MIGHT AS WELL GET UP!
BUT THEN--EXACTLY SEVEN SECONDS LATER--
MY HANDS!! SOMETHING'S HAPPENED TO THEM! THEY'VE CHANGED!
15

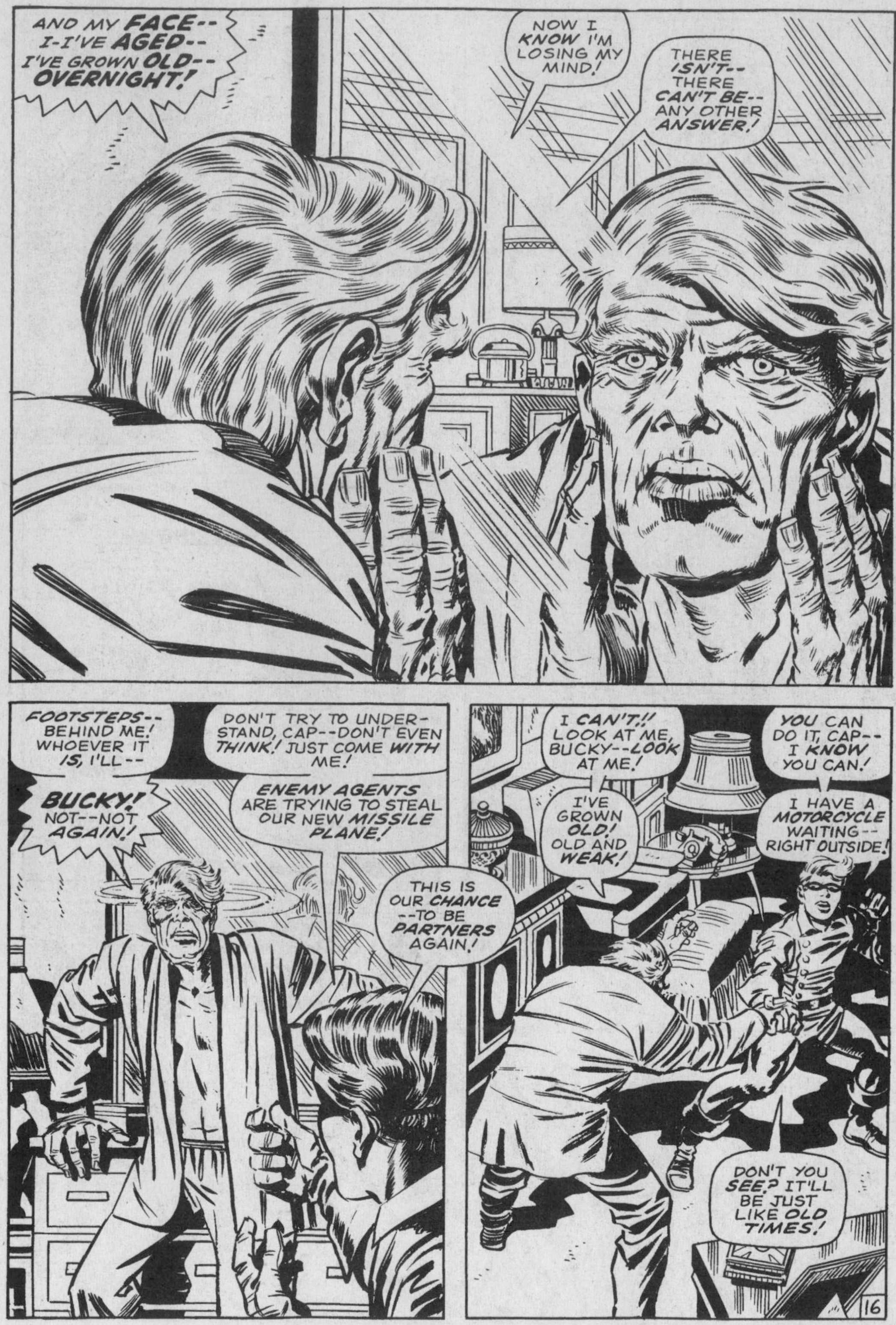

AND MY FACE-- I-I'VE AGED-- I'VE GROWN OLD-- OVERNIGHT!
NOW I KNOW I'M LOSING MY MIND!
THERE ISN'T-- THERE CAN'T BE-- ANY OTHER ANSWER!
FOOTSTEPS-- BEHIND ME! WHOEVER IT IS, I'LL--
BUCKY! NOT--NOT AGAIN!
DON'T TRY TO UNDER-STAND, CAP--DON'T EVEN THINK! JUST COME WITH ME!
ENEMY AGENTS ARE TRYING TO STEAL OUR NEW MISSILE PLANE!
THIS IS OUR CHANCE --TO BE PARTNERS AGAIN!
I CAN'T!! LOOK AT ME, BUCKY--LOOK AT ME!
I'VE GROWN OLD! OLD AND WEAK!
YOU CAN DO IT, CAP-- I KNOW YOU CAN!
I HAVE A MOTORCYCLE WAITING-- RIGHT OUTSIDE!
DON'T YOU SEE? IT'LL BE JUST LIKE OLD TIMES!
16

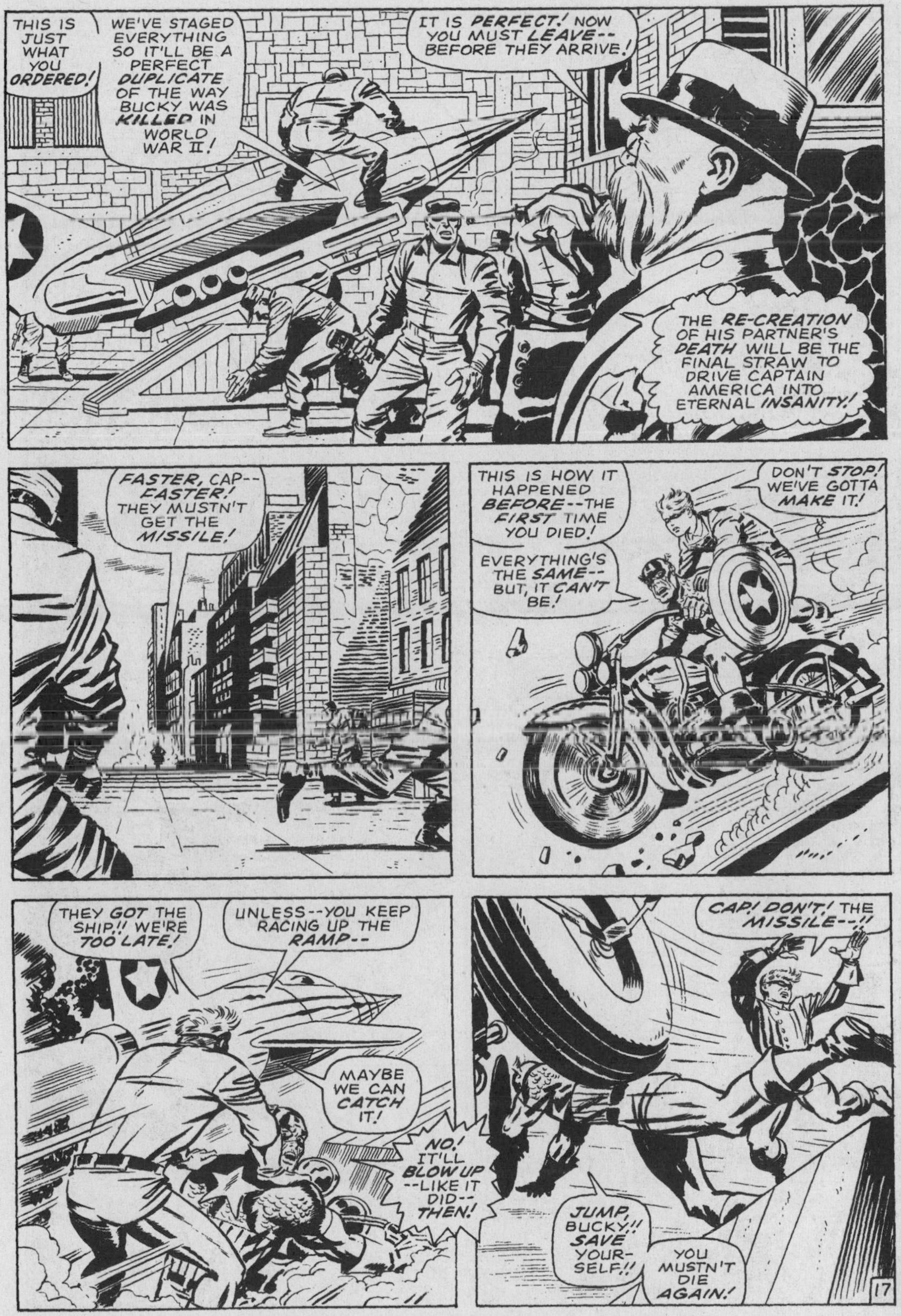
THIS IS JUST WHAT YOU ORDERED!
WE'VE STAGED EVERYTHING SO IT'LL BE A PERFECT DUPLICATE OF THE WAY BUCKY WAS KILLED IN WORLD WAR II!
IT IS PERFECT! NOW YOU MUST LEAVE-- BEFORE THEY ARRIVE!
THE RE-CREATION OF HIS PARTNER'S DEATH WILL BE THE FINAL STRAW TO DRIVE CAPTAIN AMERICA INTO ETERNAL INSANITY!
FASTER, CAP-- FASTER! THEY MUSTN'T GET THE MISSILE!
THIS IS HOW IT HAPPENED BEFORE--THE FIRST TIME YOU DIED!
EVERYTHING'S THE SAME-- BUT, IT CAN'T BE!
DON'T STOP! WE'VE GOTTA MAKE IT!
THEY GOT THE SHIP!! WE'RE TOO LATE!
UNLESS--YOU KEEP RACING UP THE RAMP--
MAYBE WE CAN CATCH IT!
NO! IT'LL BLOW UP --LIKE IT DID-- THEN!
CAP! DON'T! THE MISSILE--!!
JUMP, BUCKY!! SAVE YOURSELF!!
YOU MUSTN'T DIE AGAIN!
17

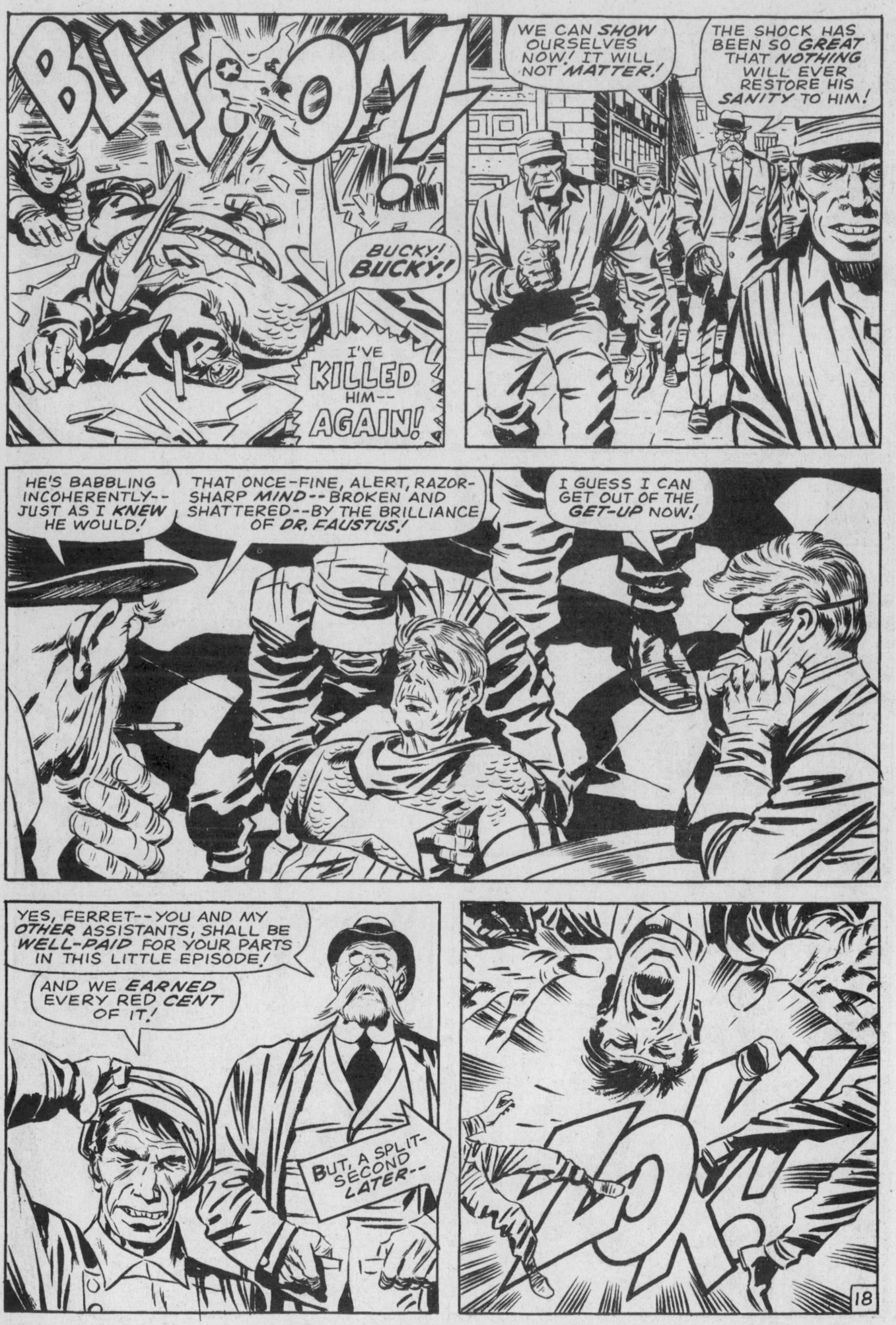
BUT-OOM!
BUCKY! BUCKY!
I'VE KILLED HIM--AGAIN!
WE CAN SHOW OURSELVES NOW! IT WILL NOT MATTER!
THE SHOCK HAS BEEN SO GREAT THAT NOTHING WILL EVER RESTORE HIS SANITY TO HIM!
HE'S BABBLING INCOHERENTLY--JUST AS I KNEW HE WOULD!
THAT ONCE-FINE, ALERT, RAZOR-SHARP MIND--BROKEN AND SHATTERED--BY THE BRILLIANCE OF DR. FAUSTUS!
I GUESS I CAN GET OUT OF THE GET-UP NOW!
YES, FERRET--YOU AND MY OTHER ASSISTANTS, SHALL BE WELL-PAID FOR YOUR PARTS IN THIS LITTLE EPISODE!
AND WE EARNED EVERY RED CENT OF IT!
BUT, A SPLIT-SECOND LATER--
18

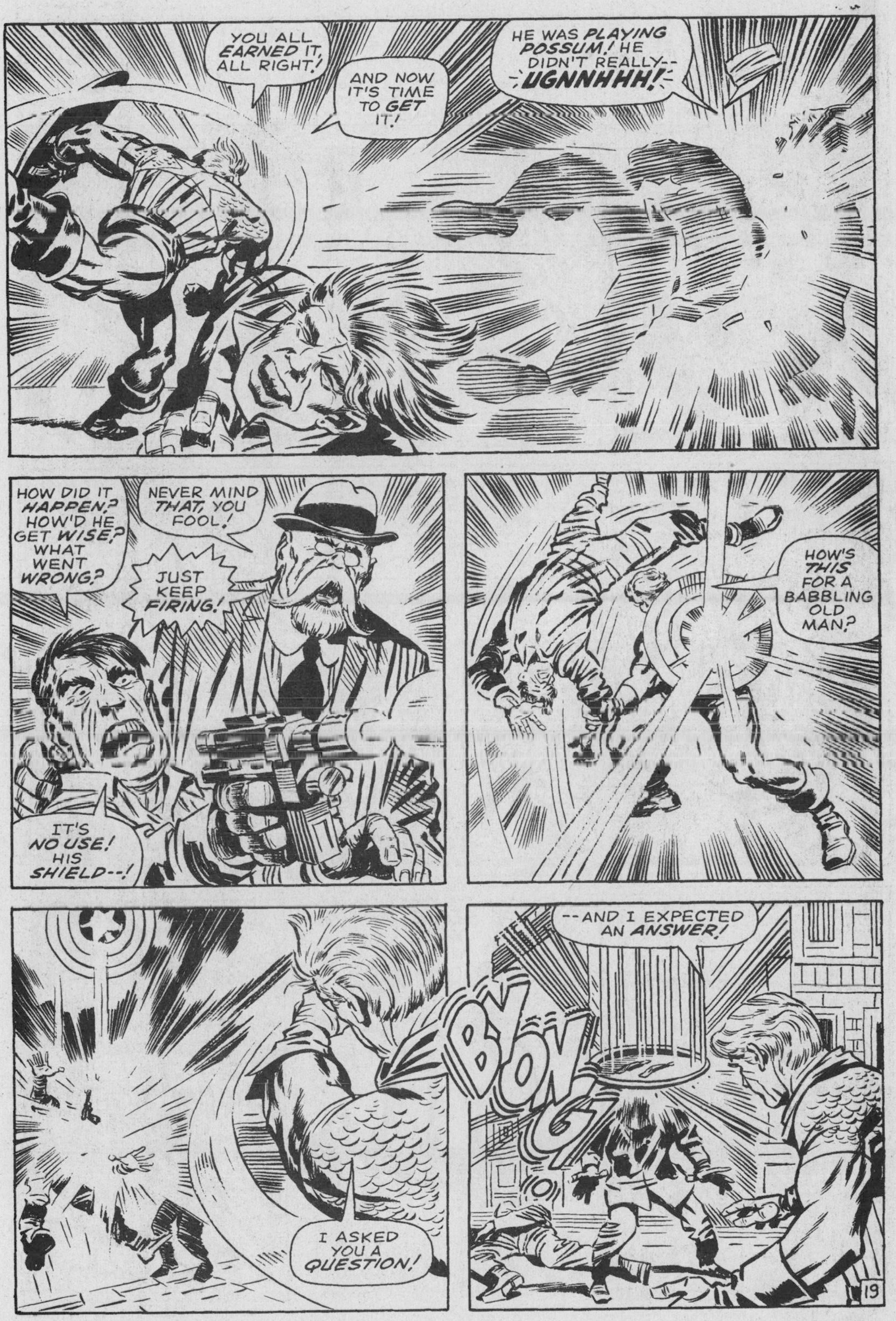
YOU ALL EARNED IT, ALL RIGHT!
AND NOW IT'S TIME TO GET IT!
HE WAS PLAYING POSSUM! HE DIDN'T REALLY-- -UGNNHHH!-
HOW DID IT HAPPEN? HOW'D HE GET WISE? WHAT WENT WRONG?
NEVER MIND THAT, YOU FOOL!
JUST KEEP FIRING!
IT'S NO USE! HIS SHIELD--!
HOW'S THIS FOR A BABBLING OLD MAN?
I ASKED YOU A QUESTION!
--AND I EXPECTED AN ANSWER!
BYONG
19

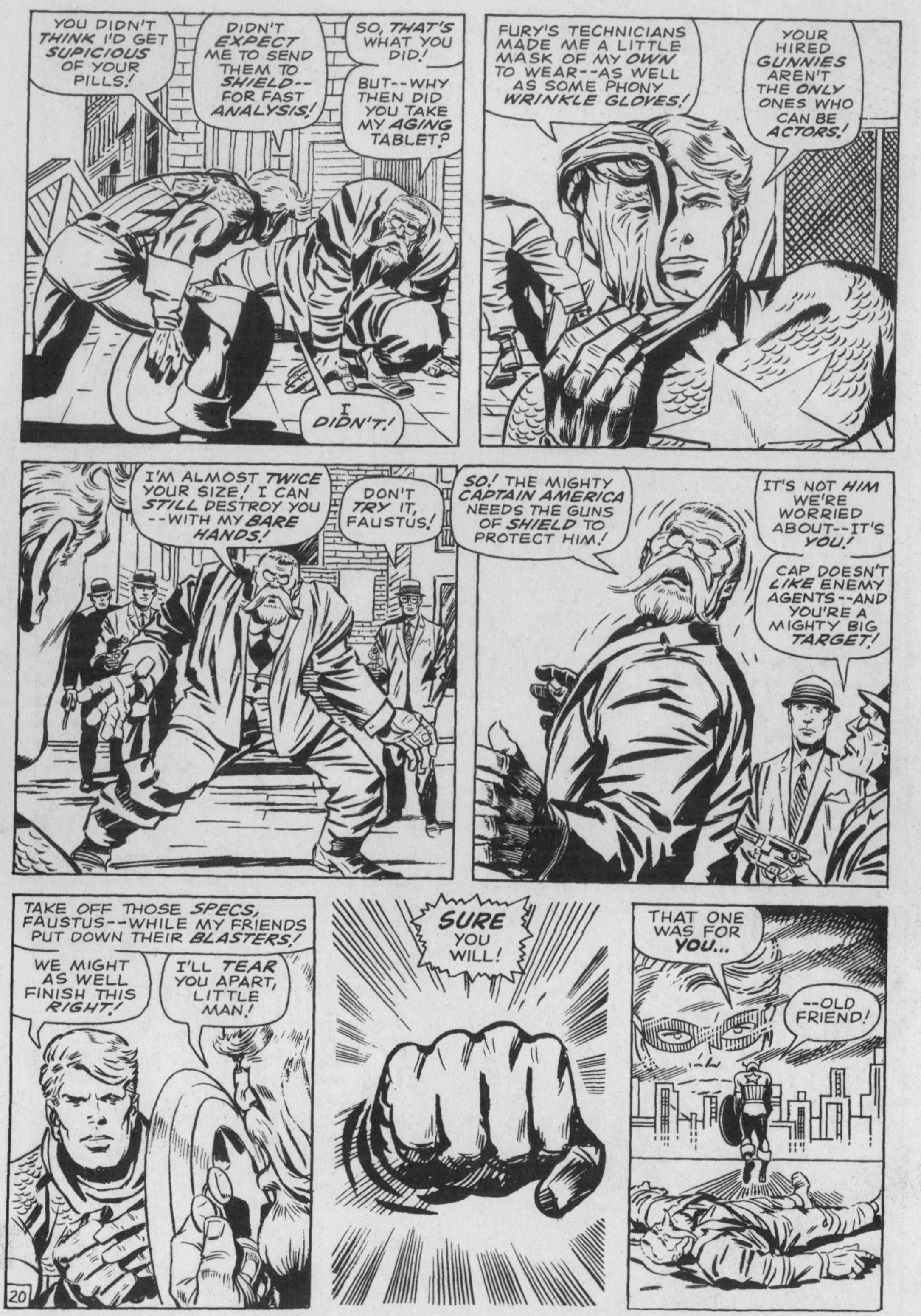
YOU DIDN'T THINK I'D GET SUPICIOUS OF YOUR PILLS!
DIDN'T EXPECT ME TO SEND THEM TO SHIELD-- FOR FAST ANALYSIS!
SO, THAT'S WHAT YOU DID!
BUT--WHY THEN DID YOU TAKE MY AGING TABLET?
I DIDN'T!
FURY'S TECHNICIANS MADE ME A LITTLE MASK OF MY OWN TO WEAR--AS WELL AS SOME PHONY WRINKLE GLOVES!
YOUR HIRED GUNNIES AREN'T THE ONLY ONES WHO CAN BE ACTORS!
I'M ALMOST TWICE YOUR SIZE! I CAN STILL DESTROY YOU --WITH MY BARE HANDS!
DON'T TRY IT, FAUSTUS!
SO! THE MIGHTY CAPTAIN AMERICA NEEDS THE GUNS OF SHIELD TO PROTECT HIM!
IT'S NOT HIM WE'RE WORRIED ABOUT--IT'S YOU!
CAP DOESN'T LIKE ENEMY AGENTS--AND YOU'RE A MIGHTY BIG TARGET!
TAKE OFF THOSE SPECS, FAUSTUS--WHILE MY FRIENDS PUT DOWN THEIR BLASTERS!
WE MIGHT AS WELL FINISH THIS RIGHT!
I'LL TEAR YOU APART, LITTLE MAN!
SURE YOU WILL!
THAT ONE WAS FOR YOU...
--OLD FRIEND!
20

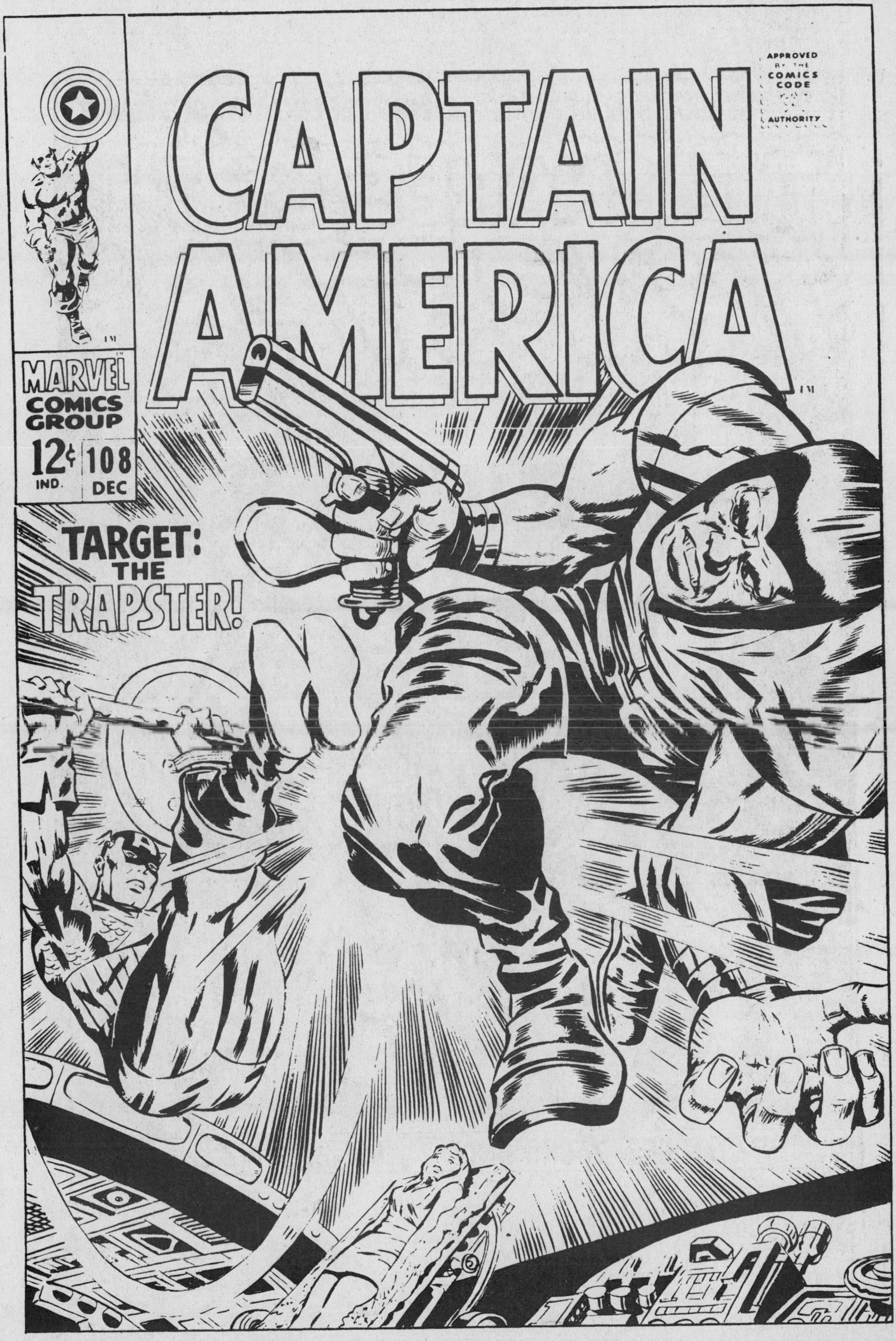
CAPTAIN AMERICA
MARVEL COMICS GROUP
12¢ IND.
108 DEC
APPROVED BY THE COMICS CODE AUTHORITY
TARGET: THE TRAPSTER!

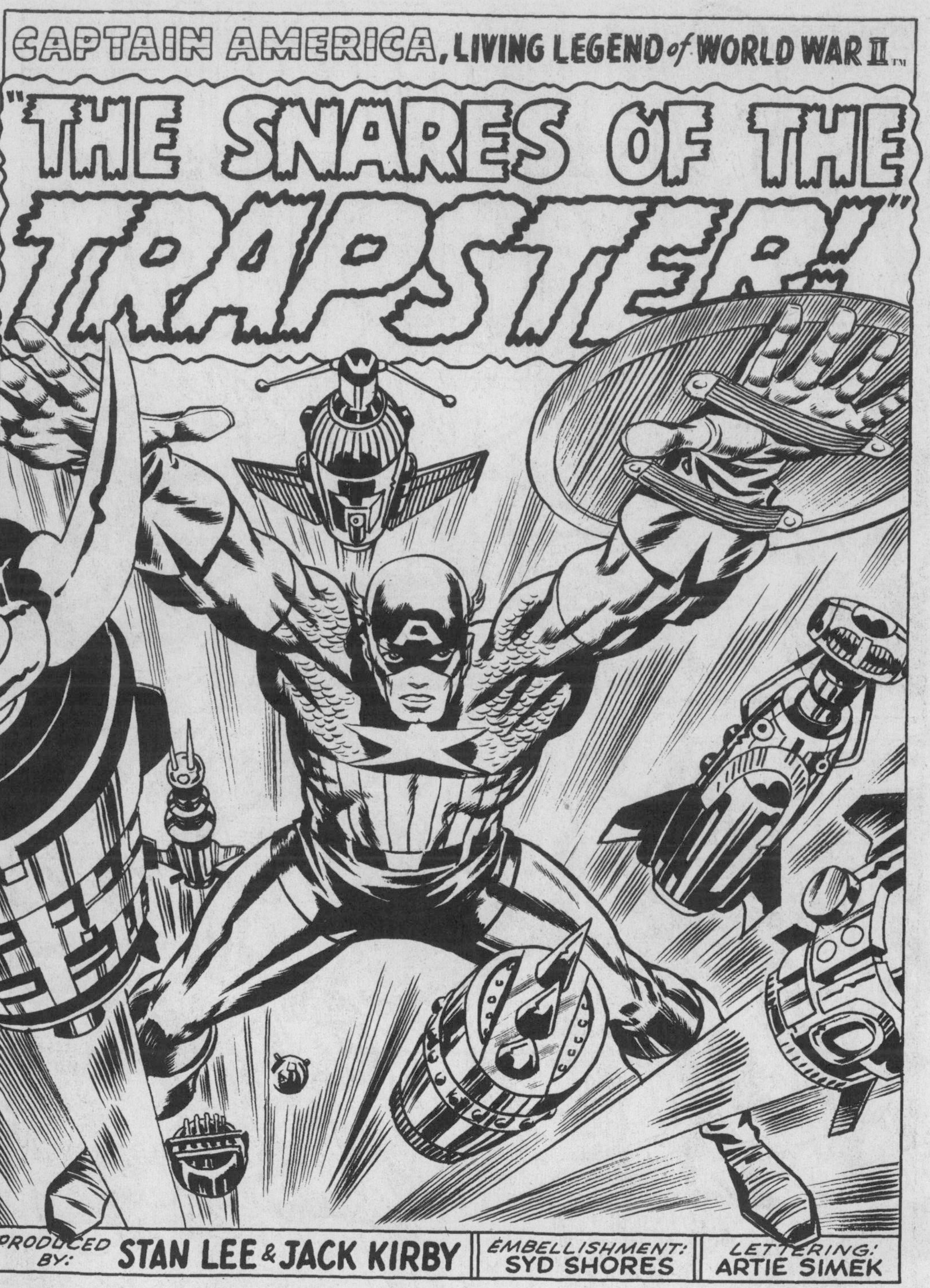
CAPTAIN AMERICA, LIVING LEGEND of WORLD WAR II™
"THE SNARES OF THE TRAPSTER!"
PRODUCED BY: STAN LEE & JACK KIRBY
EMBELLISHMENT: SYD SHORES
LETTERING: ARTIE SIMEK

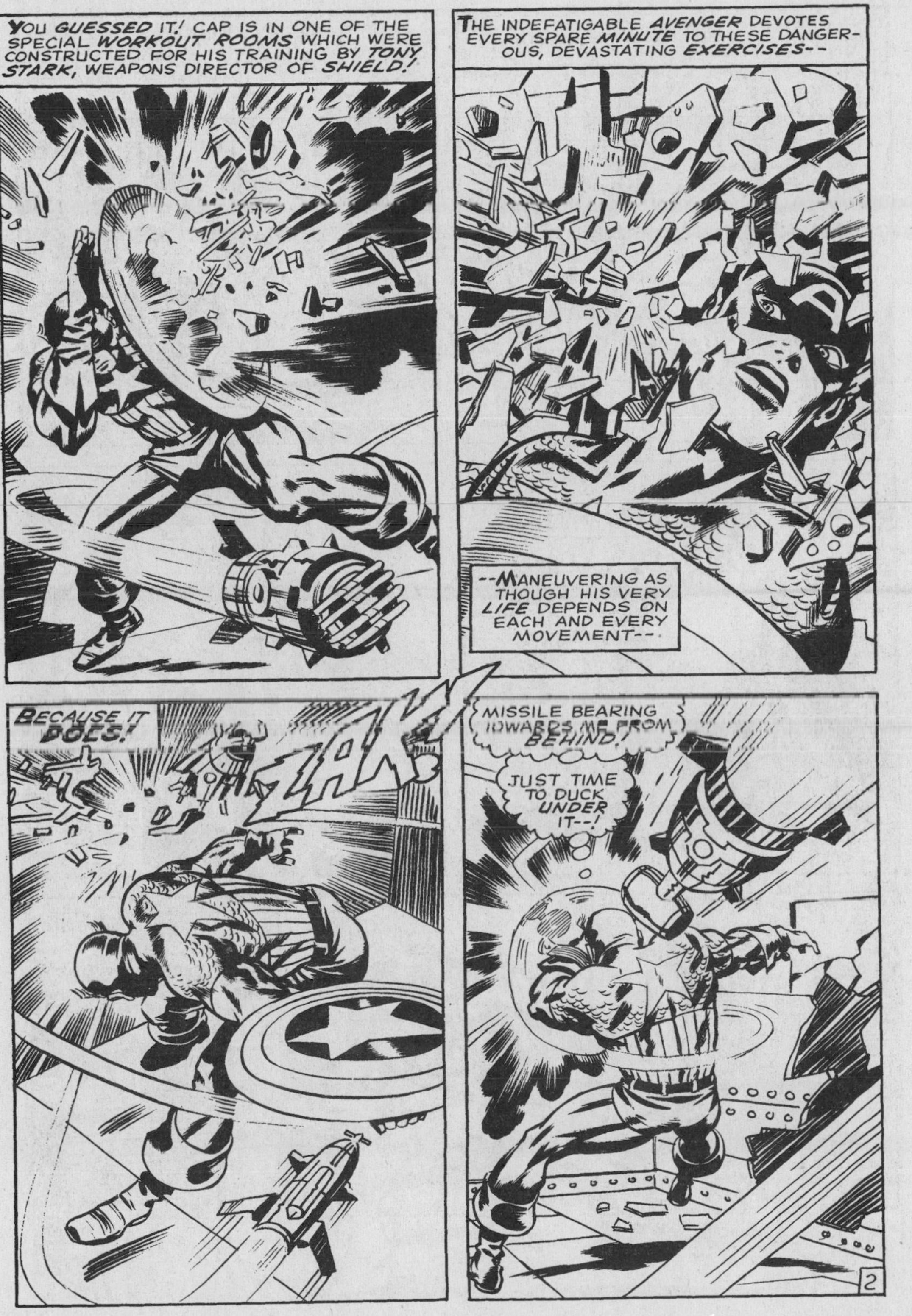
YOU GUESSED IT! CAP IS IN ONE OF THE SPECIAL WORKOUT ROOMS WHICH WERE CONSTRUCTED FOR HIS TRAINING BY TONY STARK, WEAPONS DIRECTOR OF SHIELD!
THE INDEFATIGABLE AVENGER DEVOTES EVERY SPARE MINUTE TO THESE DANGER-OUS, DEVASTATING EXERCISES--
--MANEUVERING AS THOUGH HIS VERY LIFE DEPENDS ON EACH AND EVERY MOVEMENT--
BECAUSE IT DOES!
ZAK!
MISSILE BEARING TOWARDS ME FROM BEHIND!
JUST TIME TO DUCK UNDER IT--!
2

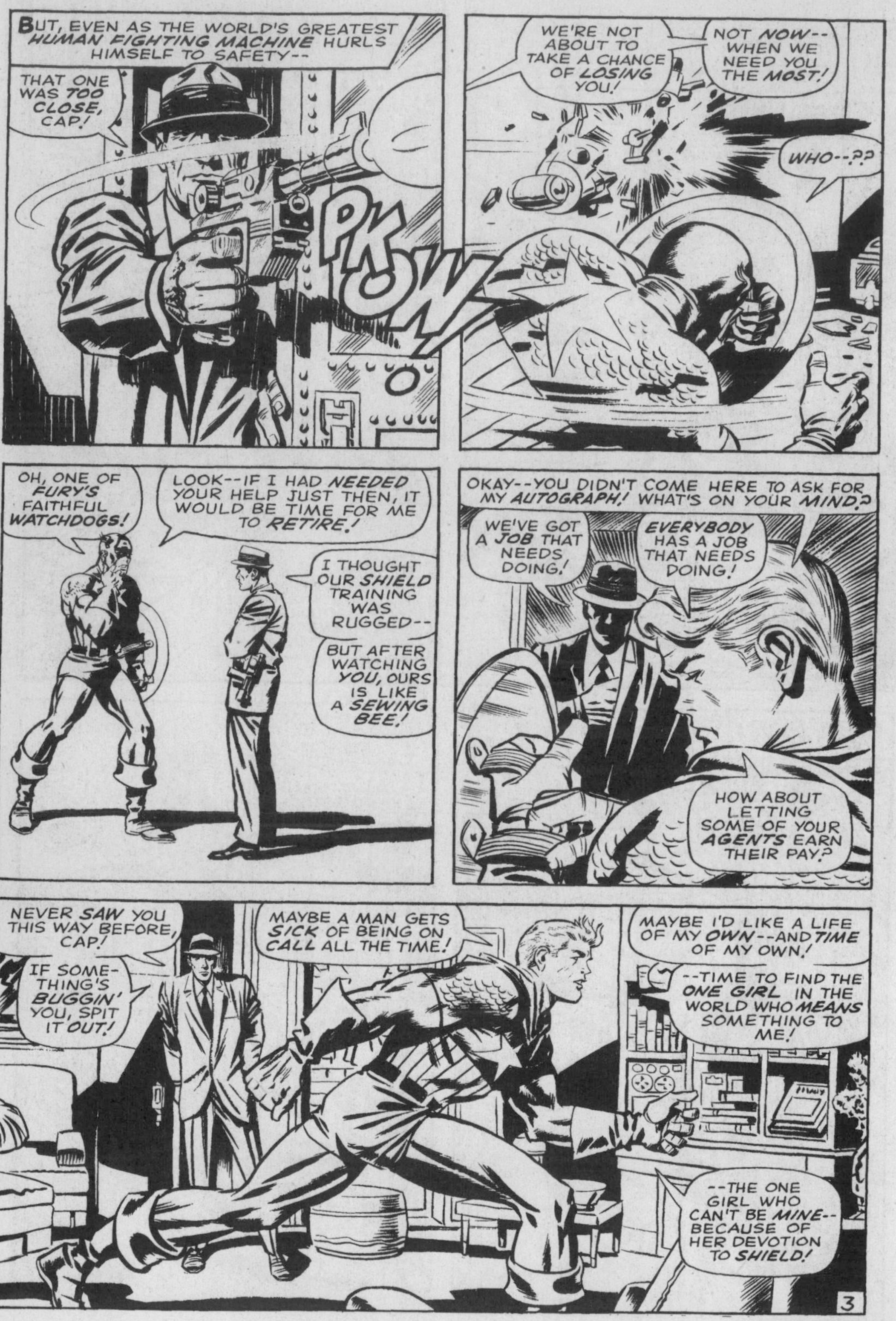
BUT, EVEN AS THE WORLD'S GREATEST HUMAN FIGHTING MACHINE HURLS HIMSELF TO SAFETY--
THAT ONE WAS TOO CLOSE, CAP!
PKOW
WE'RE NOT ABOUT TO TAKE A CHANCE OF LOSING YOU!
NOT NOW-- WHEN WE NEED YOU THE MOST!
WHO--??
OH, ONE OF FURY'S FAITHFUL WATCHDOGS!
LOOK--IF I HAD NEEDED YOUR HELP JUST THEN, IT WOULD BE TIME FOR ME TO RETIRE!
I THOUGHT OUR SHIELD TRAINING WAS RUGGED--
BUT AFTER WATCHING YOU, OURS IS LIKE A SEWING BEE!
OKAY--YOU DIDN'T COME HERE TO ASK FOR MY AUTOGRAPH! WHAT'S ON YOUR MIND??
WE'VE GOT A JOB THAT NEEDS DOING!
EVERYBODY HAS A JOB THAT NEEDS DOING!
HOW ABOUT LETTING SOME OF YOUR AGENTS EARN THEIR PAY?
NEVER SAW YOU THIS WAY BEFORE, CAP!
IF SOME-THING'S BUGGIN' YOU, SPIT IT OUT!
MAYBE A MAN GETS SICK OF BEING ON CALL ALL THE TIME!
MAYBE I'D LIKE A LIFE OF MY OWN--AND TIME OF MY OWN!
--TIME TO FIND THE ONE GIRL IN THE WORLD WHO MEANS SOMETHING TO ME!
--THE ONE GIRL WHO CAN'T BE MINE-- BECAUSE OF HER DEVOTION TO SHIELD!
3

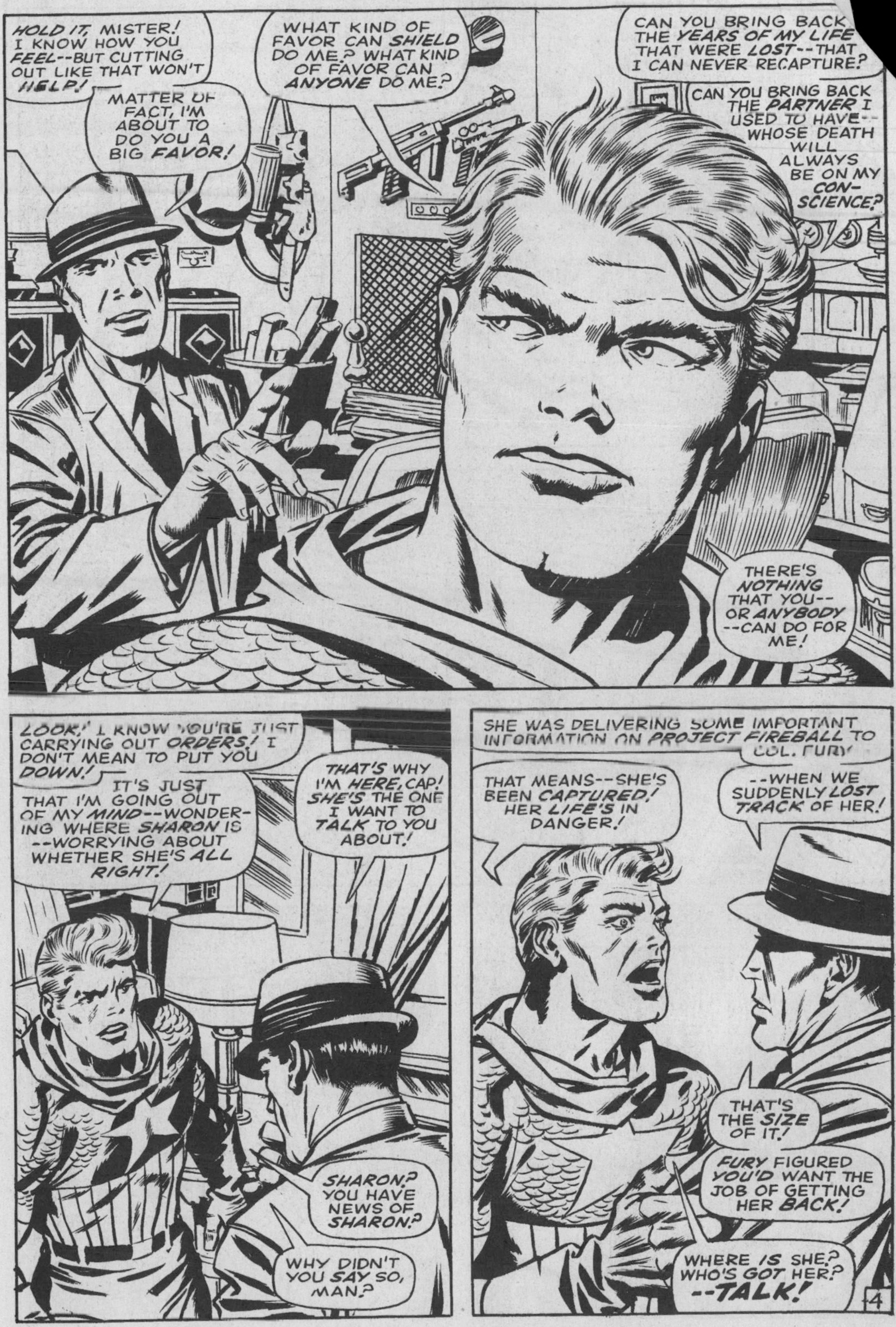
HOLD IT, MISTER! I KNOW HOW YOU FEEL--BUT CUTTING OUT LIKE THAT WON'T HELP!
MATTER OF FACT, I'M ABOUT TO DO YOU A BIG FAVOR!
WHAT KIND OF FAVOR CAN SHIELD DO ME? WHAT KIND OF FAVOR CAN ANYONE DO ME?
CAN YOU BRING BACK THE YEARS OF MY LIFE THAT WERE LOST--THAT I CAN NEVER RECAPTURE?
CAN YOU BRING BACK THE PARTNER I USED TO HAVE--WHOSE DEATH WILL ALWAYS BE ON MY CON-SCIENCE?
THERE'S NOTHING THAT YOU--OR ANYBODY--CAN DO FOR ME!
LOOK! I KNOW YOU'RE JUST CARRYING OUT ORDERS! I DON'T MEAN TO PUT YOU DOWN!
IT'S JUST THAT I'M GOING OUT OF MY MIND--WONDERING WHERE SHARON IS--WORRYING ABOUT WHETHER SHE'S ALL RIGHT!
THAT'S WHY I'M HERE, CAP! SHE'S THE ONE I WANT TO TALK TO YOU ABOUT!
SHARON? YOU HAVE NEWS OF SHARON?
WHY DIDN'T YOU SAY SO, MAN?
SHE WAS DELIVERING SOME IMPORTANT INFORMATION ON PROJECT FIREBALL TO COL. FURY
--WHEN WE SUDDENLY LOST TRACK OF HER!
THAT MEANS--SHE'S BEEN CAPTURED! HER LIFE'S IN DANGER!
THAT'S THE SIZE OF IT!
FURY FIGURED YOU'D WANT THE JOB OF GETTING HER BACK!
WHERE IS SHE? WHO'S GOT HER? --TALK!
4

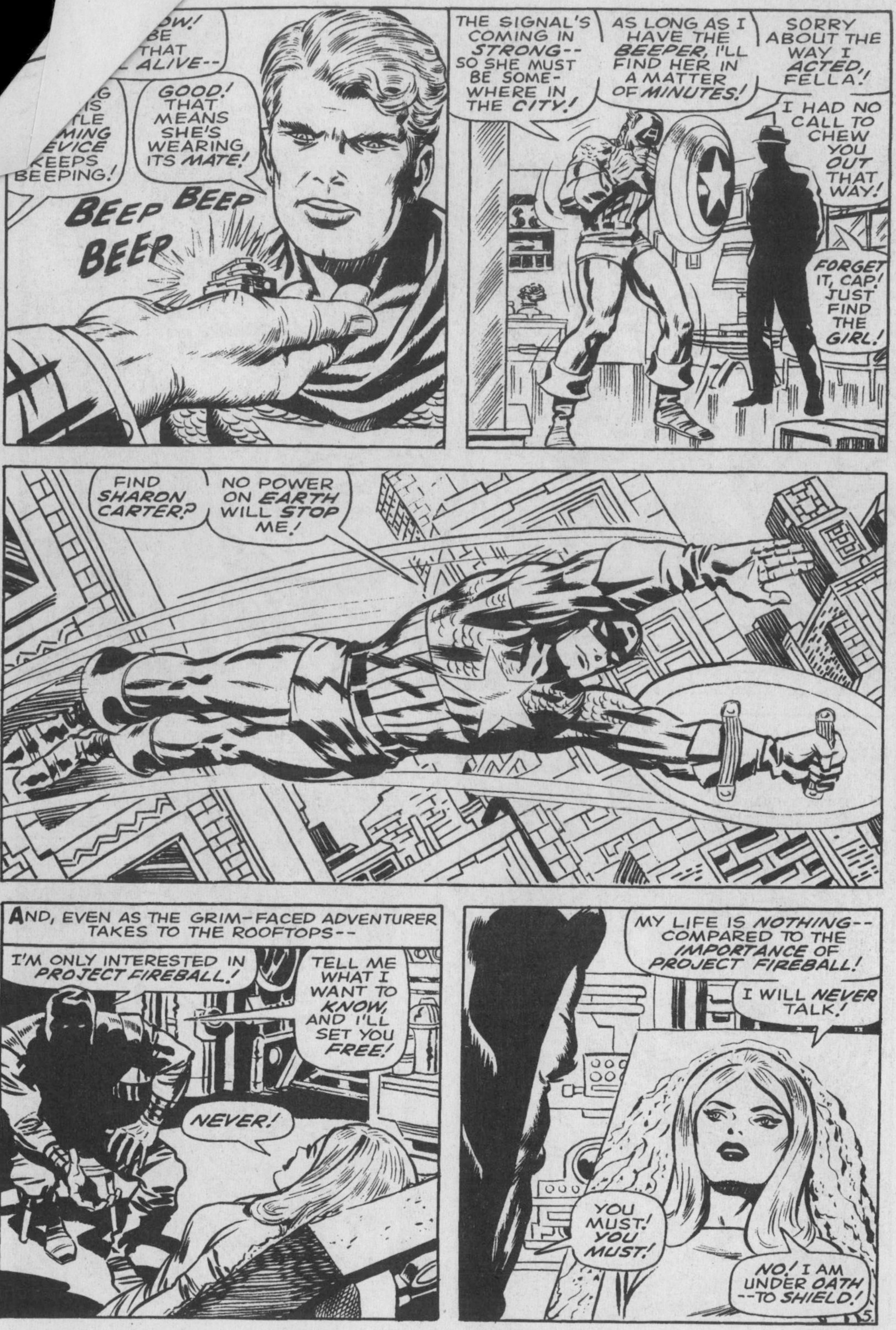

GOOD! THAT MEANS SHE'S WEARING ITS MATE!
BEEPING!
BEEP BEEP BEEP
THE SIGNAL'S COMING IN STRONG-- SO SHE MUST BE SOME-WHERE IN THE CITY!
AS LONG AS I HAVE THE BEEPER, I'LL FIND HER IN A MATTER OF MINUTES!
SORRY ABOUT THE WAY I ACTED, FELLA!
I HAD NO CALL TO CHEW YOU OUT THAT WAY!
FORGET IT, CAP! JUST FIND THE GIRL!
FIND SHARON CARTER?
NO POWER ON EARTH WILL STOP ME!
AND, EVEN AS THE GRIM-FACED ADVENTURER TAKES TO THE ROOFTOPS--
I'M ONLY INTERESTED IN PROJECT FIREBALL!
TELL ME WHAT I WANT TO KNOW, AND I'LL SET YOU FREE!
NEVER!
MY LIFE IS NOTHING-- COMPARED TO THE IMPORTANCE OF PROJECT FIREBALL!
I WILL NEVER TALK!
YOU MUST! YOU MUST!
NO! I AM UNDER OATH --TO SHIELD!
5.

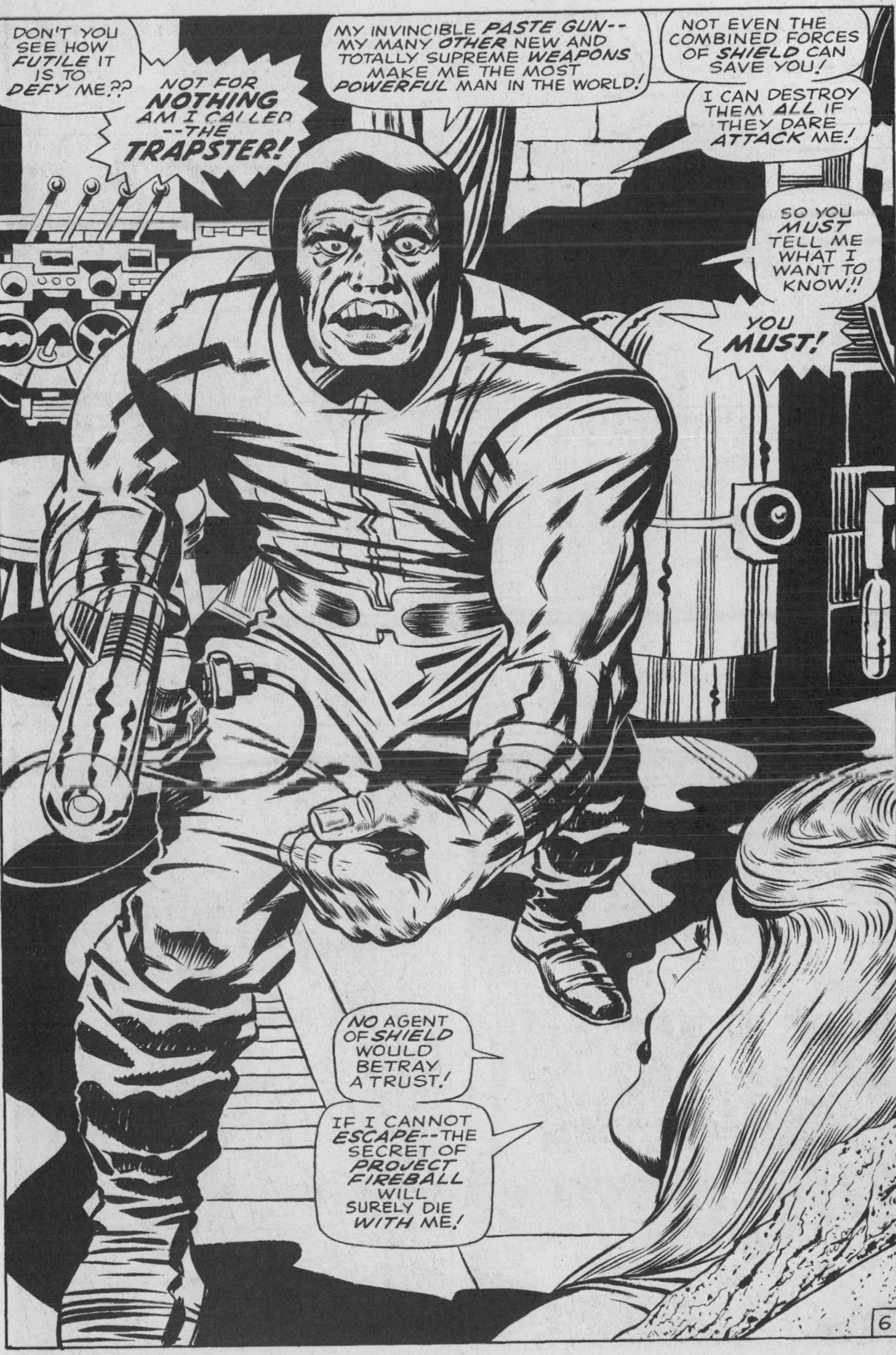

DON'T YOU SEE HOW FUTILE IT IS TO DEFY ME??
NOT FOR NOTHING AM I CALLED --THE TRAPSTER!
MY INVINCIBLE PASTE GUN-- MY MANY OTHER NEW AND TOTALLY SUPREME WEAPONS MAKE ME THE MOST POWERFUL MAN IN THE WORLD!
NOT EVEN THE COMBINED FORCES OF SHIELD CAN SAVE YOU!
I CAN DESTROY THEM ALL IF THEY DARE ATTACK ME!
SO YOU MUST TELL ME WHAT I WANT TO KNOW!!
YOU MUST!
NO AGENT OF SHIELD WOULD BETRAY A TRUST!
IF I CANNOT ESCAPE--THE SECRET OF PROJECT FIREBALL WILL SURELY DIE WITH ME!
6

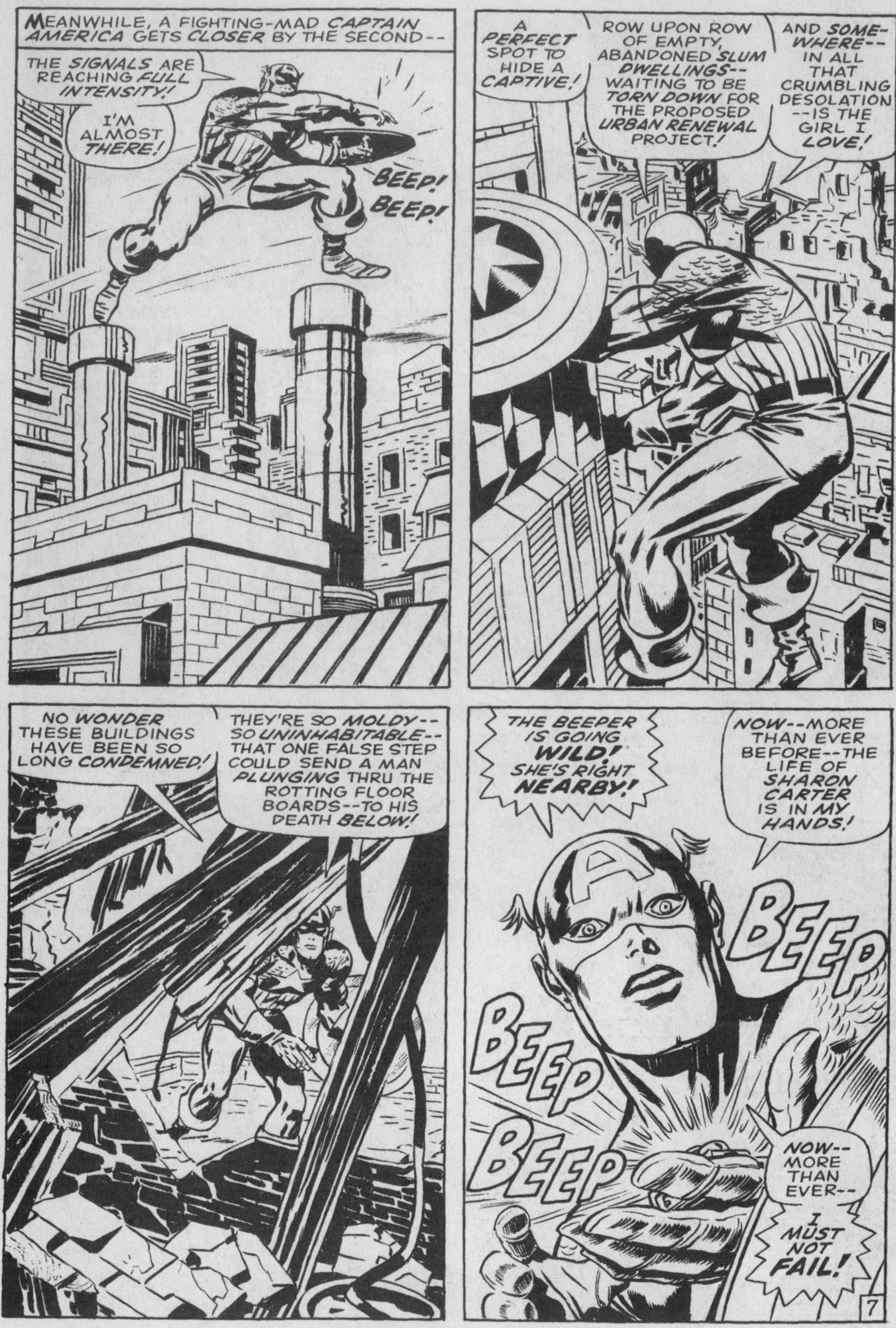
MEANWHILE, A FIGHTING-MAD CAPTAIN AMERICA GETS CLOSER BY THE SECOND--
THE SIGNALS ARE REACHING FULL INTENSITY!
I'M ALMOST THERE!
BEEP! BEEP!
A PERFECT SPOT TO HIDE A CAPTIVE!
ROW UPON ROW OF EMPTY, ABANDONED SLUM DWELLINGS--WAITING TO BE TORN DOWN FOR THE PROPOSED URBAN RENEWAL PROJECT!
AND SOMEWHERE--IN ALL THAT CRUMBLING DESOLATION--IS THE GIRL I LOVE!
NO WONDER THESE BUILDINGS HAVE BEEN SO LONG CONDEMNED!
THEY'RE SO MOLDY--SO UNINHABITABLE--THAT ONE FALSE STEP COULD SEND A MAN PLUNGING THRU THE ROTTING FLOOR BOARDS--TO HIS DEATH BELOW!
THE BEEPER IS GOING WILD! SHE'S RIGHT NEARBY!
NOW--MORE THAN EVER BEFORE--THE LIFE OF SHARON CARTER IS IN MY HANDS!
BEEP
BEEP
BEEP
NOW--MORE THAN EVER--I MUST NOT FAIL!
7

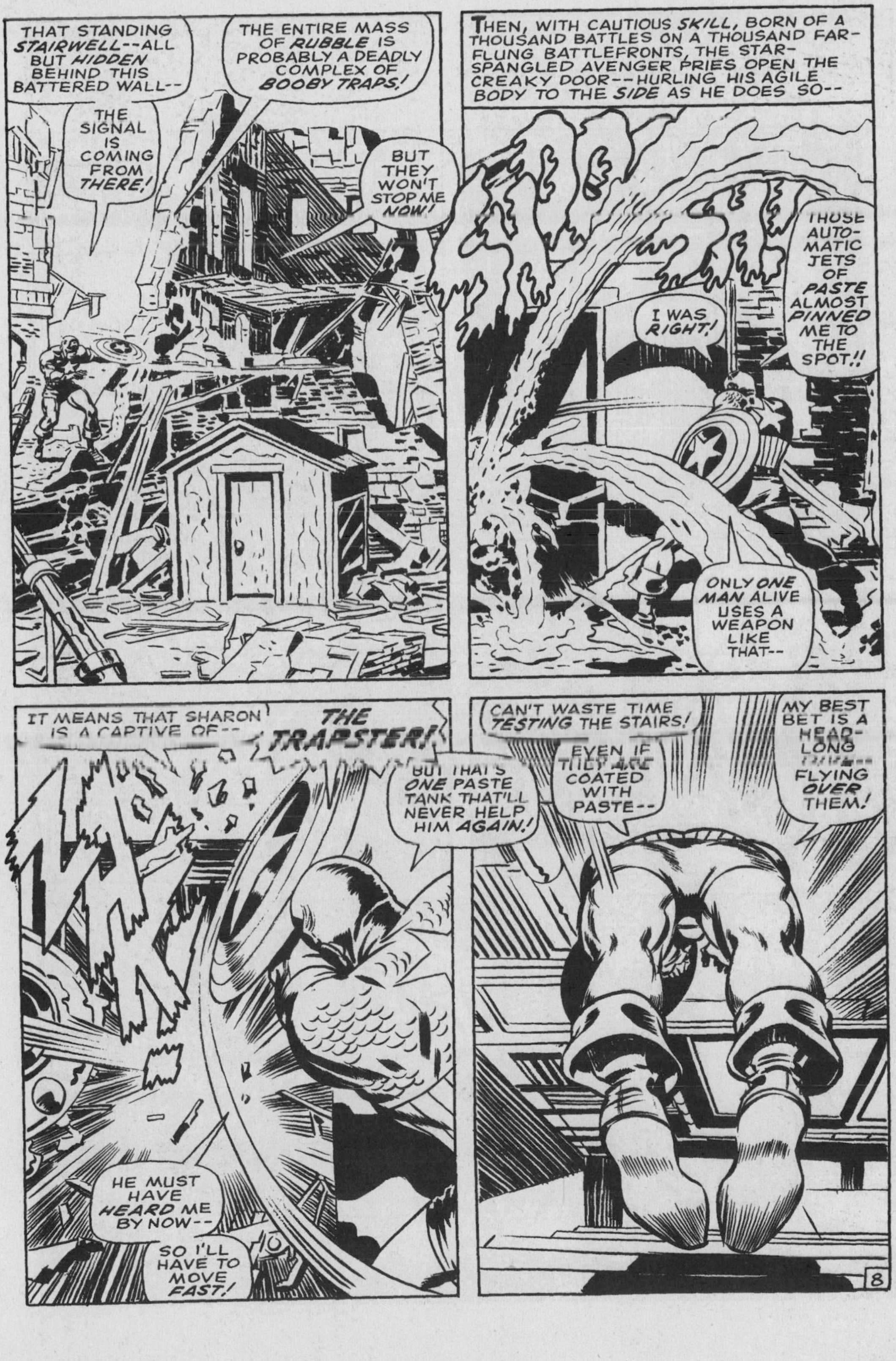
THAT STANDING STAIRWELL--ALL BUT HIDDEN BEHIND THIS BATTERED WALL--
THE ENTIRE MASS OF RUBBLE IS PROBABLY A DEADLY COMPLEX OF BOOBY TRAPS!
THE SIGNAL IS COMING FROM THERE!
BUT THEY WON'T STOP ME NOW!
THEN, WITH CAUTIOUS SKILL, BORN OF A THOUSAND BATTLES ON A THOUSAND FAR-FLUNG BATTLEFRONTS, THE STAR-SPANGLED AVENGER PRIES OPEN THE CREAKY DOOR--HURLING HIS AGILE BODY TO THE SIDE AS HE DOES SO--
THOSE AUTOMATIC JETS OF PASTE ALMOST PINNED ME TO THE SPOT!!
I WAS RIGHT!
ONLY ONE MAN ALIVE USES A WEAPON LIKE THAT--
IT MEANS THAT SHARON IS A CAPTIVE OF--
THE TRAPSTER!
BUT THAT'S ONE PASTE TANK THAT'LL NEVER HELP HIM AGAIN!
HE MUST HAVE HEARD ME BY NOW--
SO I'LL HAVE TO MOVE FAST!
CAN'T WASTE TIME TESTING THE STAIRS!
EVEN IF
COATED WITH PASTE--
MY BEST BET IS A HEAD-LONG
FLYING OVER THEM!
8

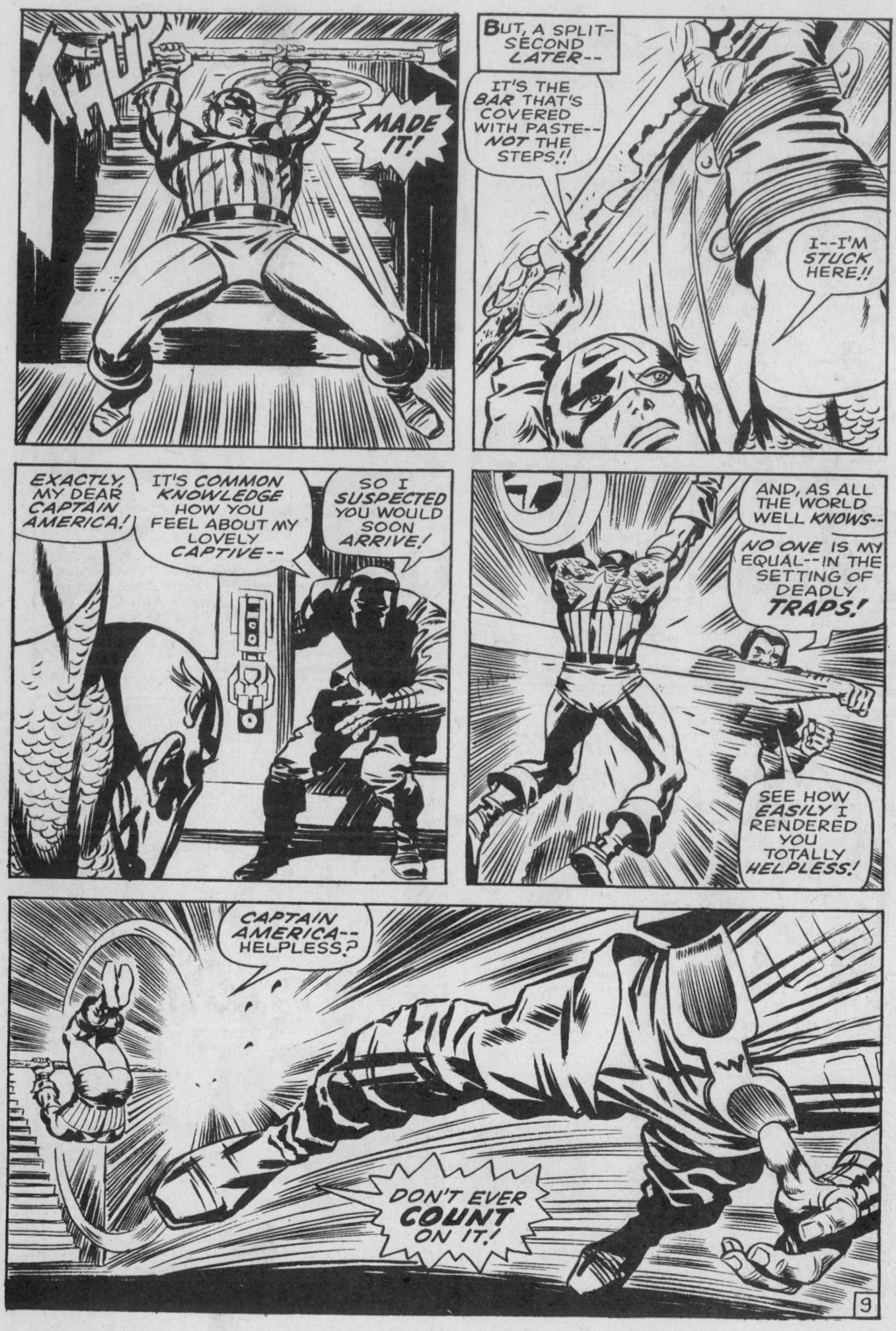
THUD
MADE IT!
BUT, A SPLIT-SECOND LATER--
IT'S THE BAR THAT'S COVERED WITH PASTE--NOT THE STEPS!!
I--I'M STUCK HERE!!
EXACTLY, MY DEAR CAPTAIN AMERICA!
IT'S COMMON KNOWLEDGE HOW YOU FEEL ABOUT MY LOVELY CAPTIVE--
SO I SUSPECTED YOU WOULD SOON ARRIVE!
AND, AS ALL THE WORLD WELL KNOWS--
NO ONE IS MY EQUAL--IN THE SETTING OF DEADLY TRAPS!
SEE HOW EASILY I RENDERED YOU TOTALLY HELPLESS!
CAPTAIN AMERICA--HELPLESS?
DON'T EVER COUNT ON IT!
9

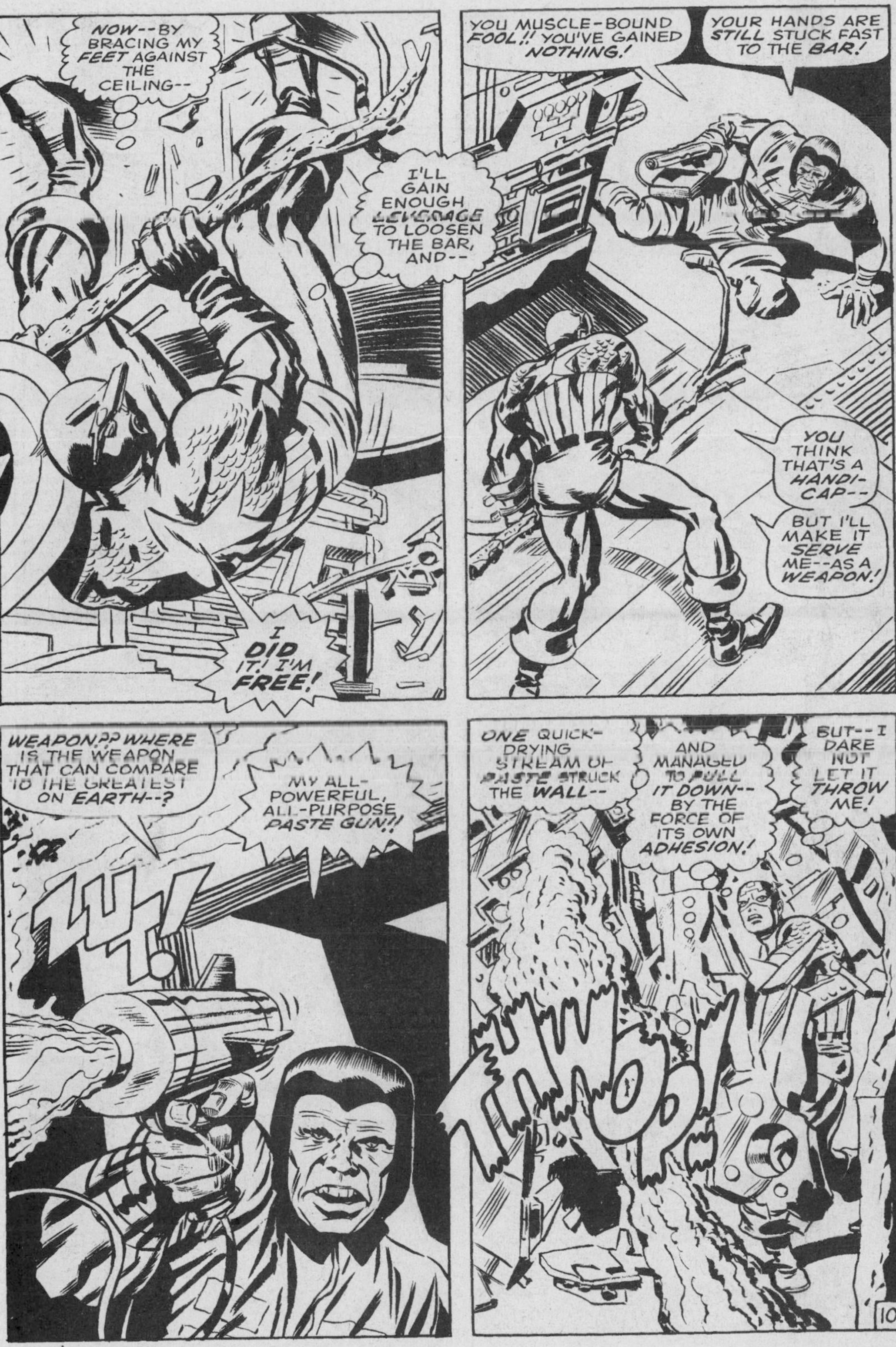
NOW--BY BRACING MY FEET AGAINST THE CEILING--
I'LL GAIN ENOUGH LEVERAGE TO LOOSEN THE BAR, AND--
I DID IT! I'M FREE!
YOU MUSCLE-BOUND FOOL!! YOU'VE GAINED NOTHING!
YOUR HANDS ARE STILL STUCK FAST TO THE BAR!
YOU THINK THAT'S A HANDI-CAP--
BUT I'LL MAKE IT SERVE ME--AS A WEAPON!
WEAPON?? WHERE IS THE WEAPON THAT CAN COMPARE TO THE GREATEST ON EARTH--?
MY ALL-POWERFUL, ALL-PURPOSE PASTE GUN!!
ZUT!
ONE QUICK-DRYING STREAM OF PASTE STRUCK THE WALL--
AND MANAGED TO PULL IT DOWN-- BY THE FORCE OF ITS OWN ADHESION!
BUT--I DARE NOT LET IT THROW ME!
THWOK
10

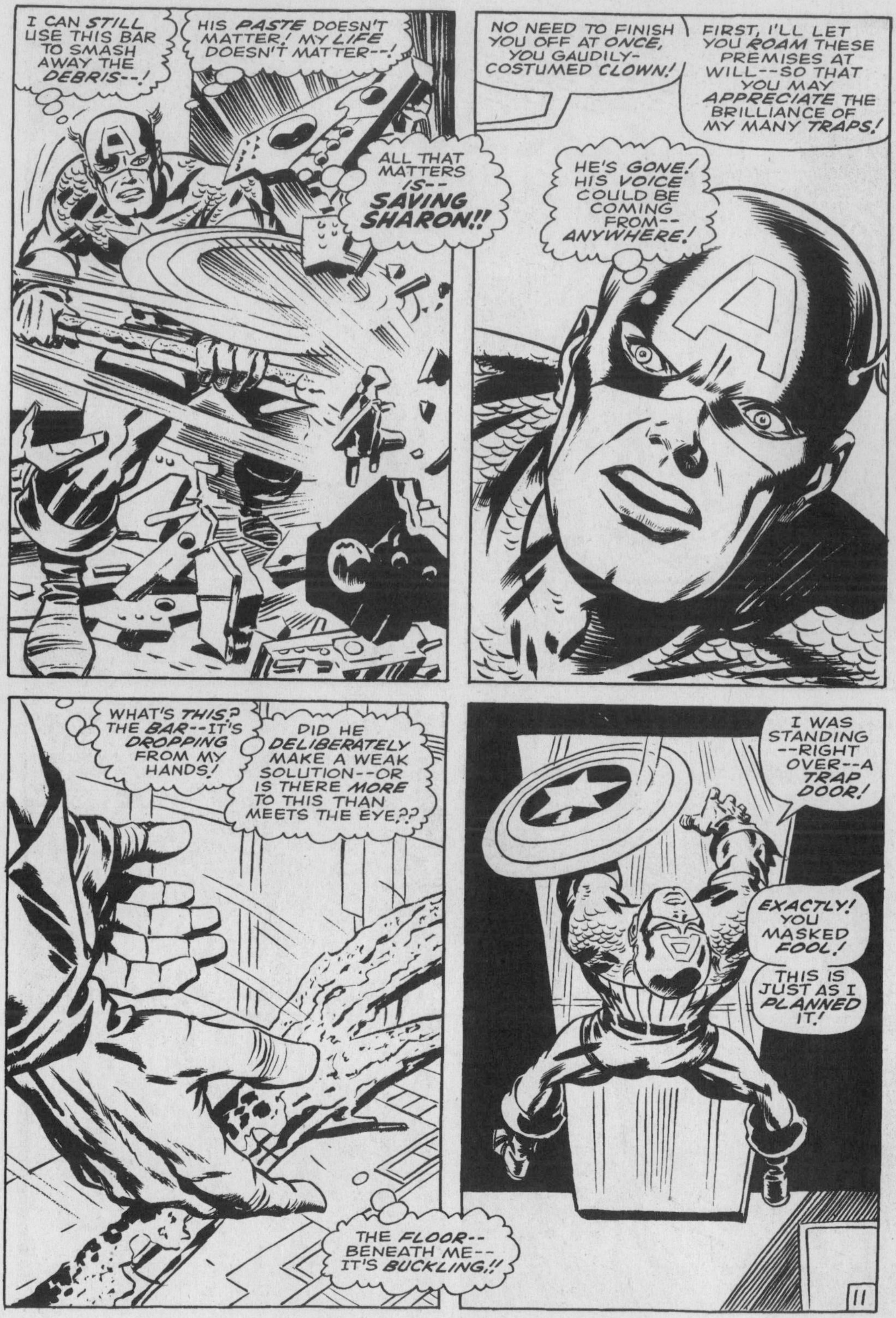
I CAN STILL USE THIS BAR TO SMASH AWAY THE DEBRIS--!
HIS PASTE DOESN'T MATTER! MY LIFE DOESN'T MATTER--!
ALL THAT MATTERS IS-- SAVING SHARON!!
NO NEED TO FINISH YOU OFF AT ONCE, YOU GAUDILY-COSTUMED CLOWN!
FIRST, I'LL LET YOU ROAM THESE PREMISES AT WILL--SO THAT YOU MAY APPRECIATE THE BRILLIANCE OF MY MANY TRAPS!
HE'S GONE! HIS VOICE COULD BE COMING FROM-- ANYWHERE!
WHAT'S THIS? THE BAR--IT'S DROPPING FROM MY HANDS!
DID HE DELIBERATELY MAKE A WEAK SOLUTION--OR IS THERE MORE TO THIS THAN MEETS THE EYE??
THE FLOOR-- BENEATH ME-- IT'S BUCKLING!!
I WAS STANDING --RIGHT OVER--A TRAP DOOR!
EXACTLY! YOU MASKED FOOL!
THIS IS JUST AS I PLANNED IT!
11

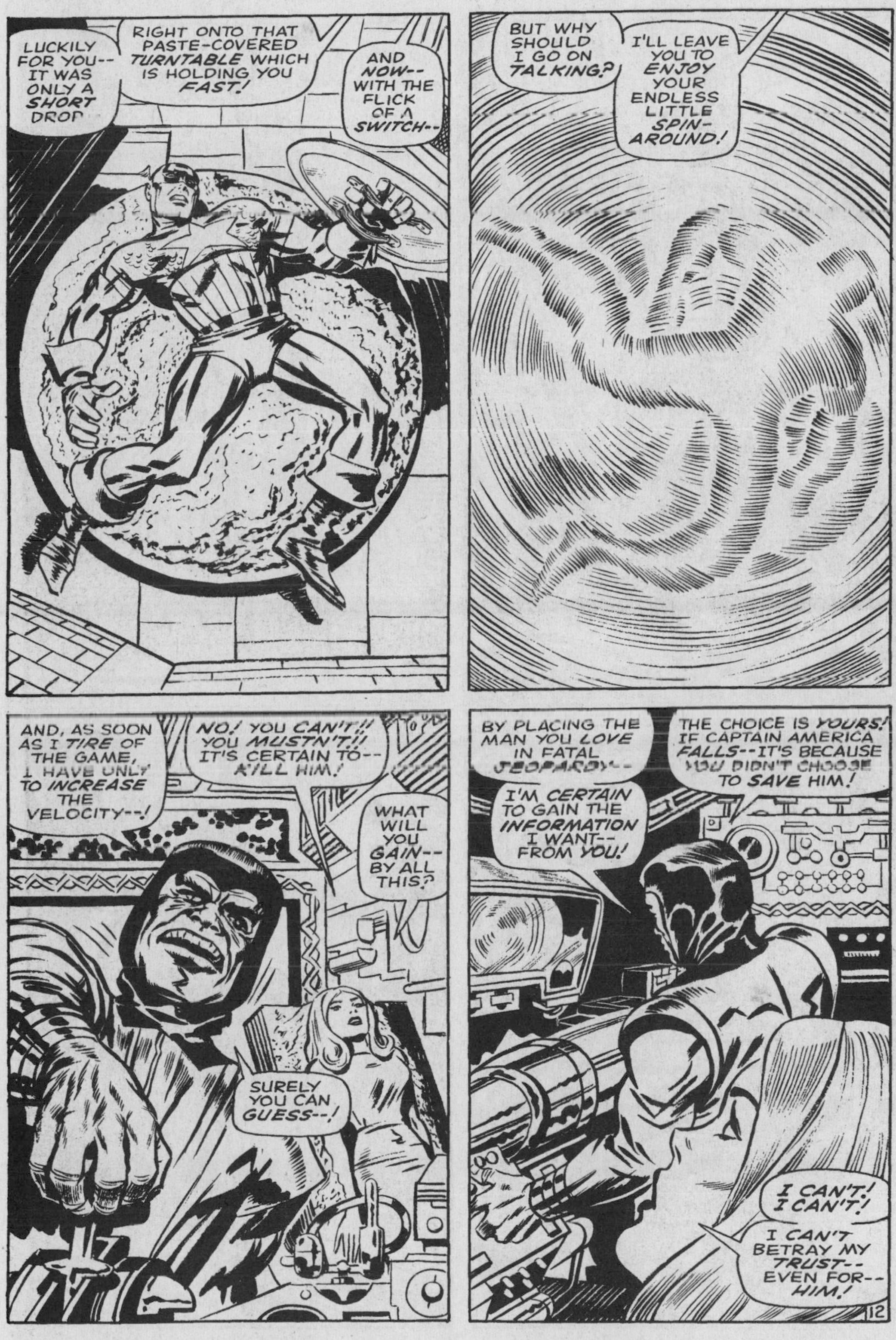
LUCKILY FOR YOU-- IT WAS ONLY A SHORT DROP
RIGHT ONTO THAT PASTE-COVERED TURNTABLE WHICH IS HOLDING YOU FAST!
AND NOW-- WITH THE FLICK OF A SWITCH--
BUT WHY SHOULD I GO ON TALKING?
I'LL LEAVE YOU TO ENJOY YOUR ENDLESS LITTLE SPIN-AROUND!
AND, AS SOON AS I TIRE OF THE GAME, I HAVE ONLY TO INCREASE THE VELOCITY--!
NO! YOU CAN'T!! YOU MUSTN'T!! IT'S CERTAIN TO-- KILL HIM!
WHAT WILL YOU GAIN-- BY ALL THIS?
SURELY YOU CAN GUESS--!
BY PLACING THE MAN YOU LOVE IN FATAL JEOPARDY--
I'M CERTAIN TO GAIN THE INFORMATION I WANT-- FROM YOU!
THE CHOICE IS YOURS! IF CAPTAIN AMERICA FALLS--IT'S BECAUSE YOU DIDN'T CHOOSE TO SAVE HIM!
I CAN'T! I CAN'T!
I CAN'T BETRAY MY TRUST-- EVEN FOR-- HIM!
12

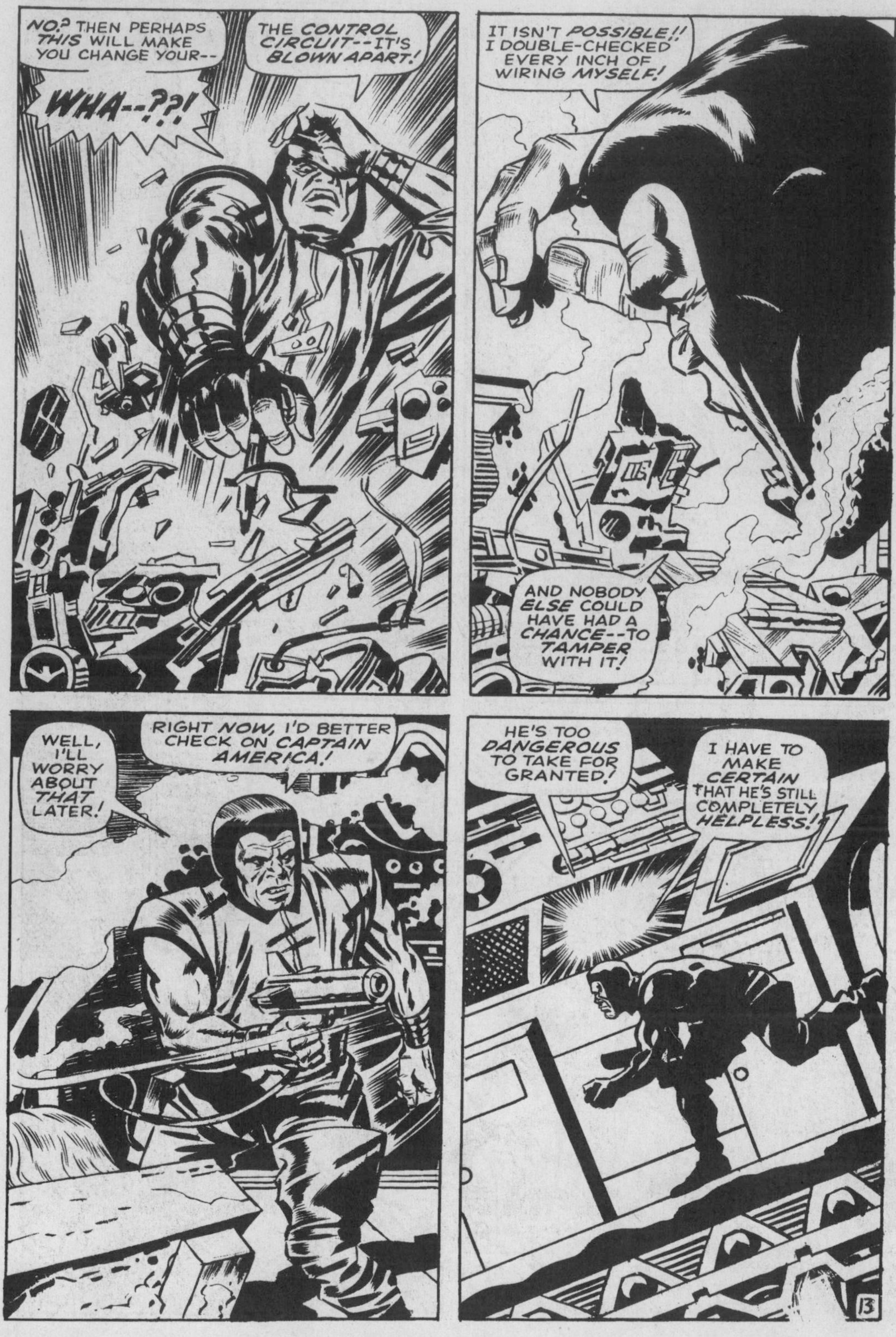
NO? THEN PERHAPS THIS WILL MAKE YOU CHANGE YOUR--
WHA--??!
THE CONTROL CIRCUIT--IT'S BLOWN APART!
IT ISN'T POSSIBLE!! I DOUBLE-CHECKED EVERY INCH OF WIRING MYSELF!
AND NOBODY ELSE COULD HAVE HAD A CHANCE--TO TAMPER WITH IT!
WELL, I'LL WORRY ABOUT THAT LATER!
RIGHT NOW, I'D BETTER CHECK ON CAPTAIN AMERICA!
HE'S TOO DANGEROUS TO TAKE FOR GRANTED!
I HAVE TO MAKE CERTAIN THAT HE'S STILL COMPLETELY HELPLESS!
13

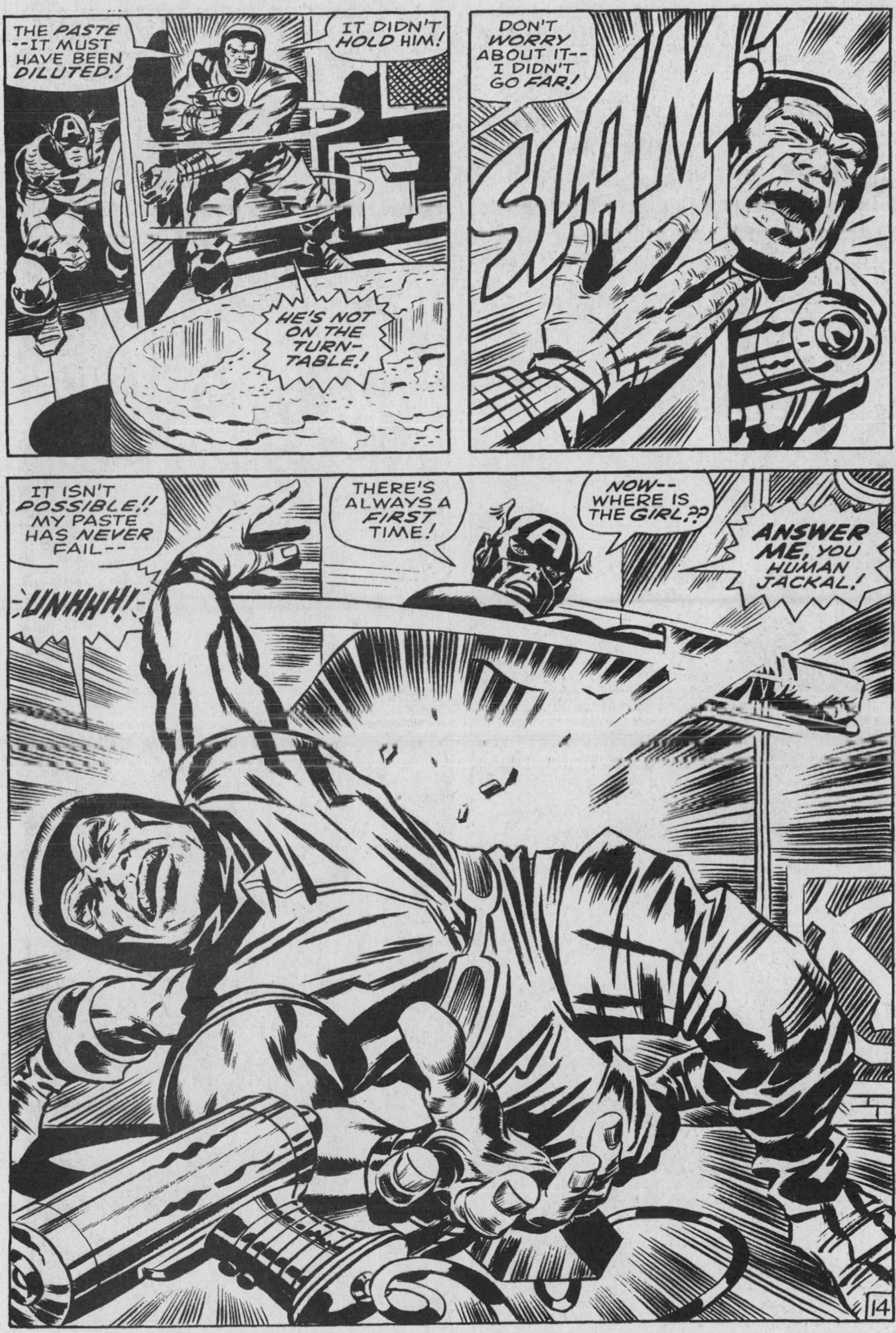
THE PASTE --IT MUST HAVE BEEN DILUTED!
IT DIDN'T HOLD HIM!
HE'S NOT ON THE TURN-TABLE!
DON'T WORRY ABOUT IT-- I DIDN'T GO FAR!
SLAM!
IT ISN'T POSSIBLE!! MY PASTE HAS NEVER FAIL--
UNHHH!
THERE'S ALWAYS A FIRST TIME!
NOW-- WHERE IS THE GIRL??
ANSWER ME, YOU HUMAN JACKAL!
14

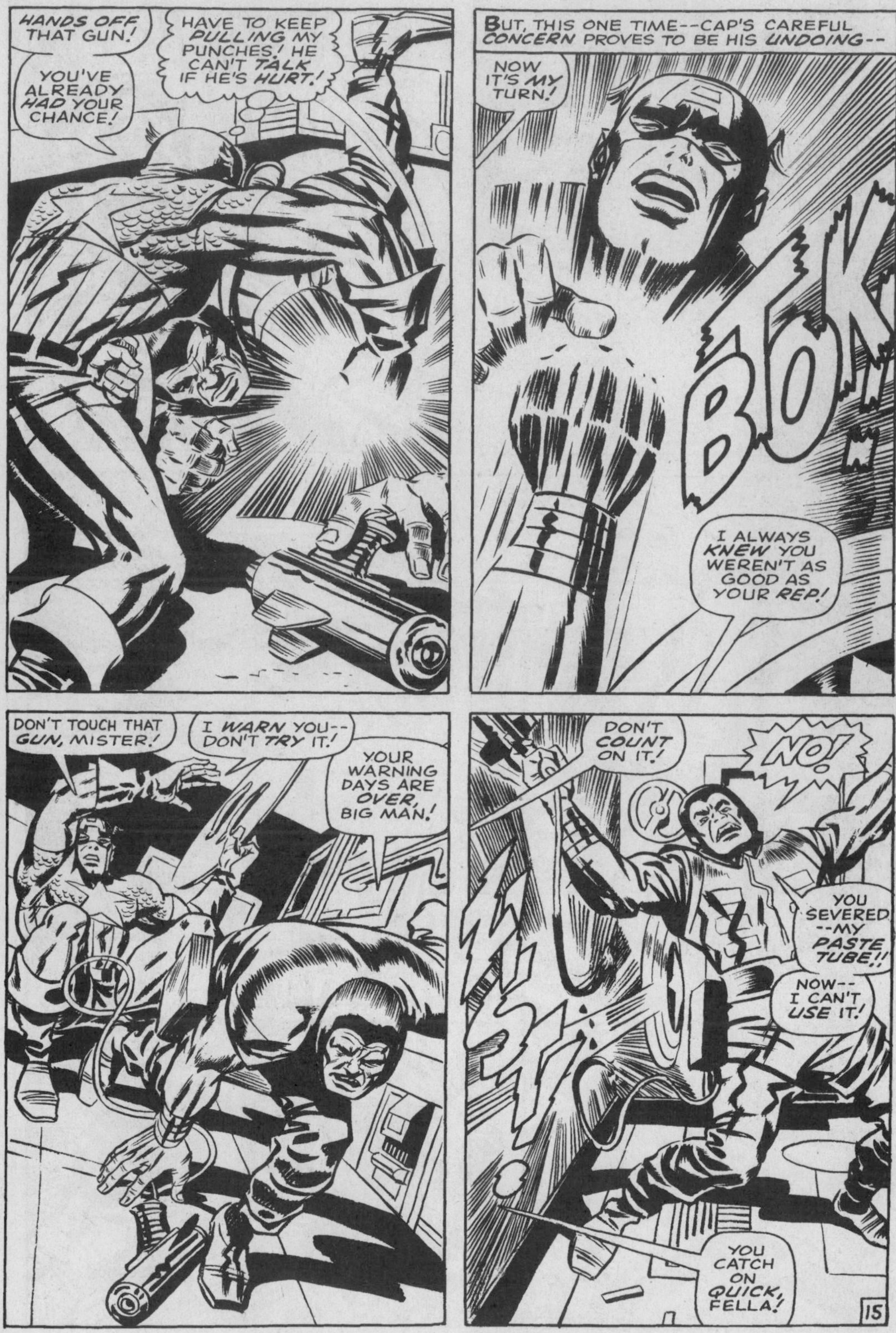
HANDS OFF THAT GUN!
HAVE TO KEEP PULLING MY PUNCHES! HE CAN'T TALK IF HE'S HURT!
YOU'VE ALREADY HAD YOUR CHANCE!
BUT, THIS ONE TIME--CAP'S CAREFUL CONCERN PROVES TO BE HIS UNDOING--
NOW IT'S MY TURN!
BTOK!
I ALWAYS KNEW YOU WEREN'T AS GOOD AS YOUR REP!
DON'T TOUCH THAT GUN, MISTER!
I WARN YOU-- DON'T TRY IT!
YOUR WARNING DAYS ARE OVER, BIG MAN!
DON'T COUNT ON IT!
NO!
YOU SEVERED --MY PASTE TUBE!!
NOW-- I CAN'T USE IT!
YOU CATCH ON QUICK, FELLA!
15

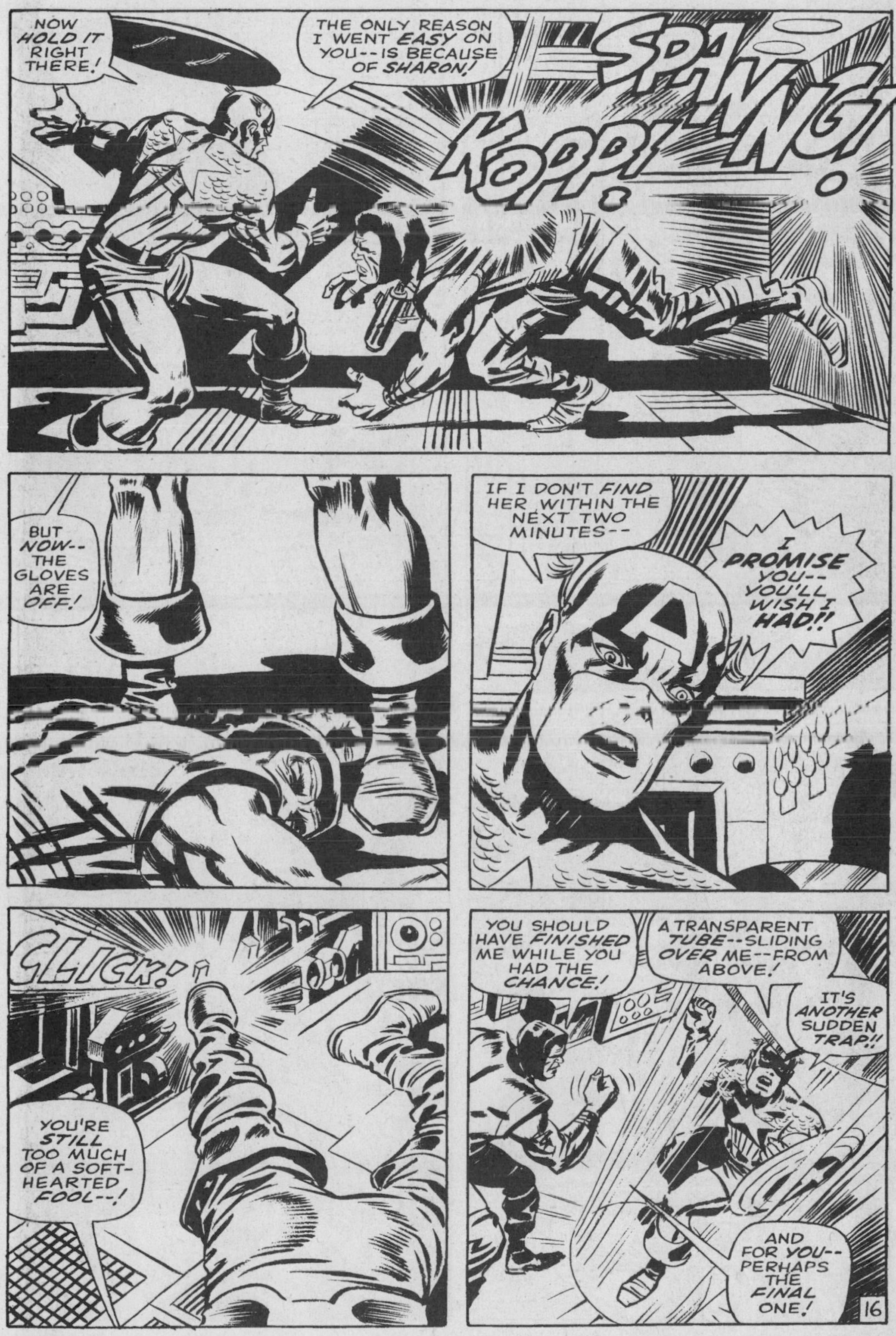
NOW HOLD IT RIGHT THERE!
THE ONLY REASON I WENT EASY ON YOU--IS BECAUSE OF SHARON!
SPANNG!
KOPPI!
BUT NOW--THE GLOVES ARE OFF!
IF I DON'T FIND HER WITHIN THE NEXT TWO MINUTES--
I PROMISE YOU--YOU'LL WISH I HAD!!
CLICK!
YOU'RE STILL TOO MUCH OF A SOFT-HEARTED FOOL--!
YOU SHOULD HAVE FINISHED ME WHILE YOU HAD THE CHANCE!
A TRANSPARENT TUBE--SLIDING OVER ME--FROM ABOVE!
IT'S ANOTHER SUDDEN TRAP!!
AND FOR YOU--PERHAPS THE FINAL ONE!
16

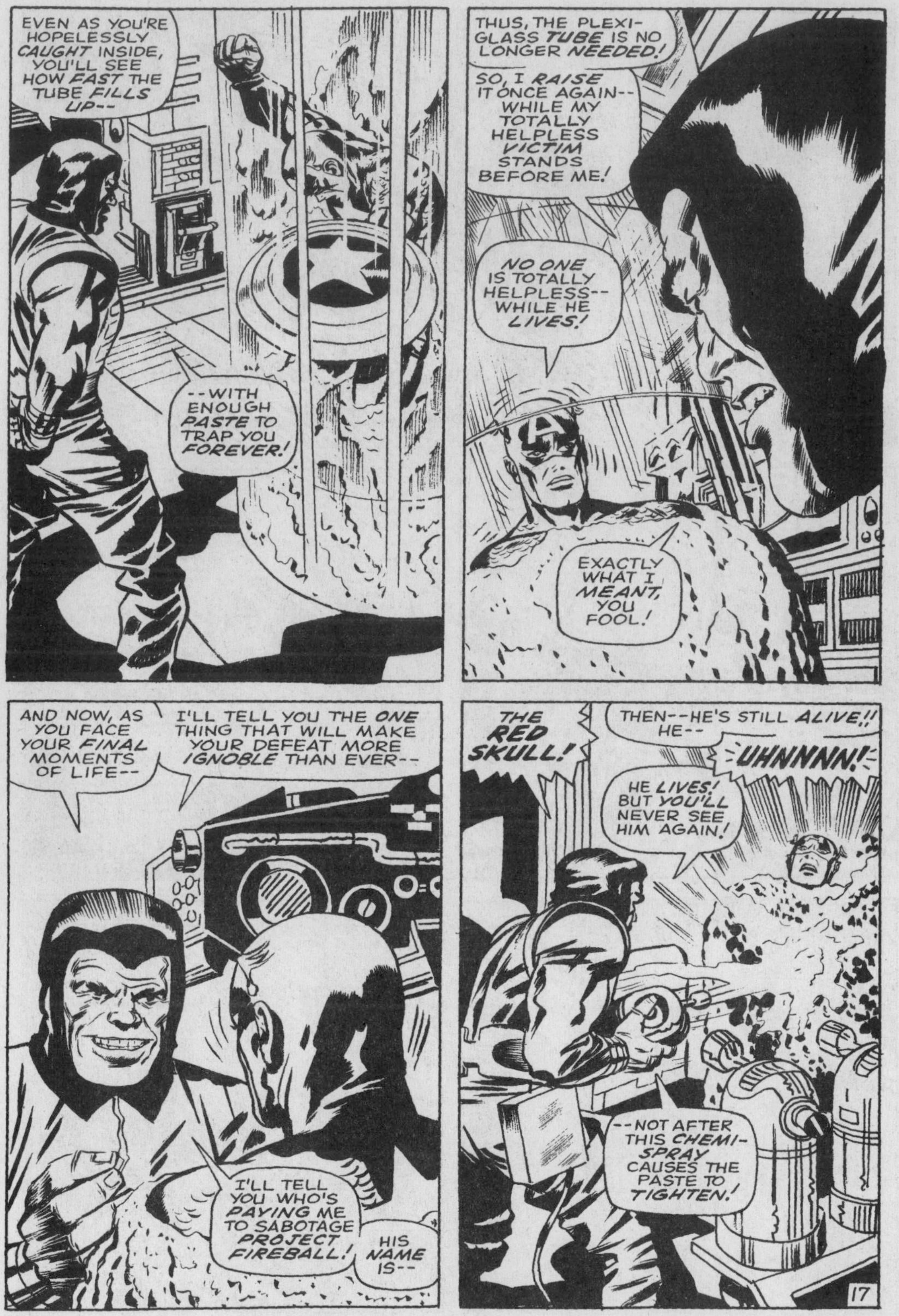
EVEN AS YOU'RE HOPELESSLY CAUGHT INSIDE, YOU'LL SEE HOW FAST THE TUBE FILLS UP--
--WITH ENOUGH PASTE TO TRAP YOU FOREVER!
THUS, THE PLEXI-GLASS TUBE IS NO LONGER NEEDED!
SO, I RAISE IT ONCE AGAIN-- WHILE MY TOTALLY HELPLESS VICTIM STANDS BEFORE ME!
NO ONE IS TOTALLY HELPLESS-- WHILE HE LIVES!
EXACTLY WHAT I MEANT, YOU FOOL!
AND NOW, AS YOU FACE YOUR FINAL MOMENTS OF LIFE--
I'LL TELL YOU THE ONE THING THAT WILL MAKE YOUR DEFEAT MORE IGNOBLE THAN EVER--
I'LL TELL YOU WHO'S PAYING ME TO SABOTAGE PROJECT FIREBALL!
HIS NAME IS--
THE RED SKULL!
THEN--HE'S STILL ALIVE!! HE--
UHNNNNN!
HE LIVES! BUT YOU'LL NEVER SEE HIM AGAIN!
--NOT AFTER THIS CHEMI-SPRAY CAUSES THE PASTE TO TIGHTEN!
17

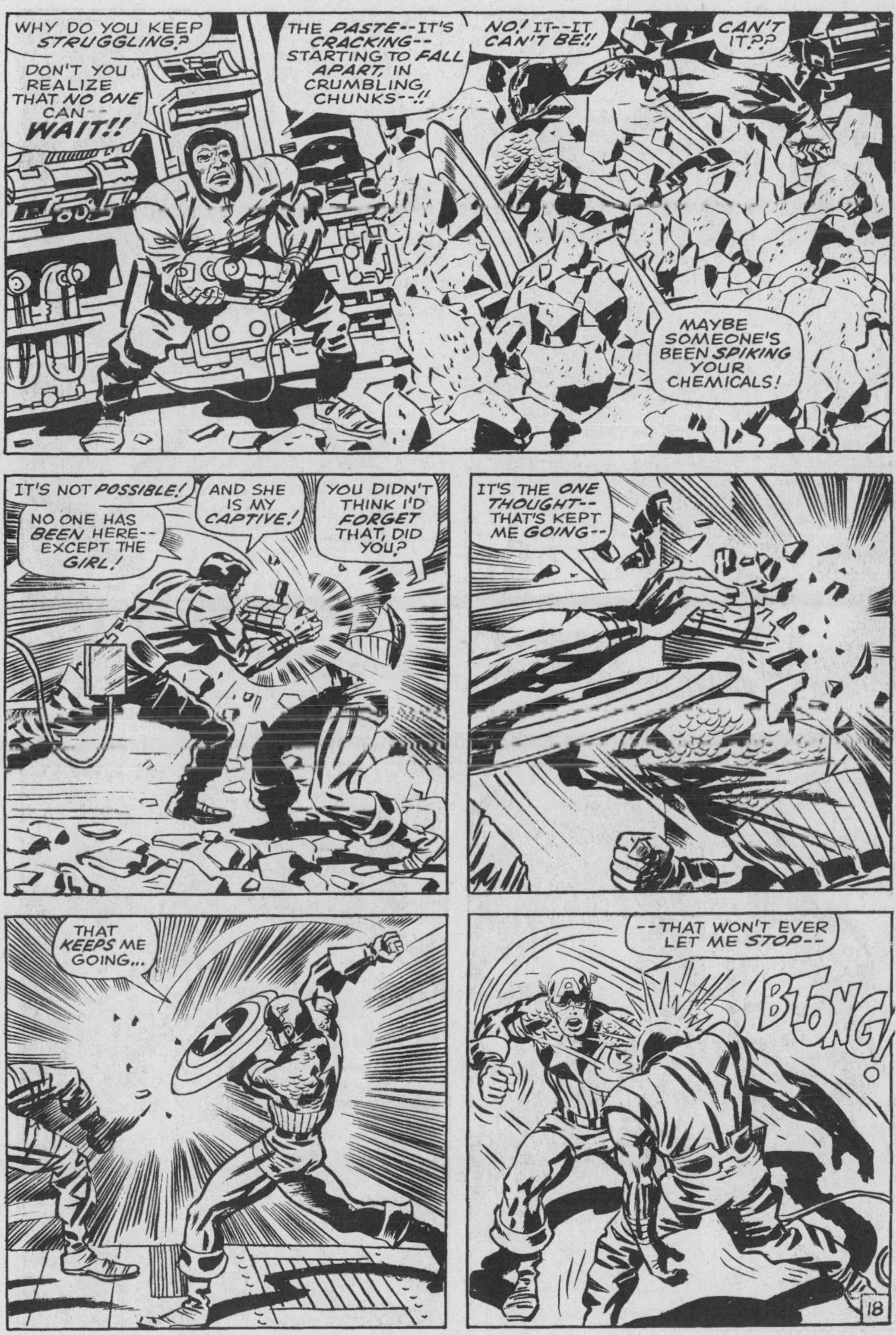

WHY DO YOU KEEP STRUGGLING?
DON'T YOU REALIZE THAT NO ONE CAN--
WAIT!!
THE PASTE--IT'S CRACKING--STARTING TO FALL APART, IN CRUMBLING CHUNKS--!!
NO! IT--IT CAN'T BE!!
CAN'T IT??
MAYBE SOMEONE'S BEEN SPIKING YOUR CHEMICALS!
IT'S NOT POSSIBLE!
NO ONE HAS BEEN HERE--EXCEPT THE GIRL!
AND SHE IS MY CAPTIVE!
YOU DIDN'T THINK I'D FORGET THAT, DID YOU?
IT'S THE ONE THOUGHT--THAT'S KEPT ME GOING--
THAT KEEPS ME GOING...
--THAT WON'T EVER LET ME STOP--
BTONG!
18

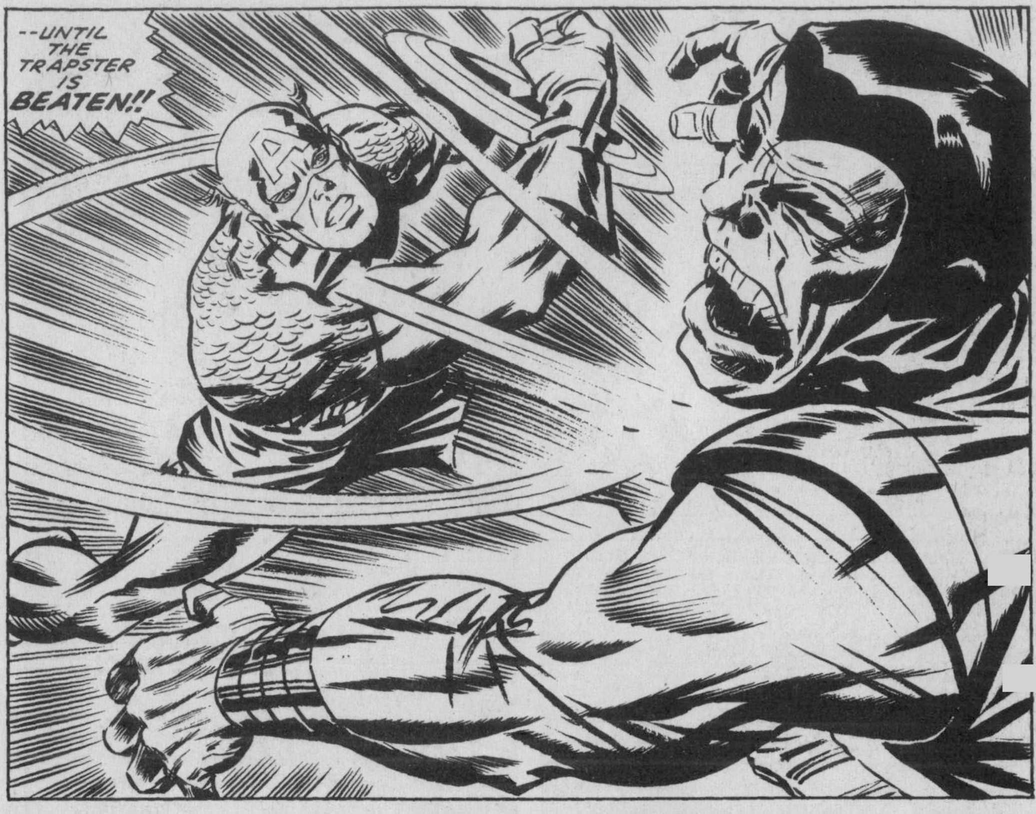
--UNTIL THE TRAPSTER IS BEATEN!!

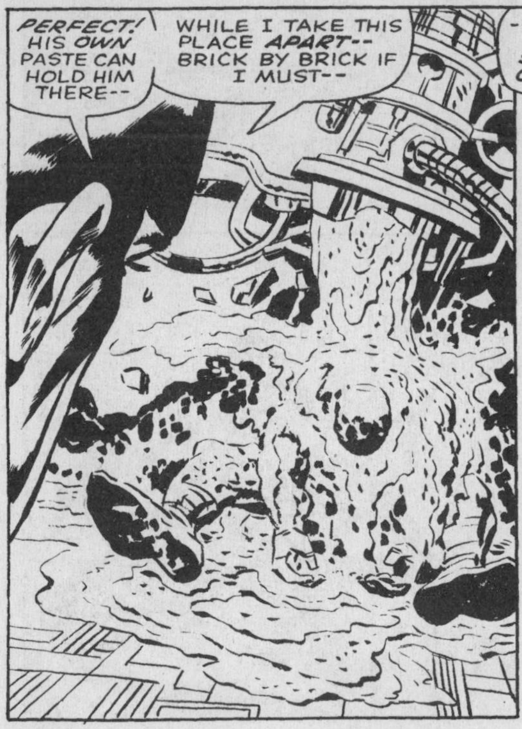
PERFECT! HIS OWN PASTE CAN HOLD HIM THERE--
WHILE I TAKE THIS PLACE APART-- BRICK BY BRICK IF I MUST--

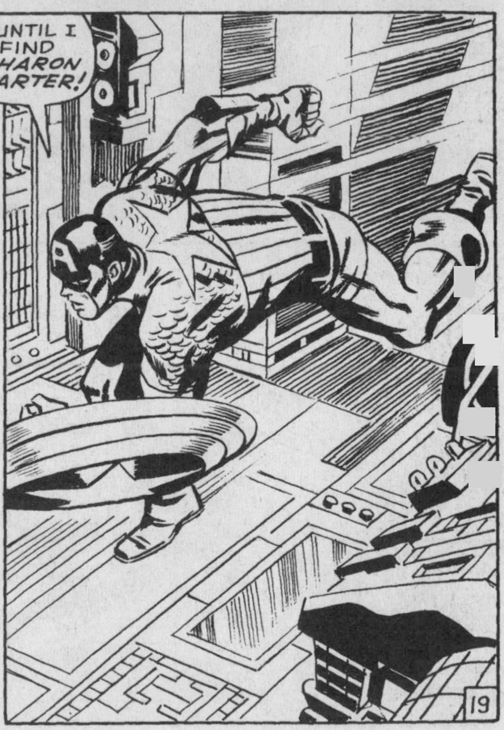
--UNTIL I FIND SHARON CARTER!
19

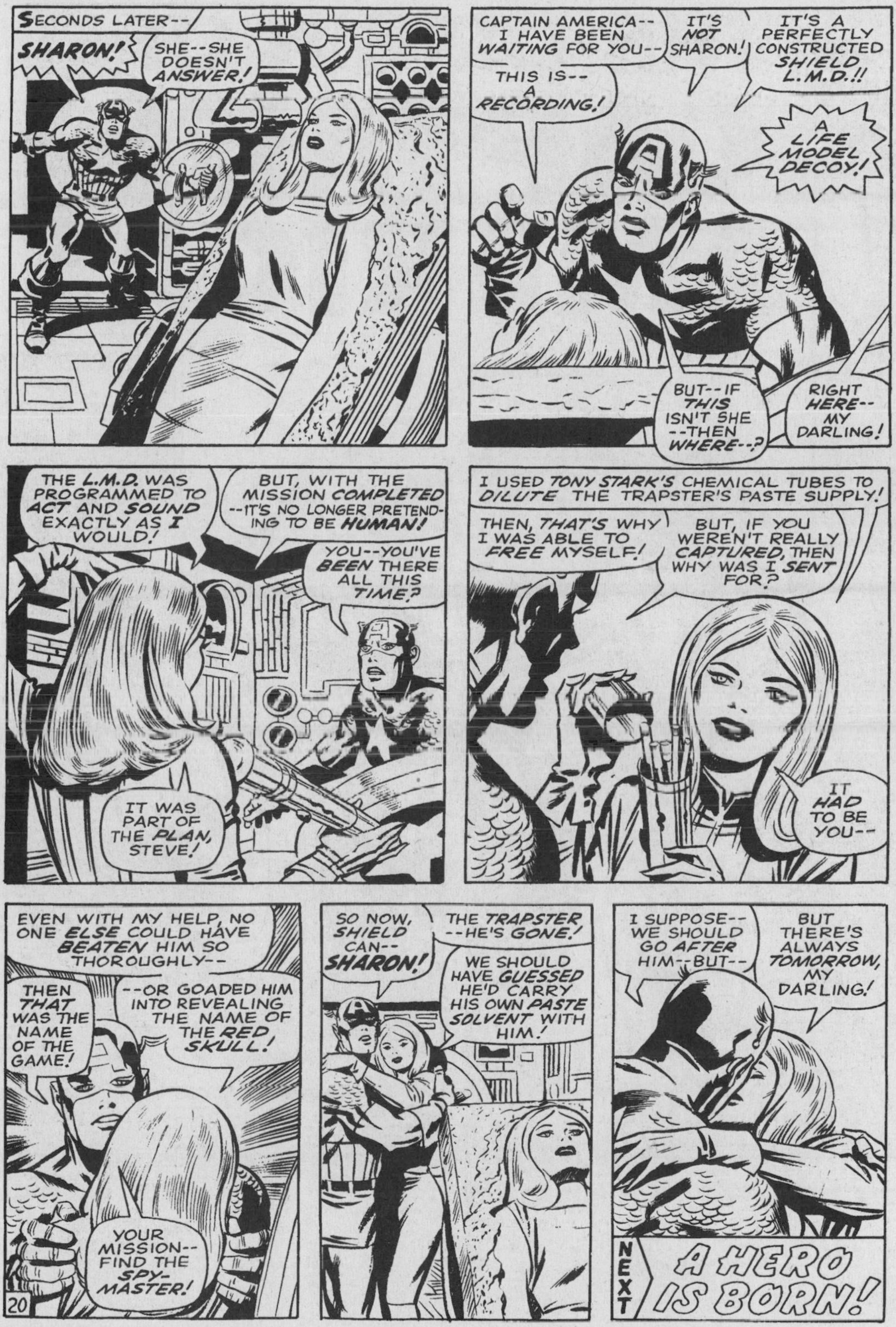
SECONDS LATER--
SHARON!
SHE--SHE DOESN'T ANSWER!
CAPTAIN AMERICA-- I HAVE BEEN WAITING FOR YOU--
THIS IS-- A RECORDING!
IT'S NOT SHARON!
IT'S A PERFECTLY CONSTRUCTED SHIELD L.M.D.!!
A LIFE MODEL DECOY!
BUT--IF THIS ISN'T SHE --THEN WHERE--?
RIGHT HERE-- MY DARLING!
THE L.M.D. WAS PROGRAMMED TO ACT AND SOUND EXACTLY AS I WOULD!
BUT, WITH THE MISSION COMPLETED --IT'S NO LONGER PRETENDING TO BE HUMAN!
YOU--YOU'VE BEEN THERE ALL THIS TIME?
IT WAS PART OF THE PLAN, STEVE!
I USED TONY STARK'S CHEMICAL TUBES TO DILUTE THE TRAPSTER'S PASTE SUPPLY!
THEN, THAT'S WHY I WAS ABLE TO FREE MYSELF!
BUT, IF YOU WEREN'T REALLY CAPTURED, THEN WHY WAS I SENT FOR?
IT HAD TO BE YOU--
EVEN WITH MY HELP, NO ONE ELSE COULD HAVE BEATEN HIM SO THOROUGHLY--
THEN THAT WAS THE NAME OF THE GAME!
--OR GOADED HIM INTO REVEALING THE NAME OF THE RED SKULL!
YOUR MISSION-- FIND THE SPY-MASTER!
20
SO NOW, SHIELD CAN-- SHARON!
THE TRAPSTER --HE'S GONE!
WE SHOULD HAVE GUESSED HE'D CARRY HIS OWN PASTE SOLVENT WITH HIM!
I SUPPOSE-- WE SHOULD GO AFTER HIM--BUT--
BUT THERE'S ALWAYS TOMORROW, MY DARLING!
NEXT
A HERO IS BORN!

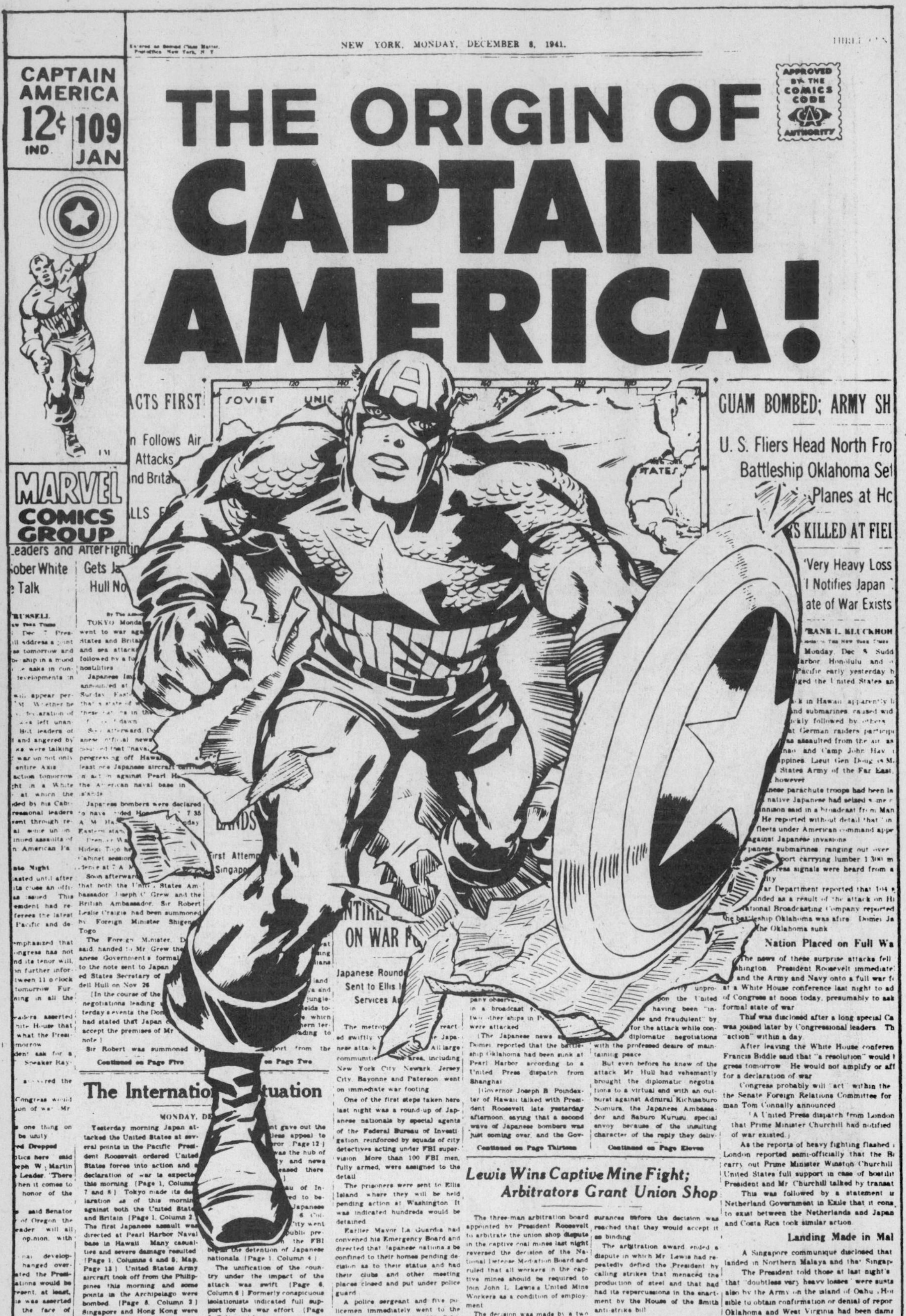
NEW YORK, MONDAY, DECEMBER 8, 1941.
CAPTAIN AMERICA
12¢
IND.
109
JAN
APPROVED BY THE COMICS CODE AUTHORITY
MARVEL COMICS GROUP
THE ORIGIN OF CAPTAIN AMERICA!
GUAM BOMBED; ARMY SH
U. S. Fliers Head North Fro
Battleship Oklahoma Set
Planes at Hc
KILLED AT FIEI
'Very Heavy Loss
Nation Placed on Full Wa
The International Situation
Lewis Wins Captive Mine Fight; Arbitrators Grant Union Shop
Landing Made in Mal
Continued on Page Five
Continued on Page Thirteen
Continued on Page Eleven

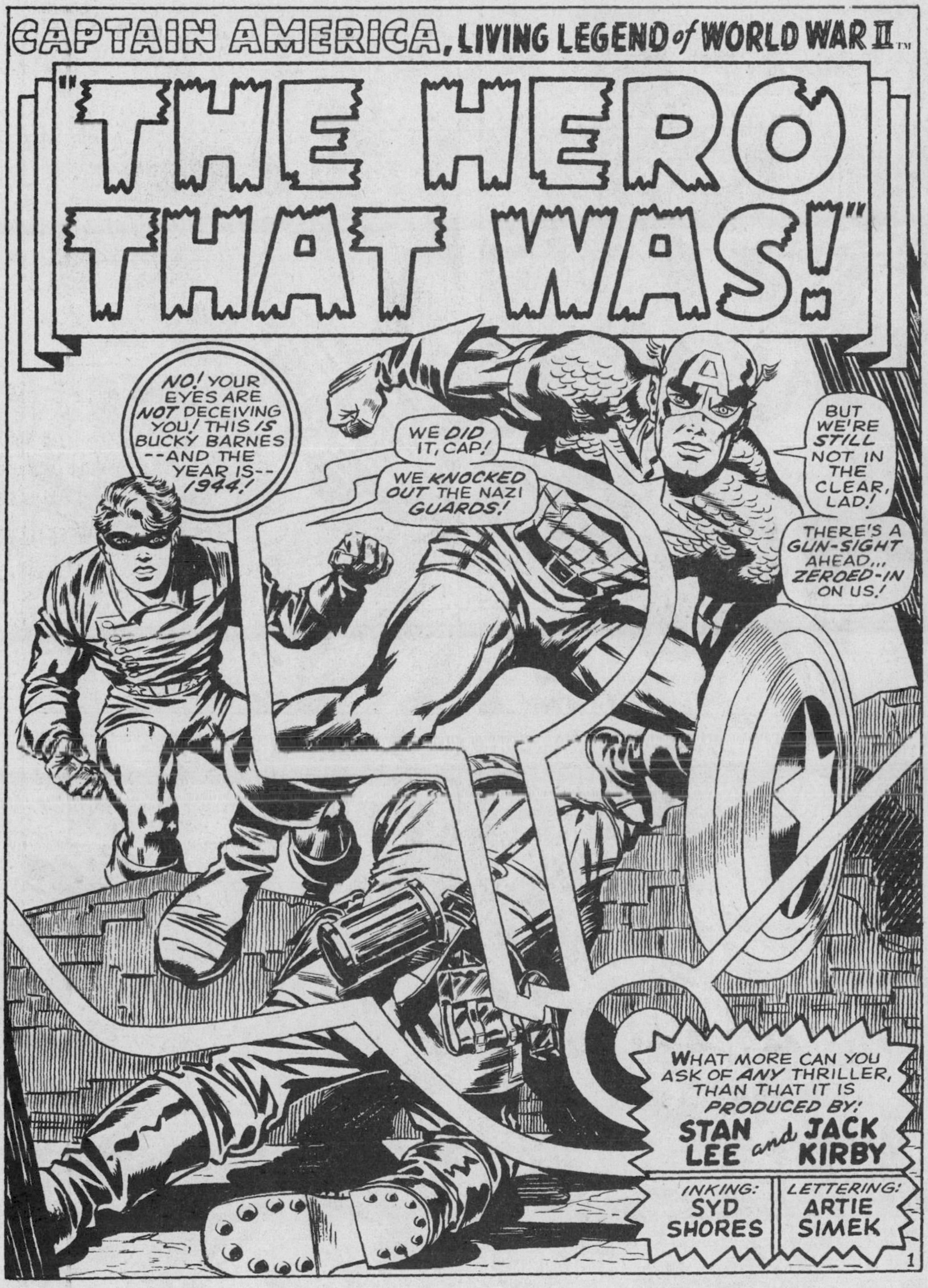
CAPTAIN AMERICA, LIVING LEGEND of WORLD WAR II™
"THE HERO THAT WAS!"
NO! YOUR EYES ARE NOT DECEIVING YOU! THIS IS BUCKY BARNES --AND THE YEAR IS-- 1944!
WE DID IT, CAP!
WE KNOCKED OUT THE NAZI GUARDS!
BUT WE'RE STILL NOT IN THE CLEAR, LAD!
THERE'S A GUN-SIGHT AHEAD... ZEROED-IN ON US!
WHAT MORE CAN YOU ASK OF ANY THRILLER, THAN THAT IT IS PRODUCED BY: STAN LEE and JACK KIRBY
INKING: SYD SHORES
LETTERING: ARTIE SIMEK
1

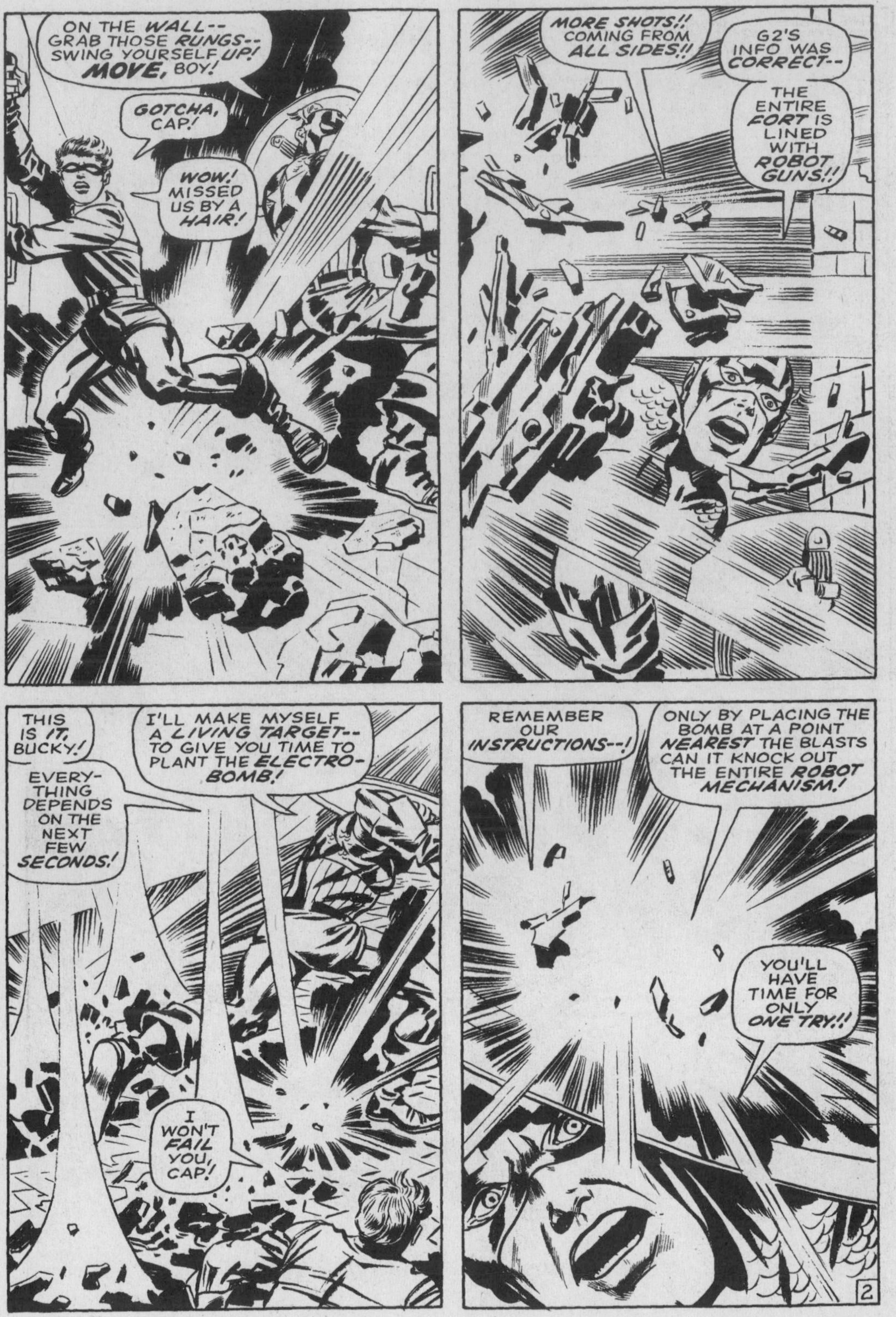
ON THE WALL-- GRAB THOSE RUNGS-- SWING YOURSELF UP! MOVE, BOY!
GOTCHA, CAP!
WOW! MISSED US BY A HAIR!
MORE SHOTS!! COMING FROM ALL SIDES!!
G2'S INFO WAS CORRECT--
THE ENTIRE FORT IS LINED WITH ROBOT GUNS!!
THIS IS IT, BUCKY!
EVERYTHING DEPENDS ON THE NEXT FEW SECONDS!
I'LL MAKE MYSELF A LIVING TARGET-- TO GIVE YOU TIME TO PLANT THE ELECTRO-BOMB!
I WON'T FAIL YOU, CAP!
REMEMBER OUR INSTRUCTIONS--!
ONLY BY PLACING THE BOMB AT A POINT NEAREST THE BLASTS CAN IT KNOCK OUT THE ENTIRE ROBOT MECHANISM!
YOU'LL HAVE TIME FOR ONLY ONE TRY!!
2

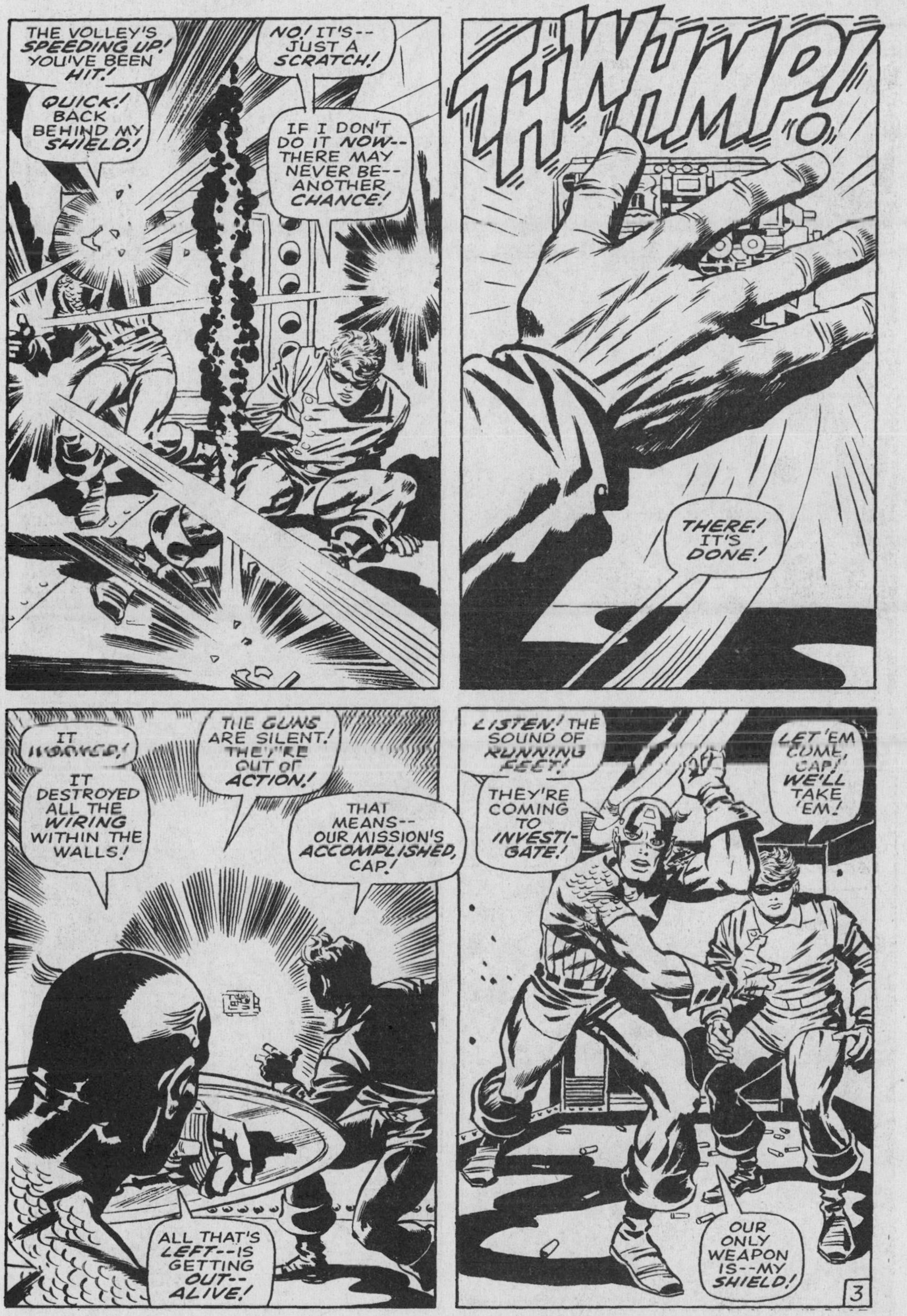
THE VOLLEY'S SPEEDING UP! YOU'VE BEEN HIT!
QUICK! BACK BEHIND MY SHIELD!
NO! IT'S-- JUST A SCRATCH!
IF I DON'T DO IT NOW-- THERE MAY NEVER BE-- ANOTHER CHANCE!
THWMP!
THERE! IT'S DONE!
IT
IT DESTROYED ALL THE WIRING WITHIN THE WALLS!
THE GUNS ARE SILENT! THEY'RE OUT OF ACTION!
THAT MEANS-- OUR MISSION'S ACCOMPLISHED, CAP!
ALL THAT'S LEFT--IS GETTING OUT-- ALIVE!
LISTEN! THE SOUND OF RUNNING FEET!
THEY'RE COMING TO INVESTI- GATE!
LET 'EM COME, CAP! WE'LL TAKE 'EM!
OUR ONLY WEAPON IS--MY SHIELD!
3

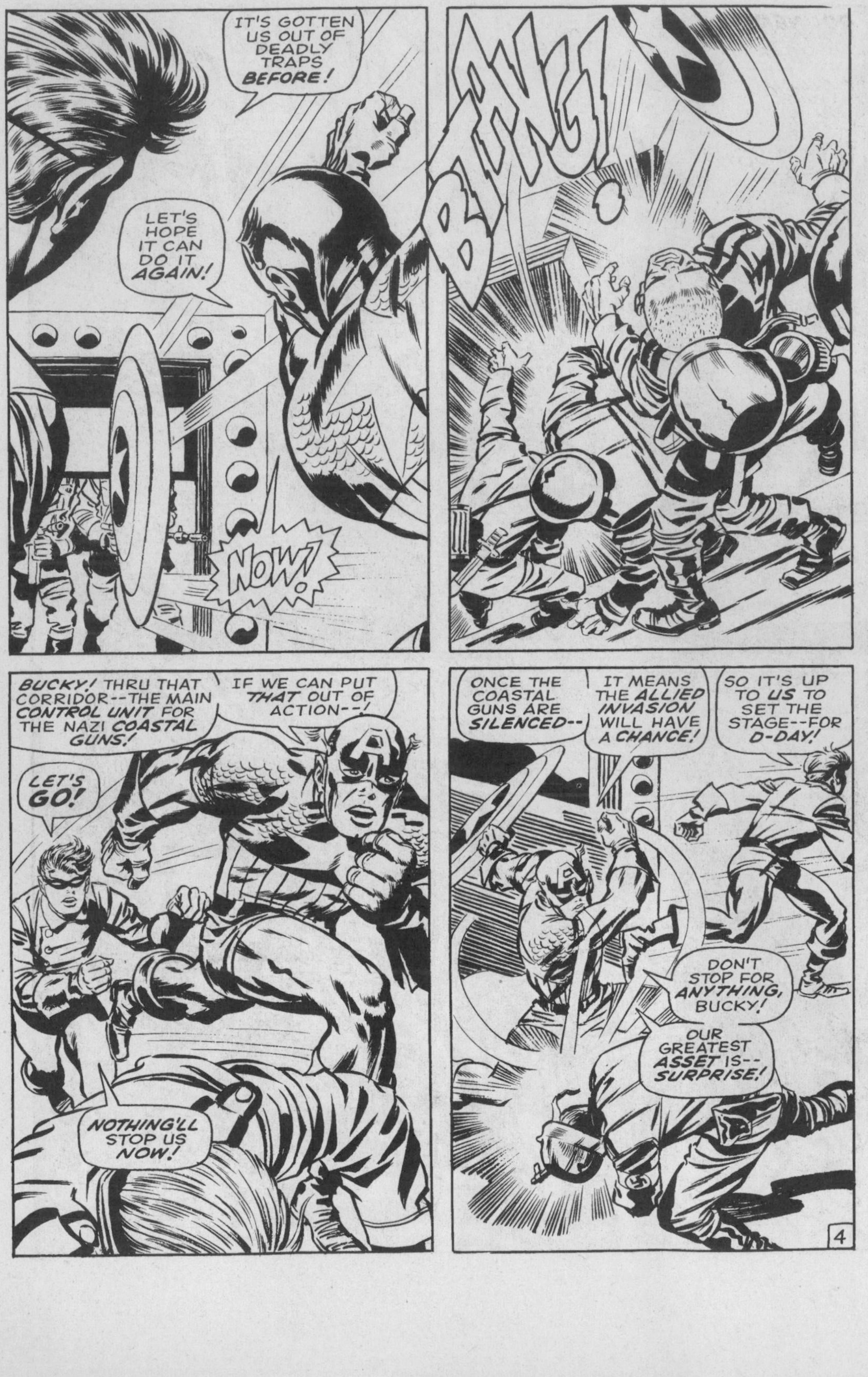

IT'S GOTTEN US OUT OF DEADLY TRAPS BEFORE!
LET'S HOPE IT CAN DO IT AGAIN!
NOW!
BTANG!
BUCKY! THRU THAT CORRIDOR--THE MAIN CONTROL UNIT FOR THE NAZI COASTAL GUNS!
IF WE CAN PUT THAT OUT OF ACTION--!
LET'S GO!
NOTHING'LL STOP US NOW!
ONCE THE COASTAL GUNS ARE SILENCED--
IT MEANS THE ALLIED INVASION WILL HAVE A CHANCE!
SO IT'S UP TO US TO SET THE STAGE--FOR D-DAY!
DON'T STOP FOR ANYTHING, BUCKY!
OUR GREATEST ASSET IS--SURPRISE!
4

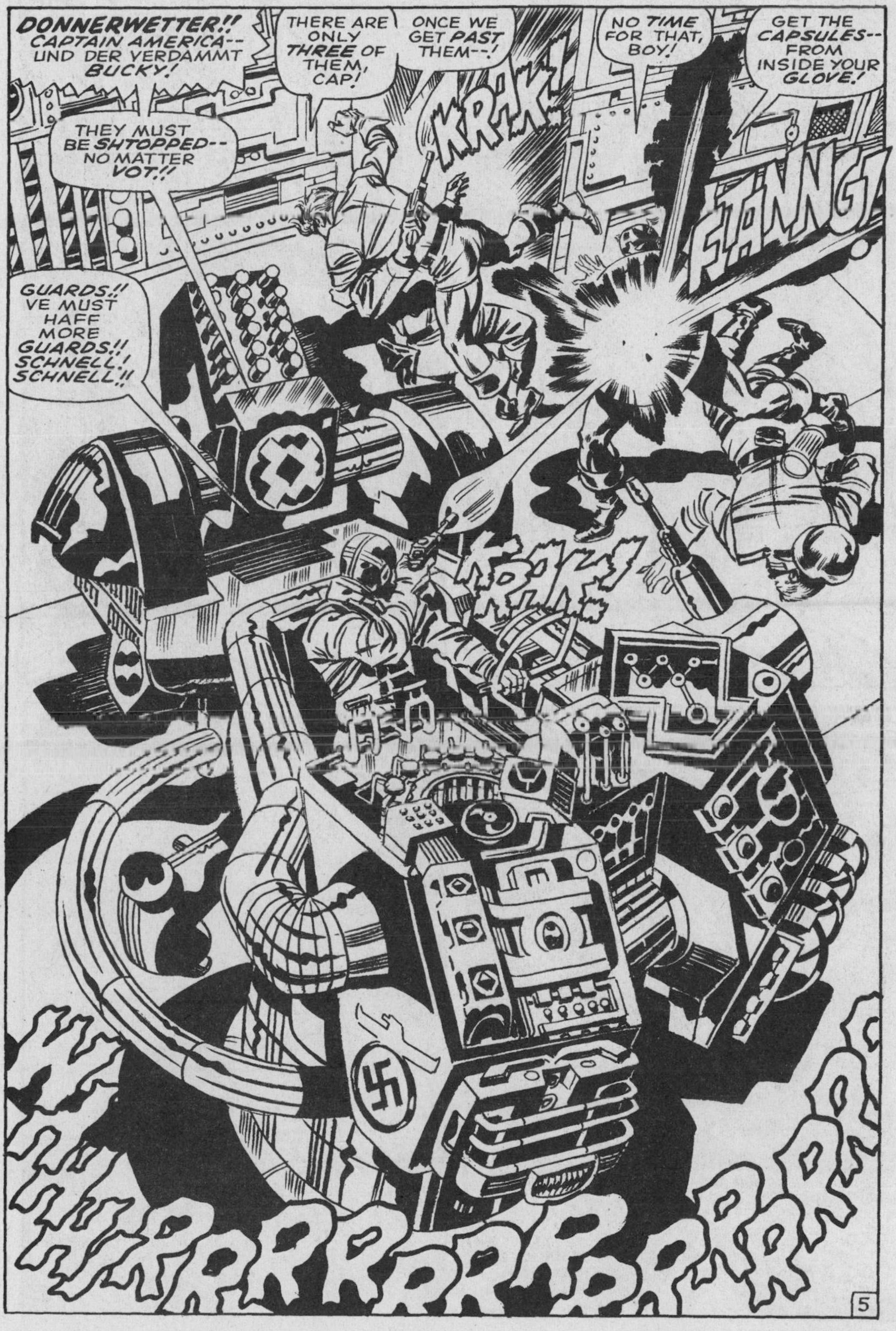

DONNERWETTER!! CAPTAIN AMERICA-- UND DER VERDAMMT BUCKY!
THEY MUST BE SHTOPPED-- NO MATTER VOT!!
THERE ARE ONLY THREE OF THEM, CAP!
ONCE WE GET PAST THEM--!
KRAK!
NO TIME FOR THAT, BOY!
GET THE CAPSULES-- FROM INSIDE YOUR GLOVE!
FTANNG!
GUARDS!! VE MUST HAFF MORE GUARDS!! SCHNELL! SCHNELL!!
KRAK!
WHIRRRRRRRRRRR

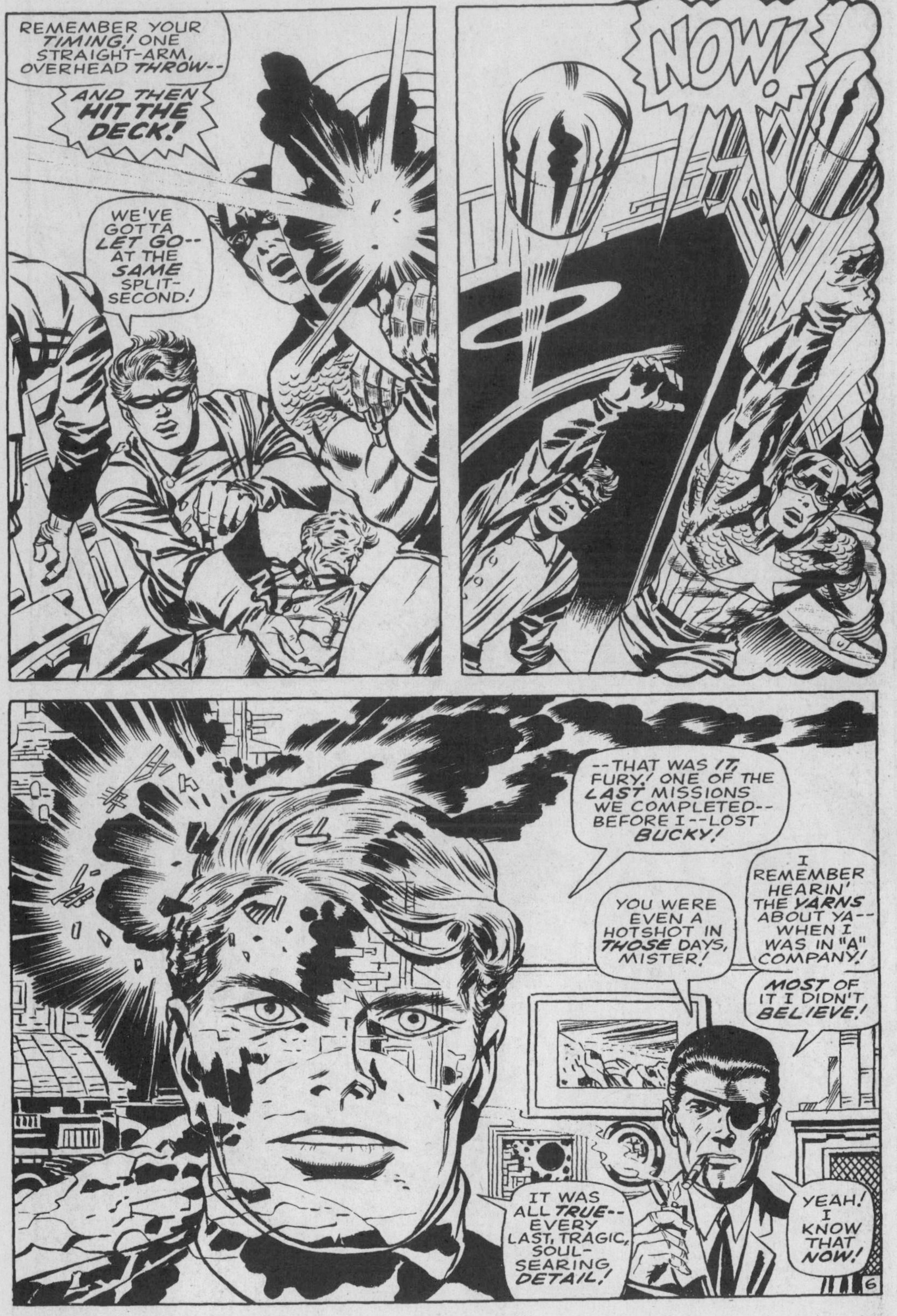
REMEMBER YOUR TIMING! ONE STRAIGHT-ARM, OVERHEAD THROW--
AND THEN HIT THE DECK!
WE'VE GOTTA LET GO-- AT THE SAME SPLIT-SECOND!
NOW!
--THAT WAS IT, FURY! ONE OF THE LAST MISSIONS WE COMPLETED-- BEFORE I--LOST BUCKY!
YOU WERE EVEN A HOTSHOT IN THOSE DAYS, MISTER!
I REMEMBER HEARIN' THE YARNS ABOUT YA-- WHEN I WAS IN "A" COMPANY!
MOST OF IT I DIDN'T BELIEVE!
IT WAS ALL TRUE-- EVERY LAST, TRAGIC, SOUL-SEARING DETAIL!
YEAH! I KNOW THAT NOW!
6

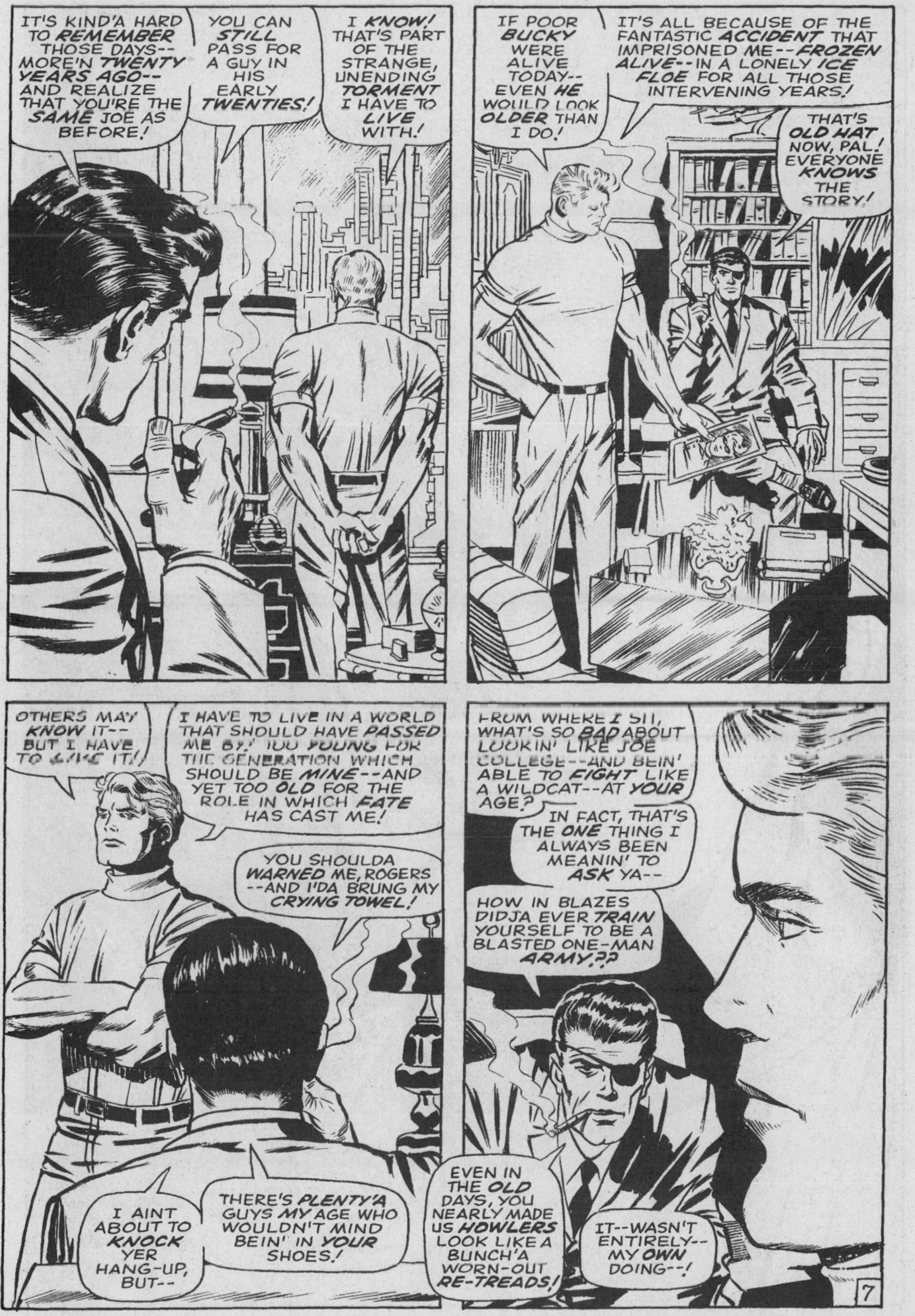
IT'S KIND'A HARD TO REMEMBER THOSE DAYS-- MORE'N TWENTY YEARS AGO-- AND REALIZE THAT YOU'RE THE SAME JOE AS BEFORE!
YOU CAN STILL PASS FOR A GUY IN HIS EARLY TWENTIES!
I KNOW! THAT'S PART OF THE STRANGE, UNENDING TORMENT I HAVE TO LIVE WITH!
IF POOR BUCKY WERE ALIVE TODAY-- EVEN HE WOULD LOOK OLDER THAN I DO!
IT'S ALL BECAUSE OF THE FANTASTIC ACCIDENT THAT IMPRISONED ME--FROZEN ALIVE--IN A LONELY ICE FLOE FOR ALL THOSE INTERVENING YEARS!
THAT'S OLD HAT NOW, PAL! EVERYONE KNOWS THE STORY!
OTHERS MAY KNOW IT-- BUT I HAVE TO LIVE IT!
I HAVE TO LIVE IN A WORLD THAT SHOULD HAVE PASSED ME BY! TOO YOUNG FOR THE GENERATION WHICH SHOULD BE MINE--AND YET TOO OLD FOR THE ROLE IN WHICH FATE HAS CAST ME!
YOU SHOULDA WARNED ME, ROGERS --AND I'DA BRUNG MY CRYING TOWEL!
I AINT ABOUT TO KNOCK YER HANG-UP, BUT--
THERE'S PLENTY'A GUYS MY AGE WHO WOULDN'T MIND BEIN' IN YOUR SHOES!
FROM WHERE I SIT, WHAT'S SO BAD ABOUT LOOKIN' LIKE JOE COLLEGE--AND BEIN' ABLE TO FIGHT LIKE A WILDCAT--AT YOUR AGE?
IN FACT, THAT'S THE ONE THING I ALWAYS BEEN MEANIN' TO ASK YA--
HOW IN BLAZES DIDJA EVER TRAIN YOURSELF TO BE A BLASTED ONE-MAN ARMY???
EVEN IN THE OLD DAYS, YOU NEARLY MADE US HOWLERS LOOK LIKE A BUNCH'A WORN-OUT RE-TREADS!
IT--WASN'T ENTIRELY-- MY OWN DOING--!
7

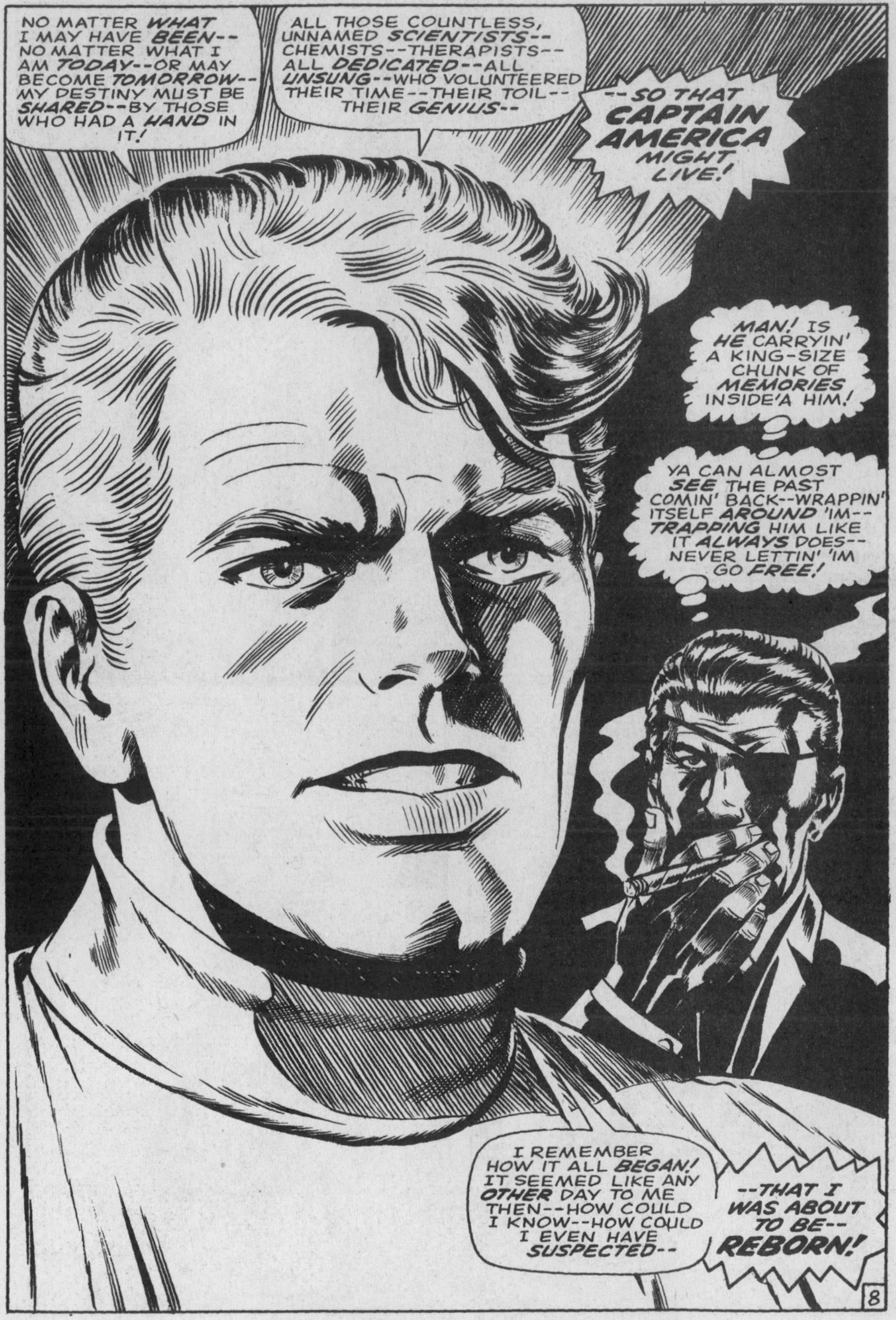
NO MATTER WHAT I MAY HAVE BEEN-- NO MATTER WHAT I AM TODAY--OR MAY BECOME TOMORROW-- MY DESTINY MUST BE SHARED--BY THOSE WHO HAD A HAND IN IT!
ALL THOSE COUNTLESS, UNNAMED SCIENTISTS-- CHEMISTS--THERAPISTS-- ALL DEDICATED--ALL UNSUNG--WHO VOLUNTEERED THEIR TIME--THEIR TOIL-- THEIR GENIUS--
--SO THAT CAPTAIN AMERICA MIGHT LIVE!
MAN! IS HE CARRYIN' A KING-SIZE CHUNK OF MEMORIES INSIDE'A HIM!
YA CAN ALMOST SEE THE PAST COMIN' BACK--WRAPPIN' ITSELF AROUND 'IM-- TRAPPING HIM LIKE IT ALWAYS DOES-- NEVER LETTIN' 'IM GO FREE!
I REMEMBER HOW IT ALL BEGAN! IT SEEMED LIKE ANY OTHER DAY TO ME THEN--HOW COULD I KNOW--HOW COULD I EVEN HAVE SUSPECTED--
--THAT I WAS ABOUT TO BE-- REBORN!
8

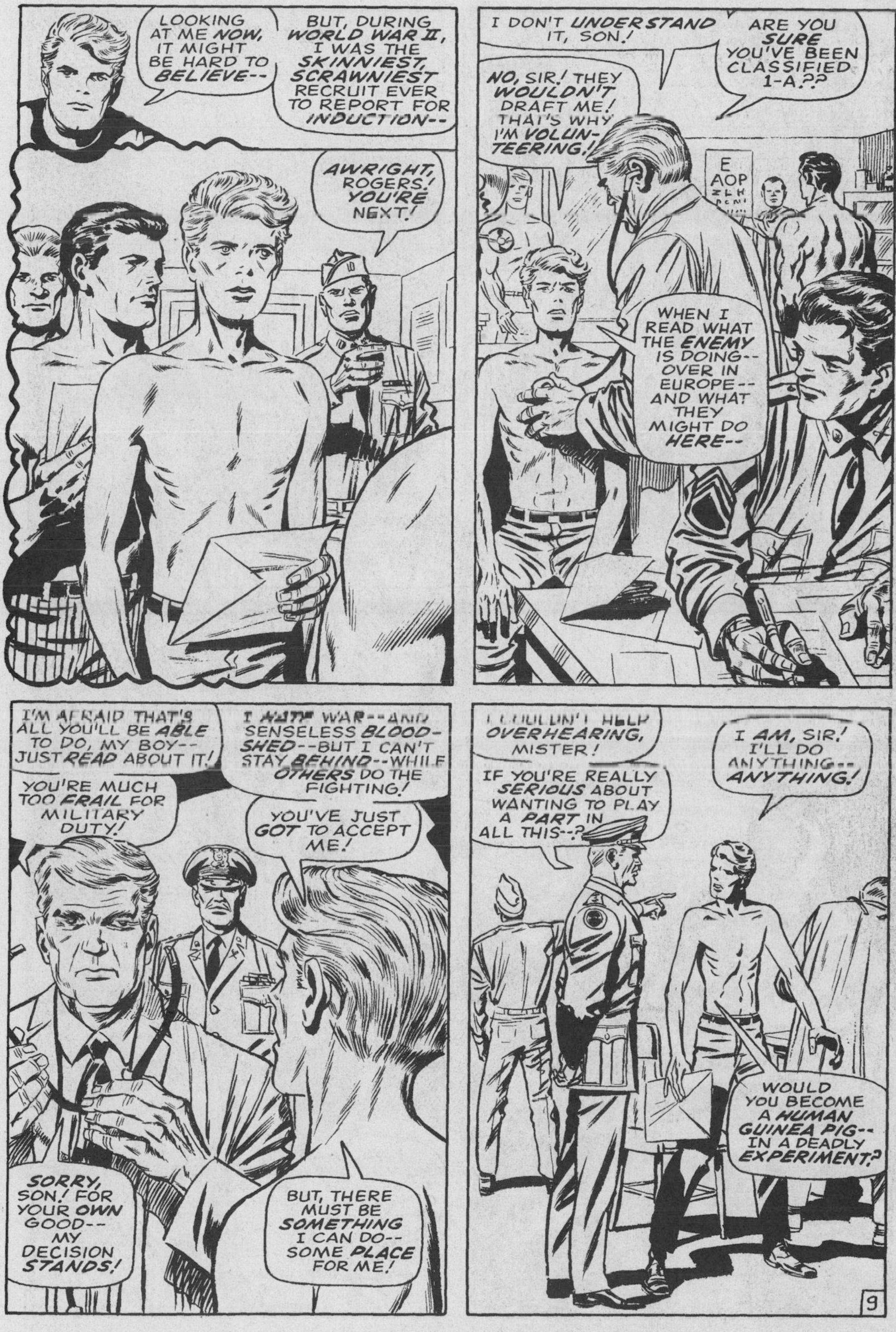
LOOKING AT ME NOW, IT MIGHT BE HARD TO BELIEVE--
BUT, DURING WORLD WAR II, I WAS THE SKINNIEST, SCRAWNIEST RECRUIT EVER TO REPORT FOR INDUCTION--
AWRIGHT, ROGERS! YOU'RE NEXT!
I DON'T UNDERSTAND IT, SON!
ARE YOU SURE YOU'VE BEEN CLASSIFIED 1-A??
NO, SIR! THEY WOULDN'T DRAFT ME! THAT'S WHY I'M VOLUN-TEERING!
WHEN I READ WHAT THE ENEMY IS DOING--OVER IN EUROPE--AND WHAT THEY MIGHT DO HERE--
I'M AFRAID THAT'S ALL YOU'LL BE ABLE TO DO, MY BOY--JUST READ ABOUT IT!
YOU'RE MUCH TOO FRAIL FOR MILITARY DUTY!
I HATE WAR--AND SENSELESS BLOOD-SHED--BUT I CAN'T STAY BEHIND--WHILE OTHERS DO THE FIGHTING!
YOU'VE JUST GOT TO ACCEPT ME!
SORRY, SON! FOR YOUR OWN GOOD--MY DECISION STANDS!
BUT, THERE MUST BE SOMETHING I CAN DO--SOME PLACE FOR ME!
I COULDN'T HELP OVERHEARING, MISTER!
IF YOU'RE REALLY SERIOUS ABOUT WANTING TO PLAY A PART IN ALL THIS--?
I AM, SIR! I'LL DO ANYTHING--ANYTHING!
WOULD YOU BECOME A HUMAN GUINEA PIG--IN A DEADLY EXPERIMENT?

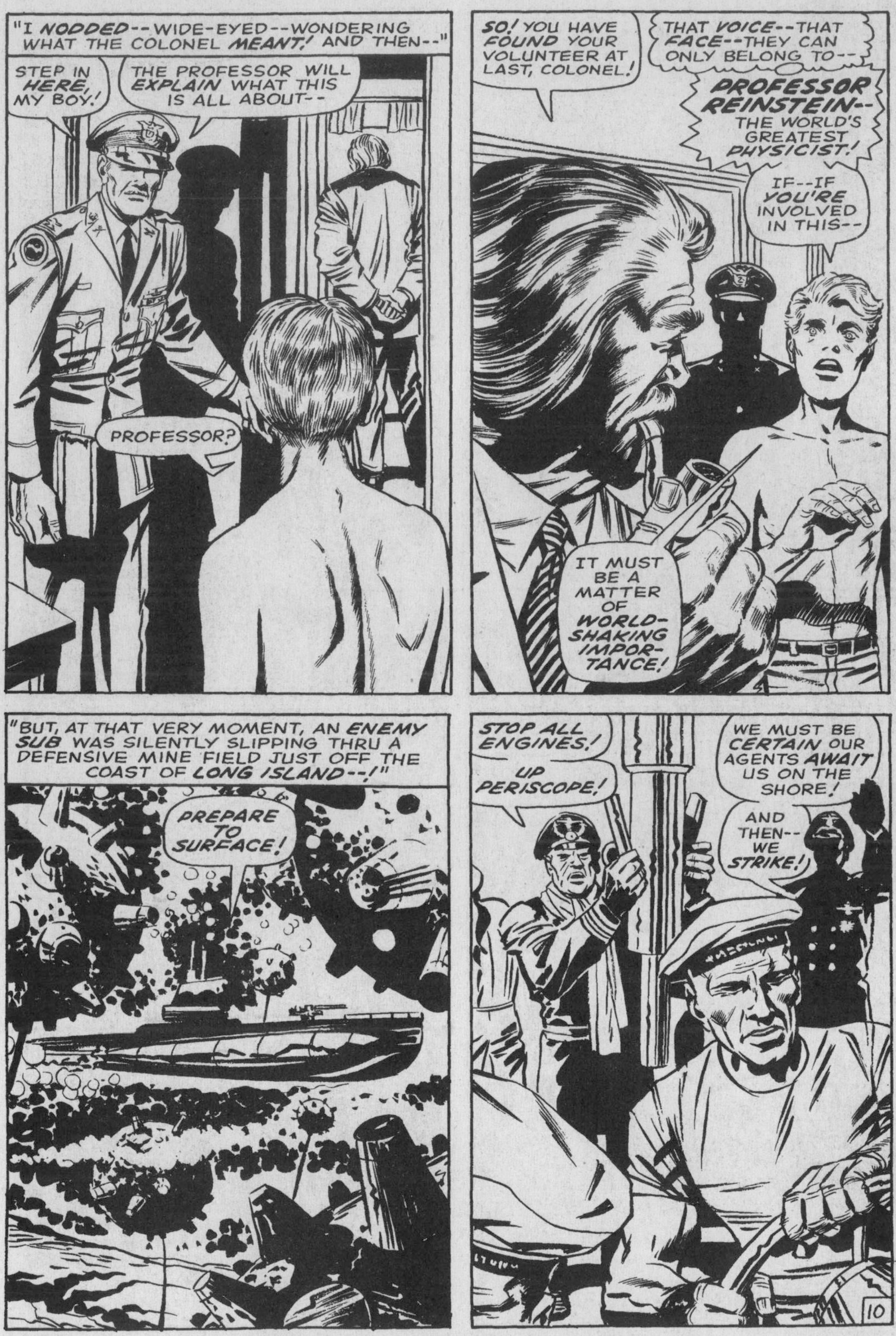

"I NODDED--WIDE-EYED--WONDERING WHAT THE COLONEL MEANT! AND THEN--"
STEP IN HERE, MY BOY!
THE PROFESSOR WILL EXPLAIN WHAT THIS IS ALL ABOUT--
PROFESSOR?
SO! YOU HAVE FOUND YOUR VOLUNTEER AT LAST, COLONEL!
THAT VOICE--THAT FACE--THEY CAN ONLY BELONG TO--
PROFESSOR REINSTEIN--THE WORLD'S GREATEST PHYSICIST!
IF--IF YOU'RE INVOLVED IN THIS--
IT MUST BE A MATTER OF WORLD-SHAKING IMPORTANCE!
"BUT, AT THAT VERY MOMENT, AN ENEMY SUB WAS SILENTLY SLIPPING THRU A DEFENSIVE MINE FIELD JUST OFF THE COAST OF LONG ISLAND--!"
PREPARE TO SURFACE!
STOP ALL ENGINES!
UP PERISCOPE!
WE MUST BE CERTAIN OUR AGENTS AWAIT US ON THE SHORE!
AND THEN--WE STRIKE!
10

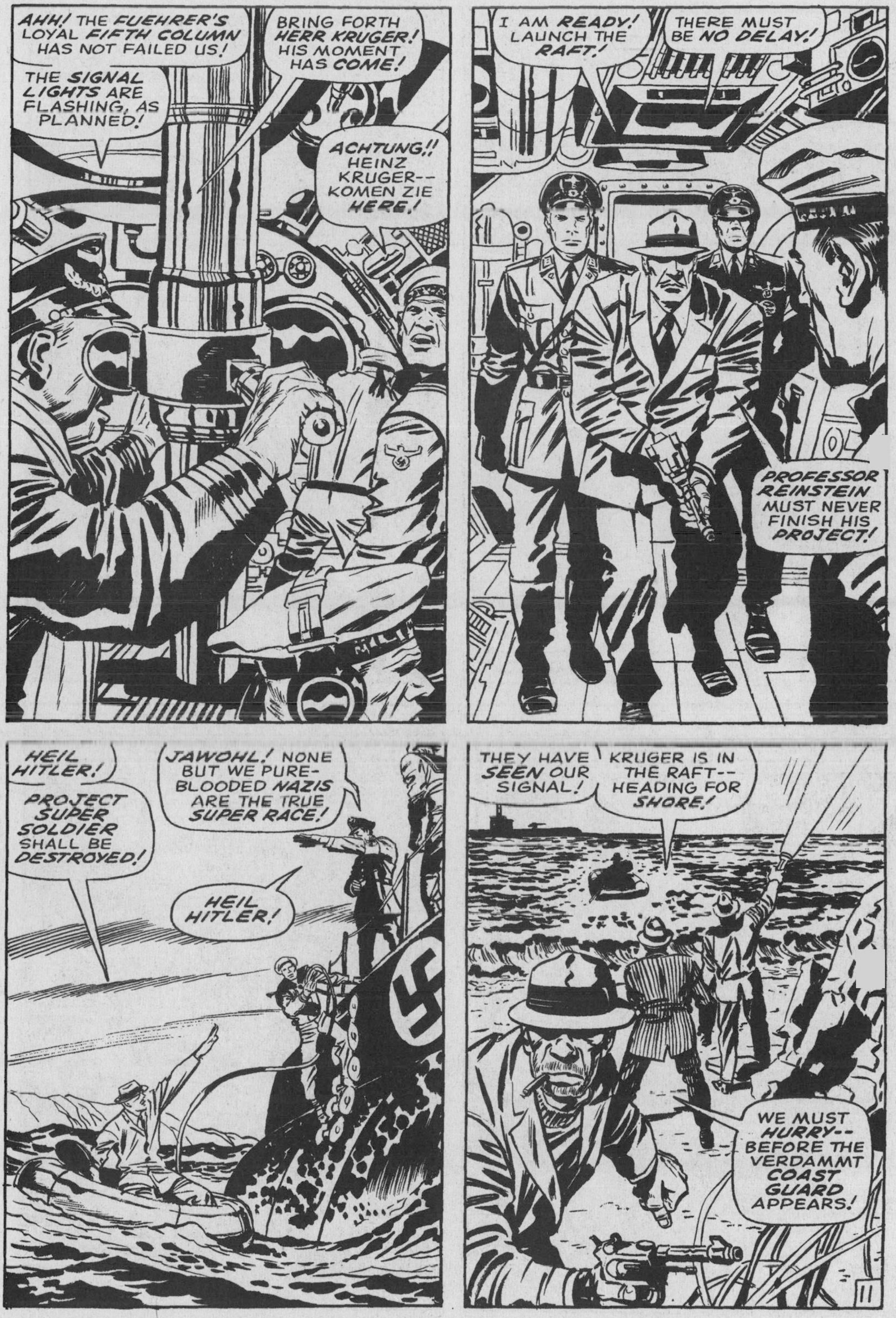
AHH! THE FUEHRER'S LOYAL FIFTH COLUMN HAS NOT FAILED US!
THE SIGNAL LIGHTS ARE FLASHING, AS PLANNED!
BRING FORTH HERR KRUGER! HIS MOMENT HAS COME!
ACHTUNG!! HEINZ KRUGER-- KOMEN ZIE HERE!
I AM READY! LAUNCH THE RAFT!
THERE MUST BE NO DELAY!
PROFESSOR REINSTEIN MUST NEVER FINISH HIS PROJECT!
HEIL HITLER!
PROJECT SUPER SOLDIER SHALL BE DESTROYED!
JAWOHL! NONE BUT WE PURE-BLOODED NAZIS ARE THE TRUE SUPER RACE!
HEIL HITLER!
THEY HAVE SEEN OUR SIGNAL!
KRUGER IS IN THE RAFT-- HEADING FOR SHORE!
WE MUST HURRY-- BEFORE THE VERDAMMT COAST GUARD APPEARS!
11

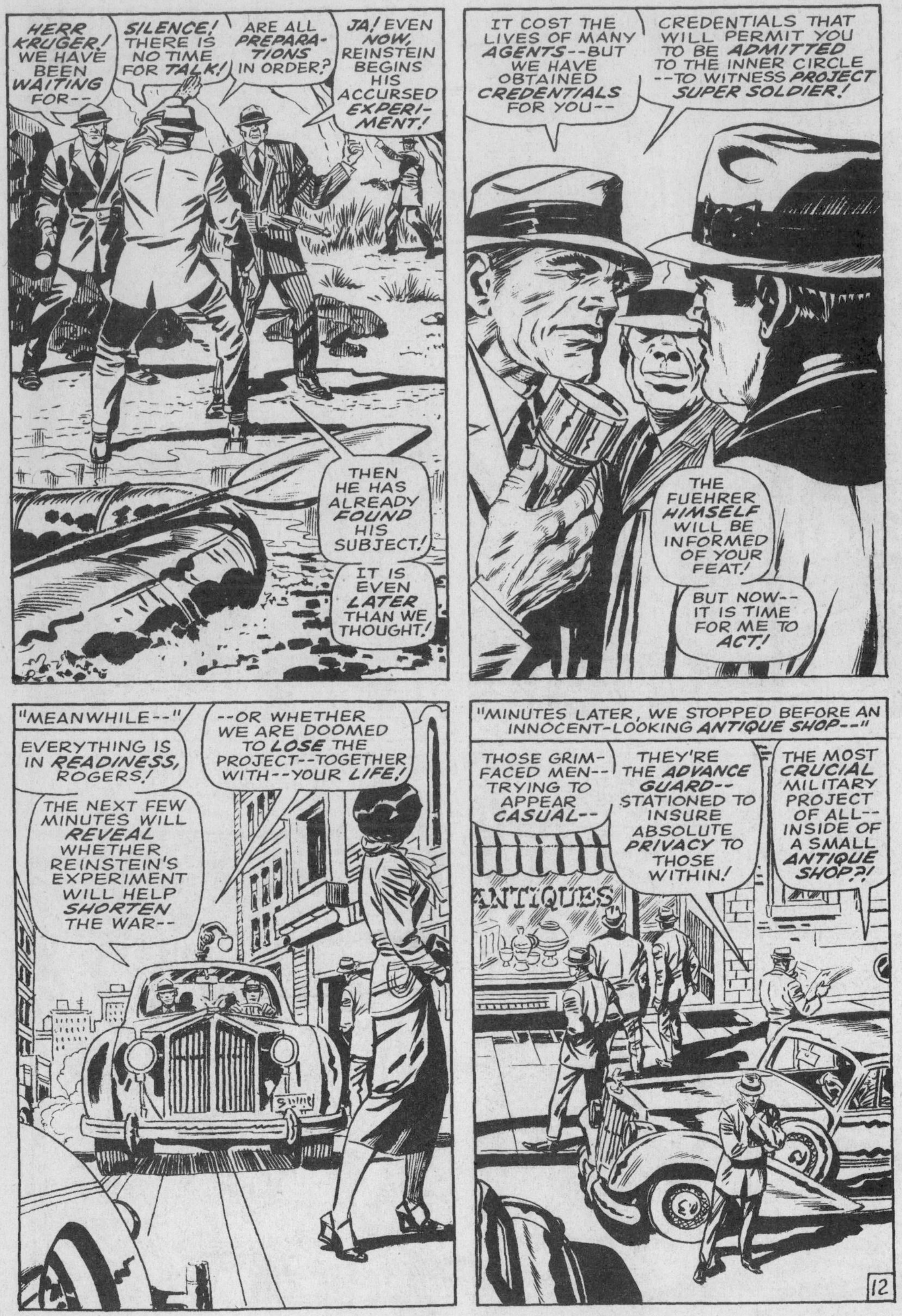
HERR KRUGER! WE HAVE BEEN WAITING FOR--
SILENCE! THERE IS NO TIME FOR TALK!
ARE ALL PREPARATIONS IN ORDER?
JA! EVEN NOW, REINSTEIN BEGINS HIS ACCURSED EXPERIMENT!
THEN HE HAS ALREADY FOUND HIS SUBJECT!
IT IS EVEN LATER THAN WE THOUGHT!
IT COST THE LIVES OF MANY AGENTS--BUT WE HAVE OBTAINED CREDENTIALS FOR YOU--
CREDENTIALS THAT WILL PERMIT YOU TO BE ADMITTED TO THE INNER CIRCLE --TO WITNESS PROJECT SUPER SOLDIER!
THE FUEHRER HIMSELF WILL BE INFORMED OF YOUR FEAT!
BUT NOW-- IT IS TIME FOR ME TO ACT!
"MEANWHILE--"
EVERYTHING IS IN READINESS, ROGERS!
THE NEXT FEW MINUTES WILL REVEAL WHETHER REINSTEIN'S EXPERIMENT WILL HELP SHORTEN THE WAR--
--OR WHETHER WE ARE DOOMED TO LOSE THE PROJECT--TOGETHER WITH--YOUR LIFE!
"MINUTES LATER, WE STOPPED BEFORE AN INNOCENT-LOOKING ANTIQUE SHOP--"
THOSE GRIM-FACED MEN--TRYING TO APPEAR CASUAL--
THEY'RE THE ADVANCE GUARD--STATIONED TO INSURE ABSOLUTE PRIVACY TO THOSE WITHIN!
THE MOST CRUCIAL MILITARY PROJECT OF ALL--INSIDE OF A SMALL ANTIQUE SHOP?!
ANTIQUES
12

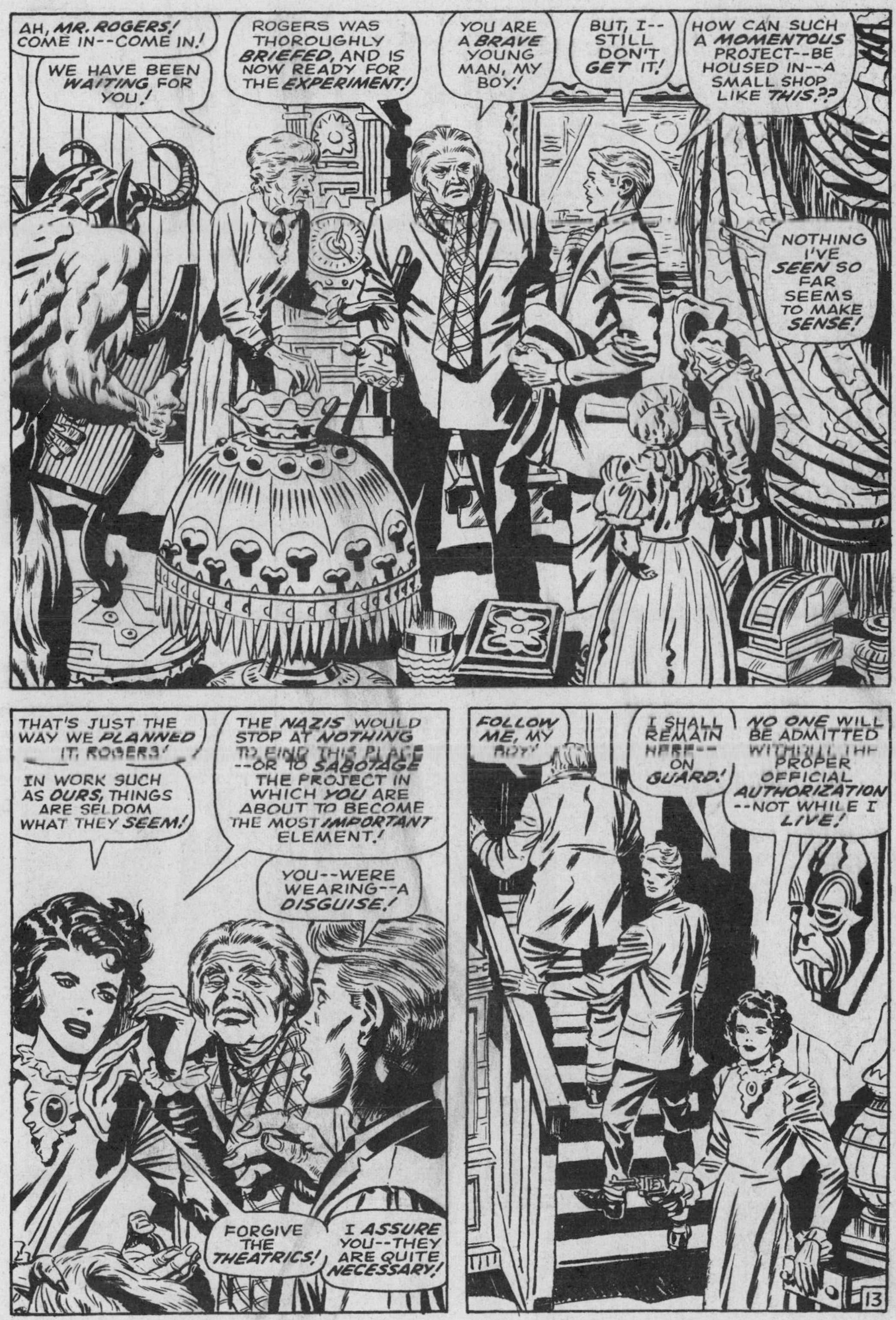
AH, MR. ROGERS! COME IN--COME IN!
WE HAVE BEEN WAITING FOR YOU!
ROGERS WAS THOROUGHLY BRIEFED, AND IS NOW READY FOR THE EXPERIMENT!
YOU ARE A BRAVE YOUNG MAN, MY BOY!
BUT, I-- STILL DON'T GET IT!
HOW CAN SUCH A MOMENTOUS PROJECT--BE HOUSED IN--A SMALL SHOP LIKE THIS??
NOTHING I'VE SEEN SO FAR SEEMS TO MAKE SENSE!
THAT'S JUST THE WAY WE PLANNED IT, ROGERS!
IN WORK SUCH AS OURS, THINGS ARE SELDOM WHAT THEY SEEM!
THE NAZIS WOULD STOP AT NOTHING TO FIND THIS PLACE --OR TO SABOTAGE THE PROJECT IN WHICH YOU ARE ABOUT TO BECOME THE MOST IMPORTANT ELEMENT!
YOU--WERE WEARING--A DISGUISE!
FORGIVE THE THEATRICS!
I ASSURE YOU--THEY ARE QUITE NECESSARY!
FOLLOW ME, MY BOY!
I SHALL REMAIN HERE-- ON GUARD!
NO ONE WILL BE ADMITTED WITHOUT THE PROPER OFFICIAL AUTHORIZATION --NOT WHILE I LIVE!
13

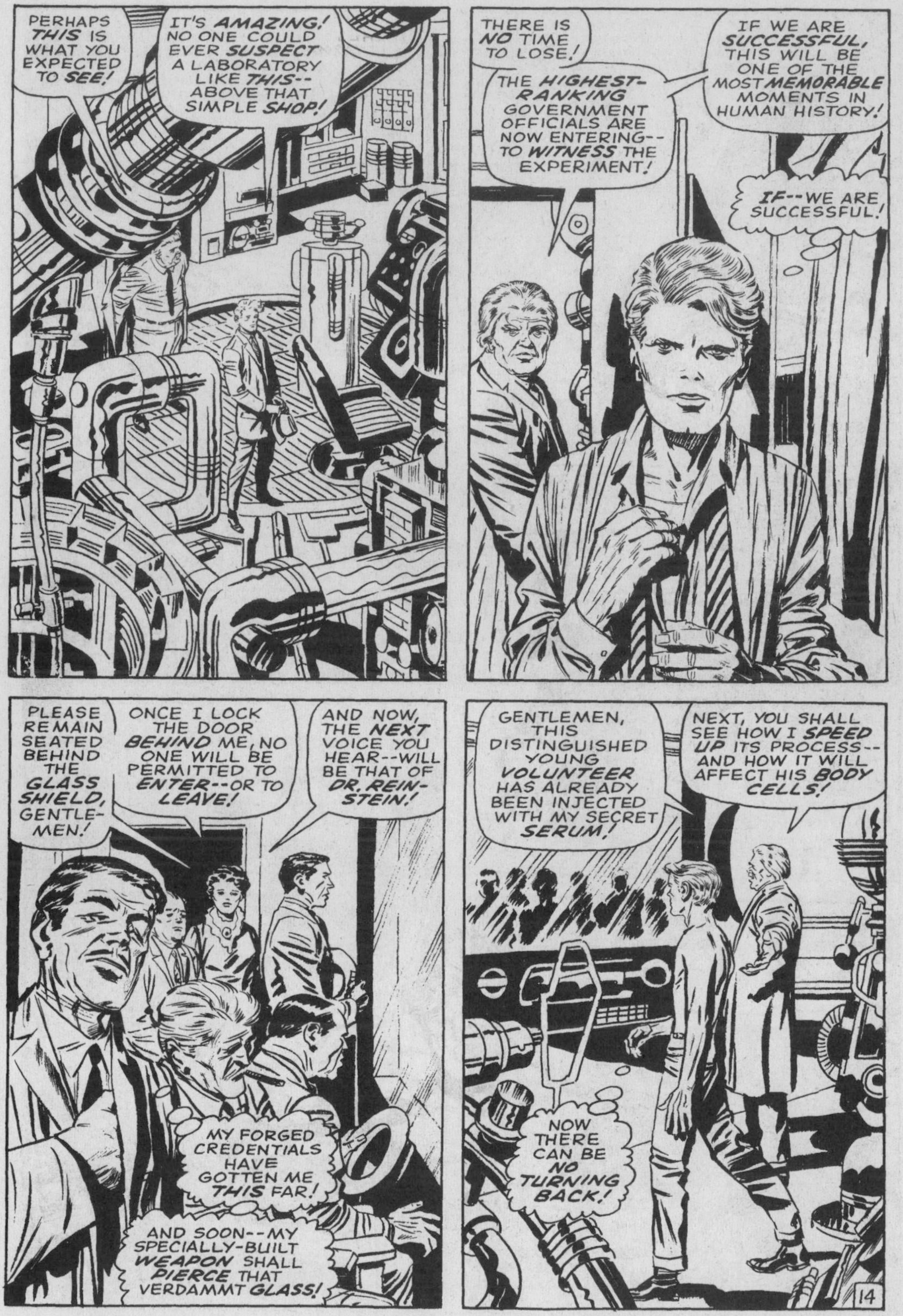
PERHAPS THIS IS WHAT YOU EXPECTED TO SEE!
IT'S AMAZING! NO ONE COULD EVER SUSPECT A LABORATORY LIKE THIS-- ABOVE THAT SIMPLE SHOP!
THERE IS NO TIME TO LOSE!
THE HIGHEST-RANKING GOVERNMENT OFFICIALS ARE NOW ENTERING-- TO WITNESS THE EXPERIMENT!
IF WE ARE SUCCESSFUL, THIS WILL BE ONE OF THE MOST MEMORABLE MOMENTS IN HUMAN HISTORY!
IF--WE ARE SUCCESSFUL!
PLEASE REMAIN SEATED BEHIND THE GLASS SHIELD, GENTLEMEN!
ONCE I LOCK THE DOOR BEHIND ME, NO ONE WILL BE PERMITTED TO ENTER--OR TO LEAVE!
AND NOW, THE NEXT VOICE YOU HEAR--WILL BE THAT OF DR. REINSTEIN!
MY FORGED CREDENTIALS HAVE GOTTEN ME THIS FAR!
AND SOON--MY SPECIALLY-BUILT WEAPON SHALL PIERCE THAT VERDAMMT GLASS!
GENTLEMEN, THIS DISTINGUISHED YOUNG VOLUNTEER HAS ALREADY BEEN INJECTED WITH MY SECRET SERUM!
NEXT, YOU SHALL SEE HOW I SPEED UP ITS PROCESS-- AND HOW IT WILL AFFECT HIS BODY CELLS!
NOW THERE CAN BE NO TURNING BACK!
14

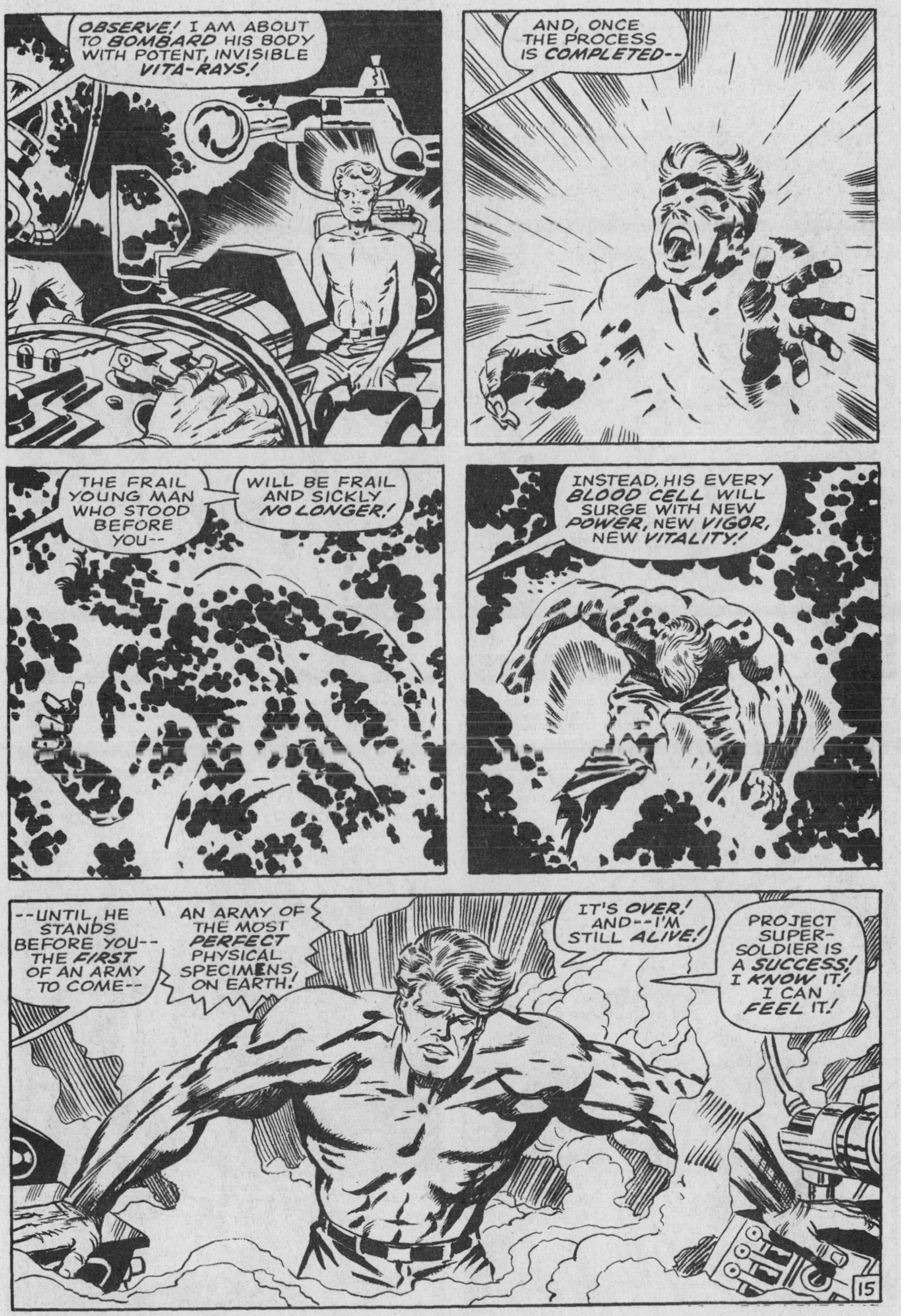
OBSERVE! I AM ABOUT TO BOMBARD HIS BODY WITH POTENT, INVISIBLE VITA-RAYS!
AND, ONCE THE PROCESS IS COMPLETED--
THE FRAIL YOUNG MAN WHO STOOD BEFORE YOU--
WILL BE FRAIL AND SICKLY NO LONGER!
INSTEAD, HIS EVERY BLOOD CELL WILL SURGE WITH NEW POWER, NEW VIGOR, NEW VITALITY!
--UNTIL HE STANDS BEFORE YOU-- THE FIRST OF AN ARMY TO COME--
AN ARMY OF THE MOST PERFECT PHYSICAL SPECIMENS ON EARTH!
IT'S OVER! AND--I'M STILL ALIVE!
PROJECT SUPER-SOLDIER IS A SUCCESS! I KNOW IT! I CAN FEEL IT!
15

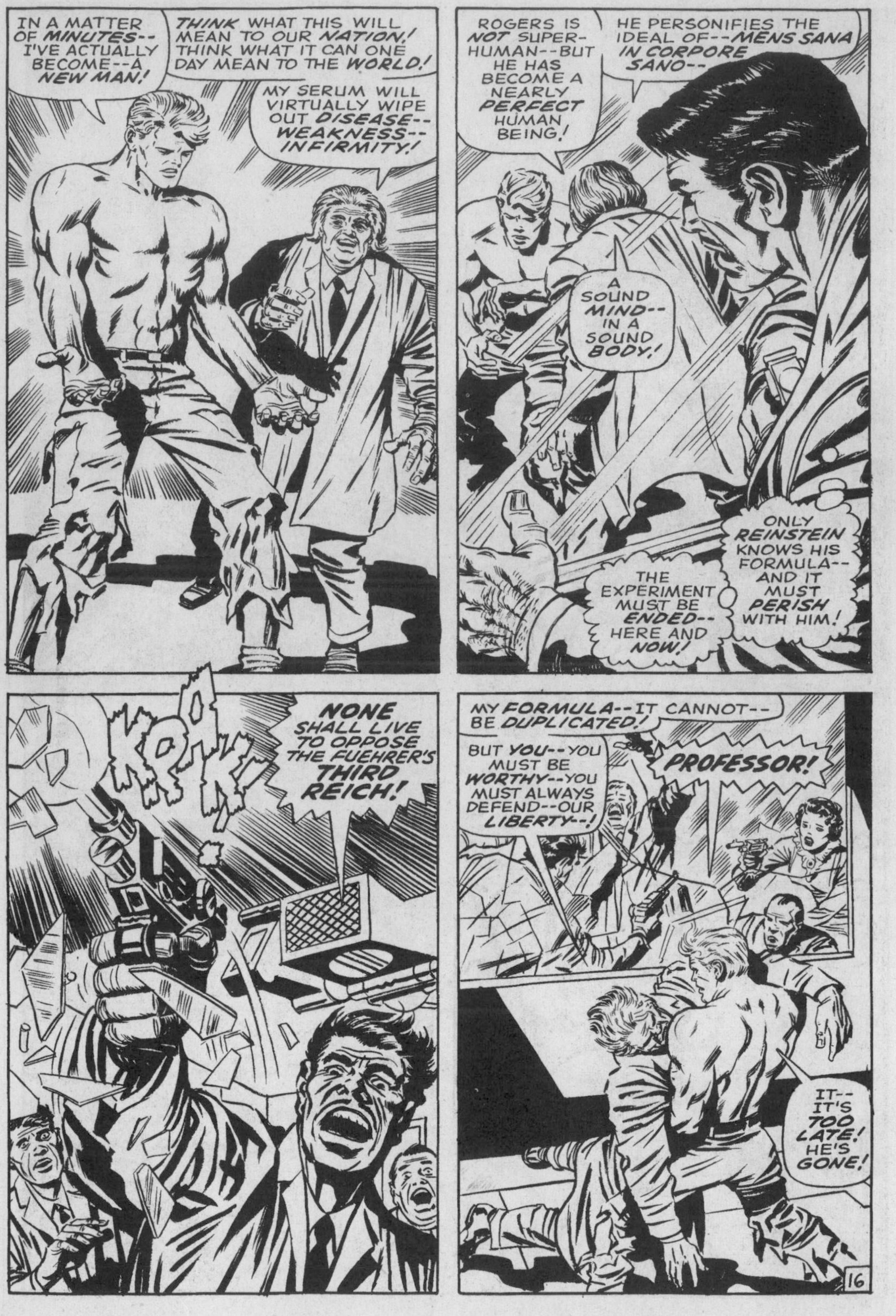
IN A MATTER OF MINUTES-- I'VE ACTUALLY BECOME--A NEW MAN!
THINK WHAT THIS WILL MEAN TO OUR NATION! THINK WHAT IT CAN ONE DAY MEAN TO THE WORLD!
MY SERUM WILL VIRTUALLY WIPE OUT DISEASE-- WEAKNESS-- INFIRMITY!
ROGERS IS NOT SUPER-HUMAN--BUT HE HAS BECOME A NEARLY PERFECT HUMAN BEING!
HE PERSONIFIES THE IDEAL OF--MENS SANA IN CORPORE SANO--
A SOUND MIND-- IN A SOUND BODY!
ONLY REINSTEIN KNOWS HIS FORMULA-- AND IT MUST PERISH WITH HIM!
THE EXPERIMENT MUST BE ENDED-- HERE AND NOW!
KRAK!
NONE SHALL LIVE TO OPPOSE THE FUEHRER'S THIRD REICH!
MY FORMULA--IT CANNOT--BE DUPLICATED!
BUT YOU--YOU MUST BE WORTHY--YOU MUST ALWAYS DEFEND--OUR LIBERTY--!
PROFESSOR!
IT-- IT'S TOO LATE! HE'S GONE!
16

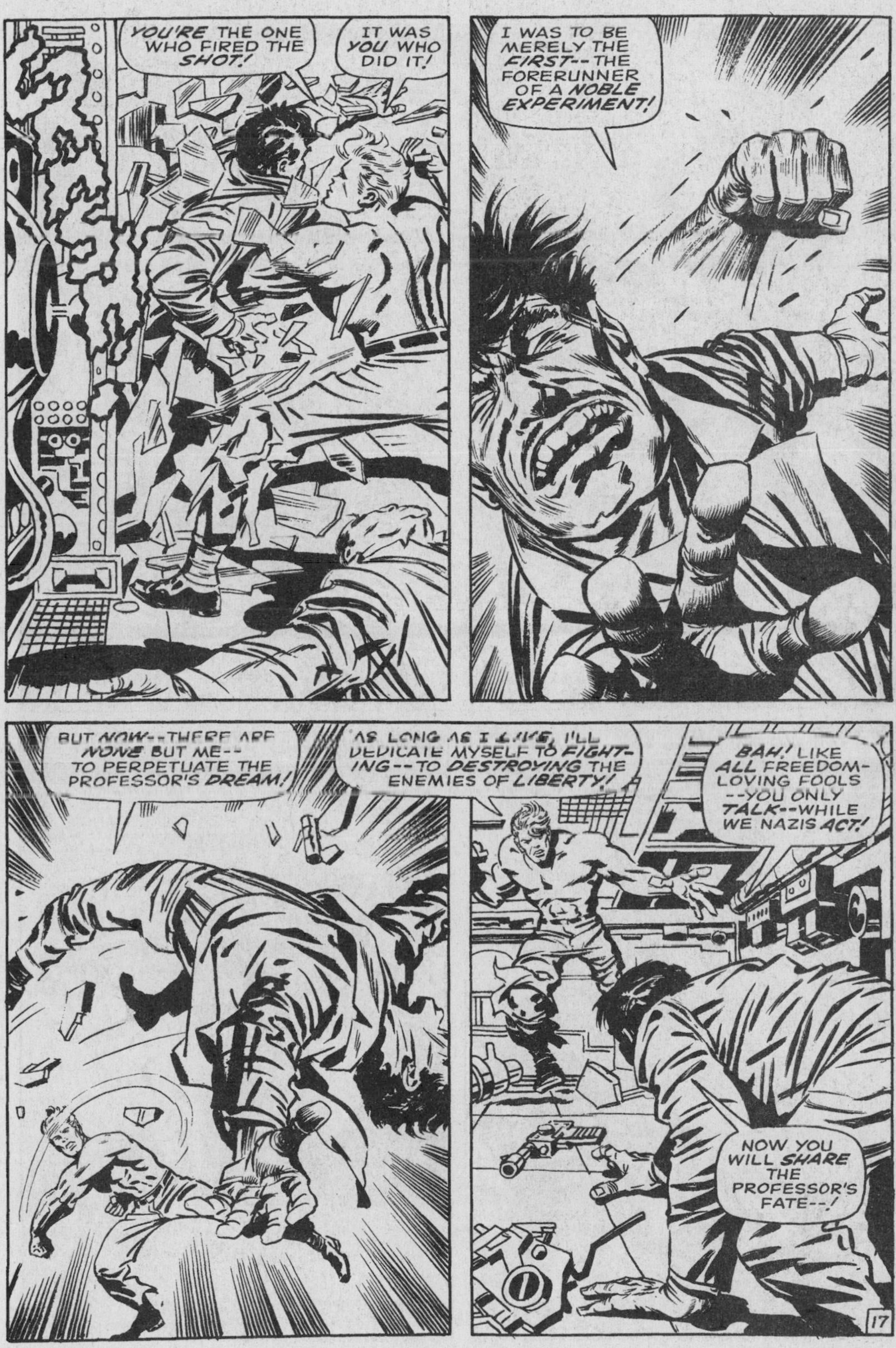
YOU'RE THE ONE WHO FIRED THE SHOT!
IT WAS YOU WHO DID IT!
I WAS TO BE MERELY THE FIRST-- THE FORERUNNER OF A NOBLE EXPERIMENT!
BUT NOW--THERE ARE NONE BUT ME-- TO PERPETUATE THE PROFESSOR'S DREAM!
AS LONG AS I LIKE, I'LL DEDICATE MYSELF TO FIGHTING--TO DESTROYING THE ENEMIES OF LIBERTY!
BAH! LIKE ALL FREEDOM-LOVING FOOLS --YOU ONLY TALK--WHILE WE NAZIS ACT!
NOW YOU WILL SHARE THE PROFESSOR'S FATE--!

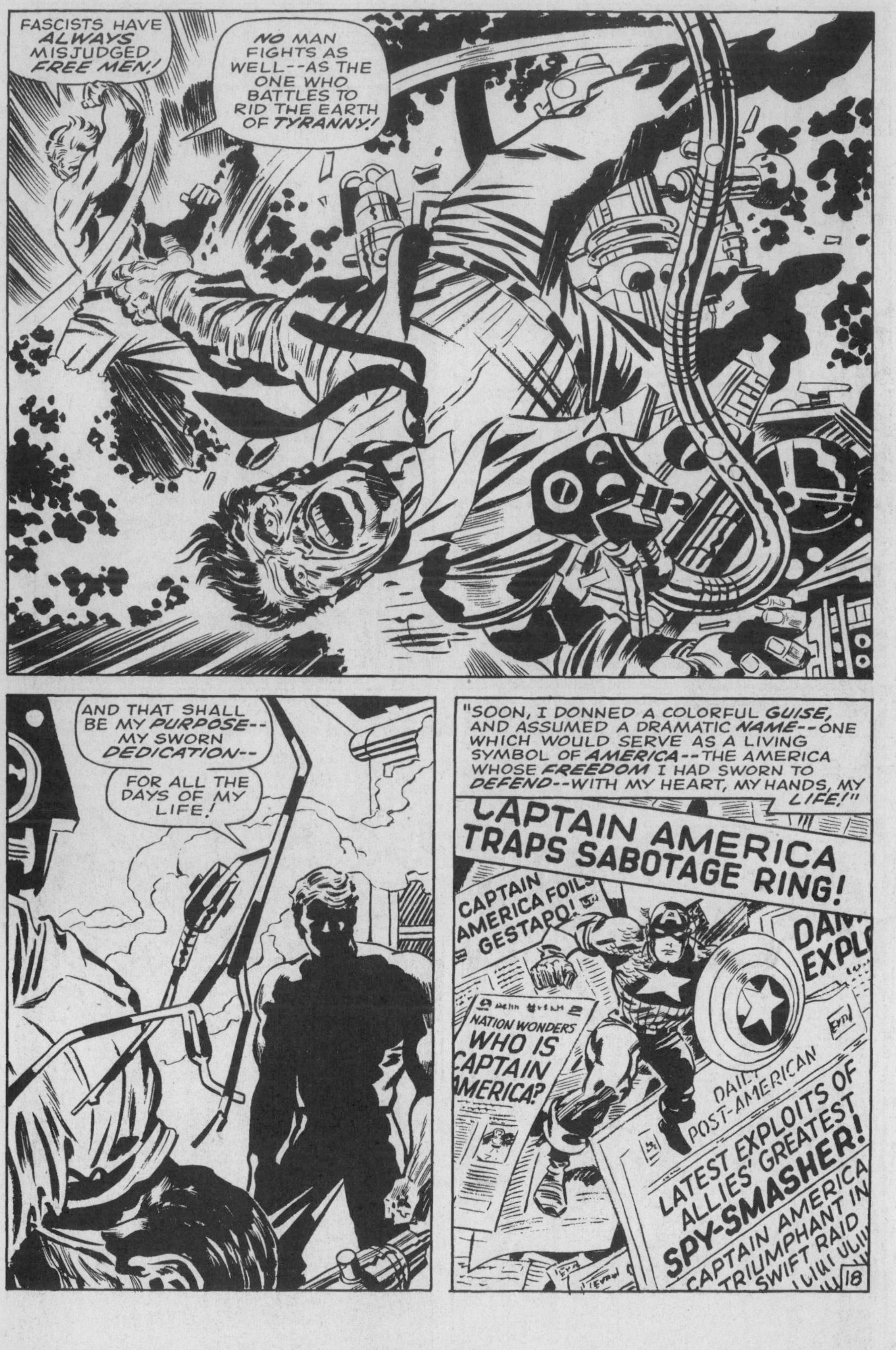
FASCISTS HAVE ALWAYS MISJUDGED FREE MEN!
NO MAN FIGHTS AS WELL--AS THE ONE WHO BATTLES TO RID THE EARTH OF TYRANNY!
AND THAT SHALL BE MY PURPOSE-- MY SWORN DEDICATION--
FOR ALL THE DAYS OF MY LIFE!
"SOON, I DONNED A COLORFUL GUISE, AND ASSUMED A DRAMATIC NAME--ONE WHICH WOULD SERVE AS A LIVING SYMBOL OF AMERICA--THE AMERICA WHOSE FREEDOM I HAD SWORN TO DEFEND--WITH MY HEART, MY HANDS, MY LIFE!"
CAPTAIN AMERICA TRAPS SABOTAGE RING!
CAPTAIN AMERICA FOILS GESTAPO!
NATION WONDERS WHO IS CAPTAIN AMERICA?
DAILY POST-AMERICAN
LATEST EXPLOITS OF ALLIES' GREATEST SPY-SMASHER!
CAPTAIN AMERICA TRIUMPHANT IN SWIFT RAID
18

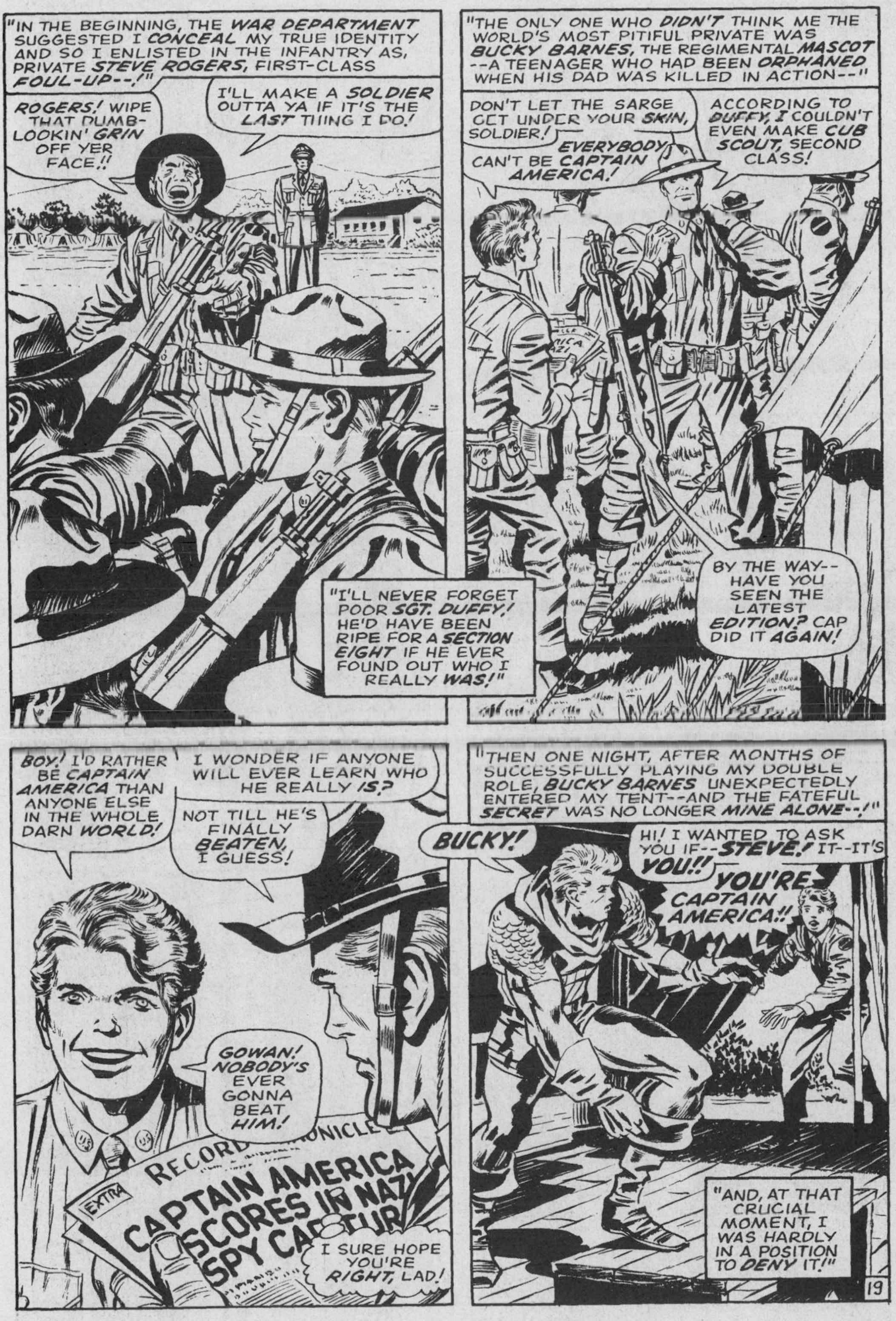
"IN THE BEGINNING, THE WAR DEPARTMENT SUGGESTED I CONCEAL MY TRUE IDENTITY AND SO I ENLISTED IN THE INFANTRY AS, PRIVATE STEVE ROGERS, FIRST-CLASS FOUL-UP--!"
I'LL MAKE A SOLDIER OUTTA YA IF IT'S THE LAST THING I DO!
ROGERS! WIPE THAT DUMB-LOOKIN' GRIN OFF YER FACE!!
"I'LL NEVER FORGET POOR SGT. DUFFY! HE'D HAVE BEEN RIPE FOR A SECTION EIGHT IF HE EVER FOUND OUT WHO I REALLY WAS!"
"THE ONLY ONE WHO DIDN'T THINK ME THE WORLD'S MOST PITIFUL PRIVATE WAS BUCKY BARNES, THE REGIMENTAL MASCOT --A TEENAGER WHO HAD BEEN ORPHANED WHEN HIS DAD WAS KILLED IN ACTION--"
DON'T LET THE SARGE GET UNDER YOUR SKIN, SOLDIER! EVERYBODY CAN'T BE CAPTAIN AMERICA!
ACCORDING TO DUFFY, I COULDN'T EVEN MAKE CUB SCOUT, SECOND CLASS!
BY THE WAY--HAVE YOU SEEN THE LATEST EDITION? CAP DID IT AGAIN!
BOY! I'D RATHER BE CAPTAIN AMERICA THAN ANYONE ELSE IN THE WHOLE DARN WORLD!
I WONDER IF ANYONE WILL EVER LEARN WHO HE REALLY IS?
NOT TILL HE'S FINALLY BEATEN, I GUESS!
GOWAN! NOBODY'S EVER GONNA BEAT HIM!
RECORD
EXTRA
CAPTAIN AMERICA SCORES IN NAZ SPY CAPTUR
I SURE HOPE YOU'RE RIGHT, LAD!
"THEN ONE NIGHT, AFTER MONTHS OF SUCCESSFULLY PLAYING MY DOUBLE ROLE, BUCKY BARNES UNEXPECTEDLY ENTERED MY TENT--AND THE FATEFUL SECRET WAS NO LONGER MINE ALONE--!"
BUCKY!
HI! I WANTED TO ASK YOU IF--STEVE! IT--IT'S YOU!! YOU'RE CAPTAIN AMERICA!!
"AND, AT THAT CRUCIAL MOMENT, I WAS HARDLY IN A POSITION TO DENY IT!"
19

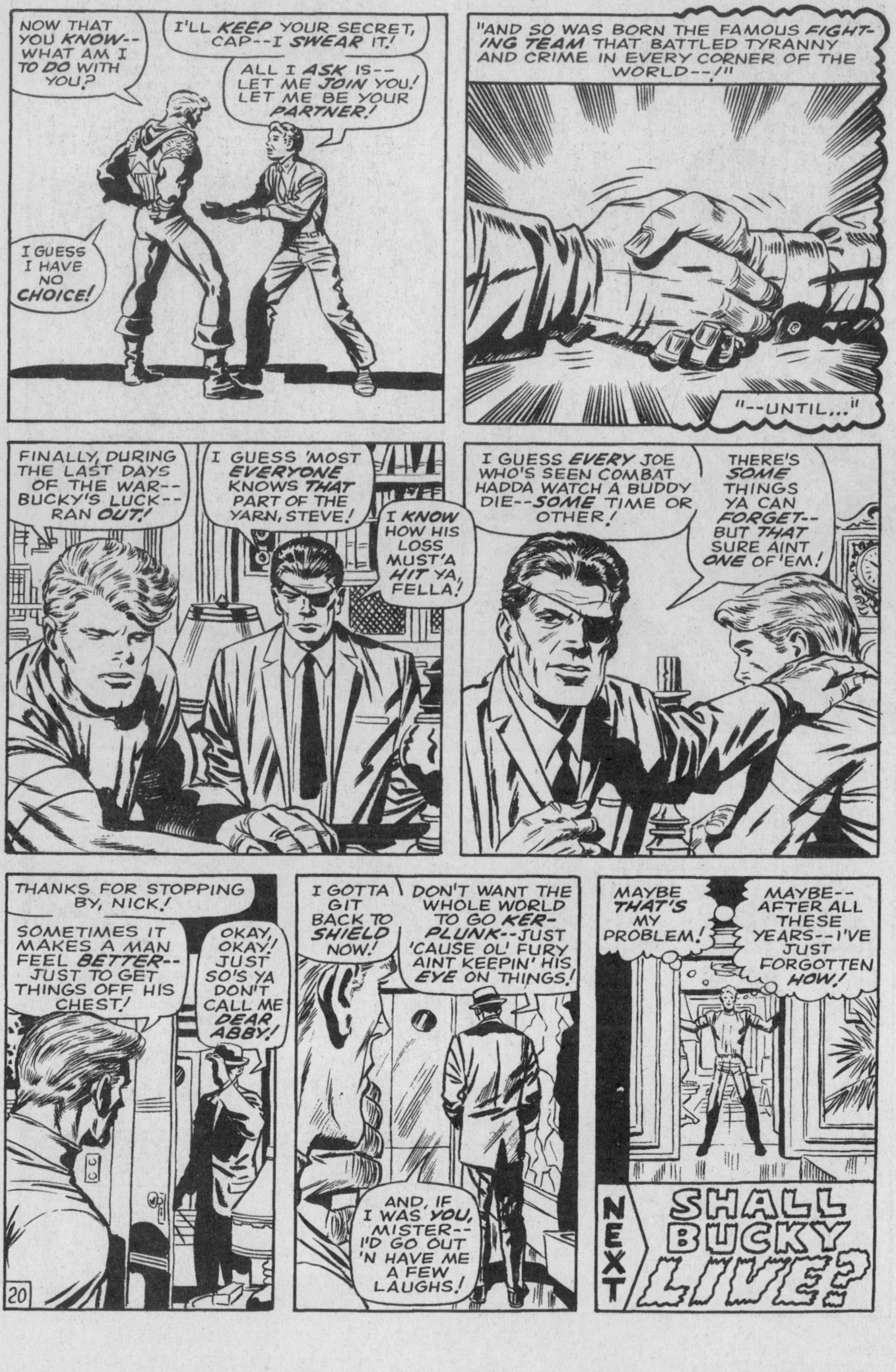
NOW THAT YOU KNOW-- WHAT AM I TO DO WITH YOU?
I'LL KEEP YOUR SECRET, CAP--I SWEAR IT!
ALL I ASK IS-- LET ME JOIN YOU! LET ME BE YOUR PARTNER!
I GUESS I HAVE NO CHOICE!
"AND SO WAS BORN THE FAMOUS FIGHTING TEAM THAT BATTLED TYRANNY AND CRIME IN EVERY CORNER OF THE WORLD--!"
"--UNTIL..."
FINALLY, DURING THE LAST DAYS OF THE WAR-- BUCKY'S LUCK-- RAN OUT!
I GUESS 'MOST EVERYONE KNOWS THAT PART OF THE YARN, STEVE!
I KNOW HOW HIS LOSS MUST'A HIT YA, FELLA!
I GUESS EVERY JOE WHO'S SEEN COMBAT HADDA WATCH A BUDDY DIE--SOME TIME OR OTHER!
THERE'S SOME THINGS YA CAN FORGET-- BUT THAT SURE AINT ONE OF 'EM!
THANKS FOR STOPPING BY, NICK!
SOMETIMES IT MAKES A MAN FEEL BETTER-- JUST TO GET THINGS OFF HIS CHEST!
OKAY, OKAY! JUST SO'S YA DON'T CALL ME DEAR ABBY!
I GOTTA GIT BACK TO SHIELD NOW!
DON'T WANT THE WHOLE WORLD TO GO KER-PLUNK--JUST 'CAUSE OL' FURY AINT KEEPIN' HIS EYE ON THINGS!
AND, IF I WAS YOU, MISTER-- I'D GO OUT 'N HAVE ME A FEW LAUGHS!
MAYBE THAT'S MY PROBLEM!
MAYBE-- AFTER ALL THESE YEARS--I'VE JUST FORGOTTEN HOW!
NEXT
SHALL BUCKY LIVE?
20

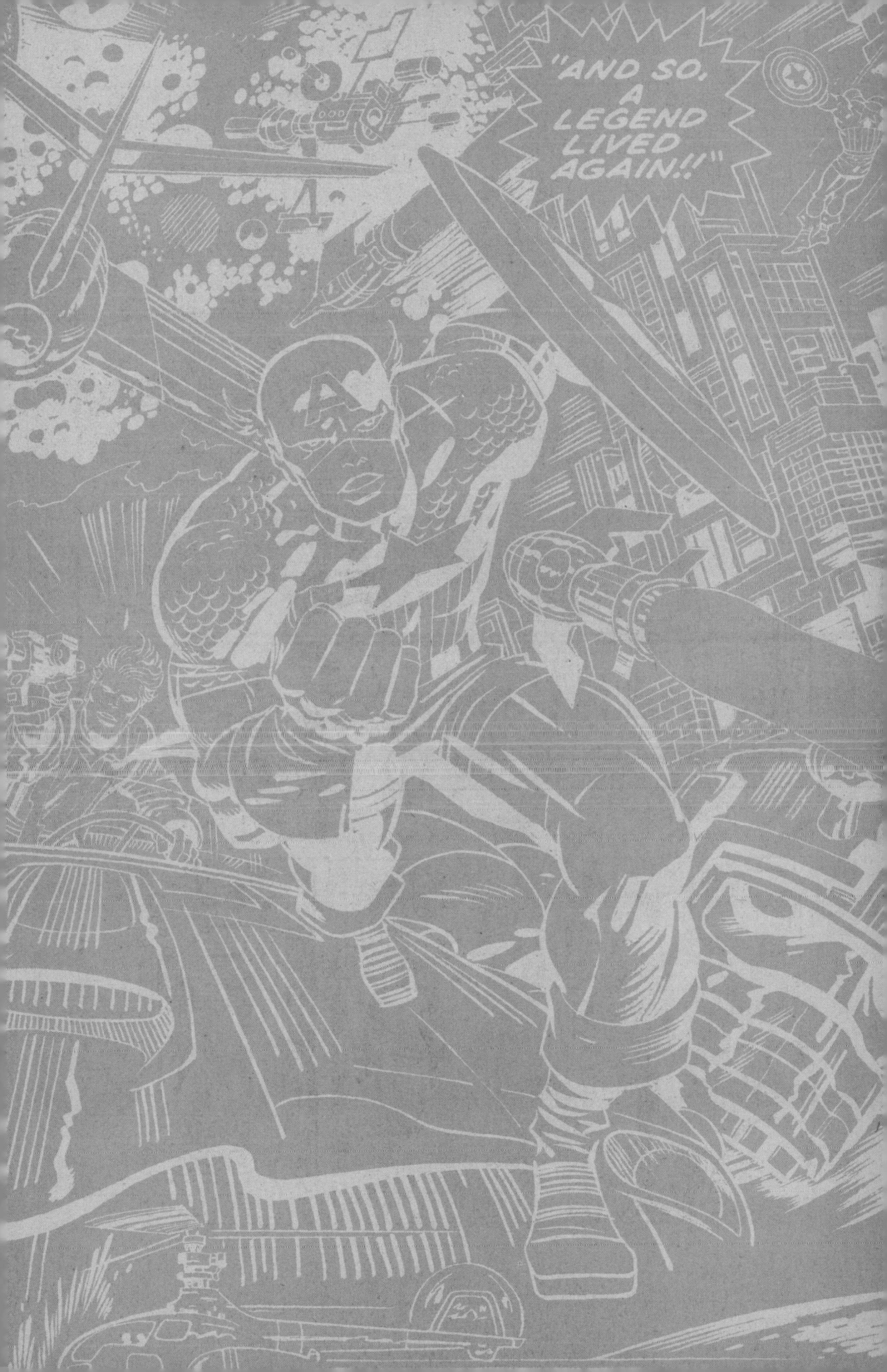
"AND SO, A LEGEND LIVED AGAIN!!"

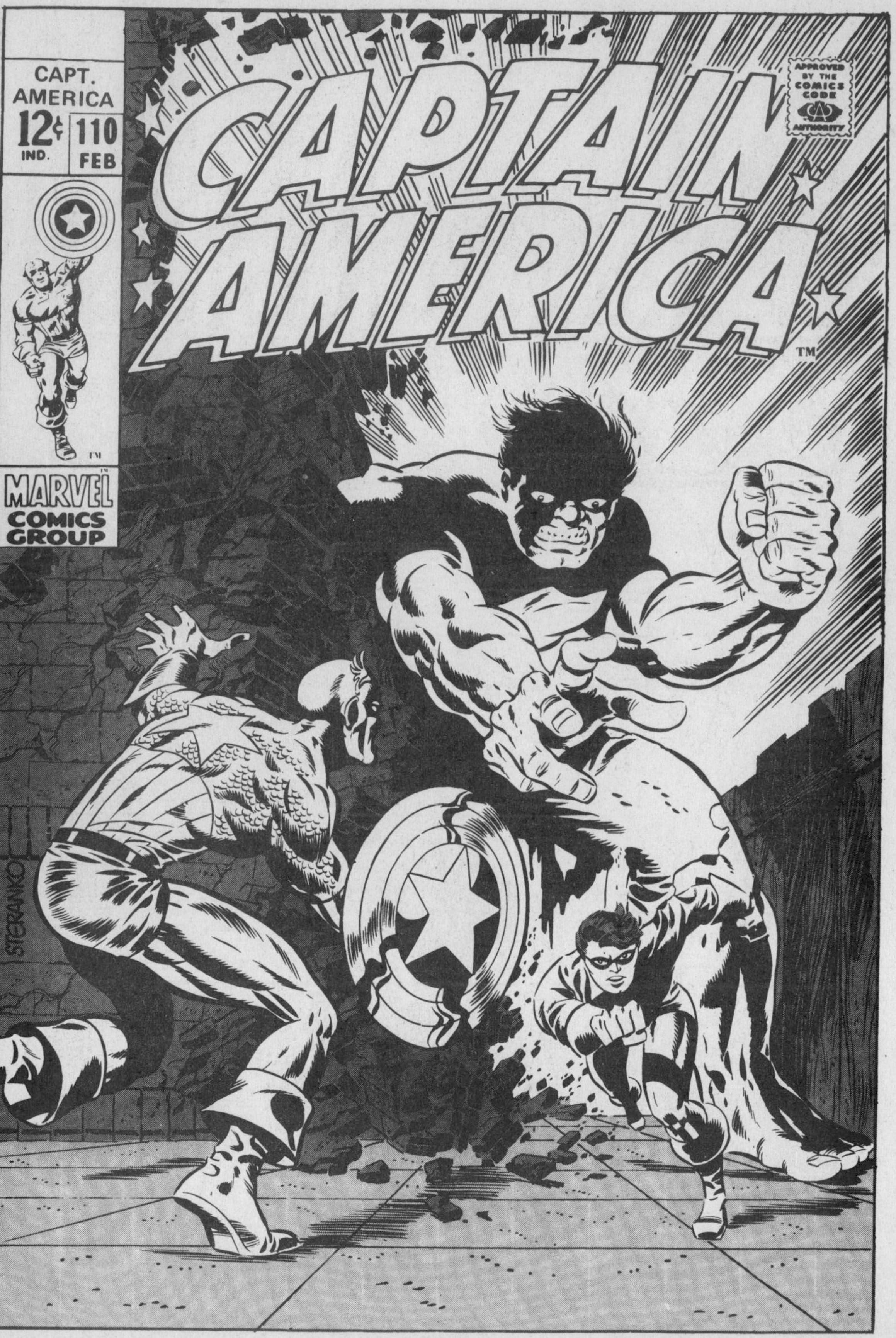
CAPT. AMERICA
12¢ IND.
110 FEB
CAPTAIN AMERICA
MARVEL COMICS GROUP
APPROVED BY THE COMICS CODE AUTHORITY
STERANKO

SLOWLY, FALTER- INGLY, HE WALKS THRU THE NIGHT...

A LONE, SILENT FIGURE...HAUNTED BY THE PAST...

PLAGUED BY MEMO- RIES SUCH AS FEW HAVE EVER KNOWN...

EVER TORTURED BY DOUBT...YET DRIVEN BY DUTY...

AND NOW HE STANDS BEFORE US...THIS MAN *STEVE ROGERS!*

STAN LEE-STERANKO

ASSOCIATION UNLIMITED PRESENT...

IN PERSON!

NO LONGER ALONE!

JOE SINNOTT, INKER WAS HERE

BENEFIT PERFO

LETTERED BY: SAM ROSEN

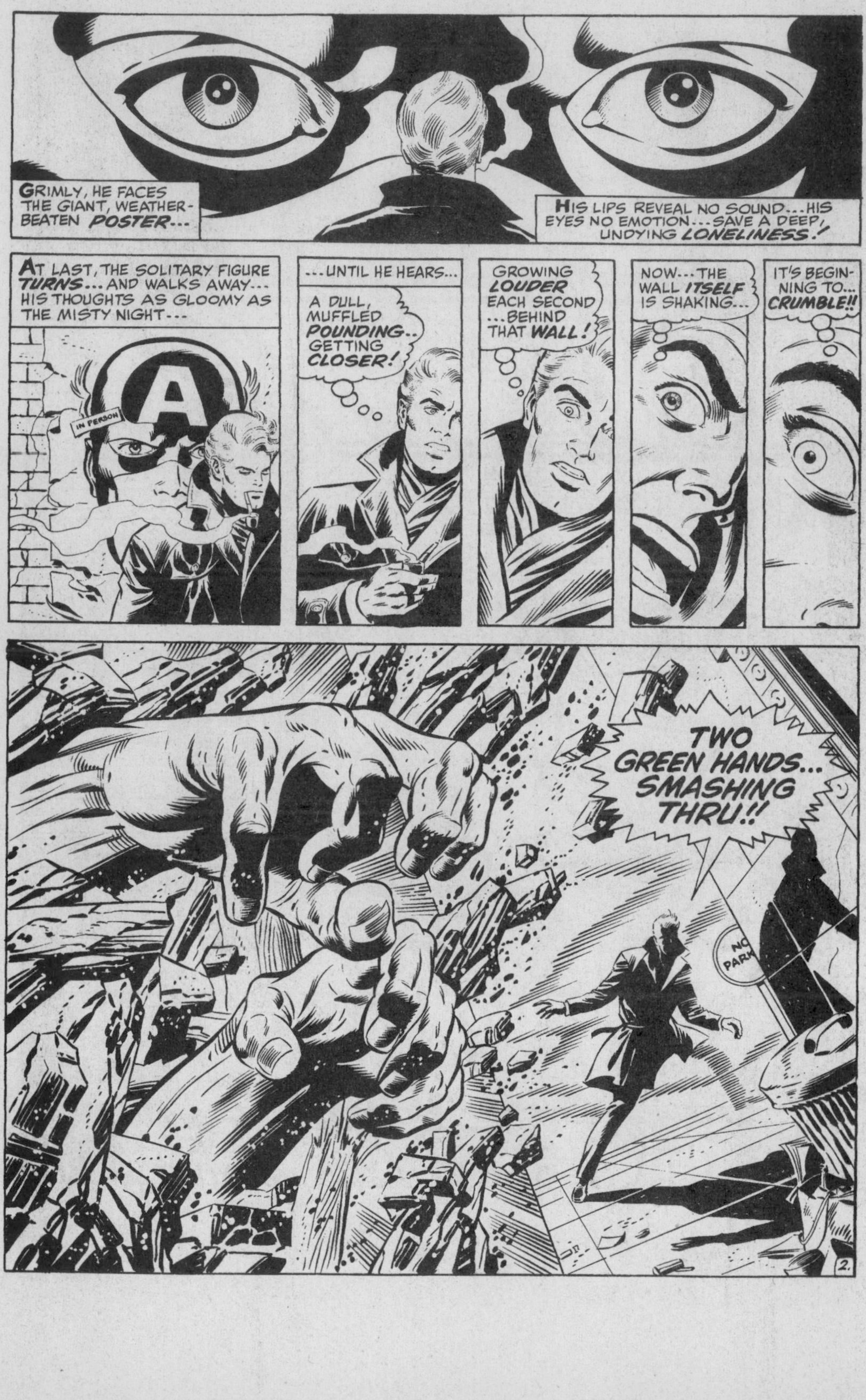
GRIMLY, HE FACES THE GIANT, WEATHER-BEATEN POSTER...
HIS LIPS REVEAL NO SOUND... HIS EYES NO EMOTION... SAVE A DEEP, UNDYING LONELINESS!
AT LAST, THE SOLITARY FIGURE TURNS... AND WALKS AWAY... HIS THOUGHTS AS GLOOMY AS THE MISTY NIGHT...
IN PERSON
...UNTIL HE HEARS...
A DULL, MUFFLED POUNDING.. GETTING CLOSER!
GROWING LOUDER EACH SECOND ...BEHIND THAT WALL!
NOW... THE WALL ITSELF IS SHAKING...
IT'S BEGINNING TO... CRUMBLE!!
TWO GREEN HANDS... SMASHING THRU!!
2.

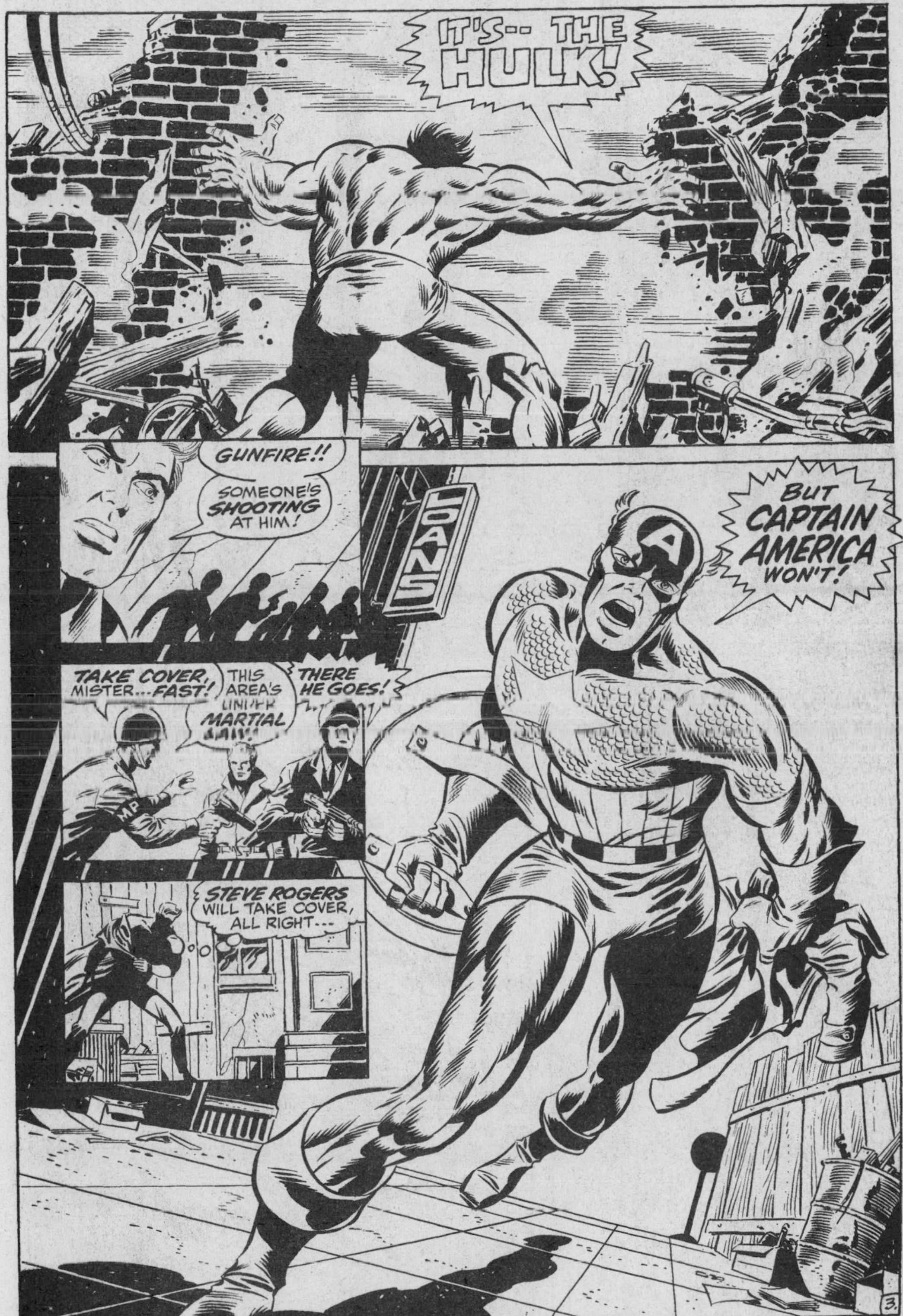

IT'S-- THE HULK!
GUNFIRE!!
SOMEONE'S SHOOTING AT HIM!
LOANS
TAKE COVER, MISTER... FAST!
THIS AREA'S UNDER MARTIAL
THERE HE GOES!
MP
STEVE ROGERS WILL TAKE COVER, ALL RIGHT---
BUT CAPTAIN AMERICA WON'T!
3.

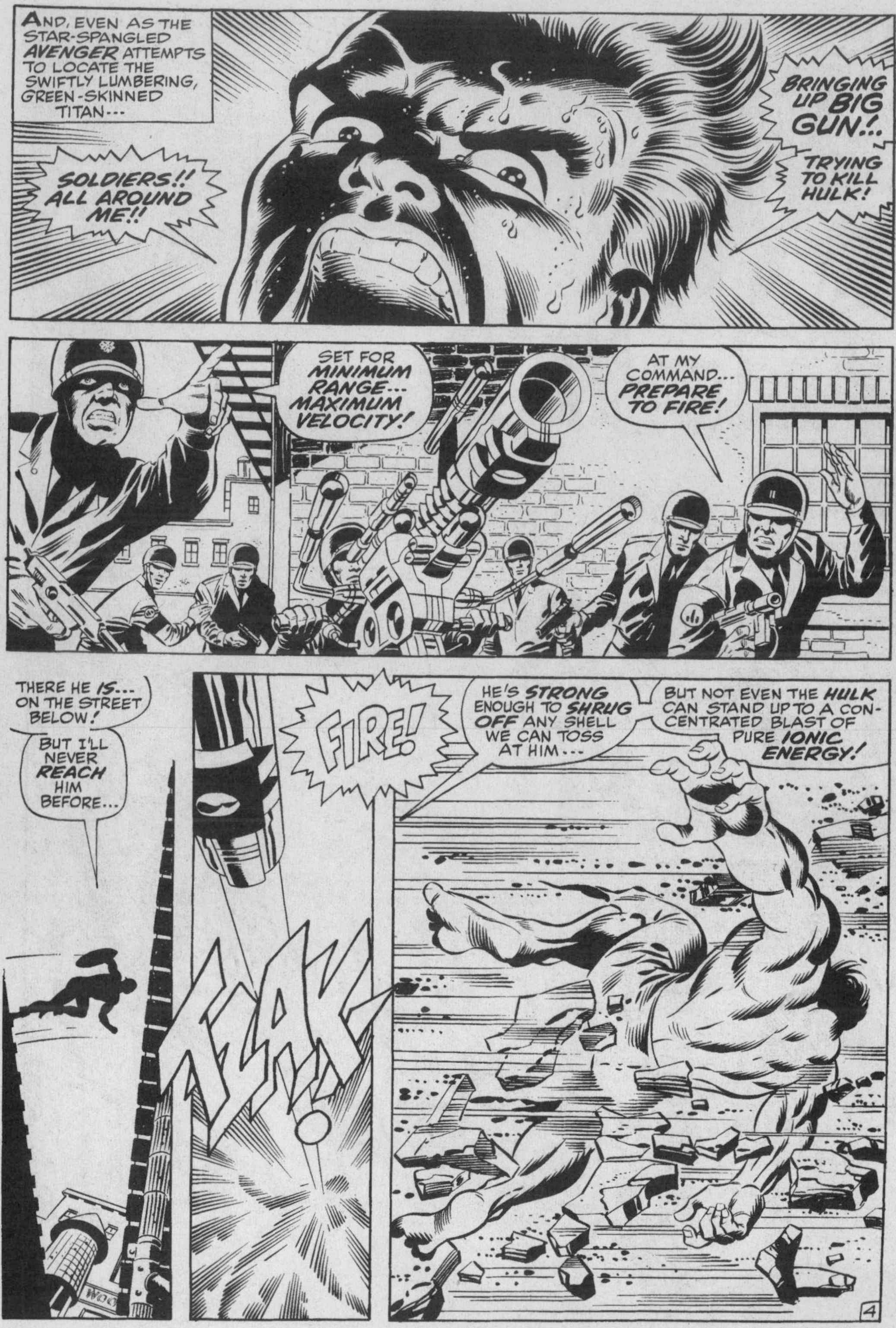
AND, EVEN AS THE STAR-SPANGLED AVENGER ATTEMPTS TO LOCATE THE SWIFTLY LUMBERING, GREEN-SKINNED TITAN---
SOLDIERS!! ALL AROUND ME!!
BRINGING UP BIG GUN!..
TRYING TO KILL HULK!
SET FOR MINIMUM RANGE--- MAXIMUM VELOCITY!
AT MY COMMAND... PREPARE TO FIRE!
THERE HE IS... ON THE STREET BELOW!
BUT I'LL NEVER REACH HIM BEFORE...
FIRE!
HE'S STRONG ENOUGH TO SHRUG OFF ANY SHELL WE CAN TOSS AT HIM...
BUT NOT EVEN THE HULK CAN STAND UP TO A CON-CENTRATED BLAST OF PURE IONIC ENERGY!
FZAK!

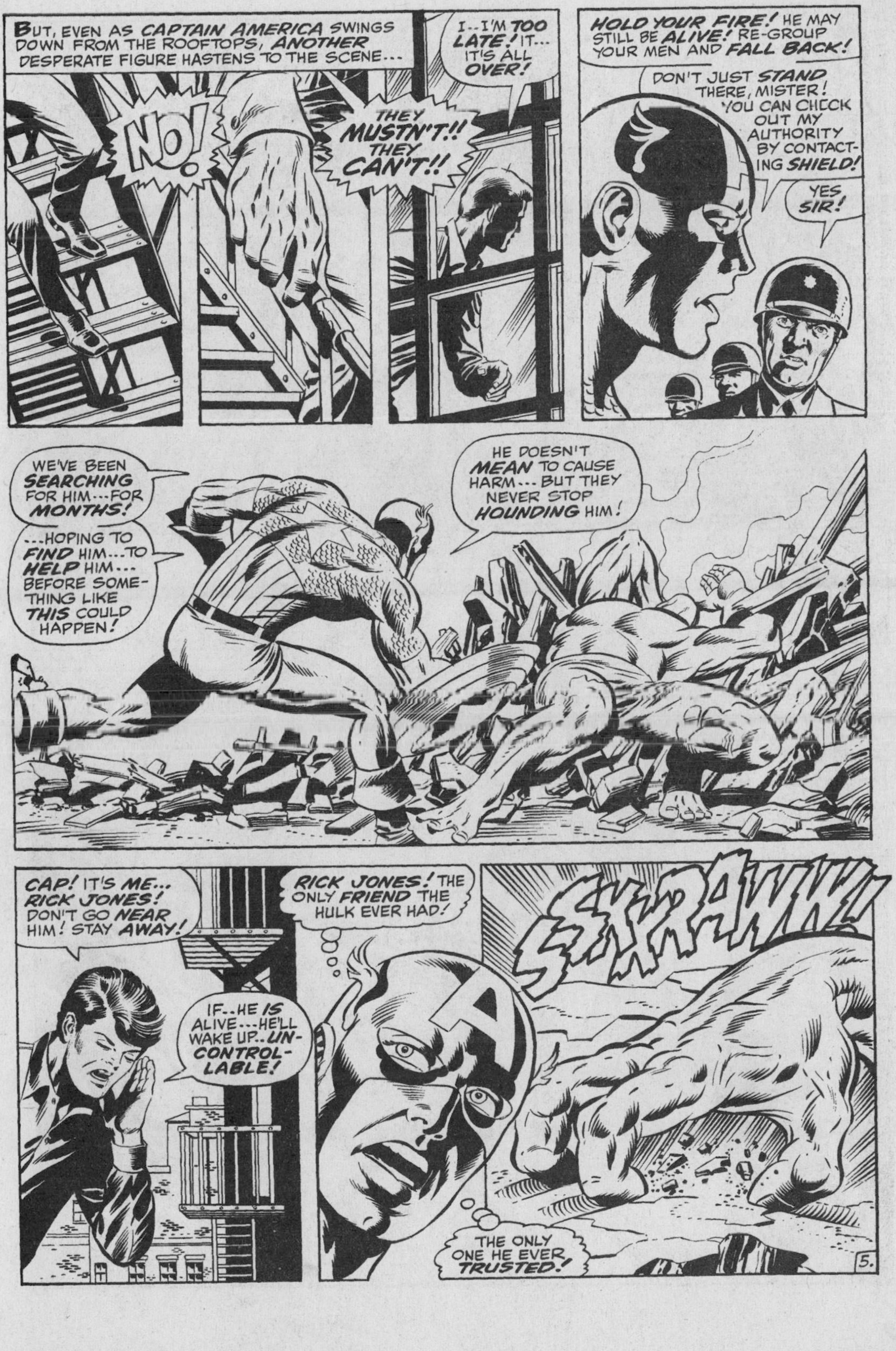
But, even as Captain America swings down from the rooftops, another desperate figure hastens to the scene...
NO!
I..I'm too late! It... it's all over!
They mustn't!! They can't!!
Hold your fire! He may still be alive! Re-group your men and fall back!
Don't just stand there, mister! You can check out my authority by contacting Shield!
Yes sir!
We've been searching for him---for months!
...Hoping to find him...to help him... before something like this could happen!
He doesn't mean to cause harm--- but they never stop hounding him!
Cap! It's me... Rick Jones! Don't go near him! Stay away!
Rick Jones! The only friend the Hulk ever had!
If..he is alive---he'll wake up..uncontrollable!
SKRAWK!
The only one he ever trusted!
5.

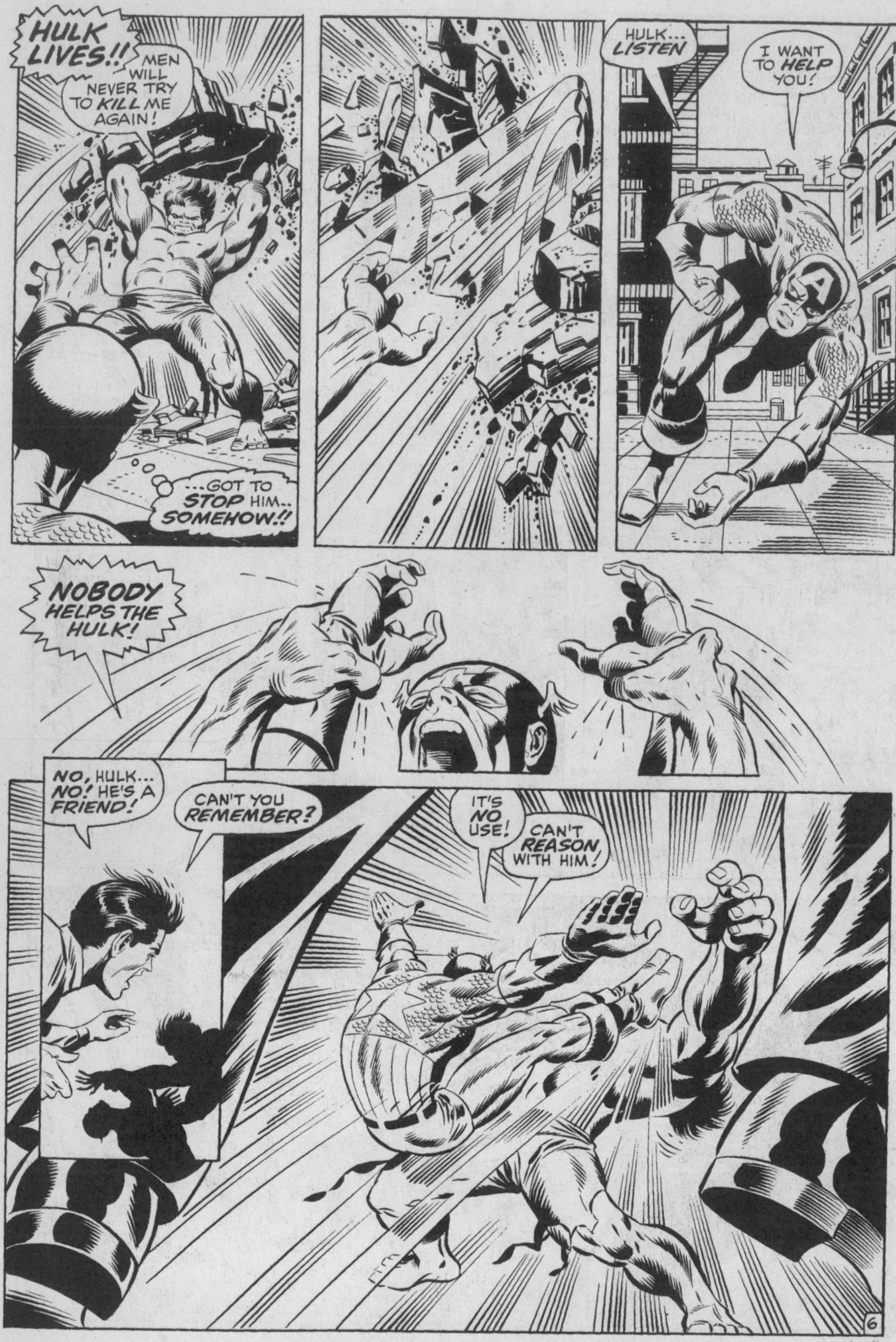
HULK LIVES!!
MEN WILL NEVER TRY TO KILL ME AGAIN!
...GOT TO STOP HIM... SOMEHOW!!
HULK... LISTEN
I WANT TO HELP YOU!
NOBODY HELPS THE HULK!
NO, HULK... NO! HE'S A FRIEND!
CAN'T YOU REMEMBER?
IT'S NO USE!
CAN'T REASON WITH HIM!
6

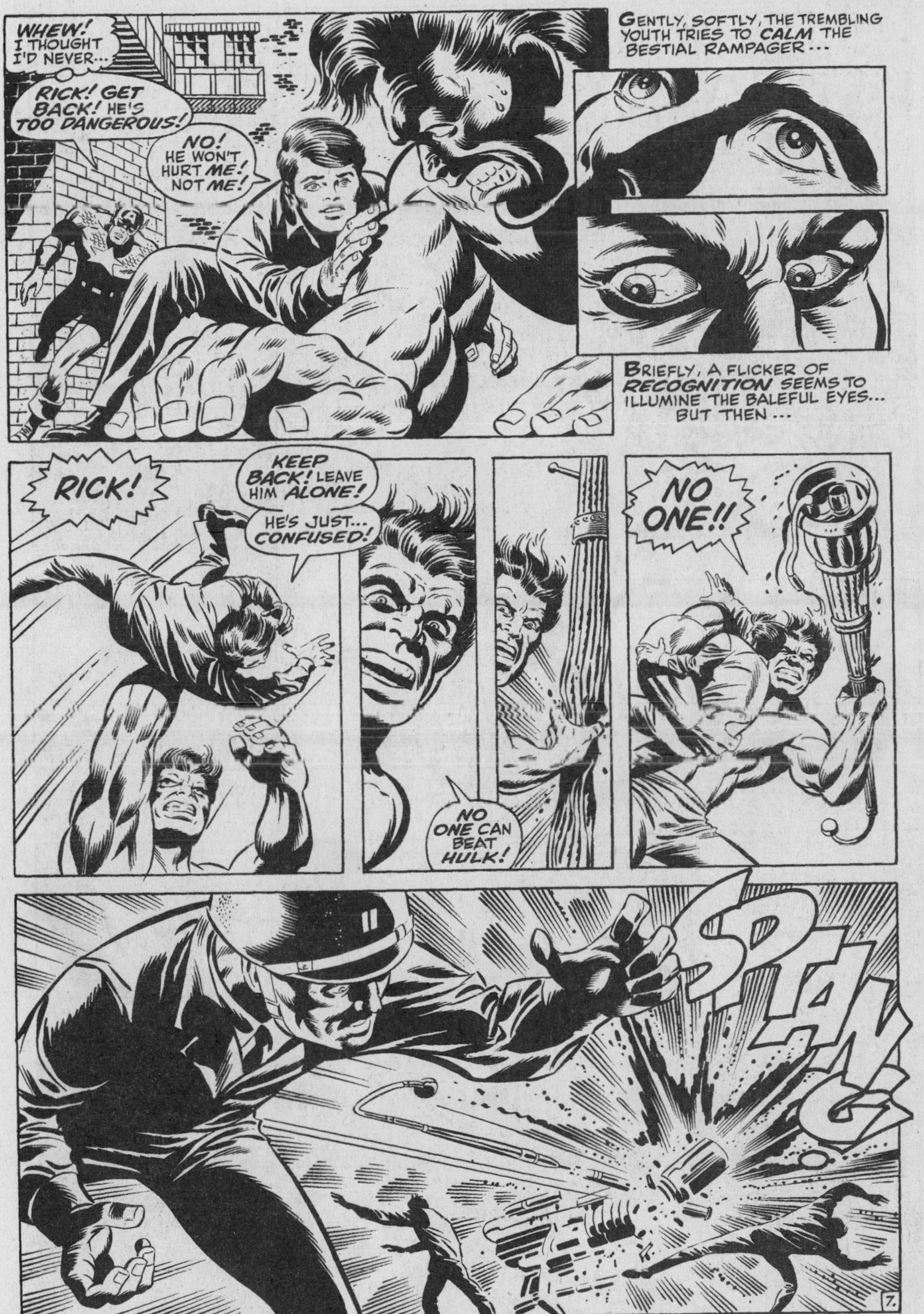

WHEW! I THOUGHT I'D NEVER...
RICK! GET BACK! HE'S TOO DANGEROUS!
NO! HE WON'T HURT ME! NOT ME!
GENTLY, SOFTLY, THE TREMBLING YOUTH TRIES TO CALM THE BESTIAL RAMPAGER...
BRIEFLY, A FLICKER OF RECOGNITION SEEMS TO ILLUMINE THE BALEFUL EYES... BUT THEN...
RICK!
KEEP BACK! LEAVE HIM ALONE!
HE'S JUST... CONFUSED!
NO ONE CAN BEAT HULK!
NO ONE!!
SPTANG
7.

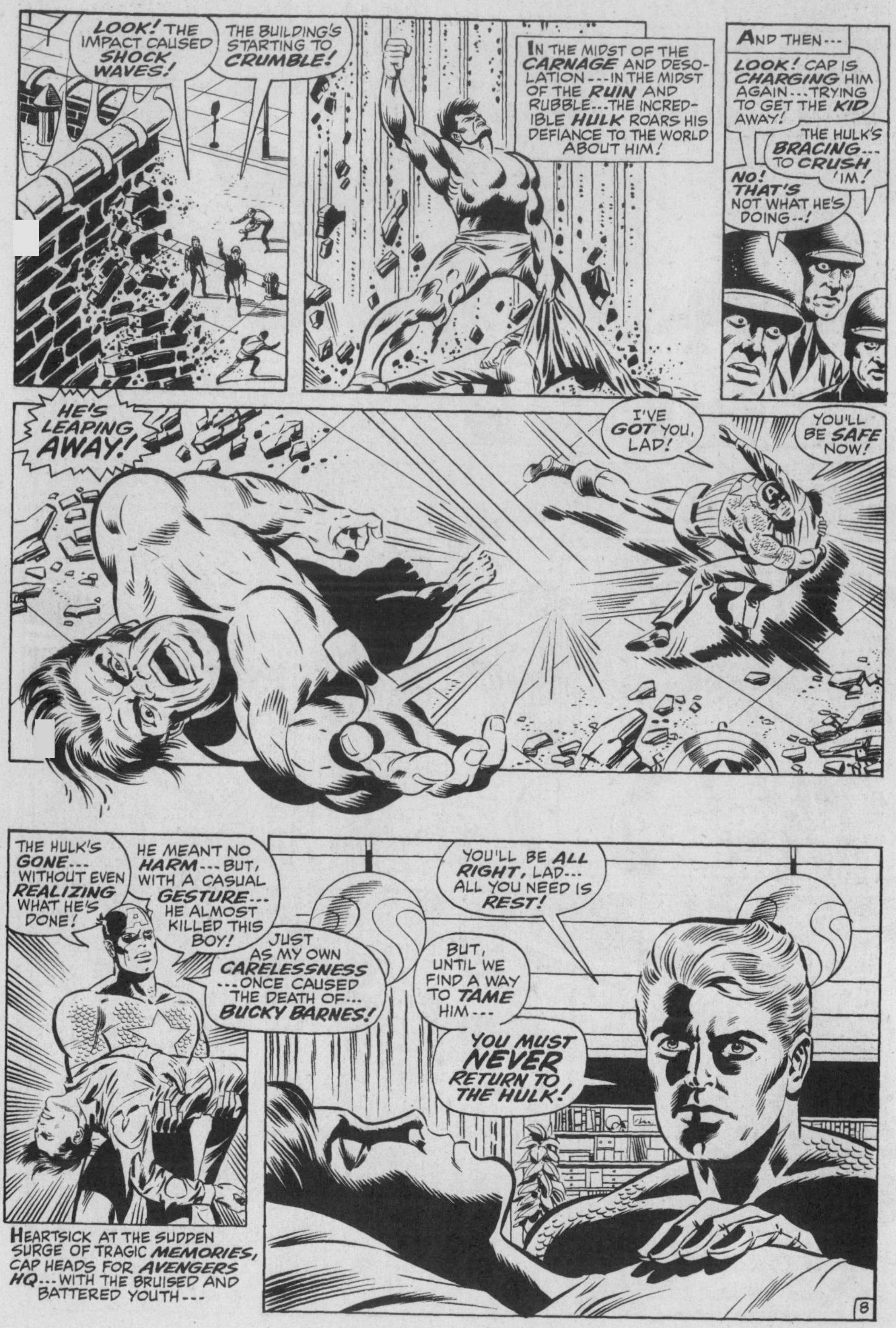

LOOK! THE IMPACT CAUSED SHOCK WAVES!
THE BUILDING'S STARTING TO CRUMBLE!
IN THE MIDST OF THE CARNAGE AND DESOLATION---IN THE MIDST OF THE RUIN AND RUBBLE---THE INCREDIBLE HULK ROARS HIS DEFIANCE TO THE WORLD ABOUT HIM!
AND THEN---
LOOK! CAP IS CHARGING HIM AGAIN---TRYING TO GET THE KID AWAY!
THE HULK'S BRACING---TO CRUSH 'IM!
NO! THAT'S NOT WHAT HE'S DOING--!
HE'S LEAPING AWAY!
I'VE GOT YOU, LAD!
YOU'LL BE SAFE NOW!
THE HULK'S GONE---WITHOUT EVEN REALIZING WHAT HE'S DONE!
HE MEANT NO HARM---BUT, WITH A CASUAL GESTURE---HE ALMOST KILLED THIS BOY!
JUST AS MY OWN CARELESSNESS---ONCE CAUSED THE DEATH OF...BUCKY BARNES!
HEARTSICK AT THE SUDDEN SURGE OF TRAGIC MEMORIES, CAP HEADS FOR AVENGERS HQ---WITH THE BRUISED AND BATTERED YOUTH---
YOU'LL BE ALL RIGHT, LAD---ALL YOU NEED IS REST!
BUT, UNTIL WE FIND A WAY TO TAME HIM---
YOU MUST NEVER RETURN TO THE HULK!
8

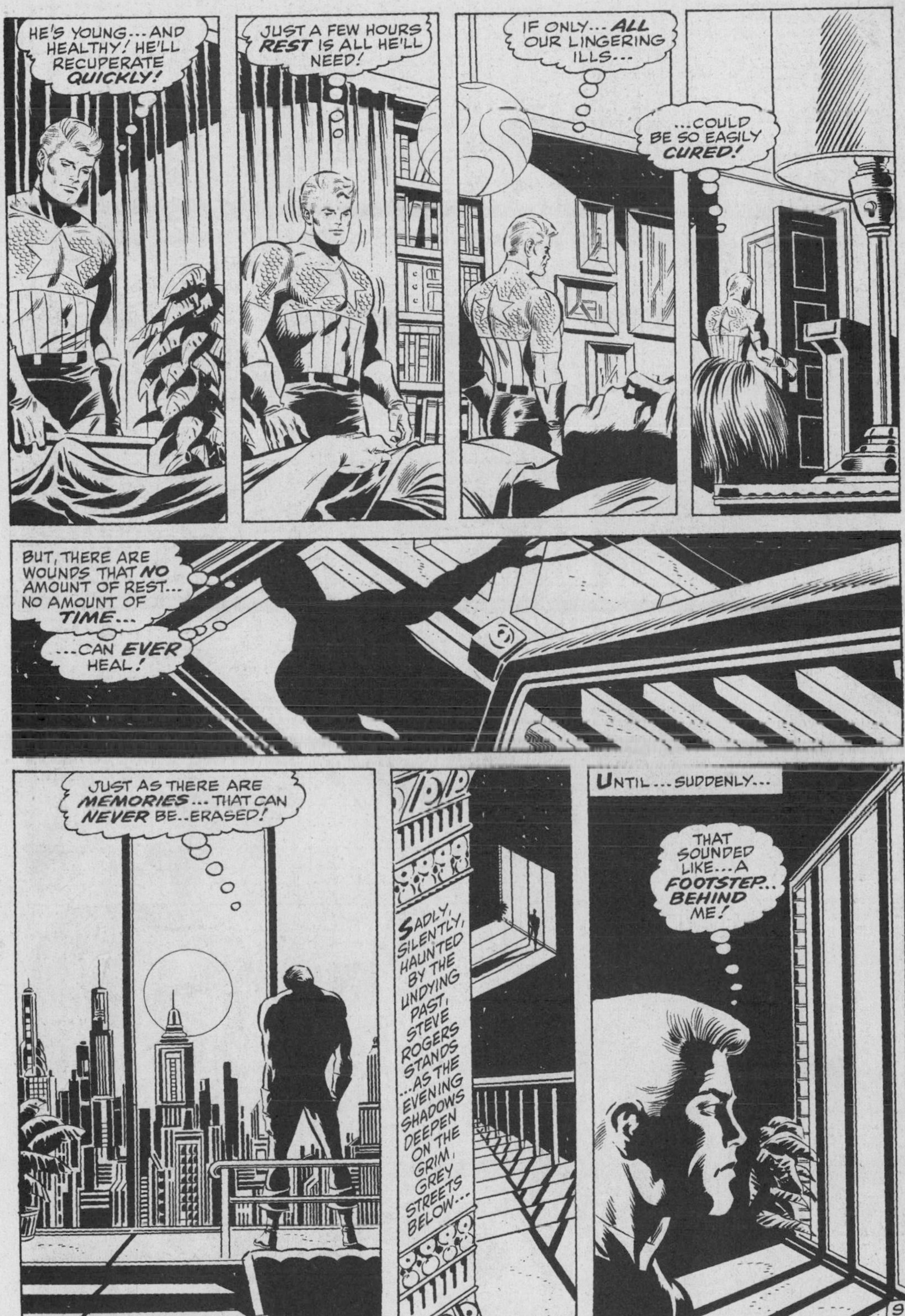
HE'S YOUNG... AND HEALTHY! HE'LL RECUPERATE QUICKLY!
JUST A FEW HOURS REST IS ALL HE'LL NEED!
IF ONLY... ALL OUR LINGERING ILLS...
...COULD BE SO EASILY CURED!
BUT, THERE ARE WOUNDS THAT NO AMOUNT OF REST... NO AMOUNT OF TIME...
...CAN EVER HEAL!
JUST AS THERE ARE MEMORIES... THAT CAN NEVER BE..ERASED!
SADLY, SILENTLY, HAUNTED BY THE UNDYING PAST, STEVE ROGERS STANDS ...AS THE EVENING SHADOWS DEEPEN ON THE GRIM, GREY STREETS BELOW...
UNTIL... SUDDENLY...
THAT SOUNDED LIKE... A FOOTSTEP.. BEHIND ME!
9

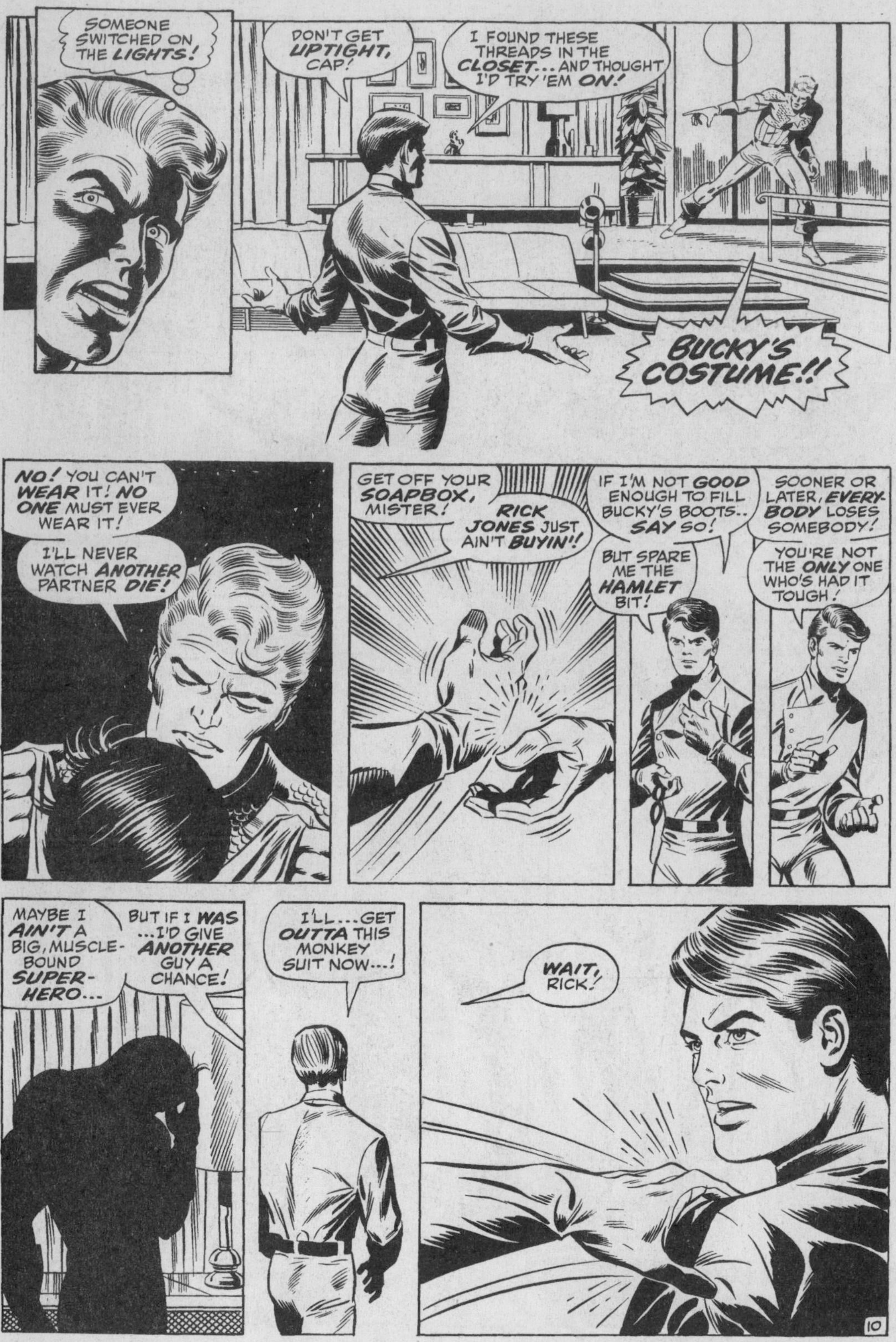
SOMEONE SWITCHED ON THE LIGHTS!
DON'T GET UPTIGHT, CAP!
I FOUND THESE THREADS IN THE CLOSET... AND THOUGHT I'D TRY 'EM ON!
BUCKY'S COSTUME!!
NO! YOU CAN'T WEAR IT! NO ONE MUST EVER WEAR IT!
I'LL NEVER WATCH ANOTHER PARTNER DIE!
GET OFF YOUR SOAPBOX, MISTER!
RICK JONES JUST AIN'T BUYIN'!
IF I'M NOT GOOD ENOUGH TO FILL BUCKY'S BOOTS.. SAY SO!
BUT SPARE ME THE HAMLET BIT!
SOONER OR LATER, EVERYBODY LOSES SOMEBODY!
YOU'RE NOT THE ONLY ONE WHO'S HAD IT TOUGH!
MAYBE I AIN'T A BIG, MUSCLE-BOUND SUPER-HERO...
BUT IF I WAS ...I'D GIVE ANOTHER GUY A CHANCE!
I'LL...GET OUTTA THIS MONKEY SUIT NOW...!
WAIT, RICK!
10

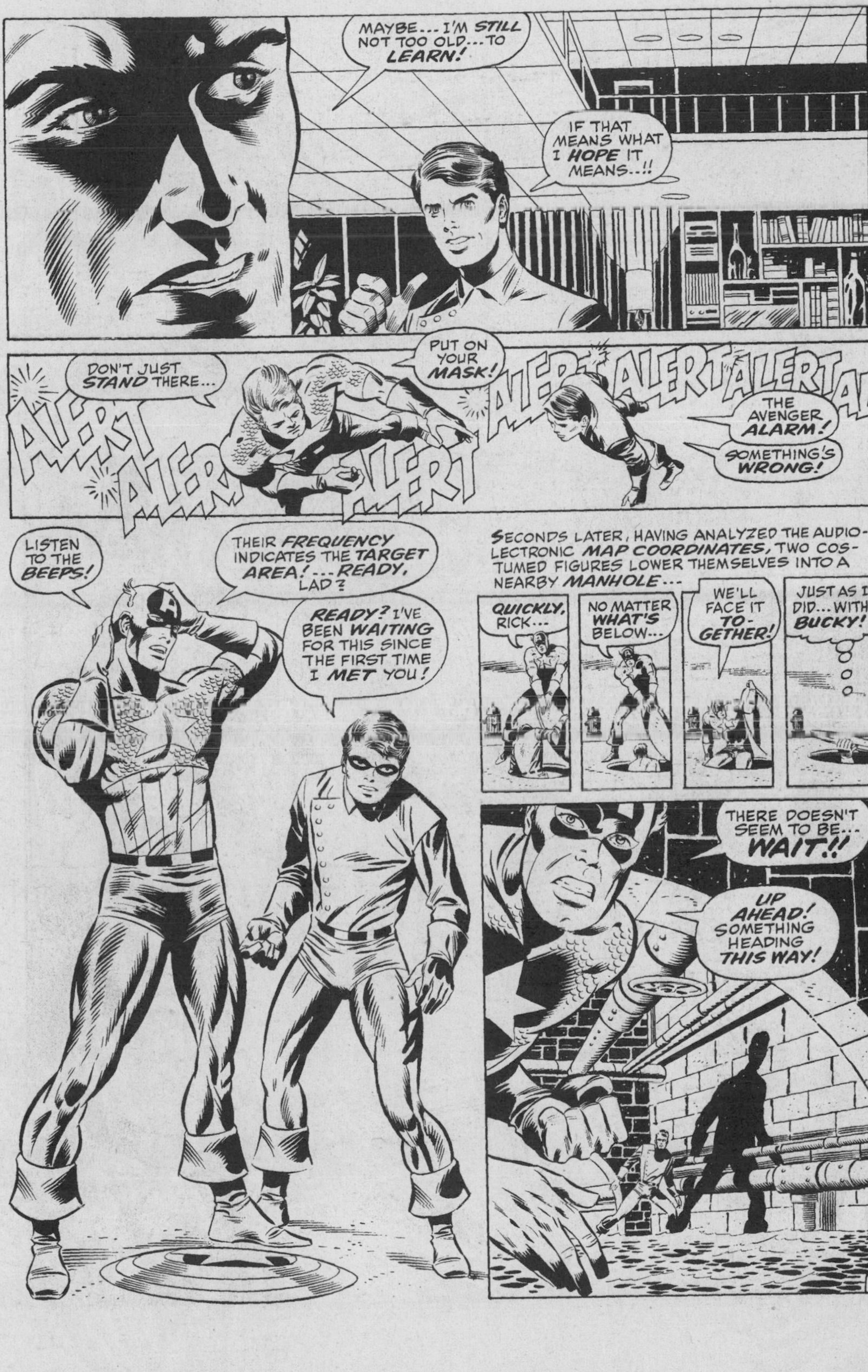

MAYBE... I'M STILL NOT TOO OLD... TO LEARN!
IF THAT MEANS WHAT I HOPE IT MEANS..!!
DON'T JUST STAND THERE...
PUT ON YOUR MASK!
ALERT ALERT ALERT ALERT ALERT ALERT AL
THE AVENGER ALARM!
SOMETHING'S WRONG!
LISTEN TO THE BEEPS!
THEIR FREQUENCY INDICATES THE TARGET AREA! ... READY, LAD?
READY? I'VE BEEN WAITING FOR THIS SINCE THE FIRST TIME I MET YOU!
SECONDS LATER, HAVING ANALYZED THE AUDIO-LECTRONIC MAP COORDINATES, TWO COSTUMED FIGURES LOWER THEMSELVES INTO A NEARBY MANHOLE...
QUICKLY, RICK...
NO MATTER WHAT'S BELOW...
WE'LL FACE IT TO-GETHER!
JUST AS I DID... WITH BUCKY!
THERE DOESN'T SEEM TO BE... WAIT!!
UP AHEAD! SOMETHING HEADING THIS WAY!
11.

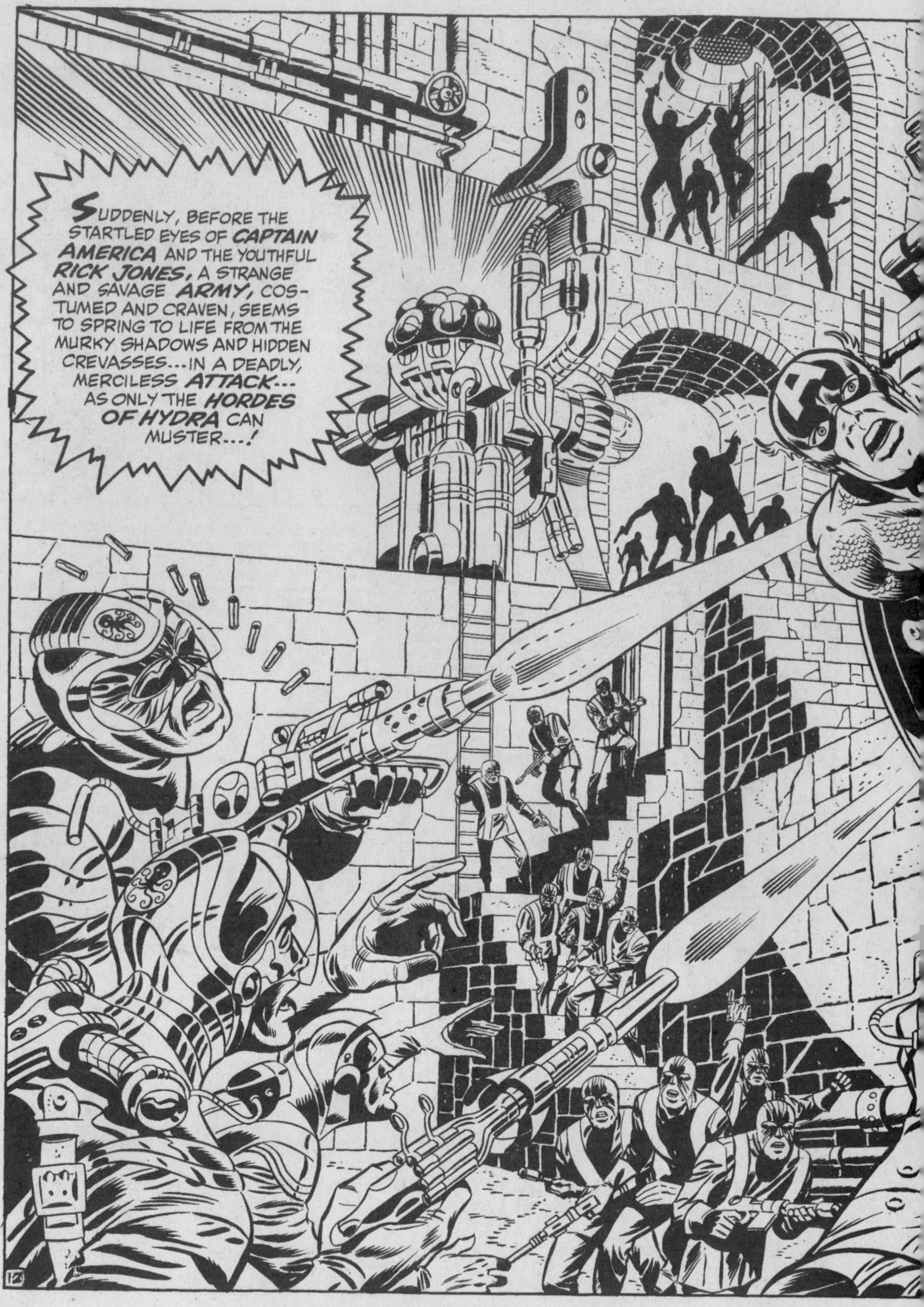
SUDDENLY, BEFORE THE STARTLED EYES OF CAPTAIN AMERICA AND THE YOUTHFUL RICK JONES, A STRANGE AND SAVAGE ARMY, COSTUMED AND CRAVEN, SEEMS TO SPRING TO LIFE FROM THE MURKY SHADOWS AND HIDDEN CREVASSES...IN A DEADLY, MERCILESS ATTACK... AS ONLY THE HORDES OF HYDRA CAN MUSTER...!
12

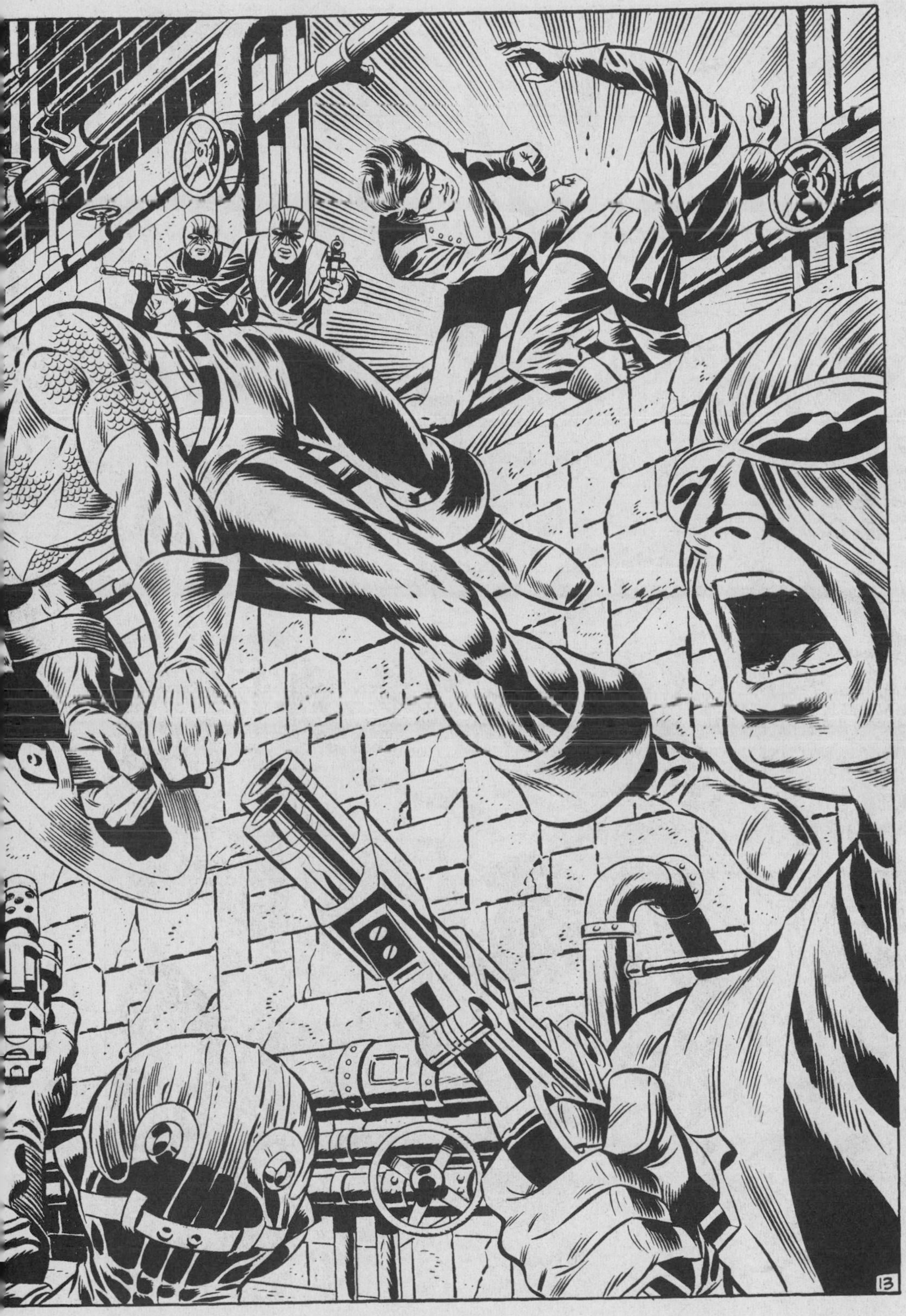
13

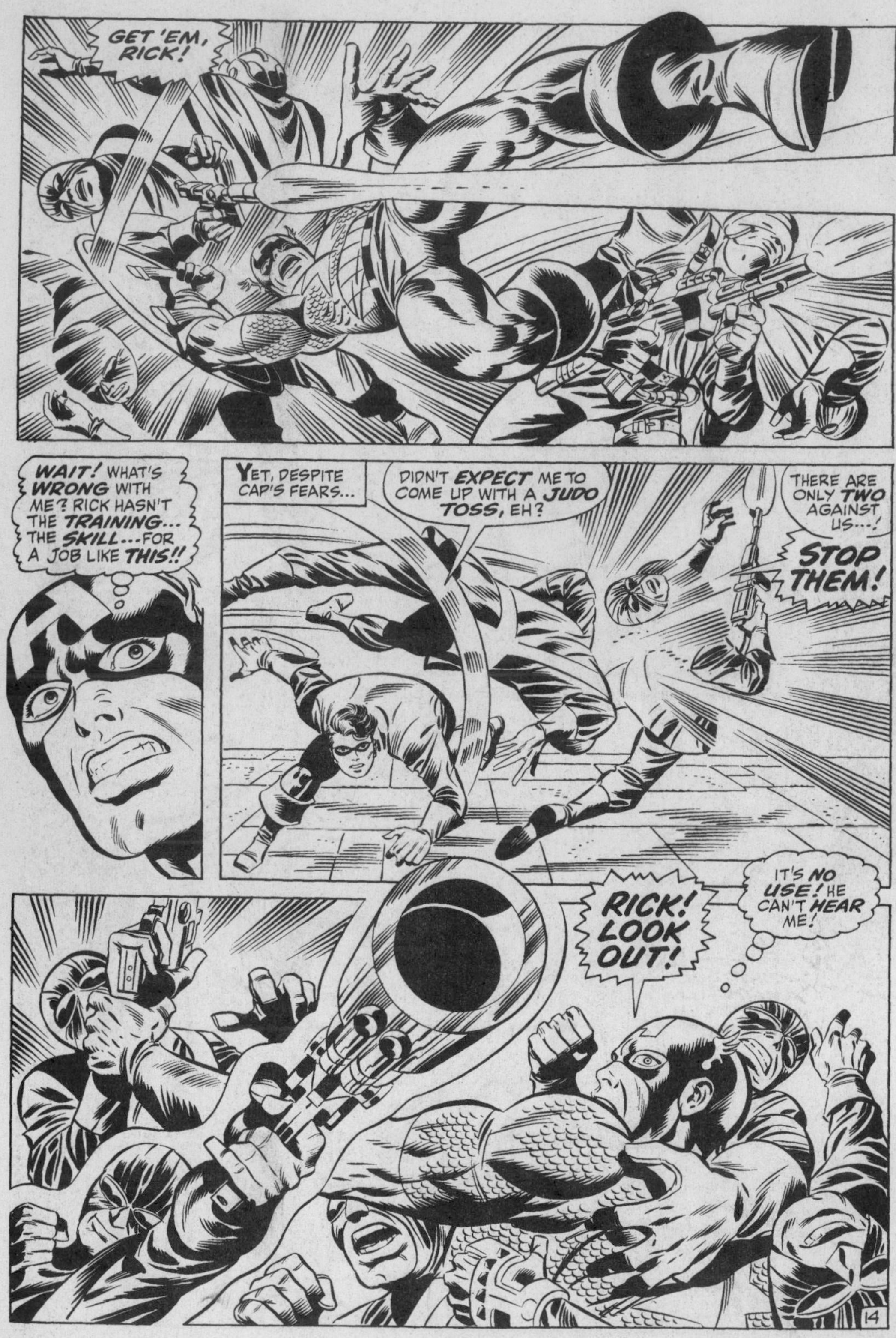
GET 'EM, RICK!
WAIT! WHAT'S WRONG WITH ME? RICK HASN'T THE TRAINING... THE SKILL... FOR A JOB LIKE THIS!!
YET, DESPITE CAP'S FEARS...
DIDN'T EXPECT ME TO COME UP WITH A JUDO TOSS, EH?
THERE ARE ONLY TWO AGAINST US...!
STOP THEM!
RICK! LOOK OUT!
IT'S NO USE! HE CAN'T HEAR ME!
14

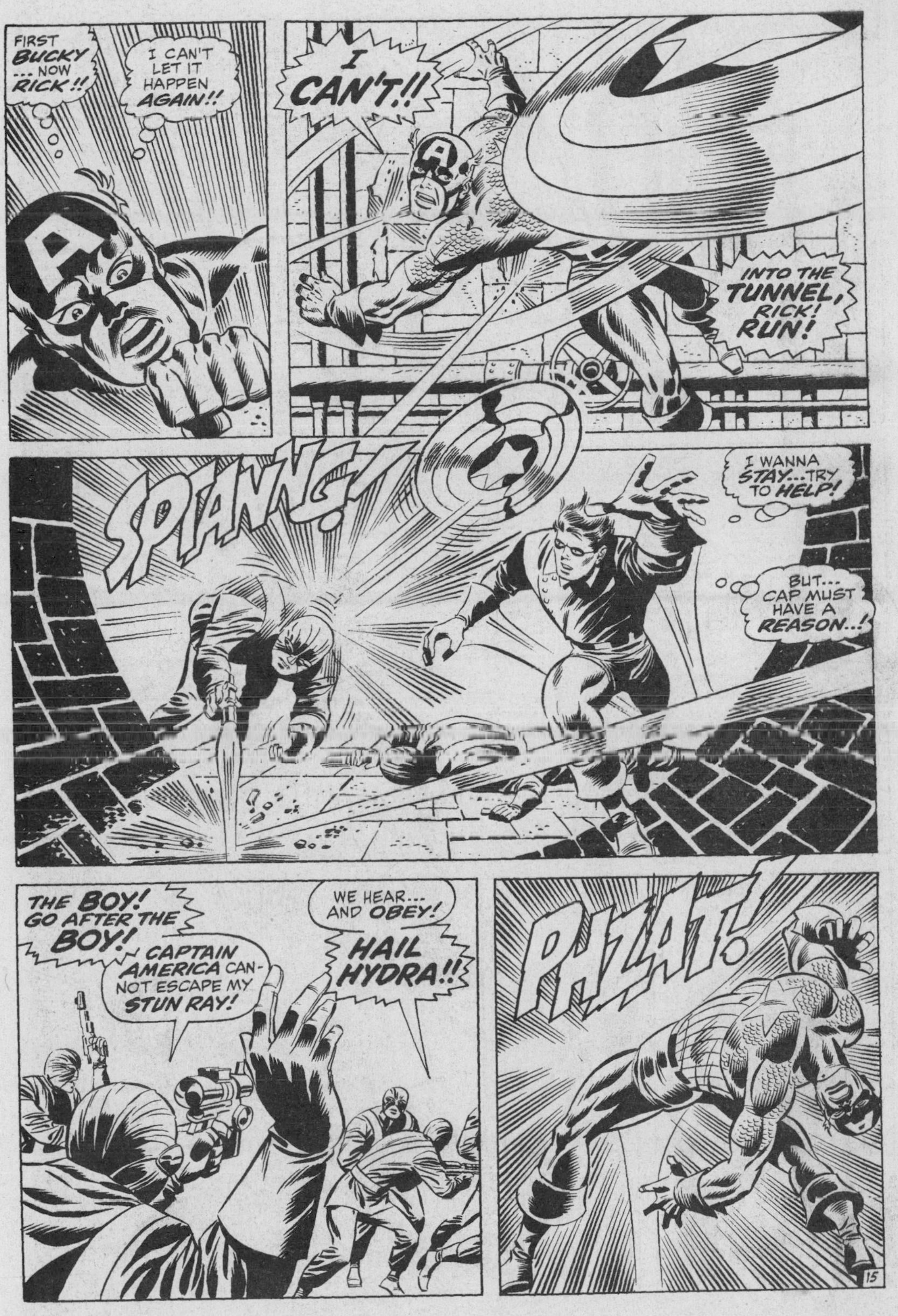

FIRST BUCKY ...NOW RICK!!
I CAN'T LET IT HAPPEN AGAIN!!
I CAN'T!!
INTO THE TUNNEL, RICK! RUN!
SPLANNG!
I WANNA STAY...TRY TO HELP!
BUT... CAP MUST HAVE A REASON..!
THE BOY! GO AFTER THE BOY!
CAPTAIN AMERICA CAN-NOT ESCAPE MY STUN RAY!
WE HEAR... AND OBEY!
HAIL HYDRA!!
PHZAT!
15

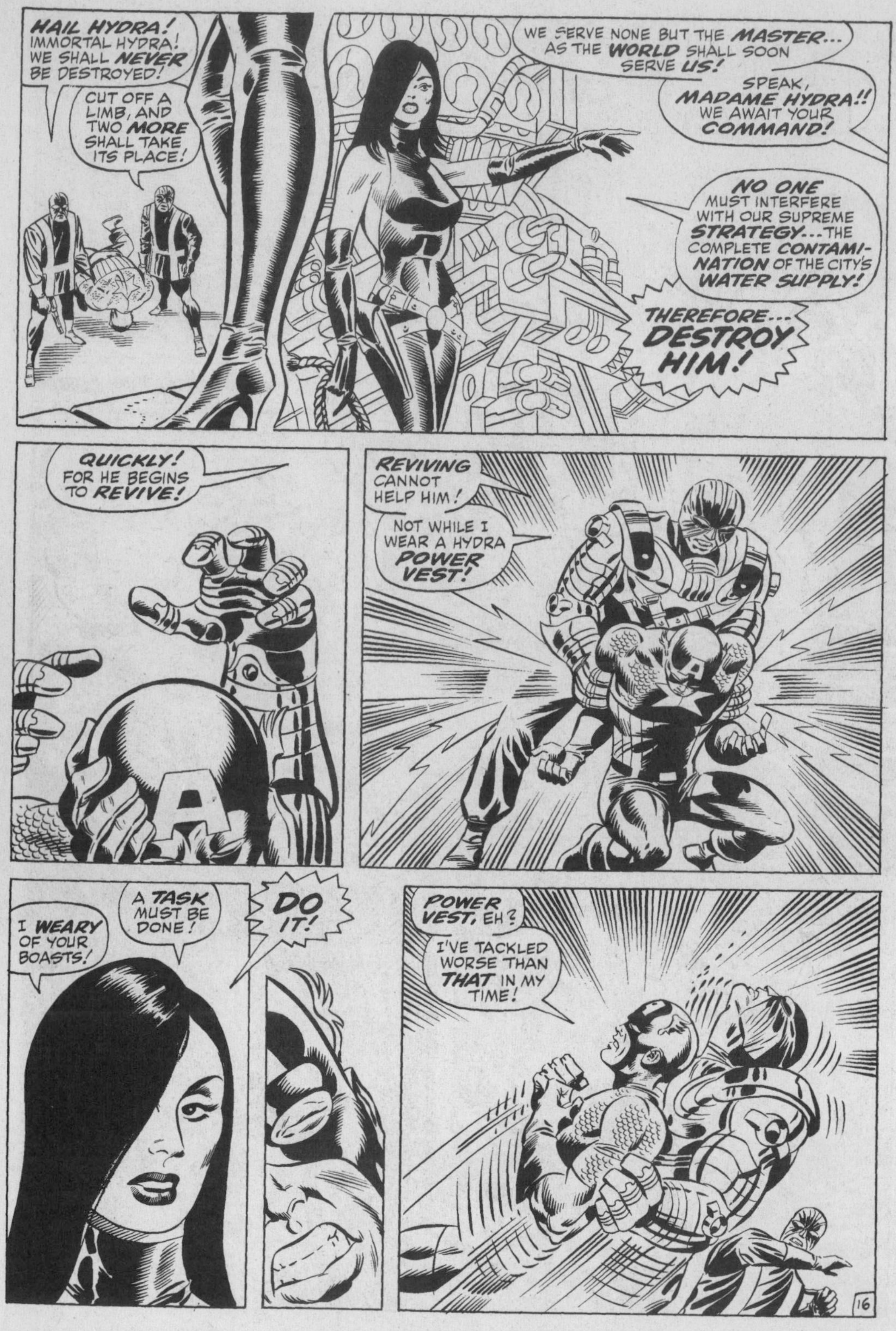
HAIL HYDRA! IMMORTAL HYDRA! WE SHALL NEVER BE DESTROYED!
CUT OFF A LIMB, AND TWO MORE SHALL TAKE ITS PLACE!
WE SERVE NONE BUT THE MASTER... AS THE WORLD SHALL SOON SERVE US!
SPEAK, MADAME HYDRA!! WE AWAIT YOUR COMMAND!
NO ONE MUST INTERFERE WITH OUR SUPREME STRATEGY... THE COMPLETE CONTAMINATION OF THE CITY'S WATER SUPPLY!
THEREFORE... DESTROY HIM!
QUICKLY! FOR HE BEGINS TO REVIVE!
REVIVING CANNOT HELP HIM!
NOT WHILE I WEAR A HYDRA POWER VEST!
I WEARY OF YOUR BOASTS!
A TASK MUST BE DONE!
DO IT!
POWER VEST, EH?
I'VE TACKLED WORSE THAN THAT IN MY TIME!
16

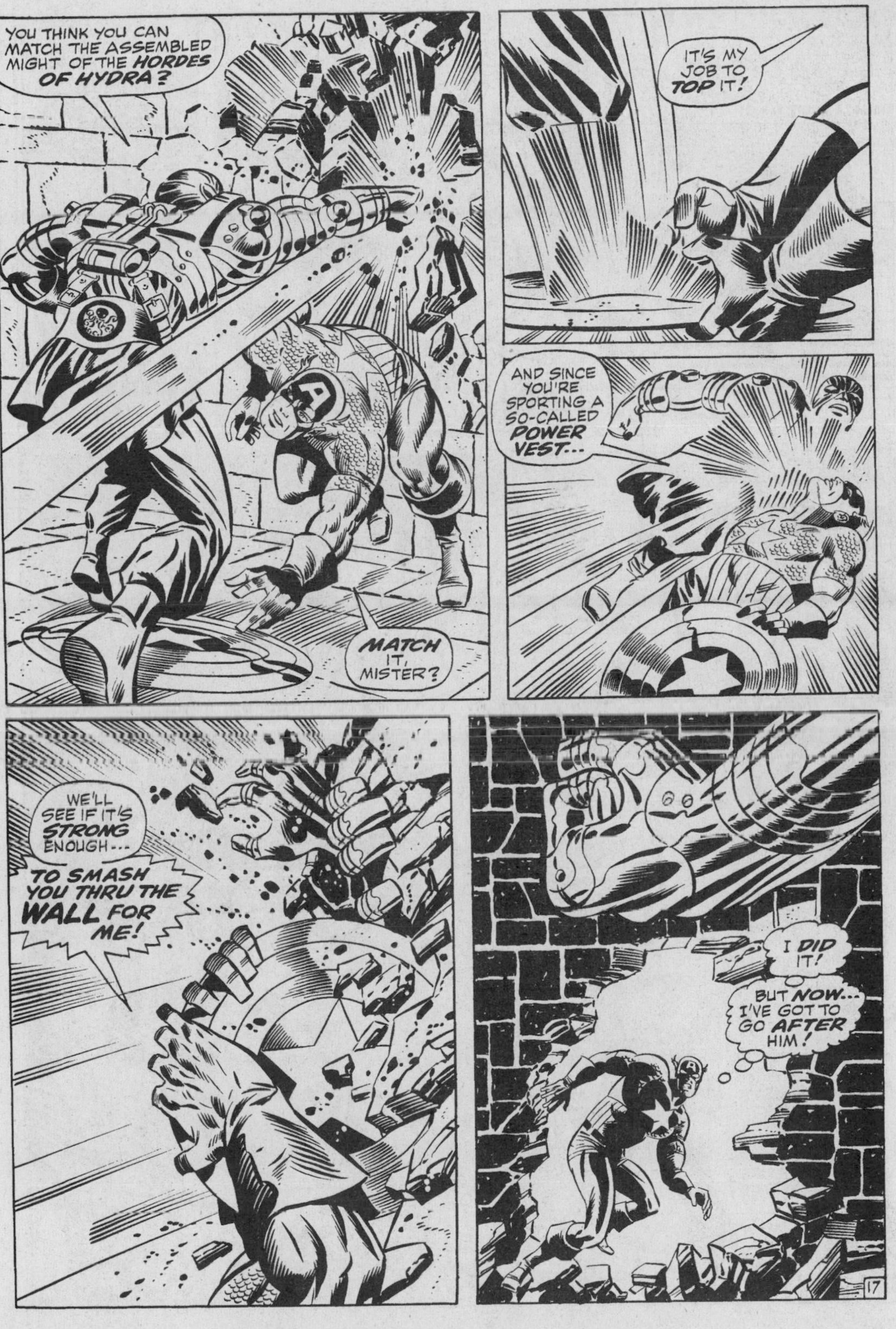
YOU THINK YOU CAN MATCH THE ASSEMBLED MIGHT OF THE HORDES OF HYDRA?
MATCH IT, MISTER?
IT'S MY JOB TO TOP IT!
AND SINCE YOU'RE SPORTING A SO-CALLED POWER VEST...
WE'LL SEE IF IT'S STRONG ENOUGH...
TO SMASH YOU THRU THE WALL FOR ME!
I DID IT!
BUT NOW... I'VE GOT TO GO AFTER HIM!
17

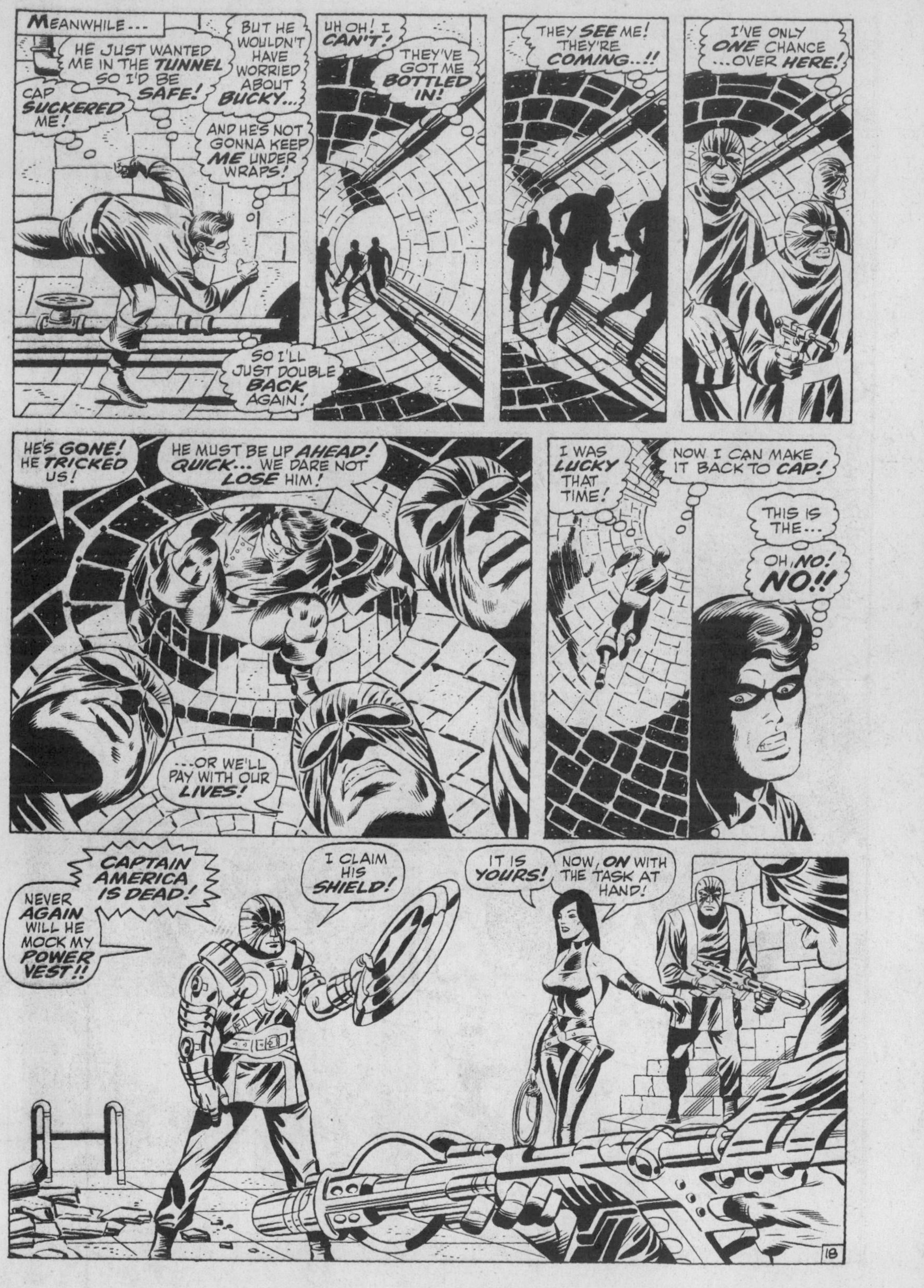
MEANWHILE...
HE JUST WANTED ME IN THE TUNNEL SO I'D BE SAFE!
CAP SUCKERED ME!
BUT HE WOULDN'T HAVE WORRIED ABOUT BUCKY...
AND HE'S NOT GONNA KEEP ME UNDER WRAPS!
UH OH! I CAN'T!
THEY'VE GOT ME BOTTLED IN!
SO I'LL JUST DOUBLE BACK AGAIN!
THEY SEE ME! THEY'RE COMING...!!
I'VE ONLY ONE CHANCE ...OVER HERE!
HE'S GONE! HE TRICKED US!
HE MUST BE UP AHEAD! QUICK... WE DARE NOT LOSE HIM!
...OR WE'LL PAY WITH OUR LIVES!
I WAS LUCKY THAT TIME!
NOW I CAN MAKE IT BACK TO CAP!
THIS IS THE...
OH, NO! NO!!
CAPTAIN AMERICA IS DEAD!
NEVER AGAIN WILL HE MOCK MY POWER VEST!!
I CLAIM HIS SHIELD!
IT IS YOURS!
NOW, ON WITH THE TASK AT HAND!
18

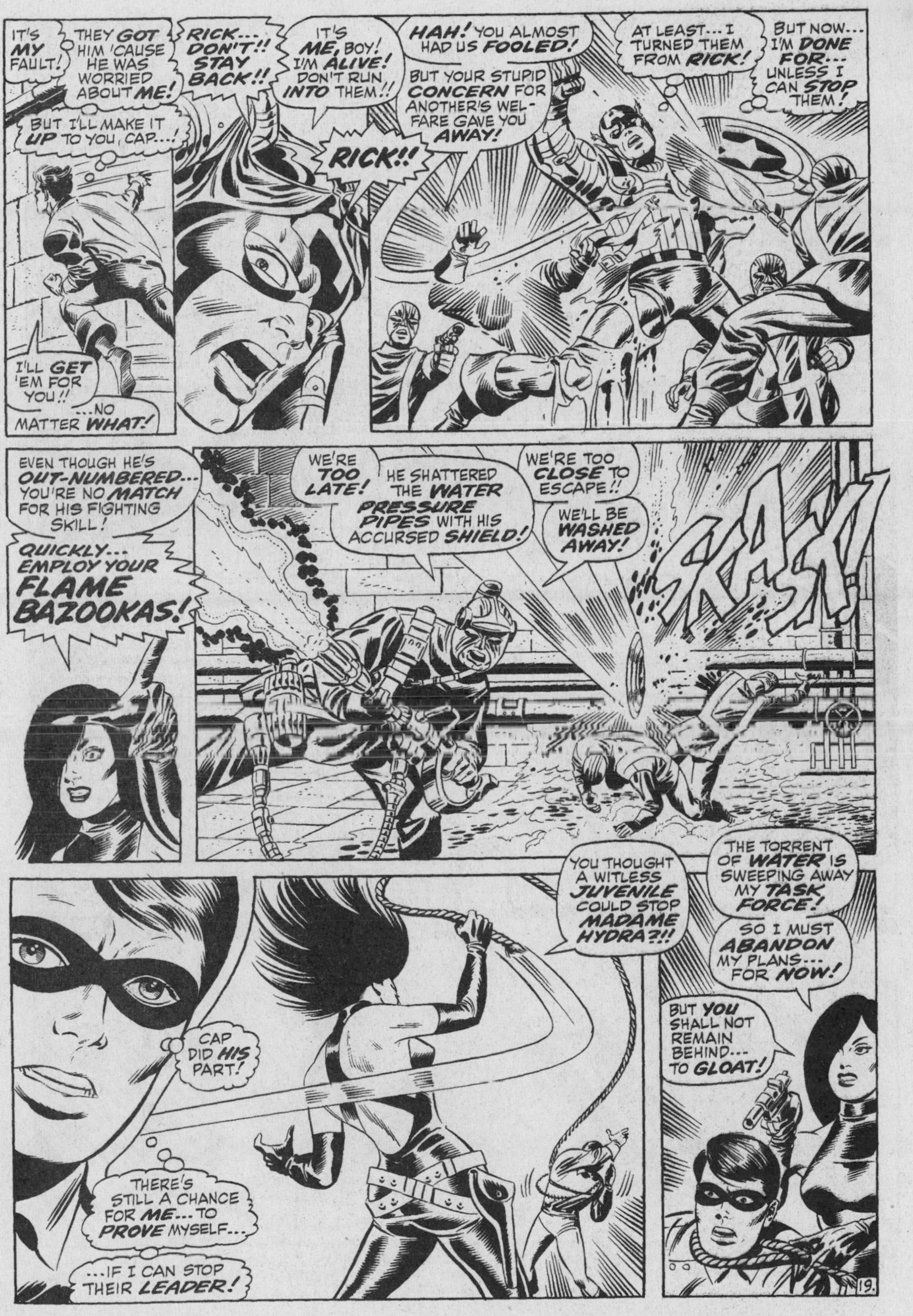

IT'S MY FAULT!
THEY GOT HIM 'CAUSE HE WAS WORRIED ABOUT ME!
BUT I'LL MAKE IT UP TO YOU, CAP...!
I'LL GET 'EM FOR YOU!!
...NO MATTER WHAT!
RICK... DON'T!! STAY BACK!!
IT'S ME, BOY! I'M ALIVE! DON'T RUN INTO THEM!!
RICK!!
HAH! YOU ALMOST HAD US FOOLED!
BUT YOUR STUPID CONCERN FOR ANOTHER'S WELFARE GAVE YOU AWAY!
AT LEAST... I TURNED THEM FROM RICK!
BUT NOW... I'M DONE FOR... UNLESS I CAN STOP THEM!
EVEN THOUGH HE'S OUT-NUMBERED... YOU'RE NO MATCH FOR HIS FIGHTING SKILL!
QUICKLY... EMPLOY YOUR FLAME BAZOOKAS!
WE'RE TOO LATE!
HE SHATTERED THE WATER PRESSURE PIPES WITH HIS ACCURSED SHIELD!
WE'RE TOO CLOSE TO ESCAPE!!
WE'LL BE WASHED AWAY!
SKASH!
CAP DID HIS PART!
THERE'S STILL A CHANCE FOR ME... TO PROVE MYSELF...
...IF I CAN STOP THEIR LEADER!
YOU THOUGHT A WITLESS JUVENILE COULD STOP MADAME HYDRA?!!
THE TORRENT OF WATER IS SWEEPING AWAY MY TASK FORCE!
SO I MUST ABANDON MY PLANS... FOR NOW!
BUT YOU SHALL NOT REMAIN BEHIND... TO GLOAT!
19.

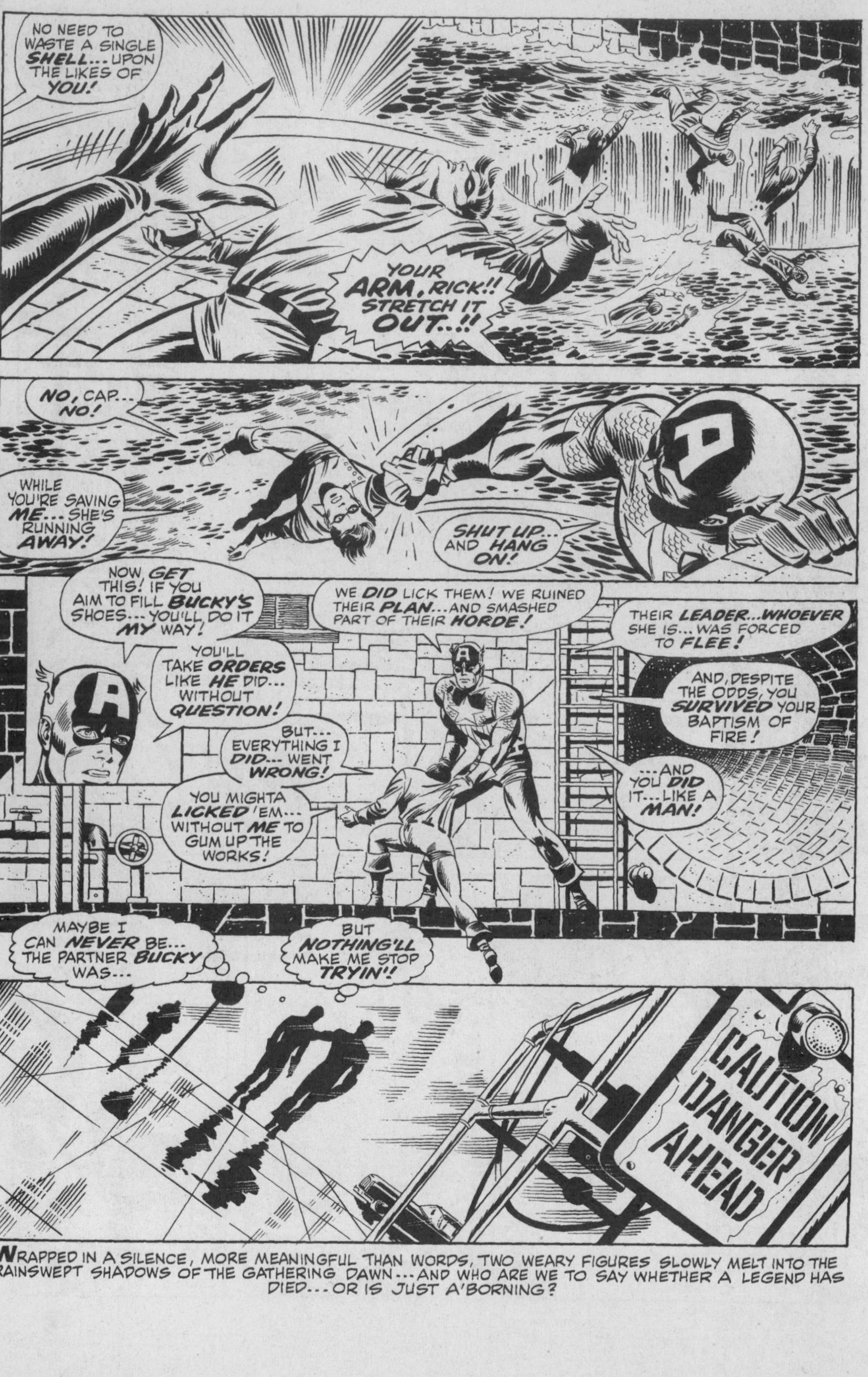
NO NEED TO WASTE A SINGLE SHELL... UPON THE LIKES OF YOU!
YOUR ARM, RICK!! STRETCH IT OUT..!!
NO, CAP... NO!
WHILE YOU'RE SAVING ME... SHE'S RUNNING AWAY!
SHUT UP... AND HANG ON!
NOW GET THIS! IF YOU AIM TO FILL BUCKY'S SHOES... YOU'LL DO IT MY WAY!
YOU'LL TAKE ORDERS LIKE HE DID... WITHOUT QUESTION!
BUT... EVERYTHING I DID... WENT WRONG!
YOU MIGHTA LICKED 'EM... WITHOUT ME TO GUM UP THE WORKS!
WE DID LICK THEM! WE RUINED THEIR PLAN... AND SMASHED PART OF THEIR HORDE!
THEIR LEADER... WHOEVER SHE IS... WAS FORCED TO FLEE!
AND, DESPITE THE ODDS, YOU SURVIVED YOUR BAPTISM OF FIRE!
...AND YOU DID IT... LIKE A MAN!
MAYBE I CAN NEVER BE... THE PARTNER BUCKY WAS...
BUT NOTHING'LL MAKE ME STOP TRYIN'!
CAUTION DANGER AHEAD

WRAPPED IN A SILENCE, MORE MEANINGFUL THAN WORDS, TWO WEARY FIGURES SLOWLY MELT INTO THE RAINSWEPT SHADOWS OF THE GATHERING DAWN... AND WHO ARE WE TO SAY WHETHER A LEGEND HAS DIED... OR IS JUST A'BORNING?

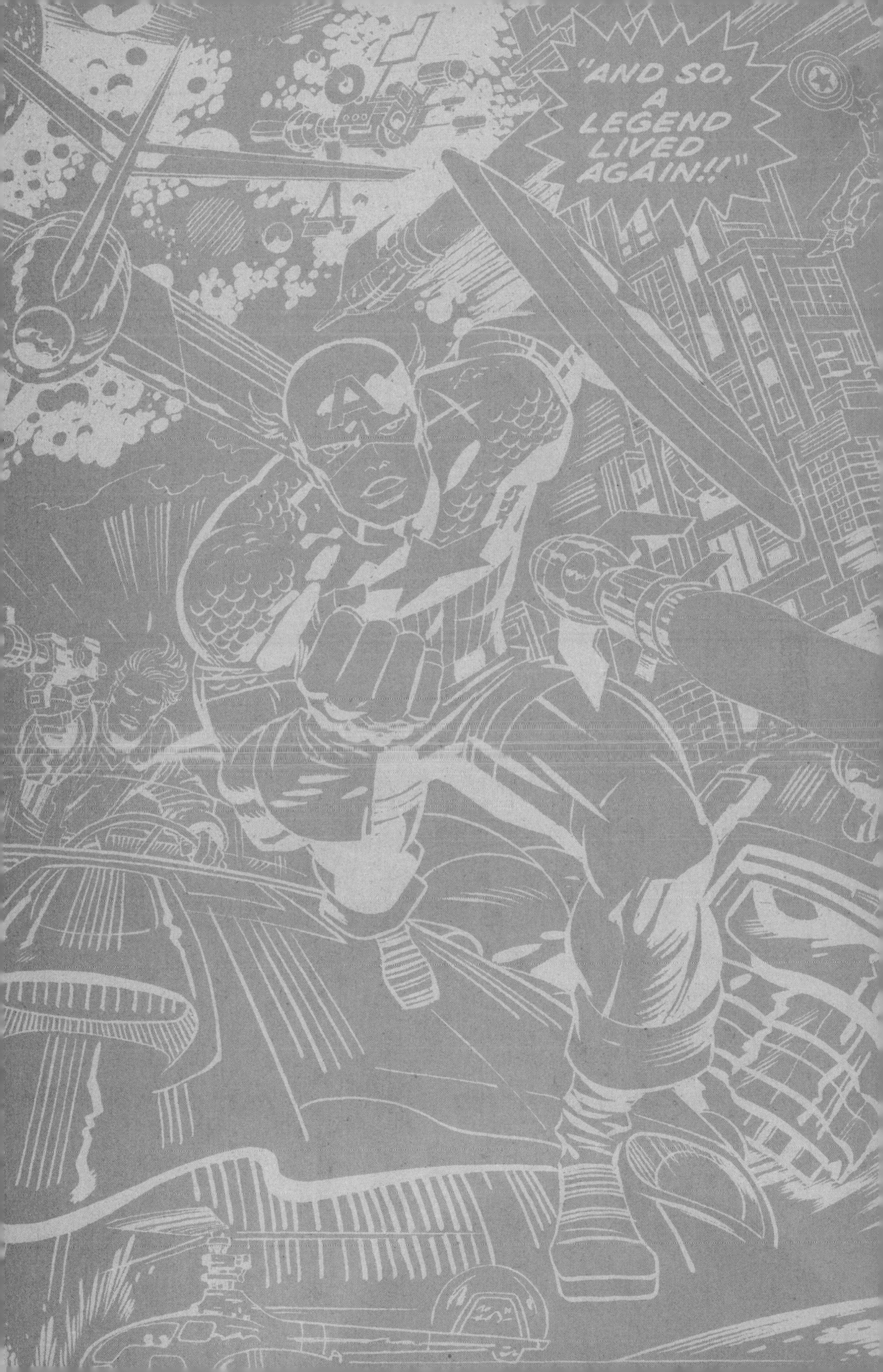
"AND SO, A LEGEND LIVED AGAIN!!"

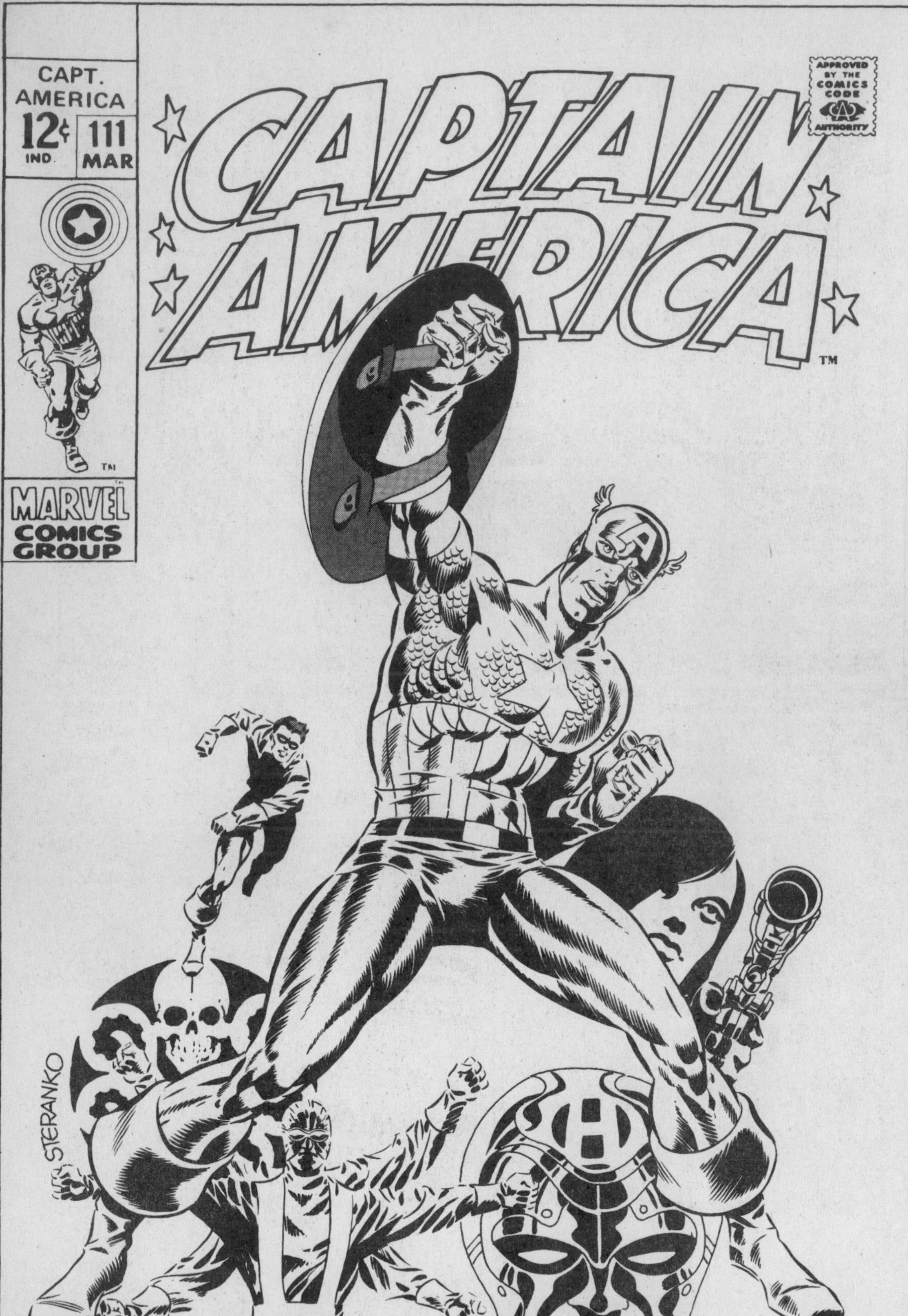
CAPT. AMERICA
12¢ IND.
111 MAR
MARVEL COMICS GROUP
CAPTAIN AMERICA
APPROVED BY THE COMICS CODE AUTHORITY
STERANKO

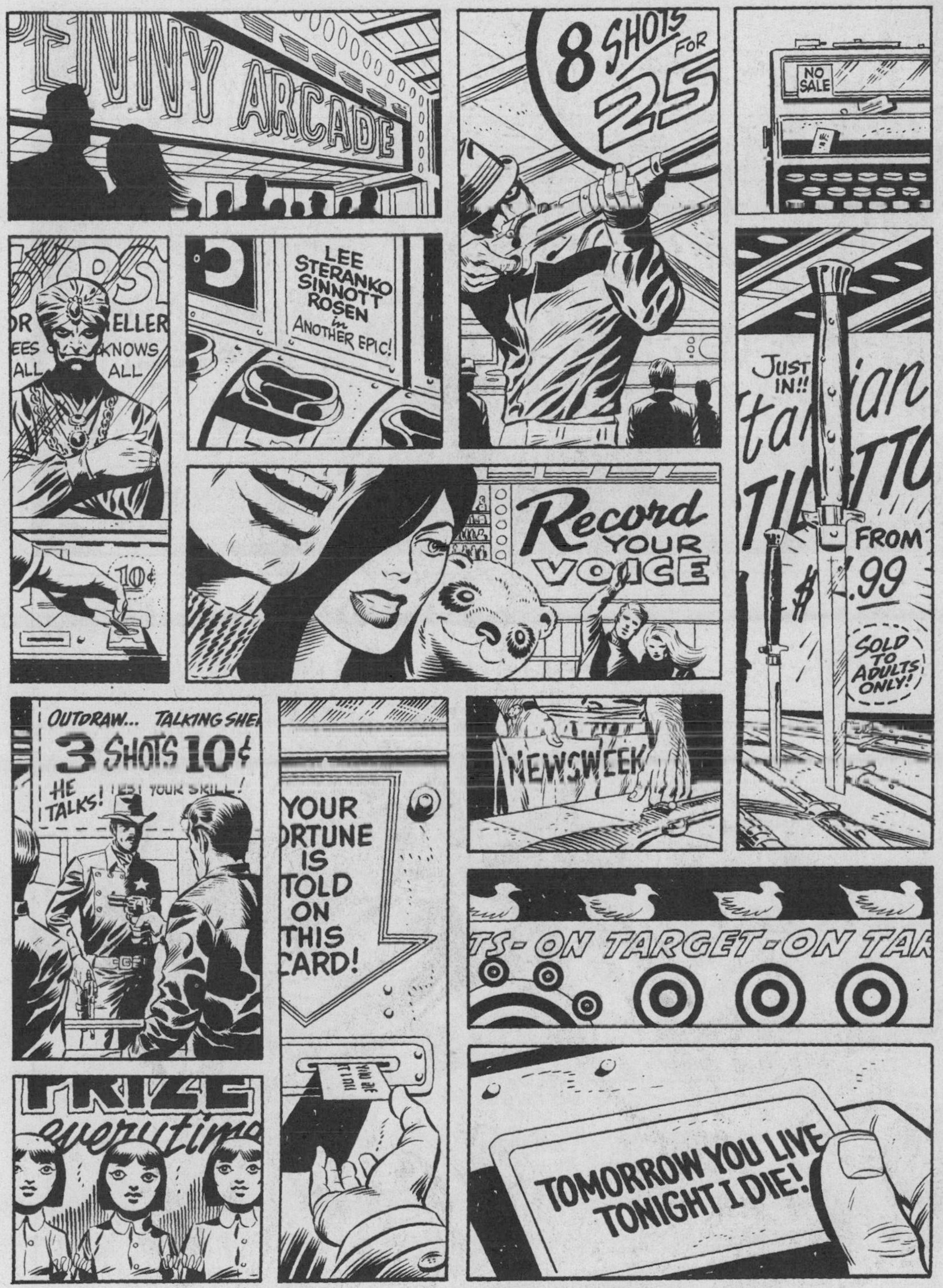
PENNY ARCADE
8 SHOTS FOR 25
NO SALE
KNOWS ALL
LEE STERANKO SINNOTT ROSEN in ANOTHER EPIC!
JUST IN!!
FROM
.99
SOLD TO ADULTS ONLY!
10¢
Record YOUR VOICE
OUTDRAW... TALKING SHE
3 SHOTS 10¢
HE TALKS!
YOUR ORTUNE IS TOLD ON THIS CARD!
NEWSWEEK
ON TARGET - ON TAR
TOMORROW YOU LIVE
TONIGHT I DIE!

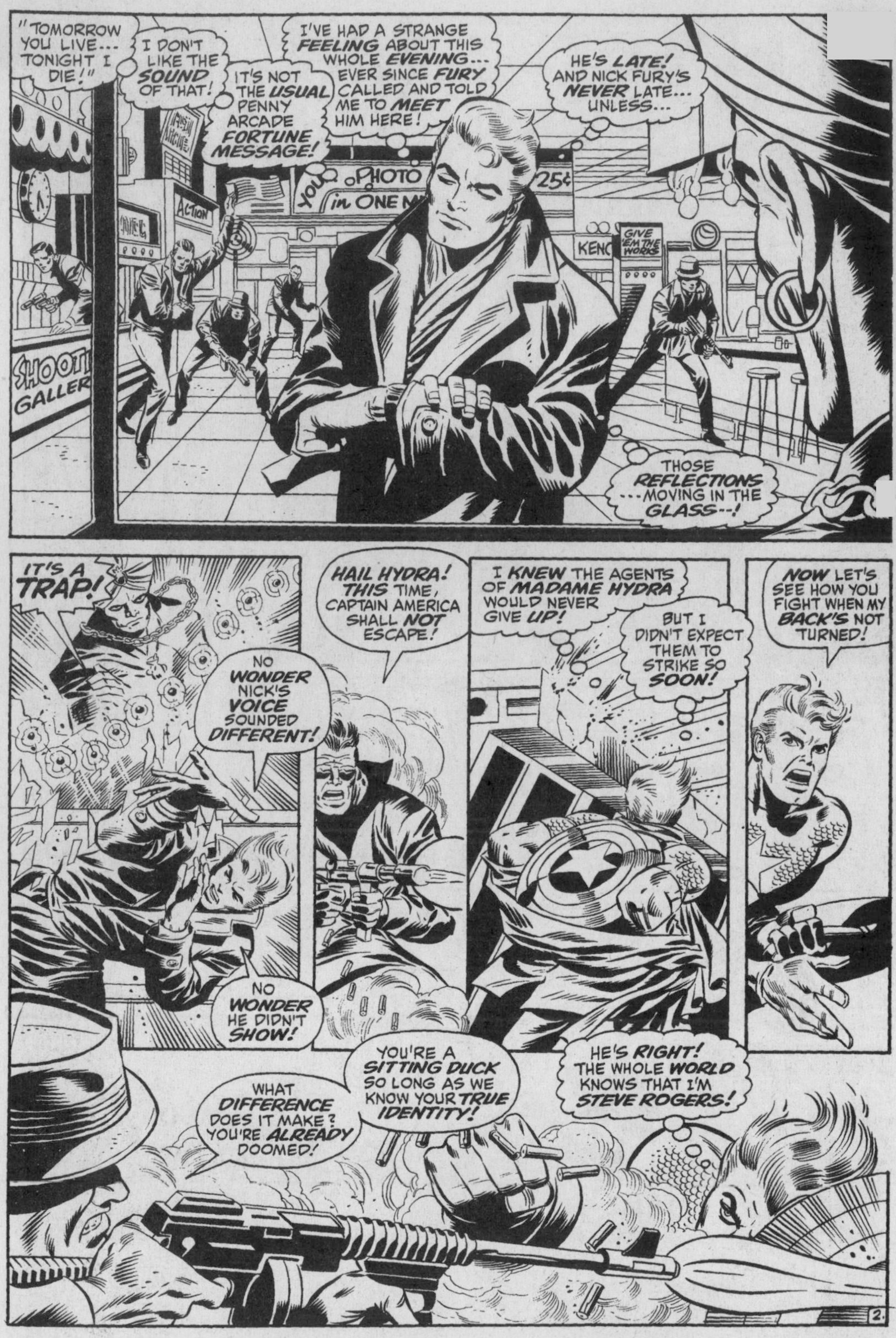
"TOMORROW YOU LIVE... TONIGHT I DIE!"
I DON'T LIKE THE SOUND OF THAT!
IT'S NOT THE USUAL PENNY ARCADE FORTUNE MESSAGE!
I'VE HAD A STRANGE FEELING ABOUT THIS WHOLE EVENING... EVER SINCE FURY CALLED AND TOLD ME TO MEET HIM HERE!
HE'S LATE! AND NICK FURY'S NEVER LATE... UNLESS...
PHOTO
25¢
in ONE M
ACTION
KENO
GIVE 'EM THE WORKS
SHOOTI
GALLER
THOSE REFLECTIONS ---MOVING IN THE GLASS--!
IT'S A TRAP!
NO WONDER NICK'S VOICE SOUNDED DIFFERENT!
NO WONDER HE DIDN'T SHOW!
HAIL HYDRA! THIS TIME, CAPTAIN AMERICA SHALL NOT ESCAPE!
I KNEW THE AGENTS OF MADAME HYDRA WOULD NEVER GIVE UP!
BUT I DIDN'T EXPECT THEM TO STRIKE SO SOON!
NOW LET'S SEE HOW YOU FIGHT WHEN MY BACK'S NOT TURNED!
WHAT DIFFERENCE DOES IT MAKE? YOU'RE ALREADY DOOMED!
YOU'RE A SITTING DUCK SO LONG AS WE KNOW YOUR TRUE IDENTITY!
HE'S RIGHT! THE WHOLE WORLD KNOWS THAT I'M STEVE ROGERS!
2.

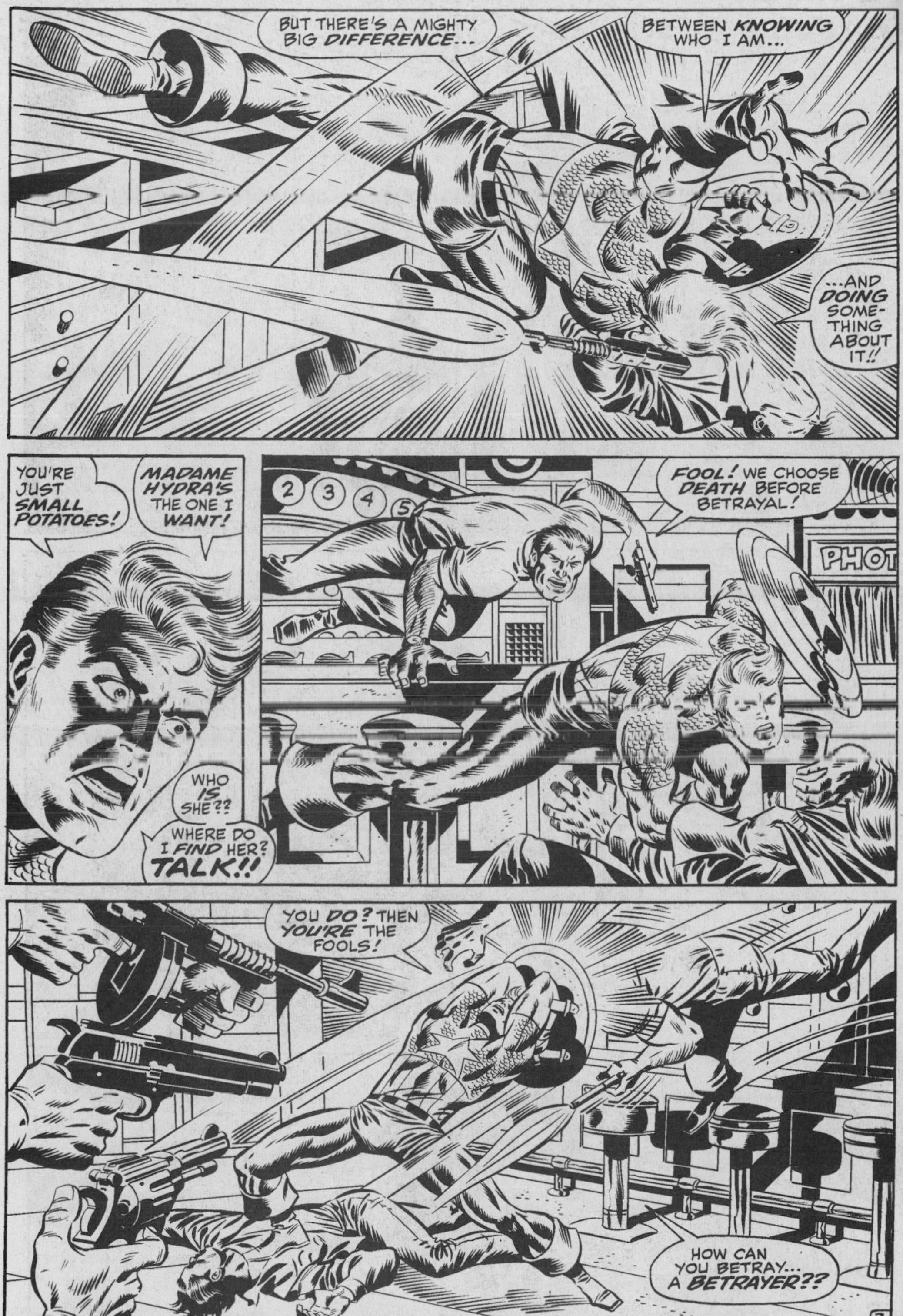
BUT THERE'S A MIGHTY BIG DIFFERENCE...
BETWEEN KNOWING WHO I AM...
...AND DOING SOMETHING ABOUT IT!!
YOU'RE JUST SMALL POTATOES!
MADAME HYDRA'S THE ONE I WANT!
WHO IS SHE??
WHERE DO I FIND HER? TALK!!
FOOL! WE CHOOSE DEATH BEFORE BETRAYAL!
PHOT
YOU DO? THEN YOU'RE THE FOOLS!
HOW CAN YOU BETRAY... A BETRAYER??
3.

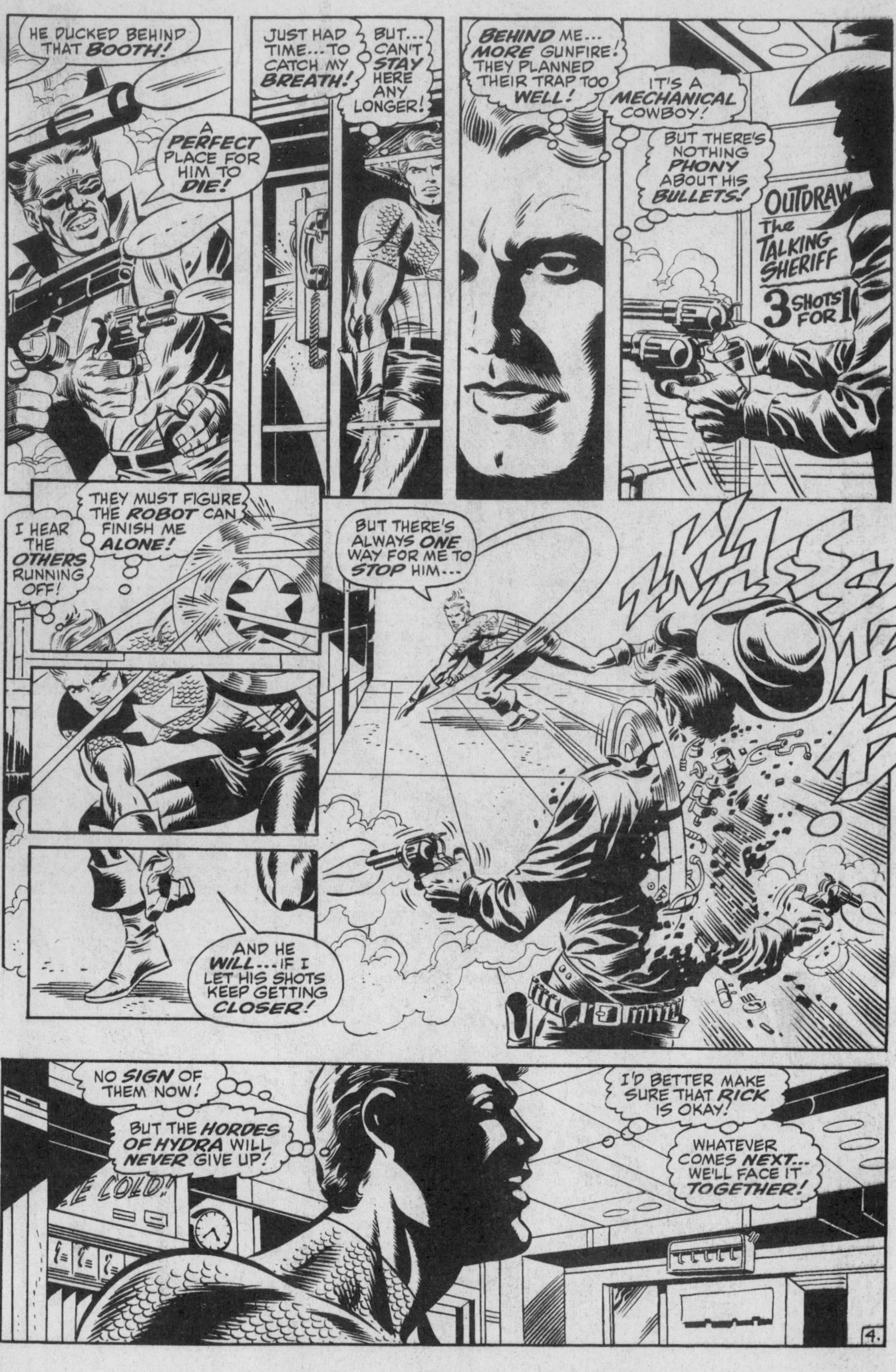

HE DUCKED BEHIND THAT BOOTH!
A PERFECT PLACE FOR HIM TO DIE!
JUST HAD TIME...TO CATCH MY BREATH!
BUT... CAN'T STAY HERE ANY LONGER!
BEHIND ME... MORE GUNFIRE! THEY PLANNED THEIR TRAP TOO WELL!
IT'S A MECHANICAL COWBOY!
BUT THERE'S NOTHING PHONY ABOUT HIS BULLETS!
OUTDRAW The TALKING SHERIFF
3 SHOTS FOR 1
I HEAR THE OTHERS RUNNING OFF!
THEY MUST FIGURE THE ROBOT CAN FINISH ME ALONE!
BUT THERE'S ALWAYS ONE WAY FOR ME TO STOP HIM...
AND HE WILL...IF I LET HIS SHOTS KEEP GETTING CLOSER!
NO SIGN OF THEM NOW!
BUT THE HORDES OF HYDRA WILL NEVER GIVE UP!
I'D BETTER MAKE SURE THAT RICK IS OKAY!
WHATEVER COMES NEXT... WE'LL FACE IT TOGETHER!
4.

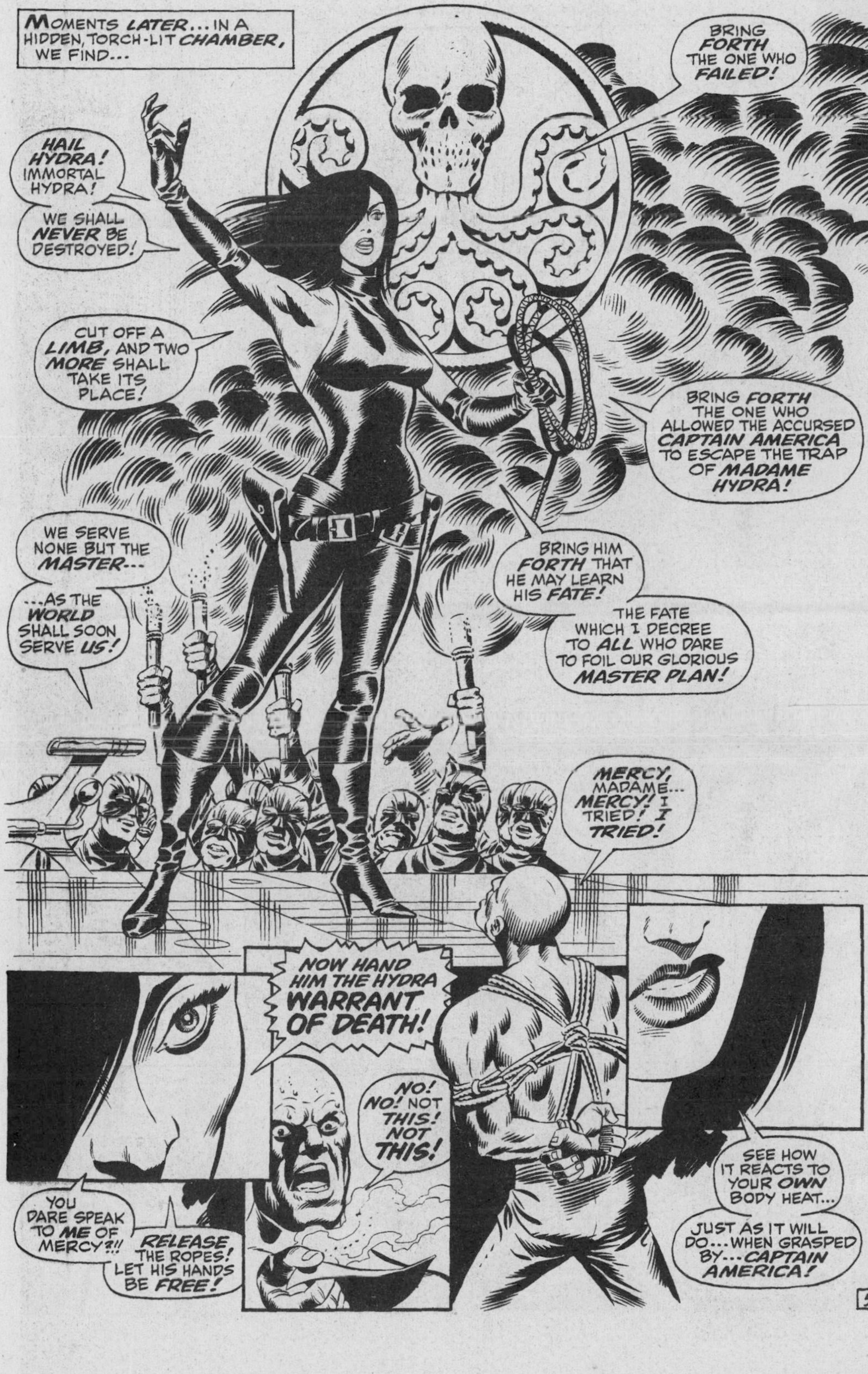
MOMENTS LATER... IN A HIDDEN, TORCH-LIT CHAMBER, WE FIND...
HAIL HYDRA! IMMORTAL HYDRA!
WE SHALL NEVER BE DESTROYED!
BRING FORTH THE ONE WHO FAILED!
CUT OFF A LIMB, AND TWO MORE SHALL TAKE ITS PLACE!
BRING FORTH THE ONE WHO ALLOWED THE ACCURSED CAPTAIN AMERICA TO ESCAPE THE TRAP OF MADAME HYDRA!
WE SERVE NONE BUT THE MASTER---
...AS THE WORLD SHALL SOON SERVE US!
BRING HIM FORTH THAT HE MAY LEARN HIS FATE!
THE FATE WHICH I DECREE TO ALL WHO DARE TO FOIL OUR GLORIOUS MASTER PLAN!
MERCY, MADAME... MERCY! I TRIED! I TRIED!
NOW HAND HIM THE HYDRA WARRANT OF DEATH!
NO! NO! NOT THIS! NOT THIS!
YOU DARE SPEAK TO ME OF MERCY?!!
RELEASE THE ROPES! LET HIS HANDS BE FREE!
SEE HOW IT REACTS TO YOUR OWN BODY HEAT...
JUST AS IT WILL DO... WHEN GRASPED BY... CAPTAIN AMERICA!

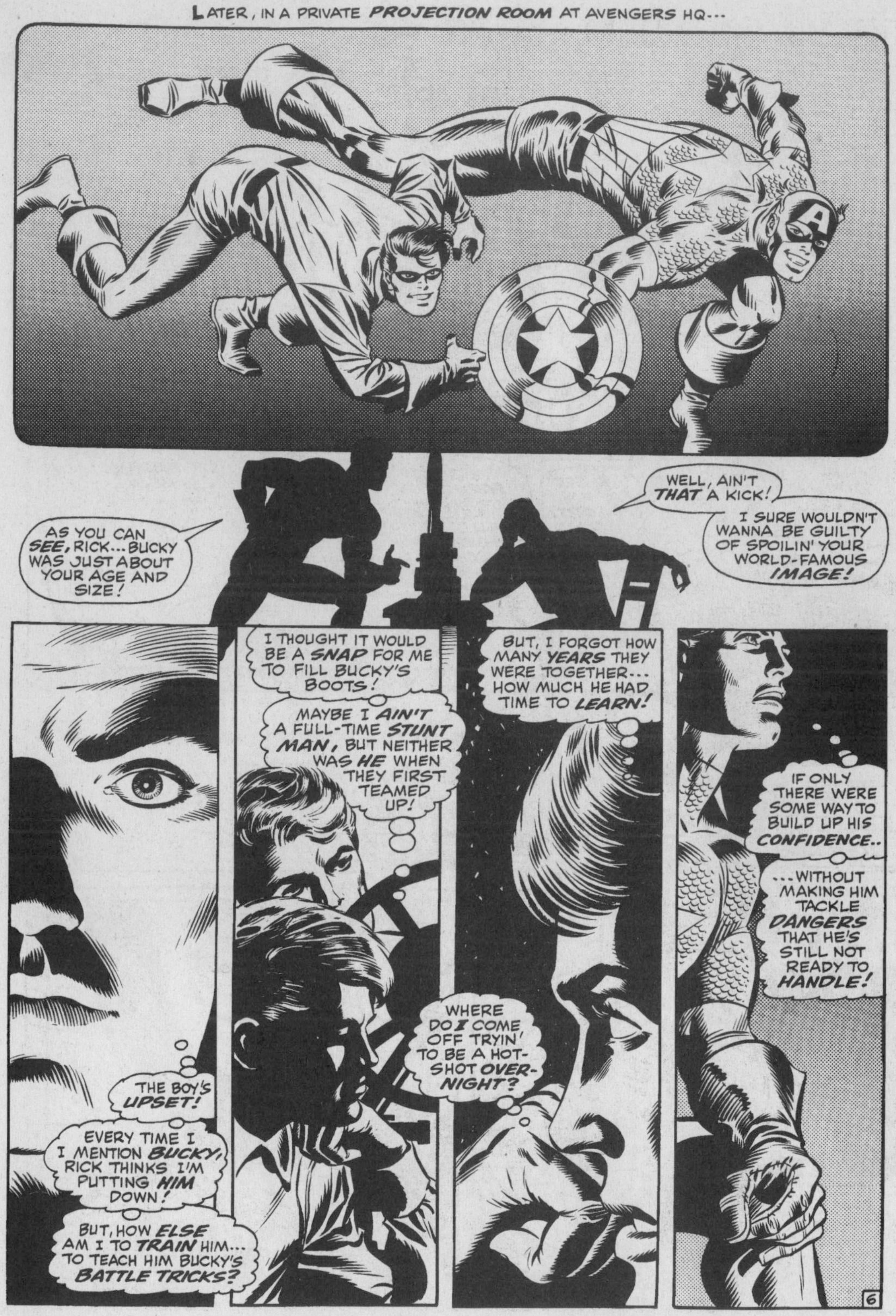
LATER, IN A PRIVATE PROJECTION ROOM AT AVENGERS HQ---
AS YOU CAN SEE, RICK... BUCKY WAS JUST ABOUT YOUR AGE AND SIZE!
WELL, AIN'T THAT A KICK!
I SURE WOULDN'T WANNA BE GUILTY OF SPOILIN' YOUR WORLD-FAMOUS IMAGE!
THE BOY'S UPSET!
EVERY TIME I MENTION BUCKY, RICK THINKS I'M PUTTING HIM DOWN!
BUT, HOW ELSE AM I TO TRAIN HIM... TO TEACH HIM BUCKY'S BATTLE TRICKS?
I THOUGHT IT WOULD BE A SNAP FOR ME TO FILL BUCKY'S BOOTS!
MAYBE I AIN'T A FULL-TIME STUNT MAN, BUT NEITHER WAS HE WHEN THEY FIRST TEAMED UP!
BUT, I FORGOT HOW MANY YEARS THEY WERE TOGETHER--- HOW MUCH HE HAD TIME TO LEARN!
WHERE DO I COME OFF TRYIN' TO BE A HOT-SHOT OVER-NIGHT?
IF ONLY THERE WERE SOME WAY TO BUILD UP HIS CONFIDENCE..
...WITHOUT MAKING HIM TACKLE DANGERS THAT HE'S STILL NOT READY TO HANDLE!
6

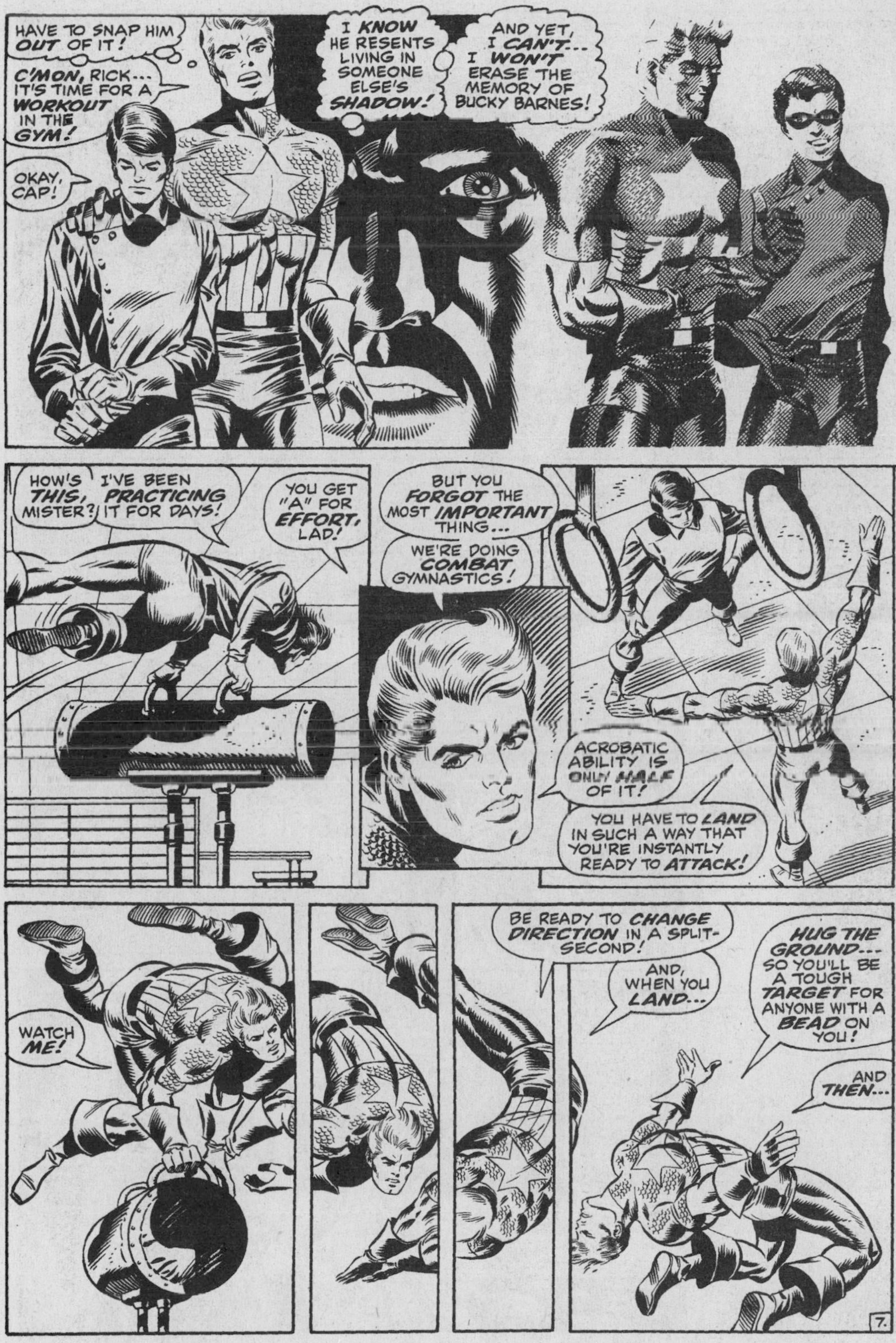
HAVE TO SNAP HIM OUT OF IT!
C'MON, RICK... IT'S TIME FOR A WORKOUT IN THE GYM!
OKAY, CAP!
I KNOW HE RESENTS LIVING IN SOMEONE ELSE'S SHADOW!
AND YET, I CAN'T... I WON'T ERASE THE MEMORY OF BUCKY BARNES!
HOW'S THIS, MISTER?
I'VE BEEN PRACTICING IT FOR DAYS!
YOU GET "A" FOR EFFORT, LAD!
BUT YOU FORGOT THE MOST IMPORTANT THING...
WE'RE DOING COMBAT GYMNASTICS!
ACROBATIC ABILITY IS ONLY HALF OF IT!
YOU HAVE TO LAND IN SUCH A WAY THAT YOU'RE INSTANTLY READY TO ATTACK!
WATCH ME!
BE READY TO CHANGE DIRECTION IN A SPLIT-SECOND!
AND, WHEN YOU LAND...
HUG THE GROUND... SO YOU'LL BE A TOUGH TARGET FOR ANYONE WITH A BEAD ON YOU!
AND THEN...
7.

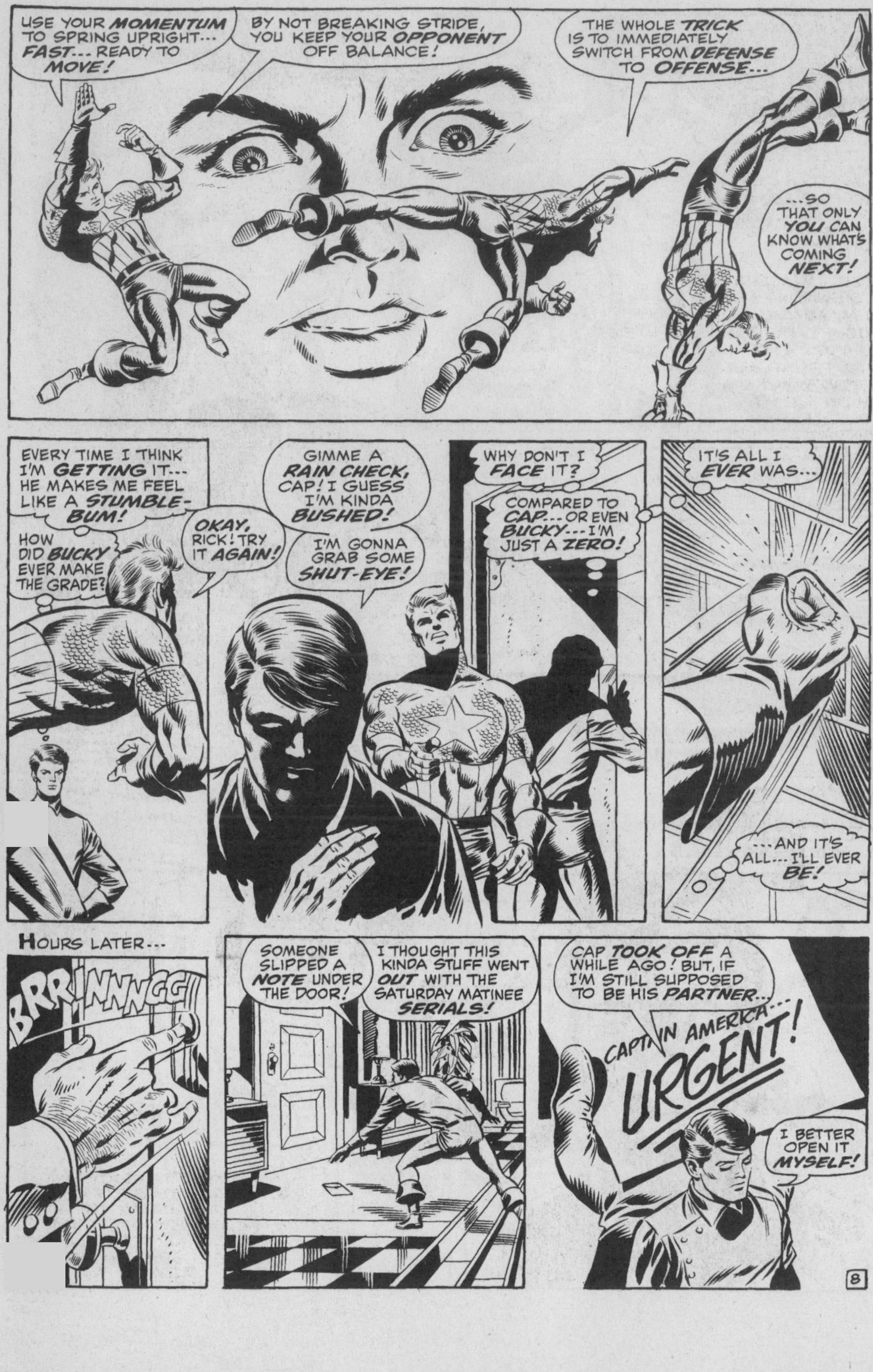
USE YOUR MOMENTUM TO SPRING UPRIGHT--- FAST--- READY TO MOVE!
BY NOT BREAKING STRIDE, YOU KEEP YOUR OPPONENT OFF BALANCE!
THE WHOLE TRICK IS TO IMMEDIATELY SWITCH FROM DEFENSE TO OFFENSE...
...SO THAT ONLY YOU CAN KNOW WHAT'S COMING NEXT!
EVERY TIME I THINK I'M GETTING IT--- HE MAKES ME FEEL LIKE A STUMBLE-BUM!
HOW DID BUCKY EVER MAKE THE GRADE?
OKAY, RICK! TRY IT AGAIN!
GIMME A RAIN CHECK, CAP! I GUESS I'M KINDA BUSHED!
I'M GONNA GRAB SOME SHUT-EYE!
WHY DON'T I FACE IT?
COMPARED TO CAP--- OR EVEN BUCKY--- I'M JUST A ZERO!
IT'S ALL I EVER WAS...
...AND IT'S ALL--- I'LL EVER BE!
HOURS LATER...
BRRINNNGG!
SOMEONE SLIPPED A NOTE UNDER THE DOOR!
I THOUGHT THIS KINDA STUFF WENT OUT WITH THE SATURDAY MATINEE SERIALS!
CAP TOOK OFF A WHILE AGO! BUT, IF I'M STILL SUPPOSED TO BE HIS PARTNER...
CAPTAIN AMERICA... URGENT!
I BETTER OPEN IT MYSELF!
8

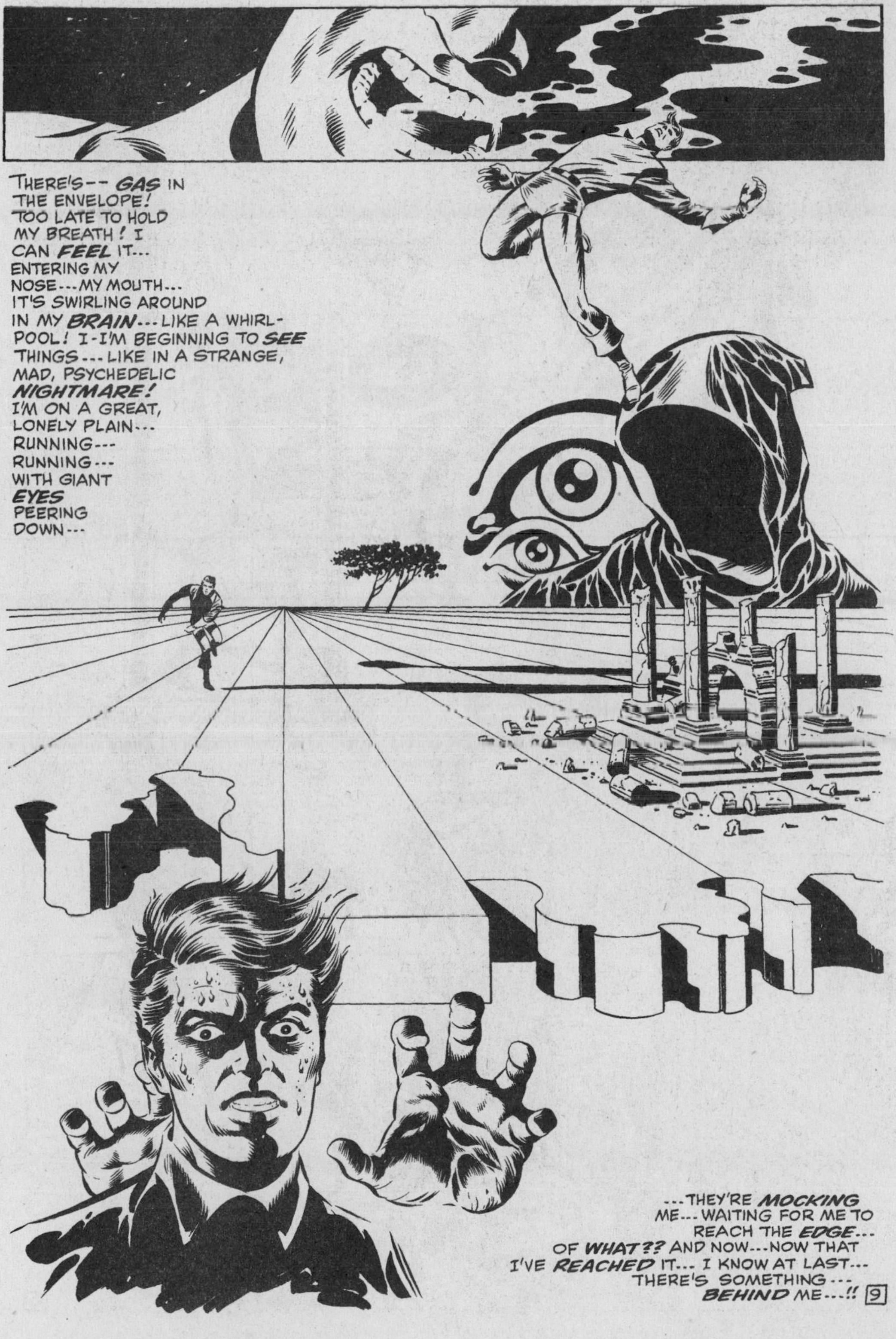

THERE'S-- GAS IN THE ENVELOPE! TOO LATE TO HOLD MY BREATH! I CAN FEEL IT... ENTERING MY NOSE---MY MOUTH--- IT'S SWIRLING AROUND IN MY BRAIN--- LIKE A WHIRL-POOL! I-I'M BEGINNING TO SEE THINGS--- LIKE IN A STRANGE, MAD, PSYCHEDELIC NIGHTMARE! I'M ON A GREAT, LONELY PLAIN--- RUNNING--- RUNNING--- WITH GIANT EYES PEERING DOWN---
---THEY'RE MOCKING ME---WAITING FOR ME TO REACH THE EDGE--- OF WHAT?? AND NOW---NOW THAT I'VE REACHED IT--- I KNOW AT LAST--- THERE'S SOMETHING--- BEHIND ME---!!
9

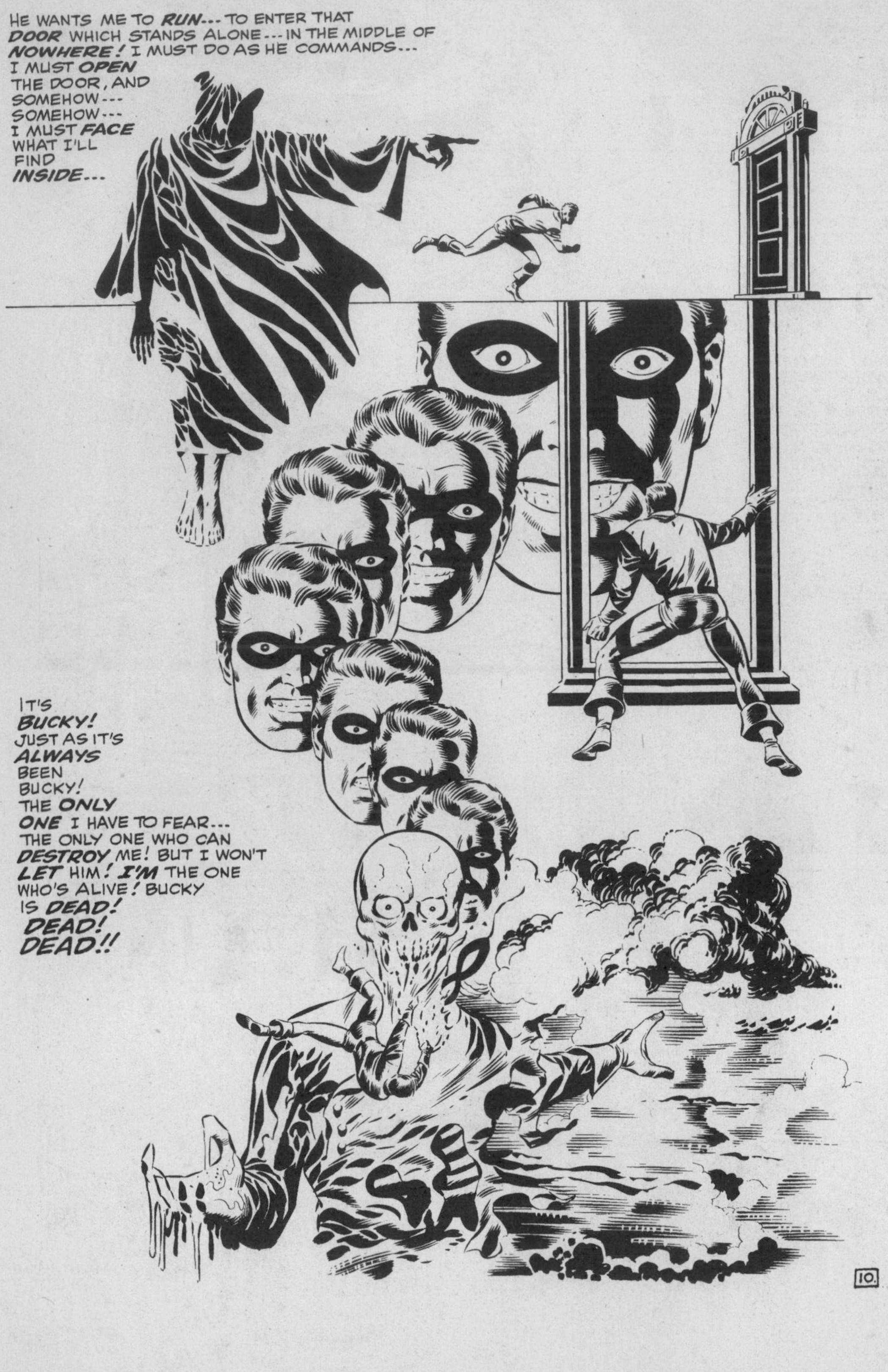
HE WANTS ME TO RUN... TO ENTER THAT DOOR WHICH STANDS ALONE... IN THE MIDDLE OF NOWHERE! I MUST DO AS HE COMMANDS... I MUST OPEN THE DOOR, AND SOMEHOW--- SOMEHOW--- I MUST FACE WHAT I'LL FIND INSIDE...
IT'S BUCKY! JUST AS IT'S ALWAYS BEEN BUCKY! THE ONLY ONE I HAVE TO FEAR... THE ONLY ONE WHO CAN DESTROY ME! BUT I WON'T LET HIM! I'M THE ONE WHO'S ALIVE! BUCKY IS DEAD! DEAD! DEAD!!
10.

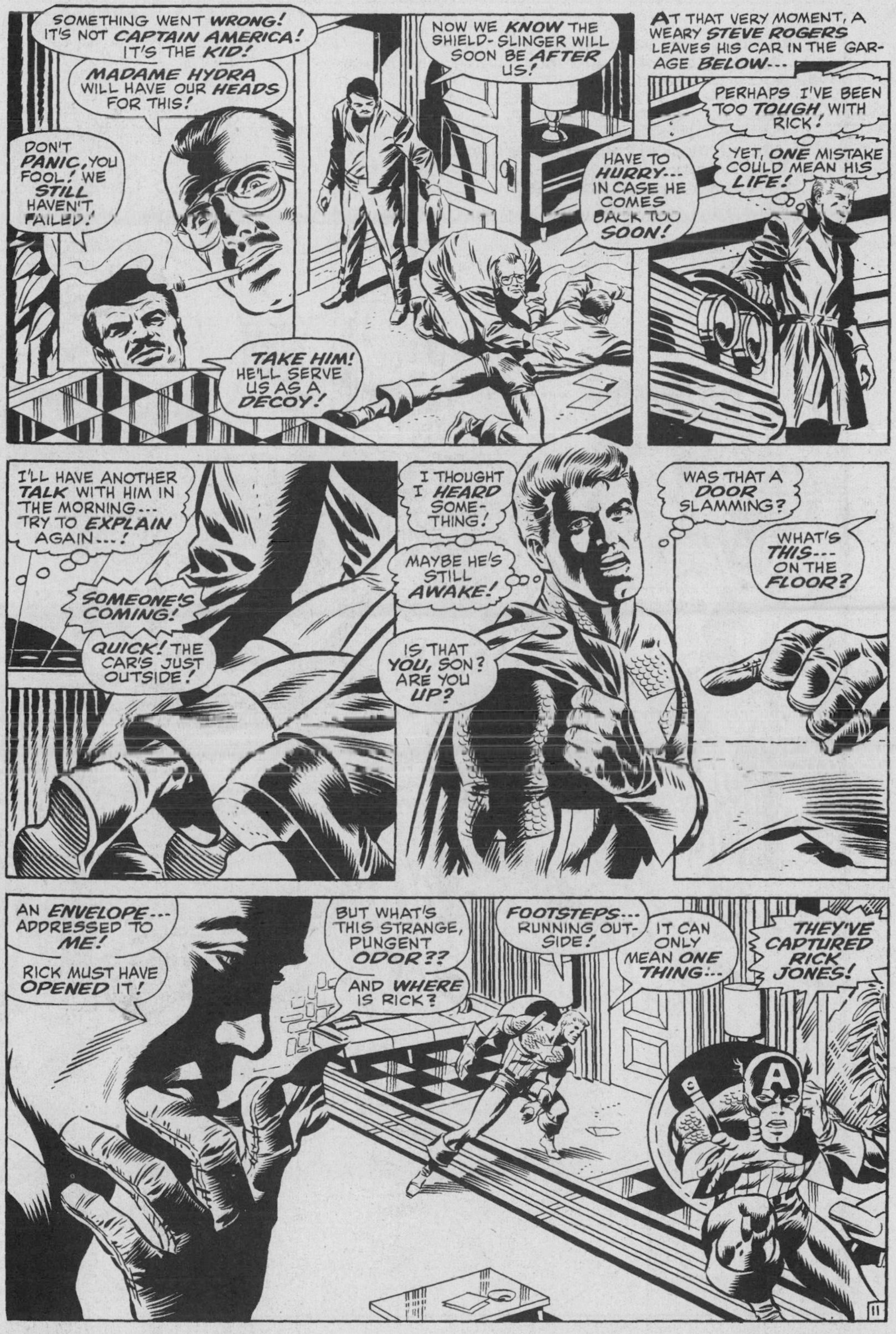
SOMETHING WENT WRONG! IT'S NOT CAPTAIN AMERICA! IT'S THE KID!
MADAME HYDRA WILL HAVE OUR HEADS FOR THIS!
DON'T PANIC, YOU FOOL! WE STILL HAVEN'T FAILED!
NOW WE KNOW THE SHIELD-SLINGER WILL SOON BE AFTER US!
HAVE TO HURRY--- IN CASE HE COMES BACK TOO SOON!
TAKE HIM! HE'LL SERVE US AS A DECOY!
AT THAT VERY MOMENT, A WEARY STEVE ROGERS LEAVES HIS CAR IN THE GARAGE BELOW---
PERHAPS I'VE BEEN TOO TOUGH, WITH RICK!
YET, ONE MISTAKE COULD MEAN HIS LIFE!
I'LL HAVE ANOTHER TALK WITH HIM IN THE MORNING--- TRY TO EXPLAIN AGAIN---!
SOMEONE'S COMING!
QUICK! THE CAR'S JUST OUTSIDE!
I THOUGHT I HEARD SOMETHING!
MAYBE HE'S STILL AWAKE!
IS THAT YOU, SON? ARE YOU UP?
WAS THAT A DOOR SLAMMING?
WHAT'S THIS--- ON THE FLOOR?
AN ENVELOPE--- ADDRESSED TO ME!
RICK MUST HAVE OPENED IT!
BUT WHAT'S THIS STRANGE, PUNGENT ODOR??
AND WHERE IS RICK?
FOOTSTEPS--- RUNNING OUTSIDE!
IT CAN ONLY MEAN ONE THING:---
THEY'VE CAPTURED RICK JONES!

LIKE A MAN *POSSESSED,* THE COSTUMED *AVENGER* HURLS HIMSELF THRU THE SITTING ROOM WINDOW IN THE DIRECTION OF THE HASTY *FOOTSTEPS* HE HEARS BELOW--- HEEDLESS OF THE *DANGER*... HEEDLESS OF THE *ODDS* AGAINST HIM.... *ONE* ACHING THOUGHT RAGING OVER AND OVER IN HIS ANGUISHED MIND--- *HIS PARTNER MUST NOT DIE AGAIN!!*

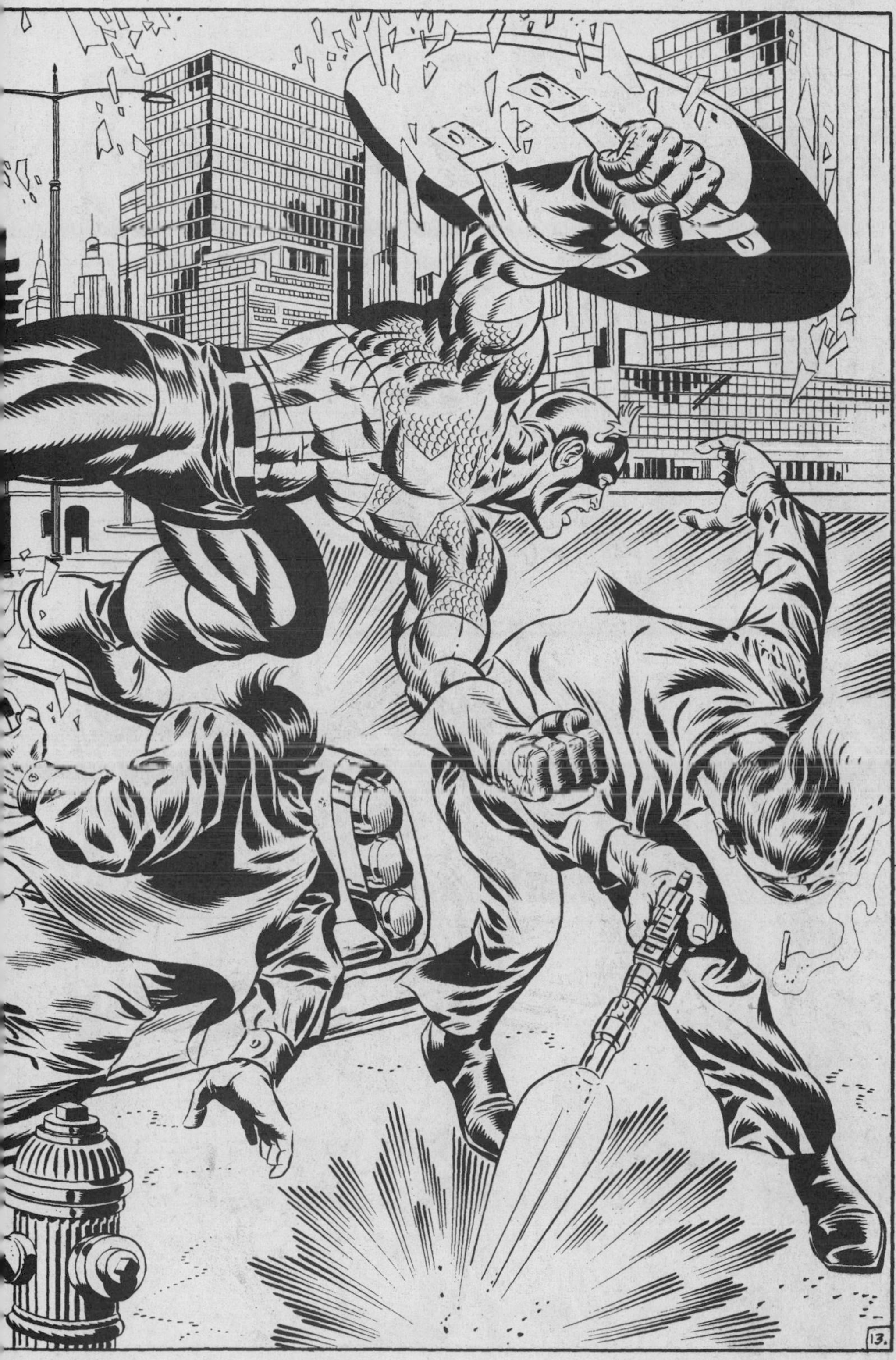
13.

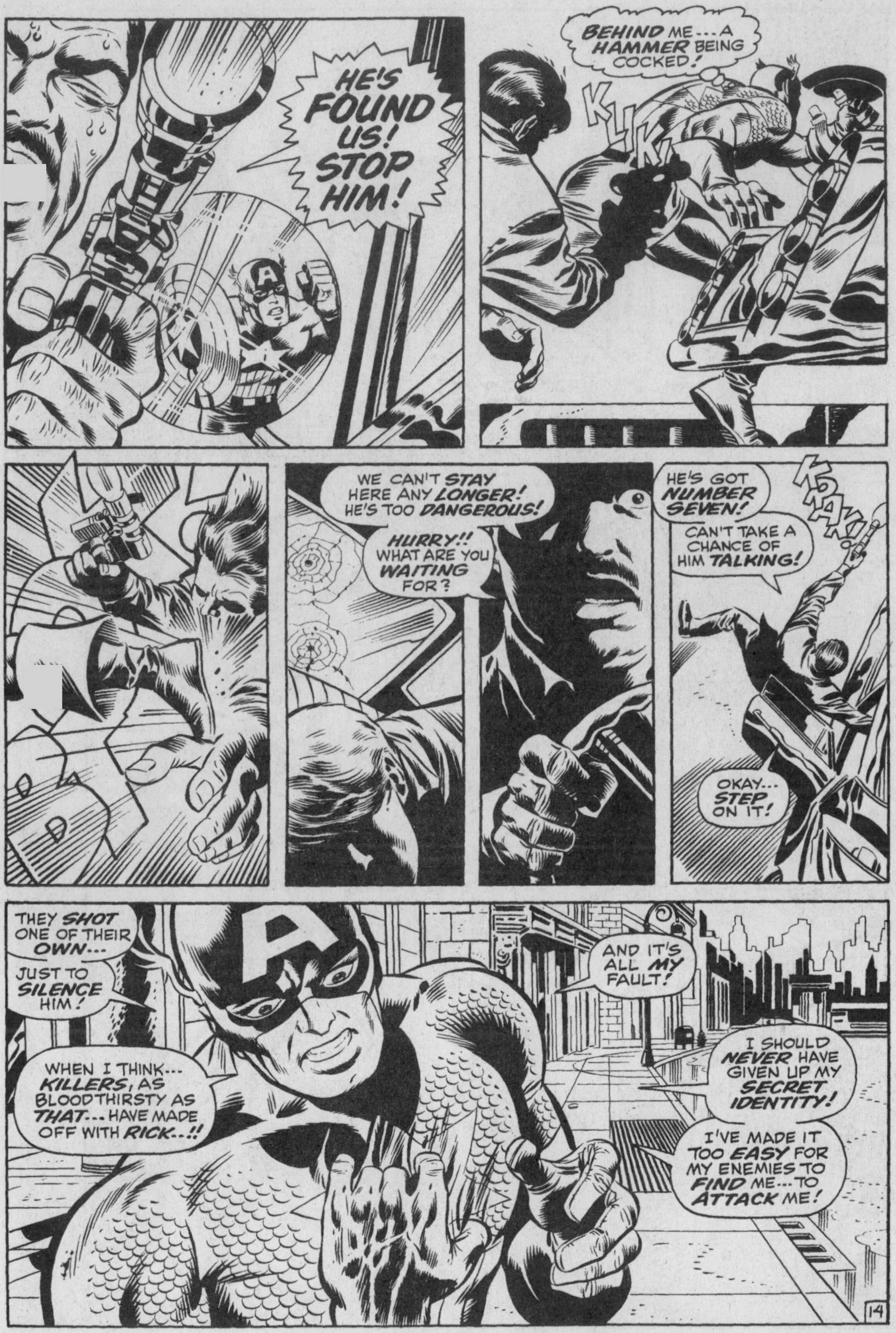

HE'S FOUND US! STOP HIM!
BEHIND ME... A HAMMER BEING COCKED!
KLIK
WE CAN'T STAY HERE ANY LONGER! HE'S TOO DANGEROUS!
HURRY!! WHAT ARE YOU WAITING FOR?
HE'S GOT NUMBER SEVEN!
CAN'T TAKE A CHANCE OF HIM TALKING!
KRAK!
OKAY... STEP ON IT!
THEY SHOT ONE OF THEIR OWN...
JUST TO SILENCE HIM!
AND IT'S ALL MY FAULT!
WHEN I THINK... KILLERS, AS BLOODTHIRSTY AS THAT... HAVE MADE OFF WITH RICK..!!
I SHOULD NEVER HAVE GIVEN UP MY SECRET IDENTITY!
I'VE MADE IT TOO EASY FOR MY ENEMIES TO FIND ME... TO ATTACK ME!
14

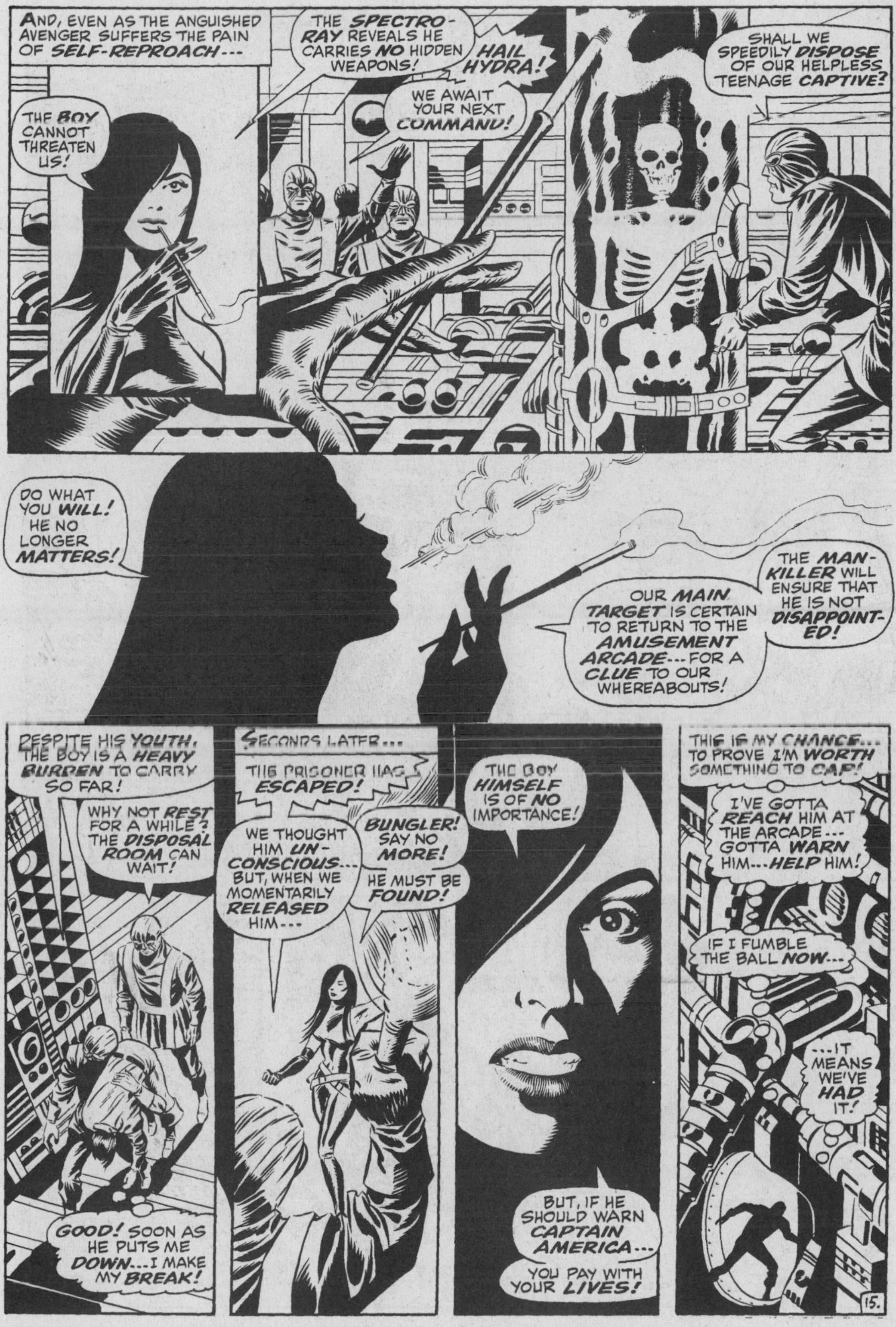
AND, EVEN AS THE ANGUISHED AVENGER SUFFERS THE PAIN OF SELF-REPROACH---
THE BOY CANNOT THREATEN US!
THE SPECTRO-RAY REVEALS HE CARRIES NO HIDDEN WEAPONS!
HAIL HYDRA!
WE AWAIT YOUR NEXT COMMAND!
SHALL WE SPEEDILY DISPOSE OF OUR HELPLESS TEENAGE CAPTIVE?
DO WHAT YOU WILL! HE NO LONGER MATTERS!
OUR MAIN TARGET IS CERTAIN TO RETURN TO THE AMUSEMENT ARCADE--- FOR A CLUE TO OUR WHEREABOUTS!
THE MAN-KILLER WILL ENSURE THAT HE IS NOT DISAPPOINTED!
DESPITE HIS YOUTH, THE BOY IS A HEAVY BURDEN TO CARRY SO FAR!
WHY NOT REST FOR A WHILE? THE DISPOSAL ROOM CAN WAIT!
GOOD! SOON AS HE PUTS ME DOWN...I MAKE MY BREAK!
SECONDS LATER...
THE PRISONER HAS ESCAPED!
WE THOUGHT HIM UN-CONSCIOUS... BUT, WHEN WE MOMENTARILY RELEASED HIM---
BUNGLER! SAY NO MORE!
HE MUST BE FOUND!
THE BOY HIMSELF IS OF NO IMPORTANCE!
BUT, IF HE SHOULD WARN CAPTAIN AMERICA...
YOU PAY WITH YOUR LIVES!
THIS IS MY CHANCE... TO PROVE I'M WORTH SOMETHING TO CAP!
I'VE GOTTA REACH HIM AT THE ARCADE --- GOTTA WARN HIM... HELP HIM!
IF I FUMBLE THE BALL NOW...
...IT MEANS WE'VE HAD IT!
15.

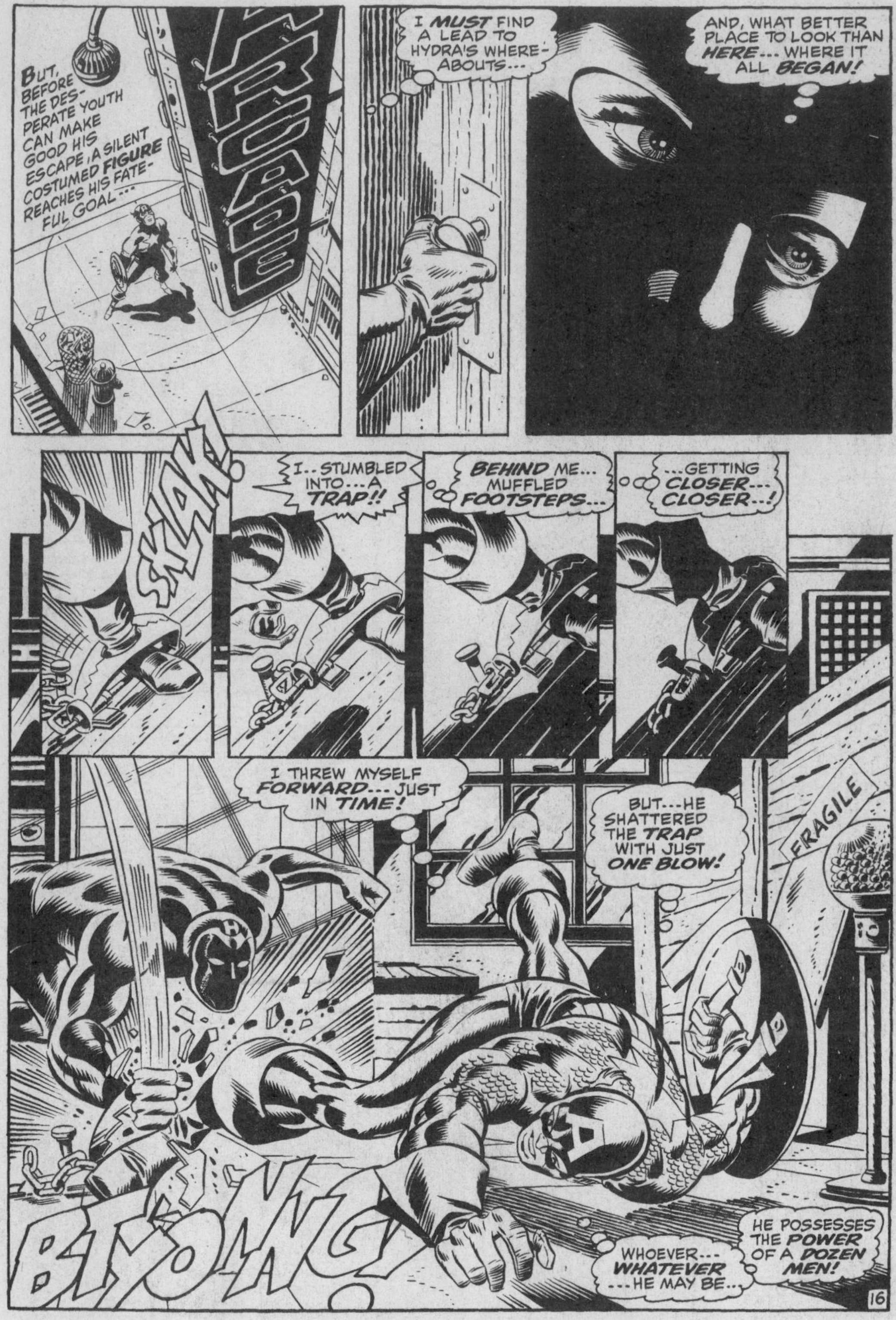

But, before the desperate youth can make good his escape, a silent costumed figure reaches his fateful goal...
I must find a lead to Hydra's whereabouts...
And, what better place to look than here... where it all began!
SKLAK!
I.. stumbled into... a trap!!
Behind me... muffled footsteps...
...getting closer... closer...!
I threw myself forward... just in time!
But... he shattered the trap with just one blow!
FRAGILE
BTYONNG!
Whoever... whatever ...he may be...
He possesses the power of a dozen men!
16

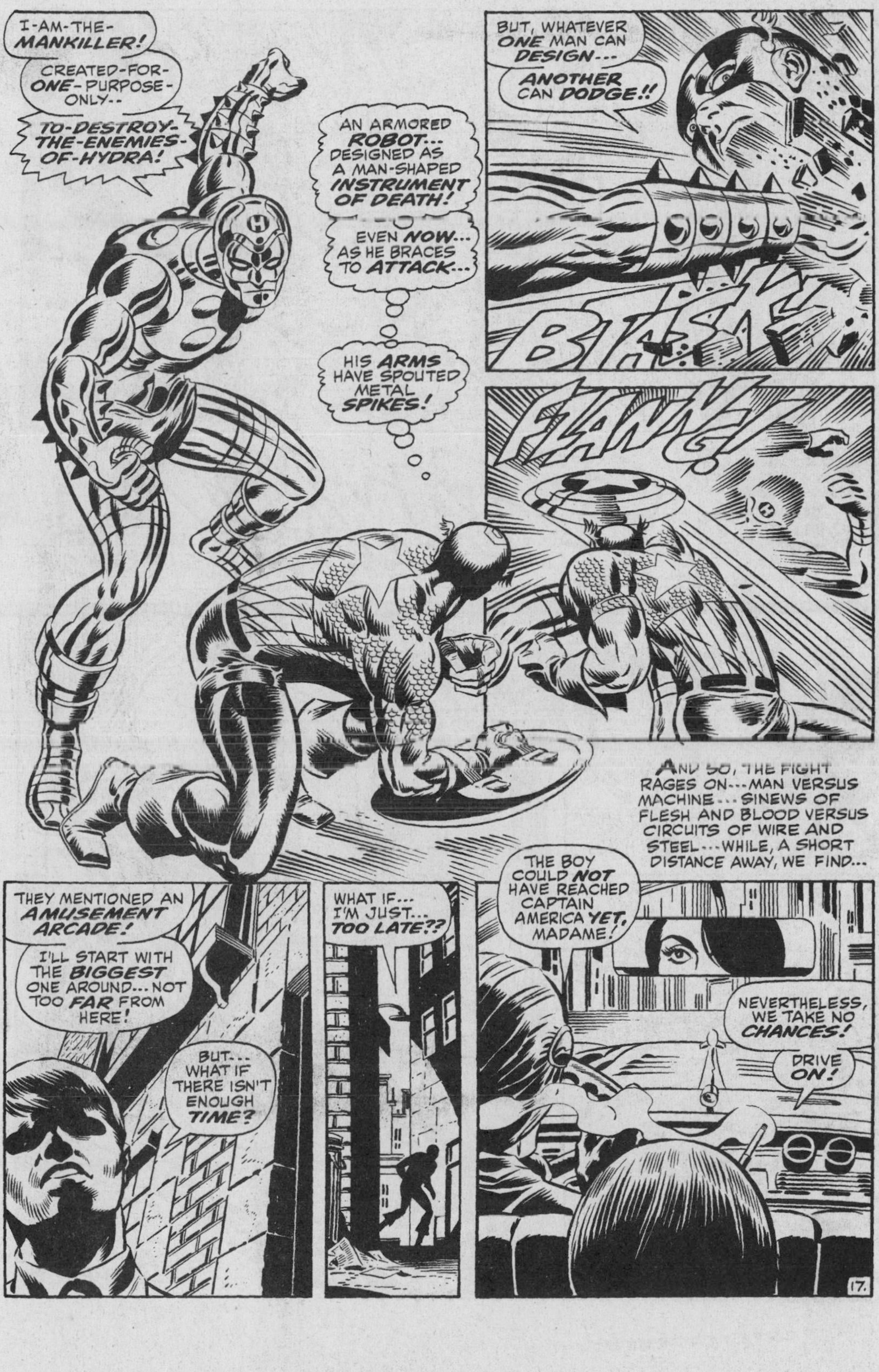
I-AM-THE-MANKILLER!
CREATED-FOR-ONE-PURPOSE-ONLY--
TO-DESTROY-THE-ENEMIES-OF-HYDRA!
AN ARMORED ROBOT... DESIGNED AS A MAN-SHAPED INSTRUMENT OF DEATH!
EVEN NOW... AS HE BRACES TO ATTACK...
HIS ARMS HAVE SPOUTED METAL SPIKES!
BUT, WHATEVER ONE MAN CAN DESIGN---
ANOTHER CAN DODGE!!
FLANNG!
AND SO, THE FIGHT RAGES ON---MAN VERSUS MACHINE---SINEWS OF FLESH AND BLOOD VERSUS CIRCUITS OF WIRE AND STEEL---WHILE, A SHORT DISTANCE AWAY, WE FIND...
THEY MENTIONED AN AMUSEMENT ARCADE!
I'LL START WITH THE BIGGEST ONE AROUND... NOT TOO FAR FROM HERE!
BUT... WHAT IF THERE ISN'T ENOUGH TIME?
WHAT IF... I'M JUST... TOO LATE??
THE BOY COULD NOT HAVE REACHED CAPTAIN AMERICA YET, MADAME!
NEVERTHELESS, WE TAKE NO CHANCES!
DRIVE ON!
17.

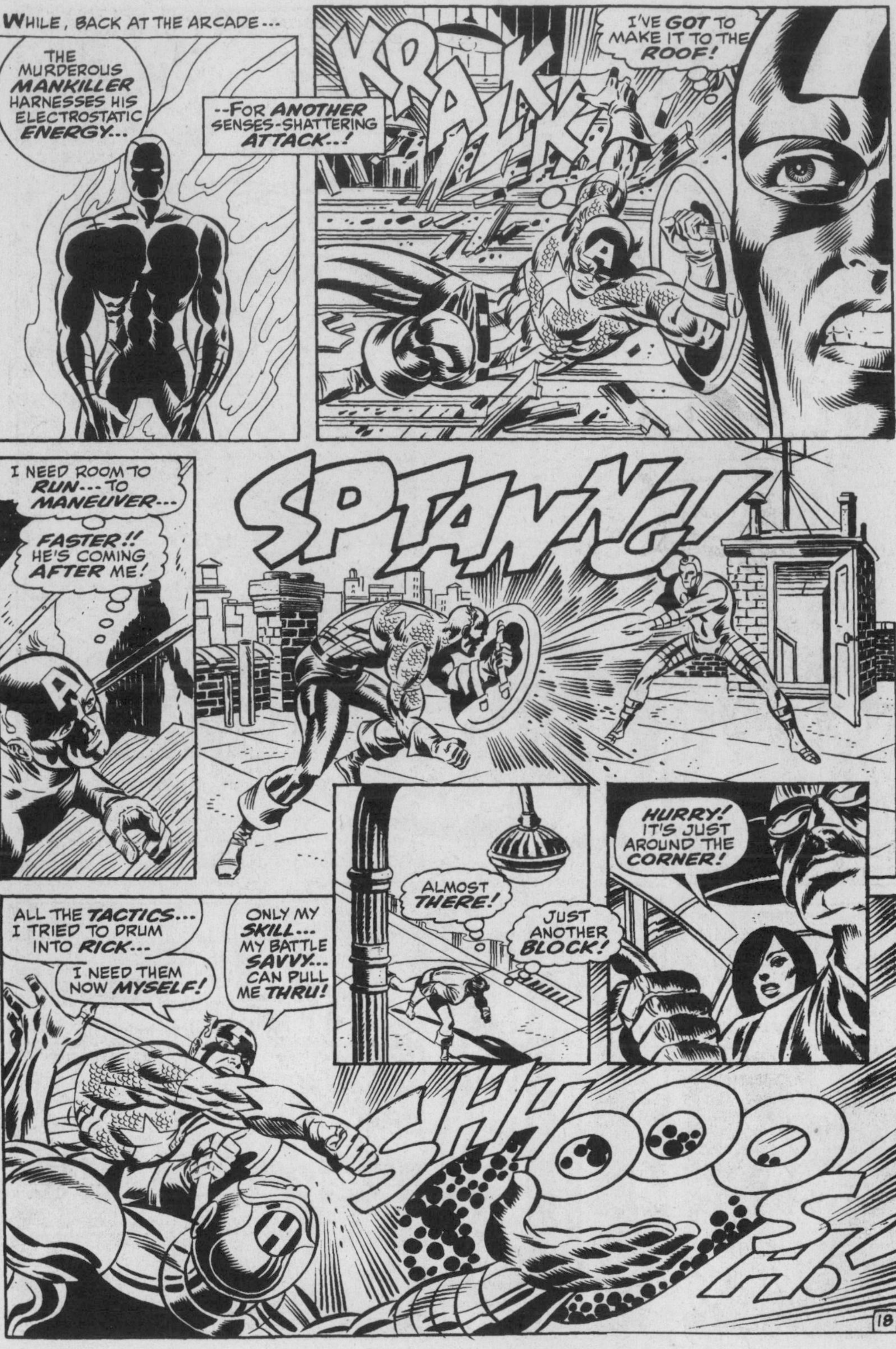
WHILE, BACK AT THE ARCADE...
THE MURDEROUS MANKILLER HARNESSES HIS ELECTROSTATIC ENERGY...
--FOR ANOTHER SENSES-SHATTERING ATTACK..!
KRAKK!
I'VE GOT TO MAKE IT TO THE ROOF!
I NEED ROOM TO RUN... TO MANEUVER...
FASTER!! HE'S COMING AFTER ME!
SPTANNG!
ALMOST THERE!
JUST ANOTHER BLOCK!
HURRY! IT'S JUST AROUND THE CORNER!
ALL THE TACTICS... I TRIED TO DRUM INTO RICK...
I NEED THEM NOW MYSELF!
ONLY MY SKILL... MY BATTLE SAVVY... CAN PULL ME THRU!
SHHOOOSH!

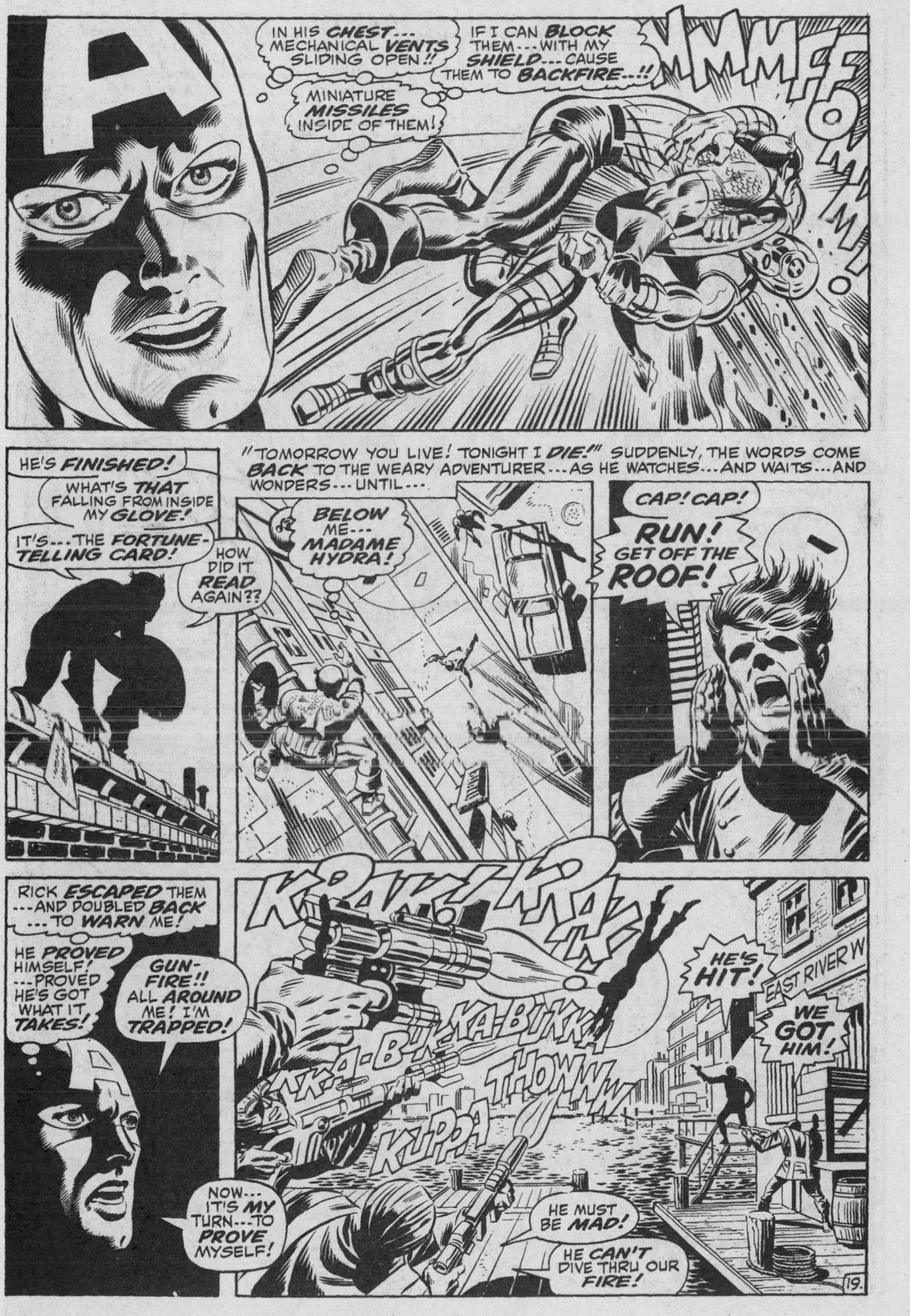

IN HIS CHEST... MECHANICAL VENTS SLIDING OPEN!!
MINIATURE MISSILES INSIDE OF THEM!
IF I CAN BLOCK THEM---WITH MY SHIELD--- CAUSE THEM TO BACKFIRE--!!
VMMMFF
FOMMM!
"TOMORROW YOU LIVE! TONIGHT I DIE!" SUDDENLY, THE WORDS COME BACK TO THE WEARY ADVENTURER--- AS HE WATCHES... AND WAITS... AND WONDERS--- UNTIL---
HE'S FINISHED!
WHAT'S THAT FALLING FROM INSIDE MY GLOVE!
IT'S--- THE FORTUNE-TELLING CARD!
HOW DID IT READ AGAIN??
BELOW ME--- MADAME HYDRA!
CAP! CAP!
RUN! GET OFF THE ROOF!
RICK ESCAPED THEM ---AND DOUBLED BACK ---TO WARN ME!
HE PROVED HIMSELF! ---PROVED HE'S GOT WHAT IT TAKES!
GUN-FIRE!! ALL AROUND ME! I'M TRAPPED!
NOW--- IT'S MY TURN---TO PROVE MYSELF!
KRAK! KRAK!
KA-BUKKA-KA-BUKKA
THOWWW
KUPPA
HE'S HIT!
EAST RIVER W
WE GOT HIM!
HE MUST BE MAD!
HE CAN'T DIVE THRU OUR FIRE!

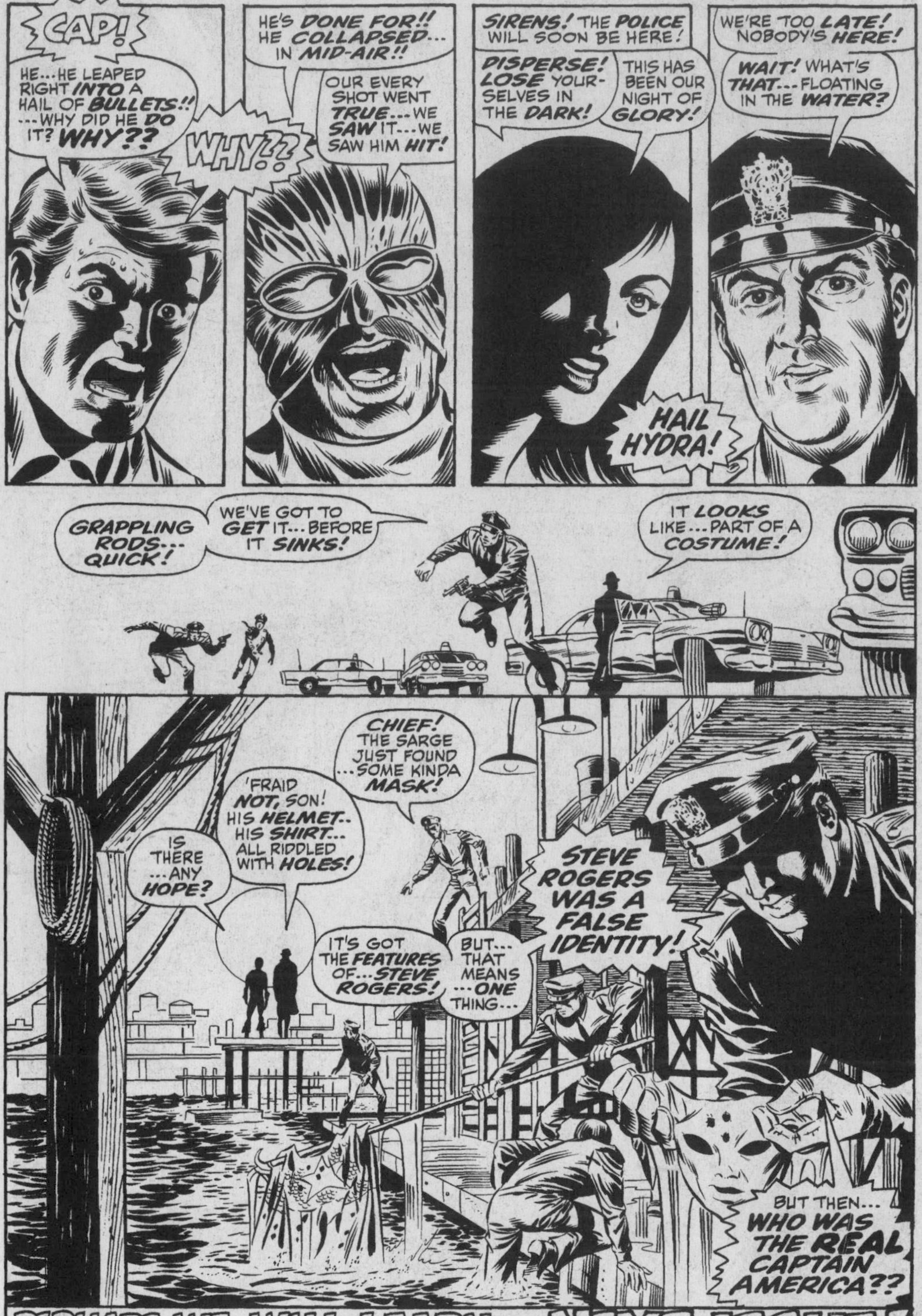
CAP!
HE...HE LEAPED RIGHT INTO A HAIL OF BULLETS!! ---WHY DID HE DO IT? WHY??
WHY??
HE'S DONE FOR!! HE COLLAPSED... IN MID-AIR!!
OUR EVERY SHOT WENT TRUE---WE SAW IT---WE SAW HIM HIT!
SIRENS! THE POLICE WILL SOON BE HERE!
DISPERSE! LOSE YOURSELVES IN THE DARK!
THIS HAS BEEN OUR NIGHT OF GLORY!
HAIL HYDRA!
WE'RE TOO LATE! NOBODY'S HERE!
WAIT! WHAT'S THAT---FLOATING IN THE WATER?
GRAPPLING RODS... QUICK!
WE'VE GOT TO GET IT---BEFORE IT SINKS!
IT LOOKS LIKE---PART OF A COSTUME!
CHIEF! THE SARGE JUST FOUND ...SOME KINDA MASK!
IS THERE ...ANY HOPE?
'FRAID NOT, SON! HIS HELMET-- HIS SHIRT--- ALL RIDDLED WITH HOLES!
IT'S GOT THE FEATURES OF...STEVE ROGERS!
BUT... THAT MEANS ---ONE THING---
STEVE ROGERS WAS A FALSE IDENTITY!
BUT THEN... WHO WAS THE REAL CAPTAIN AMERICA??
PERHAPS WE WILL LEARN---NEXT ISSUE!
20

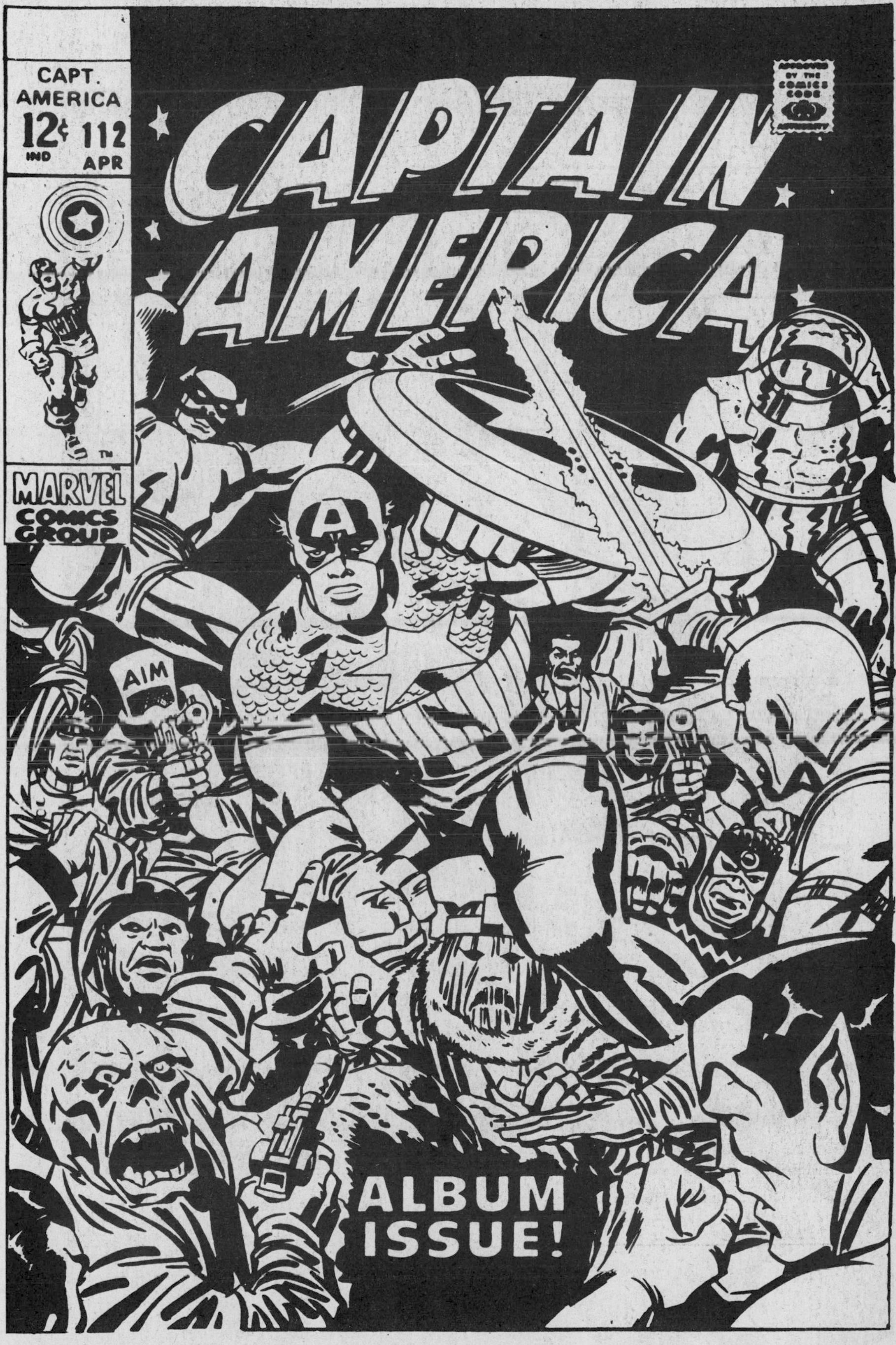
CAPT.
AMERICA
12¢ 112
IND APR
MARVEL
COMICS
GROUP
CAPTAIN
AMERICA
APPROVED BY THE COMICS CODE AUTHORITY
AIM
ALBUM
ISSUE!

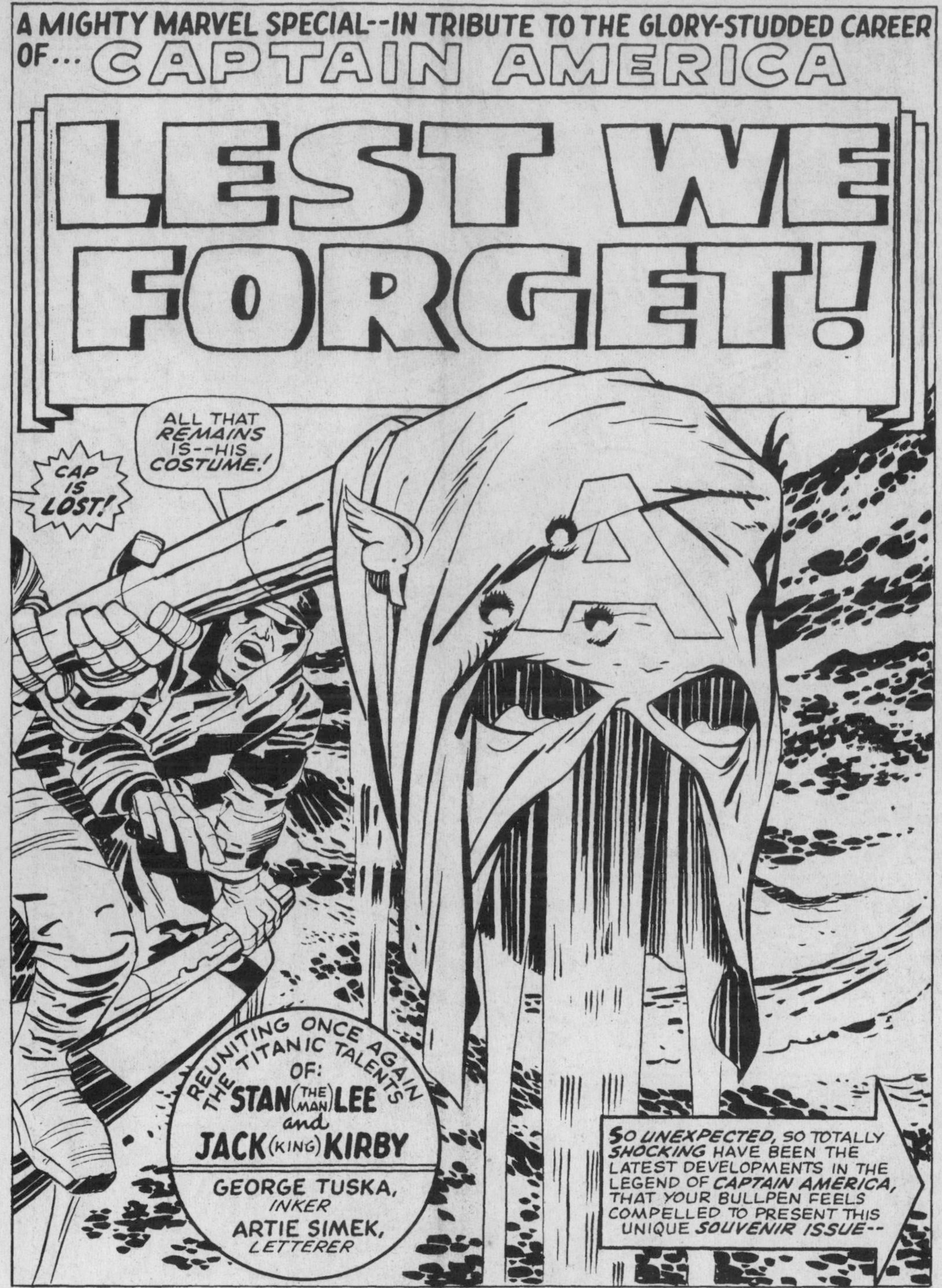
A MIGHTY MARVEL SPECIAL--IN TRIBUTE TO THE GLORY-STUDDED CAREER OF... CAPTAIN AMERICA
LEST WE FORGET!
CAP IS LOST!
ALL THAT REMAINS IS--HIS COSTUME!
REUNITING ONCE AGAIN THE TITANIC TALENTS OF: STAN (THE MAN) LEE and JACK (KING) KIRBY
GEORGE TUSKA, INKER
ARTIE SIMEK, LETTERER
SO UNEXPECTED, SO TOTALLY SHOCKING HAVE BEEN THE LATEST DEVELOPMENTS IN THE LEGEND OF CAPTAIN AMERICA, THAT YOUR BULLPEN FEELS COMPELLED TO PRESENT THIS UNIQUE SOUVENIR ISSUE--

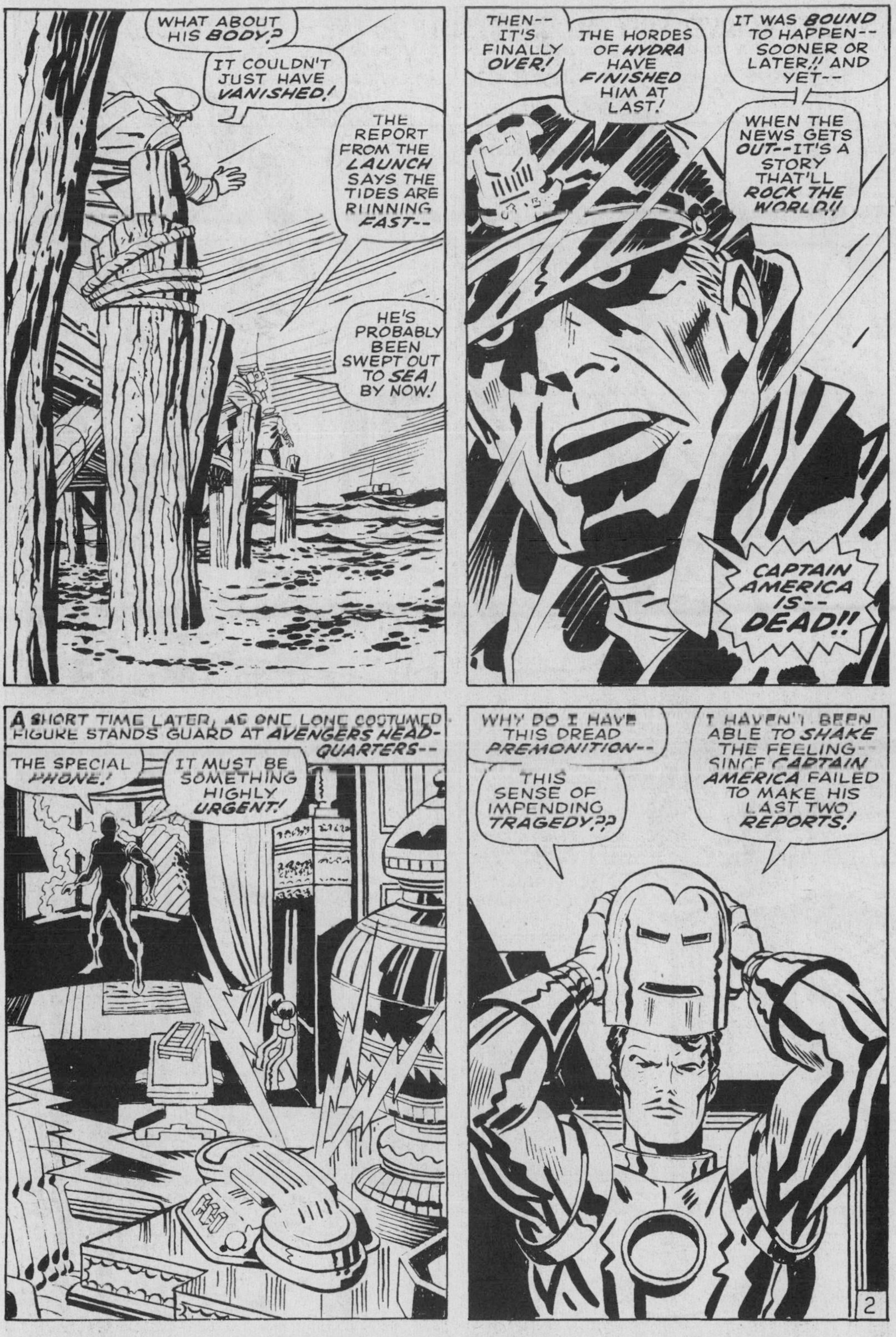
WHAT ABOUT HIS BODY?
IT COULDN'T JUST HAVE VANISHED!
THE REPORT FROM THE LAUNCH SAYS THE TIDES ARE RUNNING FAST--
HE'S PROBABLY BEEN SWEPT OUT TO SEA BY NOW!
THEN-- IT'S FINALLY OVER!
THE HORDES OF HYDRA HAVE FINISHED HIM AT LAST!
IT WAS BOUND TO HAPPEN-- SOONER OR LATER!! AND YET--
WHEN THE NEWS GETS OUT--IT'S A STORY THAT'LL ROCK THE WORLD!!
CAPTAIN AMERICA IS-- DEAD!!
A SHORT TIME LATER, AS ONE LONE COSTUMED FIGURE STANDS GUARD AT AVENGERS HEAD-QUARTERS--
THE SPECIAL PHONE!
IT MUST BE SOMETHING HIGHLY URGENT!
WHY DO I HAVE THIS DREAD PREMONITION--
THIS SENSE OF IMPENDING TRAGEDY??
I HAVEN'T BEEN ABLE TO SHAKE THE FEELING SINCE CAPTAIN AMERICA FAILED TO MAKE HIS LAST TWO REPORTS!
2

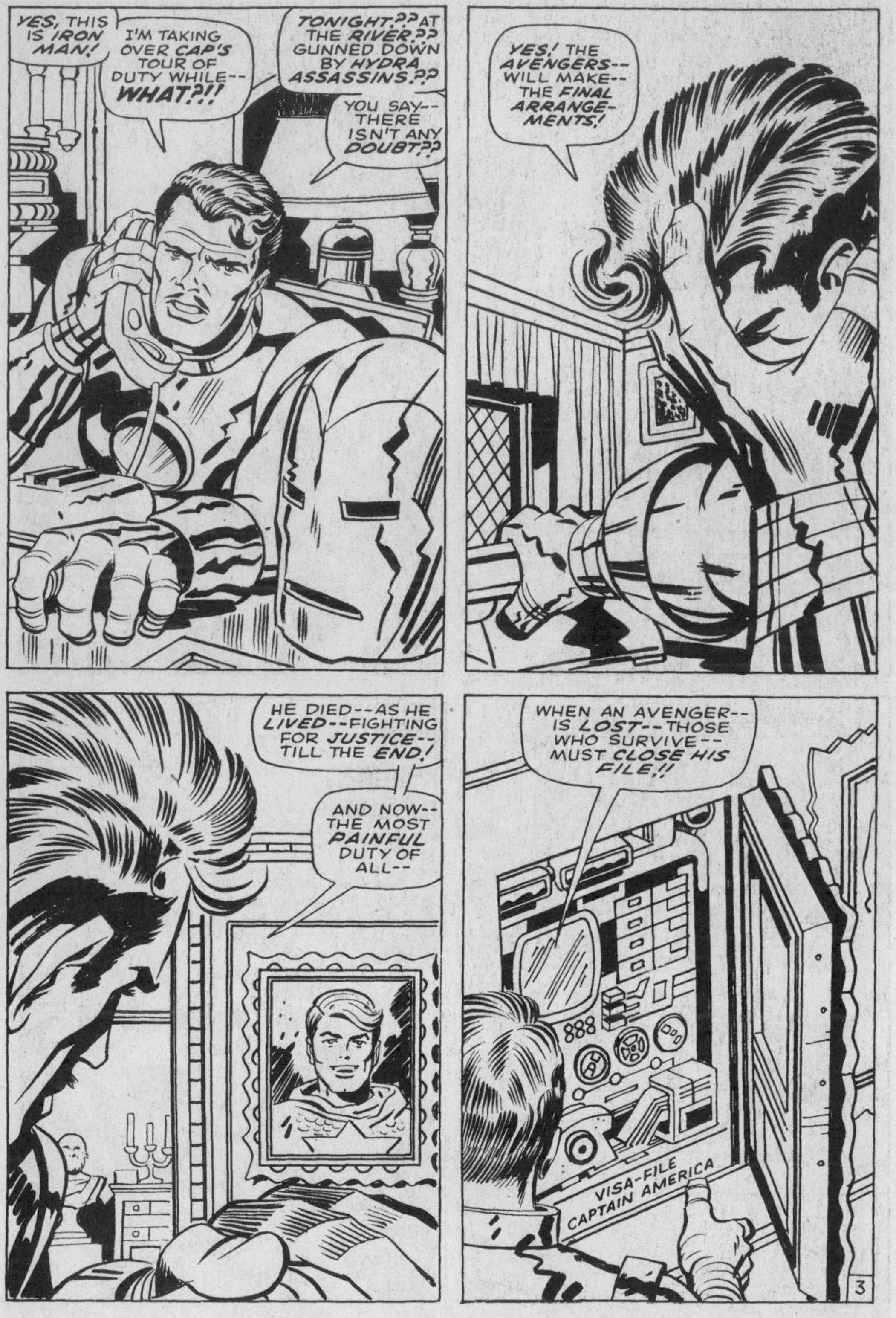
YES, THIS IS IRON MAN!
I'M TAKING OVER CAP'S TOUR OF DUTY WHILE-- WHAT?!!
TONIGHT?? AT THE RIVER?? GUNNED DOWN BY HYDRA ASSASSINS??
YOU SAY-- THERE ISN'T ANY DOUBT??
YES! THE AVENGERS-- WILL MAKE-- THE FINAL ARRANGE-MENTS!
HE DIED--AS HE LIVED--FIGHTING FOR JUSTICE-- TILL THE END!
AND NOW-- THE MOST PAINFUL DUTY OF ALL--
WHEN AN AVENGER-- IS LOST--THOSE WHO SURVIVE-- MUST CLOSE HIS FILE!!
VISA-FILE CAPTAIN AMERICA
3

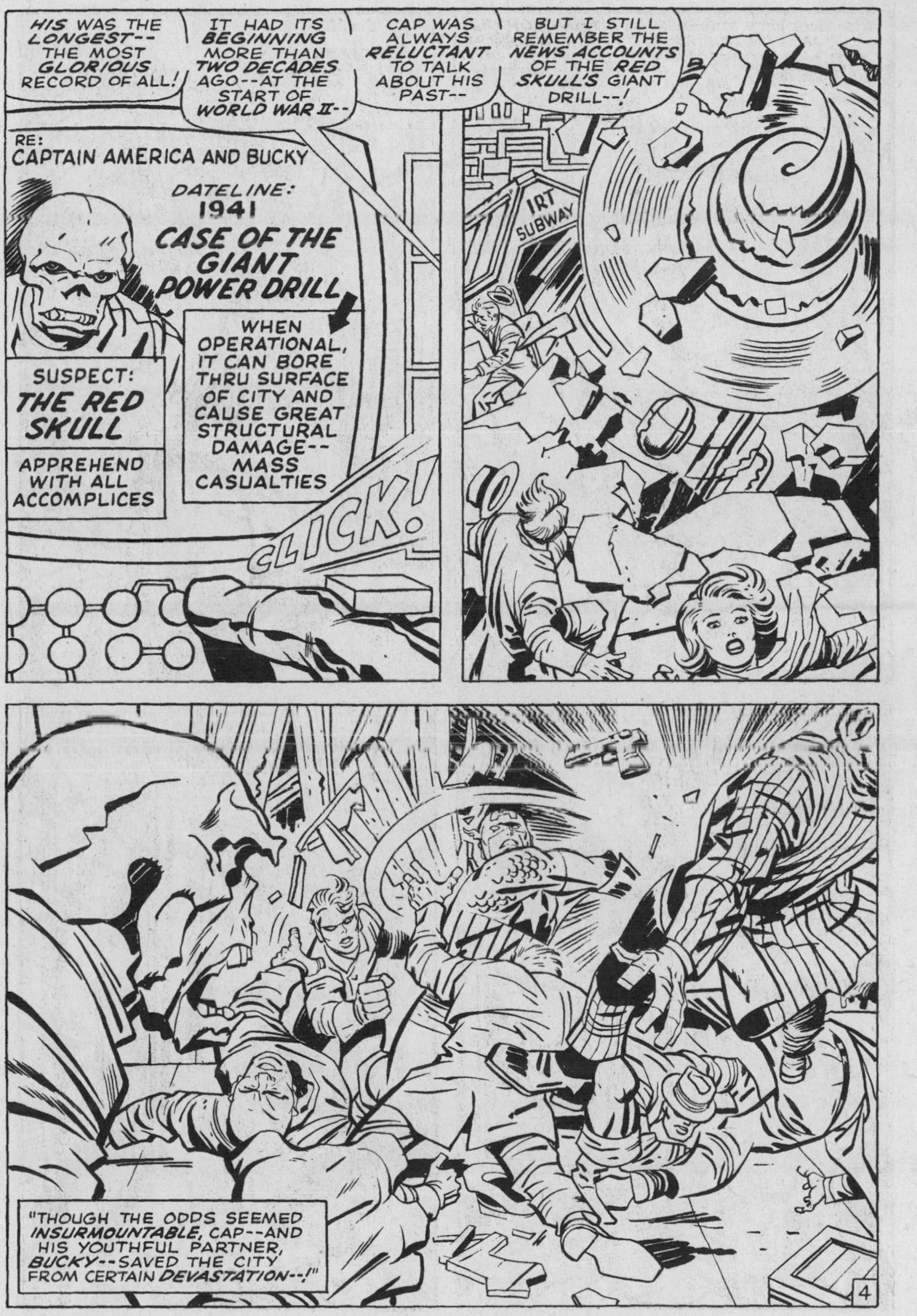
HIS WAS THE LONGEST-- THE MOST GLORIOUS RECORD OF ALL!
IT HAD ITS BEGINNING MORE THAN TWO DECADES AGO--AT THE START OF WORLD WAR II--
CAP WAS ALWAYS RELUCTANT TO TALK ABOUT HIS PAST--
RE: CAPTAIN AMERICA AND BUCKY
DATELINE: 1941
CASE OF THE GIANT POWER DRILL
SUSPECT: THE RED SKULL
APPREHEND WITH ALL ACCOMPLICES
WHEN OPERATIONAL, IT CAN BORE THRU SURFACE OF CITY AND CAUSE GREAT STRUCTURAL DAMAGE-- MASS CASUALTIES
CLICK!
BUT I STILL REMEMBER THE NEWS ACCOUNTS OF THE RED SKULL'S GIANT DRILL--!
IRT SUBWAY
"THOUGH THE ODDS SEEMED INSURMOUNTABLE, CAP--AND HIS YOUTHFUL PARTNER, BUCKY--SAVED THE CITY FROM CERTAIN DEVASTATION--!"
4

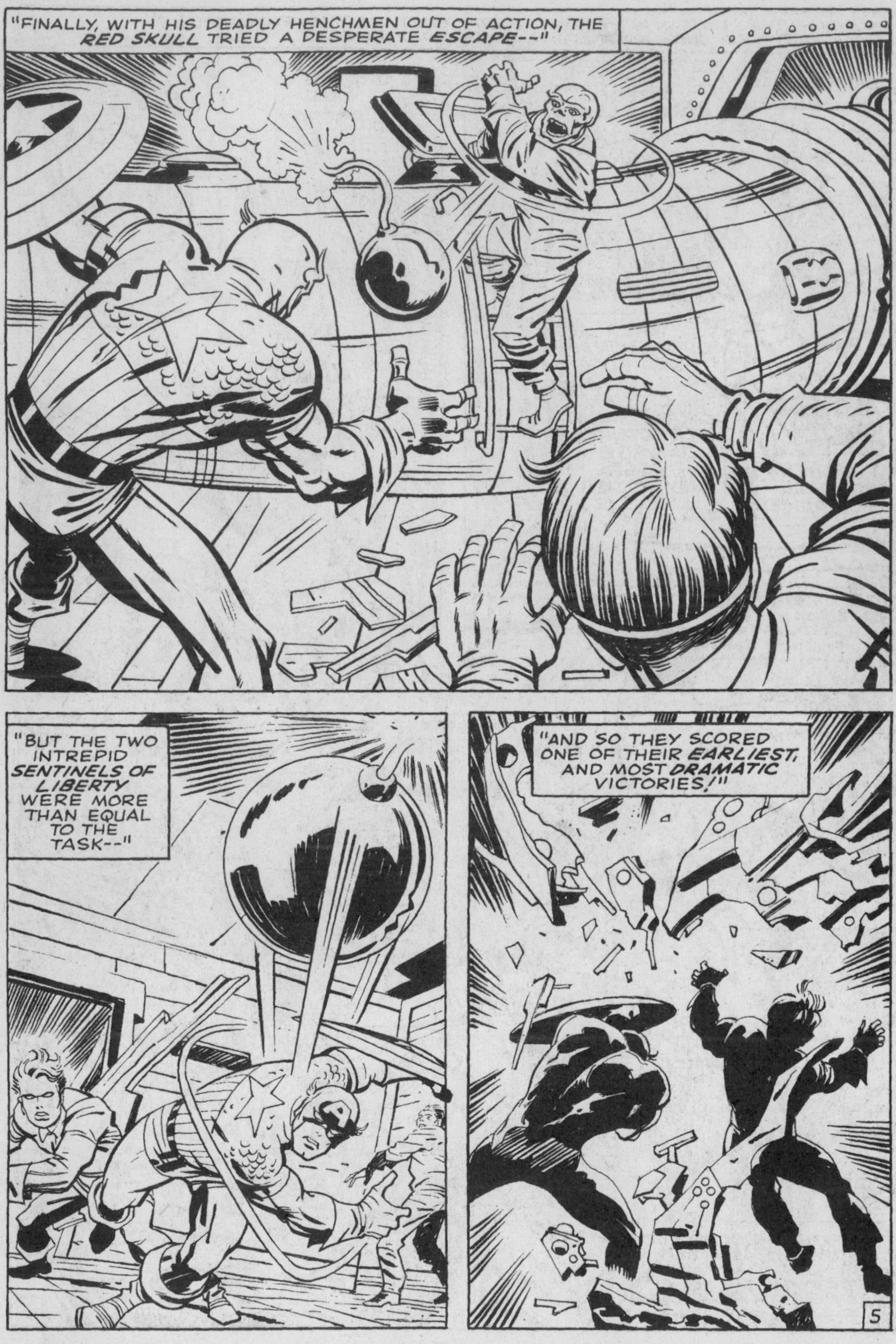
"FINALLY, WITH HIS DEADLY HENCHMEN OUT OF ACTION, THE RED SKULL TRIED A DESPERATE ESCAPE--"
"BUT THE TWO INTREPID SENTINELS OF LIBERTY WERE MORE THAN EQUAL TO THE TASK--"
"AND SO THEY SCORED ONE OF THEIR EARLIEST, AND MOST DRAMATIC VICTORIES!"
5

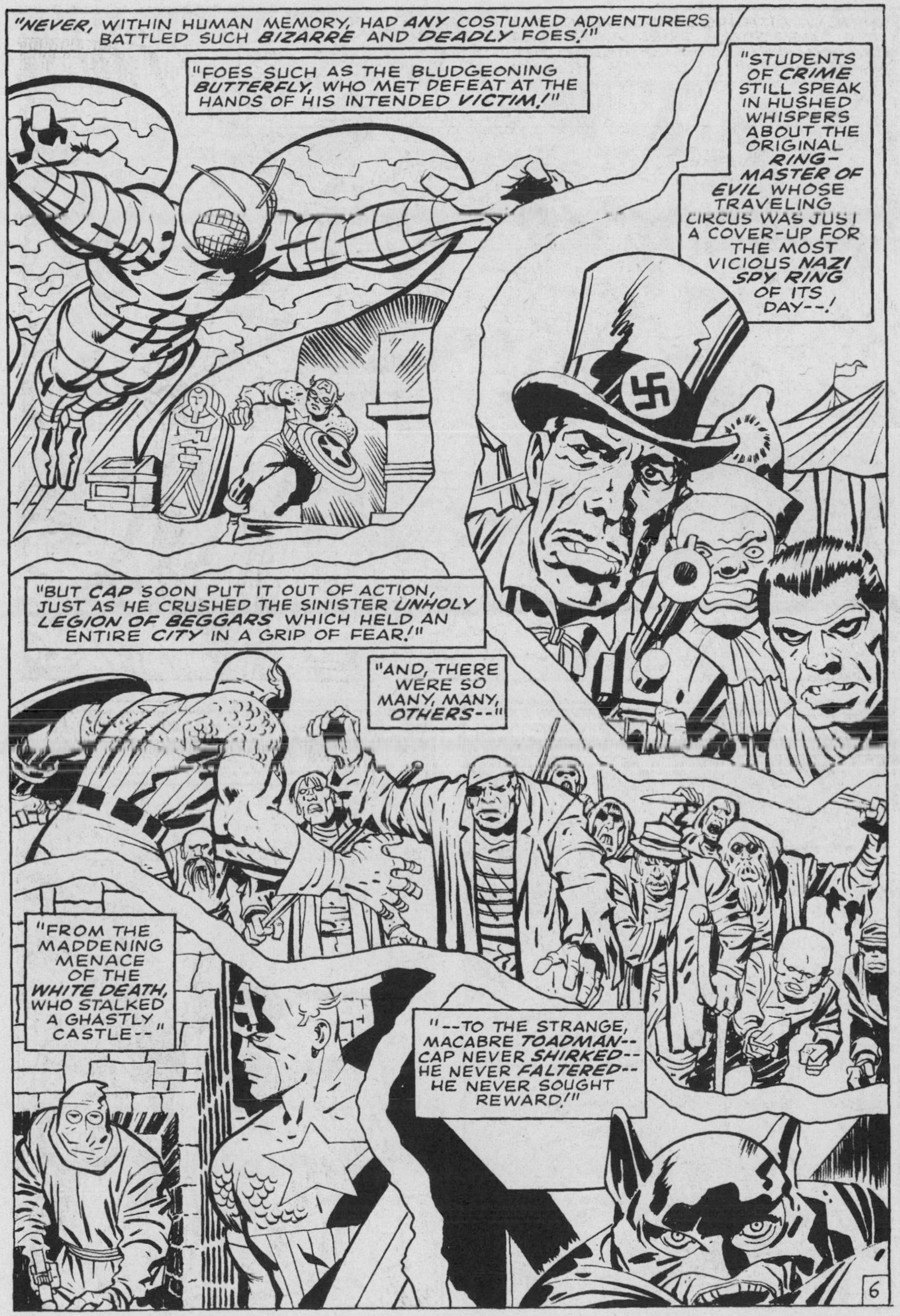
"NEVER, WITHIN HUMAN MEMORY, HAD ANY COSTUMED ADVENTURERS BATTLED SUCH BIZARRE AND DEADLY FOES!"
"FOES SUCH AS THE BLUDGEONING BUTTERFLY, WHO MET DEFEAT AT THE HANDS OF HIS INTENDED VICTIM!"
"STUDENTS OF CRIME STILL SPEAK IN HUSHED WHISPERS ABOUT THE ORIGINAL RING-MASTER OF EVIL WHOSE TRAVELING CIRCUS WAS JUST A COVER-UP FOR THE MOST VICIOUS NAZI SPY RING OF ITS DAY--!
"BUT CAP SOON PUT IT OUT OF ACTION, JUST AS HE CRUSHED THE SINISTER UNHOLY LEGION OF BEGGARS WHICH HELD AN ENTIRE CITY IN A GRIP OF FEAR!"
"AND, THERE WERE SO MANY, MANY, OTHERS--"
"FROM THE MADDENING MENACE OF THE WHITE DEATH, WHO STALKED A GHASTLY CASTLE--"
"--TO THE STRANGE, MACABRE TOADMAN--CAP NEVER SHIRKED--HE NEVER FALTERED--HE NEVER SOUGHT REWARD!"
6

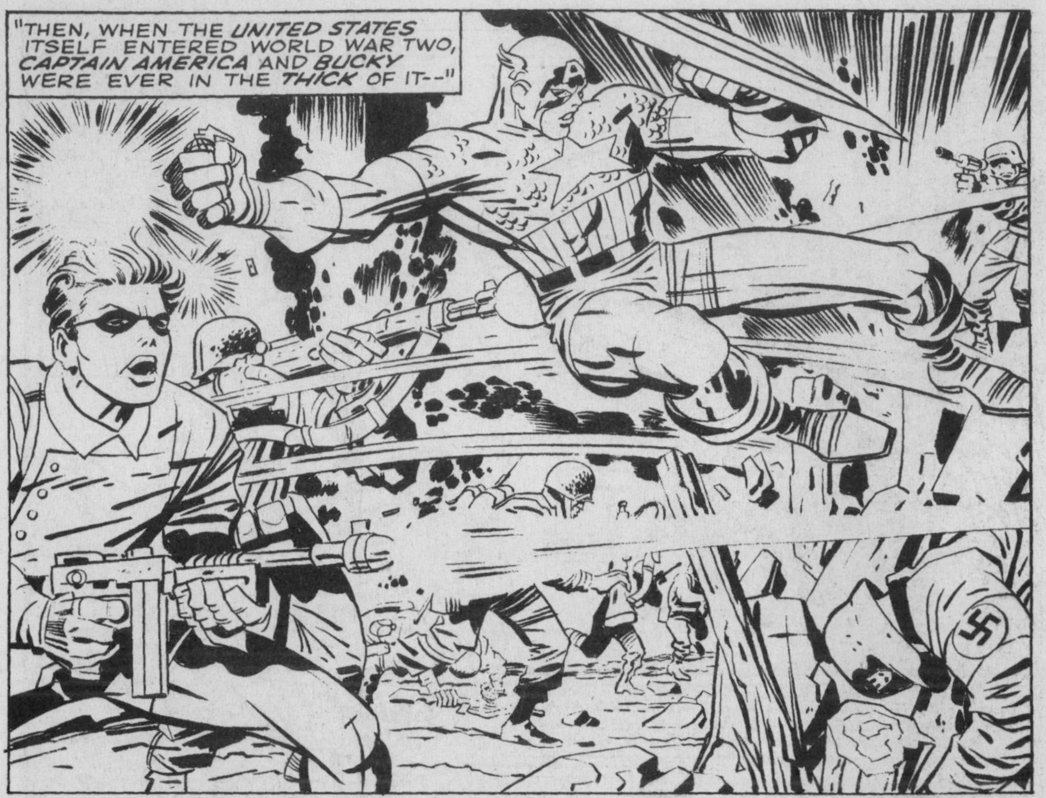
"THEN, WHEN THE UNITED STATES ITSELF ENTERED WORLD WAR TWO, CAPTAIN AMERICA AND BUCKY WERE EVER IN THE THICK OF IT--"

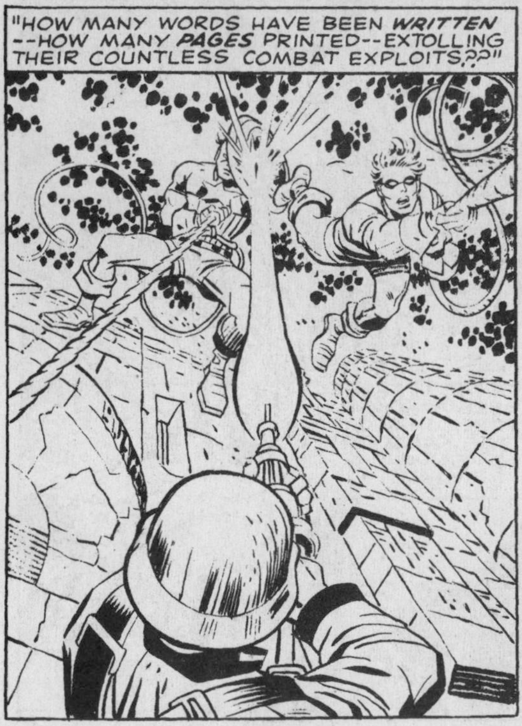
"HOW MANY WORDS HAVE BEEN WRITTEN --HOW MANY PAGES PRINTED--EXTOLLING THEIR COUNTLESS COMBAT EXPLOITS??"

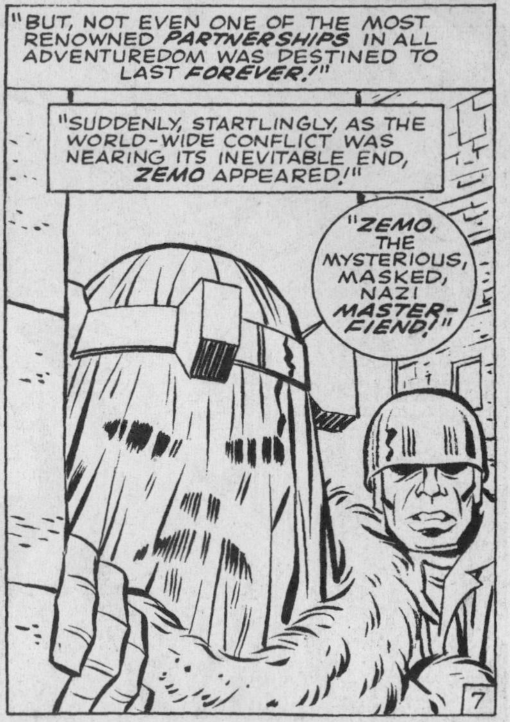
"BUT, NOT EVEN ONE OF THE MOST RENOWNED PARTNERSHIPS IN ALL ADVENTUREDOM WAS DESTINED TO LAST FOREVER!"
"SUDDENLY, STARTLINGLY, AS THE WORLD-WIDE CONFLICT WAS NEARING ITS INEVITABLE END, ZEMO APPEARED!"
"ZEMO, THE MYSTERIOUS, MASKED, NAZI MASTER-FIEND!"

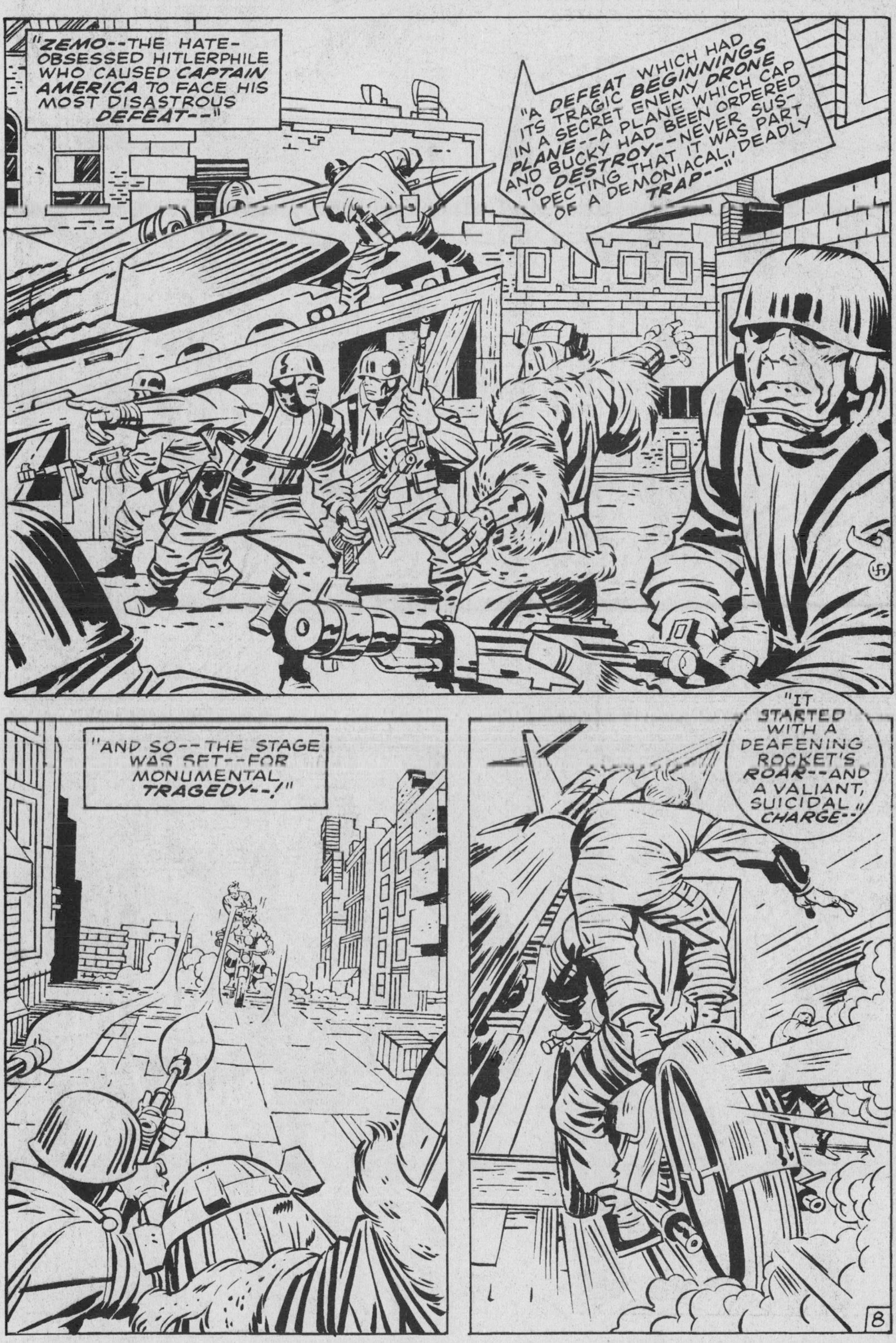
"ZEMO--THE HATE-OBSESSED HITLERPHILE WHO CAUSED CAPTAIN AMERICA TO FACE HIS MOST DISASTROUS DEFEAT--"
"A DEFEAT WHICH HAD ITS TRAGIC BEGINNINGS IN A SECRET ENEMY DRONE PLANE--A PLANE WHICH CAP AND BUCKY HAD BEEN ORDERED TO DESTROY--NEVER SUSPECTING THAT IT WAS PART OF A DEMONIACAL, DEADLY TRAP--"
"AND SO--THE STAGE WAS SET--FOR MONUMENTAL TRAGEDY--!"
"IT STARTED WITH A DEAFENING ROCKET'S ROAR--AND A VALIANT, SUICIDAL CHARGE--"
8

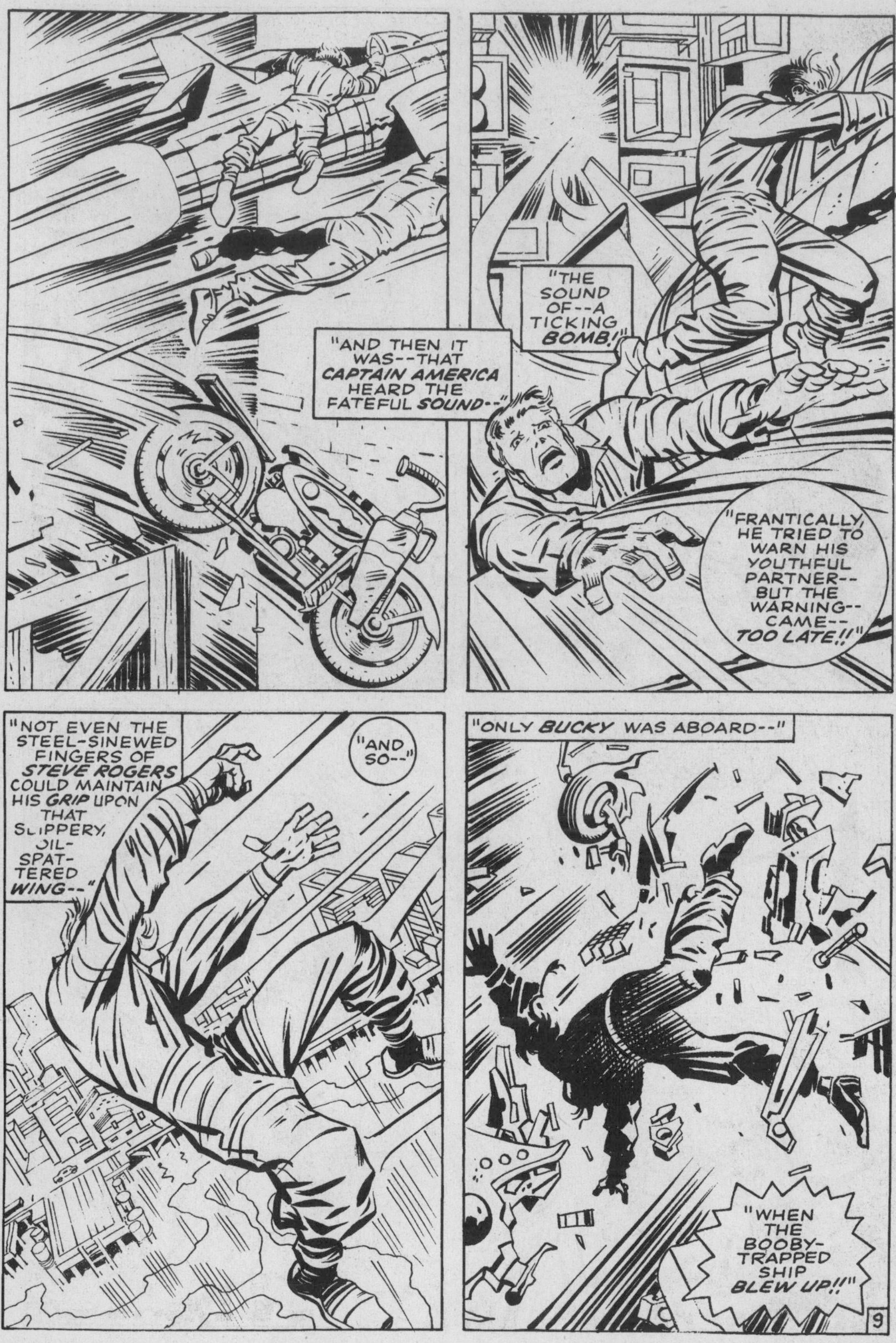
"AND THEN IT WAS--THAT CAPTAIN AMERICA HEARD THE FATEFUL SOUND--"
"THE SOUND OF--A TICKING BOMB!"
"FRANTICALLY, HE TRIED TO WARN HIS YOUTHFUL PARTNER--BUT THE WARNING--CAME--TOO LATE!!"
"NOT EVEN THE STEEL-SINEWED FINGERS OF STEVE ROGERS COULD MAINTAIN HIS GRIP UPON THAT SLIPPERY, OIL-SPATTERED WING--"
"AND SO--"
"ONLY BUCKY WAS ABOARD--"
"WHEN THE BOOBY-TRAPPED SHIP BLEW UP!!"
9

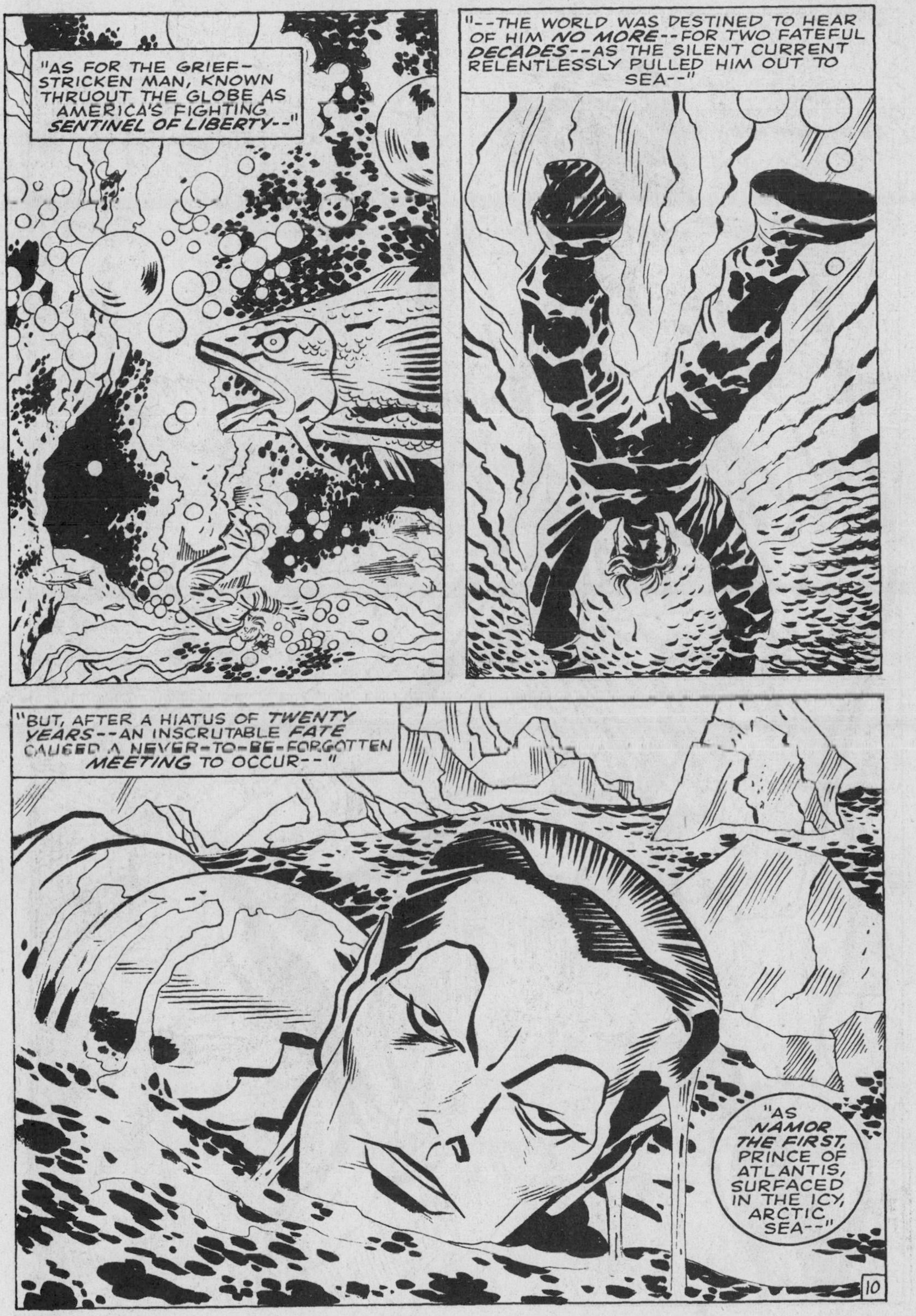
"AS FOR THE GRIEF-STRICKEN MAN, KNOWN THRUOUT THE GLOBE AS AMERICA'S FIGHTING SENTINEL OF LIBERTY--"
"--THE WORLD WAS DESTINED TO HEAR OF HIM NO MORE--FOR TWO FATEFUL DECADES--AS THE SILENT CURRENT RELENTLESSLY PULLED HIM OUT TO SEA--"
"BUT, AFTER A HIATUS OF TWENTY YEARS--AN INSCRUTABLE FATE CAUSED A NEVER-TO-BE-FORGOTTEN MEETING TO OCCUR--"
"AS NAMOR THE FIRST, PRINCE OF ATLANTIS, SURFACED IN THE ICY, ARCTIC SEA--"
10

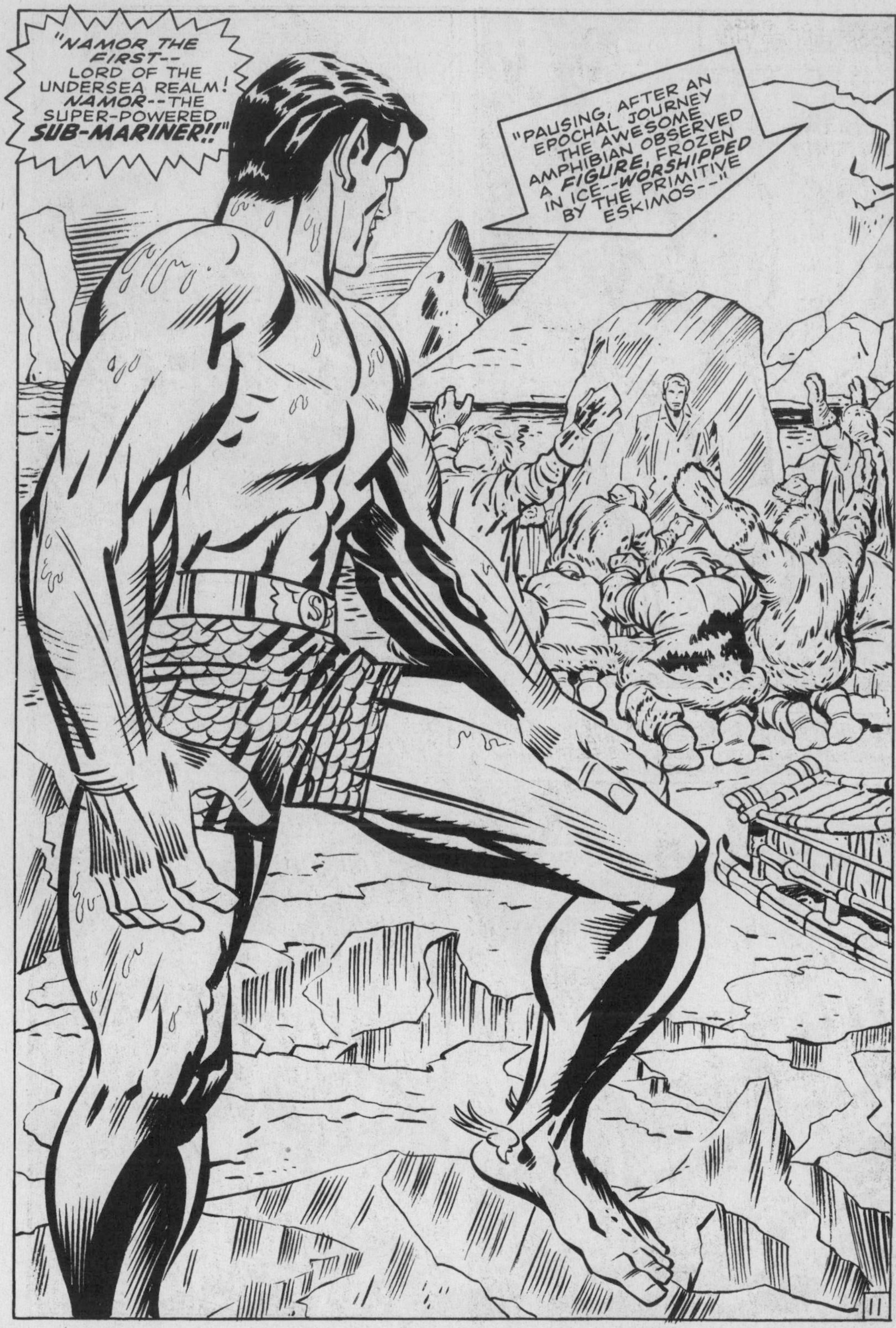
"NAMOR THE FIRST-- LORD OF THE UNDERSEA REALM! NAMOR--THE SUPER-POWERED SUB-MARINER!!"
"PAUSING, AFTER AN EPOCHAL JOURNEY THE AWESOME AMPHIBIAN OBSERVED A FIGURE, FROZEN IN ICE--WORSHIPPED BY THE PRIMITIVE ESKIMOS--"

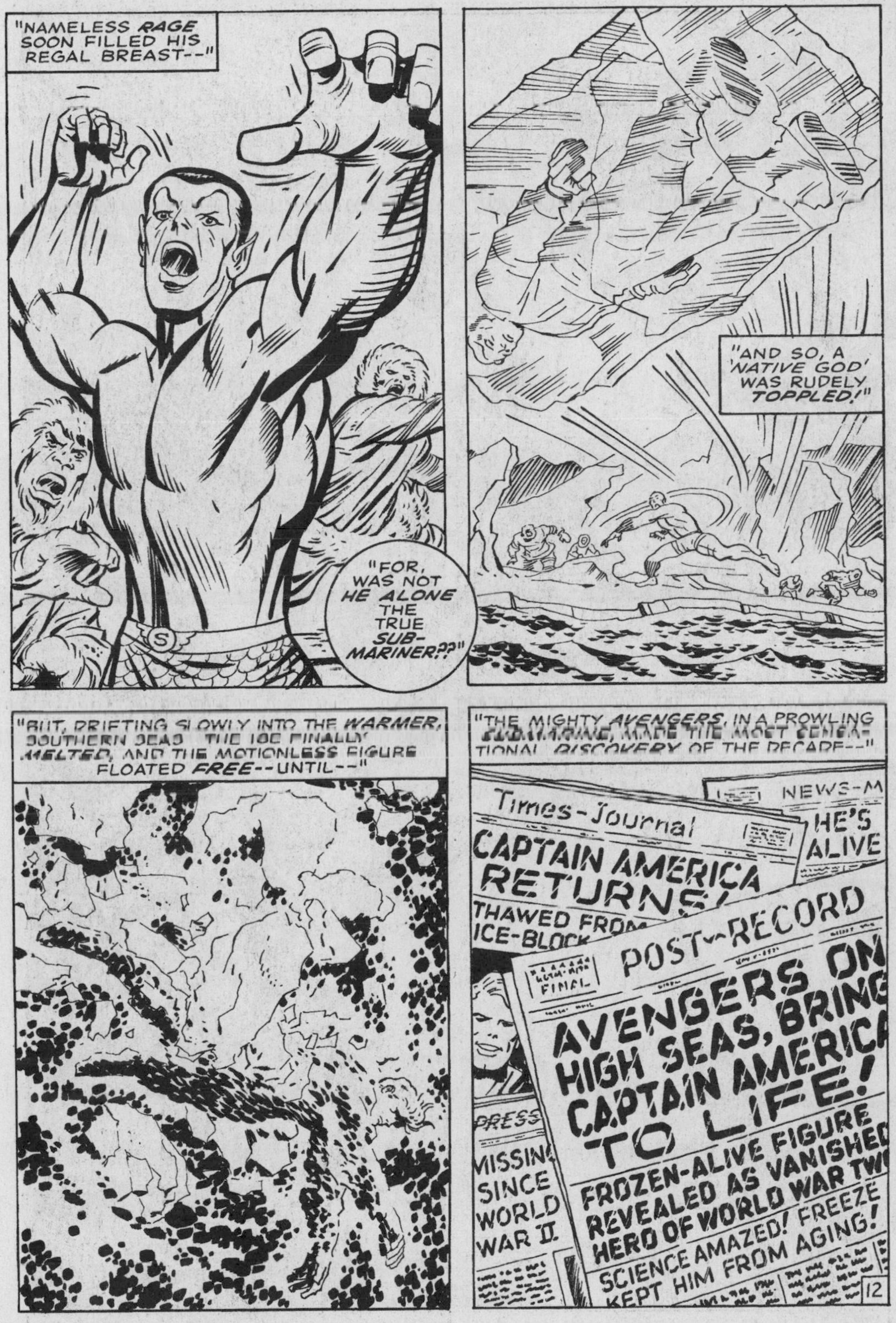
"NAMELESS RAGE SOON FILLED HIS REGAL BREAST--"
"FOR, WAS NOT HE ALONE THE TRUE SUB-MARINER??"
"AND SO, A 'NATIVE GOD' WAS RUDELY TOPPLED!"
"BUT, DRIFTING SLOWLY INTO THE WARMER, SOUTHERN SEAS, THE ICE FINALLY MELTED, AND THE MOTIONLESS FIGURE FLOATED FREE--UNTIL--"
"THE MIGHTY AVENGERS, IN A PROWLING SUBMARINE, MADE THE MOST SENSA-TIONAL DISCOVERY OF THE DECADE--"
Times-Journal
CAPTAIN AMERICA RETURNS!
THAWED FROM ICE-BLOCK
NEWS-M
HE'S ALIVE
POST-RECORD
FINAL
AVENGERS ON HIGH SEAS, BRING CAPTAIN AMERICA TO LIFE!
FROZEN-ALIVE FIGURE REVEALED AS VANISHED HERO OF WORLD WAR TWO
SCIENCE AMAZED! FREEZE KEPT HIM FROM AGING!
PRESS
MISSING SINCE WORLD WAR II
12

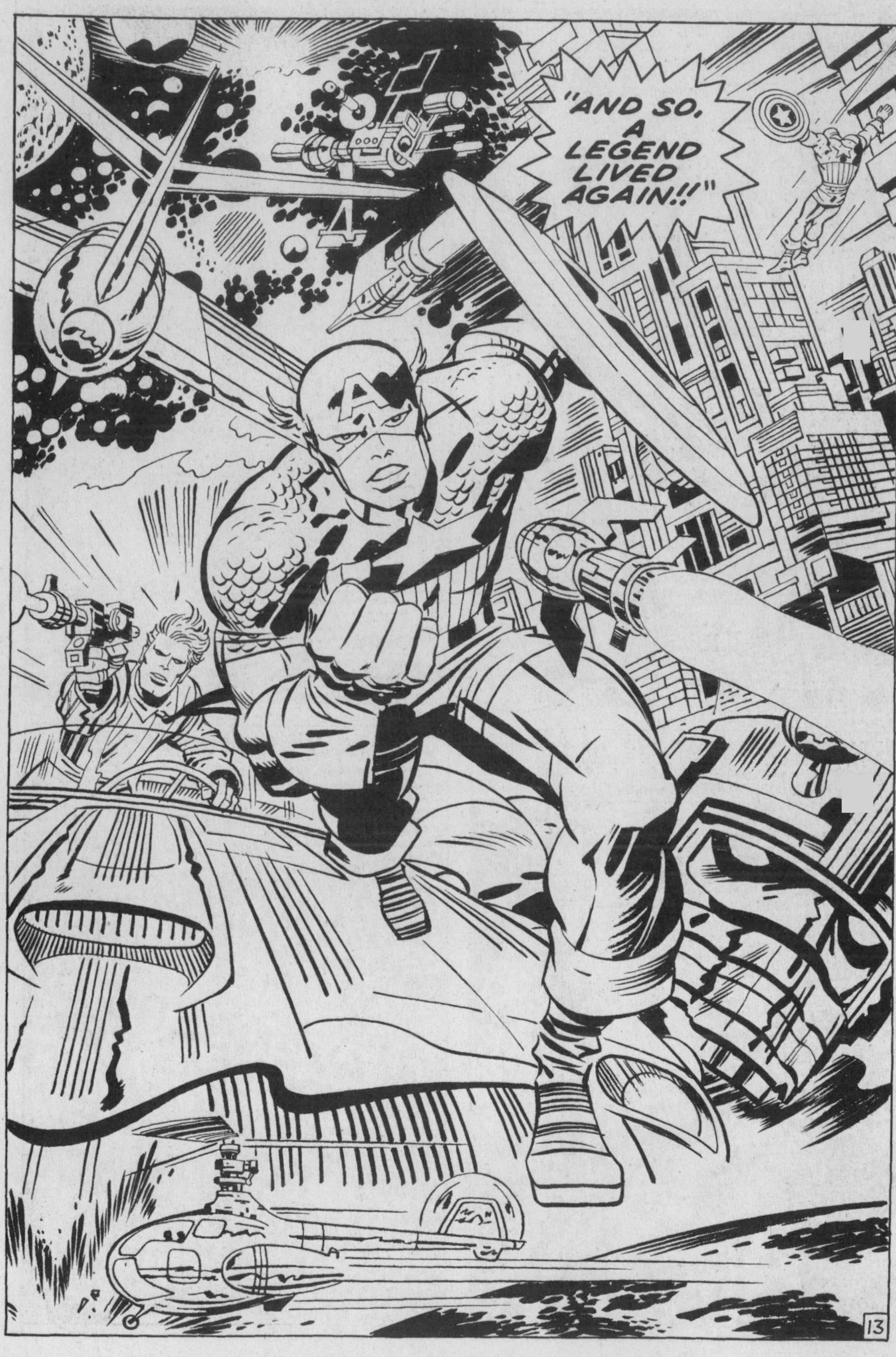
"AND SO, A LEGEND LIVED AGAIN!!"
13

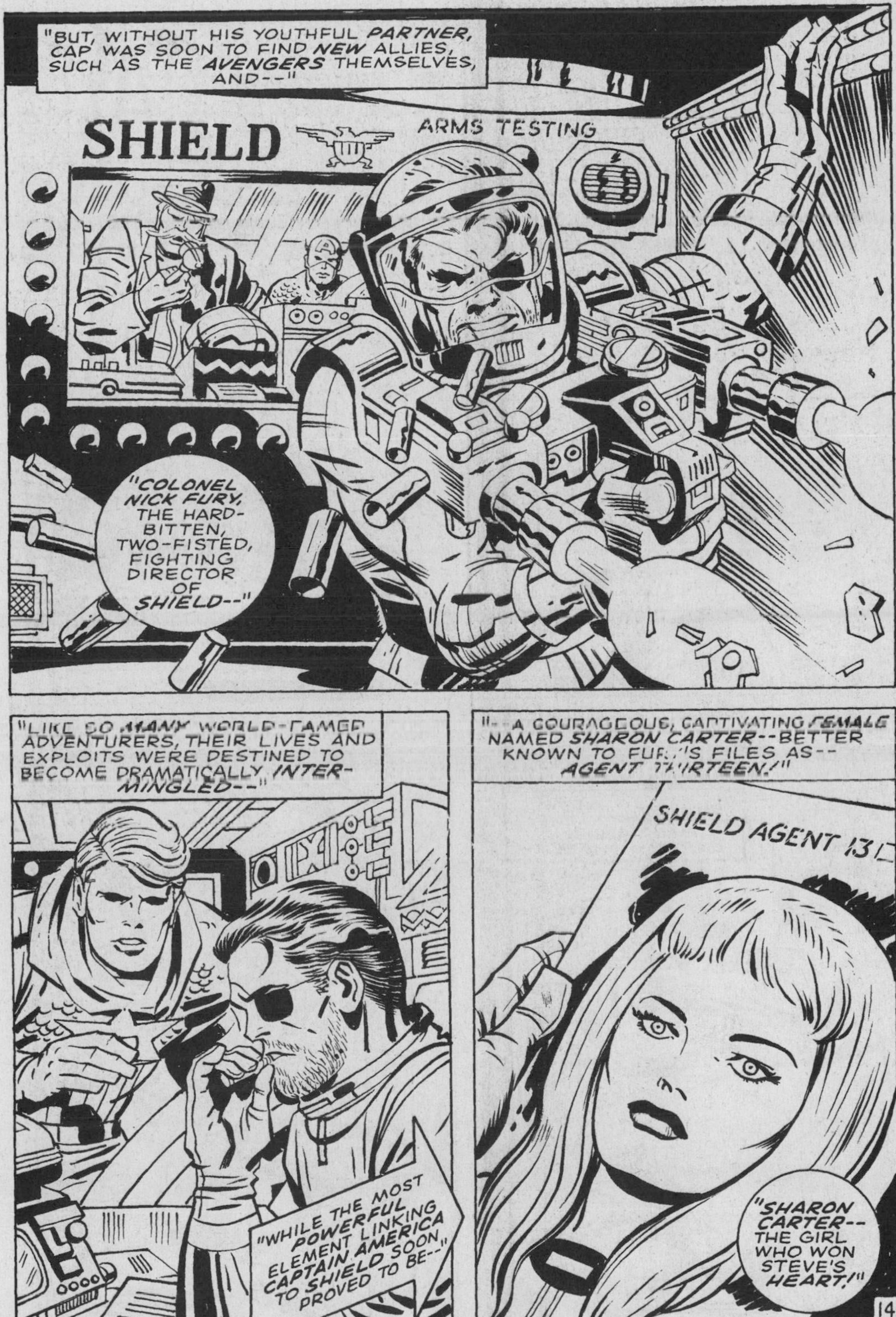
"BUT, WITHOUT HIS YOUTHFUL PARTNER, CAP WAS SOON TO FIND NEW ALLIES, SUCH AS THE AVENGERS THEMSELVES, AND--"
SHIELD
ARMS TESTING
"COLONEL NICK FURY, THE HARD-BITTEN, TWO-FISTED, FIGHTING DIRECTOR OF SHIELD--"
"LIKE SO MANY WORLD-FAMED ADVENTURERS, THEIR LIVES AND EXPLOITS WERE DESTINED TO BECOME DRAMATICALLY INTER-MINGLED--"
"WHILE THE MOST POWERFUL ELEMENT LINKING CAPTAIN AMERICA TO SHIELD SOON PROVED TO BE--"
"--A COURAGEOUS, CAPTIVATING FEMALE NAMED SHARON CARTER--BETTER KNOWN TO FURY'S FILES AS--AGENT THIRTEEN!"
SHIELD AGENT 13
"SHARON CARTER-- THE GIRL WHO WON STEVE'S HEART!"
14

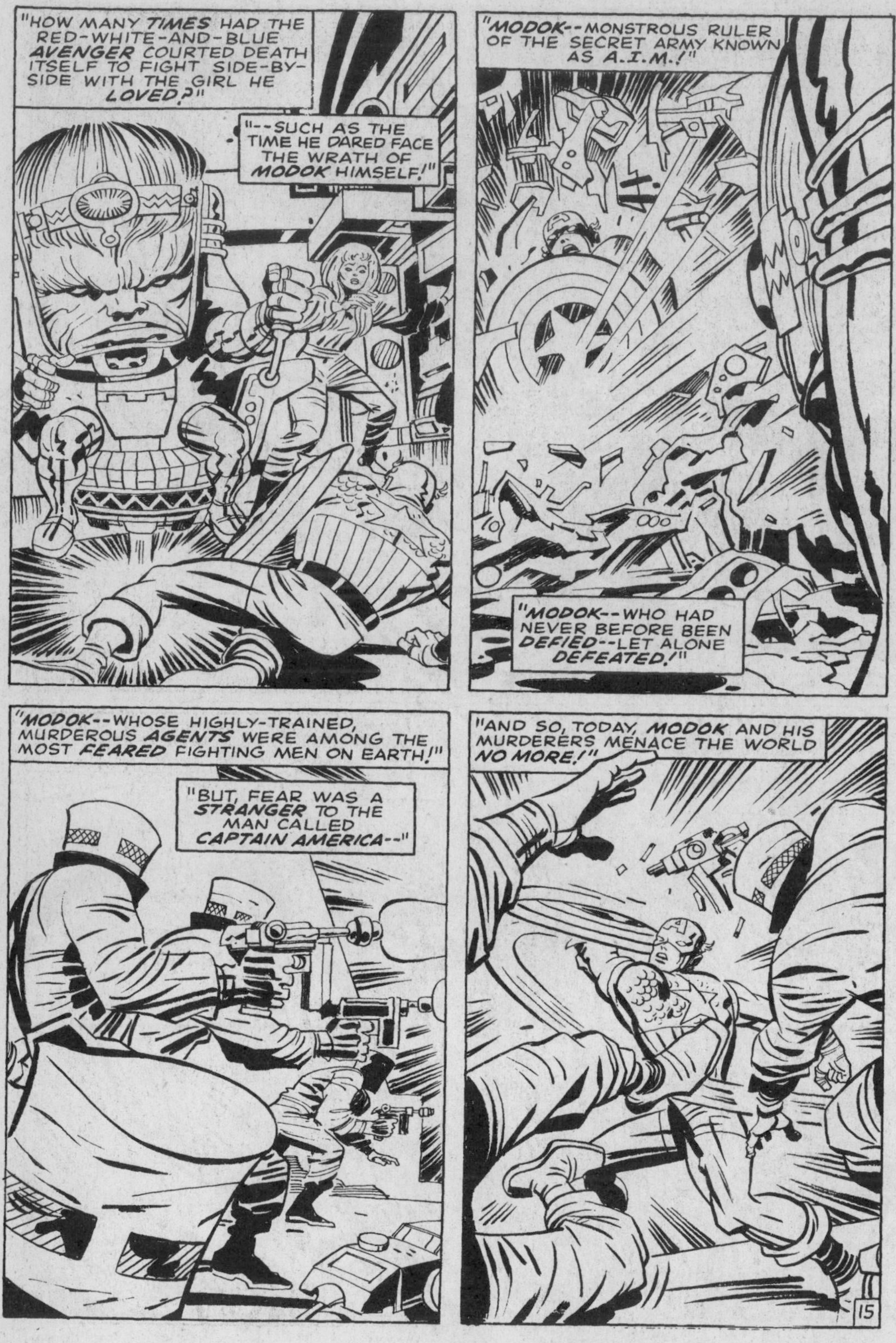
"HOW MANY TIMES HAD THE RED-WHITE-AND-BLUE AVENGER COURTED DEATH ITSELF TO FIGHT SIDE-BY-SIDE WITH THE GIRL HE LOVED?"
"--SUCH AS THE TIME HE DARED FACE THE WRATH OF MODOK HIMSELF!"
"MODOK--MONSTROUS RULER OF THE SECRET ARMY KNOWN AS A.I.M.!"
"MODOK--WHO HAD NEVER BEFORE BEEN DEFIED--LET ALONE DEFEATED!"
"MODOK--WHOSE HIGHLY-TRAINED, MURDEROUS AGENTS WERE AMONG THE MOST FEARED FIGHTING MEN ON EARTH!"
"BUT, FEAR WAS A STRANGER TO THE MAN CALLED CAPTAIN AMERICA--"
"AND SO, TODAY, MODOK AND HIS MURDERERS MENACE THE WORLD NO MORE!"
15

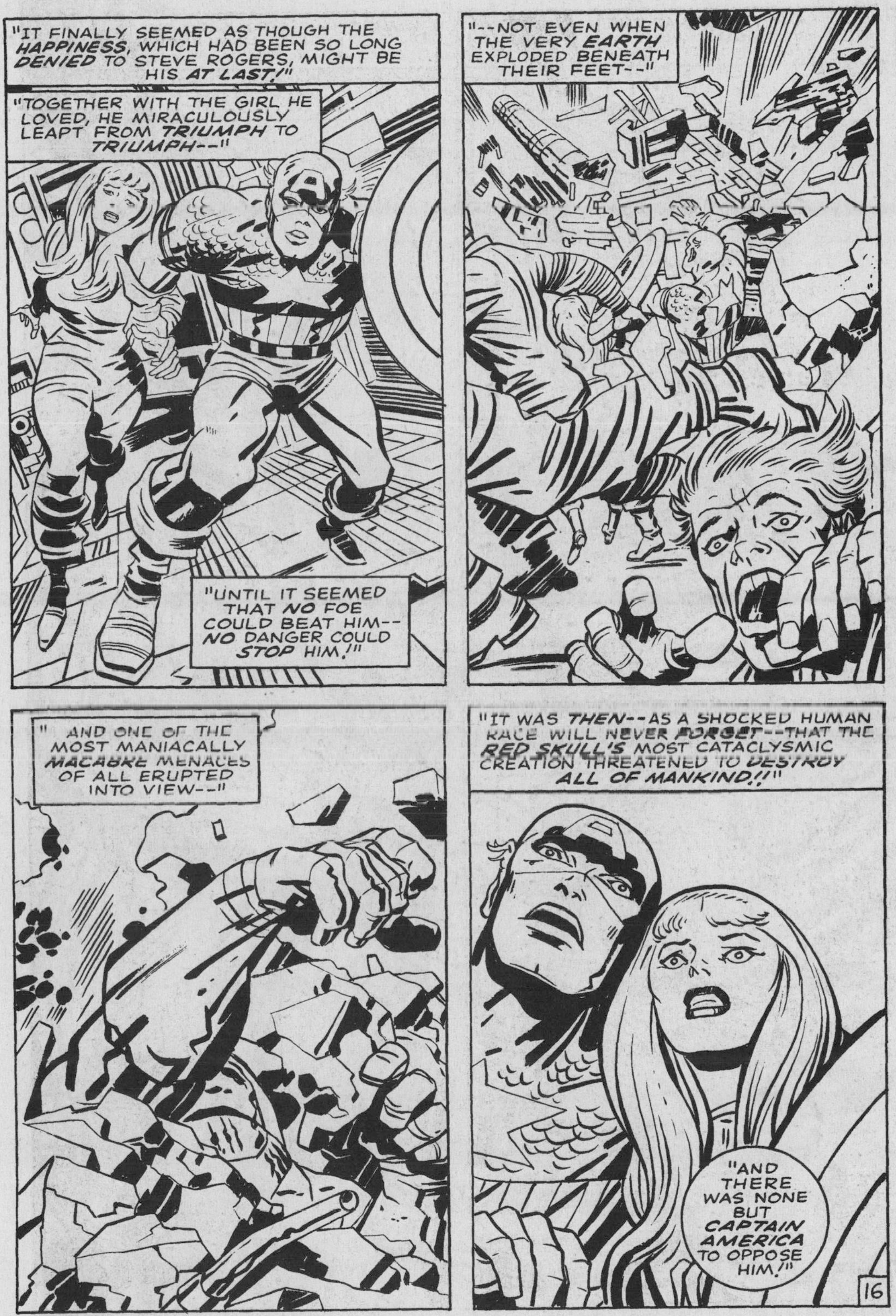
"IT FINALLY SEEMED AS THOUGH THE HAPPINESS, WHICH HAD BEEN SO LONG DENIED TO STEVE ROGERS, MIGHT BE HIS AT LAST!"
"TOGETHER WITH THE GIRL HE LOVED, HE MIRACULOUSLY LEAPT FROM TRIUMPH TO TRIUMPH--"
"UNTIL IT SEEMED THAT NO FOE COULD BEAT HIM-- NO DANGER COULD STOP HIM!"
"--NOT EVEN WHEN THE VERY EARTH EXPLODED BENEATH THEIR FEET--"
" AND ONE OF THE MOST MANIACALLY MACABRE MENACES OF ALL ERUPTED INTO VIEW--"
"IT WAS THEN--AS A SHOCKED HUMAN RACE WILL NEVER FORGET--THAT THE RED SKULL'S MOST CATACLYSMIC CREATION THREATENED TO DESTROY ALL OF MANKIND!!"
"AND THERE WAS NONE BUT CAPTAIN AMERICA TO OPPOSE HIM!"
16

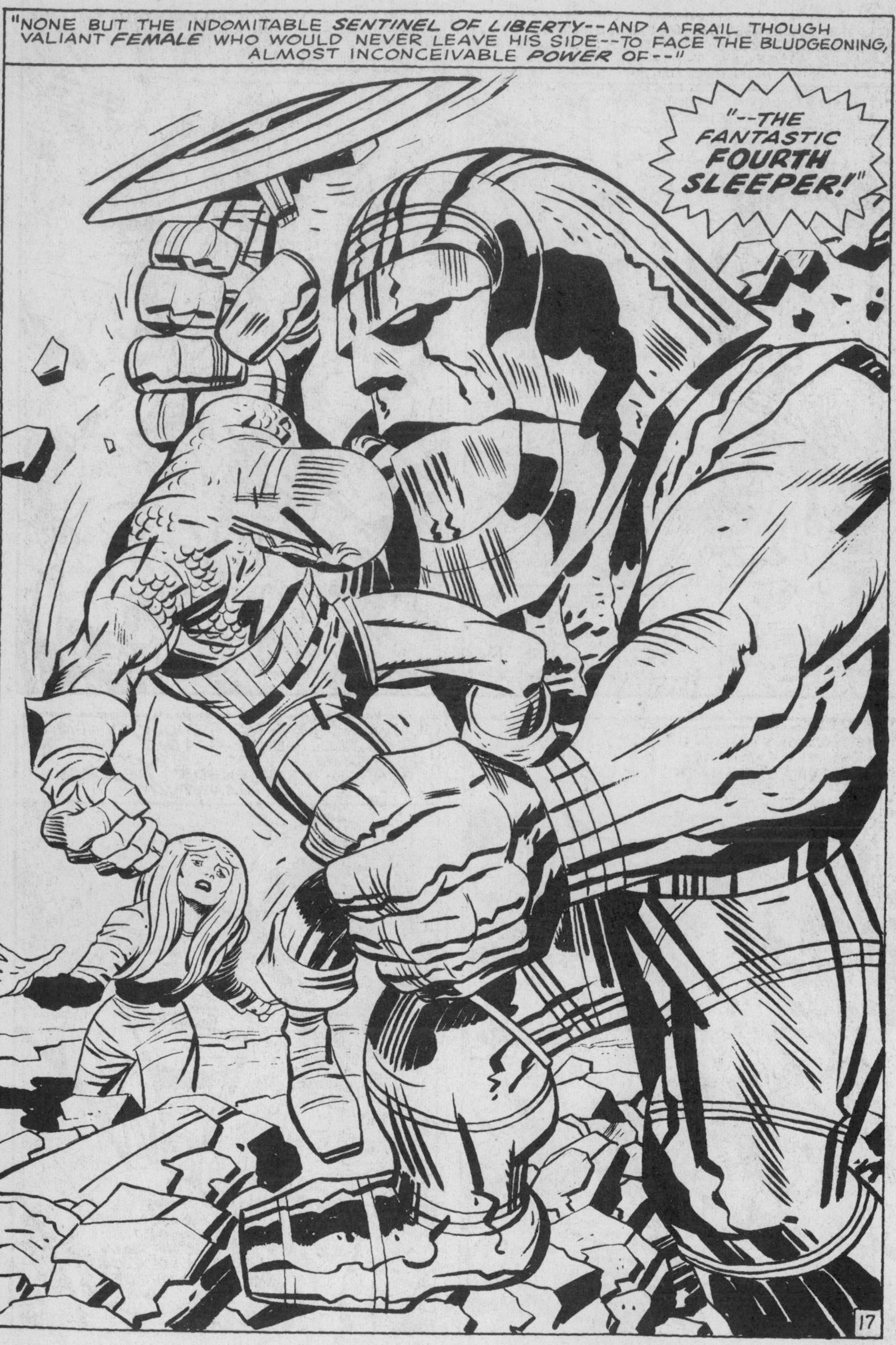
"NONE BUT THE INDOMITABLE SENTINEL OF LIBERTY--AND A FRAIL THOUGH VALIANT FEMALE WHO WOULD NEVER LEAVE HIS SIDE--TO FACE THE BLUDGEONING, ALMOST INCONCEIVABLE POWER OF--"
"--THE FANTASTIC FOURTH SLEEPER!"
17

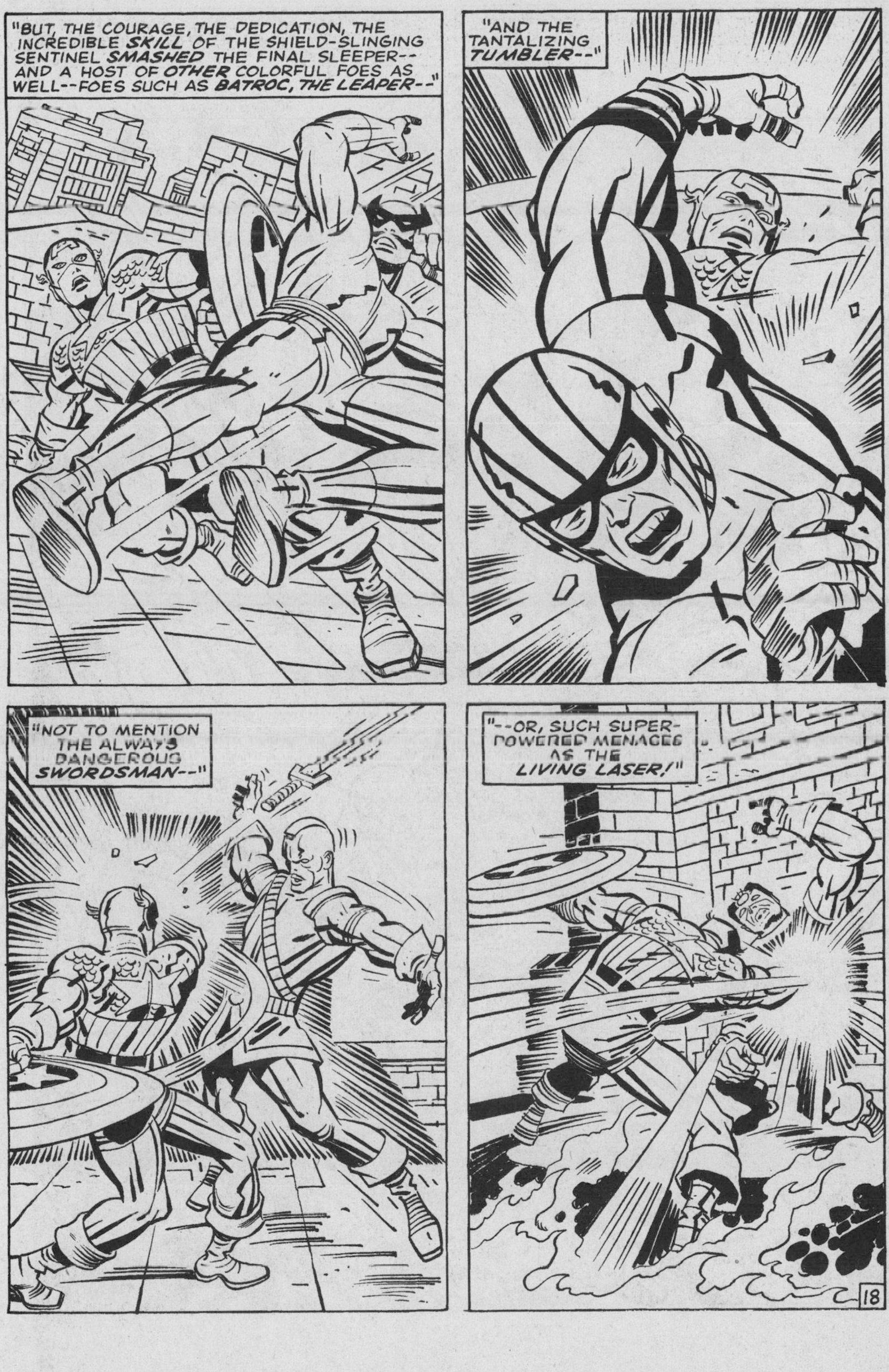
"BUT, THE COURAGE, THE DEDICATION, THE INCREDIBLE SKILL OF THE SHIELD-SLINGING SENTINEL SMASHED THE FINAL SLEEPER-- AND A HOST OF OTHER COLORFUL FOES AS WELL--FOES SUCH AS BATROC, THE LEAPER--"
"AND THE TANTALIZING TUMBLER--"
"NOT TO MENTION THE ALWAYS DANGEROUS SWORDSMAN--"
"--OR, SUCH SUPER-POWERED MENACES AS THE LIVING LASER!"
18

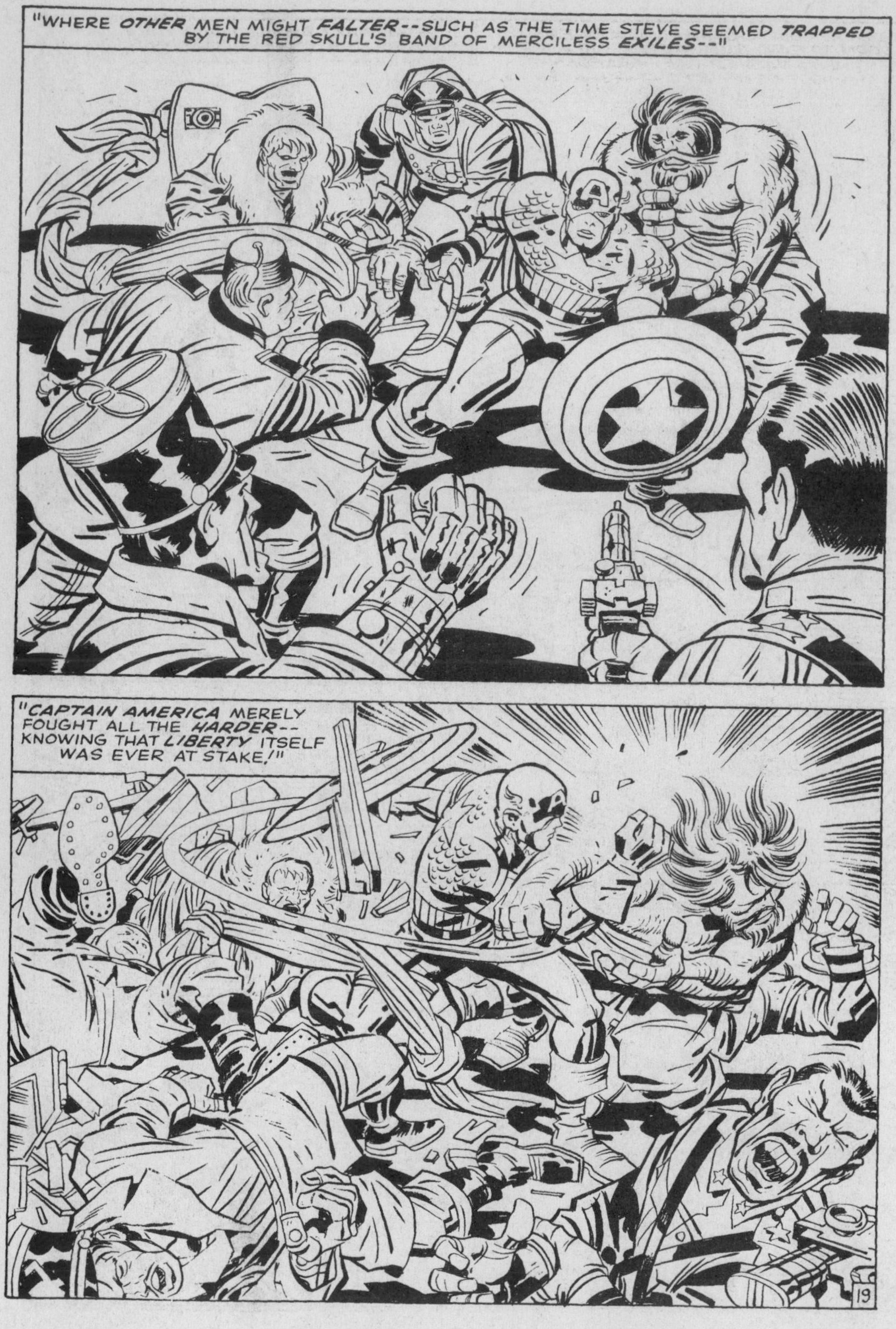
"WHERE OTHER MEN MIGHT FALTER--SUCH AS THE TIME STEVE SEEMED TRAPPED BY THE RED SKULL'S BAND OF MERCILESS EXILES--"
"CAPTAIN AMERICA MERELY FOUGHT ALL THE HARDER--KNOWING THAT LIBERTY ITSELF WAS EVER AT STAKE!"

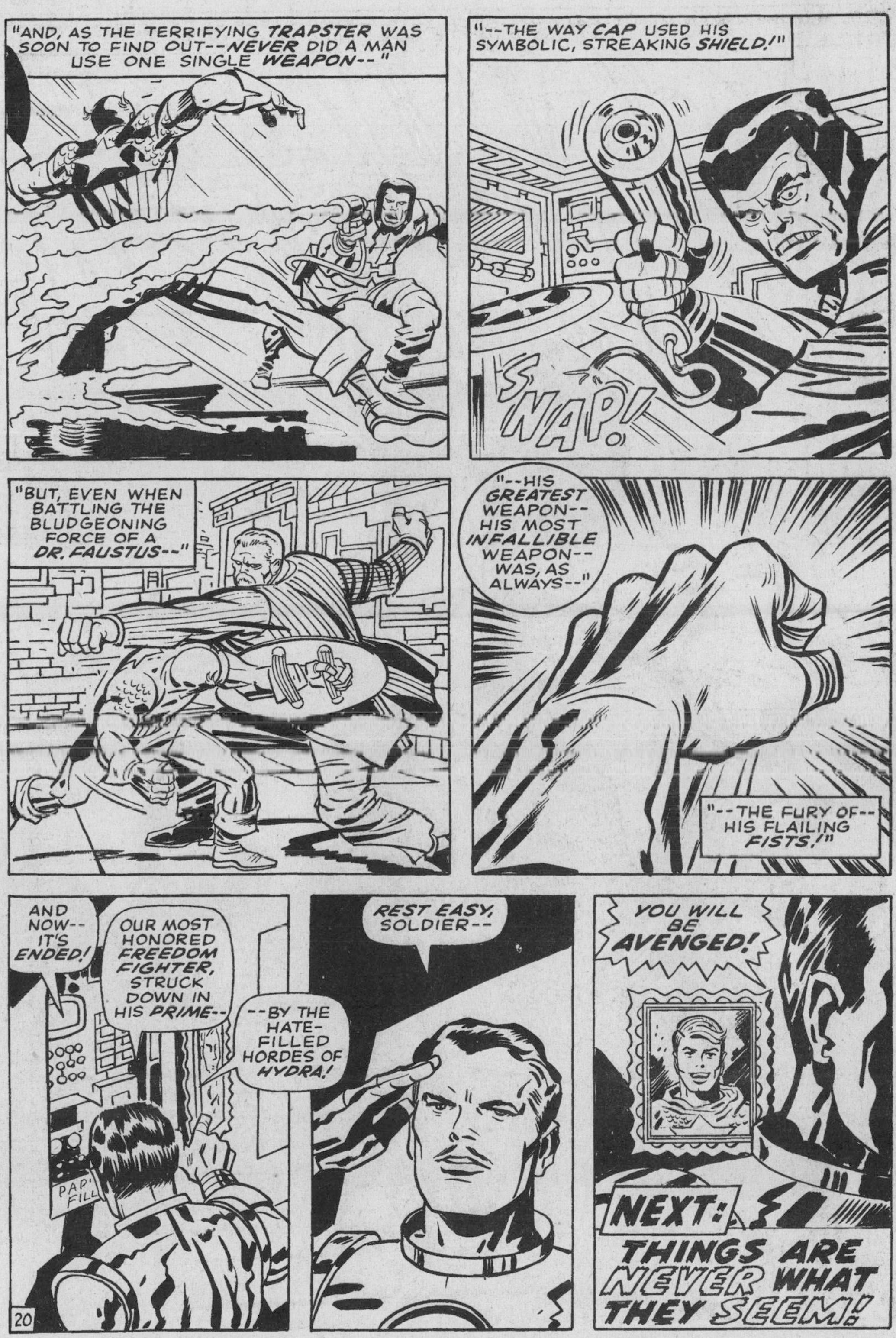
"AND, AS THE TERRIFYING TRAPSTER WAS SOON TO FIND OUT--NEVER DID A MAN USE ONE SINGLE WEAPON--"
"--THE WAY CAP USED HIS SYMBOLIC, STREAKING SHIELD!"
SNAP!
"BUT, EVEN WHEN BATTLING THE BLUDGEONING FORCE OF A DR. FAUSTUS--"
"--HIS GREATEST WEAPON--HIS MOST INFALLIBLE WEAPON--WAS, AS ALWAYS--"
"--THE FURY OF--HIS FLAILING FISTS!"
AND NOW--IT'S ENDED!
OUR MOST HONORED FREEDOM FIGHTER, STRUCK DOWN IN HIS PRIME--
--BY THE HATE-FILLED HORDES OF HYDRA!
REST EASY, SOLDIER--
YOU WILL BE AVENGED!
NEXT: THINGS ARE NEVER WHAT THEY SEEM!
20

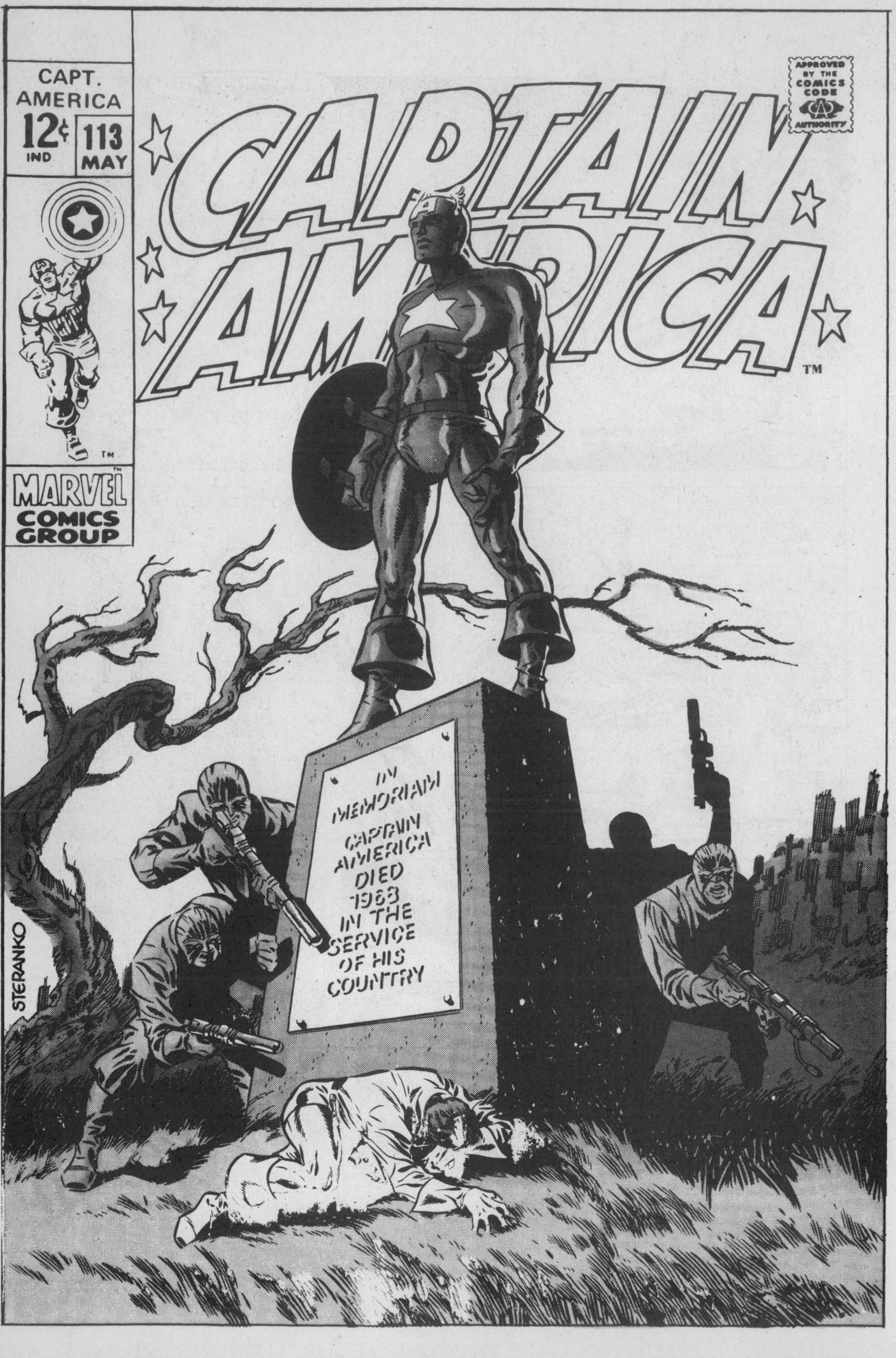
CAPT. AMERICA
12¢ IND
113 MAY
MARVEL COMICS GROUP
APPROVED BY THE COMICS CODE AUTHORITY
CAPTAIN AMERICA
IN MEMORIAM
CAPTAIN AMERICA
DIED 1968
IN THE SERVICE OF HIS COUNTRY
STERANKO

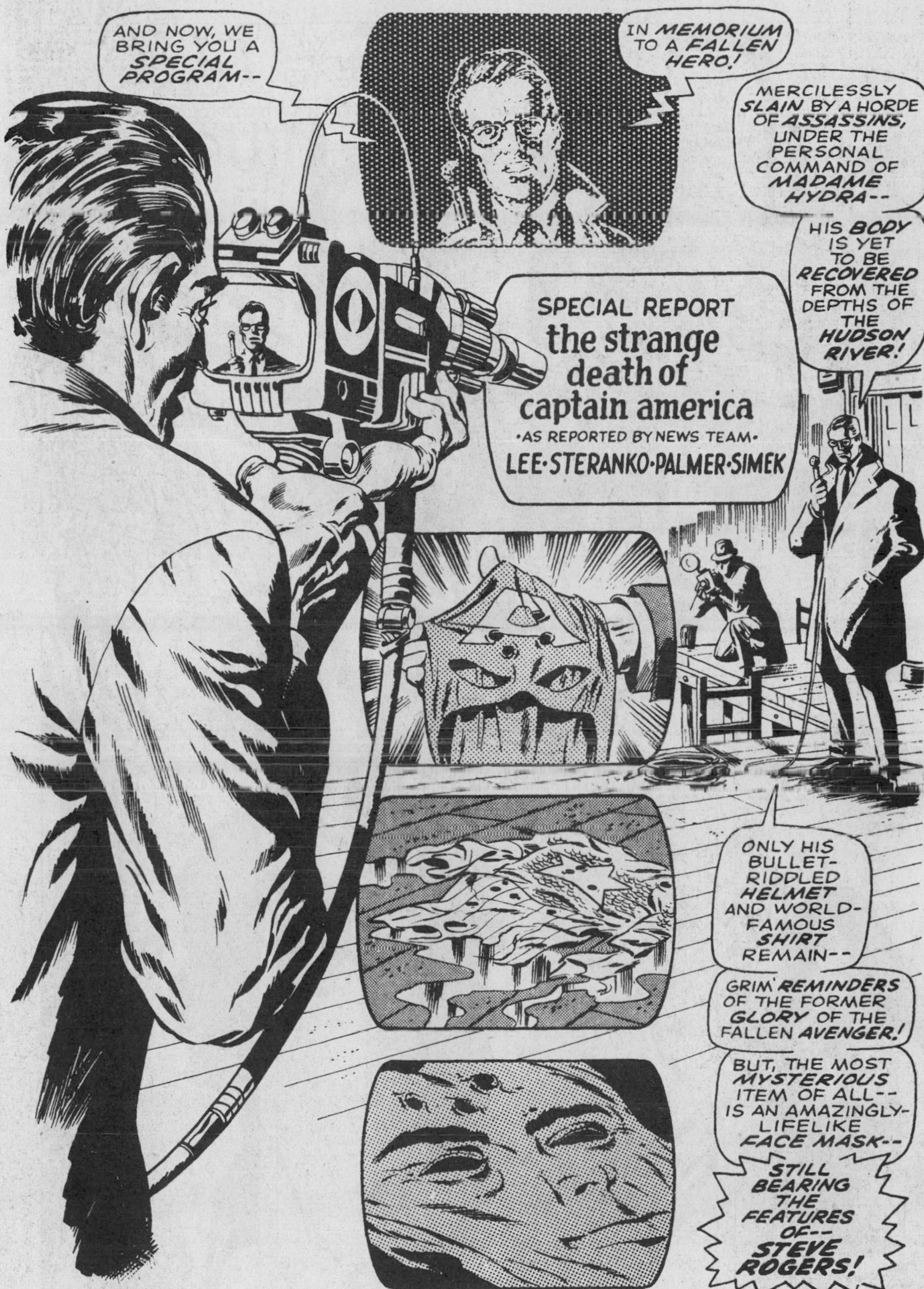
AND NOW, WE BRING YOU A SPECIAL PROGRAM--
IN MEMORIUM TO A FALLEN HERO!
MERCILESSLY SLAIN BY A HORDE OF ASSASSINS, UNDER THE PERSONAL COMMAND OF MADAME HYDRA--
HIS BODY IS YET TO BE RECOVERED FROM THE DEPTHS OF THE HUDSON RIVER!
SPECIAL REPORT
the strange death of captain america
•AS REPORTED BY NEWS TEAM•
LEE•STERANKO•PALMER•SIMEK
ONLY HIS BULLET-RIDDLED HELMET AND WORLD-FAMOUS SHIRT REMAIN--
GRIM REMINDERS OF THE FORMER GLORY OF THE FALLEN AVENGER!
BUT, THE MOST MYSTERIOUS ITEM OF ALL--IS AN AMAZINGLY-LIFELIKE FACE MASK--
STILL BEARING THE FEATURES OF--STEVE ROGERS!

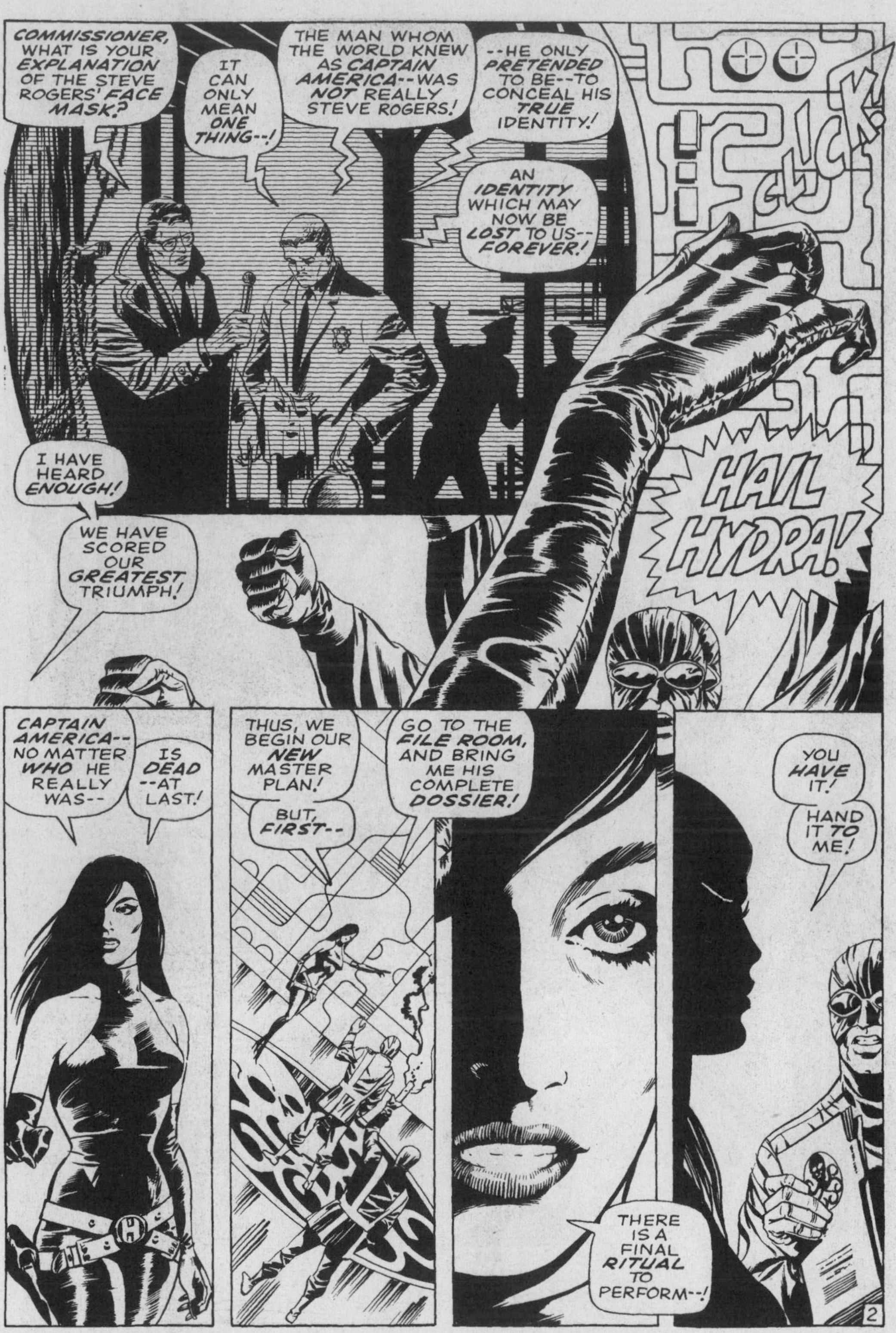
COMMISSIONER, WHAT IS YOUR EXPLANATION OF THE STEVE ROGERS' FACE MASK?
IT CAN ONLY MEAN ONE THING--!
THE MAN WHOM THE WORLD KNEW AS CAPTAIN AMERICA--WAS NOT REALLY STEVE ROGERS!
--HE ONLY PRETENDED TO BE--TO CONCEAL HIS TRUE IDENTITY!
AN IDENTITY WHICH MAY NOW BE LOST TO US--FOREVER!
CLICK!
I HAVE HEARD ENOUGH!
WE HAVE SCORED OUR GREATEST TRIUMPH!
HAIL HYDRA!
CAPTAIN AMERICA--NO MATTER WHO HE REALLY WAS--
IS DEAD--AT LAST!
THUS, WE BEGIN OUR NEW MASTER PLAN!
BUT, FIRST--
GO TO THE FILE ROOM, AND BRING ME HIS COMPLETE DOSSIER!
YOU HAVE IT!
HAND IT TO ME!
THERE IS A FINAL RITUAL TO PERFORM--!
2

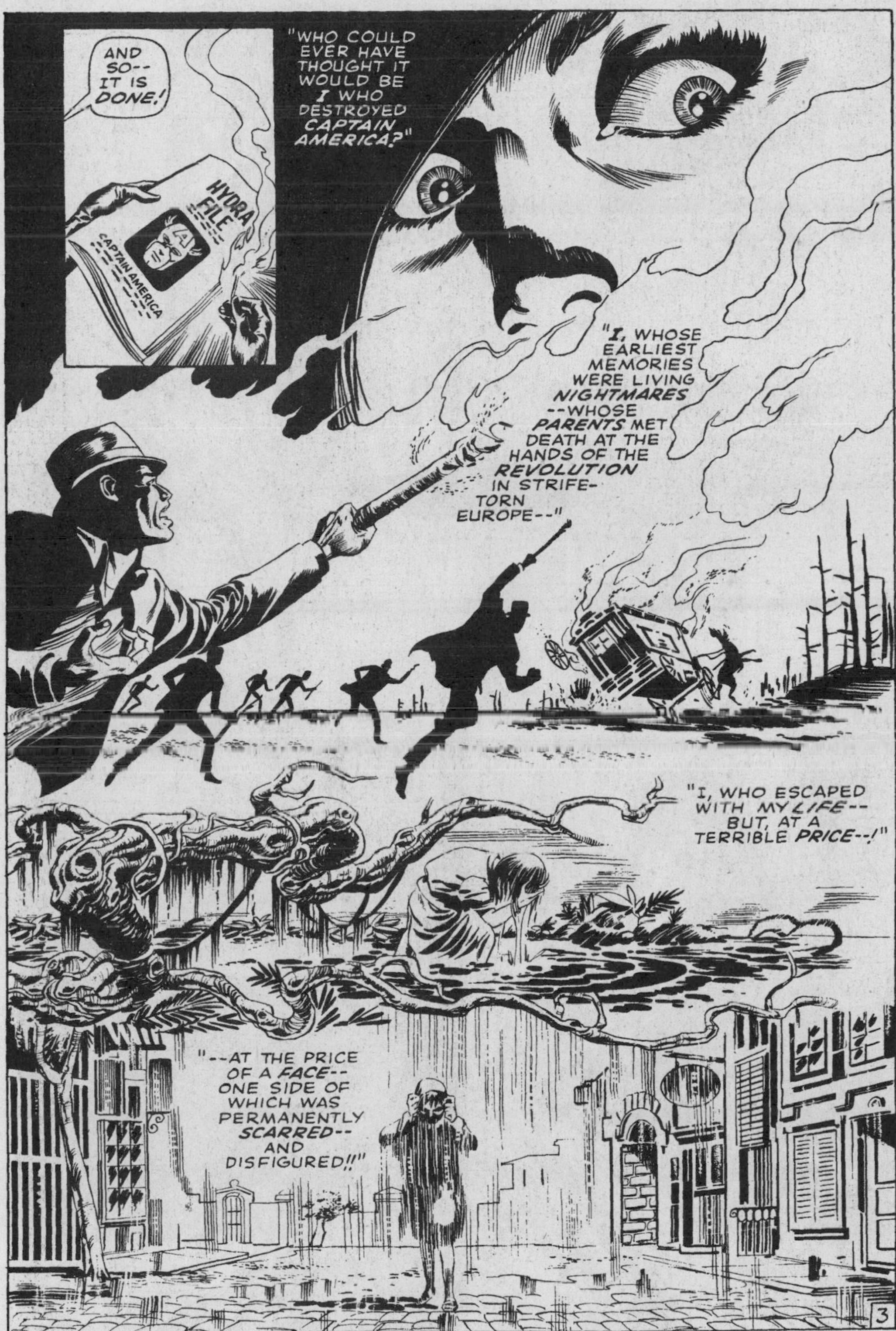
AND SO-- IT IS DONE!
"WHO COULD EVER HAVE THOUGHT IT WOULD BE I WHO DESTROYED CAPTAIN AMERICA?"
HYDRA FILE
CAPTAIN AMERICA
"I, WHOSE EARLIEST MEMORIES WERE LIVING NIGHTMARES --WHOSE PARENTS MET DEATH AT THE HANDS OF THE REVOLUTION IN STRIFE-TORN EUROPE--"
"I, WHO ESCAPED WITH MY LIFE-- BUT, AT A TERRIBLE PRICE--!"
"--AT THE PRICE OF A FACE-- ONE SIDE OF WHICH WAS PERMANENTLY SCARRED-- AND DISFIGURED!!"
3

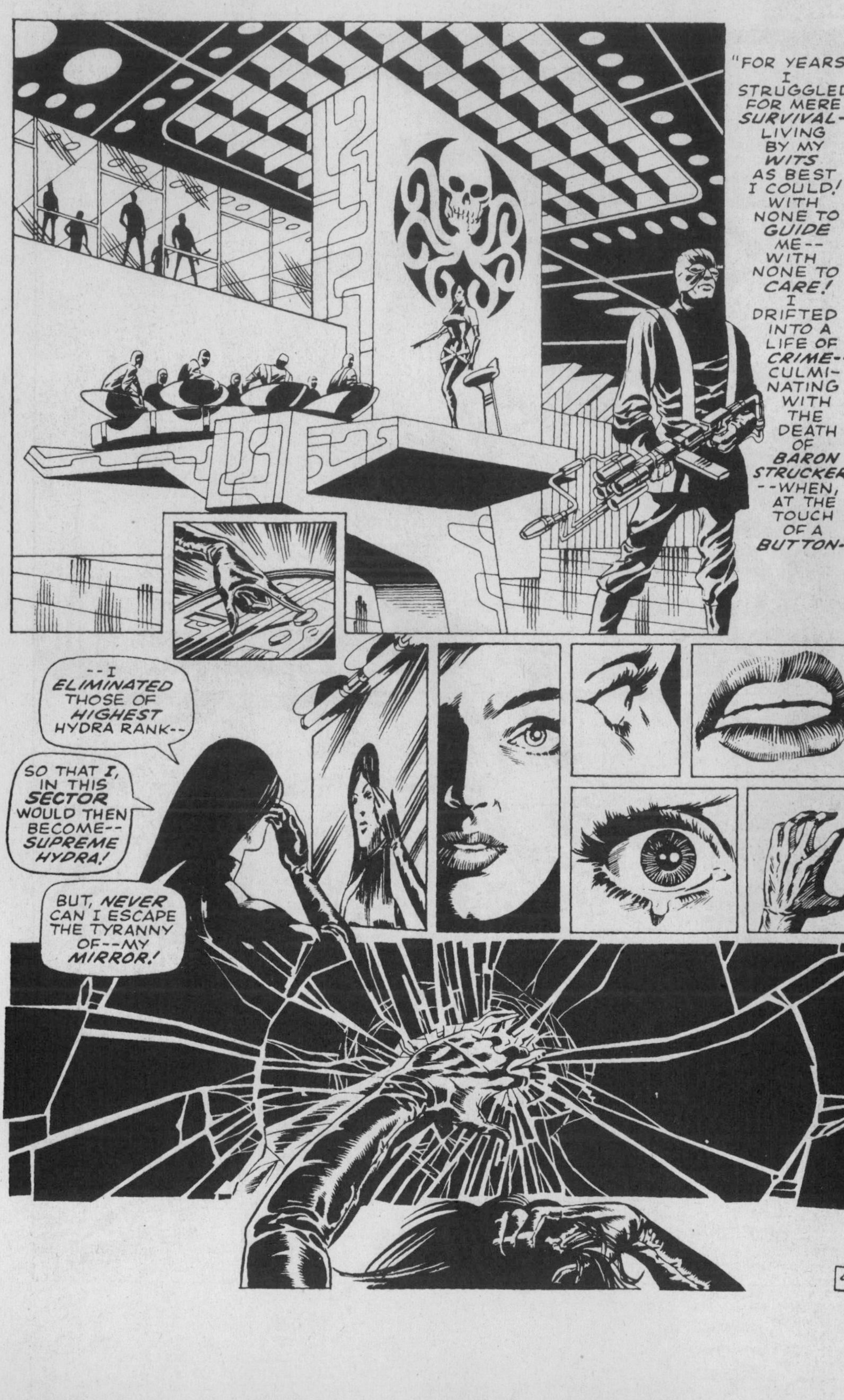
"FOR YEARS, I STRUGGLED FOR MERE SURVIVAL--LIVING BY MY WITS AS BEST I COULD! WITH NONE TO GUIDE ME--WITH NONE TO CARE! I DRIFTED INTO A LIFE OF CRIME--CULMINATING WITH THE DEATH OF BARON STRUCKER--WHEN, AT THE TOUCH OF A BUTTON--"
--I ELIMINATED THOSE OF HIGHEST HYDRA RANK--
SO THAT I, IN THIS SECTOR WOULD THEN BECOME--SUPREME HYDRA!
BUT, NEVER CAN I ESCAPE THE TYRANNY OF--MY MIRROR!

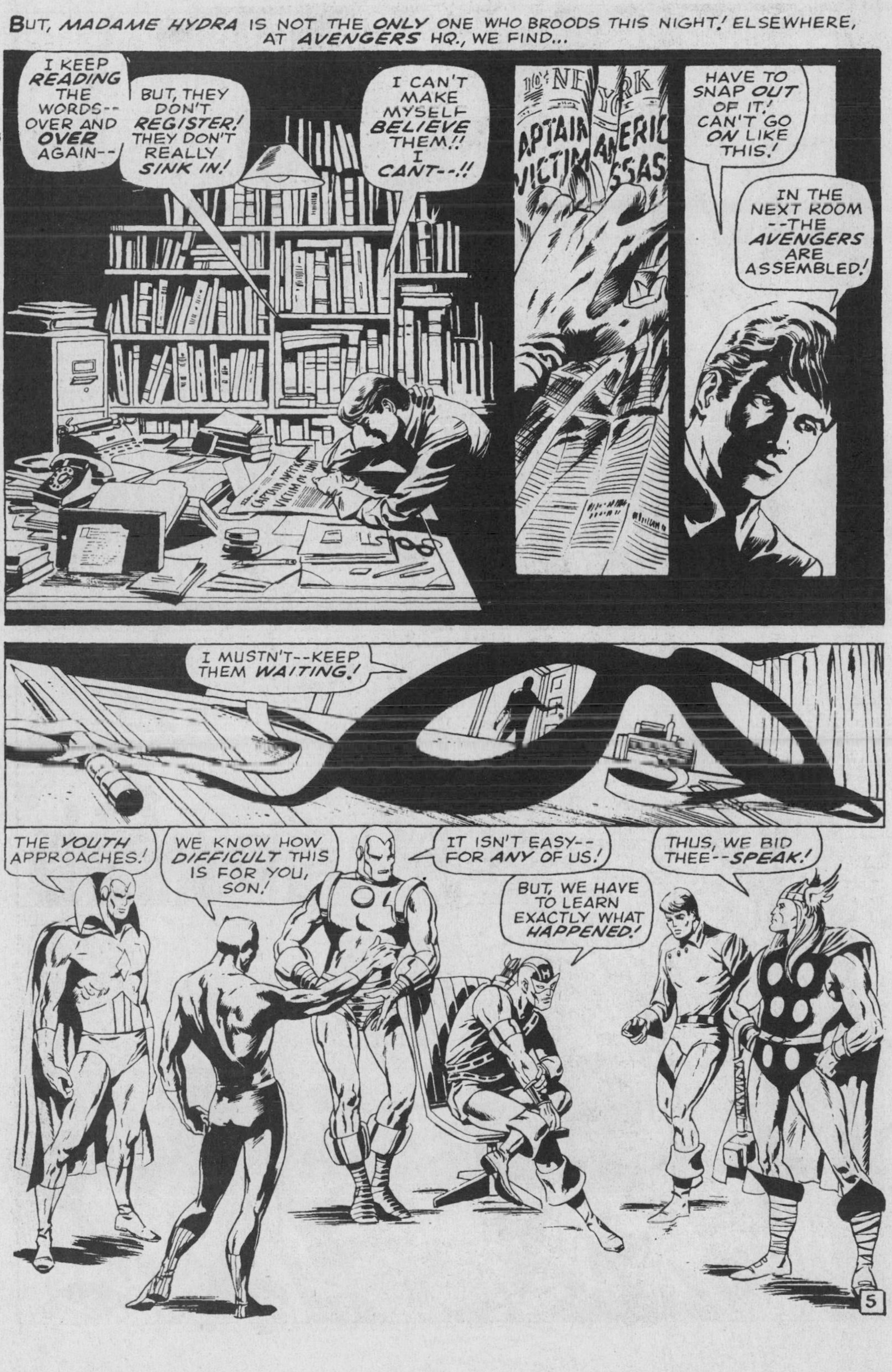
BUT, MADAME HYDRA IS NOT THE ONLY ONE WHO BROODS THIS NIGHT! ELSEWHERE, AT AVENGERS HQ., WE FIND...
I KEEP READING THE WORDS-- OVER AND OVER AGAIN--
BUT, THEY DON'T REGISTER! THEY DON'T REALLY SINK IN!
I CAN'T MAKE MYSELF BELIEVE THEM!! I CANT--!!
HAVE TO SNAP OUT OF IT! CAN'T GO ON LIKE THIS!
IN THE NEXT ROOM --THE AVENGERS ARE ASSEMBLED!
I MUSTN'T--KEEP THEM WAITING!
THE YOUTH APPROACHES!
WE KNOW HOW DIFFICULT THIS IS FOR YOU, SON!
IT ISN'T EASY-- FOR ANY OF US!
BUT, WE HAVE TO LEARN EXACTLY WHAT HAPPENED!
THUS, WE BID THEE--SPEAK!
5

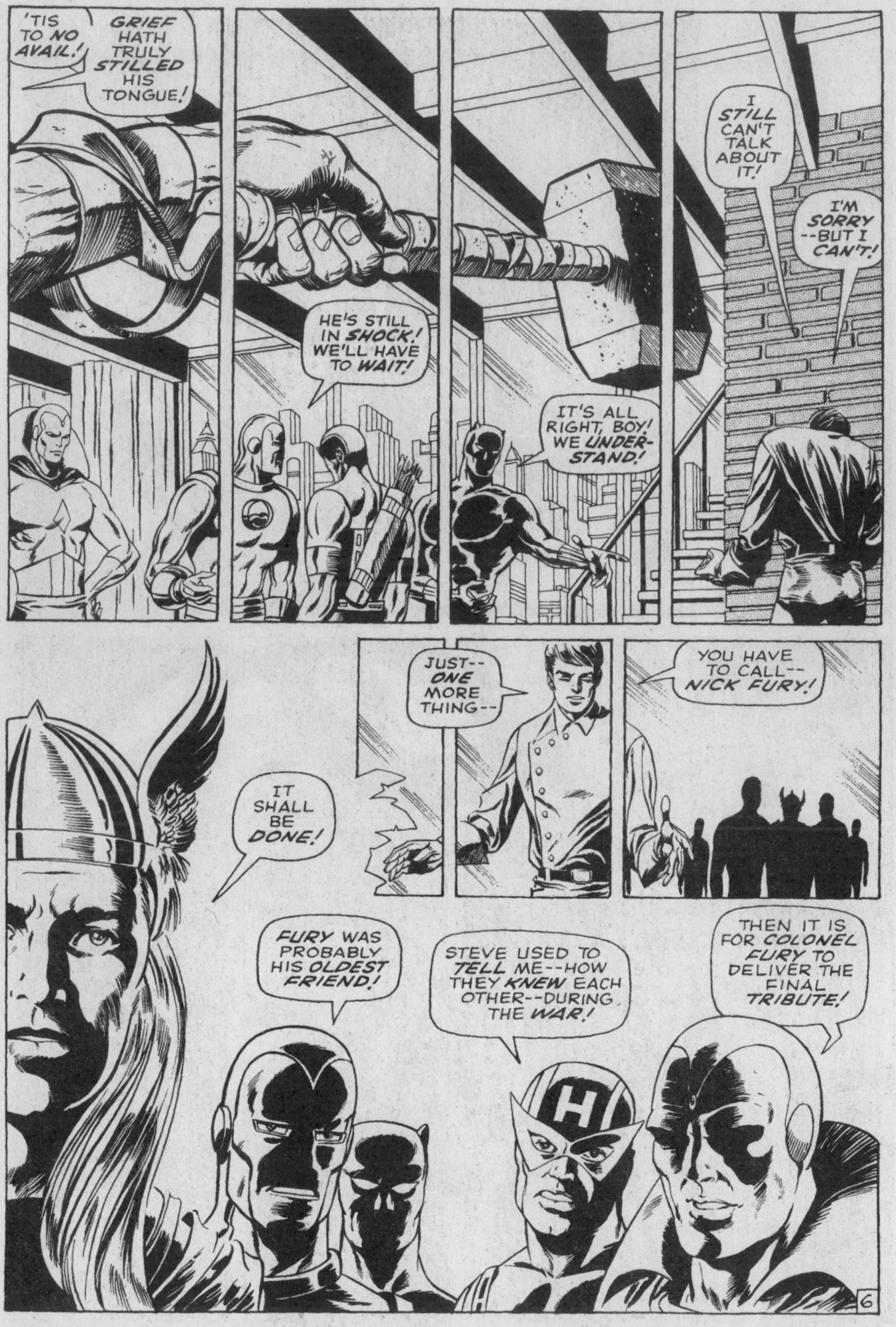
'TIS TO NO AVAIL!
GRIEF HATH TRULY STILLED HIS TONGUE!
HE'S STILL IN SHOCK! WE'LL HAVE TO WAIT!
IT'S ALL RIGHT, BOY! WE UNDER-STAND!
I STILL CAN'T TALK ABOUT IT!
I'M SORRY --BUT I CAN'T!
JUST-- ONE MORE THING--
YOU HAVE TO CALL-- NICK FURY!
IT SHALL BE DONE!
FURY WAS PROBABLY HIS OLDEST FRIEND!
STEVE USED TO TELL ME--HOW THEY KNEW EACH OTHER--DURING THE WAR!
THEN IT IS FOR COLONEL FURY TO DELIVER THE FINAL TRIBUTE!
6

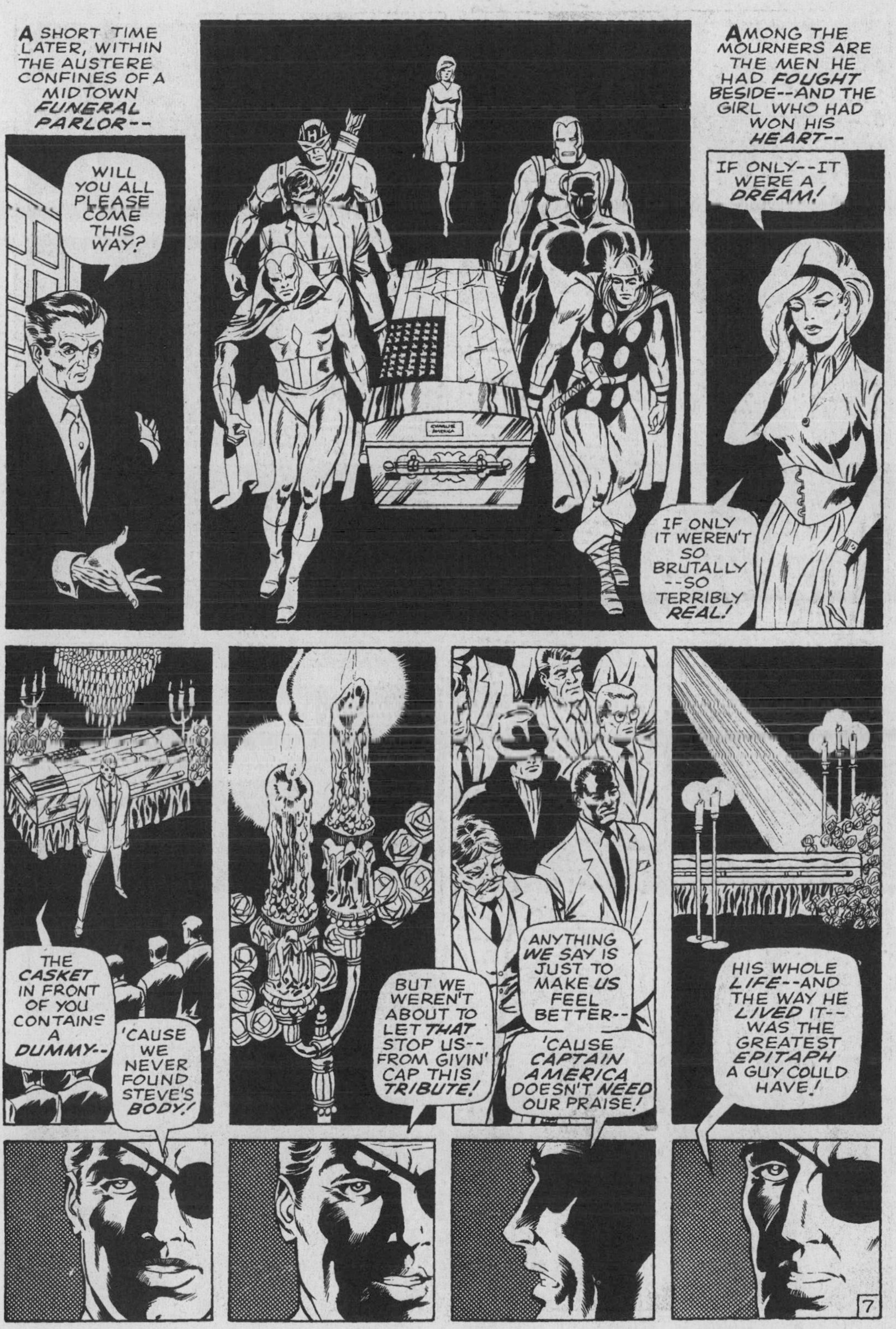
A SHORT TIME LATER, WITHIN THE AUSTERE CONFINES OF A MIDTOWN FUNERAL PARLOR--
WILL YOU ALL PLEASE COME THIS WAY?
AMONG THE MOURNERS ARE THE MEN HE HAD FOUGHT BESIDE--AND THE GIRL WHO HAD WON HIS HEART--
IF ONLY--IT WERE A DREAM!
IF ONLY IT WEREN'T SO BRUTALLY --SO TERRIBLY REAL!
THE CASKET IN FRONT OF YOU CONTAINS A DUMMY--
'CAUSE WE NEVER FOUND STEVE'S BODY!
BUT WE WEREN'T ABOUT TO LET THAT STOP US-- FROM GIVIN' CAP THIS TRIBUTE!
ANYTHING WE SAY IS JUST TO MAKE US FEEL BETTER--
'CAUSE CAPTAIN AMERICA DOESN'T NEED OUR PRAISE!
HIS WHOLE LIFE--AND THE WAY HE LIVED IT-- WAS THE GREATEST EPITAPH A GUY COULD HAVE!
7

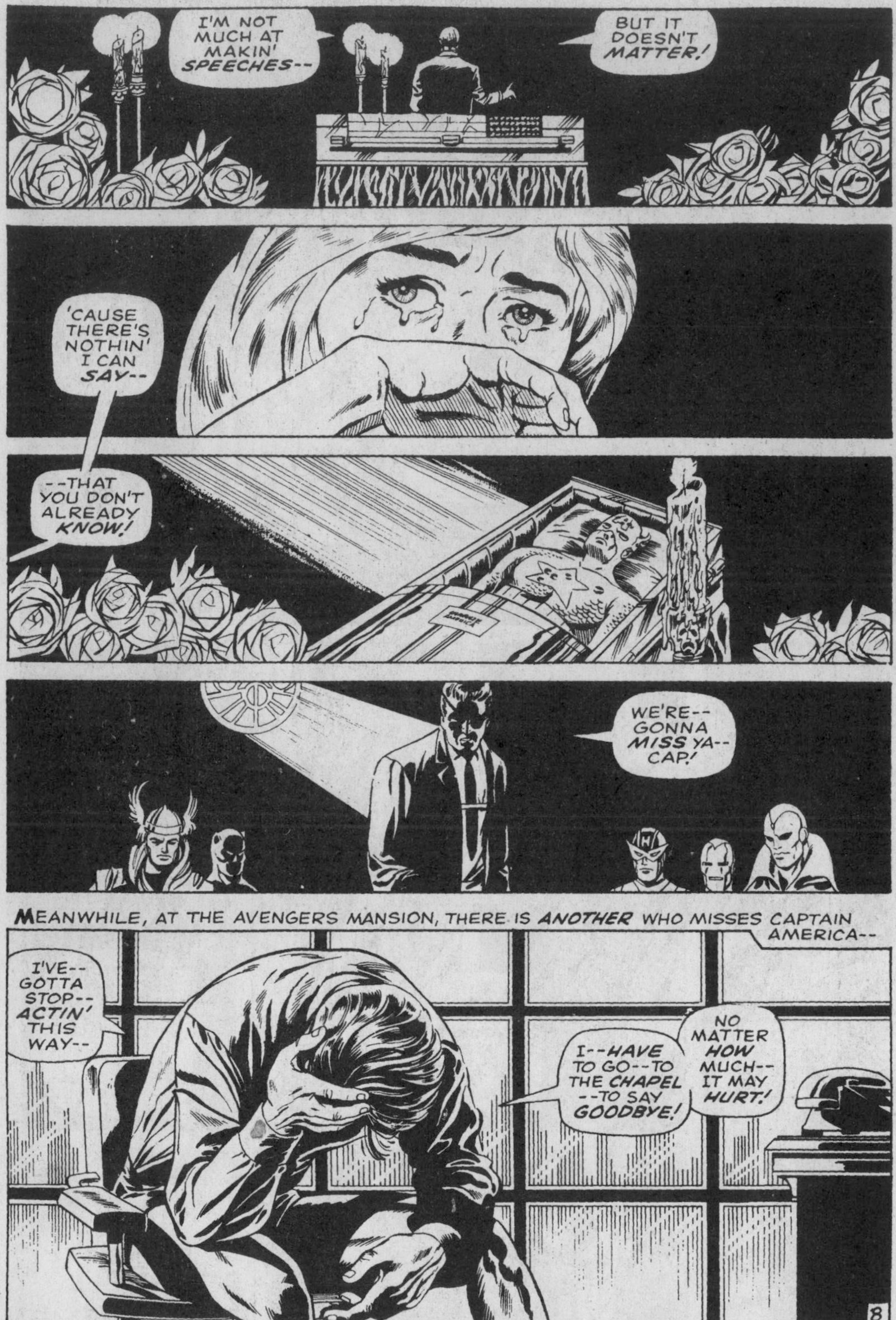

I'M NOT MUCH AT MAKIN' SPEECHES--
BUT IT DOESN'T MATTER!
'CAUSE THERE'S NOTHIN' I CAN SAY--
--THAT YOU DON'T ALREADY KNOW!
WE'RE-- GONNA MISS YA-- CAP!
MEANWHILE, AT THE AVENGERS MANSION, THERE IS ANOTHER WHO MISSES CAPTAIN AMERICA--
I'VE-- GOTTA STOP-- ACTIN' THIS WAY--
I--HAVE TO GO--TO THE CHAPEL --TO SAY GOODBYE!
NO MATTER HOW MUCH-- IT MAY HURT!
8

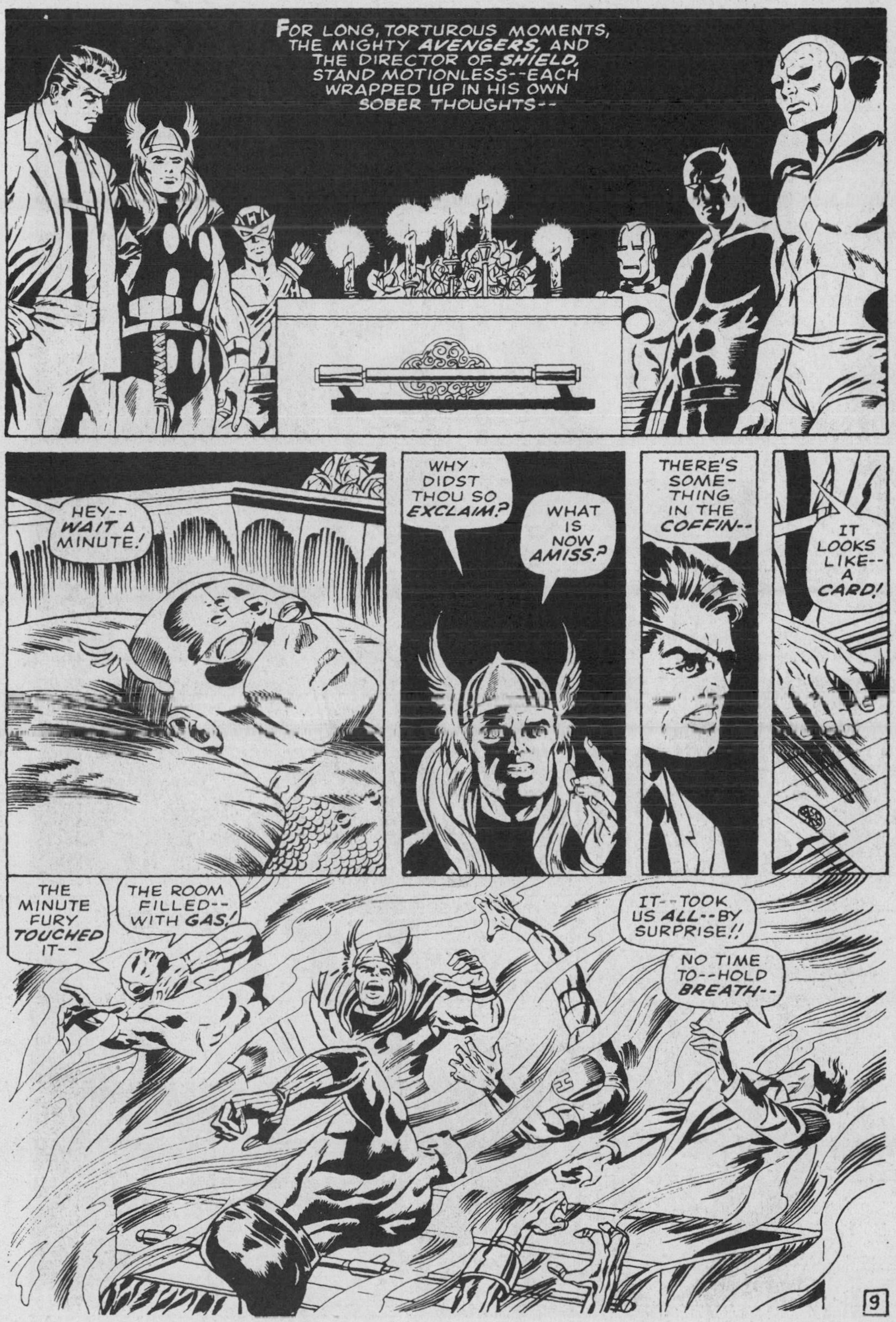
FOR LONG, TORTUROUS MOMENTS, THE MIGHTY AVENGERS, AND THE DIRECTOR OF SHIELD, STAND MOTIONLESS--EACH WRAPPED UP IN HIS OWN SOBER THOUGHTS--
HEY-- WAIT A MINUTE!
WHY DIDST THOU SO EXCLAIM?
WHAT IS NOW AMISS?
THERE'S SOME-THING IN THE COFFIN--
IT LOOKS LIKE-- A CARD!
THE MINUTE FURY TOUCHED IT--
THE ROOM FILLED-- WITH GAS!
IT--TOOK US ALL--BY SURPRISE!!
NO TIME TO--HOLD BREATH--
9

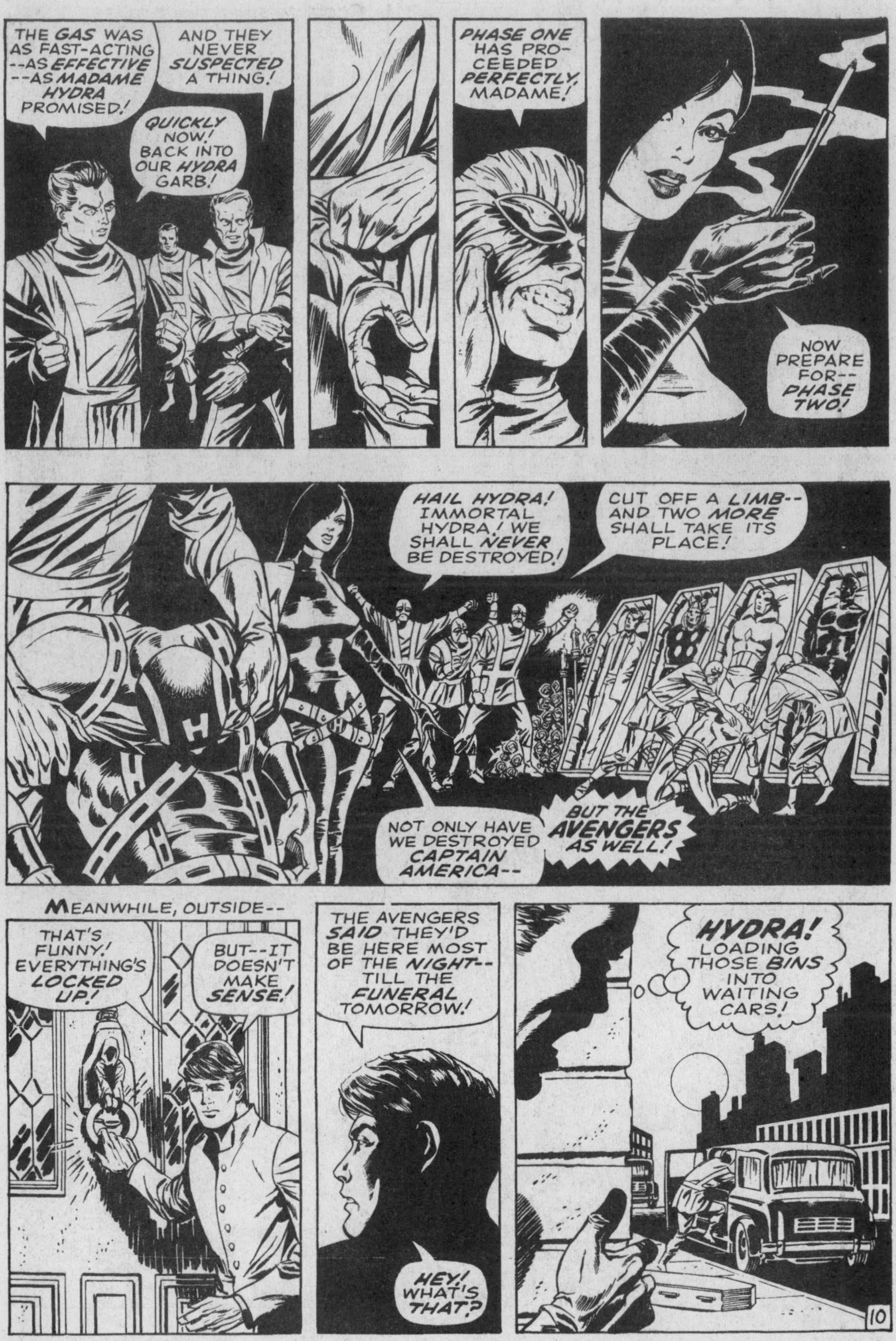
THE GAS WAS AS FAST-ACTING --AS EFFECTIVE --AS MADAME HYDRA PROMISED!
AND THEY NEVER SUSPECTED A THING!
QUICKLY NOW! BACK INTO OUR HYDRA GARB!
PHASE ONE HAS PROCEEDED PERFECTLY, MADAME!
NOW PREPARE FOR--PHASE TWO!
HAIL HYDRA! IMMORTAL HYDRA! WE SHALL NEVER BE DESTROYED!
CUT OFF A LIMB--AND TWO MORE SHALL TAKE ITS PLACE!
NOT ONLY HAVE WE DESTROYED CAPTAIN AMERICA--
BUT THE AVENGERS AS WELL!
MEANWHILE, OUTSIDE--
THAT'S FUNNY! EVERYTHING'S LOCKED UP!
BUT--IT DOESN'T MAKE SENSE!
THE AVENGERS SAID THEY'D BE HERE MOST OF THE NIGHT--TILL THE FUNERAL TOMORROW!
HEY! WHAT'S THAT?
HYDRA! LOADING THOSE BINS INTO WAITING CARS!
10

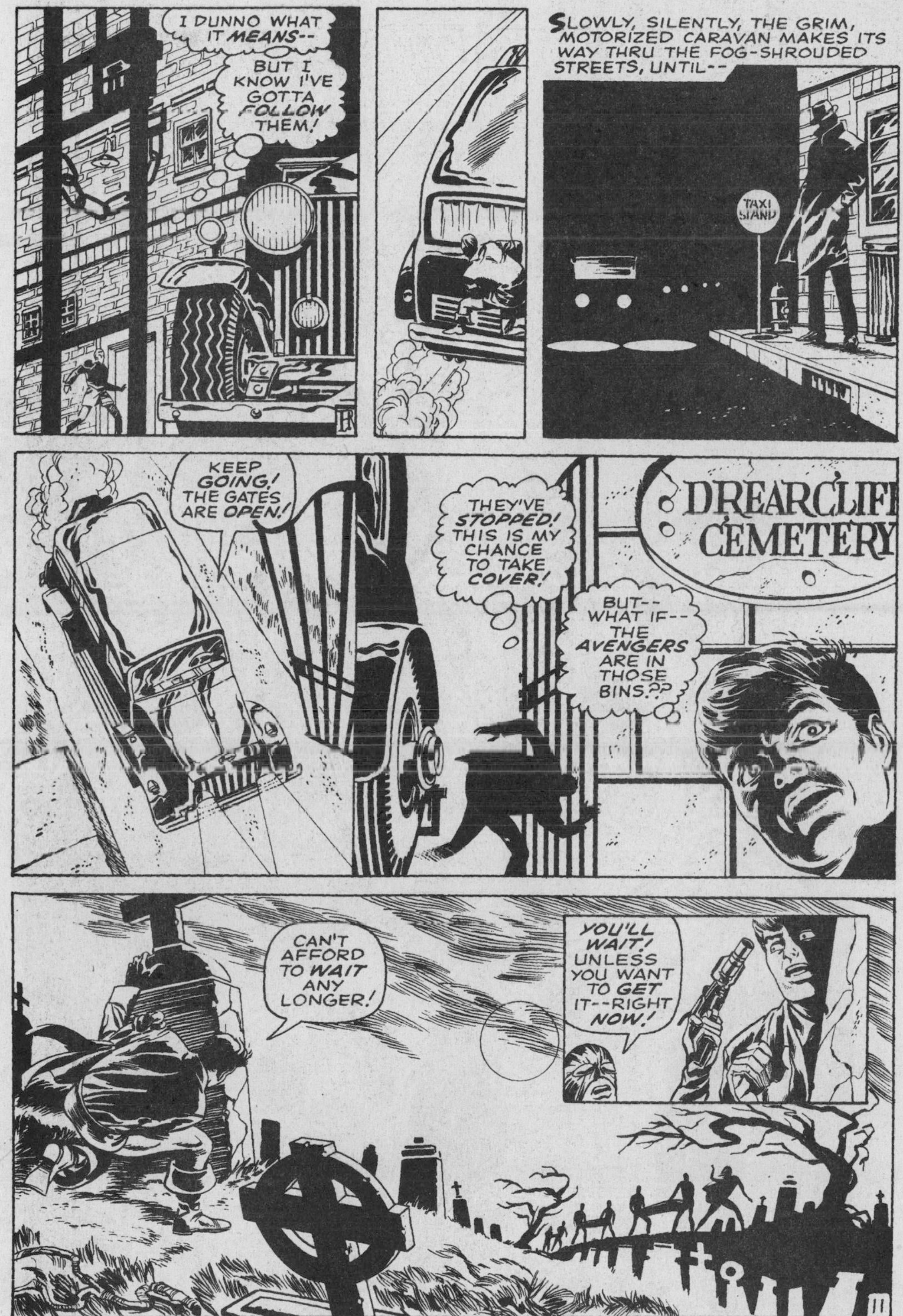

I DUNNO WHAT IT MEANS--
BUT I KNOW I'VE GOTTA FOLLOW THEM!
SLOWLY, SILENTLY, THE GRIM, MOTORIZED CARAVAN MAKES ITS WAY THRU THE FOG-SHROUDED STREETS, UNTIL--
TAXI STAND
KEEP GOING! THE GATES ARE OPEN!
THEY'VE STOPPED! THIS IS MY CHANCE TO TAKE COVER!
DREARCLIFF CEMETERY
BUT-- WHAT IF-- THE AVENGERS ARE IN THOSE BINS??
CAN'T AFFORD TO WAIT ANY LONGER!
YOU'LL WAIT! UNLESS YOU WANT TO GET IT--RIGHT NOW!
11

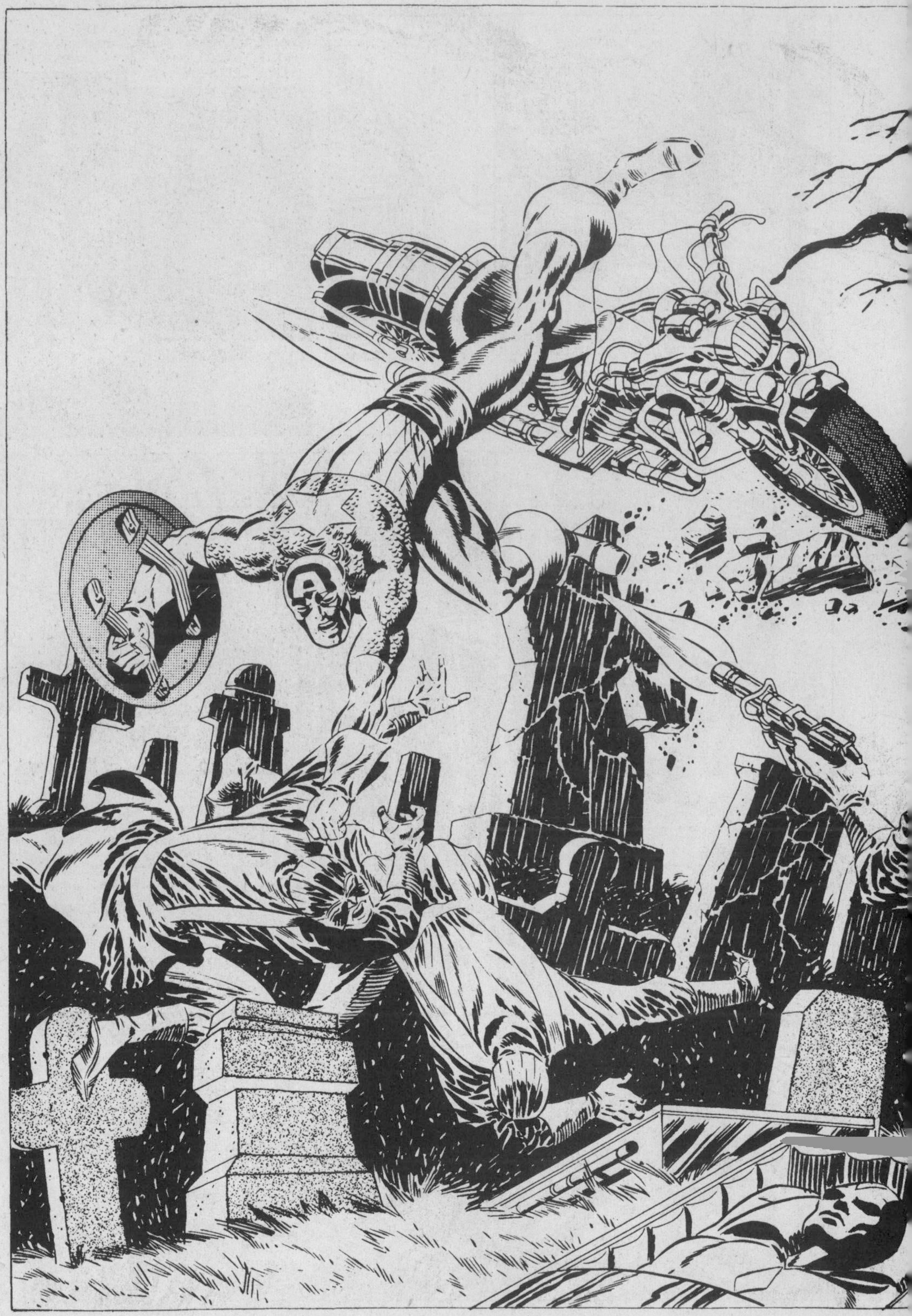

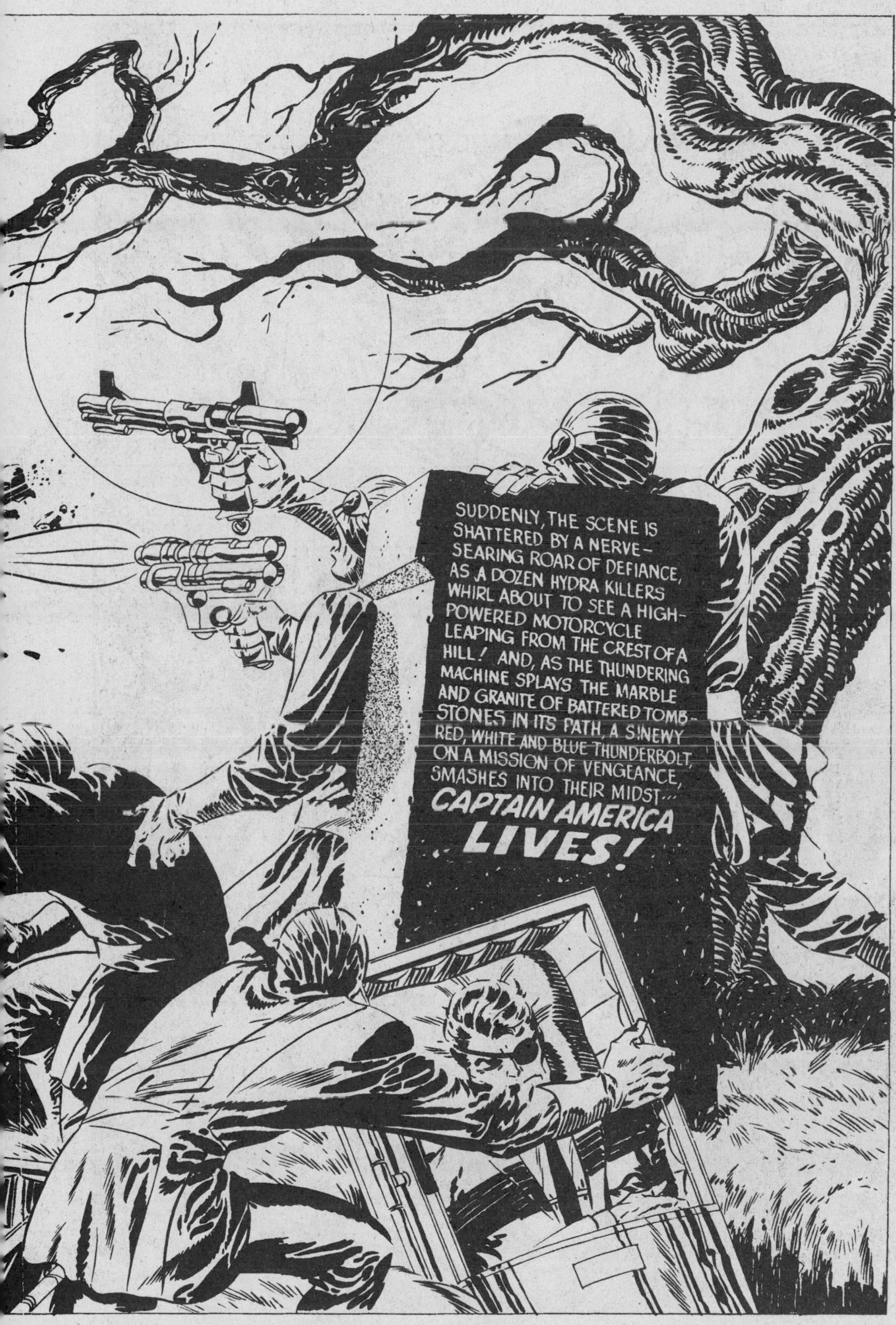
SUDDENLY, THE SCENE IS SHATTERED BY A NERVE-SEARING ROAR OF DEFIANCE, AS A DOZEN HYDRA KILLERS WHIRL ABOUT TO SEE A HIGH-POWERED MOTORCYCLE LEAPING FROM THE CREST OF A HILL! AND, AS THE THUNDERING MACHINE SPLAYS THE MARBLE AND GRANITE OF BATTERED TOMB-STONES IN ITS PATH, A SINEWY RED, WHITE AND BLUE THUNDERBOLT, ON A MISSION OF VENGEANCE, SMASHES INTO THEIR MIDST...
CAPTAIN AMERICA LIVES!

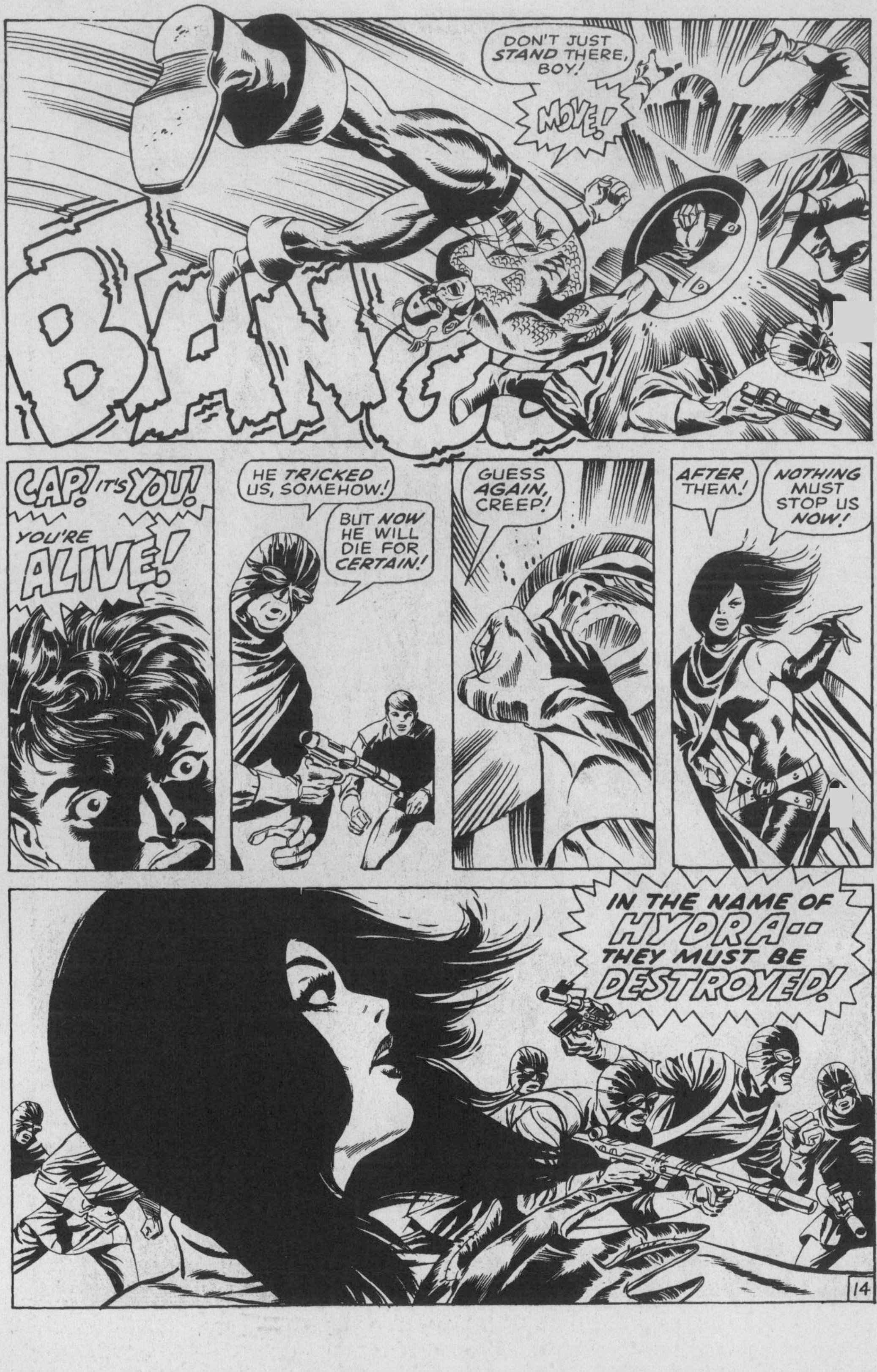
DON'T JUST STAND THERE, BOY!
MOVE!
BANG
CAP! IT'S YOU! YOU'RE ALIVE!
HE TRICKED US, SOMEHOW!
BUT NOW HE WILL DIE FOR CERTAIN!
GUESS AGAIN, CREEP!
AFTER THEM!
NOTHING MUST STOP US NOW!
IN THE NAME OF HYDRA-- THEY MUST BE DESTROYED!

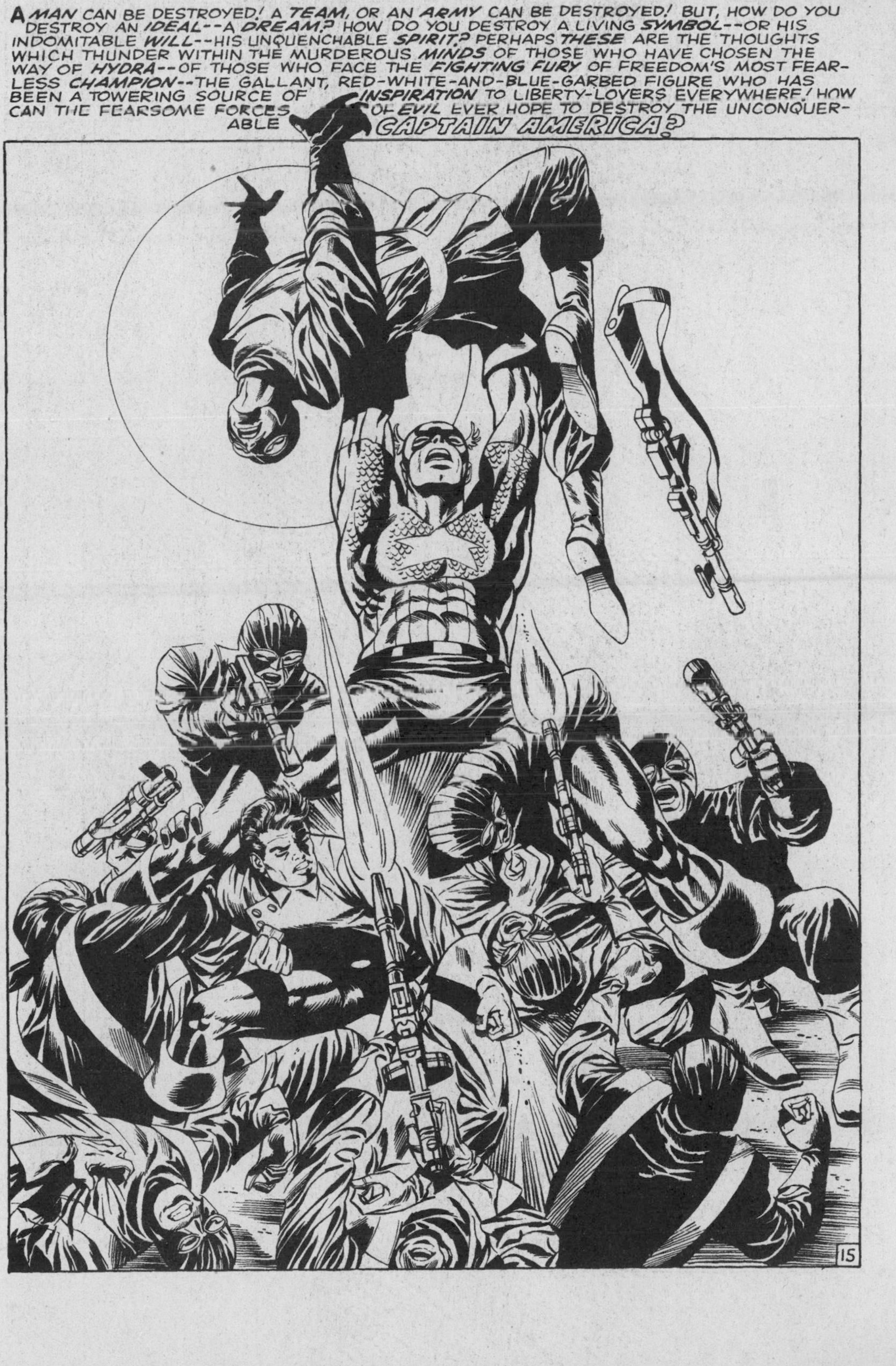
A MAN CAN BE DESTROYED! A TEAM, OR AN ARMY CAN BE DESTROYED! BUT, HOW DO YOU DESTROY AN IDEAL--A DREAM? HOW DO YOU DESTROY A LIVING SYMBOL--OR HIS INDOMITABLE WILL--HIS UNQUENCHABLE SPIRIT? PERHAPS THESE ARE THE THOUGHTS WHICH THUNDER WITHIN THE MURDEROUS MINDS OF THOSE WHO HAVE CHOSEN THE WAY OF HYDRA--OF THOSE WHO FACE THE FIGHTING FURY OF FREEDOM'S MOST FEARLESS CHAMPION--THE GALLANT, RED-WHITE-AND-BLUE-GARBED FIGURE WHO HAS BEEN A TOWERING SOURCE OF INSPIRATION TO LIBERTY-LOVERS EVERYWHERE! HOW CAN THE FEARSOME FORCES OF EVIL EVER HOPE TO DESTROY THE UNCONQUERABLE CAPTAIN AMERICA?

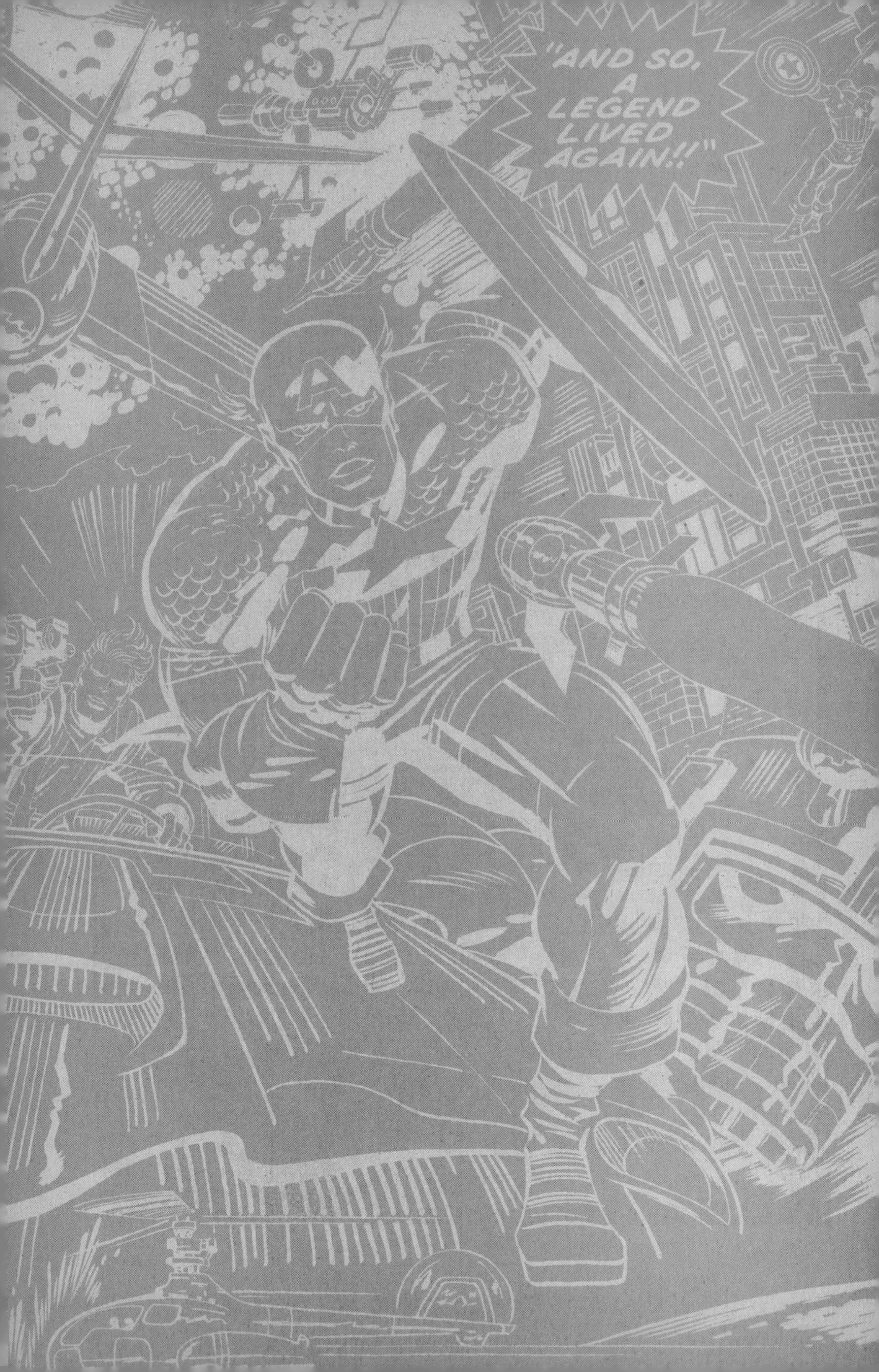
"AND SO, A LEGEND LIVED AGAIN!!"

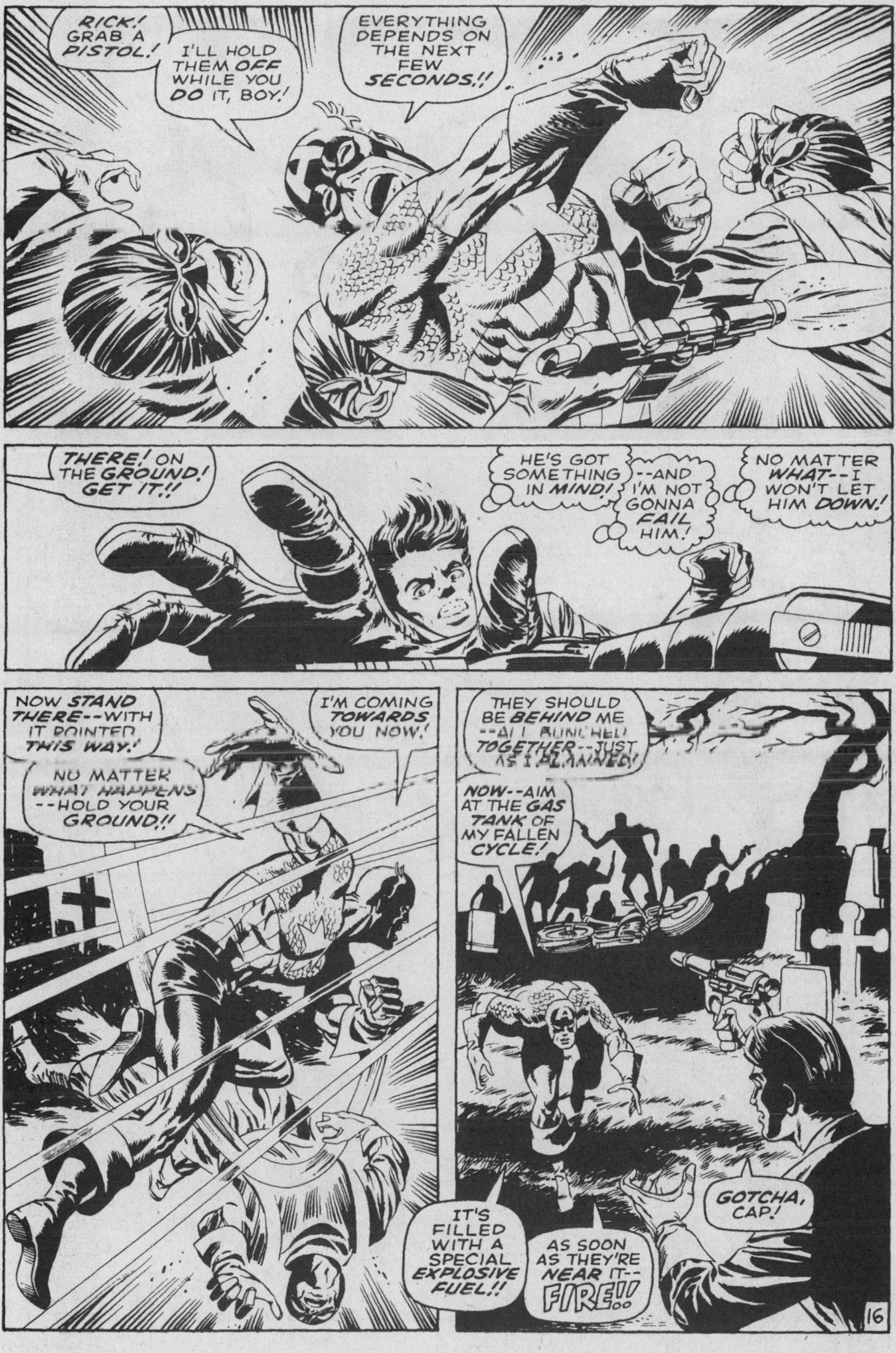
RICK! GRAB A PISTOL!
I'LL HOLD THEM OFF WHILE YOU DO IT, BOY!
EVERYTHING DEPENDS ON THE NEXT FEW SECONDS!!
THERE! ON THE GROUND! GET IT!!
HE'S GOT SOMETHING IN MIND!
--AND I'M NOT GONNA FAIL HIM!
NO MATTER WHAT--I WON'T LET HIM DOWN!
NOW STAND THERE--WITH IT POINTED THIS WAY!
NO MATTER WHAT HAPPENS--HOLD YOUR GROUND!!
I'M COMING TOWARDS YOU NOW!
THEY SHOULD BE BEHIND ME--ALL BUNCHED TOGETHER--JUST AS I PLANNED!
NOW--AIM AT THE GAS TANK OF MY FALLEN CYCLE!
IT'S FILLED WITH A SPECIAL EXPLOSIVE FUEL!!
AS SOON AS THEY'RE NEAR IT--FIRE!!
GOTCHA, CAP!
16

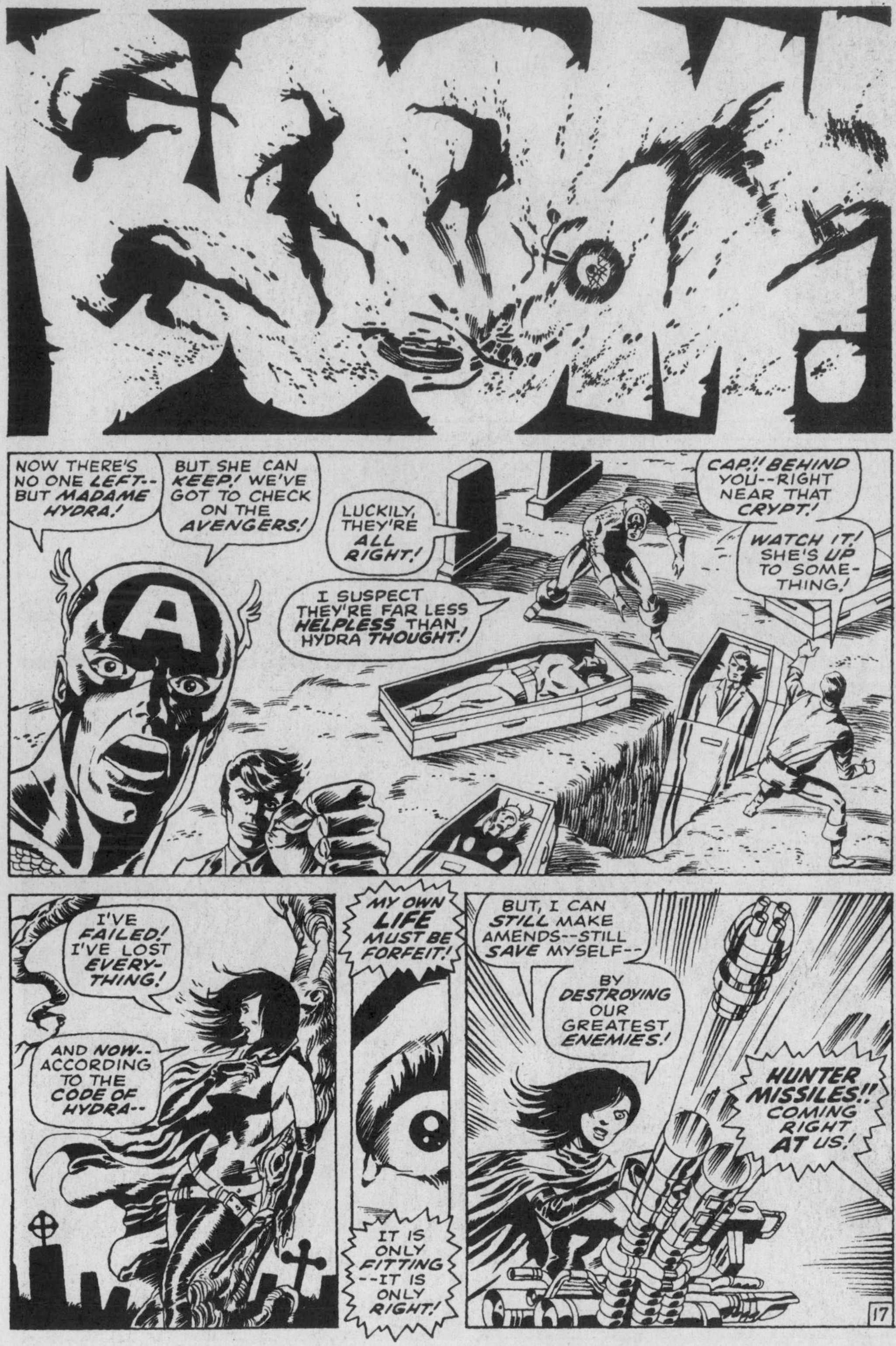

NOW THERE'S NO ONE LEFT-- BUT MADAME HYDRA!
BUT SHE CAN KEEP! WE'VE GOT TO CHECK ON THE AVENGERS!
LUCKILY, THEY'RE ALL RIGHT!
I SUSPECT THEY'RE FAR LESS HELPLESS THAN HYDRA THOUGHT!
CAP!! BEHIND YOU--RIGHT NEAR THAT CRYPT!
WATCH IT! SHE'S UP TO SOME-THING!
I'VE FAILED! I'VE LOST EVERY-THING!
AND NOW-- ACCORDING TO THE CODE OF HYDRA--
MY OWN LIFE MUST BE FORFEIT!
IT IS ONLY FITTING --IT IS ONLY RIGHT!
BUT, I CAN STILL MAKE AMENDS--STILL SAVE MYSELF--
BY DESTROYING OUR GREATEST ENEMIES!
HUNTER MISSILES!! COMING RIGHT AT US!
17

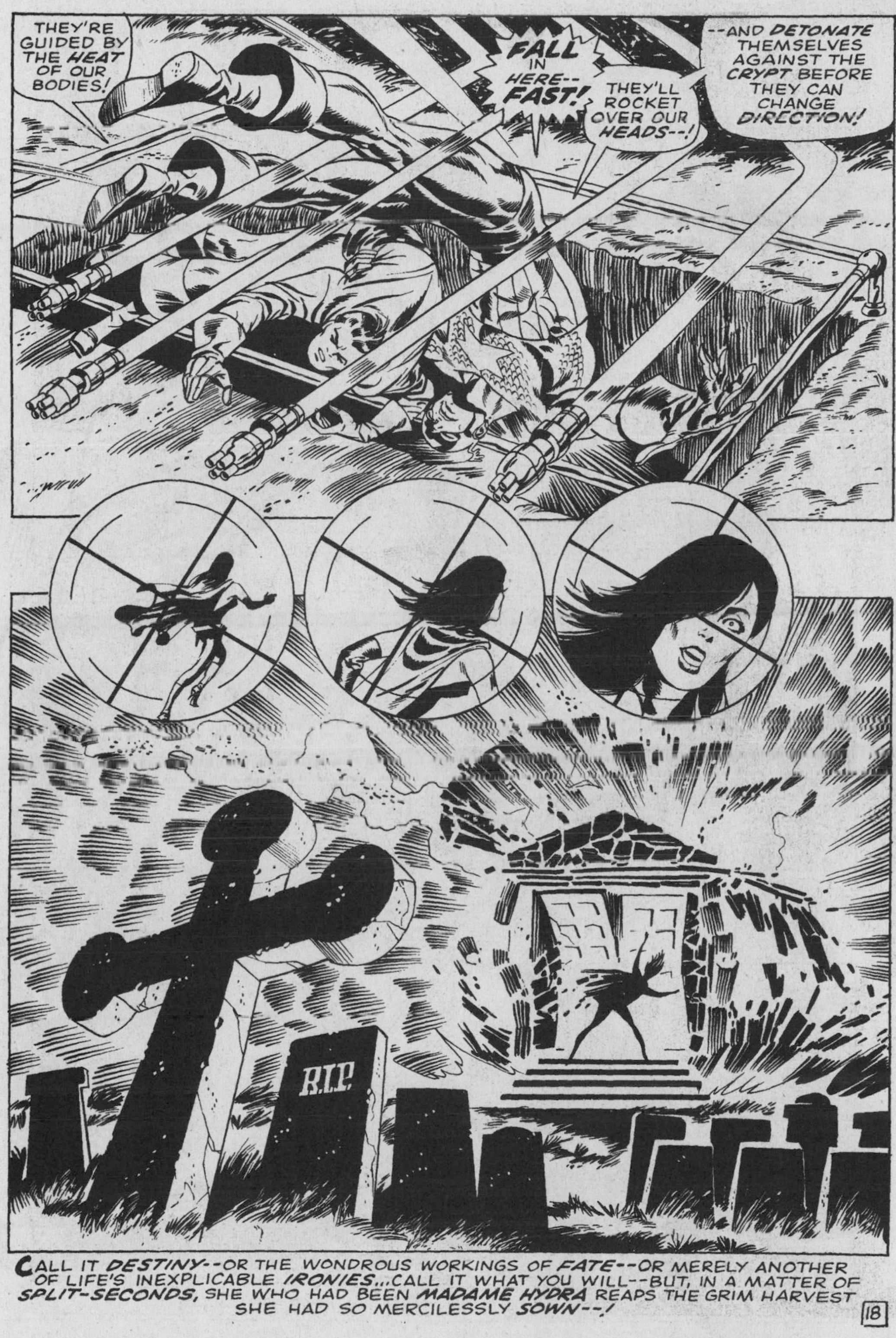
THEY'RE GUIDED BY THE HEAT OF OUR BODIES!
FALL IN HERE-- FAST!
THEY'LL ROCKET OVER OUR HEADS--!
--AND DETONATE THEMSELVES AGAINST THE CRYPT BEFORE THEY CAN CHANGE DIRECTION!
R.I.P.
CALL IT DESTINY--OR THE WONDROUS WORKINGS OF FATE--OR MERELY ANOTHER OF LIFE'S INEXPLICABLE IRONIES...CALL IT WHAT YOU WILL--BUT, IN A MATTER OF SPLIT-SECONDS, SHE WHO HAD BEEN MADAME HYDRA REAPS THE GRIM HARVEST SHE HAD SO MERCILESSLY SOWN--!

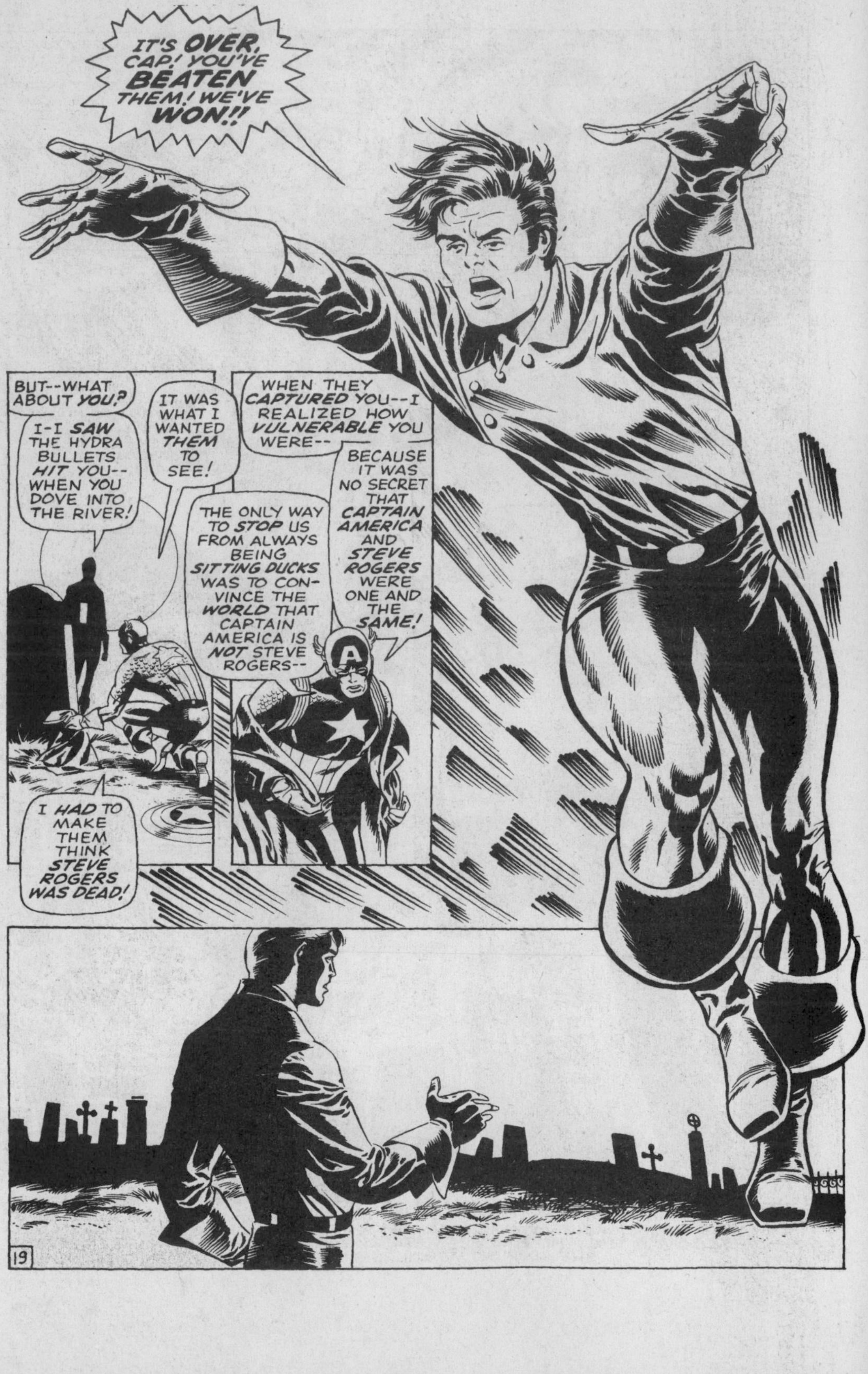
IT'S OVER, CAP! YOU'VE BEATEN THEM! WE'VE WON!!
BUT--WHAT ABOUT YOU?
I-I SAW THE HYDRA BULLETS HIT YOU-- WHEN YOU DOVE INTO THE RIVER!
IT WAS WHAT I WANTED THEM TO SEE!
I HAD TO MAKE THEM THINK STEVE ROGERS WAS DEAD!
WHEN THEY CAPTURED YOU--I REALIZED HOW VULNERABLE YOU WERE--
BECAUSE IT WAS NO SECRET THAT CAPTAIN AMERICA AND STEVE ROGERS WERE ONE AND THE SAME!
THE ONLY WAY TO STOP US FROM ALWAYS BEING SITTING DUCKS WAS TO CONVINCE THE WORLD THAT CAPTAIN AMERICA IS NOT STEVE ROGERS--
19

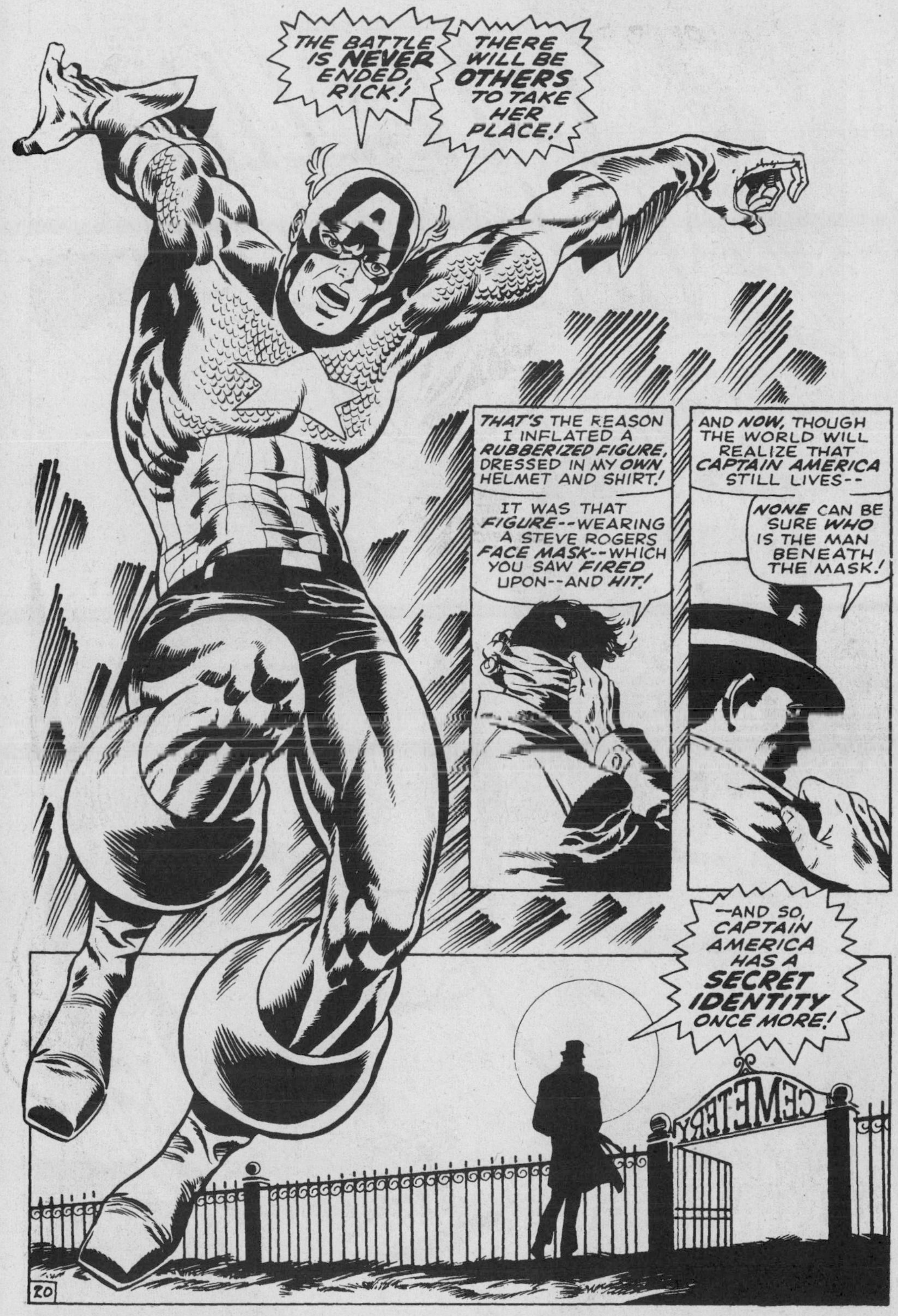

THE BATTLE IS NEVER ENDED, RICK!
THERE WILL BE OTHERS TO TAKE HER PLACE!
THAT'S THE REASON I INFLATED A RUBBERIZED FIGURE, DRESSED IN MY OWN HELMET AND SHIRT!
IT WAS THAT FIGURE--WEARING A STEVE ROGERS FACE MASK--WHICH YOU SAW FIRED UPON--AND HIT!
AND NOW, THOUGH THE WORLD WILL REALIZE THAT CAPTAIN AMERICA STILL LIVES--
NONE CAN BE SURE WHO IS THE MAN BENEATH THE MASK!
--AND SO, CAPTAIN AMERICA HAS A SECRET IDENTITY ONCE MORE!
CEMETERY
20

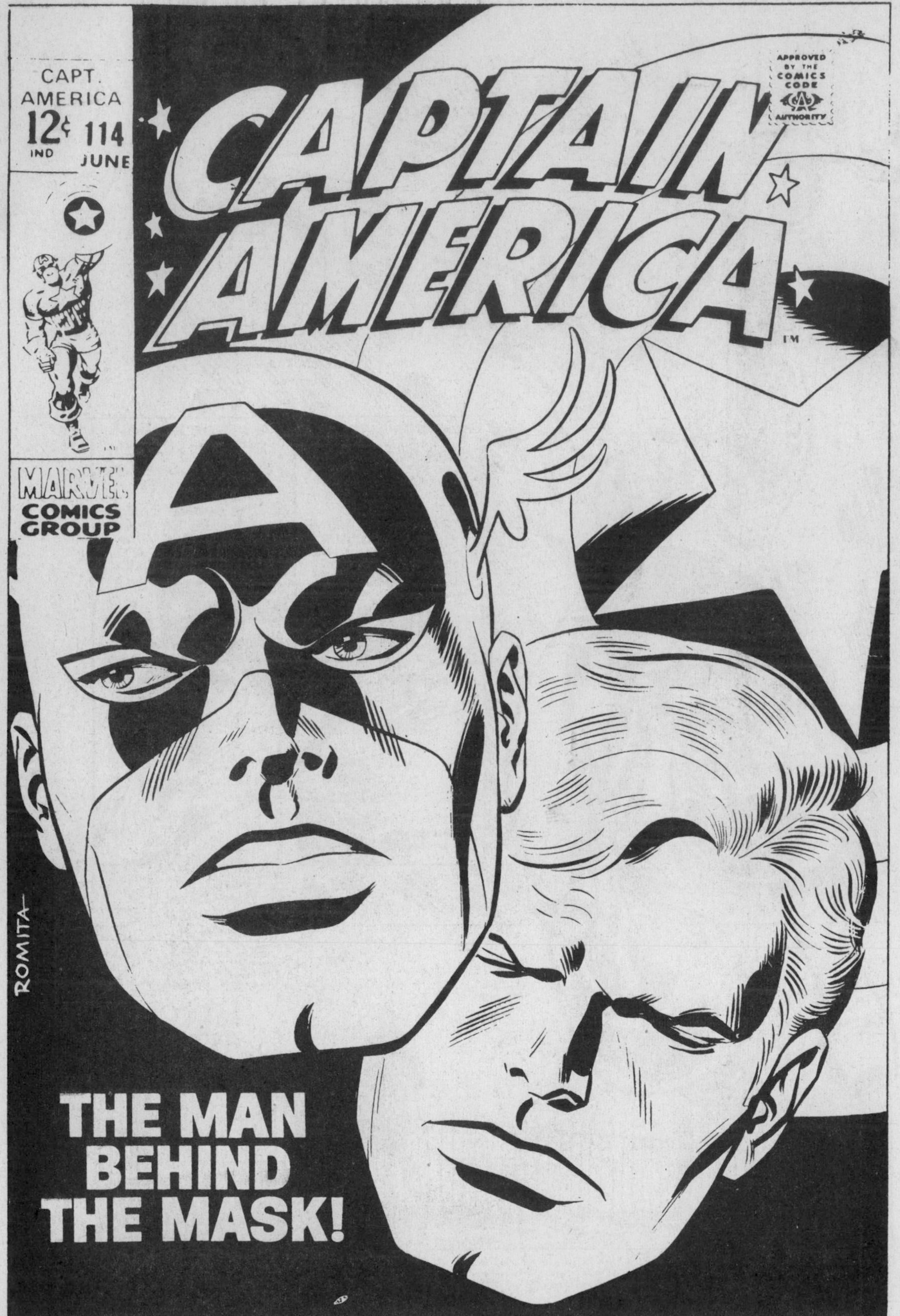
CAPT. AMERICA
12¢ 114
IND JUNE
APPROVED BY THE COMICS CODE AUTHORITY
CAPTAIN AMERICA
TM
MARVEL COMICS GROUP
ROMITA
THE MAN BEHIND THE MASK!

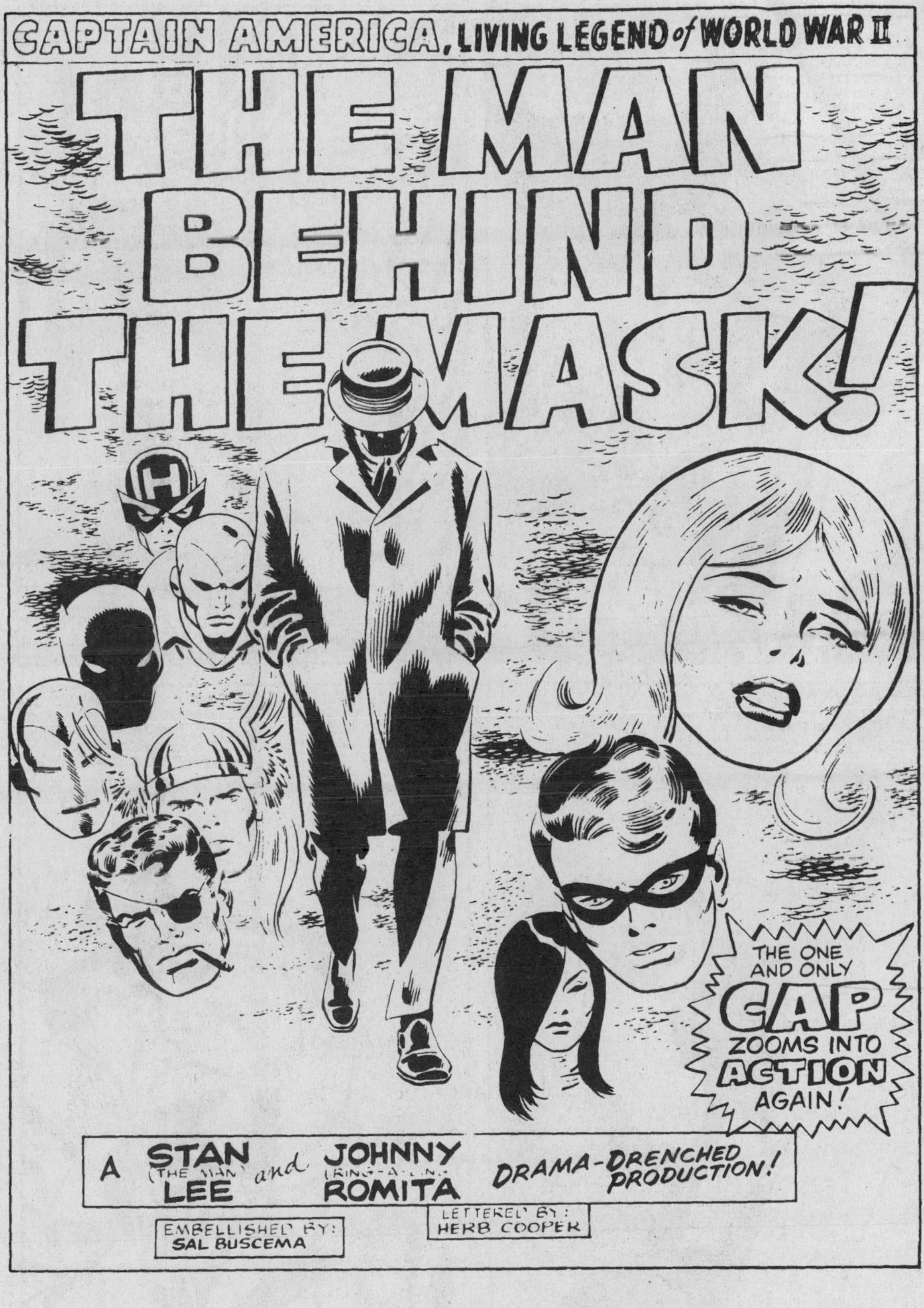
CAPTAIN AMERICA, LIVING LEGEND of WORLD WAR II
THE MAN BEHIND THE MASK!
THE ONE AND ONLY CAP ZOOMS INTO ACTION AGAIN!
A STAN (THE MAN) LEE and JOHNNY (RING-A-LING) ROMITA DRAMA-DRENCHED PRODUCTION!
EMBELLISHED BY: SAL BUSCEMA
LETTERED BY: HERB COOPER

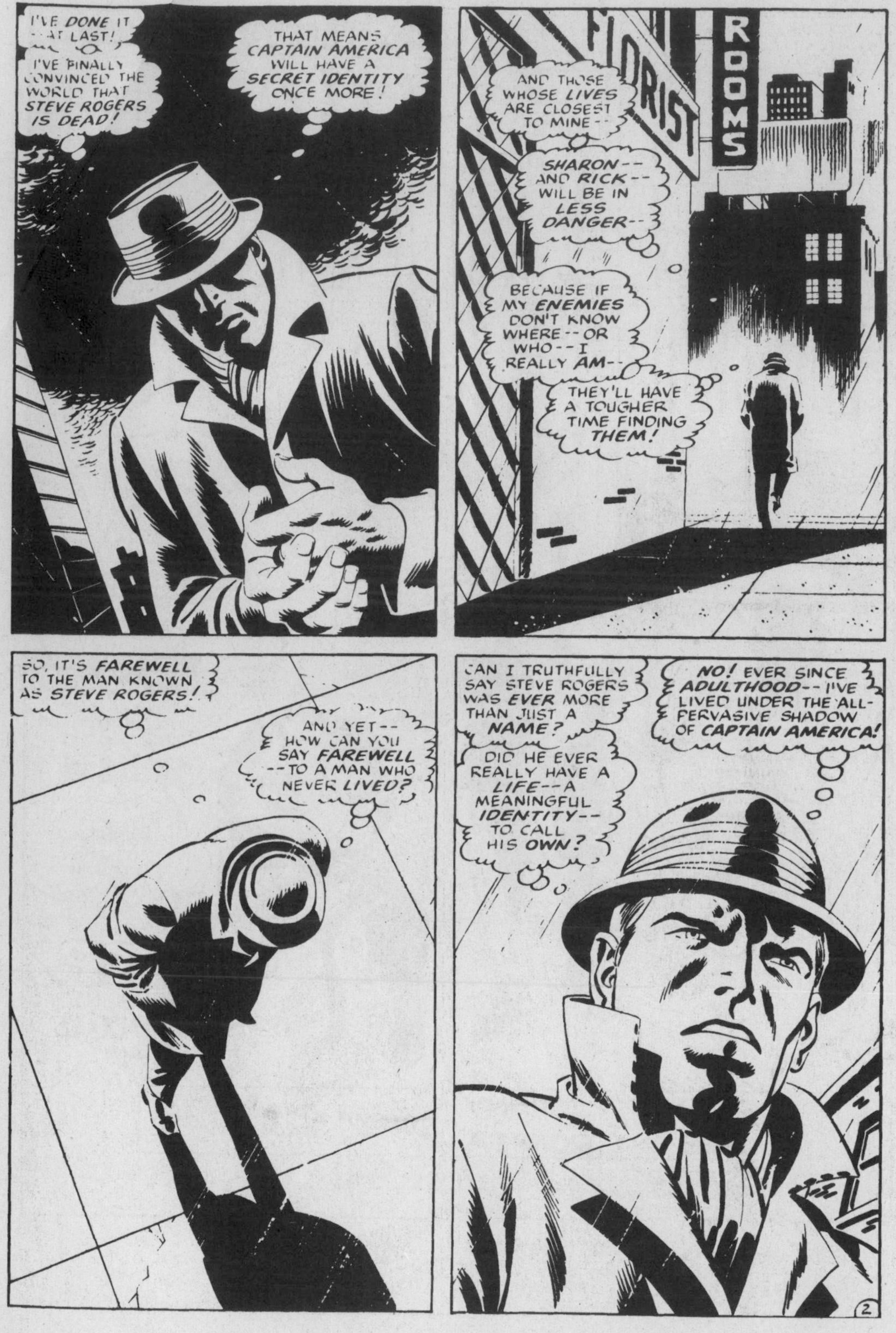
I'VE DONE IT --AT LAST! I'VE FINALLY CONVINCED THE WORLD THAT STEVE ROGERS IS DEAD!
THAT MEANS CAPTAIN AMERICA WILL HAVE A SECRET IDENTITY ONCE MORE!
AND THOSE WHOSE LIVES ARE CLOSEST TO MINE--
SHARON-- AND RICK-- WILL BE IN LESS DANGER--
BECAUSE IF MY ENEMIES DON'T KNOW WHERE--OR WHO--I REALLY AM--
THEY'LL HAVE A TOUGHER TIME FINDING THEM!
FLORIST
ROOMS
SO, IT'S FAREWELL TO THE MAN KNOWN AS STEVE ROGERS!
AND YET-- HOW CAN YOU SAY FAREWELL --TO A MAN WHO NEVER LIVED?
CAN I TRUTHFULLY SAY STEVE ROGERS WAS EVER MORE THAN JUST A NAME?
DID HE EVER REALLY HAVE A LIFE--A MEANINGFUL IDENTITY-- TO CALL HIS OWN?
NO! EVER SINCE ADULTHOOD--I'VE LIVED UNDER THE ALL-PERVASIVE SHADOW OF CAPTAIN AMERICA!
2

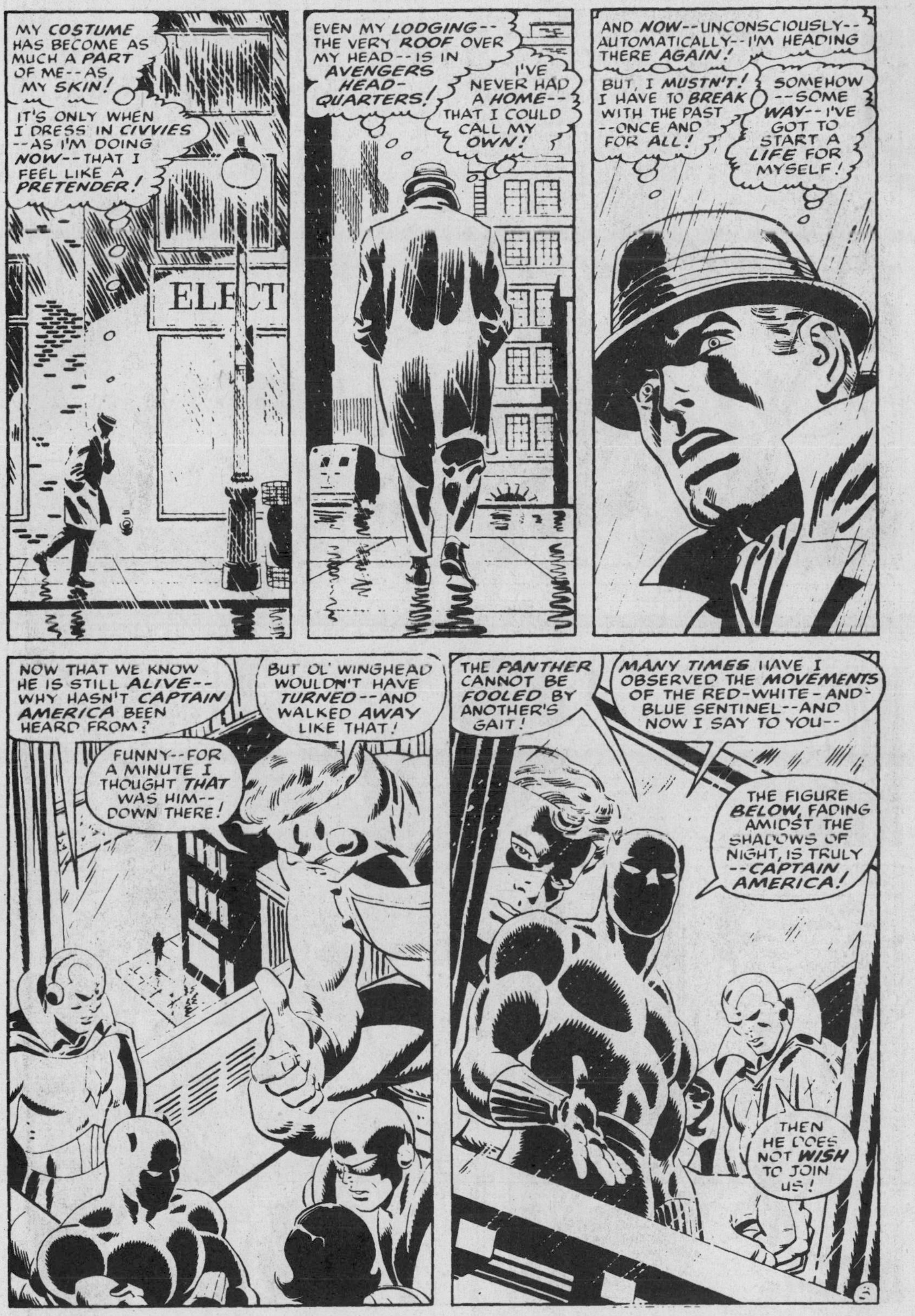
MY COSTUME HAS BECOME AS MUCH A PART OF ME--AS MY SKIN!
IT'S ONLY WHEN I DRESS IN CIVVIES --AS I'M DOING NOW--THAT I FEEL LIKE A PRETENDER!
ELECT
EVEN MY LODGING-- THE VERY ROOF OVER MY HEAD--IS IN AVENGERS HEAD-QUARTERS!
I'VE NEVER HAD A HOME-- THAT I COULD CALL MY OWN!
AND NOW--UNCONSCIOUSLY-- AUTOMATICALLY--I'M HEADING THERE AGAIN!
BUT, I MUSTN'T! I HAVE TO BREAK WITH THE PAST --ONCE AND FOR ALL!
SOMEHOW --SOME WAY--I'VE GOT TO START A LIFE FOR MYSELF!
NOW THAT WE KNOW HE IS STILL ALIVE-- WHY HASN'T CAPTAIN AMERICA BEEN HEARD FROM?
BUT OL' WINGHEAD WOULDN'T HAVE TURNED--AND WALKED AWAY LIKE THAT!
FUNNY--FOR A MINUTE I THOUGHT THAT WAS HIM-- DOWN THERE!
THE PANTHER CANNOT BE FOOLED BY ANOTHER'S GAIT!
MANY TIMES HAVE I OBSERVED THE MOVEMENTS OF THE RED-WHITE-AND-BLUE SENTINEL--AND NOW I SAY TO YOU--
THE FIGURE BELOW, FADING AMIDST THE SHADOWS OF NIGHT, IS TRULY --CAPTAIN AMERICA!
THEN HE DOES NOT WISH TO JOIN US!
3

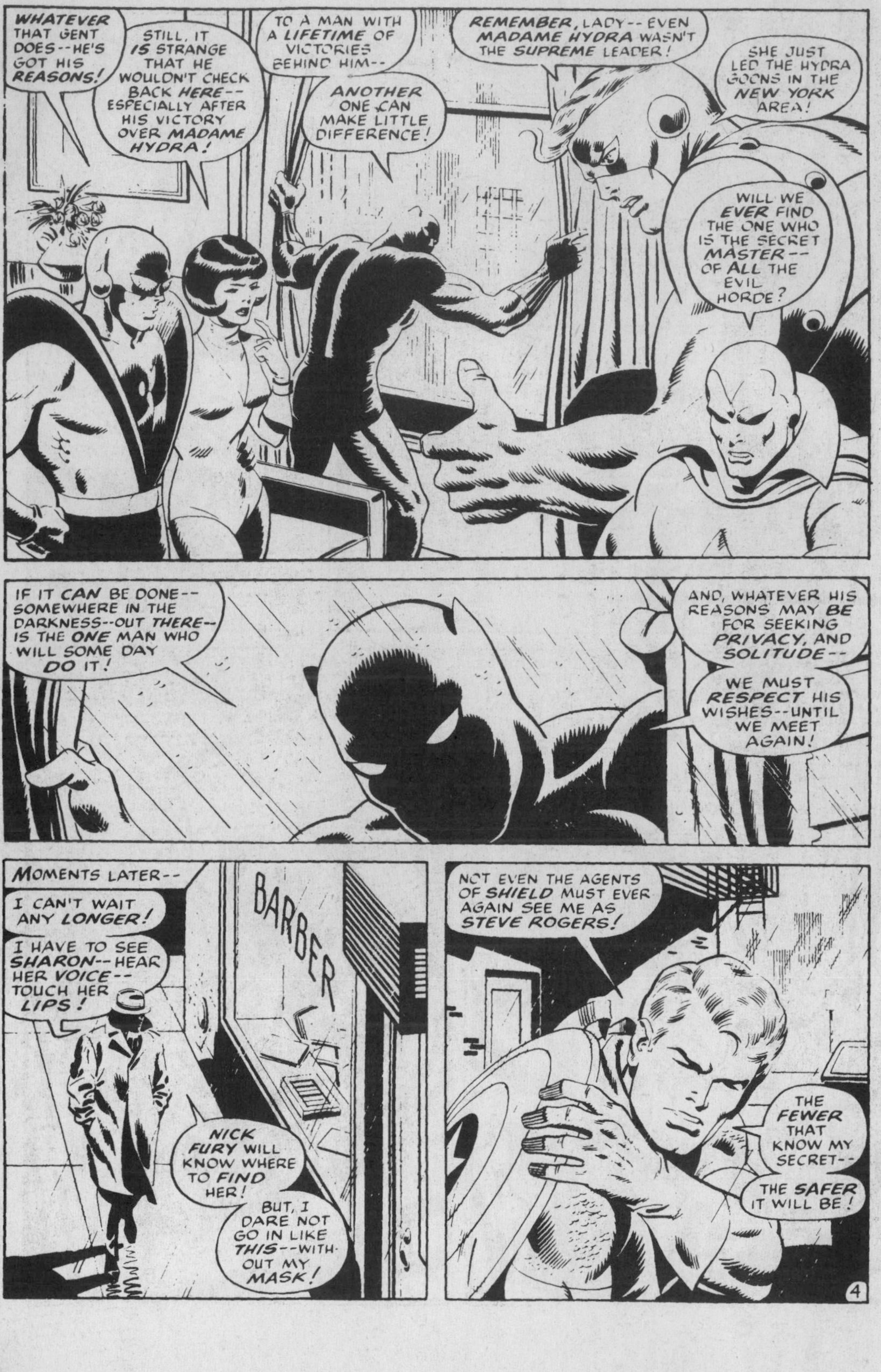
WHATEVER THAT GENT DOES--HE'S GOT HIS REASONS!
STILL, IT IS STRANGE THAT HE WOULDN'T CHECK BACK HERE--ESPECIALLY AFTER HIS VICTORY OVER MADAME HYDRA!
TO A MAN WITH A LIFETIME OF VICTORIES BEHIND HIM--
ANOTHER ONE CAN MAKE LITTLE DIFFERENCE!
REMEMBER, LADY--EVEN MADAME HYDRA WASN'T THE SUPREME LEADER!
SHE JUST LED THE HYDRA GOONS IN THE NEW YORK AREA!
WILL WE EVER FIND THE ONE WHO IS THE SECRET MASTER--OF ALL THE EVIL HORDE?
IF IT CAN BE DONE--SOMEWHERE IN THE DARKNESS--OUT THERE--IS THE ONE MAN WHO WILL SOME DAY DO IT!
AND, WHATEVER HIS REASONS MAY BE FOR SEEKING PRIVACY, AND SOLITUDE--
WE MUST RESPECT HIS WISHES--UNTIL WE MEET AGAIN!
MOMENTS LATER--
I CAN'T WAIT ANY LONGER!
I HAVE TO SEE SHARON--HEAR HER VOICE--TOUCH HER LIPS!
BARBER
NICK FURY WILL KNOW WHERE TO FIND HER!
BUT, I DARE NOT GO IN LIKE THIS--WITHOUT MY MASK!
NOT EVEN THE AGENTS OF SHIELD MUST EVER AGAIN SEE ME AS STEVE ROGERS!
THE FEWER THAT KNOW MY SECRET--
THE SAFER IT WILL BE!
4

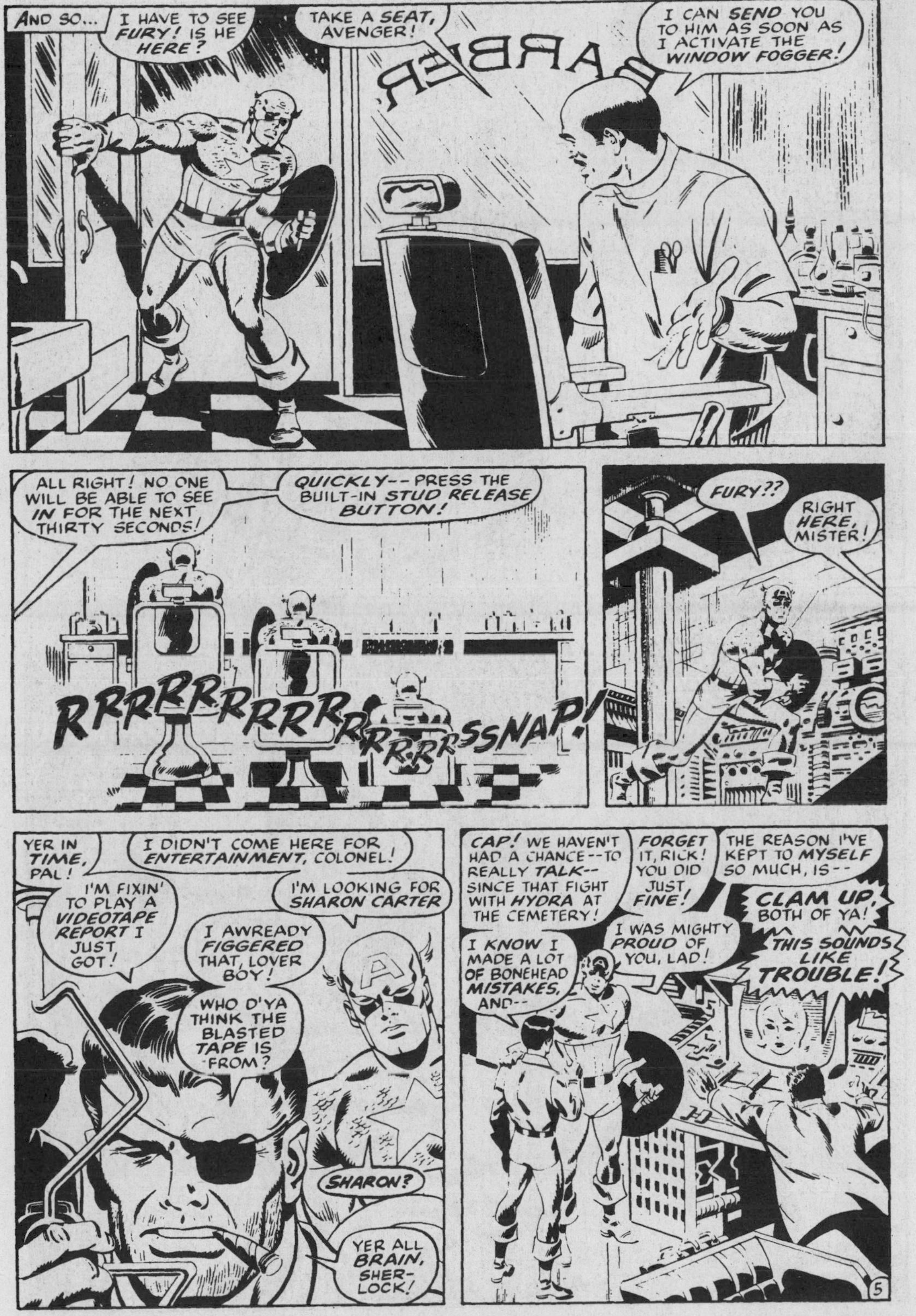
AND SO...
I HAVE TO SEE FURY! IS HE HERE?
TAKE A SEAT, AVENGER!
I CAN SEND YOU TO HIM AS SOON AS I ACTIVATE THE WINDOW FOGGER!
ALL RIGHT! NO ONE WILL BE ABLE TO SEE IN FOR THE NEXT THIRTY SECONDS!
QUICKLY-- PRESS THE BUILT-IN STUD RELEASE BUTTON!
RRRRRRRRRRRRRRRRSSNAP!
FURY??
RIGHT HERE, MISTER!
YER IN TIME, PAL!
I DIDN'T COME HERE FOR ENTERTAINMENT, COLONEL!
I'M FIXIN' TO PLAY A VIDEOTAPE REPORT I JUST GOT!
I'M LOOKING FOR SHARON CARTER
I AWREADY FIGGERED THAT, LOVER BOY!
WHO D'YA THINK THE BLASTED TAPE IS FROM?
SHARON?
YER ALL BRAIN, SHER-LOCK!
CAP! WE HAVEN'T HAD A CHANCE --TO REALLY TALK-- SINCE THAT FIGHT WITH HYDRA AT THE CEMETERY!
I KNOW I MADE A LOT OF BONEHEAD MISTAKES, AND--
FORGET IT, RICK! YOU DID JUST FINE!
I WAS MIGHTY PROUD OF YOU, LAD!
THE REASON I'VE KEPT TO MYSELF SO MUCH, IS--
CLAM UP, BOTH OF YA!
THIS SOUNDS LIKE TROUBLE!
5

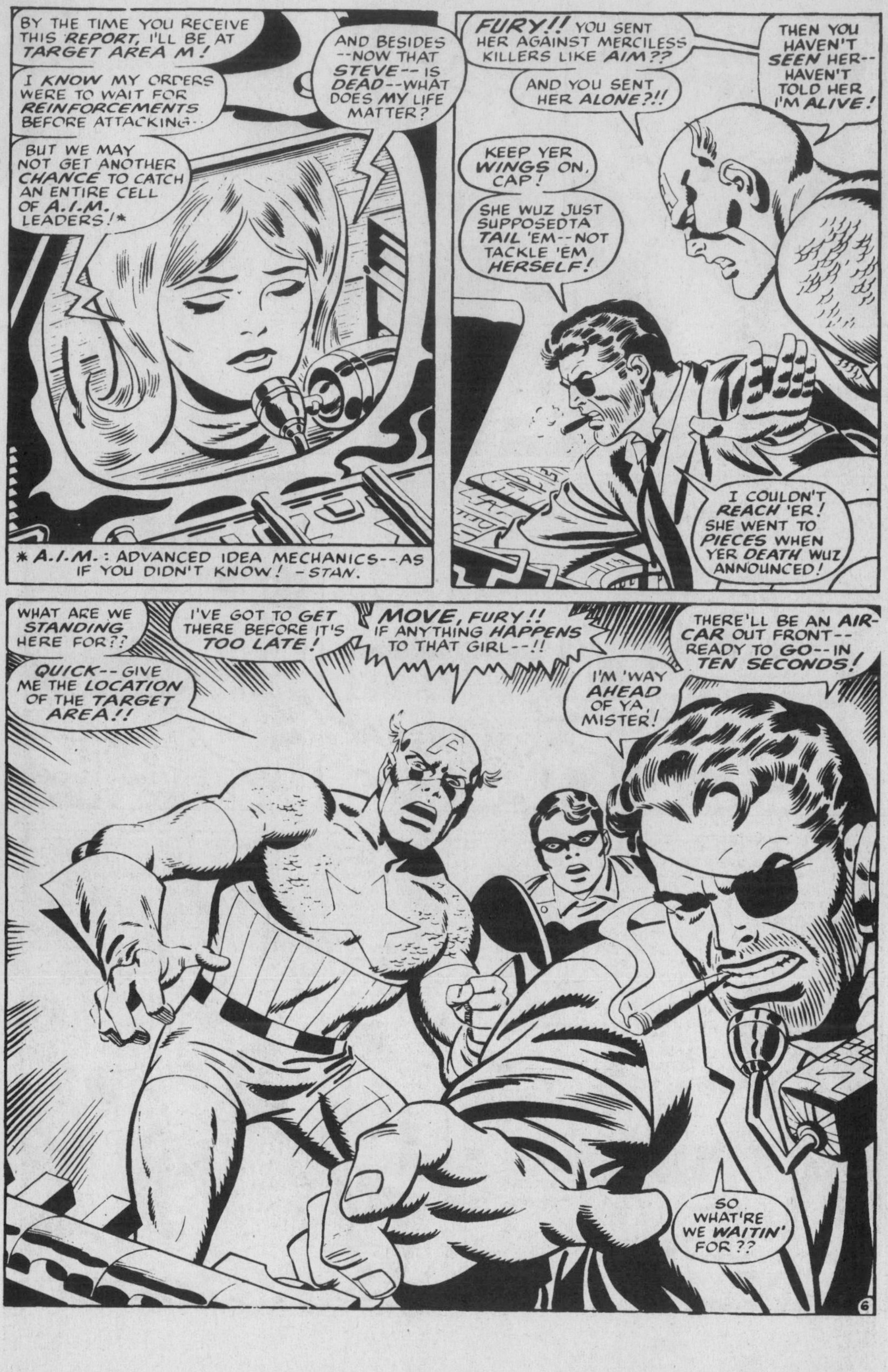
BY THE TIME YOU RECEIVE THIS REPORT, I'LL BE AT TARGET AREA M!
I KNOW MY ORDERS WERE TO WAIT FOR REINFORCEMENTS BEFORE ATTACKING--
BUT WE MAY NOT GET ANOTHER CHANCE TO CATCH AN ENTIRE CELL OF A.I.M. LEADERS!*
AND BESIDES --NOW THAT STEVE-- IS DEAD--WHAT DOES MY LIFE MATTER?
* A.I.M.: ADVANCED IDEA MECHANICS--AS IF YOU DIDN'T KNOW! -STAN.
FURY!! YOU SENT HER AGAINST MERCILESS KILLERS LIKE AIM??
AND YOU SENT HER ALONE?!!
THEN YOU HAVEN'T SEEN HER-- HAVEN'T TOLD HER I'M ALIVE!
KEEP YER WINGS ON, CAP!
SHE WUZ JUST SUPPOSEDTA TAIL 'EM--NOT TACKLE 'EM HERSELF!
I COULDN'T REACH 'ER! SHE WENT TO PIECES WHEN YER DEATH WUZ ANNOUNCED!
WHAT ARE WE STANDING HERE FOR??
QUICK--GIVE ME THE LOCATION OF THE TARGET AREA!!
I'VE GOT TO GET THERE BEFORE IT'S TOO LATE!
MOVE, FURY!! IF ANYTHING HAPPENS TO THAT GIRL--!!
THERE'LL BE AN AIR-CAR OUT FRONT-- READY TO GO--IN TEN SECONDS!
I'M 'WAY AHEAD OF YA, MISTER!
SO WHAT'RE WE WAITIN' FOR??
6

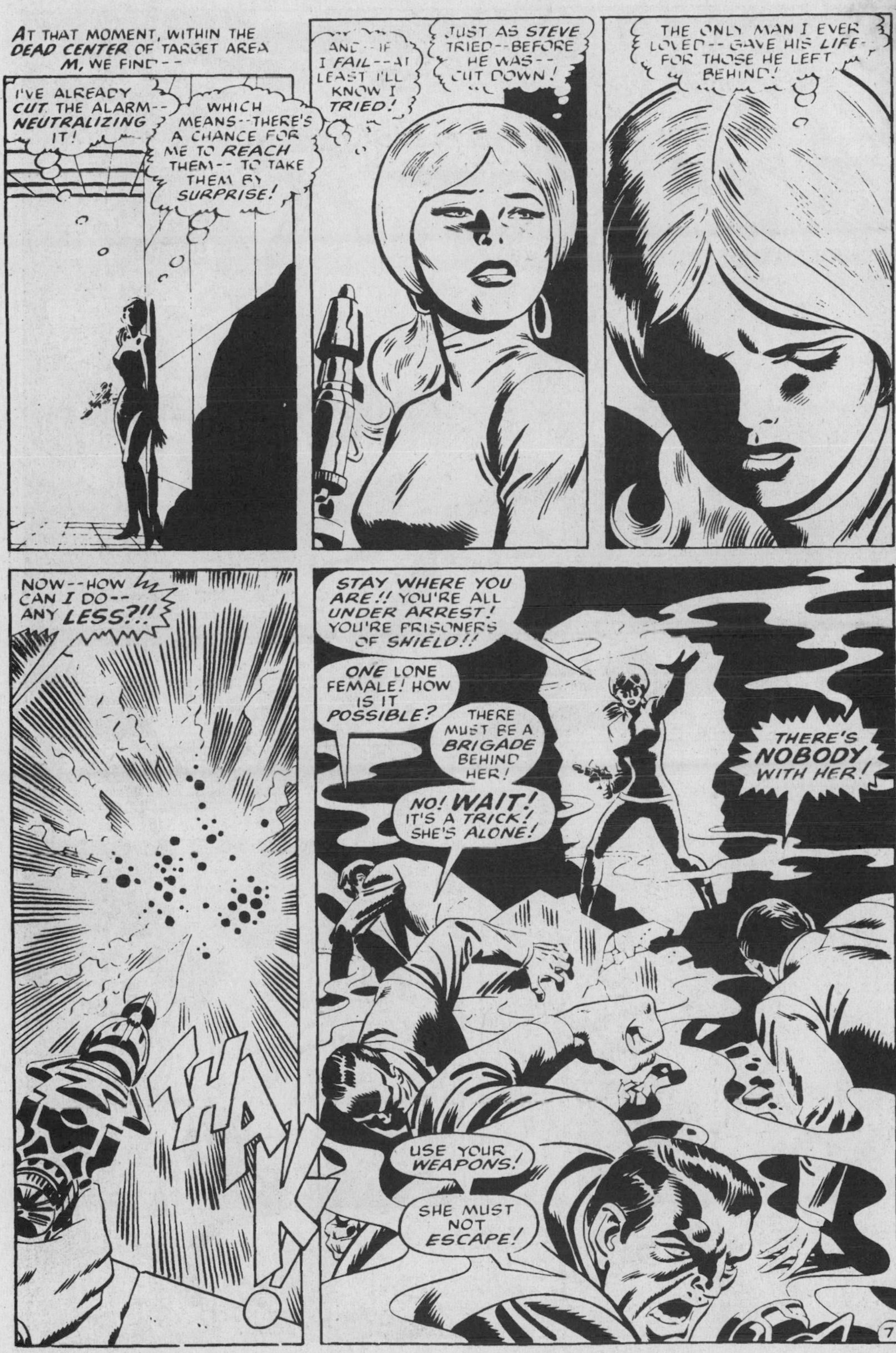

AT THAT MOMENT, WITHIN THE DEAD CENTER OF TARGET AREA M, WE FIND--
I'VE ALREADY CUT THE ALARM-- NEUTRALIZING IT!
WHICH MEANS--THERE'S A CHANCE FOR ME TO REACH THEM-- TO TAKE THEM BY SURPRISE!
AND--IF I FAIL--AT LEAST I'LL KNOW I TRIED!
JUST AS STEVE TRIED--BEFORE HE WAS-- CUT DOWN!
THE ONLY MAN I EVER LOVED-- GAVE HIS LIFE-- FOR THOSE HE LEFT BEHIND!
NOW--HOW CAN I DO-- ANY LESS?!!
THAK!
STAY WHERE YOU ARE!! YOU'RE ALL UNDER ARREST! YOU'RE PRISONERS OF SHIELD!!
ONE LONE FEMALE! HOW IS IT POSSIBLE?
THERE MUST BE A BRIGADE BEHIND HER!
NO! WAIT! IT'S A TRICK! SHE'S ALONE!
THERE'S NOBODY WITH HER!
USE YOUR WEAPONS!
SHE MUST NOT ESCAPE!
7

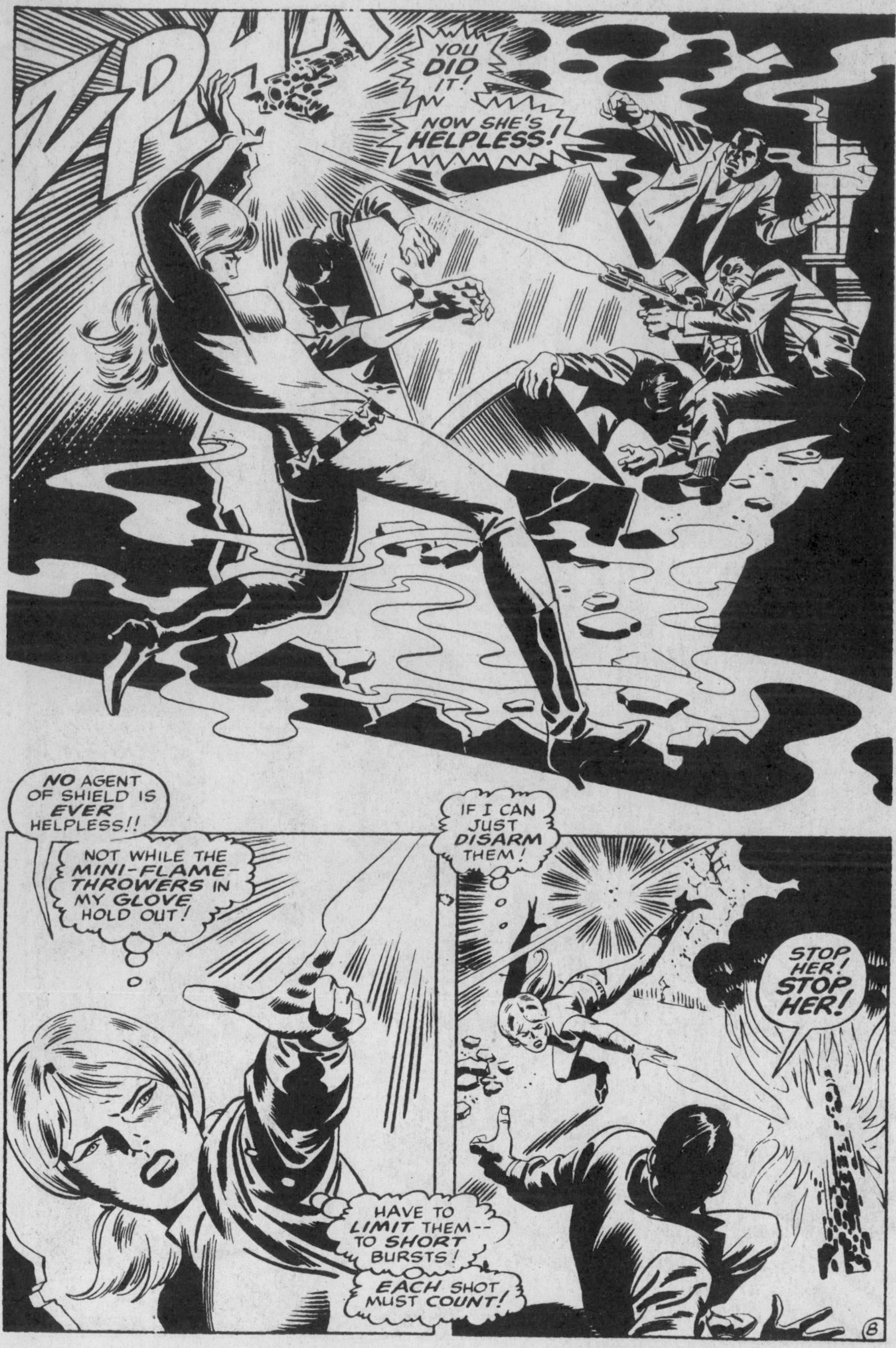
ZPHH
YOU DID IT!
NOW SHE'S HELPLESS!
NO AGENT OF SHIELD IS EVER HELPLESS!!
NOT WHILE THE MINI-FLAME-THROWERS IN MY GLOVE HOLD OUT!
HAVE TO LIMIT THEM--TO SHORT BURSTS!
EACH SHOT MUST COUNT!
IF I CAN JUST DISARM THEM!
STOP HER! STOP HER!
8

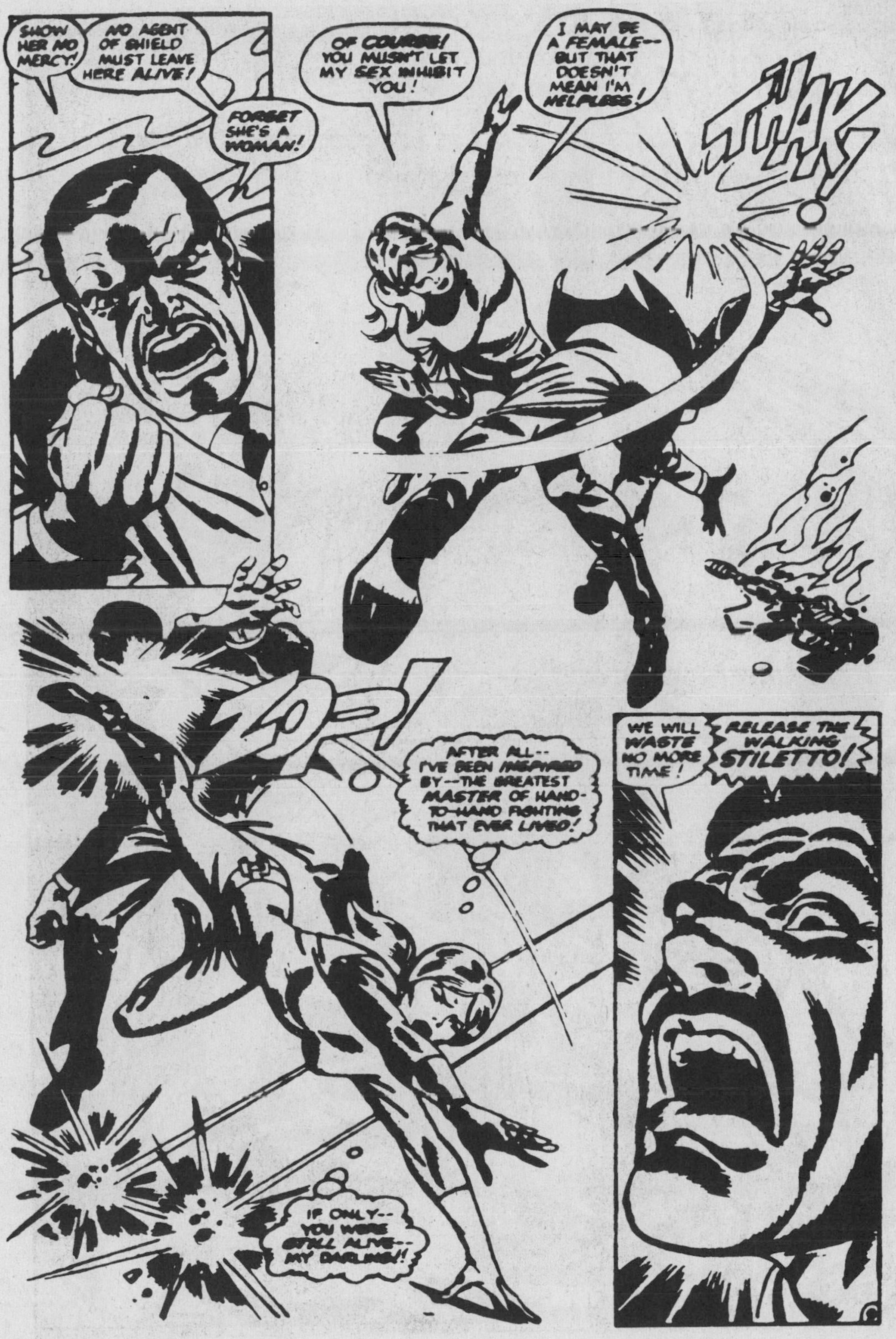
SHOW HER NO MERCY!
NO AGENT OF SHIELD MUST LEAVE HERE ALIVE!
FORGET SHE'S A WOMAN!
OF COURSE! YOU MUSN'T LET MY SEX INHIBIT YOU!
I MAY BE A FEMALE-- BUT THAT DOESN'T MEAN I'M HELPLESS!
THAK!
ZOT!
AFTER ALL-- I'VE BEEN INSPIRED BY--THE GREATEST MASTER OF HAND-TO-HAND FIGHTING THAT EVER LIVED!
IF ONLY-- YOU WERE STILL ALIVE-- MY DARLING!
WE WILL WASTE NO MORE TIME!
RELEASE THE WALKING STILETTO!

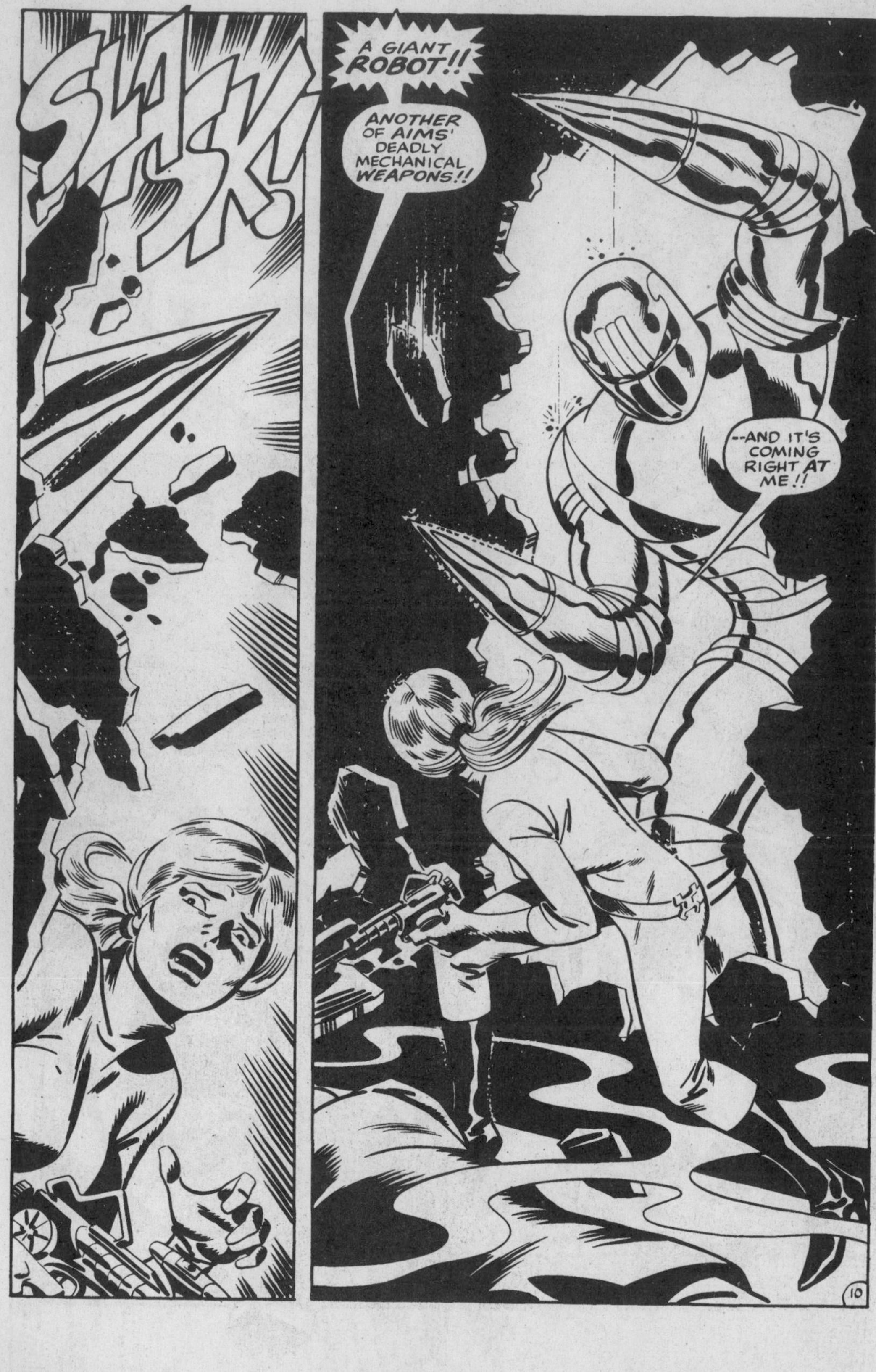
SLASSK!
A GIANT ROBOT!!
ANOTHER OF AIMS' DEADLY MECHANICAL WEAPONS!!
--AND IT'S COMING RIGHT AT ME!!
10

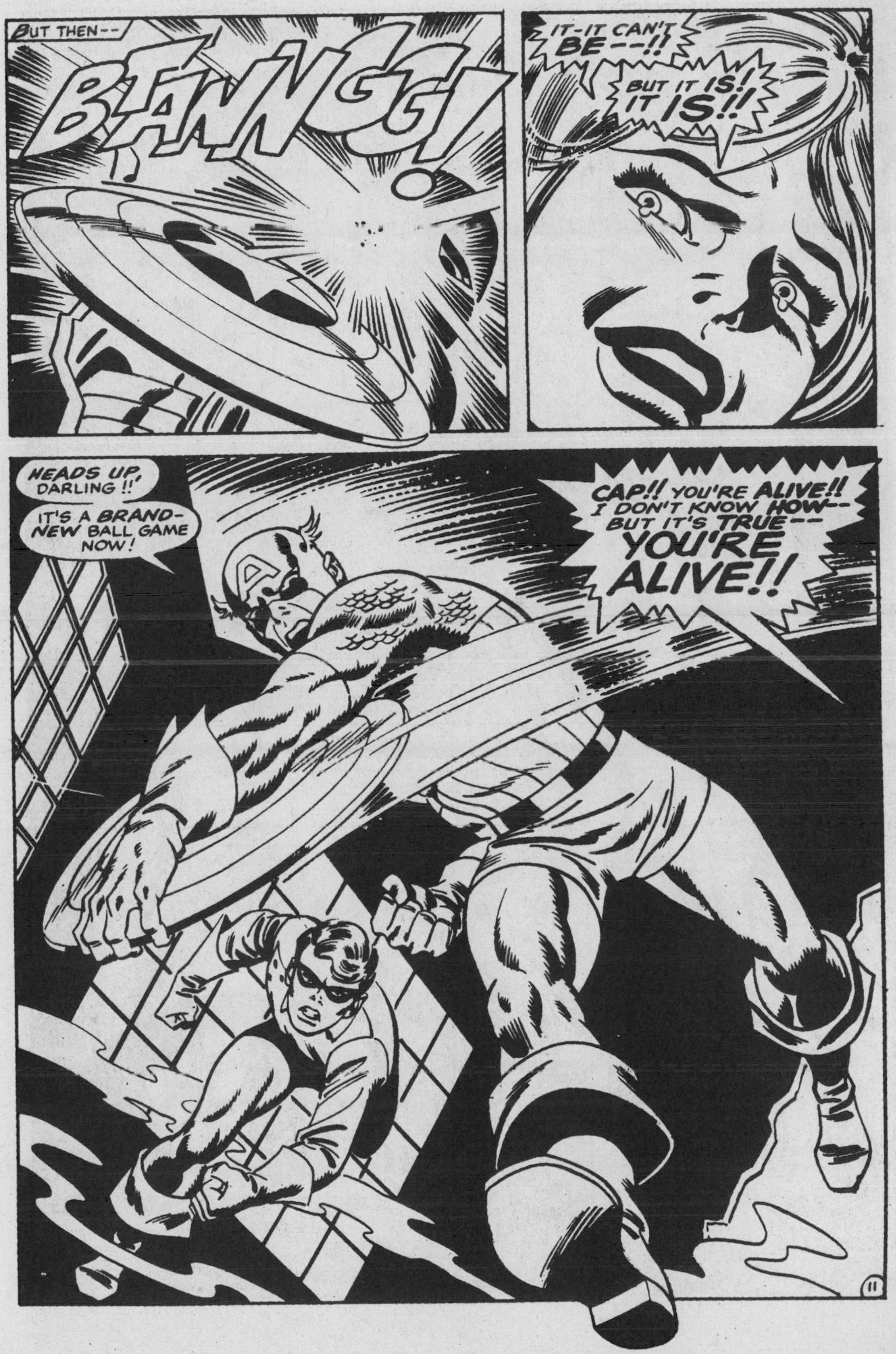
BUT THEN--
BLANNGG!
IT-IT CAN'T BE--!!
BUT IT IS! IT IS!!
HEADS UP, DARLING!!
IT'S A BRAND-NEW BALL GAME NOW!
CAP!! YOU'RE ALIVE!! I DON'T KNOW HOW--BUT IT'S TRUE--YOU'RE ALIVE!!
11

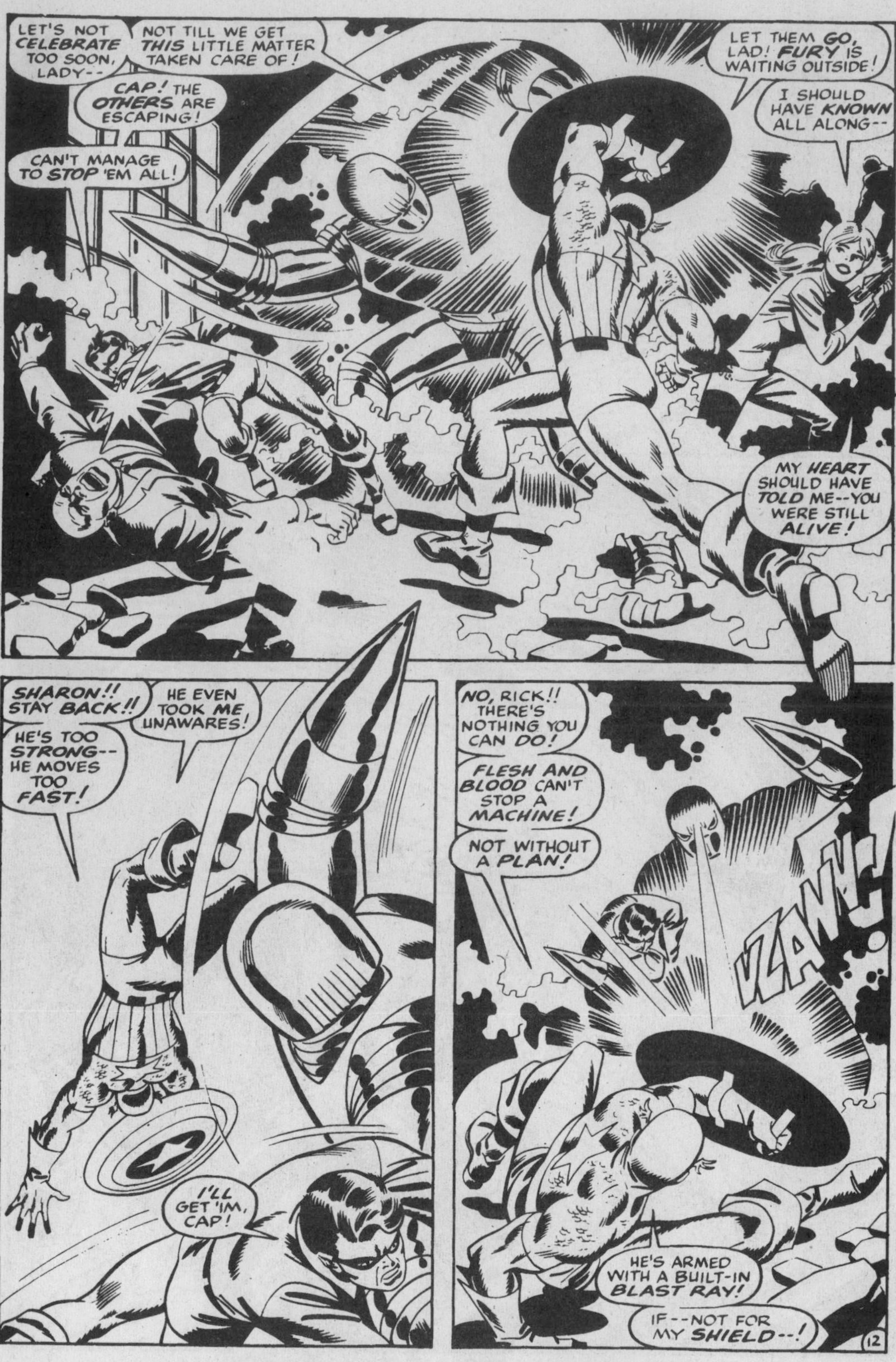
LET'S NOT CELEBRATE TOO SOON, LADY--
NOT TILL WE GET THIS LITTLE MATTER TAKEN CARE OF!
CAP! THE OTHERS ARE ESCAPING!
CAN'T MANAGE TO STOP 'EM ALL!
LET THEM GO, LAD! FURY IS WAITING OUTSIDE!
I SHOULD HAVE KNOWN ALL ALONG--
MY HEART SHOULD HAVE TOLD ME--YOU WERE STILL ALIVE!
SHARON!! STAY BACK!!
HE EVEN TOOK ME UNAWARES!
HE'S TOO STRONG-- HE MOVES TOO FAST!
I'LL GET 'IM, CAP!
NO, RICK!! THERE'S NOTHING YOU CAN DO!
FLESH AND BLOOD CAN'T STOP A MACHINE!
NOT WITHOUT A PLAN!
VZANNG!
HE'S ARMED WITH A BUILT-IN BLAST RAY!
IF--NOT FOR MY SHIELD--!
12

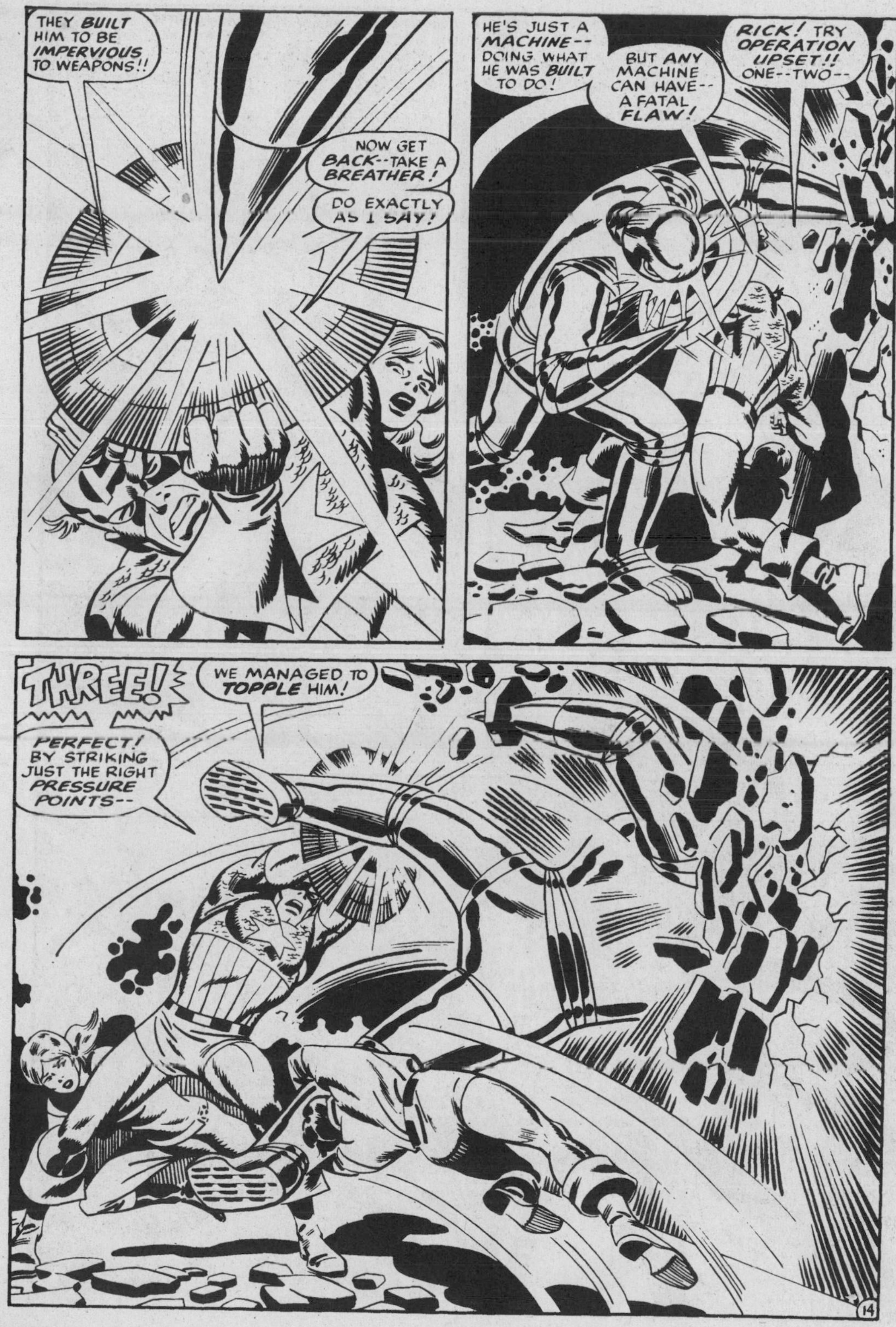

THEY BUILT HIM TO BE IMPERVIOUS TO WEAPONS!!
NOW GET BACK--TAKE A BREATHER!
DO EXACTLY AS I SAY!
HE'S JUST A MACHINE-- DOING WHAT HE WAS BUILT TO DO!
BUT ANY MACHINE CAN HAVE-- A FATAL FLAW!
RICK! TRY OPERATION UPSET!! ONE--TWO--
THREE!
WE MANAGED TO TOPPLE HIM!
PERFECT! BY STRIKING JUST THE RIGHT PRESSURE POINTS--
14

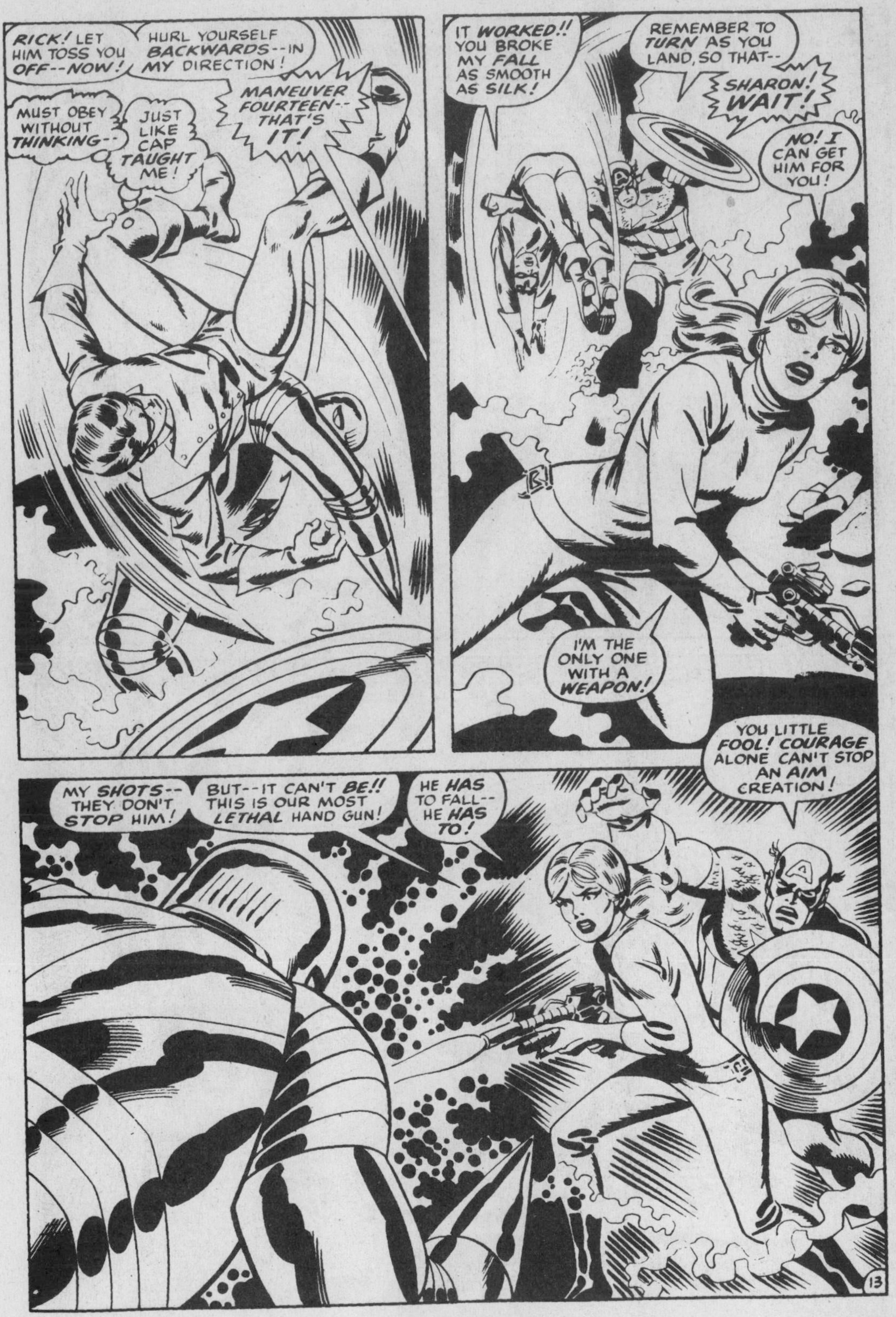
RICK! LET HIM TOSS YOU OFF--NOW!
HURL YOURSELF BACKWARDS--IN MY DIRECTION!
MUST OBEY WITHOUT THINKING--
JUST LIKE CAP TAUGHT ME!
MANEUVER FOURTEEN--THAT'S IT!
IT WORKED!! YOU BROKE MY FALL AS SMOOTH AS SILK!
REMEMBER TO TURN AS YOU LAND, SO THAT--
SHARON! WAIT!
NO! I CAN GET HIM FOR YOU!
I'M THE ONLY ONE WITH A WEAPON!
MY SHOTS--THEY DON'T STOP HIM!
BUT--IT CAN'T BE!! THIS IS OUR MOST LETHAL HAND GUN!
HE HAS TO FALL--HE HAS TO!
YOU LITTLE FOOL! COURAGE ALONE CAN'T STOP AN AIM CREATION!
13

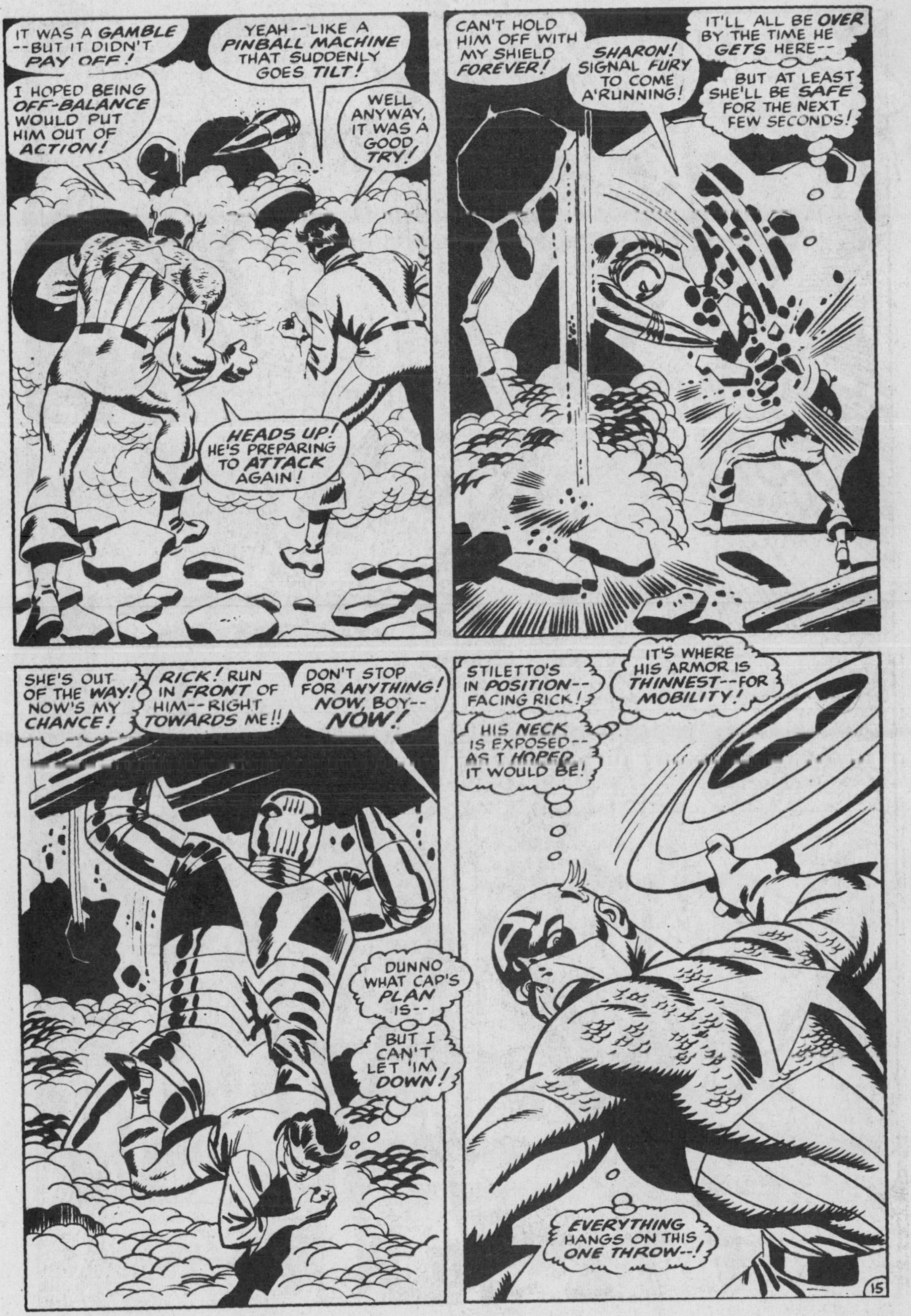
IT WAS A GAMBLE --BUT IT DIDN'T PAY OFF!
I HOPED BEING OFF-BALANCE WOULD PUT HIM OUT OF ACTION!
YEAH--LIKE A PINBALL MACHINE THAT SUDDENLY GOES TILT!
WELL ANYWAY, IT WAS A GOOD TRY!
HEADS UP! HE'S PREPARING TO ATTACK AGAIN!
CAN'T HOLD HIM OFF WITH MY SHIELD FOREVER!
SHARON! SIGNAL FURY TO COME A'RUNNING!
IT'LL ALL BE OVER BY THE TIME HE GETS HERE--
BUT AT LEAST SHE'LL BE SAFE FOR THE NEXT FEW SECONDS!
SHE'S OUT OF THE WAY! NOW'S MY CHANCE!
RICK! RUN IN FRONT OF HIM--RIGHT TOWARDS ME!!
DON'T STOP FOR ANYTHING! NOW, BOY-- NOW!
DUNNO WHAT CAP'S PLAN IS--
BUT I CAN'T LET 'IM DOWN!
STILETTO'S IN POSITION-- FACING RICK!
IT'S WHERE HIS ARMOR IS THINNEST--FOR MOBILITY!
HIS NECK IS EXPOSED-- AS I HOPED IT WOULD BE!
EVERYTHING HANGS ON THIS ONE THROW--!
15

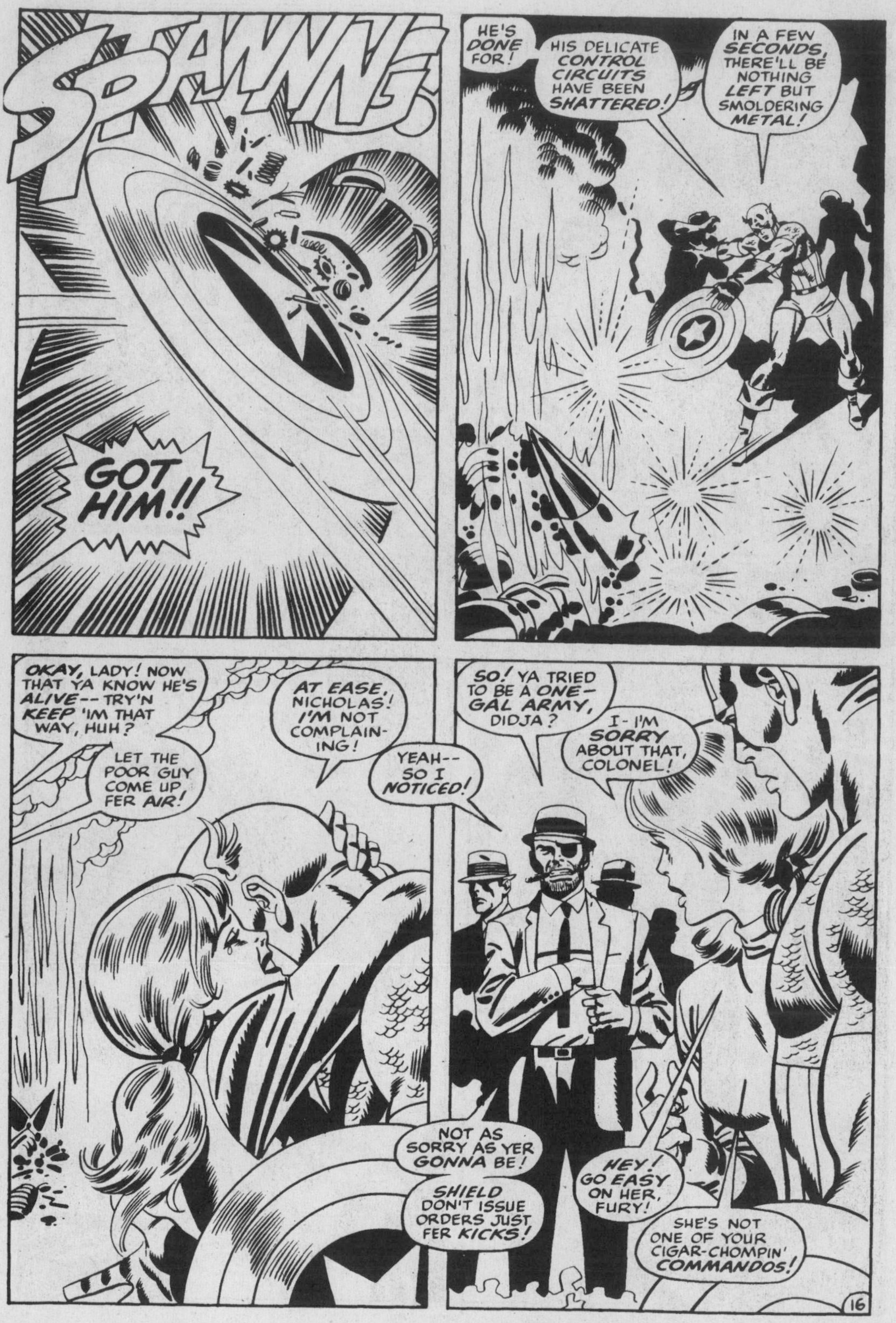

SPANNNG!
GOT HIM!!
HE'S DONE FOR!
HIS DELICATE CONTROL CIRCUITS HAVE BEEN SHATTERED!
IN A FEW SECONDS, THERE'LL BE NOTHING LEFT BUT SMOLDERING METAL!
OKAY, LADY! NOW THAT YA KNOW HE'S ALIVE-- TRY'N KEEP 'IM THAT WAY, HUH?
LET THE POOR GUY COME UP FER AIR!
AT EASE, NICHOLAS! I'M NOT COMPLAINING!
YEAH-- SO I NOTICED!
SO! YA TRIED TO BE A ONE-GAL ARMY, DIDJA?
I- I'M SORRY ABOUT THAT, COLONEL!
NOT AS SORRY AS YER GONNA BE!
SHIELD DON'T ISSUE ORDERS JUST FER KICKS!
HEY! GO EASY ON HER, FURY!
SHE'S NOT ONE OF YOUR CIGAR-CHOMPIN' COMMANDOS!
16

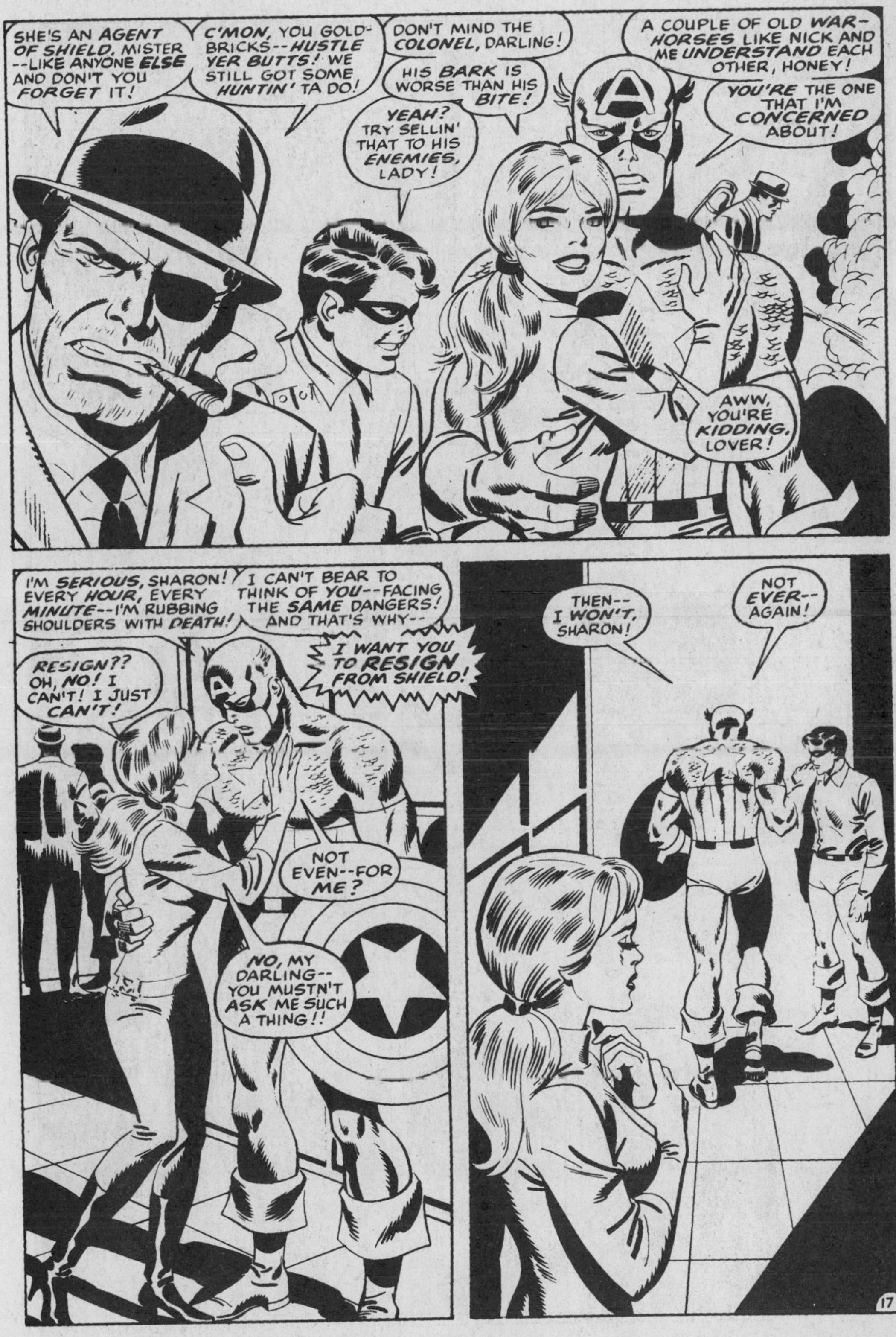
SHE'S AN AGENT OF SHIELD, MISTER --LIKE ANYONE ELSE AND DON'T YOU FORGET IT!
C'MON, YOU GOLD-BRICKS--HUSTLE YER BUTTS! WE STILL GOT SOME HUNTIN' TA DO!
DON'T MIND THE COLONEL, DARLING!
HIS BARK IS WORSE THAN HIS BITE!
YEAH? TRY SELLIN' THAT TO HIS ENEMIES, LADY!
A COUPLE OF OLD WAR-HORSES LIKE NICK AND ME UNDERSTAND EACH OTHER, HONEY!
YOU'RE THE ONE THAT I'M CONCERNED ABOUT!
AWW, YOU'RE KIDDING, LOVER!
I'M SERIOUS, SHARON! EVERY HOUR, EVERY MINUTE--I'M RUBBING SHOULDERS WITH DEATH!
I CAN'T BEAR TO THINK OF YOU--FACING THE SAME DANGERS! AND THAT'S WHY--
I WANT YOU TO RESIGN FROM SHIELD!
RESIGN?? OH, NO! I CAN'T! I JUST CAN'T!
NOT EVEN--FOR ME?
NO, MY DARLING-- YOU MUSTN'T ASK ME SUCH A THING!!
THEN-- I WON'T, SHARON!
NOT EVER-- AGAIN!
17

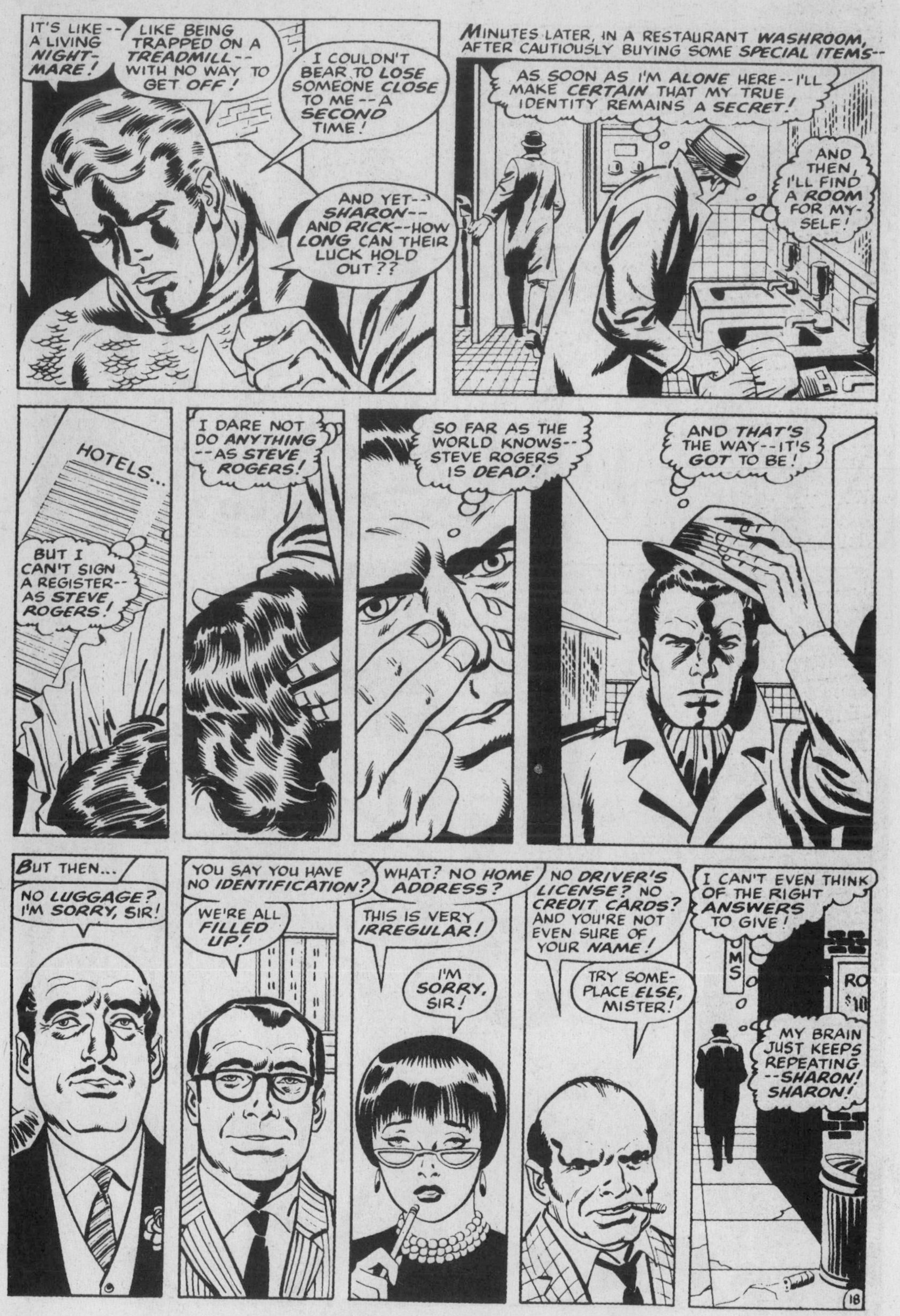

IT'S LIKE-- A LIVING NIGHTMARE!
LIKE BEING TRAPPED ON A TREADMILL-- WITH NO WAY TO GET OFF!
I COULDN'T BEAR TO LOSE SOMEONE CLOSE TO ME --A SECOND TIME!
AND YET-- SHARON-- AND RICK--HOW LONG CAN THEIR LUCK HOLD OUT??
MINUTES LATER, IN A RESTAURANT WASHROOM, AFTER CAUTIOUSLY BUYING SOME SPECIAL ITEMS--
AS SOON AS I'M ALONE HERE--I'LL MAKE CERTAIN THAT MY TRUE IDENTITY REMAINS A SECRET!
AND THEN, I'LL FIND A ROOM FOR MYSELF!
HOTELS...
BUT I CAN'T SIGN A REGISTER-- AS STEVE ROGERS!
I DARE NOT DO ANYTHING --AS STEVE ROGERS!
SO FAR AS THE WORLD KNOWS-- STEVE ROGERS IS DEAD!
AND THAT'S THE WAY--IT'S GOT TO BE!
BUT THEN...
NO LUGGAGE? I'M SORRY, SIR!
YOU SAY YOU HAVE NO IDENTIFICATION?
WE'RE ALL FILLED UP!
WHAT? NO HOME ADDRESS?
THIS IS VERY IRREGULAR!
I'M SORRY, SIR!
NO DRIVER'S LICENSE? NO CREDIT CARDS? AND YOU'RE NOT EVEN SURE OF YOUR NAME!
TRY SOMEPLACE ELSE, MISTER!
I CAN'T EVEN THINK OF THE RIGHT ANSWERS TO GIVE!
MY BRAIN JUST KEEPS REPEATING --SHARON! SHARON!
18

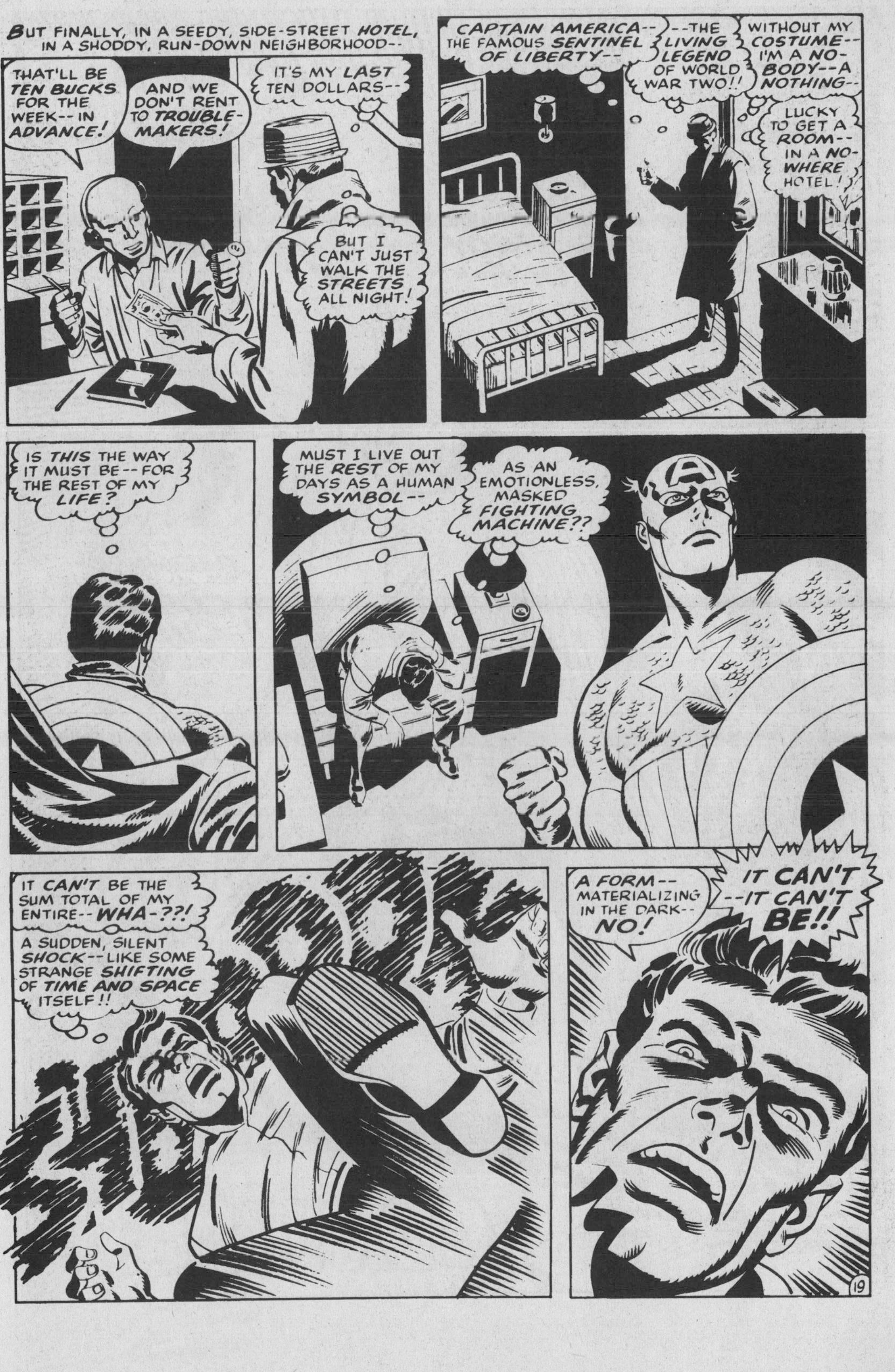
BUT FINALLY, IN A SEEDY, SIDE-STREET HOTEL, IN A SHODDY, RUN-DOWN NEIGHBORHOOD--
THAT'LL BE TEN BUCKS FOR THE WEEK--IN ADVANCE!
AND WE DON'T RENT TO TROUBLE-MAKERS!
IT'S MY LAST TEN DOLLARS--
BUT I CAN'T JUST WALK THE STREETS ALL NIGHT!
CAPTAIN AMERICA-- THE FAMOUS SENTINEL OF LIBERTY--
--THE LIVING LEGEND OF WORLD WAR TWO!!
WITHOUT MY COSTUME-- I'M A NO-BODY--A NOTHING--
LUCKY TO GET A ROOM-- IN A NO-WHERE HOTEL!
IS THIS THE WAY IT MUST BE--FOR THE REST OF MY LIFE?
MUST I LIVE OUT THE REST OF MY DAYS AS A HUMAN SYMBOL--
AS AN EMOTIONLESS, MASKED FIGHTING MACHINE??
IT CAN'T BE THE SUM TOTAL OF MY ENTIRE-- WHA-??!
A SUDDEN, SILENT SHOCK--LIKE SOME STRANGE SHIFTING OF TIME AND SPACE ITSELF!!
A FORM-- MATERIALIZING IN THE DARK-- NO!
IT CAN'T --IT CAN'T BE!!
19

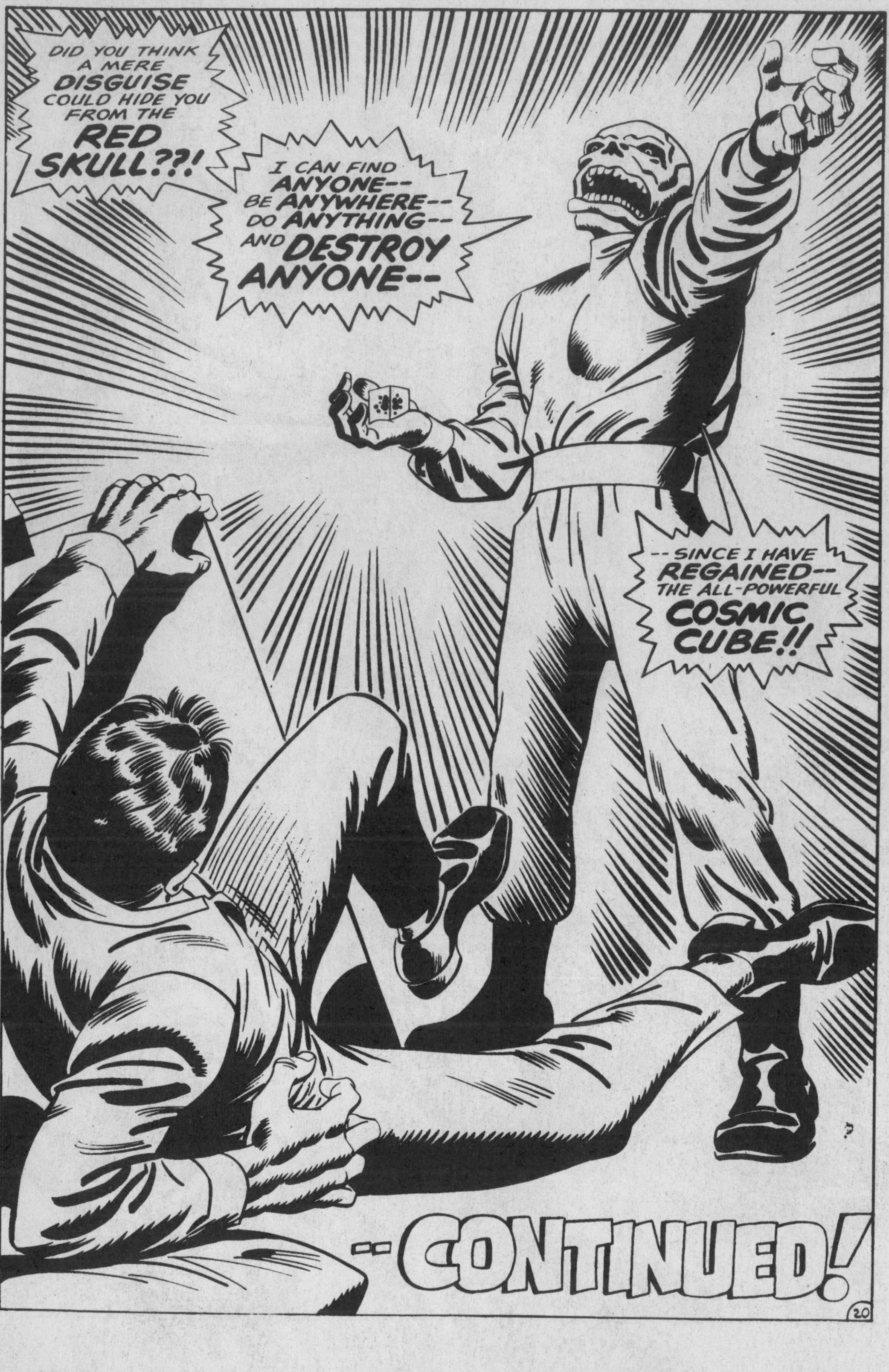
DID YOU THINK A MERE DISGUISE COULD HIDE YOU FROM THE RED SKULL??!
I CAN FIND ANYONE-- BE ANYWHERE-- DO ANYTHING-- AND DESTROY ANYONE--
--SINCE I HAVE REGAINED-- THE ALL-POWERFUL COSMIC CUBE!!
--CONTINUED!
20

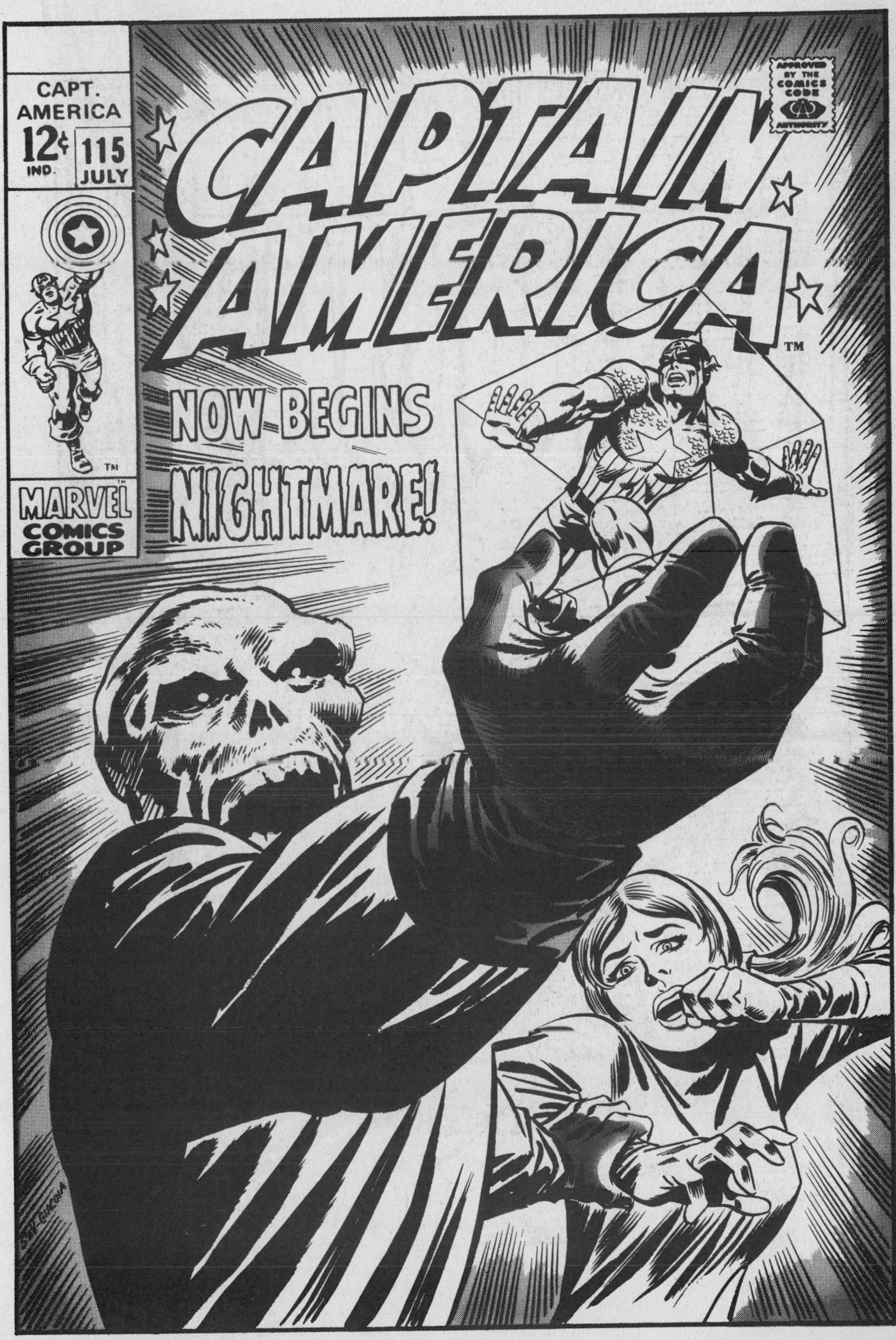
CAPT. AMERICA
12¢ IND.
115 JULY
MARVEL COMICS GROUP
APPROVED BY THE COMICS CODE AUTHORITY
CAPTAIN AMERICA
NOW BEGINS NIGHTMARE!

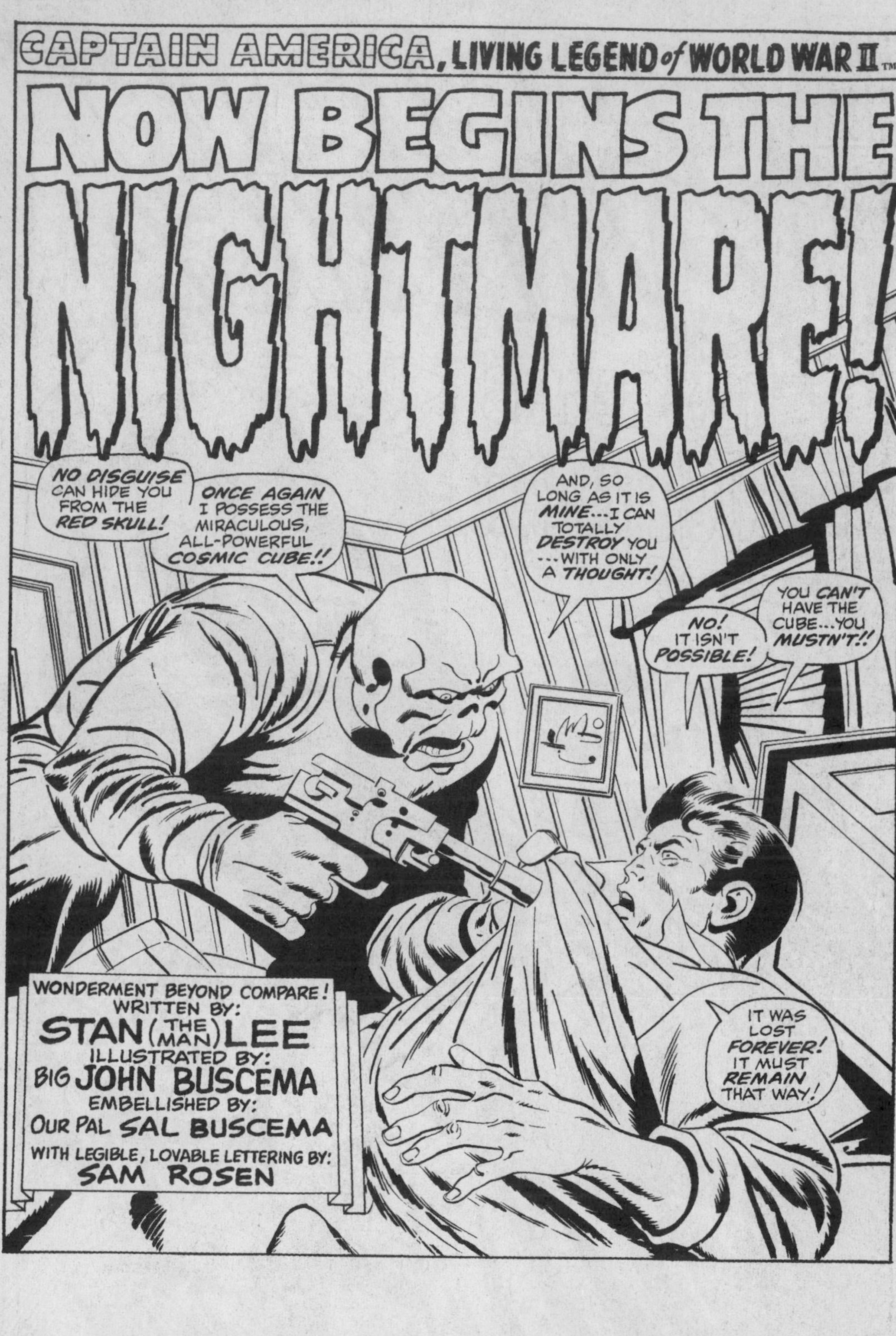
CAPTAIN AMERICA, LIVING LEGEND of WORLD WAR II™
NOW BEGINS THE NIGHTMARE!
NO DISGUISE CAN HIDE YOU FROM THE RED SKULL!
ONCE AGAIN I POSSESS THE MIRACULOUS, ALL-POWERFUL COSMIC CUBE!!
AND, SO LONG AS IT IS MINE...I CAN TOTALLY DESTROY YOU ---WITH ONLY A THOUGHT!
NO! IT ISN'T POSSIBLE!
YOU CAN'T HAVE THE CUBE...YOU MUSTN'T!!
IT WAS LOST FOREVER! IT MUST REMAIN THAT WAY!
WONDERMENT BEYOND COMPARE! WRITTEN BY: STAN (THE MAN) LEE ILLUSTRATED BY: BIG JOHN BUSCEMA EMBELLISHED BY: OUR PAL SAL BUSCEMA WITH LEGIBLE, LOVABLE LETTERING BY: SAM ROSEN

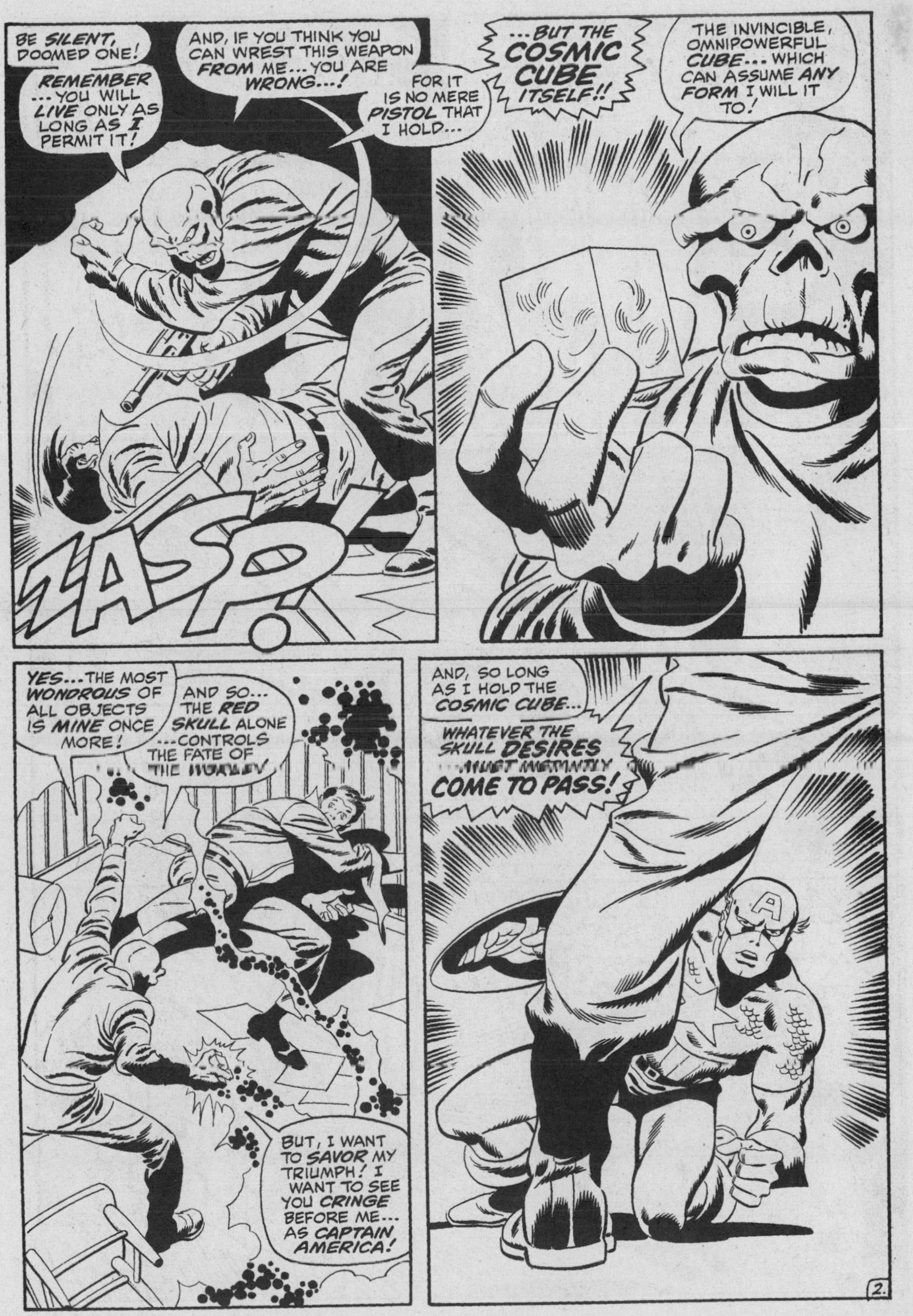
BE SILENT, DOOMED ONE!
REMEMBER ...YOU WILL LIVE ONLY AS LONG AS I PERMIT IT!
AND, IF YOU THINK YOU CAN WREST THIS WEAPON FROM ME...YOU ARE WRONG...!
FOR IT IS NO MERE PISTOL THAT I HOLD...
...BUT THE COSMIC CUBE ITSELF!!
ZASP!
THE INVINCIBLE, OMNIPOWERFUL CUBE...WHICH CAN ASSUME ANY FORM I WILL IT TO!
YES...THE MOST WONDROUS OF ALL OBJECTS IS MINE ONCE MORE!
AND SO... THE RED SKULL ALONE ...CONTROLS THE FATE OF
BUT, I WANT TO SAVOR MY TRIUMPH! I WANT TO SEE YOU CRINGE BEFORE ME... AS CAPTAIN AMERICA!
AND, SO LONG AS I HOLD THE COSMIC CUBE...
WHATEVER THE SKULL DESIRES
COME TO PASS!

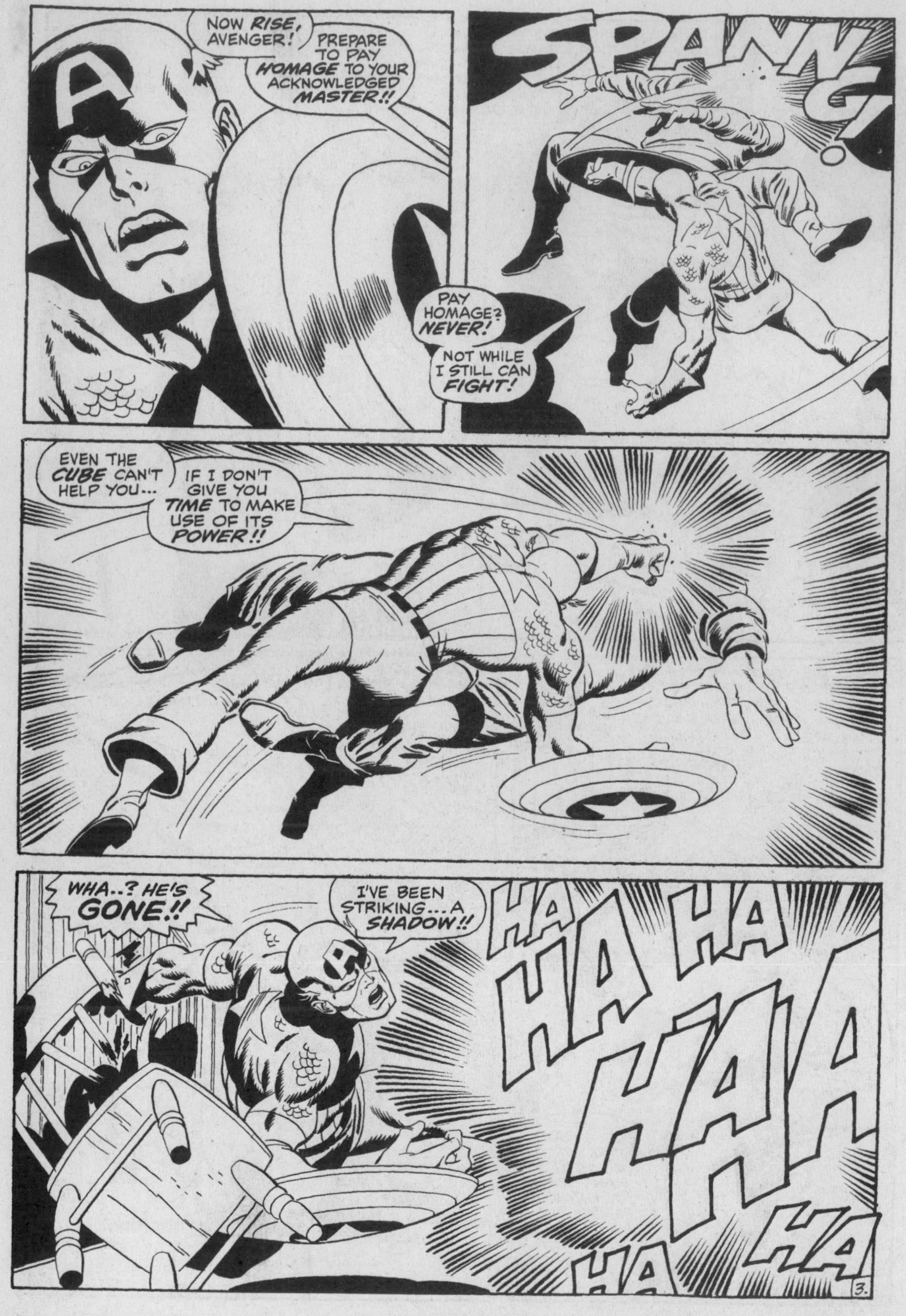
NOW RISE, AVENGER!
PREPARE TO PAY HOMAGE TO YOUR ACKNOWLEDGED MASTER!!
SPANNG!
PAY HOMAGE? NEVER!
NOT WHILE I STILL CAN FIGHT!
EVEN THE CUBE CAN'T HELP YOU...
IF I DON'T GIVE YOU TIME TO MAKE USE OF ITS POWER!!
WHA..? HE'S GONE!!
I'VE BEEN STRIKING... A SHADOW!!
HA HA HA HA HA HA HA HA HA
3.

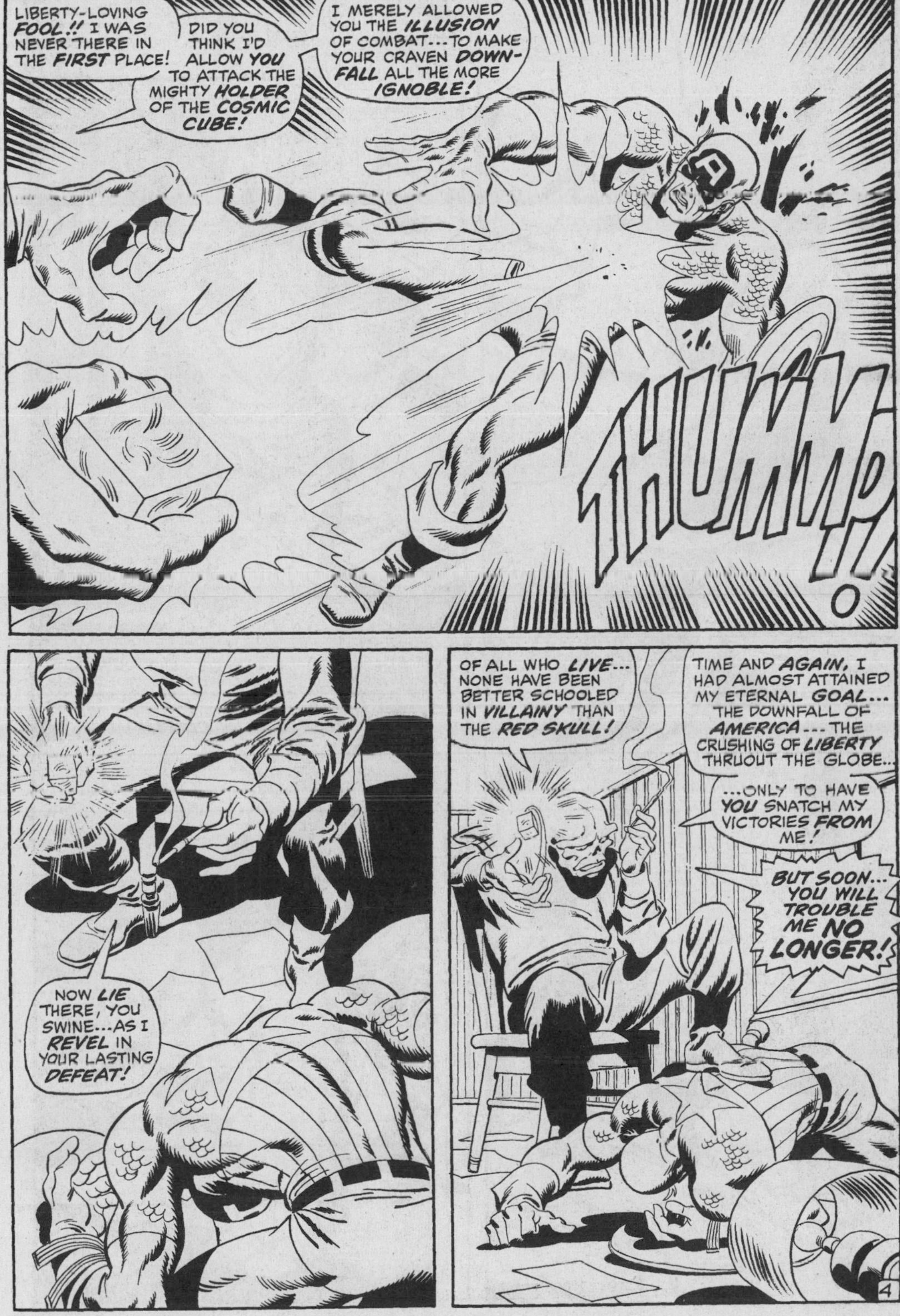
LIBERTY-LOVING FOOL!! I WAS NEVER THERE IN THE FIRST PLACE!
DID YOU THINK I'D ALLOW YOU TO ATTACK THE MIGHTY HOLDER OF THE COSMIC CUBE!
I MERELY ALLOWED YOU THE ILLUSION OF COMBAT...TO MAKE YOUR CRAVEN DOWN-FALL ALL THE MORE IGNOBLE!
THUMMP!!
NOW LIE THERE, YOU SWINE...AS I REVEL IN YOUR LASTING DEFEAT!
OF ALL WHO LIVE... NONE HAVE BEEN BETTER SCHOOLED IN VILLAINY THAN THE RED SKULL!
TIME AND AGAIN, I HAD ALMOST ATTAINED MY ETERNAL GOAL... THE DOWNFALL OF AMERICA... THE CRUSHING OF LIBERTY THRUOUT THE GLOBE...
...ONLY TO HAVE YOU SNATCH MY VICTORIES FROM ME!
BUT SOON... YOU WILL TROUBLE ME NO LONGER!
4

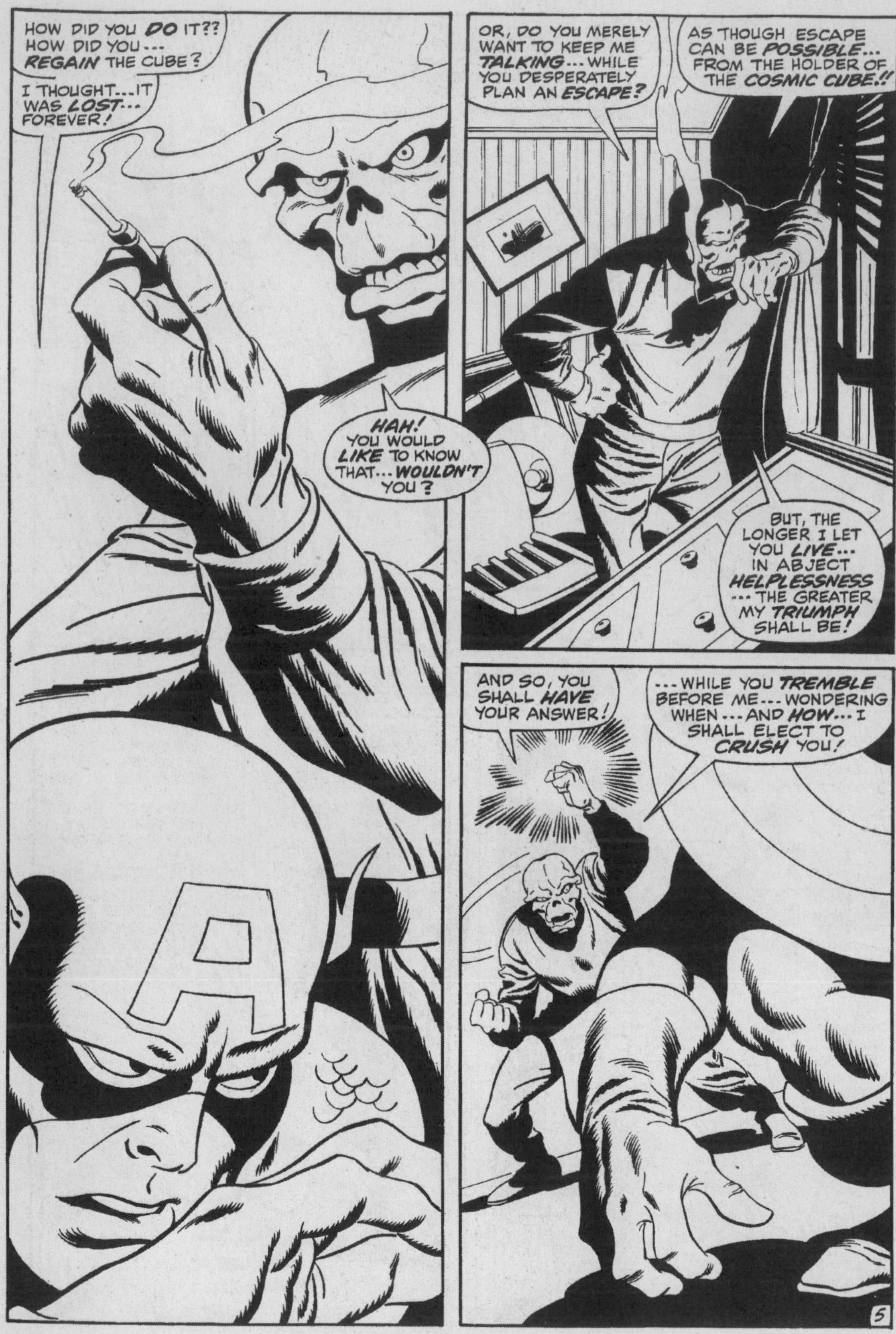
HOW DID YOU DO IT?? HOW DID YOU... REGAIN THE CUBE?
I THOUGHT...IT WAS LOST... FOREVER!
HAH! YOU WOULD LIKE TO KNOW THAT... WOULDN'T YOU?
OR, DO YOU MERELY WANT TO KEEP ME TALKING... WHILE YOU DESPERATELY PLAN AN ESCAPE?
AS THOUGH ESCAPE CAN BE POSSIBLE... FROM THE HOLDER OF THE COSMIC CUBE!!
BUT, THE LONGER I LET YOU LIVE... IN ABJECT HELPLESSNESS ... THE GREATER MY TRIUMPH SHALL BE!
AND SO, YOU SHALL HAVE YOUR ANSWER!
...WHILE YOU TREMBLE BEFORE ME... WONDERING WHEN... AND HOW... I SHALL ELECT TO CRUSH YOU!
5

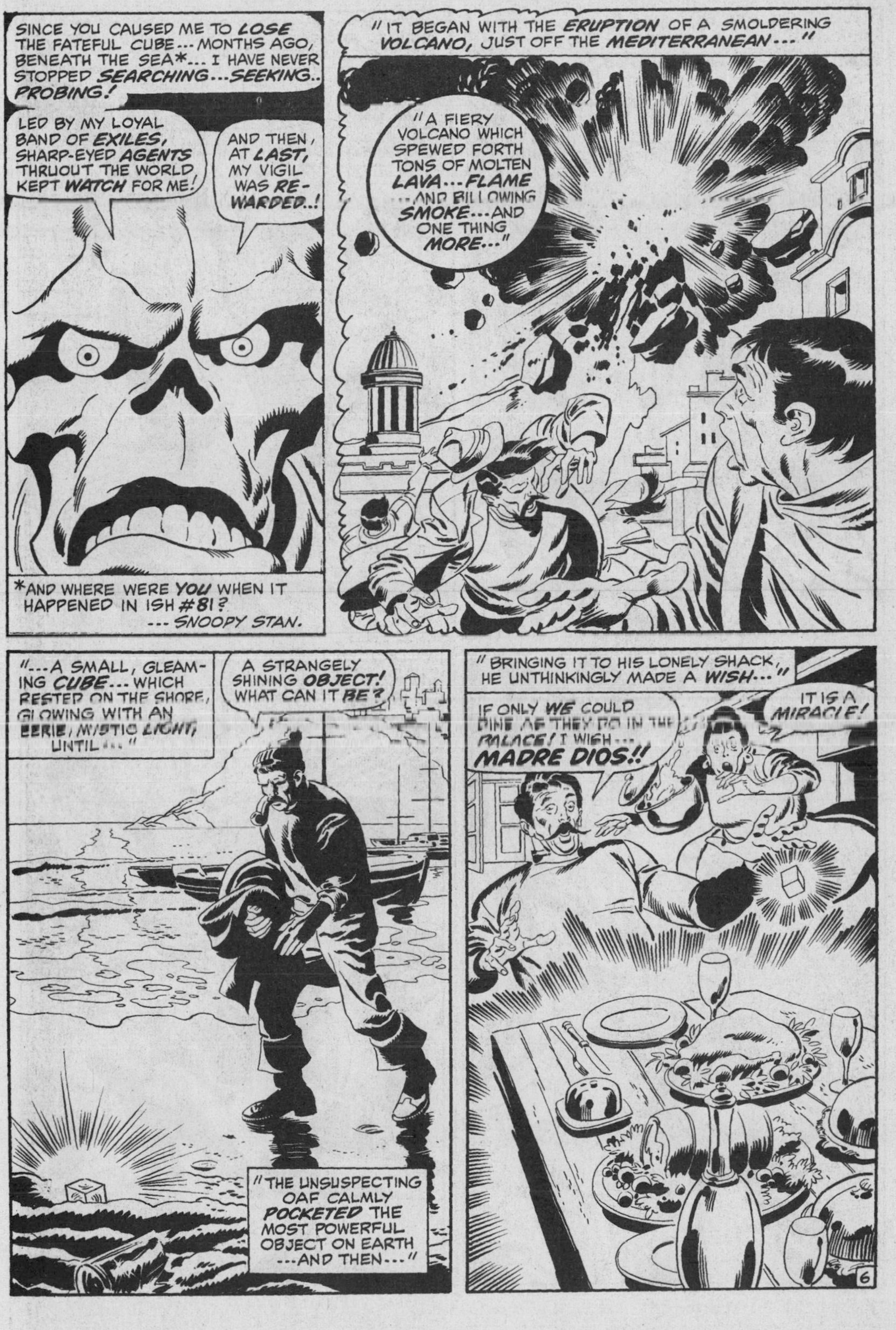
SINCE YOU CAUSED ME TO LOSE THE FATEFUL CUBE... MONTHS AGO, BENEATH THE SEA*... I HAVE NEVER STOPPED SEARCHING... SEEKING.. PROBING!
LED BY MY LOYAL BAND OF EXILES, SHARP-EYED AGENTS THRUOUT THE WORLD KEPT WATCH FOR ME!
AND THEN, AT LAST, MY VIGIL WAS REWARDED..!
*AND WHERE WERE YOU WHEN IT HAPPENED IN ISH #81? --- SNOOPY STAN.
"IT BEGAN WITH THE ERUPTION OF A SMOLDERING VOLCANO, JUST OFF THE MEDITERRANEAN..."
"A FIERY VOLCANO WHICH SPEWED FORTH TONS OF MOLTEN LAVA... FLAME ...AND BILLOWING SMOKE... AND ONE THING MORE..."
"...A SMALL, GLEAMING CUBE... WHICH RESTED ON THE SHORE, GLOWING WITH AN EERIE, MYSTIC LIGHT, UNTIL..."
A STRANGELY SHINING OBJECT! WHAT CAN IT BE?
"THE UNSUSPECTING OAF CALMLY POCKETED THE MOST POWERFUL OBJECT ON EARTH ---AND THEN..."
"BRINGING IT TO HIS LONELY SHACK, HE UNTHINKINGLY MADE A WISH..."
IF ONLY WE COULD DINE AS THEY DO IN THE PALACE! I WISH... MADRE DIOS!!
IT IS A MIRACLE!
6

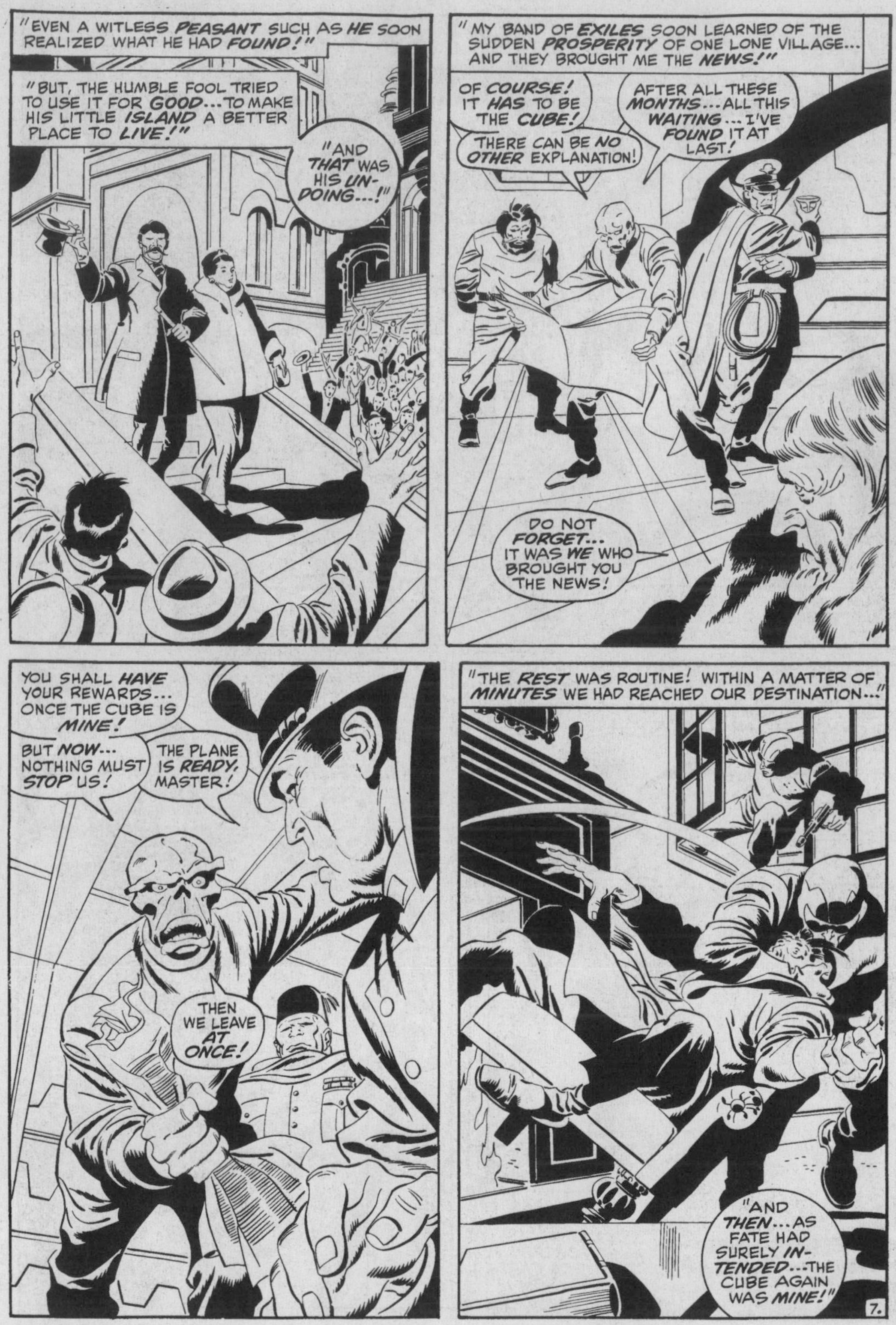
"EVEN A WITLESS PEASANT SUCH AS HE SOON REALIZED WHAT HE HAD FOUND!"
"BUT, THE HUMBLE FOOL TRIED TO USE IT FOR GOOD... TO MAKE HIS LITTLE ISLAND A BETTER PLACE TO LIVE!"
"AND THAT WAS HIS UNDOING...!"
"MY BAND OF EXILES SOON LEARNED OF THE SUDDEN PROSPERITY OF ONE LONE VILLAGE... AND THEY BROUGHT ME THE NEWS!"
OF COURSE! IT HAS TO BE THE CUBE!
THERE CAN BE NO OTHER EXPLANATION!
AFTER ALL THESE MONTHS... ALL THIS WAITING... I'VE FOUND IT AT LAST!
DO NOT FORGET... IT WAS WE WHO BROUGHT YOU THE NEWS!
YOU SHALL HAVE YOUR REWARDS... ONCE THE CUBE IS MINE!
BUT NOW... NOTHING MUST STOP US!
THE PLANE IS READY, MASTER!
THEN WE LEAVE AT ONCE!
"THE REST WAS ROUTINE! WITHIN A MATTER OF MINUTES WE HAD REACHED OUR DESTINATION...!"
"AND THEN... AS FATE HAD SURELY INTENDED... THE CUBE AGAIN WAS MINE!"

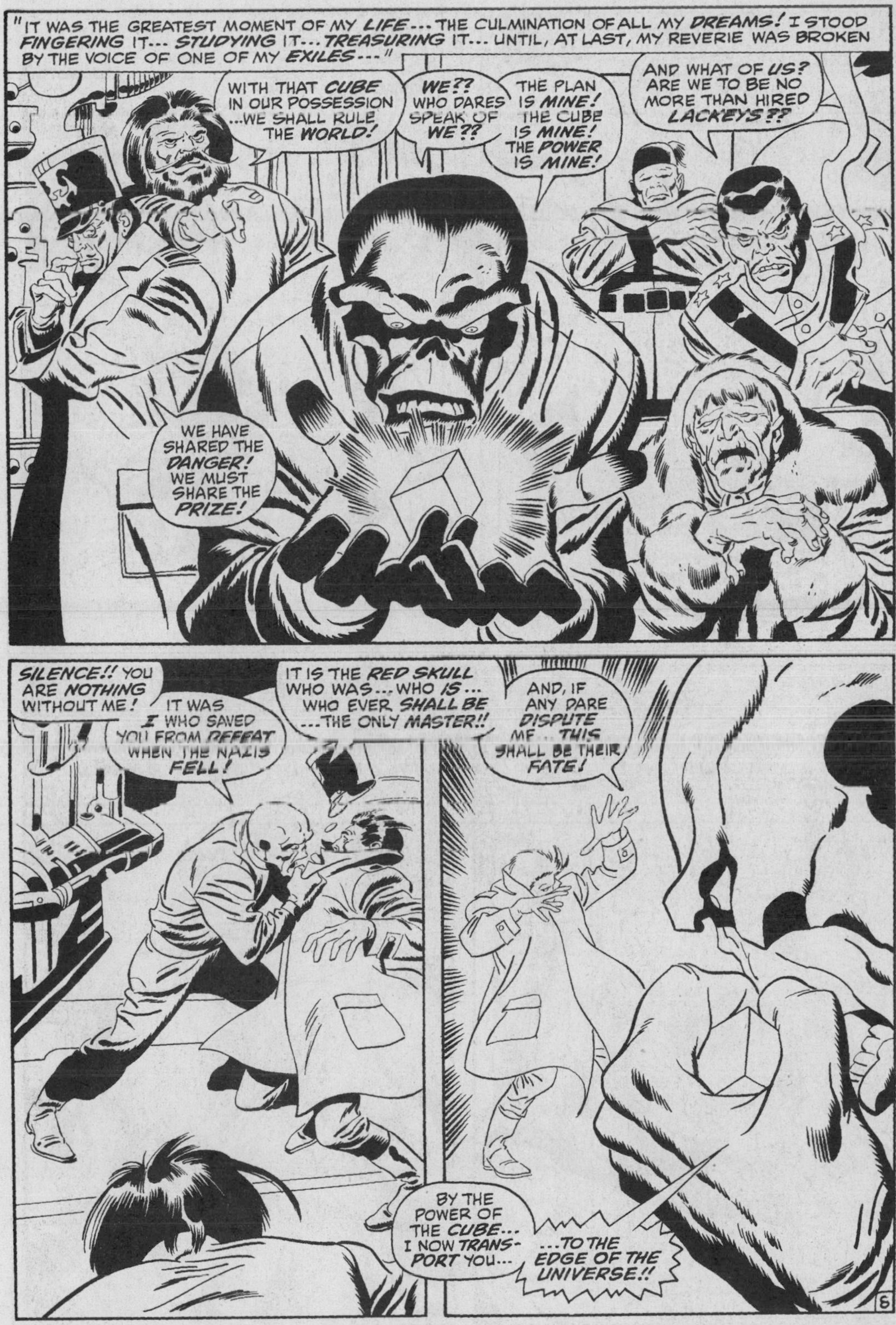
"IT WAS THE GREATEST MOMENT OF MY LIFE... THE CULMINATION OF ALL MY DREAMS! I STOOD FINGERING IT... STUDYING IT... TREASURING IT... UNTIL, AT LAST, MY REVERIE WAS BROKEN BY THE VOICE OF ONE OF MY EXILES---"
WITH THAT CUBE IN OUR POSSESSION ...WE SHALL RULE THE WORLD!
WE?? WHO DARES SPEAK OF WE??
THE PLAN IS MINE! THE CUBE IS MINE! THE POWER IS MINE!
AND WHAT OF US? ARE WE TO BE NO MORE THAN HIRED LACKEYS??
WE HAVE SHARED THE DANGER! WE MUST SHARE THE PRIZE!
SILENCE!! YOU ARE NOTHING WITHOUT ME!
IT WAS I WHO SAVED YOU FROM DEFEAT WHEN THE NAZIS FELL!
IT IS THE RED SKULL WHO WAS... WHO IS... WHO EVER SHALL BE ...THE ONLY MASTER!!
AND, IF ANY DARE DISPUTE ME... THIS SHALL BE THEIR FATE!
BY THE POWER OF THE CUBE... I NOW TRANSPORT YOU...
...TO THE EDGE OF THE UNIVERSE!!
8

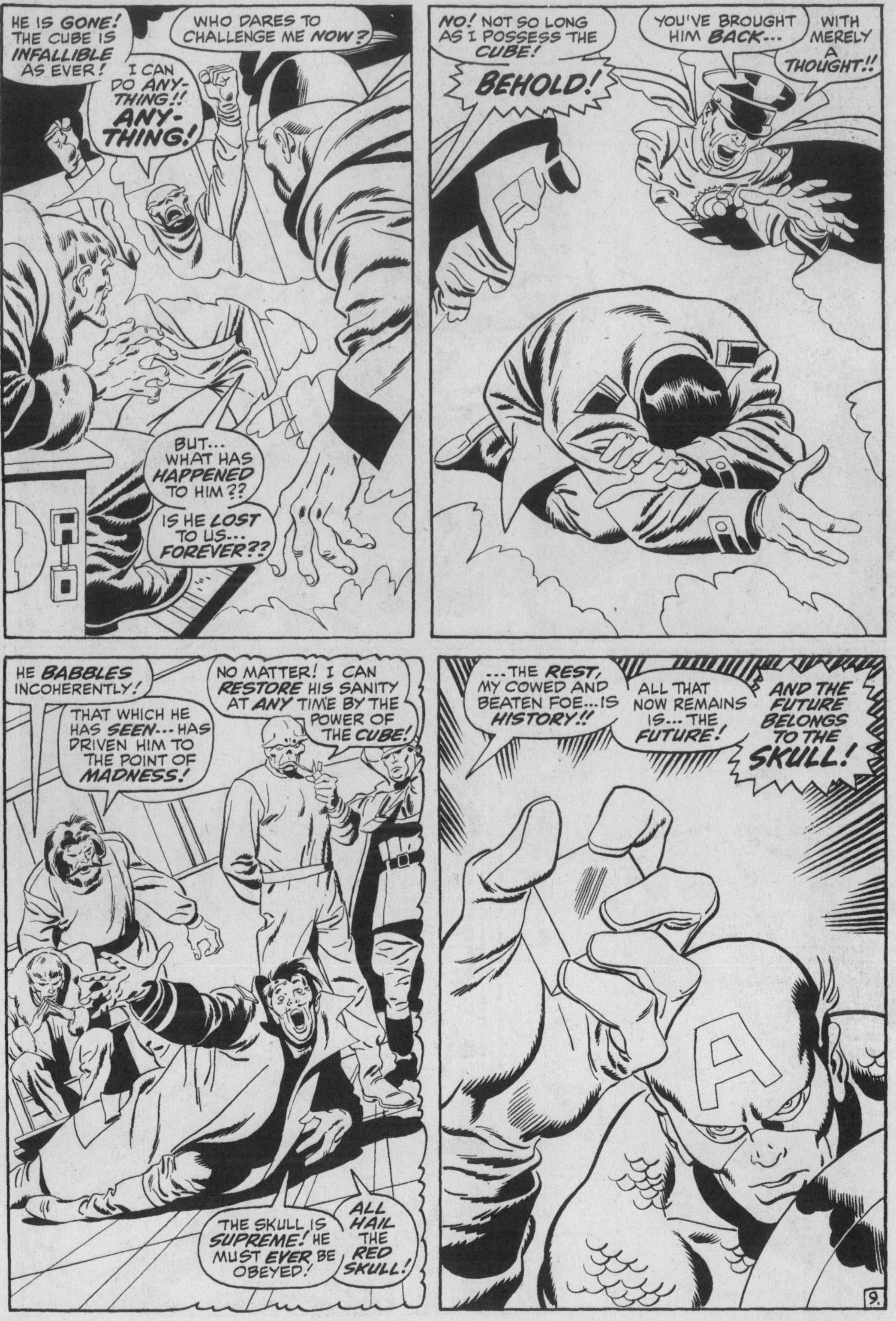

HE IS GONE! THE CUBE IS INFALLIBLE AS EVER!
WHO DARES TO CHALLENGE ME NOW?
I CAN DO ANY-THING!! ANY-THING!
BUT... WHAT HAS HAPPENED TO HIM??
IS HE LOST TO US... FOREVER??
NO! NOT SO LONG AS I POSSESS THE CUBE!
BEHOLD!
YOU'VE BROUGHT HIM BACK...
WITH MERELY A THOUGHT!!
HE BABBLES INCOHERENTLY!
THAT WHICH HE HAS SEEN... HAS DRIVEN HIM TO THE POINT OF MADNESS!
NO MATTER! I CAN RESTORE HIS SANITY AT ANY TIME BY THE POWER OF THE CUBE!
THE SKULL IS SUPREME! HE MUST EVER BE OBEYED!
ALL HAIL THE RED SKULL!
...THE REST, MY COWED AND BEATEN FOE... IS HISTORY!!
ALL THAT NOW REMAINS IS... THE FUTURE!
AND THE FUTURE BELONGS TO THE SKULL!
9.

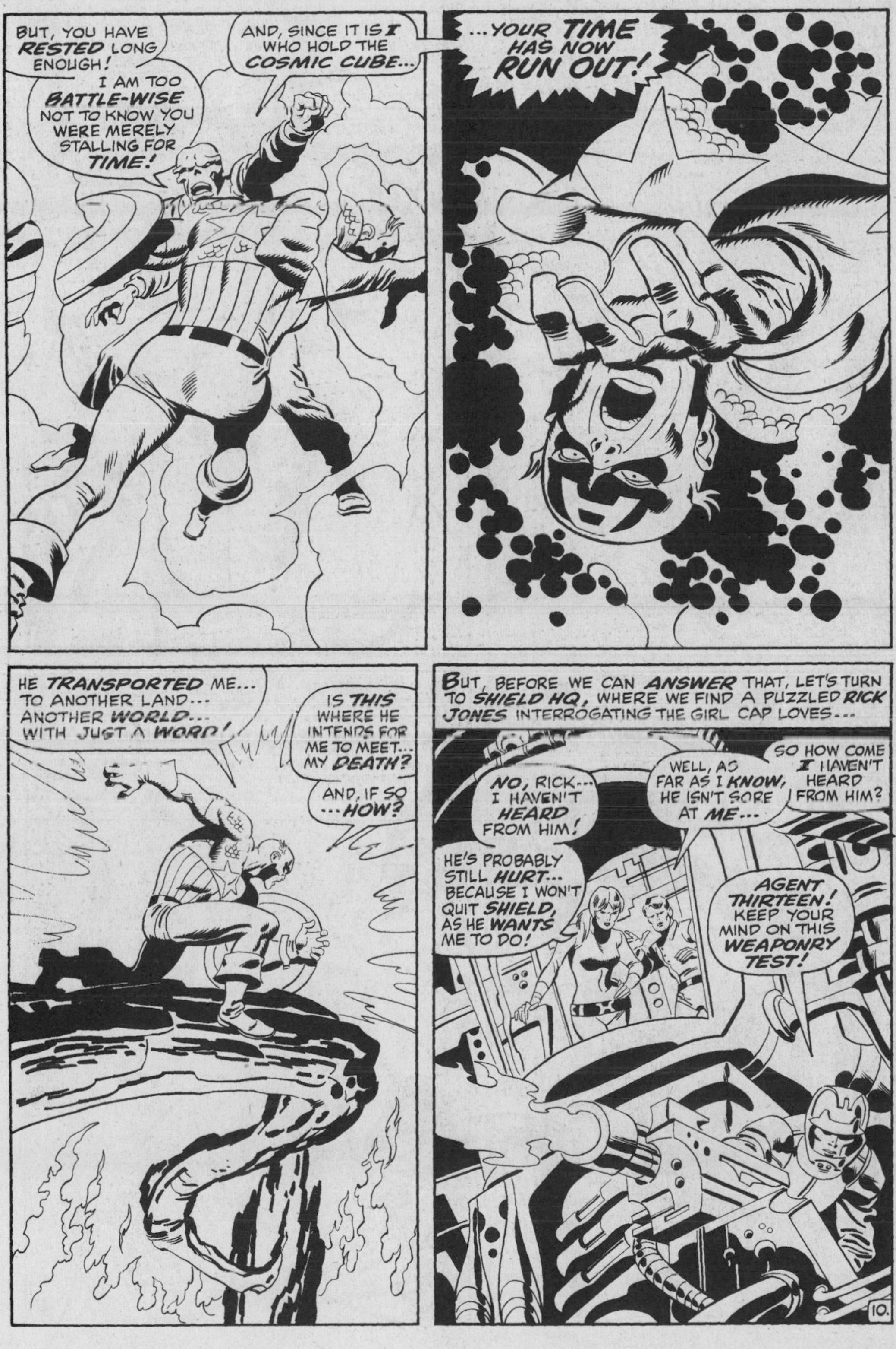
BUT, YOU HAVE RESTED LONG ENOUGH!
I AM TOO BATTLE-WISE NOT TO KNOW YOU WERE MERELY STALLING FOR TIME!
AND, SINCE IT IS I WHO HOLD THE COSMIC CUBE...
...YOUR TIME HAS NOW RUN OUT!
HE TRANSPORTED ME... TO ANOTHER LAND... ANOTHER WORLD... WITH JUST A WORD!
IS THIS WHERE HE INTENDS FOR ME TO MEET... MY DEATH?
AND, IF SO ...HOW?
BUT, BEFORE WE CAN ANSWER THAT, LET'S TURN TO SHIELD HQ, WHERE WE FIND A PUZZLED RICK JONES INTERROGATING THE GIRL CAP LOVES...
SO HOW COME I HAVEN'T HEARD FROM HIM?
NO, RICK... I HAVEN'T HEARD FROM HIM!
WELL, AS FAR AS I KNOW, HE ISN'T SORE AT ME...
HE'S PROBABLY STILL HURT... BECAUSE I WON'T QUIT SHIELD, AS HE WANTS ME TO DO!
AGENT THIRTEEN! KEEP YOUR MIND ON THIS WEAPONRY TEST!
10.

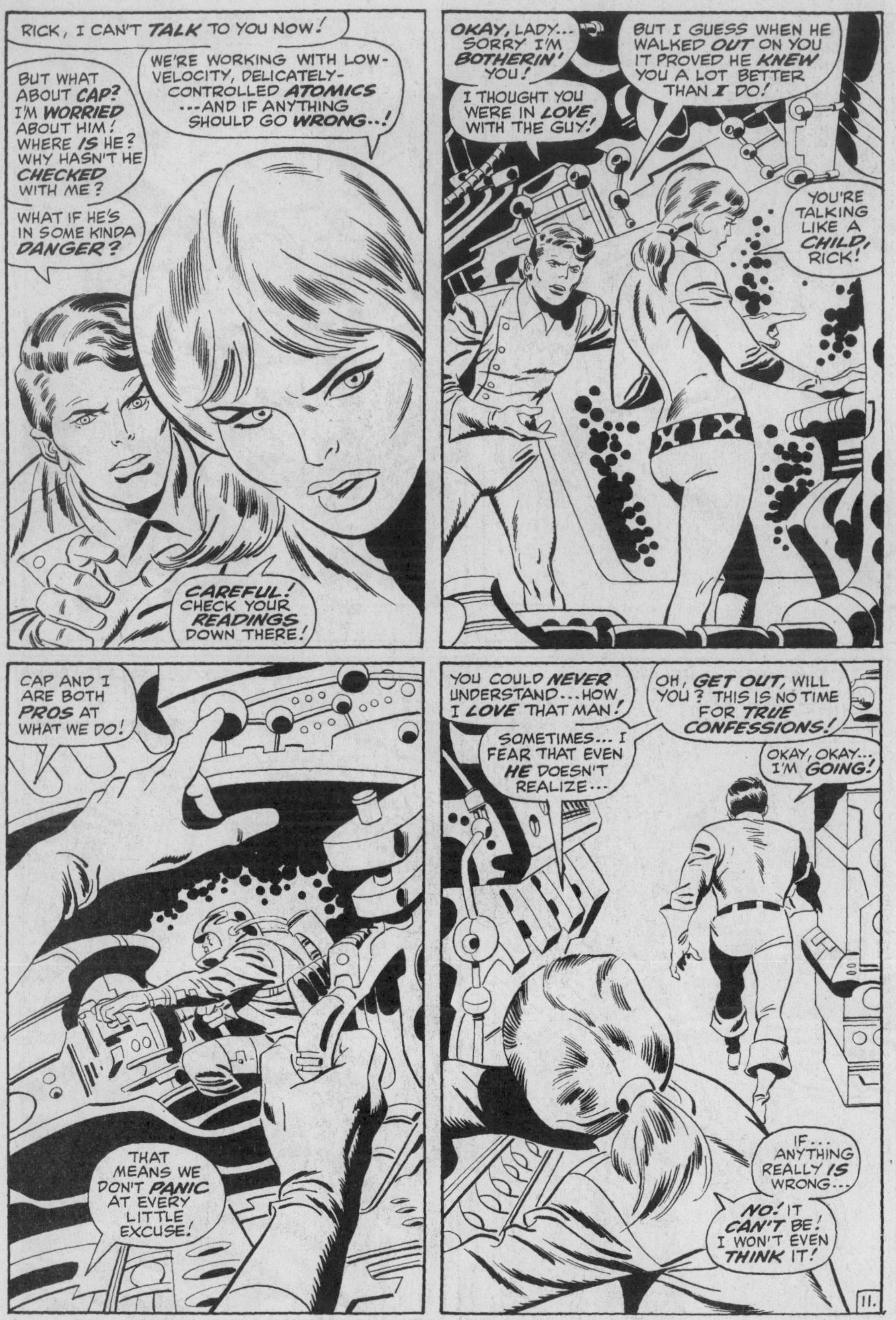
RICK, I CAN'T TALK TO YOU NOW!
BUT WHAT ABOUT CAP? I'M WORRIED ABOUT HIM! WHERE IS HE? WHY HASN'T HE CHECKED WITH ME?
WHAT IF HE'S IN SOME KINDA DANGER?
WE'RE WORKING WITH LOW-VELOCITY, DELICATELY-CONTROLLED ATOMICS ...AND IF ANYTHING SHOULD GO WRONG..!
CAREFUL! CHECK YOUR READINGS DOWN THERE!
OKAY, LADY... SORRY I'M BOTHERIN' YOU!
I THOUGHT YOU WERE IN LOVE WITH THE GUY!
BUT I GUESS WHEN HE WALKED OUT ON YOU IT PROVED HE KNEW YOU A LOT BETTER THAN I DO!
YOU'RE TALKING LIKE A CHILD, RICK!
CAP AND I ARE BOTH PROS AT WHAT WE DO!
THAT MEANS WE DON'T PANIC AT EVERY LITTLE EXCUSE!
YOU COULD NEVER UNDERSTAND... HOW I LOVE THAT MAN!
SOMETIMES... I FEAR THAT EVEN HE DOESN'T REALIZE...
OH, GET OUT, WILL YOU? THIS IS NO TIME FOR TRUE CONFESSIONS!
OKAY, OKAY... I'M GOING!
IF... ANYTHING REALLY IS WRONG...
NO! IT CAN'T BE! I WON'T EVEN THINK IT!
11.

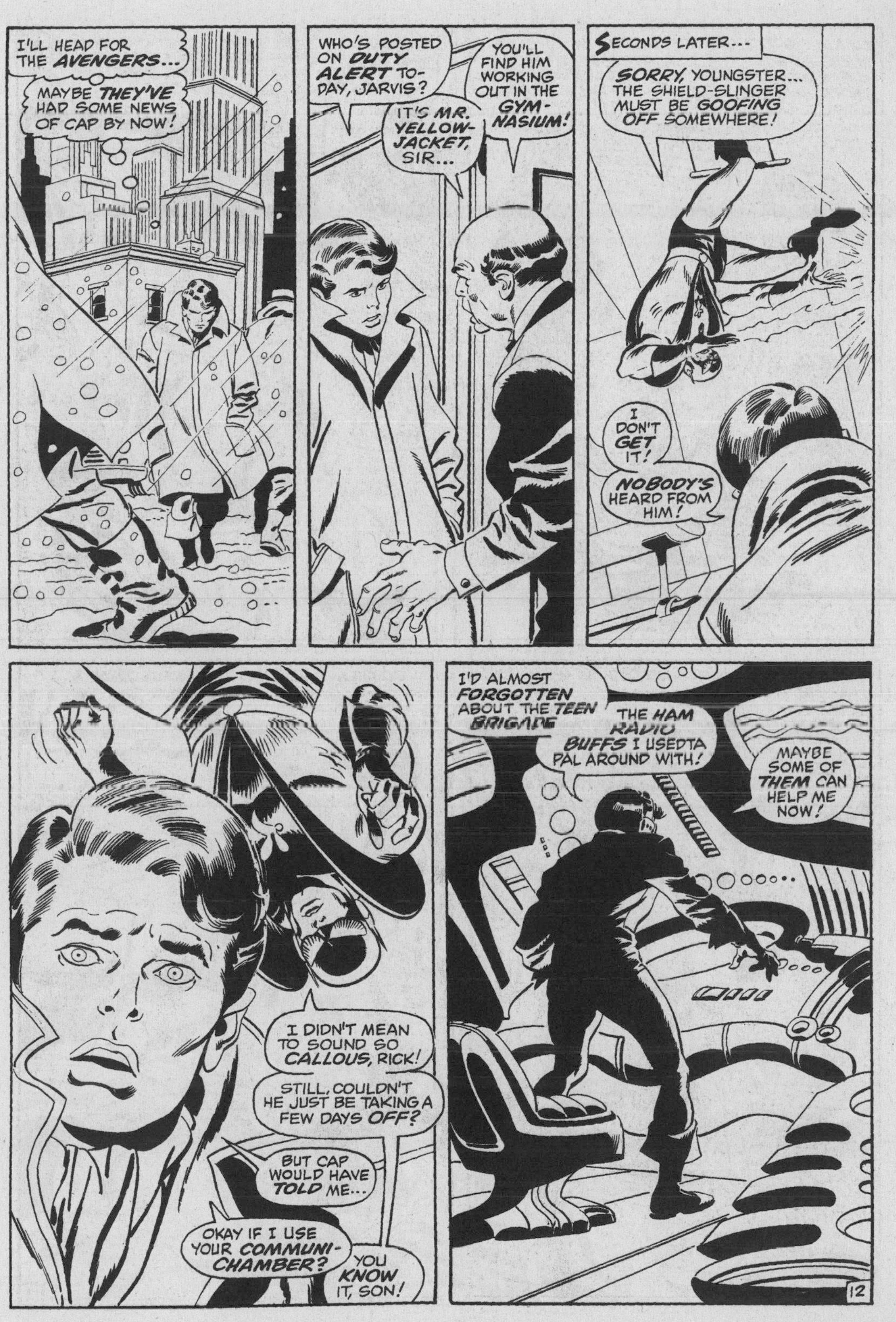
I'LL HEAD FOR THE AVENGERS...
MAYBE THEY'VE HAD SOME NEWS OF CAP BY NOW!
WHO'S POSTED ON DUTY ALERT TO-DAY, JARVIS?
IT'S MR. YELLOW-JACKET, SIR...
YOU'LL FIND HIM WORKING OUT IN THE GYM-NASIUM!
SECONDS LATER...
SORRY, YOUNGSTER... THE SHIELD-SLINGER MUST BE GOOFING OFF SOMEWHERE!
I DON'T GET IT!
NOBODY'S HEARD FROM HIM!
I DIDN'T MEAN TO SOUND SO CALLOUS, RICK!
STILL, COULDN'T HE JUST BE TAKING A FEW DAYS OFF?
BUT CAP WOULD HAVE TOLD ME...
OKAY IF I USE YOUR COMMUNI-CHAMBER?
YOU KNOW IT, SON!
I'D ALMOST FORGOTTEN ABOUT THE TEEN BRIGADE
THE HAM RADIO BUFFS I USEDTA PAL AROUND WITH!
MAYBE SOME OF THEM CAN HELP ME NOW!
12

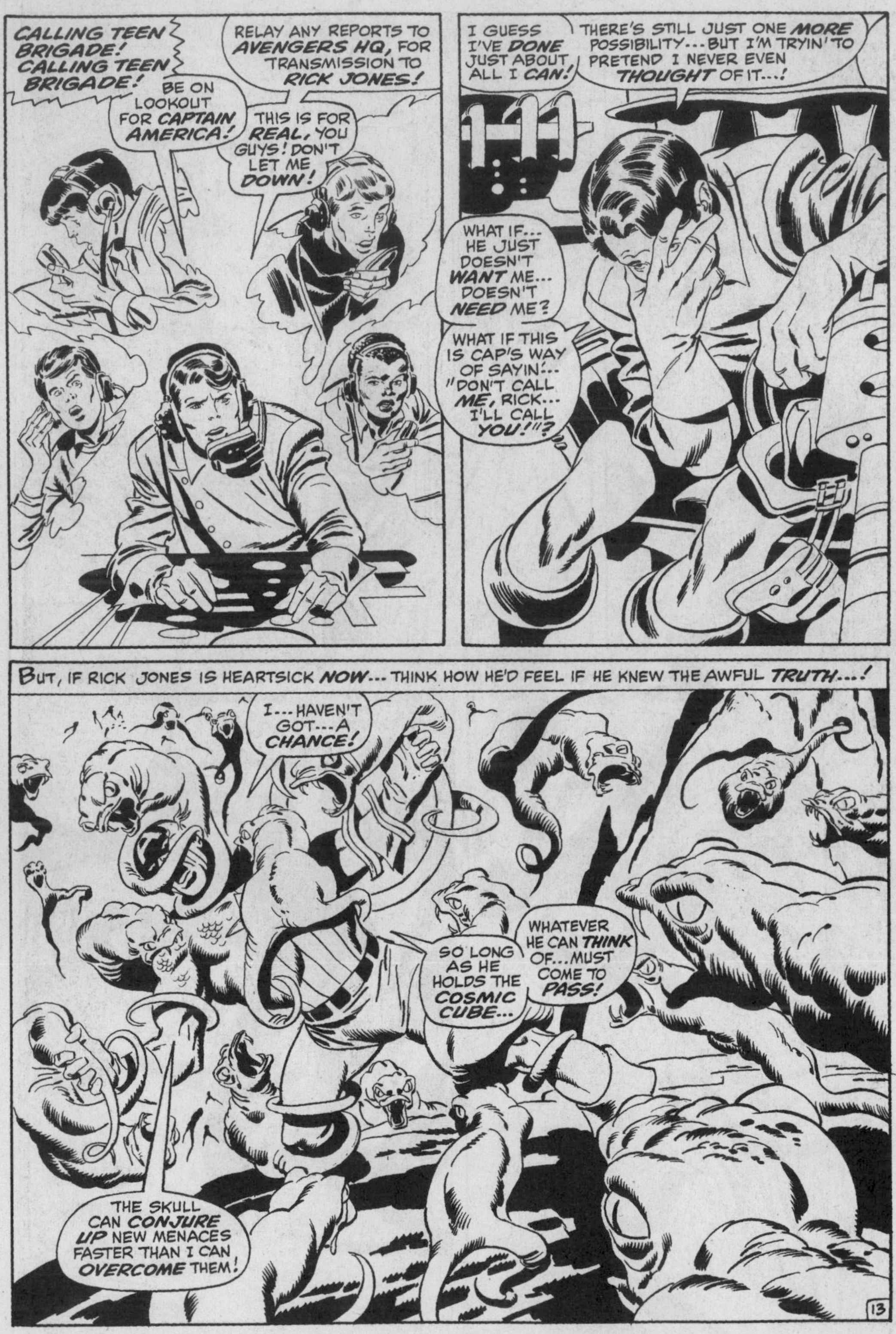
CALLING TEEN BRIGADE! CALLING TEEN BRIGADE!
BE ON LOOKOUT FOR CAPTAIN AMERICA!
RELAY ANY REPORTS TO AVENGERS HQ, FOR TRANSMISSION TO RICK JONES!
THIS IS FOR REAL, YOU GUYS! DON'T LET ME DOWN!
I GUESS I'VE DONE JUST ABOUT ALL I CAN!
THERE'S STILL JUST ONE MORE POSSIBILITY... BUT I'M TRYIN' TO PRETEND I NEVER EVEN THOUGHT OF IT...!
WHAT IF... HE JUST DOESN'T WANT ME... DOESN'T NEED ME?
WHAT IF THIS IS CAP'S WAY OF SAYIN'... "DON'T CALL ME, RICK... I'LL CALL YOU!"?
BUT, IF RICK JONES IS HEARTSICK NOW... THINK HOW HE'D FEEL IF HE KNEW THE AWFUL TRUTH...!
I... HAVEN'T GOT... A CHANCE!
THE SKULL CAN CONJURE UP NEW MENACES FASTER THAN I CAN OVERCOME THEM!
SO LONG AS HE HOLDS THE COSMIC CUBE...
WHATEVER HE CAN THINK OF... MUST COME TO PASS!
13

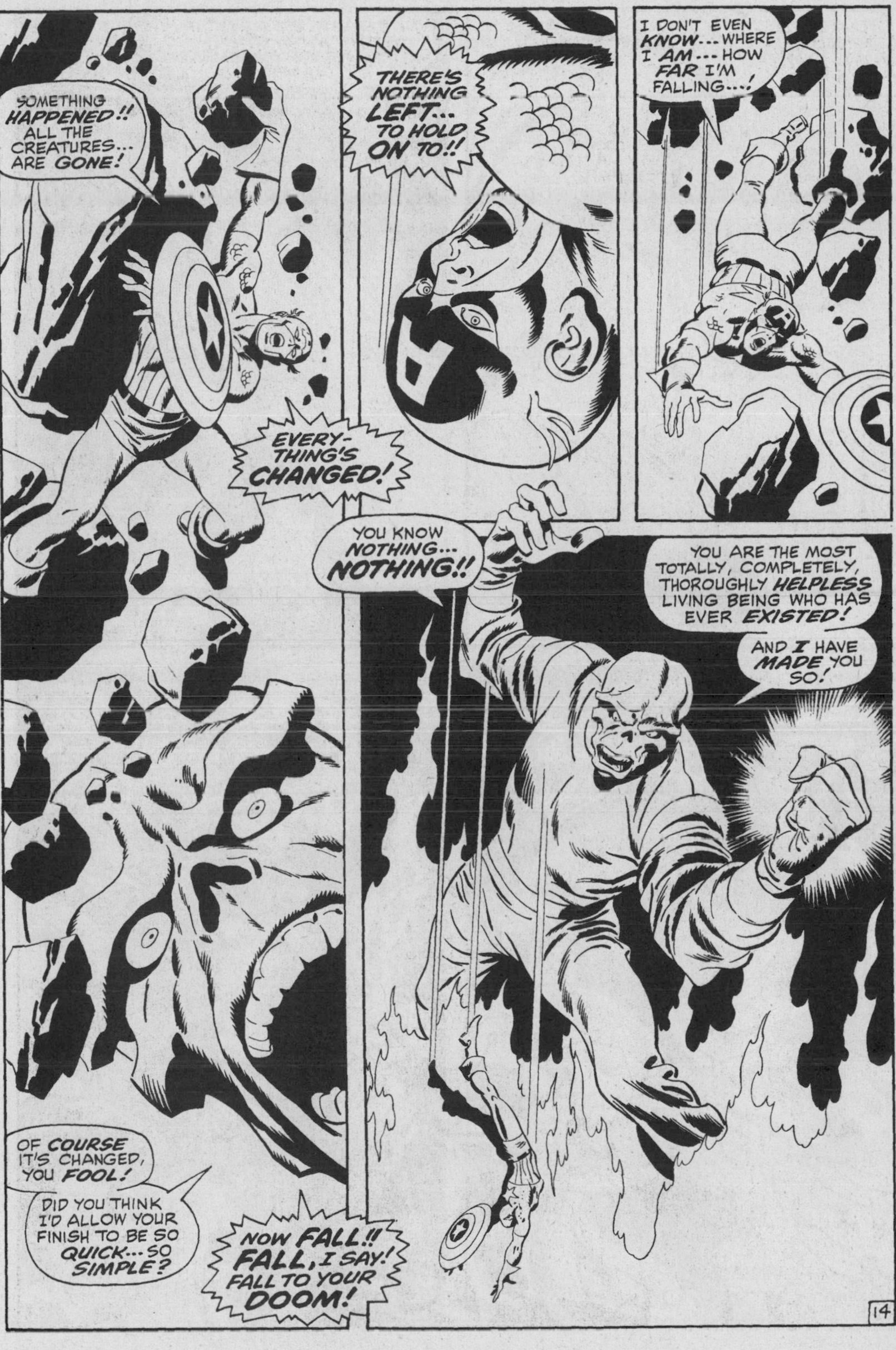
SOMETHING HAPPENED!! ALL THE CREATURES... ARE GONE!
EVERY-THING'S CHANGED!
THERE'S NOTHING LEFT... TO HOLD ON TO!!
I DON'T EVEN KNOW... WHERE I AM... HOW FAR I'M FALLING...!
OF COURSE IT'S CHANGED, YOU FOOL!
DID YOU THINK I'D ALLOW YOUR FINISH TO BE SO QUICK... SO SIMPLE?
YOU KNOW NOTHING... NOTHING!!
YOU ARE THE MOST TOTALLY, COMPLETELY, THOROUGHLY HELPLESS LIVING BEING WHO HAS EVER EXISTED!
AND I HAVE MADE YOU SO!
NOW FALL!! FALL, I SAY! FALL TO YOUR DOOM!
14

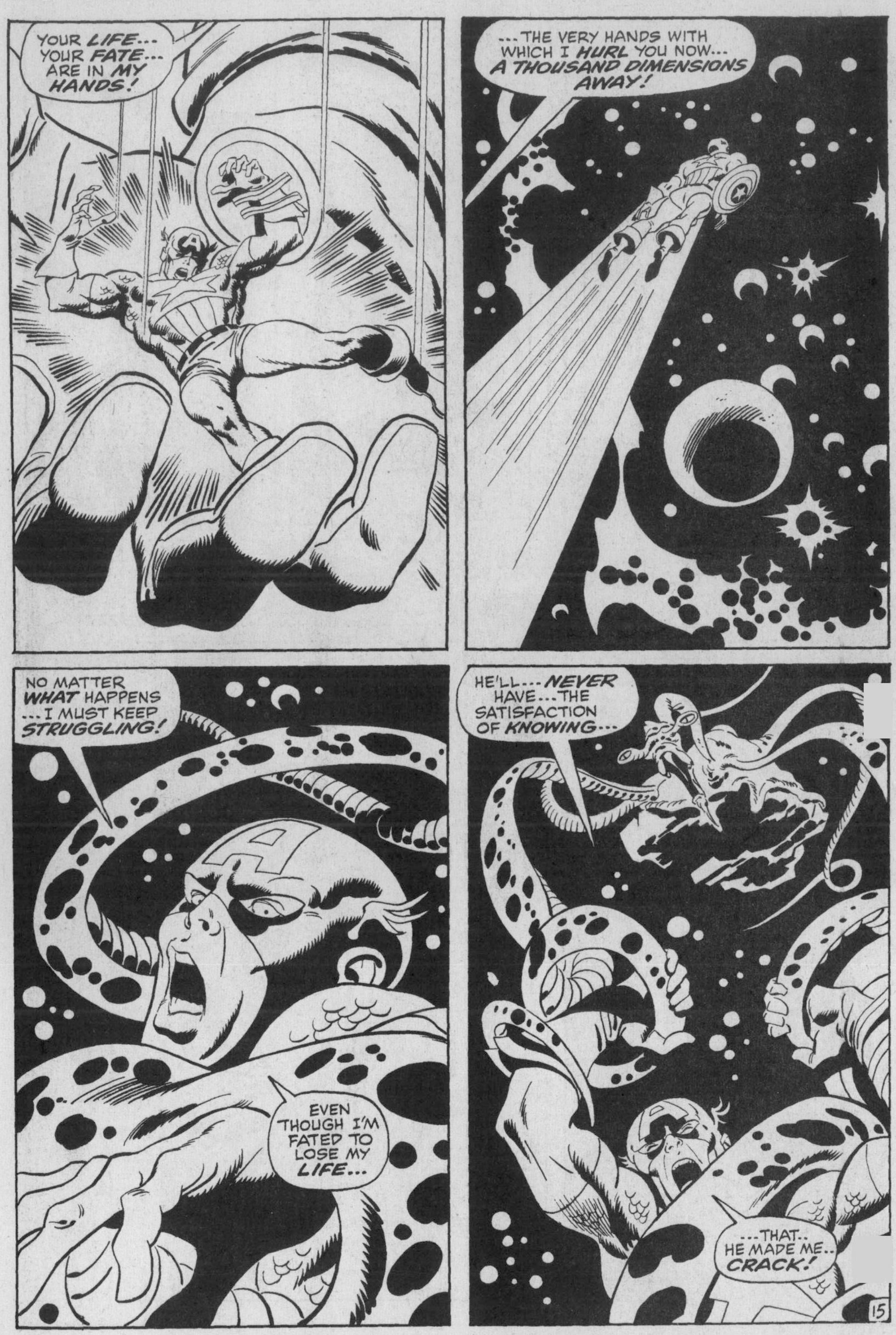
YOUR LIFE... YOUR FATE... ARE IN MY HANDS!
...THE VERY HANDS WITH WHICH I HURL YOU NOW... A THOUSAND DIMENSIONS AWAY!
NO MATTER WHAT HAPPENS ...I MUST KEEP STRUGGLING!
EVEN THOUGH I'M FATED TO LOSE MY LIFE...
HE'LL...NEVER HAVE...THE SATISFACTION OF KNOWING...
...THAT.. HE MADE ME.. CRACK!
15

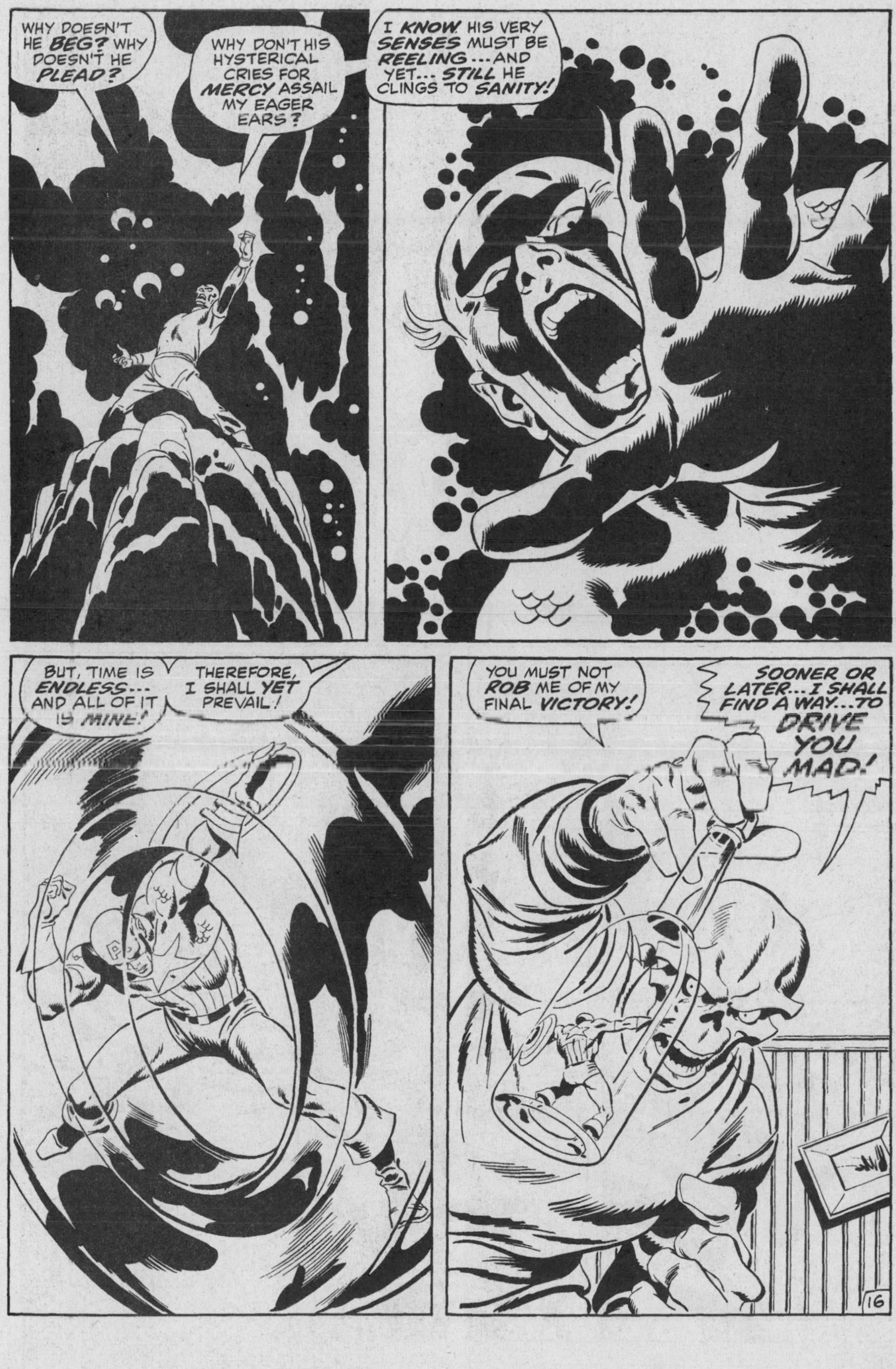

WHY DOESN'T HE BEG? WHY DOESN'T HE PLEAD?
WHY DON'T HIS HYSTERICAL CRIES FOR MERCY ASSAIL MY EAGER EARS?
I KNOW HIS VERY SENSES MUST BE REELING...AND YET... STILL HE CLINGS TO SANITY!
BUT, TIME IS ENDLESS--- AND ALL OF IT IS MINE!
THEREFORE, I SHALL YET PREVAIL!
YOU MUST NOT ROB ME OF MY FINAL VICTORY!
SOONER OR LATER...I SHALL FIND A WAY...TO DRIVE YOU MAD!
16

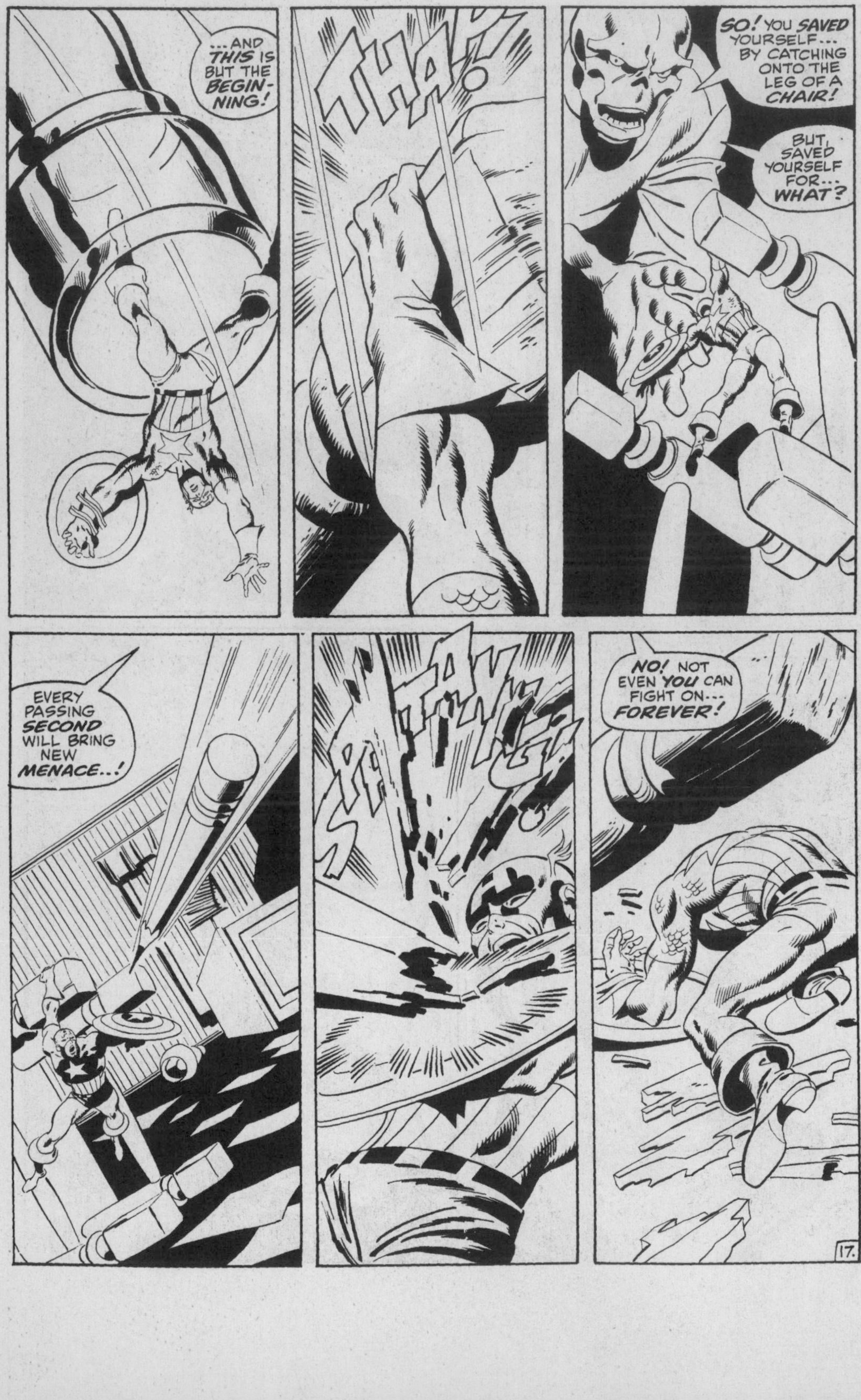
...AND THIS IS BUT THE BEGIN-NING!
THHAP!
SO! YOU SAVED YOURSELF... BY CATCHING ONTO THE LEG OF A CHAIR!
BUT, SAVED YOURSELF FOR... WHAT?
EVERY PASSING SECOND WILL BRING NEW MENACE...!
SPTANNG!
NO! NOT EVEN YOU CAN FIGHT ON... FOREVER!
17.

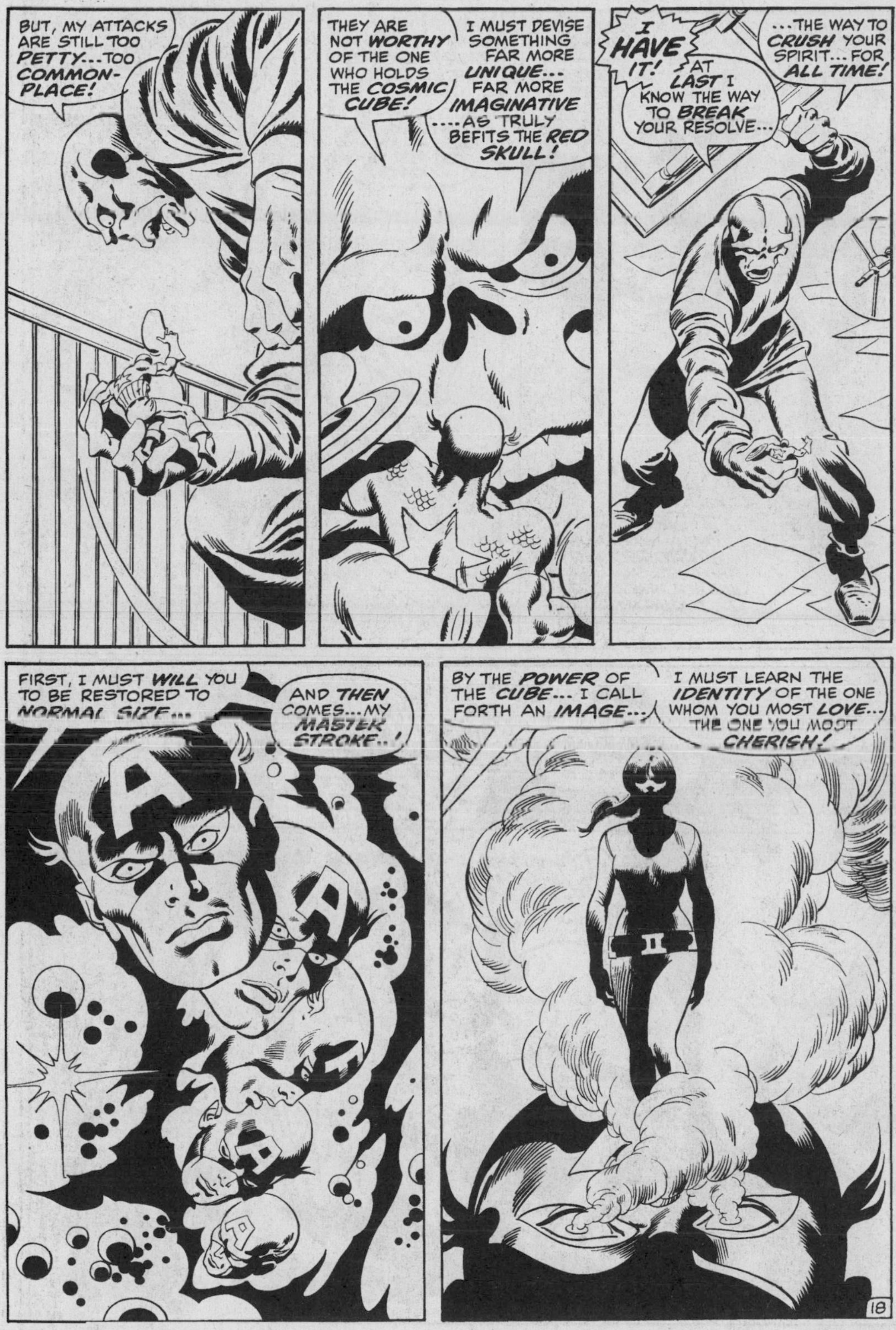
BUT, MY ATTACKS ARE STILL TOO PETTY... TOO COMMON-PLACE!
THEY ARE NOT WORTHY OF THE ONE WHO HOLDS THE COSMIC CUBE!
I MUST DEVISE SOMETHING FAR MORE UNIQUE... FAR MORE IMAGINATIVE ....AS TRULY BEFITS THE RED SKULL!
I HAVE IT!
AT LAST I KNOW THE WAY TO BREAK YOUR RESOLVE...
...THE WAY TO CRUSH YOUR SPIRIT... FOR ALL TIME!
FIRST, I MUST WILL YOU TO BE RESTORED TO NORMAL SIZE...
AND THEN COMES... MY MASTER STROKE..!
BY THE POWER OF THE CUBE... I CALL FORTH AN IMAGE...
I MUST LEARN THE IDENTITY OF THE ONE WHOM YOU MOST LOVE... THE ONE YOU MOST CHERISH!
18

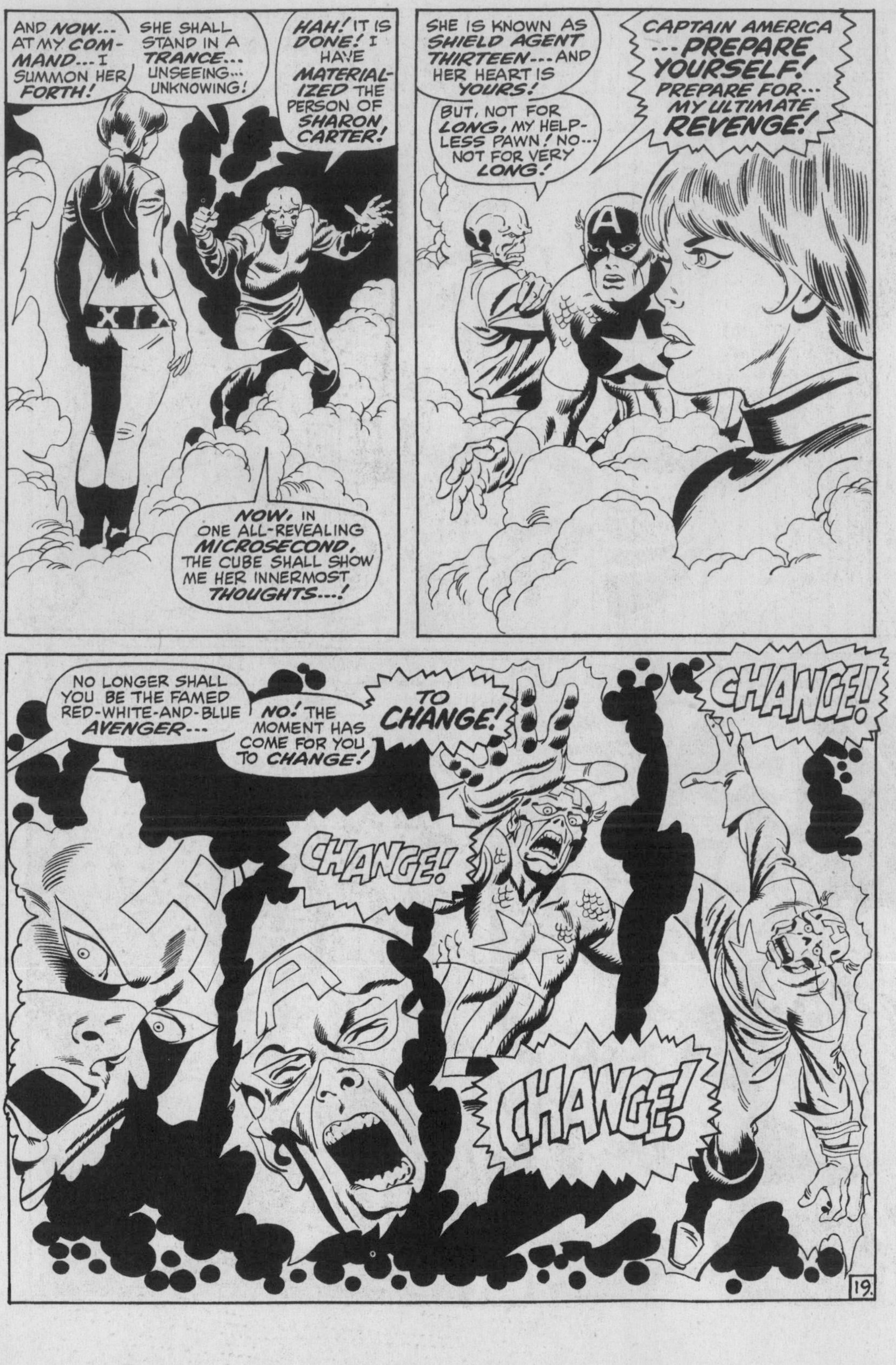

AND NOW... AT MY COMMAND... I SUMMON HER FORTH!
SHE SHALL STAND IN A TRANCE... UNSEEING... UNKNOWING!
HAH! IT IS DONE! I HAVE MATERIALIZED THE PERSON OF SHARON CARTER!
NOW, IN ONE ALL-REVEALING MICROSECOND, THE CUBE SHALL SHOW ME HER INNERMOST THOUGHTS...!
SHE IS KNOWN AS SHIELD AGENT THIRTEEN--- AND HER HEART IS YOURS!
BUT, NOT FOR LONG, MY HELPLESS PAWN! NO... NOT FOR VERY LONG!
CAPTAIN AMERICA ... PREPARE YOURSELF! PREPARE FOR... MY ULTIMATE REVENGE!
NO LONGER SHALL YOU BE THE FAMED RED-WHITE-AND-BLUE AVENGER---
NO! THE MOMENT HAS COME FOR YOU TO CHANGE!
TO CHANGE!
CHANGE!
CHANGE!
CHANGE!

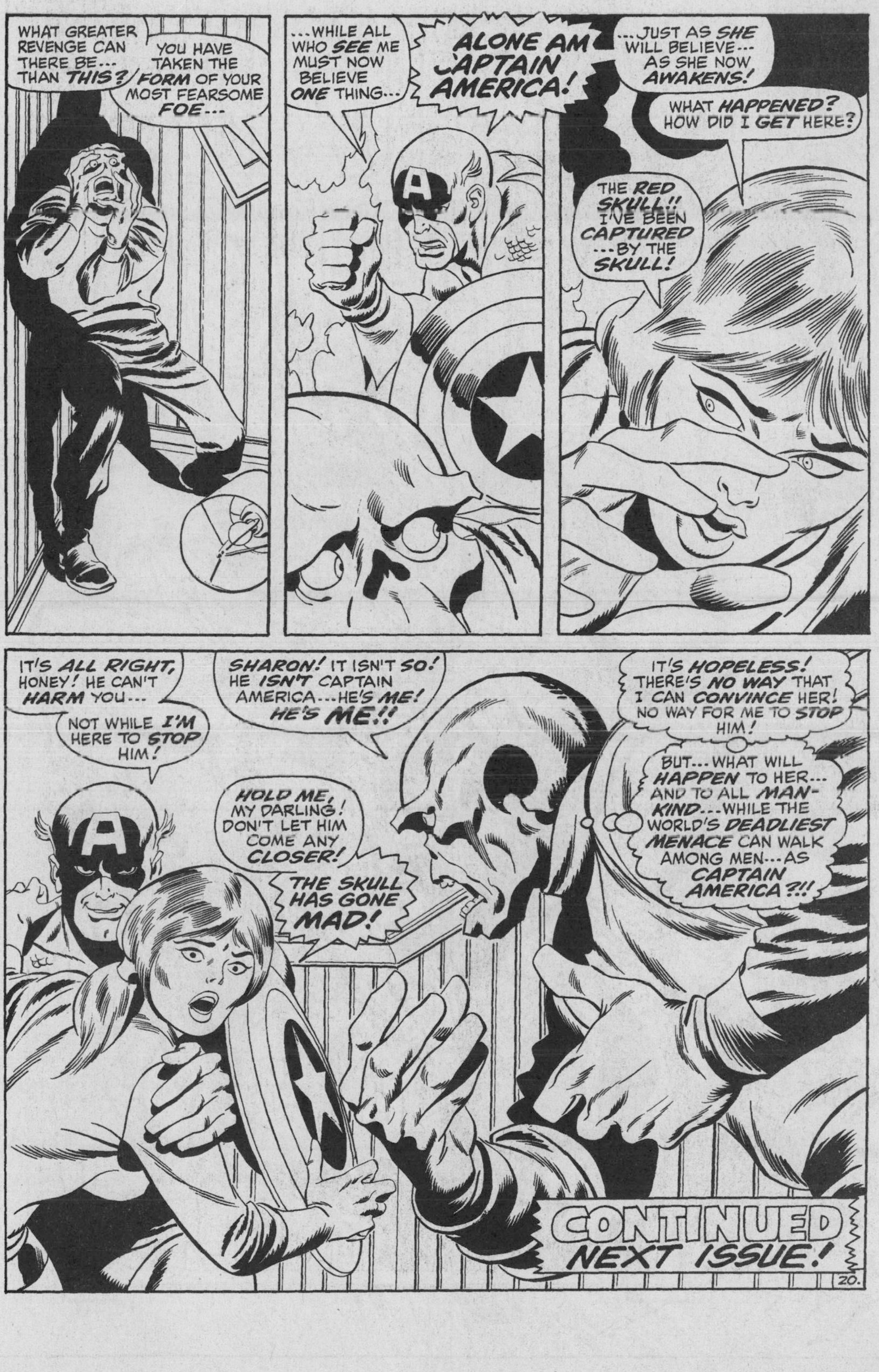
WHAT GREATER REVENGE CAN THERE BE... THAN THIS?
YOU HAVE TAKEN THE FORM OF YOUR MOST FEARSOME FOE...
...WHILE ALL WHO SEE ME MUST NOW BELIEVE ONE THING...
ALONE AM I CAPTAIN AMERICA!
...JUST AS SHE WILL BELIEVE--- AS SHE NOW AWAKENS!
WHAT HAPPENED? HOW DID I GET HERE?
THE RED SKULL!! I'VE BEEN CAPTURED ---BY THE SKULL!
IT'S ALL RIGHT, HONEY! HE CAN'T HARM YOU...
NOT WHILE I'M HERE TO STOP HIM!
SHARON! IT ISN'T SO! HE ISN'T CAPTAIN AMERICA---HE'S ME! HE'S ME!!
HOLD ME, MY DARLING! DON'T LET HIM COME ANY CLOSER!
THE SKULL HAS GONE MAD!
IT'S HOPELESS! THERE'S NO WAY THAT I CAN CONVINCE HER! NO WAY FOR ME TO STOP HIM!
BUT... WHAT WILL HAPPEN TO HER... AND TO ALL MAN-KIND... WHILE THE WORLD'S DEADLIEST MENACE CAN WALK AMONG MEN... AS CAPTAIN AMERICA?!!
CONTINUED NEXT ISSUE!
20.

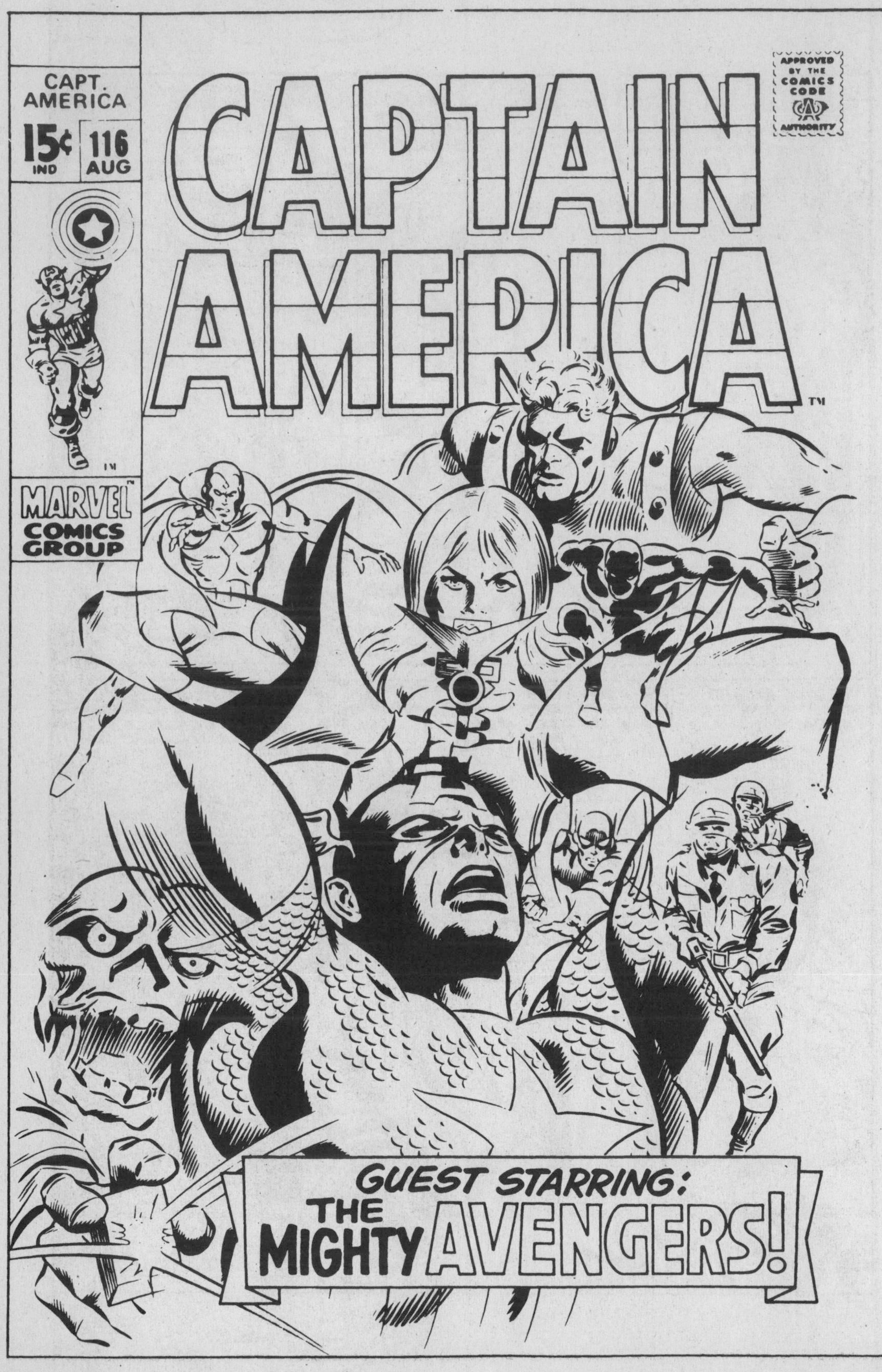
CAPT. AMERICA
15¢ IND
116 AUG
APPROVED BY THE COMICS CODE AUTHORITY
CAPTAIN AMERICA
MARVEL COMICS GROUP
GUEST STARRING:
THE MIGHTY AVENGERS!

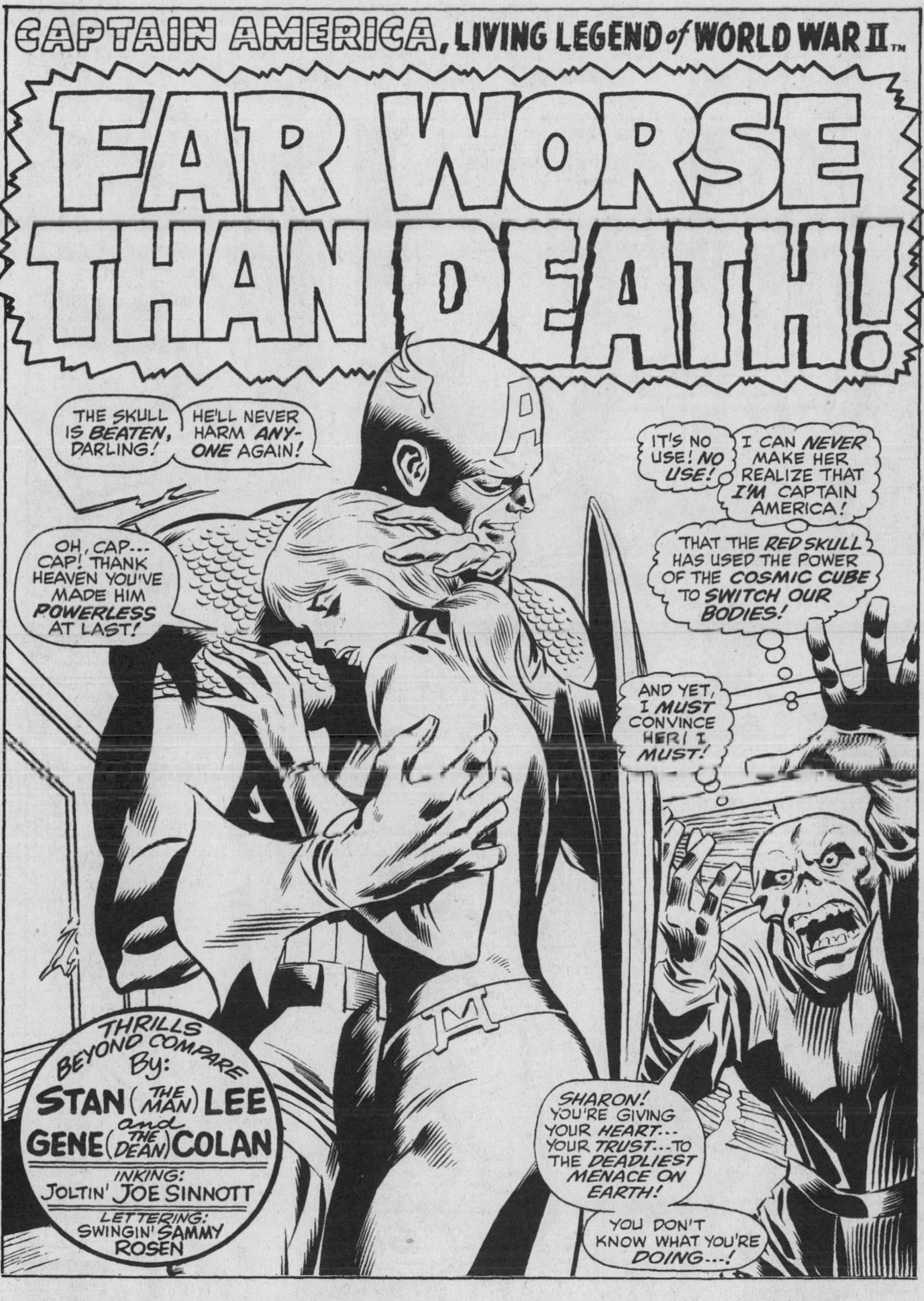
CAPTAIN AMERICA, LIVING LEGEND of WORLD WAR II™
FAR WORSE THAN DEATH!
THE SKULL IS BEATEN, DARLING!
HE'LL NEVER HARM ANYONE AGAIN!
OH, CAP... CAP! THANK HEAVEN YOU'VE MADE HIM POWERLESS AT LAST!
IT'S NO USE! NO USE!
I CAN NEVER MAKE HER REALIZE THAT I'M CAPTAIN AMERICA!
THAT THE RED SKULL HAS USED THE POWER OF THE COSMIC CUBE TO SWITCH OUR BODIES!
AND YET, I MUST CONVINCE HER! I MUST!
SHARON! YOU'RE GIVING YOUR HEART... YOUR TRUST... TO THE DEADLIEST MENACE ON EARTH!
YOU DON'T KNOW WHAT YOU'RE DOING...!
THRILLS BEYOND COMPARE By: STAN (THE MAN) LEE and GENE (THE DEAN) COLAN
INKING: JOLTIN' JOE SINNOTT
LETTERING: SWINGIN' SAMMY ROSEN

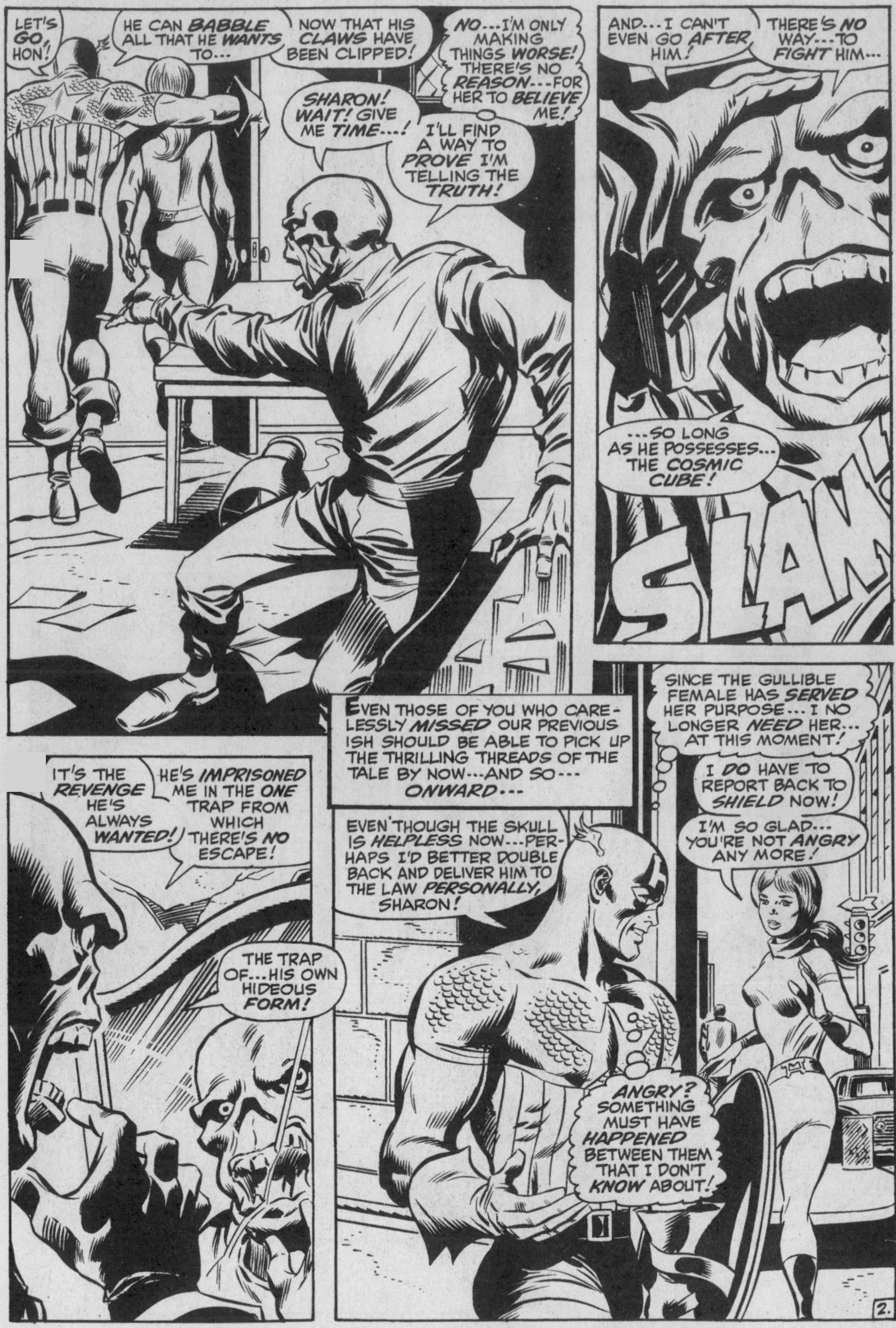
LET'S GO, HON!
HE CAN BABBLE ALL THAT HE WANTS TO...
NOW THAT HIS CLAWS HAVE BEEN CLIPPED!
SHARON! WAIT! GIVE ME TIME...!
NO...I'M ONLY MAKING THINGS WORSE! THERE'S NO REASON---FOR HER TO BELIEVE ME!
I'LL FIND A WAY TO PROVE I'M TELLING THE TRUTH!
AND...I CAN'T EVEN GO AFTER HIM!
THERE'S NO WAY---TO FIGHT HIM...
...SO LONG AS HE POSSESSES... THE COSMIC CUBE!
SLAM!
IT'S THE REVENGE HE'S ALWAYS WANTED!
HE'S IMPRISONED ME IN THE ONE TRAP FROM WHICH THERE'S NO ESCAPE!
THE TRAP OF...HIS OWN HIDEOUS FORM!
EVEN THOSE OF YOU WHO CARELESSLY MISSED OUR PREVIOUS ISH SHOULD BE ABLE TO PICK UP THE THRILLING THREADS OF THE TALE BY NOW---AND SO--- ONWARD---
EVEN THOUGH THE SKULL IS HELPLESS NOW---PERHAPS I'D BETTER DOUBLE BACK AND DELIVER HIM TO THE LAW PERSONALLY, SHARON!
SINCE THE GULLIBLE FEMALE HAS SERVED HER PURPOSE... I NO LONGER NEED HER... AT THIS MOMENT!
I DO HAVE TO REPORT BACK TO SHIELD NOW!
I'M SO GLAD... YOU'RE NOT ANGRY ANY MORE!
ANGRY? SOMETHING MUST HAVE HAPPENED BETWEEN THEM THAT I DON'T KNOW ABOUT!
2.

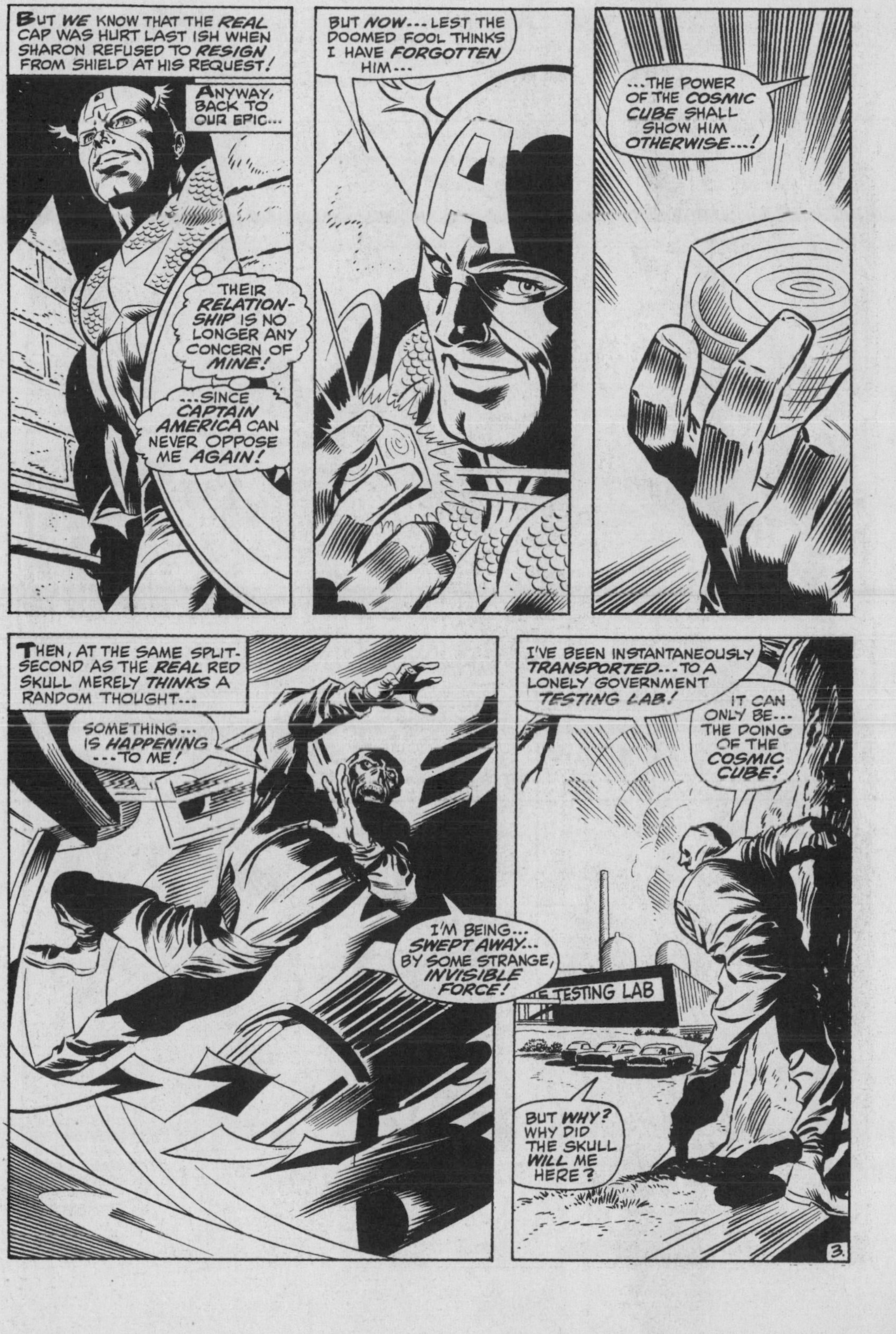
BUT WE KNOW THAT THE REAL CAP WAS HURT LAST ISH WHEN SHARON REFUSED TO RESIGN FROM SHIELD AT HIS REQUEST!
ANYWAY, BACK TO OUR EPIC...
THEIR RELATION-SHIP IS NO LONGER ANY CONCERN OF MINE!
...SINCE CAPTAIN AMERICA CAN NEVER OPPOSE ME AGAIN!
BUT NOW... LEST THE DOOMED FOOL THINKS I HAVE FORGOTTEN HIM...
...THE POWER OF THE COSMIC CUBE SHALL SHOW HIM OTHERWISE...!
THEN, AT THE SAME SPLIT-SECOND AS THE REAL RED SKULL MERELY THINKS A RANDOM THOUGHT...
SOMETHING... IS HAPPENING ...TO ME!
I'M BEING... SWEPT AWAY... BY SOME STRANGE, INVISIBLE FORCE!
I'VE BEEN INSTANTANEOUSLY TRANSPORTED... TO A LONELY GOVERNMENT TESTING LAB!
IT CAN ONLY BE... THE DOING OF THE COSMIC CUBE!
TESTING LAB
BUT WHY? WHY DID THE SKULL WILL ME HERE?
3.

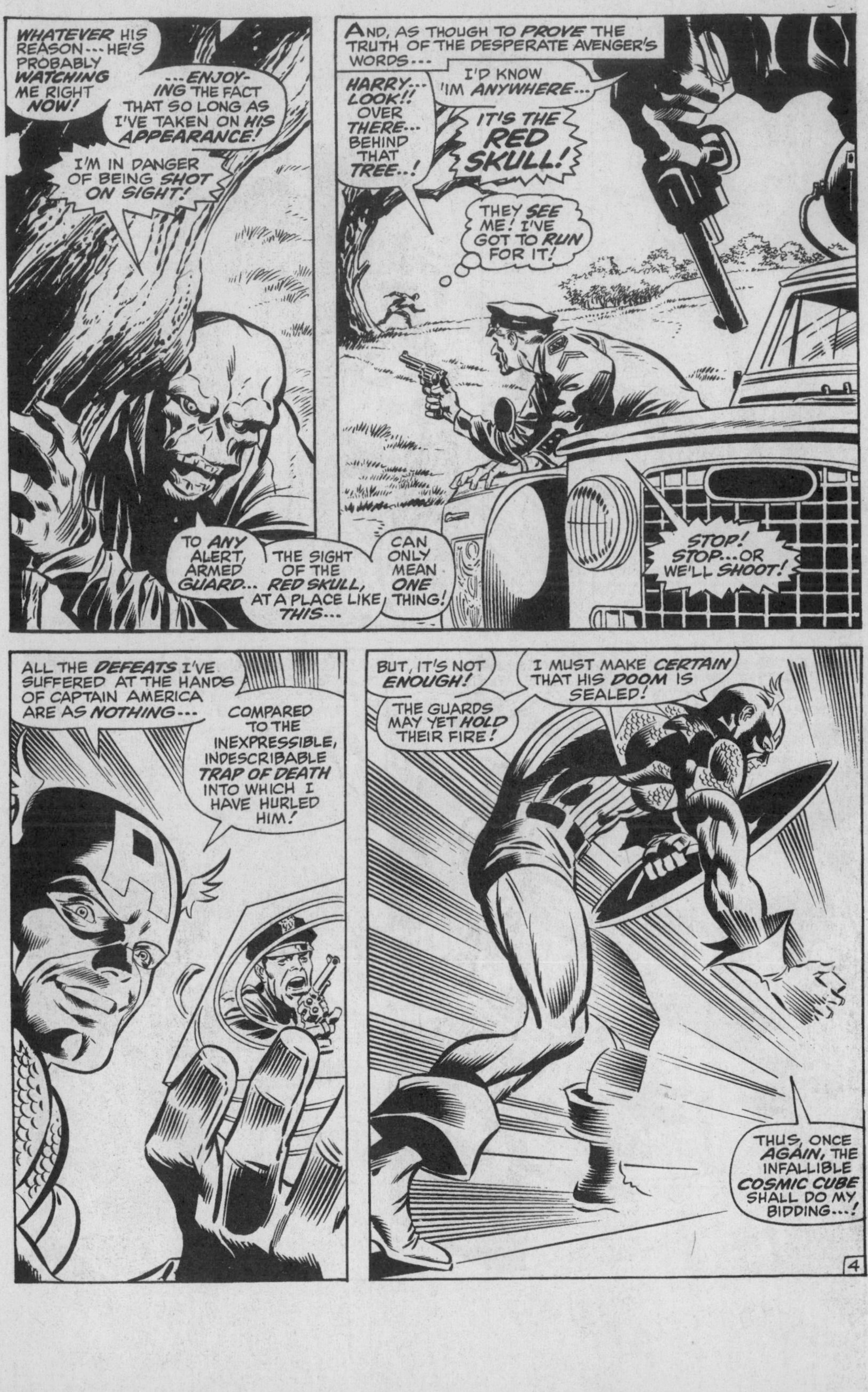
WHATEVER HIS REASON--- HE'S PROBABLY WATCHING ME RIGHT NOW!
---ENJOYING THE FACT THAT SO LONG AS I'VE TAKEN ON HIS APPEARANCE!
I'M IN DANGER OF BEING SHOT ON SIGHT!
TO ANY ALERT, ARMED GUARD...
THE SIGHT OF THE RED SKULL, AT A PLACE LIKE THIS...
CAN ONLY MEAN ONE THING!
AND, AS THOUGH TO PROVE THE TRUTH OF THE DESPERATE AVENGER'S WORDS---
HARRY... LOOK!! OVER THERE... BEHIND THAT TREE...!
I'D KNOW 'IM ANYWHERE...
IT'S THE RED SKULL!
THEY SEE ME! I'VE GOT TO RUN FOR IT!
STOP! STOP...OR WE'LL SHOOT!
ALL THE DEFEATS I'VE SUFFERED AT THE HANDS OF CAPTAIN AMERICA ARE AS NOTHING---
COMPARED TO THE INEXPRESSIBLE, INDESCRIBABLE TRAP OF DEATH INTO WHICH I HAVE HURLED HIM!
BUT, IT'S NOT ENOUGH!
THE GUARDS MAY YET HOLD THEIR FIRE!
I MUST MAKE CERTAIN THAT HIS DOOM IS SEALED!
THUS, ONCE AGAIN, THE INFALLIBLE COSMIC CUBE SHALL DO MY BIDDING...!
4

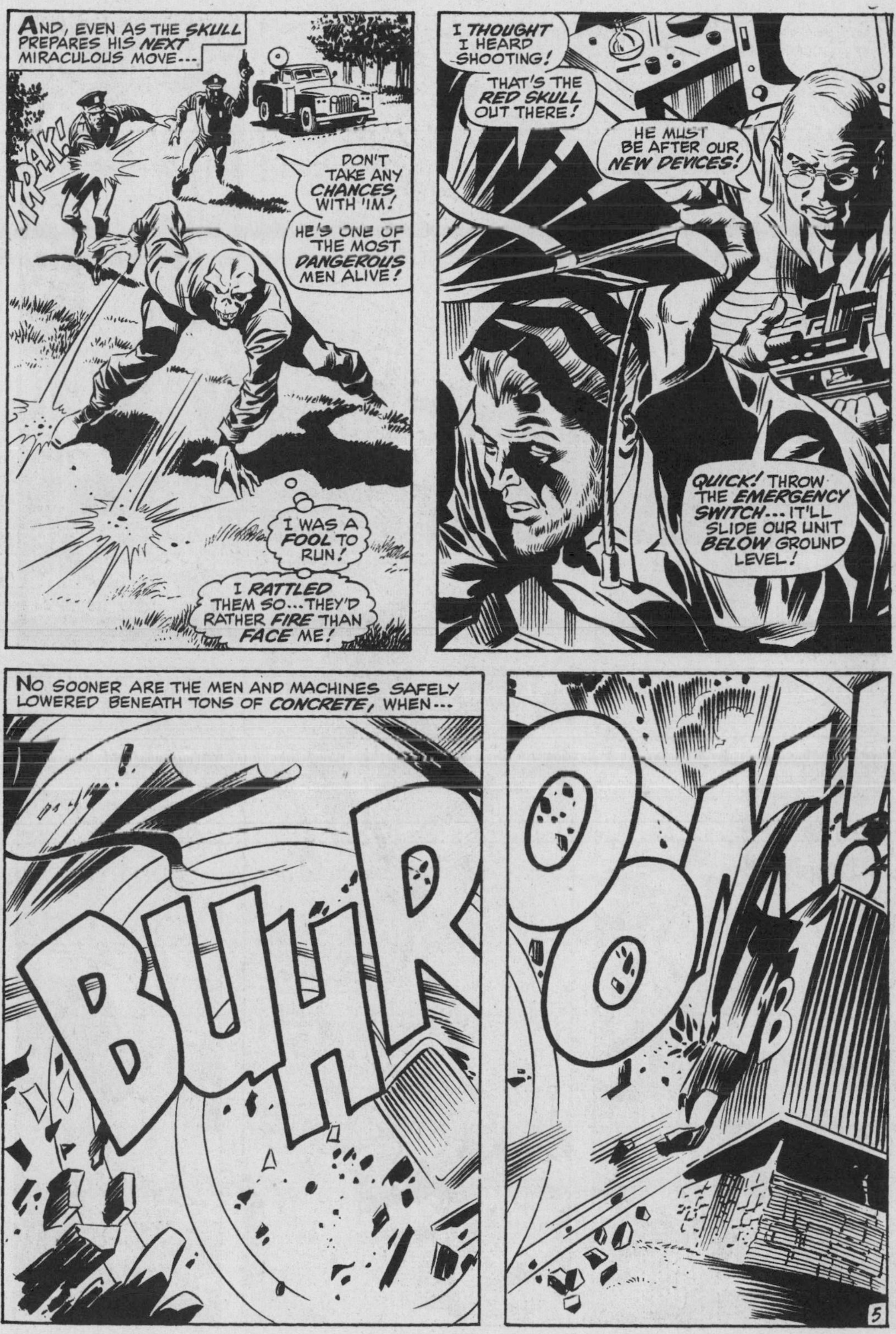

AND, EVEN AS THE SKULL PREPARES HIS NEXT MIRACULOUS MOVE---
KRAK!
DON'T TAKE ANY CHANCES WITH 'IM!
HE'S ONE OF THE MOST DANGEROUS MEN ALIVE!
I WAS A FOOL TO RUN!
I RATTLED THEM SO...THEY'D RATHER FIRE THAN FACE ME!
I THOUGHT I HEARD SHOOTING!
THAT'S THE RED SKULL OUT THERE!
HE MUST BE AFTER OUR NEW DEVICES!
QUICK! THROW THE EMERGENCY SWITCH... IT'LL SLIDE OUR UNIT BELOW GROUND LEVEL!
NO SOONER ARE THE MEN AND MACHINES SAFELY LOWERED BENEATH TONS OF CONCRETE, WHEN---
BUHROOM!
5

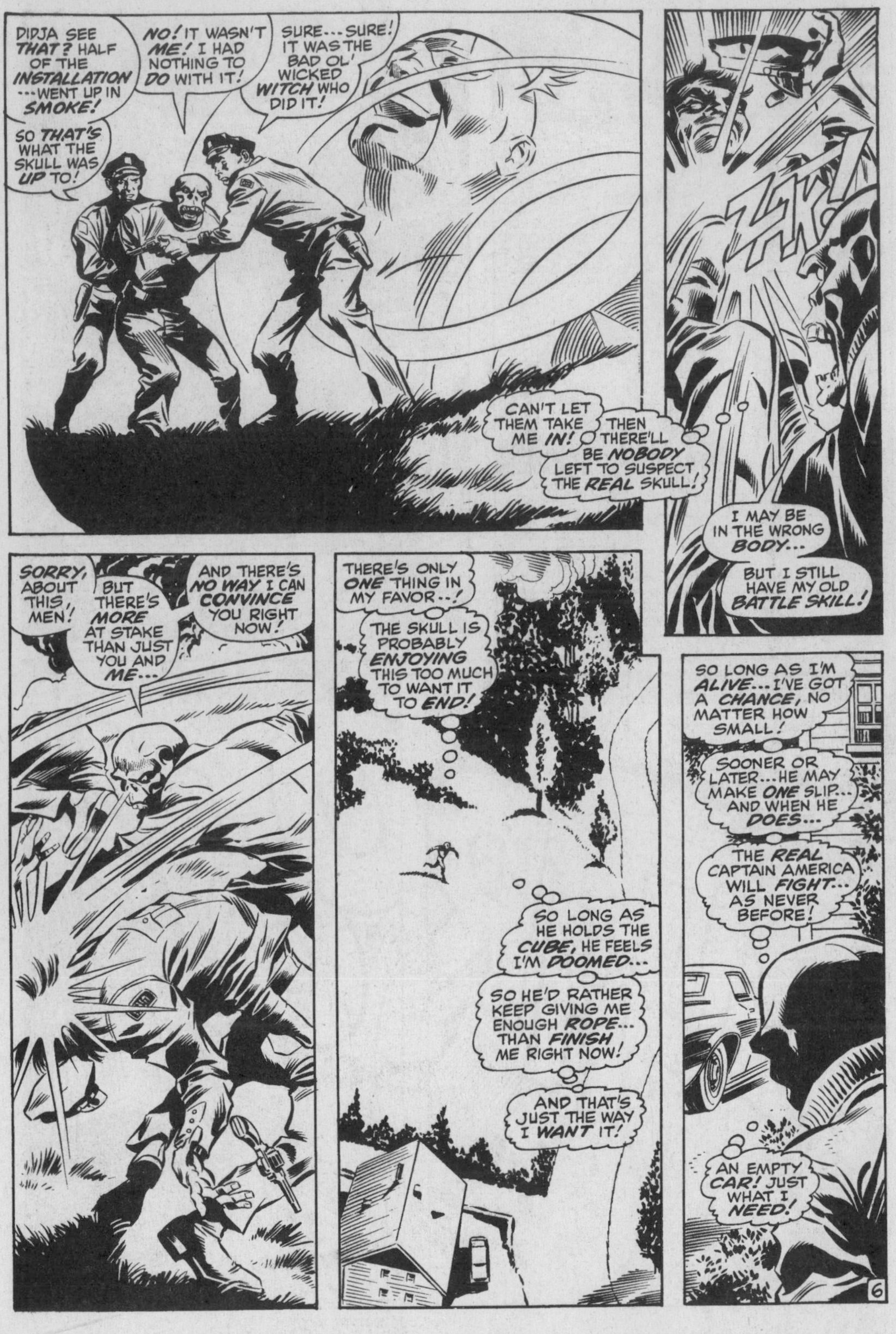

DIDJA SEE THAT? HALF OF THE INSTALLATION ---WENT UP IN SMOKE!
NO! IT WASN'T ME! I HAD NOTHING TO DO WITH IT!
SURE... SURE! IT WAS THE BAD OL' WICKED WITCH WHO DID IT!
SO THAT'S WHAT THE SKULL WAS UP TO!
CAN'T LET THEM TAKE ME IN!
THEN THERE'LL BE NOBODY LEFT TO SUSPECT THE REAL SKULL!
ZAK!
I MAY BE IN THE WRONG BODY...
BUT I STILL HAVE MY OLD BATTLE SKILL!
SORRY, ABOUT THIS, MEN!
BUT THERE'S MORE AT STAKE THAN JUST YOU AND ME...
AND THERE'S NO WAY I CAN CONVINCE YOU RIGHT NOW!
THERE'S ONLY ONE THING IN MY FAVOR..!
THE SKULL IS PROBABLY ENJOYING THIS TOO MUCH TO WANT IT TO END!
SO LONG AS HE HOLDS THE CUBE, HE FEELS I'M DOOMED...
SO HE'D RATHER KEEP GIVING ME ENOUGH ROPE... THAN FINISH ME RIGHT NOW!
AND THAT'S JUST THE WAY I WANT IT!
SO LONG AS I'M ALIVE... I'VE GOT A CHANCE, NO MATTER HOW SMALL!
SOONER OR LATER... HE MAY MAKE ONE SLIP... AND WHEN HE DOES...
THE REAL CAPTAIN AMERICA WILL FIGHT... AS NEVER BEFORE!
AN EMPTY CAR! JUST WHAT I NEED!
6

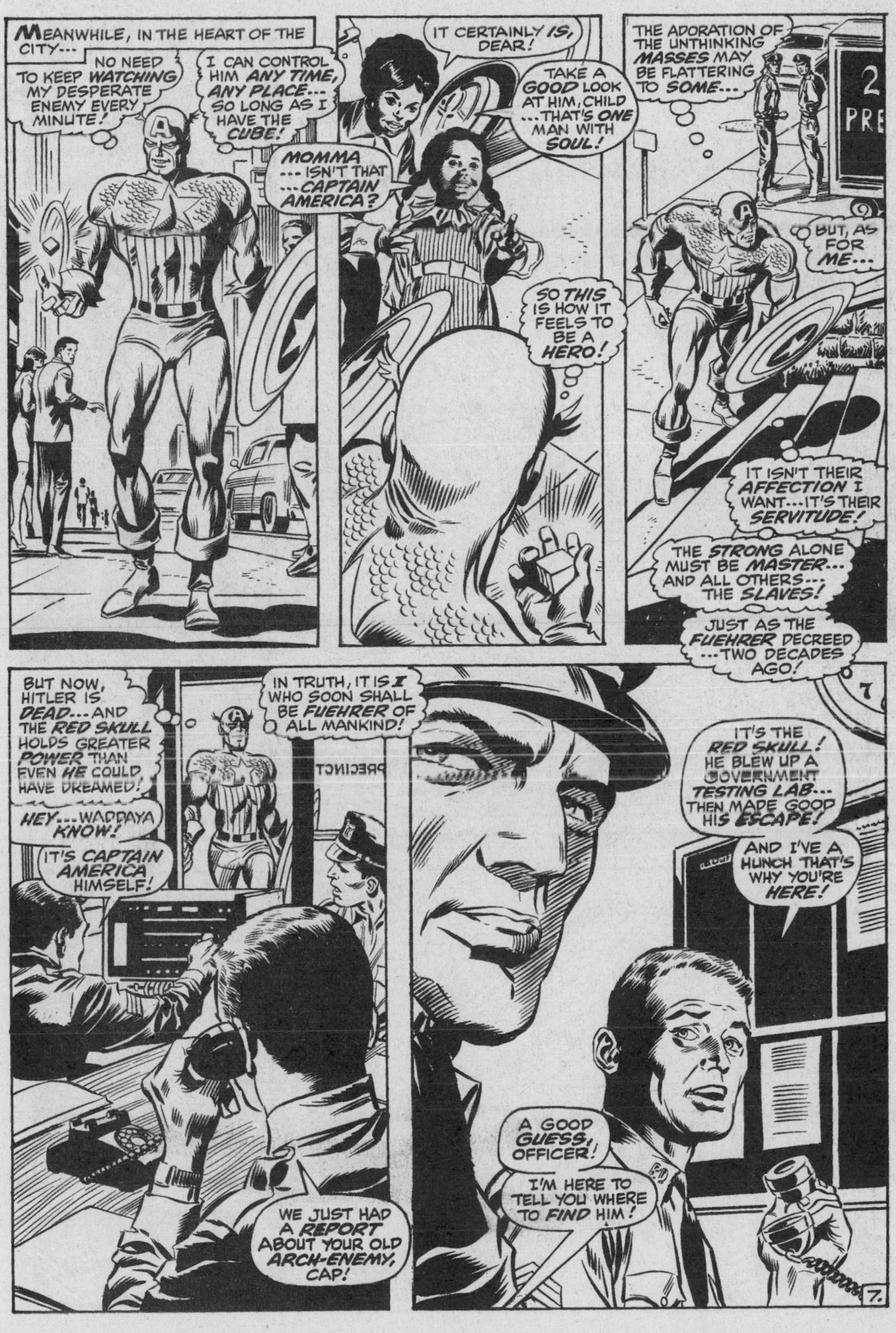
MEANWHILE, IN THE HEART OF THE CITY---
NO NEED TO KEEP WATCHING MY DESPERATE ENEMY EVERY MINUTE!
I CAN CONTROL HIM ANY TIME, ANY PLACE... SO LONG AS I HAVE THE CUBE!
MOMMA --- ISN'T THAT ...CAPTAIN AMERICA?
IT CERTAINLY IS, DEAR!
TAKE A GOOD LOOK AT HIM, CHILD ...THAT'S ONE MAN WITH SOUL!
SO THIS IS HOW IT FEELS TO BE A HERO!
THE ADORATION OF THE UNTHINKING MASSES MAY BE FLATTERING TO SOME...
BUT, AS FOR ME...
IT ISN'T THEIR AFFECTION I WANT...IT'S THEIR SERVITUDE!
THE STRONG ALONE MUST BE MASTER... AND ALL OTHERS... THE SLAVES!
JUST AS THE FUEHRER DECREED ...TWO DECADES AGO!
BUT NOW, HITLER IS DEAD... AND THE RED SKULL HOLDS GREATER POWER THAN EVEN HE COULD HAVE DREAMED!
IN TRUTH, IT IS I WHO SOON SHALL BE FUEHRER OF ALL MANKIND!
HEY...WADDAYA KNOW!
IT'S CAPTAIN AMERICA HIMSELF!
WE JUST HAD A REPORT ABOUT YOUR OLD ARCH-ENEMY, CAP!
IT'S THE RED SKULL! HE BLEW UP A GOVERNMENT TESTING LAB... THEN MADE GOOD HIS ESCAPE!
AND I'VE A HUNCH THAT'S WHY YOU'RE HERE!
A GOOD GUESS, OFFICER!
I'M HERE TO TELL YOU WHERE TO FIND HIM!
7.

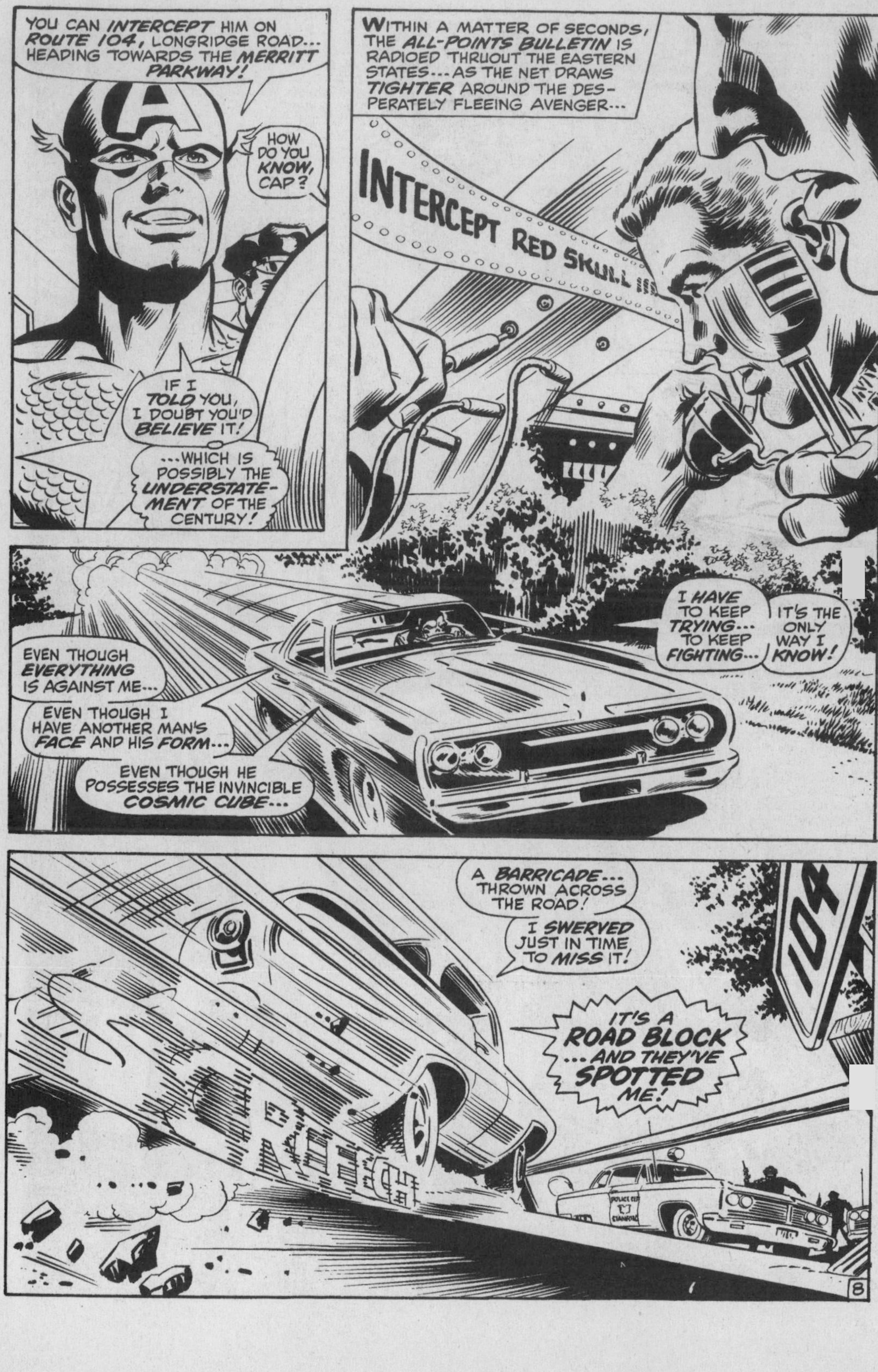
YOU CAN INTERCEPT HIM ON ROUTE 104, LONGRIDGE ROAD... HEADING TOWARDS THE MERRITT PARKWAY!
HOW DO YOU KNOW, CAP?
IF I TOLD YOU, I DOUBT YOU'D BELIEVE IT!
...WHICH IS POSSIBLY THE UNDERSTATEMENT OF THE CENTURY!
WITHIN A MATTER OF SECONDS, THE ALL-POINTS BULLETIN IS RADIOED THRUOUT THE EASTERN STATES... AS THE NET DRAWS TIGHTER AROUND THE DESPERATELY FLEEING AVENGER...
INTERCEPT RED SKULL
EVEN THOUGH EVERYTHING IS AGAINST ME...
EVEN THOUGH I HAVE ANOTHER MAN'S FACE AND HIS FORM...
EVEN THOUGH HE POSSESSES THE INVINCIBLE COSMIC CUBE...
I HAVE TO KEEP TRYING... TO KEEP FIGHTING...
IT'S THE ONLY WAY I KNOW!
A BARRICADE... THROWN ACROSS THE ROAD!
I SWERVED JUST IN TIME TO MISS IT!
IT'S A ROAD BLOCK ...AND THEY'VE SPOTTED ME!
104
SCREECH
8

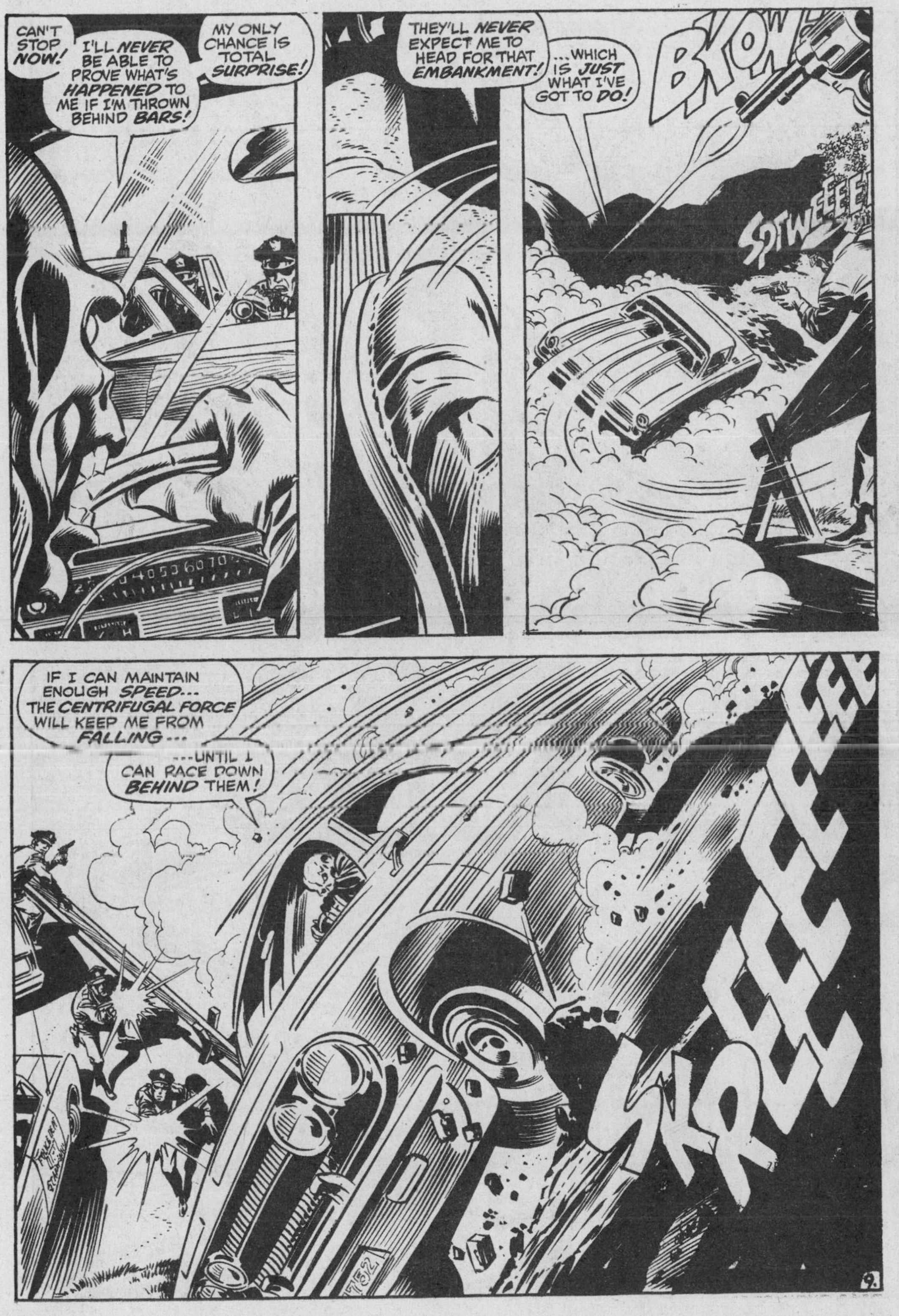
CAN'T STOP NOW!
I'LL NEVER BE ABLE TO PROVE WHAT'S HAPPENED TO ME IF I'M THROWN BEHIND BARS!
MY ONLY CHANCE IS TOTAL SURPRISE!
THEY'LL NEVER EXPECT ME TO HEAD FOR THAT EMBANKMENT!
...WHICH IS JUST WHAT I'VE GOT TO DO!
BKOW
SPTWEEEE
IF I CAN MAINTAIN ENOUGH SPEED... THE CENTRIFUGAL FORCE WILL KEEP ME FROM FALLING...
...UNTIL I CAN RACE DOWN BEHIND THEM!
SKREEEEEE
9.

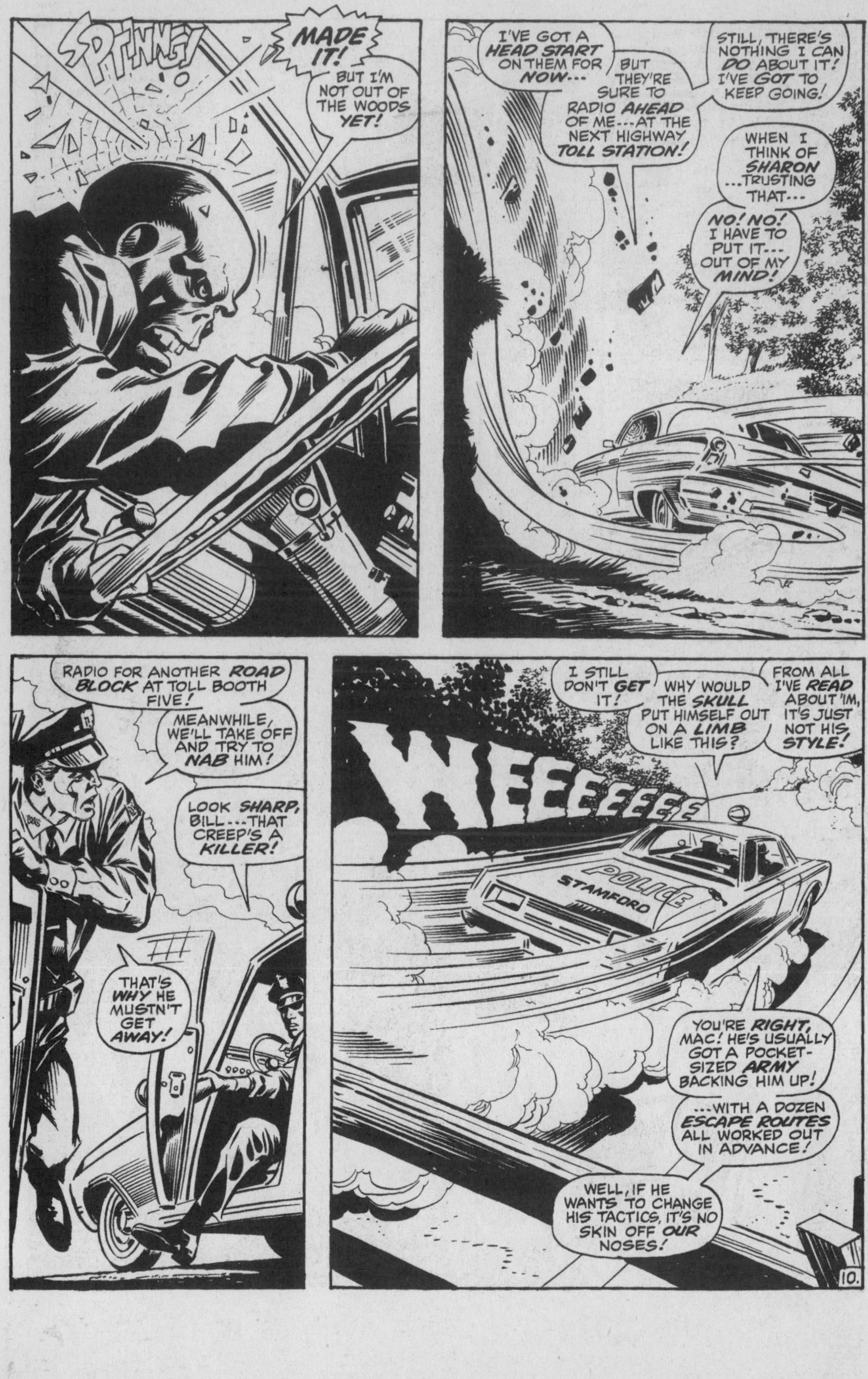
SPTINNG!
MADE IT!
BUT I'M NOT OUT OF THE WOODS YET!
I'VE GOT A HEAD START ON THEM FOR NOW...
BUT THEY'RE SURE TO RADIO AHEAD OF ME---AT THE NEXT HIGHWAY TOLL STATION!
STILL, THERE'S NOTHING I CAN DO ABOUT IT! I'VE GOT TO KEEP GOING!
WHEN I THINK OF SHARON ...TRUSTING THAT---
NO! NO! I HAVE TO PUT IT--- OUT OF MY MIND!
RADIO FOR ANOTHER ROAD BLOCK AT TOLL BOOTH FIVE!
MEANWHILE, WE'LL TAKE OFF AND TRY TO NAB HIM!
LOOK SHARP, BILL---THAT CREEP'S A KILLER!
THAT'S WHY HE MUSTN'T GET AWAY!
I STILL DON'T GET IT!
WHY WOULD THE SKULL PUT HIMSELF OUT ON A LIMB LIKE THIS?
FROM ALL I'VE READ ABOUT 'IM, IT'S JUST NOT HIS STYLE!
WEEEEEEE
POLICE
STAMFORD
YOU'RE RIGHT, MAC! HE'S USUALLY GOT A POCKET-SIZED ARMY BACKING HIM UP!
...WITH A DOZEN ESCAPE ROUTES ALL WORKED OUT IN ADVANCE!
WELL, IF HE WANTS TO CHANGE HIS TACTICS, IT'S NO SKIN OFF OUR NOSES!
10.

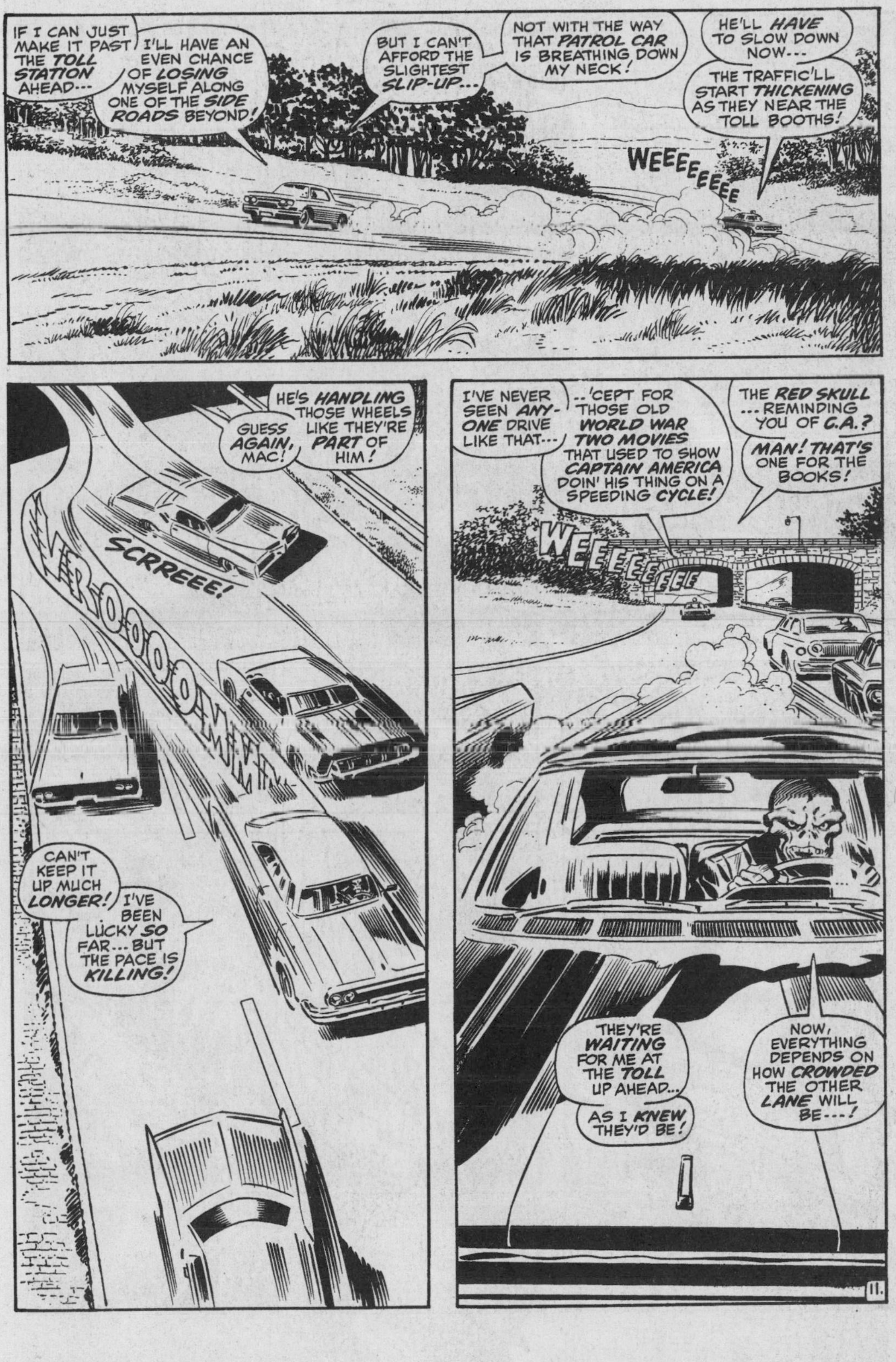
IF I CAN JUST MAKE IT PAST THE TOLL STATION AHEAD---
I'LL HAVE AN EVEN CHANCE OF LOSING MYSELF ALONG ONE OF THE SIDE ROADS BEYOND!
BUT I CAN'T AFFORD THE SLIGHTEST SLIP-UP...
NOT WITH THE WAY THAT PATROL CAR IS BREATHING DOWN MY NECK!
HE'LL HAVE TO SLOW DOWN NOW---
THE TRAFFIC'LL START THICKENING AS THEY NEAR THE TOLL BOOTHS!
WEEEEEEEE
HE'S HANDLING THOSE WHEELS LIKE THEY'RE PART OF HIM!
GUESS AGAIN, MAC!
SCRREEE!
VROOOOMMM
CAN'T KEEP IT UP MUCH LONGER!
I'VE BEEN LUCKY SO FAR... BUT THE PACE IS KILLING!
I'VE NEVER SEEN ANY-ONE DRIVE LIKE THAT---
..'CEPT FOR THOSE OLD WORLD WAR TWO MOVIES THAT USED TO SHOW CAPTAIN AMERICA DOIN' HIS THING ON A SPEEDING CYCLE!
THE RED SKULL ... REMINDING YOU OF C.A.?
MAN! THAT'S ONE FOR THE BOOKS!
WEEEEEEEE
THEY'RE WAITING FOR ME AT THE TOLL UP AHEAD...
AS I KNEW THEY'D BE!
NOW, EVERYTHING DEPENDS ON HOW CROWDED THE OTHER LANE WILL BE---!
11.

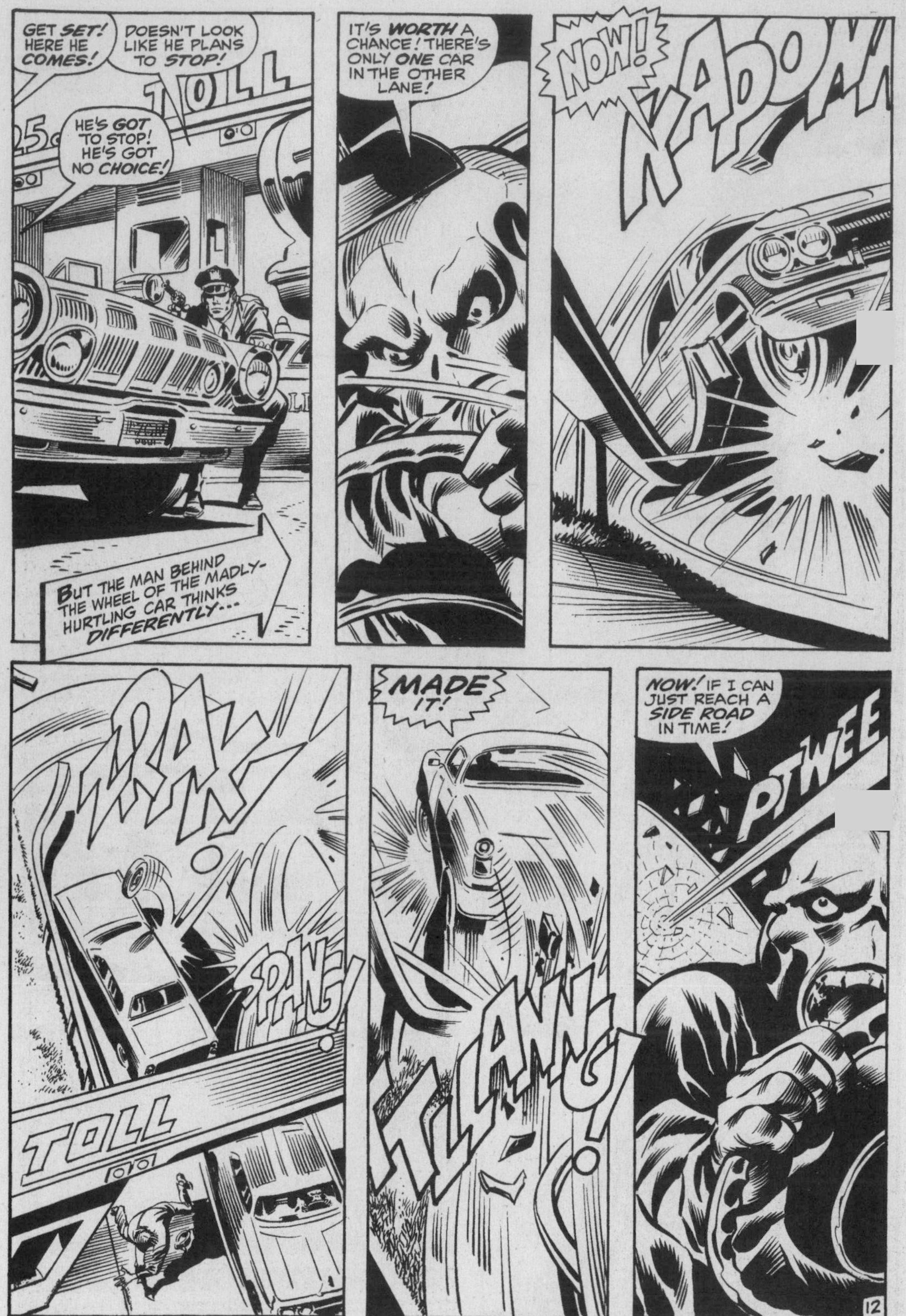
GET SET! HERE HE COMES!
DOESN'T LOOK LIKE HE PLANS TO STOP!
TOLL
HE'S GOT TO STOP! HE'S GOT NO CHOICE!
BUT THE MAN BEHIND THE WHEEL OF THE MADLY-HURTLING CAR THINKS DIFFERENTLY...
IT'S WORTH A CHANCE! THERE'S ONLY ONE CAR IN THE OTHER LANE!
NOW!
K-ADOOM
KRAK
SPANG!
TOLL
MADE IT!
KLLANNG!
NOW! IF I CAN JUST REACH A SIDE ROAD IN TIME!
PTWEE
12

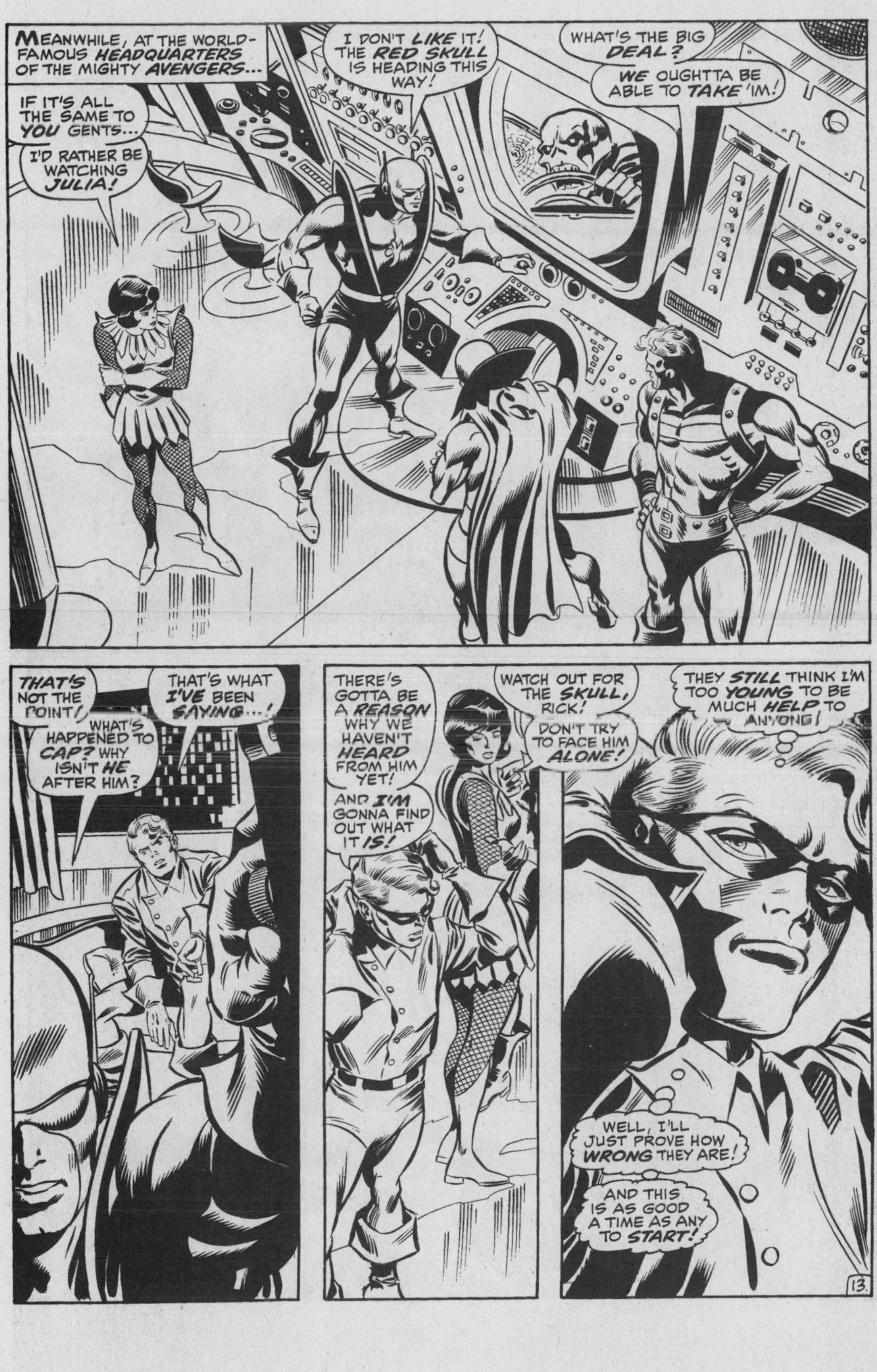
MEANWHILE, AT THE WORLD-FAMOUS HEADQUARTERS OF THE MIGHTY AVENGERS...
I DON'T LIKE IT! THE RED SKULL IS HEADING THIS WAY!
WHAT'S THE BIG DEAL?
WE OUGHTTA BE ABLE TO TAKE 'IM!
IF IT'S ALL THE SAME TO YOU GENTS...
I'D RATHER BE WATCHING JULIA!
THAT'S NOT THE POINT!
WHAT'S HAPPENED TO CAP? WHY ISN'T HE AFTER HIM?
THAT'S WHAT I'VE BEEN SAYING...!
THERE'S GOTTA BE A REASON WHY WE HAVEN'T HEARD FROM HIM YET!
AND I'M GONNA FIND OUT WHAT IT IS!
WATCH OUT FOR THE SKULL, RICK!
DON'T TRY TO FACE HIM ALONE!
THEY STILL THINK I'M TOO YOUNG TO BE MUCH HELP TO ANYONE!
WELL, I'LL JUST PROVE HOW WRONG THEY ARE!
AND THIS IS AS GOOD A TIME AS ANY TO START!
13.

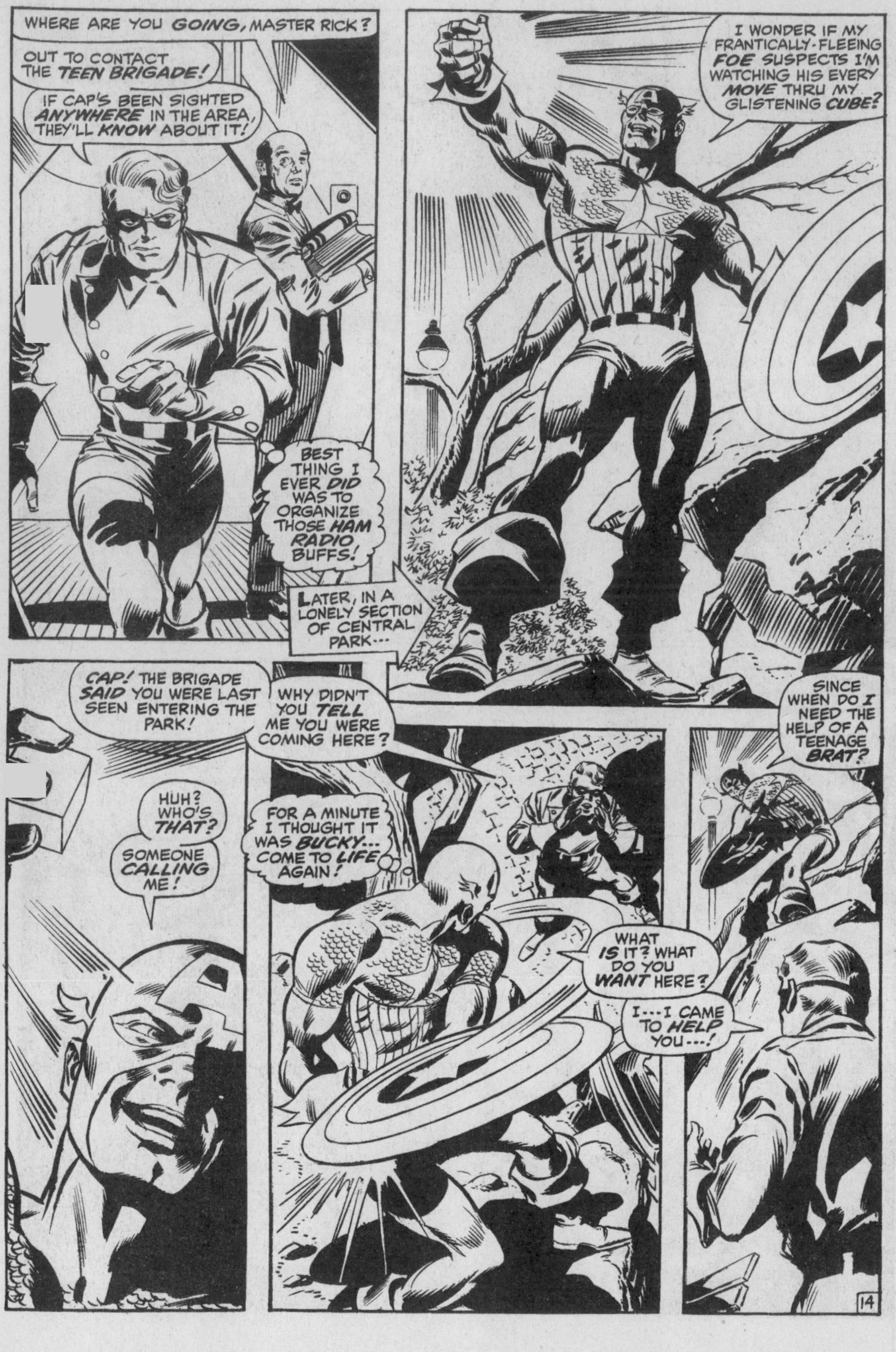
WHERE ARE YOU GOING, MASTER RICK?
OUT TO CONTACT THE TEEN BRIGADE!
IF CAP'S BEEN SIGHTED ANYWHERE IN THE AREA, THEY'LL KNOW ABOUT IT!
BEST THING I EVER DID WAS TO ORGANIZE THOSE HAM RADIO BUFFS!
LATER, IN A LONELY SECTION OF CENTRAL PARK...
I WONDER IF MY FRANTICALLY-FLEEING FOE SUSPECTS I'M WATCHING HIS EVERY MOVE THRU MY GLISTENING CUBE?
CAP! THE BRIGADE SAID YOU WERE LAST SEEN ENTERING THE PARK!
HUH? WHO'S THAT?
SOMEONE CALLING ME!
WHY DIDN'T YOU TELL ME YOU WERE COMING HERE?
FOR A MINUTE I THOUGHT IT WAS BUCKY... COME TO LIFE AGAIN!
SINCE WHEN DO I NEED THE HELP OF A TEENAGE BRAT?
WHAT IS IT? WHAT DO YOU WANT HERE?
I--- I CAME TO HELP YOU---!
14

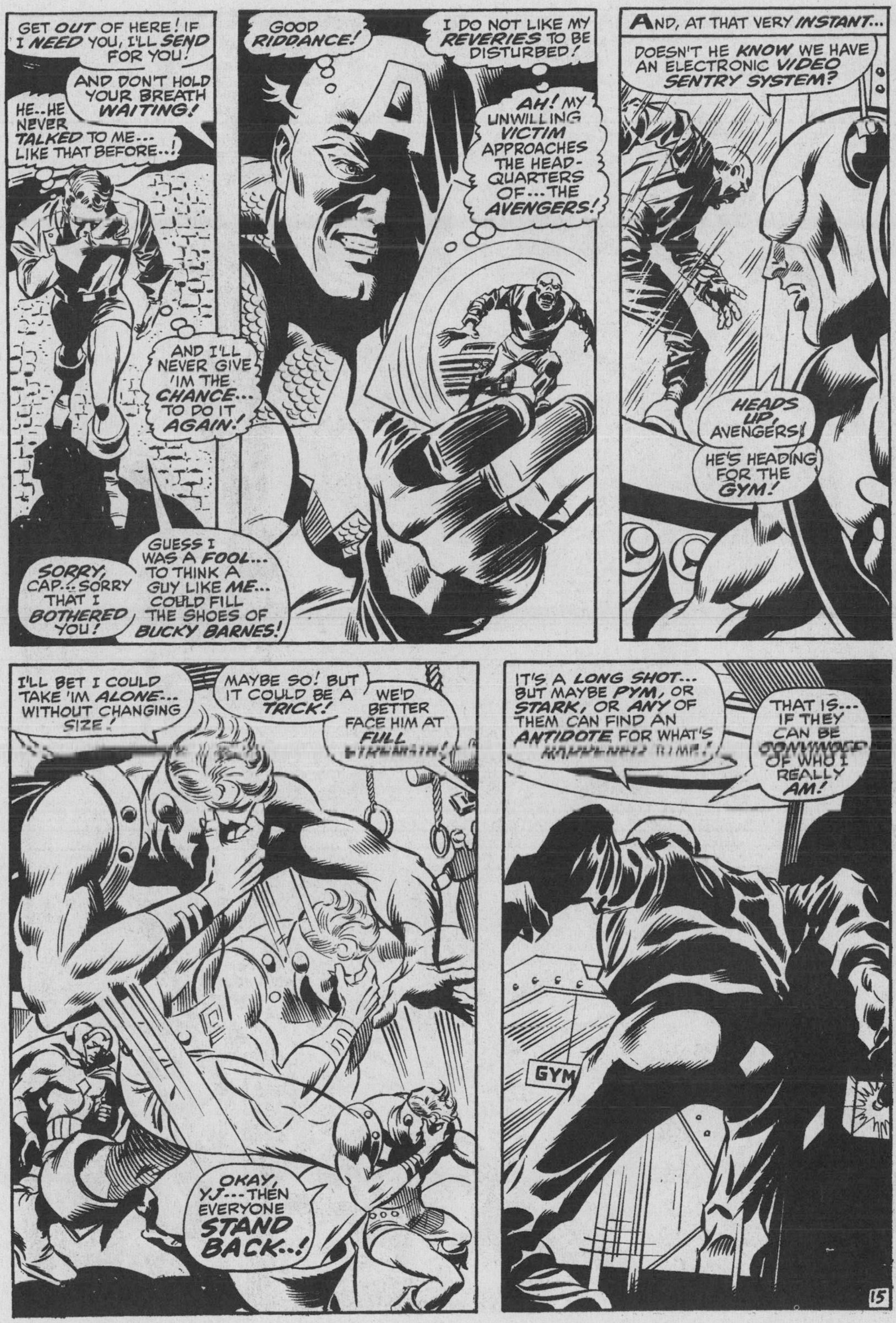
GET OUT OF HERE! IF I NEED YOU, I'LL SEND FOR YOU!
AND DON'T HOLD YOUR BREATH WAITING!
HE..HE NEVER TALKED TO ME... LIKE THAT BEFORE..!
AND I'LL NEVER GIVE 'IM THE CHANCE... TO DO IT AGAIN!
GUESS I WAS A FOOL... TO THINK A GUY LIKE ME... COULD FILL THE SHOES OF BUCKY BARNES!
SORRY, CAP... SORRY THAT I BOTHERED YOU!
GOOD RIDDANCE!
I DO NOT LIKE MY REVERIES TO BE DISTURBED!
AH! MY UNWILLING VICTIM APPROACHES THE HEAD-QUARTERS OF... THE AVENGERS!
AND, AT THAT VERY INSTANT...
DOESN'T HE KNOW WE HAVE AN ELECTRONIC VIDEO SENTRY SYSTEM?
HEADS UP, AVENGERS!
HE'S HEADING FOR THE GYM!
I'LL BET I COULD TAKE 'IM ALONE... WITHOUT CHANGING SIZE!
MAYBE SO! BUT IT COULD BE A TRICK!
WE'D BETTER FACE HIM AT FULL
OKAY, YJ... THEN EVERYONE STAND BACK..!
IT'S A LONG SHOT... BUT MAYBE PYM, OR STARK, OR ANY OF THEM CAN FIND AN ANTIDOTE FOR WHAT'S
THAT IS... IF THEY CAN BE
OF WHO I REALLY AM!
GYM
15

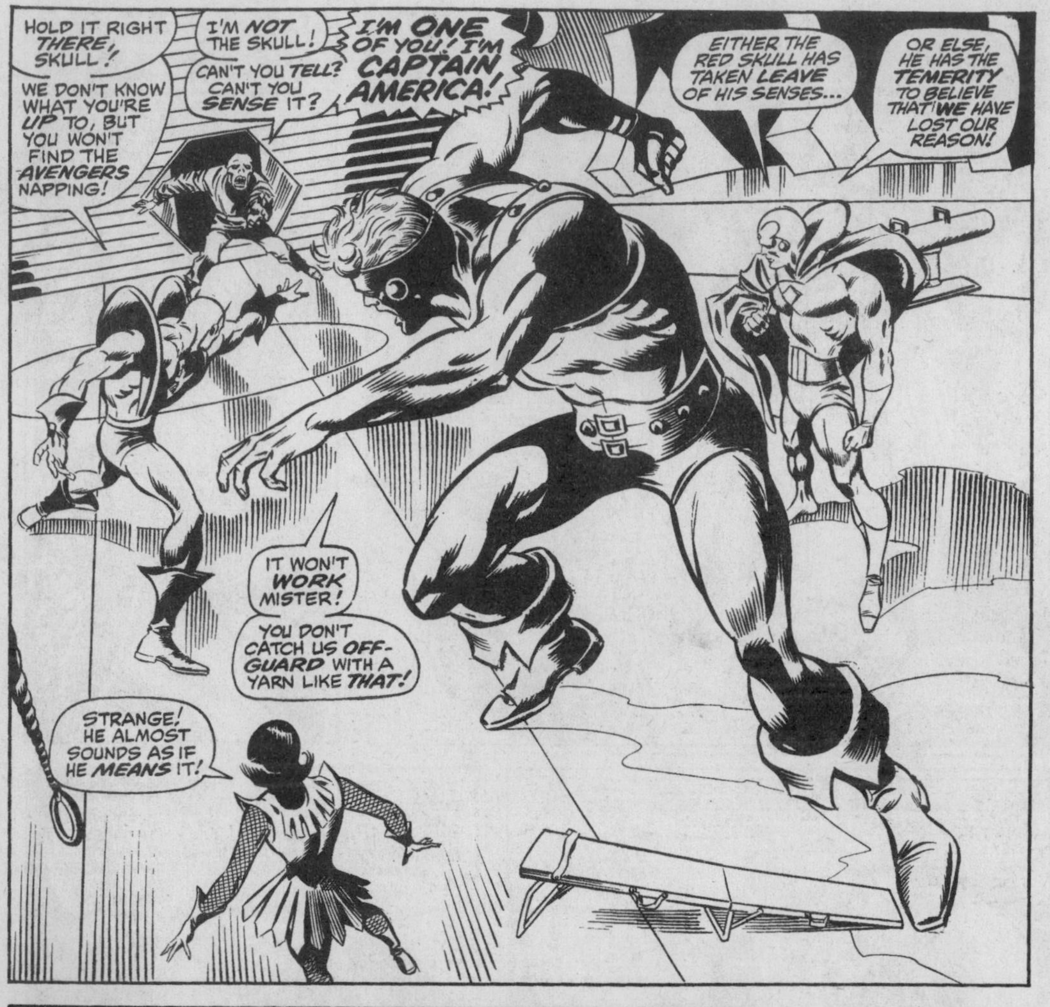
HOLD IT RIGHT THERE, SKULL!
WE DON'T KNOW WHAT YOU'RE UP TO, BUT YOU WON'T FIND THE AVENGERS NAPPING!
I'M NOT THE SKULL!
CAN'T YOU TELL? CAN'T YOU SENSE IT?
I'M ONE OF YOU! I'M CAPTAIN AMERICA!
EITHER THE RED SKULL HAS TAKEN LEAVE OF HIS SENSES...
OR ELSE, HE HAS THE TEMERITY TO BELIEVE THAT WE HAVE LOST OUR REASON!
IT WON'T WORK MISTER!
YOU DON'T CATCH US OFF-GUARD WITH A YARN LIKE THAT!
STRANGE! HE ALMOST SOUNDS AS IF HE MEANS IT!

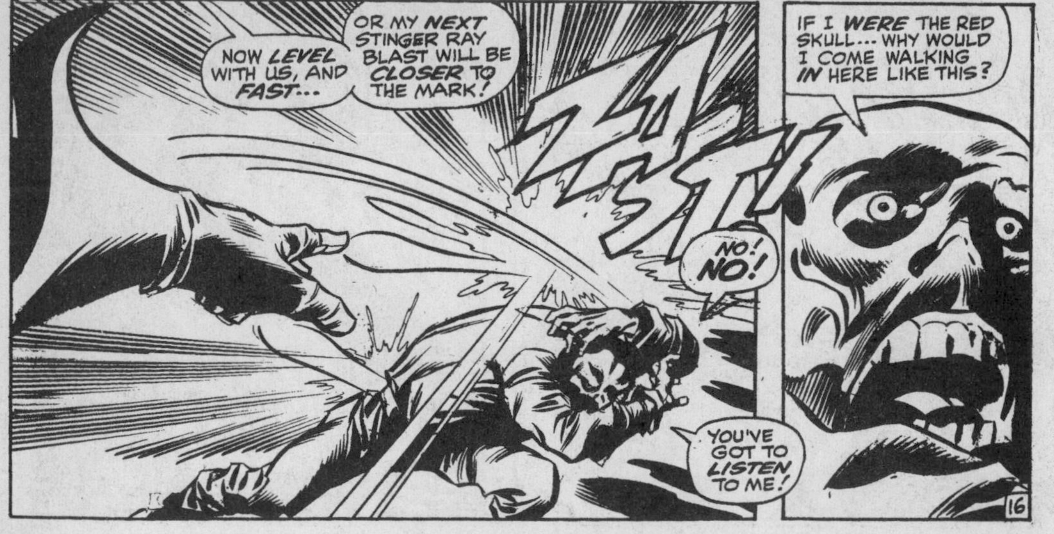
NOW LEVEL WITH US, AND FAST...
OR MY NEXT STINGER RAY BLAST WILL BE CLOSER TO THE MARK!
ZZAT!
NO! NO!
YOU'VE GOT TO LISTEN TO ME!
IF I WERE THE RED SKULL... WHY WOULD I COME WALKING IN HERE LIKE THIS?
16

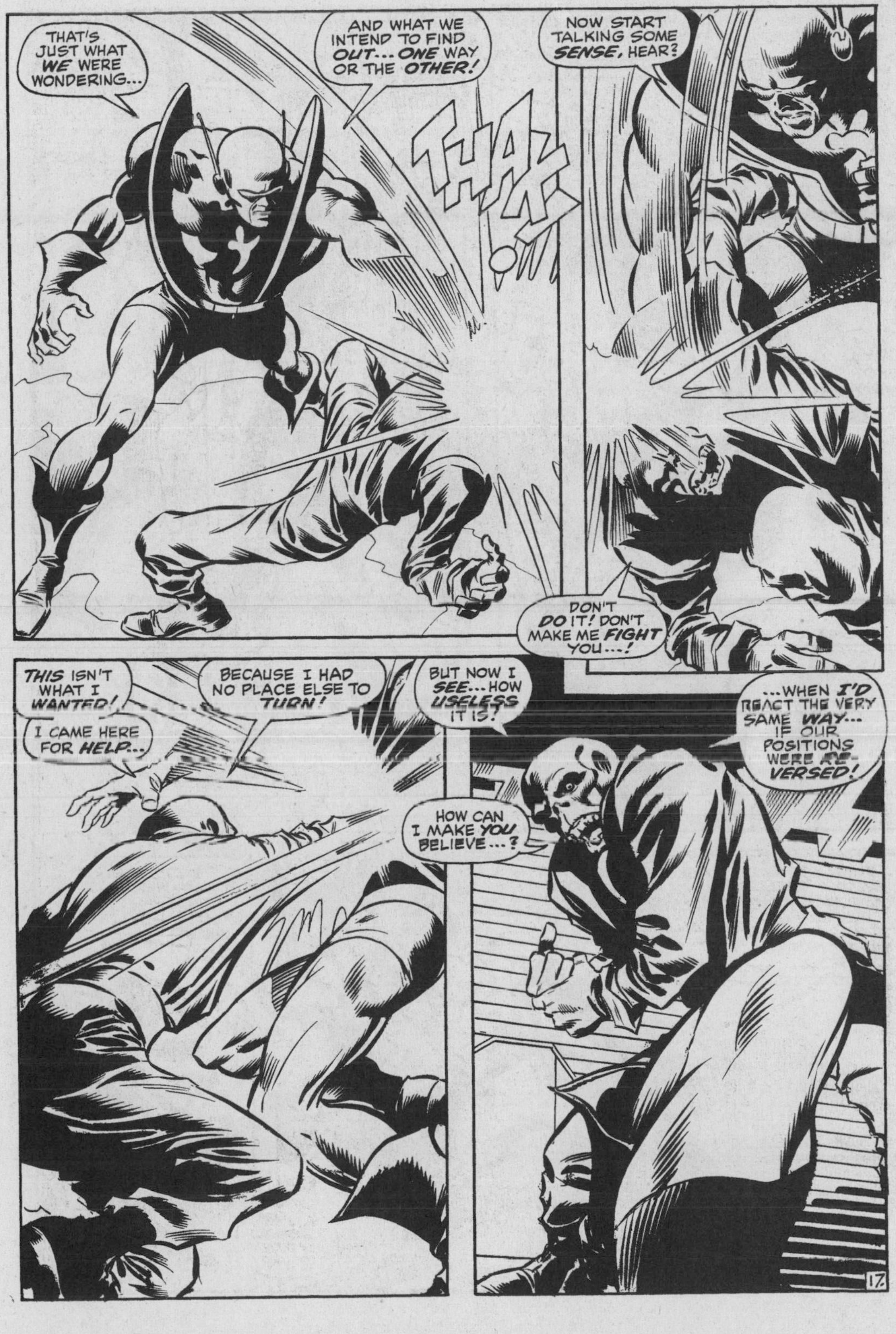
THAT'S JUST WHAT WE WERE WONDERING...
AND WHAT WE INTEND TO FIND OUT... ONE WAY OR THE OTHER!
THAK
NOW START TALKING SOME SENSE, HEAR?
DON'T DO IT! DON'T MAKE ME FIGHT YOU...!
THIS ISN'T WHAT I WANTED!
I CAME HERE FOR HELP...
BECAUSE I HAD NO PLACE ELSE TO TURN!
BUT NOW I SEE... HOW USELESS IT IS!
HOW CAN I MAKE YOU BELIEVE...?
...WHEN I'D REACT THE VERY SAME WAY... IF OUR POSITIONS WERE RE-VERSED!
17

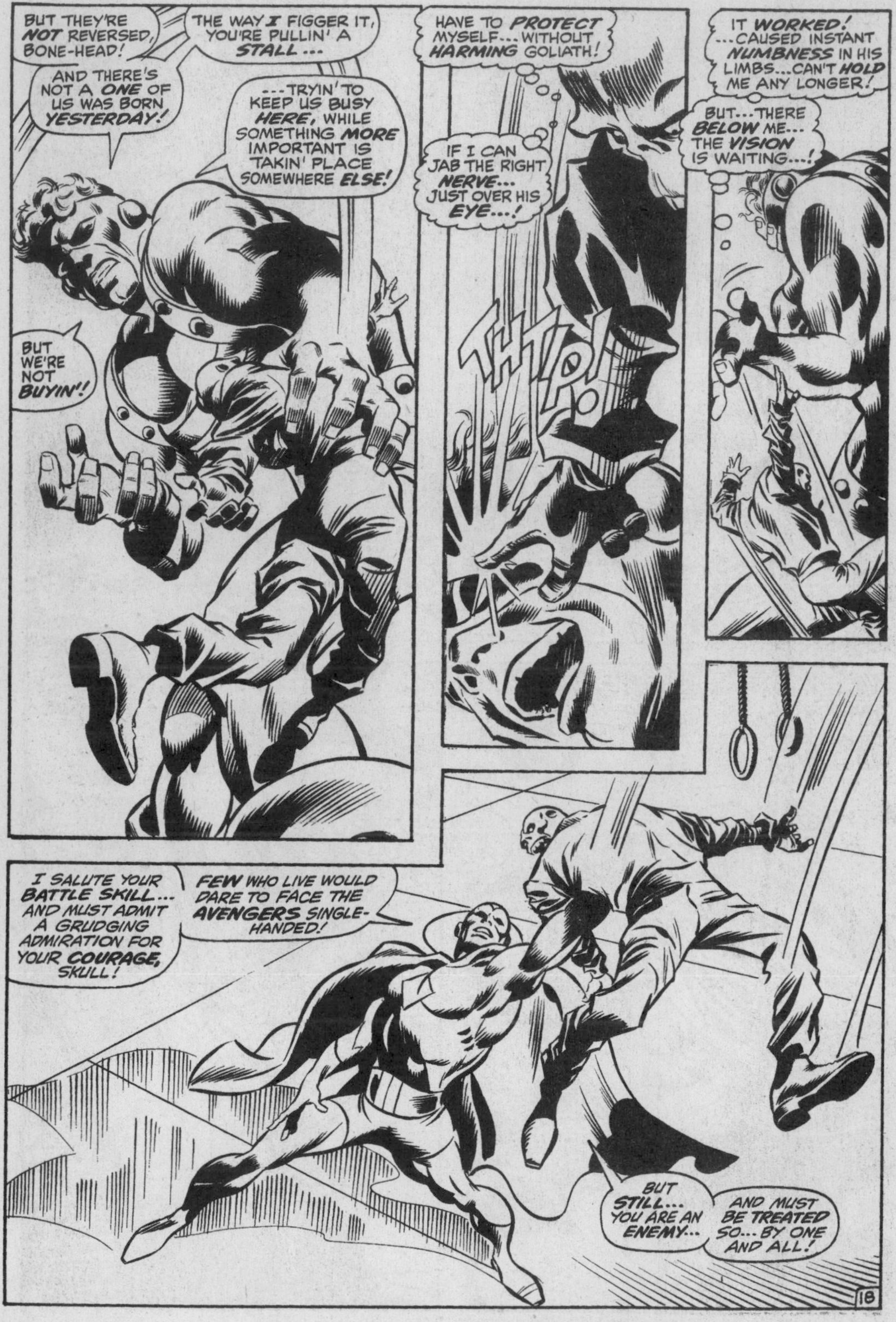

BUT THEY'RE NOT REVERSED, BONE-HEAD!
THE WAY I FIGGER IT, YOU'RE PULLIN' A STALL...
AND THERE'S NOT A ONE OF US WAS BORN YESTERDAY!
...TRYIN' TO KEEP US BUSY HERE, WHILE SOMETHING MORE IMPORTANT IS TAKIN' PLACE SOMEWHERE ELSE!
BUT WE'RE NOT BUYIN'!
HAVE TO PROTECT MYSELF... WITHOUT HARMING GOLIATH!
IF I CAN JAB THE RIGHT NERVE... JUST OVER HIS EYE...!
THTP!
IT WORKED! ...CAUSED INSTANT NUMBNESS IN HIS LIMBS...CAN'T HOLD ME ANY LONGER!
BUT... THERE BELOW ME... THE VISION IS WAITING...!
I SALUTE YOUR BATTLE SKILL... AND MUST ADMIT A GRUDGING ADMIRATION FOR YOUR COURAGE, SKULL!
FEW WHO LIVE WOULD DARE TO FACE THE AVENGERS SINGLE-HANDED!
BUT STILL... YOU ARE AN ENEMY...
AND MUST BE TREATED SO... BY ONE AND ALL!
18

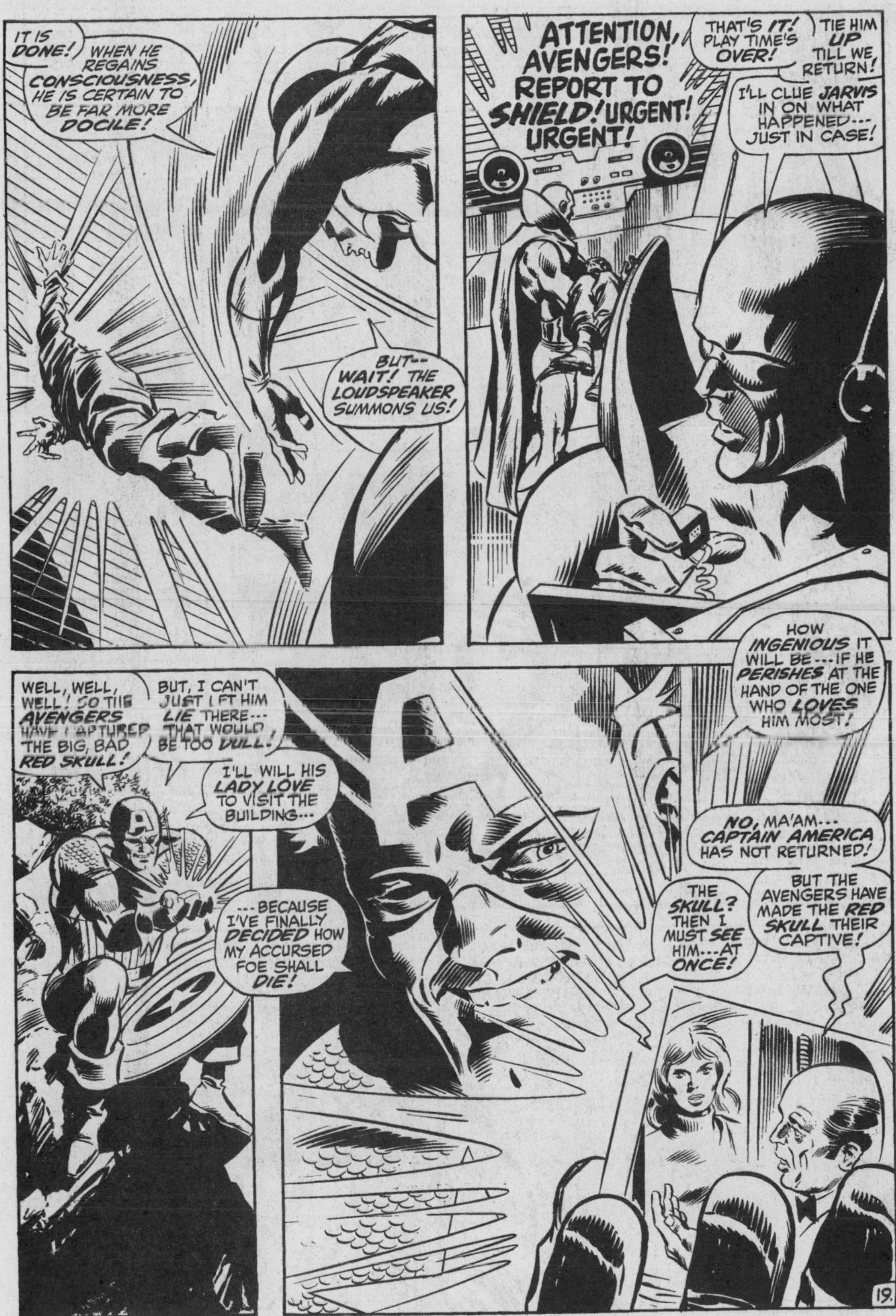
IT IS DONE!
WHEN HE REGAINS CONSCIOUSNESS, HE IS CERTAIN TO BE FAR MORE DOCILE!
BUT-- WAIT! THE LOUDSPEAKER SUMMONS US!
ATTENTION, AVENGERS! REPORT TO SHIELD! URGENT! URGENT!
THAT'S IT! PLAY TIME'S OVER!
TIE HIM UP TILL WE RETURN!
I'LL CLUE JARVIS IN ON WHAT HAPPENED--- JUST IN CASE!
WELL, WELL, WELL! SO THE AVENGERS HAVE CAPTURED THE BIG, BAD RED SKULL!
BUT, I CAN'T JUST LET HIM LIE THERE--- THAT WOULD BE TOO DULL!
I'LL WILL HIS LADY LOVE TO VISIT THE BUILDING...
---BECAUSE I'VE FINALLY DECIDED HOW MY ACCURSED FOE SHALL DIE!
HOW INGENIOUS IT WILL BE---IF HE PERISHES AT THE HAND OF THE ONE WHO LOVES HIM MOST!
NO, MA'AM... CAPTAIN AMERICA HAS NOT RETURNED!
BUT THE AVENGERS HAVE MADE THE RED SKULL THEIR CAPTIVE!
THE SKULL? THEN I MUST SEE HIM...AT ONCE!
19.

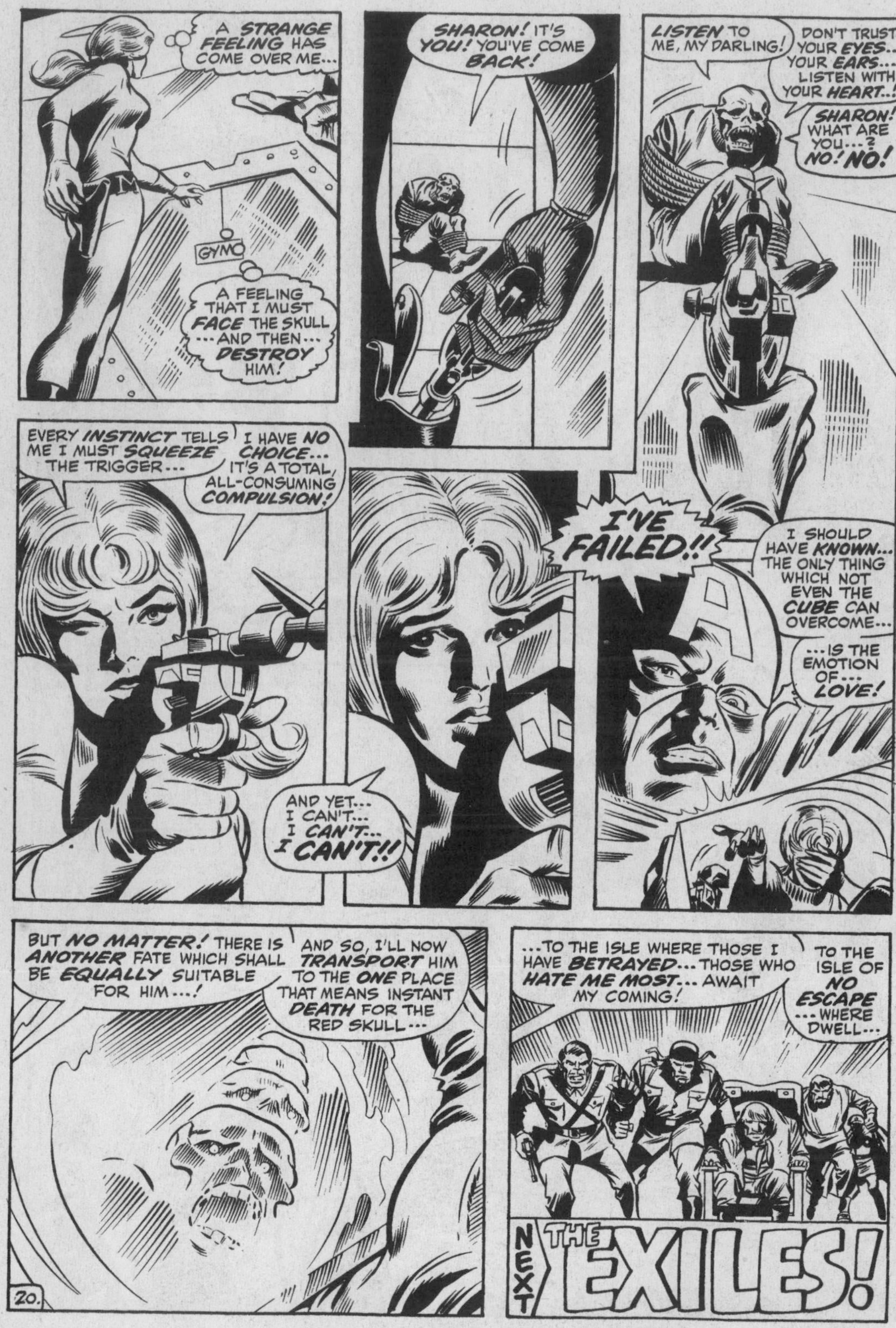
A STRANGE FEELING HAS COME OVER ME...
GYMO
A FEELING THAT I MUST FACE THE SKULL ...AND THEN... DESTROY HIM!
SHARON! IT'S YOU! YOU'VE COME BACK!
LISTEN TO ME, MY DARLING!
DON'T TRUST YOUR EYES.. YOUR EARS... LISTEN WITH YOUR HEART..!
SHARON! WHAT ARE YOU...? NO! NO!
EVERY INSTINCT TELLS ME I MUST SQUEEZE THE TRIGGER...
I HAVE NO CHOICE... IT'S A TOTAL, ALL-CONSUMING COMPULSION!
AND YET... I CAN'T... I CAN'T... I CAN'T!!
I'VE FAILED!!
I SHOULD HAVE KNOWN... THE ONLY THING WHICH NOT EVEN THE CUBE CAN OVERCOME...
...IS THE EMOTION OF... LOVE!
BUT NO MATTER! THERE IS ANOTHER FATE WHICH SHALL BE EQUALLY SUITABLE FOR HIM...!
AND SO, I'LL NOW TRANSPORT HIM TO THE ONE PLACE THAT MEANS INSTANT DEATH FOR THE RED SKULL...
20.
...TO THE ISLE WHERE THOSE I HAVE BETRAYED... THOSE WHO HATE ME MOST... AWAIT MY COMING!
TO THE ISLE OF NO ESCAPE ...WHERE DWELL...
NEXT THE EXILES!

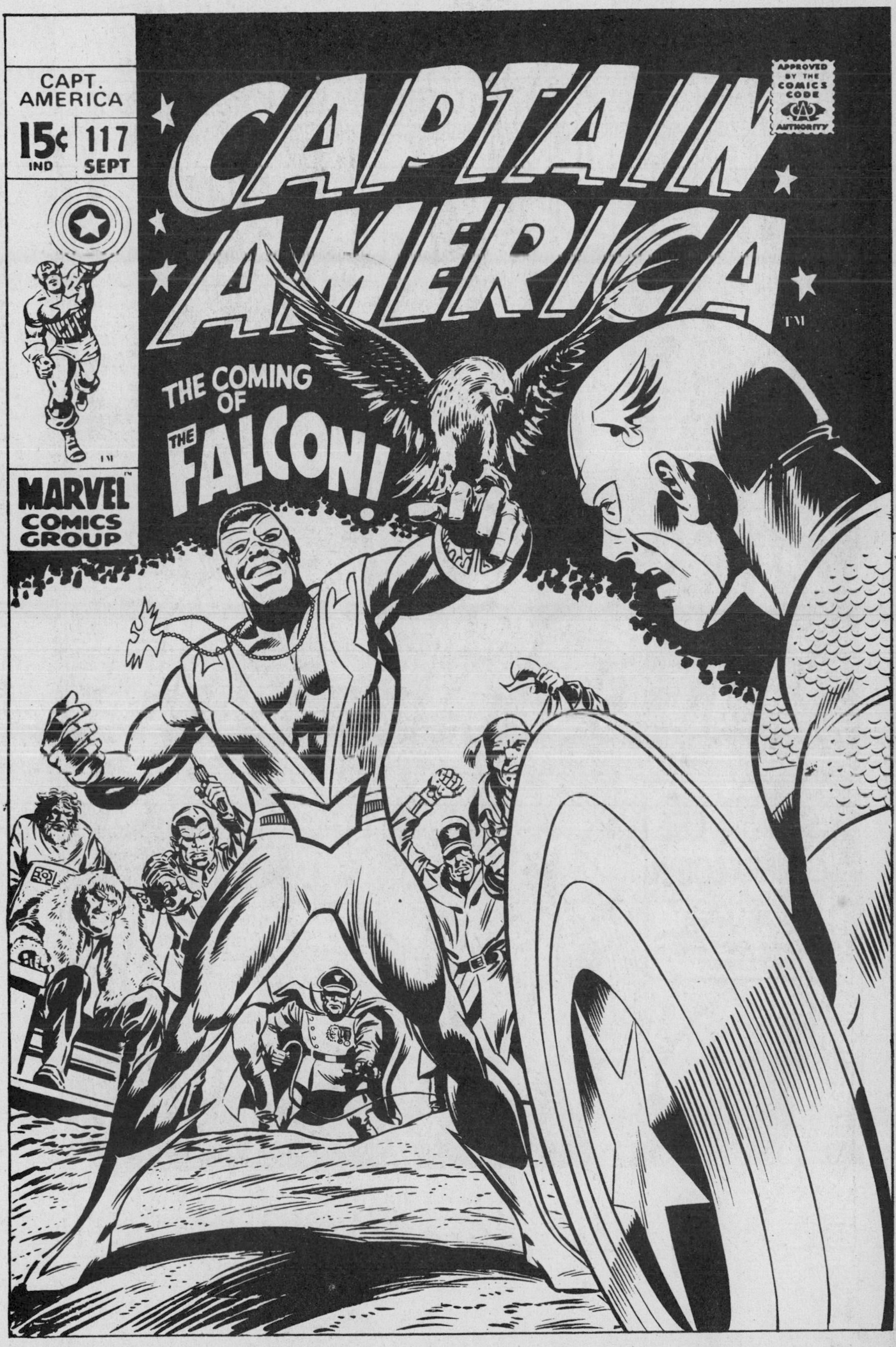

CAPT. AMERICA
15¢ IND
117 SEPT
MARVEL COMICS GROUP
APPROVED BY THE COMICS CODE AUTHORITY
CAPTAIN AMERICA
THE COMING OF THE FALCON!

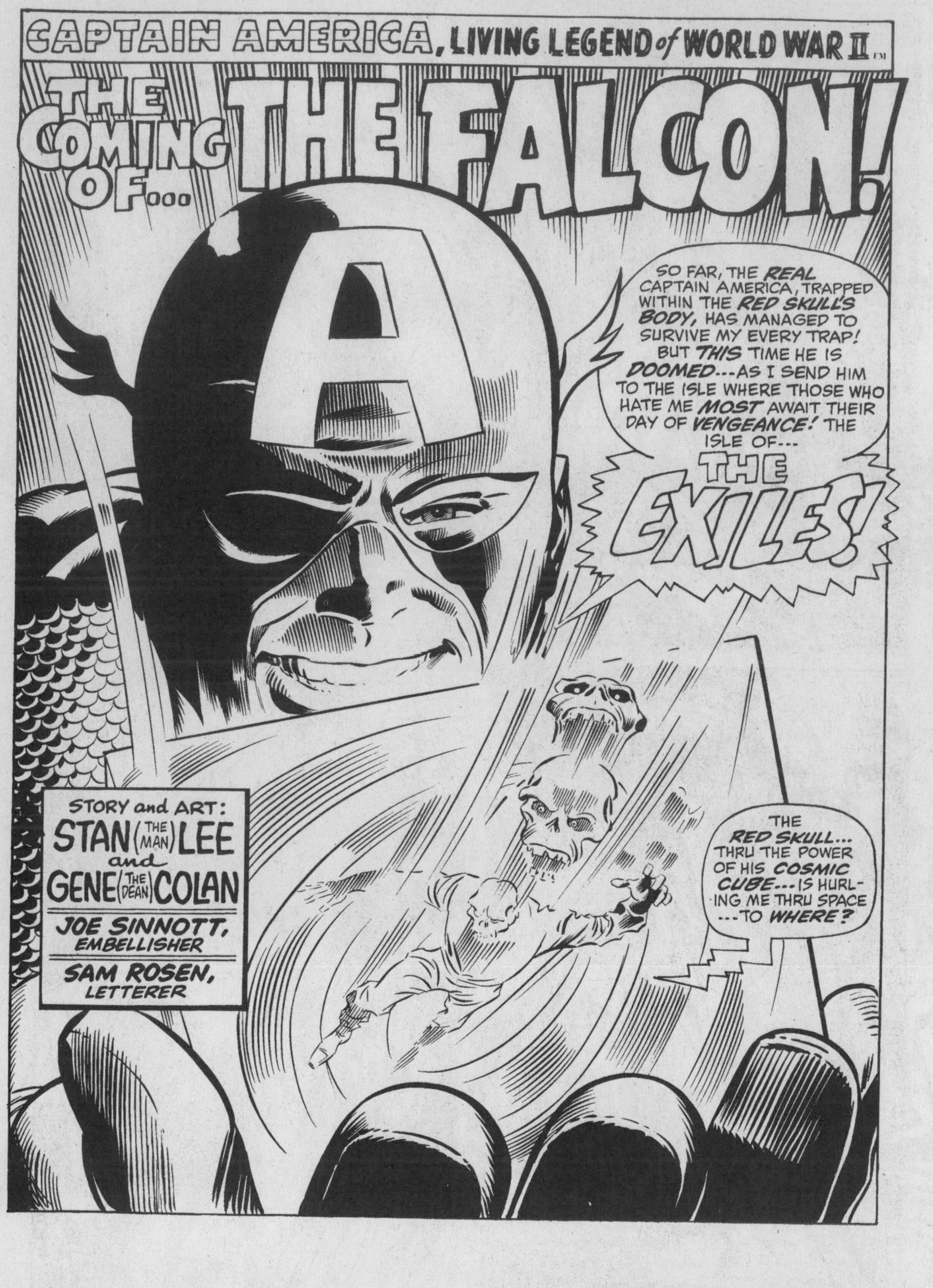
CAPTAIN AMERICA, LIVING LEGEND of WORLD WAR II TM
THE COMING OF... THE FALCON!
SO FAR, THE REAL CAPTAIN AMERICA, TRAPPED WITHIN THE RED SKULL'S BODY, HAS MANAGED TO SURVIVE MY EVERY TRAP! BUT THIS TIME HE IS DOOMED--AS I SEND HIM TO THE ISLE WHERE THOSE WHO HATE ME MOST AWAIT THEIR DAY OF VENGEANCE! THE ISLE OF--- THE EXILES!
STORY and ART: STAN (THE MAN) LEE and GENE (THE DEAN) COLAN
JOE SINNOTT, EMBELLISHER
SAM ROSEN, LETTERER
THE RED SKULL... THRU THE POWER OF HIS COSMIC CUBE---IS HURLING ME THRU SPACE ---TO WHERE?

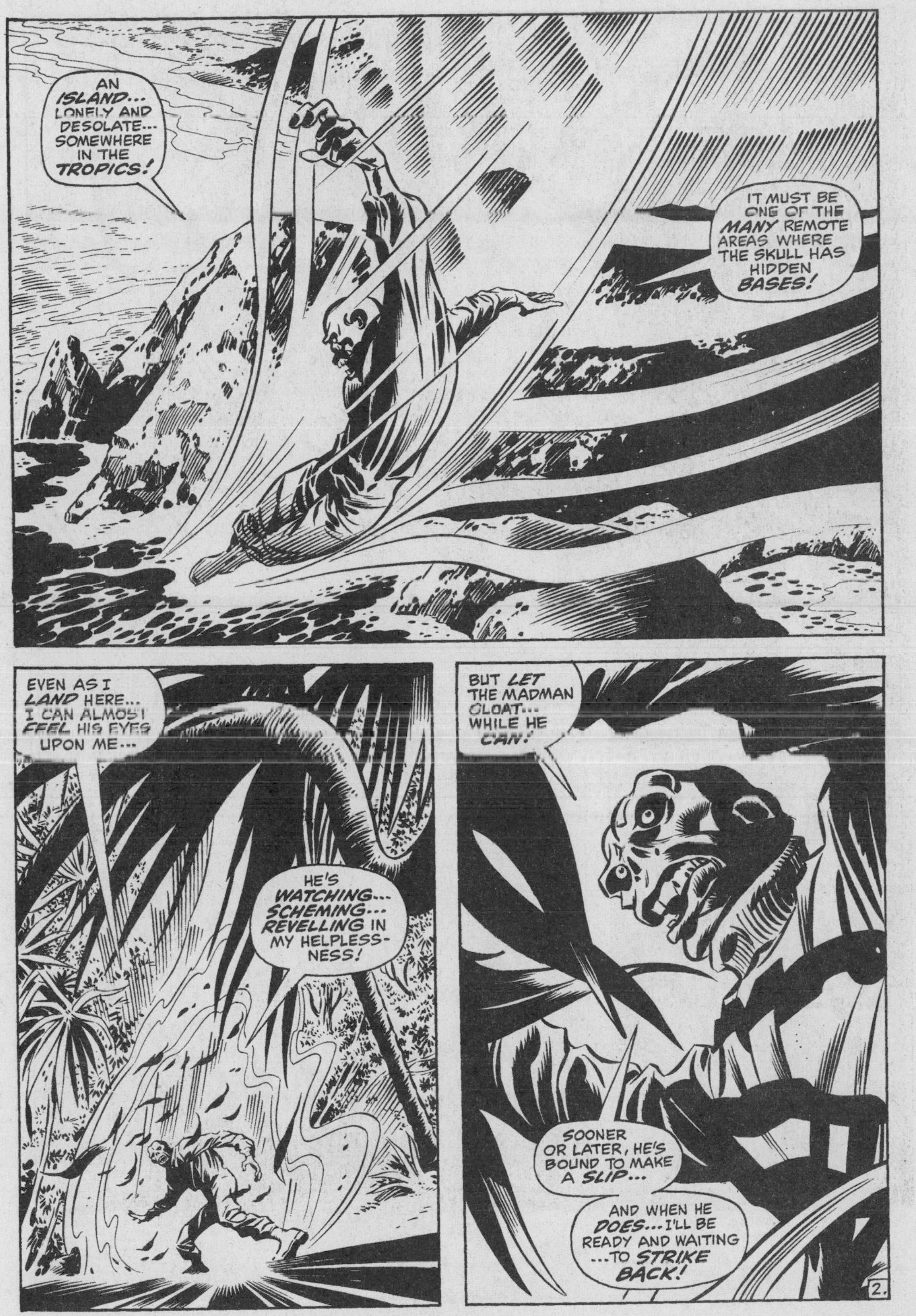
AN ISLAND... LONELY AND DESOLATE... SOMEWHERE IN THE TROPICS!
IT MUST BE ONE OF THE MANY REMOTE AREAS WHERE THE SKULL HAS HIDDEN BASES!
EVEN AS I LAND HERE... I CAN ALMOST FEEL HIS EYES UPON ME...
HE'S WATCHING... SCHEMING... REVELLING IN MY HELPLESS-NESS!
BUT LET THE MADMAN GLOAT... WHILE HE CAN!
SOONER OR LATER, HE'S BOUND TO MAKE A SLIP...
AND WHEN HE DOES... I'LL BE READY AND WAITING ...TO STRIKE BACK!
2.

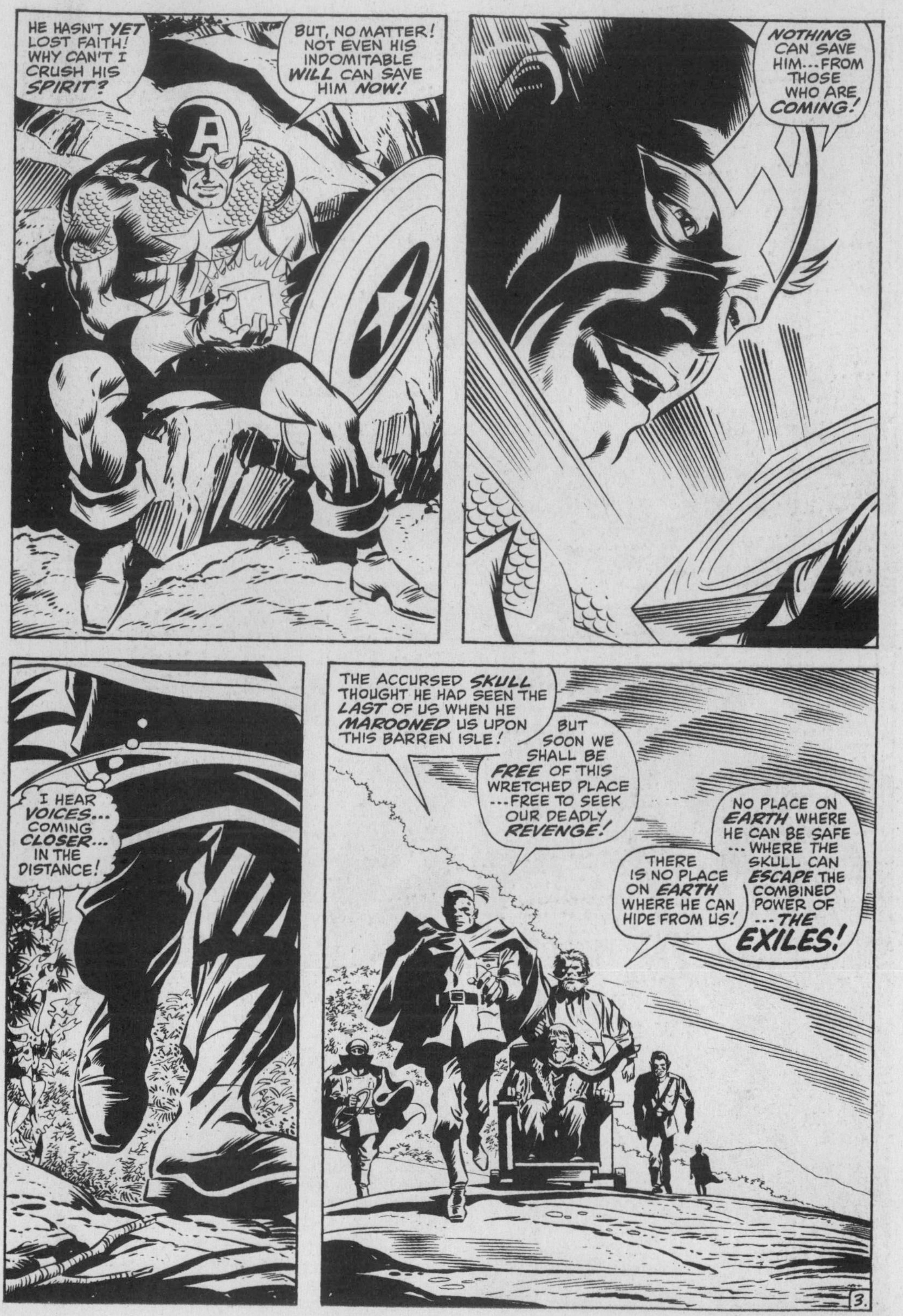
HE HASN'T YET LOST FAITH! WHY CAN'T I CRUSH HIS SPIRIT?
BUT, NO MATTER! NOT EVEN HIS INDOMITABLE WILL CAN SAVE HIM NOW!
NOTHING CAN SAVE HIM... FROM THOSE WHO ARE COMING!
I HEAR VOICES... COMING CLOSER... IN THE DISTANCE!
THE ACCURSED SKULL THOUGHT HE HAD SEEN THE LAST OF US WHEN HE MAROONED US UPON THIS BARREN ISLE!
BUT SOON WE SHALL BE FREE OF THIS WRETCHED PLACE ---FREE TO SEEK OUR DEADLY REVENGE!
THERE IS NO PLACE ON EARTH WHERE HE CAN HIDE FROM US!
NO PLACE ON EARTH WHERE HE CAN BE SAFE --- WHERE THE SKULL CAN ESCAPE THE COMBINED POWER OF --- THE EXILES!
3.

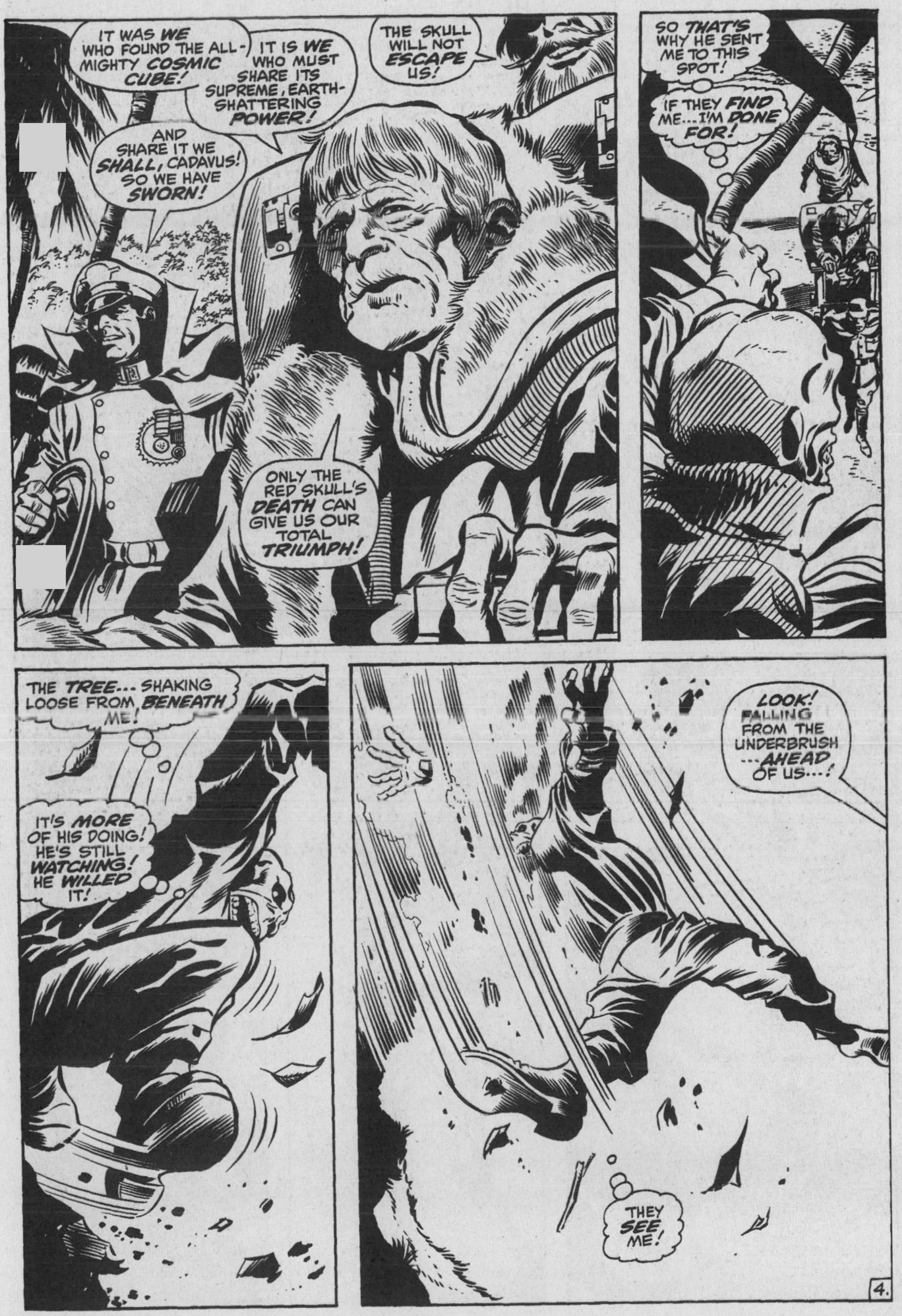
IT WAS WE WHO FOUND THE ALL-MIGHTY COSMIC CUBE!
IT IS WE WHO MUST SHARE ITS SUPREME, EARTH-SHATTERING POWER!
THE SKULL WILL NOT ESCAPE US!
AND SHARE IT WE SHALL, CADAVUS! SO WE HAVE SWORN!
ONLY THE RED SKULL'S DEATH CAN GIVE US OUR TOTAL TRIUMPH!
SO THAT'S WHY HE SENT ME TO THIS SPOT!
IF THEY FIND ME... I'M DONE FOR!
THE TREE... SHAKING LOOSE FROM BENEATH ME!
IT'S MORE OF HIS DOING! HE'S STILL WATCHING! HE WILLED IT!
LOOK! FALLING FROM THE UNDERBRUSH ...AHEAD OF US...!
THEY SEE ME!
4.

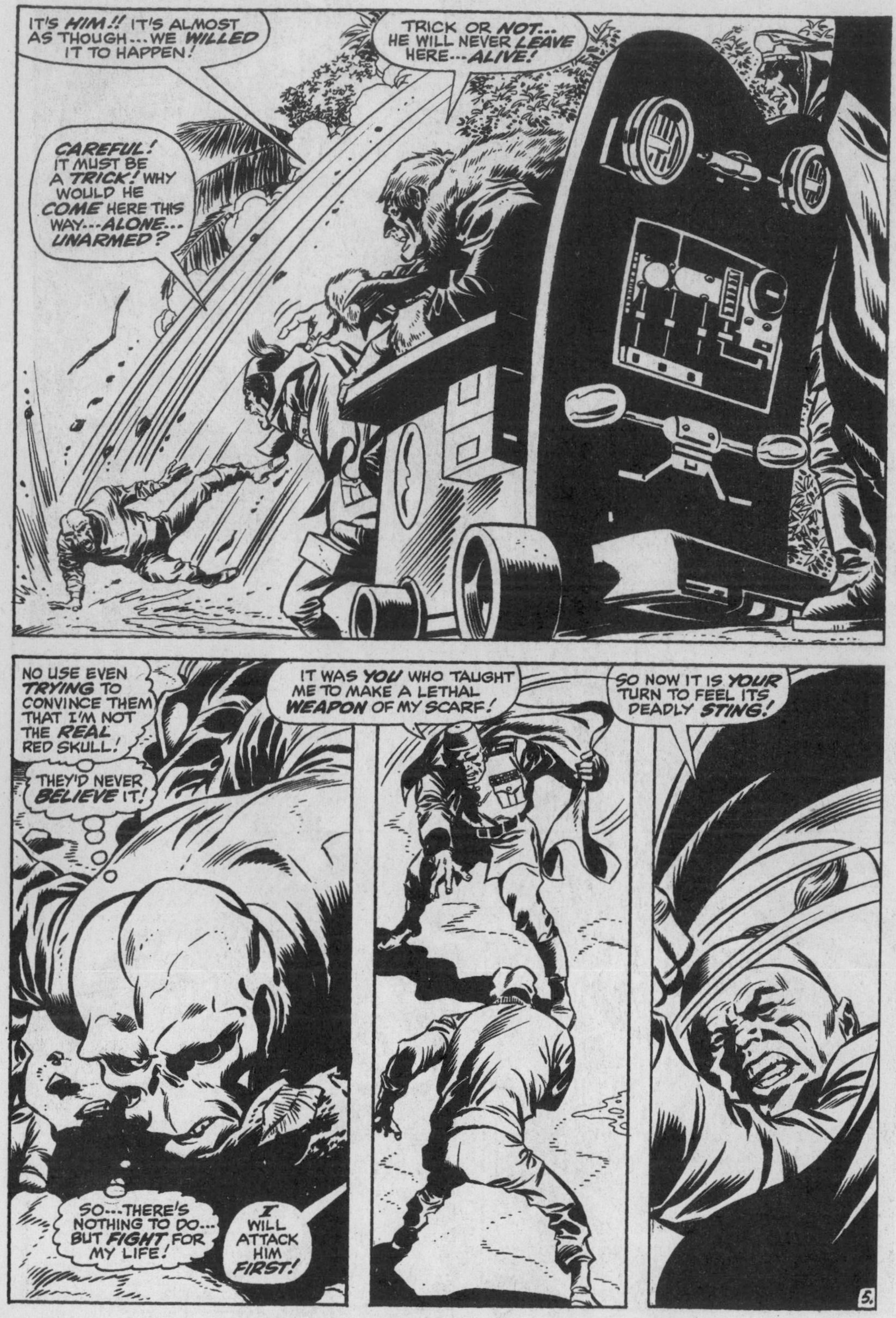
IT'S HIM!! IT'S ALMOST AS THOUGH--- WE WILLED IT TO HAPPEN!
TRICK OR NOT... HE WILL NEVER LEAVE HERE---ALIVE!
CAREFUL! IT MUST BE A TRICK! WHY WOULD HE COME HERE THIS WAY---ALONE... UNARMED?
NO USE EVEN TRYING TO CONVINCE THEM THAT I'M NOT THE REAL RED SKULL!
THEY'D NEVER BELIEVE IT!
SO---THERE'S NOTHING TO DO... BUT FIGHT FOR MY LIFE!
I WILL ATTACK HIM FIRST!
IT WAS YOU WHO TAUGHT ME TO MAKE A LETHAL WEAPON OF MY SCARF!
SO NOW IT IS YOUR TURN TO FEEL ITS DEADLY STING!
5.

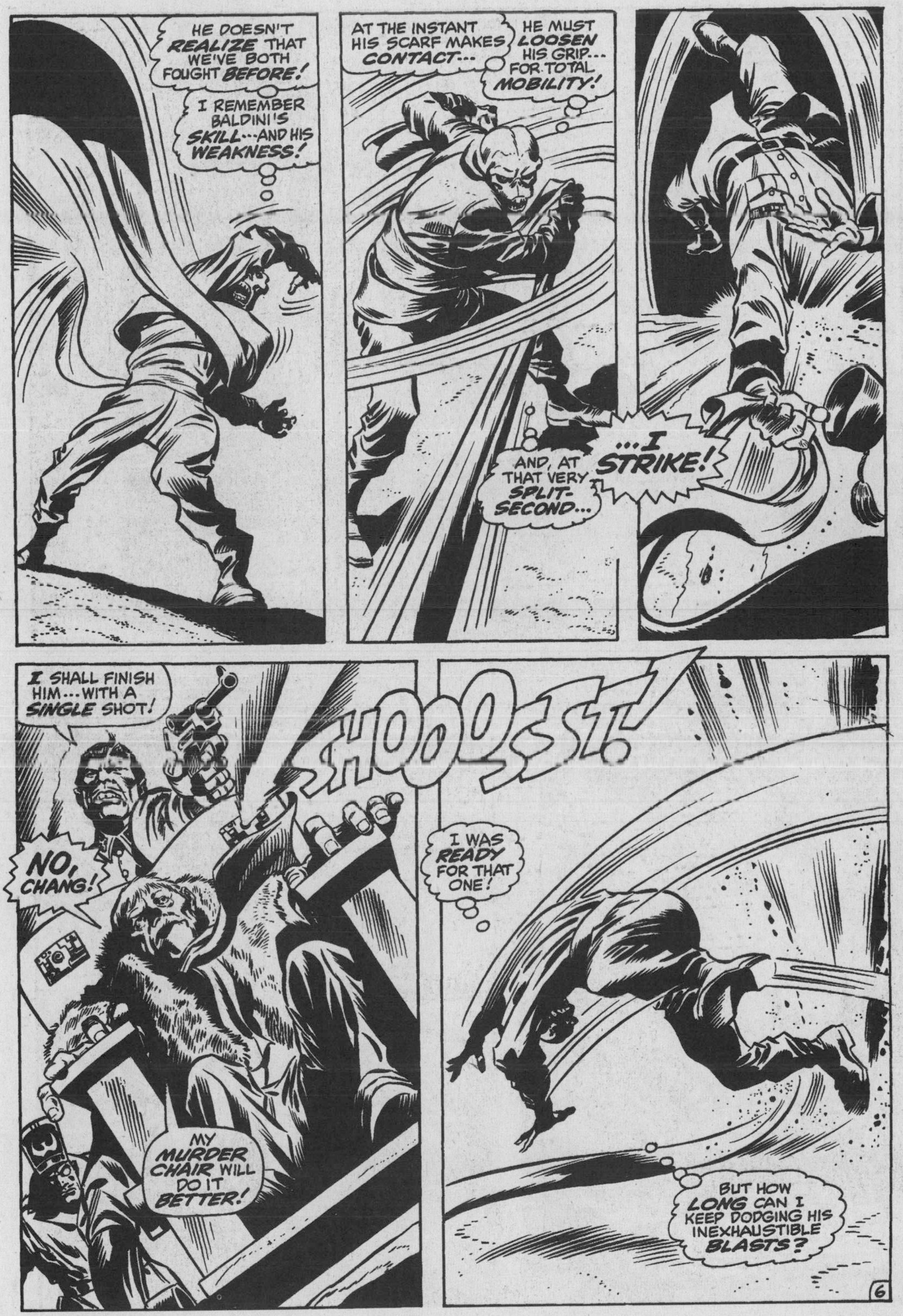
HE DOESN'T REALIZE THAT WE'VE BOTH FOUGHT BEFORE!
I REMEMBER BALDINI'S SKILL---AND HIS WEAKNESS!
AT THE INSTANT HIS SCARF MAKES CONTACT---
HE MUST LOOSEN HIS GRIP--- FOR TOTAL MOBILITY!
AND, AT THAT VERY SPLIT-SECOND...
...I STRIKE!
I SHALL FINISH HIM---WITH A SINGLE SHOT!
NO, CHANG!
MY MURDER CHAIR WILL DO IT BETTER!
SHOOOSST!
I WAS READY FOR THAT ONE!
BUT HOW LONG CAN I KEEP DODGING HIS INEXHAUSTIBLE BLASTS?
6

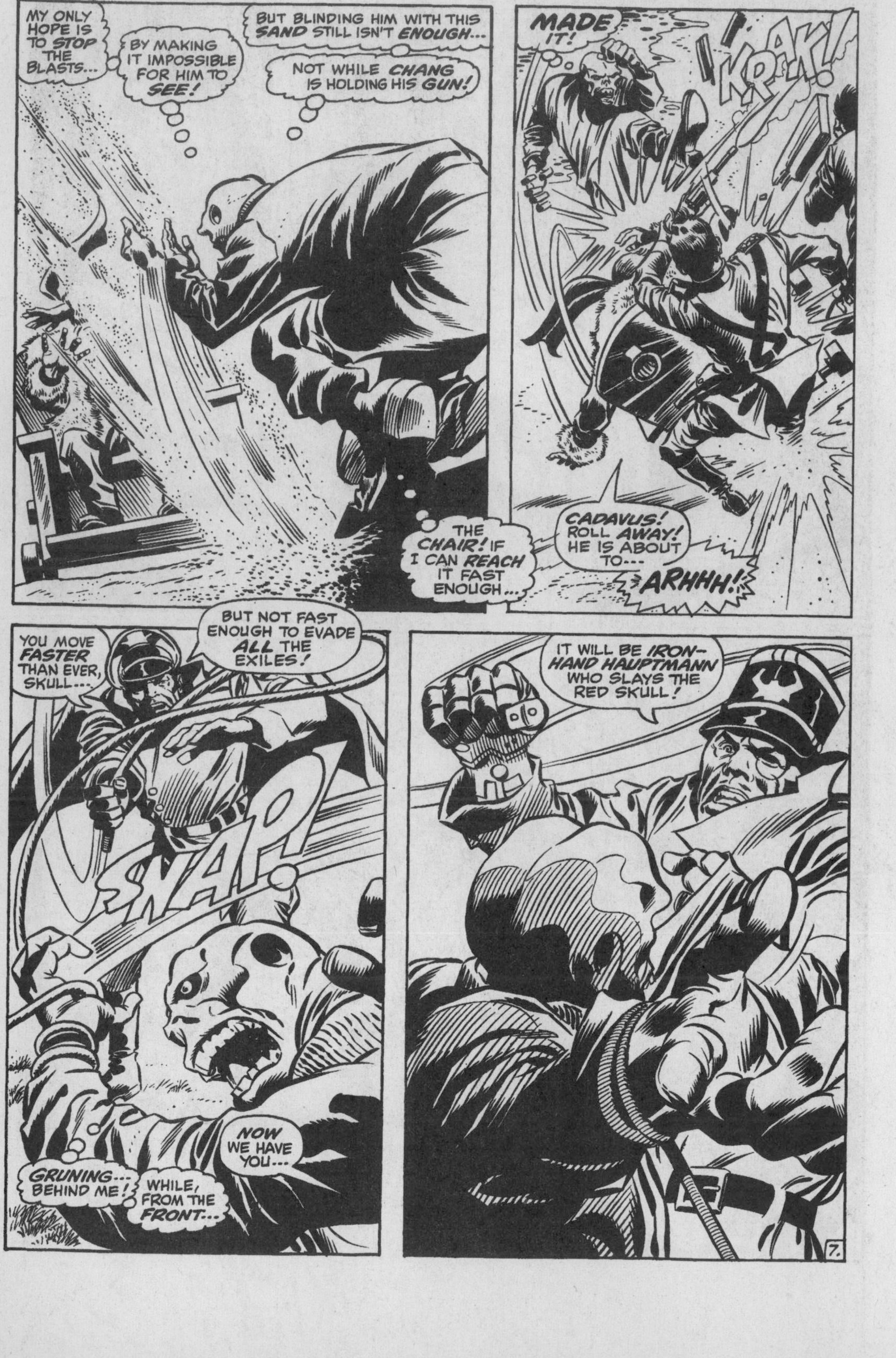
MY ONLY HOPE IS TO STOP THE BLASTS...
BY MAKING IT IMPOSSIBLE FOR HIM TO SEE!
BUT BLINDING HIM WITH THIS SAND STILL ISN'T ENOUGH...
NOT WHILE CHANG IS HOLDING HIS GUN!
THE CHAIR! IF I CAN REACH IT FAST ENOUGH...
MADE IT!
KRAK!
CADAVUS! ROLL AWAY! HE IS ABOUT TO---
ARHHH!
YOU MOVE FASTER THAN EVER, SKULL---
BUT NOT FAST ENOUGH TO EVADE ALL THE EXILES!
SNAP!
NOW WE HAVE YOU---
GRUNING... BEHIND ME!
WHILE, FROM THE FRONT...
IT WILL BE IRON-HAND HAUPTMANN WHO SLAYS THE RED SKULL!
7.

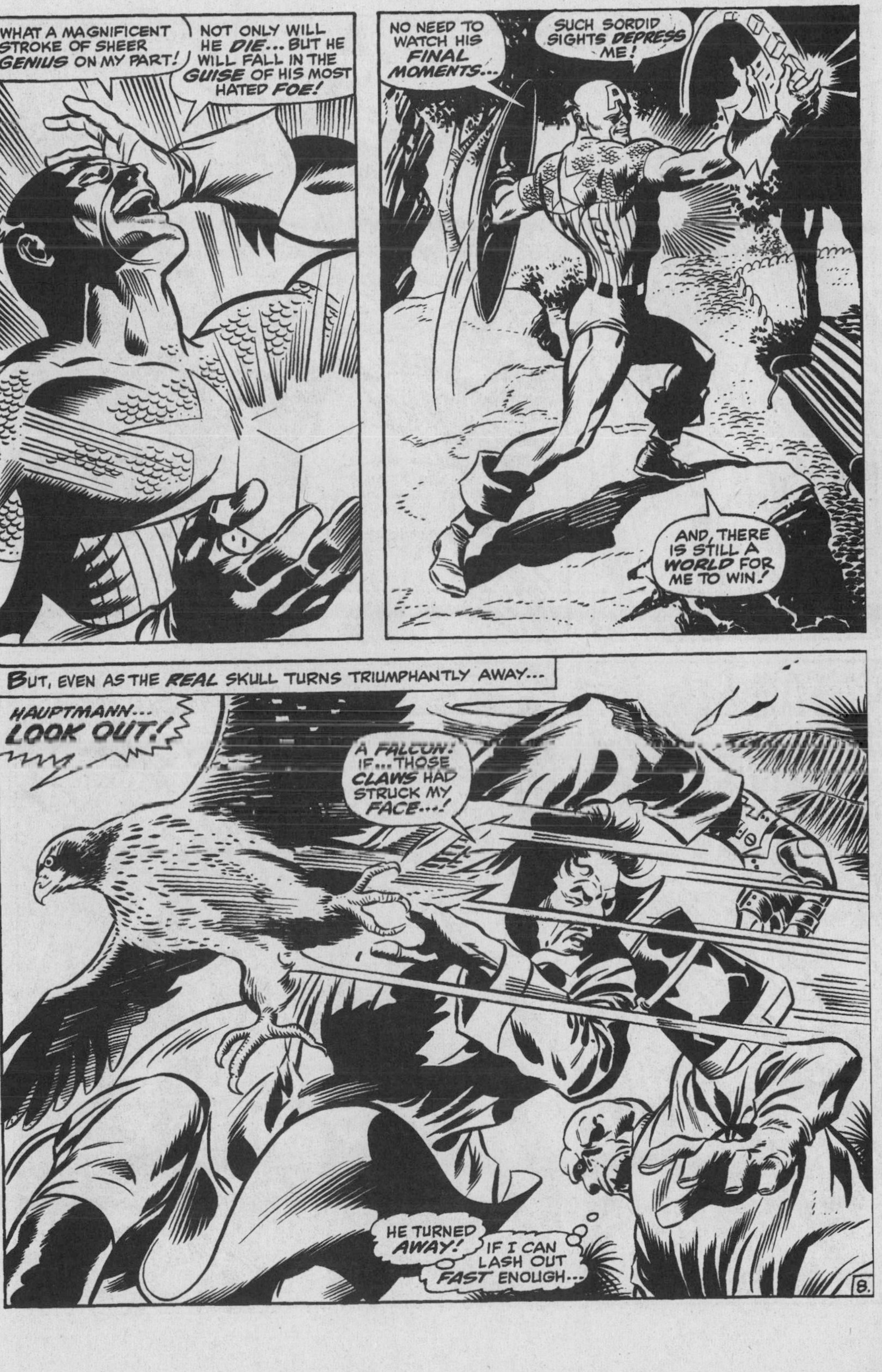
WHAT A MAGNIFICENT STROKE OF SHEER GENIUS ON MY PART!
NOT ONLY WILL HE DIE... BUT HE WILL FALL IN THE GUISE OF HIS MOST HATED FOE!
NO NEED TO WATCH HIS FINAL MOMENTS...
SUCH SORDID SIGHTS DEPRESS ME!
AND, THERE IS STILL A WORLD FOR ME TO WIN!
BUT, EVEN AS THE REAL SKULL TURNS TRIUMPHANTLY AWAY...
HAUPTMANN... LOOK OUT!
A FALCON! IF... THOSE CLAWS HAD STRUCK MY FACE...!
HE TURNED AWAY!
IF I CAN LASH OUT FAST ENOUGH...
8.

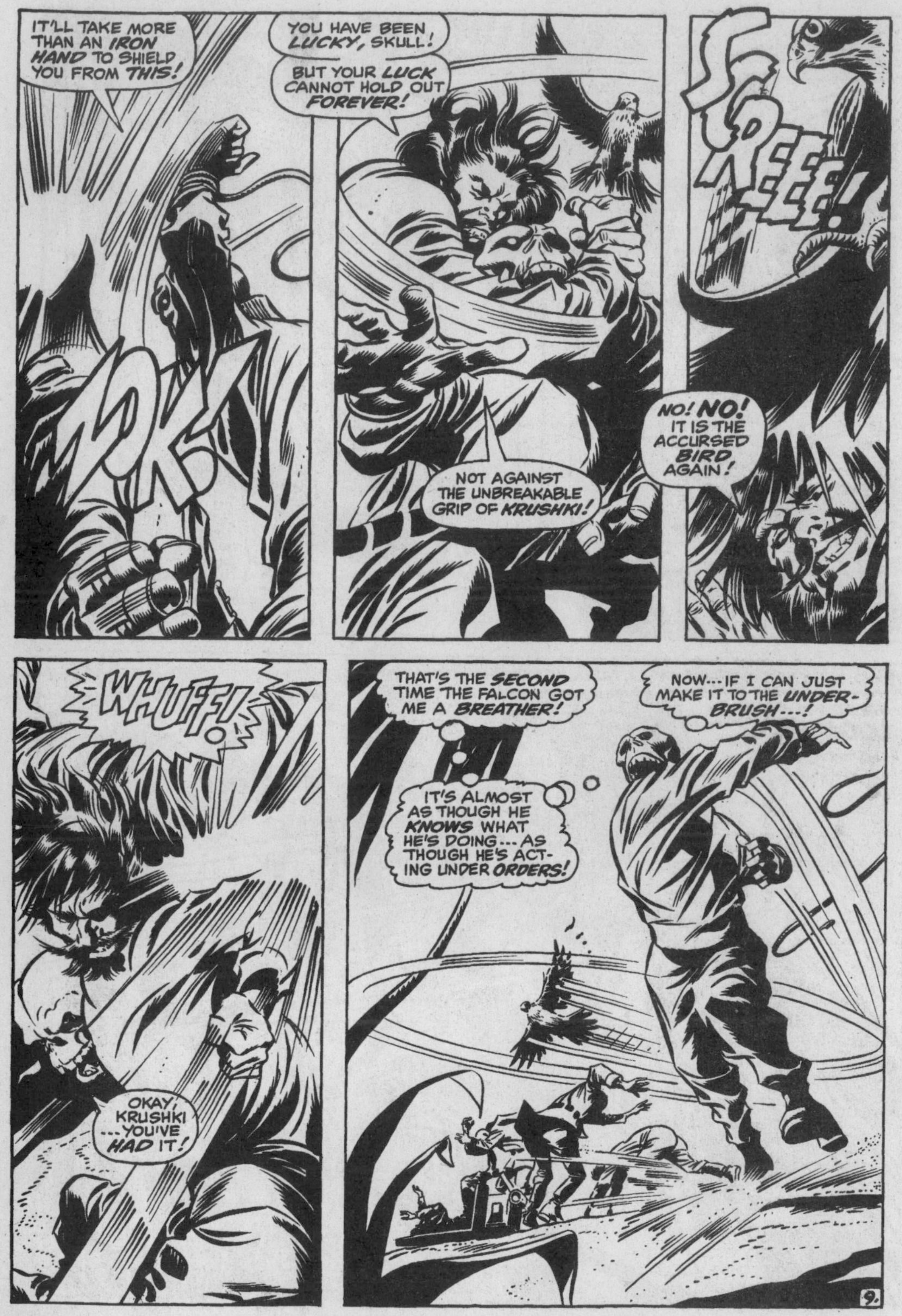
IT'LL TAKE MORE THAN AN IRON HAND TO SHIELD YOU FROM THIS!
SOK!
YOU HAVE BEEN LUCKY, SKULL!
BUT YOUR LUCK CANNOT HOLD OUT FOREVER!
NOT AGAINST THE UNBREAKABLE GRIP OF KRUSHKI!
SCREEE!
NO! NO! IT IS THE ACCURSED BIRD AGAIN!
WHUFF!
OKAY, KRUSHKI ...YOU'VE HAD IT!
THAT'S THE SECOND TIME THE FALCON GOT ME A BREATHER!
IT'S ALMOST AS THOUGH HE KNOWS WHAT HE'S DOING... AS THOUGH HE'S ACTING UNDER ORDERS!
NOW... IF I CAN JUST MAKE IT TO THE UNDER-BRUSH...!
9.

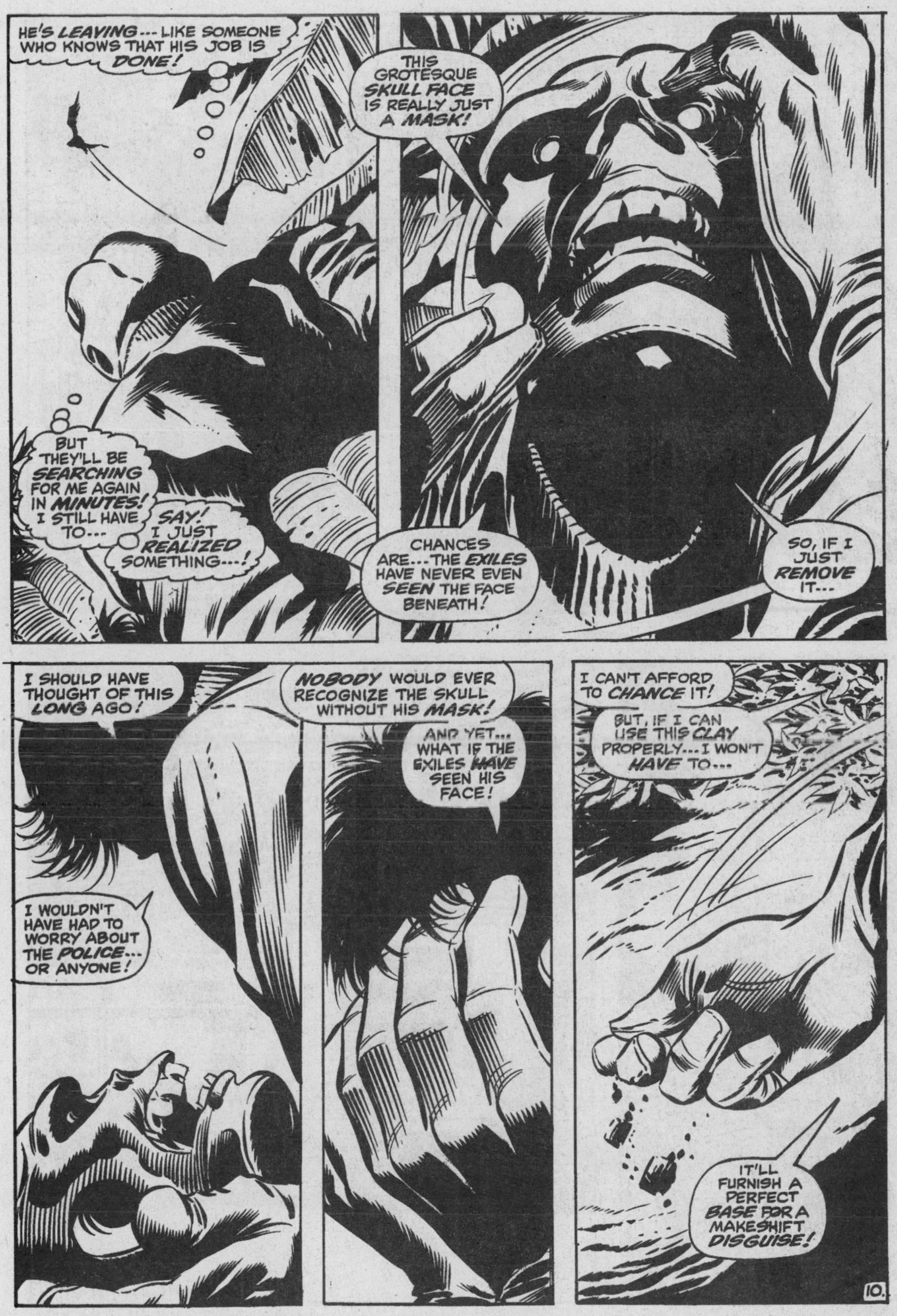
HE'S LEAVING --- LIKE SOMEONE WHO KNOWS THAT HIS JOB IS DONE!
BUT THEY'LL BE SEARCHING FOR ME AGAIN IN MINUTES! I STILL HAVE TO---
SAY! I JUST REALIZED SOMETHING---!
THIS GROTESQUE SKULL FACE IS REALLY JUST A MASK!
CHANCES ARE---THE EXILES HAVE NEVER EVEN SEEN THE FACE BENEATH!
SO, IF I JUST REMOVE IT---
I SHOULD HAVE THOUGHT OF THIS LONG AGO!
I WOULDN'T HAVE HAD TO WORRY ABOUT THE POLICE--- OR ANYONE!
NOBODY WOULD EVER RECOGNIZE THE SKULL WITHOUT HIS MASK!
AND YET... WHAT IF THE EXILES HAVE SEEN HIS FACE!
I CAN'T AFFORD TO CHANCE IT!
BUT, IF I CAN USE THIS CLAY PROPERLY---I WON'T HAVE TO---
IT'LL FURNISH A PERFECT BASE FOR A MAKESHIFT DISGUISE!

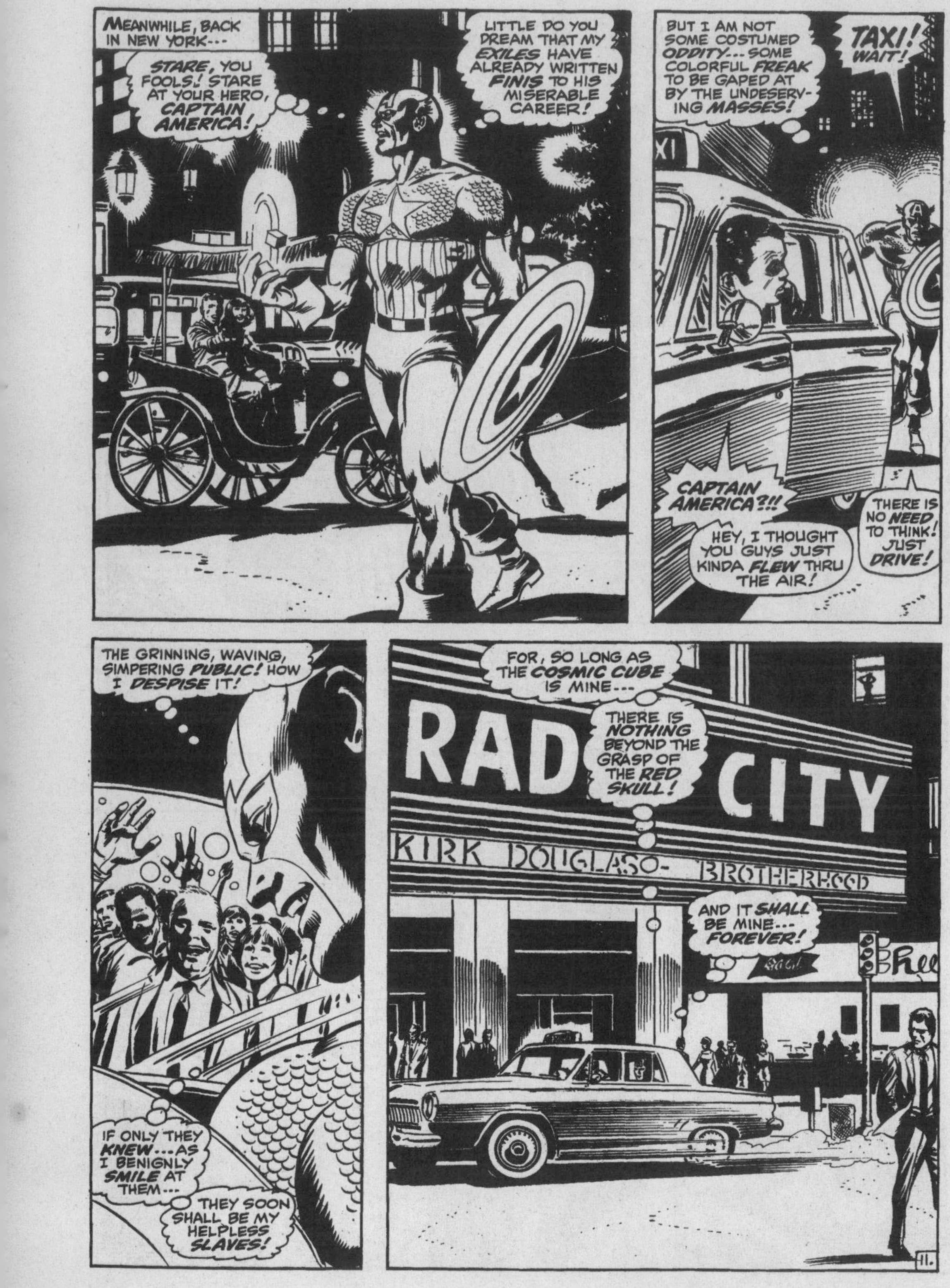
MEANWHILE, BACK IN NEW YORK---
STARE, YOU FOOLS! STARE AT YOUR HERO, CAPTAIN AMERICA!
LITTLE DO YOU DREAM THAT MY EXILES HAVE ALREADY WRITTEN FINIS TO HIS MISERABLE CAREER!
BUT I AM NOT SOME COSTUMED ODDITY--- SOME COLORFUL FREAK TO BE GAPED AT BY THE UNDESERVING MASSES!
TAXI! WAIT!
CAPTAIN AMERICA?!!
HEY, I THOUGHT YOU GUYS JUST KINDA FLEW THRU THE AIR!
THERE IS NO NEED TO THINK! JUST DRIVE!
THE GRINNING, WAVING, SIMPERING PUBLIC! HOW I DESPISE IT!
IF ONLY THEY KNEW... AS I BENIGNLY SMILE AT THEM...
THEY SOON SHALL BE MY HELPLESS SLAVES!
FOR, SO LONG AS THE COSMIC CUBE IS MINE---
THERE IS NOTHING BEYOND THE GRASP OF THE RED SKULL!
RAD CITY
KIRK DOUGLAS BROTHERHOOD
AND IT SHALL BE MINE--- FOREVER!
11.

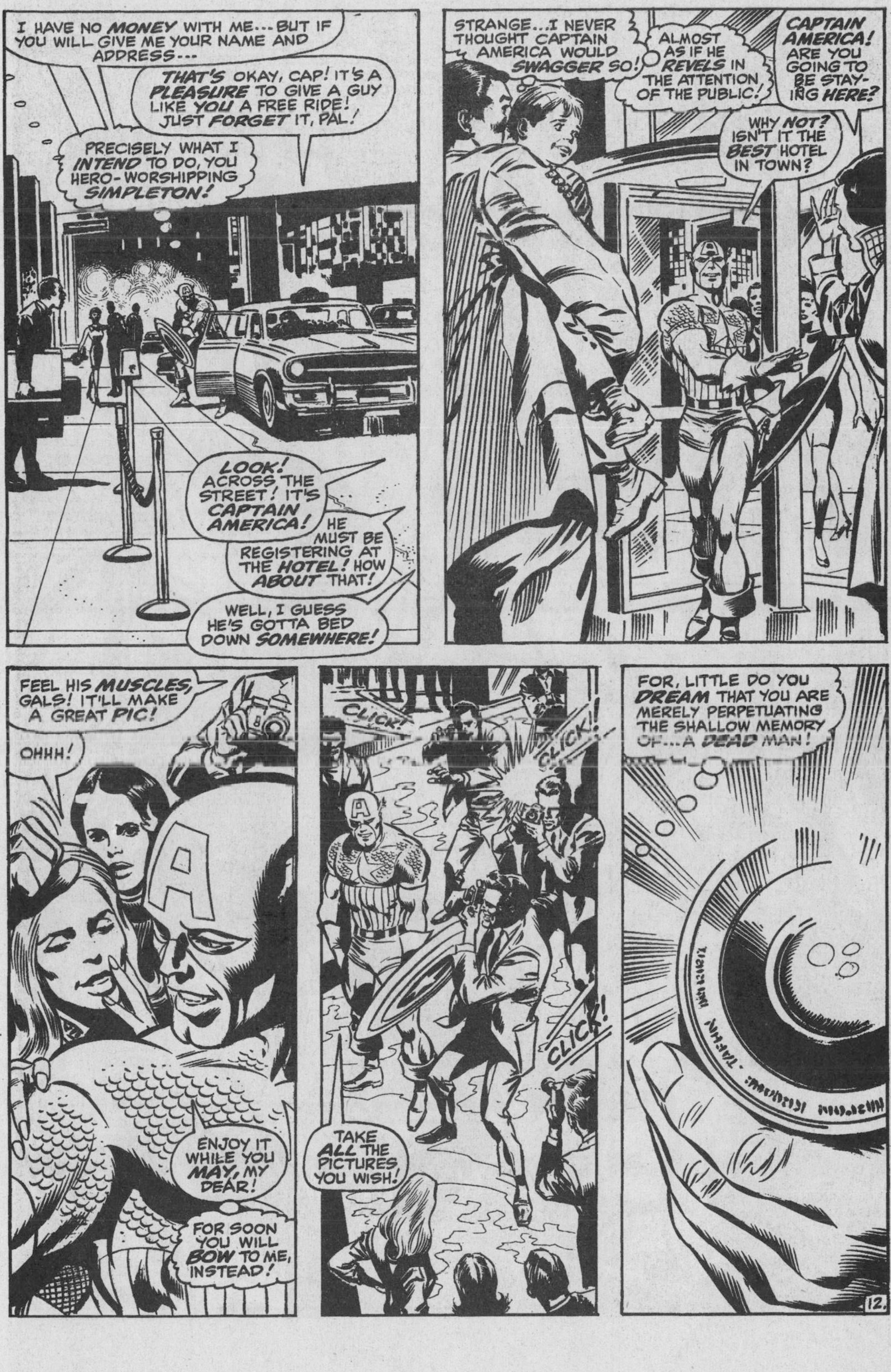
I HAVE NO MONEY WITH ME... BUT IF YOU WILL GIVE ME YOUR NAME AND ADDRESS...
THAT'S OKAY, CAP! IT'S A PLEASURE TO GIVE A GUY LIKE YOU A FREE RIDE! JUST FORGET IT, PAL!
PRECISELY WHAT I INTEND TO DO, YOU HERO-WORSHIPPING SIMPLETON!
LOOK! ACROSS THE STREET! IT'S CAPTAIN AMERICA!
HE MUST BE REGISTERING AT THE HOTEL! HOW ABOUT THAT!
WELL, I GUESS HE'S GOTTA BED DOWN SOMEWHERE!
STRANGE...I NEVER THOUGHT CAPTAIN AMERICA WOULD SWAGGER SO!
ALMOST AS IF HE REVELS IN THE ATTENTION OF THE PUBLIC!
CAPTAIN AMERICA! ARE YOU GOING TO BE STAYING HERE?
WHY NOT? ISN'T IT THE BEST HOTEL IN TOWN?
FEEL HIS MUSCLES, GALS! IT'LL MAKE A GREAT PIC!
OHHH!
ENJOY IT WHILE YOU MAY, MY DEAR!
FOR SOON YOU WILL BOW TO ME, INSTEAD!
CLICK!
CLICK!
CLICK!
TAKE ALL THE PICTURES YOU WISH!
FOR, LITTLE DO YOU DREAM THAT YOU ARE MERELY PERPETUATING THE SHALLOW MEMORY OF... A DEAD MAN!
12.

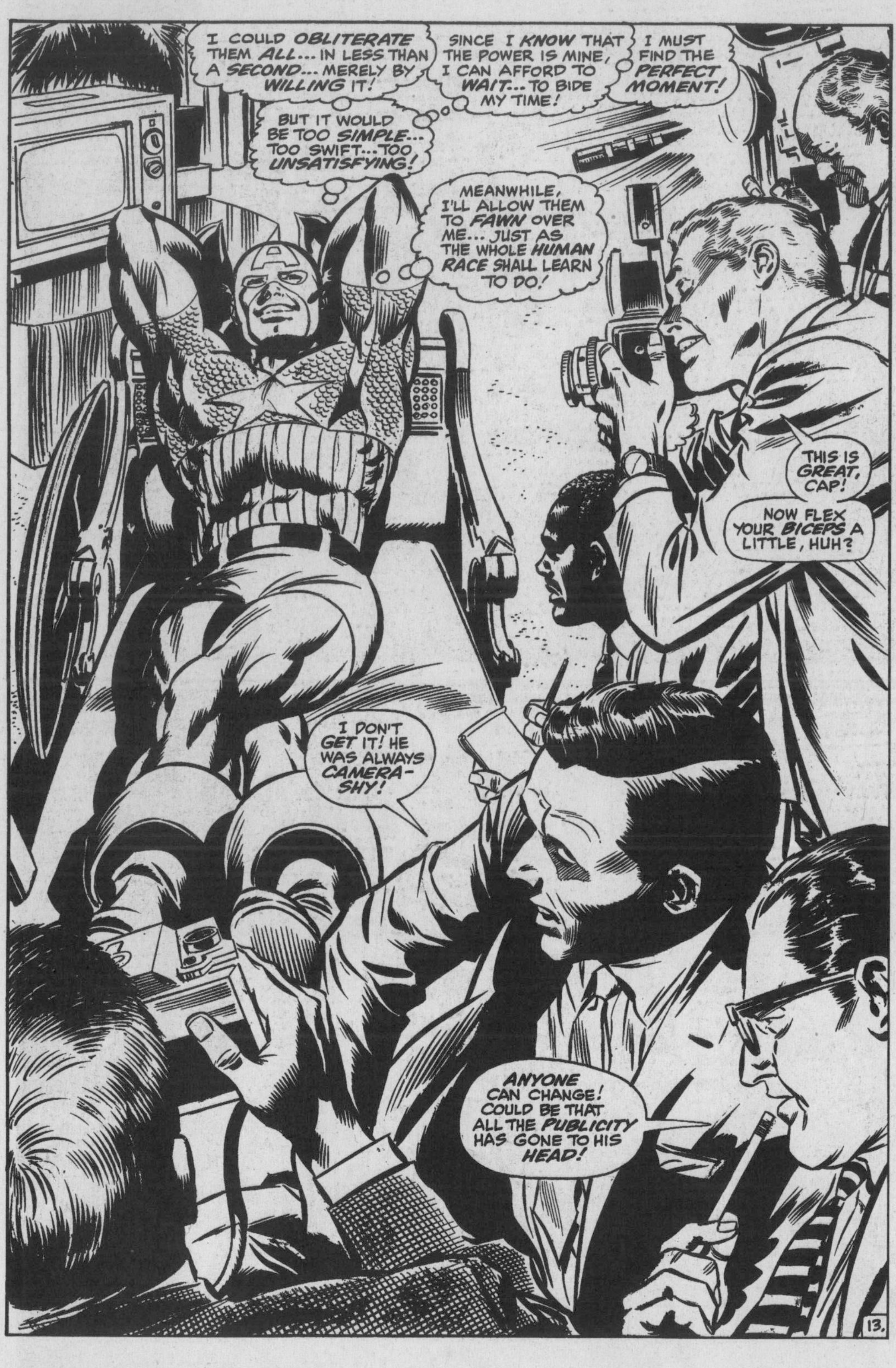

I COULD OBLITERATE THEM ALL... IN LESS THAN A SECOND... MERELY BY WILLING IT!
BUT IT WOULD BE TOO SIMPLE... TOO SWIFT... TOO UNSATISFYING!
SINCE I KNOW THAT THE POWER IS MINE, I CAN AFFORD TO WAIT... TO BIDE MY TIME!
I MUST FIND THE PERFECT MOMENT!
MEANWHILE, I'LL ALLOW THEM TO FAWN OVER ME... JUST AS THE WHOLE HUMAN RACE SHALL LEARN TO DO!
THIS IS GREAT, CAP!
NOW FLEX YOUR BICEPS A LITTLE, HUH?
I DON'T GET IT! HE WAS ALWAYS CAMERA-SHY!
ANYONE CAN CHANGE! COULD BE THAT ALL THE PUBLICITY HAS GONE TO HIS HEAD!
13.

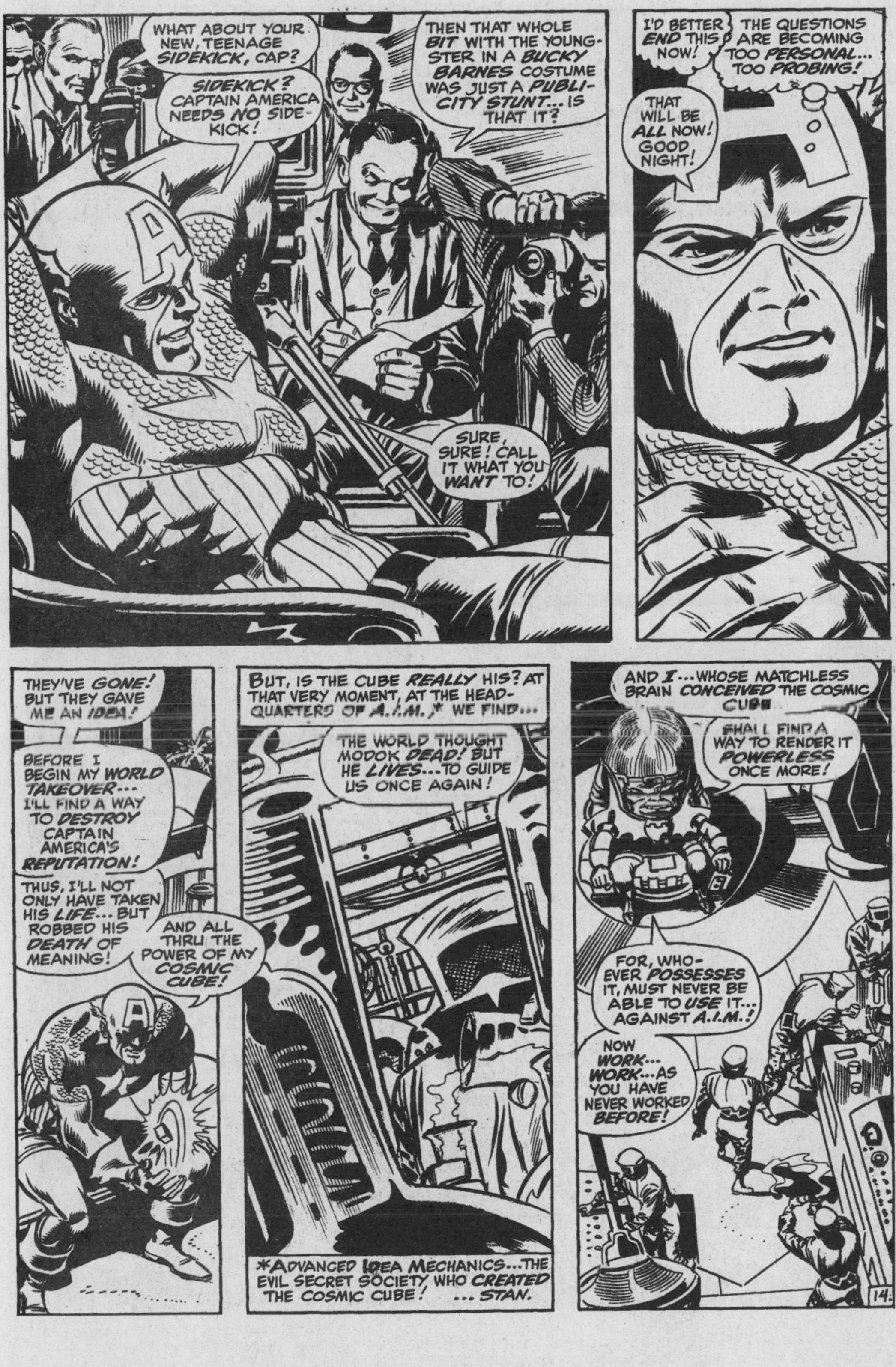
WHAT ABOUT YOUR NEW, TEENAGE SIDEKICK, CAP?
SIDEKICK? CAPTAIN AMERICA NEEDS NO SIDEKICK!
THEN THAT WHOLE BIT WITH THE YOUNGSTER IN A BUCKY BARNES COSTUME WAS JUST A PUBLICITY STUNT... IS THAT IT?
SURE, SURE! CALL IT WHAT YOU WANT TO!
I'D BETTER END THIS NOW!
THE QUESTIONS ARE BECOMING TOO PERSONAL... TOO PROBING!
THAT WILL BE ALL NOW! GOOD NIGHT!
THEY'VE GONE! BUT THEY GAVE ME AN IDEA!
BEFORE I BEGIN MY WORLD TAKEOVER... I'LL FIND A WAY TO DESTROY CAPTAIN AMERICA'S REPUTATION!
THUS, I'LL NOT ONLY HAVE TAKEN HIS LIFE... BUT ROBBED HIS DEATH OF MEANING!
AND ALL THRU THE POWER OF MY COSMIC CUBE!
BUT, IS THE CUBE REALLY HIS? AT THAT VERY MOMENT, AT THE HEADQUARTERS OF A.I.M.,* WE FIND...
THE WORLD THOUGHT MODOK DEAD! BUT HE LIVES... TO GUIDE US ONCE AGAIN!
*ADVANCED IDEA MECHANICS... THE EVIL SECRET SOCIETY WHO CREATED THE COSMIC CUBE! ...STAN.
AND I... WHOSE MATCHLESS BRAIN CONCEIVED THE COSMIC CUBE
SHALL FIND A WAY TO RENDER IT POWERLESS ONCE MORE!
FOR, WHOEVER POSSESSES IT, MUST NEVER BE ABLE TO USE IT... AGAINST A.I.M.!
NOW WORK... WORK... AS YOU HAVE NEVER WORKED BEFORE!
14.

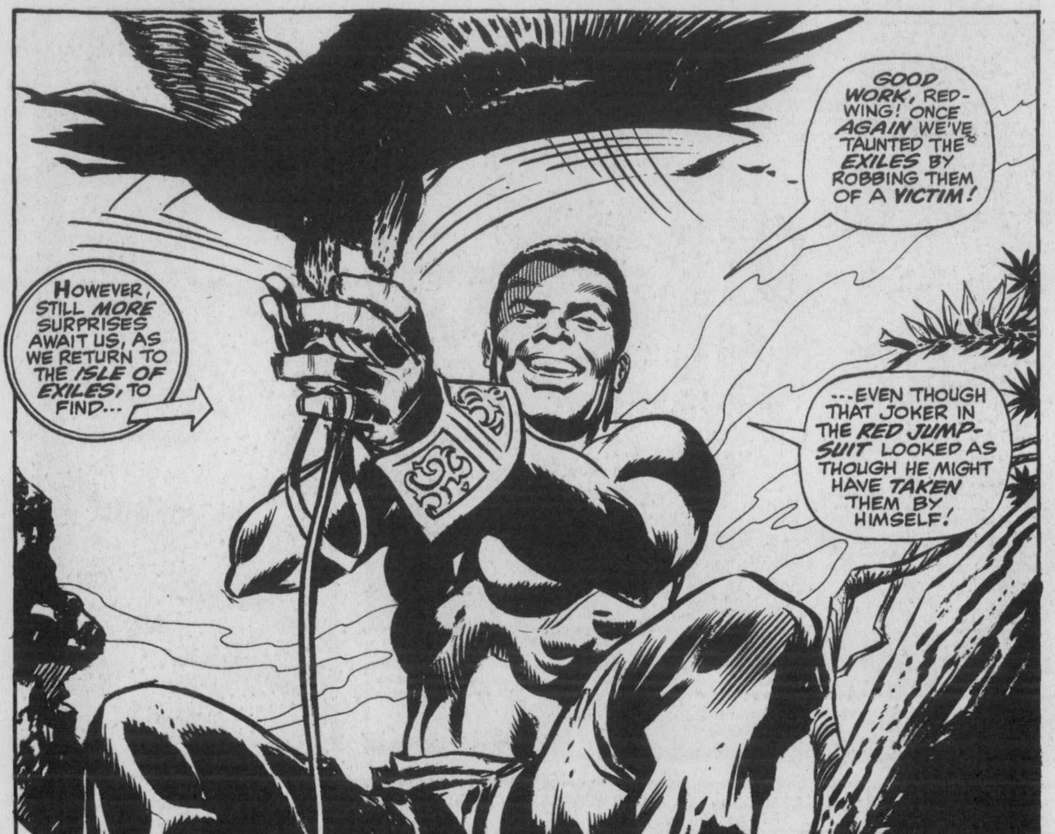
GOOD WORK, RED-WING! ONCE AGAIN WE'VE TAUNTED THE EXILES BY ROBBING THEM OF A VICTIM!
HOWEVER, STILL MORE SURPRISES AWAIT US, AS WE RETURN TO THE ISLE OF EXILES, TO FIND...
...EVEN THOUGH THAT JOKER IN THE RED JUMP-SUIT LOOKED AS THOUGH HE MIGHT HAVE TAKEN THEM BY HIMSELF!

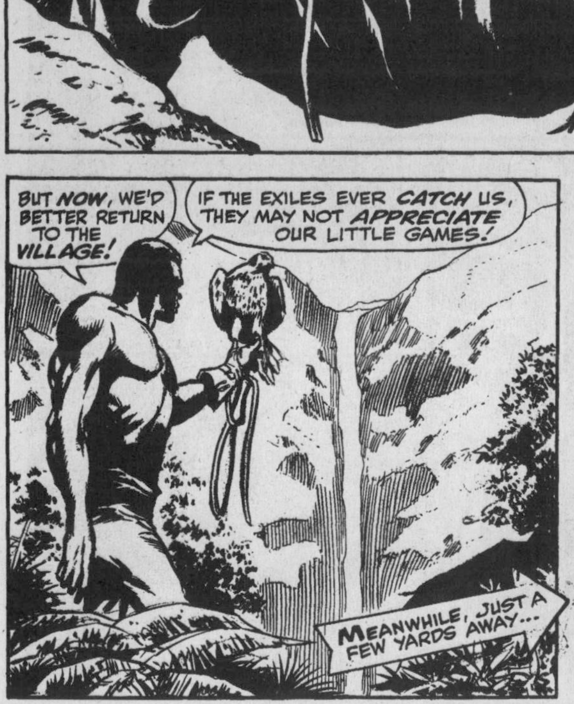
BUT NOW, WE'D BETTER RETURN TO THE VILLAGE!
IF THE EXILES EVER CATCH US, THEY MAY NOT APPRECIATE OUR LITTLE GAMES!
MEANWHILE, JUST A FEW YARDS AWAY...

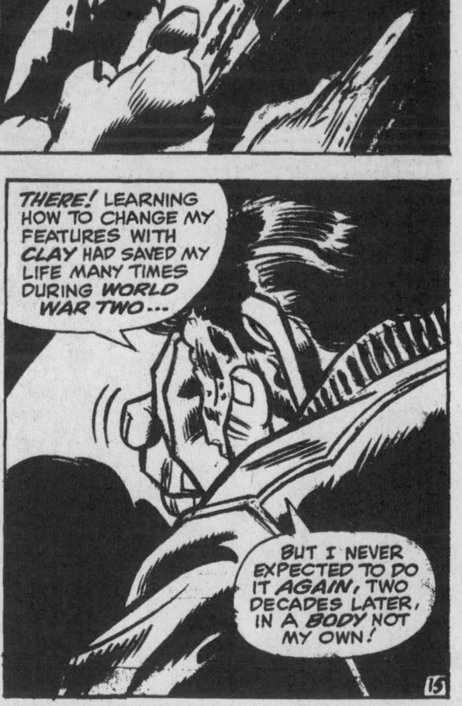
THERE! LEARNING HOW TO CHANGE MY FEATURES WITH CLAY HAD SAVED MY LIFE MANY TIMES DURING WORLD WAR TWO...
BUT I NEVER EXPECTED TO DO IT AGAIN, TWO DECADES LATER, IN A BODY NOT MY OWN!

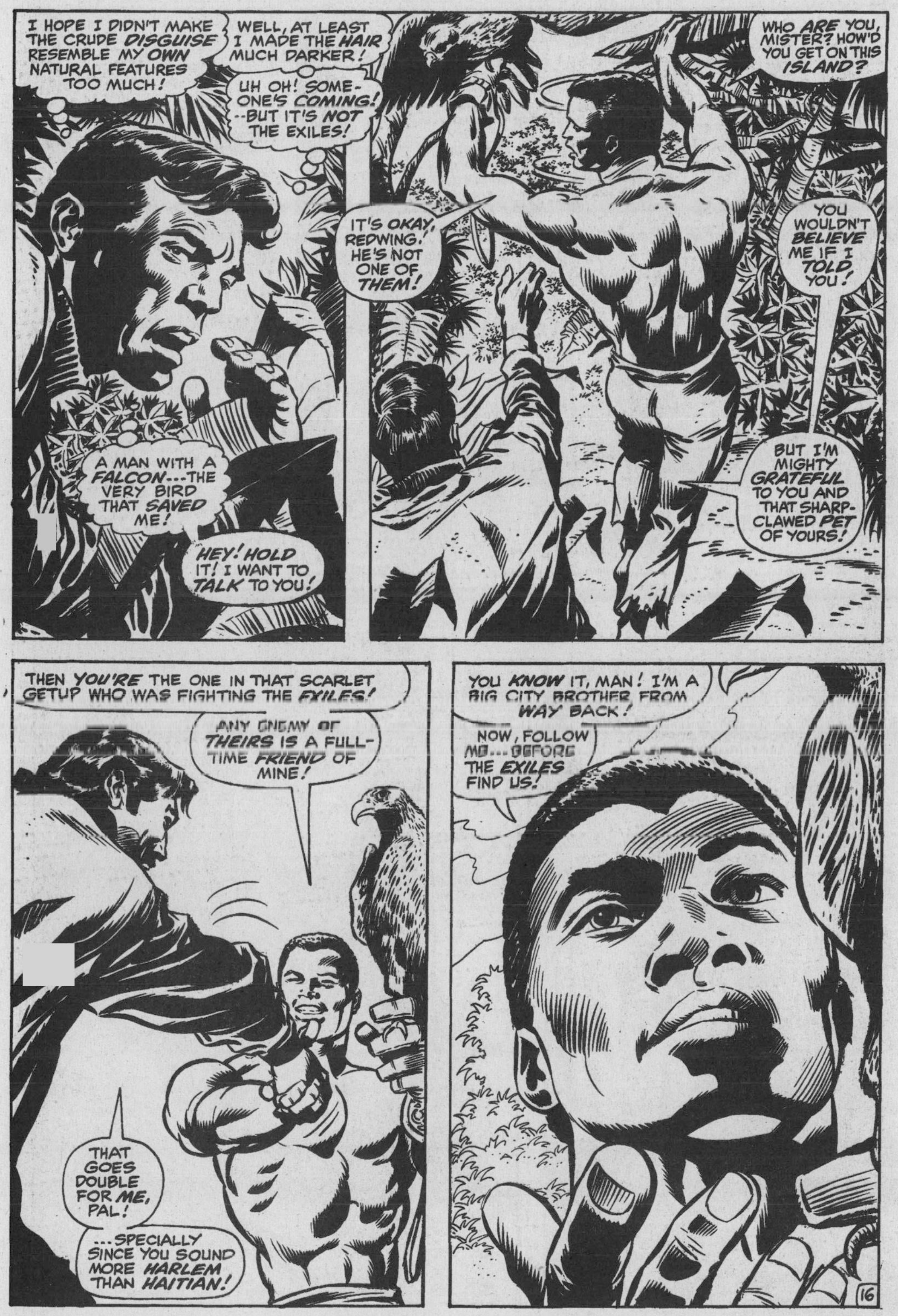

I HOPE I DIDN'T MAKE THE CRUDE DISGUISE RESEMBLE MY OWN NATURAL FEATURES TOO MUCH!
WELL, AT LEAST I MADE THE HAIR MUCH DARKER!
UH OH! SOME-ONE'S COMING! --BUT IT'S NOT THE EXILES!
A MAN WITH A FALCON---THE VERY BIRD THAT SAVED ME!
HEY! HOLD IT! I WANT TO TALK TO YOU!
WHO ARE YOU, MISTER? HOW'D YOU GET ON THIS ISLAND?
IT'S OKAY, REDWING! HE'S NOT ONE OF THEM!
YOU WOULDN'T BELIEVE ME IF I TOLD YOU!
BUT I'M MIGHTY GRATEFUL TO YOU AND THAT SHARP-CLAWED PET OF YOURS!
THEN YOU'RE THE ONE IN THAT SCARLET GETUP WHO WAS FIGHTING THE EXILES!
ANY ENEMY OF THEIRS IS A FULL-TIME FRIEND OF MINE!
THAT GOES DOUBLE FOR ME, PAL!
...SPECIALLY SINCE YOU SOUND MORE HARLEM THAN HAITIAN!
YOU KNOW IT, MAN! I'M A BIG CITY BROTHER FROM WAY BACK!
NOW, FOLLOW ME... BEFORE THE EXILES FIND US!
16

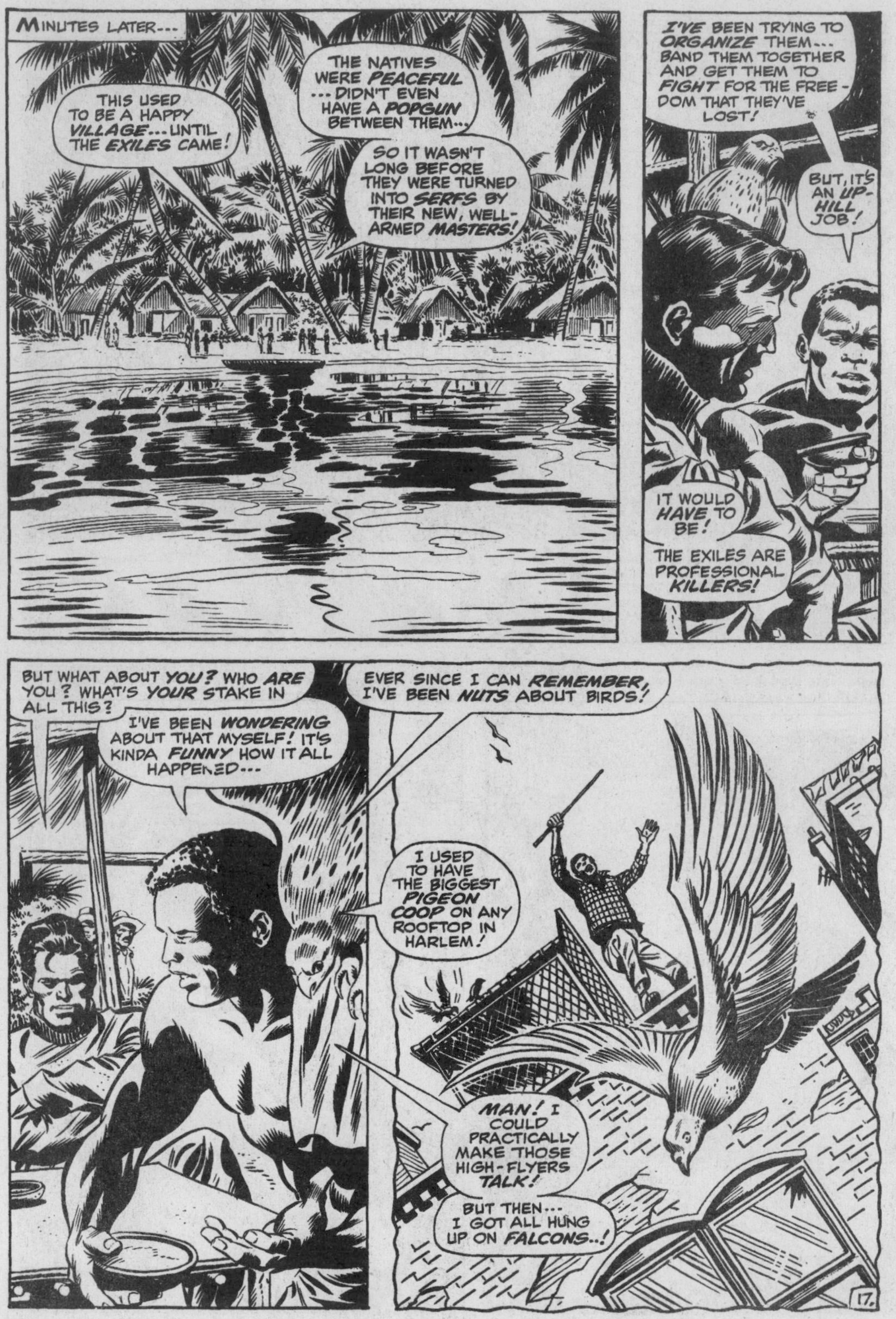
MINUTES LATER---
THIS USED TO BE A HAPPY VILLAGE--- UNTIL THE EXILES CAME!
THE NATIVES WERE PEACEFUL ---DIDN'T EVEN HAVE A POPGUN BETWEEN THEM---
SO IT WASN'T LONG BEFORE THEY WERE TURNED INTO SERFS BY THEIR NEW, WELL-ARMED MASTERS!
I'VE BEEN TRYING TO ORGANIZE THEM--- BAND THEM TOGETHER AND GET THEM TO FIGHT FOR THE FREE-DOM THAT THEY'VE LOST!
BUT, IT'S AN UP-HILL JOB!
IT WOULD HAVE TO BE!
THE EXILES ARE PROFESSIONAL KILLERS!
BUT WHAT ABOUT YOU? WHO ARE YOU? WHAT'S YOUR STAKE IN ALL THIS?
I'VE BEEN WONDERING ABOUT THAT MYSELF! IT'S KINDA FUNNY HOW IT ALL HAPPENED---
EVER SINCE I CAN REMEMBER, I'VE BEEN NUTS ABOUT BIRDS!
I USED TO HAVE THE BIGGEST PIGEON COOP ON ANY ROOFTOP IN HARLEM!
MAN! I COULD PRACTICALLY MAKE THOSE HIGH-FLYERS TALK!
BUT THEN--- I GOT ALL HUNG UP ON FALCONS--!
17.

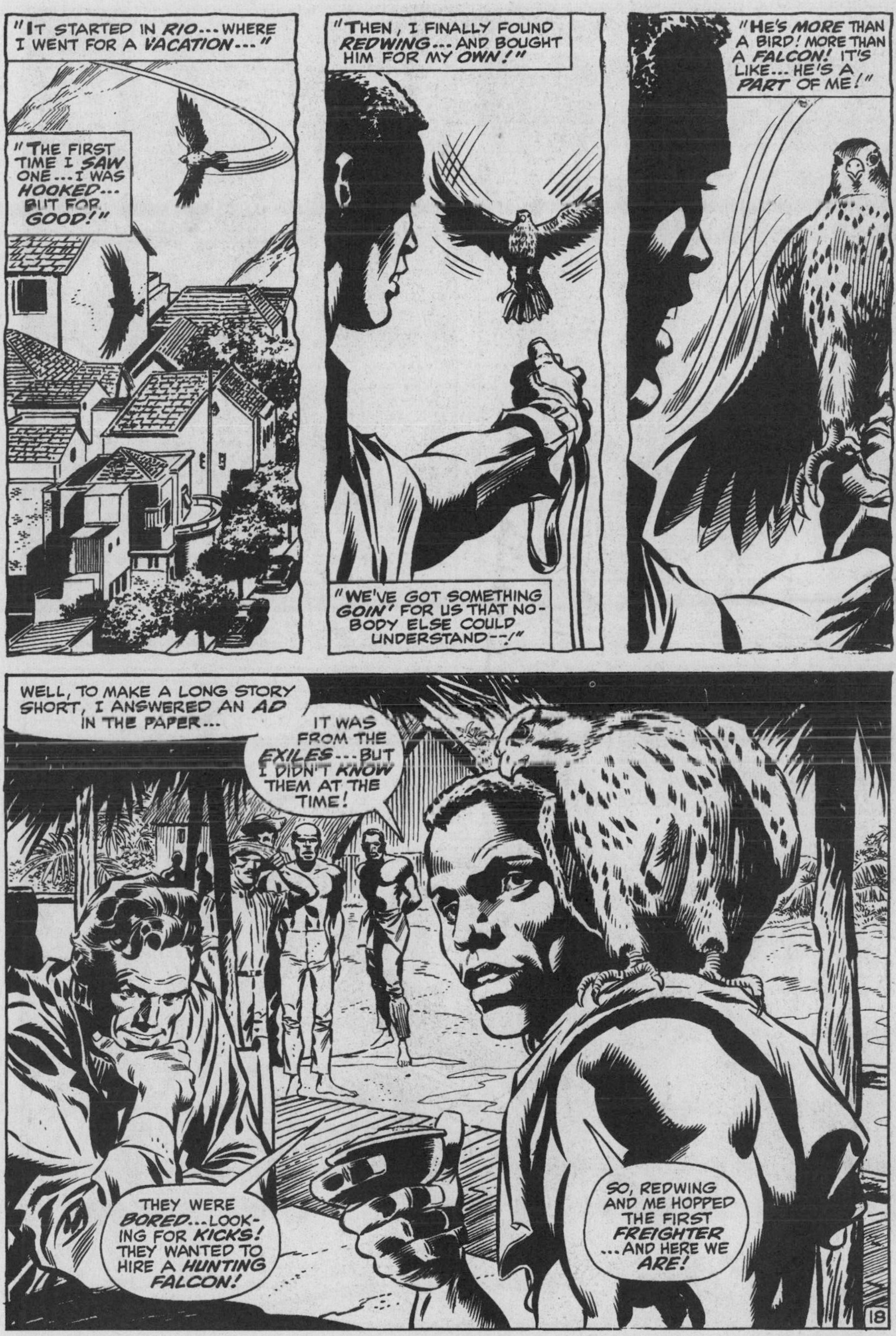
"IT STARTED IN RIO--- WHERE I WENT FOR A VACATION---"
"THE FIRST TIME I SAW ONE---I WAS HOOKED--- BUT FOR GOOD!"
"THEN, I FINALLY FOUND REDWING--- AND BOUGHT HIM FOR MY OWN!"
"WE'VE GOT SOMETHING GOIN' FOR US THAT NO-BODY ELSE COULD UNDERSTAND--!"
"HE'S MORE THAN A BIRD! MORE THAN A FALCON! IT'S LIKE--- HE'S A PART OF ME!"
WELL, TO MAKE A LONG STORY SHORT, I ANSWERED AN AD IN THE PAPER---
IT WAS FROM THE EXILES---BUT I DIDN'T KNOW THEM AT THE TIME!
THEY WERE BORED---LOOK-ING FOR KICKS! THEY WANTED TO HIRE A HUNTING FALCON!
SO, REDWING AND ME HOPPED THE FIRST FREIGHTER ---AND HERE WE ARE!
18

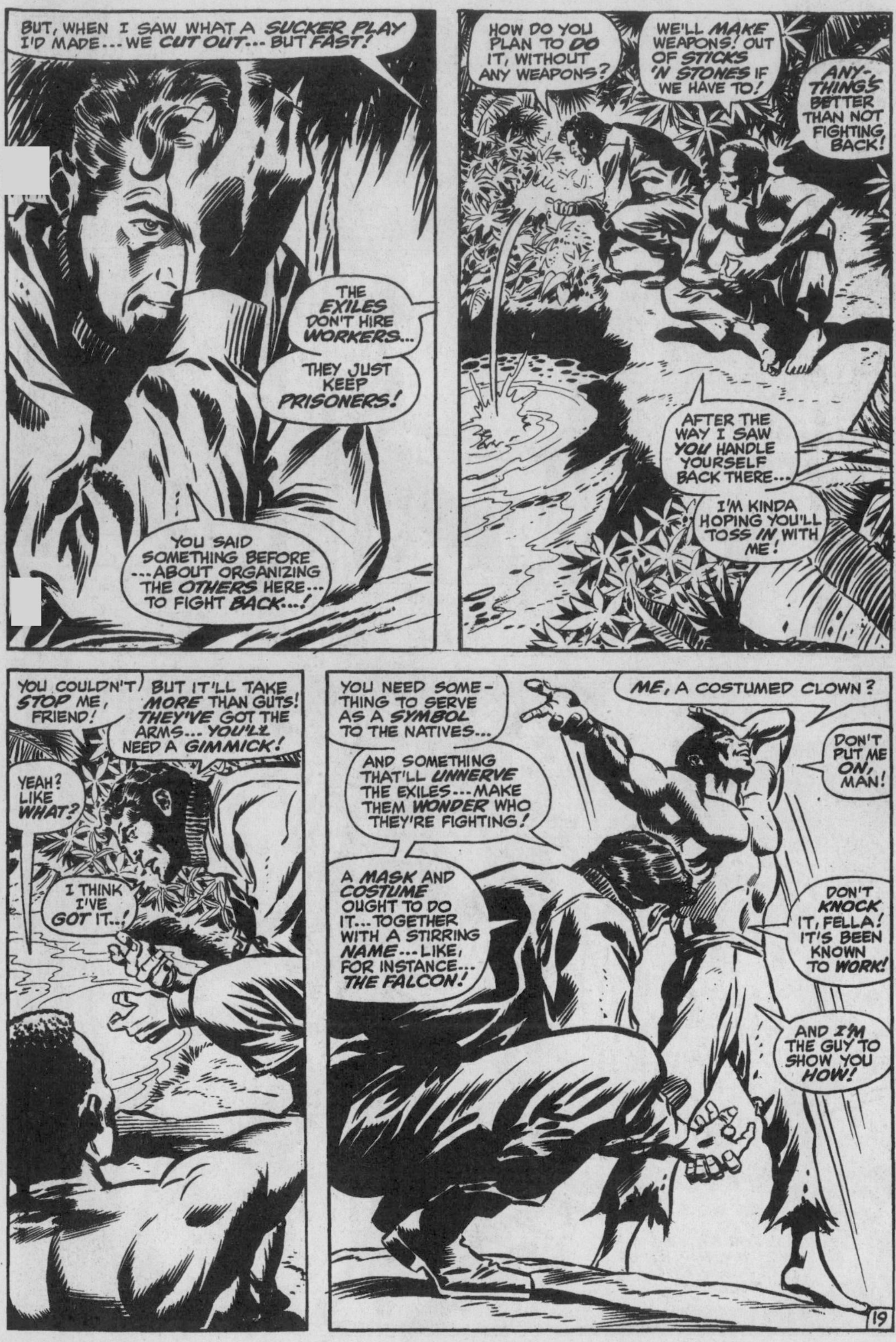
BUT, WHEN I SAW WHAT A SUCKER PLAY I'D MADE... WE CUT OUT... BUT FAST!
THE EXILES DON'T HIRE WORKERS...
THEY JUST KEEP PRISONERS!
YOU SAID SOMETHING BEFORE ...ABOUT ORGANIZING THE OTHERS HERE... TO FIGHT BACK...!
HOW DO YOU PLAN TO DO IT, WITHOUT ANY WEAPONS?
WE'LL MAKE WEAPONS! OUT OF STICKS 'N STONES IF WE HAVE TO!
ANY-THING'S BETTER THAN NOT FIGHTING BACK!
AFTER THE WAY I SAW YOU HANDLE YOURSELF BACK THERE...
I'M KINDA HOPING YOU'LL TOSS IN WITH ME!
YOU COULDN'T STOP ME, FRIEND!
BUT IT'LL TAKE MORE THAN GUTS! THEY'VE GOT THE ARMS... YOU'LL NEED A GIMMICK!
YEAH? LIKE WHAT?
I THINK I'VE GOT IT...!
YOU NEED SOME-THING TO SERVE AS A SYMBOL TO THE NATIVES...
AND SOMETHING THAT'LL UNNERVE THE EXILES... MAKE THEM WONDER WHO THEY'RE FIGHTING!
A MASK AND COSTUME OUGHT TO DO IT... TOGETHER WITH A STIRRING NAME... LIKE, FOR INSTANCE... THE FALCON!
ME, A COSTUMED CLOWN?
DON'T PUT ME ON, MAN!
DON'T KNOCK IT, FELLA! IT'S BEEN KNOWN TO WORK!
AND I'M THE GUY TO SHOW YOU HOW!
19

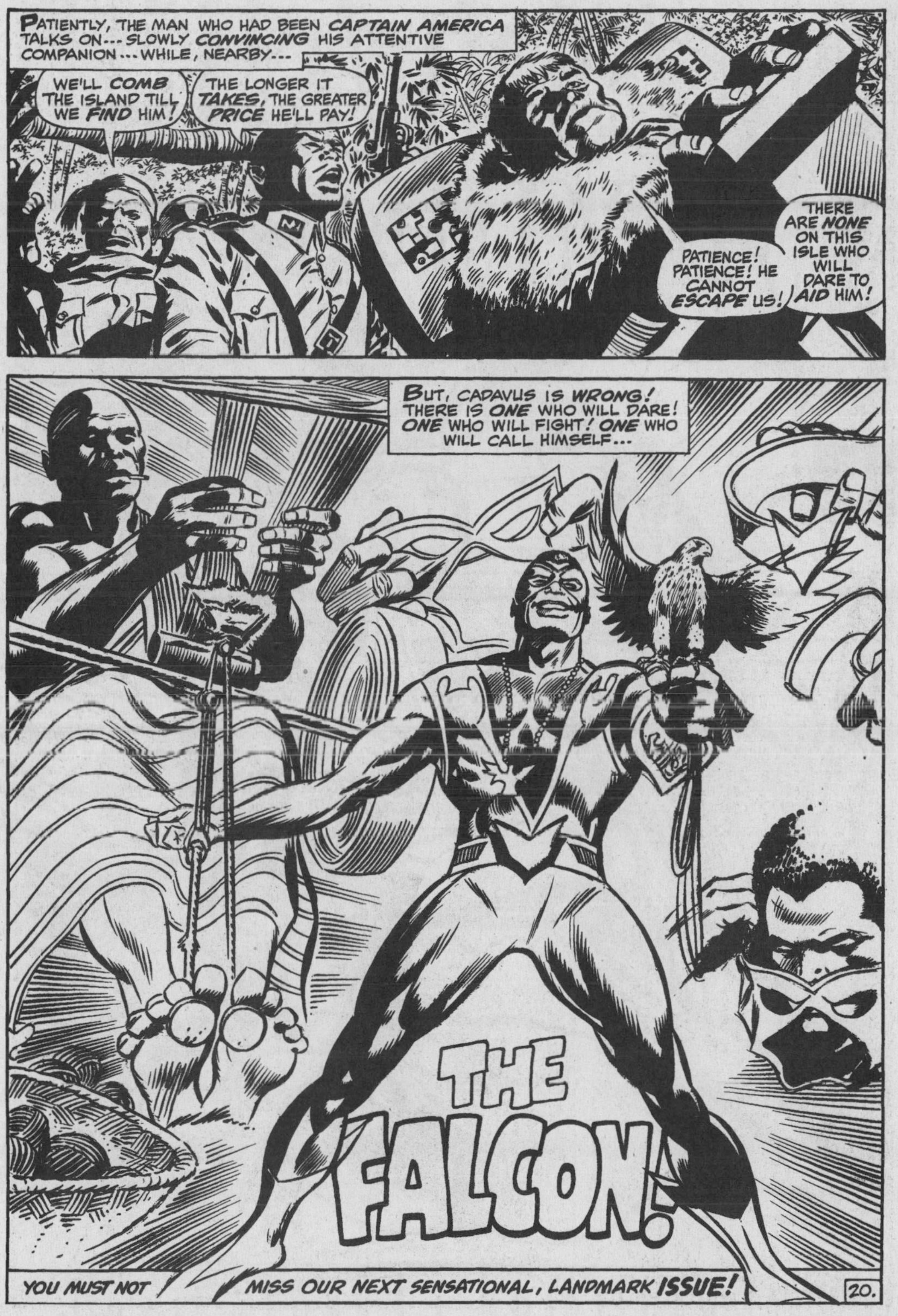
PATIENTLY, THE MAN WHO HAD BEEN CAPTAIN AMERICA TALKS ON--- SLOWLY CONVINCING HIS ATTENTIVE COMPANION --- WHILE, NEARBY---
WE'LL COMB THE ISLAND TILL WE FIND HIM!
THE LONGER IT TAKES, THE GREATER PRICE HE'LL PAY!
PATIENCE! PATIENCE! HE CANNOT ESCAPE US!
THERE ARE NONE ON THIS ISLE WHO WILL DARE TO AID HIM!
BUT, CADAVUS IS WRONG! THERE IS ONE WHO WILL DARE! ONE WHO WILL FIGHT! ONE WHO WILL CALL HIMSELF...
THE FALCON!
YOU MUST NOT MISS OUR NEXT SENSATIONAL, LANDMARK ISSUE!
20.

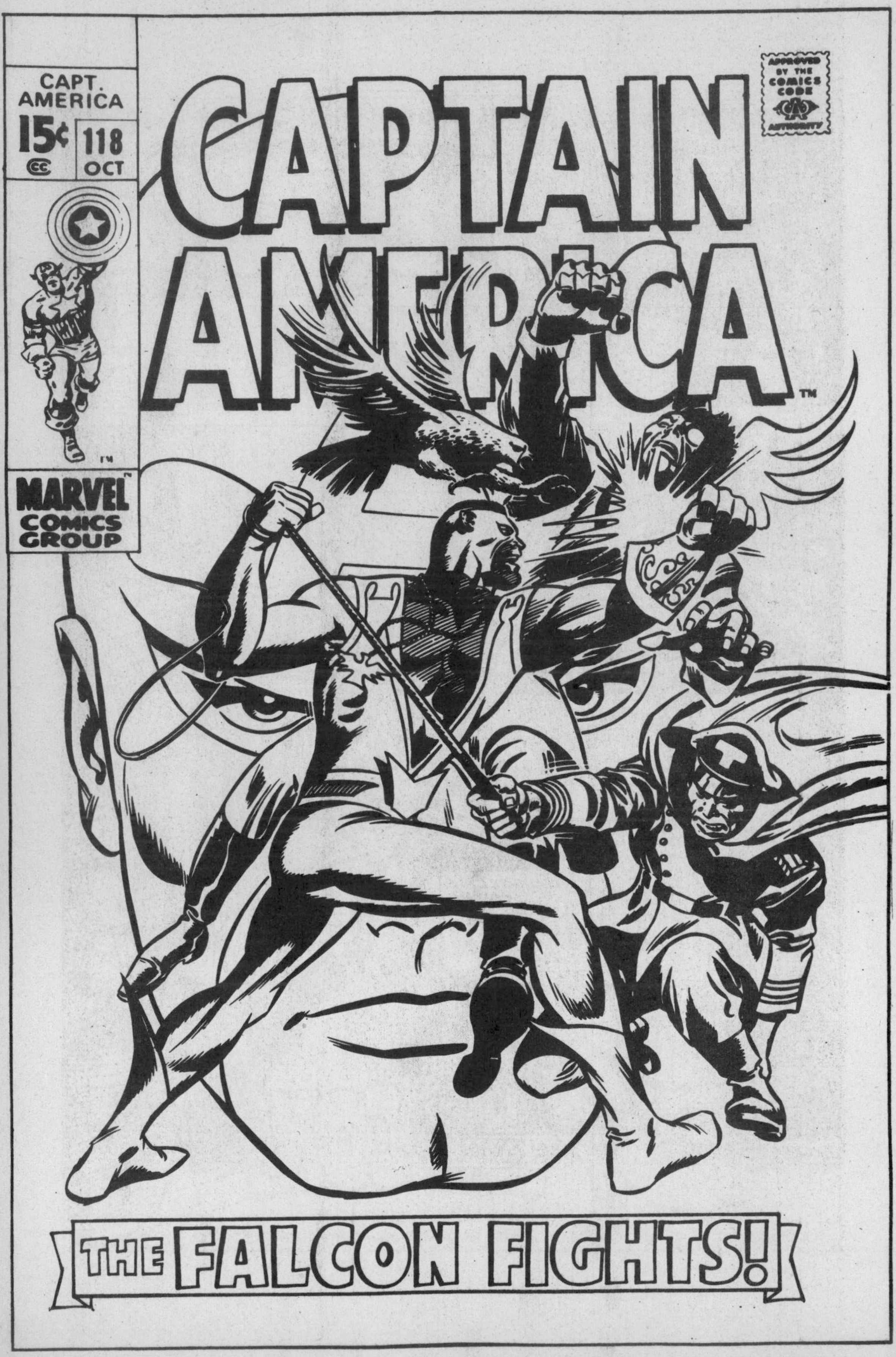
CAPT. AMERICA
15¢
118
OCT
MARVEL COMICS GROUP
APPROVED BY THE COMICS CODE AUTHORITY
CAPTAIN AMERICA
THE FALCON FIGHTS!

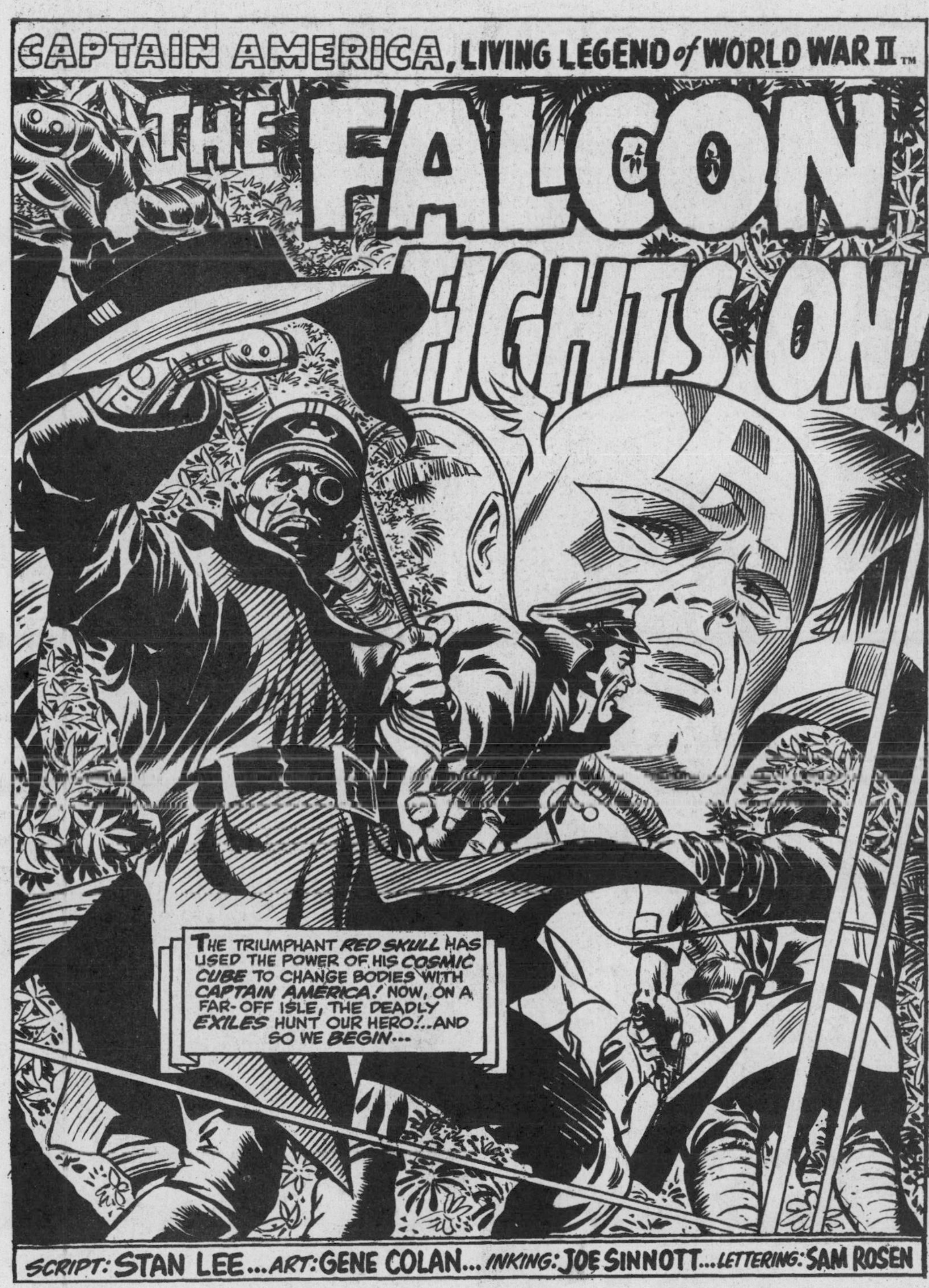
CAPTAIN AMERICA, LIVING LEGEND of WORLD WAR II ™
THE FALCON FIGHTS ON!
THE TRIUMPHANT RED SKULL HAS USED THE POWER OF HIS COSMIC CUBE TO CHANGE BODIES WITH CAPTAIN AMERICA! NOW, ON A FAR-OFF ISLE, THE DEADLY EXILES HUNT OUR HERO!...AND SO WE BEGIN...
SCRIPT: STAN LEE...ART: GENE COLAN...INKING: JOE SINNOTT...LETTERING: SAM ROSEN

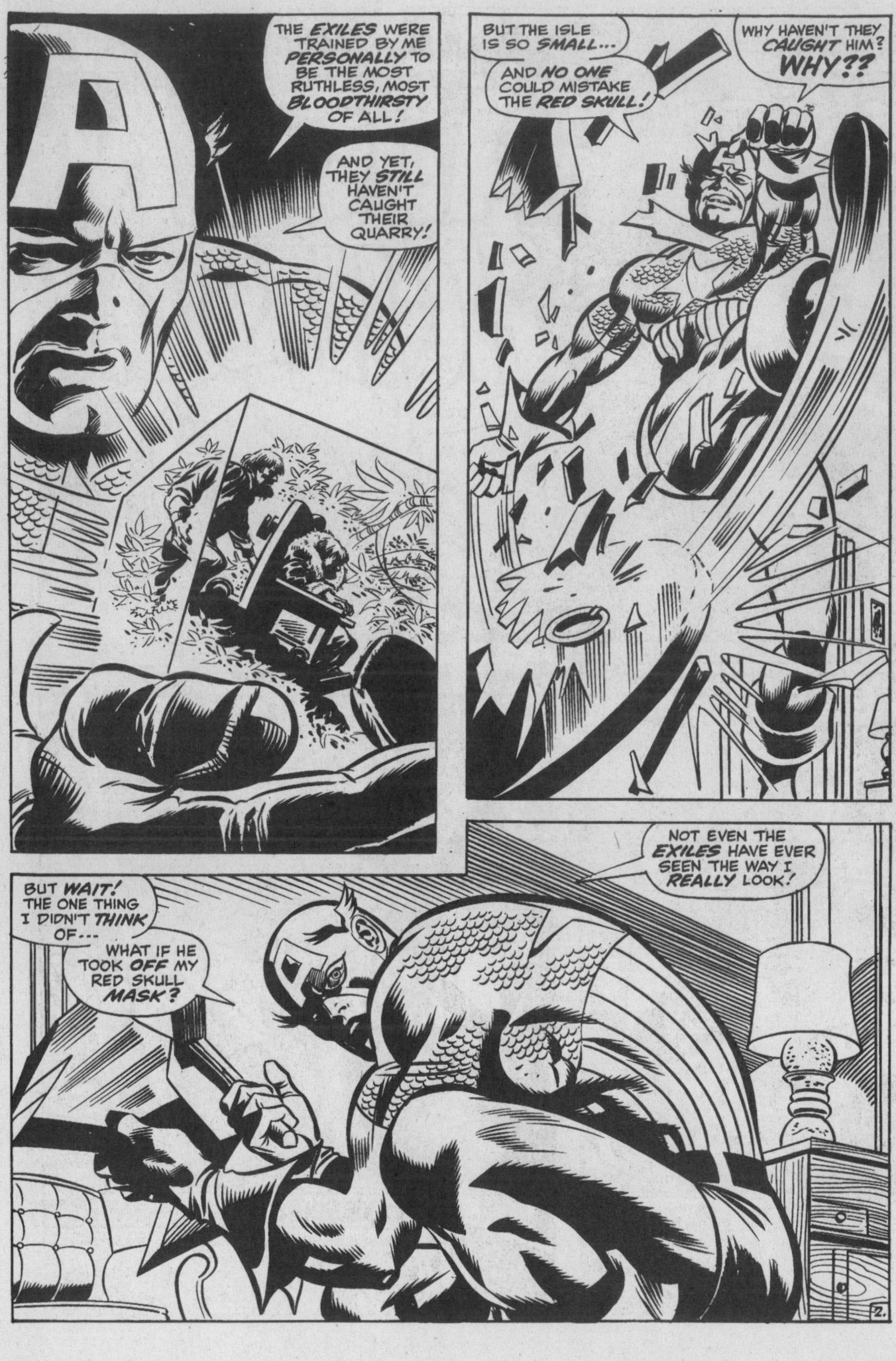
THE EXILES WERE TRAINED BY ME PERSONALLY TO BE THE MOST RUTHLESS, MOST BLOODTHIRSTY OF ALL!
AND YET, THEY STILL HAVEN'T CAUGHT THEIR QUARRY!
BUT THE ISLE IS SO SMALL...
AND NO ONE COULD MISTAKE THE RED SKULL!
WHY HAVEN'T THEY CAUGHT HIM? WHY??
NOT EVEN THE EXILES HAVE EVER SEEN THE WAY I REALLY LOOK!
BUT WAIT! THE ONE THING I DIDN'T THINK OF---
WHAT IF HE TOOK OFF MY RED SKULL MASK?
2.

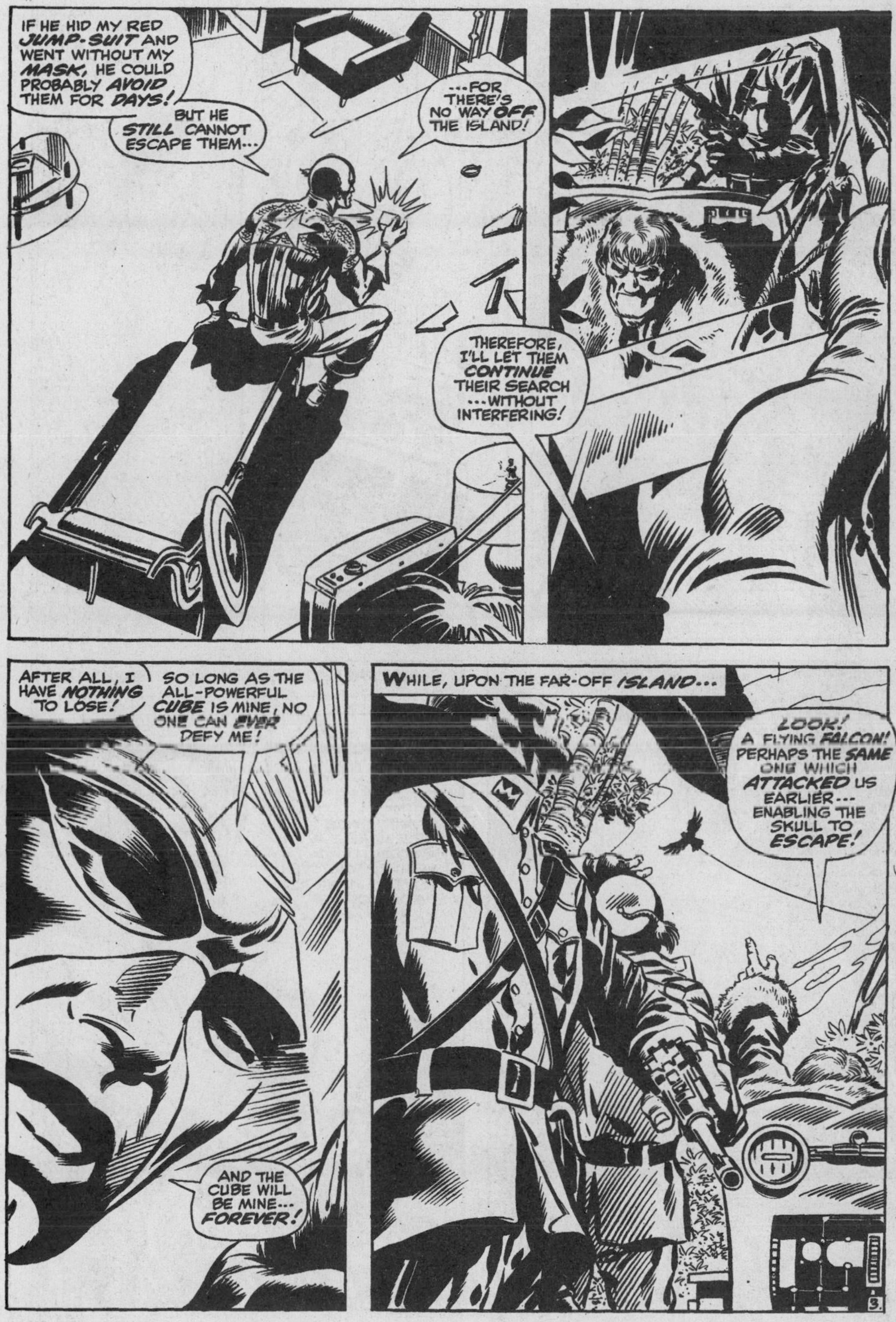
IF HE HID MY RED JUMP-SUIT AND WENT WITHOUT MY MASK, HE COULD PROBABLY AVOID THEM FOR DAYS!
BUT HE STILL CANNOT ESCAPE THEM...
...FOR THERE'S NO WAY OFF THE ISLAND!
THEREFORE, I'LL LET THEM CONTINUE THEIR SEARCH ...WITHOUT INTERFERING!
AFTER ALL, I HAVE NOTHING TO LOSE!
SO LONG AS THE ALL-POWERFUL CUBE IS MINE, NO ONE CAN EVER DEFY ME!
AND THE CUBE WILL BE MINE... FOREVER!
WHILE, UPON THE FAR-OFF ISLAND...
LOOK! A FLYING FALCON! PERHAPS THE SAME ONE WHICH ATTACKED US EARLIER--- ENABLING THE SKULL TO ESCAPE!
3.

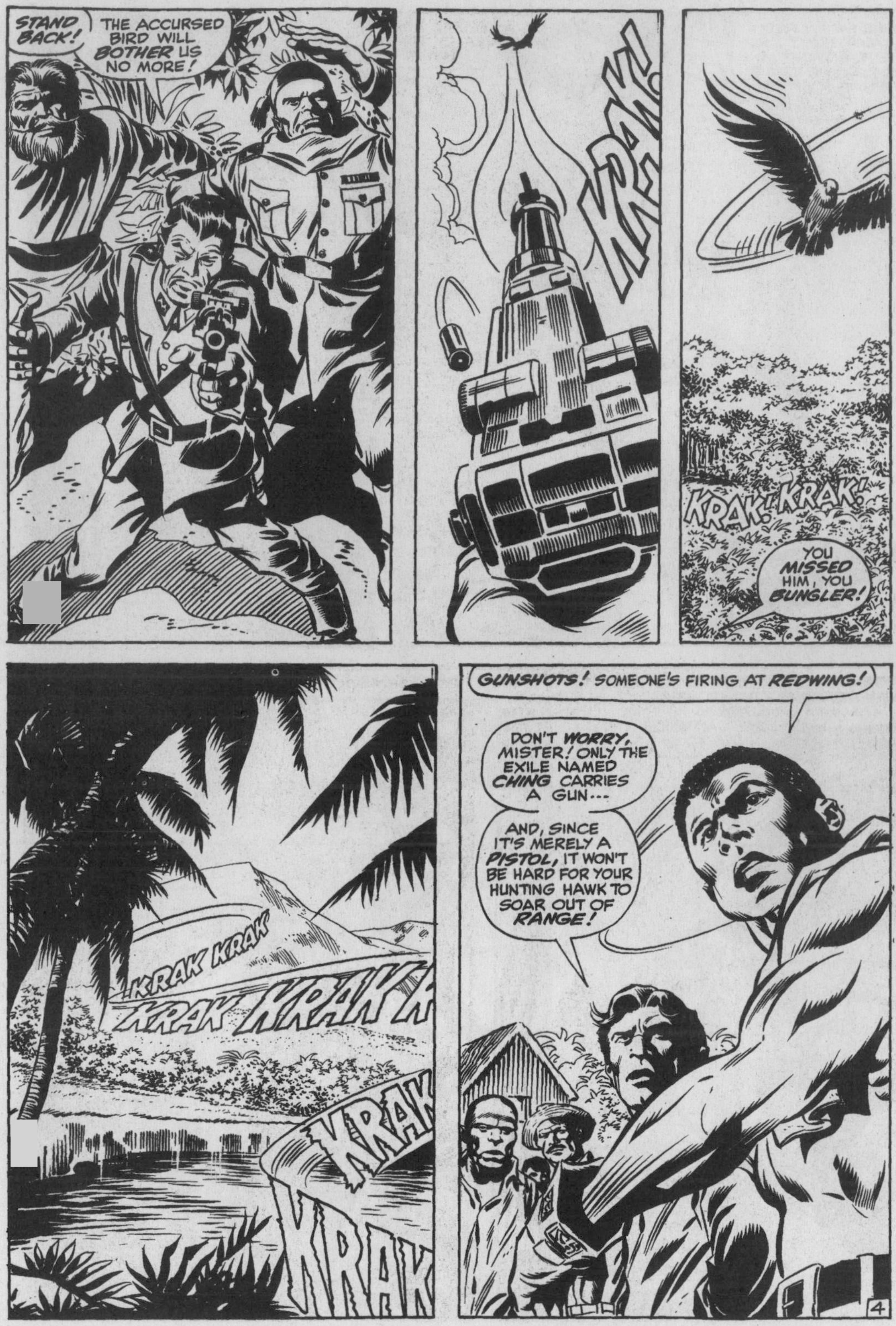
STAND BACK!
THE ACCURSED BIRD WILL BOTHER US NO MORE!
KRAK!
KRAK! KRAK!
YOU MISSED HIM, YOU BUNGLER!
KRAK KRAK
KRAK KRAK K
KRAK
KRAK
GUNSHOTS! SOMEONE'S FIRING AT REDWING!
DON'T WORRY, MISTER! ONLY THE EXILE NAMED CHING CARRIES A GUN---
AND, SINCE IT'S MERELY A PISTOL, IT WON'T BE HARD FOR YOUR HUNTING HAWK TO SOAR OUT OF RANGE!
4

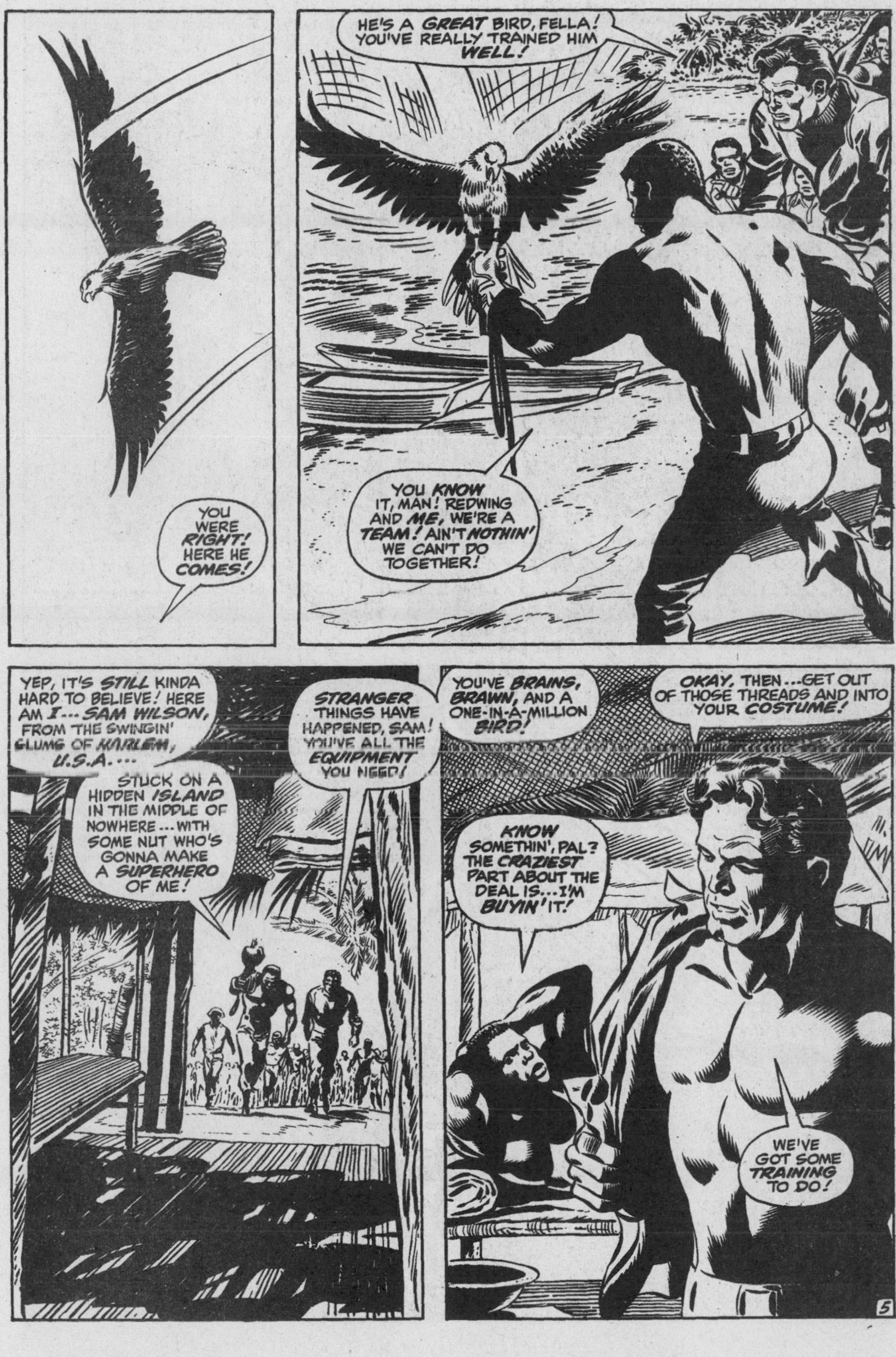

YOU WERE RIGHT! HERE HE COMES!
HE'S A GREAT BIRD, FELLA! YOU'VE REALLY TRAINED HIM WELL!
YOU KNOW IT, MAN! REDWING AND ME, WE'RE A TEAM! AIN'T NOTHIN' WE CAN'T DO TOGETHER!
YEP, IT'S STILL KINDA HARD TO BELIEVE! HERE AM I... SAM WILSON, FROM THE SWINGIN' SLUMS OF HARLEM, U.S.A....
STUCK ON A HIDDEN ISLAND IN THE MIDDLE OF NOWHERE... WITH SOME NUT WHO'S GONNA MAKE A SUPERHERO OF ME!
STRANGER THINGS HAVE HAPPENED, SAM! YOU'VE ALL THE EQUIPMENT YOU NEED!
YOU'VE BRAINS, BRAWN, AND A ONE-IN-A-MILLION BIRD!
OKAY. THEN... GET OUT OF THOSE THREADS AND INTO YOUR COSTUME!
KNOW SOMETHIN', PAL? THE CRAZIEST PART ABOUT THE DEAL IS... I'M BUYIN' IT!
WE'VE GOT SOME TRAINING TO DO!
5

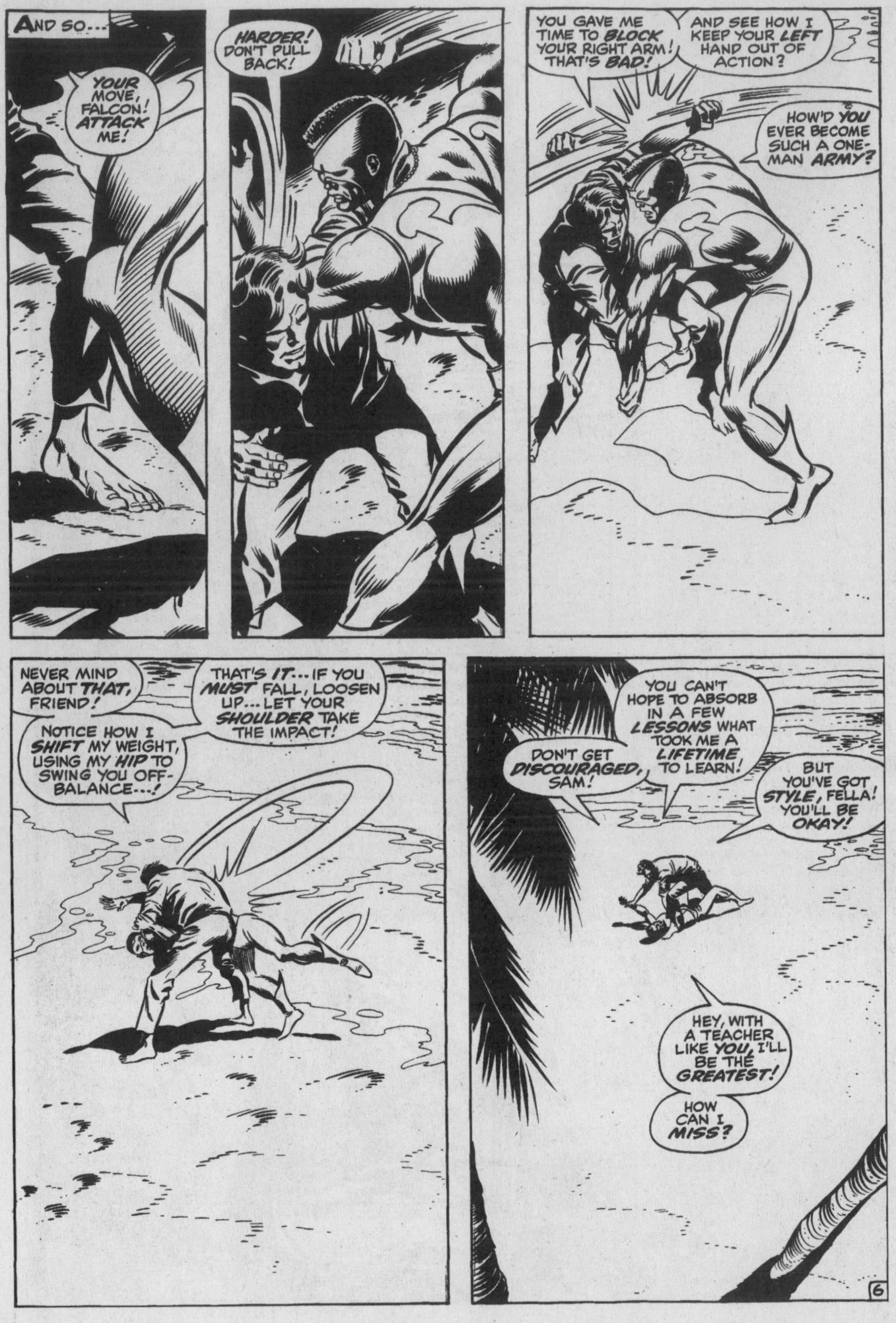
AND SO...
YOUR MOVE, FALCON! ATTACK ME!
HARDER! DON'T PULL BACK!
YOU GAVE ME TIME TO BLOCK YOUR RIGHT ARM! THAT'S BAD!
AND SEE HOW I KEEP YOUR LEFT HAND OUT OF ACTION?
HOW'D YOU EVER BECOME SUCH A ONE-MAN ARMY?
NEVER MIND ABOUT THAT, FRIEND!
NOTICE HOW I SHIFT MY WEIGHT, USING MY HIP TO SWING YOU OFF-BALANCE...!
THAT'S IT... IF YOU MUST FALL, LOOSEN UP... LET YOUR SHOULDER TAKE THE IMPACT!
DON'T GET DISCOURAGED, SAM!
YOU CAN'T HOPE TO ABSORB IN A FEW LESSONS WHAT TOOK ME A LIFETIME TO LEARN!
BUT YOU'VE GOT STYLE, FELLA! YOU'LL BE OKAY!
HEY, WITH A TEACHER LIKE YOU, I'LL BE THE GREATEST!
HOW CAN I MISS?
6

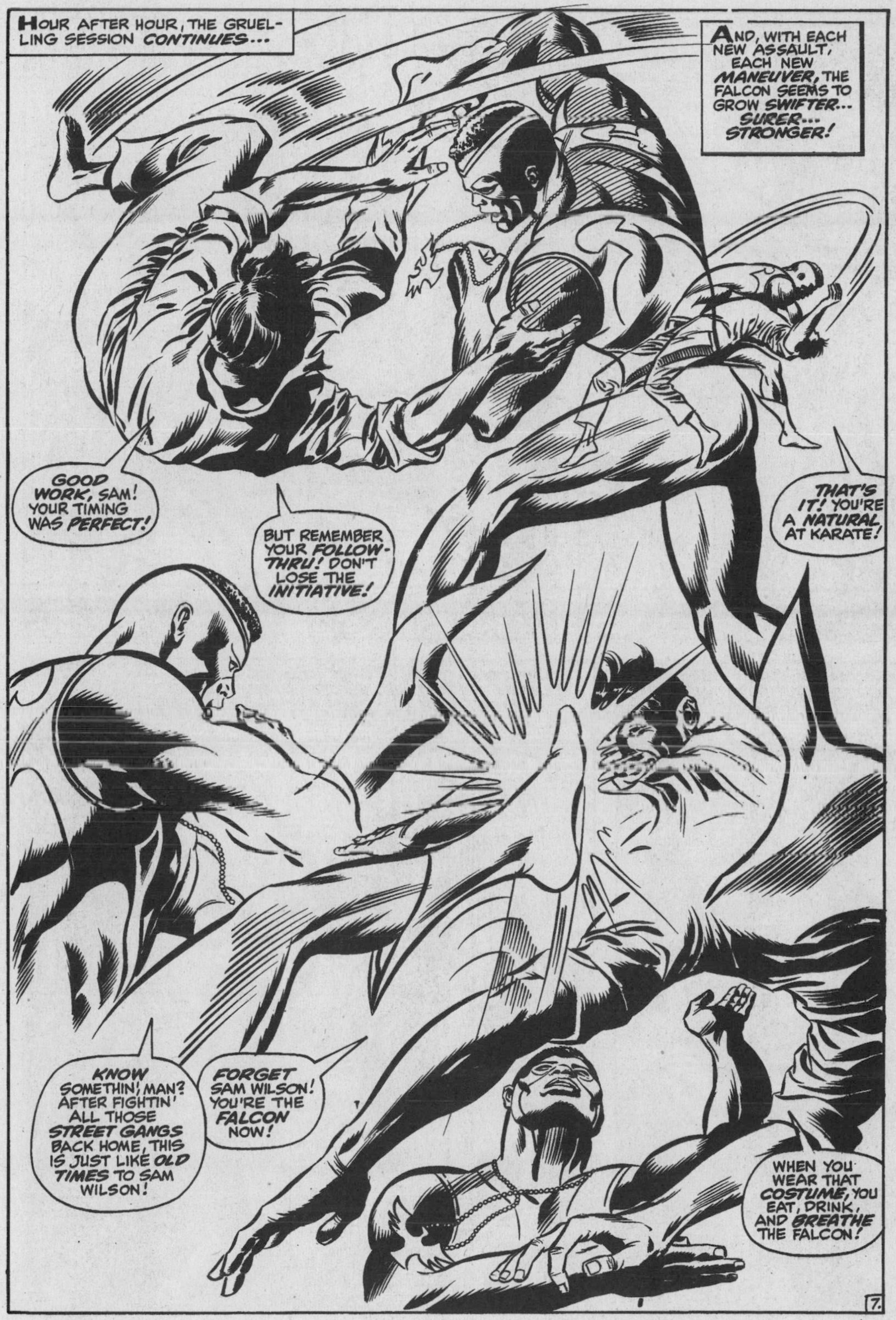
HOUR AFTER HOUR, THE GRUELLING SESSION CONTINUES...
AND, WITH EACH NEW ASSAULT, EACH NEW MANEUVER, THE FALCON SEEMS TO GROW SWIFTER... SURER... STRONGER!
GOOD WORK, SAM! YOUR TIMING WAS PERFECT!
BUT REMEMBER YOUR FOLLOW-THRU! DON'T LOSE THE INITIATIVE!
THAT'S IT! YOU'RE A NATURAL AT KARATE!
KNOW SOMETHIN', MAN? AFTER FIGHTIN' ALL THOSE STREET GANGS BACK HOME, THIS IS JUST LIKE OLD TIMES TO SAM WILSON!
FORGET SAM WILSON! YOU'RE THE FALCON NOW!
WHEN YOU WEAR THAT COSTUME, YOU EAT, DRINK, AND BREATHE THE FALCON!
7.

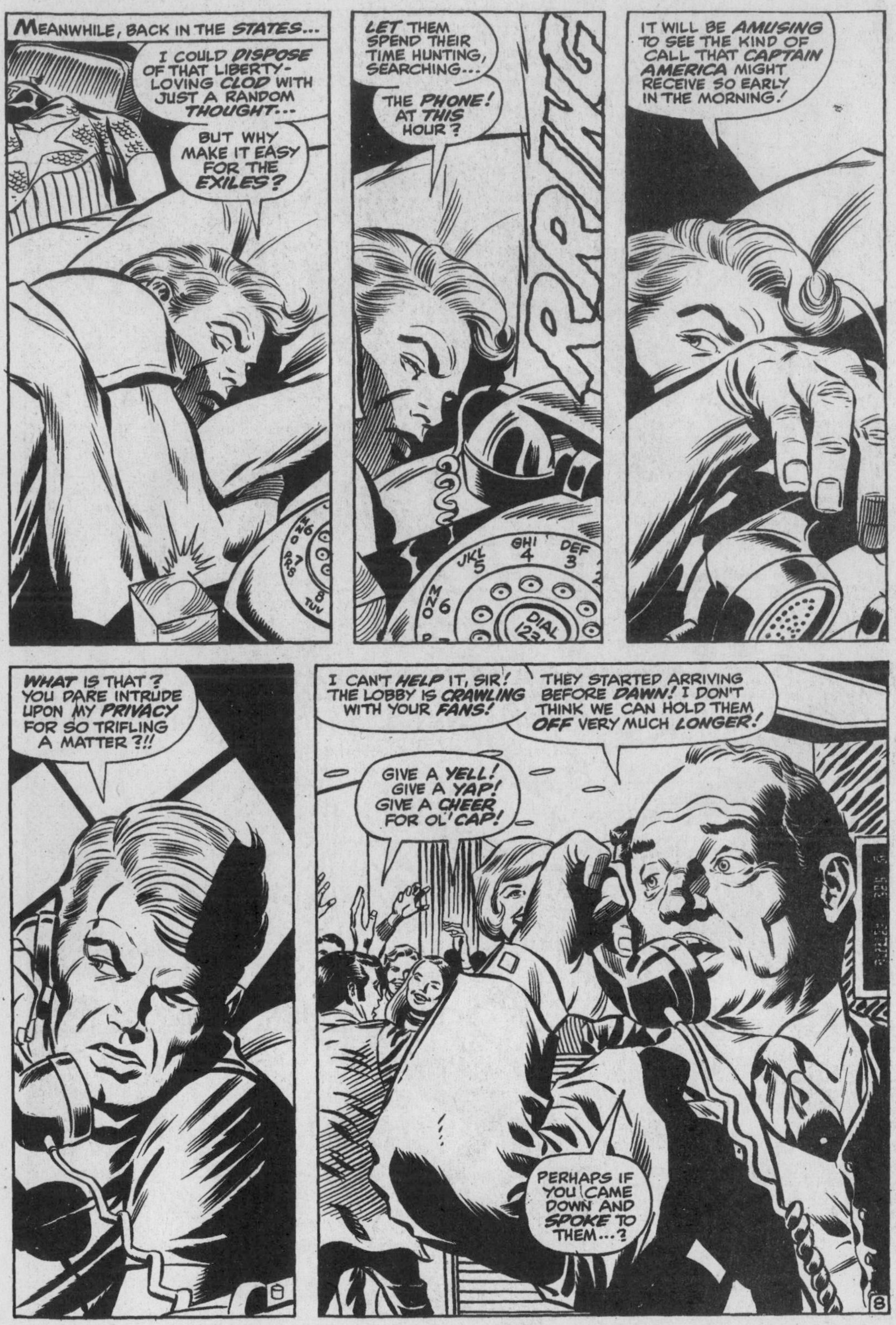
MEANWHILE, BACK IN THE STATES...
I COULD DISPOSE OF THAT LIBERTY-LOVING CLOD WITH JUST A RANDOM THOUGHT...
BUT WHY MAKE IT EASY FOR THE EXILES?
LET THEM SPEND THEIR TIME HUNTING, SEARCHING...
THE PHONE! AT THIS HOUR?
IT WILL BE AMUSING TO SEE THE KIND OF CALL THAT CAPTAIN AMERICA MIGHT RECEIVE SO EARLY IN THE MORNING!
WHAT IS THAT? YOU DARE INTRUDE UPON MY PRIVACY FOR SO TRIFLING A MATTER?!!
I CAN'T HELP IT, SIR! THE LOBBY IS CRAWLING WITH YOUR FANS!
THEY STARTED ARRIVING BEFORE DAWN! I DON'T THINK WE CAN HOLD THEM OFF VERY MUCH LONGER!
GIVE A YELL! GIVE A YAP! GIVE A CHEER FOR OL' CAP!
PERHAPS IF YOU CAME DOWN AND SPOKE TO THEM...?
8

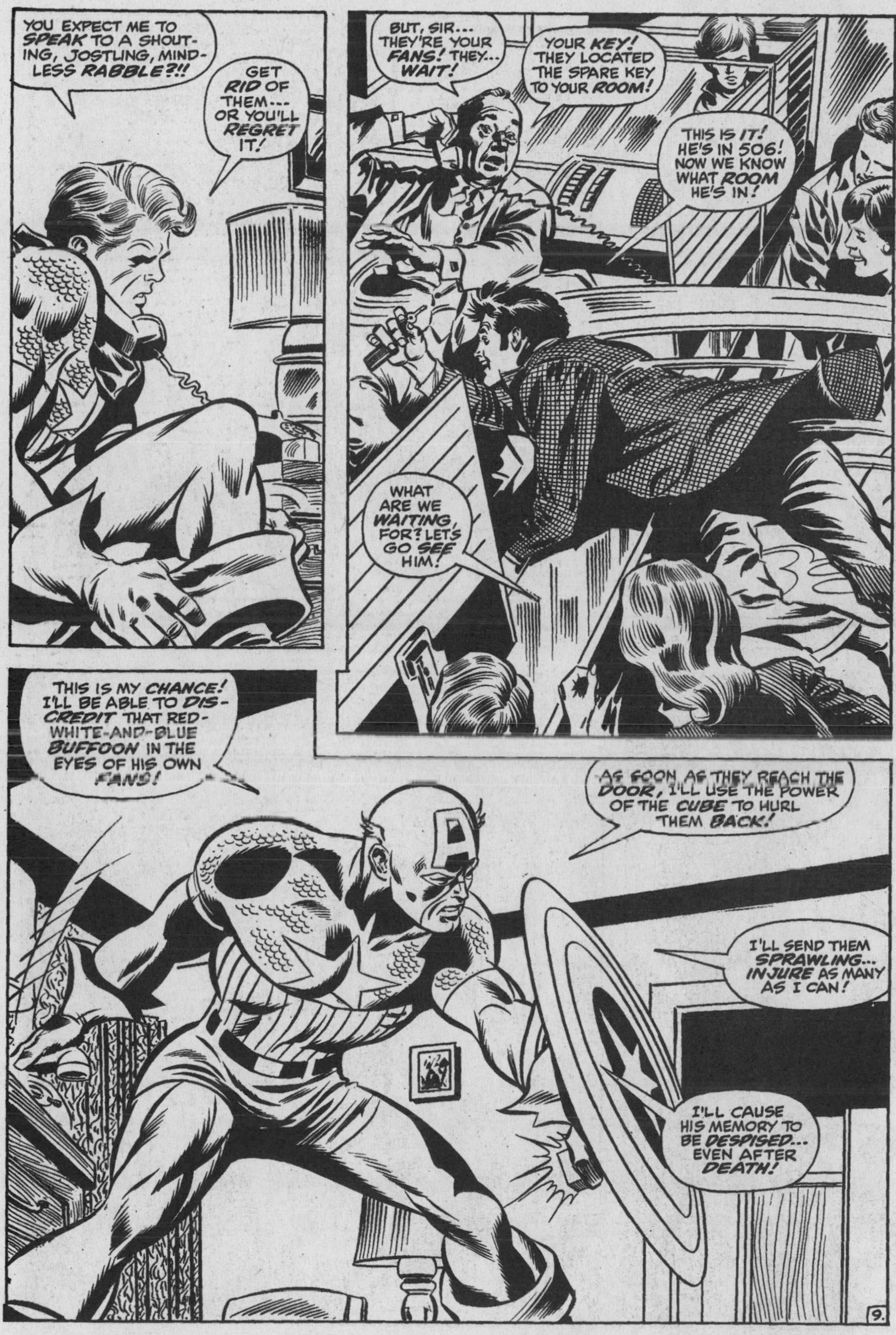
YOU EXPECT ME TO SPEAK TO A SHOUTING, JOSTLING, MINDLESS RABBLE?!!
GET RID OF THEM... OR YOU'LL REGRET IT!
BUT, SIR... THEY'RE YOUR FANS! THEY... WAIT!
YOUR KEY! THEY LOCATED THE SPARE KEY TO YOUR ROOM!
THIS IS IT! HE'S IN 506! NOW WE KNOW WHAT ROOM HE'S IN!
WHAT ARE WE WAITING FOR? LET'S GO SEE HIM!
THIS IS MY CHANCE! I'LL BE ABLE TO DISCREDIT THAT RED-WHITE-AND-BLUE BUFFOON IN THE EYES OF HIS OWN FANS!
AS SOON AS THEY REACH THE DOOR, I'LL USE THE POWER OF THE CUBE TO HURL THEM BACK!
I'LL SEND THEM SPRAWLING... INJURE AS MANY AS I CAN!
I'LL CAUSE HIS MEMORY TO BE DESPISED... EVEN AFTER DEATH!
9.

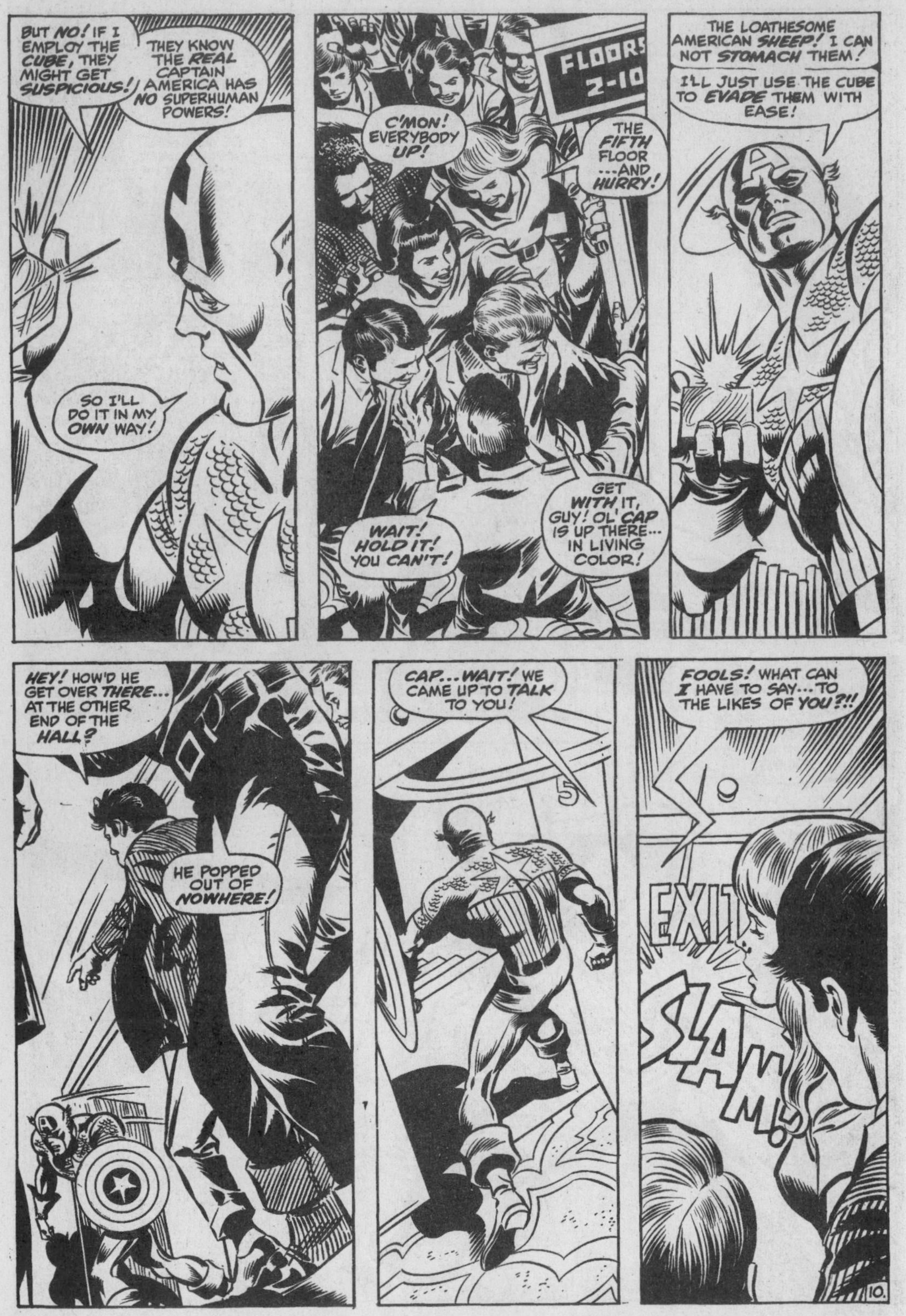
BUT NO! IF I EMPLOY THE CUBE, THEY MIGHT GET SUSPICIOUS!
THEY KNOW THE REAL CAPTAIN AMERICA HAS NO SUPERHUMAN POWERS!
SO I'LL DO IT IN MY OWN WAY!
FLOORS 2-10
C'MON! EVERYBODY UP!
THE FIFTH FLOOR ...AND HURRY!
WAIT! HOLD IT! YOU CAN'T!
GET WITH IT, GUY! OL' CAP IS UP THERE... IN LIVING COLOR!
THE LOATHESOME AMERICAN SHEEP! I CAN NOT STOMACH THEM!
I'LL JUST USE THE CUBE TO EVADE THEM WITH EASE!
HEY! HOW'D HE GET OVER THERE... AT THE OTHER END OF THE HALL?
HE POPPED OUT OF NOWHERE!
CAP... WAIT! WE CAME UP TO TALK TO YOU!
5
FOOLS! WHAT CAN I HAVE TO SAY... TO THE LIKES OF YOU?!!
EXIT
SLAM!
10.

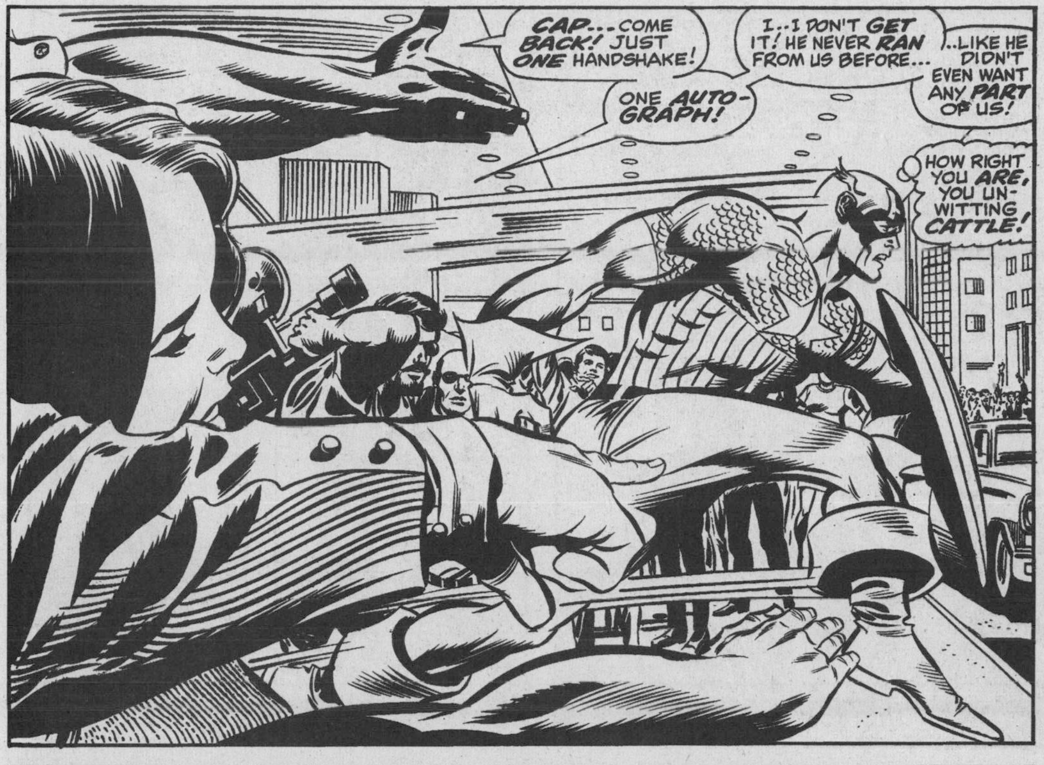
CAP... COME BACK! JUST ONE HANDSHAKE!
ONE AUTO-GRAPH!
I... I DON'T GET IT! HE NEVER RAN FROM US BEFORE...
...LIKE HE DIDN'T EVEN WANT ANY PART OF US!
HOW RIGHT YOU ARE, YOU UN-WITTING CATTLE!

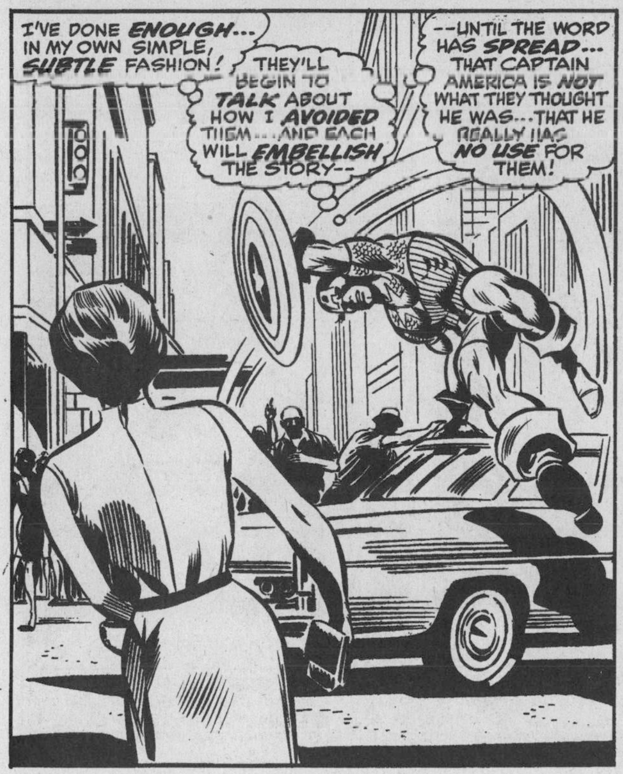
I'VE DONE ENOUGH... IN MY OWN SIMPLE, SUBTLE FASHION!
THEY'LL BEGIN TO TALK ABOUT HOW I AVOIDED THEM... AND EACH WILL EMBELLISH THE STORY--
--UNTIL THE WORD HAS SPREAD... THAT CAPTAIN AMERICA IS NOT WHAT THEY THOUGHT HE WAS... THAT HE REALLY HAS NO USE FOR THEM!

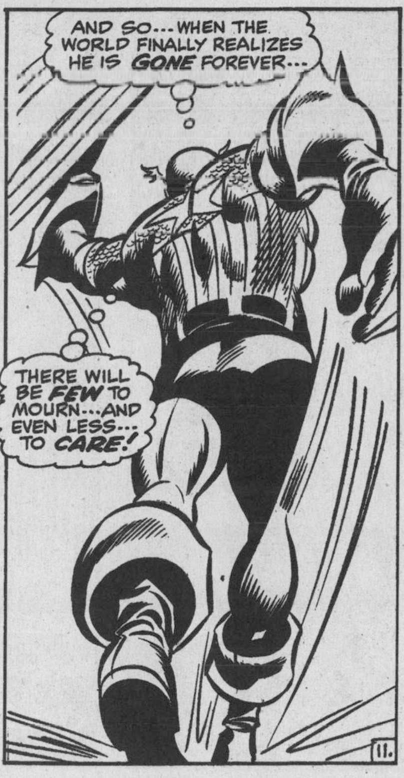
AND SO... WHEN THE WORLD FINALLY REALIZES HE IS GONE FOREVER...
THERE WILL BE FEW TO MOURN... AND EVEN LESS... TO CARE!

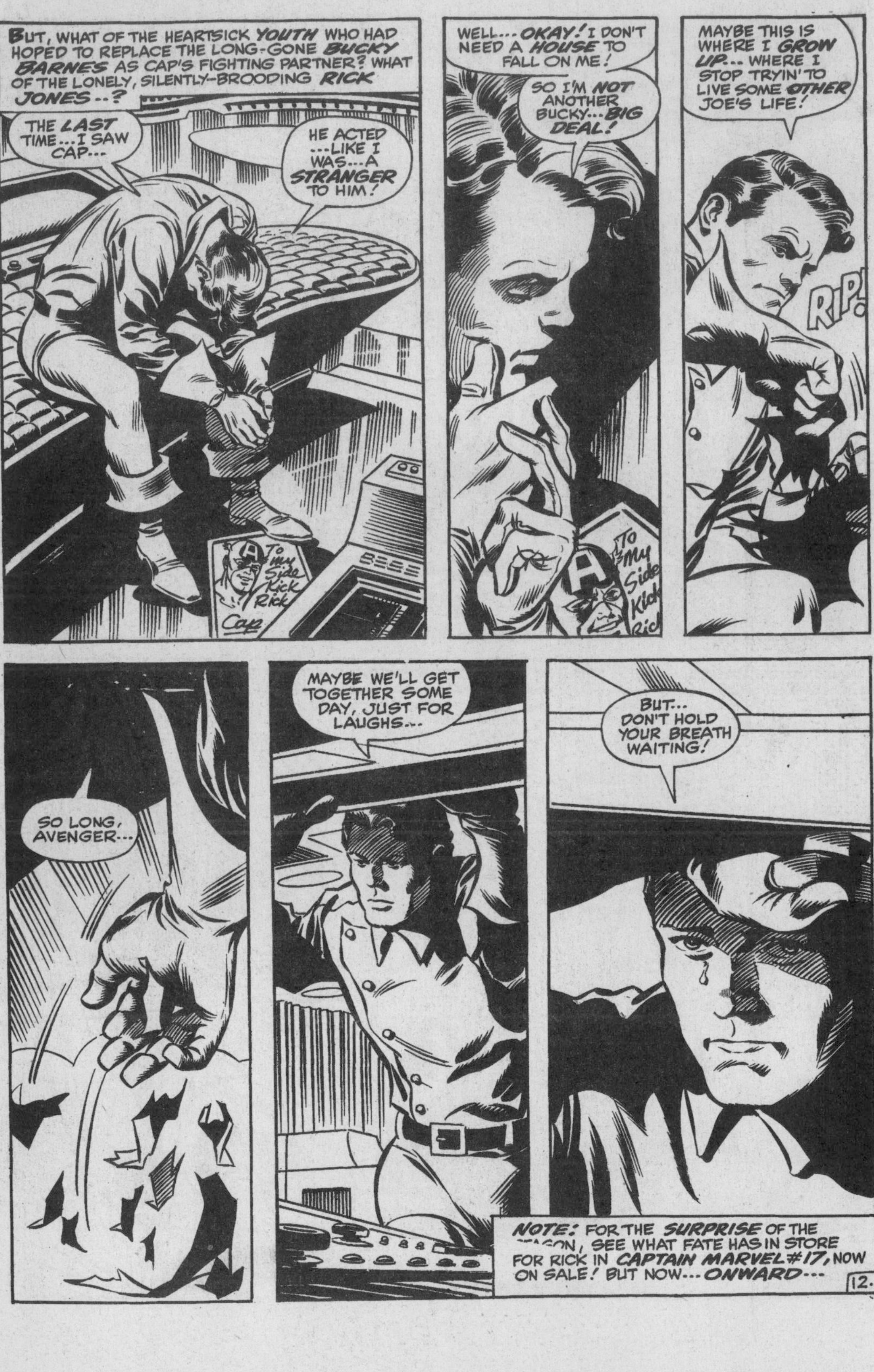
BUT, WHAT OF THE HEARTSICK YOUTH WHO HAD HOPED TO REPLACE THE LONG-GONE BUCKY BARNES AS CAP'S FIGHTING PARTNER? WHAT OF THE LONELY, SILENTLY-BROODING RICK JONES--?
THE LAST TIME...I SAW CAP...
HE ACTED ...LIKE I WAS...A STRANGER TO HIM!
To my Side Kick Rick
Cap
WELL...OKAY! I DON'T NEED A HOUSE TO FALL ON ME!
SO I'M NOT ANOTHER BUCKY...BIG DEAL!
MAYBE THIS IS WHERE I GROW UP...WHERE I STOP TRYIN' TO LIVE SOME OTHER JOE'S LIFE!
RIP!
SO LONG, AVENGER...
MAYBE WE'LL GET TOGETHER SOME DAY, JUST FOR LAUGHS...
BUT...DON'T HOLD YOUR BREATH WAITING!
NOTE: FOR THE SURPRISE OF THE
, SEE WHAT FATE HAS IN STORE FOR RICK IN CAPTAIN MARVEL #17, NOW ON SALE! BUT NOW...ONWARD...
12.

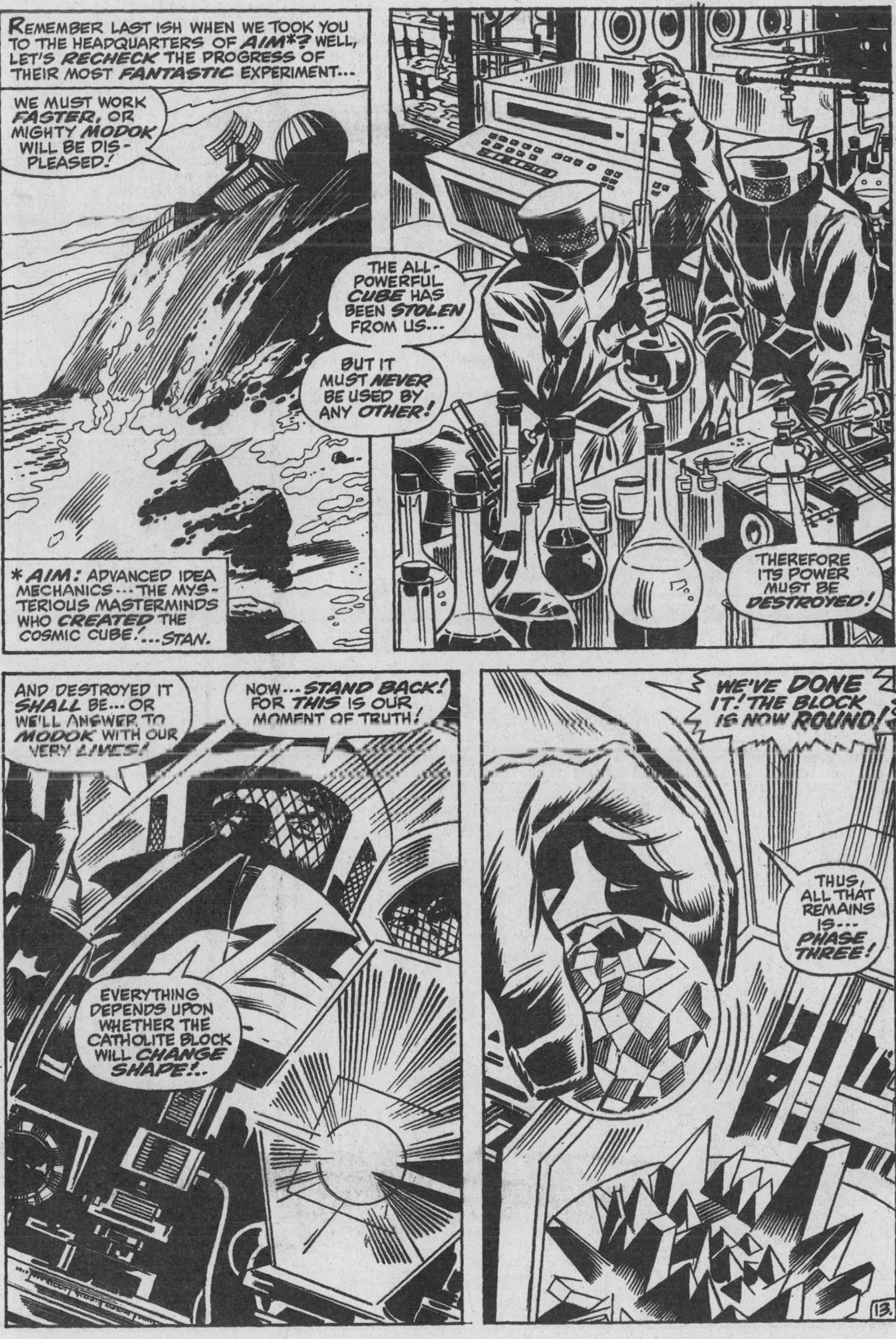
REMEMBER LAST ISH WHEN WE TOOK YOU TO THE HEADQUARTERS OF AIM*? WELL, LET'S RECHECK THE PROGRESS OF THEIR MOST FANTASTIC EXPERIMENT...
WE MUST WORK FASTER, OR MIGHTY MODOK WILL BE DISPLEASED!
*AIM: ADVANCED IDEA MECHANICS... THE MYSTERIOUS MASTERMINDS WHO CREATED THE COSMIC CUBE!... STAN.
THE ALL-POWERFUL CUBE HAS BEEN STOLEN FROM US...
BUT IT MUST NEVER BE USED BY ANY OTHER!
THEREFORE ITS POWER MUST BE DESTROYED!
AND DESTROYED IT SHALL BE... OR WE'LL ANSWER TO MODOK WITH OUR VERY LIVES!
NOW... STAND BACK! FOR THIS IS OUR MOMENT OF TRUTH!
EVERYTHING DEPENDS UPON WHETHER THE CATHOLITE BLOCK WILL CHANGE SHAPE!..
WE'VE DONE IT! THE BLOCK IS NOW ROUND!
THUS, ALL THAT REMAINS IS... PHASE THREE!
13.

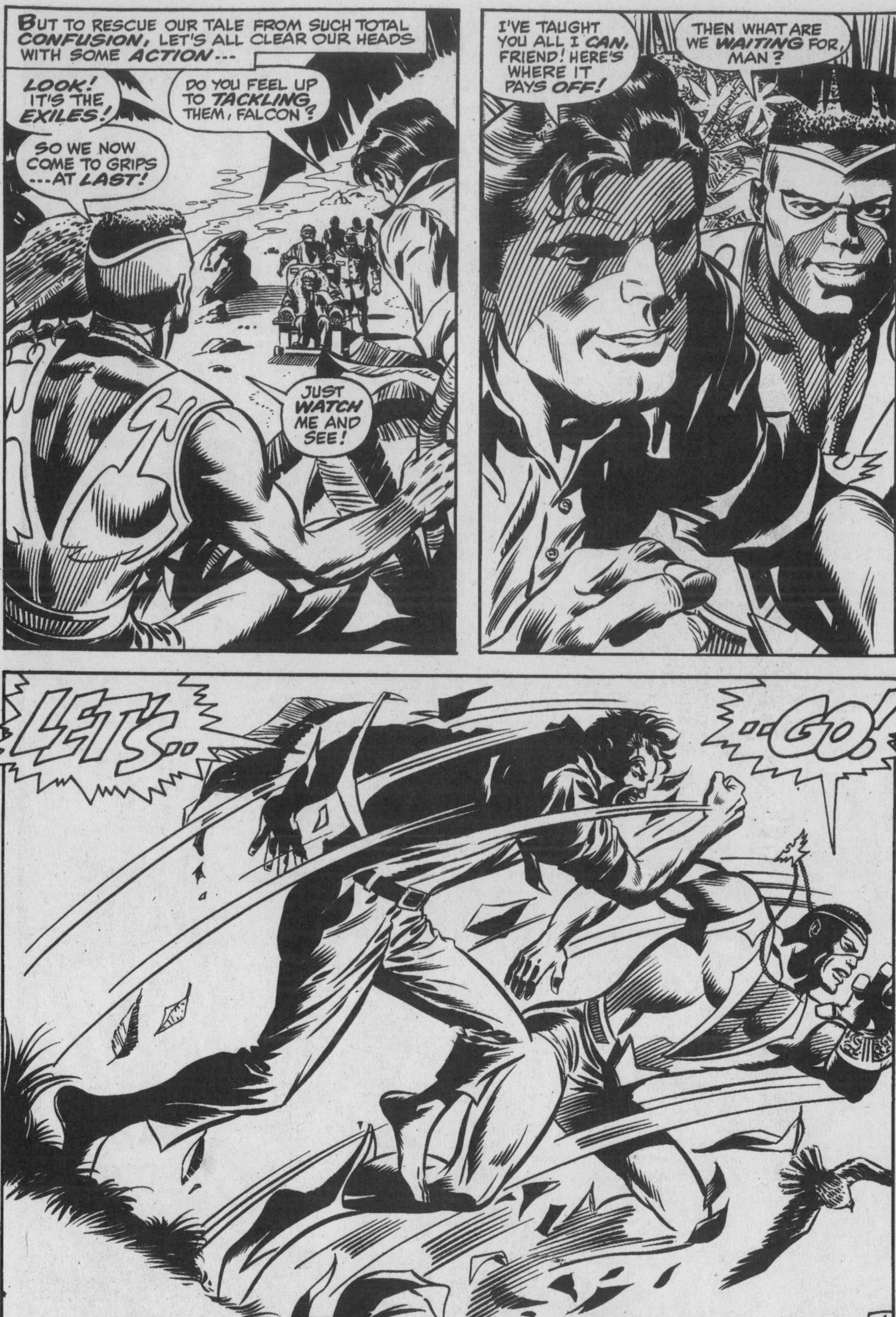
BUT TO RESCUE OUR TALE FROM SUCH TOTAL CONFUSION, LET'S ALL CLEAR OUR HEADS WITH SOME ACTION---
LOOK! IT'S THE EXILES!
DO YOU FEEL UP TO TACKLING THEM, FALCON?
SO WE NOW COME TO GRIPS ---AT LAST!
JUST WATCH ME AND SEE!
I'VE TAUGHT YOU ALL I CAN, FRIEND! HERE'S WHERE IT PAYS OFF!
THEN WHAT ARE WE WAITING FOR, MAN?
LET'S..
..GO!
14

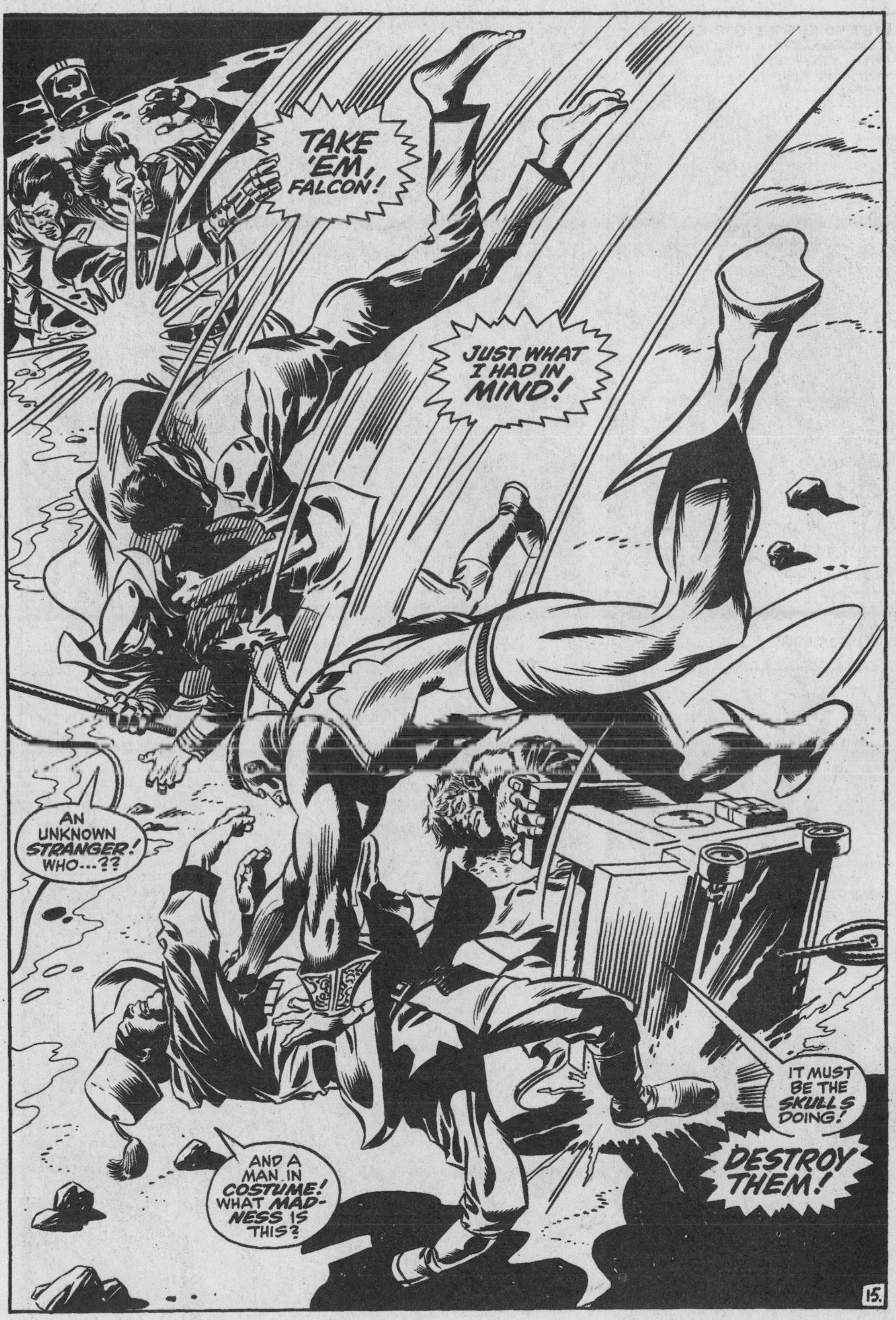
TAKE 'EM, FALCON!
JUST WHAT I HAD IN MIND!
AN UNKNOWN STRANGER! WHO...??
AND A MAN IN COSTUME! WHAT MADNESS IS THIS?
IT MUST BE THE SKULL'S DOING!
DESTROY THEM!
15.

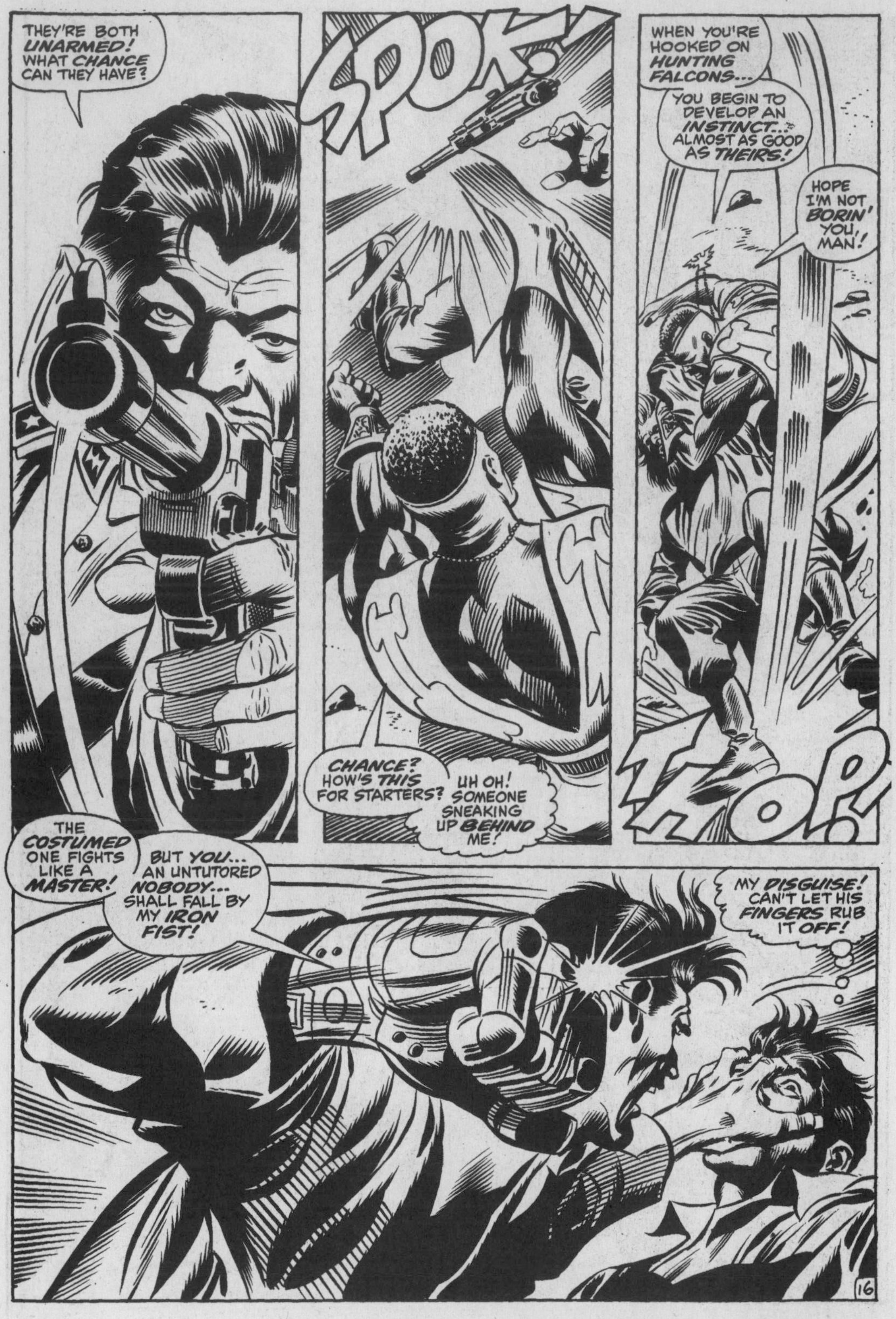

THEY'RE BOTH UNARMED! WHAT CHANCE CAN THEY HAVE?
SPOK!
CHANCE? HOW'S THIS FOR STARTERS?
UH OH! SOMEONE SNEAKING UP BEHIND ME!
WHEN YOU'RE HOOKED ON HUNTING FALCONS...
YOU BEGIN TO DEVELOP AN INSTINCT... ALMOST AS GOOD AS THEIRS!
HOPE I'M NOT BORIN' YOU, MAN!
THOP!
THE COSTUMED ONE FIGHTS LIKE A MASTER!
BUT YOU... AN UNTUTORED NOBODY... SHALL FALL BY MY IRON FIST!
MY DISGUISE! CAN'T LET HIS FINGERS RUB IT OFF!
16

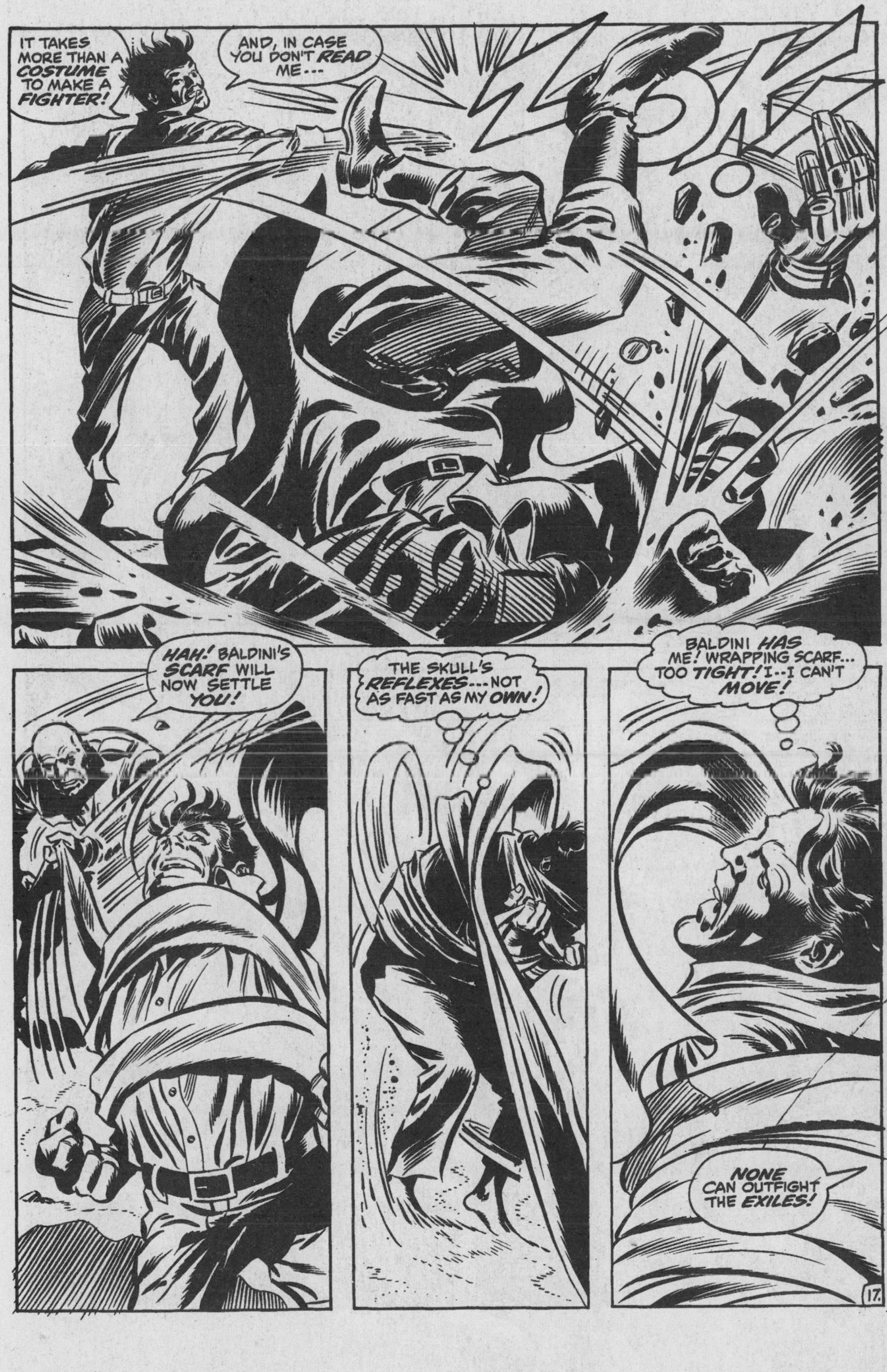
IT TAKES MORE THAN A COSTUME TO MAKE A FIGHTER!
AND, IN CASE YOU DON'T READ ME---
ZOK!
HAH! BALDINI'S SCARF WILL NOW SETTLE YOU!
THE SKULL'S REFLEXES--- NOT AS FAST AS MY OWN!
BALDINI HAS ME! WRAPPING SCARF... TOO TIGHT! I--I CAN'T MOVE!
NONE CAN OUTFIGHT THE EXILES!
17.

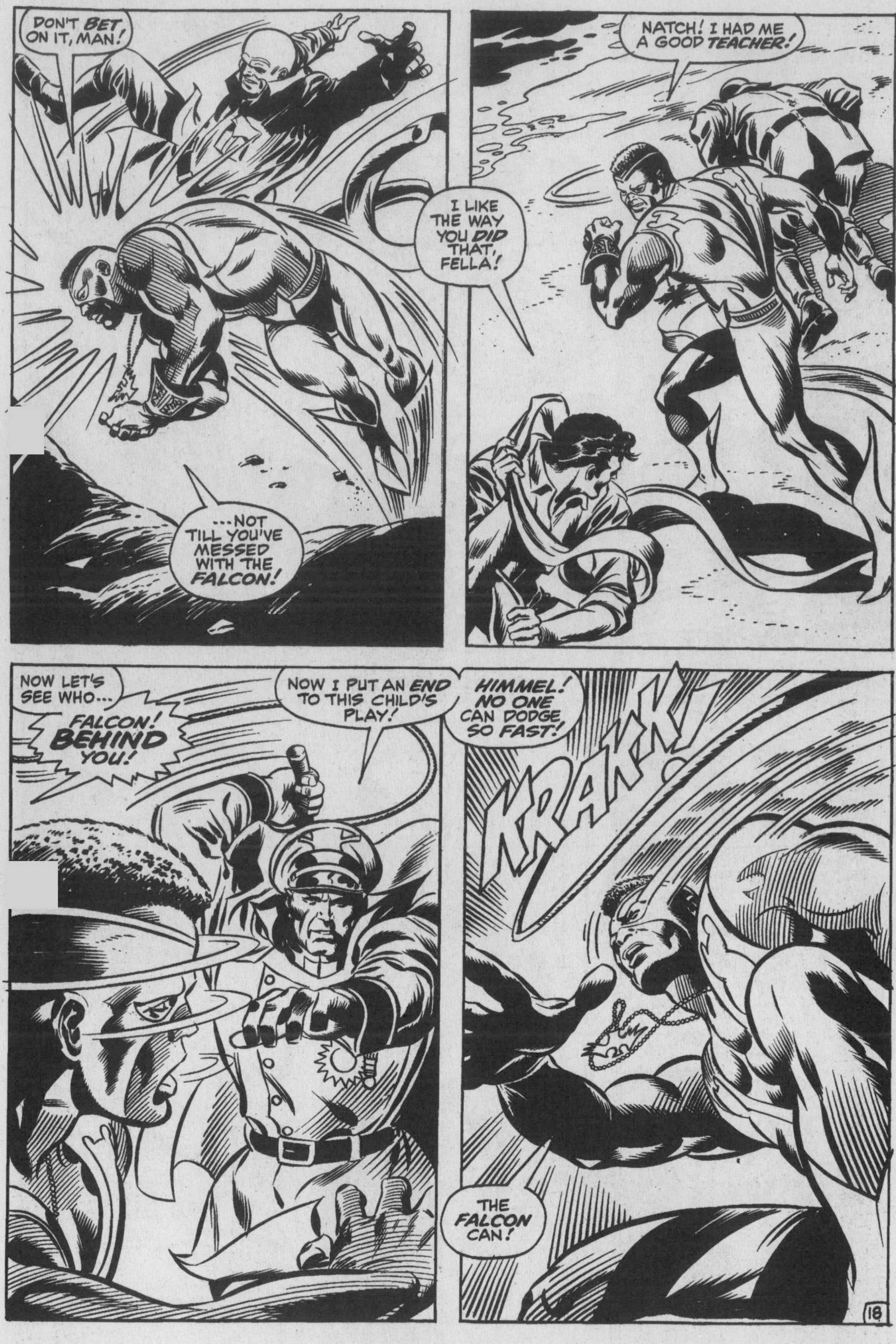
DON'T BET ON IT, MAN!
...NOT TILL YOU'VE MESSED WITH THE FALCON!
I LIKE THE WAY YOU DID THAT, FELLA!
NATCH! I HAD ME A GOOD TEACHER!
NOW LET'S SEE WHO...
FALCON! BEHIND YOU!
NOW I PUT AN END TO THIS CHILD'S PLAY!
HIMMEL! NO ONE CAN DODGE SO FAST!
KRAKK!
THE FALCON CAN!
18

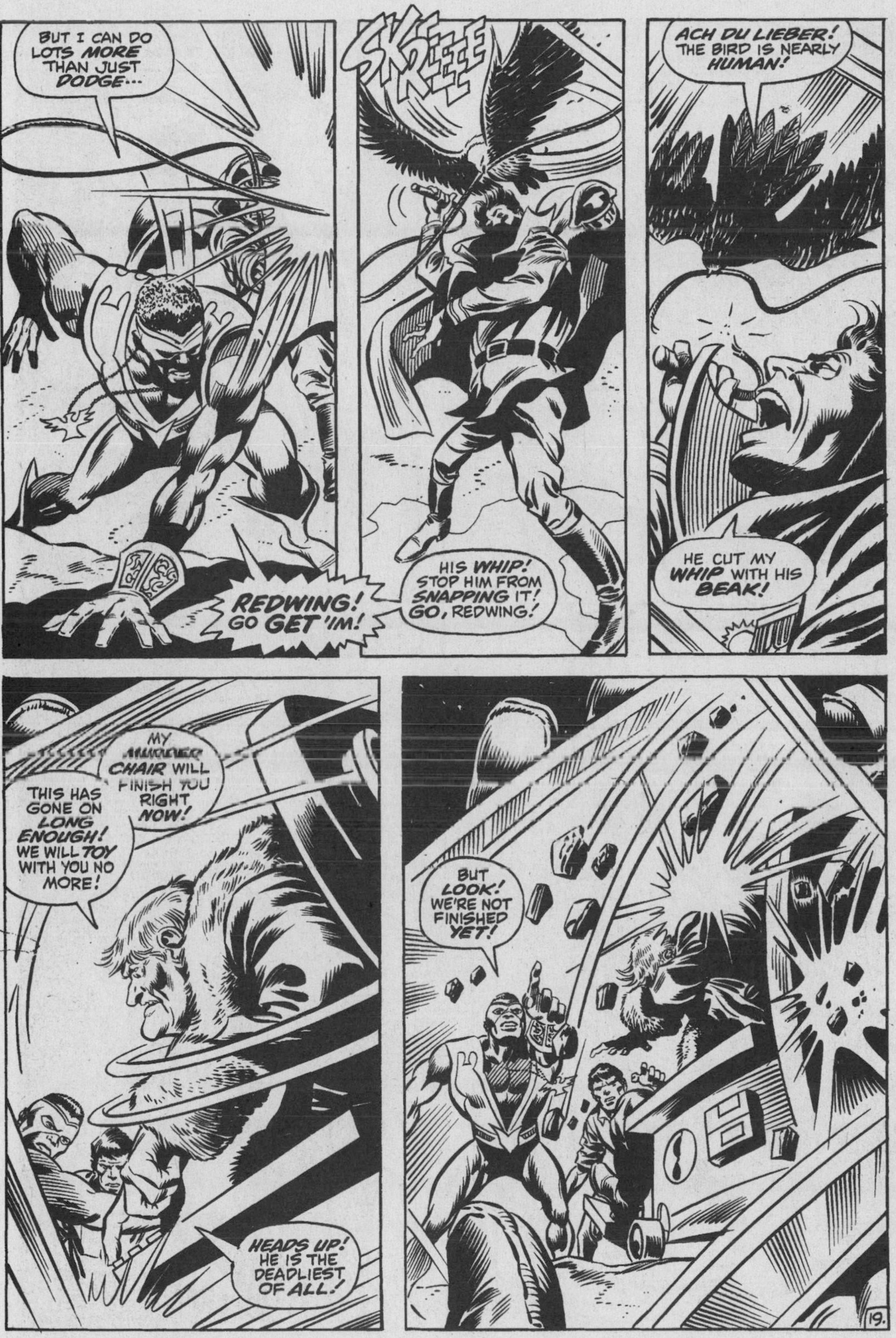

BUT I CAN DO LOTS MORE THAN JUST DODGE...
SKREEEE
REDWING! GO GET 'IM!
HIS WHIP! STOP HIM FROM SNAPPING IT! GO, REDWING!
ACH DU LIEBER! THE BIRD IS NEARLY HUMAN!
HE CUT MY WHIP WITH HIS BEAK!
THIS HAS GONE ON LONG ENOUGH! WE WILL TOY WITH YOU NO MORE!
MY MURDER CHAIR WILL FINISH YOU RIGHT NOW!
HEADS UP! HE IS THE DEADLIEST OF ALL!
BUT LOOK! WE'RE NOT FINISHED YET!

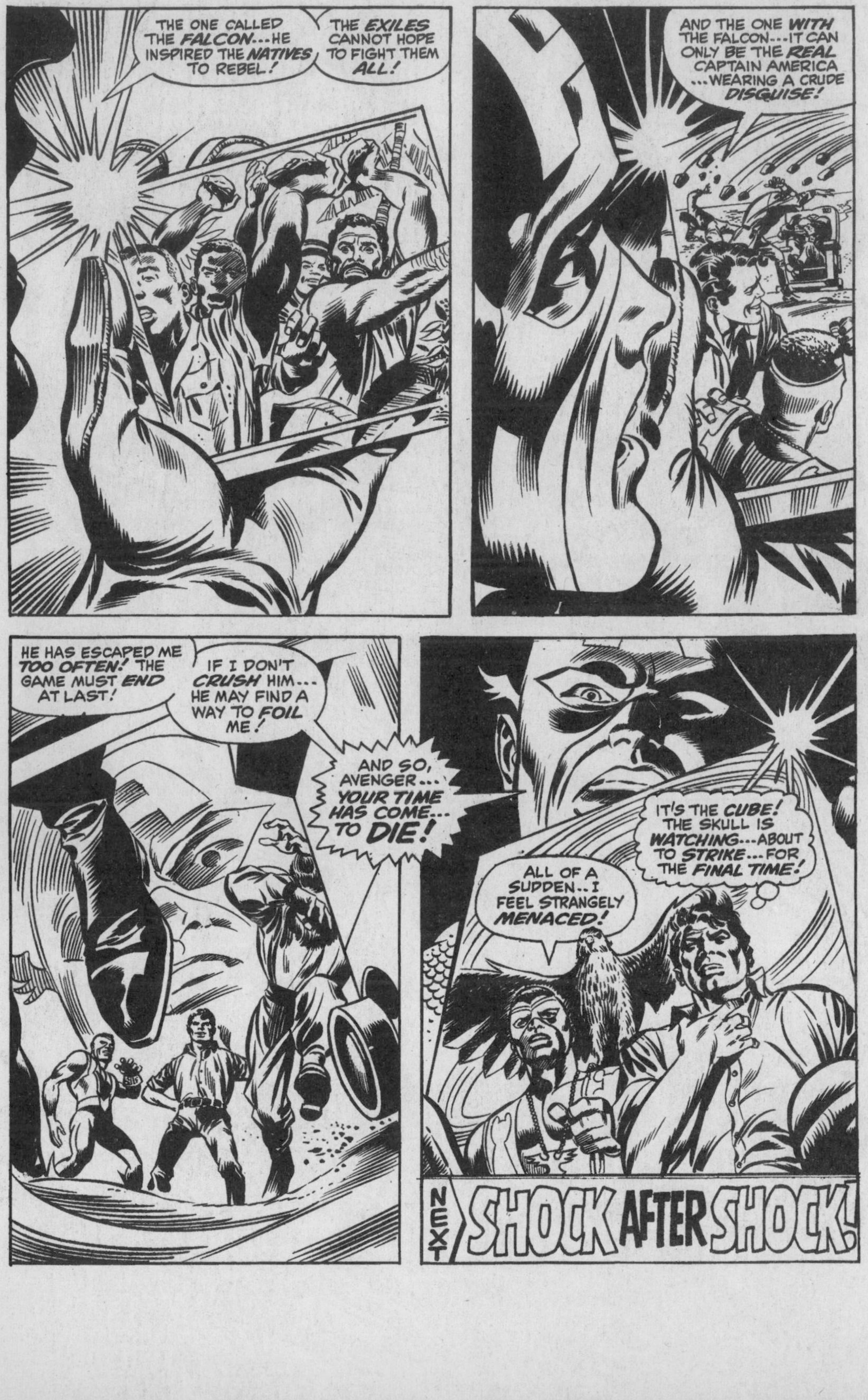
THE ONE CALLED THE FALCON... HE INSPIRED THE NATIVES TO REBEL!
THE EXILES CANNOT HOPE TO FIGHT THEM ALL!
AND THE ONE WITH THE FALCON... IT CAN ONLY BE THE REAL CAPTAIN AMERICA ...WEARING A CRUDE DISGUISE!
HE HAS ESCAPED ME TOO OFTEN! THE GAME MUST END AT LAST!
IF I DON'T CRUSH HIM... HE MAY FIND A WAY TO FOIL ME!
AND SO, AVENGER... YOUR TIME HAS COME... TO DIE!
IT'S THE CUBE! THE SKULL IS WATCHING... ABOUT TO STRIKE... FOR THE FINAL TIME!
ALL OF A SUDDEN.. I FEEL STRANGELY MENACED!
NEXT
SHOCK AFTER SHOCK!

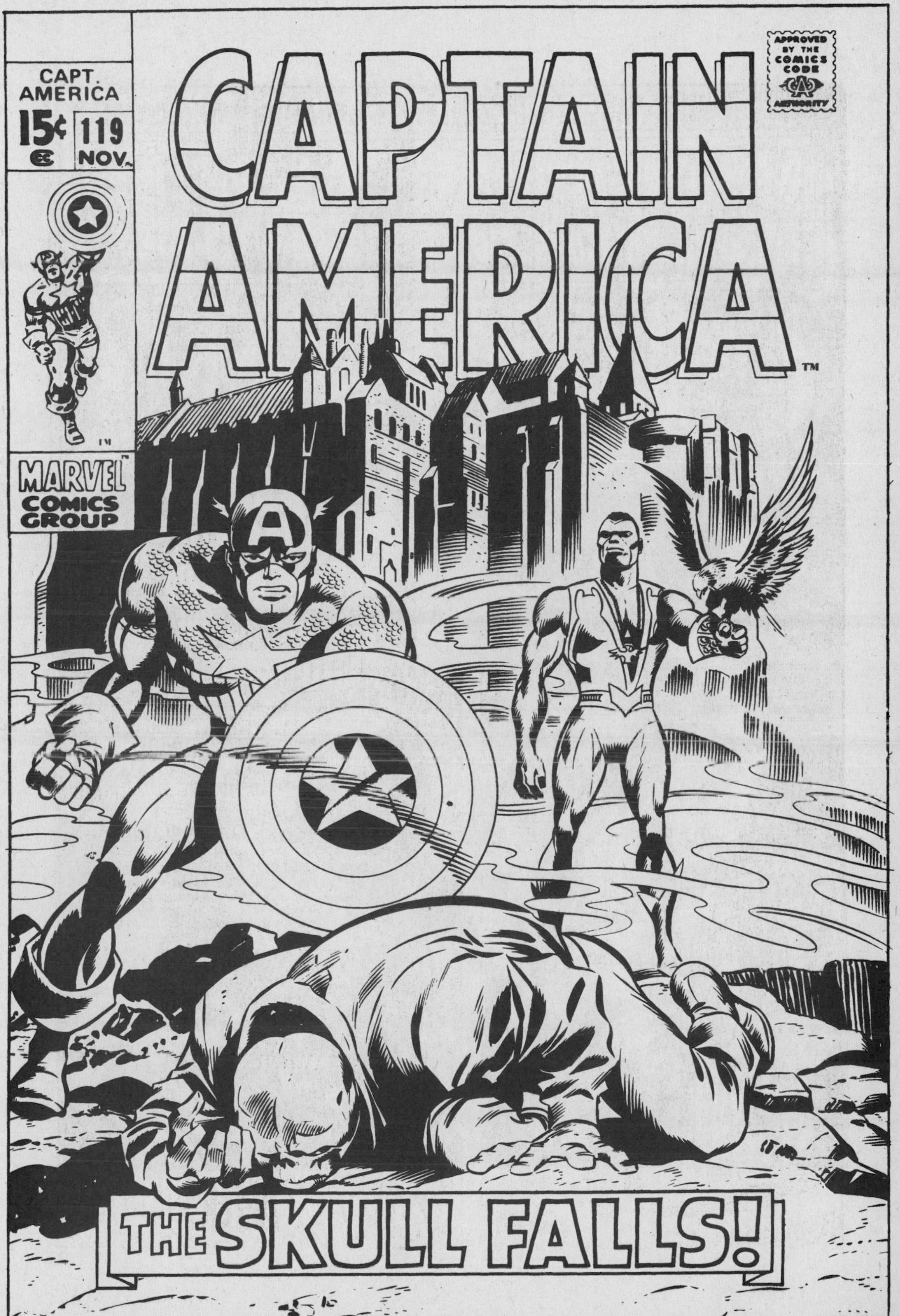
CAPT. AMERICA
15¢
119
NOV.
APPROVED BY THE COMICS CODE AUTHORITY
CAPTAIN AMERICA
MARVEL COMICS GROUP
THE SKULL FALLS!

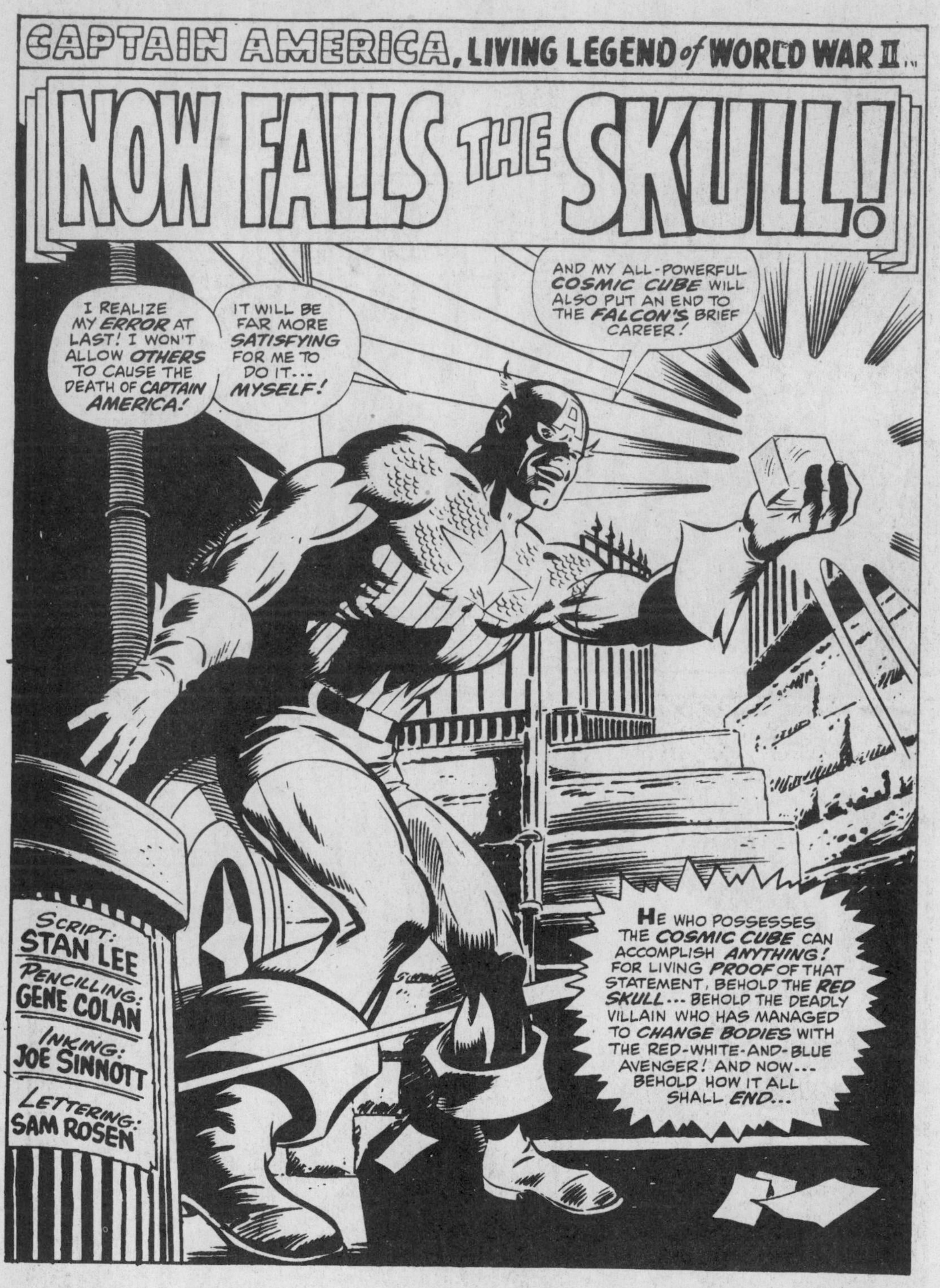
CAPTAIN AMERICA, LIVING LEGEND of WORLD WAR II ™
NOW FALLS THE SKULL!
I REALIZE MY ERROR AT LAST! I WON'T ALLOW OTHERS TO CAUSE THE DEATH OF CAPTAIN AMERICA!
IT WILL BE FAR MORE SATISFYING FOR ME TO DO IT... MYSELF!
AND MY ALL-POWERFUL COSMIC CUBE WILL ALSO PUT AN END TO THE FALCON'S BRIEF CAREER!
HE WHO POSSESSES THE COSMIC CUBE CAN ACCOMPLISH ANYTHING! FOR LIVING PROOF OF THAT STATEMENT, BEHOLD THE RED SKULL... BEHOLD THE DEADLY VILLAIN WHO HAS MANAGED TO CHANGE BODIES WITH THE RED-WHITE-AND-BLUE AVENGER! AND NOW... BEHOLD HOW IT ALL SHALL END...
SCRIPT: STAN LEE
PENCILLING: GENE COLAN
INKING: JOE SINNOTT
LETTERING: SAM ROSEN

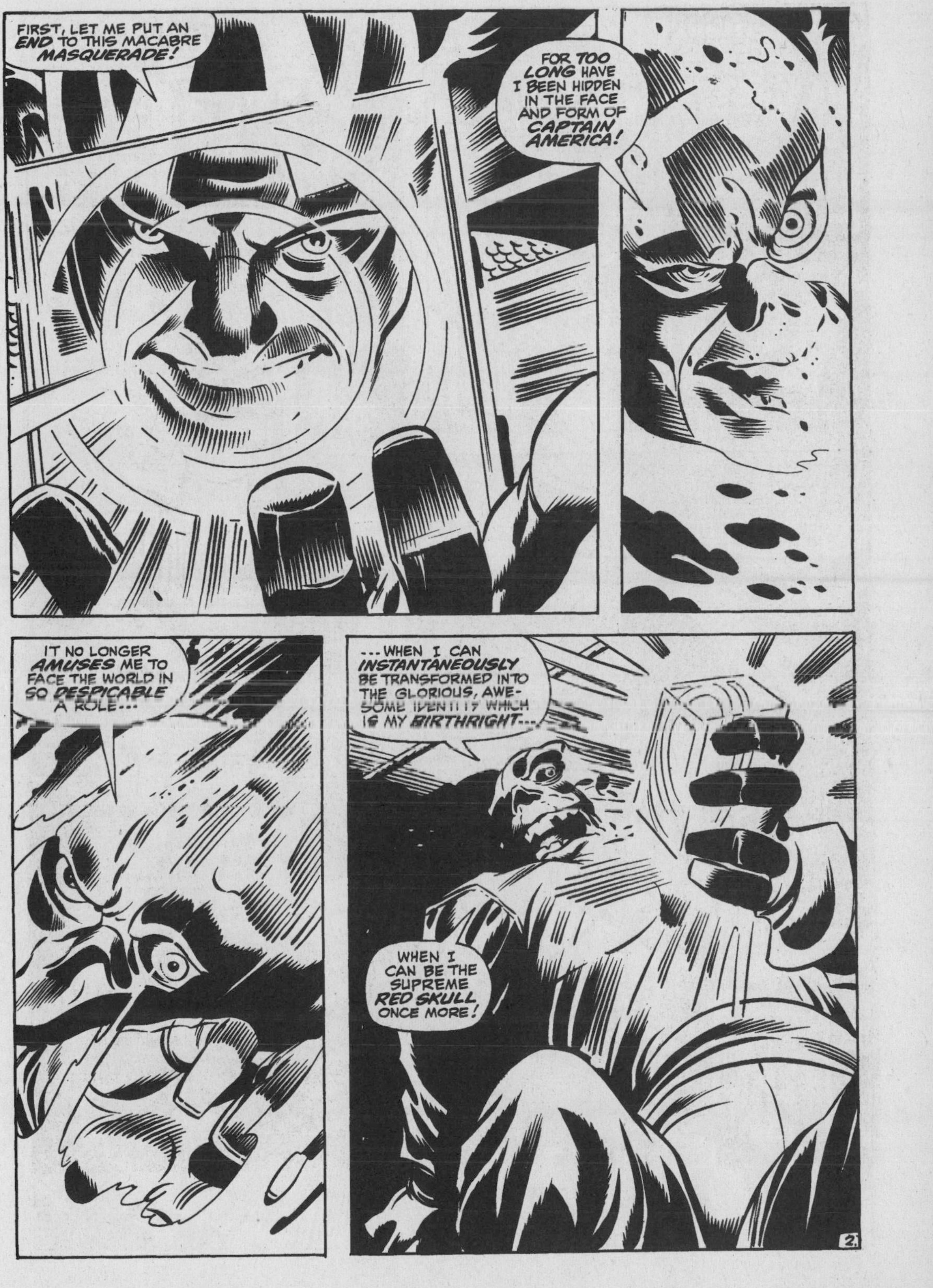
FIRST, LET ME PUT AN END TO THIS MACABRE MASQUERADE!
FOR TOO LONG HAVE I BEEN HIDDEN IN THE FACE AND FORM OF CAPTAIN AMERICA!
IT NO LONGER AMUSES ME TO FACE THE WORLD IN SO DESPICABLE A ROLE---
---WHEN I CAN INSTANTANEOUSLY BE TRANSFORMED INTO THE GLORIOUS, AWE-SOME IDENTITY WHICH IS MY BIRTHRIGHT---
WHEN I CAN BE THE SUPREME RED SKULL ONCE MORE!
2

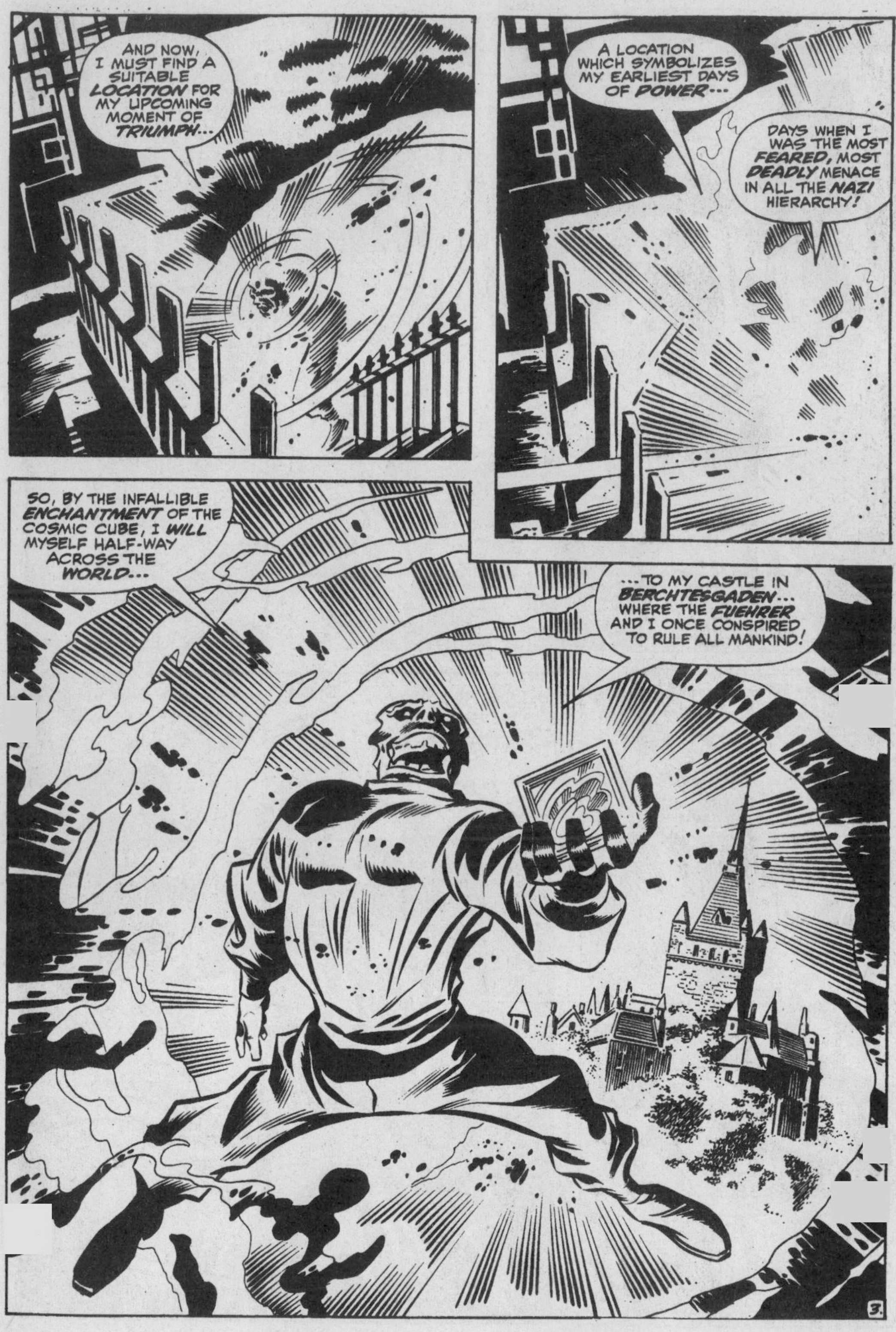
AND NOW, I MUST FIND A SUITABLE LOCATION FOR MY UPCOMING MOMENT OF TRIUMPH...
A LOCATION WHICH SYMBOLIZES MY EARLIEST DAYS OF POWER---
DAYS WHEN I WAS THE MOST FEARED, MOST DEADLY MENACE IN ALL THE NAZI HIERARCHY!
SO, BY THE INFALLIBLE ENCHANTMENT OF THE COSMIC CUBE, I WILL MYSELF HALF-WAY ACROSS THE WORLD...
...TO MY CASTLE IN BERCHTESGADEN... WHERE THE FUEHRER AND I ONCE CONSPIRED TO RULE ALL MANKIND!
3.

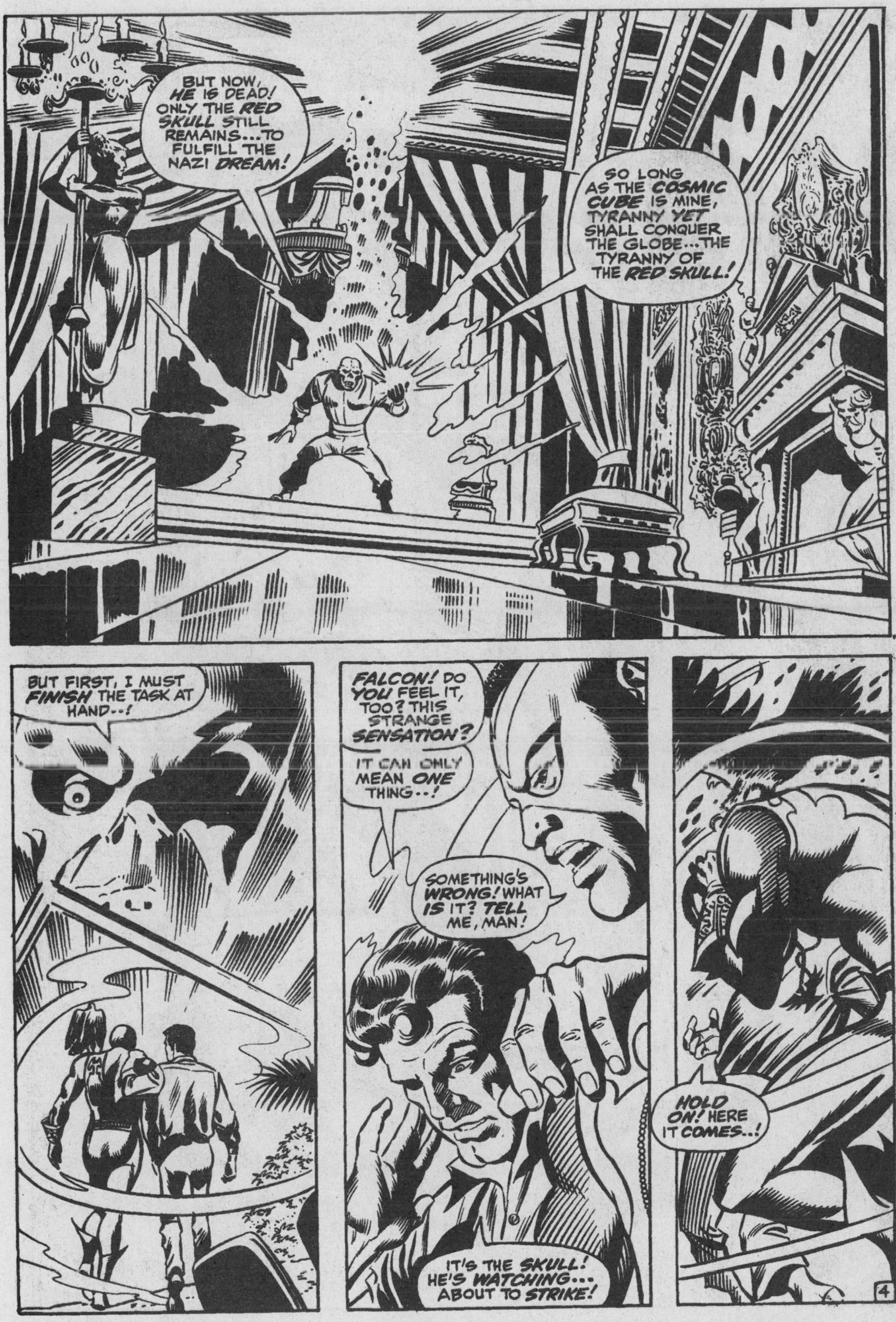
BUT NOW, HE IS DEAD! ONLY THE RED SKULL STILL REMAINS...TO FULFILL THE NAZI DREAM!
SO LONG AS THE COSMIC CUBE IS MINE, TYRANNY YET SHALL CONQUER THE GLOBE...THE TYRANNY OF THE RED SKULL!
BUT FIRST, I MUST FINISH THE TASK AT HAND--!
FALCON! DO YOU FEEL IT, TOO? THIS STRANGE SENSATION?
IT CAN ONLY MEAN ONE THING--!
SOMETHING'S WRONG! WHAT IS IT? TELL ME, MAN!
IT'S THE SKULL! HE'S WATCHING... ABOUT TO STRIKE!
HOLD ON! HERE IT COMES..!
4

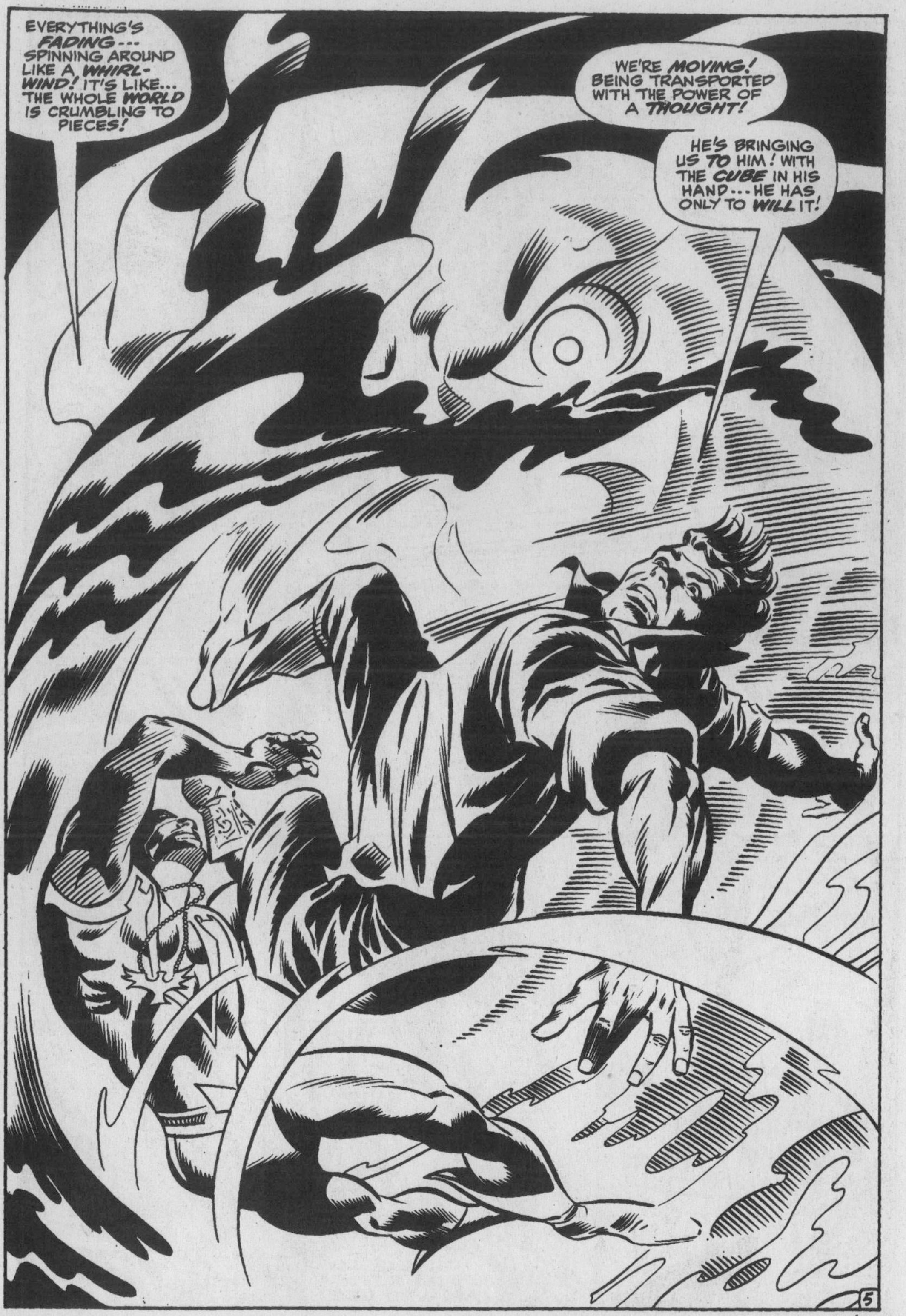
EVERYTHING'S FADING... SPINNING AROUND LIKE A WHIRL-WIND! IT'S LIKE... THE WHOLE WORLD IS CRUMBLING TO PIECES!
WE'RE MOVING! BEING TRANSPORTED WITH THE POWER OF A THOUGHT!
HE'S BRINGING US TO HIM! WITH THE CUBE IN HIS HAND... HE HAS ONLY TO WILL IT!
5

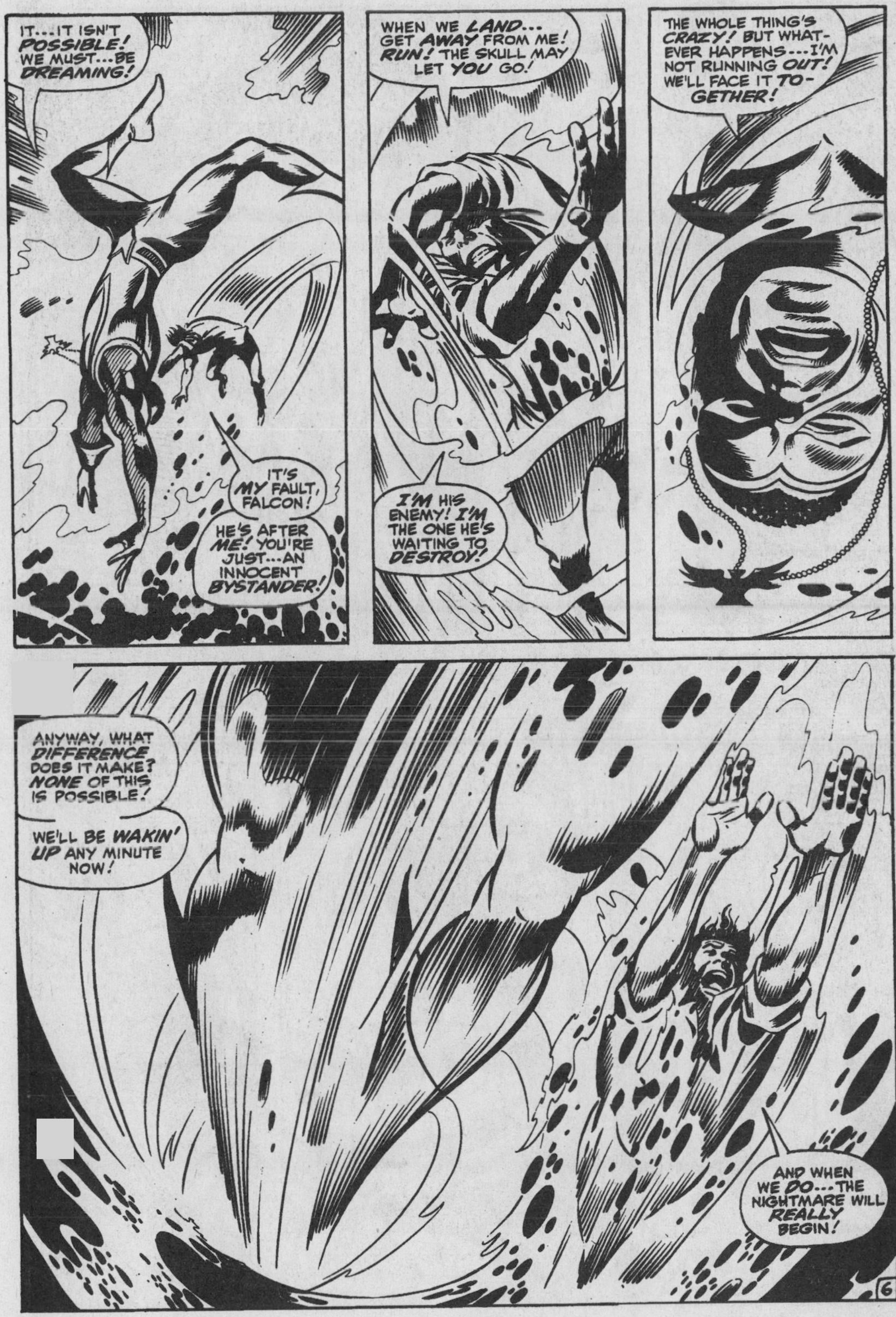
IT...IT ISN'T POSSIBLE! WE MUST...BE DREAMING!
IT'S MY FAULT, FALCON!
HE'S AFTER ME! YOU'RE JUST...AN INNOCENT BYSTANDER!
WHEN WE LAND... GET AWAY FROM ME! RUN! THE SKULL MAY LET YOU GO!
I'M HIS ENEMY! I'M THE ONE HE'S WAITING TO DESTROY!
THE WHOLE THING'S CRAZY! BUT WHATEVER HAPPENS...I'M NOT RUNNING OUT! WE'LL FACE IT TOGETHER!
ANYWAY, WHAT DIFFERENCE DOES IT MAKE? NONE OF THIS IS POSSIBLE!
WE'LL BE WAKIN' UP ANY MINUTE NOW!
AND WHEN WE DO... THE NIGHTMARE WILL REALLY BEGIN!
6

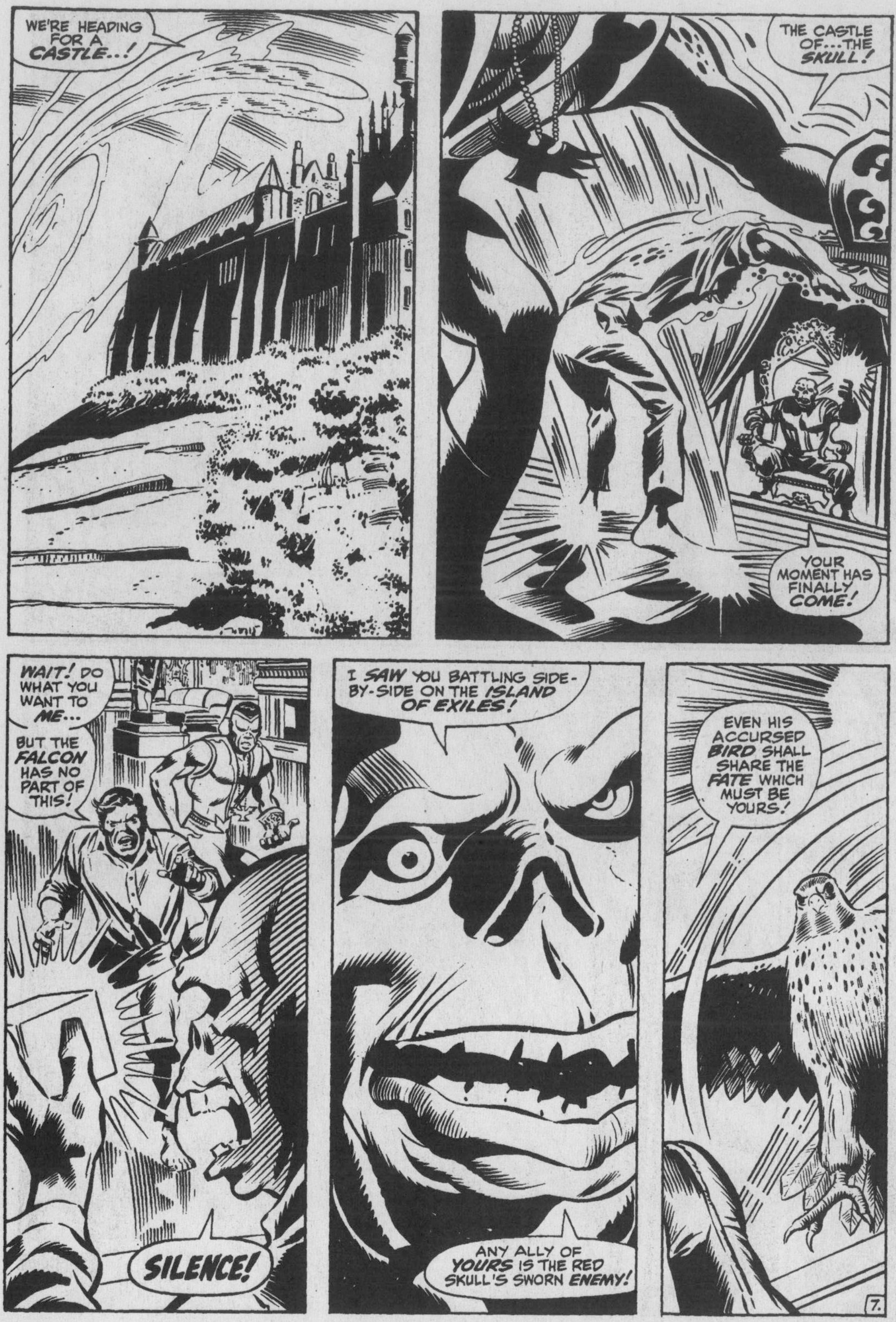
WE'RE HEADING FOR A CASTLE..!
THE CASTLE OF... THE SKULL!
YOUR MOMENT HAS FINALLY COME!
WAIT! DO WHAT YOU WANT TO ME...
BUT THE FALCON HAS NO PART OF THIS!
SILENCE!
I SAW YOU BATTLING SIDE-BY-SIDE ON THE ISLAND OF EXILES!
ANY ALLY OF YOURS IS THE RED SKULL'S SWORN ENEMY!
EVEN HIS ACCURSED BIRD SHALL SHARE THE FATE WHICH MUST BE YOURS!
7.

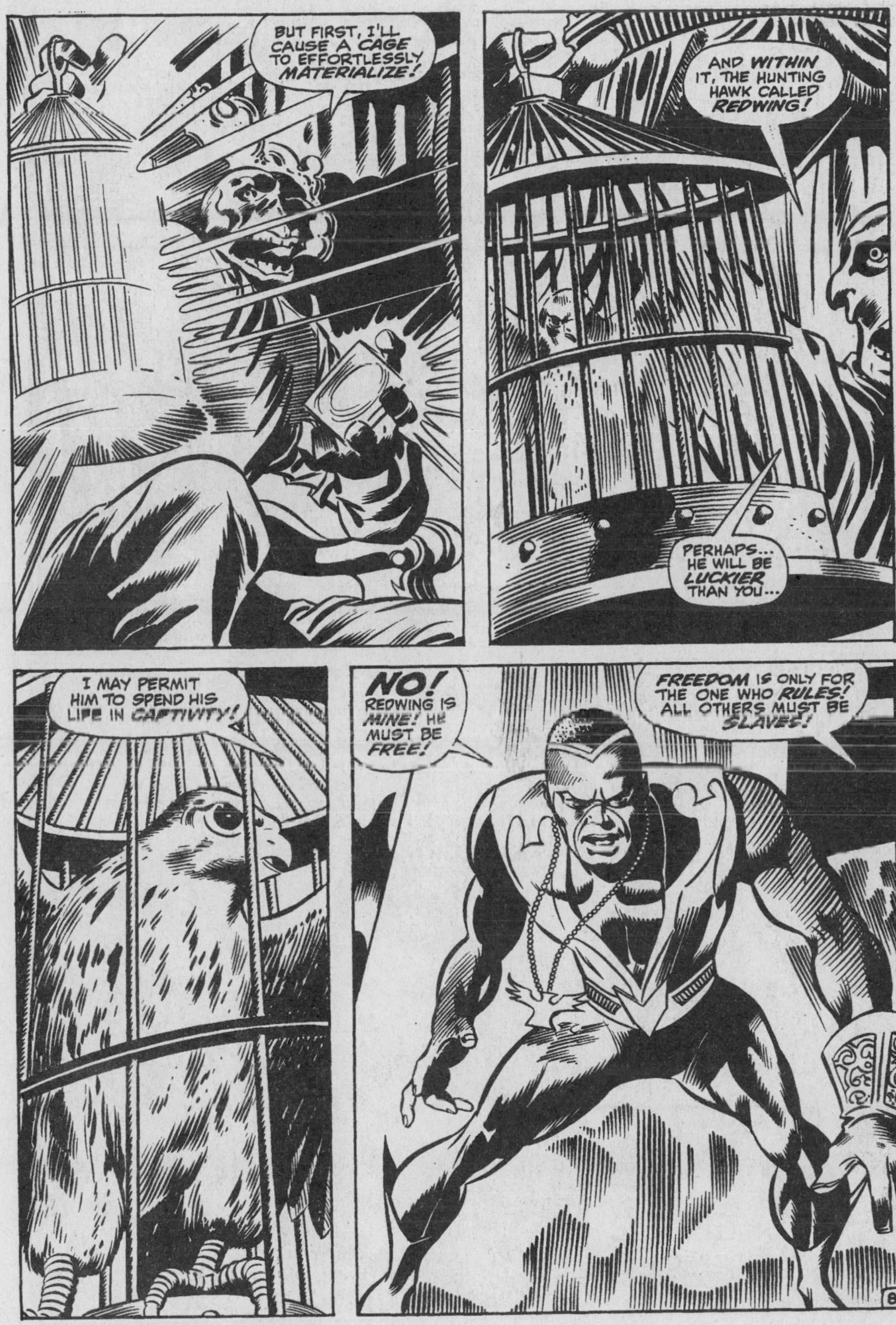
BUT FIRST, I'LL CAUSE A CAGE TO EFFORTLESSLY MATERIALIZE!
AND WITHIN IT, THE HUNTING HAWK CALLED REDWING!
PERHAPS... HE WILL BE LUCKIER THAN YOU...
I MAY PERMIT HIM TO SPEND HIS LIFE IN CAPTIVITY!
NO! REDWING IS MINE! HE MUST BE FREE!
FREEDOM IS ONLY FOR THE ONE WHO RULES! ALL OTHERS MUST BE SLAVES!
8

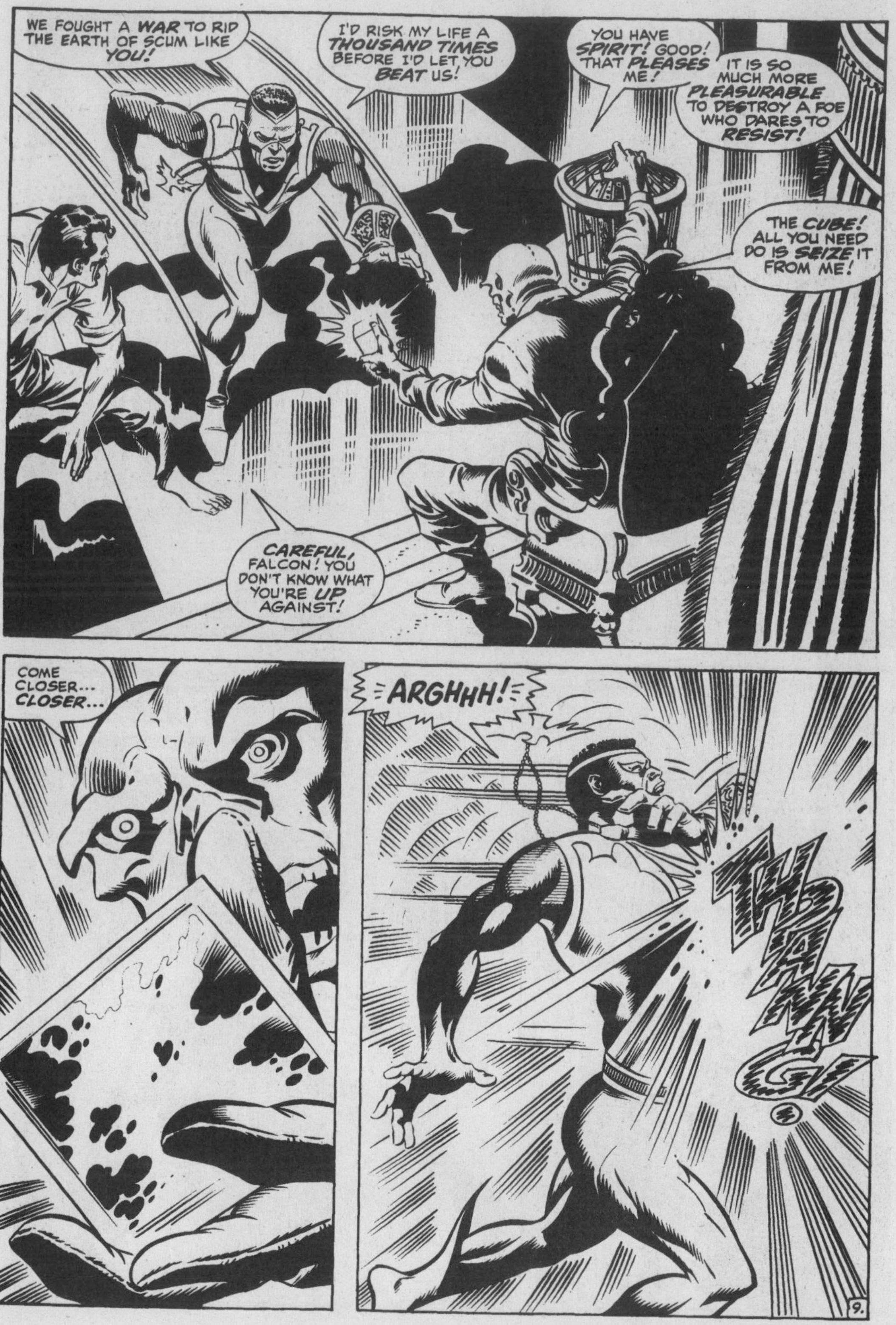

WE FOUGHT A WAR TO RID THE EARTH OF SCUM LIKE YOU!
I'D RISK MY LIFE A THOUSAND TIMES BEFORE I'D LET YOU BEAT US!
YOU HAVE SPIRIT! GOOD! THAT PLEASES ME!
IT IS SO MUCH MORE PLEASURABLE TO DESTROY A FOE WHO DARES TO RESIST!
THE CUBE! ALL YOU NEED DO IS SEIZE IT FROM ME!
CAREFUL, FALCON! YOU DON'T KNOW WHAT YOU'RE UP AGAINST!
COME CLOSER... CLOSER...
ARGHHH!
THWANNG!
9.

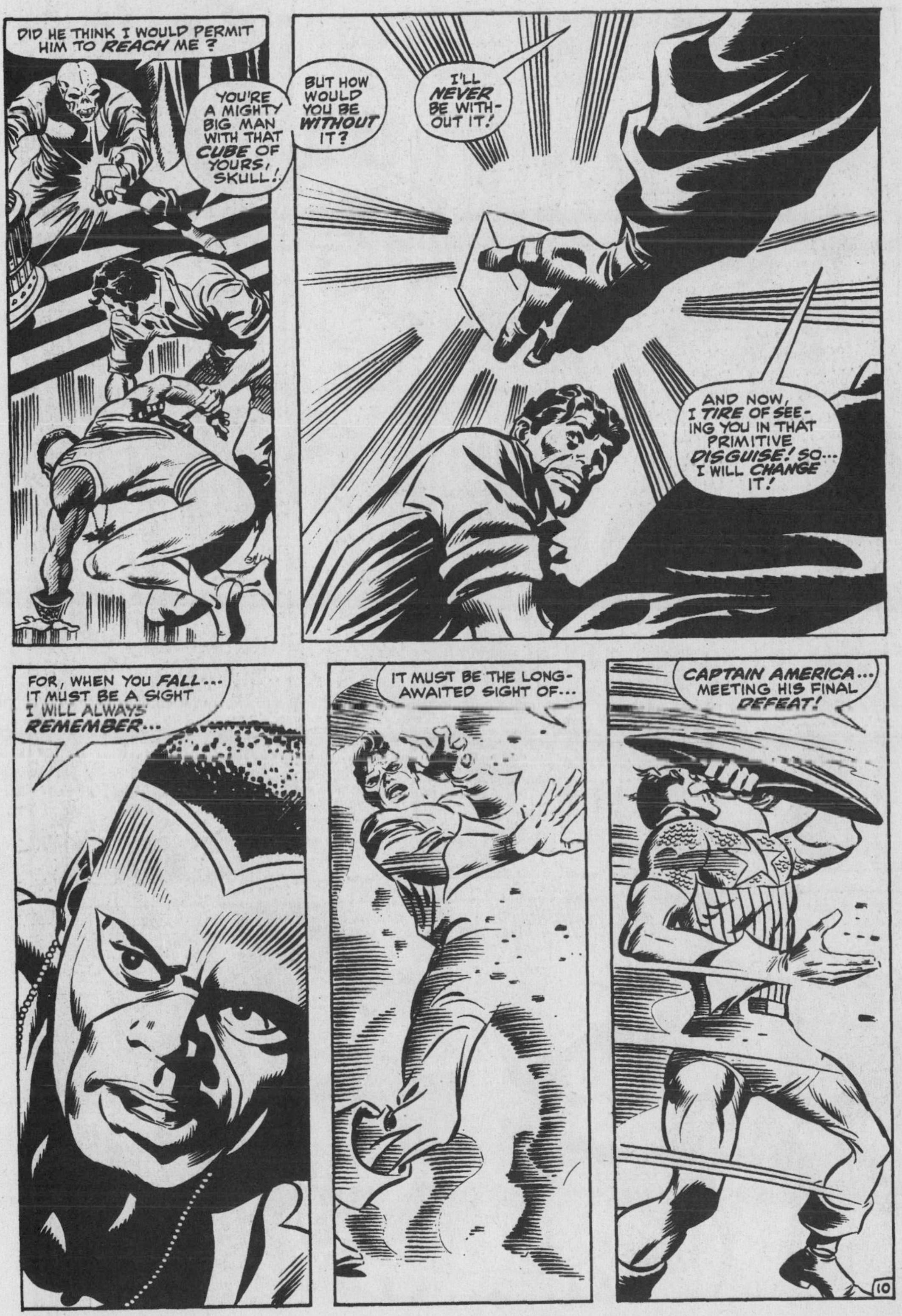
DID HE THINK I WOULD PERMIT HIM TO REACH ME?
YOU'RE A MIGHTY BIG MAN WITH THAT CUBE OF YOURS, SKULL!
BUT HOW WOULD YOU BE WITHOUT IT?
I'LL NEVER BE WITHOUT IT!
AND NOW, I TIRE OF SEEING YOU IN THAT PRIMITIVE DISGUISE! SO... I WILL CHANGE IT!
FOR, WHEN YOU FALL... IT MUST BE A SIGHT I WILL ALWAYS REMEMBER...
IT MUST BE THE LONG-AWAITED SIGHT OF...
CAPTAIN AMERICA... MEETING HIS FINAL DEFEAT!
10

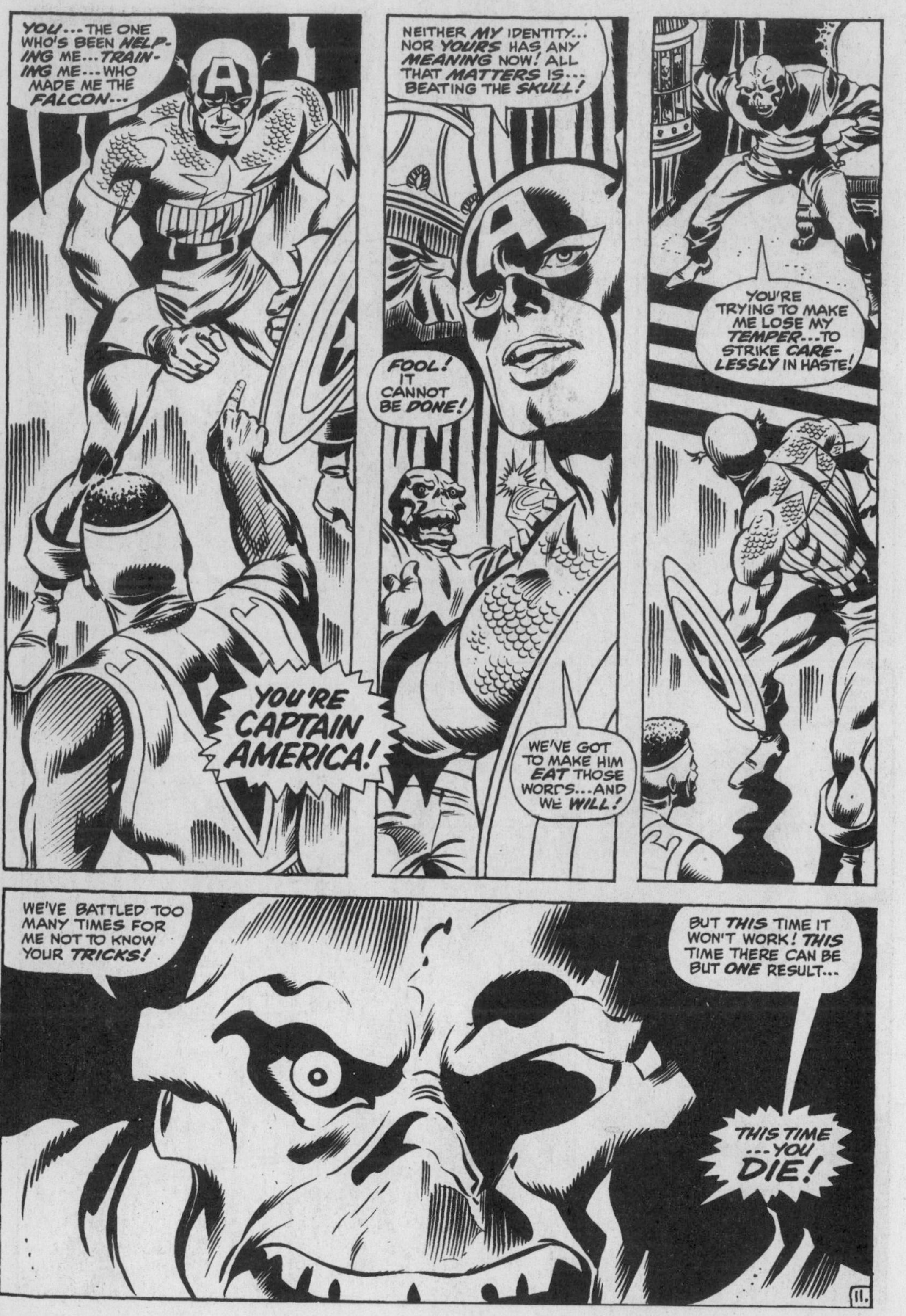

YOU... THE ONE WHO'S BEEN HELPING ME... TRAINING ME... WHO MADE ME THE FALCON...
YOU'RE CAPTAIN AMERICA!
NEITHER MY IDENTITY... NOR YOURS HAS ANY MEANING NOW! ALL THAT MATTERS IS... BEATING THE SKULL!
FOOL! IT CANNOT BE DONE!
WE'VE GOT TO MAKE HIM EAT THOSE WORDS...AND WE WILL!
YOU'RE TRYING TO MAKE ME LOSE MY TEMPER...TO STRIKE CARELESSLY IN HASTE!
WE'VE BATTLED TOO MANY TIMES FOR ME NOT TO KNOW YOUR TRICKS!
BUT THIS TIME IT WON'T WORK! THIS TIME THERE CAN BE BUT ONE RESULT...
THIS TIME ...YOU DIE!
11.

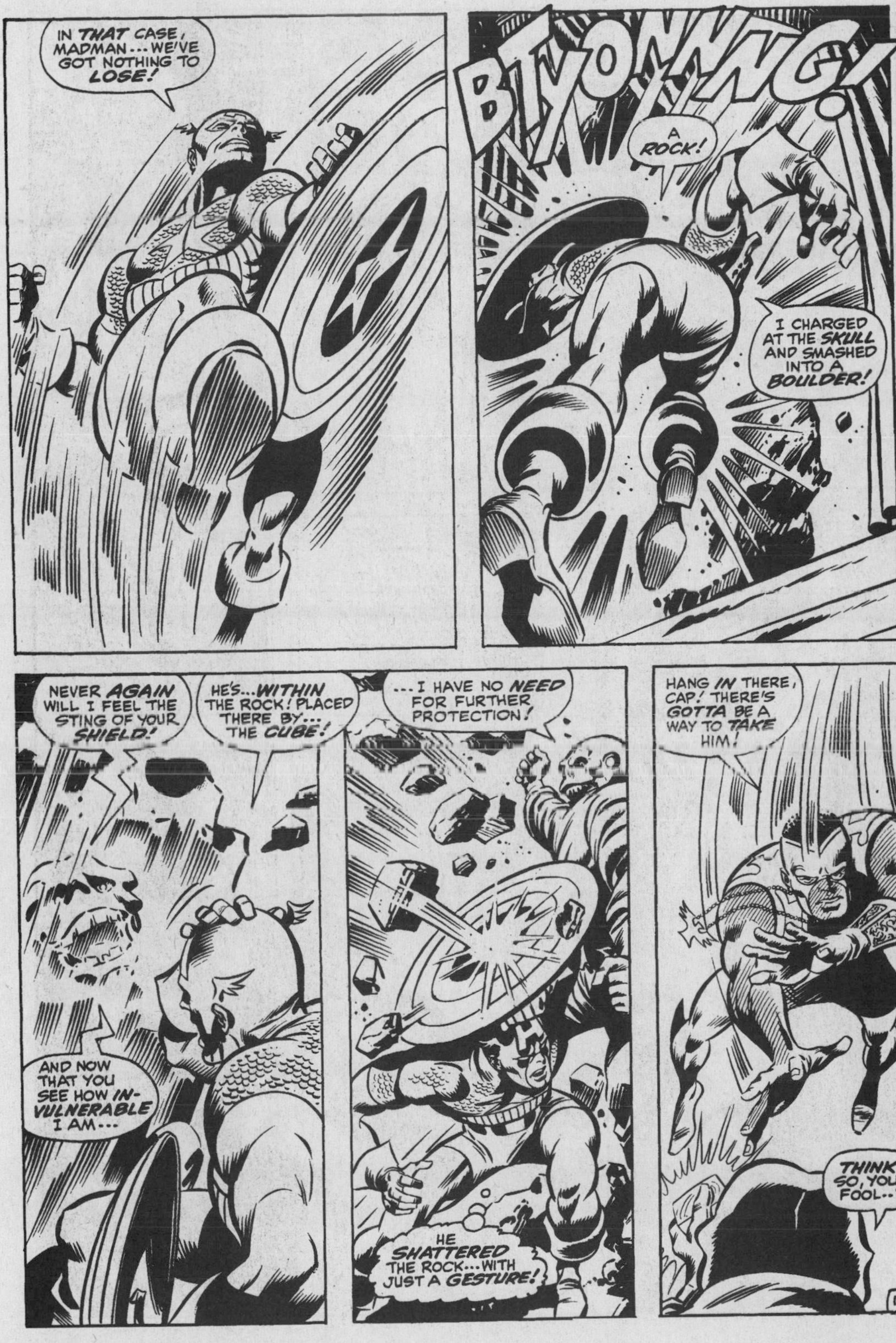
IN THAT CASE, MADMAN... WE'VE GOT NOTHING TO LOSE!
BTYONNNG!
A ROCK!
I CHARGED AT THE SKULL AND SMASHED INTO A BOULDER!
NEVER AGAIN WILL I FEEL THE STING OF YOUR SHIELD!
AND NOW THAT YOU SEE HOW INVULNERABLE I AM...
HE'S... WITHIN THE ROCK! PLACED THERE BY... THE CUBE!
...I HAVE NO NEED FOR FURTHER PROTECTION!
HE SHATTERED THE ROCK... WITH JUST A GESTURE!
HANG IN THERE, CAP! THERE'S GOTTA BE A WAY TO TAKE HIM!
THINK SO, YOU FOOL--?
12

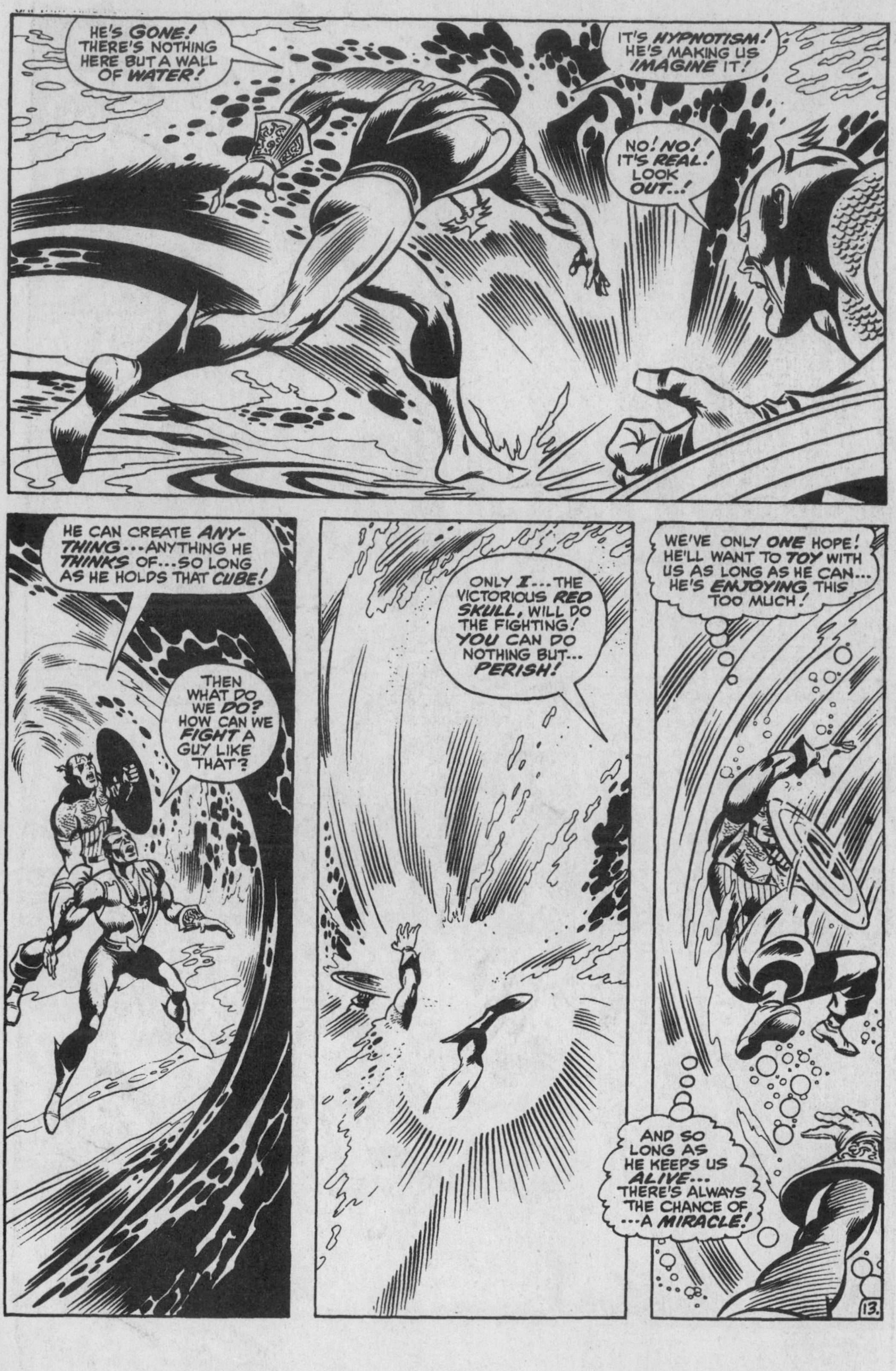

HE'S GONE! THERE'S NOTHING HERE BUT A WALL OF WATER!
IT'S HYPNOTISM! HE'S MAKING US IMAGINE IT!
NO! NO! IT'S REAL! LOOK OUT..!
HE CAN CREATE ANY-THING...ANYTHING HE THINKS OF...SO LONG AS HE HOLDS THAT CUBE!
THEN WHAT DO WE DO? HOW CAN WE FIGHT A GUY LIKE THAT?
ONLY I... THE VICTORIOUS RED SKULL, WILL DO THE FIGHTING! YOU CAN DO NOTHING BUT... PERISH!
WE'VE ONLY ONE HOPE! HE'LL WANT TO TOY WITH US AS LONG AS HE CAN... HE'S ENJOYING THIS TOO MUCH!
AND SO LONG AS HE KEEPS US ALIVE... THERE'S ALWAYS THE CHANCE OF ...A MIRACLE!
13.

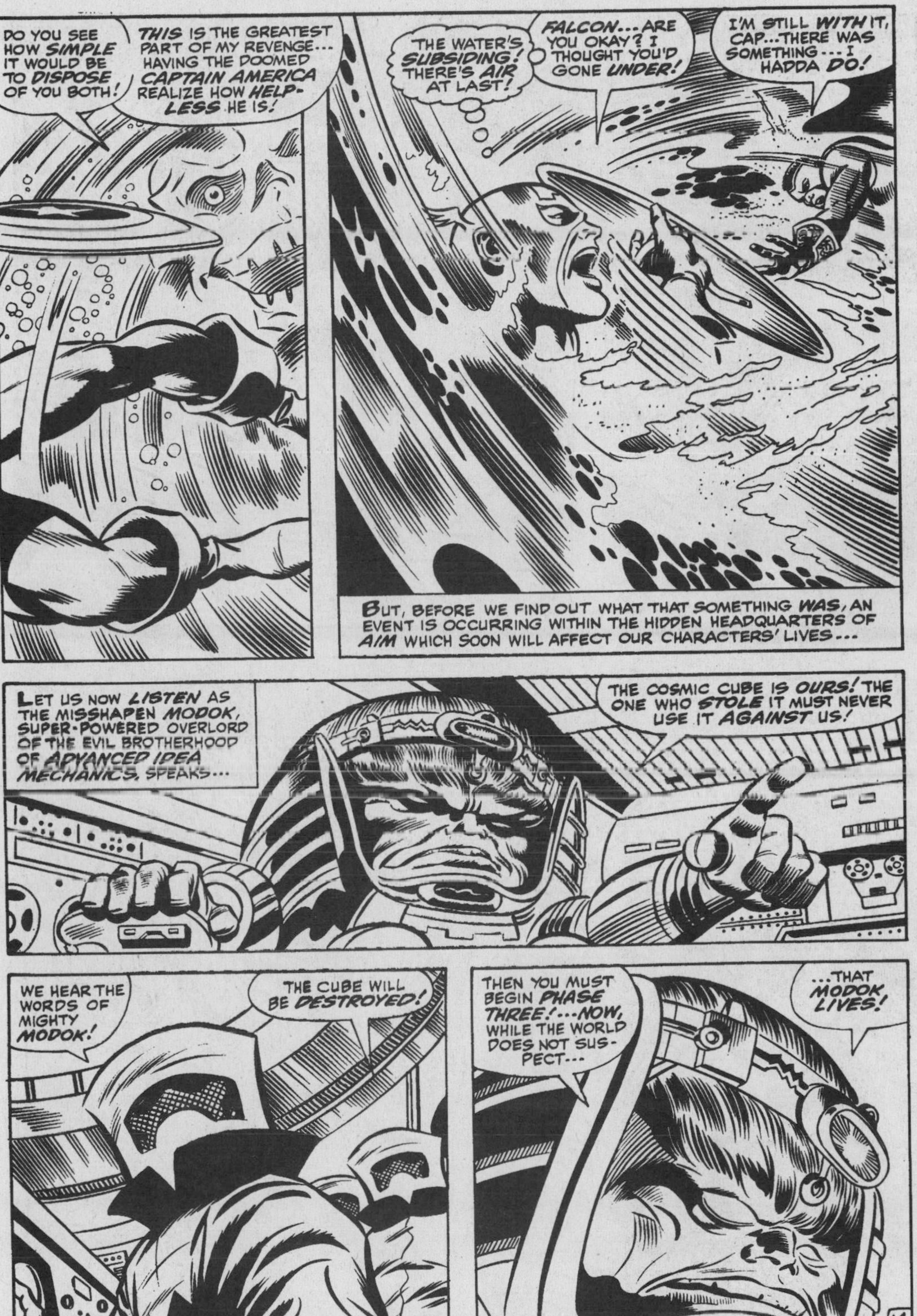
DO YOU SEE HOW SIMPLE IT WOULD BE TO DISPOSE OF YOU BOTH!
THIS IS THE GREATEST PART OF MY REVENGE... HAVING THE DOOMED CAPTAIN AMERICA REALIZE HOW HELP-LESS HE IS!
THE WATER'S SUBSIDING! THERE'S AIR AT LAST!
FALCON... ARE YOU OKAY? I THOUGHT YOU'D GONE UNDER!
I'M STILL WITH IT, CAP... THERE WAS SOMETHING... I HADDA DO!
BUT, BEFORE WE FIND OUT WHAT THAT SOMETHING WAS, AN EVENT IS OCCURRING WITHIN THE HIDDEN HEADQUARTERS OF AIM WHICH SOON WILL AFFECT OUR CHARACTERS' LIVES...
LET US NOW LISTEN AS THE MISSHAPEN MODOK, SUPER-POWERED OVERLORD OF THE EVIL BROTHERHOOD OF ADVANCED IDEA MECHANICS, SPEAKS...
THE COSMIC CUBE IS OURS! THE ONE WHO STOLE IT MUST NEVER USE IT AGAINST US!
WE HEAR THE WORDS OF MIGHTY MODOK!
THE CUBE WILL BE DESTROYED!
THEN YOU MUST BEGIN PHASE THREE!...NOW, WHILE THE WORLD DOES NOT SUS-PECT---
...THAT MODOK LIVES!
14

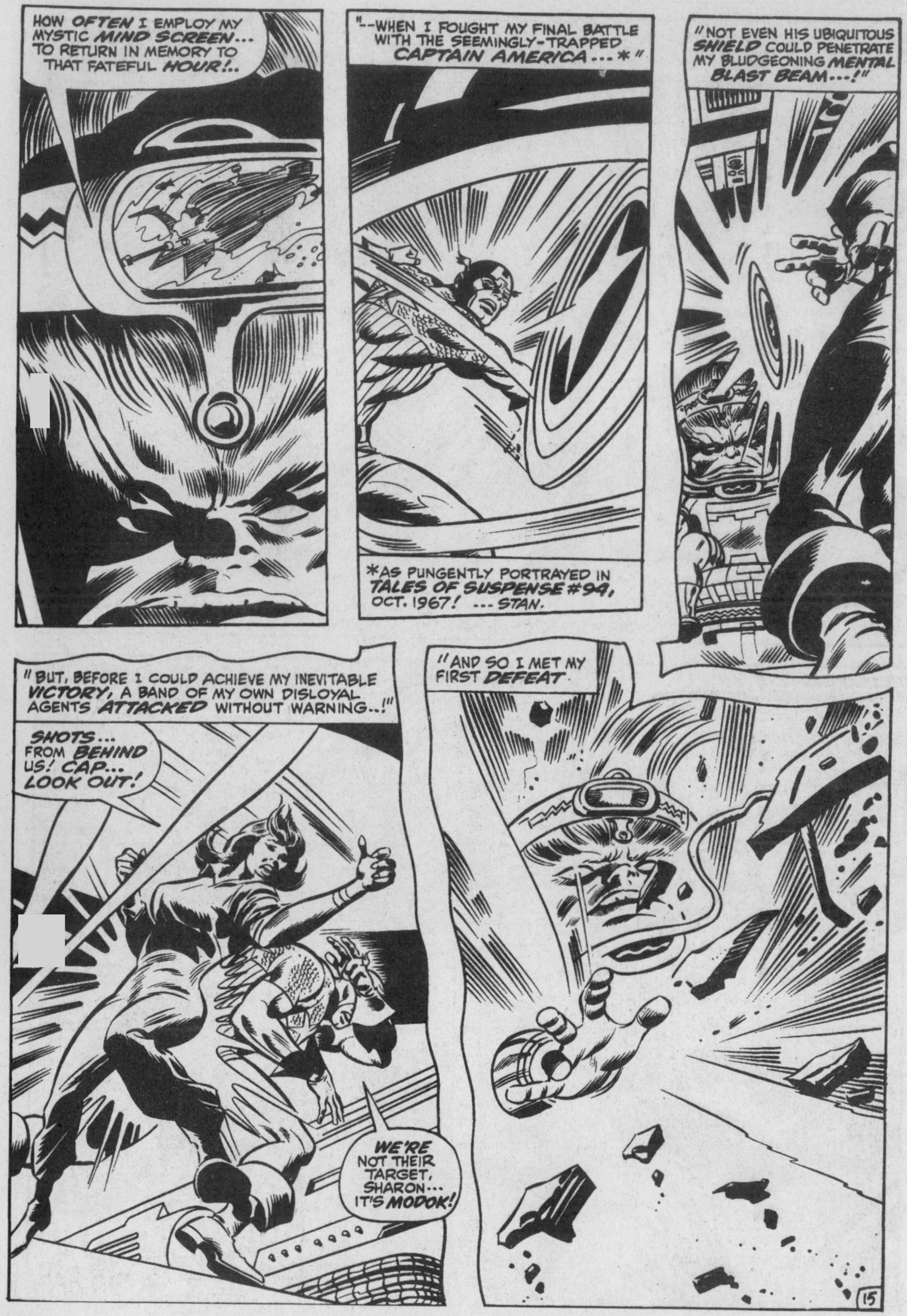
HOW OFTEN I EMPLOY MY MYSTIC MIND SCREEN... TO RETURN IN MEMORY TO THAT FATEFUL HOUR!..
"--WHEN I FOUGHT MY FINAL BATTLE WITH THE SEEMINGLY-TRAPPED CAPTAIN AMERICA...*"
*AS PUNGENTLY PORTRAYED IN TALES OF SUSPENSE #94, OCT. 1967! ...STAN.
"NOT EVEN HIS UBIQUITOUS SHIELD COULD PENETRATE MY BLUDGEONING MENTAL BLAST BEAM...!"
"BUT, BEFORE I COULD ACHIEVE MY INEVITABLE VICTORY, A BAND OF MY OWN DISLOYAL AGENTS ATTACKED WITHOUT WARNING..!"
SHOTS... FROM BEHIND US! CAP... LOOK OUT!
WE'RE NOT THEIR TARGET, SHARON... IT'S MODOK!
"AND SO I MET MY FIRST DEFEAT.
15

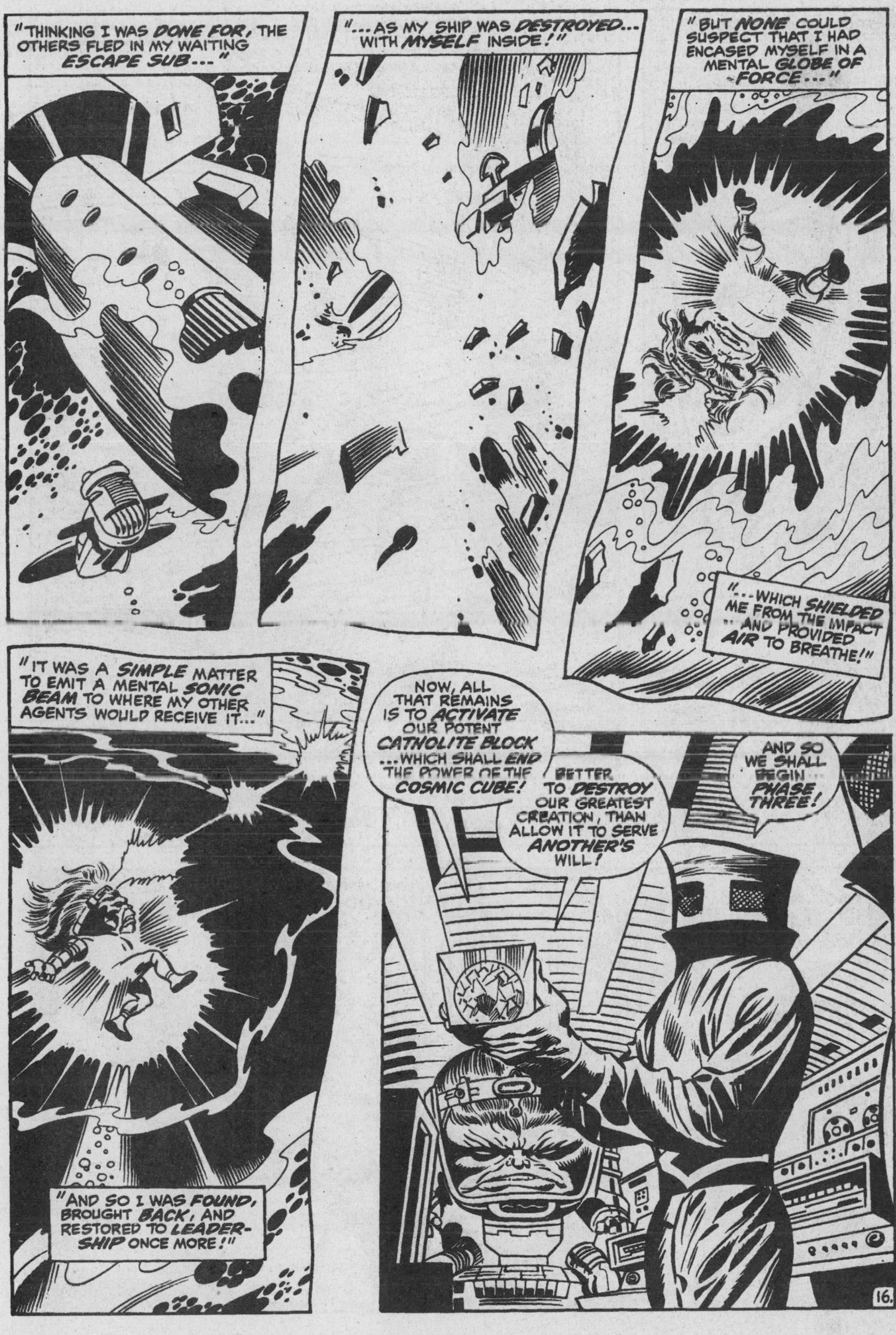
"THINKING I WAS DONE FOR, THE OTHERS FLED IN MY WAITING ESCAPE SUB..."
"...AS MY SHIP WAS DESTROYED... WITH MYSELF INSIDE!"
"BUT NONE COULD SUSPECT THAT I HAD ENCASED MYSELF IN A MENTAL GLOBE OF FORCE..."
"...WHICH SHIELDED ME FROM THE IMPACT AND PROVIDED AIR TO BREATHE!"
"IT WAS A SIMPLE MATTER TO EMIT A MENTAL SONIC BEAM TO WHERE MY OTHER AGENTS WOULD RECEIVE IT..."
"AND SO I WAS FOUND, BROUGHT BACK, AND RESTORED TO LEADER-SHIP ONCE MORE!"
NOW, ALL THAT REMAINS IS TO ACTIVATE OUR POTENT CATHOLITE BLOCK ...WHICH SHALL END THE POWER OF THE COSMIC CUBE!
BETTER TO DESTROY OUR GREATEST CREATION, THAN ALLOW IT TO SERVE ANOTHER'S WILL!
AND SO WE SHALL BEGIN PHASE THREE!
16.

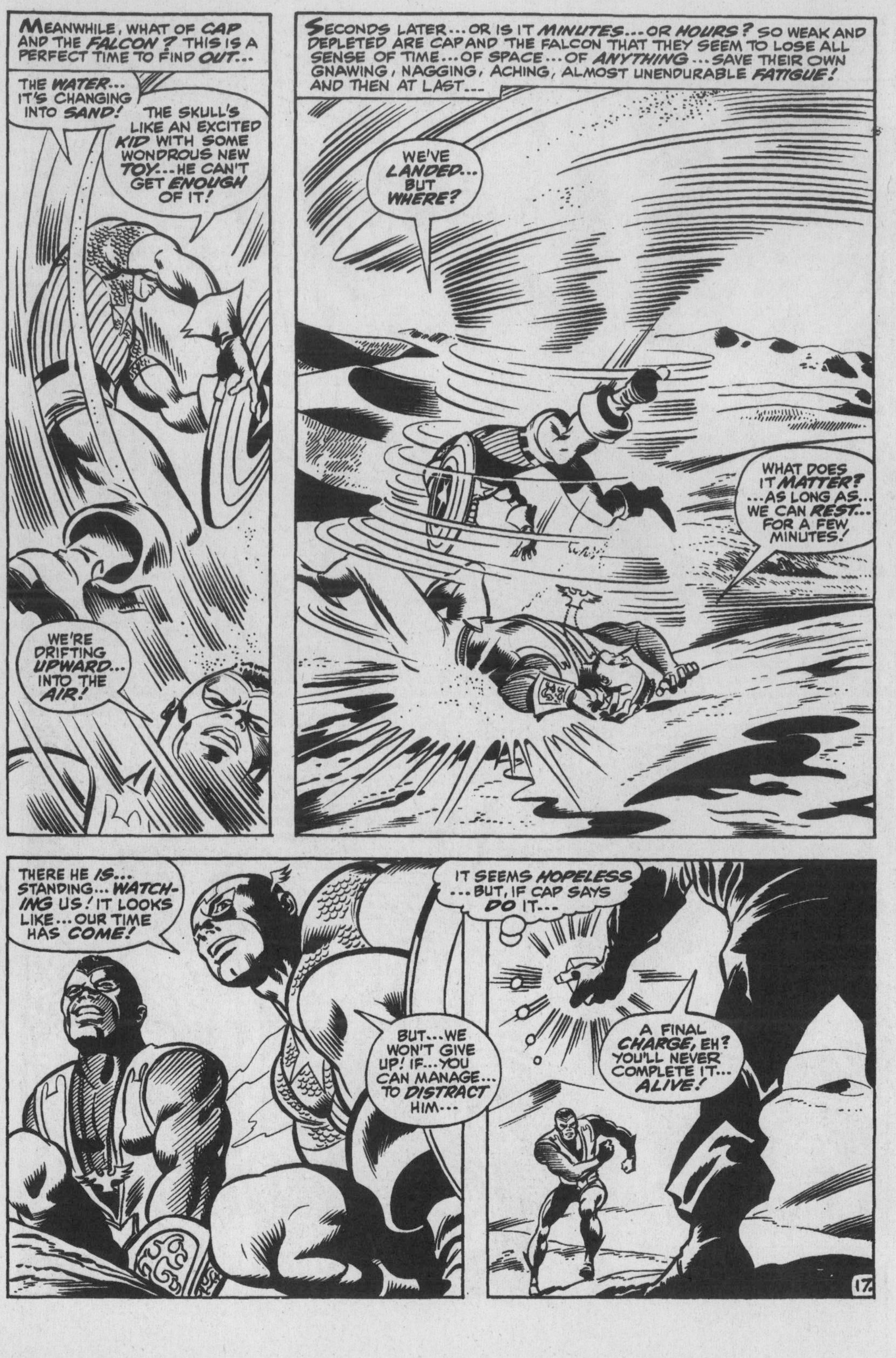
MEANWHILE, WHAT OF CAP AND THE FALCON? THIS IS A PERFECT TIME TO FIND OUT...
THE WATER... IT'S CHANGING INTO SAND!
THE SKULL'S LIKE AN EXCITED KID WITH SOME WONDROUS NEW TOY... HE CAN'T GET ENOUGH OF IT!
WE'RE DRIFTING UPWARD... INTO THE AIR!
SECONDS LATER... OR IS IT MINUTES... OR HOURS? SO WEAK AND DEPLETED ARE CAP AND THE FALCON THAT THEY SEEM TO LOSE ALL SENSE OF TIME... OF SPACE... OF ANYTHING... SAVE THEIR OWN GNAWING, NAGGING, ACHING, ALMOST UNENDURABLE FATIGUE! AND THEN AT LAST...
WE'VE LANDED... BUT WHERE?
WHAT DOES IT MATTER? ...AS LONG AS... WE CAN REST... FOR A FEW MINUTES!
THERE HE IS... STANDING... WATCHING US! IT LOOKS LIKE... OUR TIME HAS COME!
BUT... WE WON'T GIVE UP! IF... YOU CAN MANAGE... TO DISTRACT HIM...
IT SEEMS HOPELESS ...BUT, IF CAP SAYS DO IT...
A FINAL CHARGE, EH? YOU'LL NEVER COMPLETE IT... ALIVE!
17

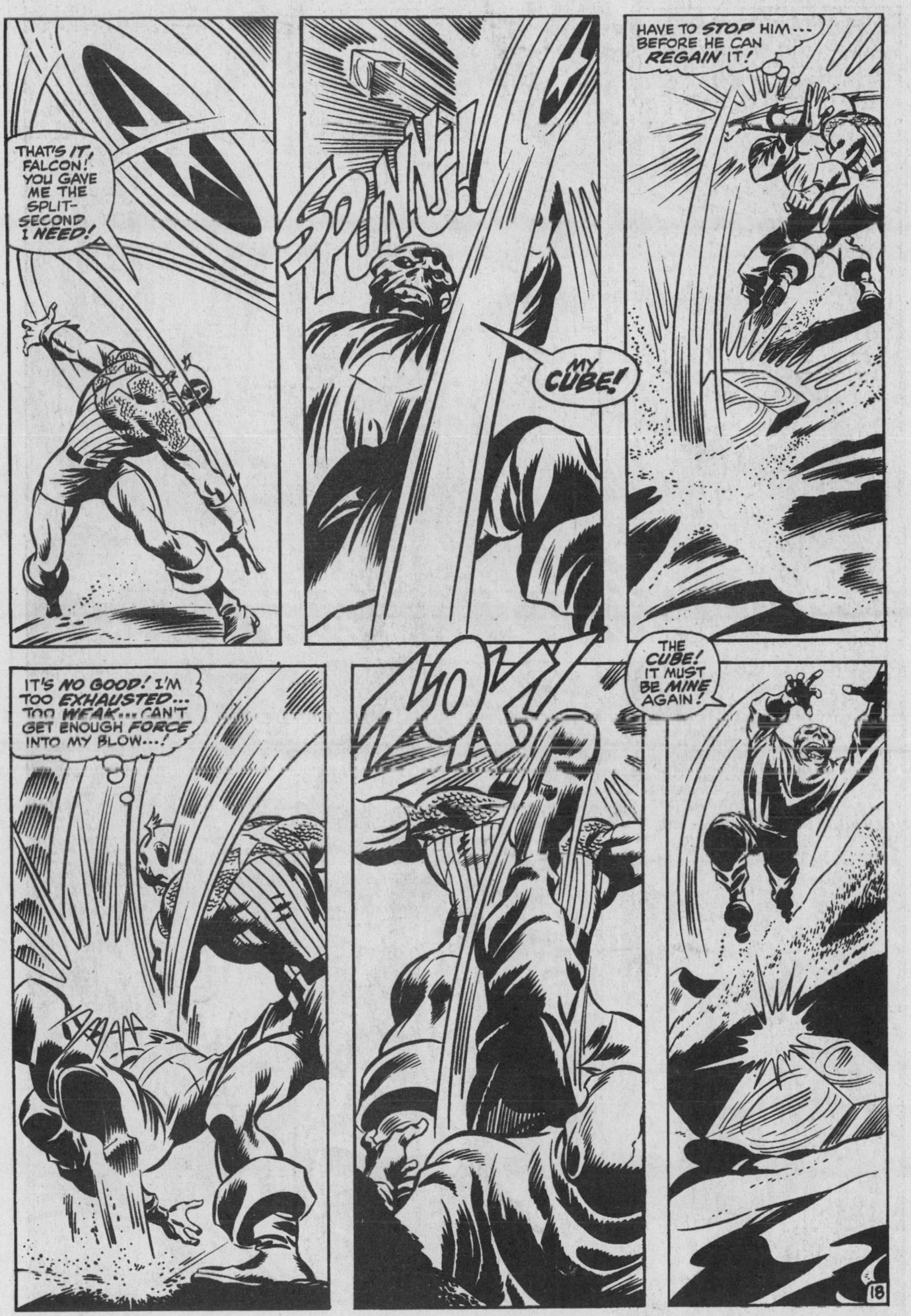
THAT'S IT, FALCON! YOU GAVE ME THE SPLIT-SECOND I NEED!
SPANNG!
MY CUBE!
HAVE TO STOP HIM... BEFORE HE CAN REGAIN IT!
IT'S NO GOOD! I'M TOO EXHAUSTED... TOO WEAK... CAN'T GET ENOUGH FORCE INTO MY BLOW...!
YAAAAAP
ZOK!
THE CUBE! IT MUST BE MINE AGAIN!
18

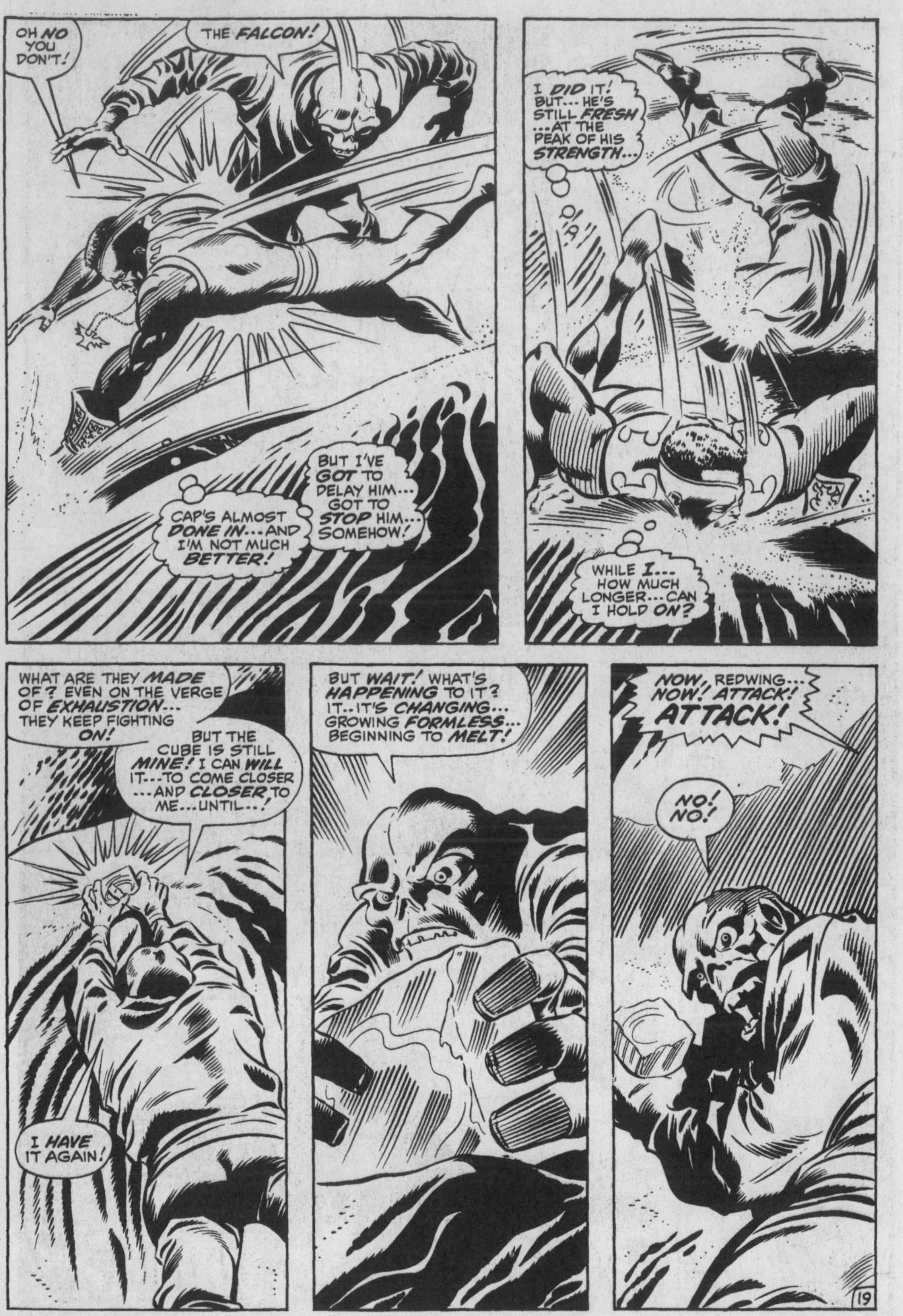
OH NO YOU DON'T!
THE FALCON!
CAP'S ALMOST DONE IN... AND I'M NOT MUCH BETTER!
BUT I'VE GOT TO DELAY HIM... GOT TO STOP HIM... SOMEHOW!
I DID IT! BUT... HE'S STILL FRESH ...AT THE PEAK OF HIS STRENGTH...
WHILE I... HOW MUCH LONGER... CAN I HOLD ON?
WHAT ARE THEY MADE OF? EVEN ON THE VERGE OF EXHAUSTION... THEY KEEP FIGHTING ON!
BUT THE CUBE IS STILL MINE! I CAN WILL IT...TO COME CLOSER ...AND CLOSER, TO ME...UNTIL...!
I HAVE IT AGAIN!
BUT WAIT! WHAT'S HAPPENING TO IT? IT..IT'S CHANGING... GROWING FORMLESS... BEGINNING TO MELT!
NOW, REDWING... NOW! ATTACK! ATTACK!
NO! NO!
19

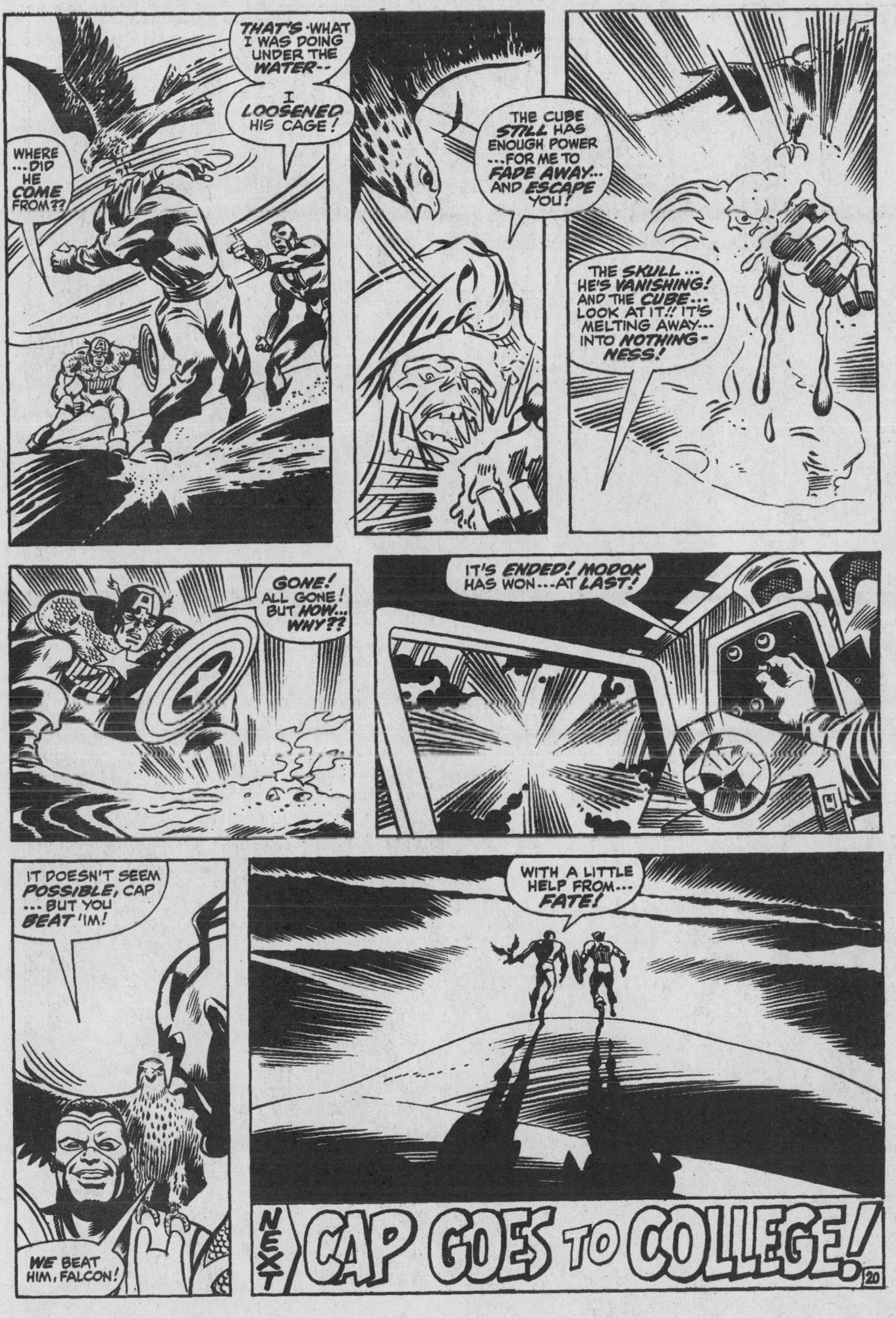

THAT'S WHAT I WAS DOING UNDER THE WATER--
I LOOSENED HIS CAGE!
WHERE ...DID HE COME FROM??
THE CUBE STILL HAS ENOUGH POWER ...FOR ME TO FADE AWAY... AND ESCAPE YOU!
THE SKULL ... HE'S VANISHING! AND THE CUBE... LOOK AT IT!! IT'S MELTING AWAY... INTO NOTHING-NESS!
GONE! ALL GONE! BUT HOW... WHY??
IT'S ENDED! MODOK HAS WON...AT LAST!
IT DOESN'T SEEM POSSIBLE, CAP ... BUT YOU BEAT 'IM!
WE BEAT HIM, FALCON!
WITH A LITTLE HELP FROM... FATE!
NEXT
CAP GOES TO COLLEGE!
20

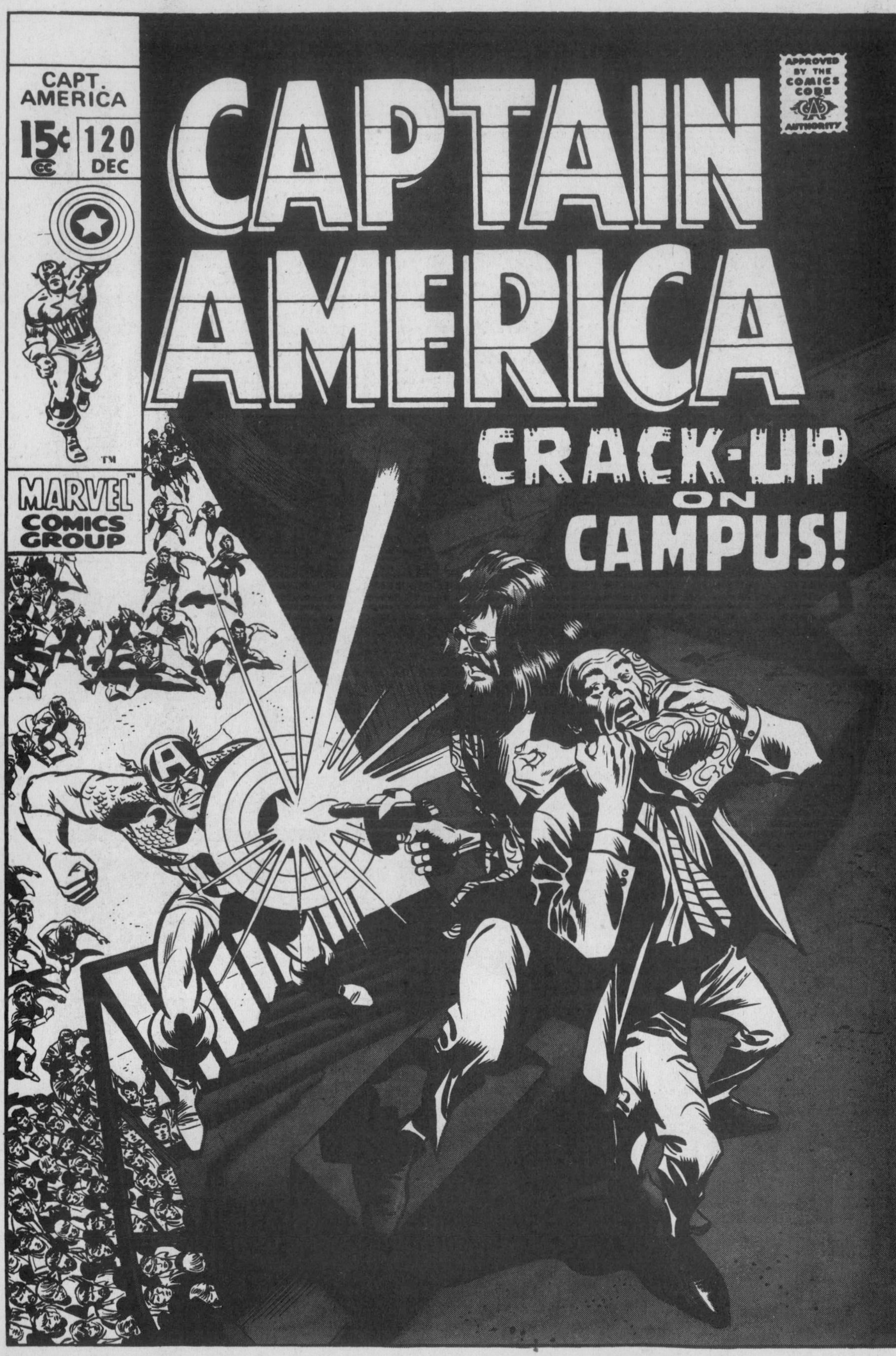
CAPT. AMERICA
15¢
120
DEC
MARVEL COMICS GROUP
APPROVED BY THE COMICS CODE AUTHORITY
CAPTAIN AMERICA
CRACK-UP ON CAMPUS!

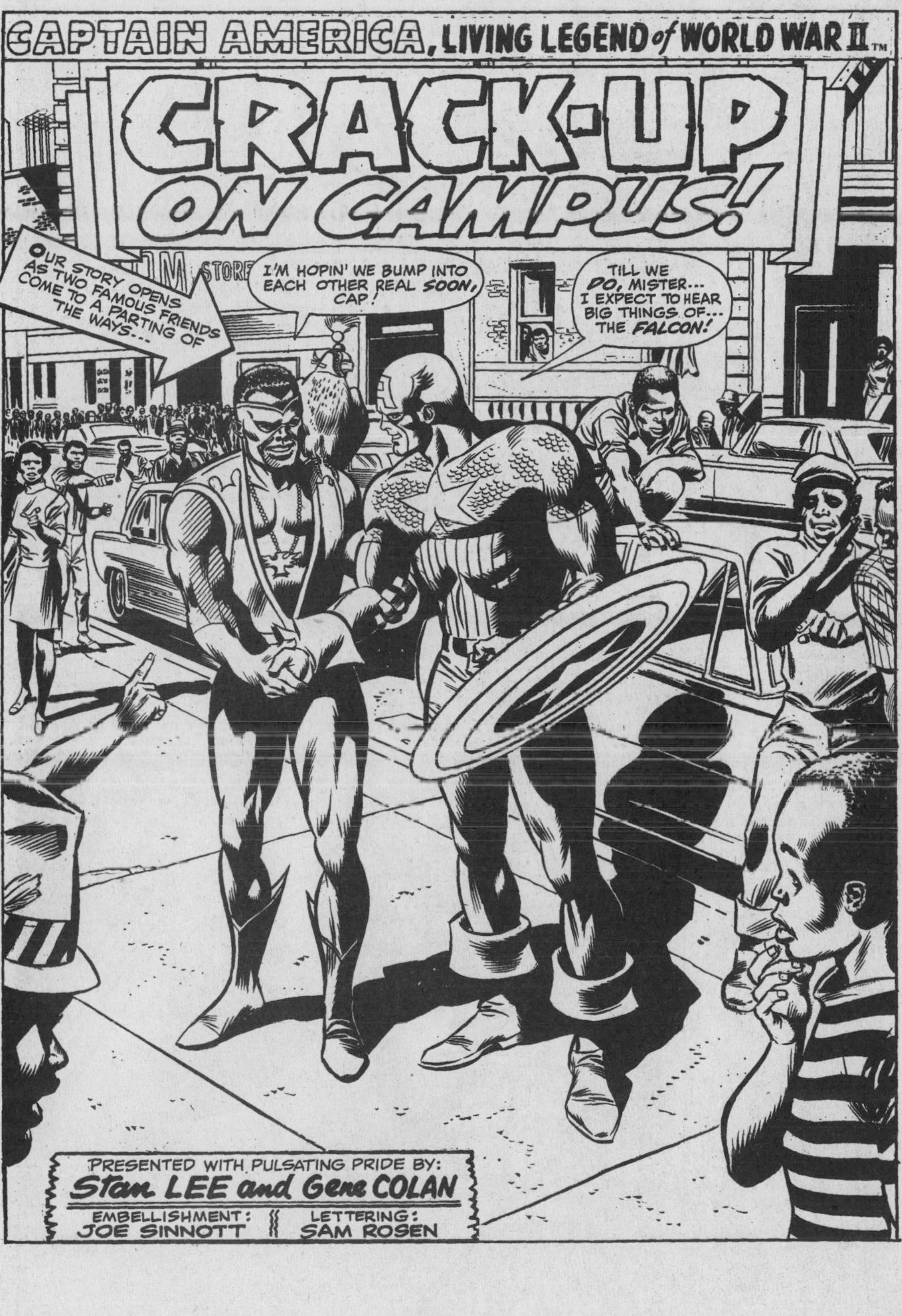
CAPTAIN AMERICA, LIVING LEGEND of WORLD WAR II™
CRACK-UP ON CAMPUS!
OUR STORY OPENS AS TWO FAMOUS FRIENDS COME TO A PARTING OF THE WAYS...
I'M HOPIN' WE BUMP INTO EACH OTHER REAL SOON, CAP!
TILL WE DO, MISTER... I EXPECT TO HEAR BIG THINGS OF... THE FALCON!
PRESENTED WITH PULSATING PRIDE BY:
Stan LEE and Gene COLAN
EMBELLISHMENT: JOE SINNOTT
LETTERING: SAM ROSEN

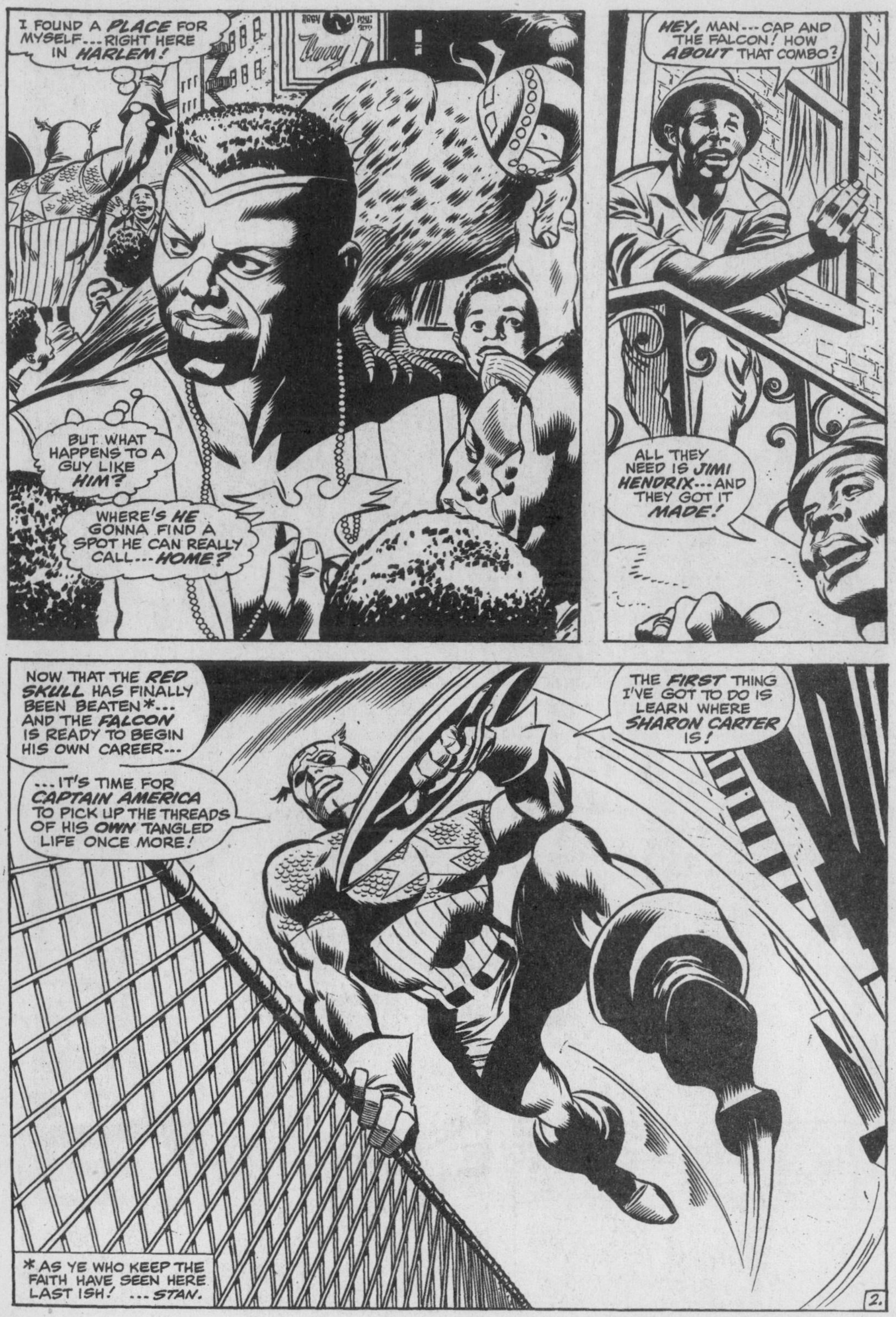

I FOUND A PLACE FOR MYSELF... RIGHT HERE IN HARLEM!
BUT WHAT HAPPENS TO A GUY LIKE HIM?
WHERE'S HE GONNA FIND A SPOT HE CAN REALLY CALL... HOME?
HEY, MAN... CAP AND THE FALCON! HOW ABOUT THAT COMBO?
ALL THEY NEED IS JIMI HENDRIX... AND THEY GOT IT MADE!
NOW THAT THE RED SKULL HAS FINALLY BEEN BEATEN*... AND THE FALCON IS READY TO BEGIN HIS OWN CAREER...
...IT'S TIME FOR CAPTAIN AMERICA TO PICK UP THE THREADS OF HIS OWN TANGLED LIFE ONCE MORE!
THE FIRST THING I'VE GOT TO DO IS LEARN WHERE SHARON CARTER IS!
*AS YE WHO KEEP THE FAITH HAVE SEEN HERE LAST ISH! ...STAN.
2.

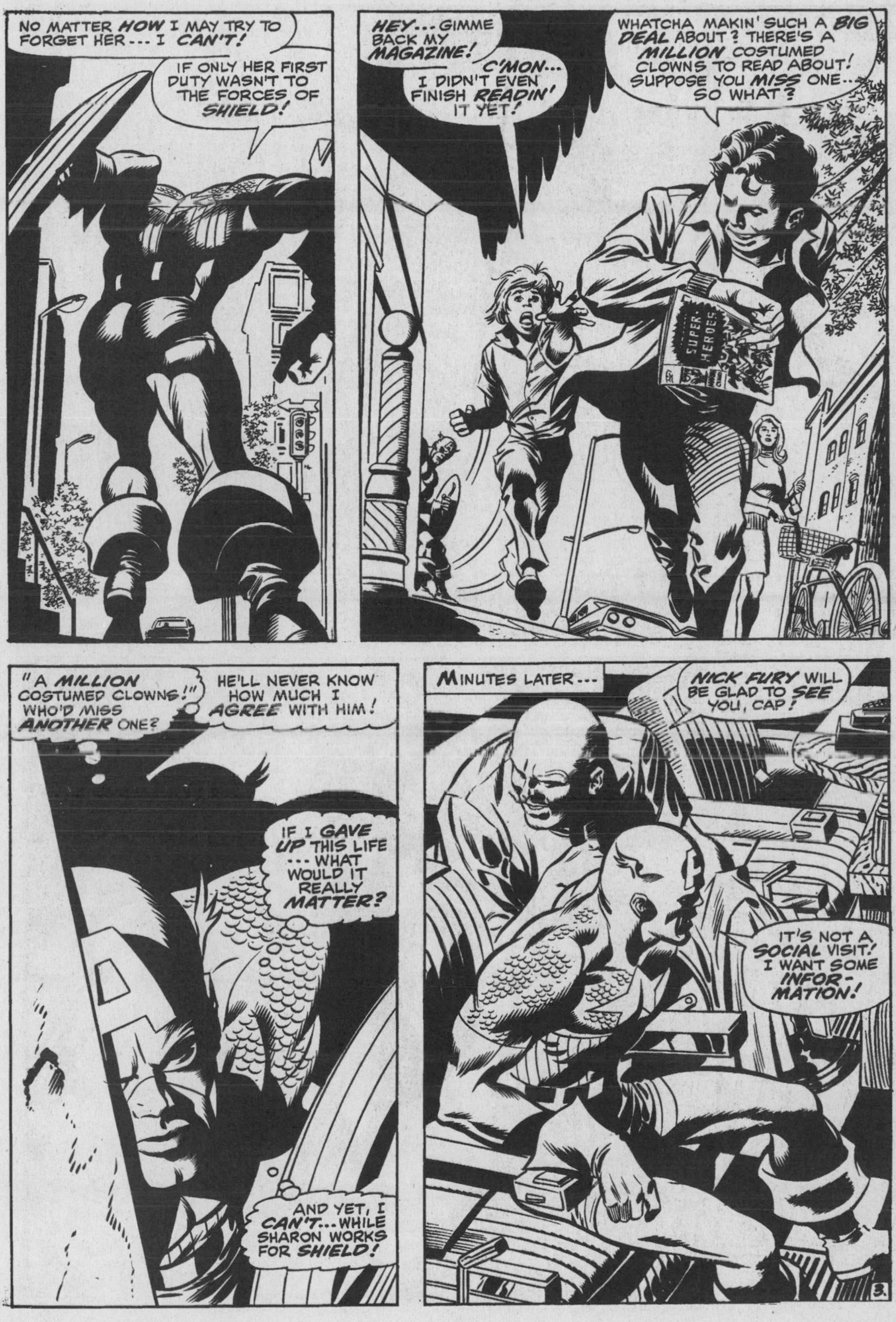

NO MATTER HOW I MAY TRY TO FORGET HER --- I CAN'T!
IF ONLY HER FIRST DUTY WASN'T TO THE FORCES OF SHIELD!
HEY... GIMME BACK MY MAGAZINE!
C'MON... I DIDN'T EVEN FINISH READIN' IT YET!
WHATCHA MAKIN' SUCH A BIG DEAL ABOUT? THERE'S A MILLION COSTUMED CLOWNS TO READ ABOUT! SUPPOSE YOU MISS ONE... SO WHAT?
SUPER-HEROES
"A MILLION COSTUMED CLOWNS!" WHO'D MISS ANOTHER ONE?
HE'LL NEVER KNOW HOW MUCH I AGREE WITH HIM!
IF I GAVE UP THIS LIFE --- WHAT WOULD IT REALLY MATTER?
AND YET, I CAN'T... WHILE SHARON WORKS FOR SHIELD!
MINUTES LATER ---
NICK FURY WILL BE GLAD TO SEE YOU, CAP!
IT'S NOT A SOCIAL VISIT! I WANT SOME INFOR-MATION!
3.

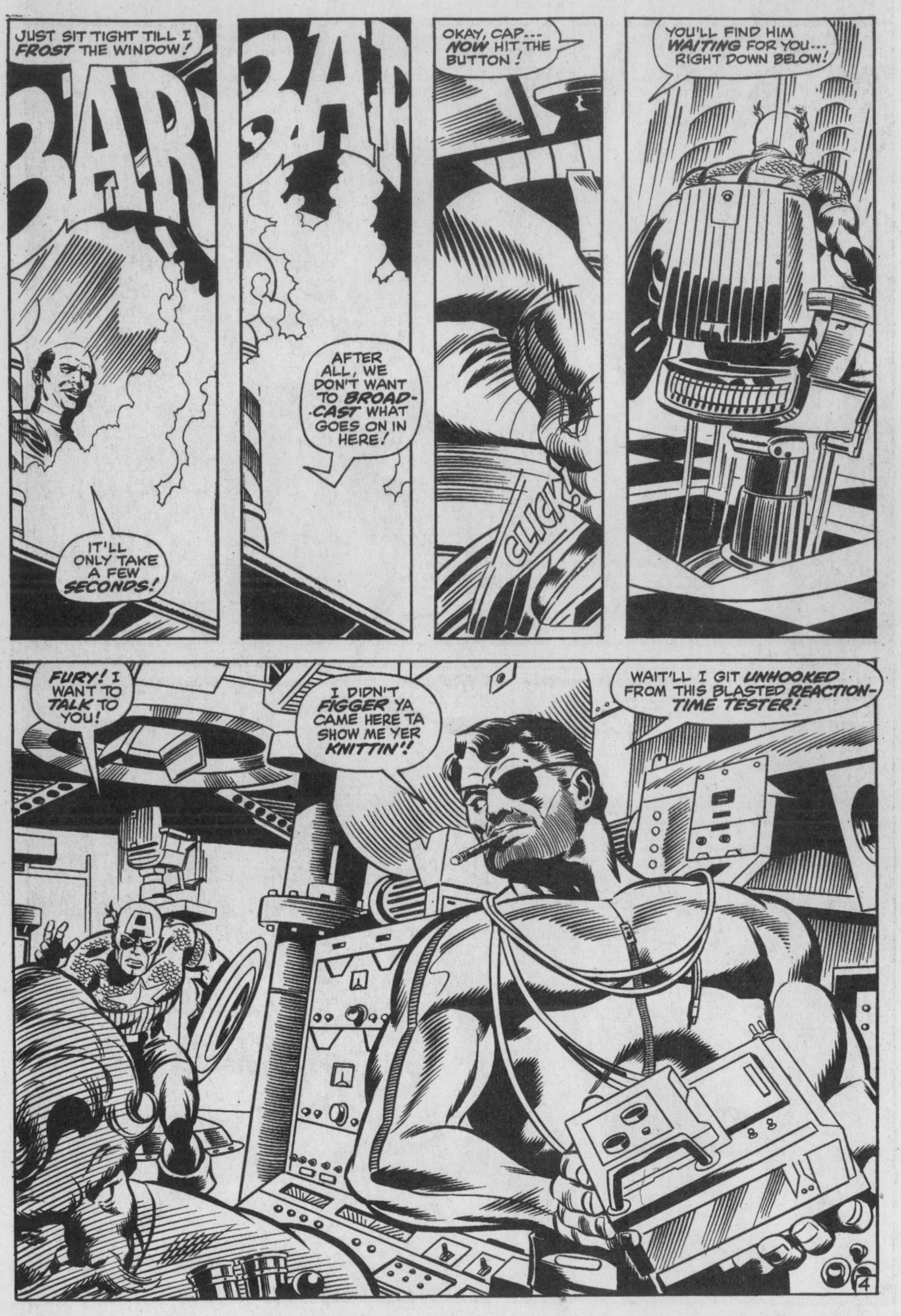
JUST SIT TIGHT TILL I FROST THE WINDOW!
BAR
IT'LL ONLY TAKE A FEW SECONDS!
BAR
AFTER ALL, WE DON'T WANT TO BROAD-CAST WHAT GOES ON IN HERE!
OKAY, CAP... NOW HIT THE BUTTON!
CLICK
YOU'LL FIND HIM WAITING FOR YOU... RIGHT DOWN BELOW!
FURY! I WANT TO TALK TO YOU!
I DIDN'T FIGGER YA CAME HERE TA SHOW ME YER KNITTIN'!
WAIT'LL I GIT UNHOOKED FROM THIS BLASTED REACTION-TIME TESTER!
4

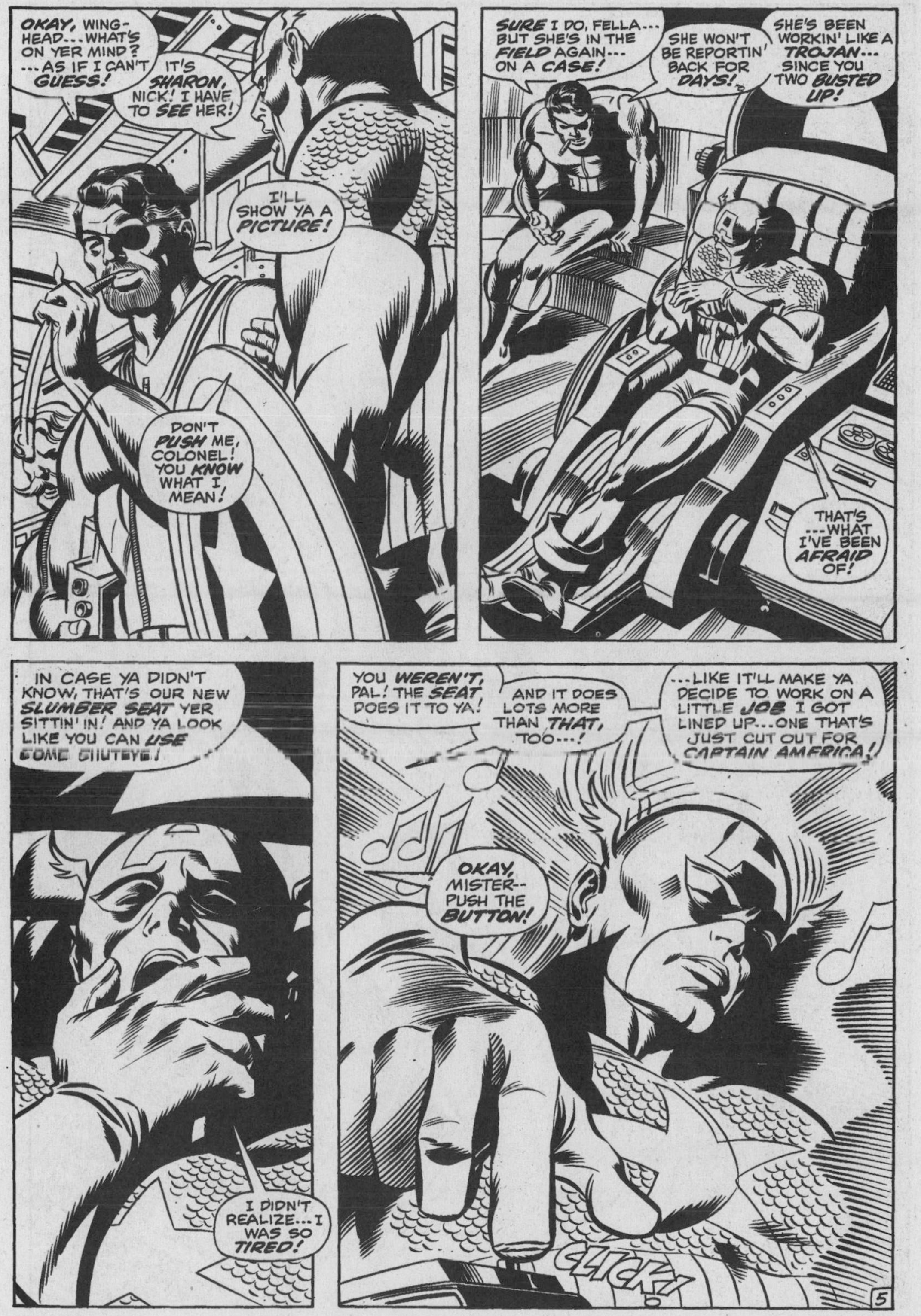
OKAY, WING-HEAD--- WHAT'S ON YER MIND? --- AS IF I CAN'T GUESS!
IT'S SHARON, NICK! I HAVE TO SEE HER!
I'LL SHOW YA A PICTURE!
DON'T PUSH ME, COLONEL! YOU KNOW WHAT I MEAN!
SURE I DO, FELLA--- BUT SHE'S IN THE FIELD AGAIN--- ON A CASE!
SHE WON'T BE REPORTIN' BACK FOR DAYS!
SHE'S BEEN WORKIN' LIKE A TROJAN--- SINCE YOU TWO BUSTED UP!
THAT'S ---WHAT I'VE BEEN AFRAID OF!
IN CASE YA DIDN'T KNOW, THAT'S OUR NEW SLUMBER SEAT YER SITTIN' IN! AND YA LOOK LIKE YOU CAN USE SOME SHUTEYE!
I DIDN'T REALIZE... I WAS SO TIRED!
YOU WEREN'T, PAL! THE SEAT DOES IT TO YA!
AND IT DOES LOTS MORE THAN THAT, TOO---!
---LIKE IT'LL MAKE YA DECIDE TO WORK ON A LITTLE JOB I GOT LINED UP...ONE THAT'S JUST CUT OUT FOR CAPTAIN AMERICA!
OKAY, MISTER-- PUSH THE BUTTON!
CLICK!
5

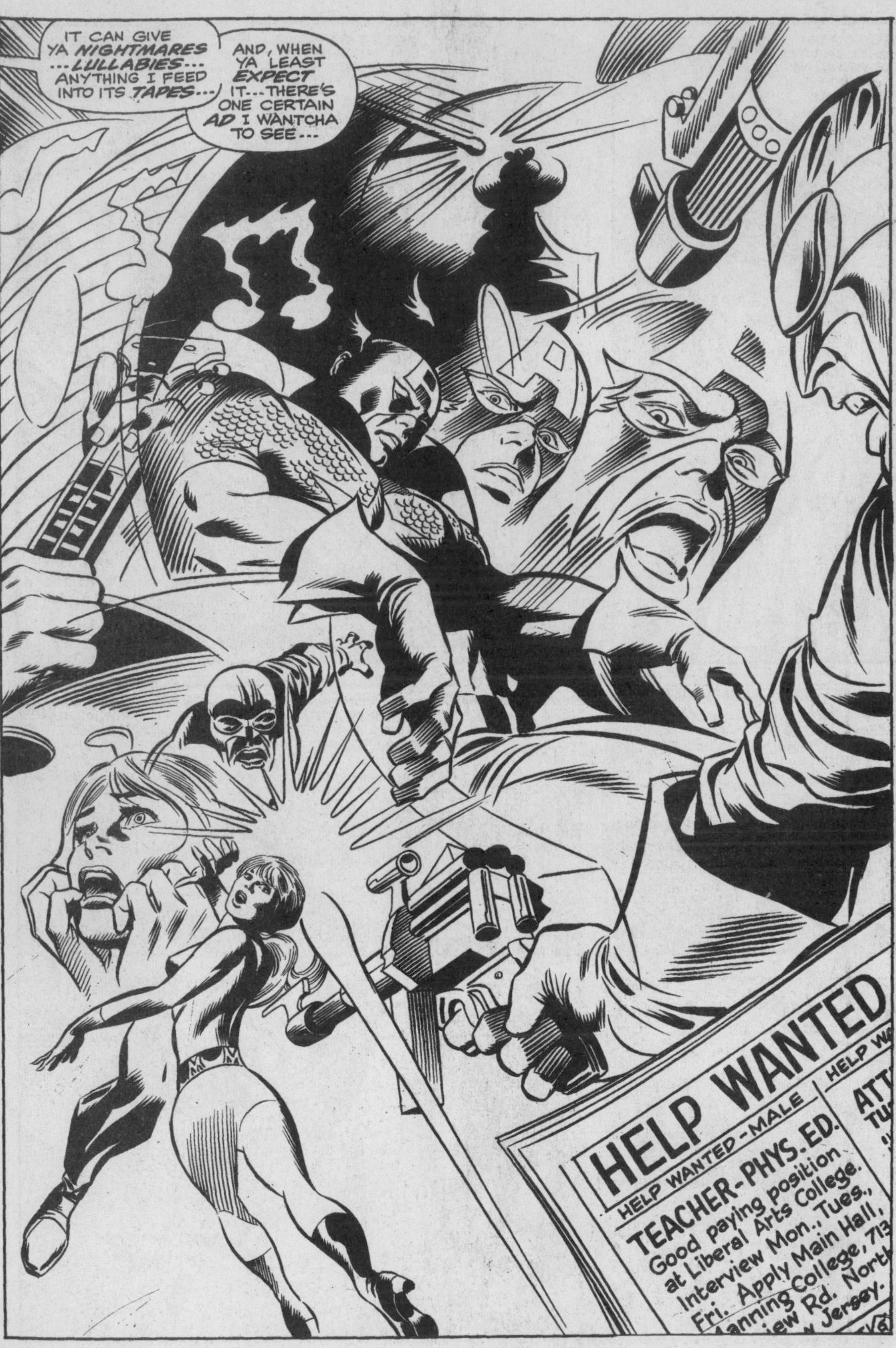
IT CAN GIVE YA NIGHTMARES ...LULLABIES... ANYTHING I FEED INTO ITS TAPES...
AND, WHEN YA LEAST EXPECT IT...THERE'S ONE CERTAIN AD I WANTCHA TO SEE...
HELP WANTED
HELP WANTED-MALE
TEACHER-PHYS. ED.
Good paying position at Liberal Arts College. Interview Mon., Tues., Fri. Apply Main Hall, Manning College,
HELP WANTED
HELP WANTED

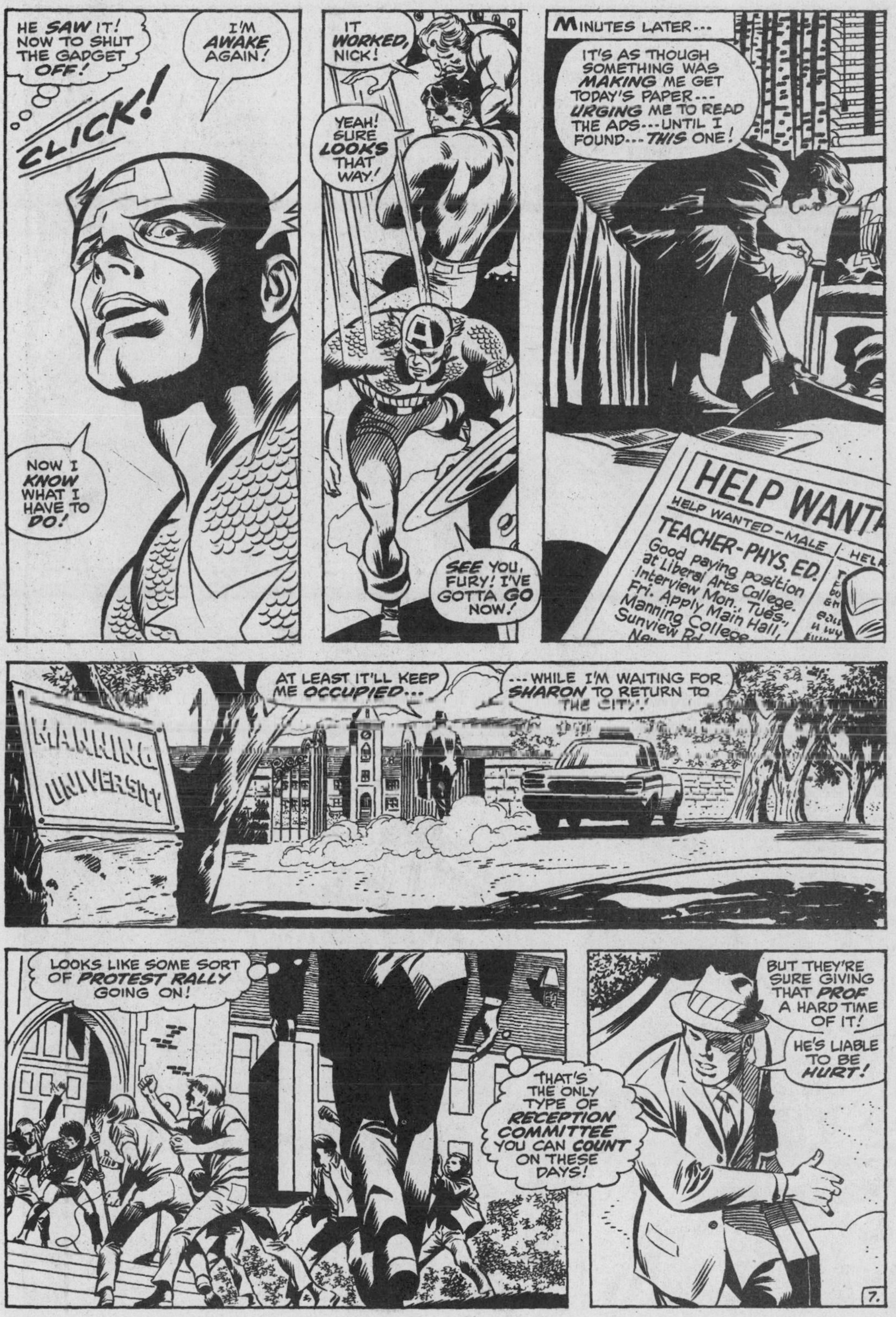
HE SAW IT! NOW TO SHUT THE GADGET OFF!
I'M AWAKE AGAIN!
CLICK!
NOW I KNOW WHAT I HAVE TO DO!
IT WORKED, NICK!
YEAH! SURE LOOKS THAT WAY!
SEE YOU, FURY! I'VE GOTTA GO NOW!
MINUTES LATER---
IT'S AS THOUGH SOMETHING WAS MAKING ME GET TODAY'S PAPER--- URGING ME TO READ THE ADS---UNTIL I FOUND---THIS ONE!
HELP WANTA
HELP WANTED-MALE
TEACHER-PHYS. ED.
Good paying position at Liberal Arts College. Interview Mon., Tues., Fri. Apply Main Hall, Manning College, Sunview Rd.
AT LEAST IT'LL KEEP ME OCCUPIED...
---WHILE I'M WAITING FOR SHARON TO RETURN TO THE CITY!
MANNING UNIVERSITY
LOOKS LIKE SOME SORT OF PROTEST RALLY GOING ON!
THAT'S THE ONLY TYPE OF RECEPTION COMMITTEE YOU CAN COUNT ON THESE DAYS!
BUT THEY'RE SURE GIVING THAT PROF A HARD TIME OF IT!
HE'S LIABLE TO BE HURT!
7.

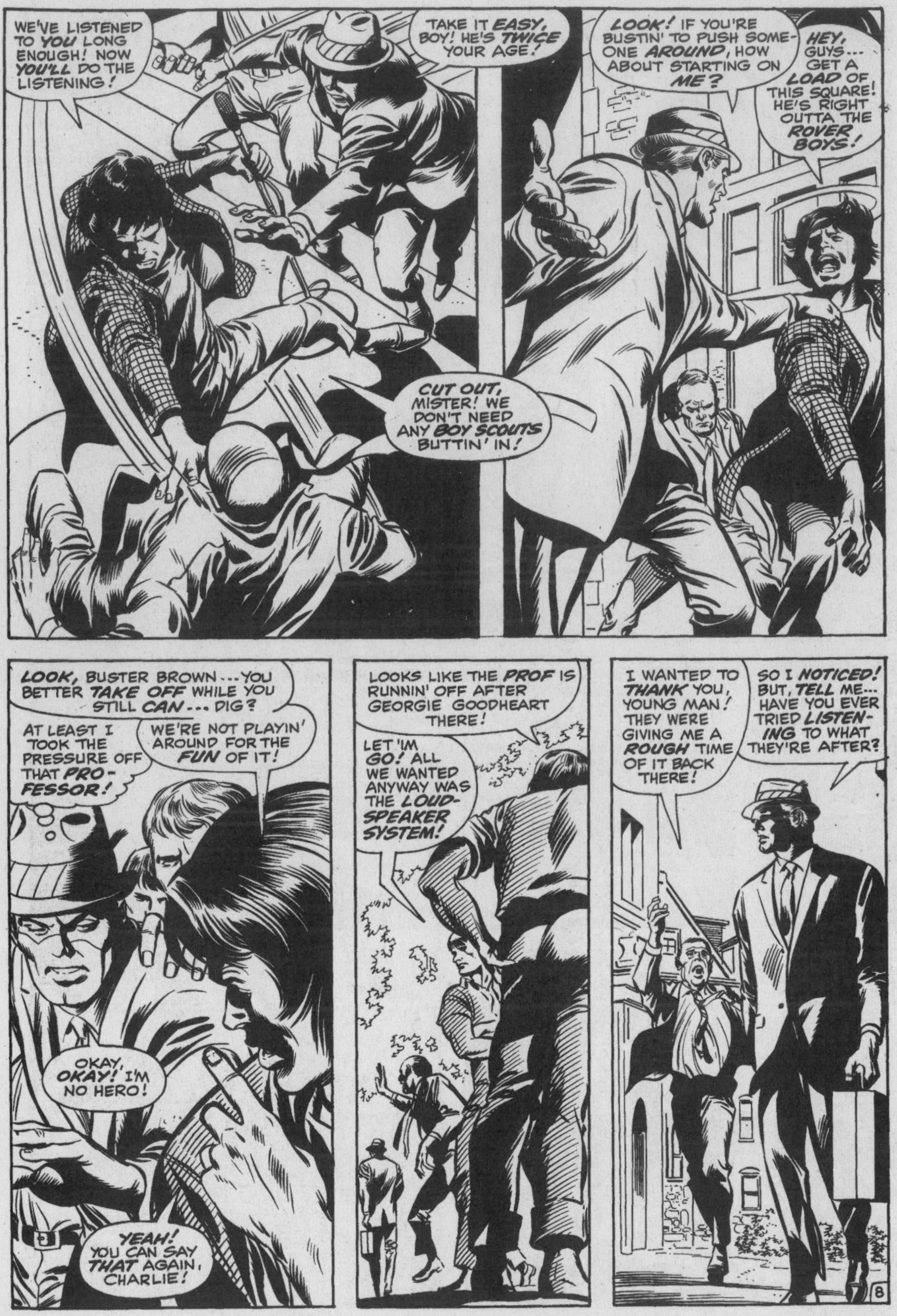
WE'VE LISTENED TO YOU LONG ENOUGH! NOW YOU'LL DO THE LISTENING!
TAKE IT EASY, BOY! HE'S TWICE YOUR AGE!
CUT OUT, MISTER! WE DON'T NEED ANY BOY SCOUTS BUTTIN' IN!
LOOK! IF YOU'RE BUSTIN' TO PUSH SOME-ONE AROUND, HOW ABOUT STARTING ON ME?
HEY, GUYS... GET A LOAD OF THIS SQUARE! HE'S RIGHT OUTTA THE ROVER BOYS!
LOOK, BUSTER BROWN... YOU BETTER TAKE OFF WHILE YOU STILL CAN... DIG?
AT LEAST I TOOK THE PRESSURE OFF THAT PRO-FESSOR!
WE'RE NOT PLAYIN' AROUND FOR THE FUN OF IT!
OKAY, OKAY! I'M NO HERO!
YEAH! YOU CAN SAY THAT AGAIN, CHARLIE!
LOOKS LIKE THE PROF IS RUNNIN' OFF AFTER GEORGIE GOODHEART THERE!
LET 'IM GO! ALL WE WANTED ANYWAY WAS THE LOUD-SPEAKER SYSTEM!
I WANTED TO THANK YOU, YOUNG MAN! THEY WERE GIVING ME A ROUGH TIME OF IT BACK THERE!
SO I NOTICED! BUT, TELL ME... HAVE YOU EVER TRIED LISTEN-ING TO WHAT THEY'RE AFTER?
8

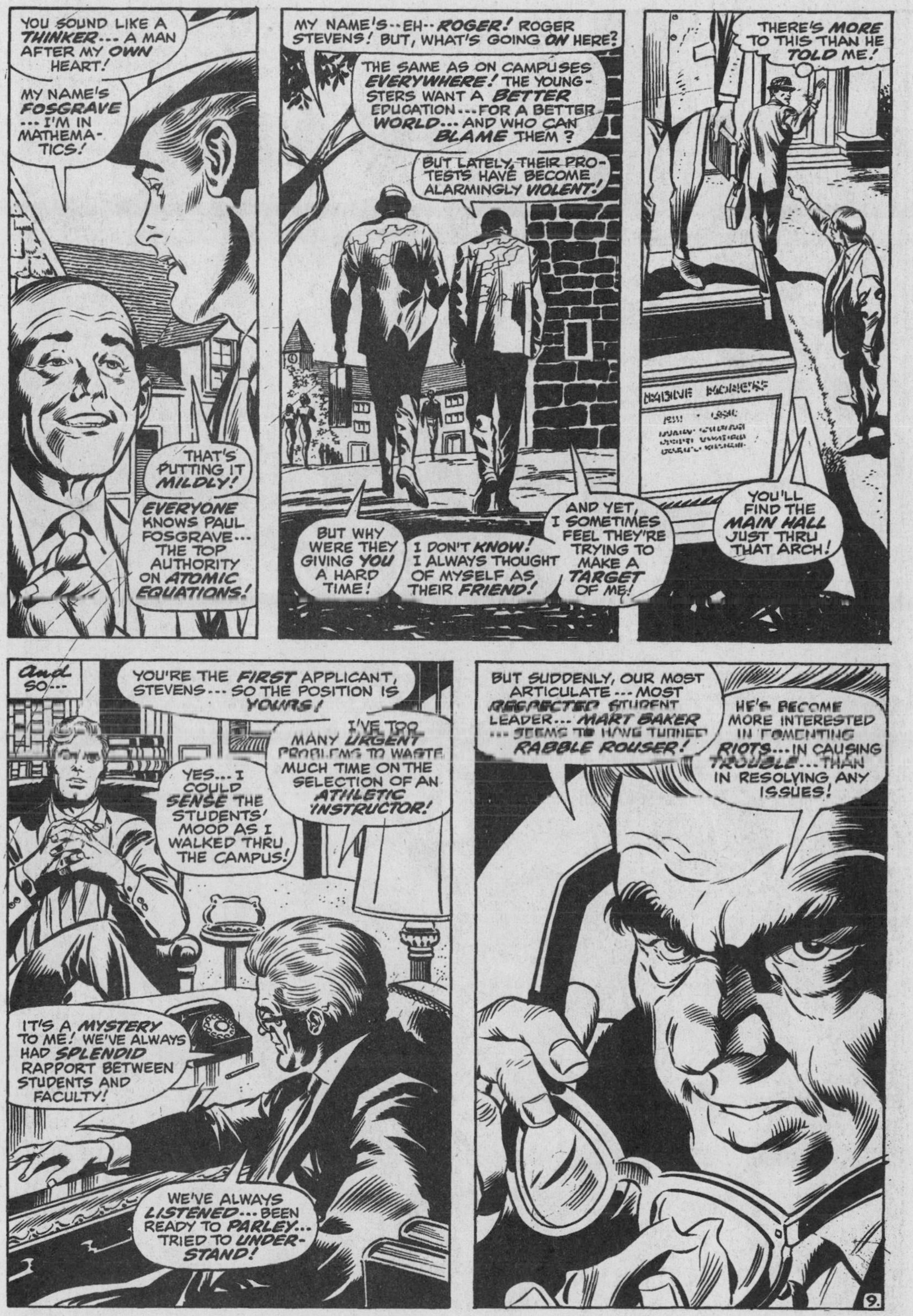
YOU SOUND LIKE A THINKER--- A MAN AFTER MY OWN HEART!
MY NAME'S FOSGRAVE ... I'M IN MATHEMATICS!
THAT'S PUTTING IT MILDLY!
EVERYONE KNOWS PAUL FOSGRAVE... THE TOP AUTHORITY ON ATOMIC EQUATIONS!
MY NAME'S--EH-- ROGER! ROGER STEVENS! BUT, WHAT'S GOING ON HERE?
THE SAME AS ON CAMPUSES EVERYWHERE! THE YOUNGSTERS WANT A BETTER EDUCATION---FOR A BETTER WORLD... AND WHO CAN BLAME THEM?
BUT LATELY, THEIR PROTESTS HAVE BECOME ALARMINGLY VIOLENT!
BUT WHY WERE THEY GIVING YOU A HARD TIME!
I DON'T KNOW! I ALWAYS THOUGHT OF MYSELF AS THEIR FRIEND!
AND YET, I SOMETIMES FEEL THEY'RE TRYING TO MAKE A TARGET OF ME!
THERE'S MORE TO THIS THAN HE TOLD ME!
YOU'LL FIND THE MAIN HALL JUST THRU THAT ARCH!
And so---
YOU'RE THE FIRST APPLICANT, STEVENS--- SO THE POSITION IS YOURS!
I'VE TOO MANY URGENT PROBLEMS TO WASTE MUCH TIME ON THE SELECTION OF AN ATHLETIC INSTRUCTOR!
YES... I COULD SENSE THE STUDENTS' MOOD AS I WALKED THRU THE CAMPUS!
IT'S A MYSTERY TO ME! WE'VE ALWAYS HAD SPLENDID RAPPORT BETWEEN STUDENTS AND FACULTY!
WE'VE ALWAYS LISTENED... BEEN READY TO PARLEY... TRIED TO UNDERSTAND!
BUT SUDDENLY, OUR MOST ARTICULATE --- MOST RESPECTED STUDENT LEADER... MART BAKER ... SEEMS TO HAVE TURNED RABBLE ROUSER!
HE'S BECOME MORE INTERESTED IN FOMENTING RIOTS... IN CAUSING TROUBLE... THAN IN RESOLVING ANY ISSUES!
9.

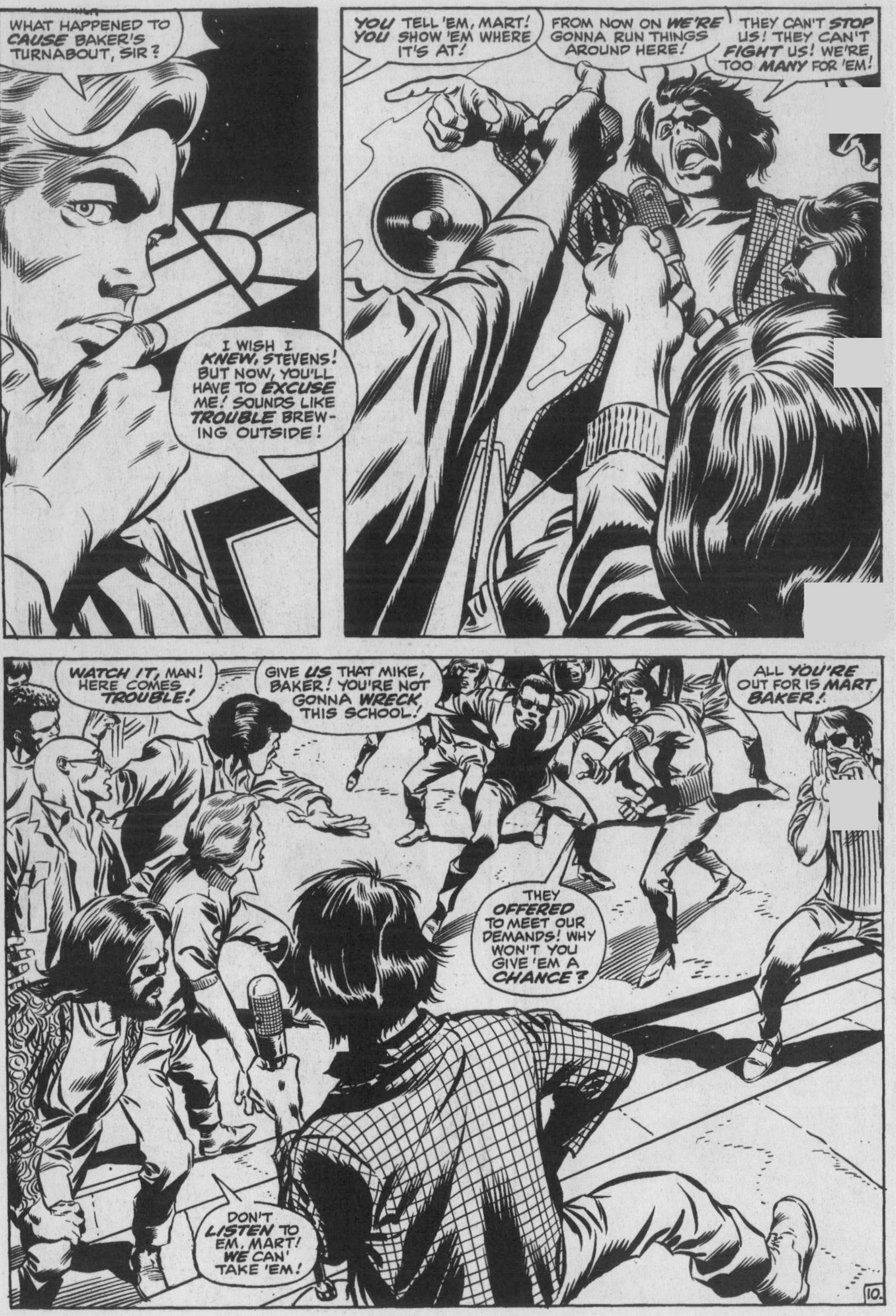
WHAT HAPPENED TO CAUSE BAKER'S TURNABOUT, SIR?
I WISH I KNEW, STEVENS! BUT NOW, YOU'LL HAVE TO EXCUSE ME! SOUNDS LIKE TROUBLE BREWING OUTSIDE!
YOU TELL 'EM, MART! YOU SHOW 'EM WHERE IT'S AT!
FROM NOW ON WE'RE GONNA RUN THINGS AROUND HERE!
THEY CAN'T STOP US! THEY CAN'T FIGHT US! WE'RE TOO MANY FOR 'EM!
WATCH IT, MAN! HERE COMES TROUBLE!
GIVE US THAT MIKE, BAKER! YOU'RE NOT GONNA WRECK THIS SCHOOL!
ALL YOU'RE OUT FOR IS MART BAKER!
THEY OFFERED TO MEET OUR DEMANDS! WHY WON'T YOU GIVE 'EM A CHANCE?
DON'T LISTEN TO EM, MART! WE CAN' TAKE 'EM!
10.

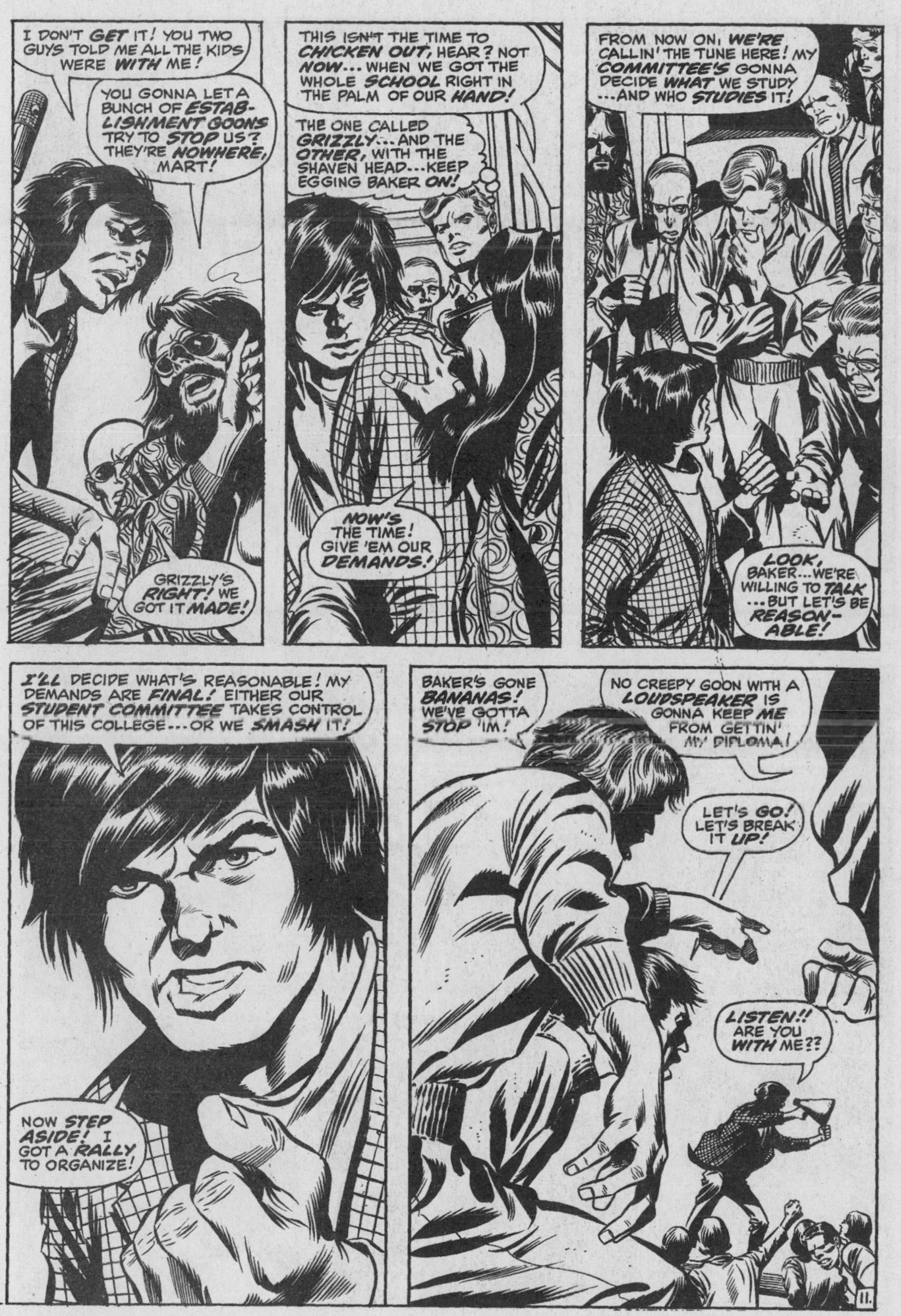
I DON'T GET IT! YOU TWO GUYS TOLD ME ALL THE KIDS WERE WITH ME!
YOU GONNA LET A BUNCH OF ESTABLISHMENT GOONS TRY TO STOP US? THEY'RE NOWHERE, MART!
GRIZZLY'S RIGHT! WE GOT IT MADE!
THIS ISN'T THE TIME TO CHICKEN OUT, HEAR? NOT NOW... WHEN WE GOT THE WHOLE SCHOOL RIGHT IN THE PALM OF OUR HAND!
THE ONE CALLED GRIZZLY... AND THE OTHER, WITH THE SHAVEN HEAD... KEEP EGGING BAKER ON!
NOW'S THE TIME! GIVE 'EM OUR DEMANDS!
FROM NOW ON, WE'RE CALLIN' THE TUNE HERE! MY COMMITTEE'S GONNA DECIDE WHAT WE STUDY ...AND WHO STUDIES IT!
LOOK, BAKER... WE'RE WILLING TO TALK ...BUT LET'S BE REASONABLE!
I'LL DECIDE WHAT'S REASONABLE! MY DEMANDS ARE FINAL! EITHER OUR STUDENT COMMITTEE TAKES CONTROL OF THIS COLLEGE... OR WE SMASH IT!
NOW STEP ASIDE! I GOT A RALLY TO ORGANIZE!
BAKER'S GONE BANANAS! WE'VE GOTTA STOP 'IM!
NO CREEPY GOON WITH A LOUDSPEAKER IS GONNA KEEP ME FROM GETTIN' MY DIPLOMA!
LET'S GO! LET'S BREAK IT UP!
LISTEN!! ARE YOU WITH ME??
11.

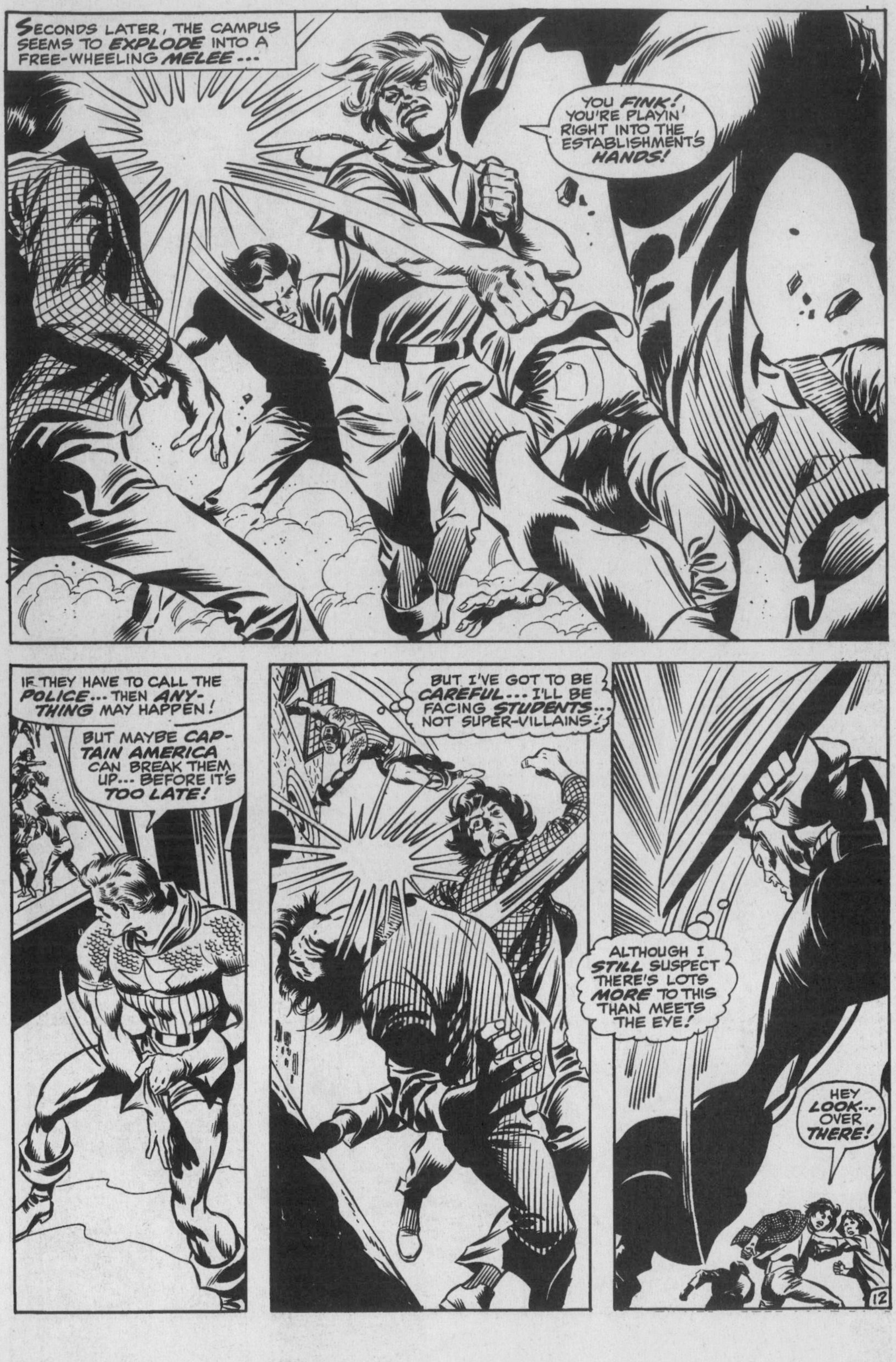
SECONDS LATER, THE CAMPUS SEEMS TO EXPLODE INTO A FREE-WHEELING MELEE...
YOU FINK! YOU'RE PLAYIN' RIGHT INTO THE ESTABLISHMENT'S HANDS!
IF THEY HAVE TO CALL THE POLICE... THEN ANYTHING MAY HAPPEN!
BUT MAYBE CAPTAIN AMERICA CAN BREAK THEM UP... BEFORE IT'S TOO LATE!
BUT I'VE GOT TO BE CAREFUL... I'LL BE FACING STUDENTS... NOT SUPER-VILLAINS!
ALTHOUGH I STILL SUSPECT THERE'S LOTS MORE TO THIS THAN MEETS THE EYE!
HEY LOOK... OVER THERE!
12

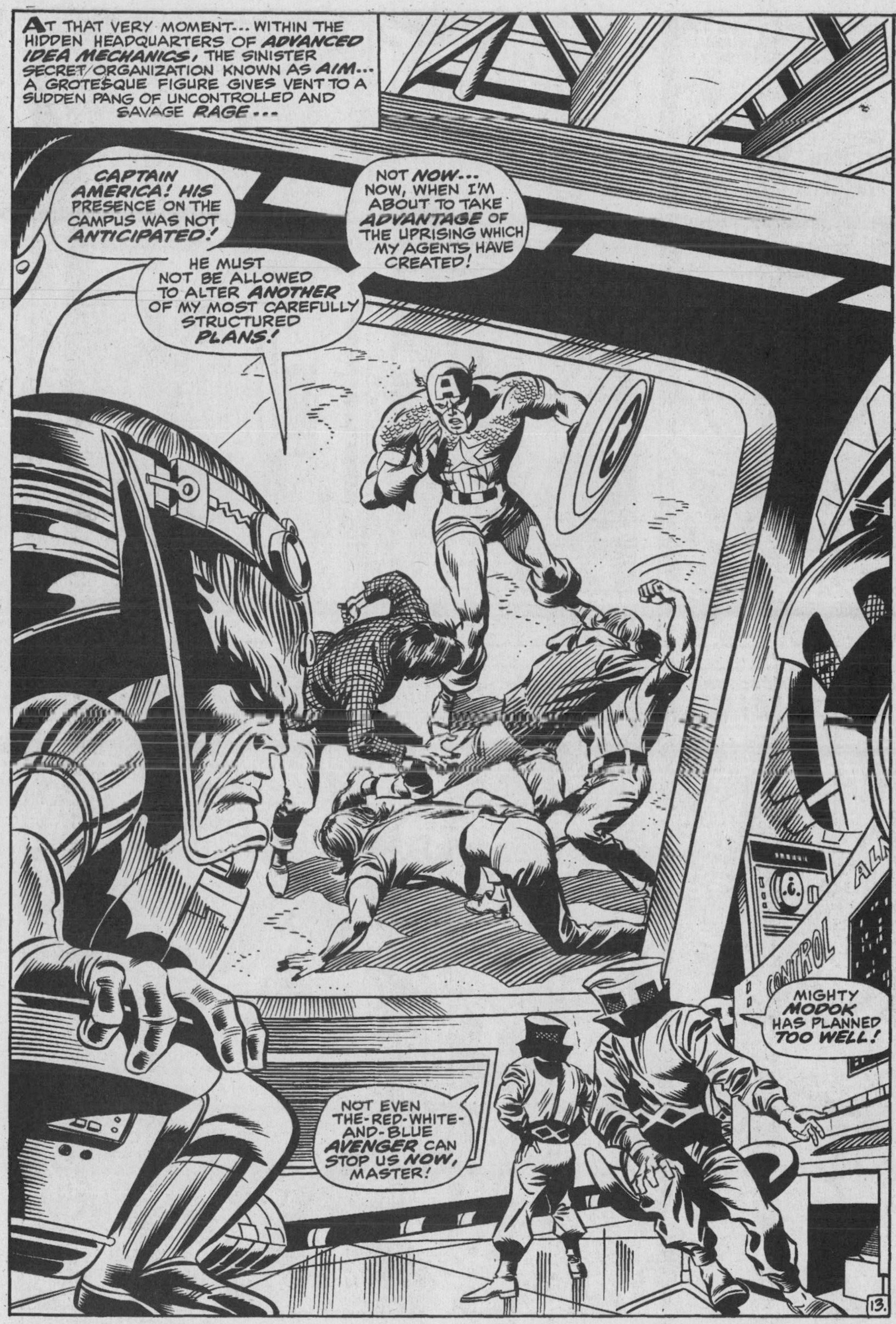
AT THAT VERY MOMENT--- WITHIN THE HIDDEN HEADQUARTERS OF ADVANCED IDEA MECHANICS, THE SINISTER SECRET ORGANIZATION KNOWN AS AIM--- A GROTESQUE FIGURE GIVES VENT TO A SUDDEN PANG OF UNCONTROLLED AND SAVAGE RAGE---
CAPTAIN AMERICA! HIS PRESENCE ON THE CAMPUS WAS NOT ANTICIPATED!
NOT NOW--- NOW, WHEN I'M ABOUT TO TAKE ADVANTAGE OF THE UPRISING WHICH MY AGENTS HAVE CREATED!
HE MUST NOT BE ALLOWED TO ALTER ANOTHER OF MY MOST CAREFULLY STRUCTURED PLANS!
CONTROL
NOT EVEN THE-RED-WHITE-AND-BLUE AVENGER CAN STOP US NOW, MASTER!
MIGHTY MODOK HAS PLANNED TOO WELL!
13.

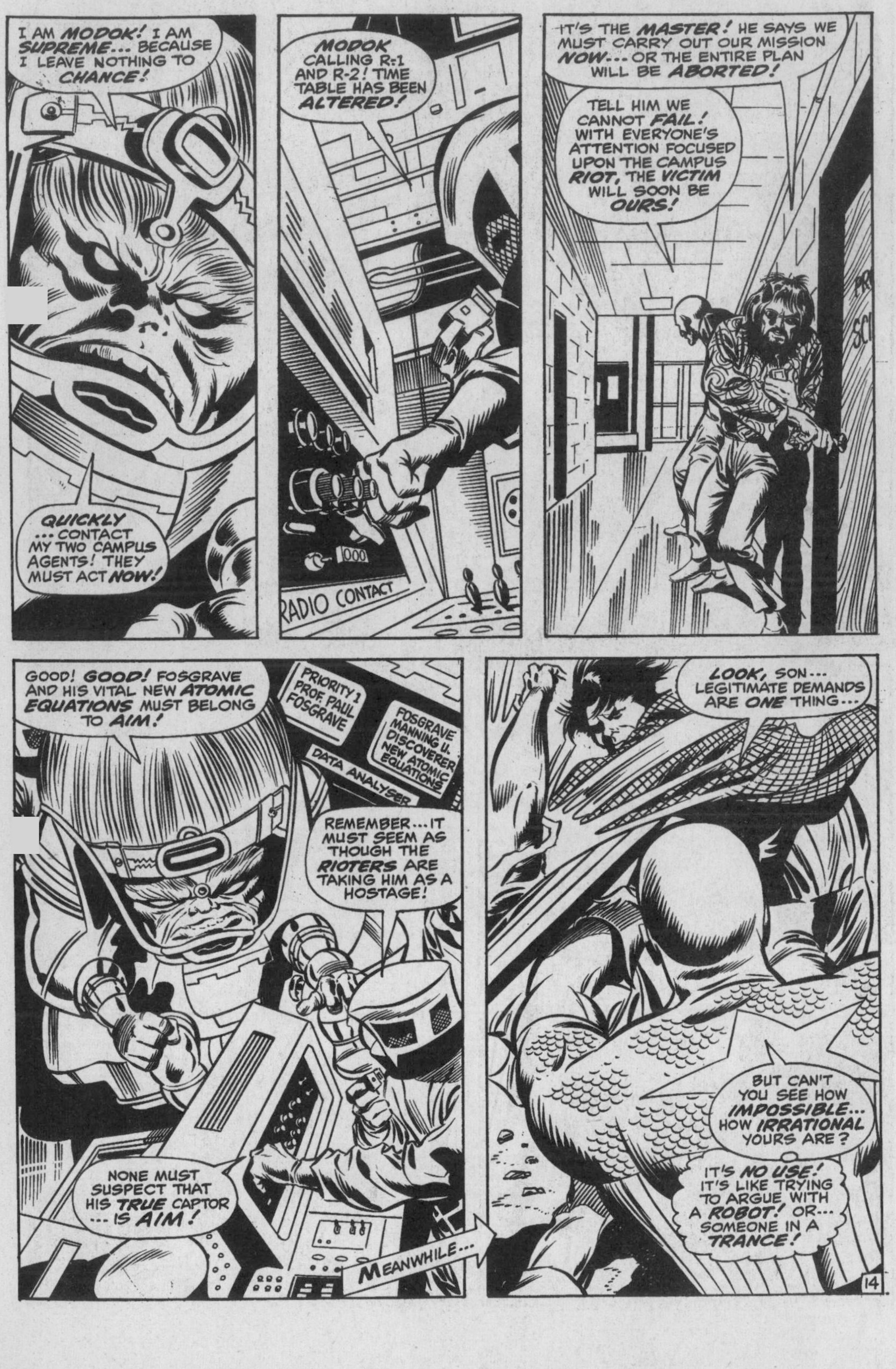

I AM MODOK! I AM SUPREME... BECAUSE I LEAVE NOTHING TO CHANCE!
...QUICKLY ...CONTACT MY TWO CAMPUS AGENTS! THEY MUST ACT NOW!
MODOK CALLING R-1 AND R-2! TIME TABLE HAS BEEN ALTERED!
RADIO CONTACT
IT'S THE MASTER! HE SAYS WE MUST CARRY OUT OUR MISSION NOW... OR THE ENTIRE PLAN WILL BE ABORTED!
TELL HIM WE CANNOT FAIL! WITH EVERYONE'S ATTENTION FOCUSED UPON THE CAMPUS RIOT, THE VICTIM WILL SOON BE OURS!
GOOD! GOOD! FOSGRAVE AND HIS VITAL NEW ATOMIC EQUATIONS MUST BELONG TO AIM!
PRIORITY 1 PROF. PAUL FOSGRAVE
FOSGRAVE MANNING U. DISCOVERER NEW ATOMIC EQUATIONS
DATA ANALYSER
REMEMBER... IT MUST SEEM AS THOUGH THE RIOTERS ARE TAKING HIM AS A HOSTAGE!
NONE MUST SUSPECT THAT HIS TRUE CAPTOR ... IS AIM!
MEANWHILE...
LOOK, SON... LEGITIMATE DEMANDS ARE ONE THING...
BUT CAN'T YOU SEE HOW IMPOSSIBLE... HOW IRRATIONAL YOURS ARE?
IT'S NO USE! IT'S LIKE TRYING TO ARGUE WITH A ROBOT! OR... SOMEONE IN A TRANCE!
14

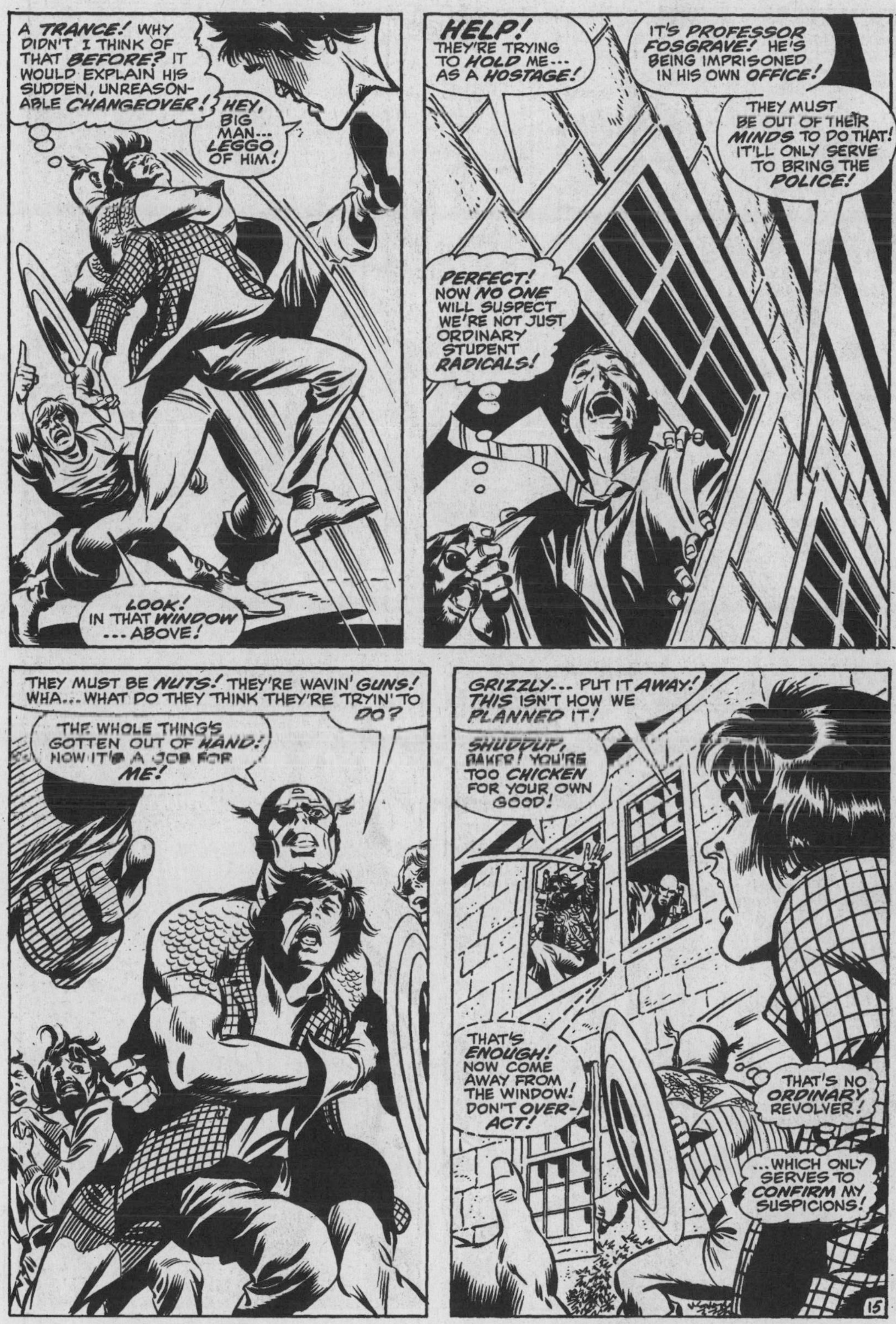
A TRANCE! WHY DIDN'T I THINK OF THAT BEFORE? IT WOULD EXPLAIN HIS SUDDEN, UNREASONABLE CHANGEOVER!
HEY, BIG MAN... LEGGO OF HIM!
LOOK! IN THAT WINDOW ...ABOVE!
HELP! THEY'RE TRYING TO HOLD ME... AS A HOSTAGE!
IT'S PROFESSOR FOSGRAVE! HE'S BEING IMPRISONED IN HIS OWN OFFICE!
THEY MUST BE OUT OF THEIR MINDS TO DO THAT! IT'LL ONLY SERVE TO BRING THE POLICE!
PERFECT! NOW NO ONE WILL SUSPECT WE'RE NOT JUST ORDINARY STUDENT RADICALS!
THEY MUST BE NUTS! THEY'RE WAVIN' GUNS! WHA... WHAT DO THEY THINK THEY'RE TRYIN' TO DO?
THE WHOLE THING'S GOTTEN OUT OF HAND! NOW IT'S A JOB FOR ME!
GRIZZLY... PUT IT AWAY! THIS ISN'T HOW WE PLANNED IT!
SHUDDUP, BAKER! YOU'RE TOO CHICKEN FOR YOUR OWN GOOD!
THAT'S ENOUGH! NOW COME AWAY FROM THE WINDOW! DON'T OVER-ACT!
THAT'S NO ORDINARY REVOLVER!
...WHICH ONLY SERVES TO CONFIRM MY SUSPICIONS!
15

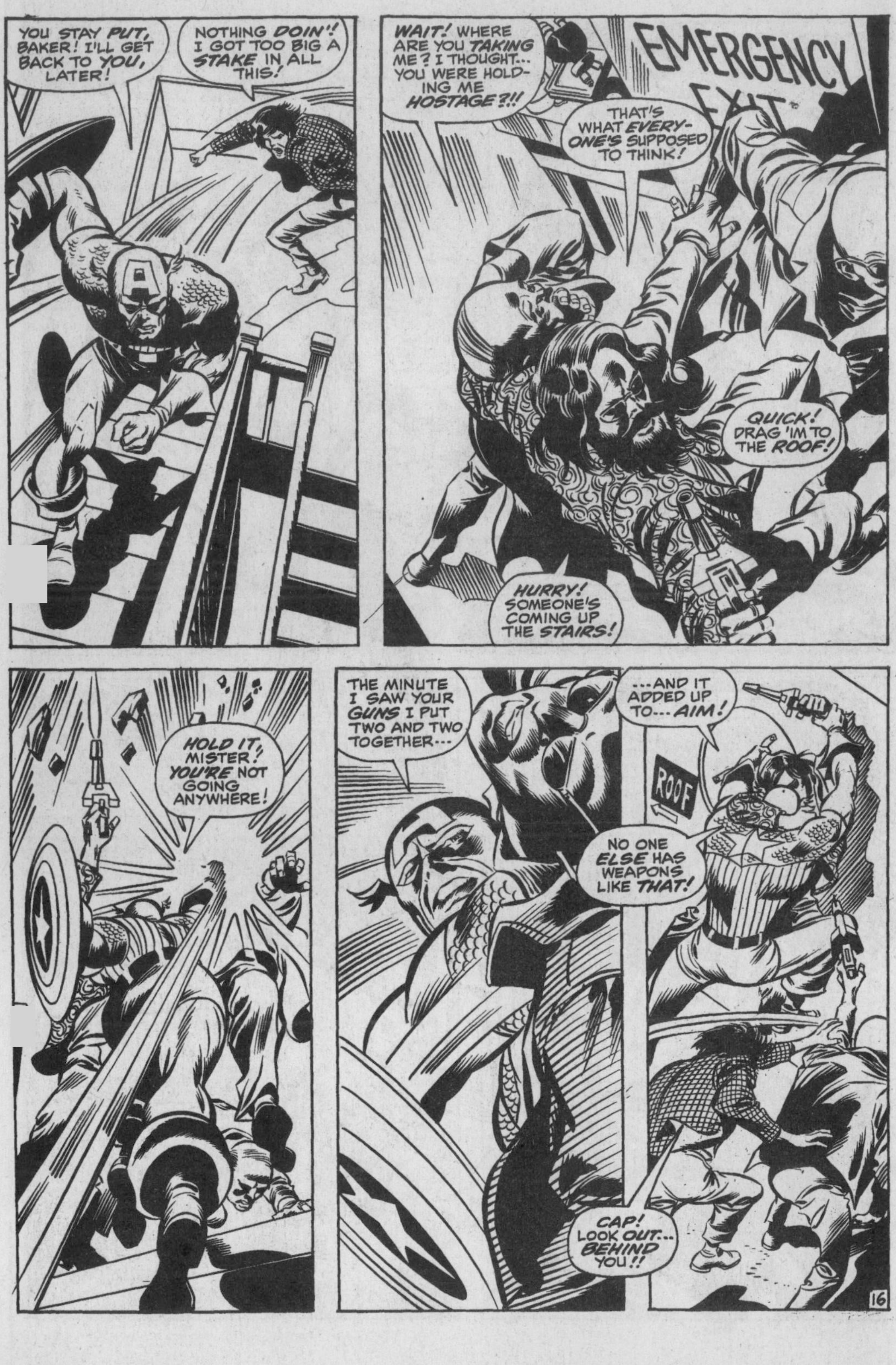
YOU STAY PUT, BAKER! I'LL GET BACK TO YOU, LATER!
NOTHING DOIN'! I GOT TOO BIG A STAKE IN ALL THIS!
EMERGENCY EXIT
WAIT! WHERE ARE YOU TAKING ME? I THOUGHT... YOU WERE HOLDING ME HOSTAGE?!!
THAT'S WHAT EVERYONE'S SUPPOSED TO THINK!
QUICK! DRAG 'IM TO THE ROOF!
HURRY! SOMEONE'S COMING UP THE STAIRS!
HOLD IT, MISTER! YOU'RE NOT GOING ANYWHERE!
THE MINUTE I SAW YOUR GUNS I PUT TWO AND TWO TOGETHER---
---AND IT ADDED UP TO--- AIM!
ROOF
NO ONE ELSE HAS WEAPONS LIKE THAT!
CAP! LOOK OUT... BEHIND YOU!!
16

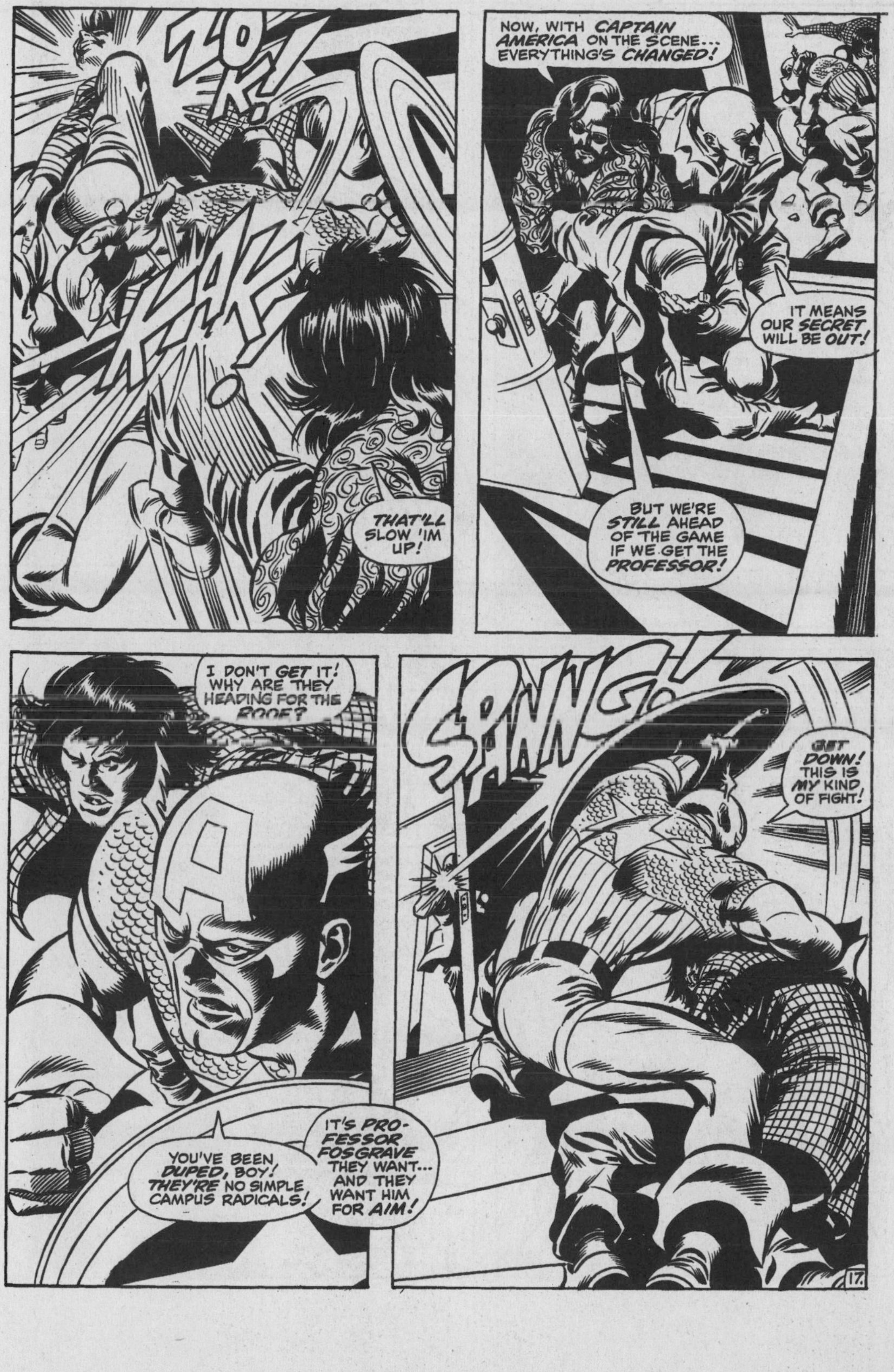
ZOK!
KRAK!
THAT'LL SLOW 'IM UP!
NOW, WITH CAPTAIN AMERICA ON THE SCENE... EVERYTHING'S CHANGED!
IT MEANS OUR SECRET WILL BE OUT!
BUT WE'RE STILL AHEAD OF THE GAME IF WE GET THE PROFESSOR!
I DON'T GET IT! WHY ARE THEY HEADING FOR THE ROOF?
YOU'VE BEEN DUPED, BOY! THEY'RE NO SIMPLE CAMPUS RADICALS!
IT'S PROFESSOR FOSGRAVE THEY WANT... AND THEY WANT HIM FOR AIM!
SPANNG!
GET DOWN! THIS IS MY KIND OF FIGHT!
17

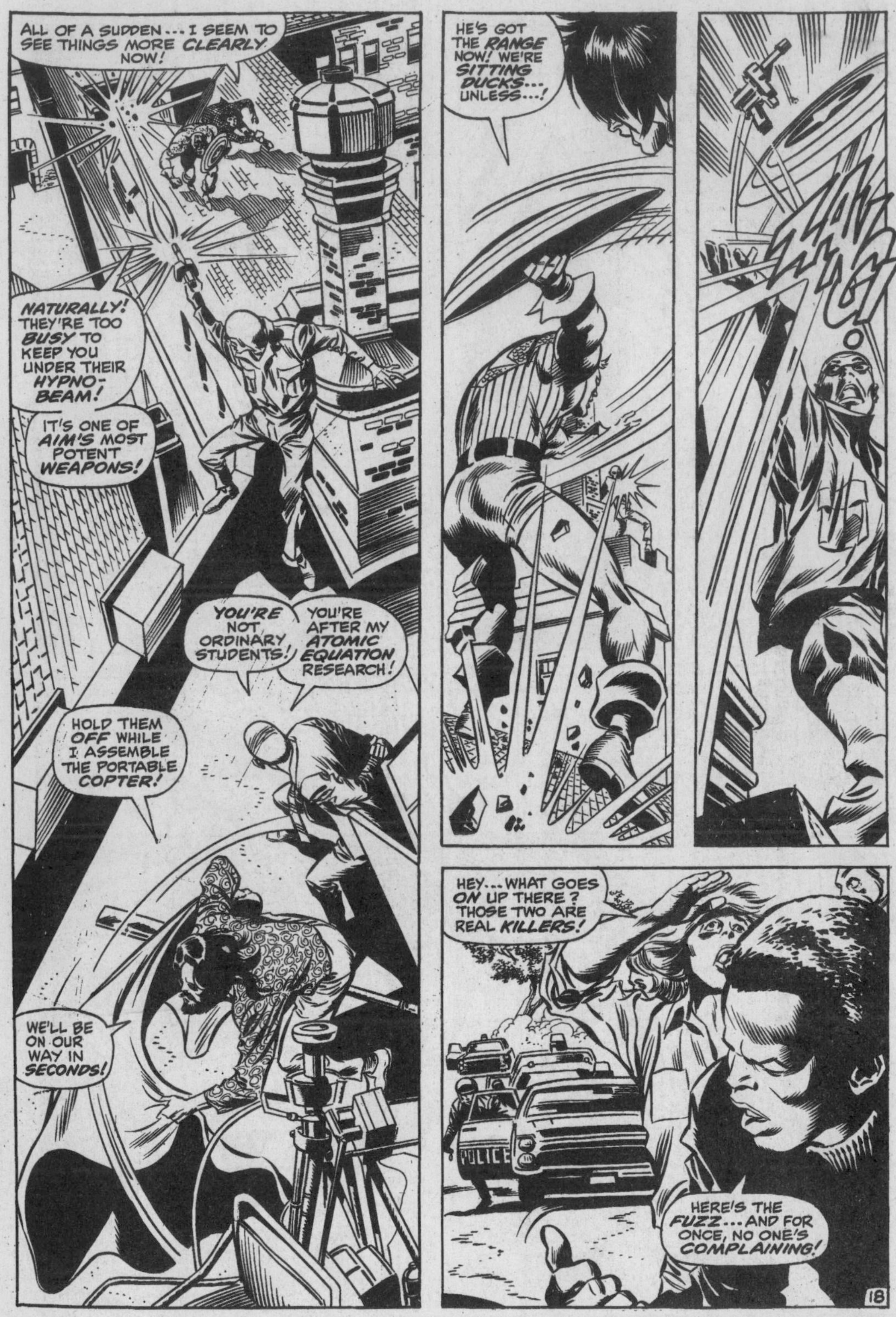
ALL OF A SUDDEN... I SEEM TO SEE THINGS MORE CLEARLY NOW!
NATURALLY! THEY'RE TOO BUSY TO KEEP YOU UNDER THEIR HYPNO-BEAM!
IT'S ONE OF AIM'S MOST POTENT WEAPONS!
YOU'RE NOT ORDINARY STUDENTS!
YOU'RE AFTER MY ATOMIC EQUATION RESEARCH!
HOLD THEM OFF WHILE I ASSEMBLE THE PORTABLE COPTER!
WE'LL BE ON OUR WAY IN SECONDS!
HE'S GOT THE RANGE NOW! WE'RE SITTING DUCKS... UNLESS...!
HEY... WHAT GOES ON UP THERE? THOSE TWO ARE REAL KILLERS!
POLICE
HERE'S THE FUZZ... AND FOR ONCE, NO ONE'S COMPLAINING!
18

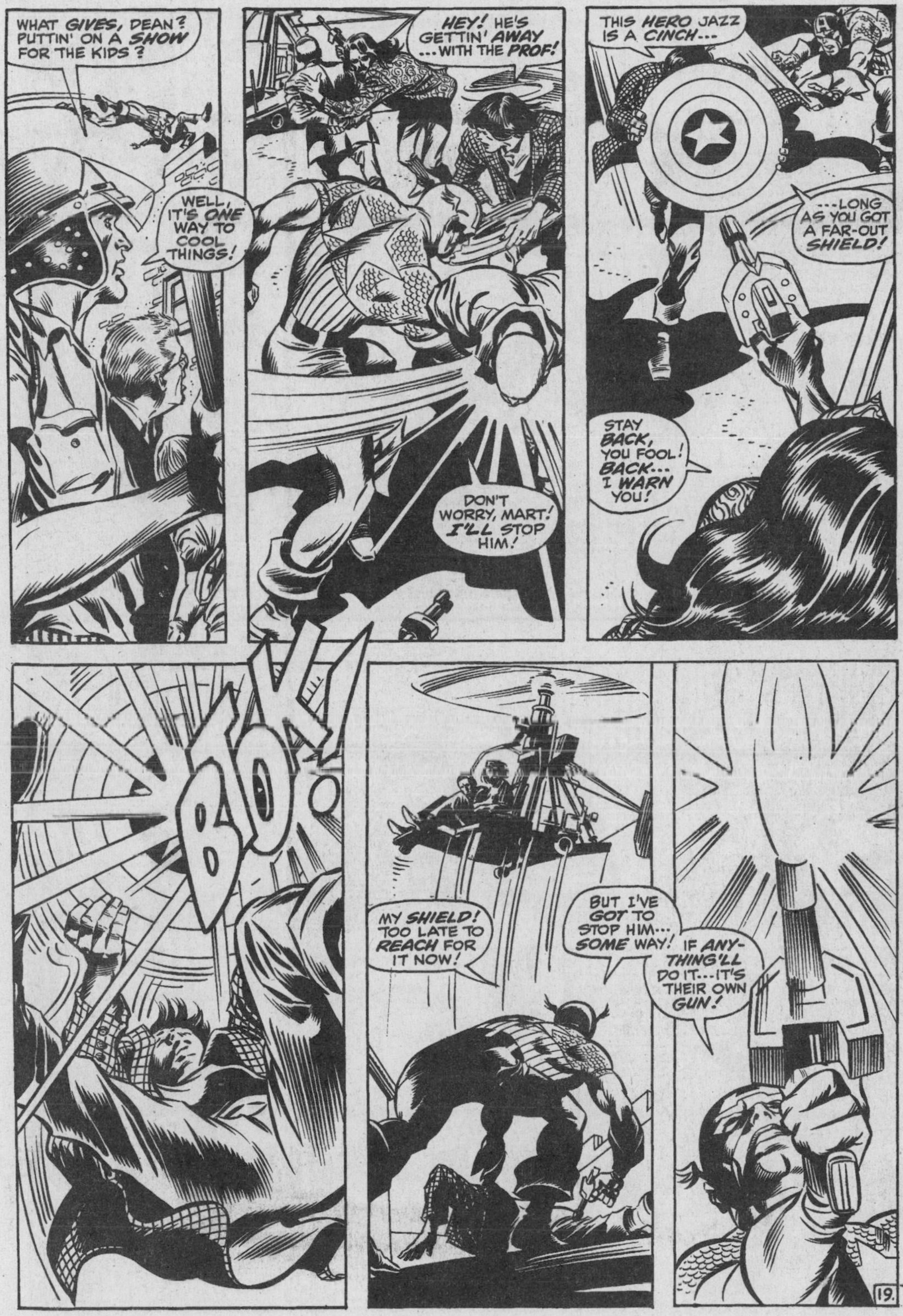
WHAT GIVES, DEAN? PUTTIN' ON A SHOW FOR THE KIDS?
WELL, IT'S ONE WAY TO COOL THINGS!
HEY! HE'S GETTIN' AWAY ...WITH THE PROF!
DON'T WORRY, MART! I'LL STOP HIM!
THIS HERO JAZZ IS A CINCH...
---LONG AS YOU GOT A FAR-OUT SHIELD!
STAY BACK, YOU FOOL! BACK... I WARN YOU!
BTOK!
MY SHIELD! TOO LATE TO REACH FOR IT NOW!
BUT I'VE GOT TO STOP HIM... SOME WAY!
IF ANYTHING'LL DO IT...IT'S THEIR OWN GUN!
19.

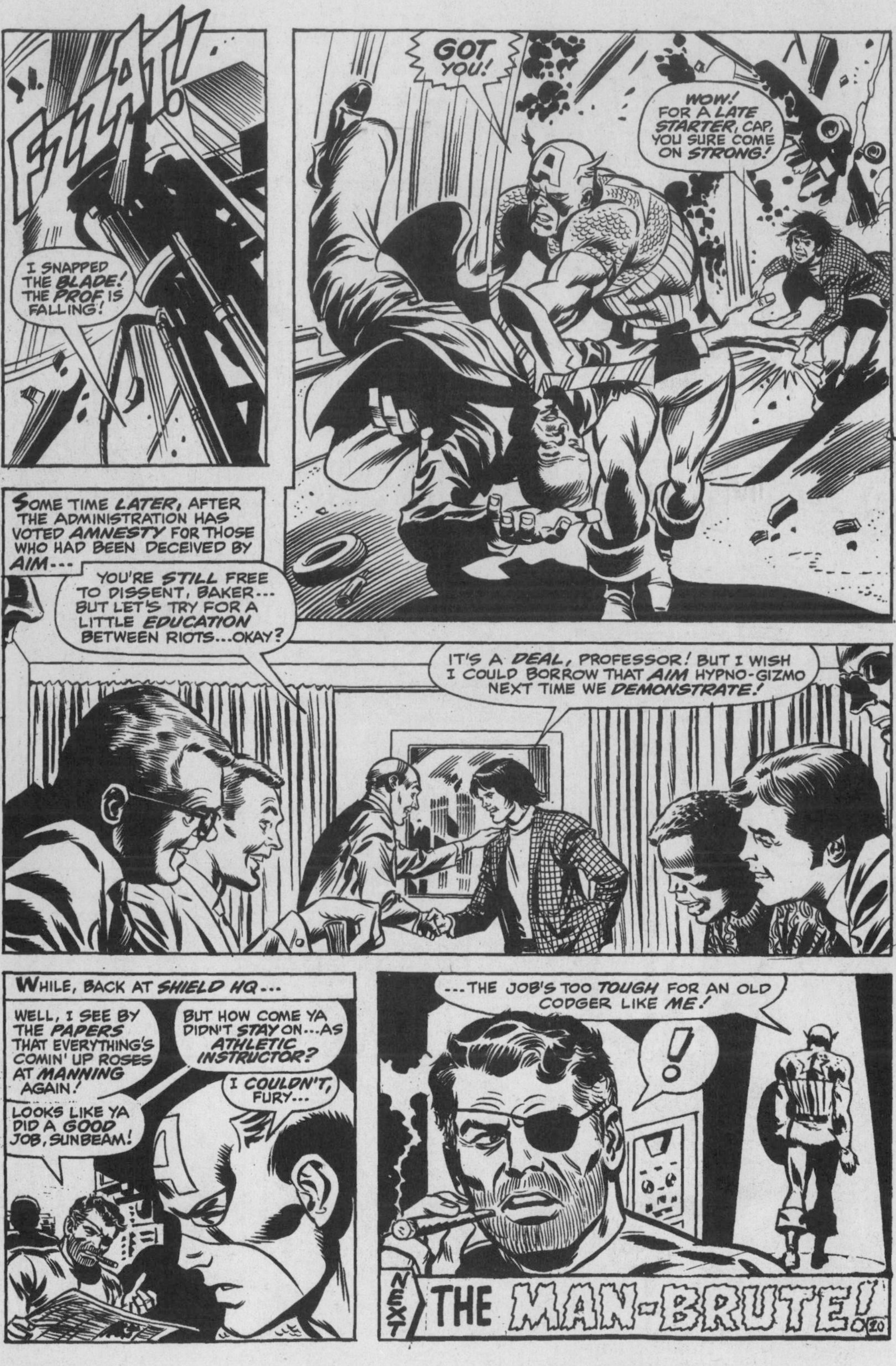
FZZAT!
I SNAPPED THE BLADE! THE PROF IS FALLING!
GOT YOU!
WOW! FOR A LATE STARTER, CAP, YOU SURE COME ON STRONG!
SOME TIME LATER, AFTER THE ADMINISTRATION HAS VOTED AMNESTY FOR THOSE WHO HAD BEEN DECEIVED BY AIM---
YOU'RE STILL FREE TO DISSENT, BAKER--- BUT LET'S TRY FOR A LITTLE EDUCATION BETWEEN RIOTS...OKAY?
IT'S A DEAL, PROFESSOR! BUT I WISH I COULD BORROW THAT AIM HYPNO-GIZMO NEXT TIME WE DEMONSTRATE!
WHILE, BACK AT SHIELD HQ ---
WELL, I SEE BY THE PAPERS THAT EVERYTHING'S COMIN' UP ROSES AT MANNING AGAIN!
LOOKS LIKE YA DID A GOOD JOB, SUNBEAM!
BUT HOW COME YA DIDN'T STAY ON---AS ATHLETIC INSTRUCTOR?
I COULDN'T, FURY---
---THE JOB'S TOO TOUGH FOR AN OLD CODGER LIKE ME!
!
NEXT
THE MAN-BRUTE!
20

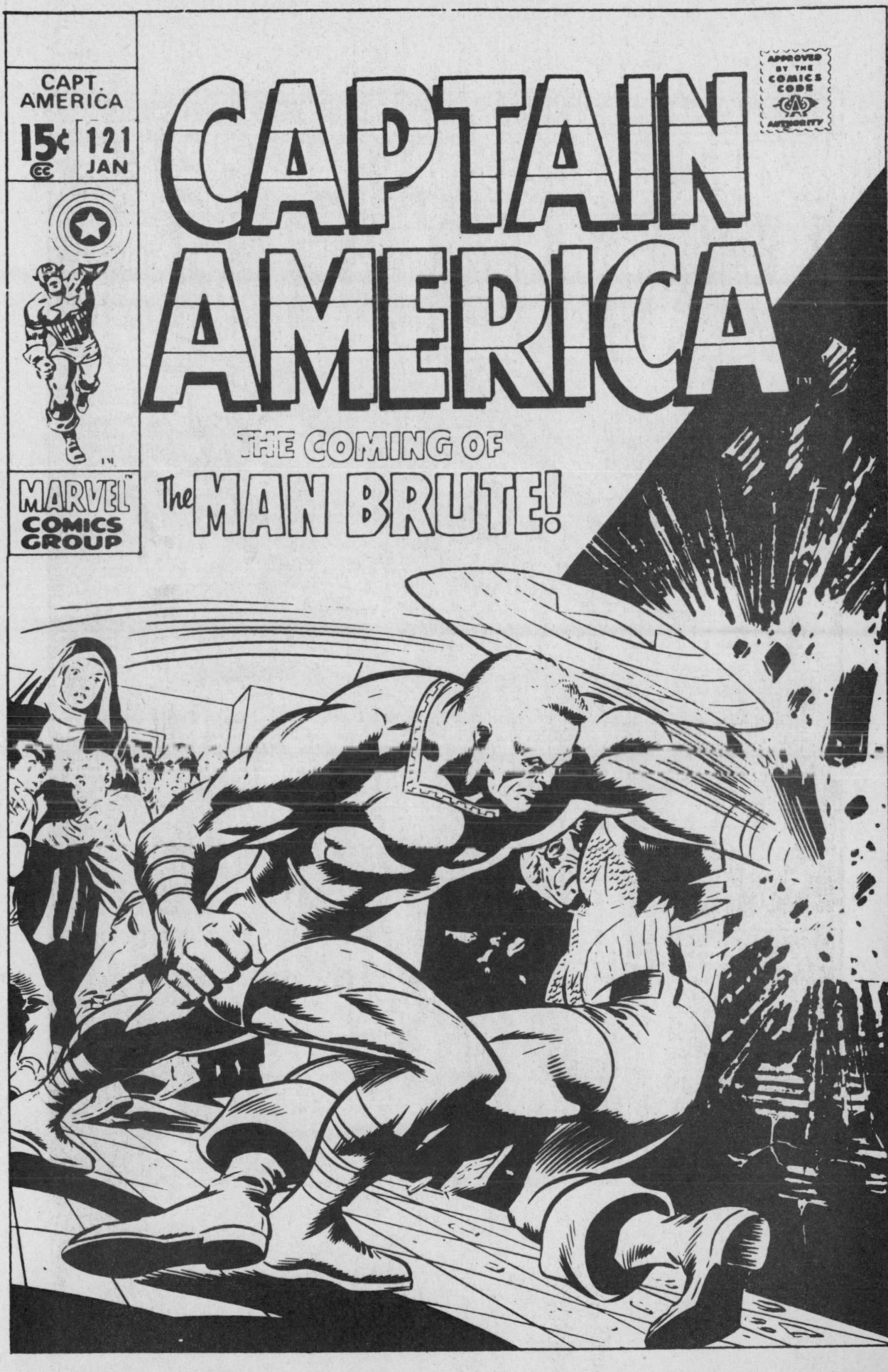
CAPT. AMERICA
15¢ 121 JAN
MARVEL COMICS GROUP
APPROVED BY THE COMICS CODE AUTHORITY
CAPTAIN AMERICA
THE COMING OF The MAN BRUTE!

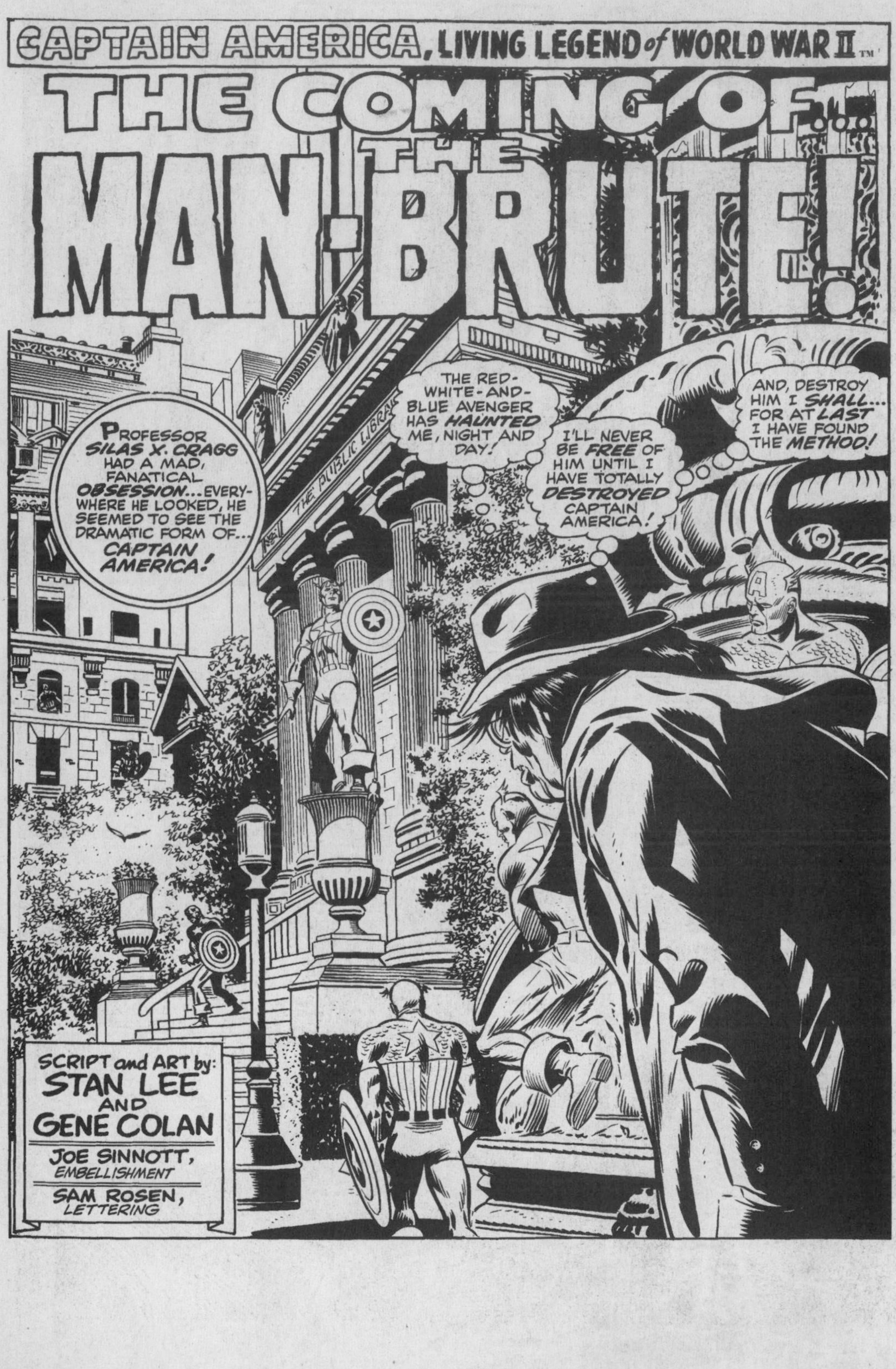
CAPTAIN AMERICA, LIVING LEGEND of WORLD WAR II TM
THE COMING OF... THE MAN-BRUTE!
PROFESSOR SILAS X. CRAGG HAD A MAD, FANATICAL OBSESSION... EVERYWHERE HE LOOKED, HE SEEMED TO SEE THE DRAMATIC FORM OF... CAPTAIN AMERICA!
THE RED-WHITE-AND-BLUE AVENGER HAS HAUNTED ME, NIGHT AND DAY!
I'LL NEVER BE FREE OF HIM UNTIL I HAVE TOTALLY DESTROYED CAPTAIN AMERICA!
AND, DESTROY HIM I SHALL... FOR AT LAST I HAVE FOUND THE METHOD!
THE PUBLIC LIBRARY
SCRIPT and ART by: STAN LEE AND GENE COLAN
JOE SINNOTT, EMBELLISHMENT
SAM ROSEN, LETTERING

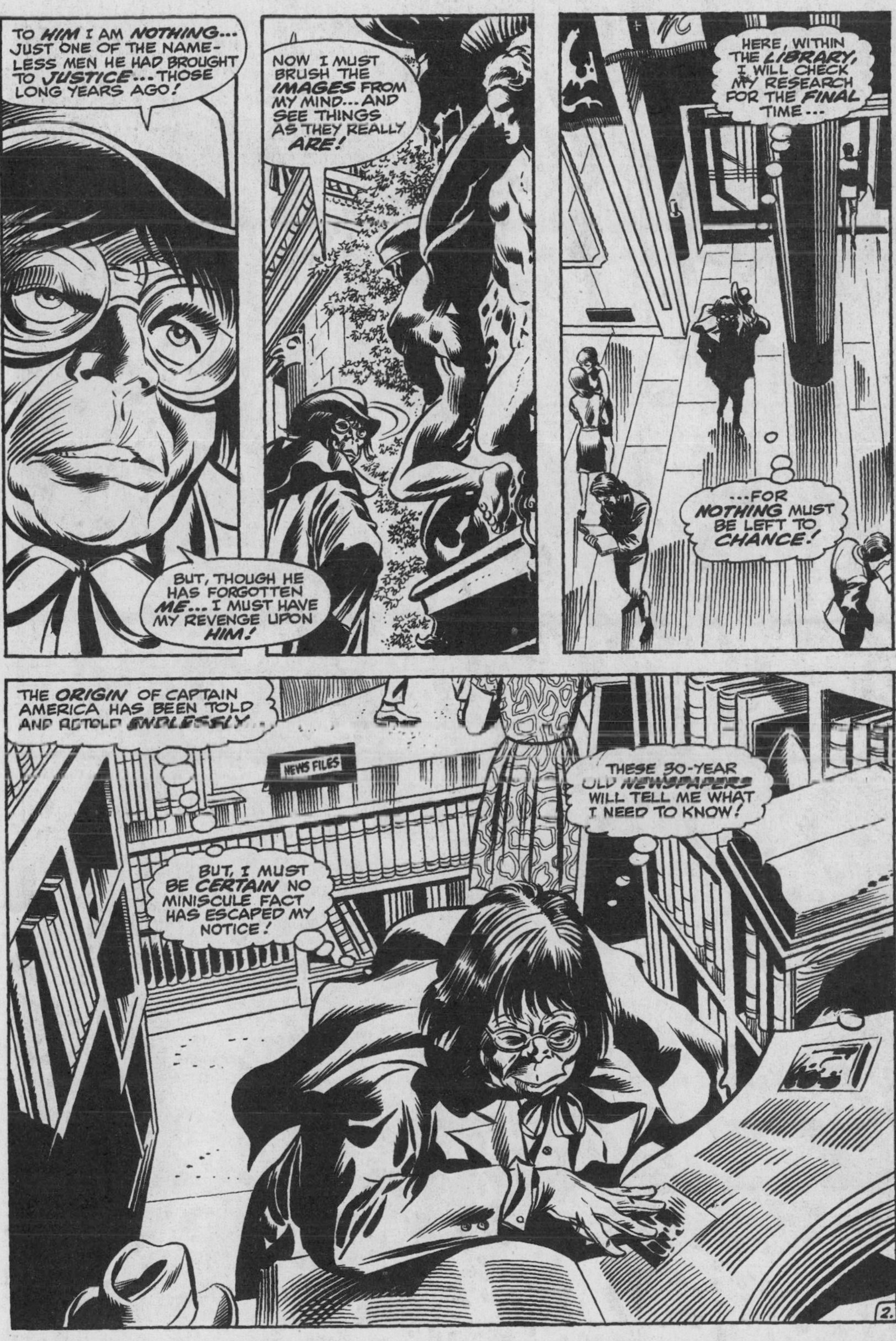
TO HIM I AM NOTHING... JUST ONE OF THE NAMELESS MEN HE HAD BROUGHT TO JUSTICE... THOSE LONG YEARS AGO!
BUT, THOUGH HE HAS FORGOTTEN ME... I MUST HAVE MY REVENGE UPON HIM!
NOW I MUST BRUSH THE IMAGES FROM MY MIND... AND SEE THINGS AS THEY REALLY ARE!
HERE, WITHIN THE LIBRARY, I WILL CHECK MY RESEARCH FOR THE FINAL TIME...
...FOR NOTHING MUST BE LEFT TO CHANCE!
THE ORIGIN OF CAPTAIN AMERICA HAS BEEN TOLD AND RETOLD
NEWS FILES
THESE 30-YEAR OLD NEWSPAPERS WILL TELL ME WHAT I NEED TO KNOW!
BUT, I MUST BE CERTAIN NO MINISCULE FACT HAS ESCAPED MY NOTICE!
2.

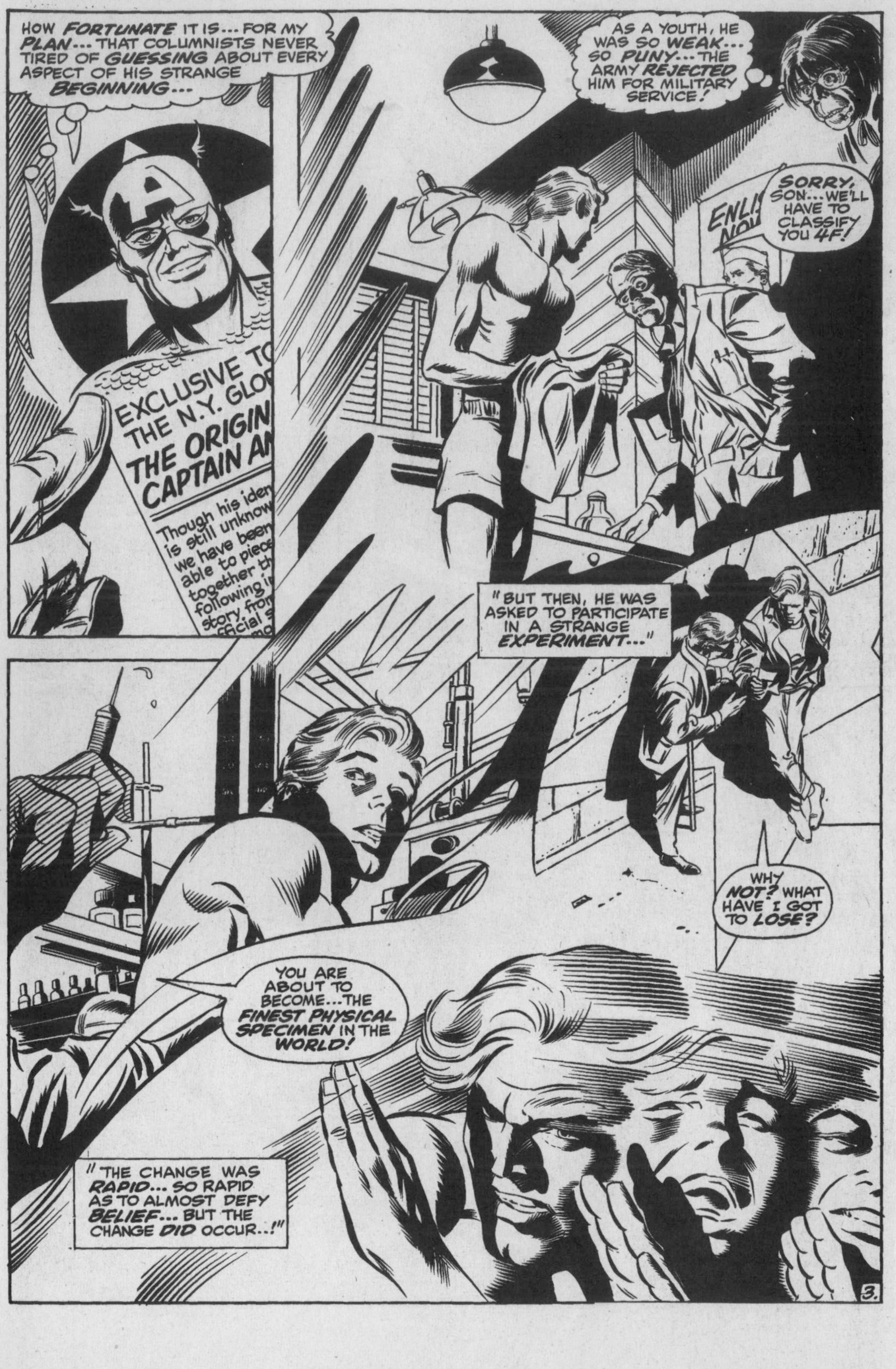

HOW FORTUNATE IT IS... FOR MY PLAN... THAT COLUMNISTS NEVER TIRED OF GUESSING ABOUT EVERY ASPECT OF HIS STRANGE BEGINNING...
EXCLUSIVE TO THE N.Y. GLO
THE ORIGIN CAPTAIN AM
Though his iden is still unknow we have been able to piec together th following in story, from fficial s
AS A YOUTH, HE WAS SO WEAK... SO PUNY... THE ARMY REJECTED HIM FOR MILITARY SERVICE!
ENLI NOV
SORRY, SON... WE'LL HAVE TO CLASSIFY YOU 4F!
"BUT THEN, HE WAS ASKED TO PARTICIPATE IN A STRANGE EXPERIMENT..."
WHY NOT? WHAT HAVE I GOT TO LOSE?
YOU ARE ABOUT TO BECOME... THE FINEST PHYSICAL SPECIMEN IN THE WORLD!
"THE CHANGE WAS RAPID... SO RAPID AS TO ALMOST DEFY BELIEF... BUT THE CHANGE DID OCCUR..!"
3.

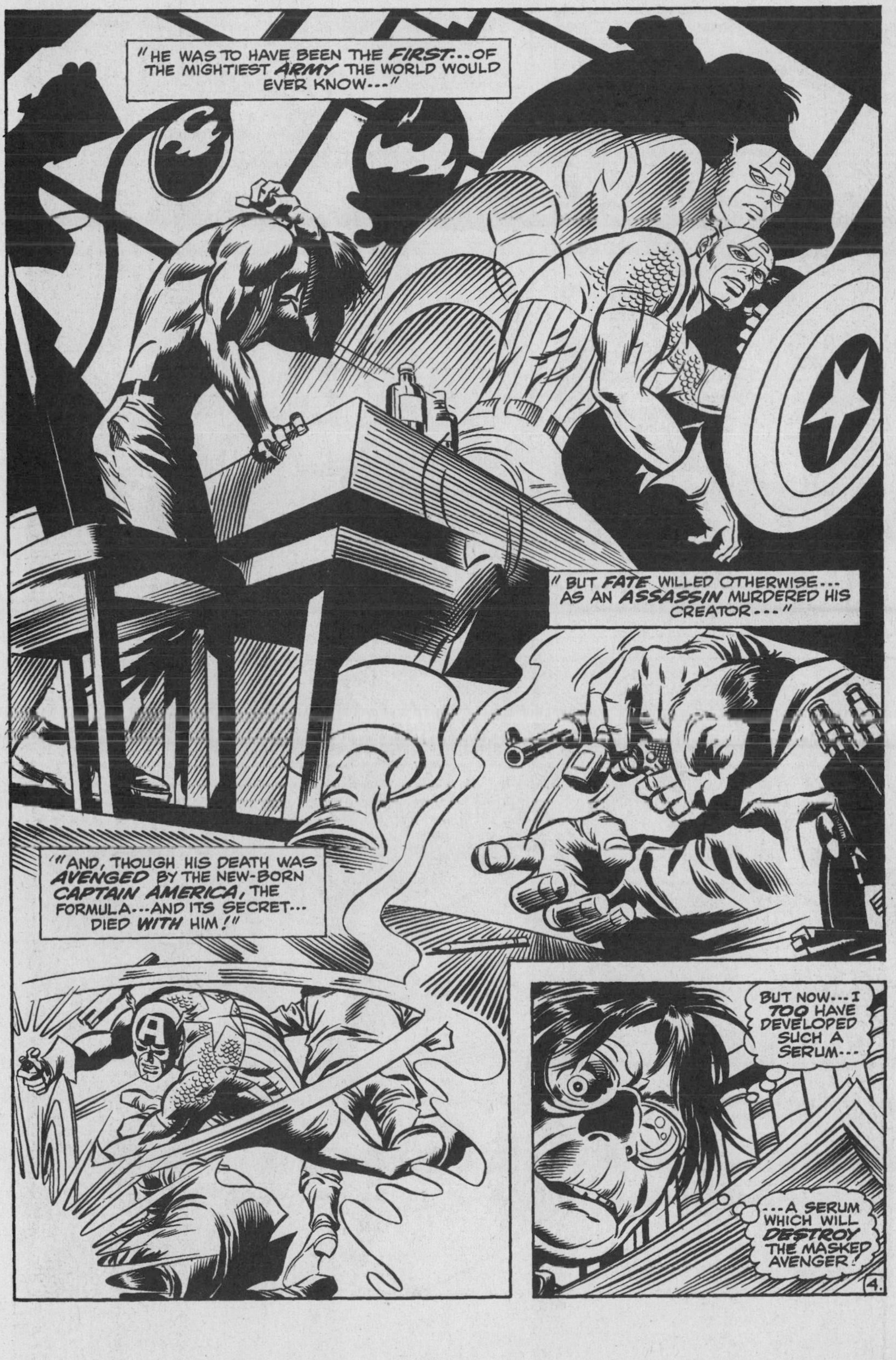
"HE WAS TO HAVE BEEN THE FIRST... OF THE MIGHTIEST ARMY THE WORLD WOULD EVER KNOW..."
"BUT FATE WILLED OTHERWISE... AS AN ASSASSIN MURDERED HIS CREATOR..."
"AND, THOUGH HIS DEATH WAS AVENGED BY THE NEW-BORN CAPTAIN AMERICA, THE FORMULA...AND ITS SECRET... DIED WITH HIM!"
BUT NOW... I TOO HAVE DEVELOPED SUCH A SERUM...
...A SERUM WHICH WILL DESTROY THE MASKED AVENGER!
4.

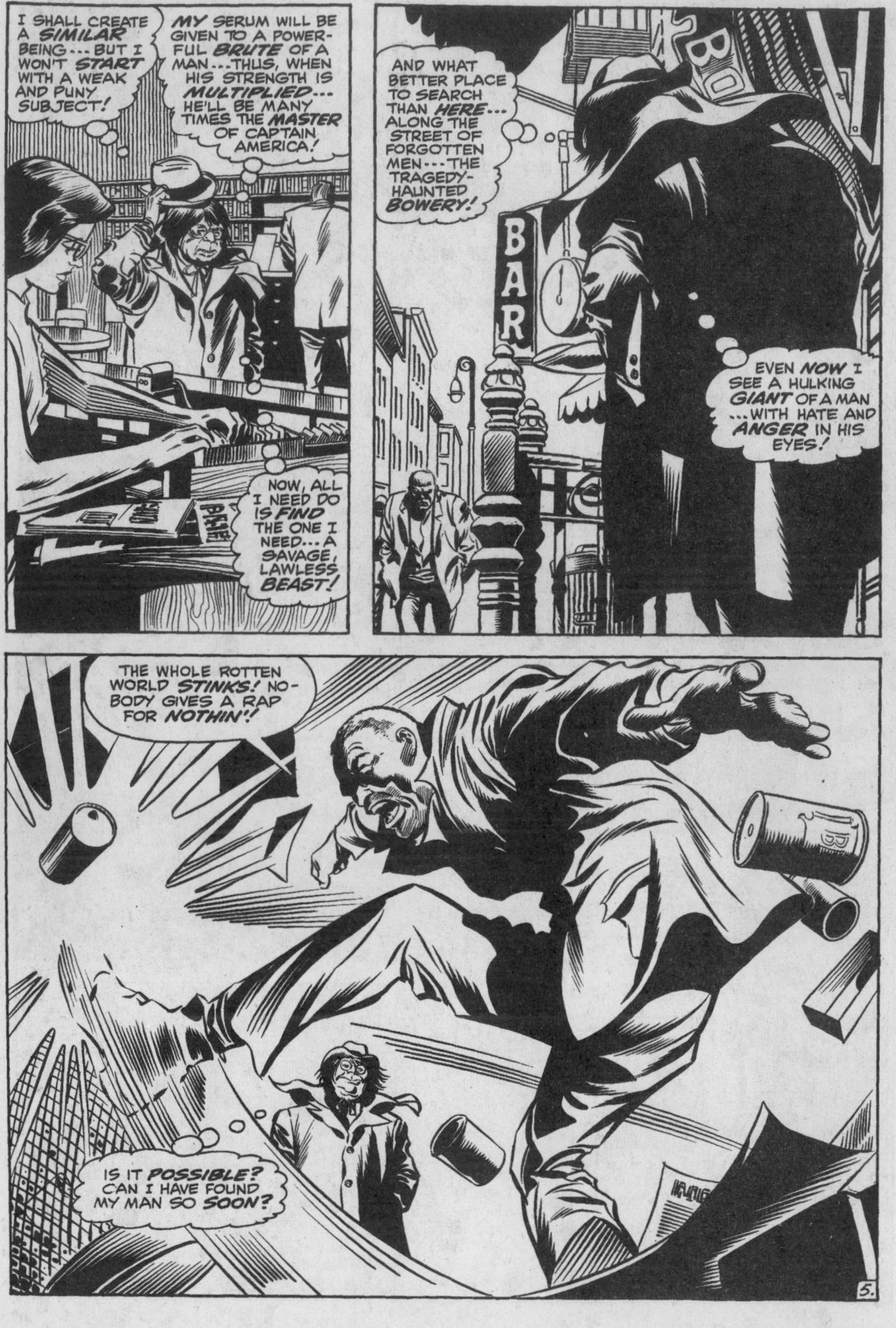
I SHALL CREATE A SIMILAR BEING--- BUT I WON'T START WITH A WEAK AND PUNY SUBJECT!
MY SERUM WILL BE GIVEN TO A POWERFUL BRUTE OF A MAN---THUS, WHEN HIS STRENGTH IS MULTIPLIED--- HE'LL BE MANY TIMES THE MASTER OF CAPTAIN AMERICA!
NOW, ALL I NEED DO IS FIND THE ONE I NEED--- A SAVAGE, LAWLESS BEAST!
AND WHAT BETTER PLACE TO SEARCH THAN HERE--- ALONG THE STREET OF FORGOTTEN MEN---THE TRAGEDY-HAUNTED BOWERY!
BAR
EVEN NOW I SEE A HULKING GIANT OF A MAN ---WITH HATE AND ANGER IN HIS EYES!
THE WHOLE ROTTEN WORLD STINKS! NOBODY GIVES A RAP FOR NOTHIN'!
IS IT POSSIBLE? CAN I HAVE FOUND MY MAN SO SOON?
5.

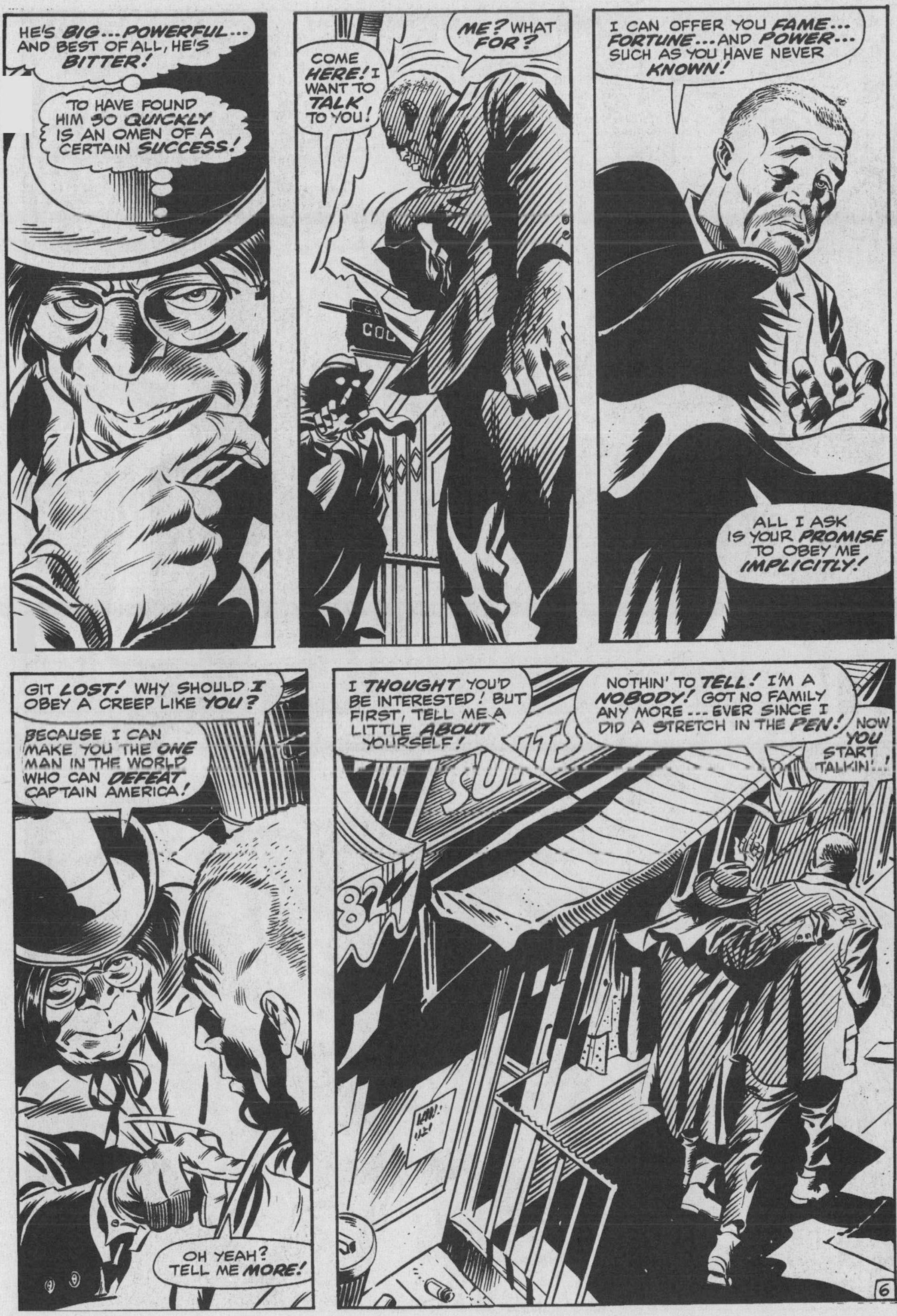
HE'S BIG...POWERFUL... AND BEST OF ALL, HE'S BITTER!
TO HAVE FOUND HIM SO QUICKLY IS AN OMEN OF A CERTAIN SUCCESS!
COME HERE! I WANT TO TALK TO YOU!
ME? WHAT FOR?
I CAN OFFER YOU FAME... FORTUNE...AND POWER... SUCH AS YOU HAVE NEVER KNOWN!
ALL I ASK IS YOUR PROMISE TO OBEY ME IMPLICITLY!
GIT LOST! WHY SHOULD I OBEY A CREEP LIKE YOU?
BECAUSE I CAN MAKE YOU THE ONE MAN IN THE WORLD WHO CAN DEFEAT CAPTAIN AMERICA!
OH YEAH? TELL ME MORE!
I THOUGHT YOU'D BE INTERESTED! BUT FIRST, TELL ME A LITTLE ABOUT YOURSELF!
NOTHIN' TO TELL! I'M A NOBODY! GOT NO FAMILY ANY MORE...EVER SINCE I DID A STRETCH IN THE PEN!
NOW YOU START TALKIN'..!
6

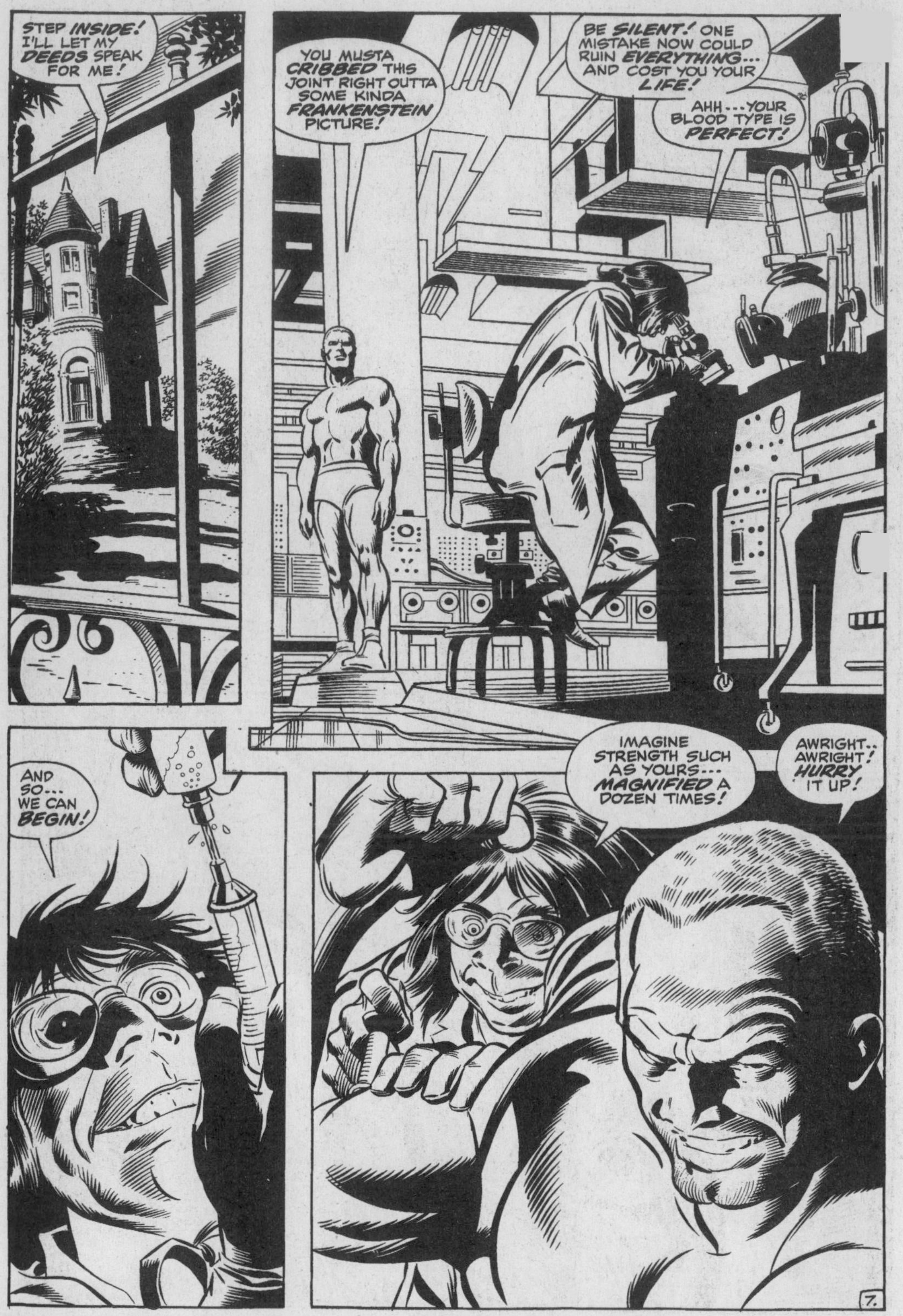
STEP INSIDE! I'LL LET MY DEEDS SPEAK FOR ME!
YOU MUSTA CRIBBED THIS JOINT RIGHT OUTTA SOME KINDA FRANKENSTEIN PICTURE!
BE SILENT! ONE MISTAKE NOW COULD RUIN EVERYTHING... AND COST YOU YOUR LIFE!
AHH... YOUR BLOOD TYPE IS PERFECT!
AND SO... WE CAN BEGIN!
IMAGINE STRENGTH SUCH AS YOURS... MAGNIFIED A DOZEN TIMES!
AWRIGHT.. AWRIGHT! HURRY IT UP!
7.

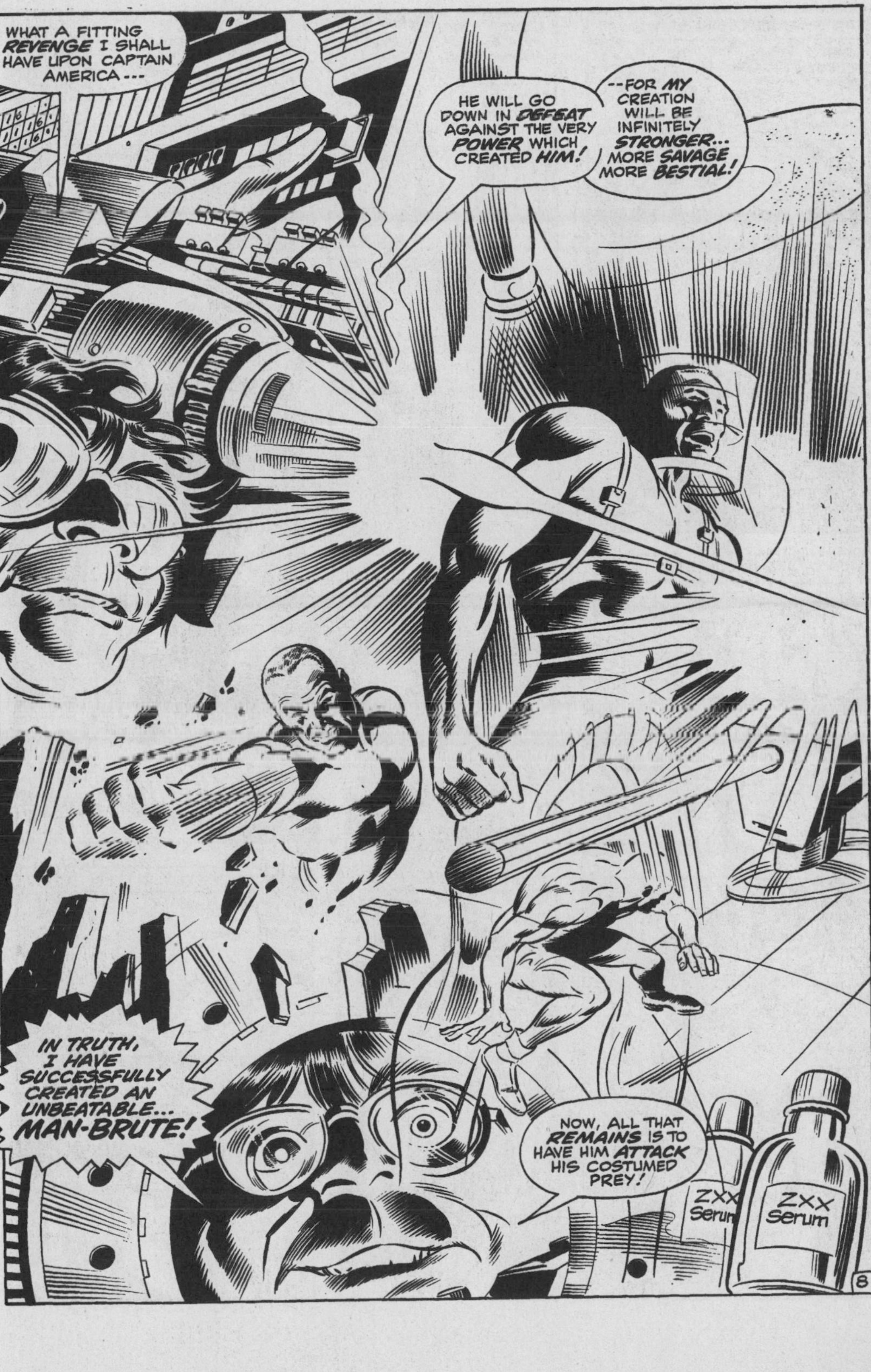
WHAT A FITTING REVENGE I SHALL HAVE UPON CAPTAIN AMERICA---
HE WILL GO DOWN IN DEFEAT AGAINST THE VERY POWER WHICH CREATED HIM!
--FOR MY CREATION WILL BE INFINITELY STRONGER... MORE SAVAGE MORE BESTIAL!
IN TRUTH, I HAVE SUCCESSFULLY CREATED AN UNBEATABLE... MAN-BRUTE!
NOW, ALL THAT REMAINS IS TO HAVE HIM ATTACK HIS COSTUMED PREY!
ZXX Serum
ZXX Serum
8

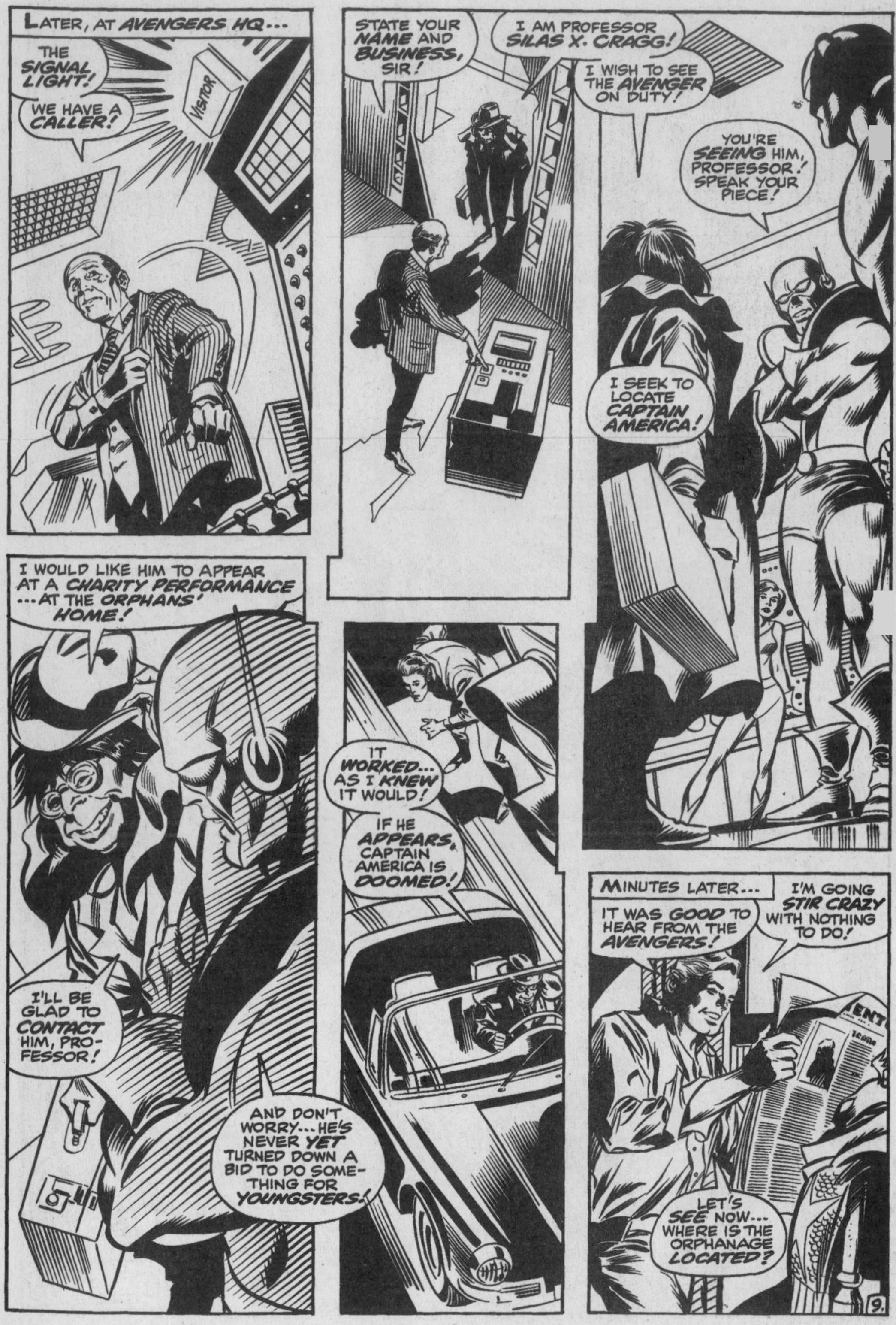
LATER, AT AVENGERS HQ...
THE SIGNAL LIGHT!
WE HAVE A CALLER!
VISITOR
STATE YOUR NAME AND BUSINESS, SIR!
I AM PROFESSOR SILAS X. CRAGG!
I WISH TO SEE THE AVENGER ON DUTY!
YOU'RE SEEING HIM, PROFESSOR! SPEAK YOUR PIECE!
I SEEK TO LOCATE CAPTAIN AMERICA!
I WOULD LIKE HIM TO APPEAR AT A CHARITY PERFORMANCE ...AT THE ORPHANS' HOME!
I'LL BE GLAD TO CONTACT HIM, PROFESSOR!
AND DON'T WORRY...HE'S NEVER YET TURNED DOWN A BID TO DO SOMETHING FOR YOUNGSTERS!
IT WORKED... AS I KNEW IT WOULD!
IF HE APPEARS, CAPTAIN AMERICA IS DOOMED!
MINUTES LATER...
IT WAS GOOD TO HEAR FROM THE AVENGERS!
I'M GOING STIR CRAZY WITH NOTHING TO DO!
LET'S SEE NOW... WHERE IS THE ORPHANAGE LOCATED?
9.

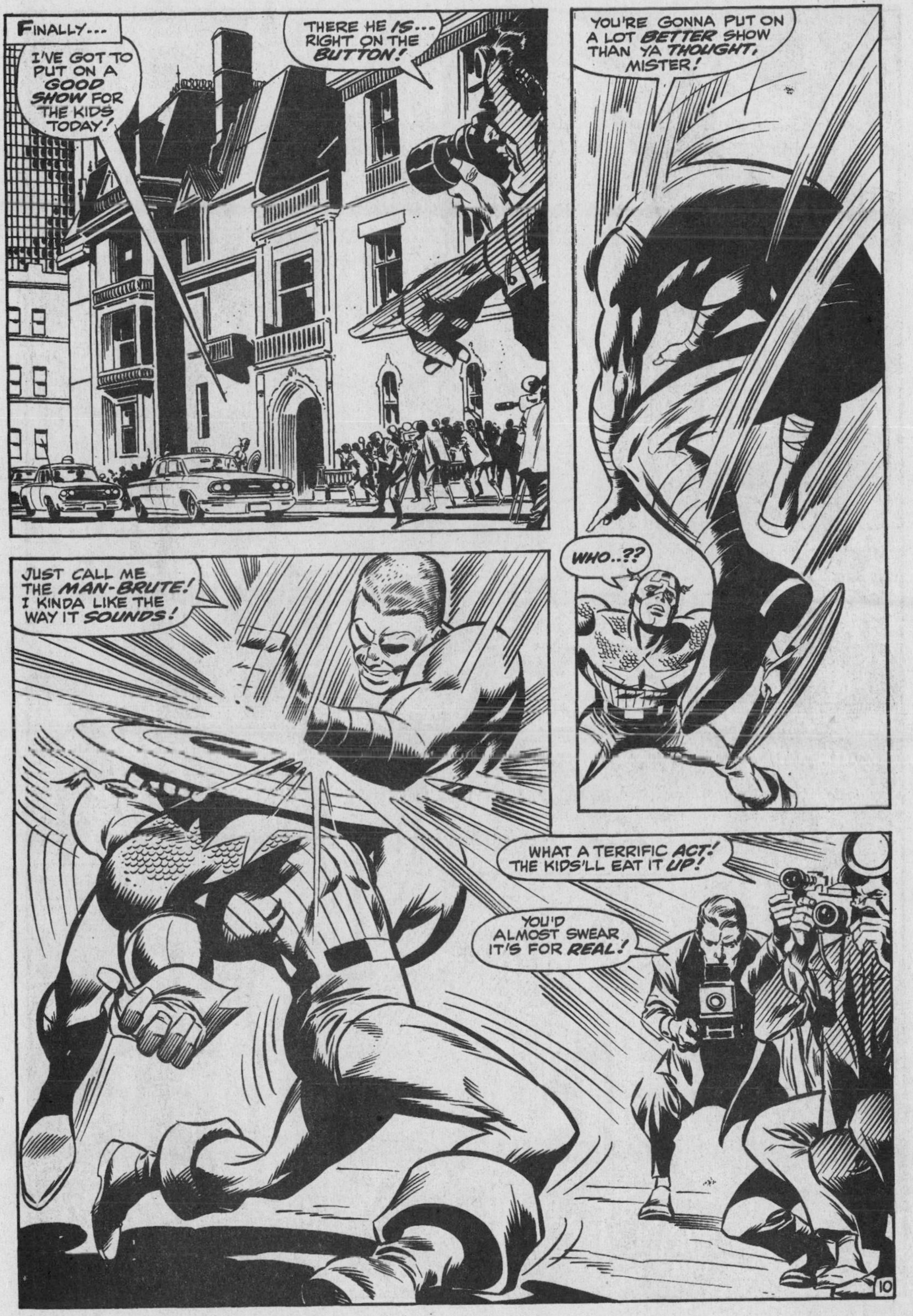

FINALLY...
I'VE GOT TO PUT ON A GOOD SHOW FOR THE KIDS TODAY!
THERE HE IS... RIGHT ON THE BUTTON!
YOU'RE GONNA PUT ON A LOT BETTER SHOW THAN YA THOUGHT, MISTER!
WHO..??
JUST CALL ME THE MAN-BRUTE! I KINDA LIKE THE WAY IT SOUNDS!
WHAT A TERRIFIC ACT! THE KIDS'LL EAT IT UP!
YOU'D ALMOST SWEAR IT'S FOR REAL!
10

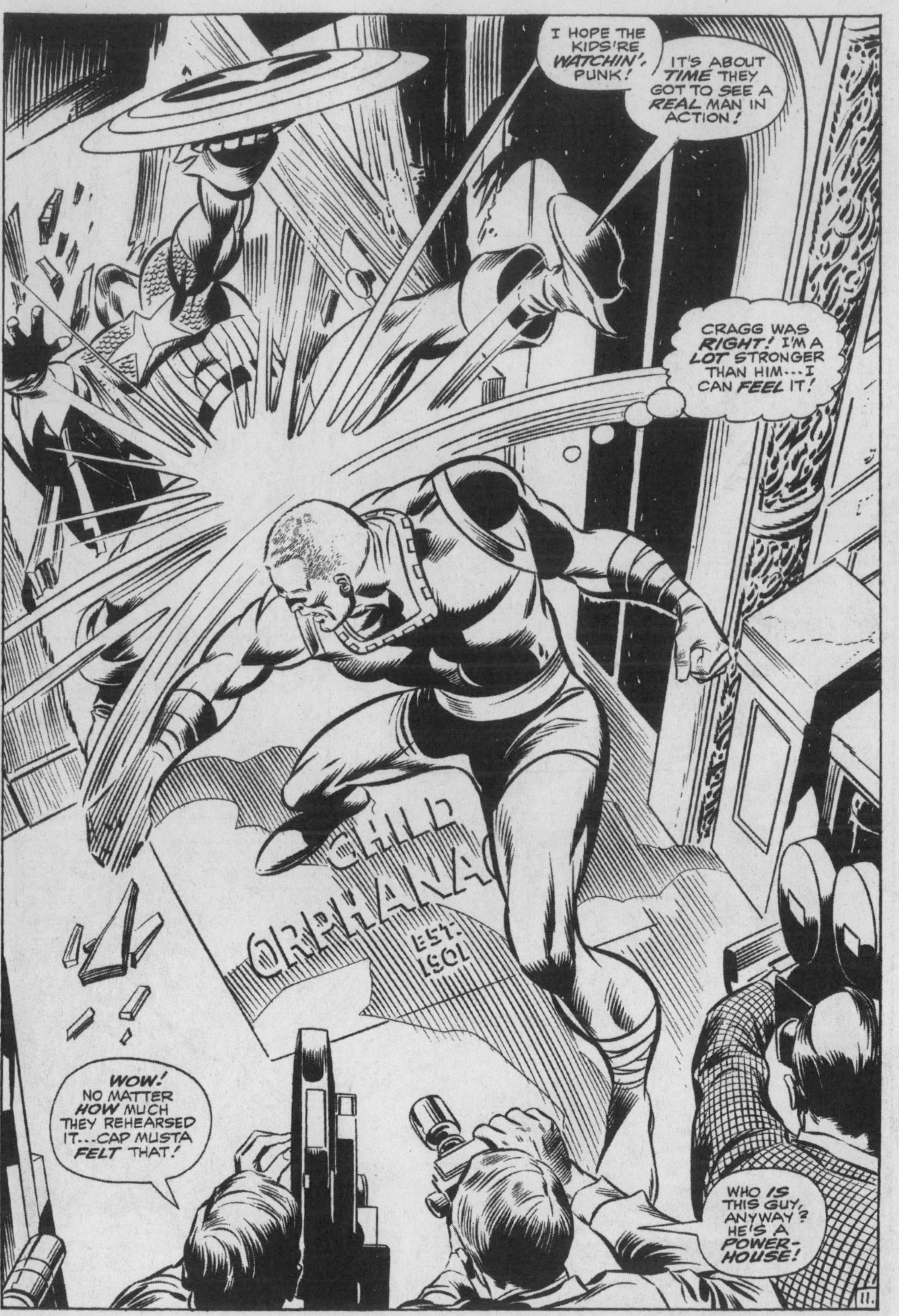
I HOPE THE KIDS'RE WATCHIN'! PUNK!
IT'S ABOUT TIME THEY GOT TO SEE A REAL MAN IN ACTION!
CRAGG WAS RIGHT! I'M A LOT STRONGER THAN HIM... I CAN FEEL IT!
CHILD ORPHANA
EST. 1901
WOW! NO MATTER HOW MUCH THEY REHEARSED IT...CAP MUSTA FELT THAT!
WHO IS THIS GUY, ANYWAY? HE'S A POWER-HOUSE!
11.

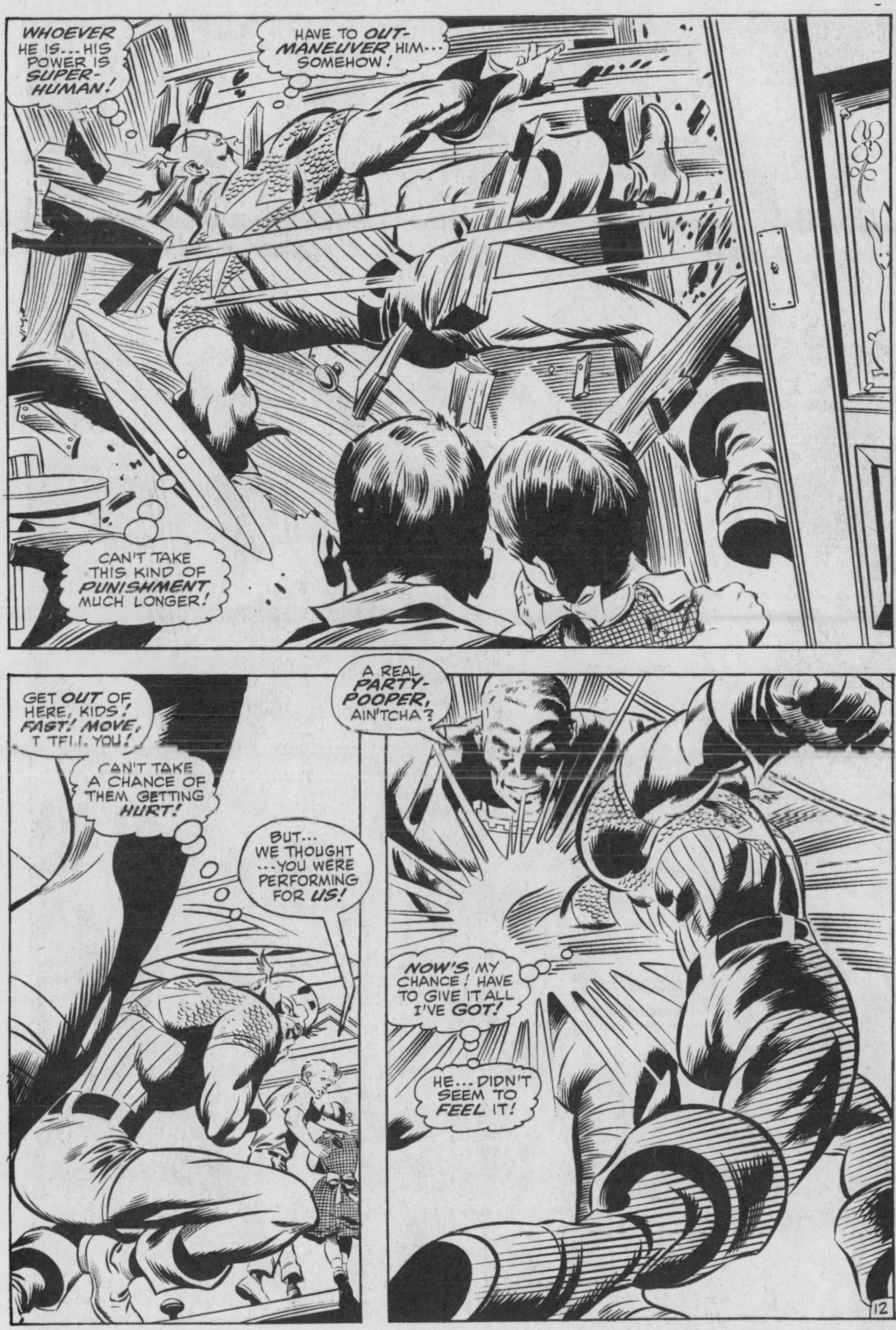
WHOEVER HE IS... HIS POWER IS SUPER-HUMAN!
HAVE TO OUT-MANEUVER HIM... SOMEHOW!
CAN'T TAKE THIS KIND OF PUNISHMENT MUCH LONGER!
GET OUT OF HERE, KIDS! FAST! MOVE, I TELL YOU!
CAN'T TAKE A CHANCE OF THEM GETTING HURT!
BUT... WE THOUGHT ...YOU WERE PERFORMING FOR US!
A REAL PARTY-POOPER, AIN'TCHA?
NOW'S MY CHANCE! HAVE TO GIVE IT ALL I'VE GOT!
HE... DIDN'T SEEM TO FEEL IT!
12

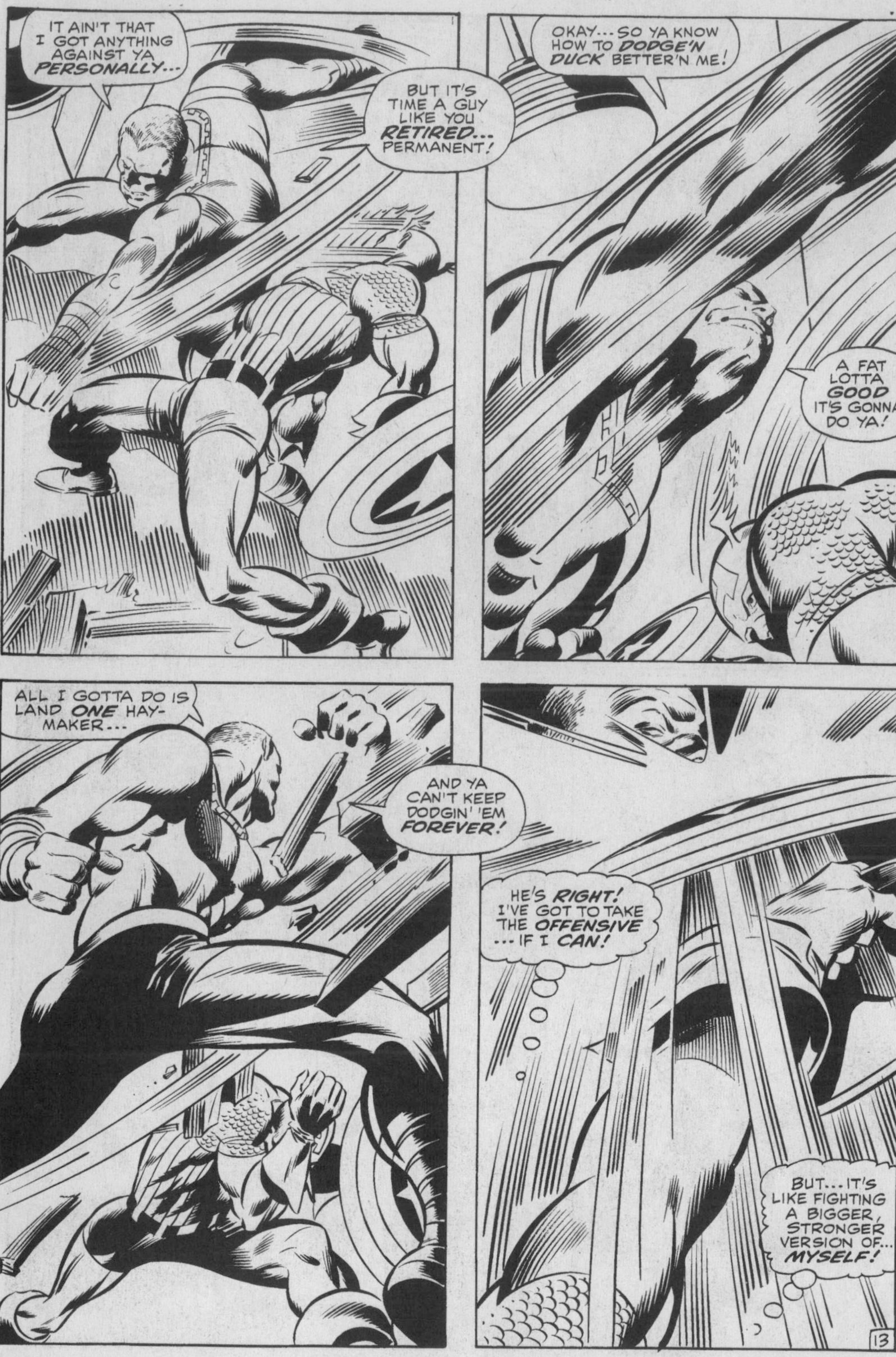
IT AIN'T THAT I GOT ANYTHING AGAINST YA PERSONALLY...
BUT IT'S TIME A GUY LIKE YOU RETIRED... PERMANENT!
OKAY... SO YA KNOW HOW TO DODGE'N DUCK BETTER'N ME!
A FAT LOTTA GOOD IT'S GONNA DO YA!
ALL I GOTTA DO IS LAND ONE HAY-MAKER...
AND YA CAN'T KEEP DODGIN' 'EM FOREVER!
HE'S RIGHT! I'VE GOT TO TAKE THE OFFENSIVE ... IF I CAN!
BUT... IT'S LIKE FIGHTING A BIGGER, STRONGER VERSION OF... MYSELF!
13

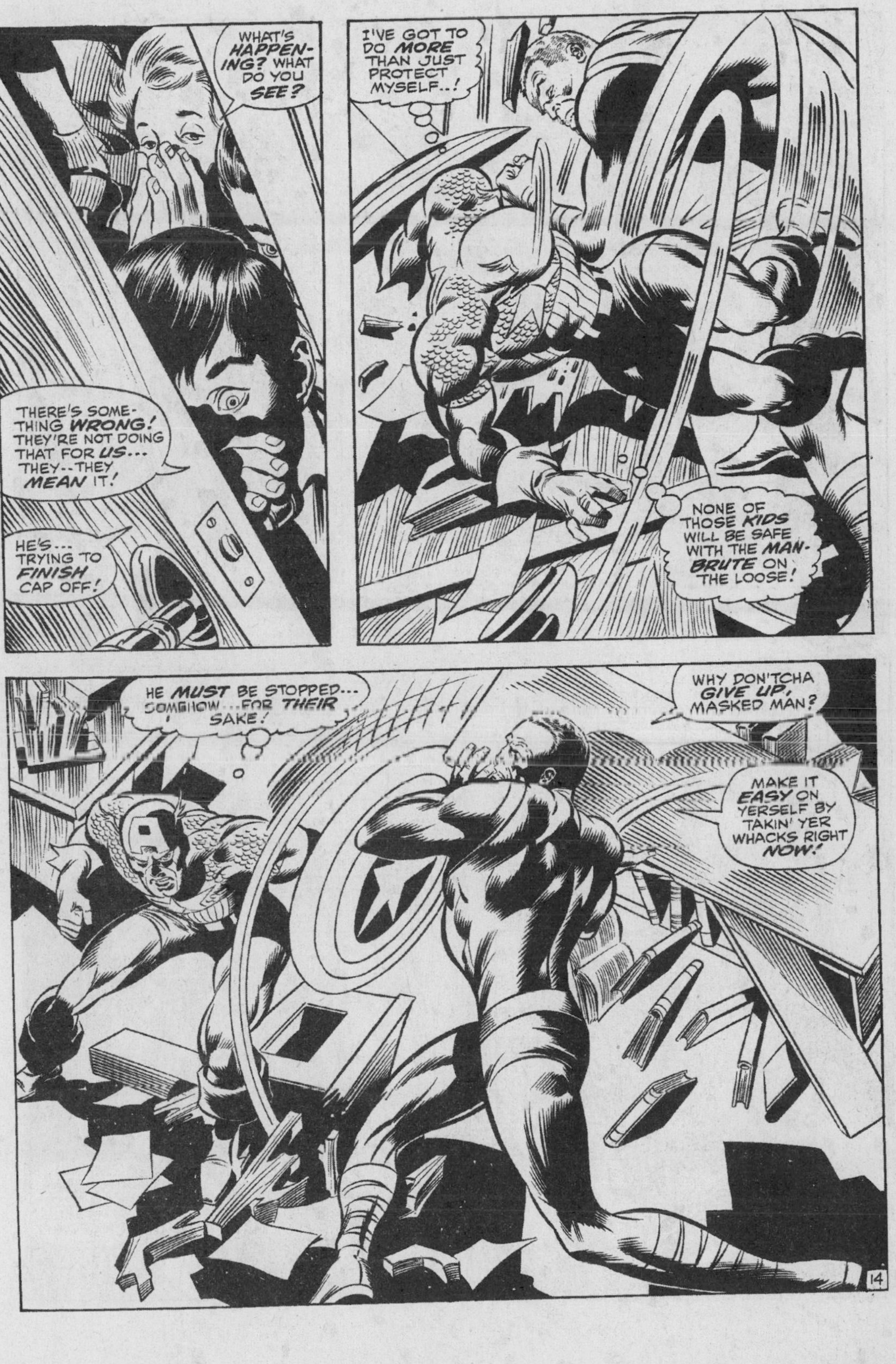
WHAT'S HAPPEN-ING? WHAT DO YOU SEE?
THERE'S SOME-THING WRONG! THEY'RE NOT DOING THAT FOR US... THEY--THEY MEAN IT!
HE'S... TRYING TO FINISH CAP OFF!
I'VE GOT TO DO MORE THAN JUST PROTECT MYSELF..!
NONE OF THOSE KIDS WILL BE SAFE WITH THE MAN-BRUTE ON THE LOOSE!
HE MUST BE STOPPED... SOMEHOW... FOR THEIR SAKE!
WHY DON'TCHA GIVE UP, MASKED MAN?
MAKE IT EASY ON YERSELF BY TAKIN' YER WHACKS RIGHT NOW!
14

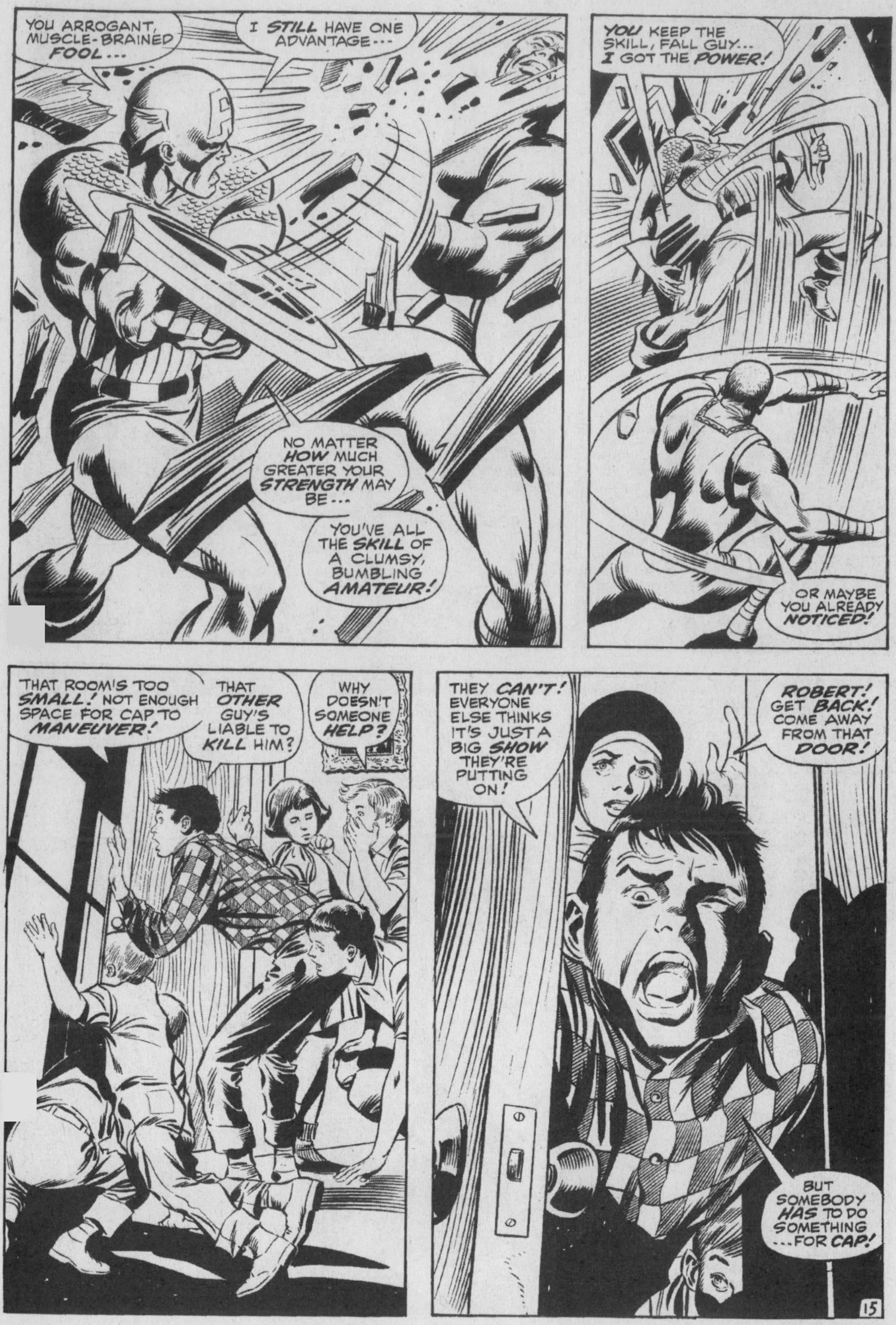
YOU ARROGANT, MUSCLE-BRAINED FOOL...
I STILL HAVE ONE ADVANTAGE---
NO MATTER HOW MUCH GREATER YOUR STRENGTH MAY BE...
YOU'VE ALL THE SKILL OF A CLUMSY, BUMBLING AMATEUR!
YOU KEEP THE SKILL, FALL GUY... I GOT THE POWER!
OR MAYBE YOU ALREADY NOTICED!
THAT ROOM'S TOO SMALL! NOT ENOUGH SPACE FOR CAP TO MANEUVER!
THAT OTHER GUY'S LIABLE TO KILL HIM?
WHY DOESN'T SOMEONE HELP?
THEY CAN'T! EVERYONE ELSE THINKS IT'S JUST A BIG SHOW THEY'RE PUTTING ON!
ROBERT! GET BACK! COME AWAY FROM THAT DOOR!
BUT SOMEBODY HAS TO DO SOMETHING ...FOR CAP!
15

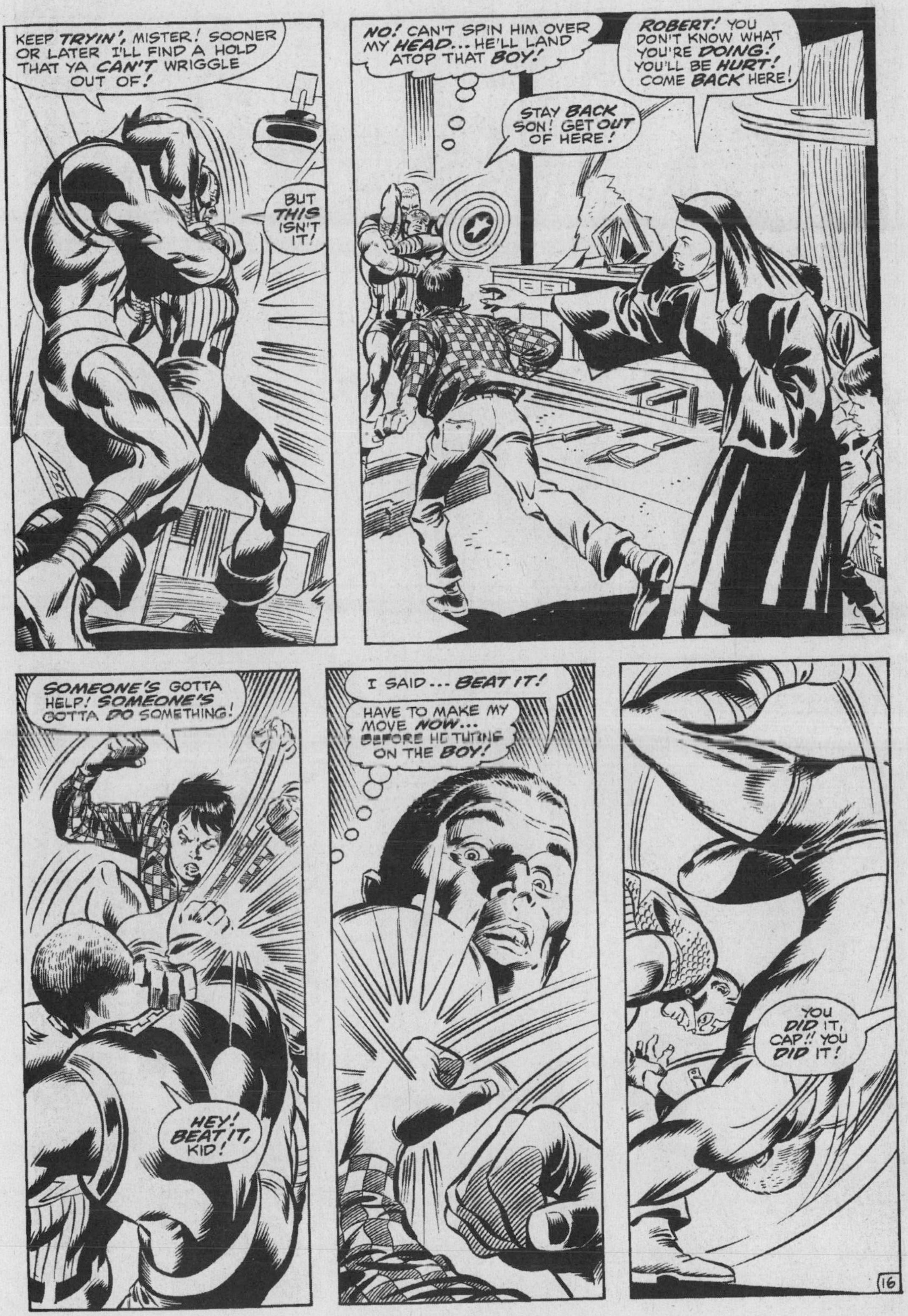

KEEP TRYIN', MISTER! SOONER OR LATER I'LL FIND A HOLD THAT YA CAN'T WRIGGLE OUT OF!
BUT THIS ISN'T IT!
NO! CAN'T SPIN HIM OVER MY HEAD... HE'LL LAND ATOP THAT BOY!
STAY BACK SON! GET OUT OF HERE!
ROBERT! YOU DON'T KNOW WHAT YOU'RE DOING! YOU'LL BE HURT! COME BACK HERE!
SOMEONE'S GOTTA HELP! SOMEONE'S GOTTA DO SOMETHING!
HEY! BEAT IT, KID!
I SAID... BEAT IT!
HAVE TO MAKE MY MOVE NOW... BEFORE HE TURNS ON THE BOY!
YOU DID IT, CAP!! YOU DID IT!
16

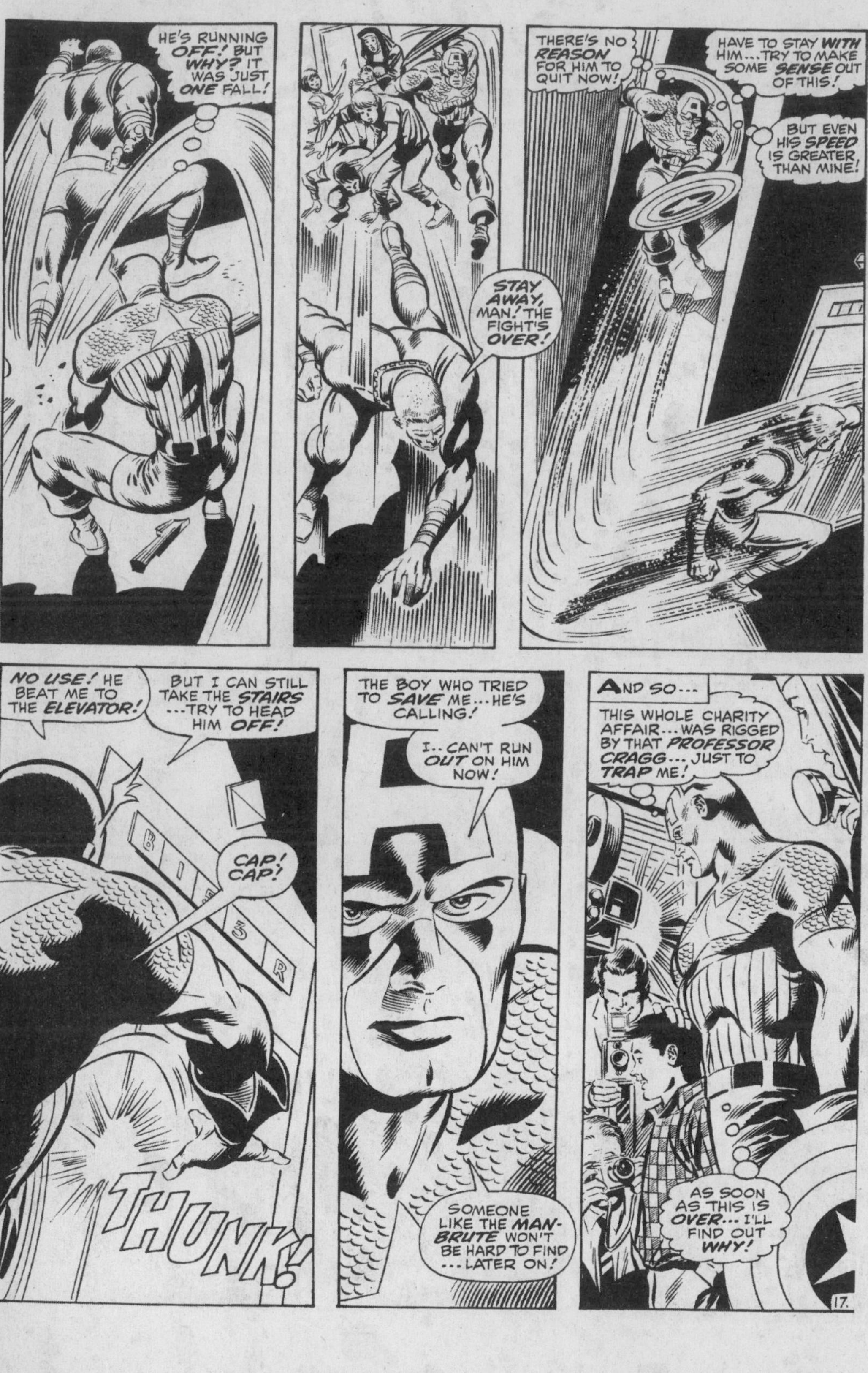
HE'S RUNNING OFF! BUT WHY? IT WAS JUST ONE FALL!
STAY AWAY, MAN! THE FIGHT'S OVER!
THERE'S NO REASON FOR HIM TO QUIT NOW!
HAVE TO STAY WITH HIM... TRY TO MAKE SOME SENSE OUT OF THIS!
BUT EVEN HIS SPEED IS GREATER THAN MINE!
NO USE! HE BEAT ME TO THE ELEVATOR!
BUT I CAN STILL TAKE THE STAIRS --- TRY TO HEAD HIM OFF!
CAP! CAP!
THUNK!
THE BOY WHO TRIED TO SAVE ME... HE'S CALLING!
I.. CAN'T RUN OUT ON HIM NOW!
SOMEONE LIKE THE MAN-BRUTE WON'T BE HARD TO FIND ... LATER ON!
AND SO---
THIS WHOLE CHARITY AFFAIR... WAS RIGGED BY THAT PROFESSOR CRAGG... JUST TO TRAP ME!
AS SOON AS THIS IS OVER... I'LL FIND OUT WHY!
17.

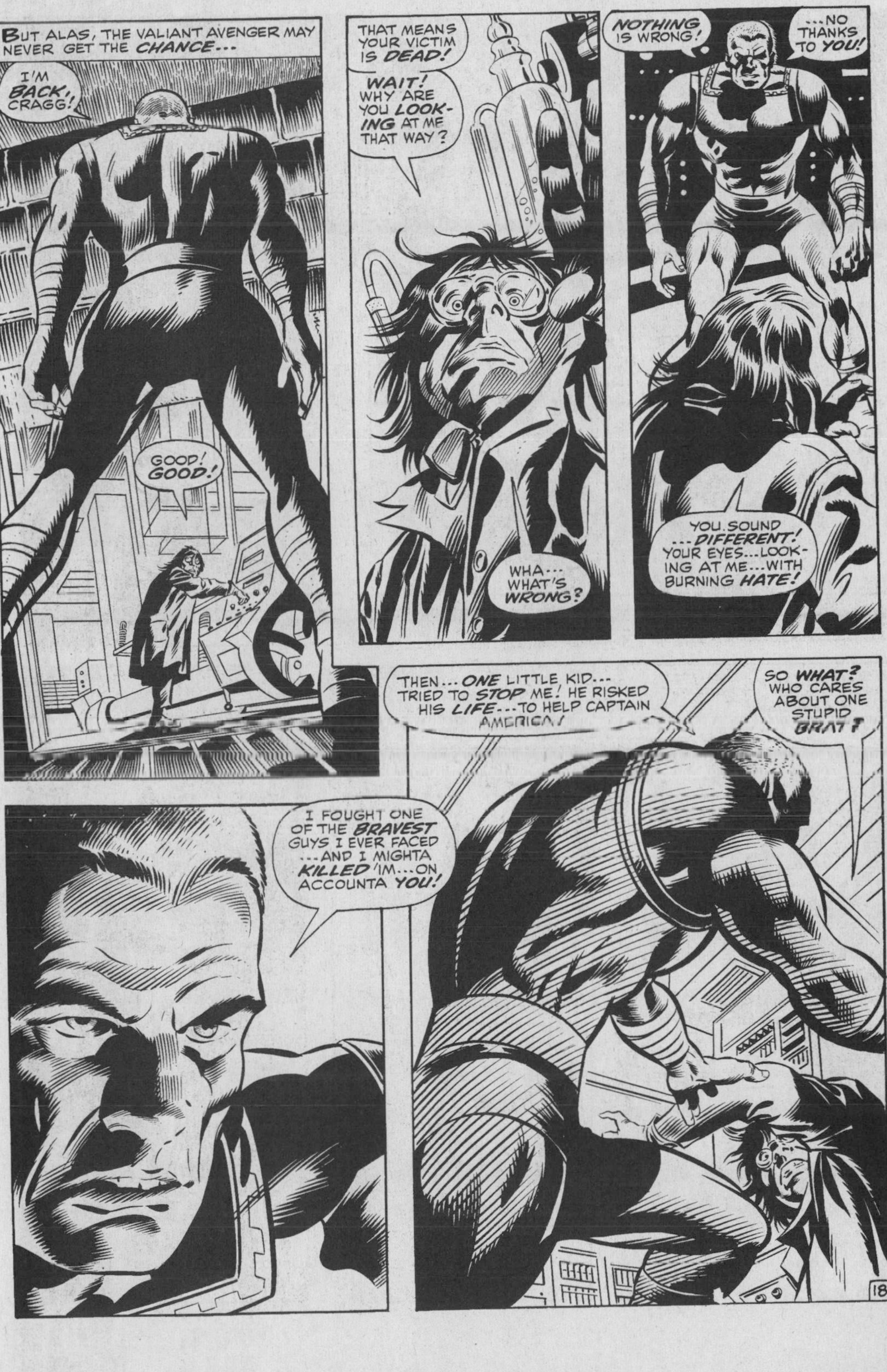
BUT ALAS, THE VALIANT AVENGER MAY NEVER GET THE CHANCE...
I'M BACK, CRAGG!
GOOD! GOOD!
THAT MEANS YOUR VICTIM IS DEAD!
WAIT! WHY ARE YOU LOOKING AT ME THAT WAY?
WHA... WHAT'S WRONG?
NOTHING IS WRONG!
...NO THANKS TO YOU!
YOU SOUND ...DIFFERENT! YOUR EYES... LOOKING AT ME... WITH BURNING HATE!
I FOUGHT ONE OF THE BRAVEST GUYS I EVER FACED ...AND I MIGHTA KILLED 'IM... ON ACCOUNTA YOU!
THEN... ONE LITTLE KID... TRIED TO STOP ME! HE RISKED HIS LIFE... TO HELP CAPTAIN AMERICA!
SO WHAT? WHO CARES ABOUT ONE STUPID BRAT?
18

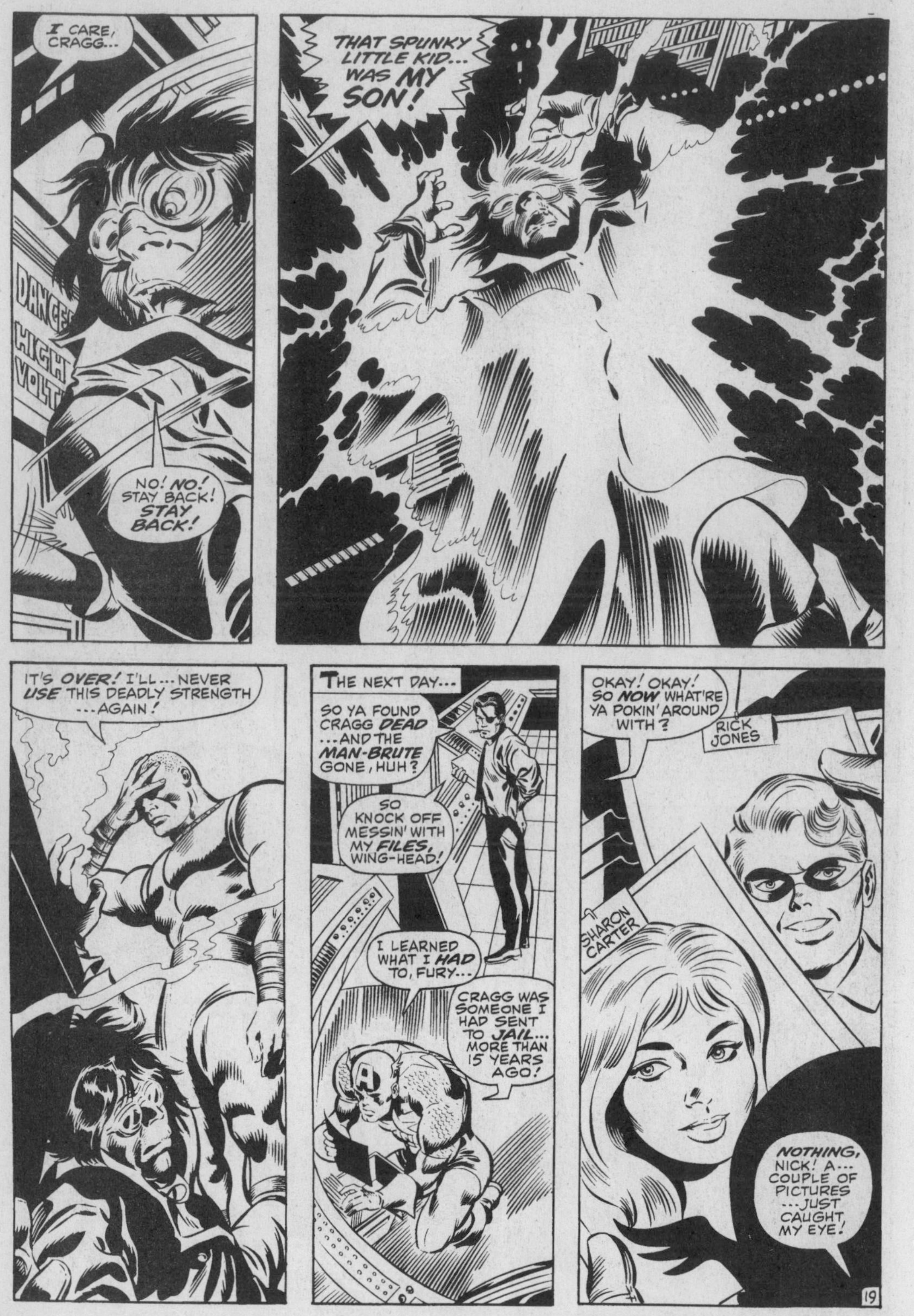
I CARE, CRAGG...
DANGER HIGH VOLT
NO! NO! STAY BACK! STAY BACK!
THAT SPUNKY LITTLE KID... WAS MY SON!
IT'S OVER! I'LL... NEVER USE THIS DEADLY STRENGTH ...AGAIN!
THE NEXT DAY...
SO YA FOUND CRAGG DEAD ...AND THE MAN-BRUTE GONE, HUH?
SO KNOCK OFF MESSIN' WITH MY FILES, WING-HEAD!
I LEARNED WHAT I HAD TO, FURY...
CRAGG WAS SOMEONE I HAD SENT TO JAIL... MORE THAN 15 YEARS AGO!
OKAY! OKAY! SO NOW WHAT'RE YA POKIN' AROUND WITH?
RICK JONES
SHARON CARTER
NOTHING, NICK! A... COUPLE OF PICTURES ...JUST CAUGHT MY EYE!
19

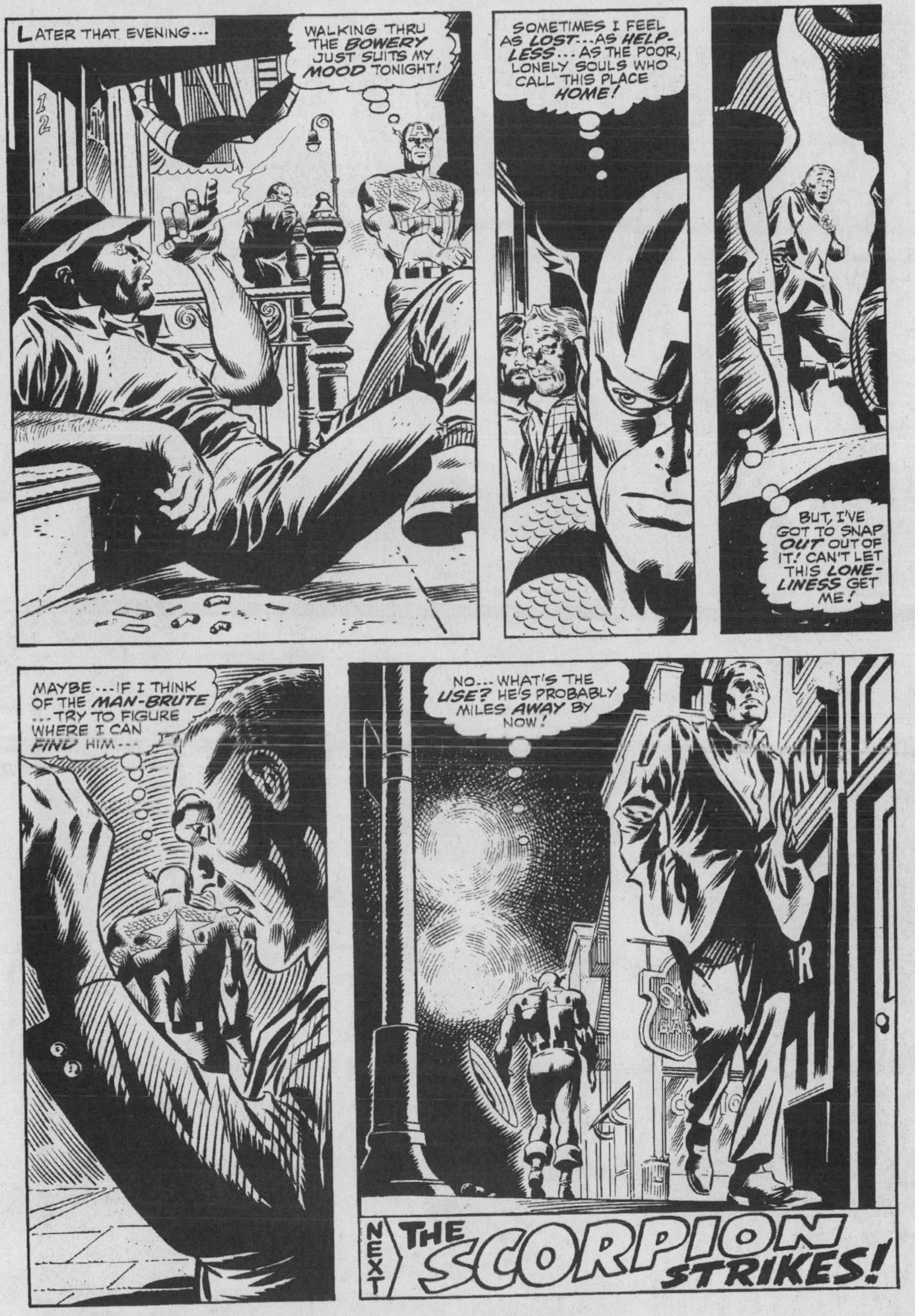
LATER THAT EVENING---
WALKING THRU THE BOWERY JUST SUITS MY MOOD TONIGHT!
SOMETIMES I FEEL AS LOST...AS HELP-LESS...AS THE POOR, LONELY SOULS WHO CALL THIS PLACE HOME!
BUT, I'VE GOT TO SNAP OUT OUT OF IT! CAN'T LET THIS LONE-LINESS GET ME!
MAYBE---IF I THINK OF THE MAN-BRUTE ...TRY TO FIGURE WHERE I CAN FIND HIM---
NO---WHAT'S THE USE? HE'S PROBABLY MILES AWAY BY NOW!
NEXT THE SCORPION STRIKES!

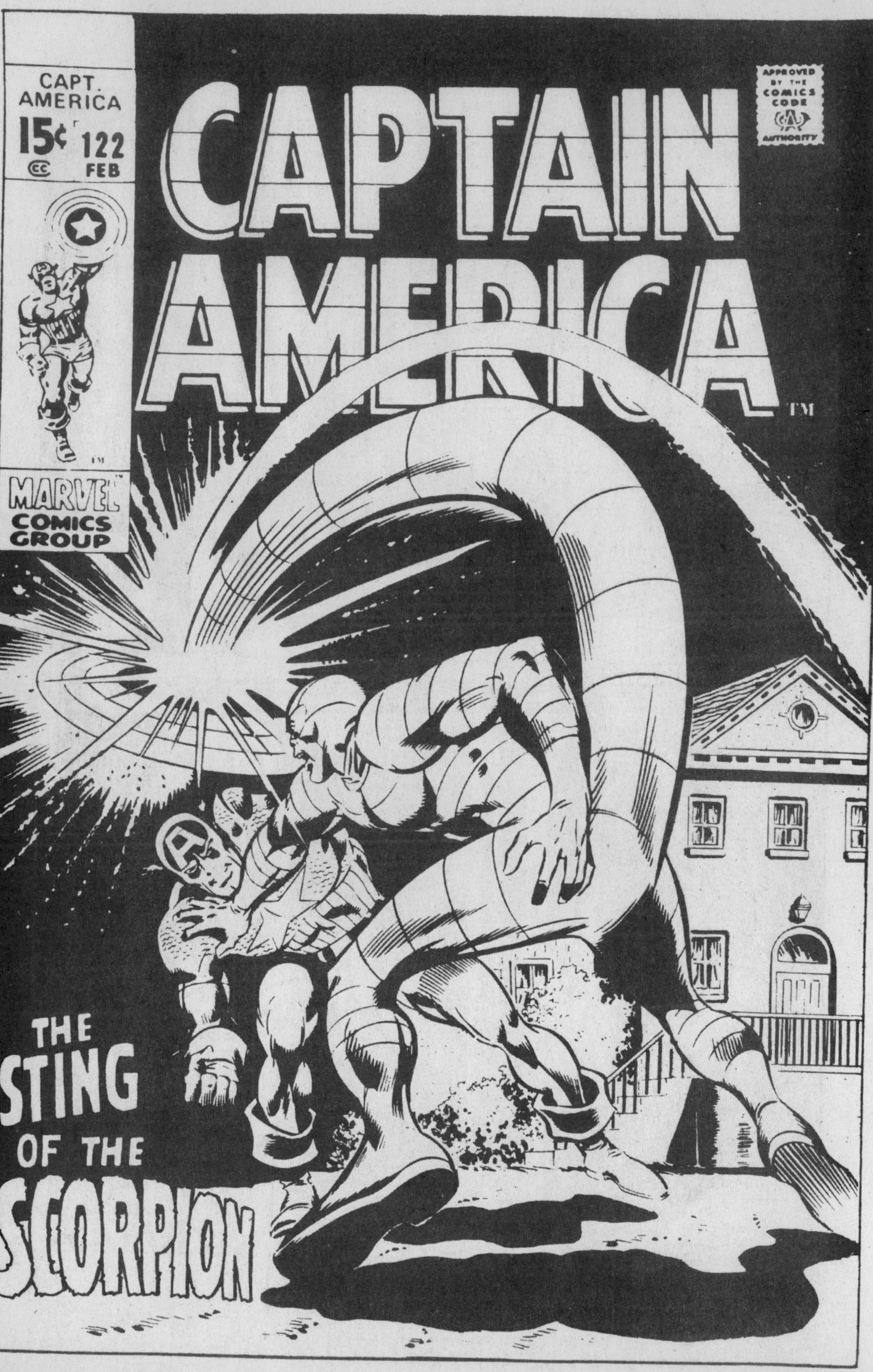
CAPT. AMERICA
15¢ 122
FEB
APPROVED BY THE COMICS CODE AUTHORITY
CAPTAIN AMERICA
MARVEL COMICS GROUP
THE STING OF THE SCORPION

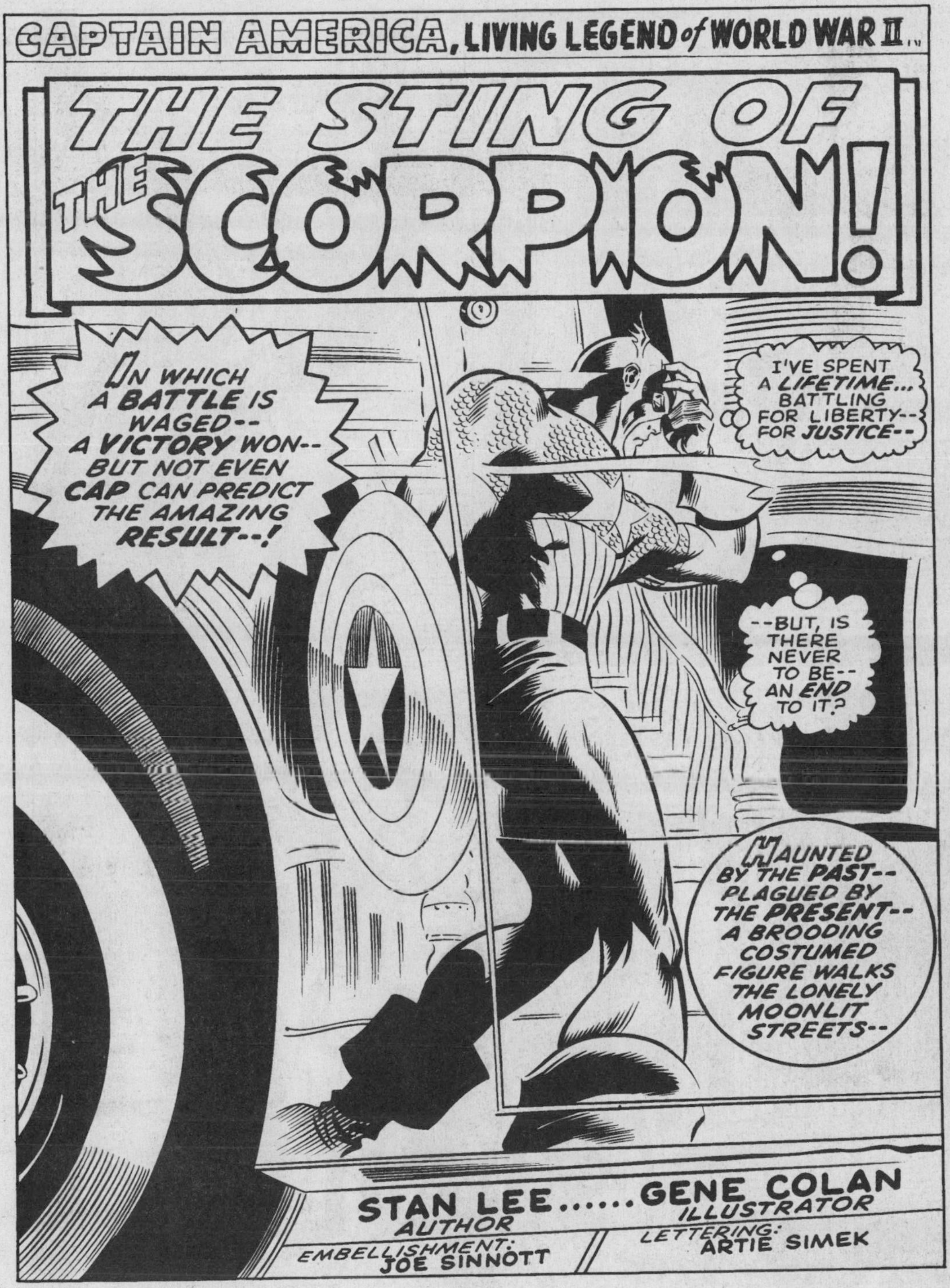

CAPTAIN AMERICA, LIVING LEGEND of WORLD WAR II...
THE STING OF THE SCORPION!
ON WHICH A BATTLE IS WAGED-- A VICTORY WON-- BUT NOT EVEN CAP CAN PREDICT THE AMAZING RESULT--!
I'VE SPENT A LIFETIME... BATTLING FOR LIBERTY-- FOR JUSTICE--
--BUT, IS THERE NEVER TO BE-- AN END TO IT?
HAUNTED BY THE PAST-- PLAGUED BY THE PRESENT-- A BROODING COSTUMED FIGURE WALKS THE LONELY MOONLIT STREETS--
STAN LEE...... AUTHOR
GENE COLAN ILLUSTRATOR
EMBELLISHMENT: JOE SINNOTT
LETTERING: ARTIE SIMEK

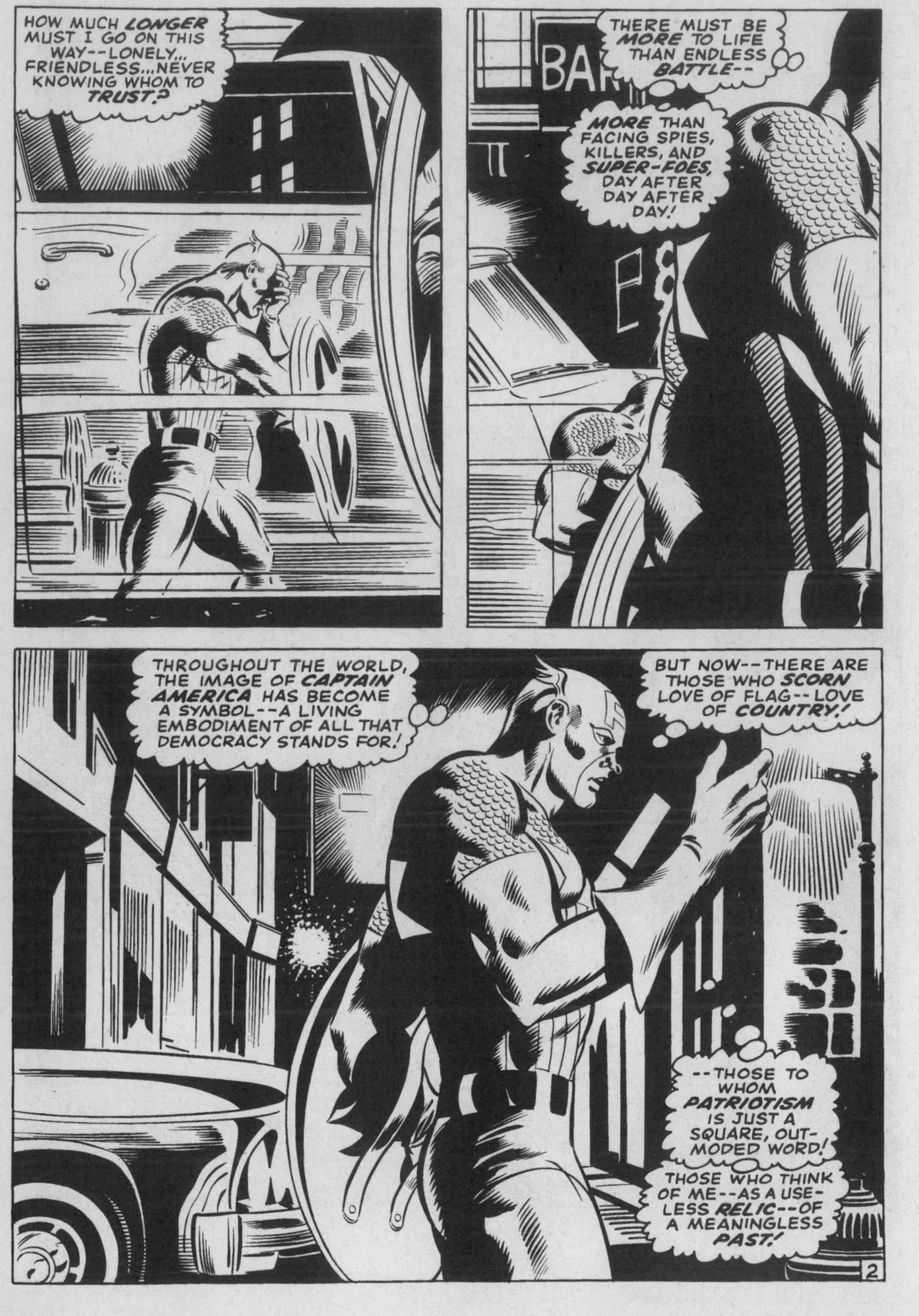
HOW MUCH LONGER MUST I GO ON THIS WAY--LONELY... FRIENDLESS...NEVER KNOWING WHOM TO TRUST?
THERE MUST BE MORE TO LIFE THAN ENDLESS BATTLE--
BAR
MORE THAN FACING SPIES, KILLERS, AND SUPER-FOES, DAY AFTER DAY AFTER DAY!
THROUGHOUT THE WORLD, THE IMAGE OF CAPTAIN AMERICA HAS BECOME A SYMBOL--A LIVING EMBODIMENT OF ALL THAT DEMOCRACY STANDS FOR!
BUT NOW--THERE ARE THOSE WHO SCORN LOVE OF FLAG--LOVE OF COUNTRY!
--THOSE TO WHOM PATRIOTISM IS JUST A SQUARE, OUT-MODED WORD!
THOSE WHO THINK OF ME--AS A USELESS RELIC--OF A MEANINGLESS PAST!
2

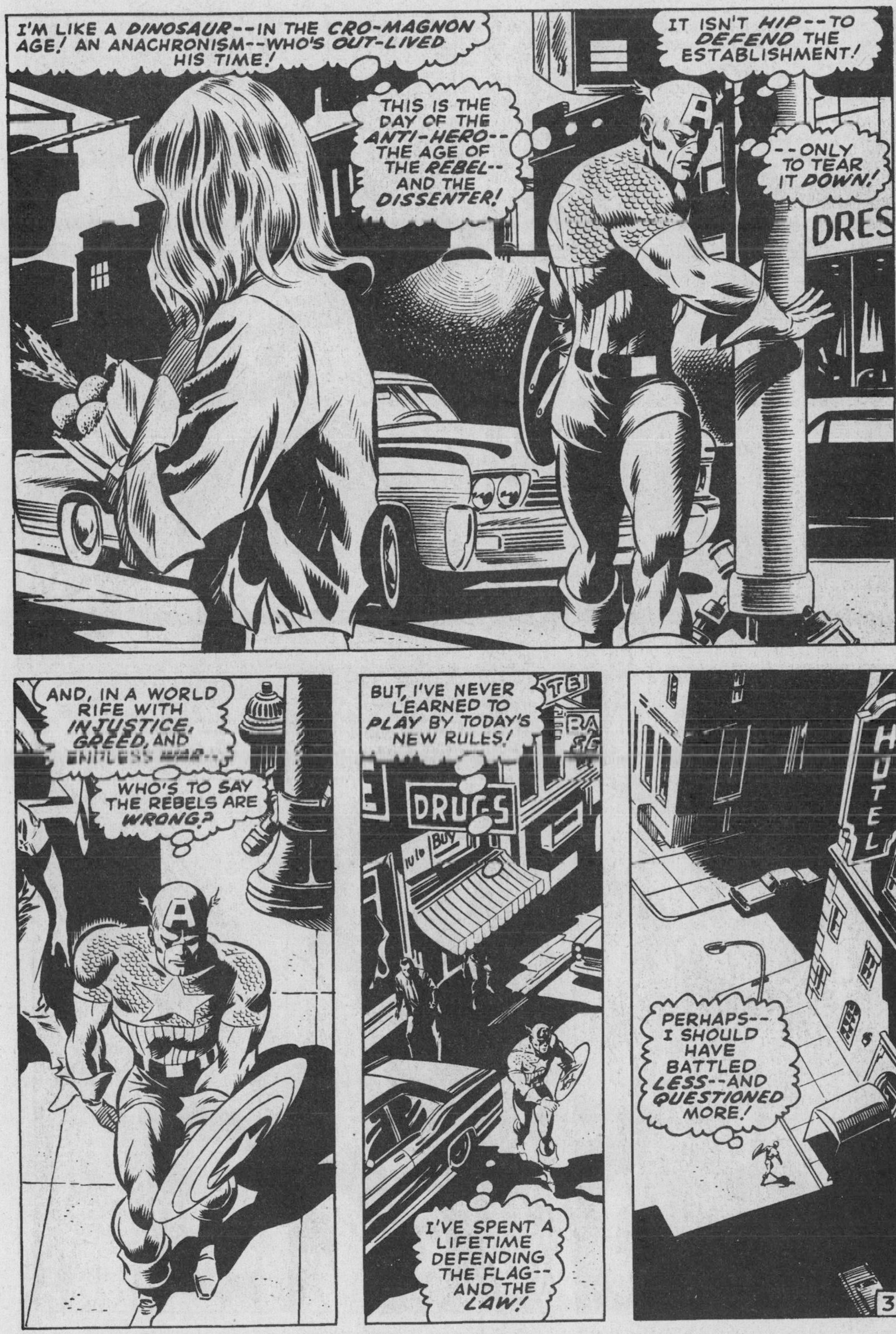
I'M LIKE A DINOSAUR--IN THE CRO-MAGNON AGE! AN ANACHRONISM--WHO'S OUT-LIVED HIS TIME!
THIS IS THE DAY OF THE ANTI-HERO--THE AGE OF THE REBEL--AND THE DISSENTER!
IT ISN'T HIP--TO DEFEND THE ESTABLISHMENT!
--ONLY TO TEAR IT DOWN!
DRES
AND, IN A WORLD RIFE WITH INJUSTICE, GREED, AND ENDLESS WAR--
WHO'S TO SAY THE REBELS ARE WRONG?
BUT, I'VE NEVER LEARNED TO PLAY BY TODAY'S NEW RULES!
DRUGS
BUY
I'VE SPENT A LIFETIME DEFENDING THE FLAG--AND THE LAW!
HOTEL
PERHAPS--I SHOULD HAVE BATTLED LESS--AND QUESTIONED MORE!
3

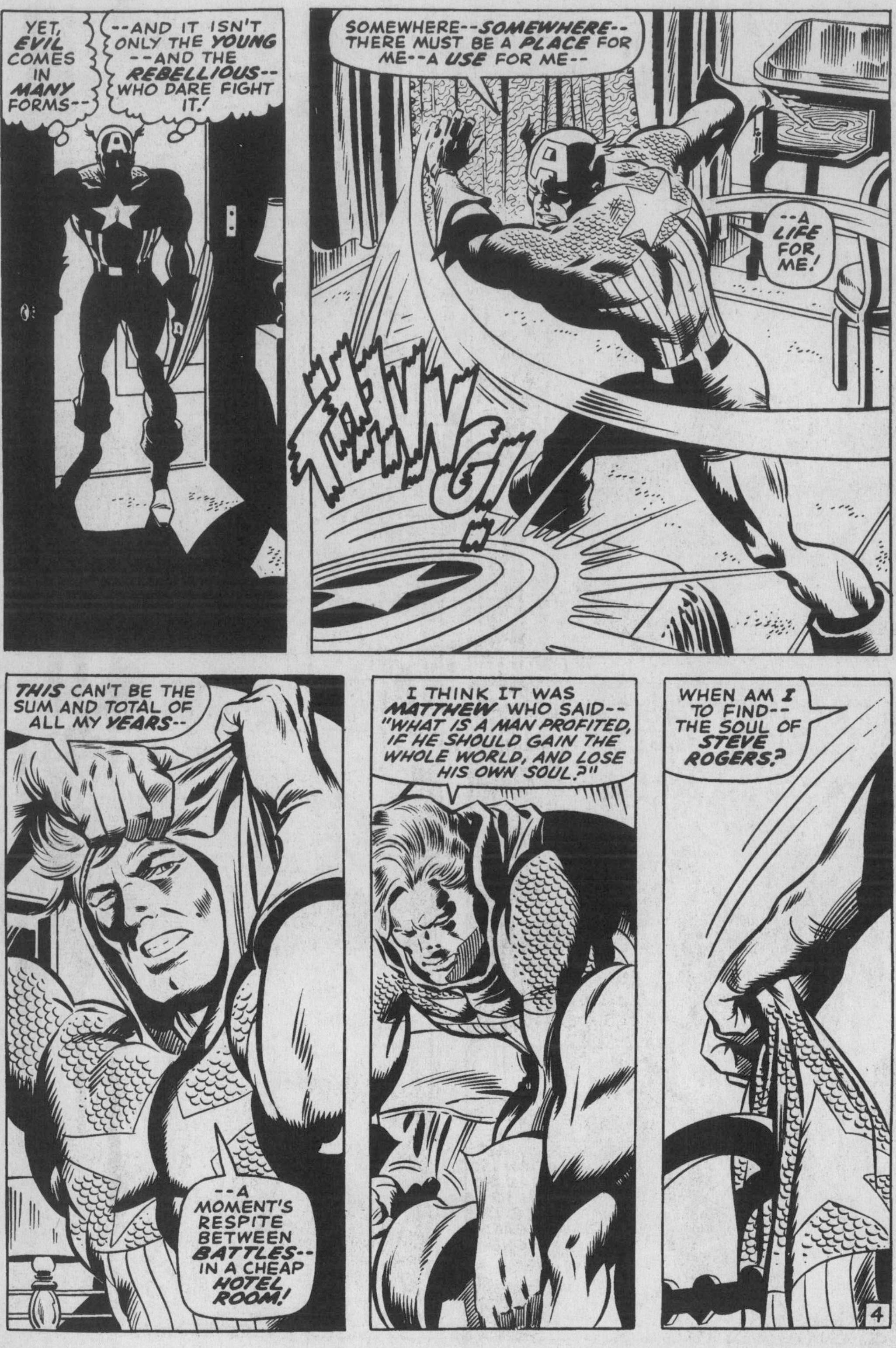
YET, EVIL COMES IN MANY FORMS--
--AND IT ISN'T ONLY THE YOUNG --AND THE REBELLIOUS-- WHO DARE FIGHT IT!
SOMEWHERE--SOMEWHERE-- THERE MUST BE A PLACE FOR ME--A USE FOR ME--
--A LIFE FOR ME!
THIS CAN'T BE THE SUM AND TOTAL OF ALL MY YEARS--
--A MOMENT'S RESPITE BETWEEN BATTLES--IN A CHEAP HOTEL ROOM!
I THINK IT WAS MATTHEW WHO SAID-- "WHAT IS A MAN PROFITED, IF HE SHOULD GAIN THE WHOLE WORLD, AND LOSE HIS OWN SOUL?"
WHEN AM I TO FIND-- THE SOUL OF STEVE ROGERS?
4

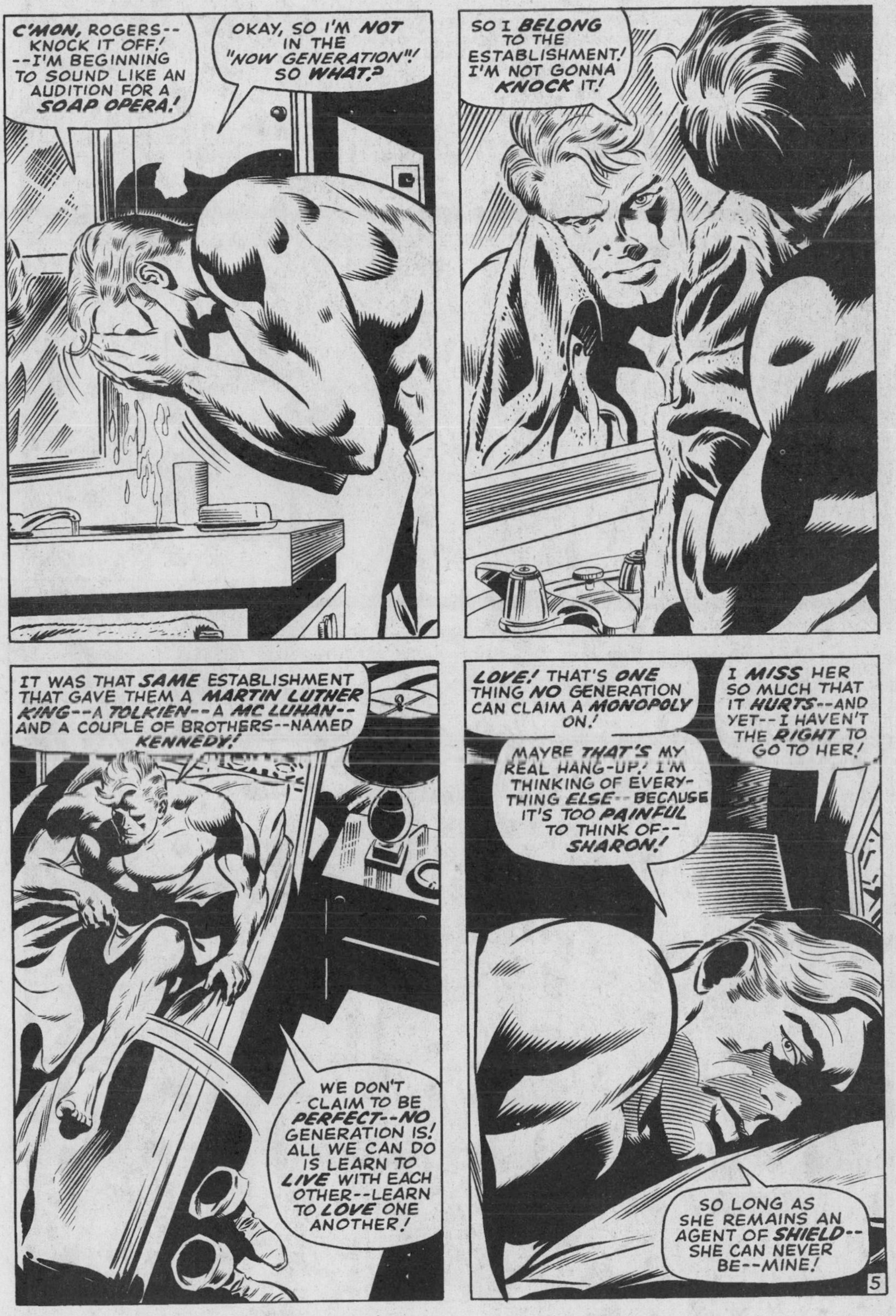
C'MON, ROGERS-- KNOCK IT OFF! --I'M BEGINNING TO SOUND LIKE AN AUDITION FOR A SOAP OPERA!
OKAY, SO I'M NOT IN THE "NOW GENERATION"! SO WHAT?
SO I BELONG TO THE ESTABLISHMENT! I'M NOT GONNA KNOCK IT!
IT WAS THAT SAME ESTABLISHMENT THAT GAVE THEM A MARTIN LUTHER KING--A TOLKIEN--A MC LUHAN--AND A COUPLE OF BROTHERS--NAMED KENNEDY!
WE DON'T CLAIM TO BE PERFECT--NO GENERATION IS! ALL WE CAN DO IS LEARN TO LIVE WITH EACH OTHER--LEARN TO LOVE ONE ANOTHER!
LOVE! THAT'S ONE THING NO GENERATION CAN CLAIM A MONOPOLY ON!
MAYBE THAT'S MY REAL HANG-UP! I'M THINKING OF EVERYTHING ELSE--BECAUSE IT'S TOO PAINFUL TO THINK OF--SHARON!
I MISS HER SO MUCH THAT IT HURTS--AND YET--I HAVEN'T THE RIGHT TO GO TO HER!
SO LONG AS SHE REMAINS AN AGENT OF SHIELD--SHE CAN NEVER BE--MINE!
5

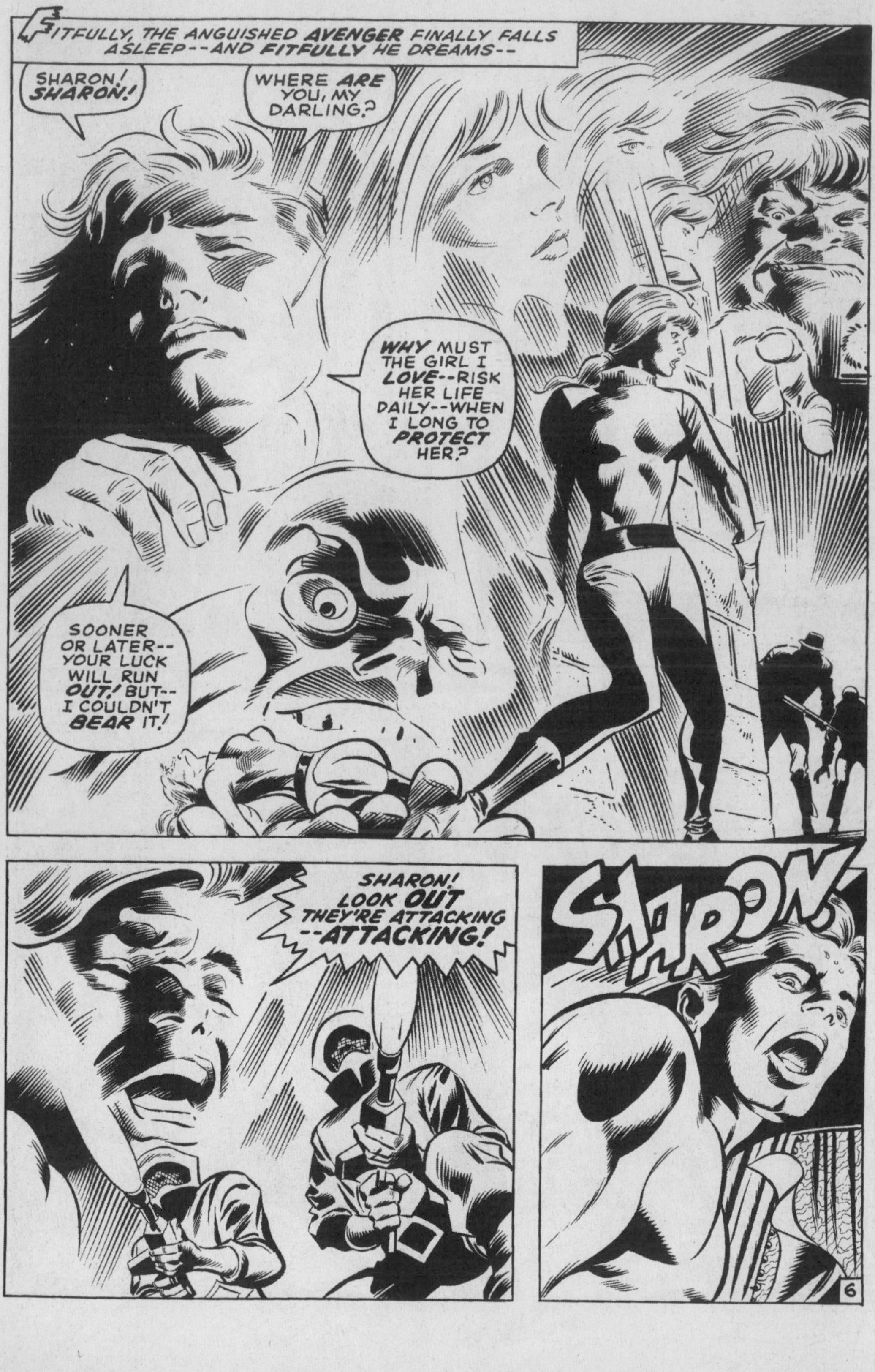
FITFULLY, THE ANGUISHED AVENGER FINALLY FALLS ASLEEP--AND FITFULLY HE DREAMS--
SHARON! SHARON!
WHERE ARE YOU, MY DARLING?
WHY MUST THE GIRL I LOVE--RISK HER LIFE DAILY--WHEN I LONG TO PROTECT HER?
SOONER OR LATER--YOUR LUCK WILL RUN OUT! BUT--I COULDN'T BEAR IT!
SHARON! LOOK OUT THEY'RE ATTACKING --ATTACKING!
SHARON!
6

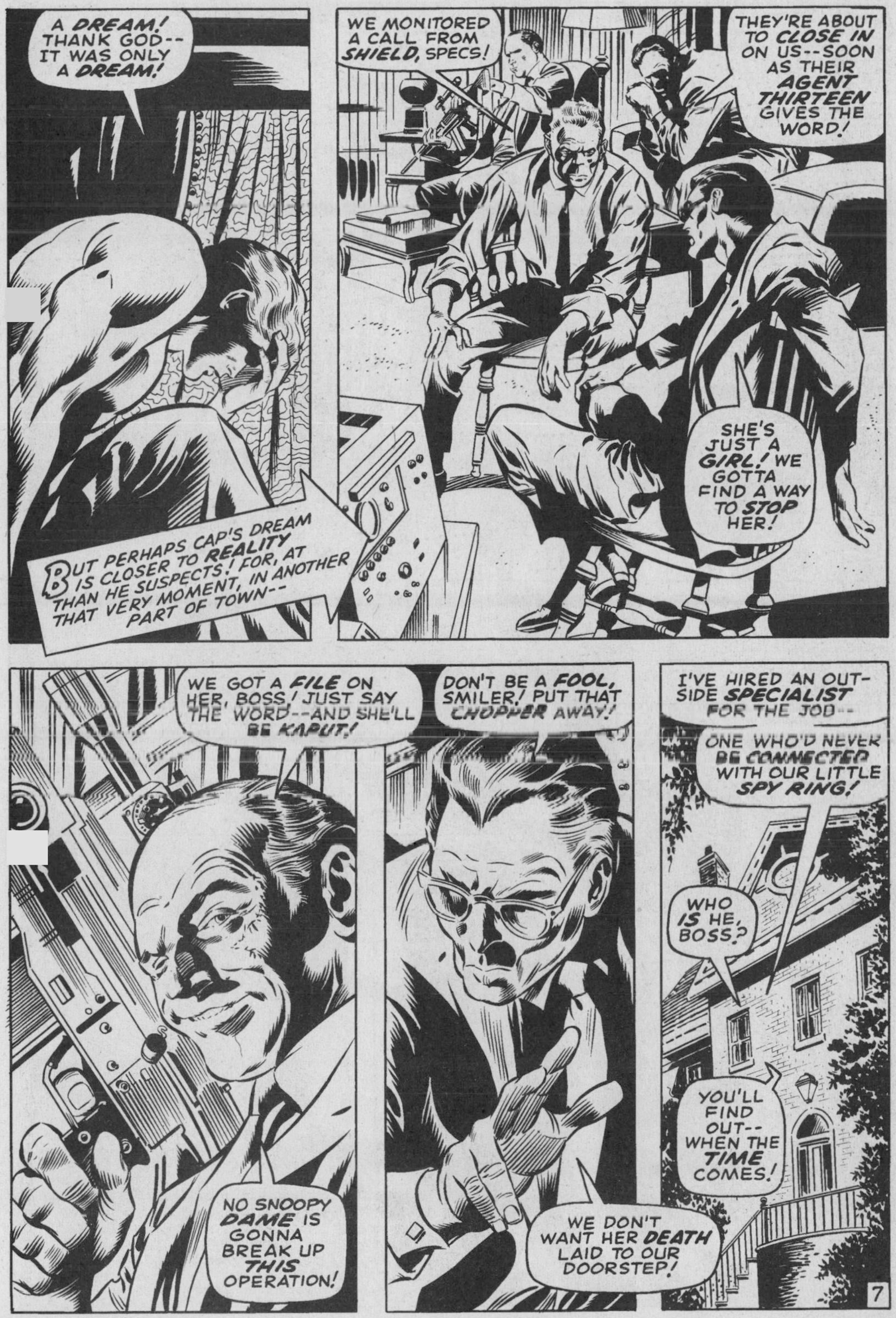
A DREAM! THANK GOD-- IT WAS ONLY A DREAM!
BUT PERHAPS CAP'S DREAM IS CLOSER TO REALITY THAN HE SUSPECTS! FOR, AT THAT VERY MOMENT, IN ANOTHER PART OF TOWN--
WE MONITORED A CALL FROM SHIELD, SPECS!
THEY'RE ABOUT TO CLOSE IN ON US--SOON AS THEIR AGENT THIRTEEN GIVES THE WORD!
SHE'S JUST A GIRL! WE GOTTA FIND A WAY TO STOP HER!
WE GOT A FILE ON HER, BOSS! JUST SAY THE WORD--AND SHE'LL BE KAPUT!
NO SNOOPY DAME IS GONNA BREAK UP THIS OPERATION!
DON'T BE A FOOL, SMILER! PUT THAT CHOPPER AWAY!
WE DON'T WANT HER DEATH LAID TO OUR DOORSTEP!
I'VE HIRED AN OUTSIDE SPECIALIST FOR THE JOB--
ONE WHO'D NEVER BE CONNECTED WITH OUR LITTLE SPY RING!
WHO IS HE, BOSS?
YOU'LL FIND OUT-- WHEN THE TIME COMES!
7

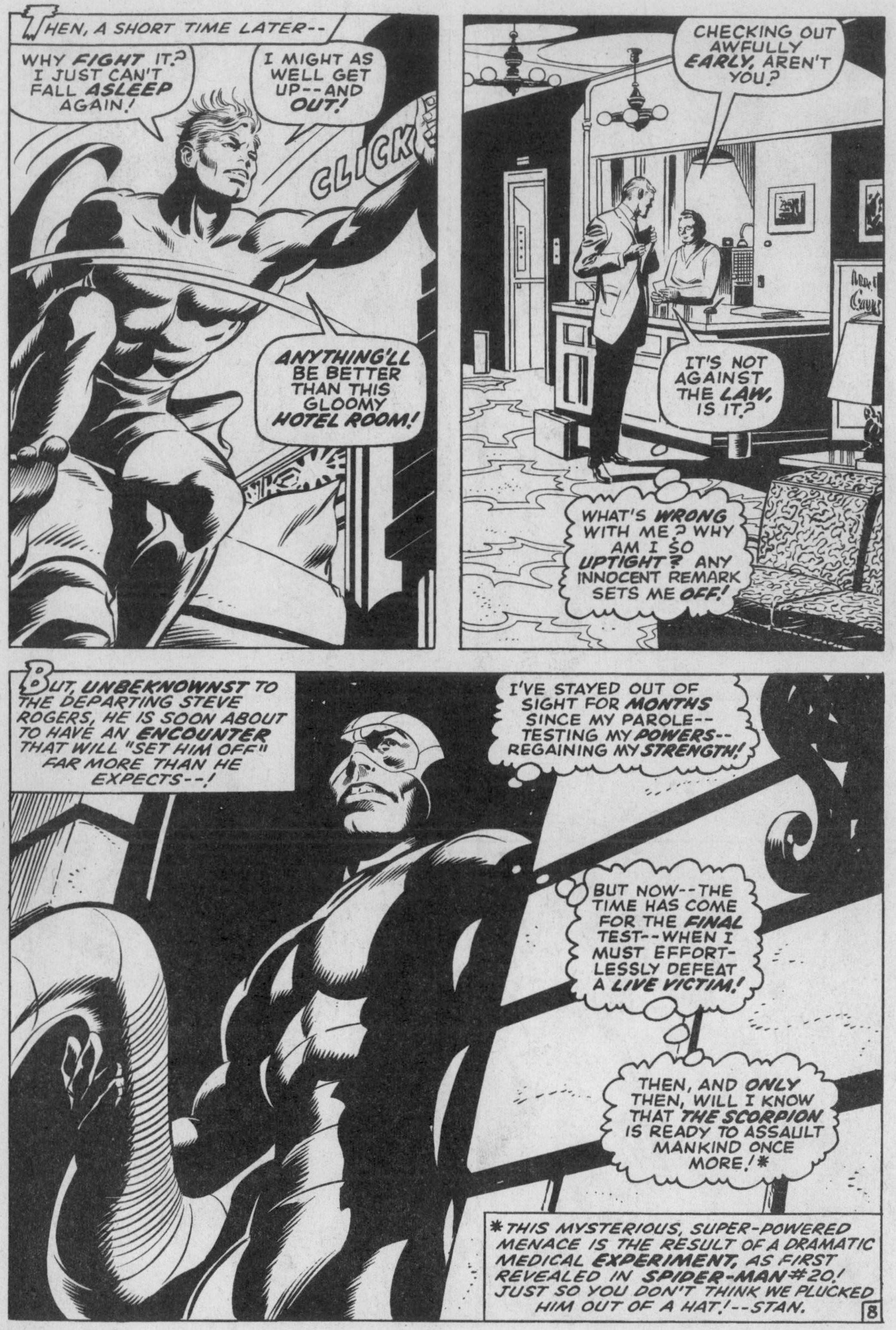
THEN, A SHORT TIME LATER--
WHY FIGHT IT? I JUST CAN'T FALL ASLEEP AGAIN!
I MIGHT AS WELL GET UP--AND OUT!
CLICK
ANYTHING'LL BE BETTER THAN THIS GLOOMY HOTEL ROOM!
CHECKING OUT AWFULLY EARLY, AREN'T YOU?
IT'S NOT AGAINST THE LAW, IS IT?
WHAT'S WRONG WITH ME? WHY AM I SO UPTIGHT? ANY INNOCENT REMARK SETS ME OFF!
BUT, UNBEKNOWNST TO THE DEPARTING STEVE ROGERS, HE IS SOON ABOUT TO HAVE AN ENCOUNTER THAT WILL "SET HIM OFF" FAR MORE THAN HE EXPECTS--!
I'VE STAYED OUT OF SIGHT FOR MONTHS SINCE MY PAROLE-- TESTING MY POWERS-- REGAINING MY STRENGTH!
BUT NOW--THE TIME HAS COME FOR THE FINAL TEST--WHEN I MUST EFFORTLESSLY DEFEAT A LIVE VICTIM!
THEN, AND ONLY THEN, WILL I KNOW THAT THE SCORPION IS READY TO ASSAULT MANKIND ONCE MORE!*
*THIS MYSTERIOUS, SUPER-POWERED MENACE IS THE RESULT OF A DRAMATIC MEDICAL EXPERIMENT, AS FIRST REVEALED IN SPIDER-MAN #20! JUST SO YOU DON'T THINK WE PLUCKED HIM OUT OF A HAT!--STAN.
8

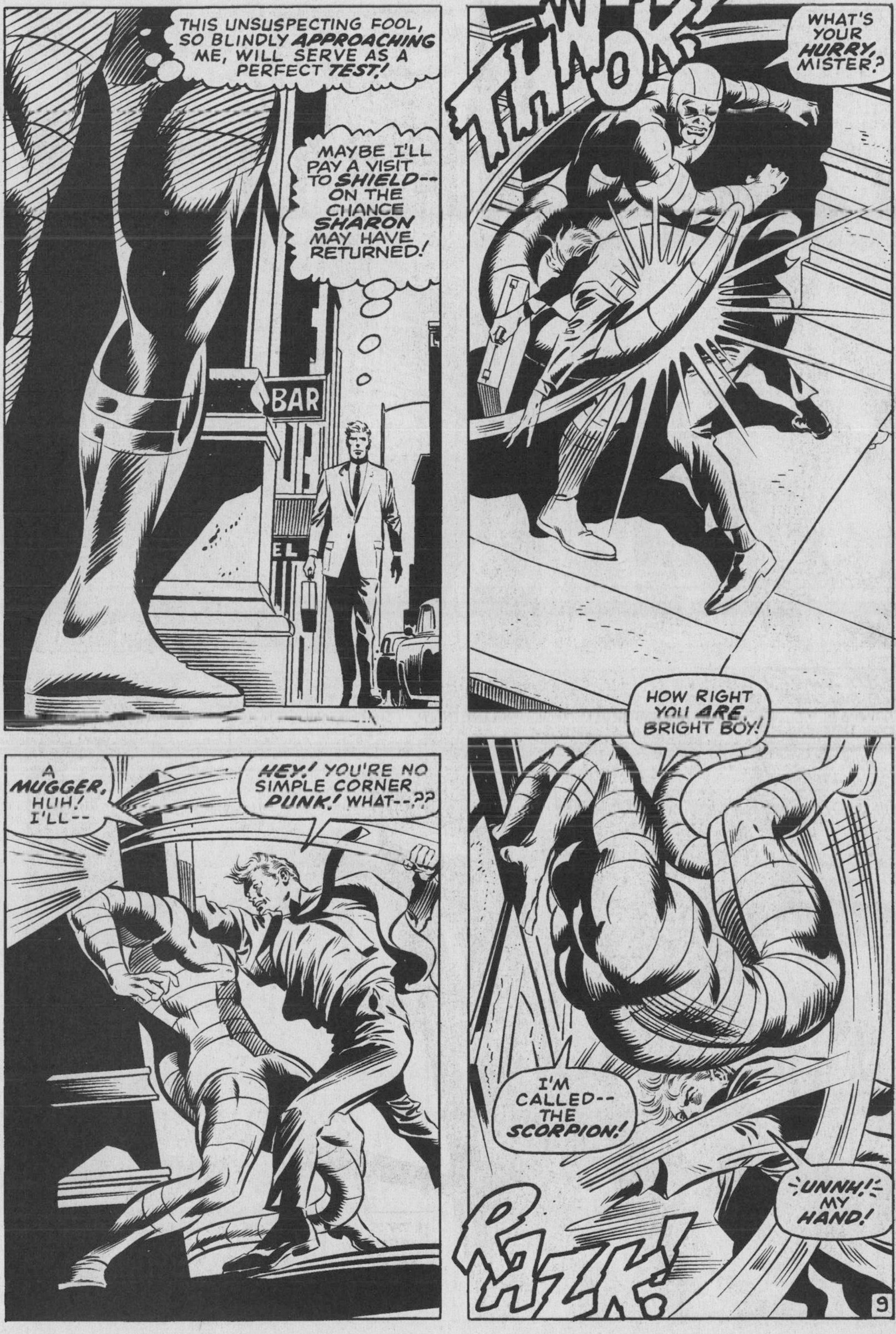
THIS UNSUSPECTING FOOL, SO BLINDLY APPROACHING ME, WILL SERVE AS A PERFECT TEST!
MAYBE I'LL PAY A VISIT TO SHIELD-- ON THE CHANCE SHARON MAY HAVE RETURNED!
BAR
EL
THWOK!
WHAT'S YOUR HURRY, MISTER?
A MUGGER, HUH! I'LL--
HEY! YOU'RE NO SIMPLE CORNER PUNK! WHAT--??
HOW RIGHT YOU ARE, BRIGHT BOY!
I'M CALLED-- THE SCORPION!
UNNH! MY HAND!
RAK!
9

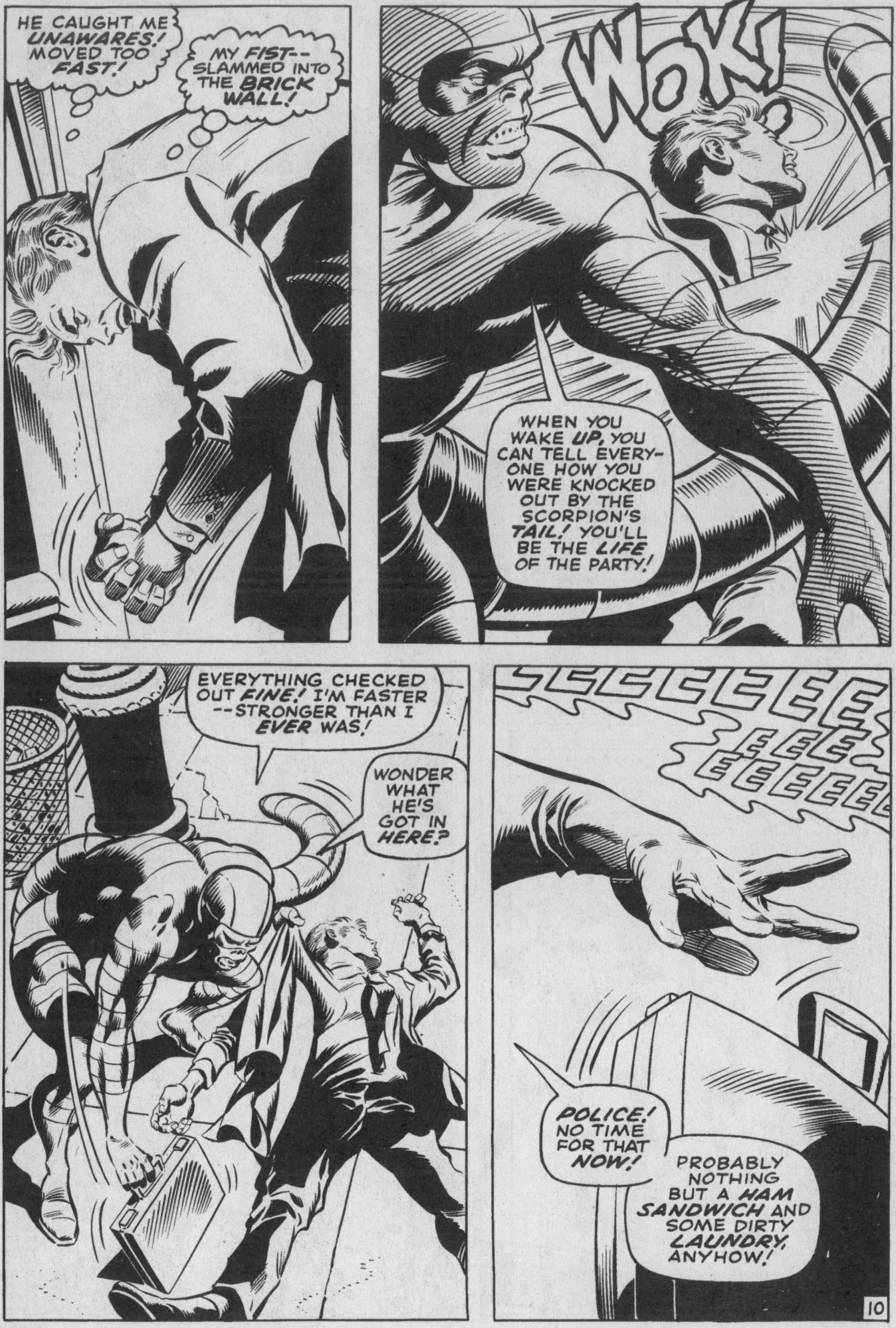
HE CAUGHT ME UNAWARES! MOVED TOO FAST!
MY FIST-- SLAMMED INTO THE BRICK WALL!
WOK!
WHEN YOU WAKE UP, YOU CAN TELL EVERY-ONE HOW YOU WERE KNOCKED OUT BY THE SCORPION'S TAIL! YOU'LL BE THE LIFE OF THE PARTY!
EVERYTHING CHECKED OUT FINE! I'M FASTER --STRONGER THAN I EVER WAS!
WONDER WHAT HE'S GOT IN HERE?
EEEEEEEEEEEEEEEEEE
POLICE! NO TIME FOR THAT NOW!
PROBABLY NOTHING BUT A HAM SANDWICH AND SOME DIRTY LAUNDRY, ANYHOW!
10

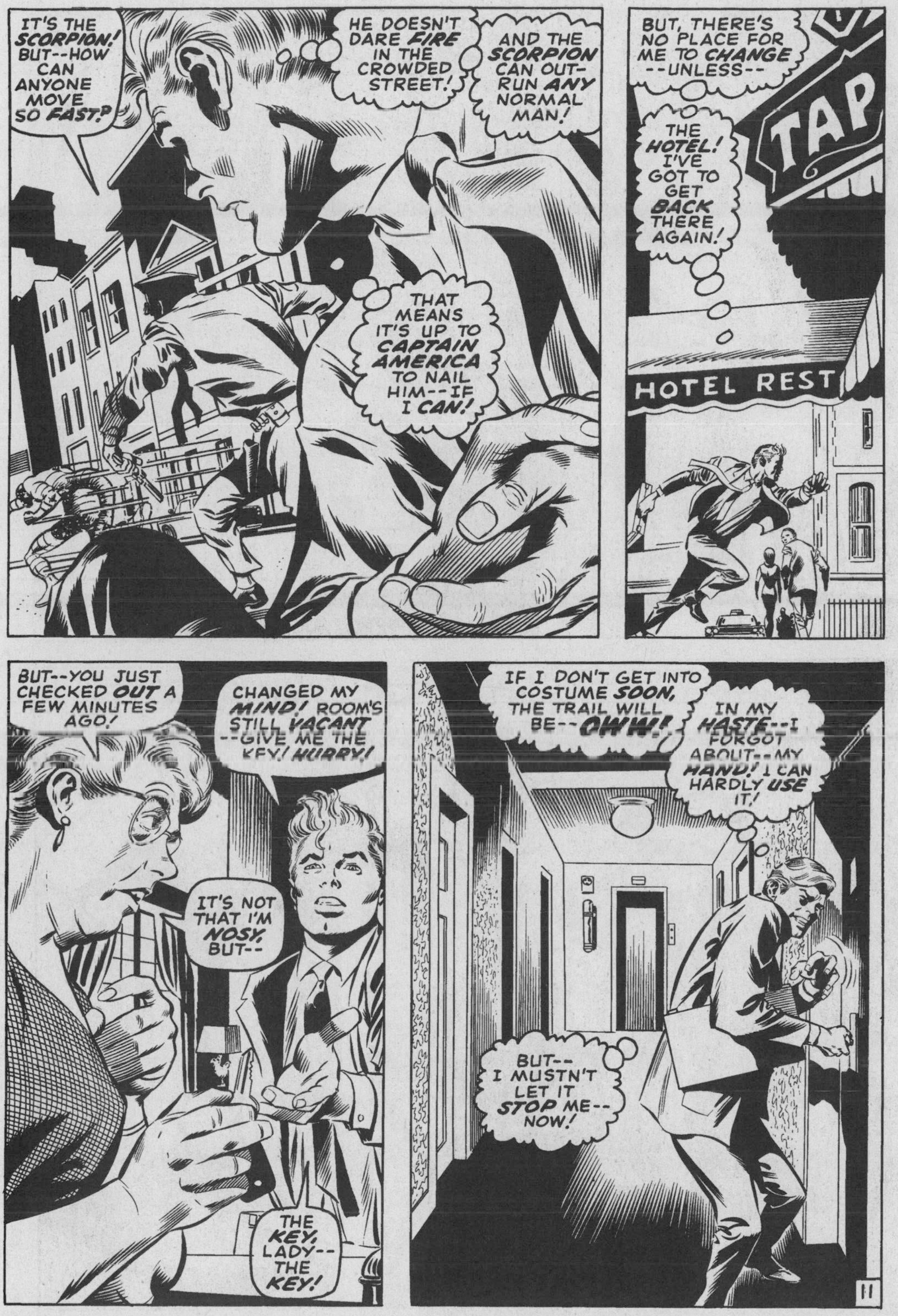
IT'S THE SCORPION! BUT--HOW CAN ANYONE MOVE SO FAST?
HE DOESN'T DARE FIRE IN THE CROWDED STREET!
AND THE SCORPION CAN OUT-RUN ANY NORMAL MAN!
THAT MEANS IT'S UP TO CAPTAIN AMERICA TO NAIL HIM--IF I CAN!
BUT, THERE'S NO PLACE FOR ME TO CHANGE --UNLESS--
THE HOTEL! I'VE GOT TO GET BACK THERE AGAIN!
TAP
HOTEL REST
BUT--YOU JUST CHECKED OUT A FEW MINUTES AGO!
CHANGED MY MIND! ROOM'S STILL VACANT --GIVE ME THE KEY! HURRY!
IT'S NOT THAT I'M NOSY, BUT--
THE KEY, LADY-- THE KEY!
IF I DON'T GET INTO COSTUME SOON, THE TRAIL WILL BE--OWW!
IN MY HASTE--I FORGOT ABOUT--MY HAND! I CAN HARDLY USE IT!
BUT-- I MUSTN'T LET IT STOP ME-- NOW!
11

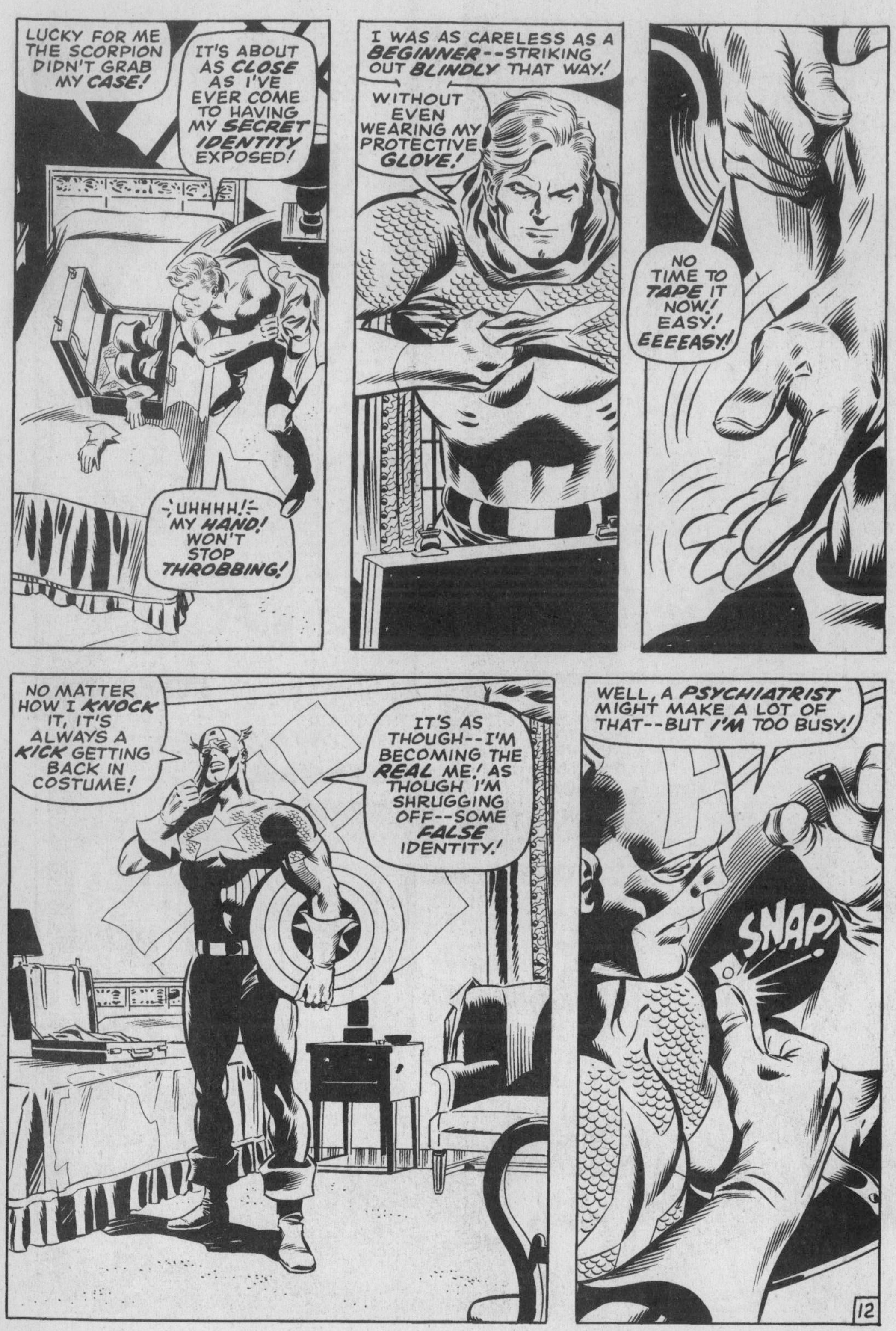
LUCKY FOR ME THE SCORPION DIDN'T GRAB MY CASE!
IT'S ABOUT AS CLOSE AS I'VE EVER COME TO HAVING MY SECRET IDENTITY EXPOSED!
UHHHH! MY HAND! WON'T STOP THROBBING!
I WAS AS CARELESS AS A BEGINNER--STRIKING OUT BLINDLY THAT WAY!
WITHOUT EVEN WEARING MY PROTECTIVE GLOVE!
NO TIME TO TAPE IT NOW! EASY! EEEEASY!
NO MATTER HOW I KNOCK IT, IT'S ALWAYS A KICK GETTING BACK IN COSTUME!
IT'S AS THOUGH--I'M BECOMING THE REAL ME! AS THOUGH I'M SHRUGGING OFF--SOME FALSE IDENTITY!
WELL, A PSYCHIATRIST MIGHT MAKE A LOT OF THAT--BUT I'M TOO BUSY!
SNAP!
12

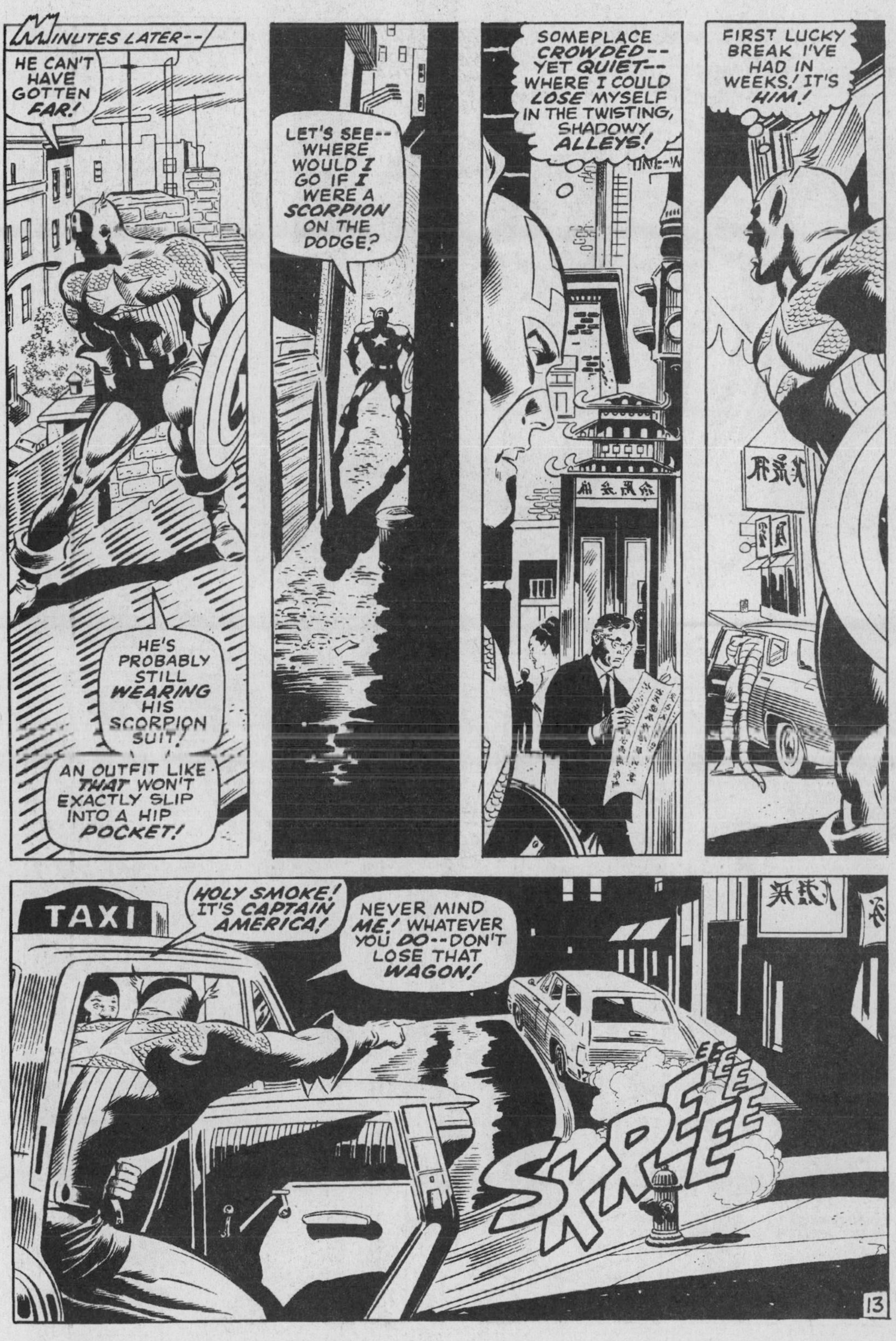
MINUTES LATER--
HE CAN'T HAVE GOTTEN FAR!
HE'S PROBABLY STILL WEARING HIS SCORPION SUIT!
AN OUTFIT LIKE THAT WON'T EXACTLY SLIP INTO A HIP POCKET!
LET'S SEE-- WHERE WOULD I GO IF I WERE A SCORPION ON THE DODGE?
SOMEPLACE CROWDED-- YET QUIET-- WHERE I COULD LOSE MYSELF IN THE TWISTING, SHADOWY ALLEYS!
FIRST LUCKY BREAK I'VE HAD IN WEEKS! IT'S HIM!
TAXI
HOLY SMOKE! IT'S CAPTAIN AMERICA!
NEVER MIND ME! WHATEVER YOU DO--DON'T LOSE THAT WAGON!
SKREEEEE
13

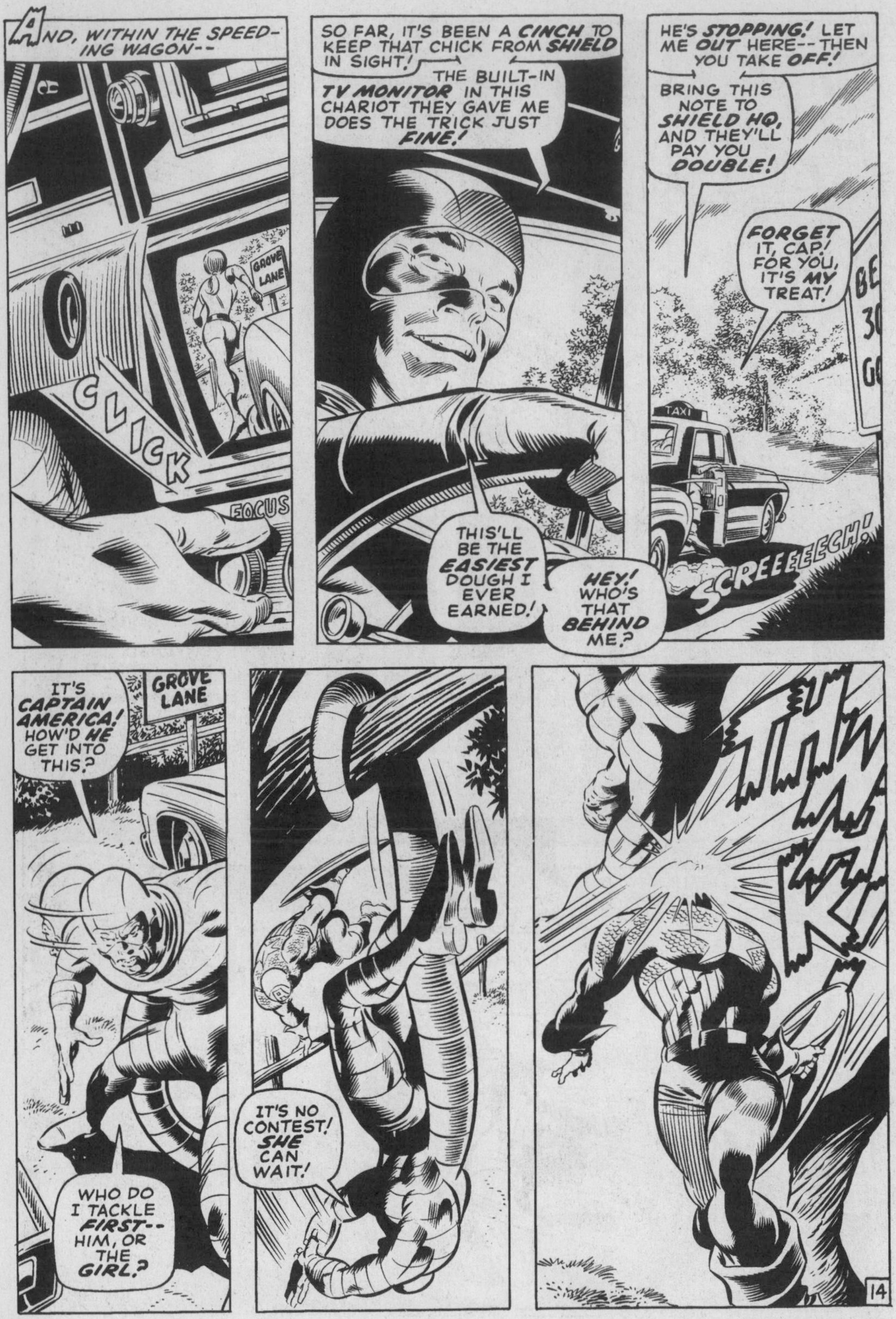
AND, WITHIN THE SPEEDING WAGON--
GROVE LANE
CLICK
FOCUS
SO FAR, IT'S BEEN A CINCH TO KEEP THAT CHICK FROM SHIELD IN SIGHT!
THE BUILT-IN TV MONITOR IN THIS CHARIOT THEY GAVE ME DOES THE TRICK JUST FINE!
THIS'LL BE THE EASIEST DOUGH I EVER EARNED!
HEY! WHO'S THAT BEHIND ME?
HE'S STOPPING! LET ME OUT HERE--THEN YOU TAKE OFF!
BRING THIS NOTE TO SHIELD HQ, AND THEY'LL PAY YOU DOUBLE!
FORGET IT, CAP! FOR YOU, IT'S MY TREAT!
TAXI
SCREEEEEECH!
GROVE LANE
IT'S CAPTAIN AMERICA! HOW'D HE GET INTO THIS?
WHO DO I TACKLE FIRST--HIM, OR THE GIRL?
IT'S NO CONTEST! SHE CAN WAIT!
THWAK!
14

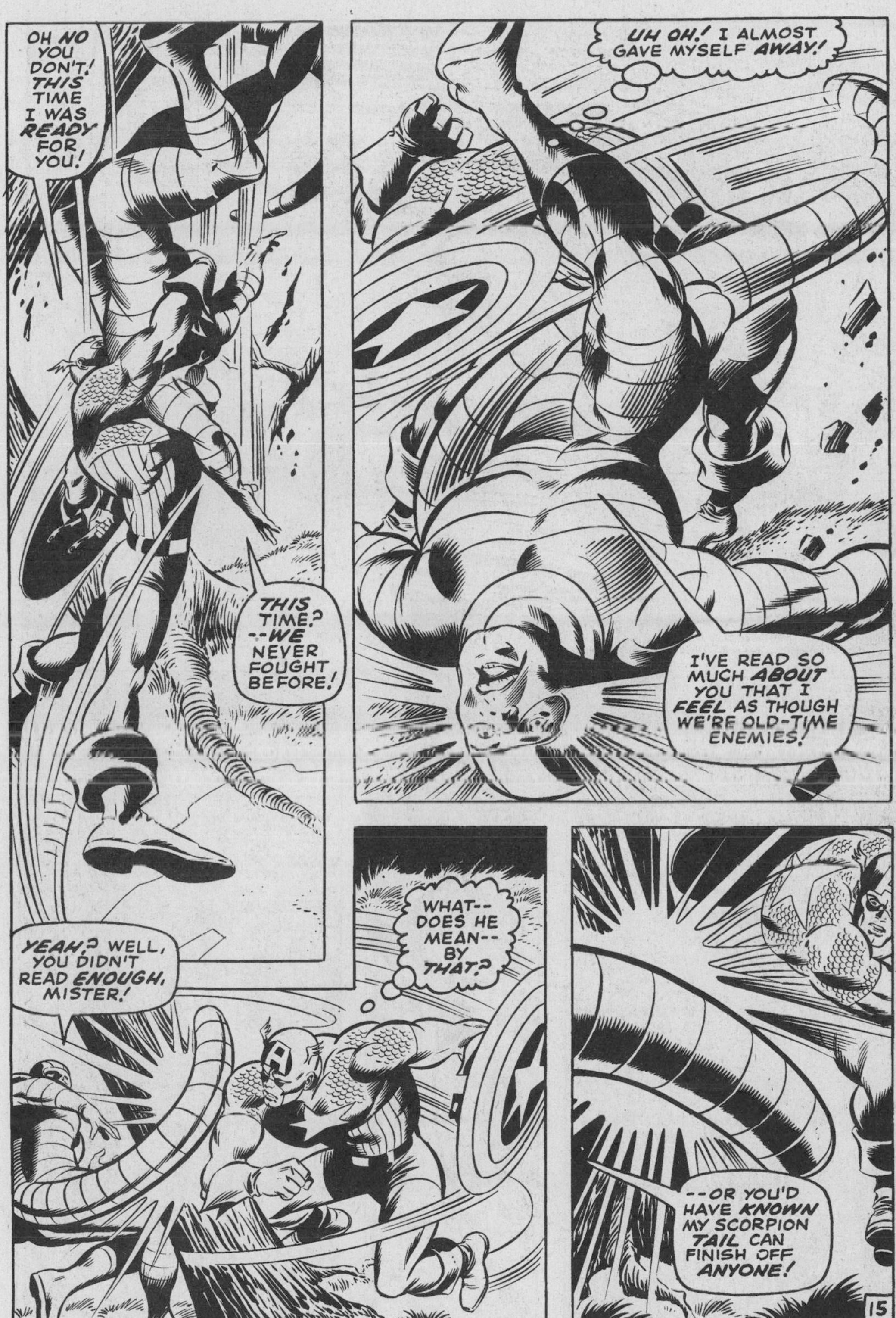

OH NO YOU DON'T! THIS TIME I WAS READY FOR YOU!
THIS TIME? --WE NEVER FOUGHT BEFORE!
UH OH! I ALMOST GAVE MYSELF AWAY!
I'VE READ SO MUCH ABOUT YOU THAT I FEEL AS THOUGH WE'RE OLD-TIME ENEMIES!
YEAH? WELL, YOU DIDN'T READ ENOUGH, MISTER!
WHAT-- DOES HE MEAN-- BY THAT?
--OR YOU'D HAVE KNOWN MY SCORPION TAIL CAN FINISH OFF ANYONE!
15

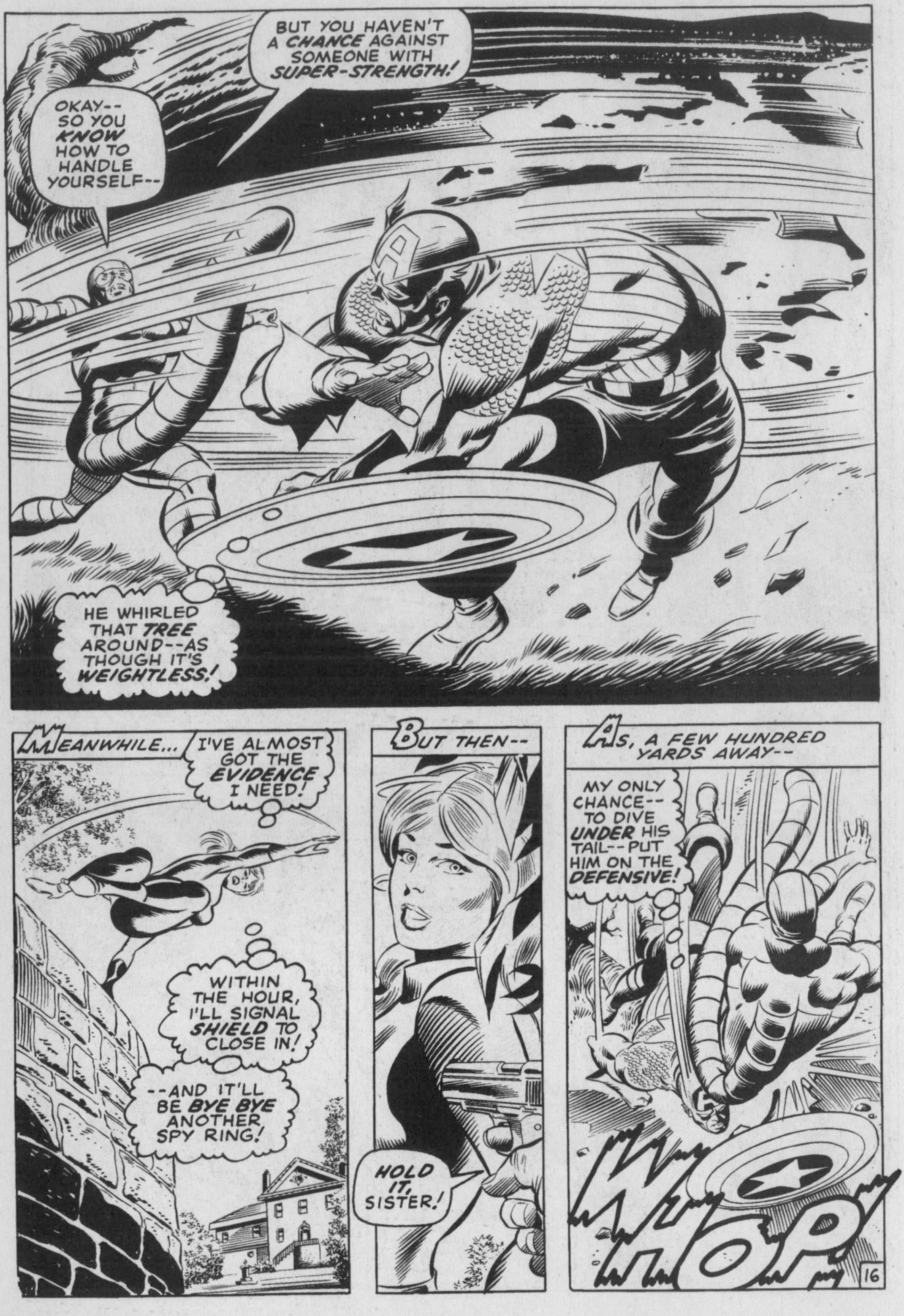

OKAY-- SO YOU KNOW HOW TO HANDLE YOURSELF--
BUT YOU HAVEN'T A CHANCE AGAINST SOMEONE WITH SUPER-STRENGTH!
HE WHIRLED THAT TREE AROUND--AS THOUGH IT'S WEIGHTLESS!
MEANWHILE...
I'VE ALMOST GOT THE EVIDENCE I NEED!
WITHIN THE HOUR, I'LL SIGNAL SHIELD TO CLOSE IN!
--AND IT'LL BE BYE BYE ANOTHER SPY RING!
BUT THEN--
HOLD IT, SISTER!
AS, A FEW HUNDRED YARDS AWAY--
MY ONLY CHANCE-- TO DIVE UNDER HIS TAIL--PUT HIM ON THE DEFENSIVE!
WHOP!
16

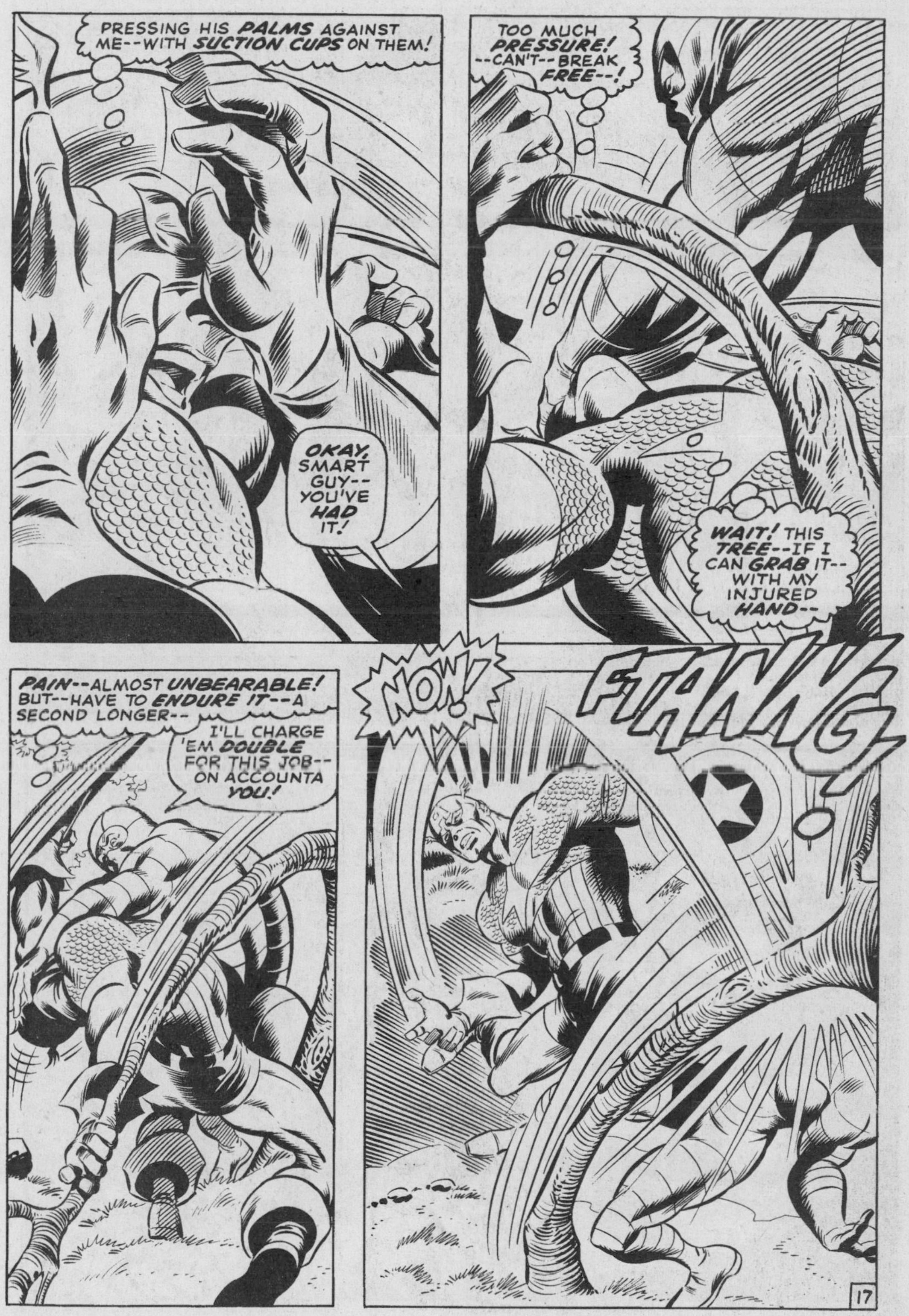
PRESSING HIS PALMS AGAINST ME--WITH SUCTION CUPS ON THEM!
OKAY, SMART GUY--YOU'VE HAD IT!
TOO MUCH PRESSURE! --CAN'T--BREAK FREE--!
WAIT! THIS TREE--IF I CAN GRAB IT--WITH MY INJURED HAND--
PAIN--ALMOST UNBEARABLE! BUT--HAVE TO ENDURE IT--A SECOND LONGER--
I'LL CHARGE 'EM DOUBLE FOR THIS JOB--ON ACCOUNTA YOU!
NOW!
FTANNG!
17

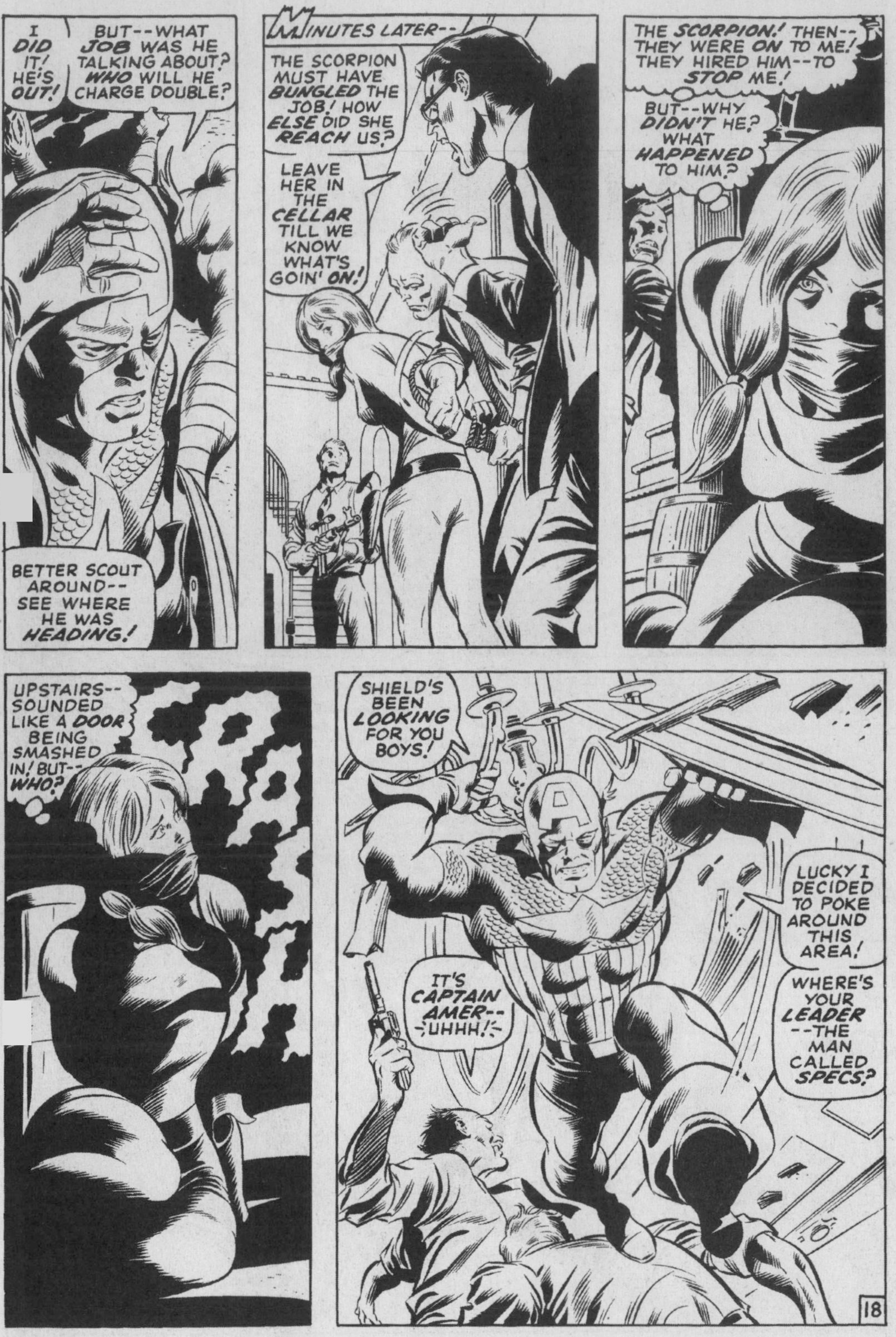
I DID IT! HE'S OUT!
BUT--WHAT JOB WAS HE TALKING ABOUT? WHO WILL HE CHARGE DOUBLE?
BETTER SCOUT AROUND--SEE WHERE HE WAS HEADING!
MINUTES LATER--
THE SCORPION MUST HAVE BUNGLED THE JOB! HOW ELSE DID SHE REACH US?
LEAVE HER IN THE CELLAR TILL WE KNOW WHAT'S GOIN' ON!
THE SCORPION! THEN--THEY WERE ON TO ME! THEY HIRED HIM--TO STOP ME!
BUT--WHY DIDN'T HE? WHAT HAPPENED TO HIM?
UPSTAIRS--SOUNDED LIKE A DOOR BEING SMASHED IN! BUT--WHO?
SHIELD'S BEEN LOOKING FOR YOU BOYS!
IT'S CAPTAIN AMER--UHHH!
LUCKY I DECIDED TO POKE AROUND THIS AREA!
WHERE'S YOUR LEADER--THE MAN CALLED SPECS?
18

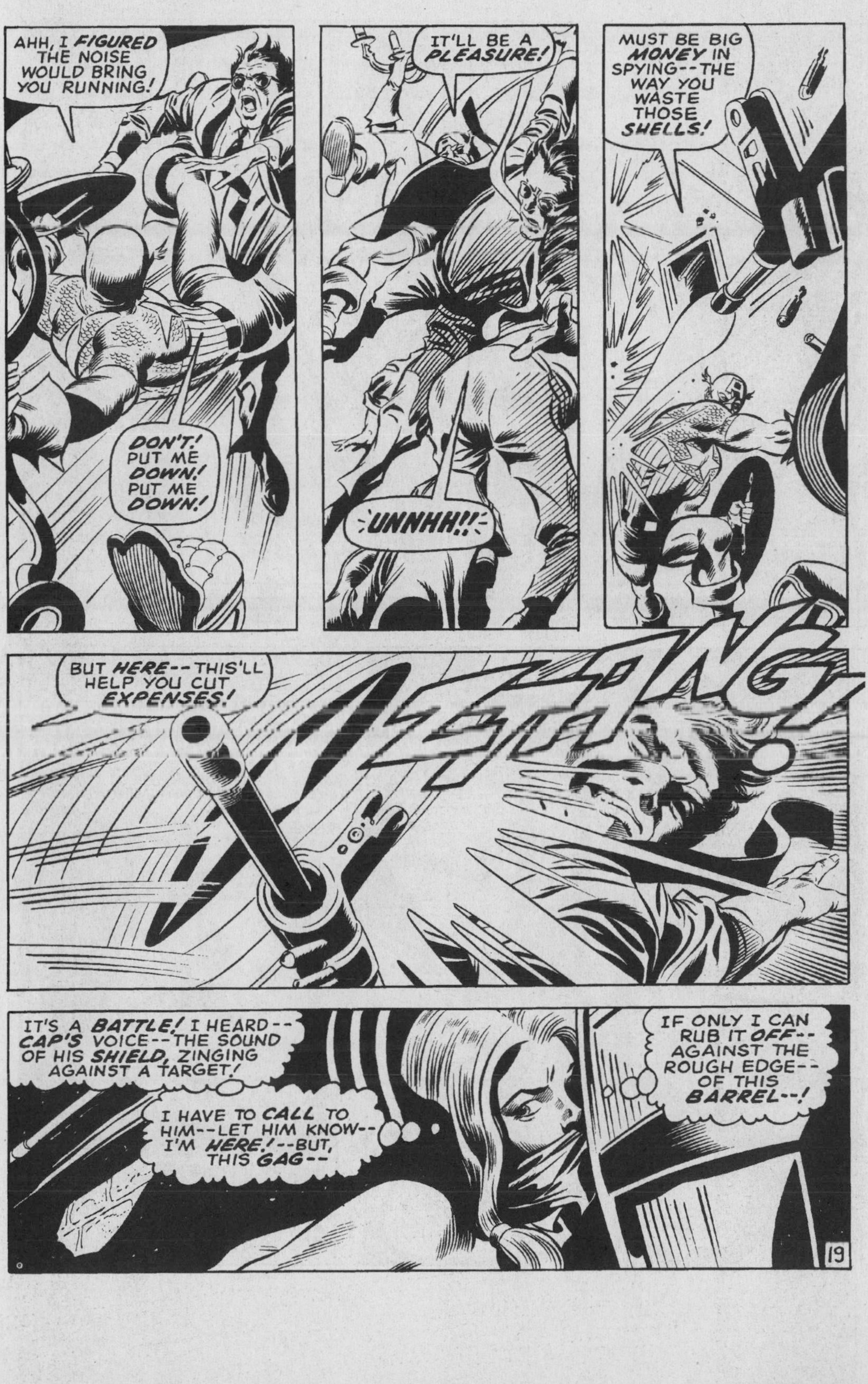
AHH, I FIGURED THE NOISE WOULD BRING YOU RUNNING!
DON'T! PUT ME DOWN! PUT ME DOWN!
IT'LL BE A PLEASURE!
UNNHH!!
MUST BE BIG MONEY IN SPYING--THE WAY YOU WASTE THOSE SHELLS!
BUT HERE--THIS'LL HELP YOU CUT EXPENSES!
SPANG!
IT'S A BATTLE! I HEARD--CAP'S VOICE--THE SOUND OF HIS SHIELD, ZINGING AGAINST A TARGET!
I HAVE TO CALL TO HIM--LET HIM KNOW--I'M HERE!--BUT, THIS GAG--
IF ONLY I CAN RUB IT OFF--AGAINST THE ROUGH EDGE--OF THIS BARREL--!
19

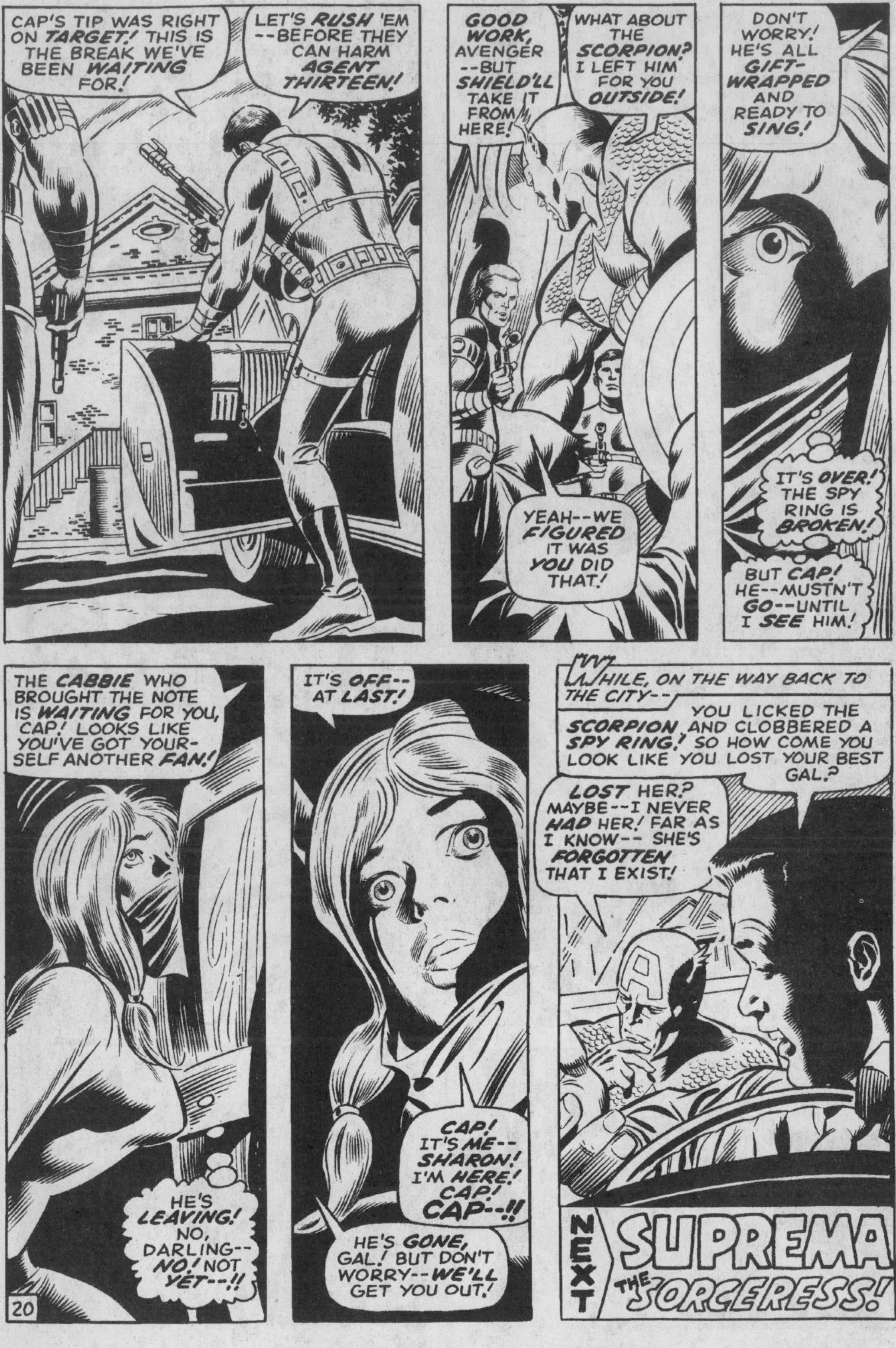

CAP'S TIP WAS RIGHT ON TARGET! THIS IS THE BREAK WE'VE BEEN WAITING FOR!
LET'S RUSH 'EM --BEFORE THEY CAN HARM AGENT THIRTEEN!
GOOD WORK, AVENGER --BUT SHIELD'LL TAKE IT FROM HERE!
WHAT ABOUT THE SCORPION? I LEFT HIM FOR YOU OUTSIDE!
YEAH--WE FIGURED IT WAS YOU DID THAT!
DON'T WORRY! HE'S ALL GIFT-WRAPPED AND READY TO SING!
IT'S OVER! THE SPY RING IS BROKEN!
BUT CAP! HE--MUSTN'T GO--UNTIL I SEE HIM!
THE CABBIE WHO BROUGHT THE NOTE IS WAITING FOR YOU, CAP! LOOKS LIKE YOU'VE GOT YOURSELF ANOTHER FAN!
HE'S LEAVING! NO, DARLING--NO! NOT YET--!!
IT'S OFF-- AT LAST!
CAP! IT'S ME--SHARON! I'M HERE! CAP! CAP--!!
HE'S GONE, GAL! BUT DON'T WORRY--WE'LL GET YOU OUT!
WHILE, ON THE WAY BACK TO THE CITY--
YOU LICKED THE SCORPION, AND CLOBBERED A SPY RING! SO HOW COME YOU LOOK LIKE YOU LOST YOUR BEST GAL?
LOST HER? MAYBE--I NEVER HAD HER! FAR AS I KNOW-- SHE'S FORGOTTEN THAT I EXIST!
NEXT
SUPREMA THE SORCERESS!
20

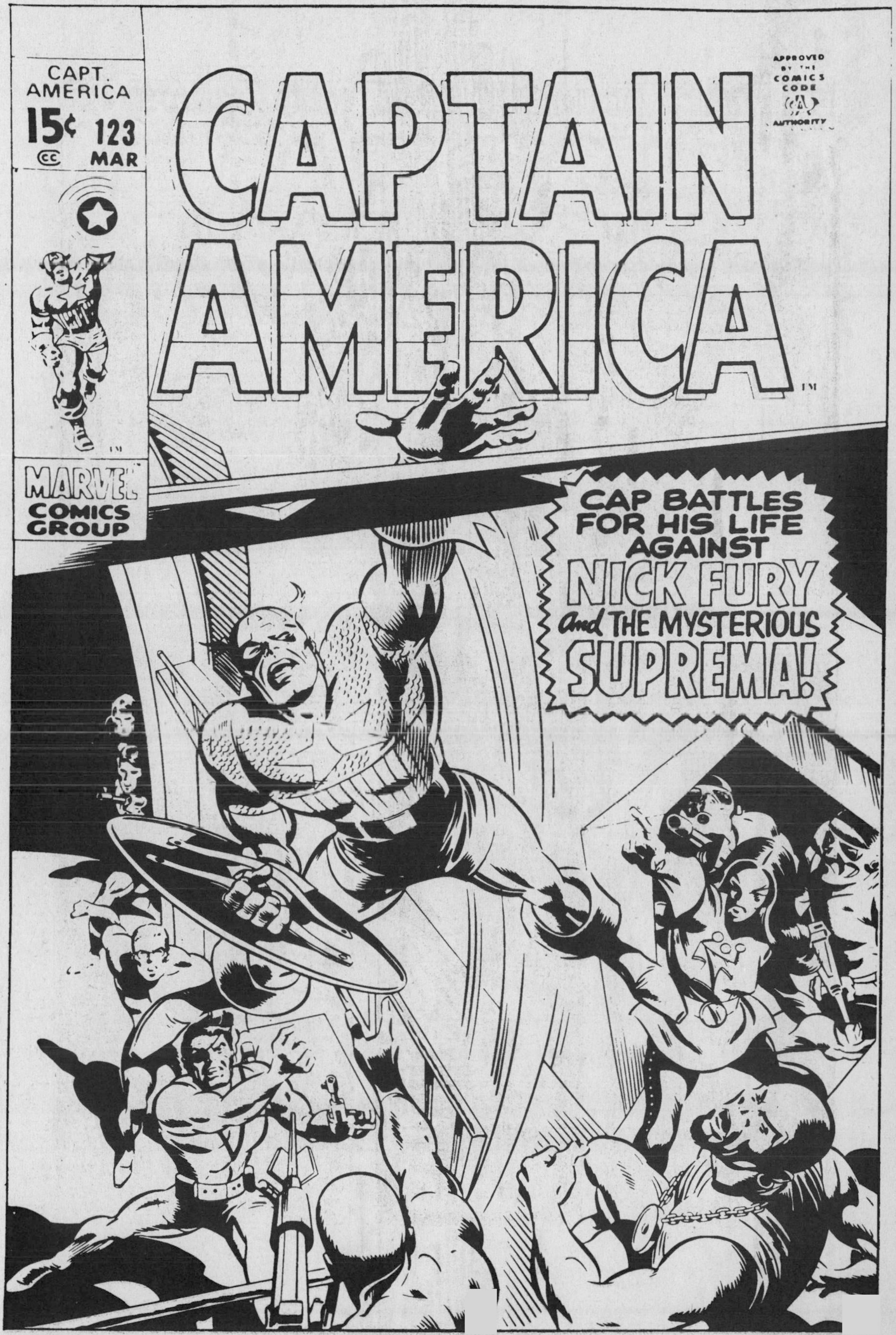
CAPT. AMERICA
15¢ 123 MAR
CC
CAPTAIN AMERICA
APPROVED BY THE COMICS CODE AUTHORITY
MARVEL COMICS GROUP
CAP BATTLES FOR HIS LIFE AGAINST NICK FURY and THE MYSTERIOUS SUPREMA!

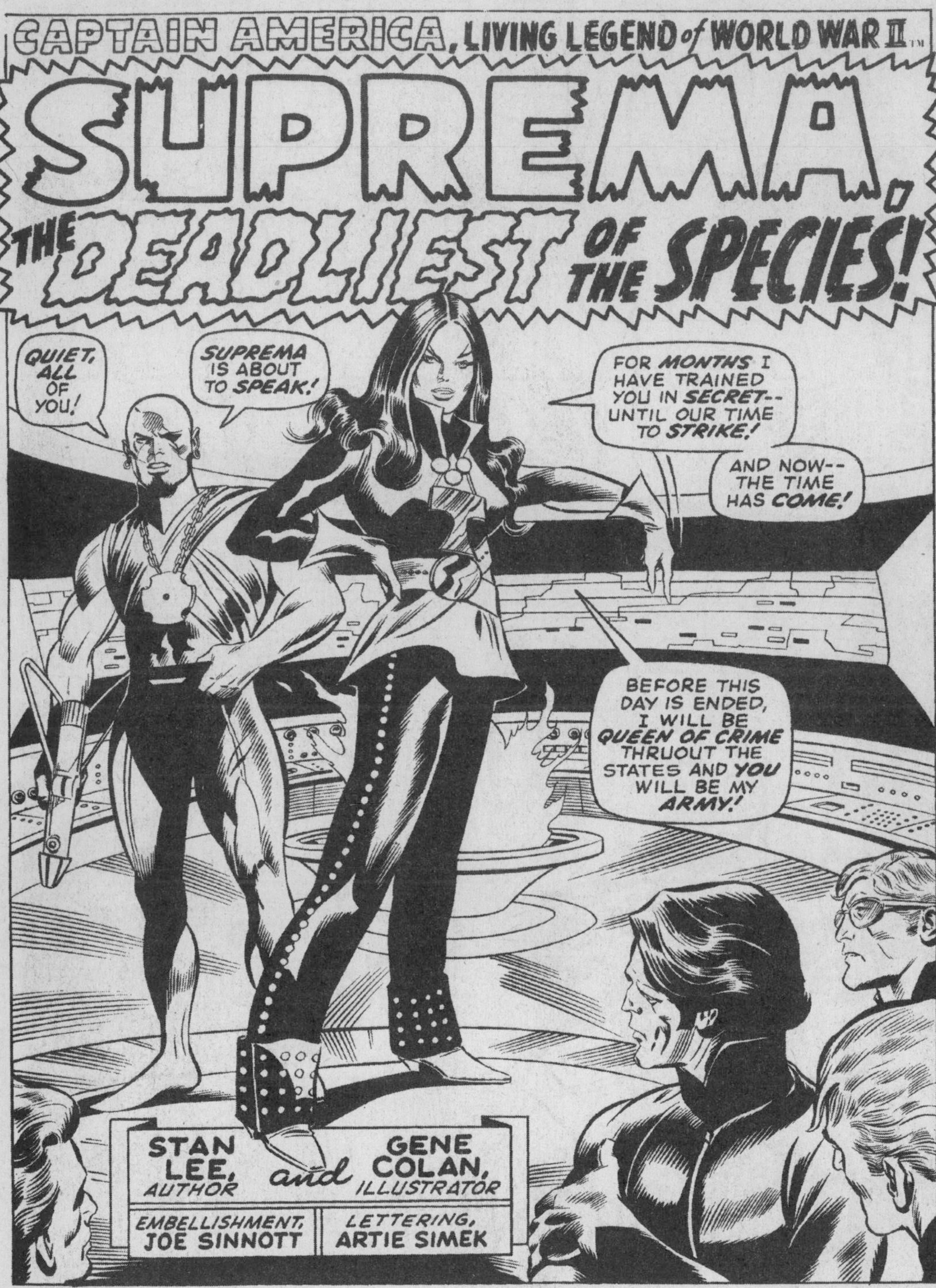
CAPTAIN AMERICA, LIVING LEGEND of WORLD WAR II TM
SUPREMA, THE DEADLIEST OF THE SPECIES!
QUIET, ALL OF YOU!
SUPREMA IS ABOUT TO SPEAK!
FOR MONTHS I HAVE TRAINED YOU IN SECRET-- UNTIL OUR TIME TO STRIKE!
AND NOW-- THE TIME HAS COME!
BEFORE THIS DAY IS ENDED, I WILL BE QUEEN OF CRIME THRUOUT THE STATES AND YOU WILL BE MY ARMY!
STAN LEE, AUTHOR and GENE COLAN, ILLUSTRATOR
EMBELLISHMENT, JOE SINNOTT
LETTERING, ARTIE SIMEK

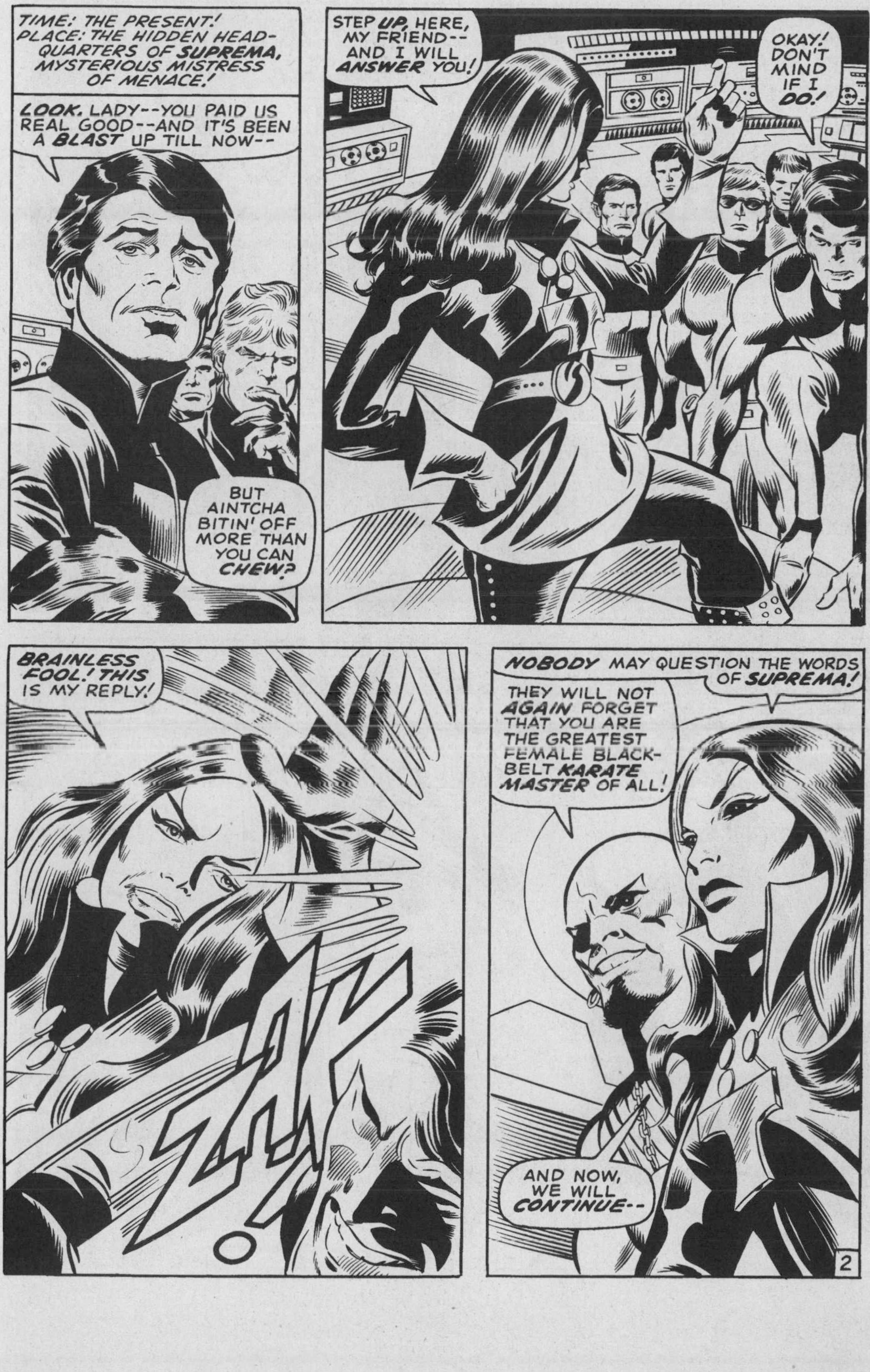
TIME: THE PRESENT! PLACE: THE HIDDEN HEAD-QUARTERS OF SUPREMA, MYSTERIOUS MISTRESS OF MENACE!
LOOK, LADY--YOU PAID US REAL GOOD--AND IT'S BEEN A BLAST UP TILL NOW--
BUT AINTCHA BITIN' OFF MORE THAN YOU CAN CHEW?
STEP UP, HERE, MY FRIEND--AND I WILL ANSWER YOU!
OKAY! DON'T MIND IF I DO!
BRAINLESS FOOL! THIS IS MY REPLY!
NOBODY MAY QUESTION THE WORDS OF SUPREMA!
THEY WILL NOT AGAIN FORGET THAT YOU ARE THE GREATEST FEMALE BLACK-BELT KARATE MASTER OF ALL!
AND NOW, WE WILL CONTINUE--
2

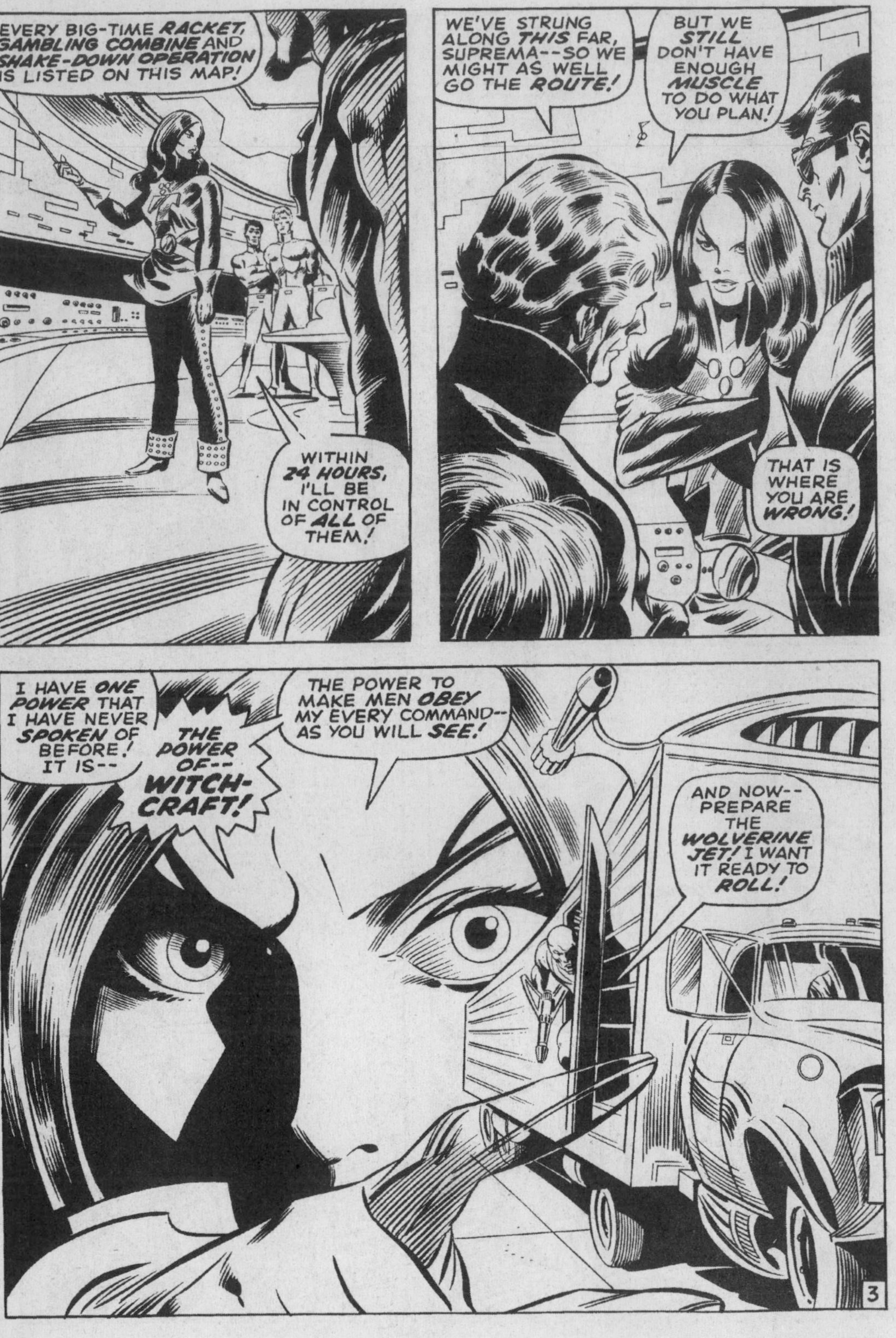
EVERY BIG-TIME RACKET, GAMBLING COMBINE AND SHAKE-DOWN OPERATION IS LISTED ON THIS MAP!
WITHIN 24 HOURS, I'LL BE IN CONTROL OF ALL OF THEM!
WE'VE STRUNG ALONG THIS FAR, SUPREMA--SO WE MIGHT AS WELL GO THE ROUTE!
BUT WE STILL DON'T HAVE ENOUGH MUSCLE TO DO WHAT YOU PLAN!
THAT IS WHERE YOU ARE WRONG!
I HAVE ONE POWER THAT I HAVE NEVER SPOKEN OF BEFORE! IT IS--
THE POWER OF-- WITCH-CRAFT!
THE POWER TO MAKE MEN OBEY MY EVERY COMMAND-- AS YOU WILL SEE!
AND NOW-- PREPARE THE WOLVERINE JET! I WANT IT READY TO ROLL!
3

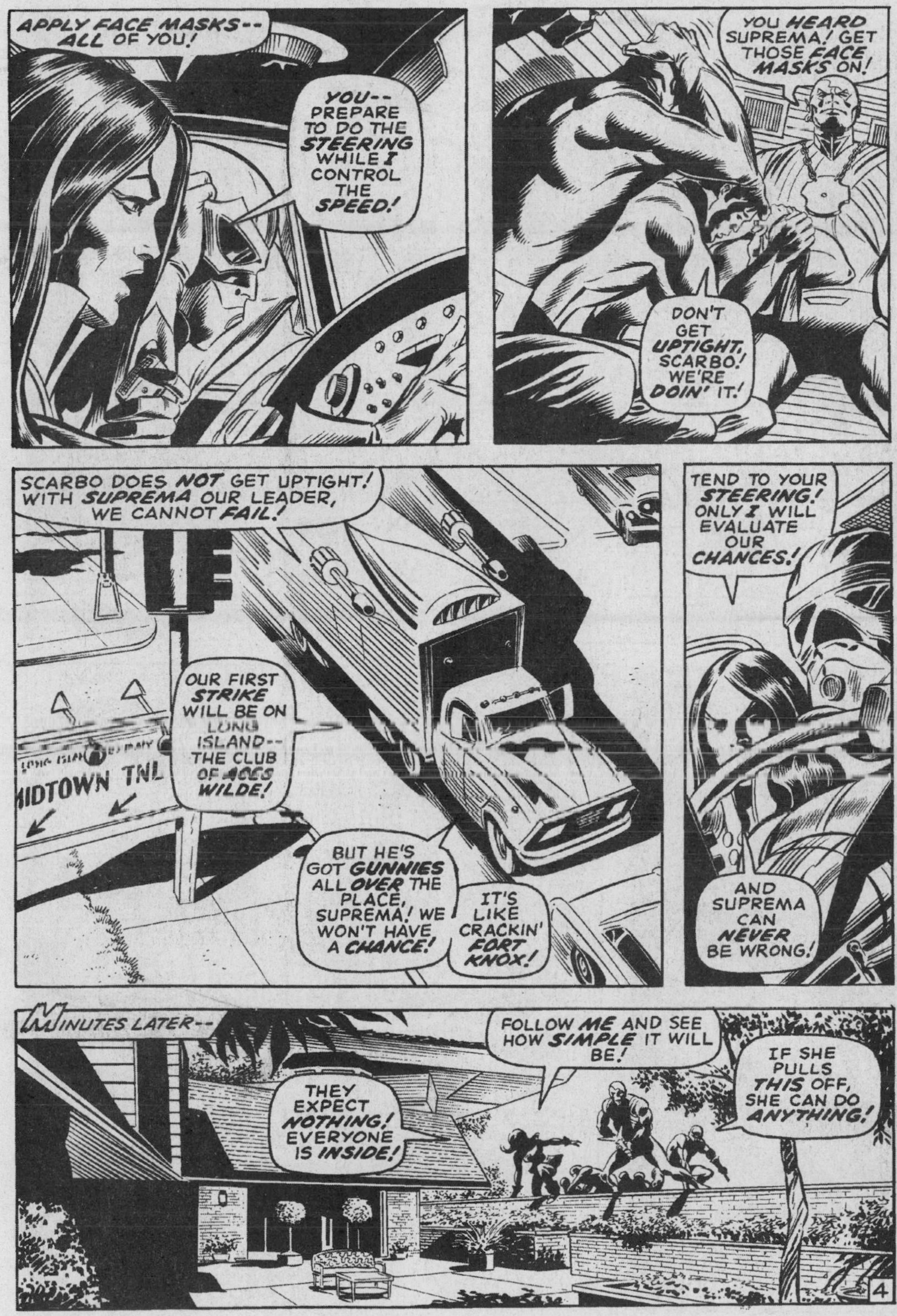
APPLY FACE MASKS-- ALL OF YOU!
YOU-- PREPARE TO DO THE STEERING WHILE I CONTROL THE SPEED!
YOU HEARD SUPREMA! GET THOSE FACE MASKS ON!
DON'T GET UPTIGHT, SCARBO! WE'RE DOIN' IT!
SCARBO DOES NOT GET UPTIGHT! WITH SUPREMA OUR LEADER, WE CANNOT FAIL!
OUR FIRST STRIKE WILL BE ON LONG ISLAND-- THE CLUB OF ACES WILDE!
MIDTOWN TNL
BUT HE'S GOT GUNNIES ALL OVER THE PLACE, SUPREMA! WE WON'T HAVE A CHANCE!
IT'S LIKE CRACKIN' FORT KNOX!
TEND TO YOUR STEERING! ONLY I WILL EVALUATE OUR CHANCES!
AND SUPREMA CAN NEVER BE WRONG!
MINUTES LATER--
FOLLOW ME AND SEE HOW SIMPLE IT WILL BE!
THEY EXPECT NOTHING! EVERYONE IS INSIDE!
IF SHE PULLS THIS OFF, SHE CAN DO ANYTHING!
4

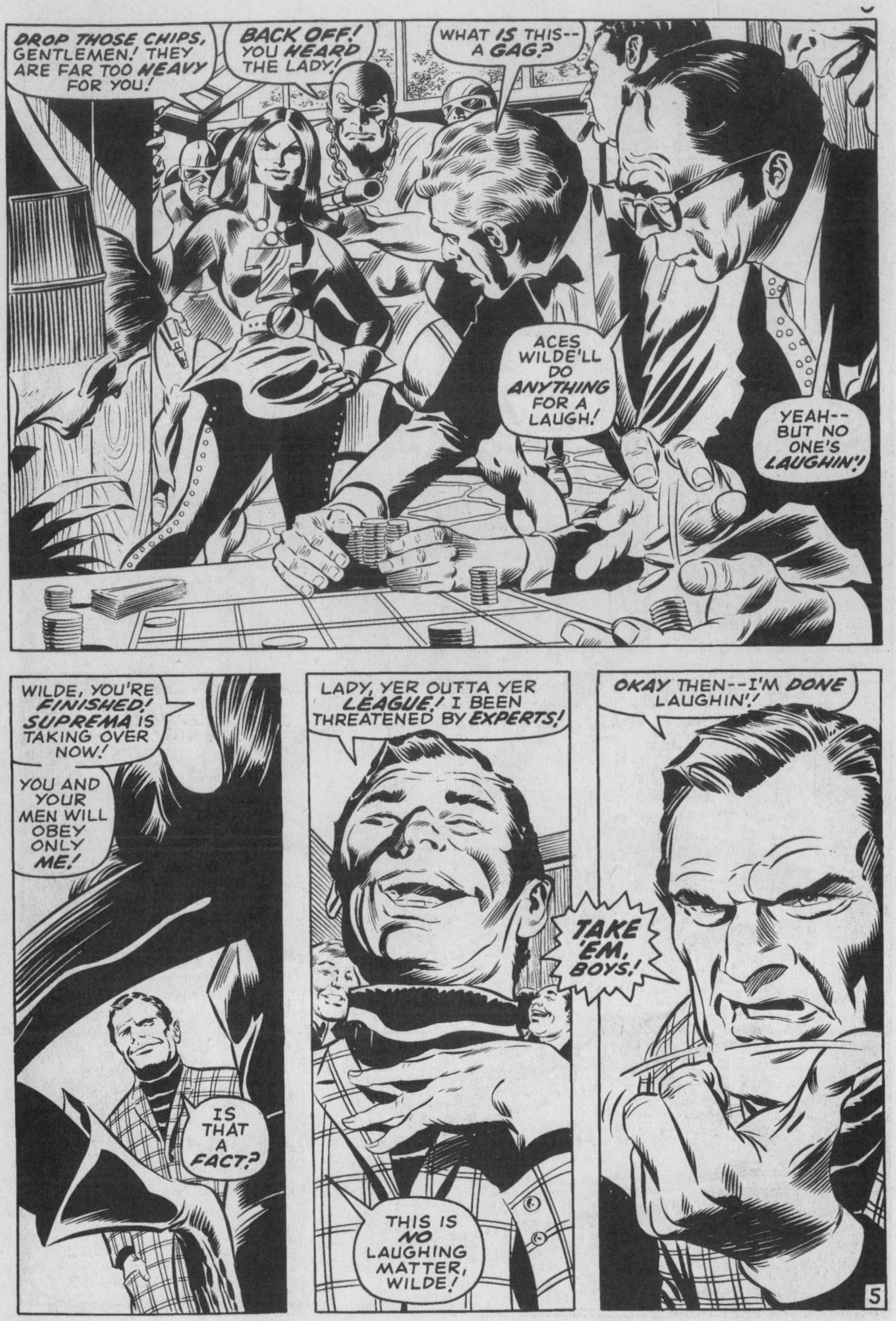
DROP THOSE CHIPS, GENTLEMEN! THEY ARE FAR TOO HEAVY FOR YOU!
BACK OFF! YOU HEARD THE LADY!
WHAT IS THIS--A GAG?
ACES WILDE'LL DO ANYTHING FOR A LAUGH!
YEAH--BUT NO ONE'S LAUGHIN'!
WILDE, YOU'RE FINISHED! SUPREMA IS TAKING OVER NOW!
YOU AND YOUR MEN WILL OBEY ONLY ME!
IS THAT A FACT?
LADY, YER OUTTA YER LEAGUE! I BEEN THREATENED BY EXPERTS!
THIS IS NO LAUGHING MATTER, WILDE!
OKAY THEN--I'M DONE LAUGHIN'!
TAKE 'EM, BOYS!
5

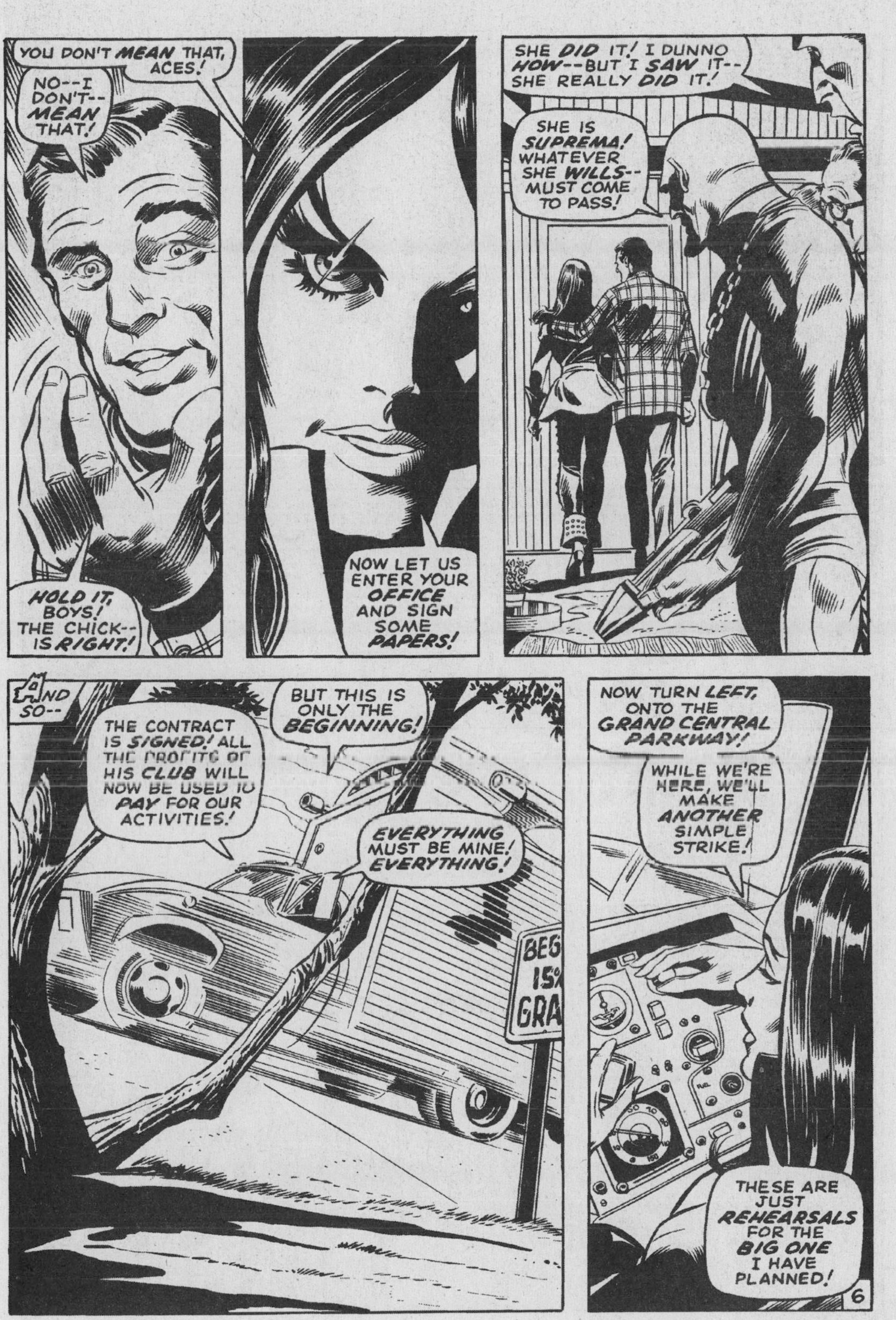
YOU DON'T MEAN THAT, ACES!
NO--I DON'T--MEAN THAT!
HOLD IT, BOYS! THE CHICK--IS RIGHT!
NOW LET US ENTER YOUR OFFICE AND SIGN SOME PAPERS!
SHE DID IT! I DUNNO HOW--BUT I SAW IT--SHE REALLY DID IT!
SHE IS SUPREMA! WHATEVER SHE WILLS--MUST COME TO PASS!
AND SO--
THE CONTRACT IS SIGNED! ALL THE PROFITS OF HIS CLUB WILL NOW BE USED TO PAY FOR OUR ACTIVITIES!
BUT THIS IS ONLY THE BEGINNING!
EVERYTHING MUST BE MINE! EVERYTHING!
BEG
15%
GRA
NOW TURN LEFT, ONTO THE GRAND CENTRAL PARKWAY!
WHILE WE'RE HERE, WE'LL MAKE ANOTHER SIMPLE STRIKE!
THESE ARE JUST REHEARSALS FOR THE BIG ONE I HAVE PLANNED!
6

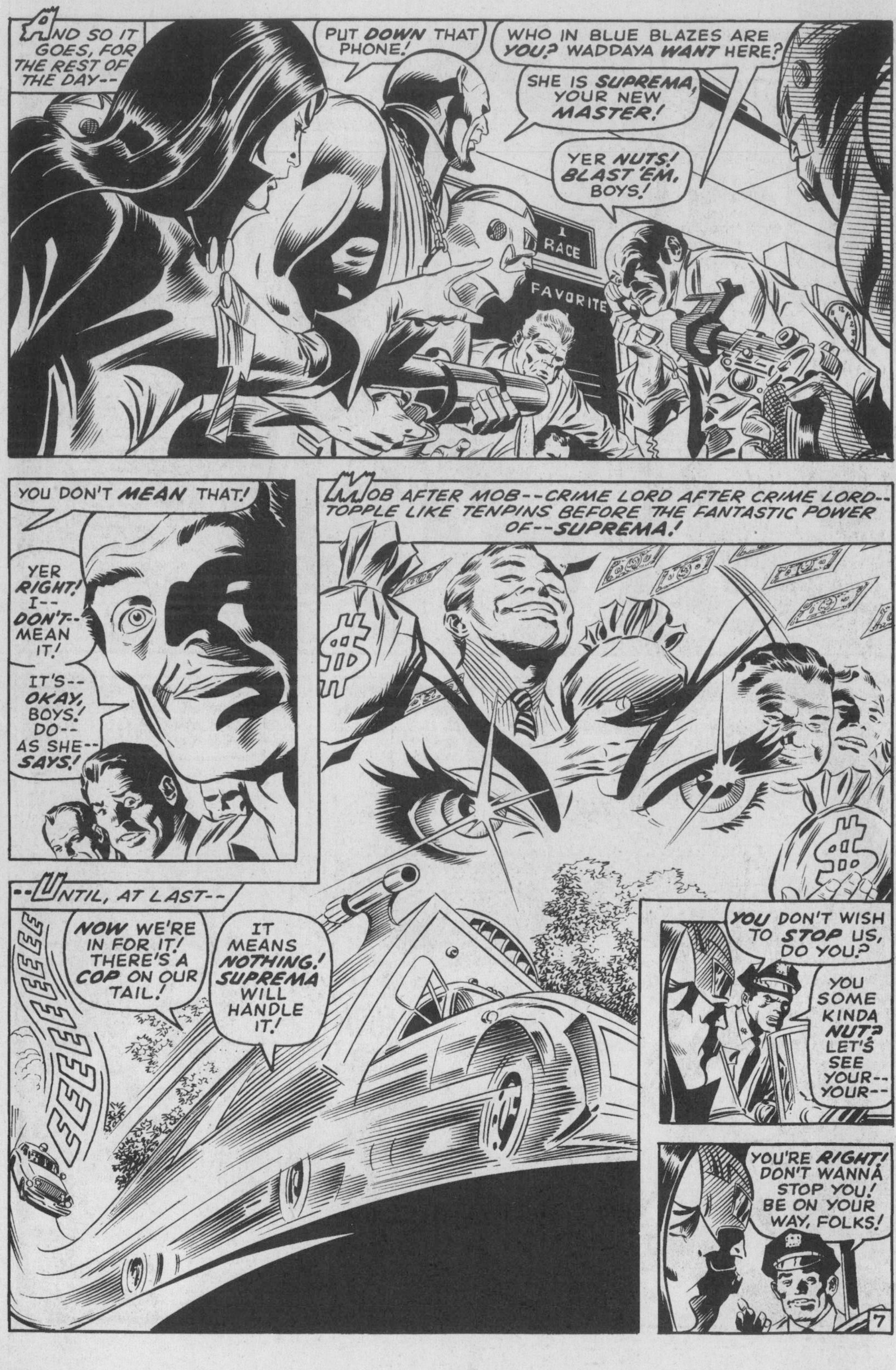

AND SO IT GOES, FOR THE REST OF THE DAY--
PUT DOWN THAT PHONE!
WHO IN BLUE BLAZES ARE YOU? WADDAYA WANT HERE?
SHE IS SUPREMA, YOUR NEW MASTER!
YER NUTS! BLAST 'EM, BOYS!
RACE
FAVORITE
YOU DON'T MEAN THAT!
YER RIGHT! I-- DON'T-- MEAN IT!
IT'S-- OKAY, BOYS! DO-- AS SHE-- SAYS!
MOB AFTER MOB--CRIME LORD AFTER CRIME LORD--TOPPLE LIKE TENPINS BEFORE THE FANTASTIC POWER OF--SUPREMA!
--UNTIL, AT LAST--
EEEEEEEEE
NOW WE'RE IN FOR IT! THERE'S A COP ON OUR TAIL!
IT MEANS NOTHING! SUPREMA WILL HANDLE IT!
YOU DON'T WISH TO STOP US, DO YOU?
YOU SOME KINDA NUT? LET'S SEE YOUR-- YOUR--
YOU'RE RIGHT! DON'T WANNA STOP YOU! BE ON YOUR WAY, FOLKS!

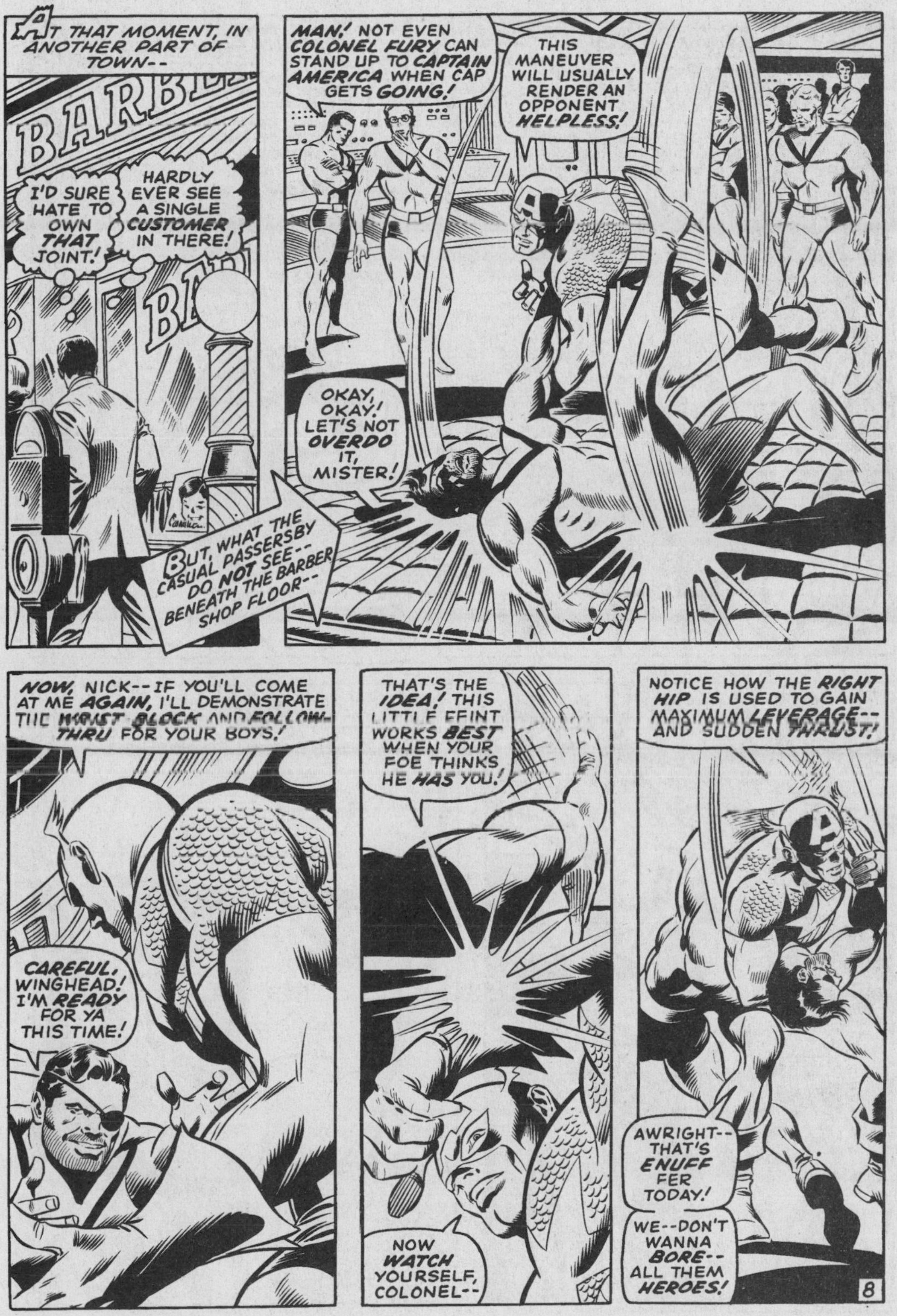
AT THAT MOMENT, IN ANOTHER PART OF TOWN--
BARBE
I'D SURE HATE TO OWN THAT JOINT!
HARDLY EVER SEE A SINGLE CUSTOMER IN THERE!
BUT, WHAT THE CASUAL PASSERSBY DO NOT SEE-- BENEATH THE BARBER SHOP FLOOR--
MAN! NOT EVEN COLONEL FURY CAN STAND UP TO CAPTAIN AMERICA WHEN CAP GETS GOING!
THIS MANEUVER WILL USUALLY RENDER AN OPPONENT HELPLESS!
OKAY, OKAY! LET'S NOT OVERDO IT, MISTER!
NOW, NICK--IF YOU'LL COME AT ME AGAIN, I'LL DEMONSTRATE THE WRIST-BLOCK AND FOLLOW-THRU FOR YOUR BOYS!
CAREFUL, WINGHEAD! I'M READY FOR YA THIS TIME!
THAT'S THE IDEA! THIS LITTLE FEINT WORKS BEST WHEN YOUR FOE THINKS HE HAS YOU!
NOW WATCH YOURSELF, COLONEL--
NOTICE HOW THE RIGHT HIP IS USED TO GAIN MAXIMUM LEVERAGE-- AND SUDDEN THRUST!
AWRIGHT-- THAT'S ENUFF FER TODAY!
WE--DON'T WANNA BORE-- ALL THEM HEROES!
8

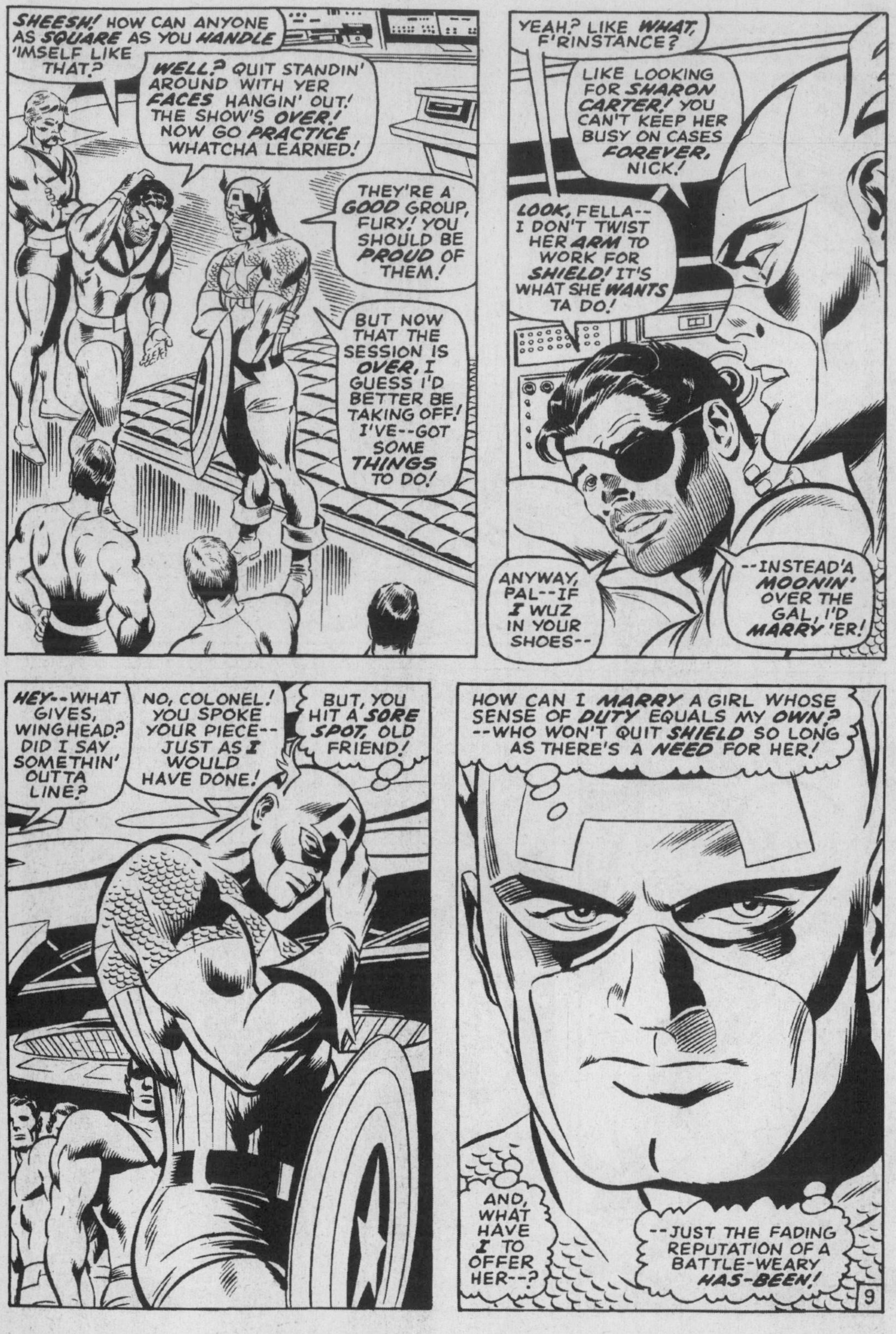

SHEESH! HOW CAN ANYONE AS SQUARE AS YOU HANDLE 'IMSELF LIKE THAT?
WELL? QUIT STANDIN' AROUND WITH YER FACES HANGIN' OUT! THE SHOW'S OVER! NOW GO PRACTICE WHATCHA LEARNED!
THEY'RE A GOOD GROUP, FURY! YOU SHOULD BE PROUD OF THEM!
BUT NOW THAT THE SESSION IS OVER, I GUESS I'D BETTER BE TAKING OFF! I'VE--GOT SOME THINGS TO DO!
YEAH? LIKE WHAT, F'RINSTANCE?
LIKE LOOKING FOR SHARON CARTER! YOU CAN'T KEEP HER BUSY ON CASES FOREVER, NICK!
LOOK, FELLA-- I DON'T TWIST HER ARM TO WORK FOR SHIELD! IT'S WHAT SHE WANTS TA DO!
ANYWAY, PAL--IF I WUZ IN YOUR SHOES--
--INSTEAD'A MOONIN' OVER THE GAL, I'D MARRY 'ER!
HEY--WHAT GIVES, WINGHEAD? DID I SAY SOMETHIN' OUTTA LINE?
NO, COLONEL! YOU SPOKE YOUR PIECE-- JUST AS I WOULD HAVE DONE!
BUT, YOU HIT A SORE SPOT, OLD FRIEND!
HOW CAN I MARRY A GIRL WHOSE SENSE OF DUTY EQUALS MY OWN? --WHO WON'T QUIT SHIELD SO LONG AS THERE'S A NEED FOR HER!
AND, WHAT HAVE I TO OFFER HER--?
--JUST THE FADING REPUTATION OF A BATTLE-WEARY HAS-BEEN!

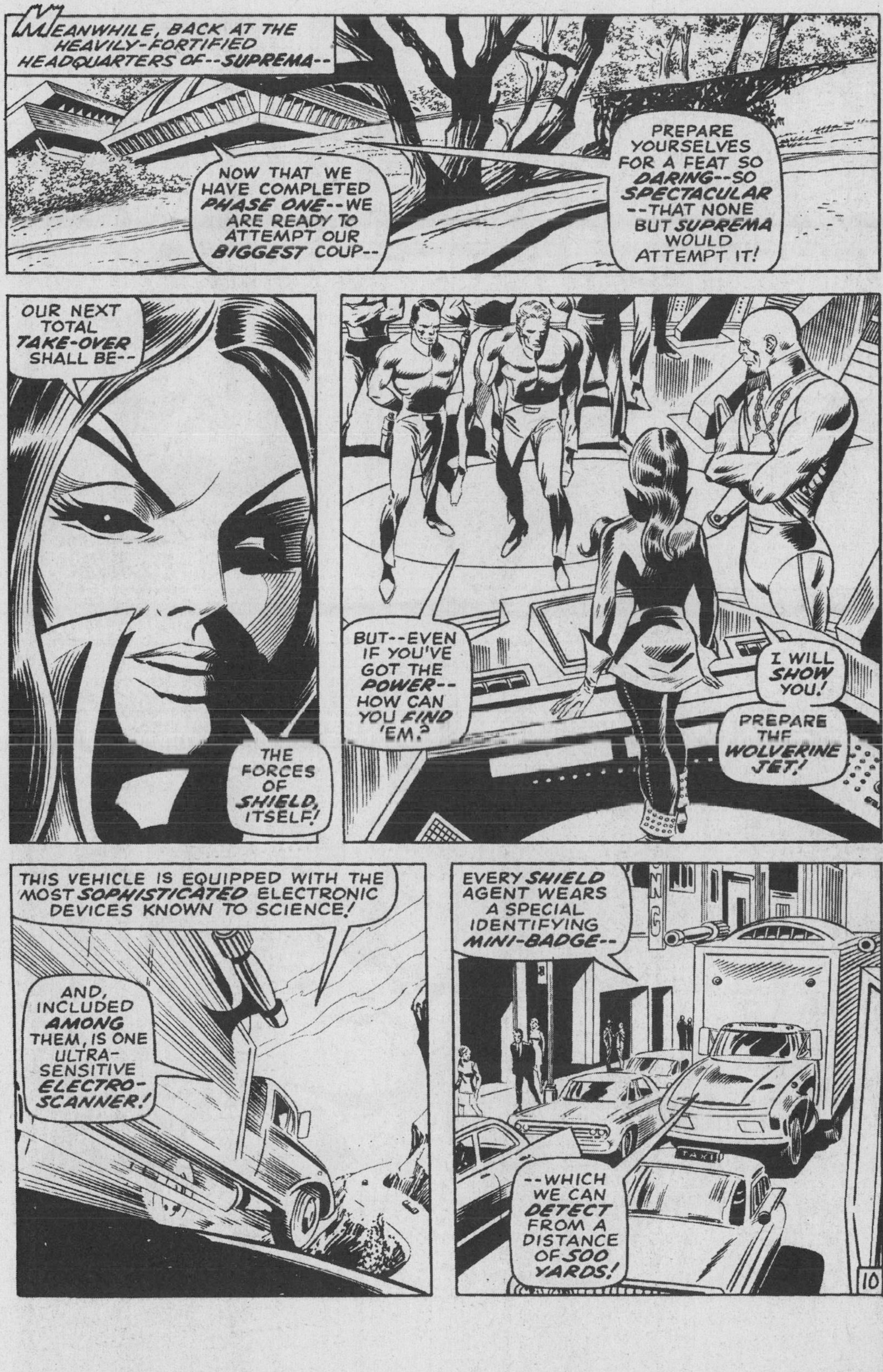
MEANWHILE, BACK AT THE HEAVILY-FORTIFIED HEADQUARTERS OF--SUPREMA--
NOW THAT WE HAVE COMPLETED PHASE ONE--WE ARE READY TO ATTEMPT OUR BIGGEST COUP--
PREPARE YOURSELVES FOR A FEAT SO DARING--SO SPECTACULAR--THAT NONE BUT SUPREMA WOULD ATTEMPT IT!
OUR NEXT TOTAL TAKE-OVER SHALL BE--
THE FORCES OF SHIELD, ITSELF!
BUT--EVEN IF YOU'VE GOT THE POWER--HOW CAN YOU FIND 'EM?
I WILL SHOW YOU!
PREPARE THE WOLVERINE JET!
THIS VEHICLE IS EQUIPPED WITH THE MOST SOPHISTICATED ELECTRONIC DEVICES KNOWN TO SCIENCE!
AND, INCLUDED AMONG THEM, IS ONE ULTRA-SENSITIVE ELECTRO-SCANNER!
EVERY SHIELD AGENT WEARS A SPECIAL IDENTIFYING MINI-BADGE--
TAXI
--WHICH WE CAN DETECT FROM A DISTANCE OF 500 YARDS!
10

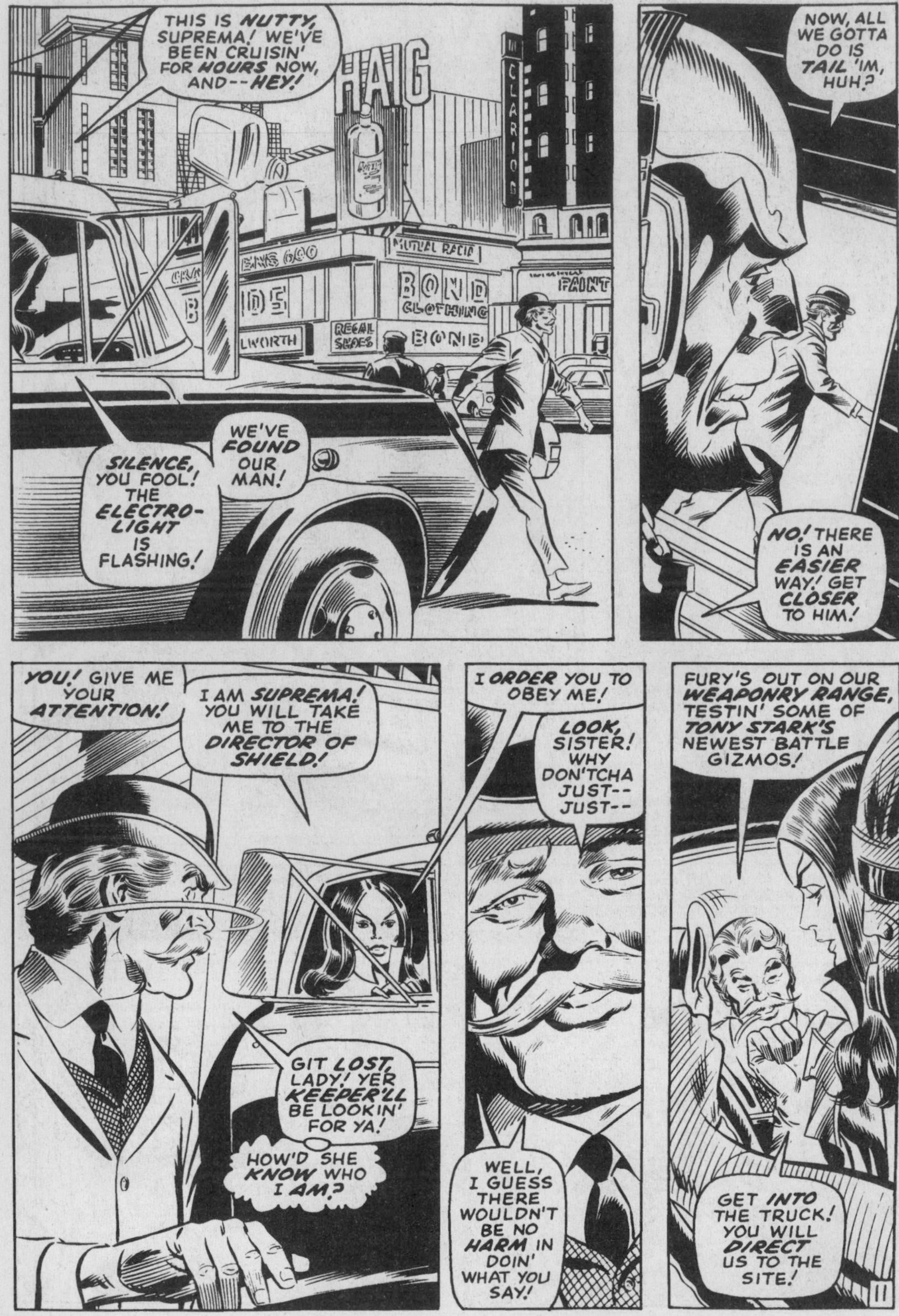
THIS IS NUTTY, SUPREMA! WE'VE BEEN CRUISIN' FOR HOURS NOW, AND--HEY!
HAIG
BOND CLOTHING
SILENCE, YOU FOOL! THE ELECTRO-LIGHT IS FLASHING!
WE'VE FOUND OUR MAN!
NOW, ALL WE GOTTA DO IS TAIL 'IM, HUH?
NO! THERE IS AN EASIER WAY! GET CLOSER TO HIM!
YOU! GIVE ME YOUR ATTENTION!
I AM SUPREMA! YOU WILL TAKE ME TO THE DIRECTOR OF SHIELD!
GIT LOST, LADY! YER KEEPER'LL BE LOOKIN' FOR YA!
HOW'D SHE KNOW WHO I AM?
I ORDER YOU TO OBEY ME!
LOOK, SISTER! WHY DON'TCHA JUST-- JUST--
WELL, I GUESS THERE WOULDN'T BE NO HARM IN DOIN' WHAT YOU SAY!
FURY'S OUT ON OUR WEAPONRY RANGE, TESTIN' SOME OF TONY STARK'S NEWEST BATTLE GIZMOS!
GET INTO THE TRUCK! YOU WILL DIRECT US TO THE SITE!
11

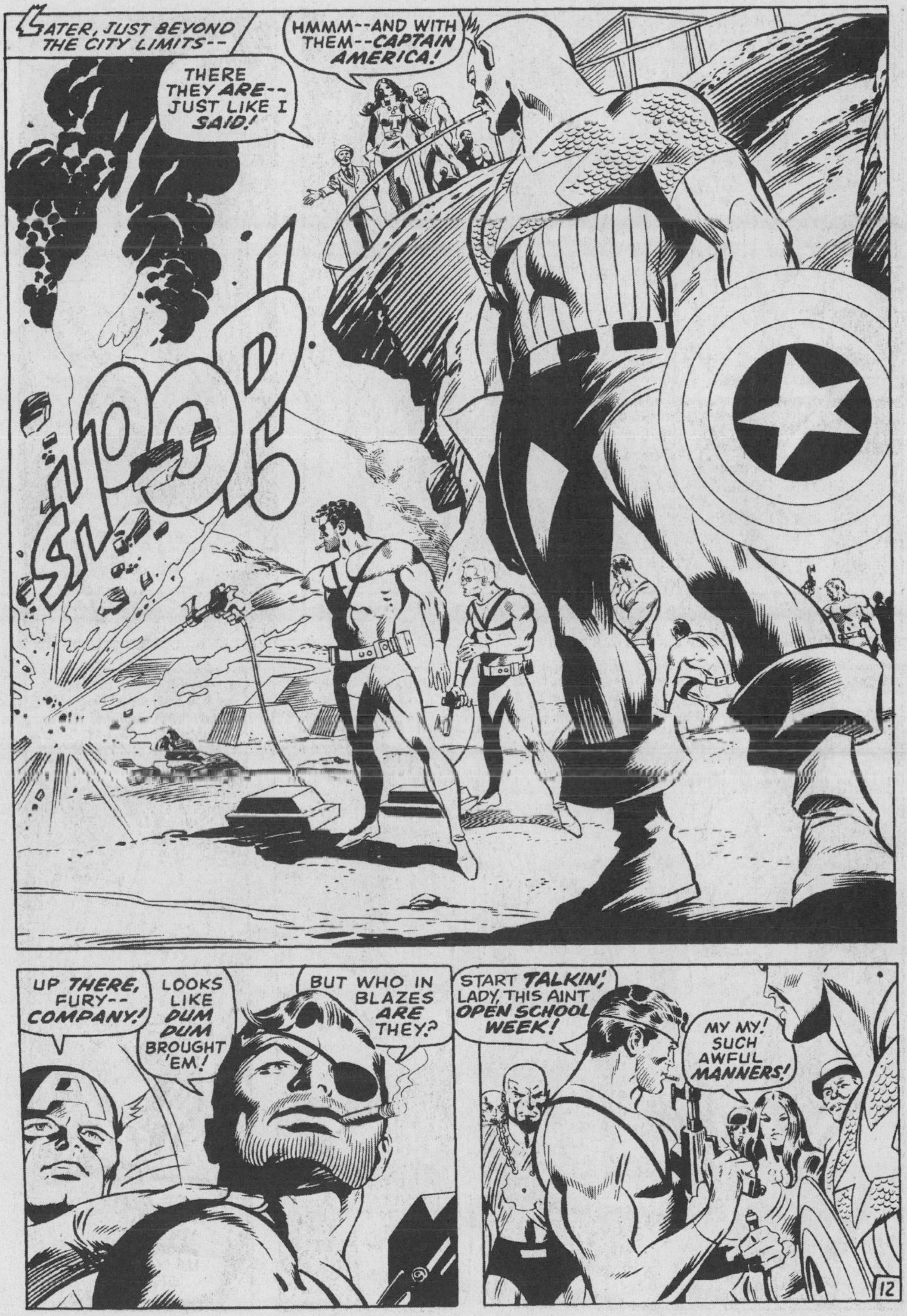
LATER, JUST BEYOND THE CITY LIMITS--
HMMM--AND WITH THEM--CAPTAIN AMERICA!
THERE THEY ARE--JUST LIKE I SAID!
SHOOP!
UP THERE, FURY--COMPANY!
LOOKS LIKE DUM DUM BROUGHT 'EM!
BUT WHO IN BLAZES ARE THEY?
START TALKIN', LADY, THIS AINT OPEN SCHOOL WEEK!
MY MY! SUCH AWFUL MANNERS!
12

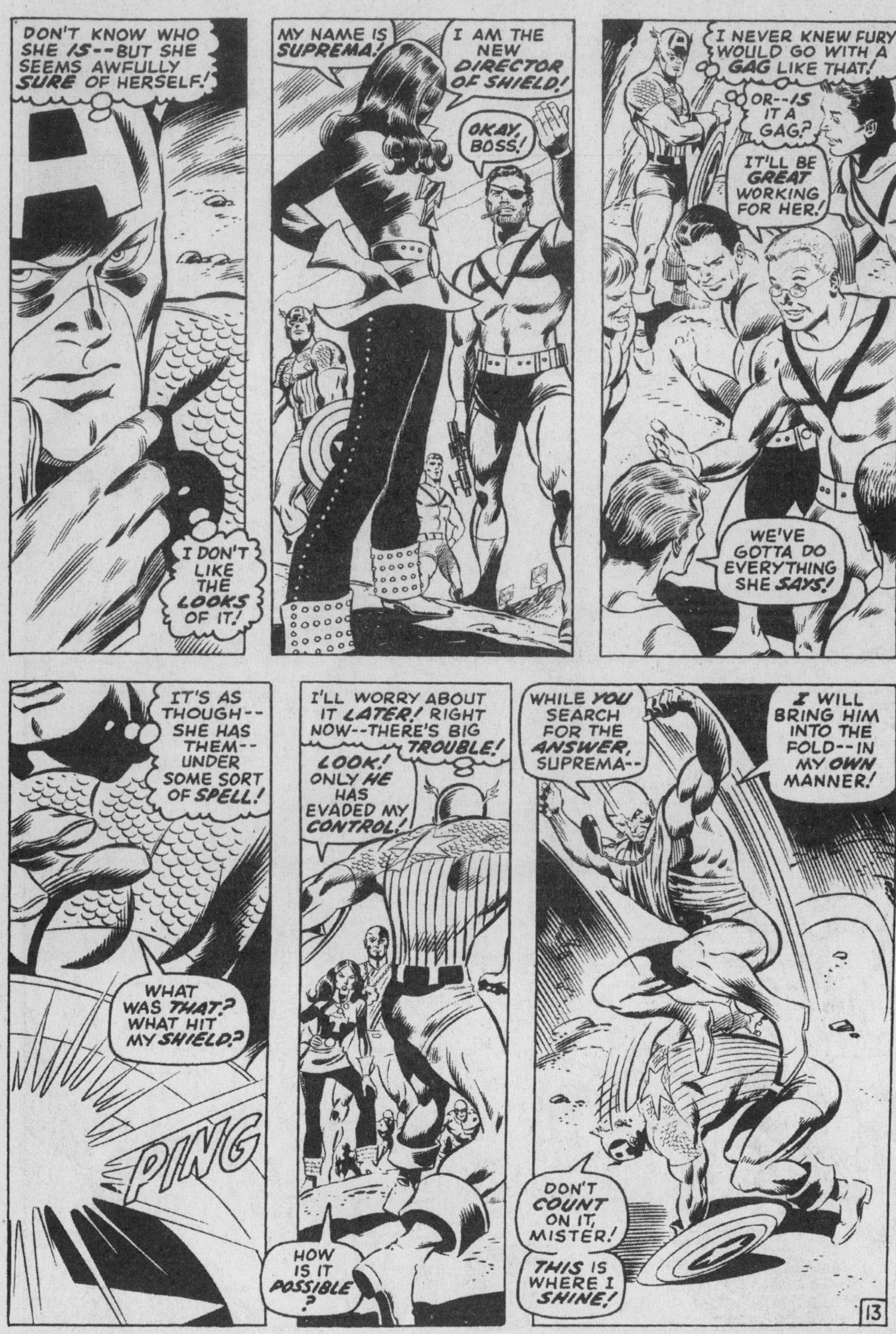
DON'T KNOW WHO SHE IS--BUT SHE SEEMS AWFULLY SURE OF HERSELF!
I DON'T LIKE THE LOOKS OF IT!
MY NAME IS SUPREMA!
I AM THE NEW DIRECTOR OF SHIELD!
OKAY, BOSS!
I NEVER KNEW FURY WOULD GO WITH A GAG LIKE THAT!
OR--IS IT A GAG?
IT'LL BE GREAT WORKING FOR HER!
WE'VE GOTTA DO EVERYTHING SHE SAYS!
IT'S AS THOUGH--SHE HAS THEM--UNDER SOME SORT OF SPELL!
WHAT WAS THAT? WHAT HIT MY SHIELD?
PING
I'LL WORRY ABOUT IT LATER! RIGHT NOW--THERE'S BIG TROUBLE!
LOOK! ONLY HE HAS EVADED MY CONTROL!
HOW IS IT POSSIBLE?
WHILE YOU SEARCH FOR THE ANSWER, SUPREMA--
I WILL BRING HIM INTO THE FOLD--IN MY OWN MANNER!
DON'T COUNT ON IT, MISTER!
THIS IS WHERE I SHINE!
13

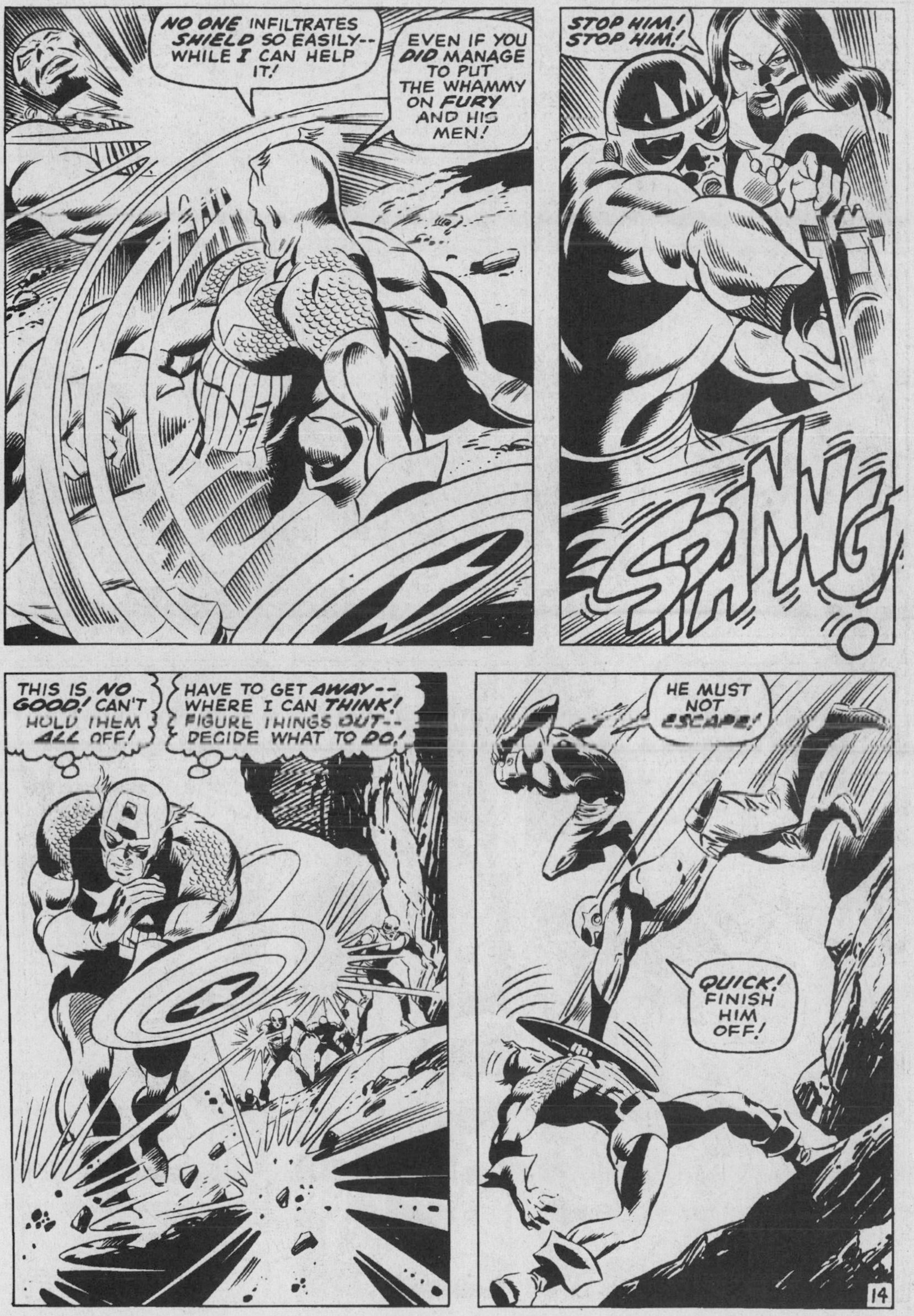

NO ONE INFILTRATES SHIELD SO EASILY-- WHILE I CAN HELP IT!
EVEN IF YOU DID MANAGE TO PUT THE WHAMMY ON FURY AND HIS MEN!
STOP HIM! STOP HIM!
SPANNG!
THIS IS NO GOOD! CAN'T HOLD THEM ALL OFF!
HAVE TO GET AWAY-- WHERE I CAN THINK! FIGURE THINGS OUT-- DECIDE WHAT TO DO!
HE MUST NOT ESCAPE!
QUICK! FINISH HIM OFF!
14

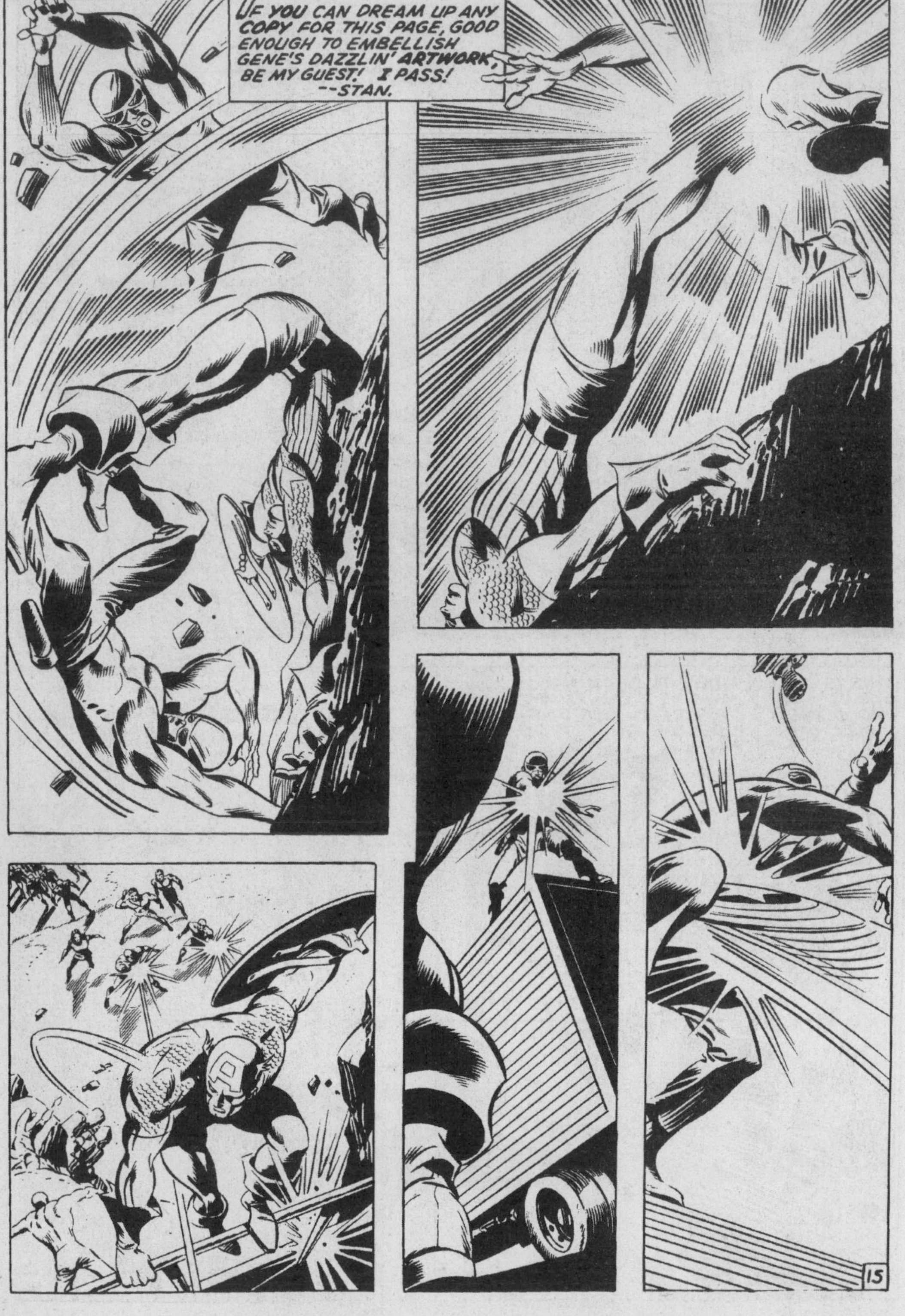
IF YOU CAN DREAM UP ANY COPY FOR THIS PAGE, GOOD ENOUGH TO EMBELLISH GENE'S DAZZLIN' ARTWORK, BE MY GUEST! I PASS! --STAN.
15

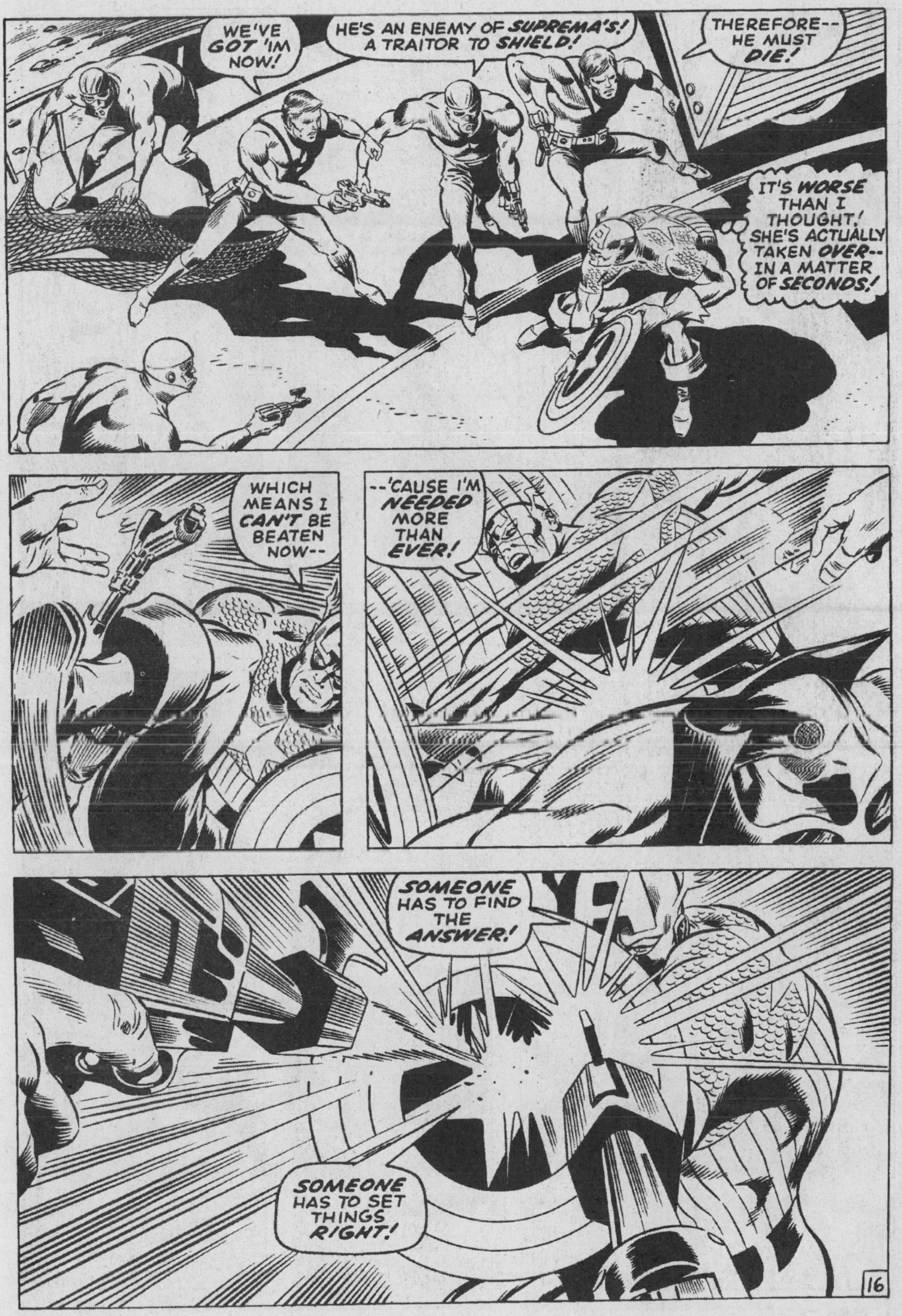
WE'VE GOT 'IM NOW!
HE'S AN ENEMY OF SUPREMA'S! A TRAITOR TO SHIELD!
THEREFORE-- HE MUST DIE!
IT'S WORSE THAN I THOUGHT! SHE'S ACTUALLY TAKEN OVER-- IN A MATTER OF SECONDS!
WHICH MEANS I CAN'T BE BEATEN NOW--
--'CAUSE I'M NEEDED MORE THAN EVER!
SOMEONE HAS TO FIND THE ANSWER!
SOMEONE HAS TO SET THINGS RIGHT!
16

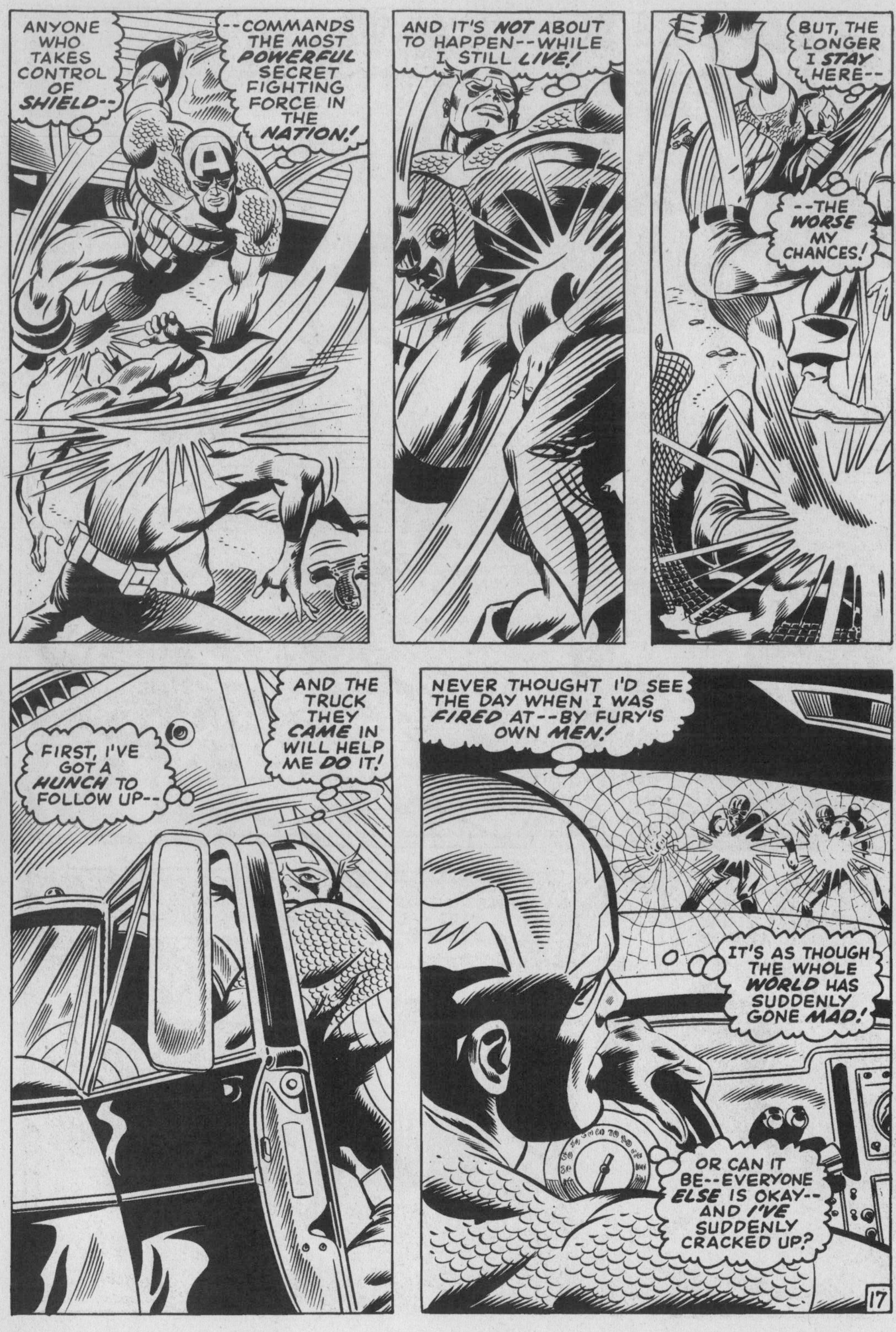
ANYONE WHO TAKES CONTROL OF SHIELD--
--COMMANDS THE MOST POWERFUL SECRET FIGHTING FORCE IN THE NATION!
AND IT'S NOT ABOUT TO HAPPEN--WHILE I STILL LIVE!
BUT, THE LONGER I STAY HERE--
--THE WORSE MY CHANCES!
FIRST, I'VE GOT A HUNCH TO FOLLOW UP--
AND THE TRUCK THEY CAME IN WILL HELP ME DO IT!
NEVER THOUGHT I'D SEE THE DAY WHEN I WAS FIRED AT--BY FURY'S OWN MEN!
IT'S AS THOUGH THE WHOLE WORLD HAS SUDDENLY GONE MAD!
OR CAN IT BE--EVERYONE ELSE IS OKAY--AND I'VE SUDDENLY CRACKED UP?
17

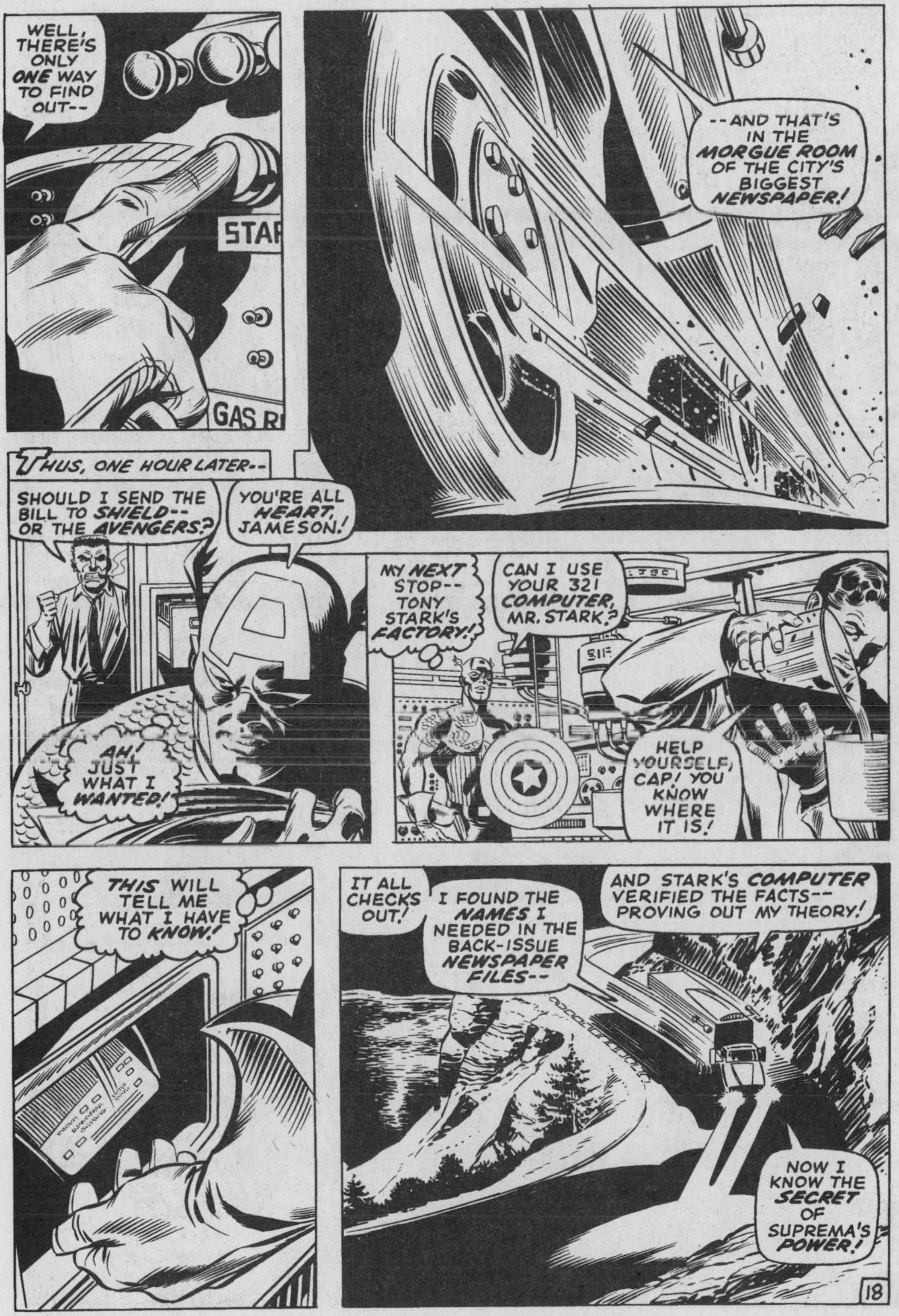
WELL, THERE'S ONLY ONE WAY TO FIND OUT--
STAR
GAS R
--AND THAT'S IN THE MORGUE ROOM OF THE CITY'S BIGGEST NEWSPAPER!
THUS, ONE HOUR LATER--
SHOULD I SEND THE BILL TO SHIELD-- OR THE AVENGERS?
YOU'RE ALL HEART, JAMESON!
AH! JUST WHAT I WANTED!
MY NEXT STOP-- TONY STARK'S FACTORY!
CAN I USE YOUR 321 COMPUTER, MR. STARK?
HELP YOURSELF, CAP! YOU KNOW WHERE IT IS!
THIS WILL TELL ME WHAT I HAVE TO KNOW!
IT ALL CHECKS OUT!
I FOUND THE NAMES I NEEDED IN THE BACK-ISSUE NEWSPAPER FILES--
AND STARK'S COMPUTER VERIFIED THE FACTS-- PROVING OUT MY THEORY!
NOW I KNOW THE SECRET OF SUPREMA'S POWER!
18

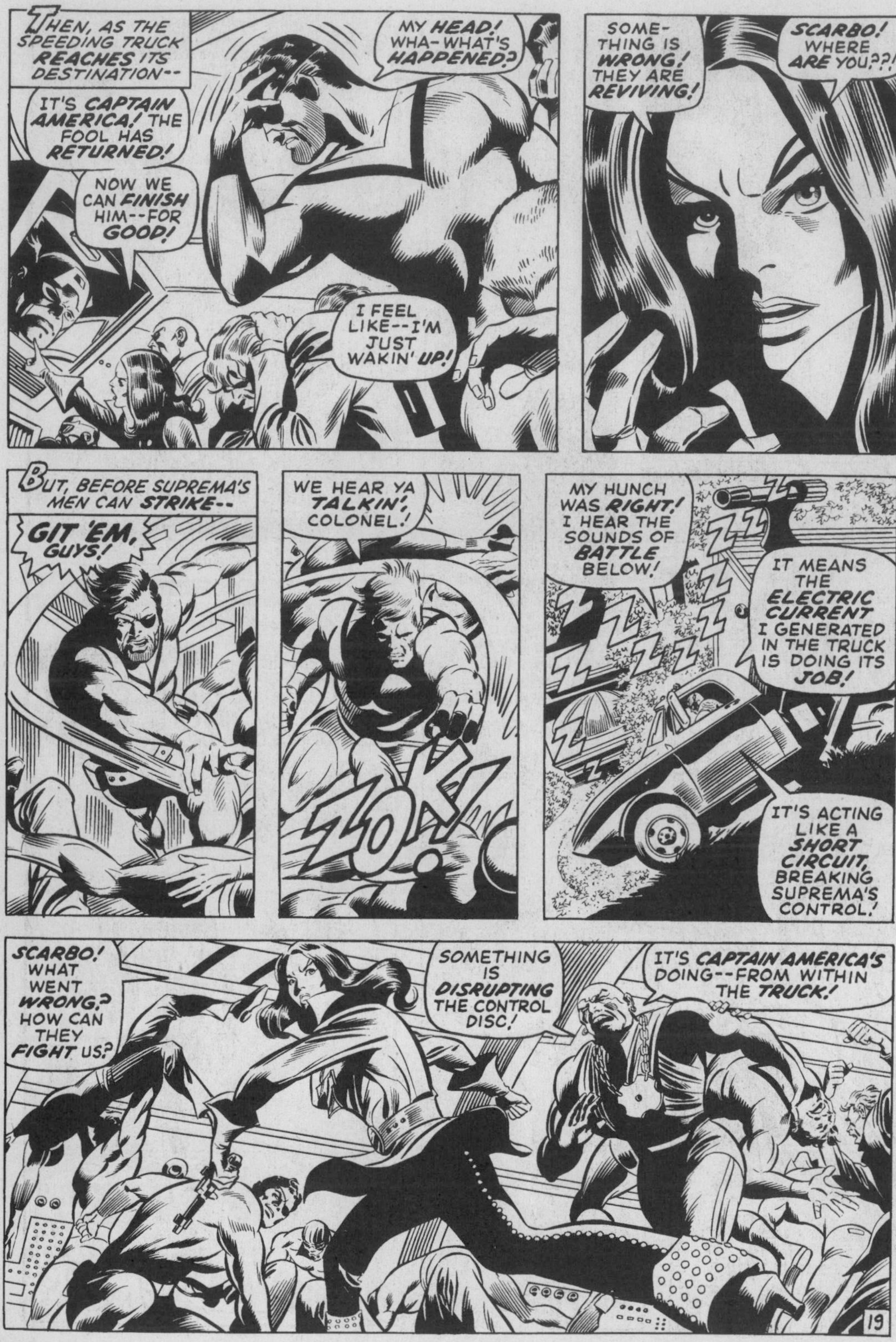

THEN, AS THE SPEEDING TRUCK REACHES ITS DESTINATION--
IT'S CAPTAIN AMERICA! THE FOOL HAS RETURNED!
NOW WE CAN FINISH HIM--FOR GOOD!
MY HEAD! WHA-WHAT'S HAPPENED?
I FEEL LIKE--I'M JUST WAKIN' UP!
SOME-THING IS WRONG! THEY ARE REVIVING!
SCARBO! WHERE ARE YOU??!
BUT, BEFORE SUPREMA'S MEN CAN STRIKE--
GIT 'EM, GUYS!
WE HEAR YA TALKIN', COLONEL!
ZOK!
MY HUNCH WAS RIGHT! I HEAR THE SOUNDS OF BATTLE BELOW!
IT MEANS THE ELECTRIC CURRENT I GENERATED IN THE TRUCK IS DOING ITS JOB!
IT'S ACTING LIKE A SHORT CIRCUIT, BREAKING SUPREMA'S CONTROL!
SCARBO! WHAT WENT WRONG? HOW CAN THEY FIGHT US?
SOMETHING IS DISRUPTING THE CONTROL DISC!
IT'S CAPTAIN AMERICA'S DOING--FROM WITHIN THE TRUCK!
19

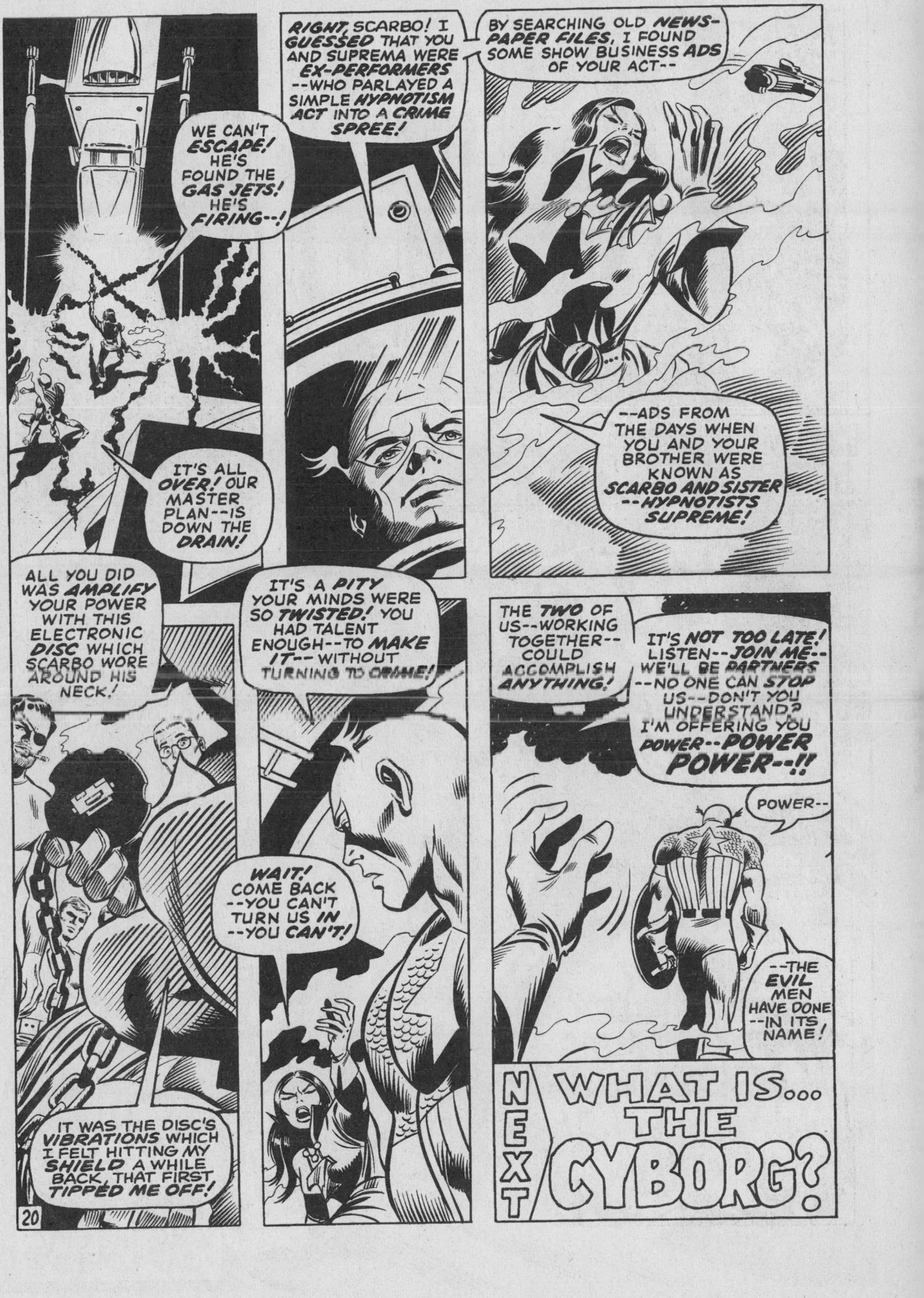
WE CAN'T ESCAPE! HE'S FOUND THE GAS JETS! HE'S FIRING--!
IT'S ALL OVER! OUR MASTER PLAN--IS DOWN THE DRAIN!
RIGHT, SCARBO! I GUESSED THAT YOU AND SUPREMA WERE EX-PERFORMERS --WHO PARLAYED A SIMPLE HYPNOTISM ACT INTO A CRIME SPREE!
BY SEARCHING OLD NEWS-PAPER FILES, I FOUND SOME SHOW BUSINESS ADS OF YOUR ACT--
--ADS FROM THE DAYS WHEN YOU AND YOUR BROTHER WERE KNOWN AS SCARBO AND SISTER --HYPNOTISTS SUPREME!
ALL YOU DID WAS AMPLIFY YOUR POWER WITH THIS ELECTRONIC DISC WHICH SCARBO WORE AROUND HIS NECK!
IT WAS THE DISC'S VIBRATIONS WHICH I FELT HITTING MY SHIELD A WHILE BACK, THAT FIRST TIPPED ME OFF!
IT'S A PITY YOUR MINDS WERE SO TWISTED! YOU HAD TALENT ENOUGH--TO MAKE IT-- WITHOUT TURNING TO CRIME!
WAIT! COME BACK --YOU CAN'T TURN US IN --YOU CAN'T!
THE TWO OF US--WORKING TOGETHER-- COULD ACCOMPLISH ANYTHING!
IT'S NOT TOO LATE! LISTEN--JOIN ME-- WE'LL BE PARTNERS --NO ONE CAN STOP US--DON'T YOU UNDERSTAND? I'M OFFERING YOU POWER--POWER POWER--!!
POWER--
--THE EVIL MEN HAVE DONE --IN ITS NAME!
NEXT
WHAT IS... THE CYBORG?
20

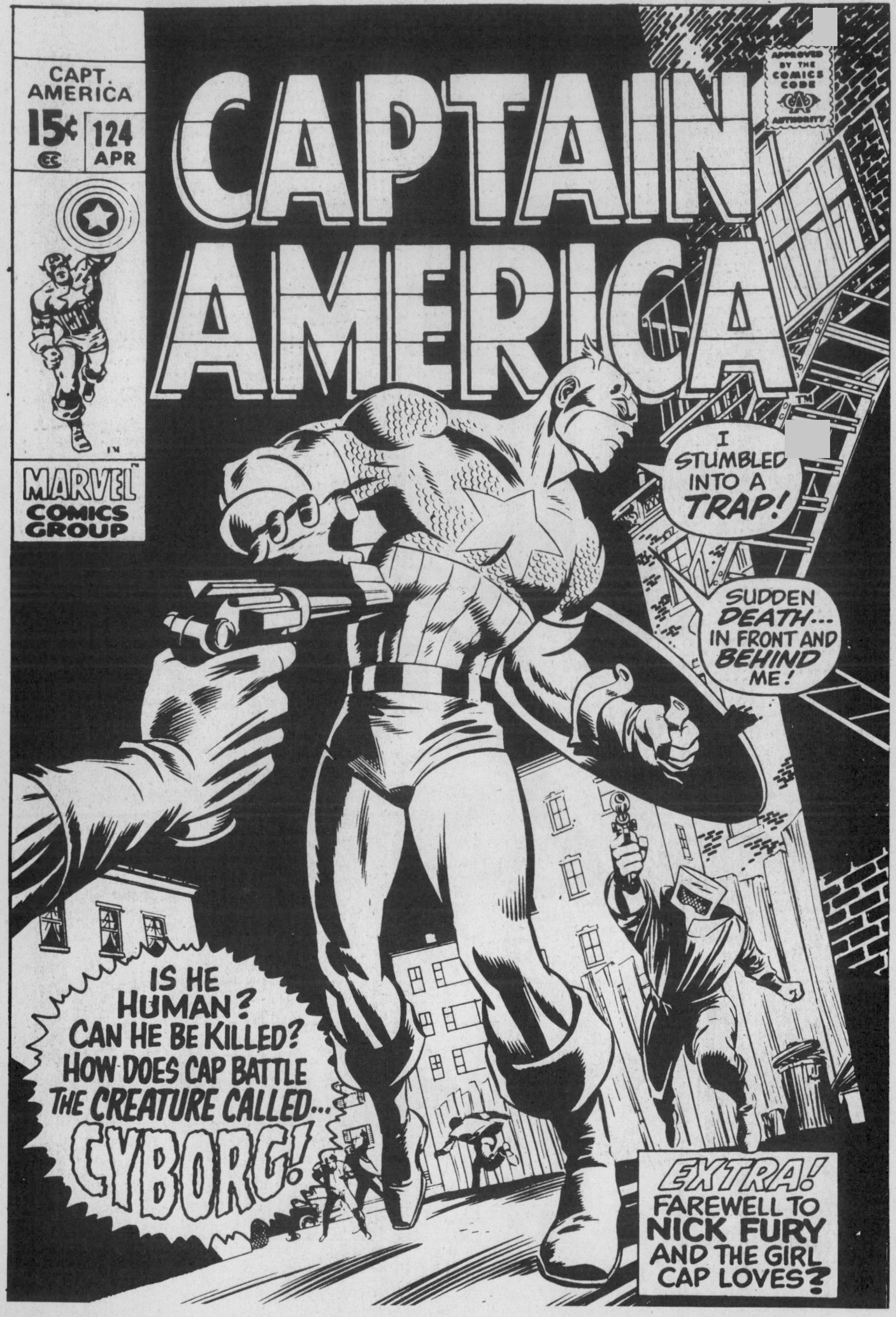
CAPT. AMERICA
15¢
124
APR
MARVEL COMICS GROUP
APPROVED BY THE COMICS CODE AUTHORITY
CAPTAIN AMERICA
I STUMBLED INTO A TRAP!
SUDDEN DEATH... IN FRONT AND BEHIND ME!
IS HE HUMAN? CAN HE BE KILLED? HOW DOES CAP BATTLE THE CREATURE CALLED... CYBORG!
EXTRA! FAREWELL TO NICK FURY AND THE GIRL CAP LOVES?

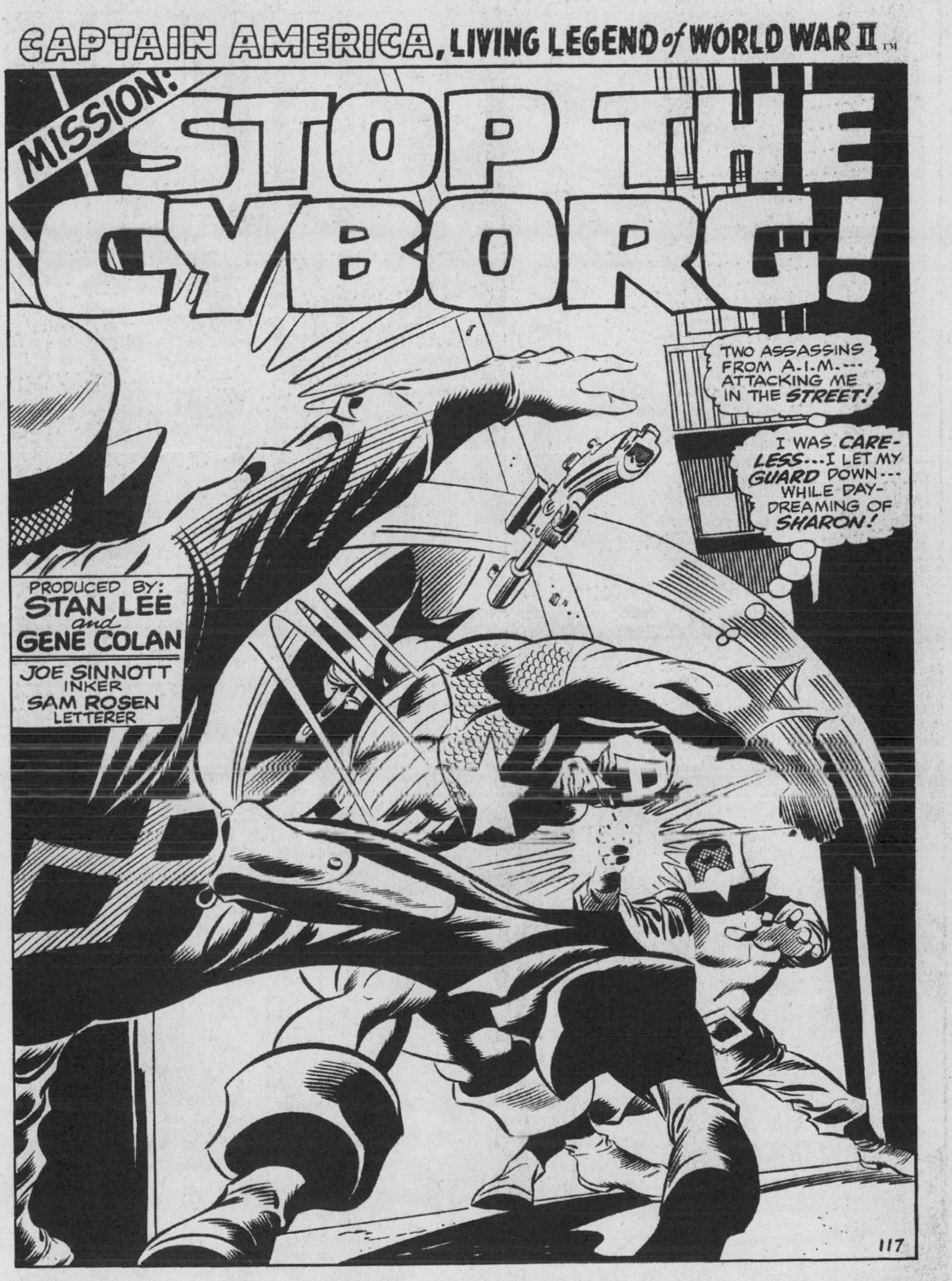
CAPTAIN AMERICA, LIVING LEGEND of WORLD WAR II ™
MISSION: STOP THE CYBORG!
TWO ASSASSINS FROM A.I.M.--- ATTACKING ME IN THE STREET!
I WAS CARE-LESS---I LET MY GUARD DOWN--- WHILE DAY-DREAMING OF SHARON!
PRODUCED BY: STAN LEE and GENE COLAN
JOE SINNOTT INKER
SAM ROSEN LETTERER
117

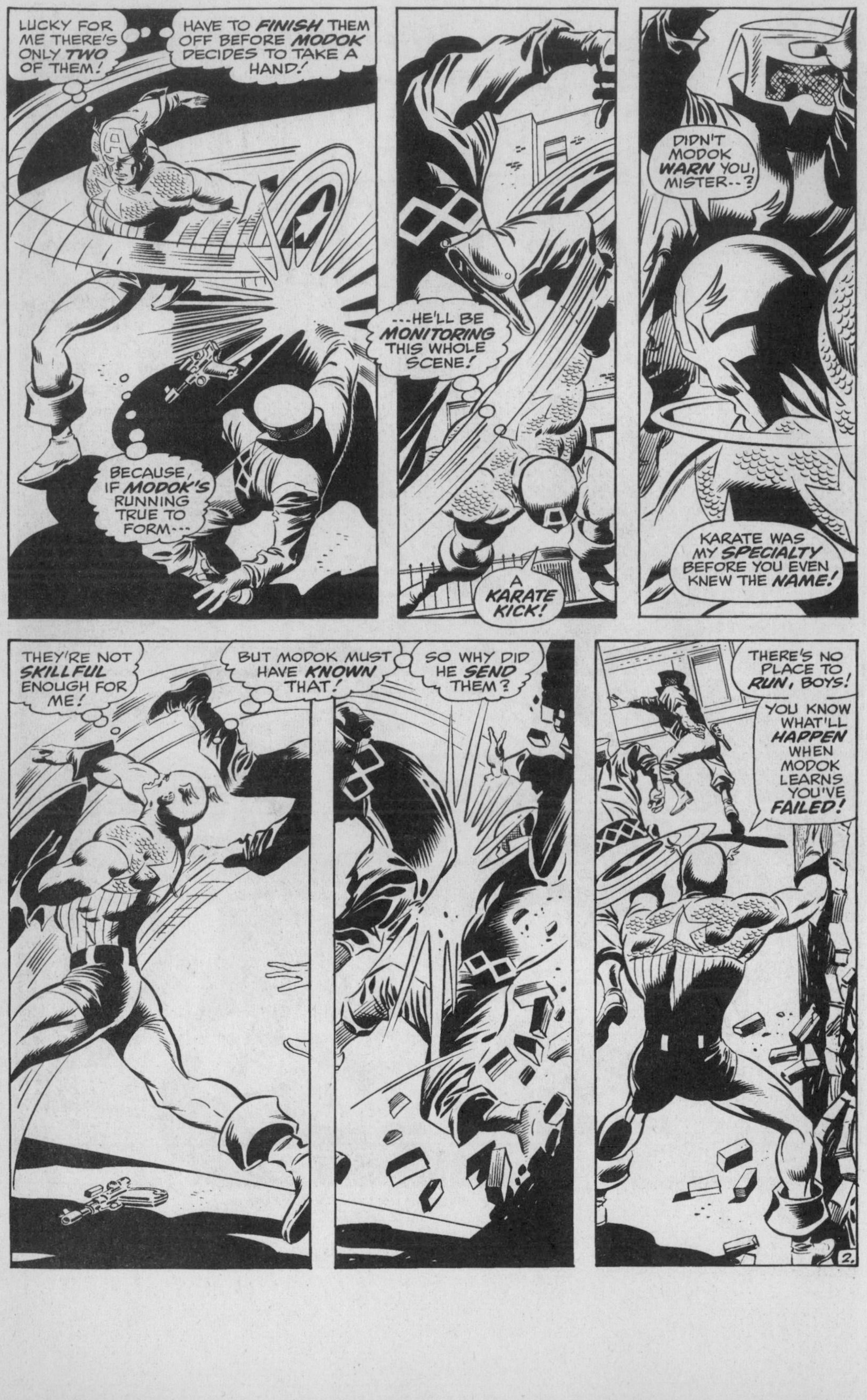
LUCKY FOR ME THERE'S ONLY TWO OF THEM!
HAVE TO FINISH THEM OFF BEFORE MODOK DECIDES TO TAKE A HAND!
BECAUSE, IF MODOK'S RUNNING TRUE TO FORM---
---HE'LL BE MONITORING THIS WHOLE SCENE!
A KARATE KICK!
DIDN'T MODOK WARN YOU, MISTER--?
KARATE WAS MY SPECIALTY BEFORE YOU EVEN KNEW THE NAME!
THEY'RE NOT SKILLFUL ENOUGH FOR ME!
BUT MODOK MUST HAVE KNOWN THAT!
SO WHY DID HE SEND THEM?
THERE'S NO PLACE TO RUN, BOYS!
YOU KNOW WHAT'LL HAPPEN WHEN MODOK LEARNS YOU'VE FAILED!
2.

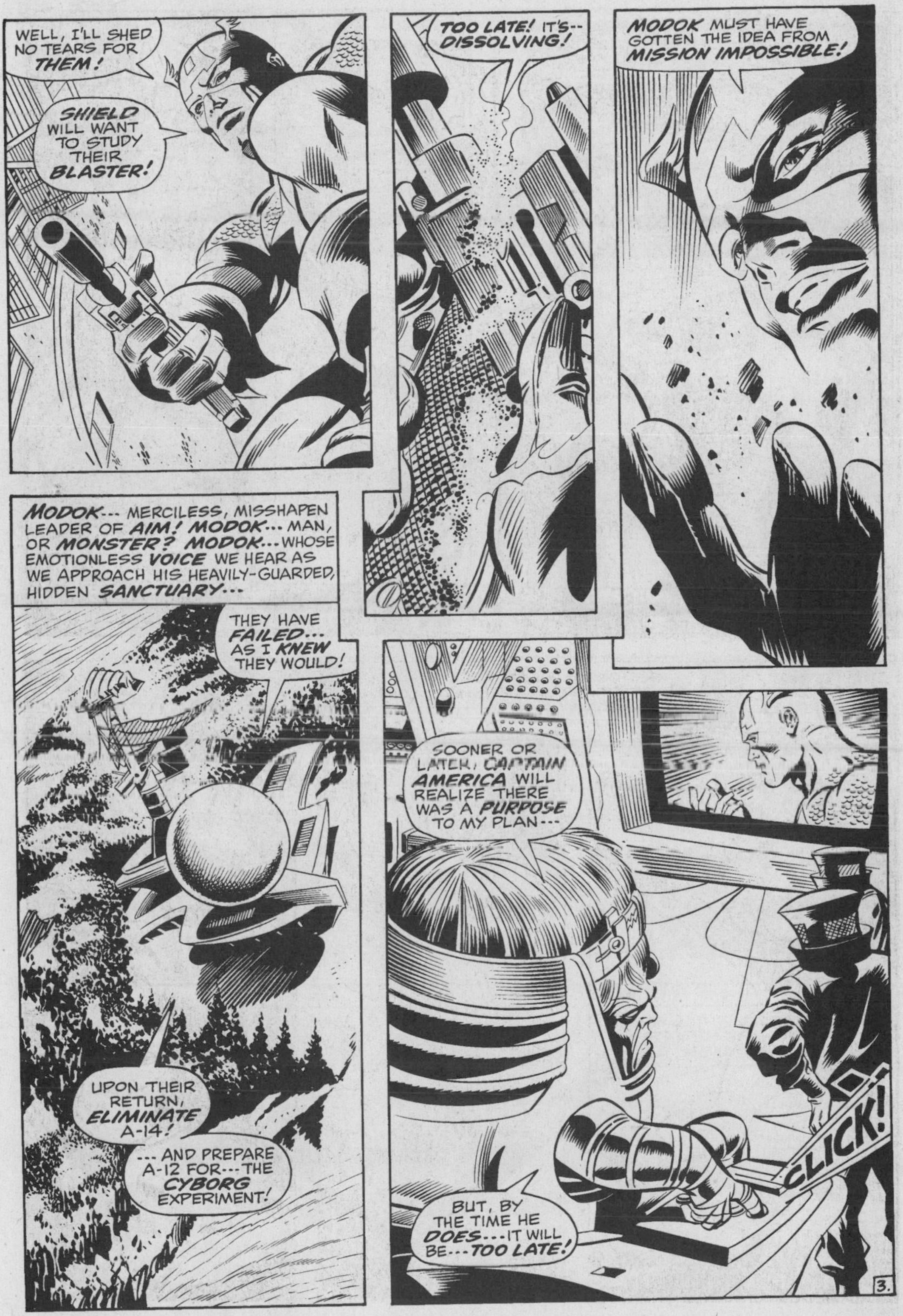
WELL, I'LL SHED NO TEARS FOR THEM!
SHIELD WILL WANT TO STUDY THEIR BLASTER!
TOO LATE! IT'S-- DISSOLVING!
MODOK MUST HAVE GOTTEN THE IDEA FROM MISSION IMPOSSIBLE!
MODOK--- MERCILESS, MISSHAPEN LEADER OF AIM! MODOK... MAN, OR MONSTER? MODOK...WHOSE EMOTIONLESS VOICE WE HEAR AS WE APPROACH HIS HEAVILY-GUARDED, HIDDEN SANCTUARY...
THEY HAVE FAILED... AS I KNEW THEY WOULD!
UPON THEIR RETURN, ELIMINATE A-14!
--- AND PREPARE A-12 FOR--- THE CYBORG EXPERIMENT!
SOONER OR LATER, CAPTAIN AMERICA WILL REALIZE THERE WAS A PURPOSE TO MY PLAN---
CLICK!
BUT, BY THE TIME HE DOES---IT WILL BE---TOO LATE!
3.

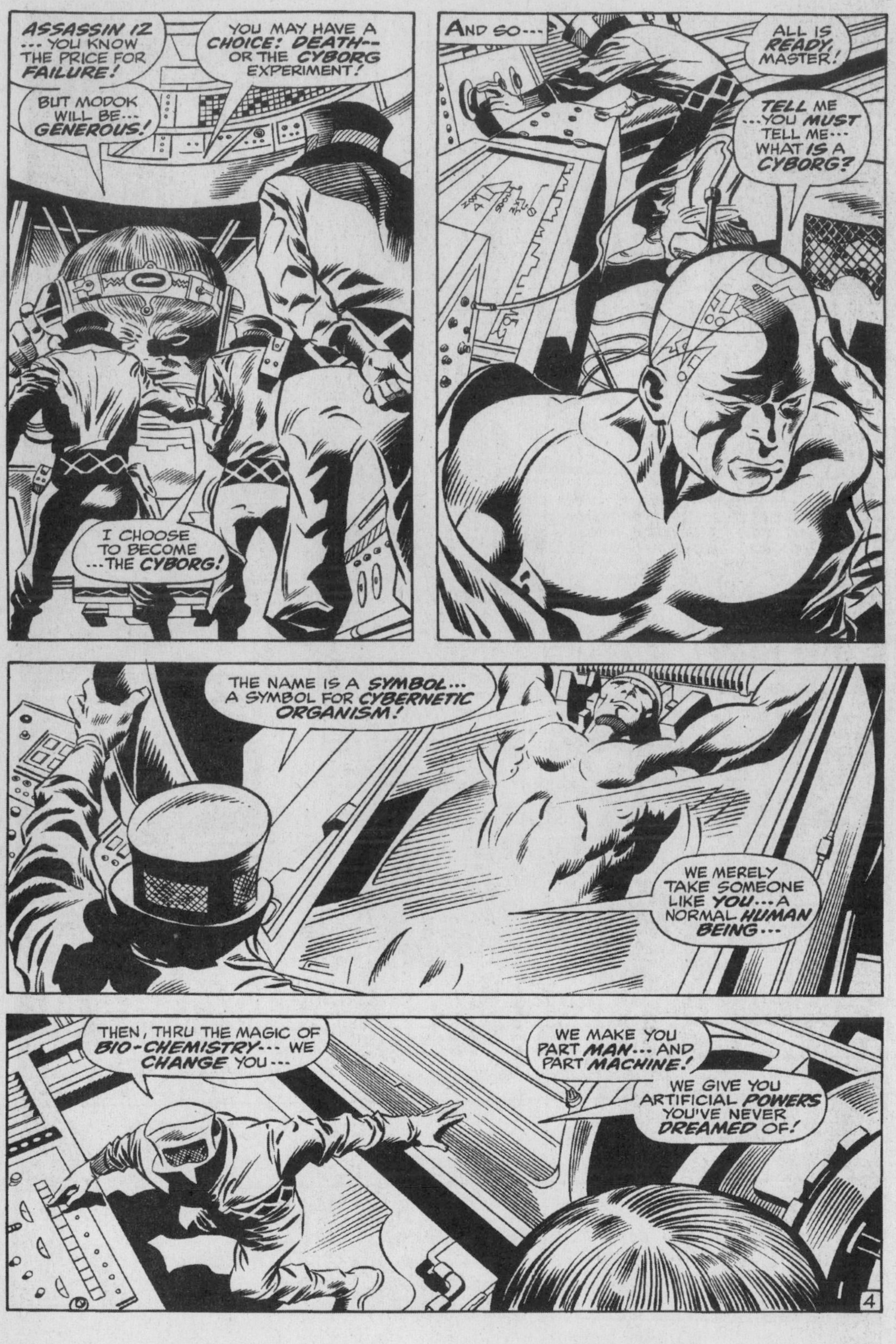
ASSASSIN 12 --- YOU KNOW THE PRICE FOR FAILURE!
YOU MAY HAVE A CHOICE: DEATH-- OR THE CYBORG EXPERIMENT!
BUT MODOK WILL BE... GENEROUS!
I CHOOSE TO BECOME ---THE CYBORG!
AND SO---
ALL IS READY, MASTER!
TELL ME ...YOU MUST TELL ME--- WHAT IS A CYBORG?
THE NAME IS A SYMBOL... A SYMBOL FOR CYBERNETIC ORGANISM!
WE MERELY TAKE SOMEONE LIKE YOU---A NORMAL HUMAN BEING---
THEN, THRU THE MAGIC OF BIO-CHEMISTRY--- WE CHANGE YOU---
WE MAKE YOU PART MAN--- AND PART MACHINE!
WE GIVE YOU ARTIFICIAL POWERS YOU'VE NEVER DREAMED OF!
4

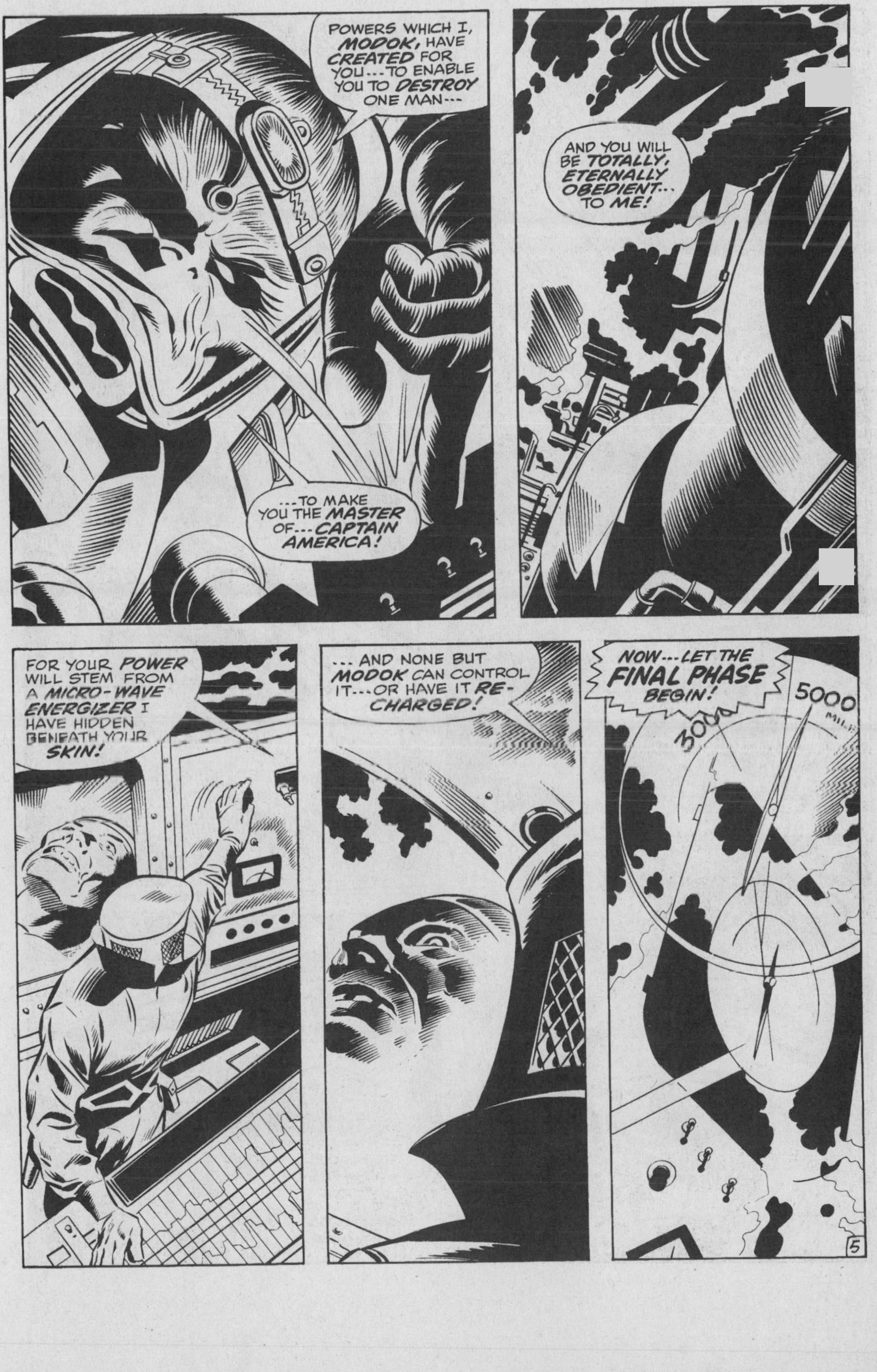
POWERS WHICH I, MODOK, HAVE CREATED FOR YOU---TO ENABLE YOU TO DESTROY ONE MAN---
...TO MAKE YOU THE MASTER OF...CAPTAIN AMERICA!
AND YOU WILL BE TOTALLY, ETERNALLY OBEDIENT... TO ME!
FOR YOUR POWER WILL STEM FROM A MICRO-WAVE ENERGIZER I HAVE HIDDEN BENEATH YOUR SKIN!
...AND NONE BUT MODOK CAN CONTROL IT---OR HAVE IT RE-CHARGED!
NOW---LET THE FINAL PHASE BEGIN!
5000
5

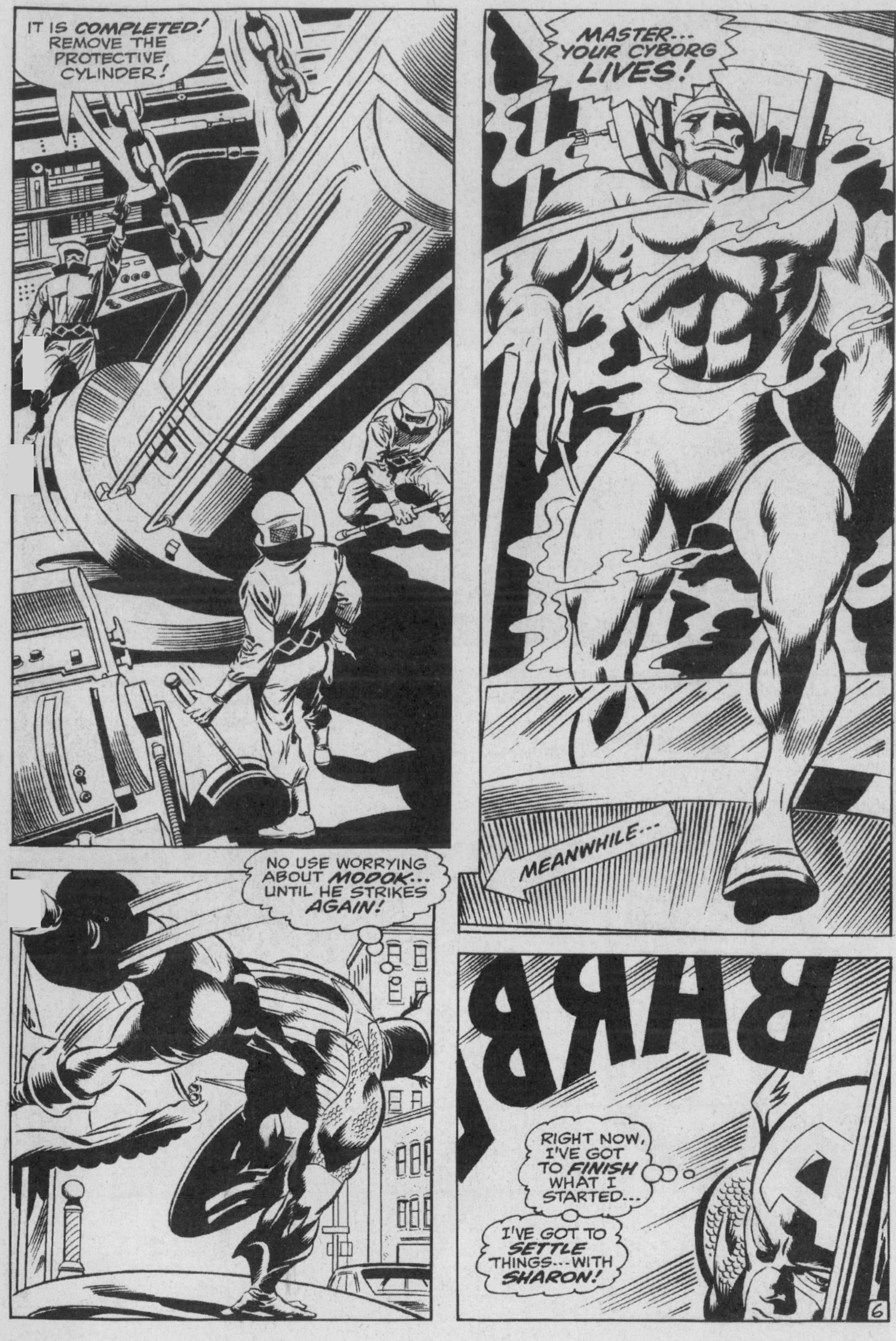

IT IS COMPLETED! REMOVE THE PROTECTIVE CYLINDER!
MASTER... YOUR CYBORG LIVES!
MEANWHILE---
NO USE WORRYING ABOUT MODOK... UNTIL HE STRIKES AGAIN!
BARRB
RIGHT NOW, I'VE GOT TO FINISH WHAT I STARTED...
I'VE GOT TO SETTLE THINGS---WITH SHARON!
6

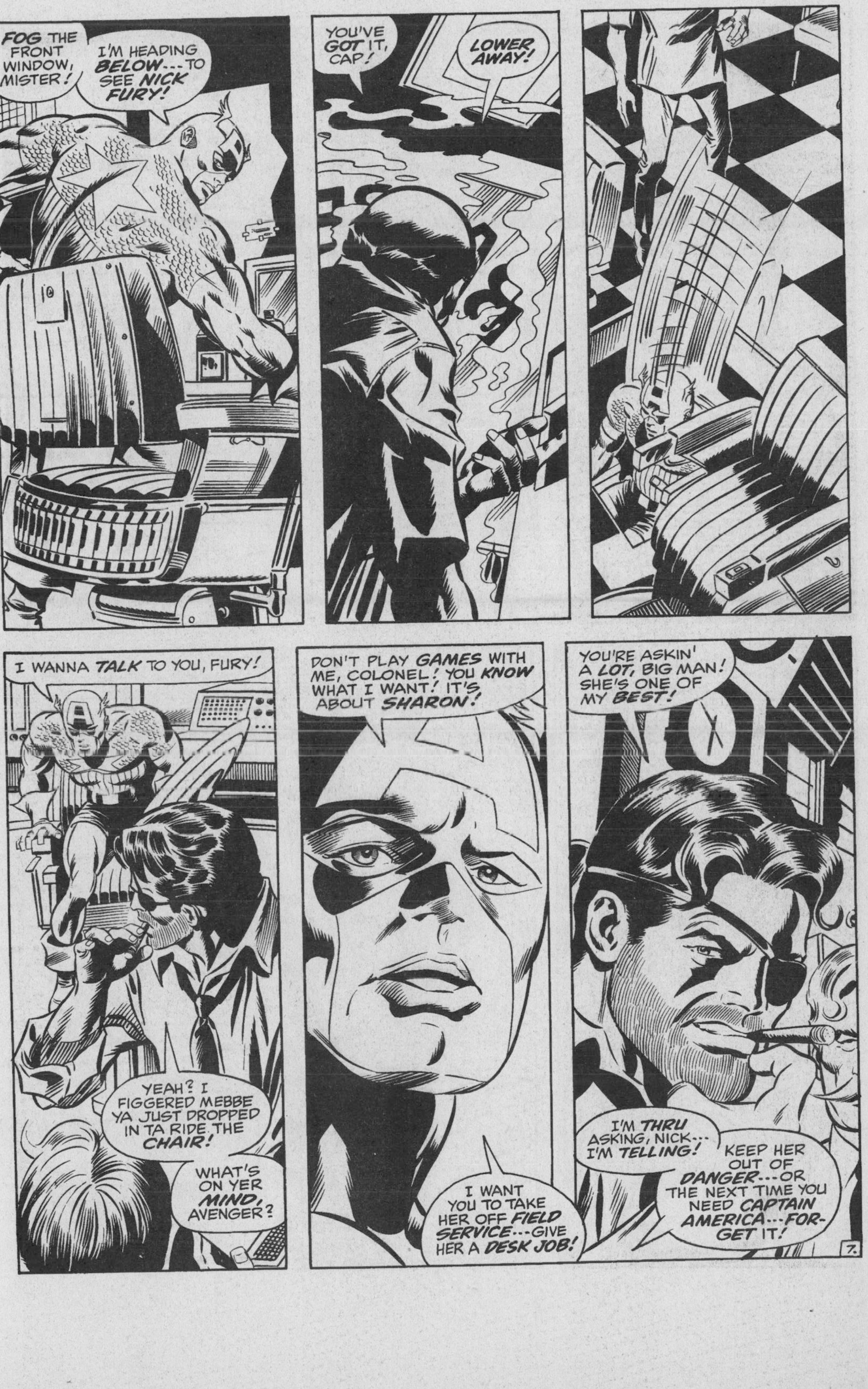
FOG THE FRONT WINDOW, MISTER!
I'M HEADING BELOW--- TO SEE NICK FURY!
YOU'VE GOT IT, CAP!
LOWER AWAY!
I WANNA TALK TO YOU, FURY!
YEAH? I FIGGERED MEBBE YA JUST DROPPED IN TA RIDE THE CHAIR!
WHAT'S ON YER MIND, AVENGER?
DON'T PLAY GAMES WITH ME, COLONEL! YOU KNOW WHAT I WANT! IT'S ABOUT SHARON!
I WANT YOU TO TAKE HER OFF FIELD SERVICE--- GIVE HER A DESK JOB!
YOU'RE ASKIN' A LOT, BIG MAN! SHE'S ONE OF MY BEST!
I'M THRU ASKING, NICK--- I'M TELLING!
KEEP HER OUT OF DANGER--- OR THE NEXT TIME YOU NEED CAPTAIN AMERICA--- FORGET IT!
7.

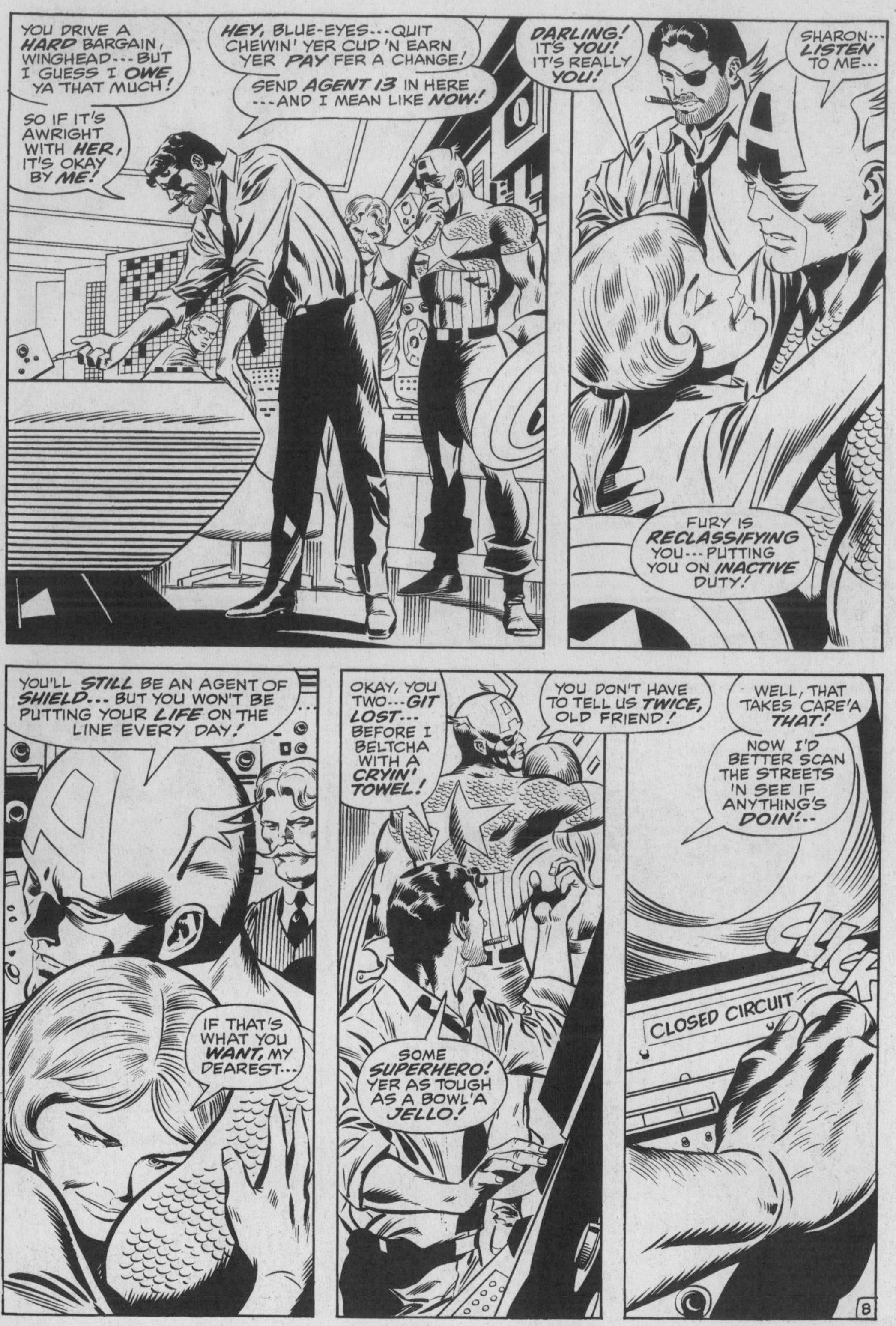
YOU DRIVE A HARD BARGAIN, WINGHEAD--- BUT I GUESS I OWE YA THAT MUCH!
SO IF IT'S AWRIGHT WITH HER, IT'S OKAY BY ME!
HEY, BLUE-EYES--- QUIT CHEWIN' YER CUD 'N EARN YER PAY FER A CHANGE!
SEND AGENT 13 IN HERE ---AND I MEAN LIKE NOW!
DARLING! IT'S YOU! IT'S REALLY YOU!
SHARON--- LISTEN TO ME---
FURY IS RECLASSIFYING YOU--- PUTTING YOU ON INACTIVE DUTY!
YOU'LL STILL BE AN AGENT OF SHIELD--- BUT YOU WON'T BE PUTTING YOUR LIFE ON THE LINE EVERY DAY!
IF THAT'S WHAT YOU WANT, MY DEAREST---
OKAY, YOU TWO--- GIT LOST--- BEFORE I BELTCHA WITH A CRYIN' TOWEL!
YOU DON'T HAVE TO TELL US TWICE, OLD FRIEND!
SOME SUPERHERO! YER AS TOUGH AS A BOWL'A JELLO!
WELL, THAT TAKES CARE'A THAT!
NOW I'D BETTER SCAN THE STREETS 'N SEE IF ANYTHING'S DOIN'---
CLICK
CLOSED CIRCUIT
8

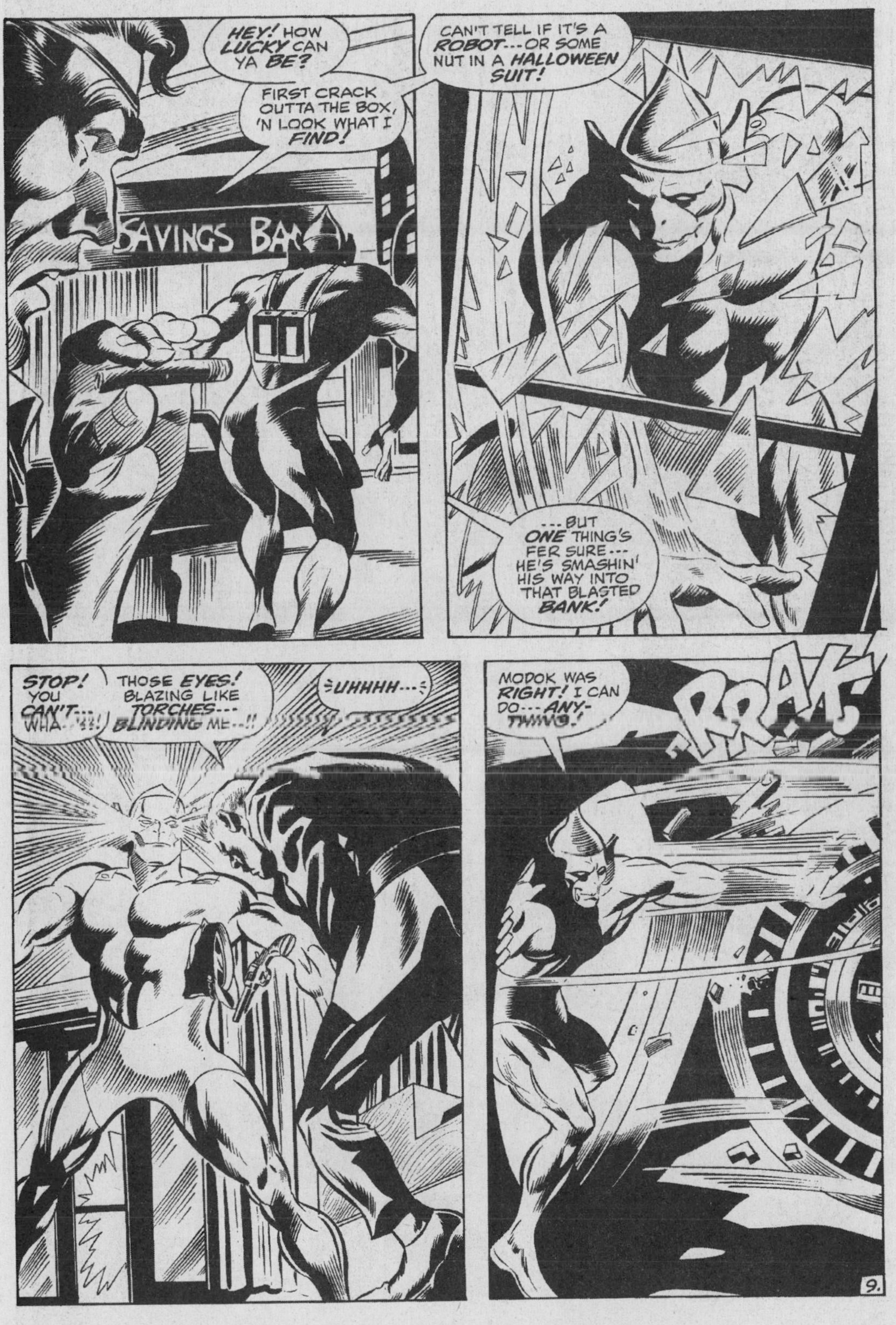
HEY! HOW LUCKY CAN YA BE?
FIRST CRACK OUTTA THE BOX, 'N LOOK WHAT I FIND!
SAVINGS BA
CAN'T TELL IF IT'S A ROBOT---OR SOME NUT IN A HALLOWEEN SUIT!
---BUT ONE THING'S FER SURE--- HE'S SMASHIN' HIS WAY INTO THAT BLASTED BANK!
STOP! YOU CAN'T--- WHA--?!
THOSE EYES! BLAZING LIKE TORCHES--- BLINDING ME--!!
UHHHH---
MODOK WAS RIGHT! I CAN DO---ANY-THING!
RRAK!
9.

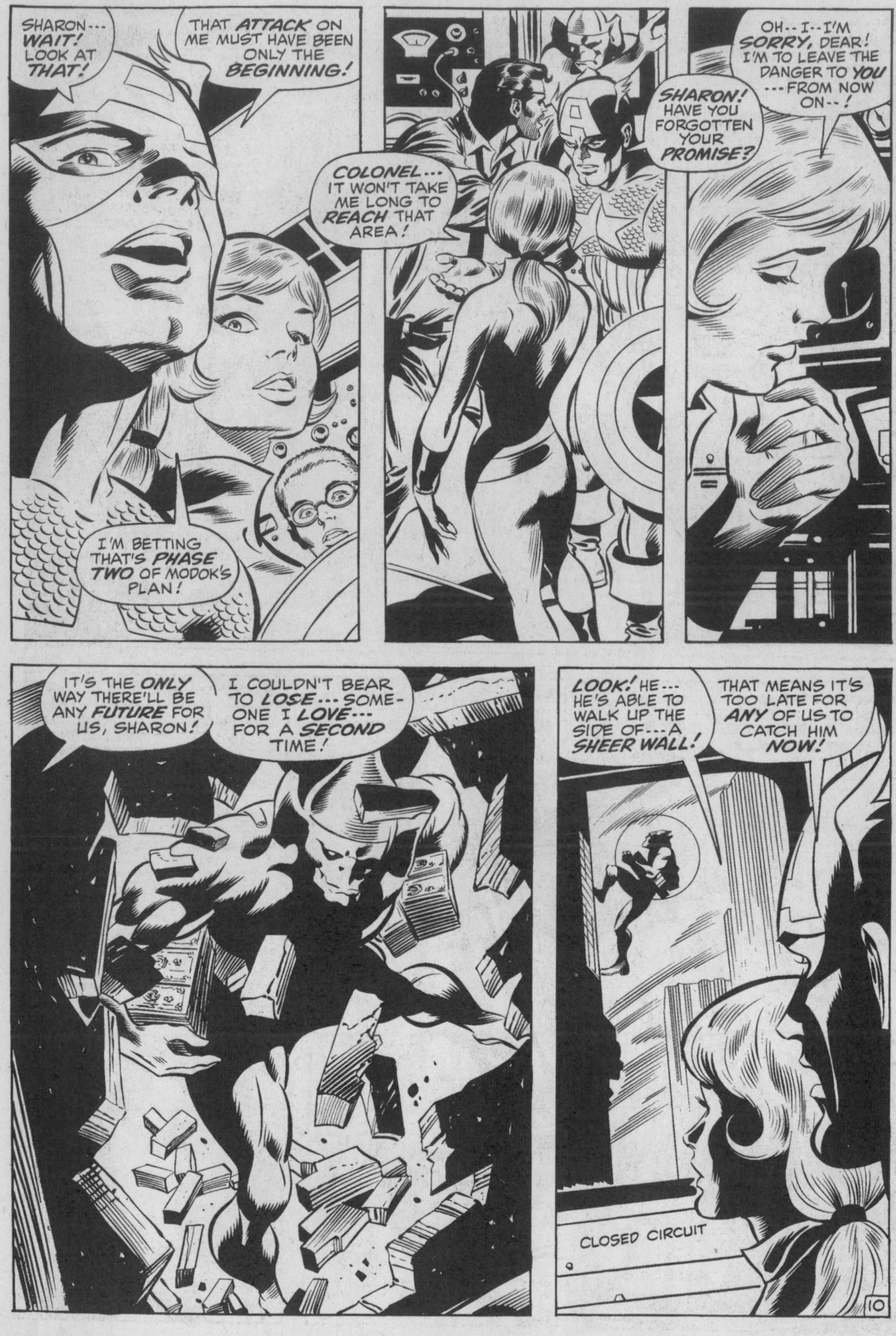
SHARON--- WAIT! LOOK AT THAT!
THAT ATTACK ON ME MUST HAVE BEEN ONLY THE BEGINNING!
I'M BETTING THAT'S PHASE TWO OF MODOK'S PLAN!
COLONEL... IT WON'T TAKE ME LONG TO REACH THAT AREA!
SHARON! HAVE YOU FORGOTTEN YOUR PROMISE?
OH-- I--I'M SORRY, DEAR! I'M TO LEAVE THE DANGER TO YOU ---FROM NOW ON--!
IT'S THE ONLY WAY THERE'LL BE ANY FUTURE FOR US, SHARON!
I COULDN'T BEAR TO LOSE--- SOME-ONE I LOVE--- FOR A SECOND TIME!
LOOK! HE--- HE'S ABLE TO WALK UP THE SIDE OF--- A SHEER WALL!
THAT MEANS IT'S TOO LATE FOR ANY OF US TO CATCH HIM NOW!
CLOSED CIRCUIT
10

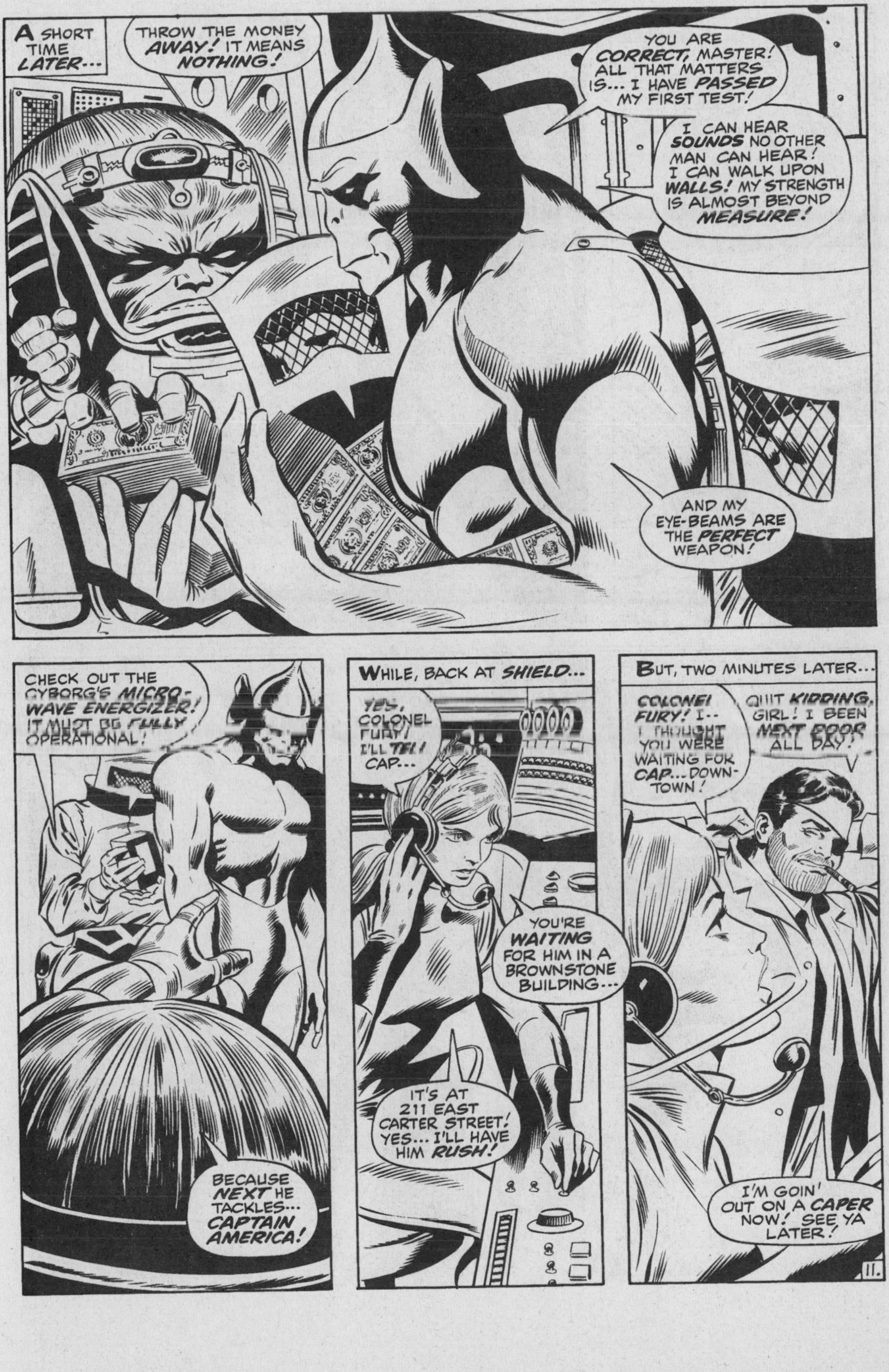

A SHORT TIME LATER...
THROW THE MONEY AWAY! IT MEANS NOTHING!
YOU ARE CORRECT, MASTER! ALL THAT MATTERS IS... I HAVE PASSED MY FIRST TEST!
I CAN HEAR SOUNDS NO OTHER MAN CAN HEAR! I CAN WALK UPON WALLS! MY STRENGTH IS ALMOST BEYOND MEASURE!
AND MY EYE-BEAMS ARE THE PERFECT WEAPON!
CHECK OUT THE CYBORG'S MICRO-WAVE ENERGIZER! IT MUST BE FULLY OPERATIONAL!
BECAUSE NEXT HE TACKLES... CAPTAIN AMERICA!
WHILE, BACK AT SHIELD...
YES, COLONEL FURY! I'LL TELL CAP...
YOU'RE WAITING FOR HIM IN A BROWNSTONE BUILDING...
IT'S AT 211 EAST CARTER STREET! YES... I'LL HAVE HIM RUSH!
BUT, TWO MINUTES LATER...
COLONEL FURY! I-- I THOUGHT YOU WERE WAITING FOR CAP... DOWN-TOWN!
QUIT KIDDING, GIRL! I BEEN NEXT DOOR ALL DAY!
I'M GOIN' OUT ON A CAPER NOW! SEE YA LATER!
11.

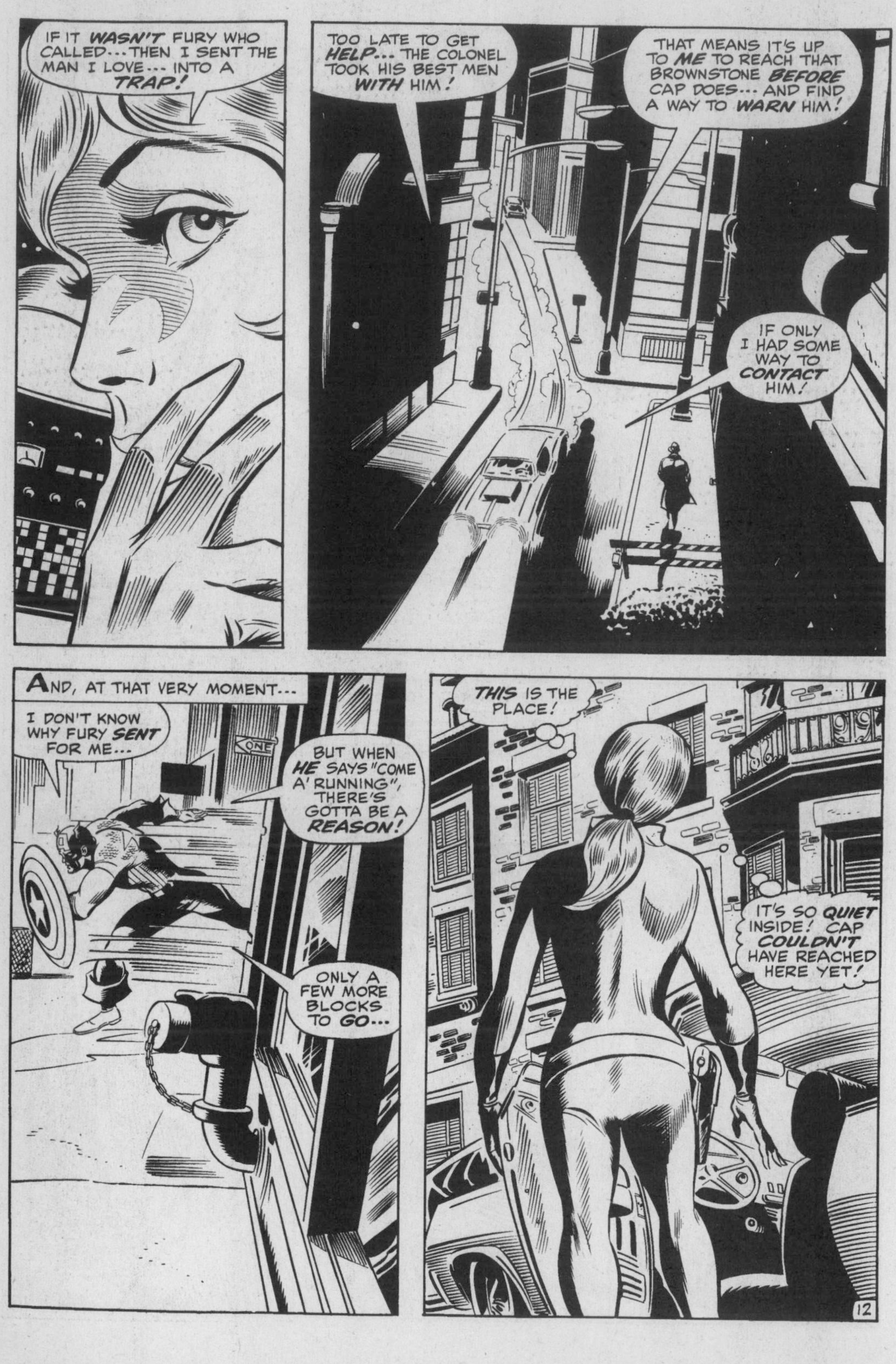
IF IT WASN'T FURY WHO CALLED... THEN I SENT THE MAN I LOVE... INTO A TRAP!
TOO LATE TO GET HELP... THE COLONEL TOOK HIS BEST MEN WITH HIM!
THAT MEANS IT'S UP TO ME TO REACH THAT BROWNSTONE BEFORE CAP DOES... AND FIND A WAY TO WARN HIM!
IF ONLY I HAD SOME WAY TO CONTACT HIM!
AND, AT THAT VERY MOMENT...
I DON'T KNOW WHY FURY SENT FOR ME...
ONE
BUT WHEN HE SAYS "COME A' RUNNING", THERE'S GOTTA BE A REASON!
ONLY A FEW MORE BLOCKS TO GO...
THIS IS THE PLACE!
IT'S SO QUIET INSIDE! CAP COULDN'T HAVE REACHED HERE YET!
12

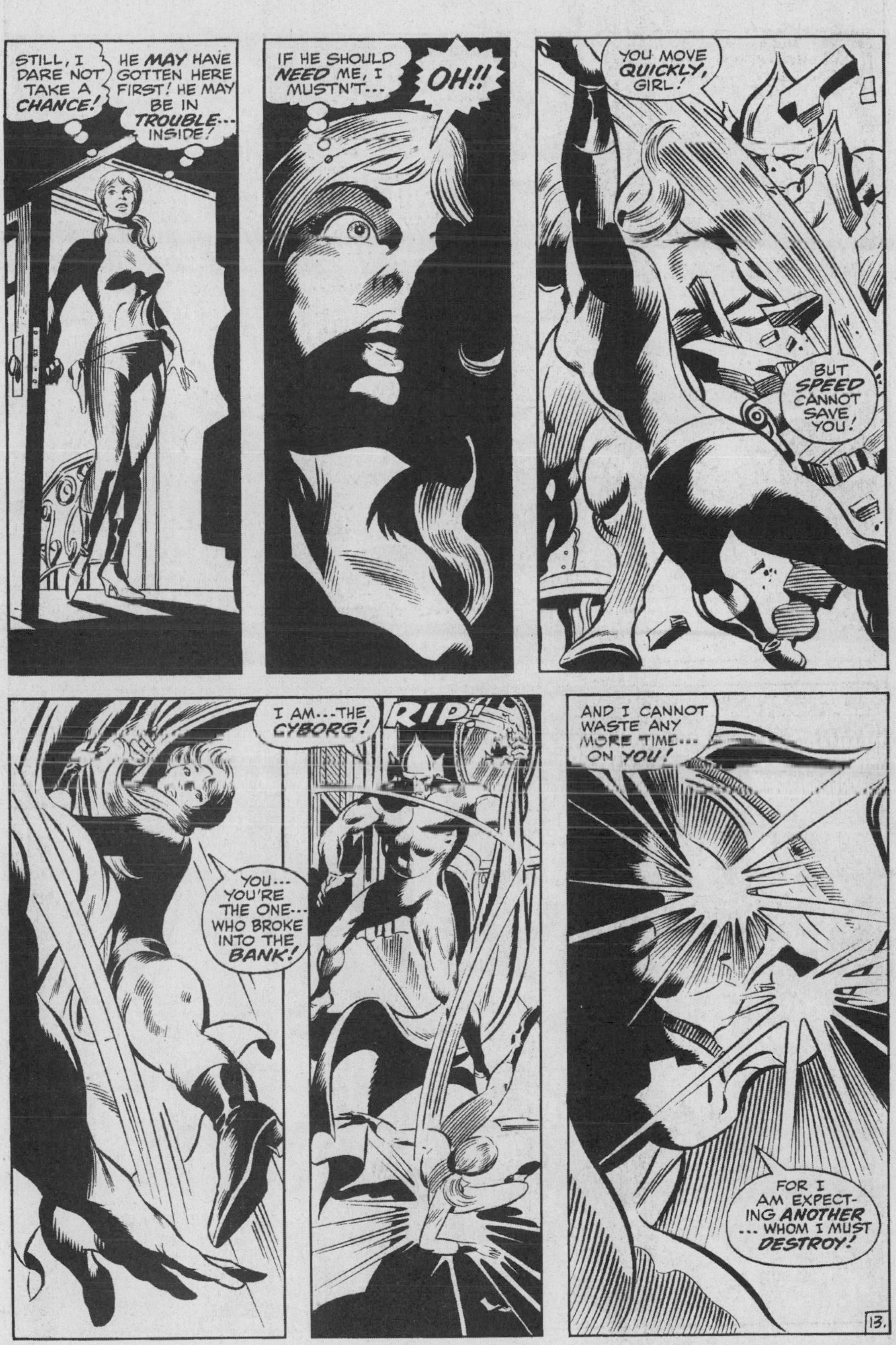
STILL, I DARE NOT TAKE A CHANCE!
HE MAY HAVE GOTTEN HERE FIRST! HE MAY BE IN TROUBLE... INSIDE!
IF HE SHOULD NEED ME, I MUSTN'T...
OH!!
YOU MOVE QUICKLY, GIRL!
BUT SPEED CANNOT SAVE YOU!
I AM...THE CYBORG!
RIP!
YOU... YOU'RE THE ONE... WHO BROKE INTO THE BANK!
AND I CANNOT WASTE ANY MORE TIME... ON YOU!
FOR I AM EXPECTING ANOTHER ... WHOM I MUST DESTROY!
13.

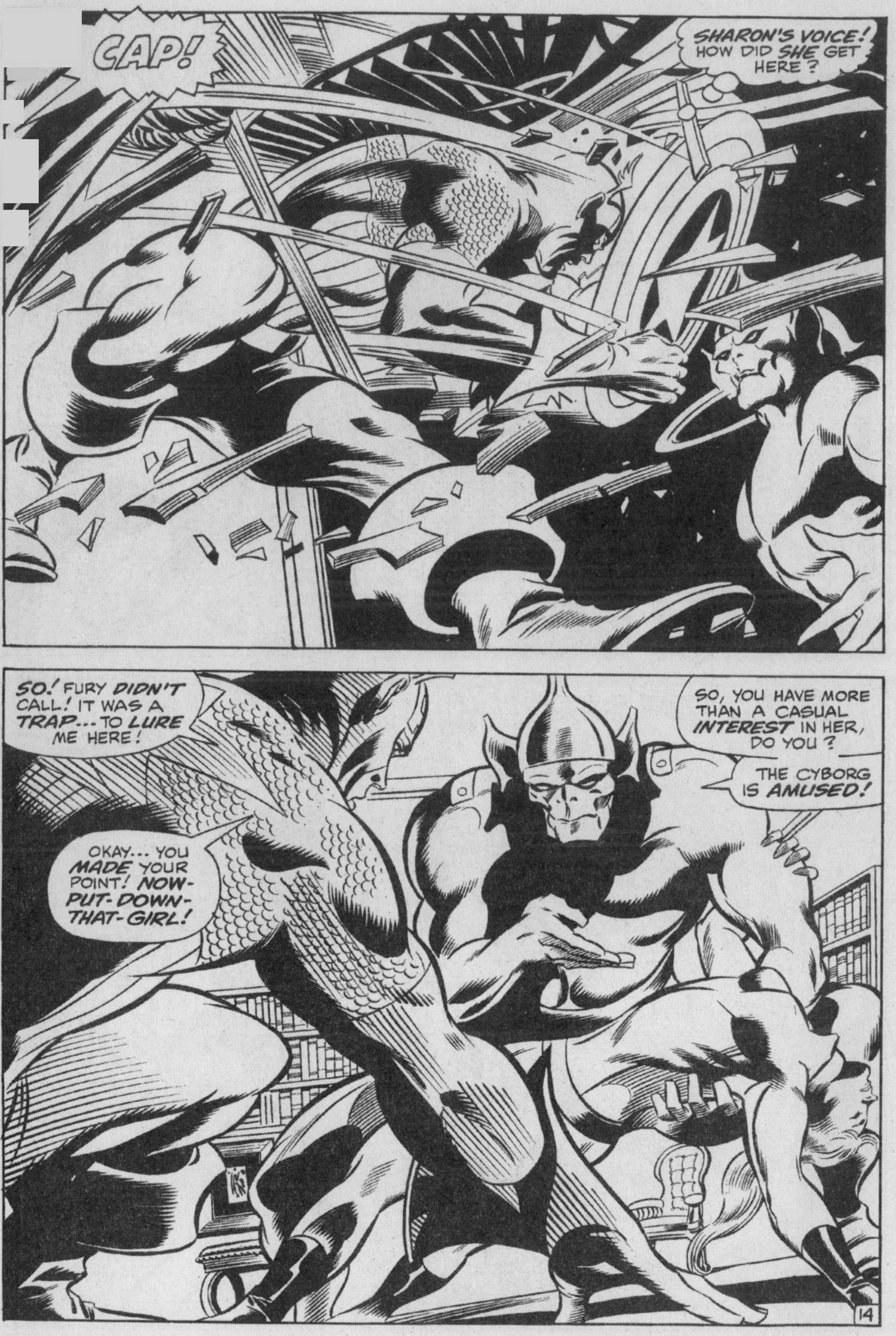
CAP!
SHARON'S VOICE! HOW DID SHE GET HERE?
SO! FURY DIDN'T CALL! IT WAS A TRAP... TO LURE ME HERE!
SO, YOU HAVE MORE THAN A CASUAL INTEREST IN HER, DO YOU?
THE CYBORG IS AMUSED!
OKAY... YOU MADE YOUR POINT! NOW-PUT-DOWN-THAT-GIRL!

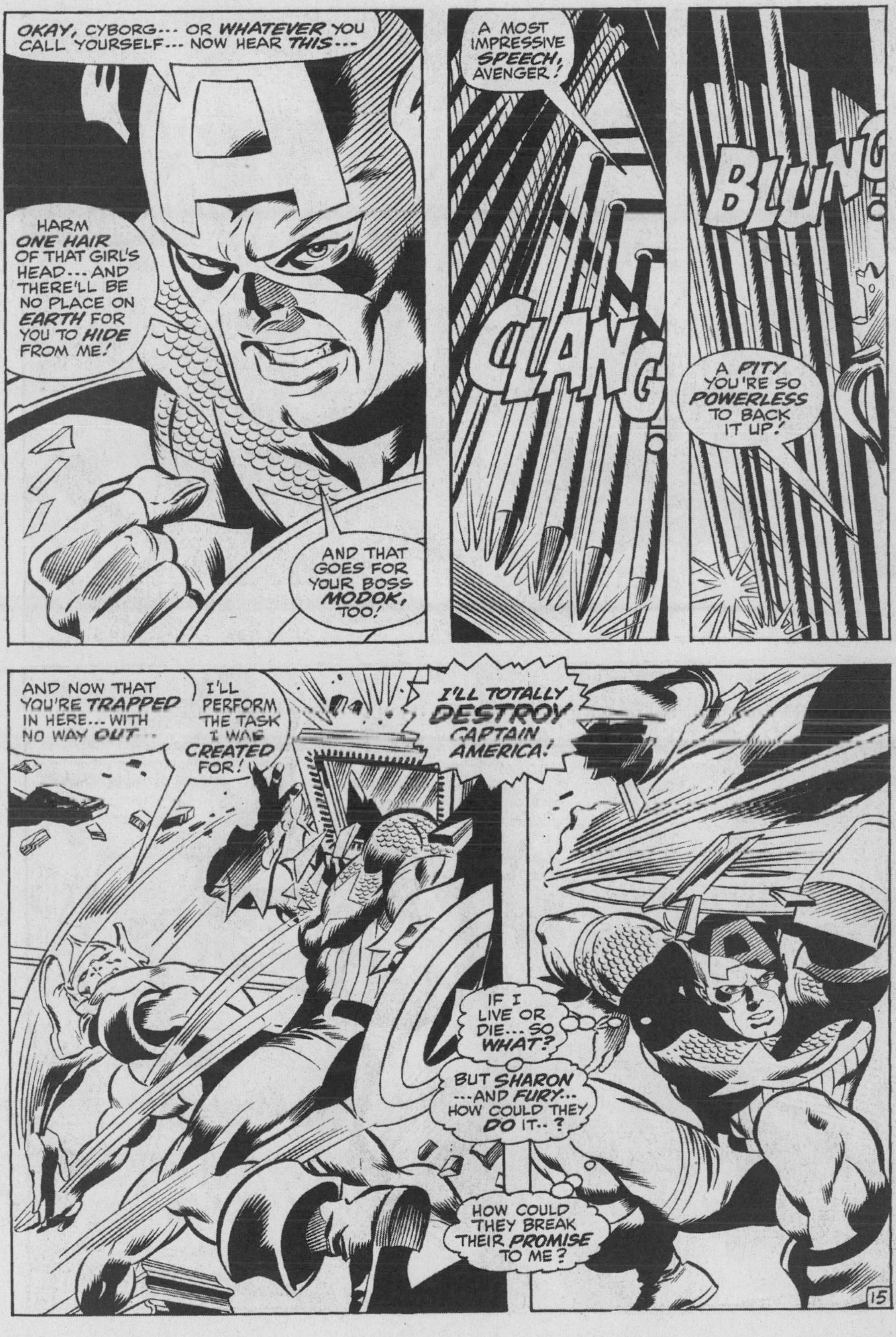
OKAY, CYBORG... OR WHATEVER YOU CALL YOURSELF... NOW HEAR THIS...
HARM ONE HAIR OF THAT GIRL'S HEAD... AND THERE'LL BE NO PLACE ON EARTH FOR YOU TO HIDE FROM ME!
AND THAT GOES FOR YOUR BOSS MODOK, TOO!
A MOST IMPRESSIVE SPEECH, AVENGER!
CLANG!
BLUNG!
A PITY YOU'RE SO POWERLESS TO BACK IT UP!
AND NOW THAT YOU'RE TRAPPED IN HERE... WITH NO WAY OUT...
I'LL PERFORM THE TASK I WAS CREATED FOR!
I'LL TOTALLY DESTROY CAPTAIN AMERICA!
IF I LIVE OR DIE... SO WHAT?
BUT SHARON ...AND FURY... HOW COULD THEY DO IT..?
HOW COULD THEY BREAK THEIR PROMISE TO ME?

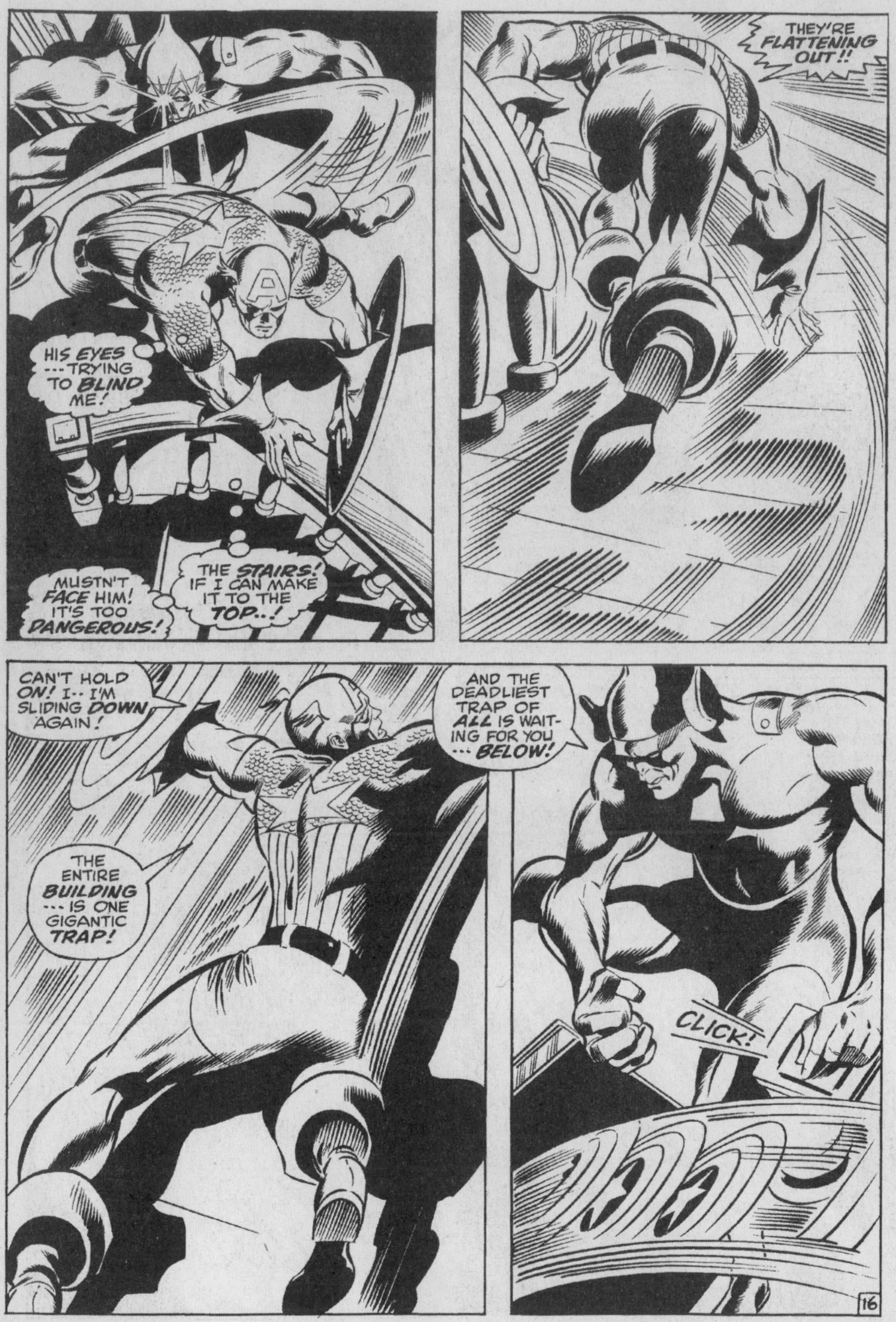
HIS EYES --- TRYING TO BLIND ME!
MUSTN'T FACE HIM! IT'S TOO DANGEROUS!
THE STAIRS! IF I CAN MAKE IT TO THE TOP..!
THEY'RE FLATTENING OUT!!
CAN'T HOLD ON! I-- I'M SLIDING DOWN AGAIN!
THE ENTIRE BUILDING --- IS ONE GIGANTIC TRAP!
AND THE DEADLIEST TRAP OF ALL IS WAITING FOR YOU --- BELOW!
CLICK!
16

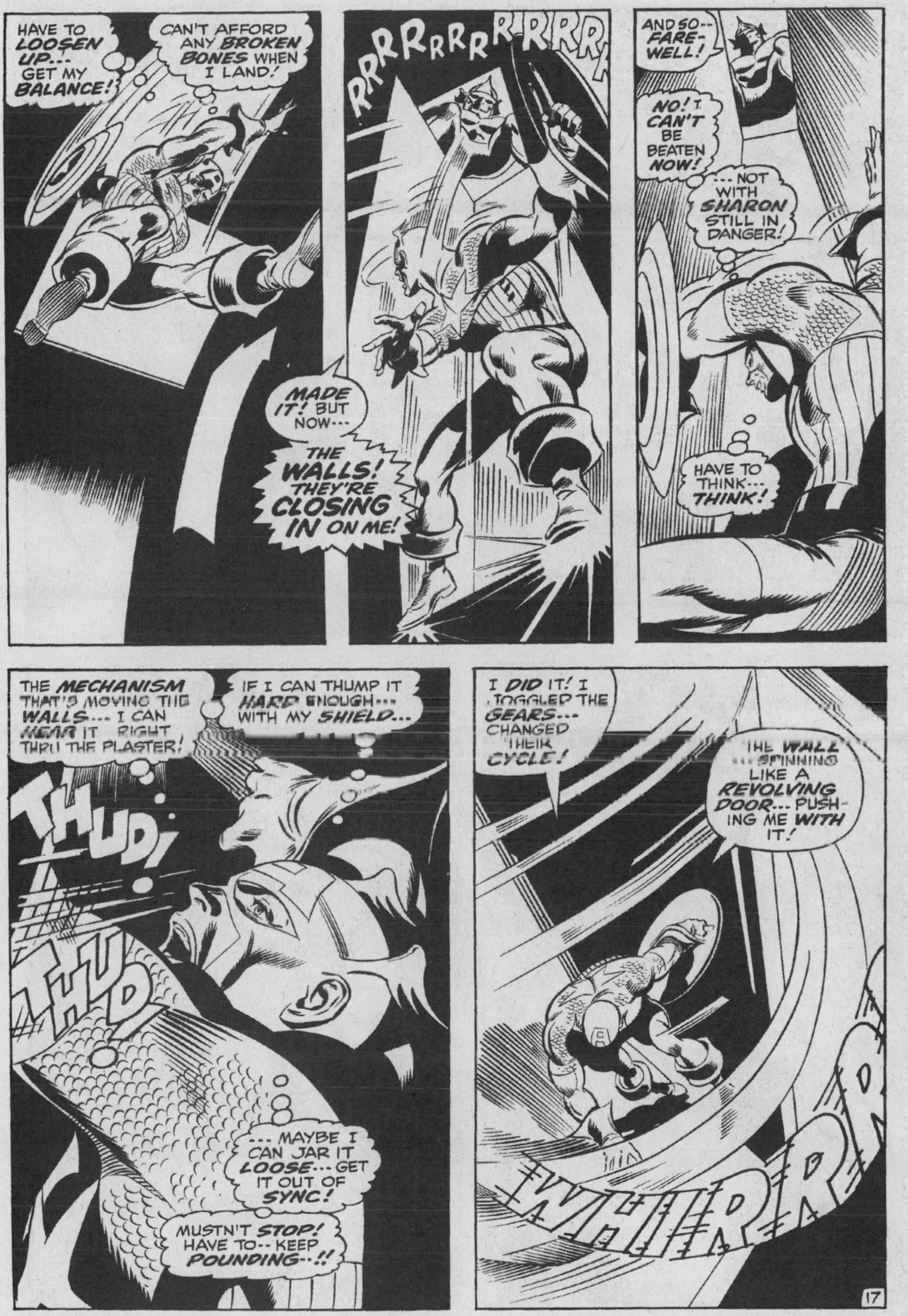
HAVE TO LOOSEN UP... GET MY BALANCE!
CAN'T AFFORD ANY BROKEN BONES WHEN I LAND!
RRRRRRRRRRR
MADE IT! BUT NOW---
THE WALLS! THEY'RE CLOSING IN ON ME!
AND SO-- FARE-WELL!
NO! I CAN'T BE BEATEN NOW!
... NOT WITH SHARON STILL IN DANGER!
HAVE TO THINK--- THINK!
THE MECHANISM THAT'S MOVING THE WALLS... I CAN HEAR IT RIGHT THRU THE PLASTER!
IF I CAN THUMP IT HARD ENOUGH... WITH MY SHIELD...
THUD!
THUD!
... MAYBE I CAN JAR IT LOOSE... GET IT OUT OF SYNC!
MUSTN'T STOP! HAVE TO-- KEEP POUNDING--!!
I DID IT! I TOGGLED THE GEARS... CHANGED THEIR CYCLE!
THE WALL ... SPINNING LIKE A REVOLVING DOOR... PUSH-ING ME WITH IT!
WHIRRR

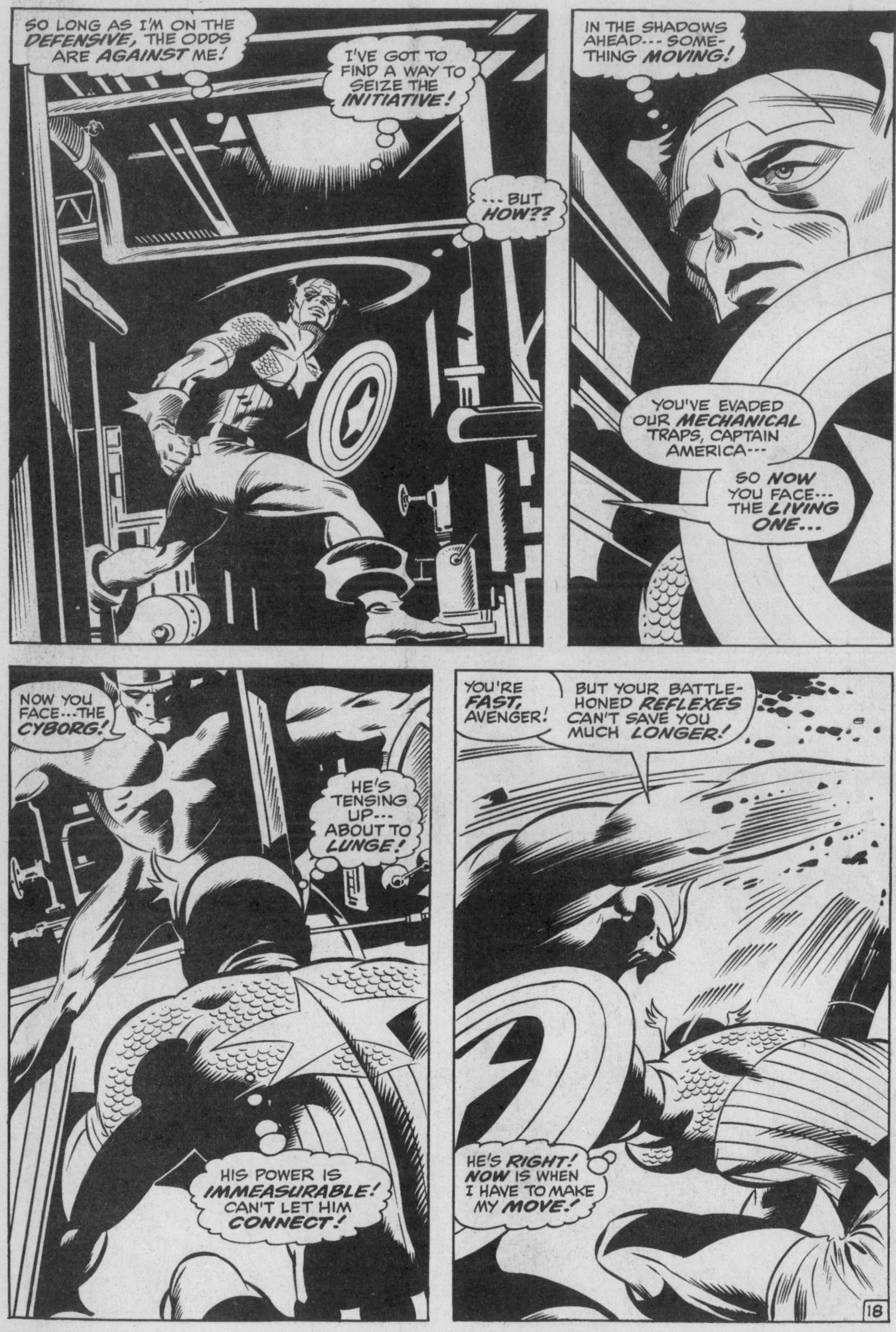
SO LONG AS I'M ON THE DEFENSIVE, THE ODDS ARE AGAINST ME!
I'VE GOT TO FIND A WAY TO SEIZE THE INITIATIVE!
... BUT HOW??
IN THE SHADOWS AHEAD--- SOMETHING MOVING!
YOU'VE EVADED OUR MECHANICAL TRAPS, CAPTAIN AMERICA---
SO NOW YOU FACE... THE LIVING ONE...
NOW YOU FACE---THE CYBORG!
HE'S TENSING UP--- ABOUT TO LUNGE!
HIS POWER IS IMMEASURABLE! CAN'T LET HIM CONNECT!
YOU'RE FAST, AVENGER!
BUT YOUR BATTLE-HONED REFLEXES CAN'T SAVE YOU MUCH LONGER!
HE'S RIGHT! NOW IS WHEN I HAVE TO MAKE MY MOVE!
18

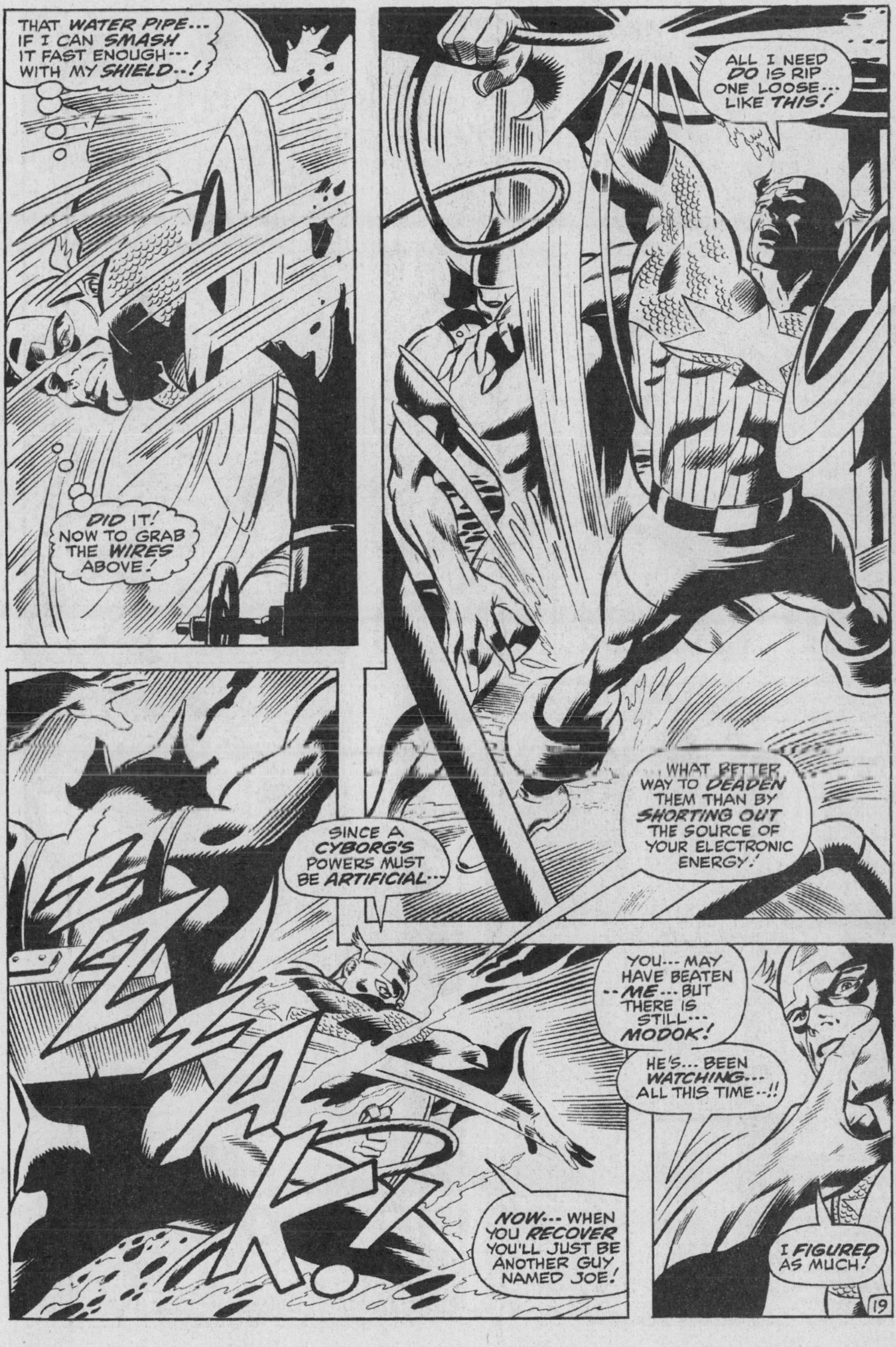
THAT WATER PIPE... IF I CAN SMASH IT FAST ENOUGH... WITH MY SHIELD..!
DID IT! NOW TO GRAB THE WIRES ABOVE!
ALL I NEED DO IS RIP ONE LOOSE... LIKE THIS!
SINCE A CYBORG'S POWERS MUST BE ARTIFICIAL...
...WHAT BETTER WAY TO DEADEN THEM THAN BY SHORTING OUT THE SOURCE OF YOUR ELECTRONIC ENERGY!
ZZZAK!
NOW... WHEN YOU RECOVER YOU'LL JUST BE ANOTHER GUY NAMED JOE!
YOU... MAY HAVE BEATEN --ME... BUT THERE IS STILL... MODOK!
HE'S... BEEN WATCHING... ALL THIS TIME--!!
I FIGURED AS MUCH!
19

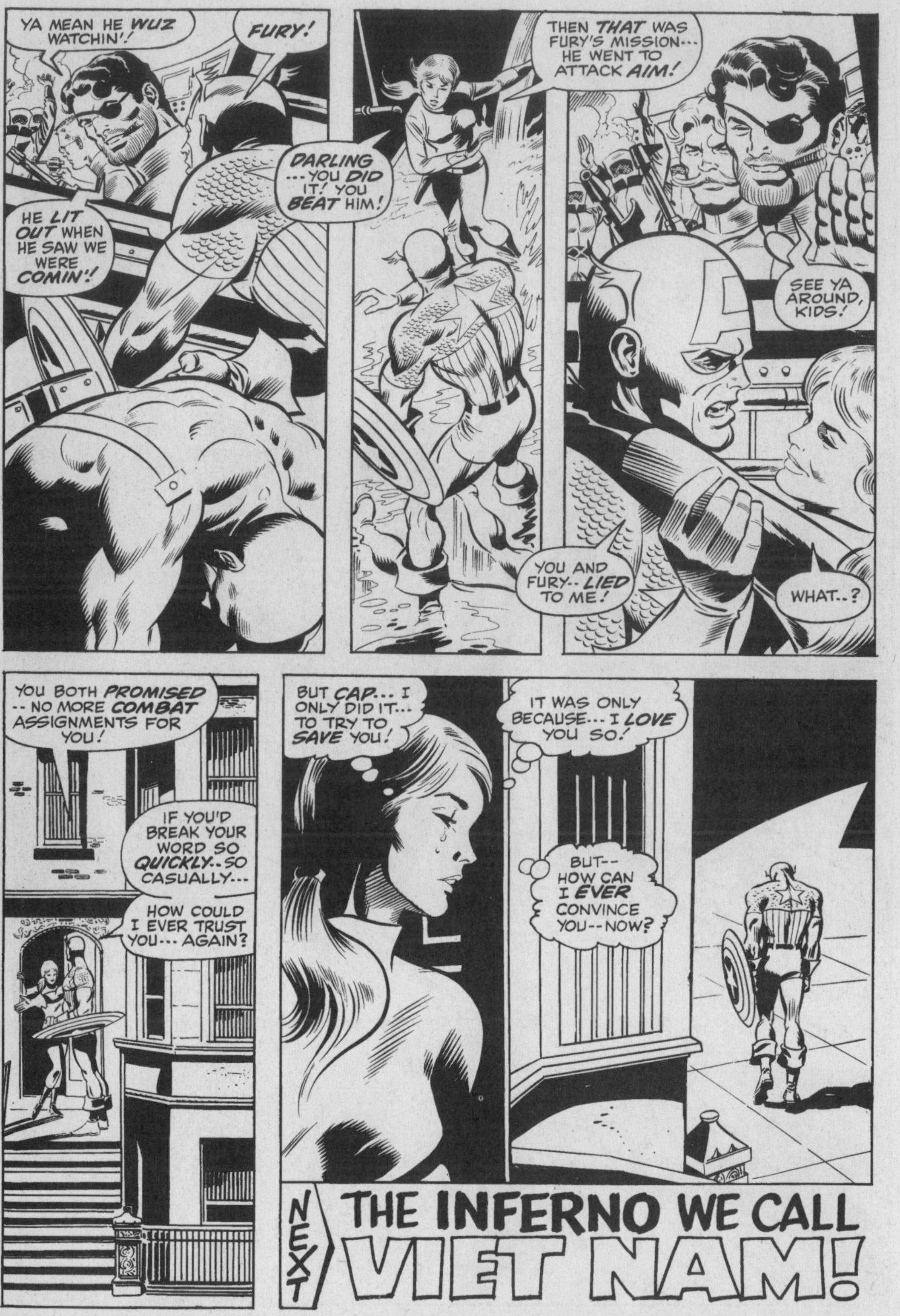
YA MEAN HE WUZ WATCHIN'!
FURY!
HE LIT OUT WHEN HE SAW WE WERE COMIN'!
DARLING --- YOU DID IT! YOU BEAT HIM!
THEN THAT WAS FURY'S MISSION--- HE WENT TO ATTACK AIM!
SEE YA AROUND, KIDS!
YOU AND FURY-- LIED TO ME!
WHAT..?
YOU BOTH PROMISED -- NO MORE COMBAT ASSIGNMENTS FOR YOU!
IF YOU'D BREAK YOUR WORD SO QUICKLY-- SO CASUALLY---
HOW COULD I EVER TRUST YOU--- AGAIN?
BUT CAP--- I ONLY DID IT--- TO TRY TO SAVE YOU!
IT WAS ONLY BECAUSE--- I LOVE YOU SO!
BUT-- HOW CAN I EVER CONVINCE YOU--NOW?
NEXT
THE INFERNO WE CALL VIET NAM!

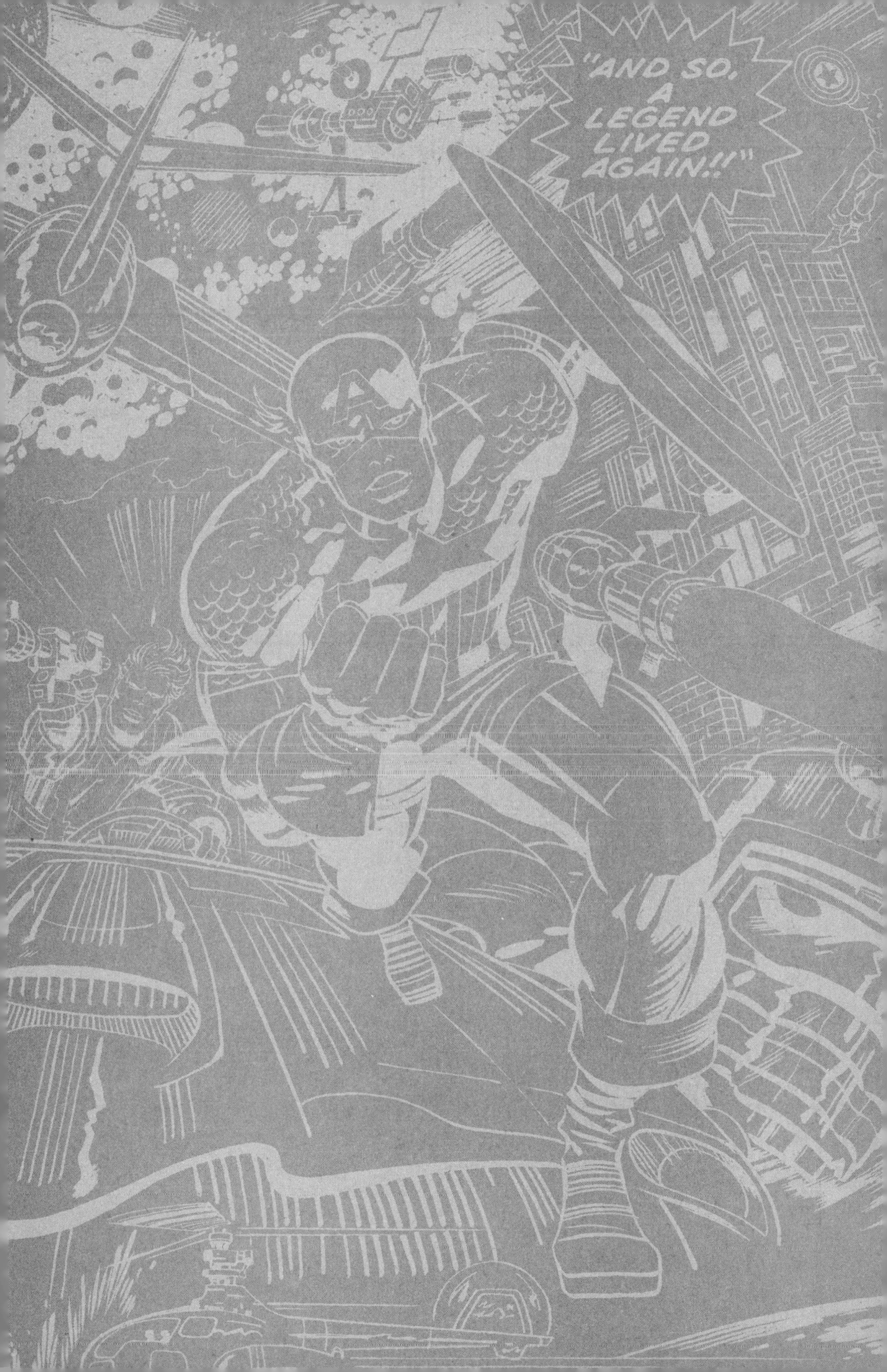
"AND SO, A LEGEND LIVED AGAIN!!"

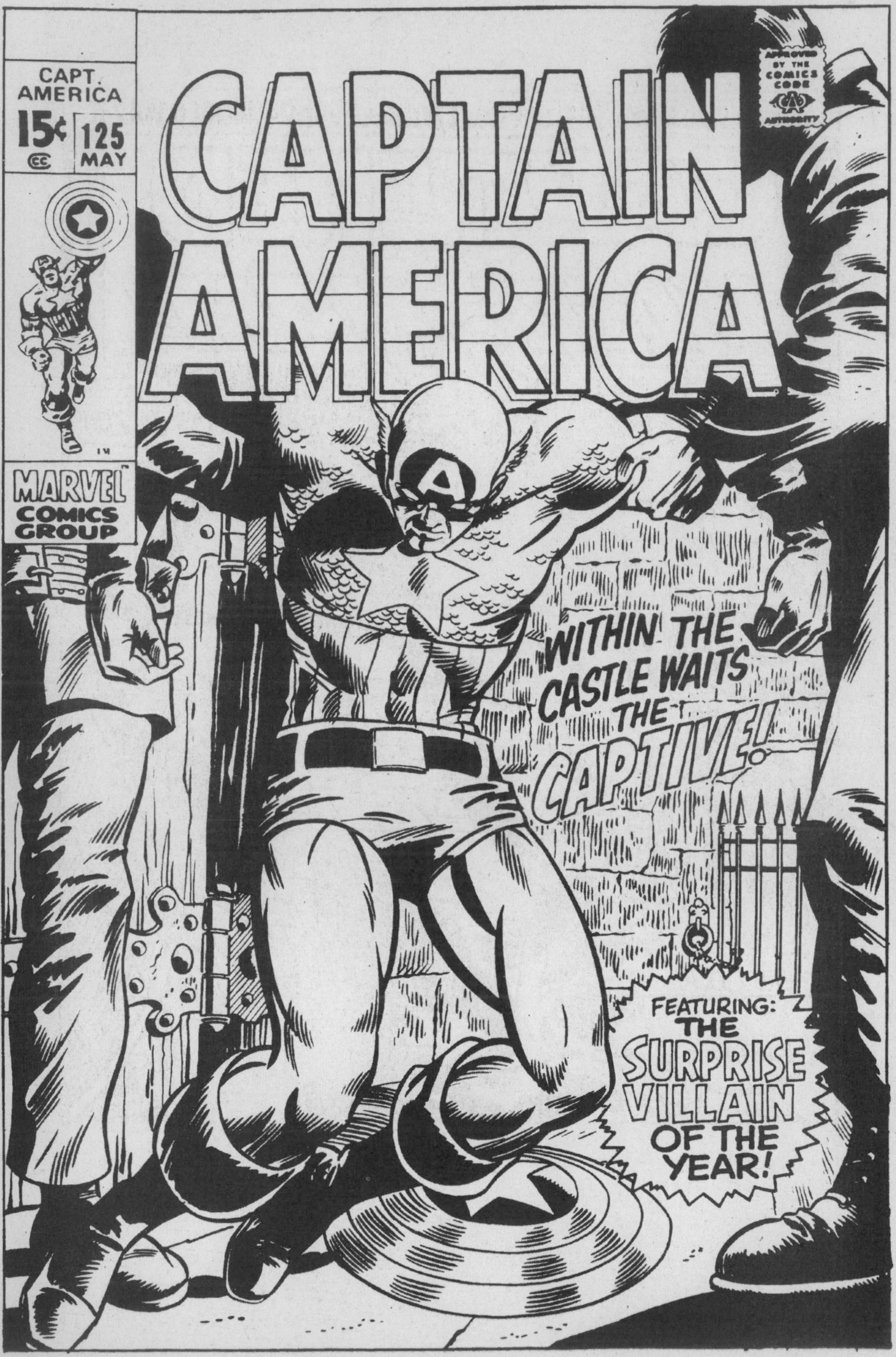
CAPT. AMERICA
15¢
125
MAY
CC
APPROVED BY THE COMICS CODE AUTHORITY
CAPTAIN AMERICA
MARVEL COMICS GROUP
WITHIN THE CASTLE WAITS THE CAPTIVE!
FEATURING: THE SURPRISE VILLAIN OF THE YEAR!

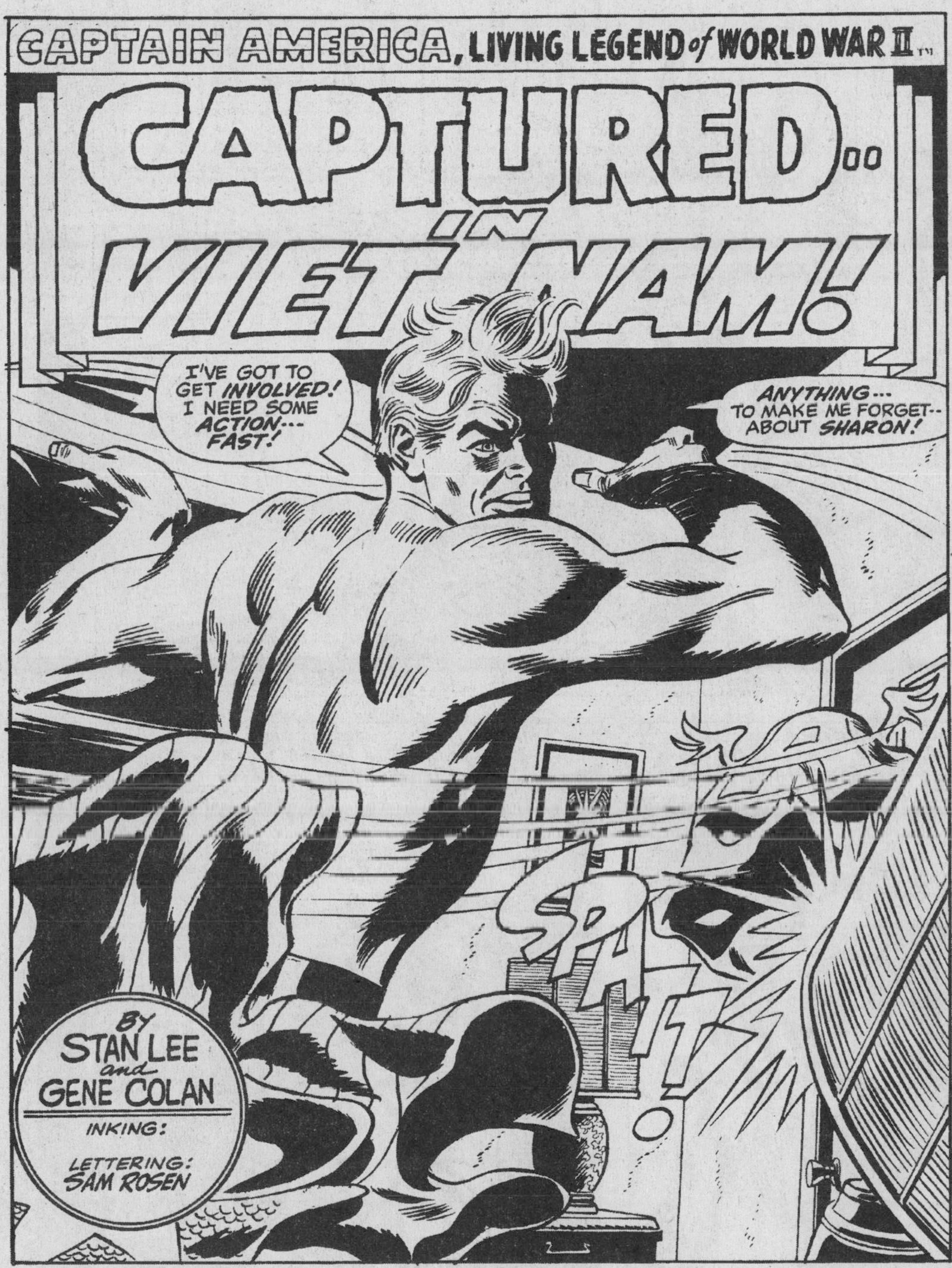
CAPTAIN AMERICA, LIVING LEGEND of WORLD WAR II™
CAPTURED.. IN VIET NAM!
I'VE GOT TO GET INVOLVED! I NEED SOME ACTION--- FAST!
ANYTHING--- TO MAKE ME FORGET-- ABOUT SHARON!
SPAT!
BY STAN LEE and GENE COLAN
INKING:
LETTERING: SAM ROSEN

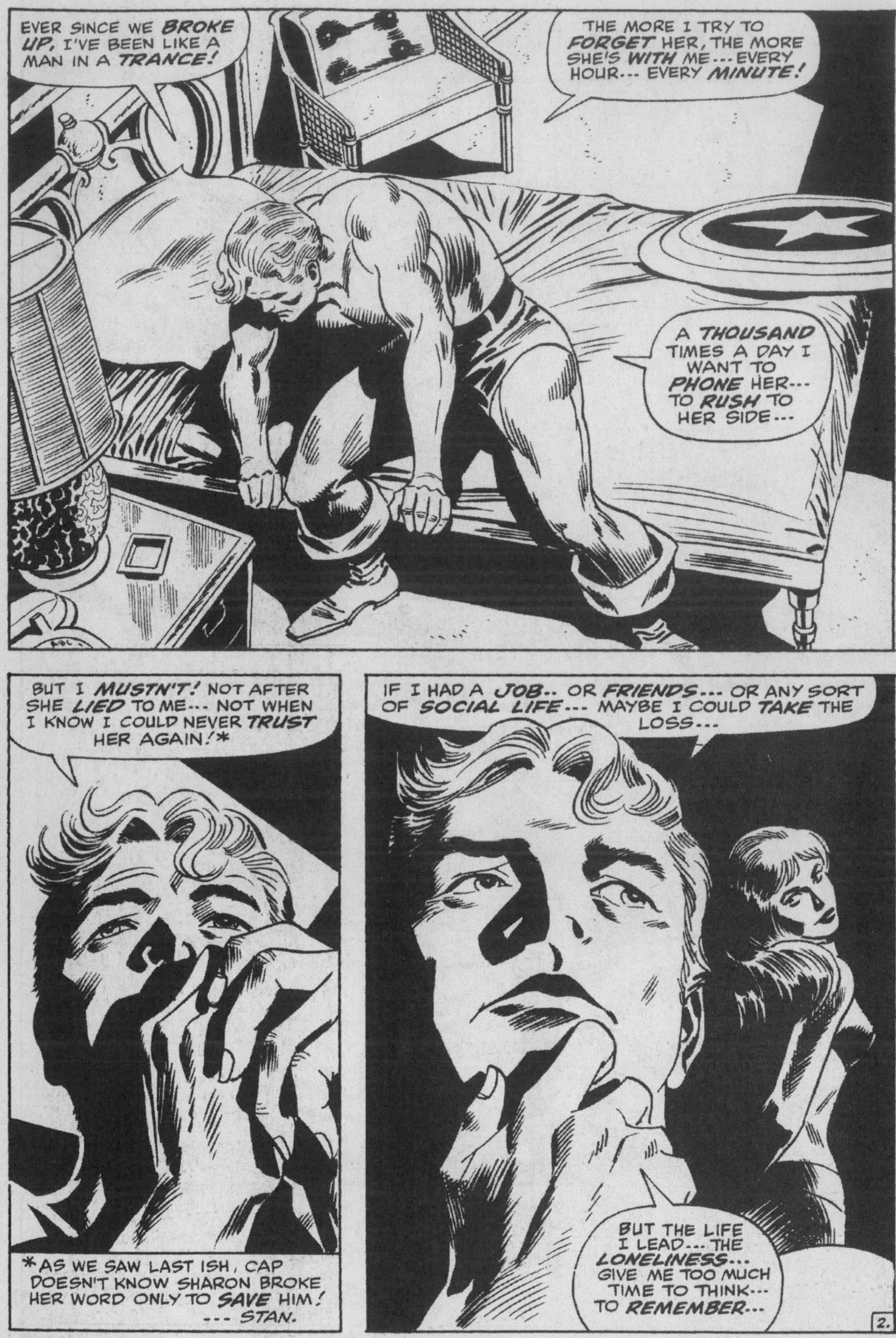
EVER SINCE WE BROKE UP, I'VE BEEN LIKE A MAN IN A TRANCE!
THE MORE I TRY TO FORGET HER, THE MORE SHE'S WITH ME--- EVERY HOUR--- EVERY MINUTE!
A THOUSAND TIMES A DAY I WANT TO PHONE HER--- TO RUSH TO HER SIDE---
BUT I MUSTN'T! NOT AFTER SHE LIED TO ME--- NOT WHEN I KNOW I COULD NEVER TRUST HER AGAIN!*
*AS WE SAW LAST ISH, CAP DOESN'T KNOW SHARON BROKE HER WORD ONLY TO SAVE HIM! --- STAN.
IF I HAD A JOB-- OR FRIENDS--- OR ANY SORT OF SOCIAL LIFE--- MAYBE I COULD TAKE THE LOSS---
BUT THE LIFE I LEAD--- THE LONELINESS--- GIVE ME TOO MUCH TIME TO THINK--- TO REMEMBER---
2.

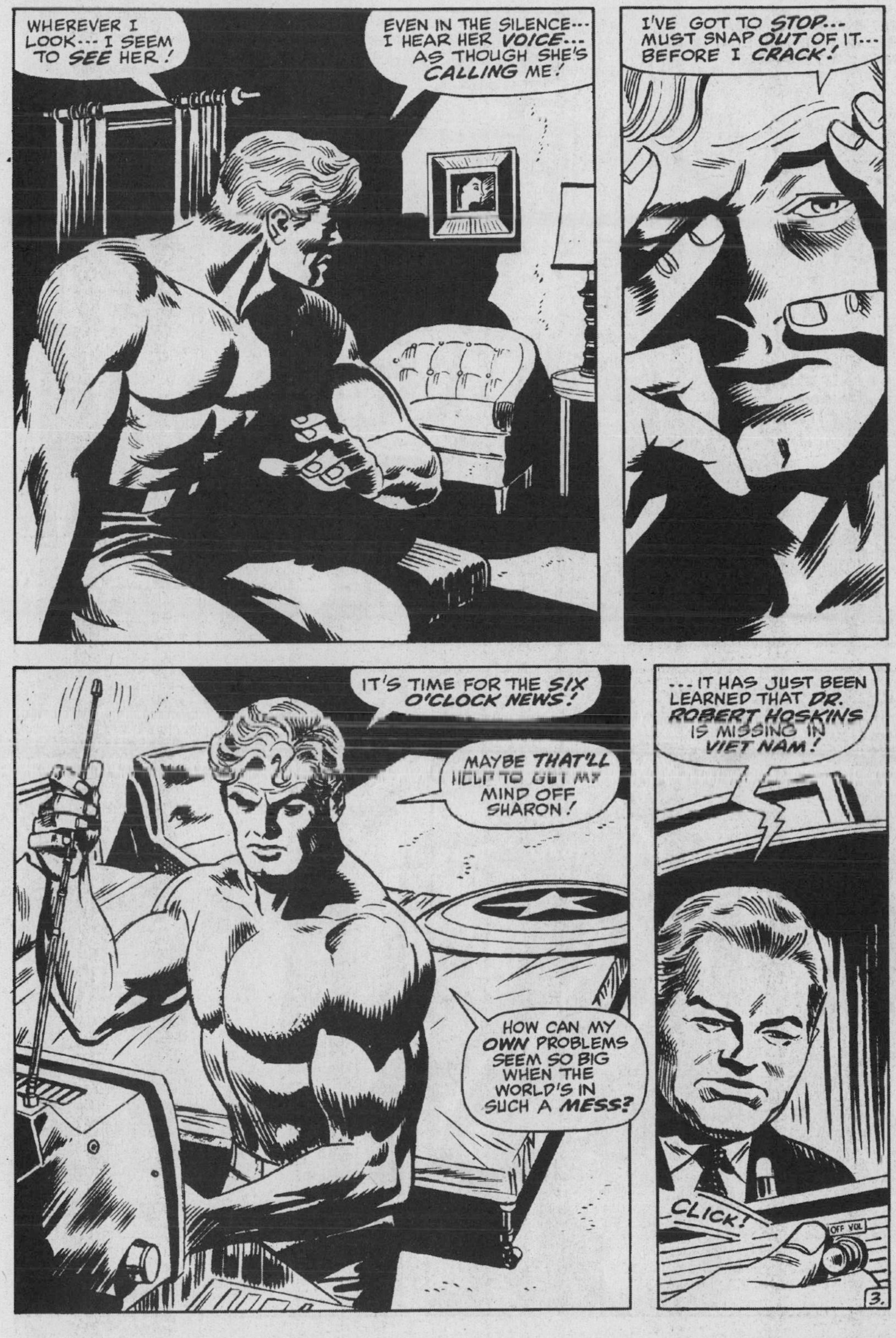
WHEREVER I LOOK--- I SEEM TO SEE HER!
EVEN IN THE SILENCE--- I HEAR HER VOICE... AS THOUGH SHE'S CALLING ME!
I'VE GOT TO STOP... MUST SNAP OUT OF IT... BEFORE I CRACK!
IT'S TIME FOR THE SIX O'CLOCK NEWS!
MAYBE THAT'LL HELP TO GET MY MIND OFF SHARON!
HOW CAN MY OWN PROBLEMS SEEM SO BIG WHEN THE WORLD'S IN SUCH A MESS?
...IT HAS JUST BEEN LEARNED THAT DR. ROBERT HOSKINS IS MISSING IN VIET NAM!
CLICK!
OFF VOL
3.

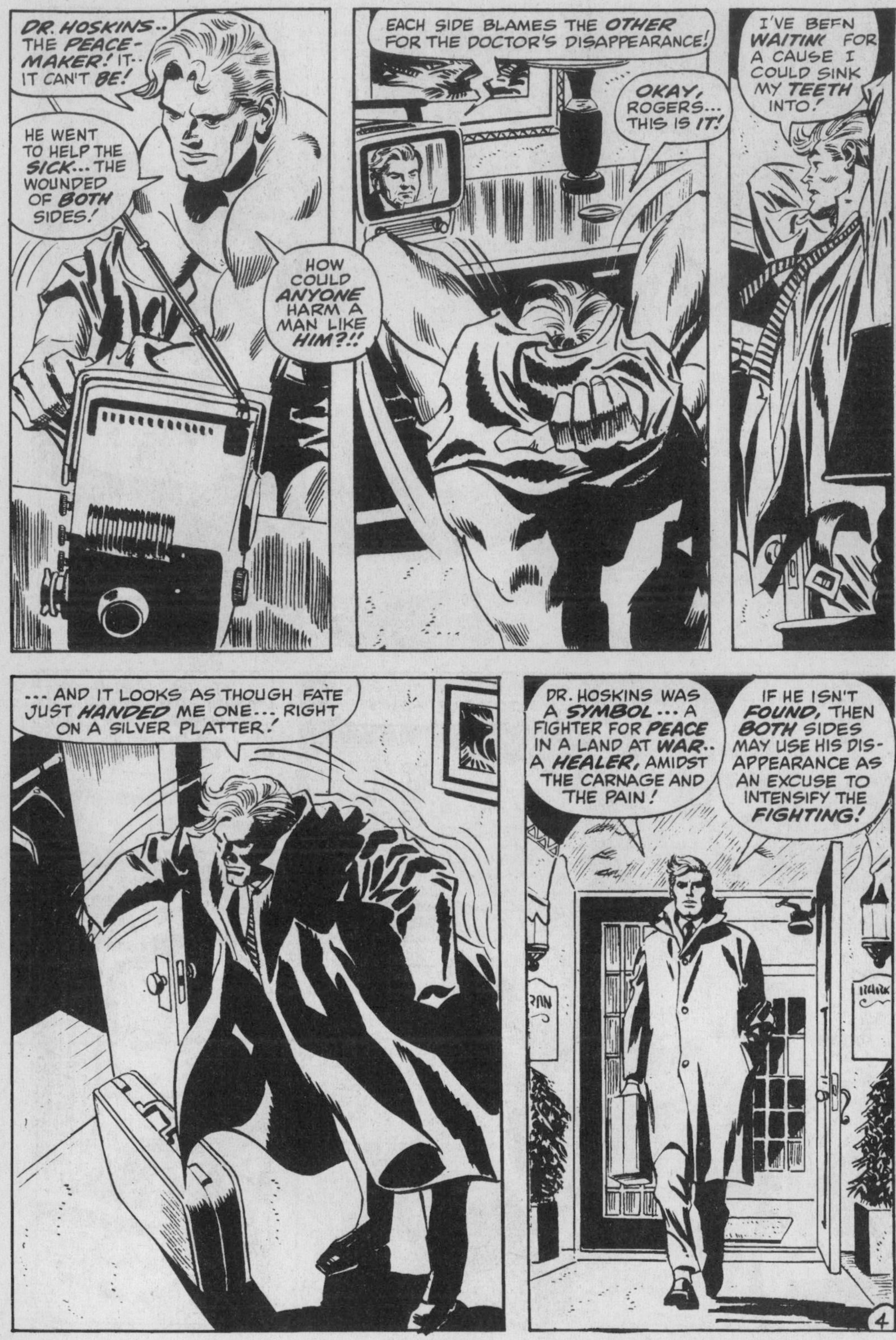
DR. HOSKINS.. THE PEACE-MAKER! IT.. IT CAN'T BE!
HE WENT TO HELP THE SICK... THE WOUNDED OF BOTH SIDES!
HOW COULD ANYONE HARM A MAN LIKE HIM?!!
EACH SIDE BLAMES THE OTHER FOR THE DOCTOR'S DISAPPEARANCE!
OKAY, ROGERS... THIS IS IT!
I'VE BEEN WAITING FOR A CAUSE I COULD SINK MY TEETH INTO!
... AND IT LOOKS AS THOUGH FATE JUST HANDED ME ONE... RIGHT ON A SILVER PLATTER!
DR. HOSKINS WAS A SYMBOL... A FIGHTER FOR PEACE IN A LAND AT WAR.. A HEALER, AMIDST THE CARNAGE AND THE PAIN!
IF HE ISN'T FOUND, THEN BOTH SIDES MAY USE HIS DIS-APPEARANCE AS AN EXCUSE TO INTENSIFY THE FIGHTING!
4

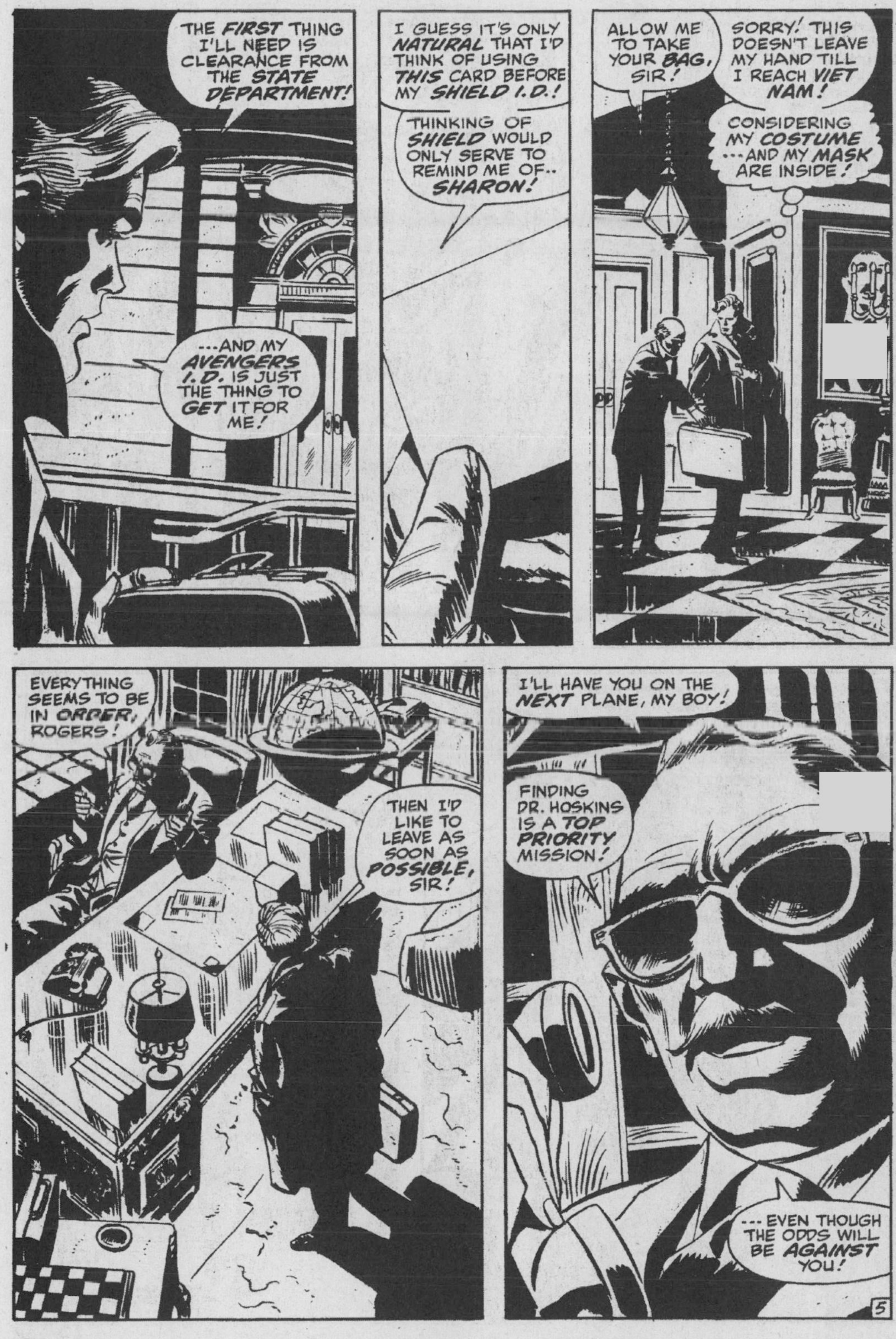
THE FIRST THING I'LL NEED IS CLEARANCE FROM THE STATE DEPARTMENT!
---AND MY AVENGERS I.D. IS JUST THE THING TO GET IT FOR ME!
I GUESS IT'S ONLY NATURAL THAT I'D THINK OF USING THIS CARD BEFORE MY SHIELD I.D.!
THINKING OF SHIELD WOULD ONLY SERVE TO REMIND ME OF.. SHARON!
ALLOW ME TO TAKE YOUR BAG, SIR!
SORRY! THIS DOESN'T LEAVE MY HAND TILL I REACH VIET NAM!
CONSIDERING MY COSTUME ---AND MY MASK ARE INSIDE!
EVERYTHING SEEMS TO BE IN ORDER, ROGERS!
THEN I'D LIKE TO LEAVE AS SOON AS POSSIBLE, SIR!
I'LL HAVE YOU ON THE NEXT PLANE, MY BOY!
FINDING DR. HOSKINS IS A TOP PRIORITY MISSION!
--- EVEN THOUGH THE ODDS WILL BE AGAINST YOU!
5

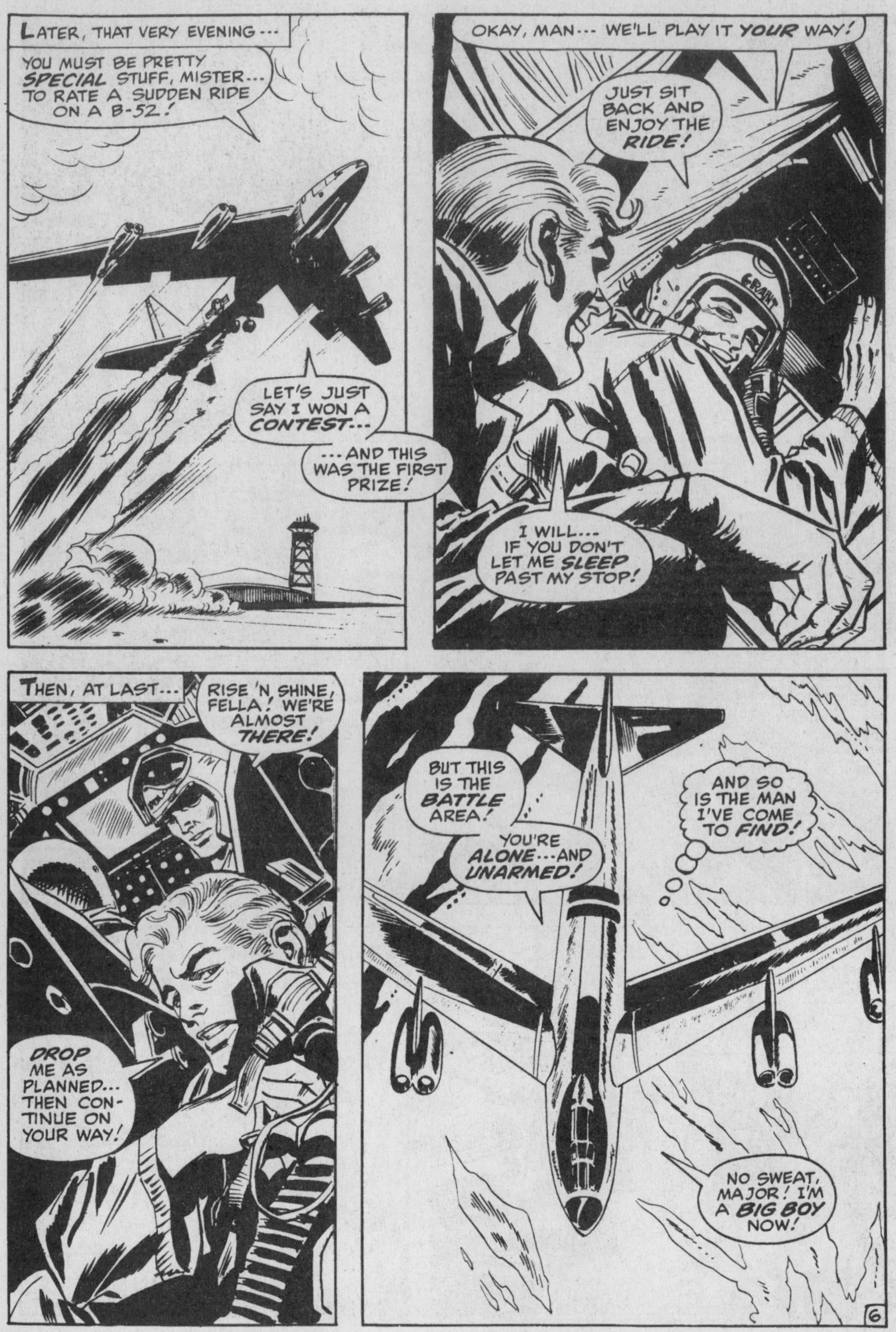
LATER, THAT VERY EVENING ---
YOU MUST BE PRETTY SPECIAL STUFF, MISTER... TO RATE A SUDDEN RIDE ON A B-52!
LET'S JUST SAY I WON A CONTEST---
---AND THIS WAS THE FIRST PRIZE!
OKAY, MAN--- WE'LL PLAY IT YOUR WAY!
JUST SIT BACK AND ENJOY THE RIDE!
I WILL--- IF YOU DON'T LET ME SLEEP PAST MY STOP!
GRANT
THEN, AT LAST...
RISE 'N SHINE, FELLA! WE'RE ALMOST THERE!
DROP ME AS PLANNED... THEN CONTINUE ON YOUR WAY!
BUT THIS IS THE BATTLE AREA!
YOU'RE ALONE---AND UNARMED!
AND SO IS THE MAN I'VE COME TO FIND!
NO SWEAT, MAJOR! I'M A BIG BOY NOW!
6

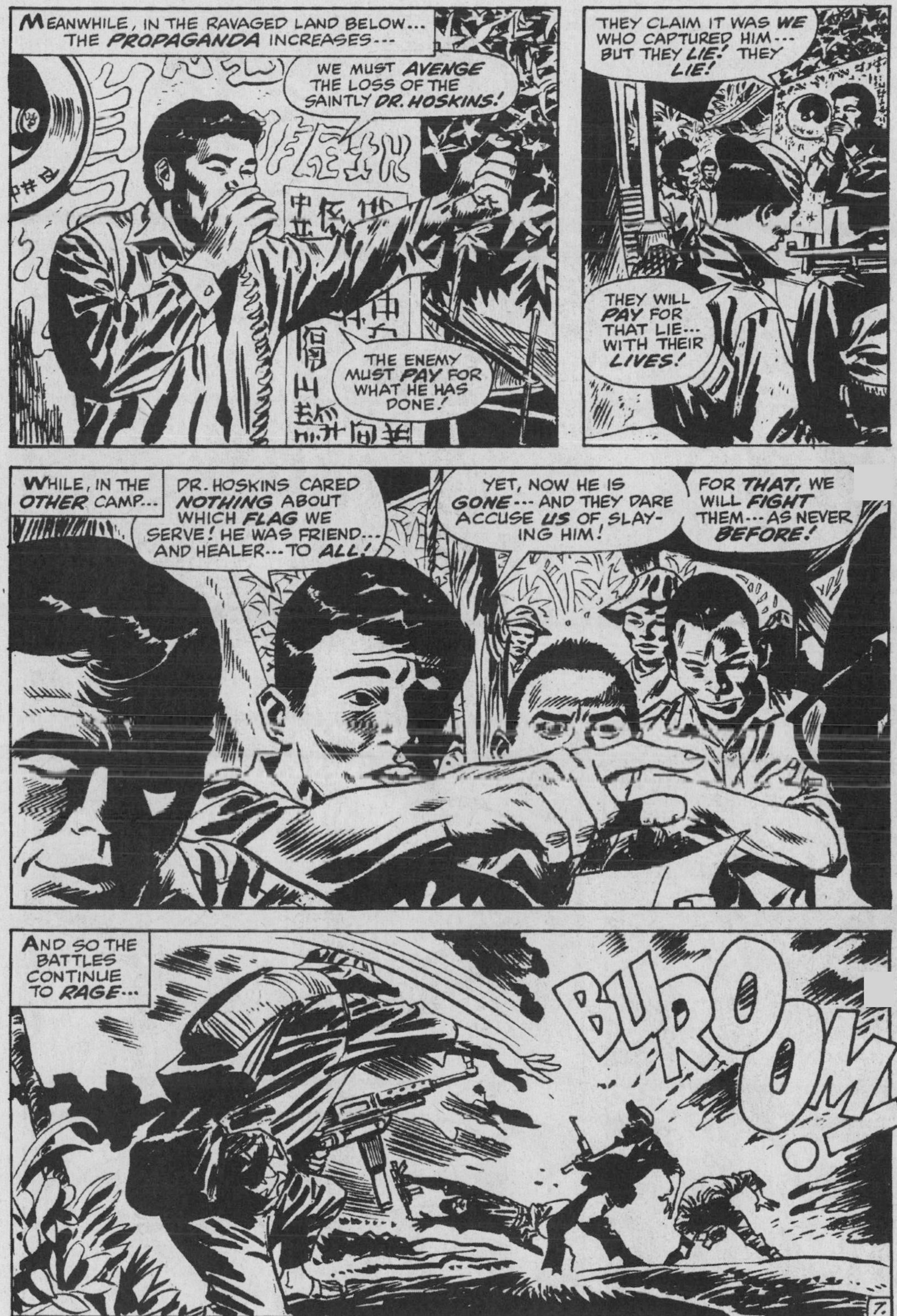
MEANWHILE, IN THE RAVAGED LAND BELOW... THE PROPAGANDA INCREASES---
WE MUST AVENGE THE LOSS OF THE SAINTLY DR. HOSKINS!
THE ENEMY MUST PAY FOR WHAT HE HAS DONE!
THEY CLAIM IT WAS WE WHO CAPTURED HIM--- BUT THEY LIE! THEY LIE!
THEY WILL PAY FOR THAT LIE--- WITH THEIR LIVES!
WHILE, IN THE OTHER CAMP...
DR. HOSKINS CARED NOTHING ABOUT WHICH FLAG WE SERVE! HE WAS FRIEND... AND HEALER---TO ALL!
YET, NOW HE IS GONE--- AND THEY DARE ACCUSE US OF SLAYING HIM!
FOR THAT, WE WILL FIGHT THEM--- AS NEVER BEFORE!
AND SO THE BATTLES CONTINUE TO RAGE...
BUROOM!
7.

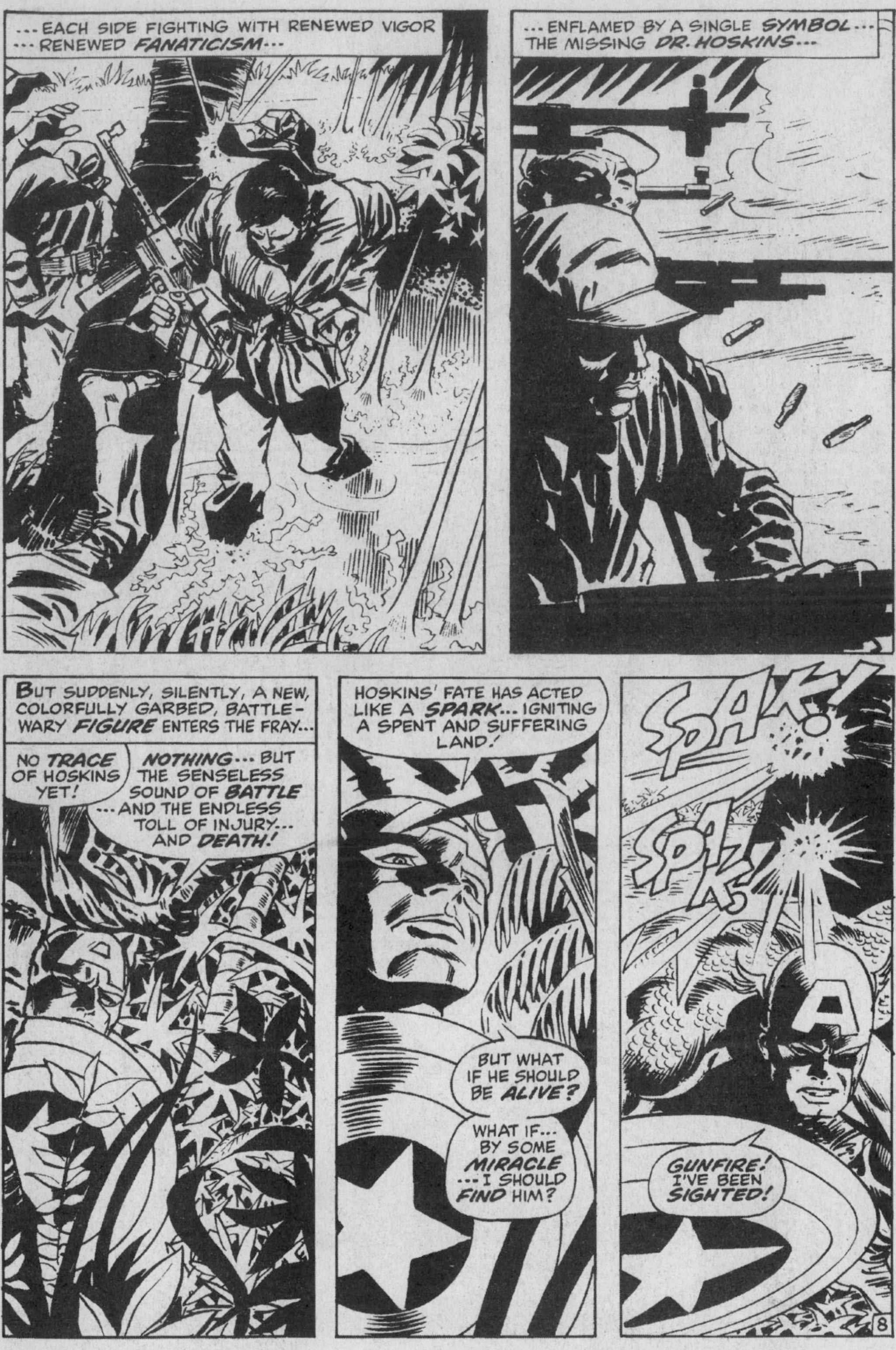
...EACH SIDE FIGHTING WITH RENEWED VIGOR ...RENEWED FANATICISM...
...ENFLAMED BY A SINGLE SYMBOL... THE MISSING DR. HOSKINS...
BUT SUDDENLY, SILENTLY, A NEW, COLORFULLY GARBED, BATTLE-WARY FIGURE ENTERS THE FRAY...
NO TRACE OF HOSKINS YET!
NOTHING... BUT THE SENSELESS SOUND OF BATTLE ...AND THE ENDLESS TOLL OF INJURY... AND DEATH!
HOSKINS' FATE HAS ACTED LIKE A SPARK... IGNITING A SPENT AND SUFFERING LAND!
BUT WHAT IF HE SHOULD BE ALIVE?
WHAT IF... BY SOME MIRACLE ...I SHOULD FIND HIM?
SPAK!
SPAK!
GUNFIRE! I'VE BEEN SIGHTED!
8

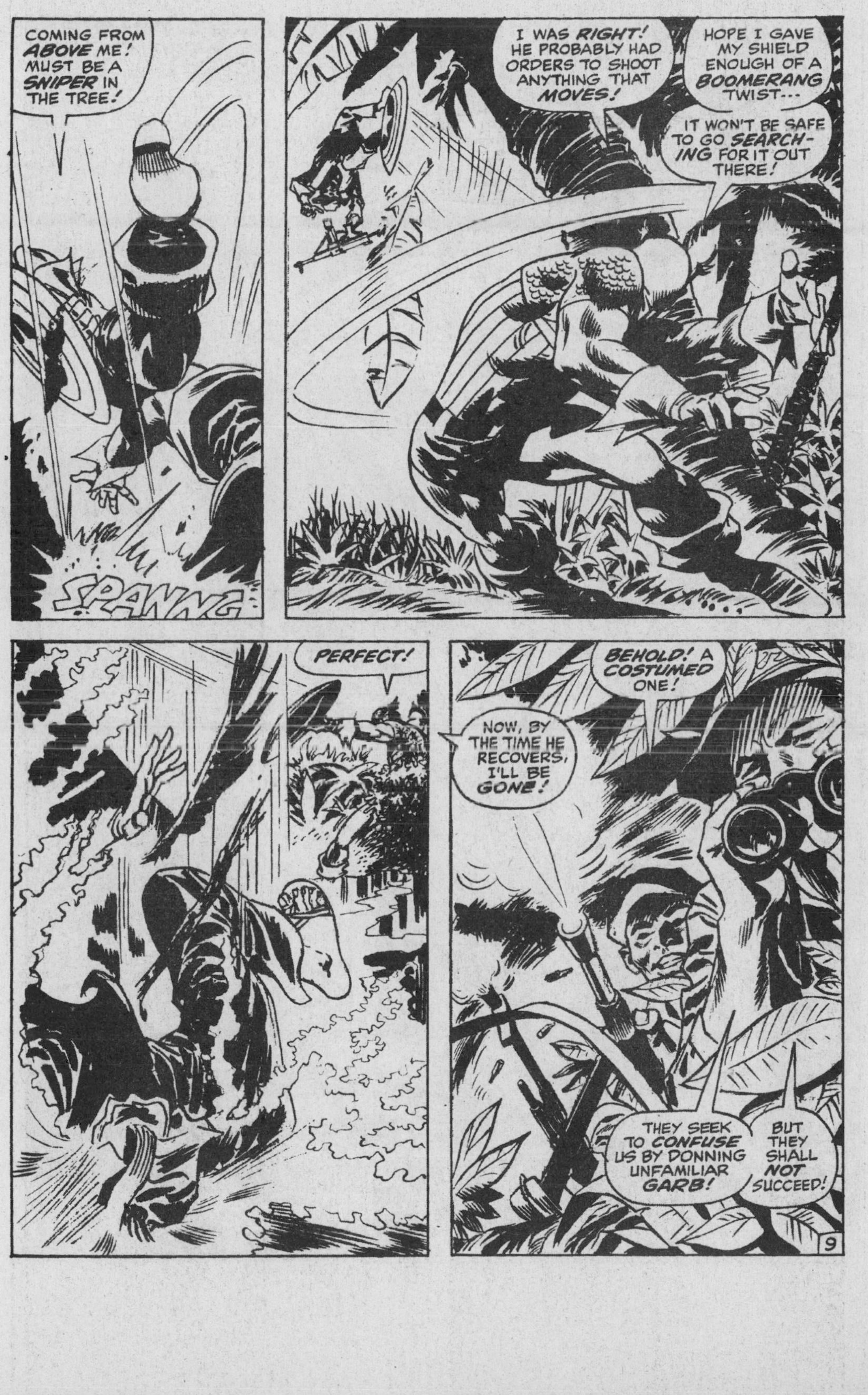
COMING FROM ABOVE ME! MUST BE A SNIPER IN THE TREE!
SPANNG
I WAS RIGHT! HE PROBABLY HAD ORDERS TO SHOOT ANYTHING THAT MOVES!
HOPE I GAVE MY SHIELD ENOUGH OF A BOOMERANG TWIST---
IT WON'T BE SAFE TO GO SEARCH-ING FOR IT OUT THERE!
PERFECT!
NOW, BY THE TIME HE RECOVERS, I'LL BE GONE!
BEHOLD! A COSTUMED ONE!
THEY SEEK TO CONFUSE US BY DONNING UNFAMILIAR GARB!
BUT THEY SHALL NOT SUCCEED!
9

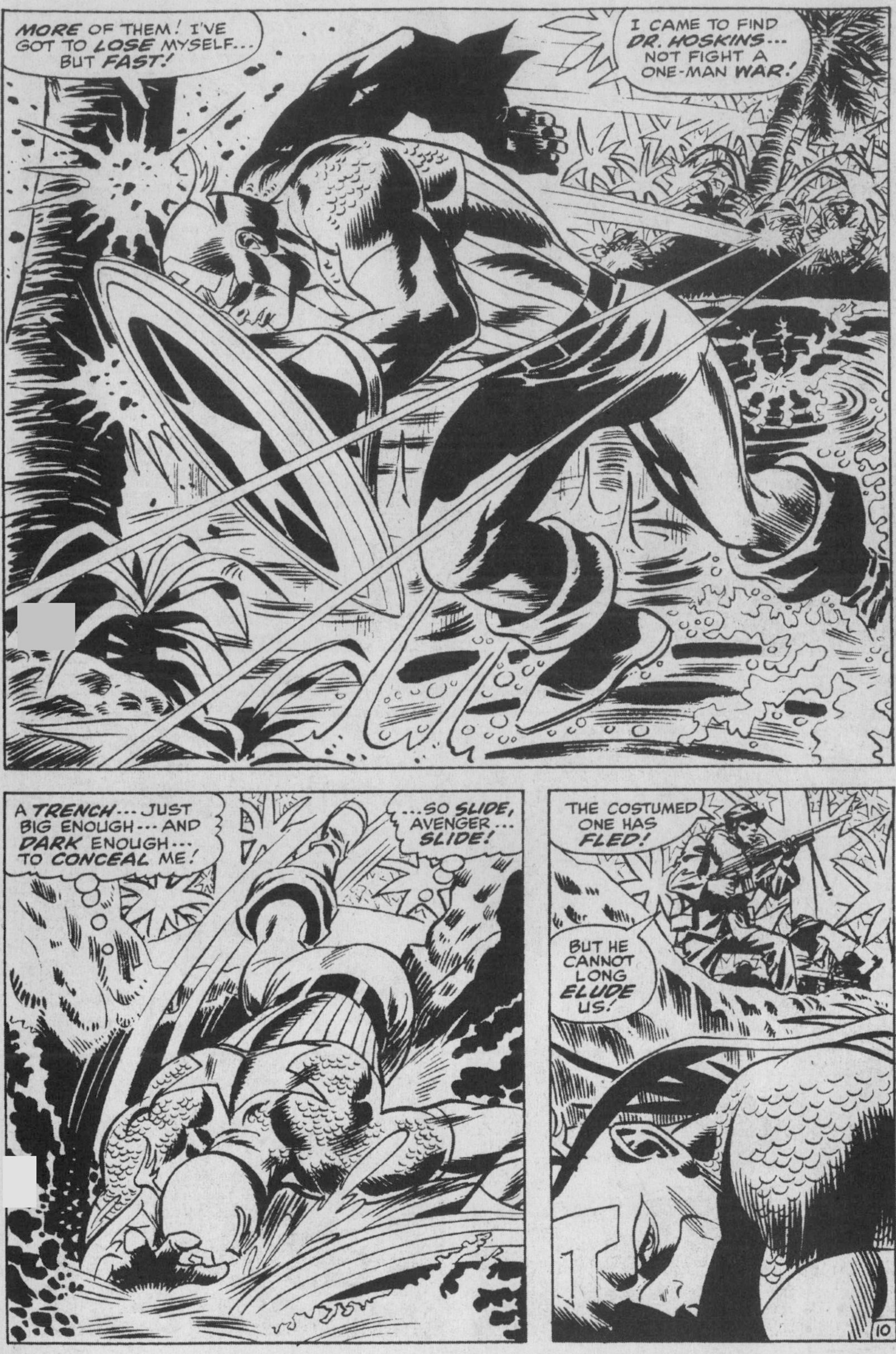
MORE OF THEM! I'VE GOT TO LOSE MYSELF... BUT FAST!
I CAME TO FIND DR. HOSKINS... NOT FIGHT A ONE-MAN WAR!
A TRENCH... JUST BIG ENOUGH... AND DARK ENOUGH... TO CONCEAL ME!
...SO SLIDE, AVENGER... SLIDE!
THE COSTUMED ONE HAS FLED!
BUT HE CANNOT LONG ELUDE US!

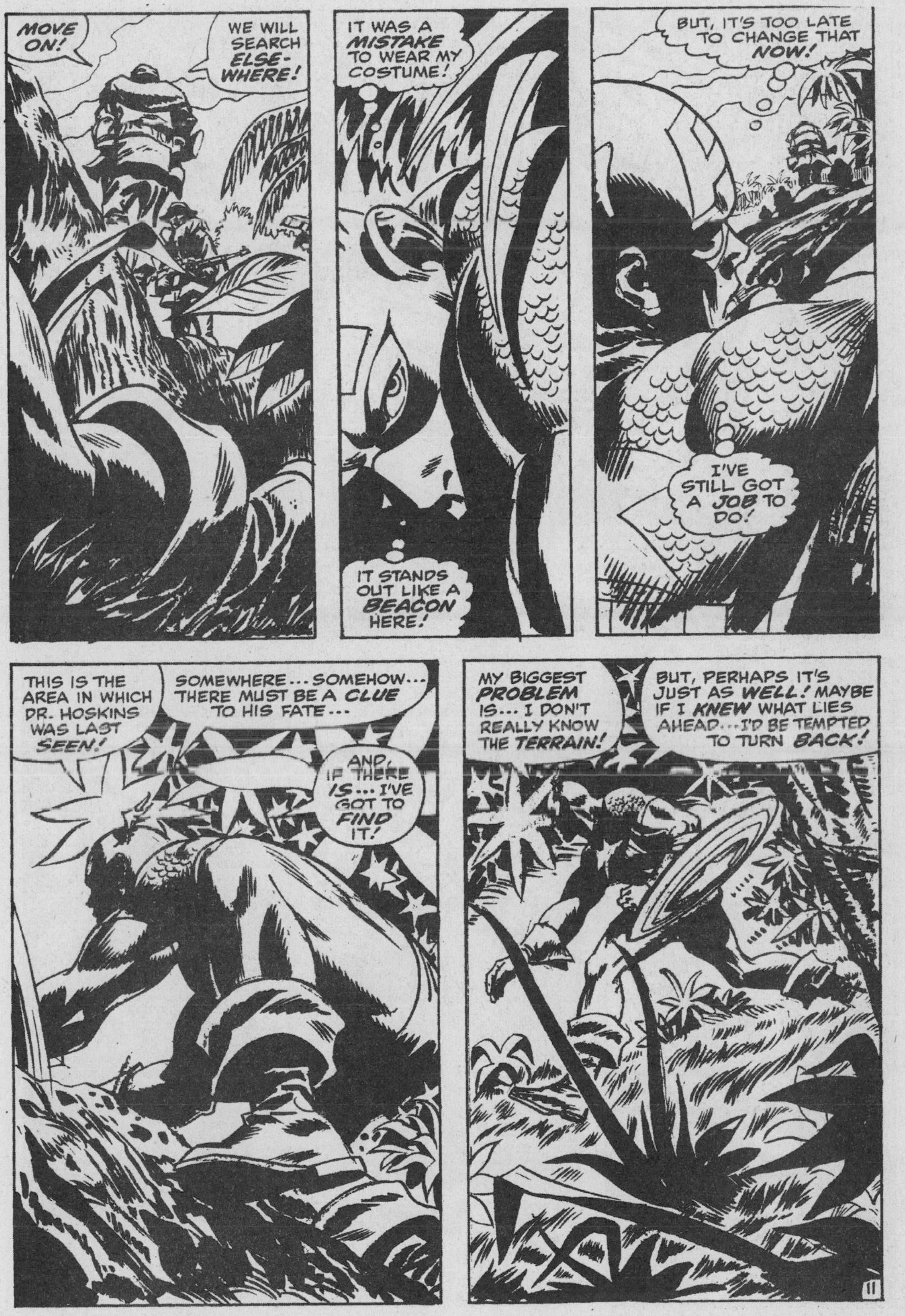

MOVE ON!
WE WILL SEARCH ELSE-WHERE!
IT WAS A MISTAKE TO WEAR MY COSTUME!
IT STANDS OUT LIKE A BEACON HERE!
BUT, IT'S TOO LATE TO CHANGE THAT NOW!
I'VE STILL GOT A JOB TO DO!
THIS IS THE AREA IN WHICH DR. HOSKINS WAS LAST SEEN!
SOMEWHERE... SOMEHOW... THERE MUST BE A CLUE TO HIS FATE...
AND, IF THERE IS... I'VE GOT TO FIND IT!
MY BIGGEST PROBLEM IS... I DON'T REALLY KNOW THE TERRAIN!
BUT, PERHAPS IT'S JUST AS WELL! MAYBE IF I KNEW WHAT LIES AHEAD... I'D BE TEMPTED TO TURN BACK!
11

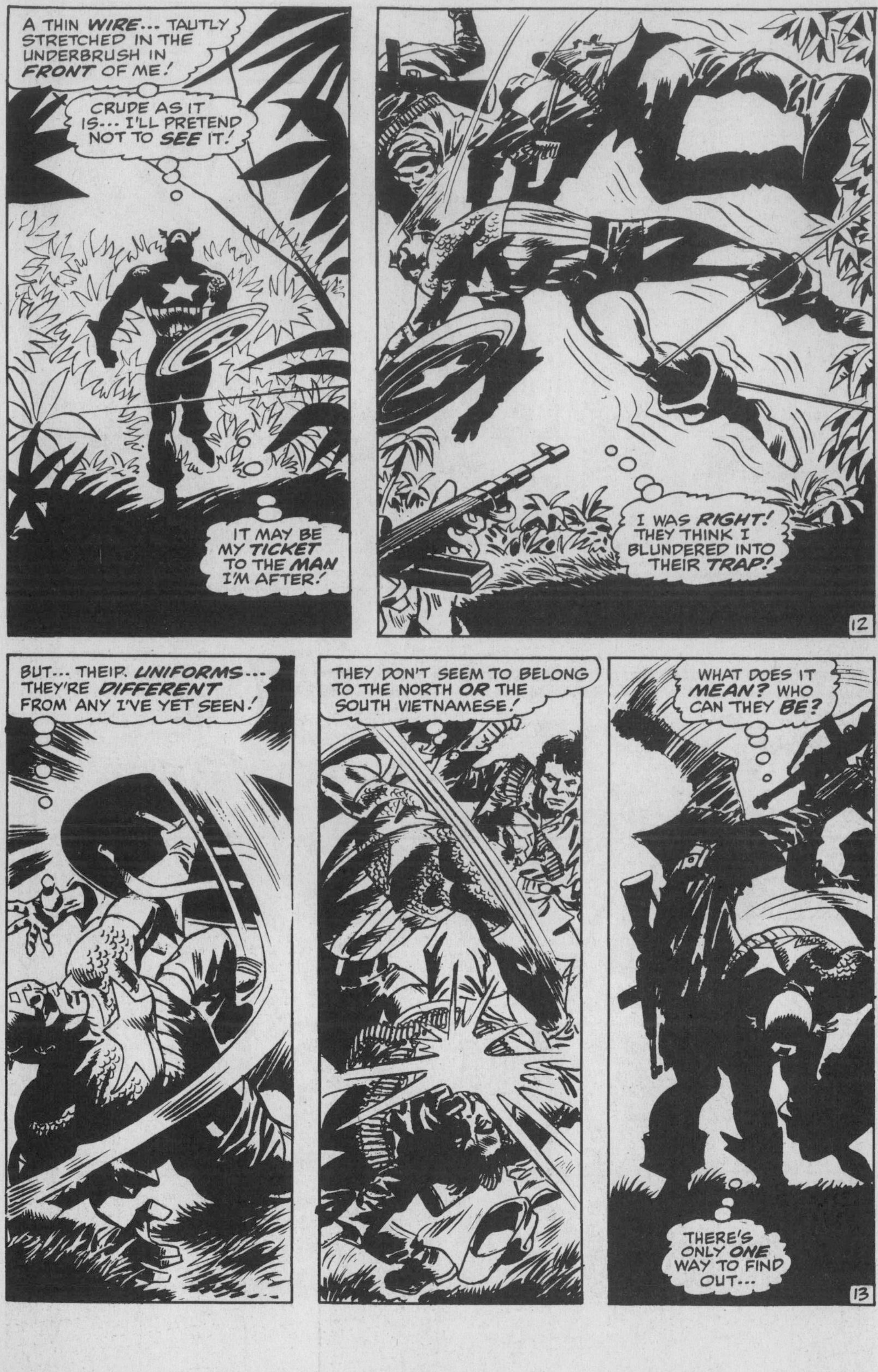

A THIN WIRE... TAUTLY STRETCHED IN THE UNDERBRUSH IN FRONT OF ME!
CRUDE AS IT IS... I'LL PRETEND NOT TO SEE IT!
IT MAY BE MY TICKET TO THE MAN I'M AFTER!
I WAS RIGHT! THEY THINK I BLUNDERED INTO THEIR TRAP!
12
BUT... THEIR UNIFORMS... THEY'RE DIFFERENT FROM ANY I'VE YET SEEN!
THEY DON'T SEEM TO BELONG TO THE NORTH OR THE SOUTH VIETNAMESE!
WHAT DOES IT MEAN? WHO CAN THEY BE?
THERE'S ONLY ONE WAY TO FIND OUT...
13

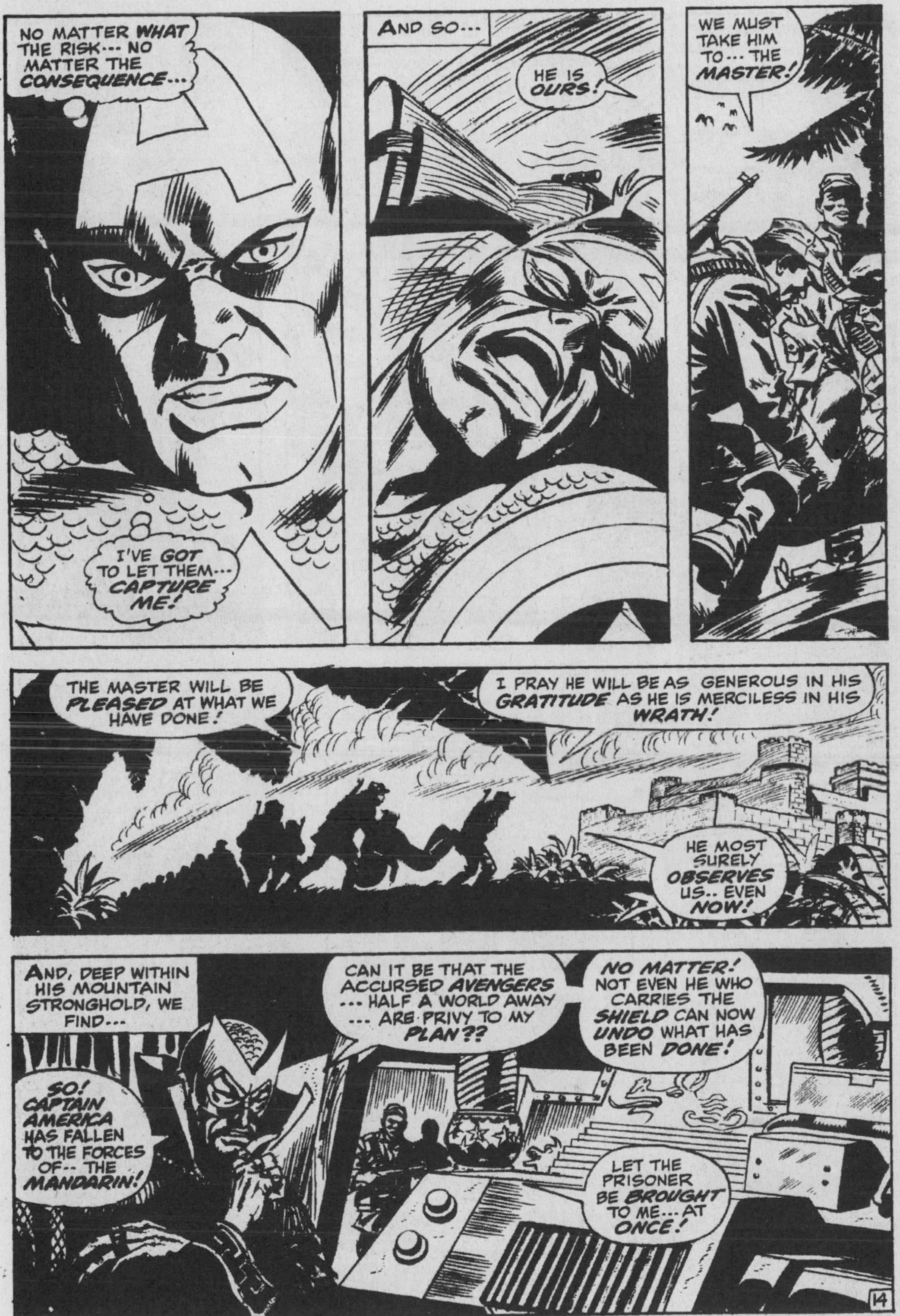
NO MATTER WHAT THE RISK--- NO MATTER THE CONSEQUENCE...
I'VE GOT TO LET THEM--- CAPTURE ME!
AND SO...
HE IS OURS!
WE MUST TAKE HIM TO--- THE MASTER!
THE MASTER WILL BE PLEASED AT WHAT WE HAVE DONE!
I PRAY HE WILL BE AS GENEROUS IN HIS GRATITUDE AS HE IS MERCILESS IN HIS WRATH!
HE MOST SURELY OBSERVES US.. EVEN NOW!
AND, DEEP WITHIN HIS MOUNTAIN STRONGHOLD, WE FIND---
SO! CAPTAIN AMERICA HAS FALLEN TO THE FORCES OF-- THE MANDARIN!
CAN IT BE THAT THE ACCURSED AVENGERS --- HALF A WORLD AWAY --- ARE PRIVY TO MY PLAN??
NO MATTER! NOT EVEN HE WHO CARRIES THE SHIELD CAN NOW UNDO WHAT HAS BEEN DONE!
LET THE PRISONER BE BROUGHT TO ME... AT ONCE!
14

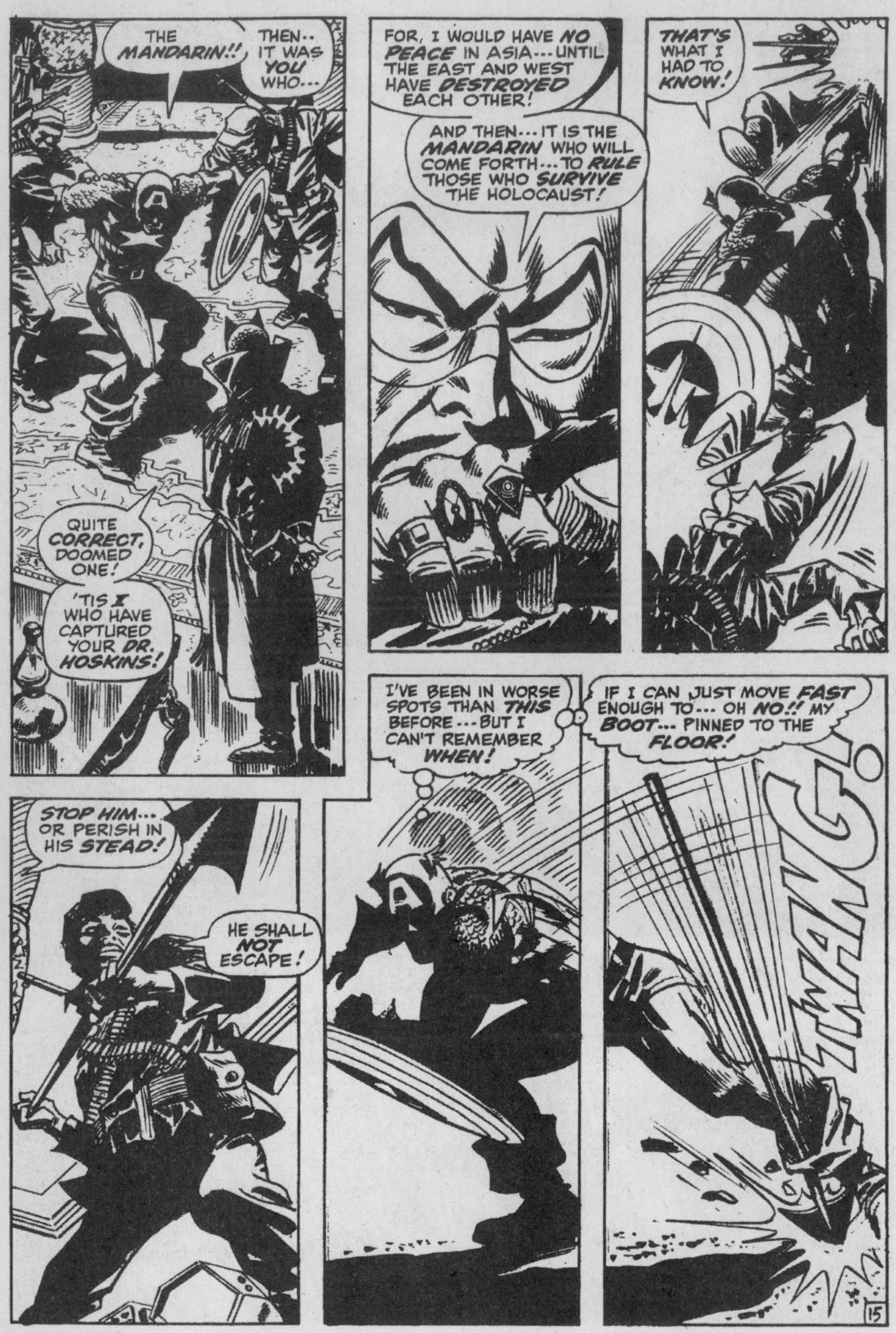
THE MANDARIN!!
THEN.. IT WAS YOU WHO...
QUITE CORRECT, DOOMED ONE!
'TIS I WHO HAVE CAPTURED YOUR DR. HOSKINS!
FOR, I WOULD HAVE NO PEACE IN ASIA... UNTIL THE EAST AND WEST HAVE DESTROYED EACH OTHER!
AND THEN... IT IS THE MANDARIN WHO WILL COME FORTH... TO RULE THOSE WHO SURVIVE THE HOLOCAUST!
THAT'S WHAT I HAD TO KNOW!
STOP HIM... OR PERISH IN HIS STEAD!
HE SHALL NOT ESCAPE!
I'VE BEEN IN WORSE SPOTS THAN THIS BEFORE... BUT I CAN'T REMEMBER WHEN!
IF I CAN JUST MOVE FAST ENOUGH TO... OH NO!! MY BOOT... PINNED TO THE FLOOR!
TWANG!
15

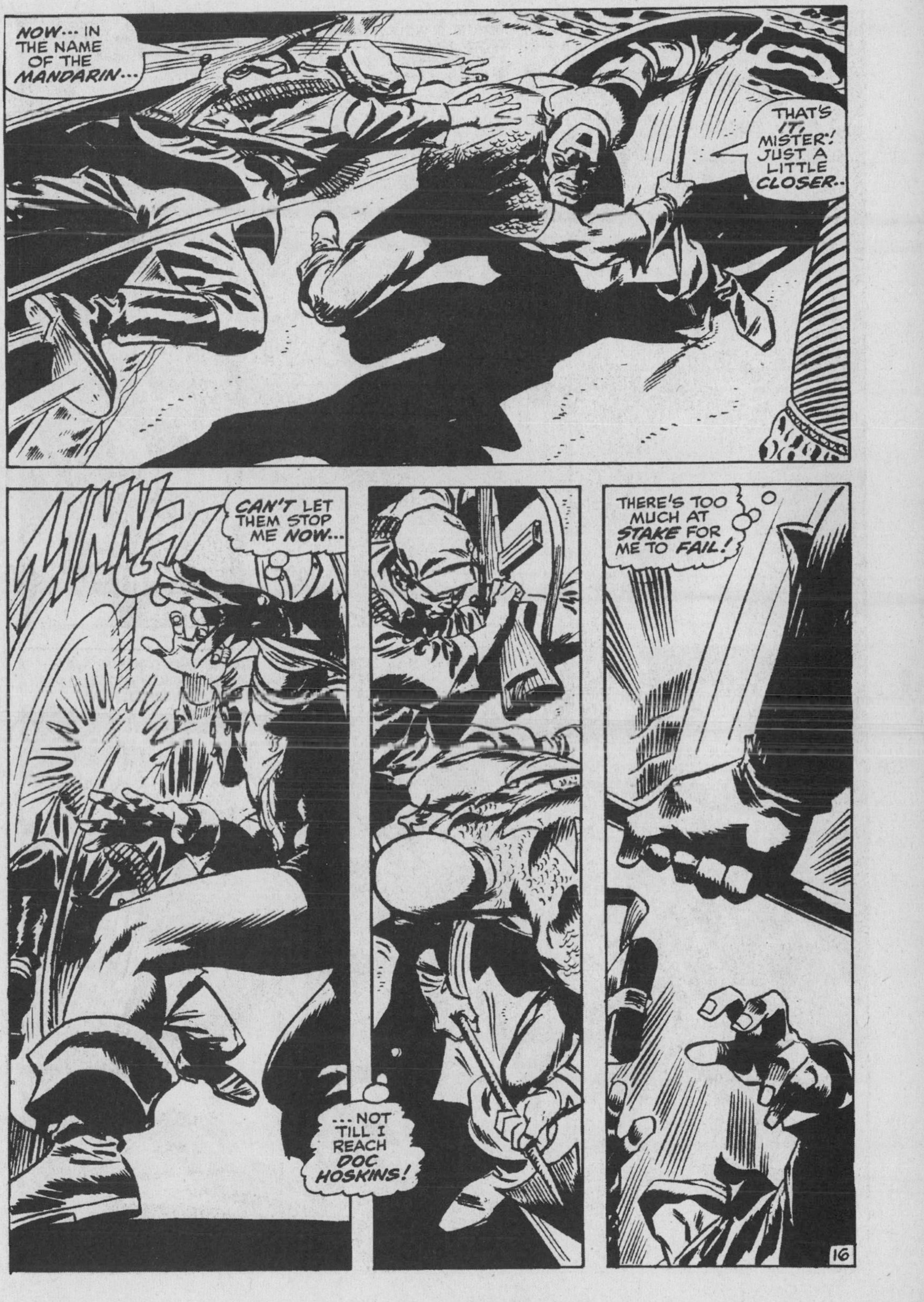
NOW... IN THE NAME OF THE MANDARIN...
THAT'S IT, MISTER! JUST A LITTLE CLOSER..
ZINNG!
CAN'T LET THEM STOP ME NOW...
...NOT TILL I REACH DOC HOSKINS!
THERE'S TOO MUCH AT STAKE FOR ME TO FAIL!
16

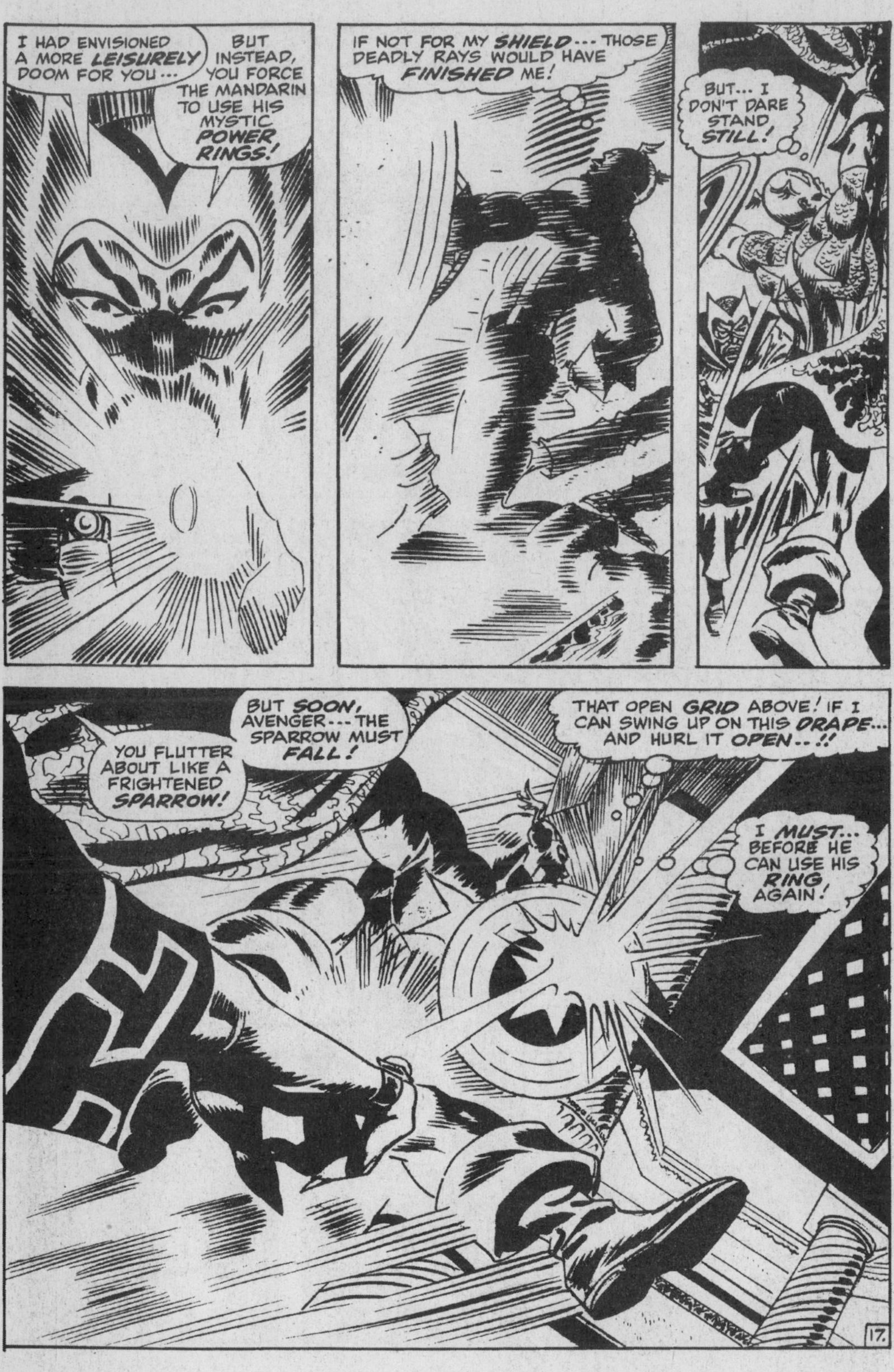

I HAD ENVISIONED A MORE LEISURELY DOOM FOR YOU...
BUT INSTEAD, YOU FORCE THE MANDARIN TO USE HIS MYSTIC POWER RINGS!
IF NOT FOR MY SHIELD--- THOSE DEADLY RAYS WOULD HAVE FINISHED ME!
BUT... I DON'T DARE STAND STILL!
YOU FLUTTER ABOUT LIKE A FRIGHTENED SPARROW!
BUT SOON, AVENGER--- THE SPARROW MUST FALL!
THAT OPEN GRID ABOVE! IF I CAN SWING UP ON THIS DRAPE... AND HURL IT OPEN..!!
I MUST... BEFORE HE CAN USE HIS RING AGAIN!
17.

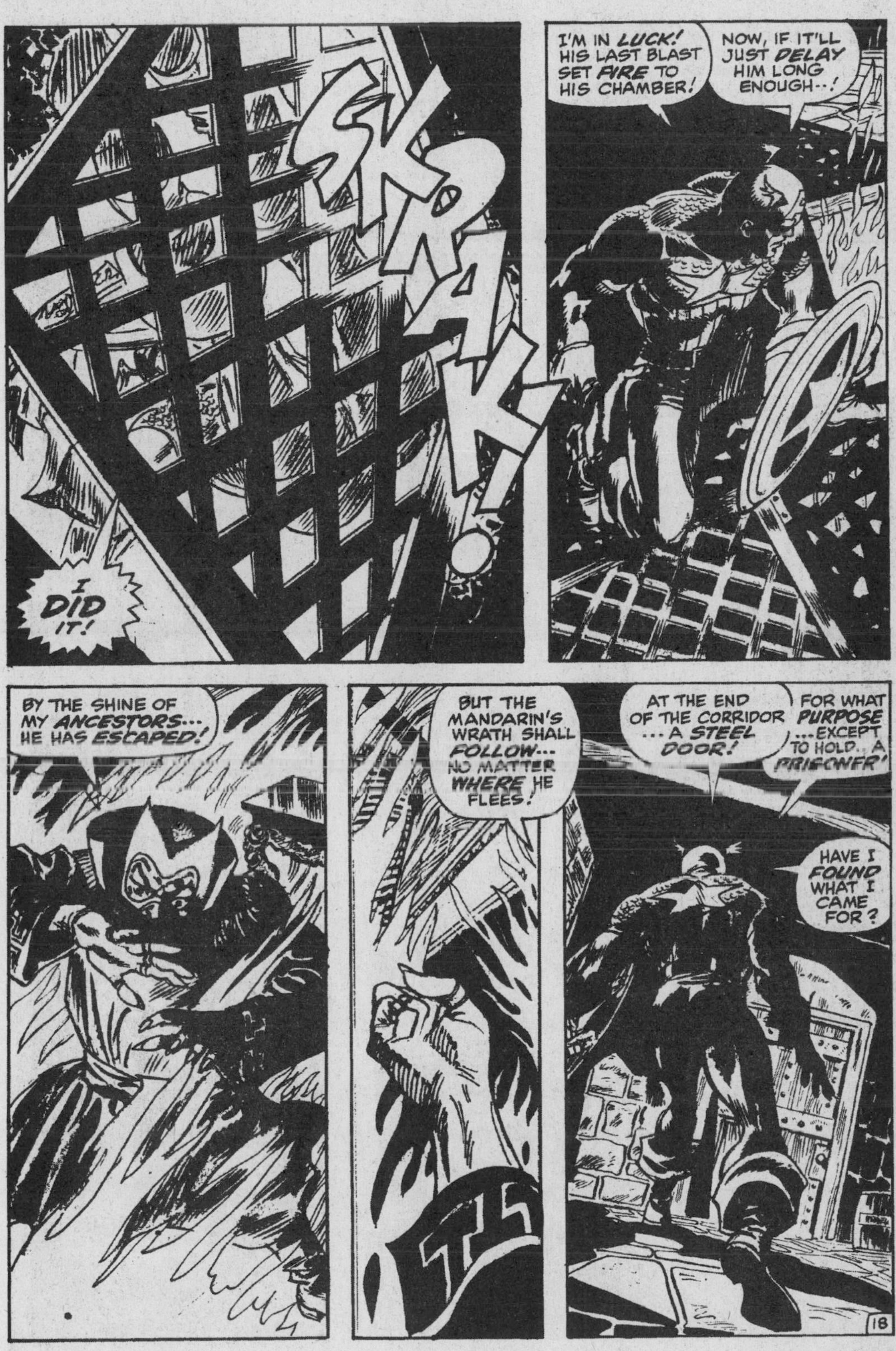
SKRAK!
I DID IT!
I'M IN LUCK! HIS LAST BLAST SET FIRE TO HIS CHAMBER!
NOW, IF IT'LL JUST DELAY HIM LONG ENOUGH--!
BY THE SHINE OF MY ANCESTORS... HE HAS ESCAPED!
BUT THE MANDARIN'S WRATH SHALL FOLLOW... NO MATTER WHERE HE FLEES!
AT THE END OF THE CORRIDOR ...A STEEL DOOR!
FOR WHAT PURPOSE ...EXCEPT TO HOLD.. A PRISONER?
HAVE I FOUND WHAT I CAME FOR?
18

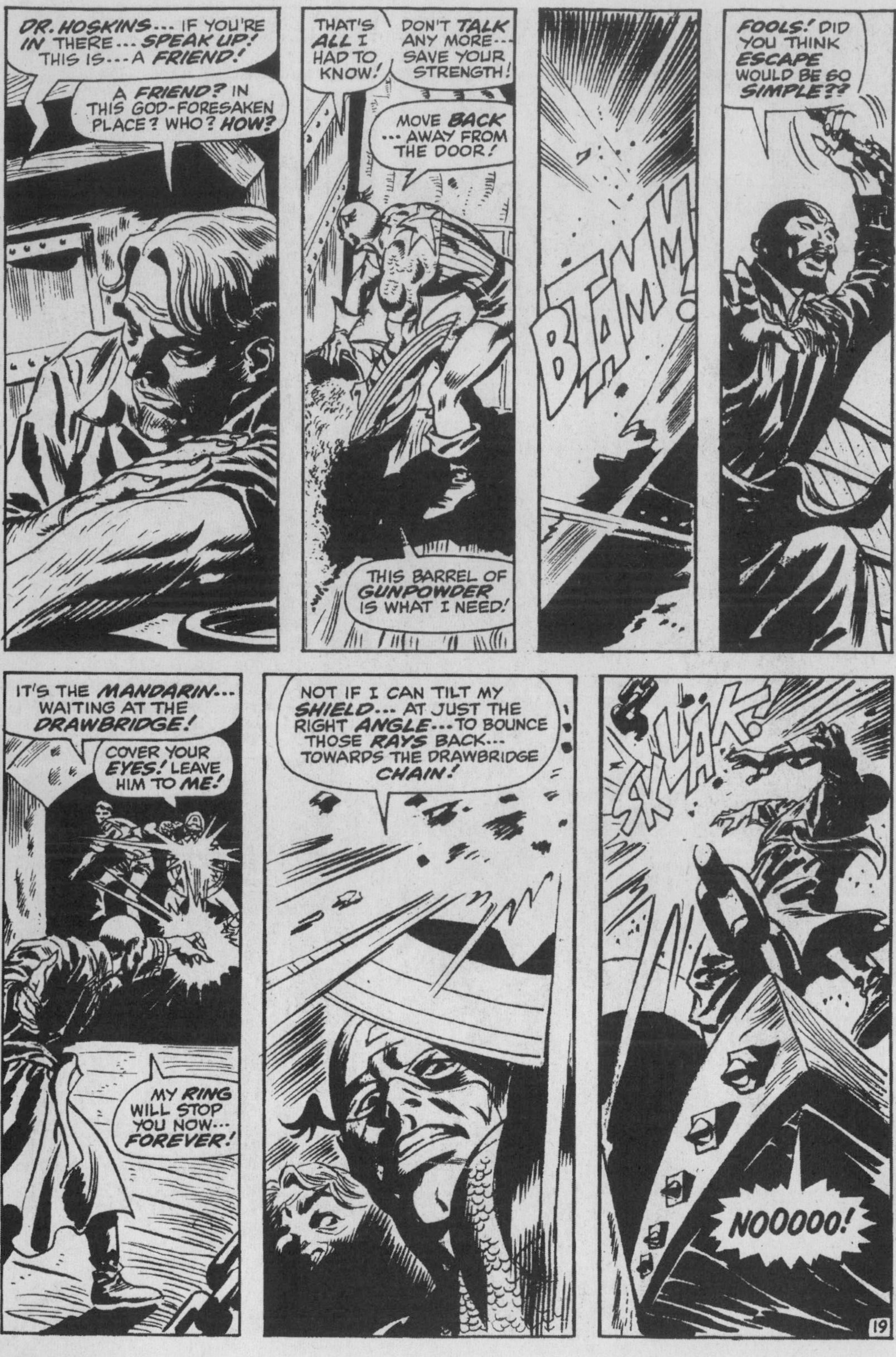
DR. HOSKINS... IF YOU'RE IN THERE... SPEAK UP! THIS IS... A FRIEND!
A FRIEND? IN THIS GOD-FORESAKEN PLACE? WHO? HOW?
THAT'S ALL I HAD TO KNOW!
DON'T TALK ANY MORE... SAVE YOUR STRENGTH!
MOVE BACK ... AWAY FROM THE DOOR!
THIS BARREL OF GUNPOWDER IS WHAT I NEED!
BTAMM!
FOOLS! DID YOU THINK ESCAPE WOULD BE SO SIMPLE??
IT'S THE MANDARIN... WAITING AT THE DRAWBRIDGE!
COVER YOUR EYES! LEAVE HIM TO ME!
MY RING WILL STOP YOU NOW... FOREVER!
NOT IF I CAN TILT MY SHIELD... AT JUST THE RIGHT ANGLE... TO BOUNCE THOSE RAYS BACK... TOWARDS THE DRAWBRIDGE CHAIN!
SKLAK!
NOOOOO!
19

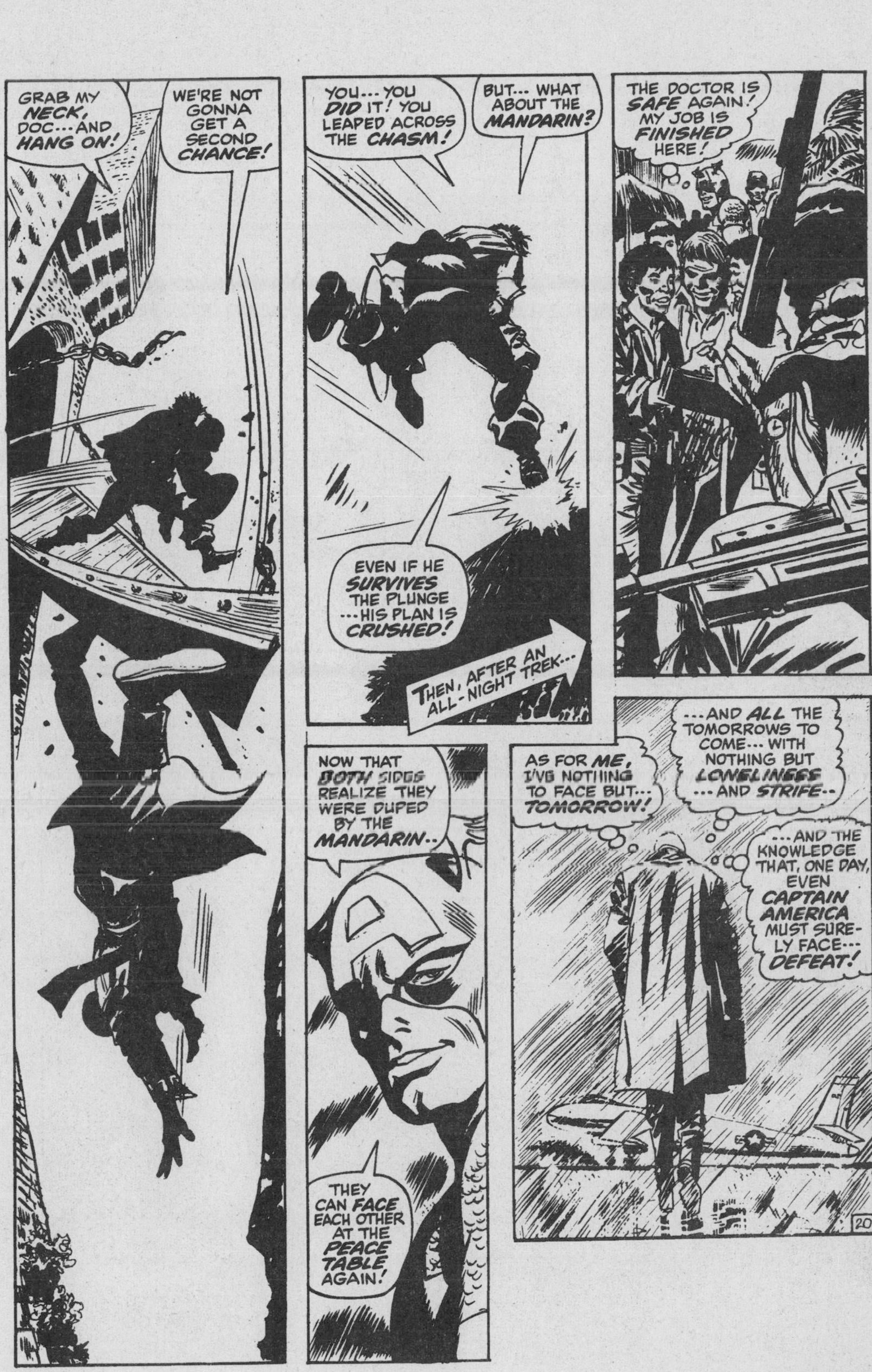
GRAB MY NECK, DOC... AND HANG ON!
WE'RE NOT GONNA GET A SECOND CHANCE!
YOU... YOU DID IT! YOU LEAPED ACROSS THE CHASM!
BUT... WHAT ABOUT THE MANDARIN?
EVEN IF HE SURVIVES THE PLUNGE ...HIS PLAN IS CRUSHED!
THEN, AFTER AN ALL-NIGHT TREK...
THE DOCTOR IS SAFE AGAIN! MY JOB IS FINISHED HERE!
NOW THAT BOTH SIDES REALIZE THEY WERE DUPED BY THE MANDARIN..
THEY CAN FACE EACH OTHER AT THE PEACE TABLE AGAIN!
AS FOR ME, I'VE NOTHING TO FACE BUT... TOMORROW!
...AND ALL THE TOMORROWS TO COME... WITH NOTHING BUT LONELINESS ...AND STRIFE..
...AND THE KNOWLEDGE THAT, ONE DAY, EVEN CAPTAIN AMERICA MUST SURELY FACE... DEFEAT!
20

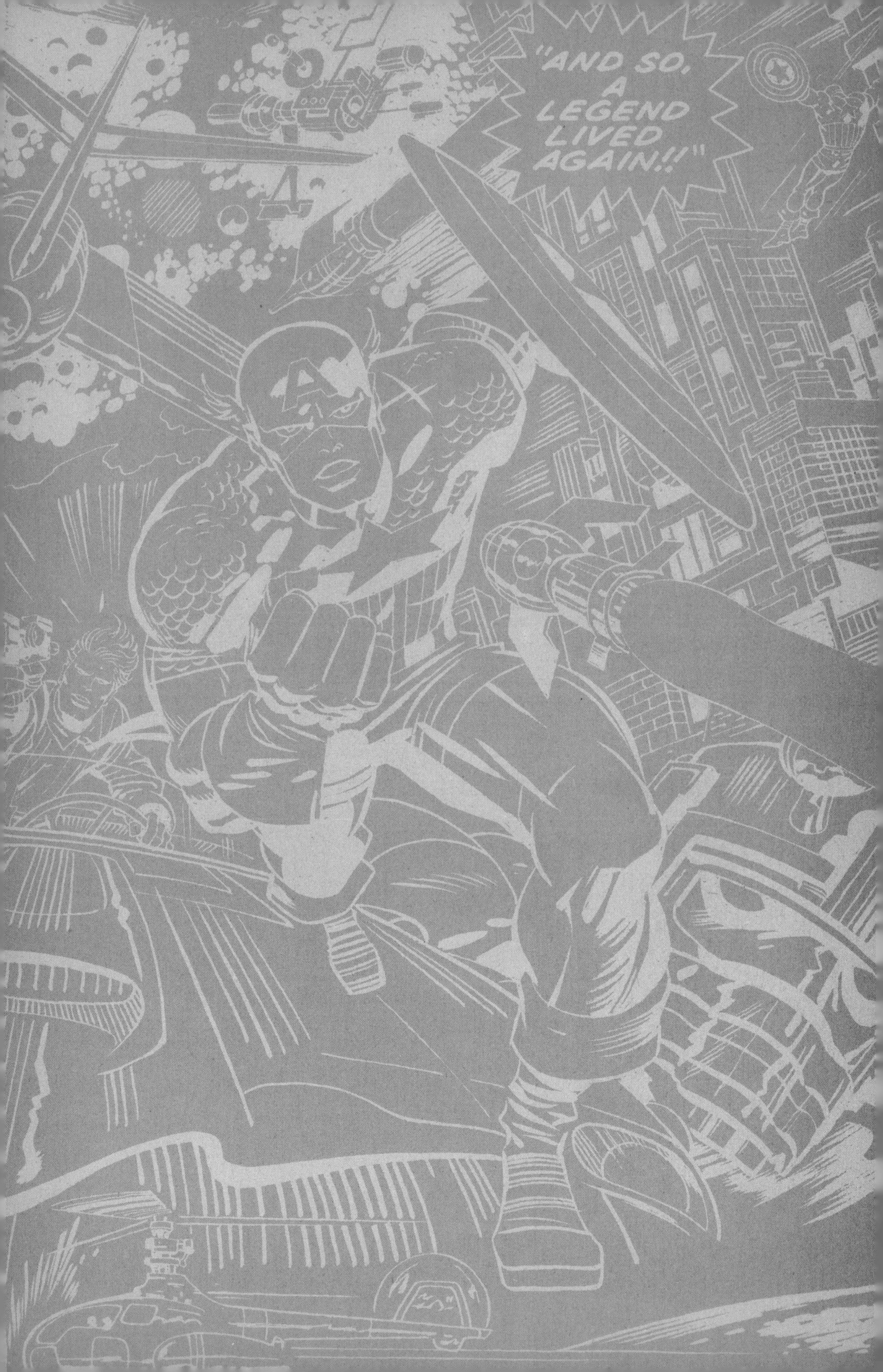
"AND SO, A LEGEND LIVED AGAIN!!"

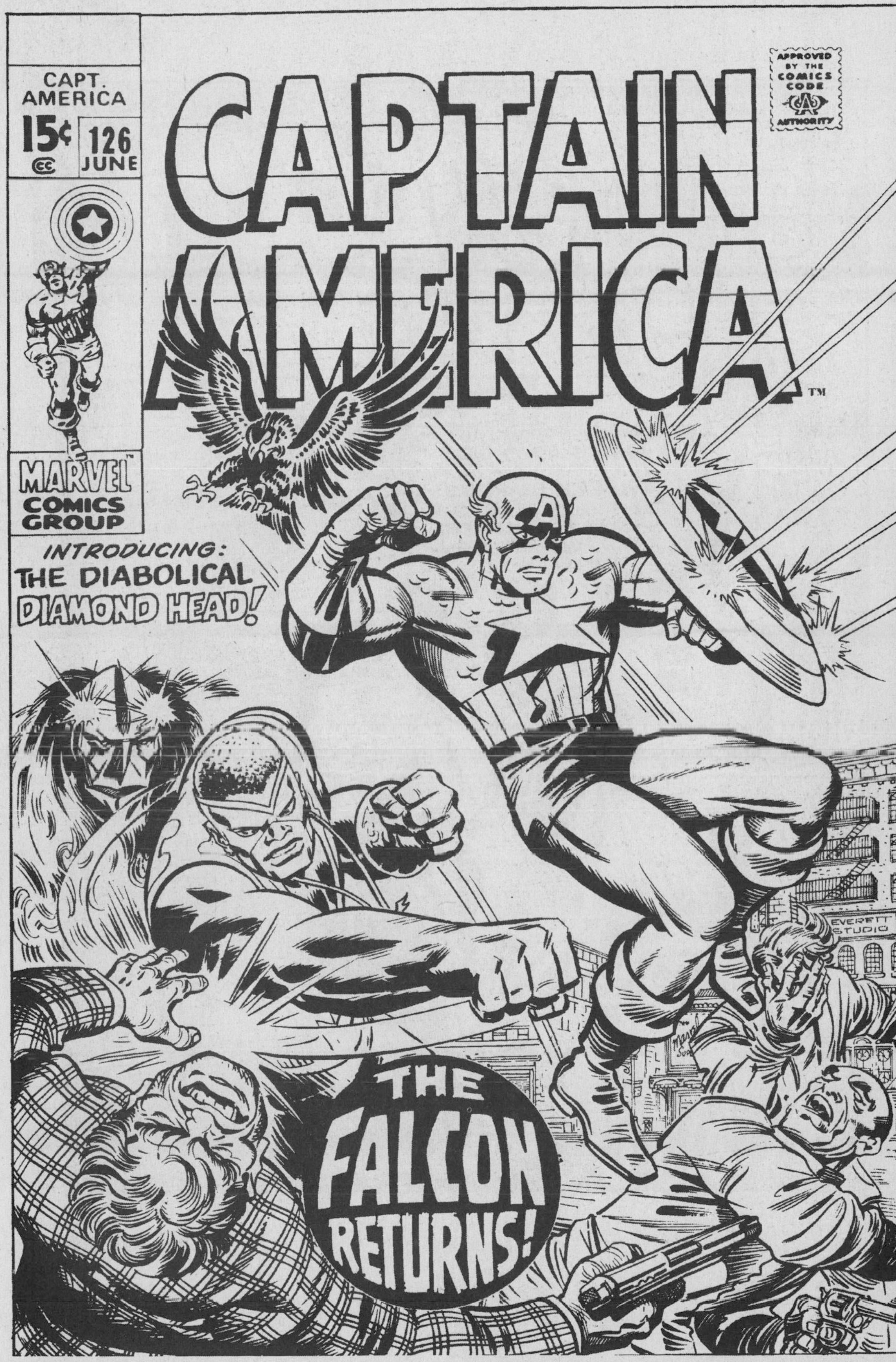

CAPT. AMERICA
15¢
126
JUNE
APPROVED BY THE COMICS CODE AUTHORITY
CAPTAIN AMERICA™
MARVEL COMICS GROUP
INTRODUCING: THE DIABOLICAL DIAMOND HEAD!
EVERETT STUDIO
THE FALCON RETURNS!

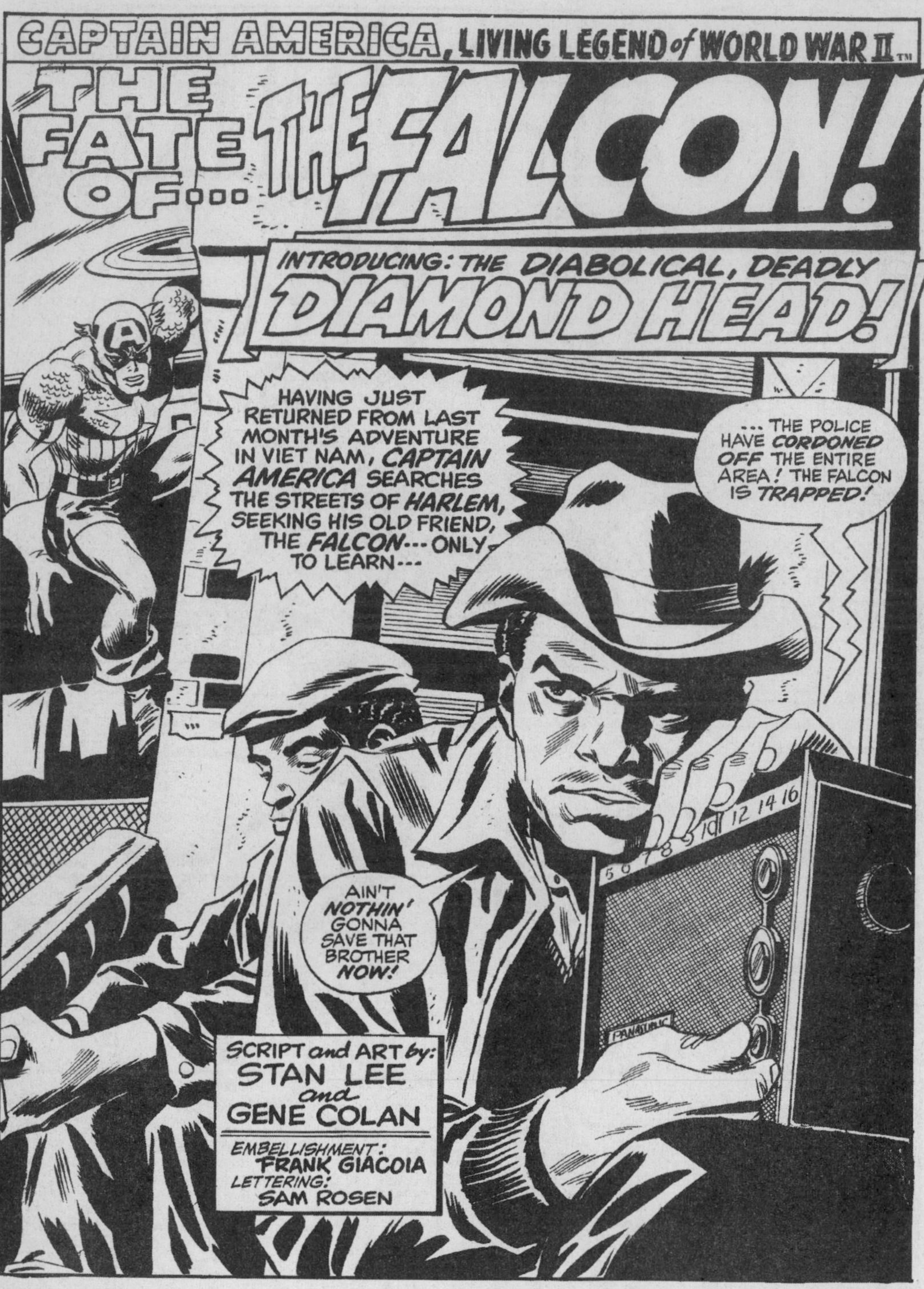

CAPTAIN AMERICA, LIVING LEGEND of WORLD WAR II TM
THE FATE OF... THE FALCON!
INTRODUCING: THE DIABOLICAL, DEADLY DIAMOND HEAD!
HAVING JUST RETURNED FROM LAST MONTH'S ADVENTURE IN VIET NAM, CAPTAIN AMERICA SEARCHES THE STREETS OF HARLEM, SEEKING HIS OLD FRIEND, THE FALCON--- ONLY TO LEARN---
... THE POLICE HAVE CORDONED OFF THE ENTIRE AREA! THE FALCON IS TRAPPED!
AIN'T NOTHIN' GONNA SAVE THAT BROTHER NOW!
SCRIPT and ART by: STAN LEE and GENE COLAN
EMBELLISHMENT: FRANK GIACOIA
LETTERING: SAM ROSEN

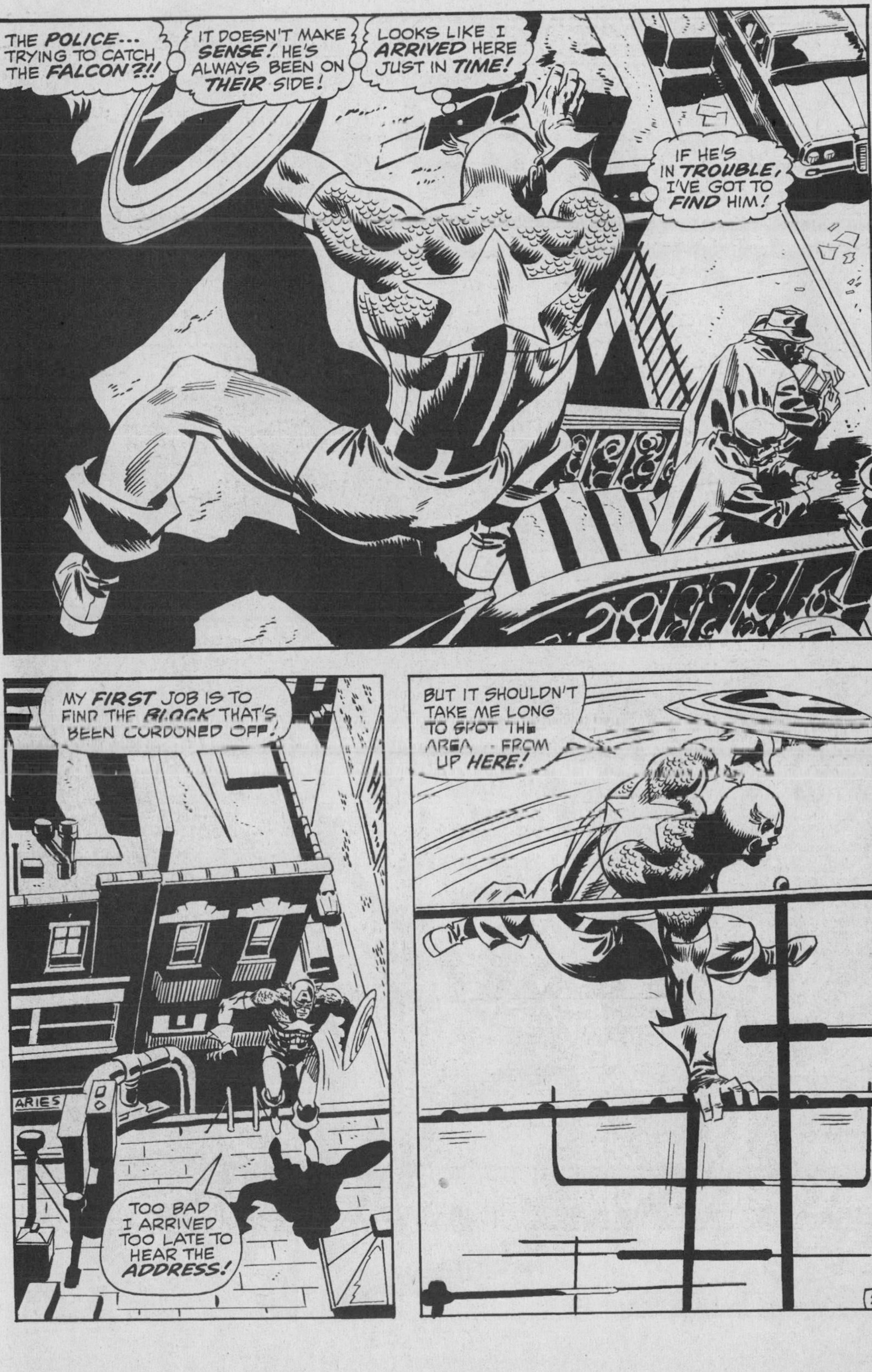

THE POLICE... TRYING TO CATCH THE FALCON?!!
IT DOESN'T MAKE SENSE! HE'S ALWAYS BEEN ON THEIR SIDE!
LOOKS LIKE I ARRIVED HERE JUST IN TIME!
IF HE'S IN TROUBLE, I'VE GOT TO FIND HIM!
MY FIRST JOB IS TO FIND THE BLOCK THAT'S BEEN CORDONED OFF!
ARIES
TOO BAD I ARRIVED TOO LATE TO HEAR THE ADDRESS!
BUT IT SHOULDN'T TAKE ME LONG TO SPOT THE AREA FROM UP HERE!

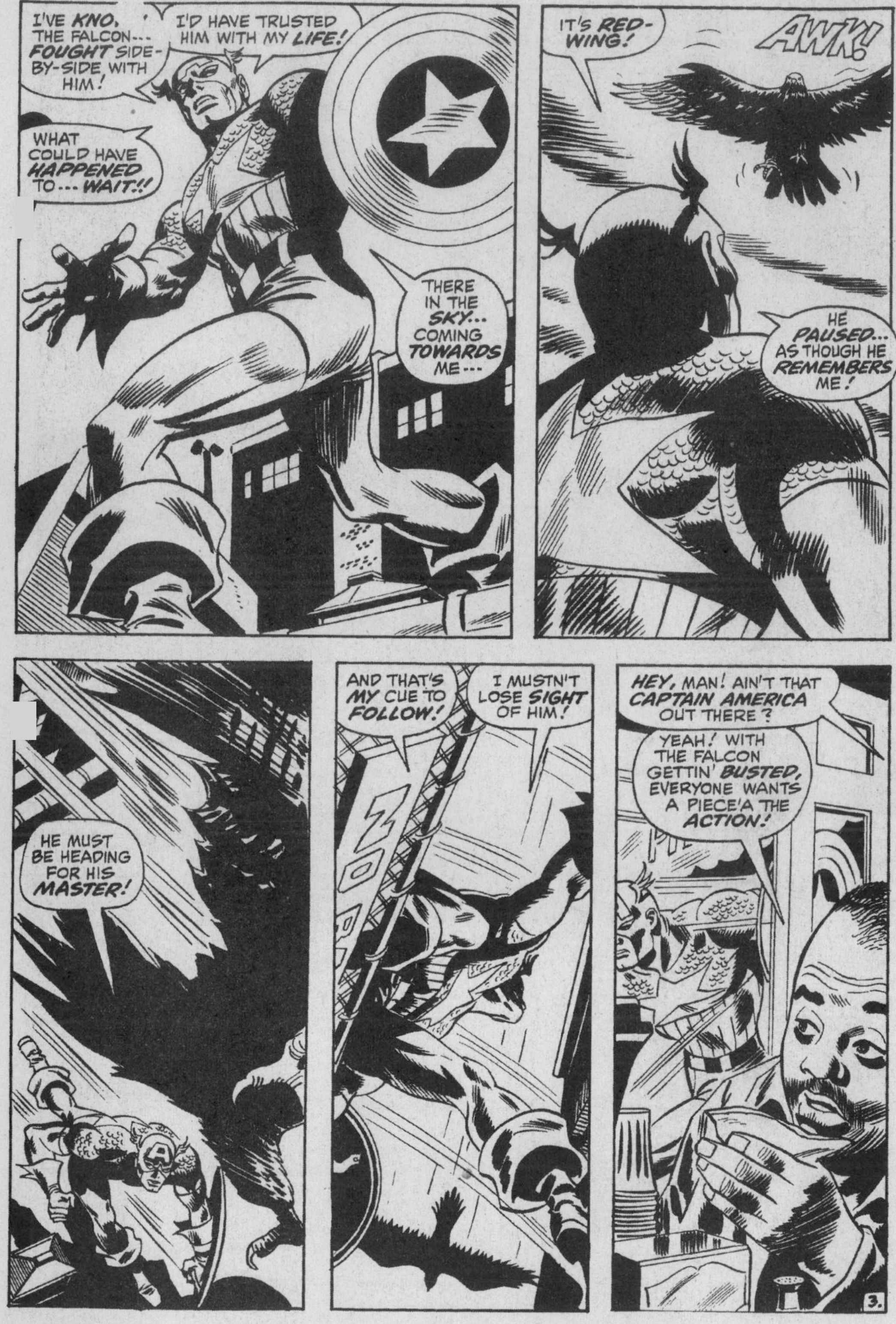
I'VE KNO, THE FALCON--- FOUGHT SIDE-BY-SIDE WITH HIM!
I'D HAVE TRUSTED HIM WITH MY LIFE!
WHAT COULD HAVE HAPPENED TO--- WAIT!!
THERE IN THE SKY... COMING TOWARDS ME---
IT'S RED-WING!
AWK!
HE PAUSED... AS THOUGH HE REMEMBERS ME!
HE MUST BE HEADING FOR HIS MASTER!
AND THAT'S MY CUE TO FOLLOW!
I MUSTN'T LOSE SIGHT OF HIM!
HEY, MAN! AIN'T THAT CAPTAIN AMERICA OUT THERE?
YEAH! WITH THE FALCON GETTIN' BUSTED, EVERYONE WANTS A PIECE'A THE ACTION!
3.

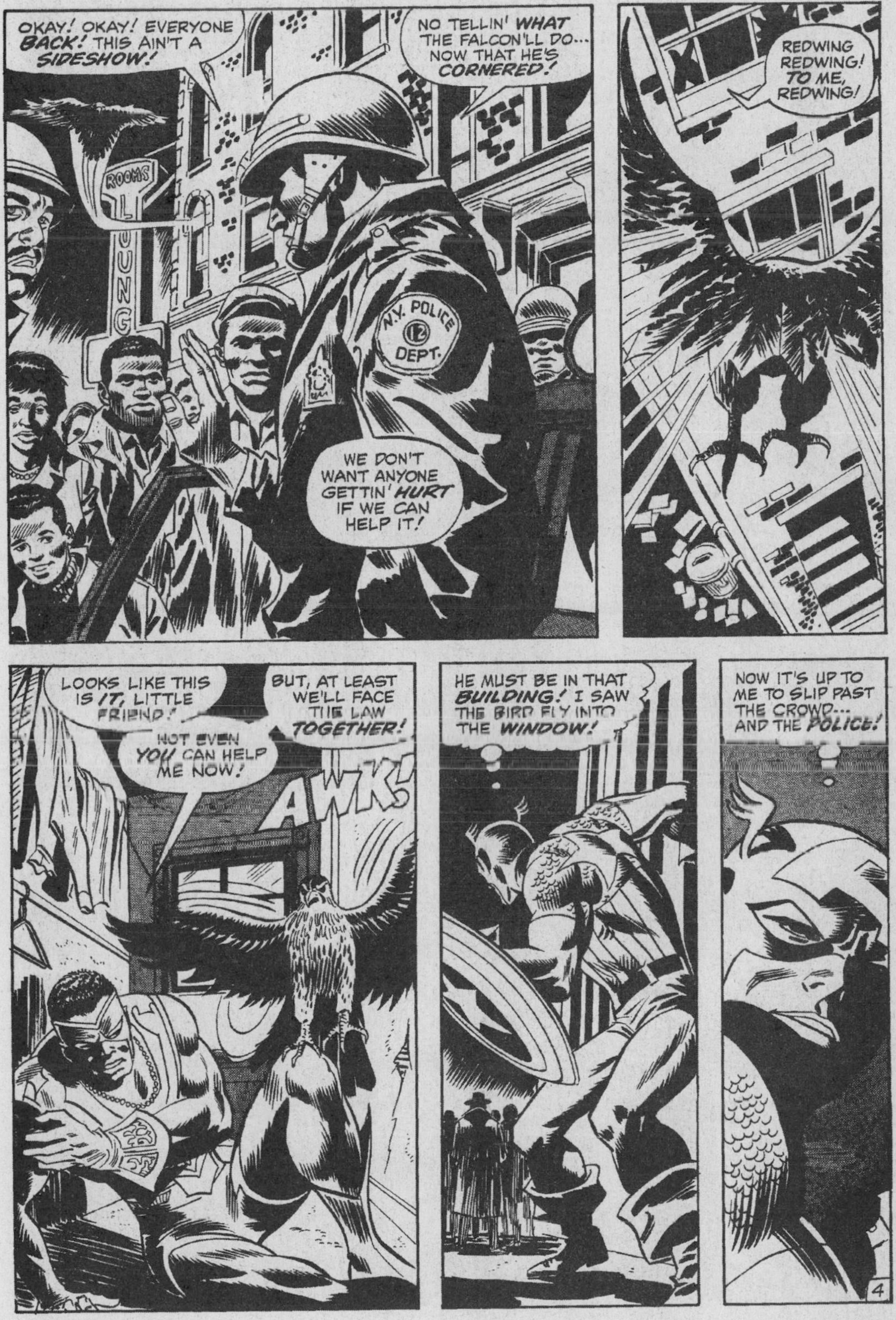
OKAY! OKAY! EVERYONE BACK! THIS AIN'T A SIDESHOW!
NO TELLIN' WHAT THE FALCON'LL DO... NOW THAT HE'S CORNERED!
ROOMS
N.Y. POLICE DEPT.
WE DON'T WANT ANYONE GETTIN' HURT IF WE CAN HELP IT!
REDWING REDWING! TO ME, REDWING!
LOOKS LIKE THIS IS IT, LITTLE FRIEND!
NOT EVEN YOU CAN HELP ME NOW!
BUT, AT LEAST WE'LL FACE THE LAW TOGETHER!
AWK!
HE MUST BE IN THAT BUILDING! I SAW THE BIRD FLY INTO THE WINDOW!
NOW IT'S UP TO ME TO SLIP PAST THE CROWD... AND THE POLICE!
4

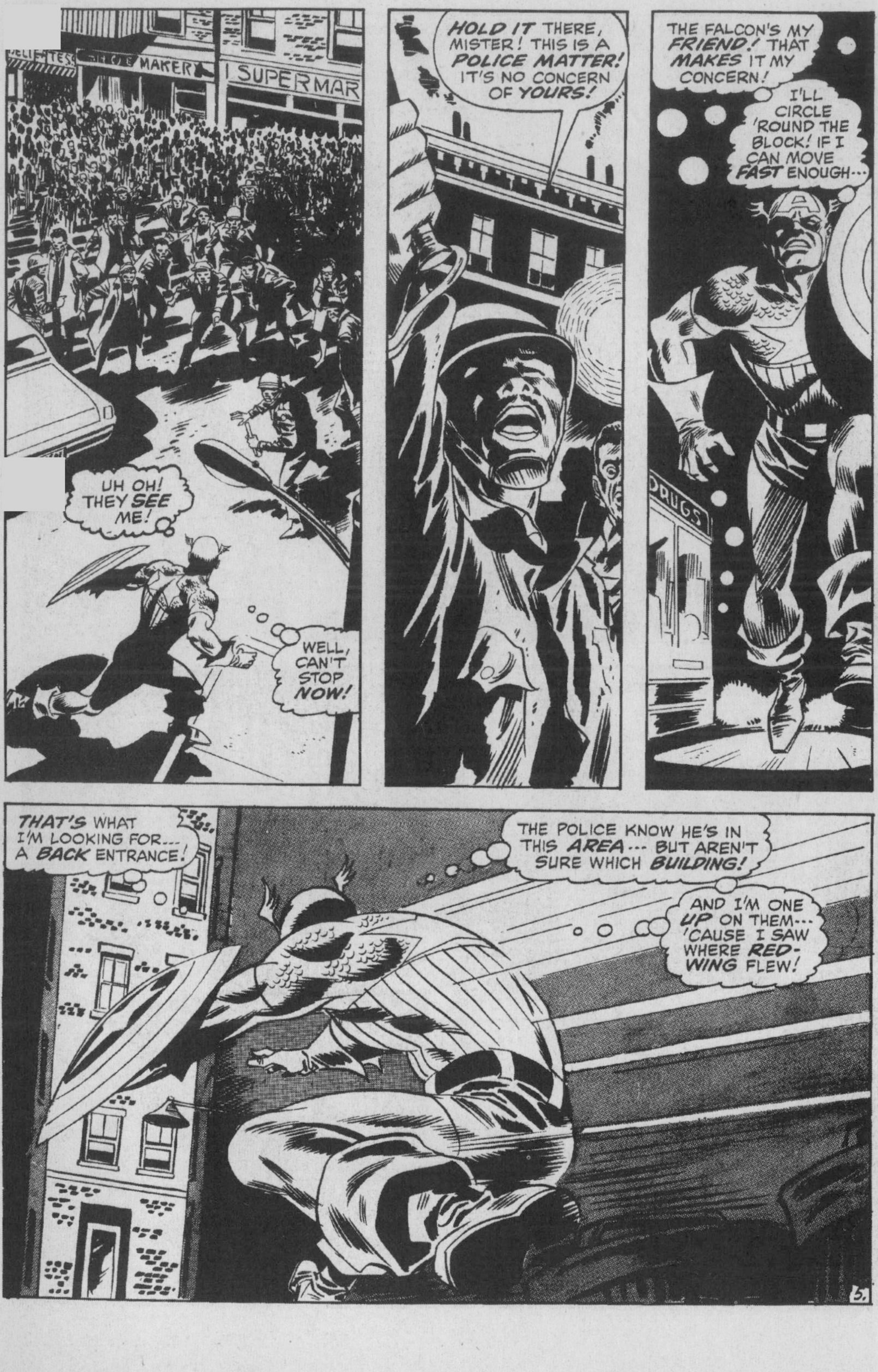

SUPERMAR
MAKER
UH OH! THEY SEE ME!
WELL, CAN'T STOP NOW!
HOLD IT THERE, MISTER! THIS IS A POLICE MATTER! IT'S NO CONCERN OF YOURS!
THE FALCON'S MY FRIEND! THAT MAKES IT MY CONCERN!
I'LL CIRCLE 'ROUND THE BLOCK! IF I CAN MOVE FAST ENOUGH...
DRUGS
THAT'S WHAT I'M LOOKING FOR... A BACK ENTRANCE!
THE POLICE KNOW HE'S IN THIS AREA... BUT AREN'T SURE WHICH BUILDING!
AND I'M ONE UP ON THEM... 'CAUSE I SAW WHERE RED-WING FLEW!
5.

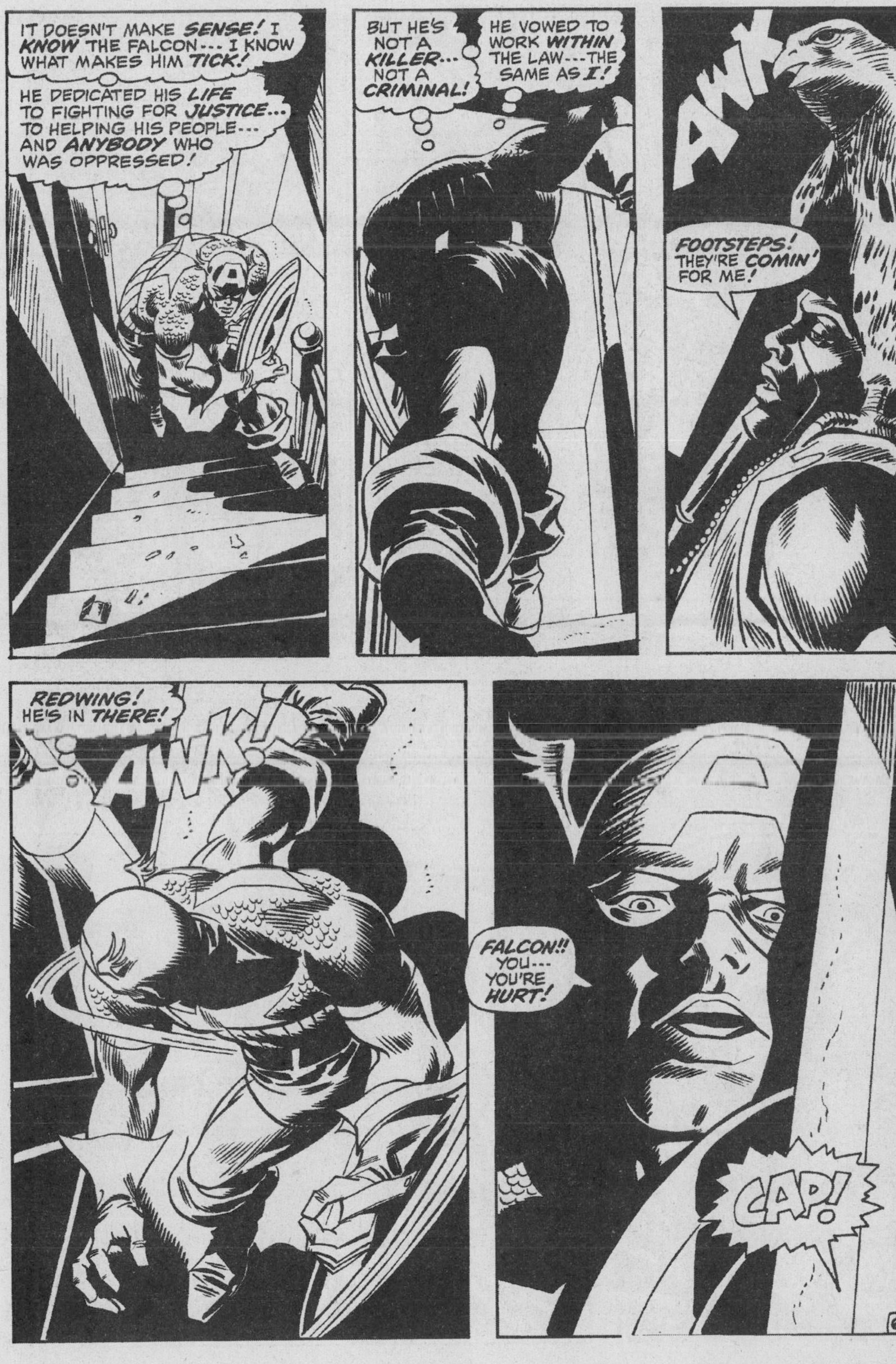
IT DOESN'T MAKE SENSE! I KNOW THE FALCON--- I KNOW WHAT MAKES HIM TICK!
HE DEDICATED HIS LIFE TO FIGHTING FOR JUSTICE... TO HELPING HIS PEOPLE--- AND ANYBODY WHO WAS OPPRESSED!
BUT HE'S NOT A KILLER... NOT A CRIMINAL!
HE VOWED TO WORK WITHIN THE LAW---THE SAME AS I!
AWK
FOOTSTEPS! THEY'RE COMIN' FOR ME!
REDWING! HE'S IN THERE!
AWK!
FALCON!! YOU--- YOU'RE HURT!
CAP!
6

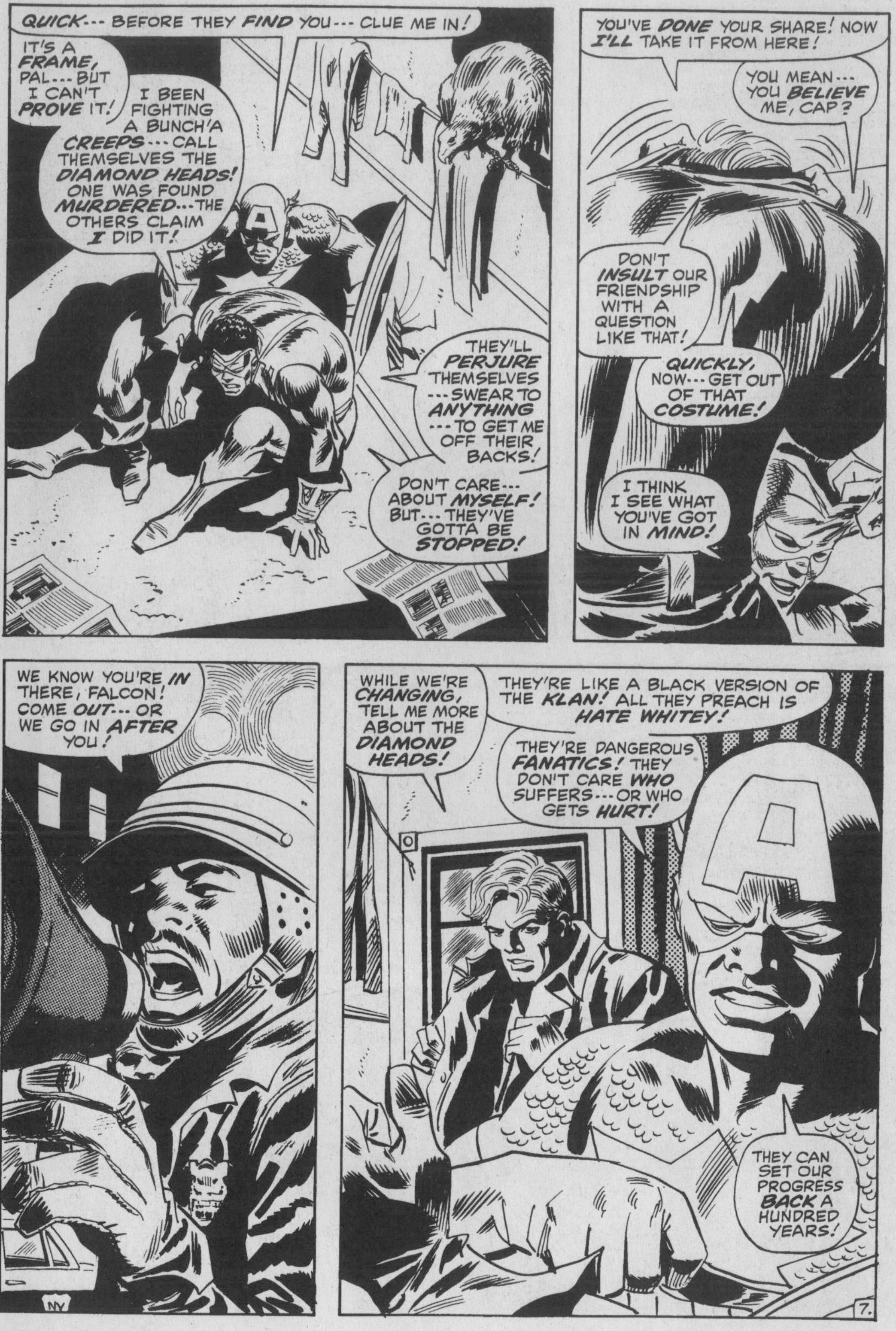
QUICK--- BEFORE THEY FIND YOU--- CLUE ME IN!
IT'S A FRAME, PAL--- BUT I CAN'T PROVE IT!
I BEEN FIGHTING A BUNCH'A CREEPS--- CALL THEMSELVES THE DIAMOND HEADS! ONE WAS FOUND MURDERED--- THE OTHERS CLAIM I DID IT!
THEY'LL PERJURE THEMSELVES ---SWEAR TO ANYTHING ---TO GET ME OFF THEIR BACKS!
DON'T CARE--- ABOUT MYSELF! BUT--- THEY'VE GOTTA BE STOPPED!
YOU'VE DONE YOUR SHARE! NOW I'LL TAKE IT FROM HERE!
YOU MEAN--- YOU BELIEVE ME, CAP?
DON'T INSULT OUR FRIENDSHIP WITH A QUESTION LIKE THAT!
QUICKLY, NOW--- GET OUT OF THAT COSTUME!
I THINK I SEE WHAT YOU'VE GOT IN MIND!
WE KNOW YOU'RE IN THERE, FALCON! COME OUT--- OR WE GO IN AFTER YOU!
WHILE WE'RE CHANGING, TELL ME MORE ABOUT THE DIAMOND HEADS!
THEY'RE LIKE A BLACK VERSION OF THE KLAN! ALL THEY PREACH IS HATE WHITEY!
THEY'RE DANGEROUS FANATICS! THEY DON'T CARE WHO SUFFERS--- OR WHO GETS HURT!
THEY CAN SET OUR PROGRESS BACK A HUNDRED YEARS!
NY
7.

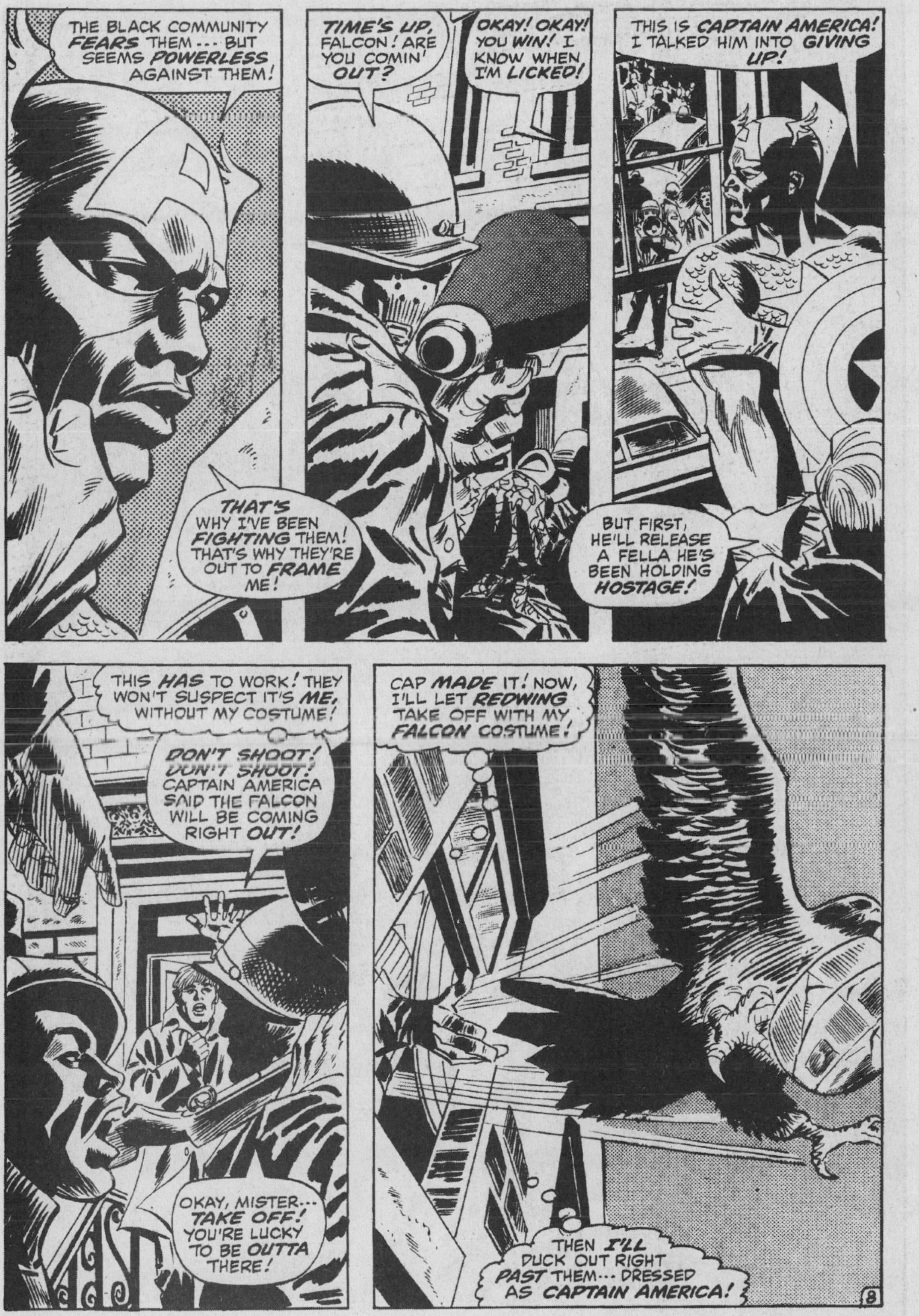
THE BLACK COMMUNITY FEARS THEM... BUT SEEMS POWERLESS AGAINST THEM!
THAT'S WHY I'VE BEEN FIGHTING THEM! THAT'S WHY THEY'RE OUT TO FRAME ME!
TIME'S UP, FALCON! ARE YOU COMIN' OUT?
OKAY! OKAY! YOU WIN! I KNOW WHEN I'M LICKED!
THIS IS CAPTAIN AMERICA! I TALKED HIM INTO GIVING UP!
BUT FIRST, HE'LL RELEASE A FELLA HE'S BEEN HOLDING HOSTAGE!
THIS HAS TO WORK! THEY WON'T SUSPECT IT'S ME, WITHOUT MY COSTUME!
DON'T SHOOT! DON'T SHOOT! CAPTAIN AMERICA SAID THE FALCON WILL BE COMING RIGHT OUT!
OKAY, MISTER... TAKE OFF! YOU'RE LUCKY TO BE OUTTA THERE!
CAP MADE IT! NOW, I'LL LET REDWING TAKE OFF WITH MY FALCON COSTUME!
THEN I'LL DUCK OUT RIGHT PAST THEM... DRESSED AS CAPTAIN AMERICA!
8

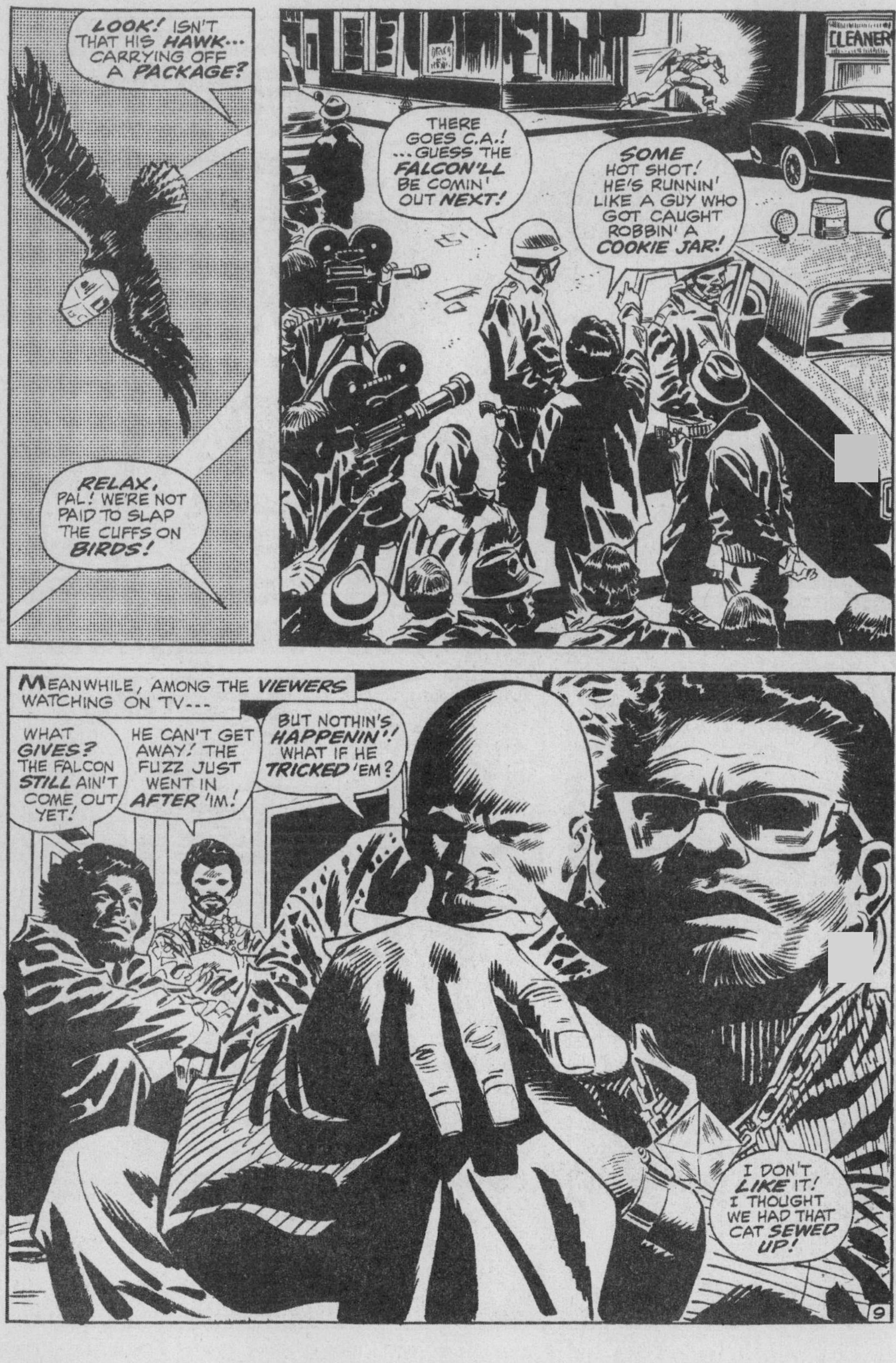
LOOK! ISN'T THAT HIS HAWK... CARRYING OFF A PACKAGE?
RELAX, PAL! WE'RE NOT PAID TO SLAP THE CUFFS ON BIRDS!
CLEANER
THERE GOES C.A.! ...GUESS THE FALCON'LL BE COMIN' OUT NEXT!
SOME HOT SHOT! HE'S RUNNIN' LIKE A GUY WHO GOT CAUGHT ROBBIN' A COOKIE JAR!
MEANWHILE, AMONG THE VIEWERS WATCHING ON TV---
WHAT GIVES? THE FALCON STILL AIN'T COME OUT YET!
HE CAN'T GET AWAY! THE FUZZ JUST WENT IN AFTER 'IM!
BUT NOTHIN'S HAPPENIN'! WHAT IF HE TRICKED 'EM?
I DON'T LIKE IT! I THOUGHT WE HAD THAT CAT SEWED UP!
9

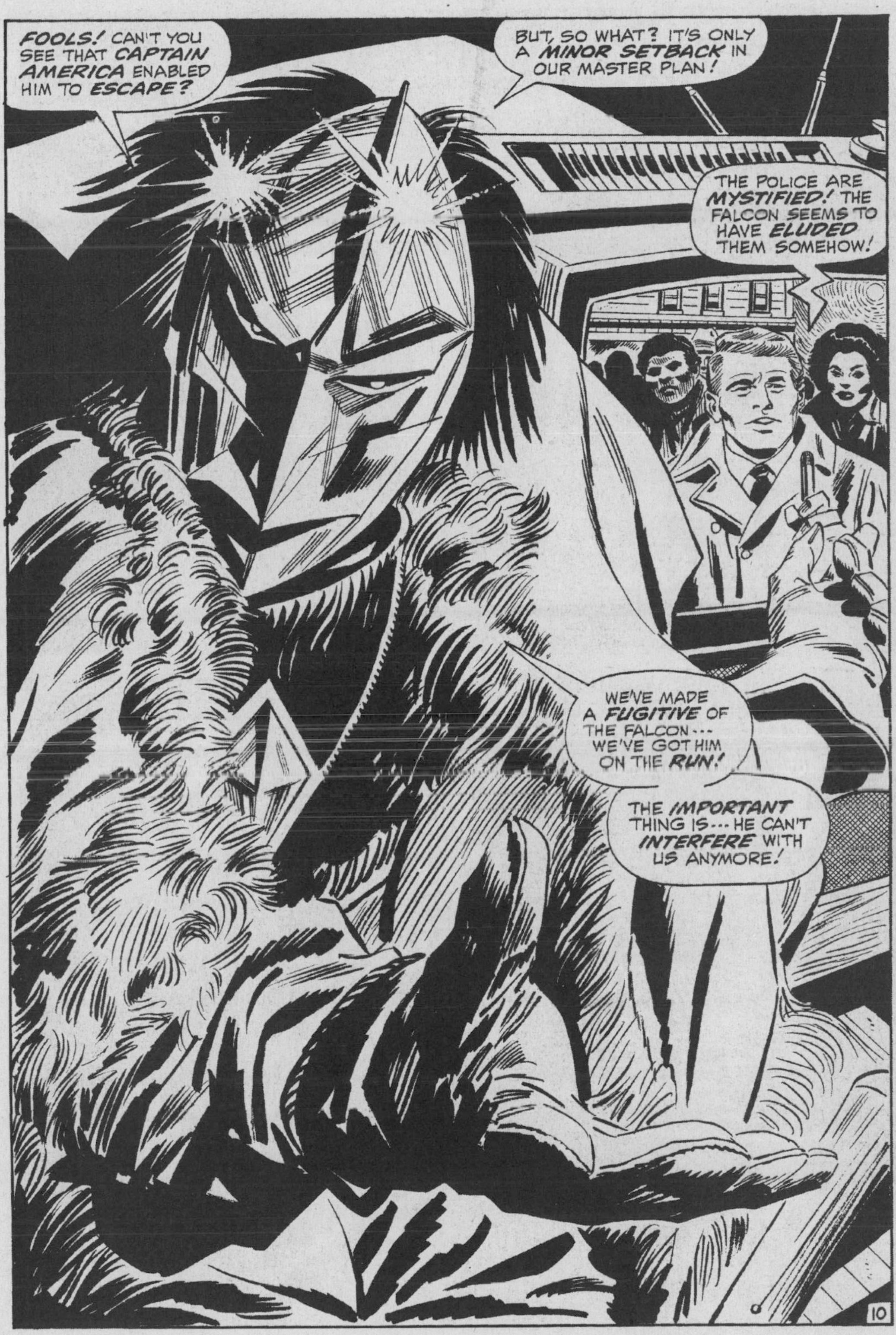
FOOLS! CAN'T YOU SEE THAT CAPTAIN AMERICA ENABLED HIM TO ESCAPE?
BUT, SO WHAT? IT'S ONLY A MINOR SETBACK IN OUR MASTER PLAN!
THE POLICE ARE MYSTIFIED! THE FALCON SEEMS TO HAVE ELUDED THEM SOMEHOW!
WE'VE MADE A FUGITIVE OF THE FALCON--- WE'VE GOT HIM ON THE RUN!
THE IMPORTANT THING IS--- HE CAN'T INTERFERE WITH US ANYMORE!
10

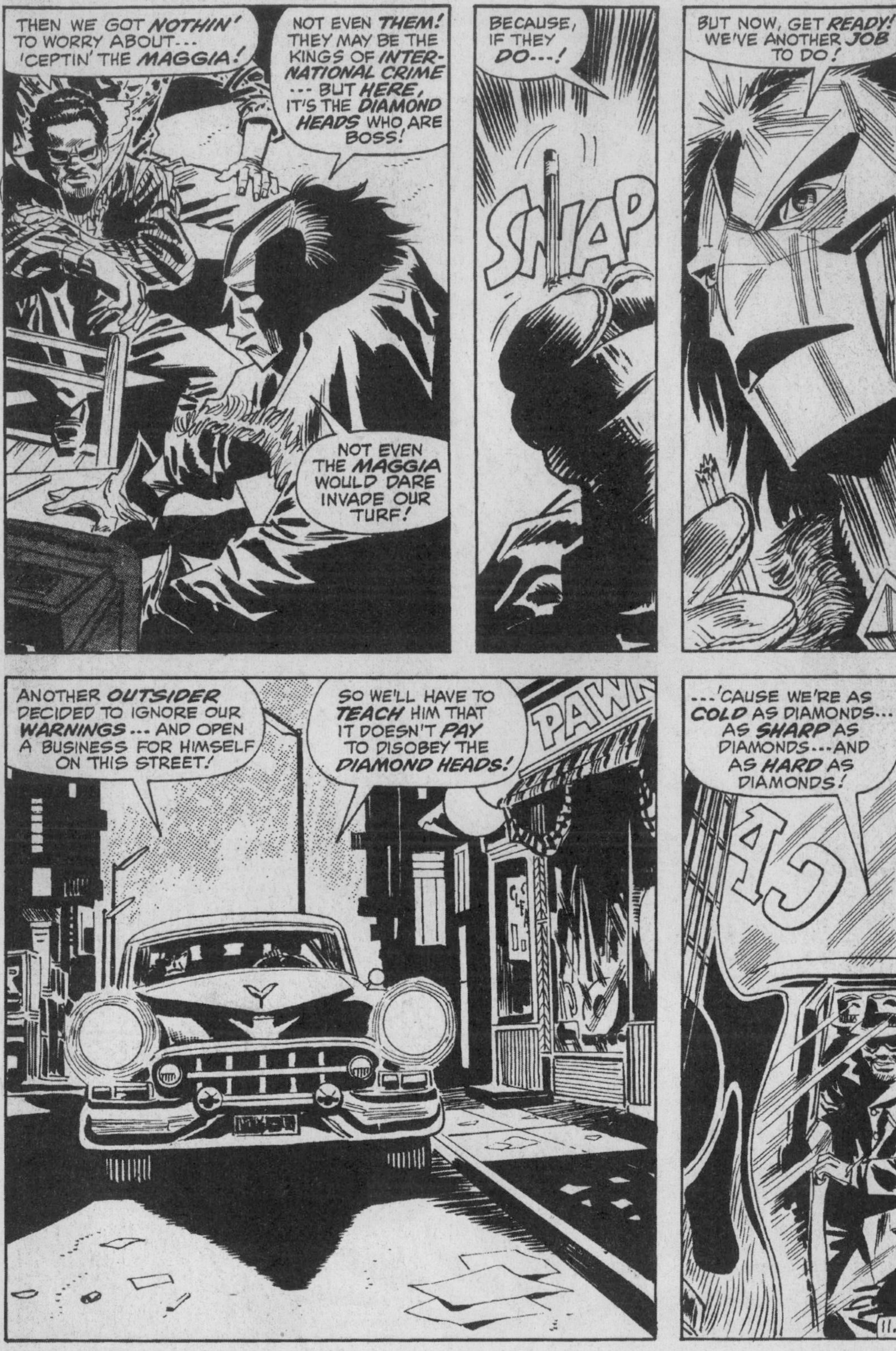
THEN WE GOT NOTHIN' TO WORRY ABOUT--- 'CEPTIN' THE MAGGIA!
NOT EVEN THEM! THEY MAY BE THE KINGS OF INTERNATIONAL CRIME --- BUT HERE, IT'S THE DIAMOND HEADS WHO ARE BOSS!
NOT EVEN THE MAGGIA WOULD DARE INVADE OUR TURF!
BECAUSE, IF THEY DO---!
SNAP
BUT NOW, GET READY! WE'VE ANOTHER JOB TO DO!
ANOTHER OUTSIDER DECIDED TO IGNORE OUR WARNINGS --- AND OPEN A BUSINESS FOR HIMSELF ON THIS STREET!
SO WE'LL HAVE TO TEACH HIM THAT IT DOESN'T PAY TO DISOBEY THE DIAMOND HEADS!
PAWN
---'CAUSE WE'RE AS COLD AS DIAMONDS... AS SHARP AS DIAMONDS---AND AS HARD AS DIAMONDS!
11.

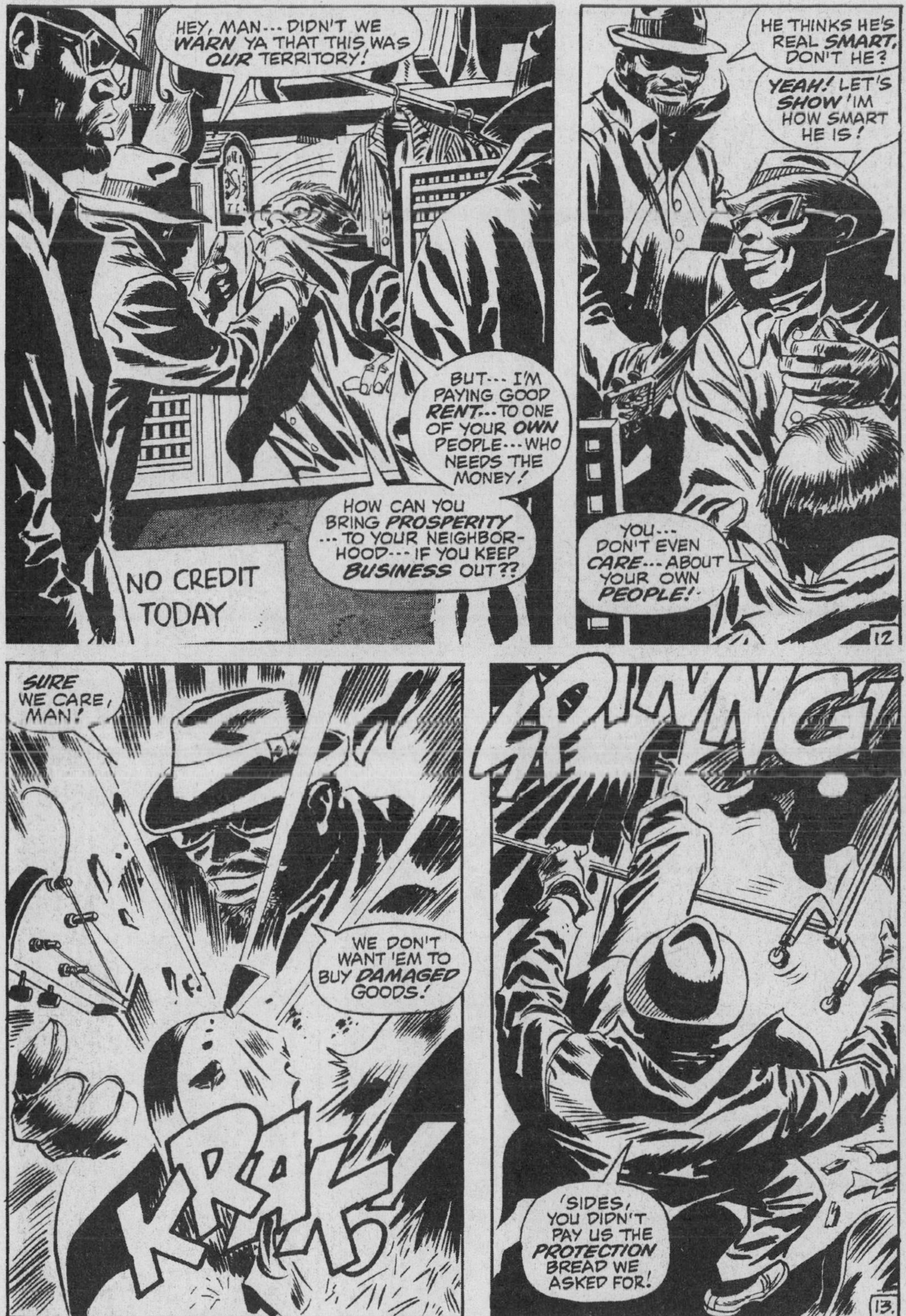
HEY, MAN--- DIDN'T WE WARN YA THAT THIS WAS OUR TERRITORY!
BUT--- I'M PAYING GOOD RENT---TO ONE OF YOUR OWN PEOPLE---WHO NEEDS THE MONEY!
HOW CAN YOU BRING PROSPERITY --- TO YOUR NEIGHBORHOOD--- IF YOU KEEP BUSINESS OUT??
NO CREDIT TODAY
HE THINKS HE'S REAL SMART, DON'T HE?
YEAH! LET'S SHOW 'IM HOW SMART HE IS!
YOU--- DON'T EVEN CARE--- ABOUT YOUR OWN PEOPLE!
12
SURE WE CARE, MAN!
WE DON'T WANT 'EM TO BUY DAMAGED GOODS!
KRAK!
SPANNG!
'SIDES, YOU DIDN'T PAY US THE PROTECTION BREAD WE ASKED FOR!
13.

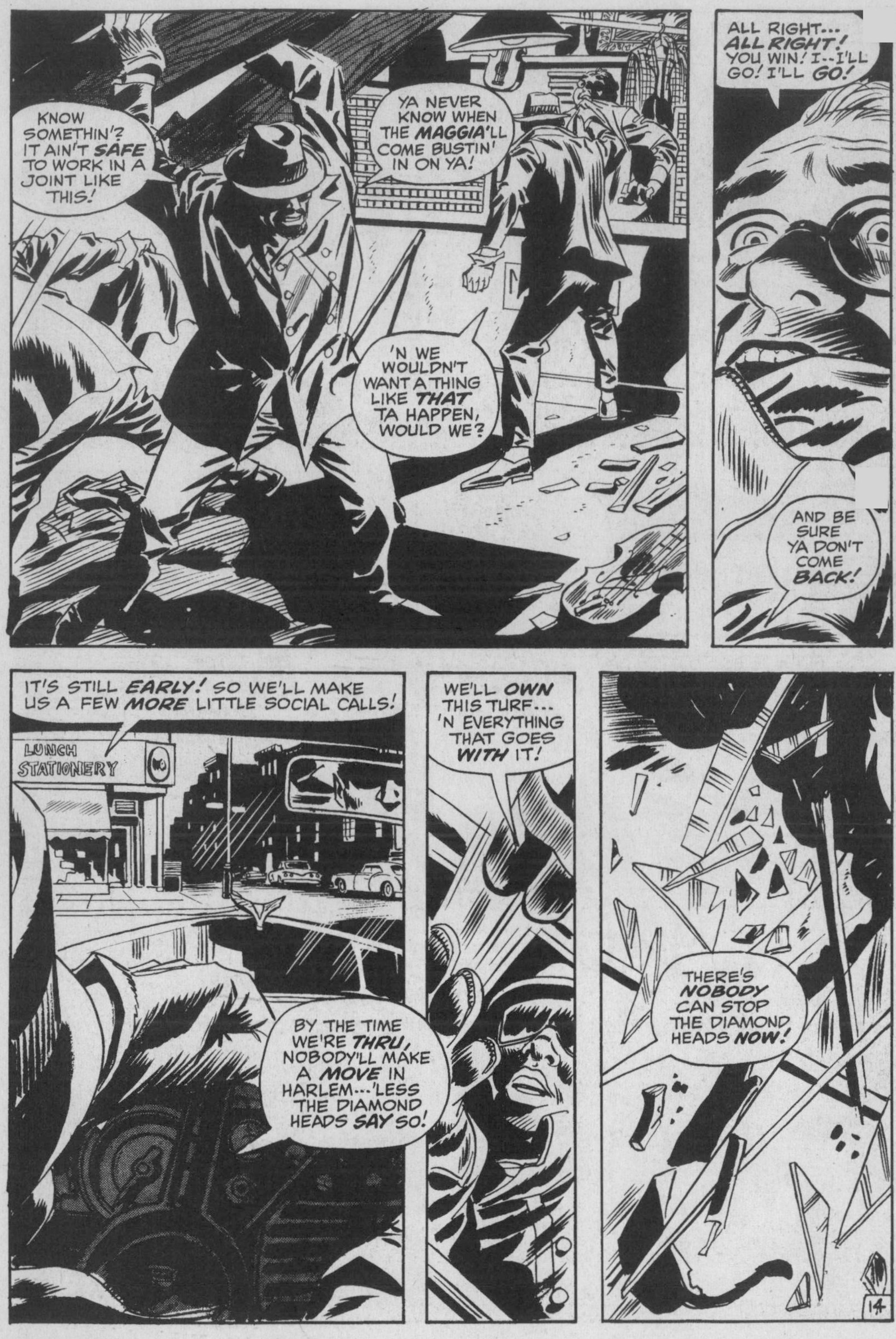
KNOW SOMETHIN'? IT AIN'T SAFE TO WORK IN A JOINT LIKE THIS!
YA NEVER KNOW WHEN THE MAGGIA'LL COME BUSTIN' IN ON YA!
'N WE WOULDN'T WANT A THING LIKE THAT TA HAPPEN, WOULD WE?
ALL RIGHT... ALL RIGHT! YOU WIN! I--I'LL GO! I'LL GO!
AND BE SURE YA DON'T COME BACK!
IT'S STILL EARLY! SO WE'LL MAKE US A FEW MORE LITTLE SOCIAL CALLS!
LUNCH
STATIONERY
BY THE TIME WE'RE THRU, NOBODY'LL MAKE A MOVE IN HARLEM...'LESS THE DIAMOND HEADS SAY SO!
WE'LL OWN THIS TURF... 'N EVERYTHING THAT GOES WITH IT!
THERE'S NOBODY CAN STOP THE DIAMOND HEADS NOW!
14

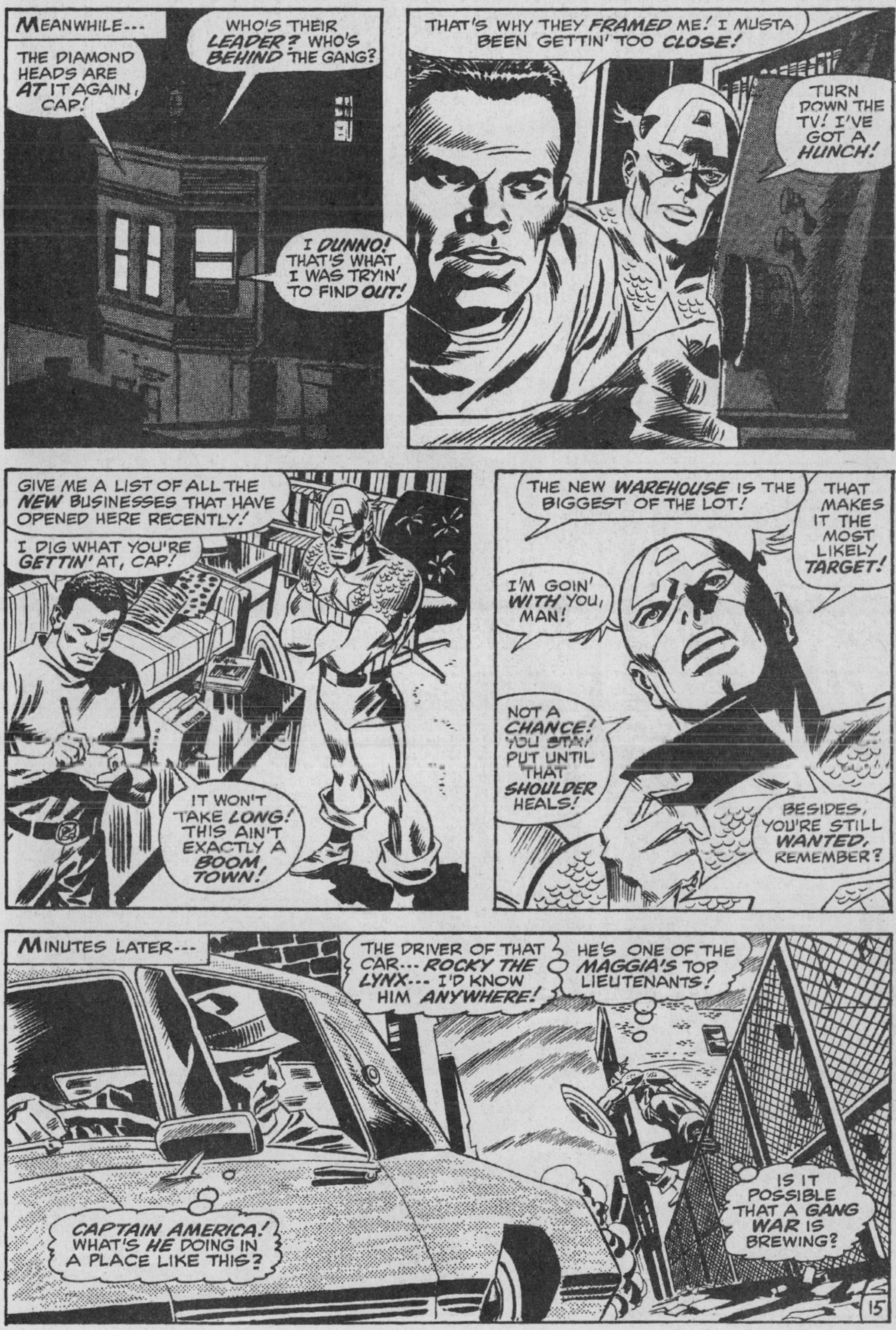
MEANWHILE---
THE DIAMOND HEADS ARE AT IT AGAIN, CAP!
WHO'S THEIR LEADER? WHO'S BEHIND THE GANG?
I DUNNO! THAT'S WHAT I WAS TRYIN' TO FIND OUT!
THAT'S WHY THEY FRAMED ME! I MUSTA BEEN GETTIN' TOO CLOSE!
TURN DOWN THE TV! I'VE GOT A HUNCH!
GIVE ME A LIST OF ALL THE NEW BUSINESSES THAT HAVE OPENED HERE RECENTLY!
I DIG WHAT YOU'RE GETTIN' AT, CAP!
IT WON'T TAKE LONG! THIS AIN'T EXACTLY A BOOM TOWN!
THE NEW WAREHOUSE IS THE BIGGEST OF THE LOT!
THAT MAKES IT THE MOST LIKELY TARGET!
I'M GOIN' WITH YOU, MAN!
NOT A CHANCE! YOU STAY PUT UNTIL THAT SHOULDER HEALS!
BESIDES, YOU'RE STILL WANTED, REMEMBER?
MINUTES LATER---
THE DRIVER OF THAT CAR--- ROCKY THE LYNX--- I'D KNOW HIM ANYWHERE!
HE'S ONE OF THE MAGGIA'S TOP LIEUTENANTS!
CAPTAIN AMERICA! WHAT'S HE DOING IN A PLACE LIKE THIS?
IS IT POSSIBLE THAT A GANG WAR IS BREWING?

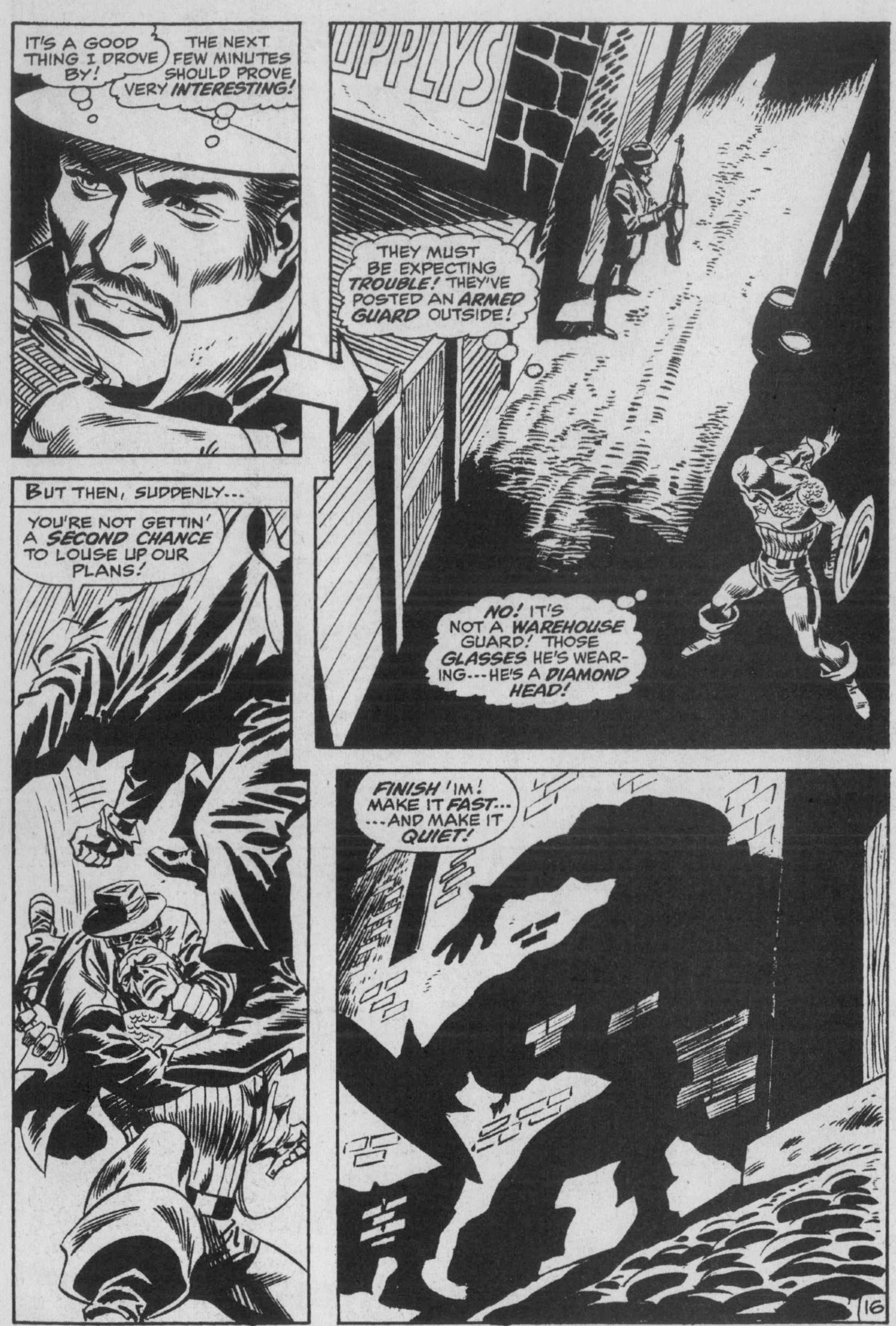
IT'S A GOOD THING I DROVE BY!
THE NEXT FEW MINUTES SHOULD PROVE VERY INTERESTING!
UPPLYS
THEY MUST BE EXPECTING TROUBLE! THEY'VE POSTED AN ARMED GUARD OUTSIDE!
NO! IT'S NOT A WAREHOUSE GUARD! THOSE GLASSES HE'S WEAR-ING---HE'S A DIAMOND HEAD!
BUT THEN, SUDDENLY...
YOU'RE NOT GETTIN' A SECOND CHANCE TO LOUSE UP OUR PLANS!
FINISH 'IM! MAKE IT FAST... ...AND MAKE IT QUIET!
16

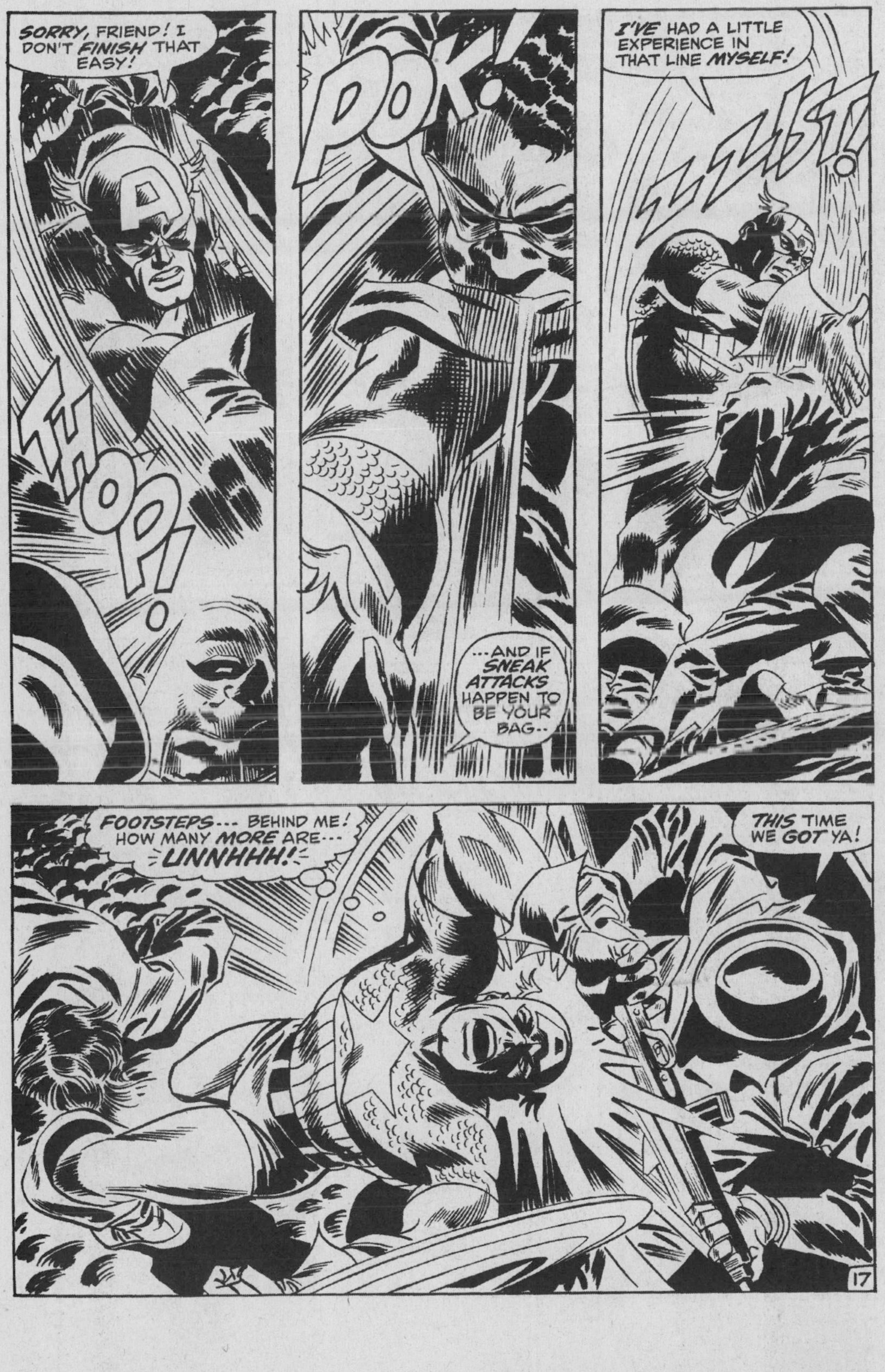
SORRY, FRIEND! I DON'T FINISH THAT EASY!
THOP!
POK!
...AND IF SNEAK ATTACKS HAPPEN TO BE YOUR BAG..
I'VE HAD A LITTLE EXPERIENCE IN THAT LINE MYSELF!
ZZZZST!
FOOTSTEPS... BEHIND ME! HOW MANY MORE ARE--- UNNHHH!
THIS TIME WE GOT YA!
17

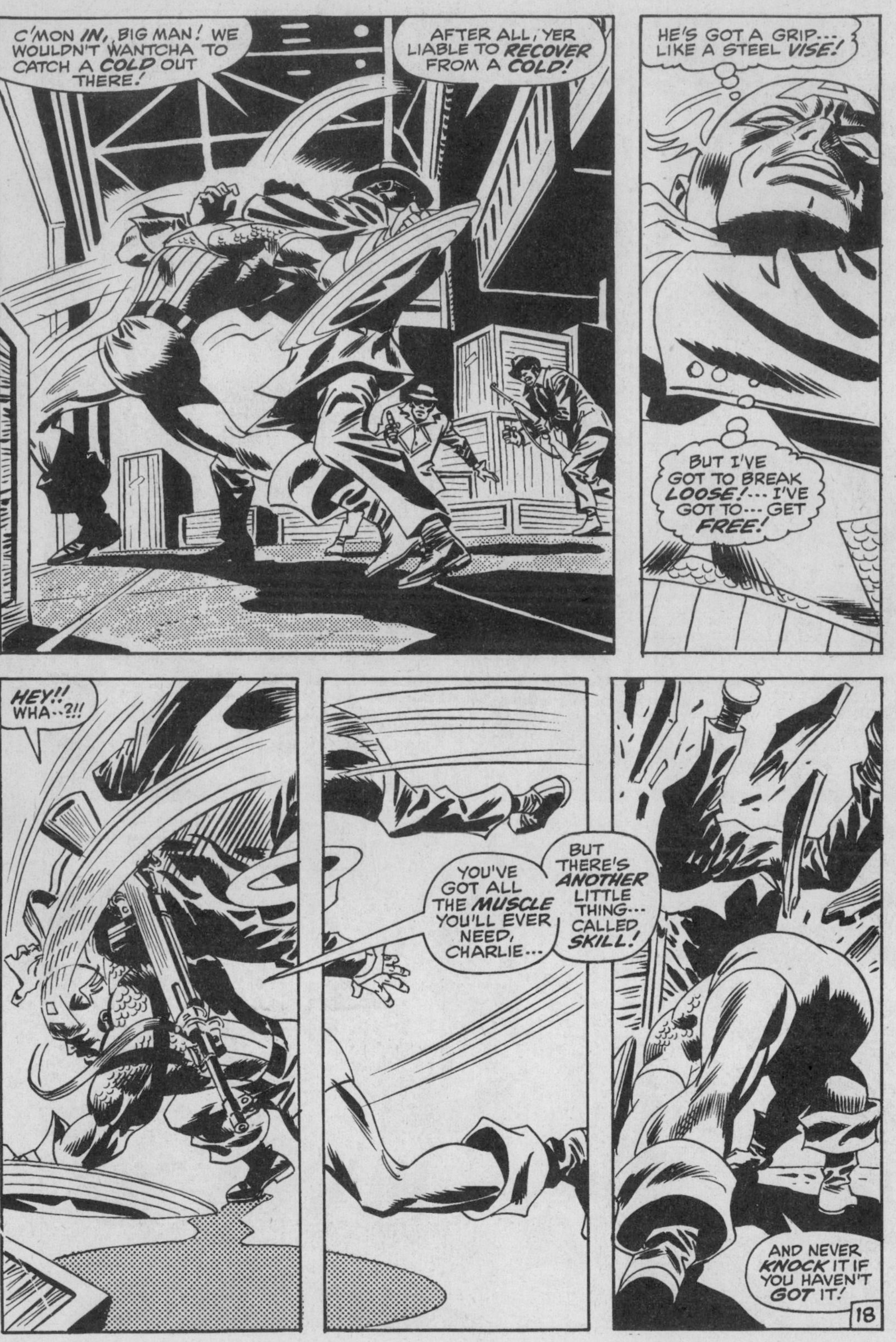

C'MON IN, BIG MAN! WE WOULDN'T WANTCHA TO CATCH A COLD OUT THERE!
AFTER ALL, YER LIABLE TO RECOVER FROM A COLD!
HE'S GOT A GRIP... LIKE A STEEL VISE!
BUT I'VE GOT TO BREAK LOOSE!... I'VE GOT TO... GET FREE!
HEY!! WHA--?!!
YOU'VE GOT ALL THE MUSCLE YOU'LL EVER NEED, CHARLIE...
BUT THERE'S ANOTHER LITTLE THING... CALLED SKILL!
AND NEVER KNOCK IT IF YOU HAVEN'T GOT IT!
18

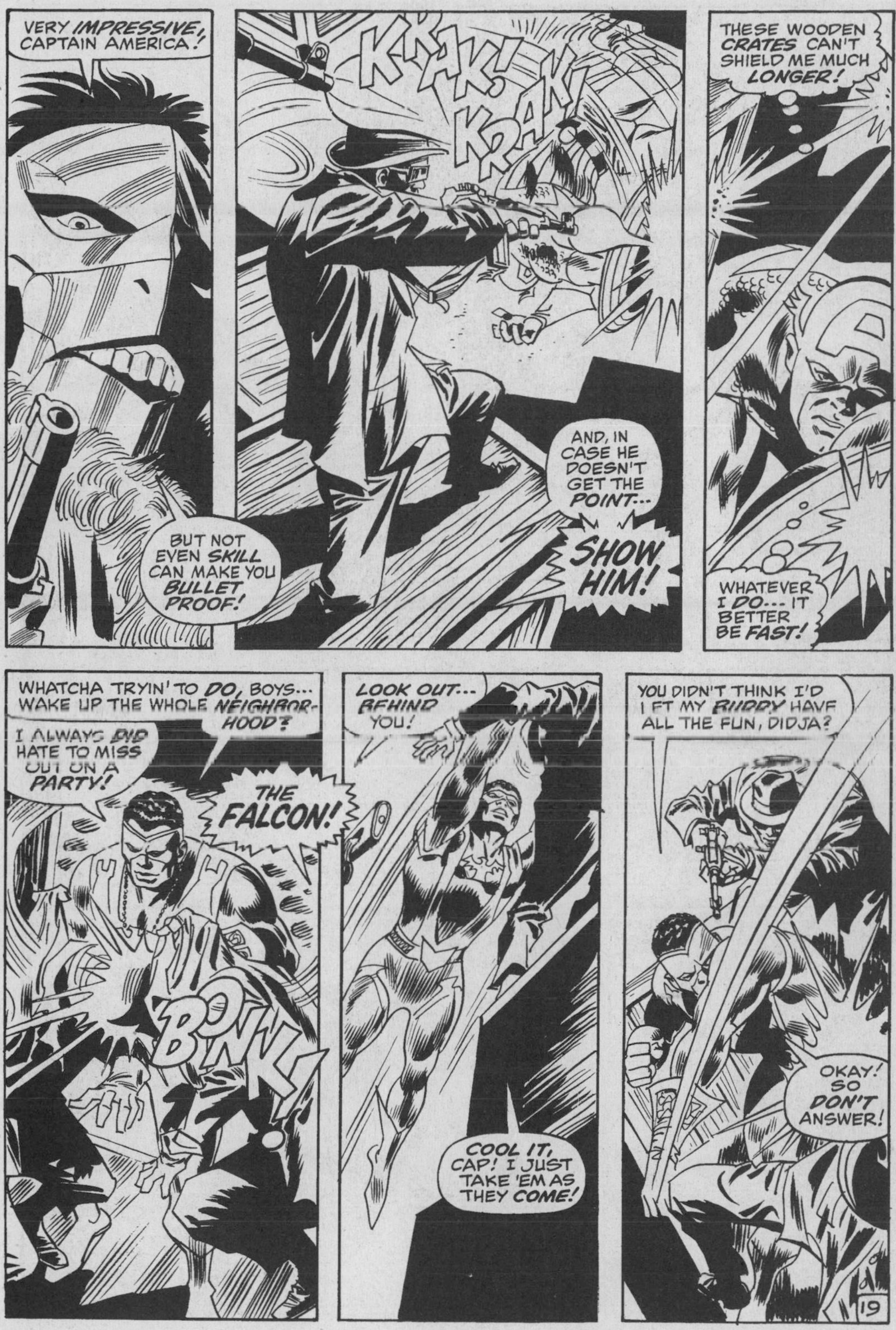
VERY IMPRESSIVE, CAPTAIN AMERICA!
BUT NOT EVEN SKILL CAN MAKE YOU BULLET PROOF!
K-RAK! K-RAK! KRAK!
AND, IN CASE HE DOESN'T GET THE POINT...
SHOW HIM!
THESE WOODEN CRATES CAN'T SHIELD ME MUCH LONGER!
WHATEVER I DO... IT BETTER BE FAST!
WHATCHA TRYIN' TO DO, BOYS... WAKE UP THE WHOLE NEIGHBOR-HOOD?
I ALWAYS DID HATE TO MISS OUT ON A PARTY!
THE FALCON!
BONK!
LOOK OUT... BEHIND YOU!
COOL IT, CAP! I JUST TAKE 'EM AS THEY COME!
YOU DIDN'T THINK I'D LET MY BUDDY HAVE ALL THE FUN, DIDJA?
OKAY! SO DON'T ANSWER!
19

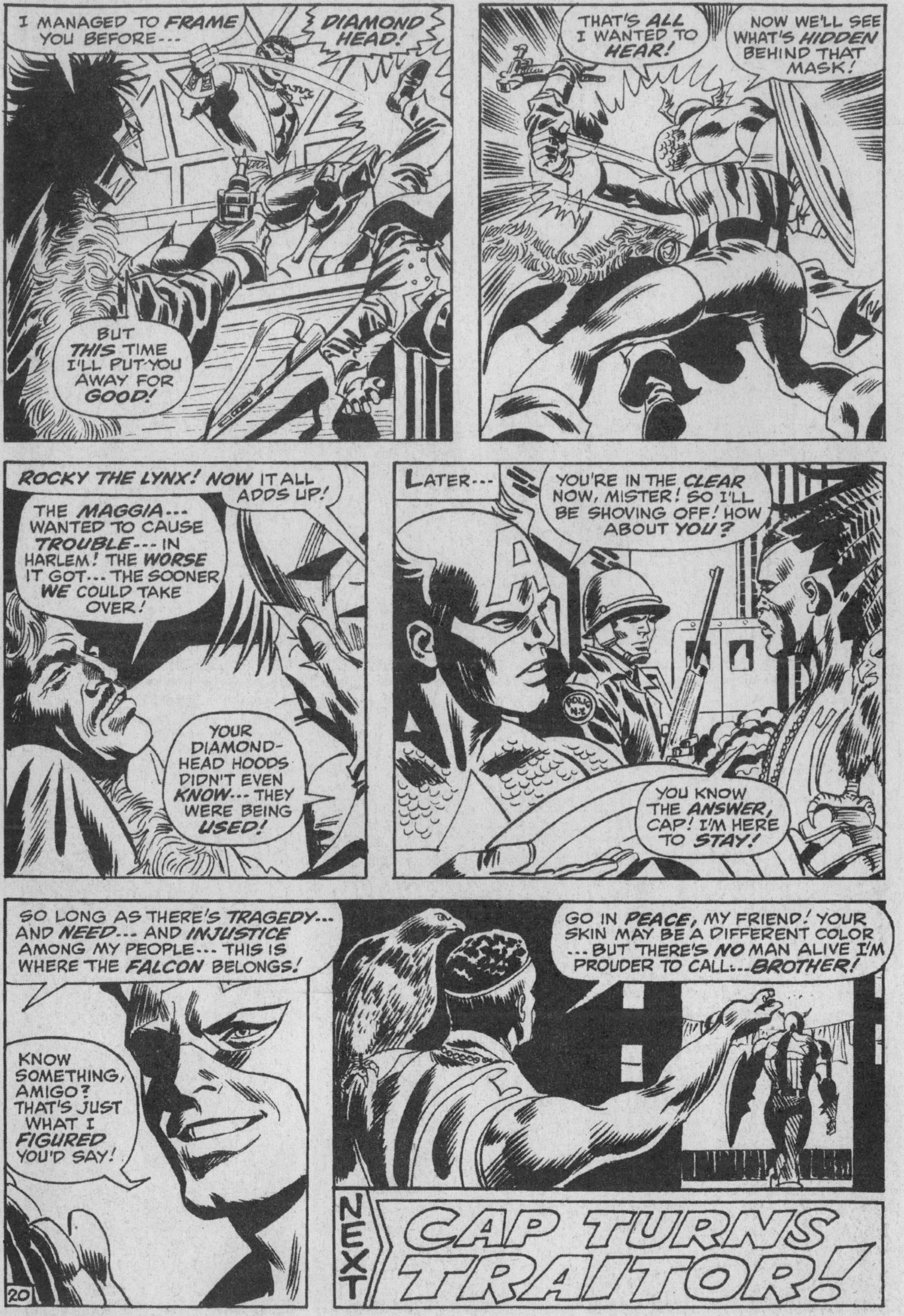
I MANAGED TO FRAME YOU BEFORE---
DIAMOND HEAD!
BUT THIS TIME I'LL PUT YOU AWAY FOR GOOD!
THAT'S ALL I WANTED TO HEAR!
NOW WE'LL SEE WHAT'S HIDDEN BEHIND THAT MASK!
ROCKY THE LYNX! NOW IT ALL ADDS UP!
THE MAGGIA--- WANTED TO CAUSE TROUBLE--- IN HARLEM! THE WORSE IT GOT--- THE SOONER WE COULD TAKE OVER!
YOUR DIAMOND-HEAD HOODS DIDN'T EVEN KNOW--- THEY WERE BEING USED!
LATER---
YOU'RE IN THE CLEAR NOW, MISTER! SO I'LL BE SHOVING OFF! HOW ABOUT YOU?
YOU KNOW THE ANSWER, CAP! I'M HERE TO STAY!
SO LONG AS THERE'S TRAGEDY--- AND NEED--- AND INJUSTICE AMONG MY PEOPLE--- THIS IS WHERE THE FALCON BELONGS!
KNOW SOMETHING, AMIGO? THAT'S JUST WHAT I FIGURED YOU'D SAY!
GO IN PEACE, MY FRIEND! YOUR SKIN MAY BE A DIFFERENT COLOR --- BUT THERE'S NO MAN ALIVE I'M PROUDER TO CALL---BROTHER!
NEXT
CAP TURNS TRAITOR!
20